American Standard Companies (p. 15)
http://www.americanstandard.com
AT&T (p. 508, p. 633)
http://www.att.com
Avcorp Industries Inc. (p. 572)
http://www.avcorp.com

Baxter International (p. 25)
http://www.baxter.com
Bell Canada Enterprises (p. 20, p. 956)
http://www.bce.ca
Boeing Inc. (p. 963)
http://www.boeing.com
Briggs & Stratton Corporation (p. 633)
http://www.briggsandstratton.com

Caterpillar (p. 562)
http://www.cat.com
Chrysler (p. 819)
http://www.chrysler.com
Coca-Cola (p. 633)
http://www.coca-cola.com
CSX (p. 633)
http://www.csx.com
Cummins Engine Company (p. 699)
http://www.cummins.com

Digital Equipment Corporation (p. 345)
http://www.digital.com
Domtar (p. 778)
http://www.domtar.com

Elgin Sweeper Company (p. 323)
http://www.elginsweeper.com
Entourage Technology Limited (p. 341)
http://www.entourage.ca
Exxon Corporation (p. 754)
http://www.exxon.com

Gelco Expense Management (p. 50)
http://www.gelconet.com
General Motors (p. 507, p. 691)
http://www.gm.com
Geneva Steel (p. 331)
http://www.geneva.com
Government of Canada (p. 685)
http://canada.gc.ca/main_e.html

Hamilton Civic Hospitals (p. 831)
http://www.hamcivhos.on.ca
Hershey Foods Corporation (p. 509)
http://www.hersheys.com
Hewlett-Packard (p. 228, p. 236)
http://www.hp.com
H.J. Heinz Co. (p. 693)
http://www.heinz.com
Hughes Aircraft (p. 861)
http://www.raytheon.com
Husky Injection Moulding (p. 778)
http://www.husky.com

IBM Canada (p. 926)
http://www.can.ibm.com
Imasco (p. 778)
http://imasco.com

Johnson Controls (p. 16)
http://www.jci.com

McCain Foods (p. 693)
http://www.mccain.com
McDonald's Corporation (p. 918)
http://www.mcdonalds.com/main
Merck & Co. (p. 771)
http://www.merck.com

Nissan Motor Company (p. 235)
http://www.nissanmotors.com
Northern Telecom (p. 244, p. 398)
http://www.nortel.com
Nova Corporation (p. 636)
http://www.nova.ca

Penril DataComm (p. 19)
http://www.penril.com
Petro-Canada (p. 569)
http://www.petro-canada.ca

Quaker Oats (p. 633, p. 634)
http://www.quakeroats.com

Rockwell International Corporation (p. 769)
http://www.rockwell.com

Sears, Roebuck & Company (p. 33)
http://www.sears.com
Siemens Electric Motor Works (p. 230)
http://www.siemens.com
Southwestern Ohio Steel (p. 706)
http://www.sosteel.com

Toronto Blue Jays (p. 449)
http://www.bluejays.ca
Toronto Transit Commission (p. 689)
http://www.city.toronto.on.ca/ttc
Toyota Motor Corporation (p. 281)
http://www.toyota.com

Ultramar (p. 325)
http://www.diasham.com
USX Corporation (p. 331)
http://www.uss.com

Volkswagen (p. 231, p. 330)
http://www.vw.com

MANAGERIAL ACCOUNTING

Concepts for
Planning, Control, Decision Making

Fourth Canadian Edition

MANAGERIAL ACCOUNTING

Concepts for Planning, Control, Decision Making

Fourth Canadian Edition

Ray H. Garrison, D.B.A., CPA
Professor Emeritus
Brigham Young University

Eric W. Noreen, Ph.D., CMA
University of Washington
and
Hong Kong University of Science & Technology

G. R. (Dick) Chesley, Ph.D., CA
St. Mary's University

Raymond F. Carroll, Ph.D., FGCA
Dalhousie University

McGraw-Hill Ryerson

Toronto New York Burr Ridge Bangkok Bogotá
Caracas Lisbon London Madrid Mexico City Milan
New Delhi Seoul Singapore Sydney Taipei

McGraw-Hill
Ryerson Limited

A Subsidiary of The McGraw·Hill Companies

Managerial Accounting: Concepts for Planning, Control, Decision Making
Fourth Canadian Edition

ISBN: 0-07-560388-8

2 3 4 5 6 7 8 9 10 GTC 8 7 6 5 4 3 2 1 0 9

Printed and bound in Canada

Sponsoring Editor: *Lisa Feil/Jennifer Dewey*
Manager, Editorial Services: *Susan Calvert*
Production Editor: *Shirley Corriveau*
Production Co-ordinator: *Nicla Dattolico*
Cover Photo: *Cirque du Soleil: Al Seib*
Costume Designer: *Dominique Lemieux*
Cover Design: *Valerie Mattocks*
Original Interior Design: *Ellen Pettengell*
Typesetter: *GAC Shepard Poorman*
Printer: *Transcontinental Printing*

Canadian Cataloguing in Publication Data
Main entry under title:
Managerial accounting: concepts for planning, control, decision making
4th Canadian ed.
Includes index.
ISBN 0-07-560388-8
1. Managerial accounting. I. Garrison, Ray H.
HF5657.4.M375 1998   658.15′11   C98-931511-8

To our students to whom we owe a great deal

ABOUT THE AUTHORS

RAY H. GARRISON

Ray H. Garrison is *emeritus* Professor of Accounting at Brigham Young University, Provo, Utah. He received his B.S. and M.S. degrees from Brigham Young University and his D.B.A. degree from Indiana University. A Certified Public Accountant, he has been involved in management consulting work with both national and regional accounting firms.

Professor Garrison has published articles in *The Accounting Review, Management Accounting,* and other professional journals. A popular teacher, he has received numerous teaching awards from students and the Karl H. Maeser Distinguished Teaching Award from Brigham Young University for innovation in the classroom.

ERIC W. NOREEN

Eric W. Noreen is a globe-trotting academic who holds appointments at institutions in the United States, Europe, and Asia. He is currently Professor of Accounting at the University of Washington; Visiting Price Waterhouse Professor of Management Information & Control at INSEAD, an international graduate school of business located in France; and Professor of Accounting at the Hong Kong University of Science and Technology. He received his B.A. degree from the University of Washington and MBA and Ph.D. degrees from Stanford University. A Certified Management Accountant, he was awarded a Certificate of Distinguished Performance by the Institute of Certified Management Accountants.

Professor Noreen has served as Associate Editor of *The Accounting Review* and the *Journal of Accounting and Economics.* He has numerous articles in academic journals including the *Journal of Accounting Research, The Accounting Review,* the *Journal of Accounting and Economics, Accounting Horizons, Accounting, Organizations and Society, Contemporary Accounting Research,* and the *Journal of Management Accounting Research.* He is a frequent presenter at workshops and conferences throughout the world.

Professor Noreen teaches management accounting at the undergraduate, masters, and doctoral levels and has won a number of awards from students for his teaching.

G. R. (DICK) CHESLEY

Dick Chesley is Professor of Accounting at Saint Mary's University in Halifax, Nova Scotia, and a Chartered Accountant. He is a graduate of Mount Allison University with a Bachelor of Commerce degree and The Ohio State University with an M.A. and a Ph.D. He has prepared and presented courses for all Canadian professional accounting associations, co-authored *Fundamentals of Financial Accounting* (Irwin), and has published articles in the *Journal of Accounting Research, Contemporary Accounting Research, The Accounting Review, CMA Magazine, CA Magazine,* and numerous proceedings. He has been a faculty member at The Wharton School, University of Pennsylvania, and Dalhousie University. As well, he has lectured throughout Canada and the United States and held visiting positions at Lingnan College and Baptist University in Hong Kong. In addition, he was awarded the 1996 Canadian Academic Accounting Association Outstanding Educator Award.

RAYMOND F. CARROLL

Raymond Carroll is a Fellow of the Certified General Accountants' Association of Canada and is Associate Professor at Dalhousie University in Halifax, Nova Scotia, where he currently teaches financial accounting, financial statement analysis, and managerial accounting. He is a graduate of St. Francis Xavier University with a Bachelor of Business Administration degree and a Bachelor of Education degree and Dalhousie University with an MBA and a Ph.D. Professor Carroll is a past president of CGA Nova Scotia and has been Chairperson of the CGA National Education Committee and a member of the CGA Canada Executive Committee. Professor Carroll is a member of the Canadian Advisory Committee (CAC) on international accounting standards. He has taught international accounting and international finance in China under the Canadian International Development Agency (CIDA) linkage program between Dalhousie University and Xiamen University and has also lectured in Hong Kong. His research interests centre on managerial accounting issues and business ethics.

CONTENTS IN BRIEF

CONTENTS

PART III THE CAPSTONE: Using Cost Data in Decision Making   681

PREFACE

A paramount objective of *Managerial Accounting* has always been to make a clear and balanced presentation of relevant subject matter. The focus on relevance continues in this fourth edition with coverage of such current topics as JIT, TQM, ABC, process reengineering, TOC, ethical issues, and quality costs and management. In recognition of the widespread application of management accounting concepts, many examples and problems in the book deal with service, not-for-profit, retail, and wholesale organizations as well as with manufacturing organizations. Also of great importance is the growing significance of the global economy. Few companies operate in a purely domestic environment, and the fourth edition provides international examples and explanations throughout. In short, the watchwords for this edition of *Managerial Accounting* are—as before—*relevance, balance,* and a continued tradition of *clarity.*

Acknowledging the greater need for a user perspective, the emphasis of *Managerial Accounting* is on uses of accounting data within an organization by its managers. Managers need information to carry out three essential functions in an organization: (1) planning operations, (2) controlling activities, and (3) making decisions. The purpose of *Managerial Accounting* is to show what kind of information is needed, where this information can be obtained, and how this information can be used by managers as they carry out their planning, controlling, and decision-making responsibilities. These three essential functions show that today's management accountant is not just a number cruncher or "corporate cop," but rather a key specialist in supporting the decision-making process.

Management accountants are now partners with other departments within an organization and engage in a wide variety of activities. These tasks range from traditional accounting work (such as financial reporting or resource management) to new types of work (such as internal consulting and process improvement). The Institute of Management Accountants (IMA) has identified the knowledge, skills, and abilities most important for entry-level accountants to have in order to perform these tasks. These skills are based on the accounting fundamentals (such as cost flows; accruals and deferrals; measurement, valuation, and presentation of revenue and expenses; and measurement, valuation, and presentation of assets and equities). *Managerial Accounting* emphasizes these accounting fundamentals in their relation to the decision-making process. Students gain an understanding of technical information and learn how to apply that information in appropriate situations.

ORGANIZATION AND CONTENT

As in prior editions, flexibility in meeting the needs of courses varying in length, content, and student composition continues to be a prime concern in the organization and content of this book. Sufficient text material is available to permit the instructor to choose topics and depth of coverage as desired. Appendixes, parts of chapters, or even (in some cases) whole chapters can be omitted without adversely affecting the continuity of the course. The Solutions Manual gives a number of alternatives for organizing the course.

New in This Edition

The fourth edition builds on the success of the third edition. The principle changes have all been motivated by a desire to make the material even more accessible and relevant to students.

Vignettes involving businesspeople in life-like settings—"Managerial Accounting in Action"—are used in many chapters to introduce core concepts and stimulate interest. These vignettes are essential to, and an integral part of, the reading and understanding of the text. Real products and services that students can relate to are used as much as possible in examples. Many more examples and problems have a distinctly international flavour. The use of "Focus on Current Practice" boxes has been expanded and updated.

As in prior editions, special attention has been given to bringing new exercise, problem, and case material into the book. Users will again find a wide range of assignment material in terms of level of difficulty. A new type of assignment material—group exercises—has been added; they appear after the case material in each chapter. These extensive group exercises allow instructors to do collaborative learning in the classroom or assign group/team work for outside the classroom. This addresses AECC and AACSB recommendations for capabilities needed by accounting and business graduates.

Many small "polishing" changes have been made throughout the book to improve flow, comprehension, and readability. However, change has not been made simply for the sake of change. Rather, the revision has been guided with a single thought in mind—to make the Fourth Canadian Edition of *Managerial Accounting* the most up-to-date and teachable book available in its field.

Specific Changes in Chapter Contents

In this fourth edition, most chapters have been improved in various ways. Chapter 1 now includes an extended discussion of the business environment, including JIT material from the third edition's Chapter 5 along with completely new material on TQM, process reengineering, and TOC. Chapter 5 is now devoted to ABC and quality management, and incorporates material that was formerly in a Quality Costs and Reports Appendix. The following table provides a summary of these and other major changes.

Chapter	Major Content Changes in This Edition
Chapter 1	This chapter now includes an extended discussion of the business environment, including JIT material from the 3rd edition's Chapter 5 along with completely new material on TQM, process reengineering, and theory of constraints.
Chapter 2	An alternate form for computing cost of goods manufactured and cost of goods sold is introduced.
Chapter 3	A vignette using a precision machine company illustrates a job-order costing system.
Chapter 4	The FIFO method of computing equivalent units of production has been moved to the FIFO appendix. A vignette about a ski manufacturer illustrates process costing concepts.

Chapter 5	This chapter is now devoted to ABC and quality management. Material that was formerly focused on service department overhead allocation has been relocated to Chapter 16 to reduce the length of the chapter. A vignette illustrates the impact of switching to an ABC system in a multi-product company.
Chapter 6	A service company vignette illustrates concepts involving fixed and variable costs.
Chapter 7	A vignette concerning a maker of automobile sound systems is used to demonstrate CVP analysis.
Chapter 8	A new vignette on a manufacturer of sweaters adds an international aspect to this chapter.
Chapter 9	Five new "Focus on Current Practice" boxes add more real world examples. A vignette centring on a maker of popsicles illustrates budgeting principles.
Chapter 10	A vignette about a maker of pewter bookends demonstrates standards and variances.
Chapter 11	A vignette about a sweatshirt manufacturer illustrates overhead control and analysis.
Chapter 12	The material on transfer pricing has been moved to an appendix. A vignette of a software company explores the issues of segment reporting and profitability analysis. Marketing analysis has been included here along with introductions to balanced scorecards, and economic value added
Chapter 13	The appendix on linear programming has been eliminated. Sunk costs are discussed using a vignette of a manufacturer of hang gliders.
Chapter 14	The discussion of investments in automated equipment has been updated.
Chapter 15	A ski resort vignette demonstrates capital budgeting decisions and depreciation. More "Focus on Current Practice" boxes have been added.
Chapter 16	Service Department costing has been relocated here to reduce the discussion materials on overhead in Chapter 5.
Chapter 17	Minimal content changes.
Appendix	Pricing details have been located here to enable a concentrated discussion for those who deem it relevant.

Features

"Focus on Current Practice" boxes contain glimpses of how actual companies use or are affected by concepts discussed in the chapter. Each chapter has from two to nine boxes, helping a student understand the uses of managerial accounting in actual business practice.

International aspects of management have become increasingly important in recent years due to the emergence of regional and global markets. Discussion and examples that have an international dimension are identified by the icon shown in the margin.

More than 100 exercise, problems, and cases requiring written solutions (identified by the logo shown in the margin) improve students' written communication skills and address educational concerns.

Ethical issues are included both in assignment material and in the text (and identified by the icon shown in the margin). End-of-chapter assignments allow students an opportunity to consider ethical issues in making managerial decisions. This user-orientation helps address AECC and AACSB recommendations related to students' abilities to make sound ethical judgments.

This edition extends the use of actual company examples and numerous examples of other realistic companies (identified by the logo shown in the margin). These companies are of all types: large and small, domestic and international, manufacturing, service, and retail. These companies and examples show how the concepts discussed in the text apply to the global business environment.

Supplements for the Instructor

The supplements listed here may accompany *Managerial Accounting*. Please contact your local McGraw-Hill Ryerson representative for details concerning policies, prices, and availability as some restrictions may apply.

Solutions Manual.   Prepared by the textbook authors, the Solutions Manual was also carefully reviewed for accuracy. This supplement contains completely worked-out solutions to all assignment material and a general discussion of the use of group exercises. In addition, the manual contains suggested course outlines and a listing of exercises, problems, and cases scaled as to difficulty.

Solutions Transparencies.   These transparencies feature completely worked-out solutions to all assignment material.

Instructor's Resource Guide.   Prepared by Andrews Oppong of Dalhousie University, the Instructor's Resource Guide contains fairly extensive chapter by chapter lecture notes, including learning objectives, that can serve as a basis for classroom presentations. The lecture notes also have suggestions for ways of presenting key concepts and ideas. Also included are an assignment grid, indicating the topics covered by each exercise, problem, and case, and teaching transparency masters.

Computerized Test Bank.   The newly revised test bank contains over 1,200 true-false and multiple-choice questions, computational problems, and essay questions, organized by chapter.

Check Figures.   A list of check figures gives key amounts for selected problems and cases.

Richard D. Irwin Managerial/Cost Video Library.   These short, action-oriented videos provide the impetus for lively classroom discussion. The *Managerial/Cost Video Library,* a series of six volumes, includes videos of international and service examples to go along with numerous manufacturing examples.

Volume I	"Behind the Bill"
	"The Vancouver Door Company"
	"How Many Bucks in a Bag"
Volume II	"Moving the Merchandise"
	"Orge Mills, After the Curtain Fell"
Volume III	"Lean Production"
	"Quality"
	"The Manufacturing Process"
Volume IV	"Computer-Integrated Manufacturing"
	"Inventory Management"
	"Service"

Volume V	"Manufacturing"
	"Supplier Development Outreach Program"
	"Accounting Careers"
Volume VI	"Atlas Foundry and Machine Company"
	"Management Accounting and Concepts"
	"International Accounting"

Video Guide.   This guide provides instructors with a brief overview of the key points and length of the video segments. It also provides questions to promote classroom discussion.

Supplements for the Student

Workbook/Study Guide.   Prepared by Andrews Oppong of Dalhousie University, this study aid provides suggestions for studying chapter material, summarizes the essential points in each chapter, and tests students' knowledge using self-test questions and exercises. The Workbook/Study Guide can be used as an efficient and effective way to prepare for exams.

Student Solutions Manual.   Answers to odd-numbered exercises and problems.

Computer Supplements

- *SPATS (Spreadsheet Applications Template Software).* This includes Lotus 1-2-3 and Excel templates for selected problems and exercises from the text. The templates gradually become more complex, requiring students to build a variety of formulas. "What if" questions are added to show the power of spreadsheets, and a simple tutorial is included. *SPATS* is included in the Instructor's Resource Guide. Copies can be made available to students for a nominal fee.
- *Tutorial Software.* Fill-in-the-blank, multiple-choice, true-false, journal entry review, and glossary review questions can be randomly accessed by students. Explanations of right and wrong answers are provided and scores are tallied.
- *Ramblewood Manufacturing, Inc.* This computerized practice set was prepared by Leland Mansuetti and Keith Weidkamp (both of Sierra College) and has been completely updated. This software simulates the operations of a company that manufactures customized fencing. It can be used to illustrate job-order costing systems with JIT inventory in a realistic setting. The entire simulation requires 10 to 14 hours to complete. A new feature prevents files from being transferred from one disk to another without detection. It is available on both 5.25″ and 3.5″ diskettes in DOS and Windows platforms. A multimedia version is available.
- *The Virtual Office.* This Windows-based multimedia software program acts as a vehicle for simulating various managerial accounting concepts and tasks. The Virtual Office provides an interactive means of gathering information pertaining to the many different scenarios facing a manager today. The Virtual Office interface allows students to launch tutorial software to enhance their subject knowledge, document their analysis by launching macro-driven spreadsheet and word-processing templates, and explore a simulated managerial accounting environment by gathering the information and performing the tasks of an actual manager.

ACKNOWLEDGEMENTS

Suggestions have been received from many of our colleagues throughout the country who have used the prior editions of *Managerial Accounting*. This is vital feedback that we rely on in revising each edition. Each of those who have offered comments and suggestions has our thanks.

The efforts of many people are needed to develop a book and improve it from edition to edition. Among these people are the reviewers who point out areas of concern, cite areas of strength, and make recommendations for change. In this regard, the following professors provided in-depth reviews that were enormously helpful in preparing the Fourth Canadian Edition of *Managerial Accounting*: Mariann Glynn, Ryerson Polytechnic University; Rob Harvey, Algonquin College; Bruce Hazelton, Sheridan College; David Hoffman, Seneca College of Applied Arts and Technology; Barbara J. MacKay, Simon Fraser University; Robert F. Madden, St. Francis Xavier University; Harvey Willows, Centennial College; and Andrew Woudstra, Athabasca University.

We acknowledge the Canadian Institute of Chartered Accountants (CICA), the Certified General Accountants Association of Canada (CGA-Canada), and the Society of Management Accountants (SMA) for permitting us to use questions and solutions from their past years' examinations. Also, appreciation is extended to the Institute of Management Accountants for the use of questions and unofficial answers from past Certified Management Accounting (CMA) examinations. Similarly, our appreciation is extended to the American Institute of Certified Public Accountants (CPA) for permission to use selected problems from its examinations. These problems bear the notations CICA, CGA-Canada, SMAC, CMA, and CPA, respectively.

G. R. (Dick) Chesley
Raymond F. Carroll

MANAGERIAL ACCOUNTING

Concepts for
Planning, Control, Decision Making

Fourth Canadian Edition

MANAGERIAL ACCOUNTING AND THE BUSINESS ENVIRONMENT

1

LEARNING OBJECTIVES

After studying Chapter 1, you should be able to:

1 Describe what managers do and why they need accounting information.

2 Identify the major differences and similarities between financial and managerial accounting.

3 Explain the basic characteristics of just-in-time (JIT).

4 Describe the total quality management (TQM) approach to continuous improvement.

5 Explain the basic ideas underlying process reengineering.

6 Describe how the theory of constraints (TOC) can be used to focus improvement efforts.

7 Discuss the impact of international competition on businesses and on managerial accounting.

8 Describe the role the controller plays in a decentralized organization.

9 Explain the importance of ethical standards in an advanced market economy.

10 Define or explain the key terms listed at the end of the chapter.

Continuous improvement through total quality management (TQM) is a key component of today's business environment. L. L. Bean provides a benchmark for processing customer orders that other companies have studied to improve their own processes.

M anagerial accounting is concerned with providing information to *managers*—
that is, to those who are *inside* an organization and who direct and control its
operations. Managerial accounting can be contrasted with **financial accounting**,
which is concerned with providing information to shareholders, creditors, and others who
are *outside* an organization. Managerial accounting provides the essential data with which
organizations are actually run. Financial accounting provides the scorecard by which a
company's past performance is judged.

Because it is manager oriented, any study of managerial accounting must be preceded
by some understanding of what managers do, the information managers need, and the
general business environment. Accordingly, the purpose of this chapter is to briefly examine these subjects.

THE WORK OF MANAGEMENT AND THE NEED FOR MANAGERIAL ACCOUNTING INFORMATION

OBJECTIVE 1
Describe what
managers do and why
they need accounting
information.

Every organization—large and small—has managers. Someone must be responsible for
laying plans, organizing resources, directing personnel, and controlling operations. This
is true of the Bank of Montreal, the Canadian Red Cross, the University of British Columbia, the Catholic Church, Husky Oil of Calgary or the local corner grocery store. In
this chapter, we will use a particular organization—Good Vibrations, Inc.—to illustrate
the work of management. What we have to say about the management of Good Vibrations, Inc., however, is very general and can be applied to virtually any organization.

Good Vibrations, Inc., runs a chain of retail outlets that sell a full range of music CDs.
The chain's stores are concentrated in Pacific Rim cities such as Sydney, Singapore, Hong
Kong, Beijing, Tokyo, and Vancouver. The company has found that the best way to generate
sales, and profits, is to create an exciting shopping environment. Consequently, the company
puts a great deal of effort into planning the layout and decor of its stores—which are often
quite large and extend over several floors in key downtown locations. Management knows
that different types of clientele are attracted to different types of music. The international
rock section is generally decorated with bold, brightly coloured graphics, and the aisles are
purposely narrow to create a crowded feeling much like one would experience at a popular
nightclub on Friday night. In contrast, the classical music section is wood panelled and fully
sound insulated, with the rich, spacious feeling of a country club meeting room.

Managers at Good Vibrations, Inc., like managers everywhere, carry out three major
activities—*planning, directing and motivating,* and *controlling.* **Planning** involves selecting a course of action and specifying how the action will be implemented. **Directing and
motivating** involves mobilizing human resources to carry out plans and run routine operations. **Controlling** involves ensuring that the plan is actually carried out and is appropriately modified as circumstances change. Management accounting information plays a
vital role in these basic management activities—but most particularly in the planning and
control functions.

Planning

The first step in planning is to identify alternatives and then to select from among the alternatives the one that does the best job of furthering the organization's objectives. The
basic objective of Good Vibrations, Inc., is to earn profits for the owners of the company
by providing superior service at competitive prices in as many markets as possible. To

further this objective, every year top management carefully considers a range of options, or alternatives, for expanding into new geographic markets. This year management is considering opening new stores in Shanghai, Bangkok, and Jakarta.

When making this and other choices, management must balance the opportunities against the demands made on the company's resources. Management knows from bitter experience that opening a store in a major new market is a big step that cannot be taken lightly. It requires enormous amounts of time and energy from the company's most experienced, talented, and busy professionals. When the company attempted to open stores in both Beijing and Hong Kong in the same year, resources were stretched too thinly. The result was that neither store opened on schedule, and operations in the rest of the company suffered. Therefore, entering new markets is planned very, very carefully.

Among other data, top management looks at the sales volumes, profit margins, and costs of the company's established stores in similar markets. These data, supplied by the management accountant, are combined with projected sales volume data at the proposed new locations to estimate the profits that would be generated by the new stores. In general, virtually all important alternatives considered by management in the planning process have some effect on revenues or costs, and management accounting data are essential in estimating those effects.

After considering all of the alternatives, Good Vibrations, Inc.'s top management decided to open a store in the burgeoning Shanghai market in the third quarter of the year, but to defer opening any other new stores to another year. As soon as this decision was made, detailed plans were drawn up for all parts of the company that would be involved in the Shanghai opening. For example, the personnel department's travel budget was increased, because it would be providing extensive on-the-site training to the new personnel hired in Shanghai.

As in the personnel department example, the plans of management are often expressed formally in **budgets**, and the term *budgeting* is applied to generally describe this part of the planning process. Budgets are usually prepared under the direction of the **controller**, who is the manager in charge of the accounting department. Typically, budgets are prepared annually and represent management's plans in specific, quantitative terms. In addition to a travel budget, the personnel department will be given goals in terms of new hires, courses taught, and detailed breakdowns of expected expenses. Similarly, the manager of each store will be given a target for sales volume, profit, expenses, pilferage losses, and employee training. These data will be collected, analyzed, and summarized for management use in the form of budgets prepared by management accountants.

Directing and Motivating

In addition to planning for the future, managers must oversee day-to-day activities and keep the organization functioning smoothly. This requires the ability to motivate and effectively direct people. Managers assign tasks to employees, arbitrate disputes, answer questions, solve on-the-spot problems, and make many small decisions that affect customers and employees. In effect, directing is that part of the managers' work that deals with the routine and the here and now. Managerial accounting data, such as daily sales reports, are often used in this type of day-to-day decision making.

Controlling

In carrying out the **control** function, managers seek to ensure that the plan is being followed. **Feedback,** which signals whether operations are on track, is the key to effective control. In sophisticated organizations this feedback is provided by detailed reports of

Information from managerial accounting can help managers control operations by comparing the performance of budgeted results with actual results.

various types. One of these reports, which compares budgeted to actual results, is called a **performance report.** Performance reports suggest where operations are not proceeding as planned and where some parts of the organization may require additional attention. For example, before the opening of the new Shanghai store in the third quarter of the year, the store's manager will be given sales volume, profit, and expense targets for the fourth quarter of the year. As the fourth quarter progresses, periodic reports will be made in which the actual sales volume, profit, and expenses are compared to the targets. If the actual results fall below the targets, top management is alerted that the Shanghai store requires more attention. Experienced personnel can be flown in to help the new manager, or top management may come to the conclusion that plans will have to be revised. As we will see in following chapters, providing this kind of feedback to managers is one of the central purposes of managerial accounting.

The End Results of Managers' Activities

As a customer enters one of the Good Vibrations' stores, the results of management's planning, directing and motivating, and control activities will be evident in the many details that make the difference between a pleasant and an irritating shopping experience. The store will be clean, fashionably decorated, and logically laid out. Featured artists' videos will be displayed on TV monitors throughout the store, and the background rock music will be loud enough to send older patrons scurrying for the classical music section. Popular CDs will be in stock, and the latest hits will be available for private listening on earphones. Specific titles will be easy to find. Regional music, such as CantoPop in Hong Kong, will be prominently featured. Checkout clerks will be alert, friendly, and efficient. In short, what the customer experiences doesn't simply happen; it is the result of the efforts of managers who must visualize and fit together the processes that are needed to get the job done.

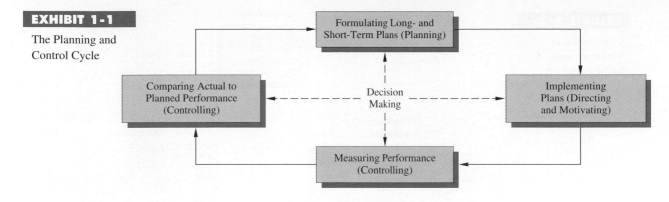

EXHIBIT 1-1

The Planning and
Control Cycle

The Planning and Control Cycle

The work of management can be summarized in a model such as the one shown in Exhibit 1–1. This model, which depicts the **planning and control cycle,** illustrates the smooth flow of management activities from planning through directing and motivating, controlling, and then back to planning again. All of these activities involve decision making, so it is depicted as the hub around which the other activities revolve.

COMPARISON OF FINANCIAL AND MANAGERIAL ACCOUNTING

OBJECTIVE 2
Identify the major differences and similarities between financial and managerial accounting.

Financial accounting reports are prepared for the use of external parties such as shareholders and creditors, whereas managerial accounting reports are intended to be used by managers inside the organization. This contrast in basic orientation results in several major differences between financial and managerial accounting, even though both financial and managerial accounting rely on the same underlying financial data. The major differences between financial and managerial accounting are summarized in Exhibit 1–2.

As shown in Exhibit 1–2, in addition to a difference in orientation of reports, financial and managerial accounting also differ in point of emphasis between the past and the future, in the type of data provided to users, and in several other ways. These differences are discussed in the following paragraphs.

Emphasis on the Future

Since *planning* is such an important part of the manager's job, managerial accounting has a strong future orientation. In contrast, financial accounting primarily provides summaries of past financial transactions. These summaries may be useful in planning, but only to a point. The difficulty with summaries of the past is that the future is not simply a reflection of what has happened in the past. Changes are constantly taking place in economic conditions, customer needs and desires, competitive conditions, and so on. All of these changes demand that the manager's planning be based in large part on estimates of what will happen rather than on summaries of what has already happened.

Comparison of
Financial and
Managerial
Accounting

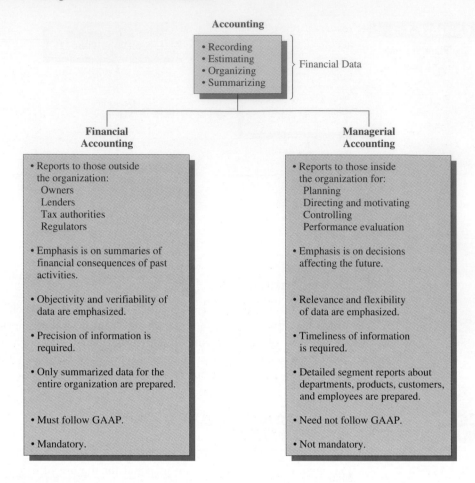

Relevance and Flexibility of Data

Financial accounting data are expected to be objective and verifiable. However, for internal uses the manager is often more concerned about receiving information that is relevant than about receiving information that is completely objective or even verifiable. By relevant, we mean *appropriate for the problem at hand.* For example, it is difficult to verify estimated sales volumes for a proposed new store at Good Vibrations, Inc., but this is exactly the type of information that is most useful to managers in their decision making. The managerial accounting information system should be flexible enough to provide whatever data are relevant for a particular decision.

Greater Emphasis on Timeliness

Timeliness is often more important than precision to managers. If a decision must be made, a manager would much rather have a good estimate now than wait a week for an answer that is more precise than is really needed. A decision involving tens of millions of dollars does not have to be based on estimates that are precise down to the penny, or even to the dollar. Estimates that are accurate to the nearest million dollars may be precise enough to make a good decision. Since precision is costly in terms of both time and resources, managerial accounting places less emphasis on precision than does financial accounting. In addition, managerial accounting places considerable weight on nonmonetary data. For example, information about customer satisfaction is of tremendous importance even though it would be difficult to express such data in a monetary form.

Segments of an Organization

Financial accounting is primarily concerned with reporting for the company as a whole. By contrast, managerial accounting focuses much more on the parts, or **segments,** of a company. These segments may be product lines, sales territories, divisions, departments, or any other categorization of the company's activities that management finds useful. Financial accounting does require some breakdowns of revenues and costs by major segments in external reports, but this is a secondary emphasis. In managerial accounting, segment reporting is the primary emphasis.

Generally Accepted Accounting Principles (GAAP)

Financial accounting statements prepared for external users must be prepared in accordance with generally accepted accounting principles (GAAP). External users must have some assurance that the reports have been prepared in accordance with some common set of ground rules. These common ground rules enhance comparability and help reduce fraud and misrepresentation, but they do not necessarily lead to the type of reports that would be most useful in internal decision making. For example, GAAP requires that land be stated at its historical cost on financial reports. However, if management is considering moving a store to a new location and then selling the land the store currently sits on, management would like to know the current market value of the land—a vital piece of information that is ignored under GAAP.

Managerial accounting is not bound by generally accepted accounting principles. Managers set their own ground rules concerning the content and form of internal reports. The only constraint is that the expected benefits from using the information should outweigh the costs of collecting, analyzing, and summarizing the data.

Managerial Accounting—Not Mandatory

Financial accounting is mandatory; that is, it must be done. Various outside parties such as the Ontario Securities Commission (OSC) and the tax authorities require periodic financial statements. Managerial accounting, on the other hand, is not mandatory. A company is completely free to do as much or as little as it wishes. There are no regulatory bodies or other outside agencies that specify what is to be done, or, for that matter, whether anything is to be done at all. Since managerial accounting is completely optional, the important question is always, "Is the information useful?" rather than, "Is the information required?"

EXPANDING ROLE OF MANAGERIAL ACCOUNTING

Managerial accounting has its roots in the Industrial Revolution of the nineteenth century. During that period, there was little need for elaborate financial accounting systems, since most firms were tightly controlled by a few owner-managers, and corporate borrowing was based largely on personal relationships. In contrast, managerial accounting was relatively sophisticated and provided the essential information needed to manage the mass production of textiles, steel, and other products.[1] After the turn of the century, several developments led to the emergence of financial accounting as the dominating force:

> The demand for financial reporting after 1900 burgeoned because of new pressures placed on corporate enterprises by capital markets, regulatory bodies, and federal taxation of income. But of all the new demands for corporate financial disclosure after 1900, the demand for financial reports audited by independent public accountants probably had the most profound and lasting influence on managerial cost accounting.
>
> . . . many firms needed to raise funds from increasingly widespread and detached suppliers of capital. To tap these vast reservoirs of outside capital, firms' managers had to supply audited financial reports. And because outside suppliers of capital relied on audited financial statements, independent accountants had a keen interest in establishing well-defined procedures for corporate financial reporting. The inventory costing procedures adopted by public accountants after the turn of the century had a profound effect on management accounting.[2]

The result of this "profound effect" was that for many years managerial accounting was subordinated to financial accounting requirements in most companies. Even today, some companies are far more concerned with inventory valuation and financial statement preparation than with information to be used for internal purposes. Fortunately, as product lines expanded and operations became more complex, forward-looking companies such as Du Pont saw a renewed need for management-oriented data that was separate from financial-oriented data.[3] Economic forces that have been unleashed in recent years have led to a renewed emphasis on the importance of management accounting.

THE CHANGING BUSINESS ENVIRONMENT

The last two decades have been a period of tremendous foment and change in the business environment. Competition in many industries has become worldwide in scope, and the pace of innovation in products and services has accelerated. This has been good news for consumers, because intensified competition has generally led to lower prices, higher quality, and more choices. However, the last two decades have been a period of wrenching change for many businesses and their employees. Many managers have learned that cherished ways of doing business no longer work and major changes must be made in how organizations are managed and in how work gets done. These changes are so great that some observers view them as a "second industrial revolution."

This revolution is having a profound effect on the practice of managerial accounting—as we will see throughout the rest of the book. First, however, it is necessary to have an appreciation of the ways in which organizations are transforming themselves to become more competitive. While many of the major improvement tools used by managers overlap, they can be classified into five major programs or approaches: just-in-time (JIT), total quality management (TQM), process reengineering, automation, and the theory of constraints (TOC). When properly implemented, these approaches can enhance quality, reduce cost, increase output, and eliminate delays in responding to customers. Each of these approaches is

---

[1]A. D. Chandler, *The Visible Hand: The Managerial Revolution in American Business* (Cambridge, Mass.: Harvard University Press, 1977).

[2]H. Thomas Johnson and Robert S. Kaplan, *Relevance Lost: The Rise and Fall of Management Accounting* (Boston, Mass.: Harvard Business School Press, 1987), pp. 129–30.

[3]H. Thomas Johnson, "Management Accounting in an Early Integrated Industrial: E. I. du Pont de Nemours Powder Company, 1903–1912," *Business History Review* (Summer 1975), pp. 186–87.

The just-in-time (JIT) approach to inventory control helped Toyota lower its overall costs of production. Those savings could then be passed on to consumers via lower prices, resulting in increased sales.

worthy of extended study, and indeed books have been written about each. For our purposes, we simply want to convey a general idea of what the approaches involve without getting into the details. Those details are best handled in operations management courses.

Just-in-Time (JIT)

OBJECTIVE 3

Explain the basic characteristics of just-in-time (JIT).

Manufacturing companies maintain three classes of inventories—*raw materials, work in process,* and *finished goods.* **Raw materials** are the materials that are used to make a product. **Work in process** inventories consist of units of product that are only partially complete and will require further work before they are ready for sale to a customer. **Finished goods** inventories consist of units of product that have been completed but have not yet been sold to customers.

Traditionally, companies have maintained large amounts of all three kinds of inventories to act as *buffers* so that operations can proceed smoothly even if there are unanticipated disruptions. Raw materials inventories provide insurance in case suppliers are late with deliveries. Work in process inventories are maintained in case a workstation is unable to operate due to a breakdown or other reason. Finished goods inventories are maintained to accommodate unanticipated fluctuations in demand.

While these inventories provide a buffer against unforeseen events, they have a cost. In addition to the money tied up in the inventory, experts argue that the presence of inventories actually encourages inefficient and sloppy work, results in too many defects, and dramatically increases the amount of time required to complete a product. None of this is obvious—if it were, companies would have long ago reduced their inventories. Managers at Toyota are credited with the insight that large inventories often create more problems than they solve, and Toyota pioneered the *just-in-time* approach. **Just-in-time (JIT)** is a production system in which materials are purchased and units are produced only as needed to meet actual customer demand. In a JIT system, inventories are reduced to the minimum and in some cases are zero. Firms such as Maax Inc., a Quebec maker of bathtubs and showers, have been able to reduce costs significantly by reducing inventory levels, and Canadian manufacturers have reduced their level of raw materials, goods in process and finished goods from $2.20 to $1.30 for every dollar of shipments.[4]

---

[4]Allan Freeman, "Why Firms Avoid Taking Inventory," *The Globe and Mail,* December 12, 1994, p. B1.

EXHIBIT 1-3   JIT Pull Approach to the Flow of Goods

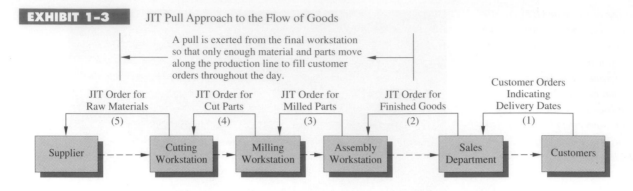

A pull is exerted from the final workstation so that only enough material and parts move along the production line to fill customer orders throughout the day.

| JIT Order for Raw Materials (5) | JIT Order for Cut Parts (4) | JIT Order for Milled Parts (3) | JIT Order for Finished Goods (2) | Customer Orders Indicating Delivery Dates (1) |

Supplier → Cutting Workstation → Milling Workstation → Assembly Workstation → Sales Department → Customers

The JIT Concept. Under ideal conditions, a company operating a just-in-time system would purchase *only* enough materials each day to meet that day's needs. Moreover, the company would have no goods still in process at the end of the day, and all goods completed during the day would be shipped immediately to customers. As this sequence suggests, "just-in-time" means that raw materials are received *just in time* to go into production, manufactured parts are completed *just in time* to be assembled into products, and products are completed *just in time* to be shipped to customers.

Although few companies have been able to reach this ideal, JIT has made it possible for many companies to reduce inventories to only a fraction of their previous levels. The result has been a substantial reduction in ordering and warehousing costs, and much more effective operations.

How does a company avoid a buildup of parts and materials at various workstations and still ensure a smooth flow of goods when JIT is in use? In a JIT environment, the flow of goods is controlled by a *pull* approach. The pull approach can be explained as follows: At the final assembly stage, a signal is sent to the preceding workstation as to the exact amount of parts and materials that will be needed *over the next few hours* to assemble products to fill customer orders, and *only* that amount of parts and materials is provided. The same signal is sent back through each preceding workstation so that a smooth flow of parts and materials is maintained with no inventory buildup at any point. Thus, all workstations respond to the pull exerted by the final assembly stage, which in turn responds to customer orders. As one worker explained, "Under a JIT system you don't produce anything, anywhere, for anybody unless they *ask* for it somewhere *down*stream. Inventories are an evil that we're taught to avoid." The pull approach to the manufacture of products is illustrated in Exhibit 1–3.

The pull approach described above can be contrasted to the *push* approach used in conventional manufacturing systems. In conventional systems, when a workstation completes its processing on a batch of units, the partially completed goods are "pushed" forward to the next workstation regardless of whether that workstation is ready to receive them. The result is an unintentional stockpiling of partially completed goods that may not be completed for days or even weeks. This ties up funds and also results in operating inefficiencies. For one thing, it becomes very difficult to keep track of where everything is when so much is scattered all over the factory floor.

With the "pull" approach final assembly can pull production each day according to changing market demand. Cimco, Canada's oldest and largest industrial refrigeration manufacturer, uses a system known as *kanban*. The purpose of this concept is to inform

the previous step in the manufacturing process to make a part. A card, label or tag accompanies each part with descriptive and identifying information such as the delivery location, reorder point on the shelf stack, and turnaround time negotiated between the users and producers in each stage of the process. Using such a system, Cimco was able to save more than $1 million by reducing inventory significantly below earlier levels and to reduce lead time by more than one-half the previous time.[5]

Another characteristic of conventional manufacturing systems is an emphasis on "keeping everyone busy" as an end in itself. This inevitably leads to excess inventories—particularly work in process inventories—for reasons that will be more fully explored in a later section on the theory of constraints. In JIT, the traditional emphasis on keeping everyone busy is abandoned in favour of producing only what customers actually want—even if that means some workers are idle.

Key Elements in a JIT System. Five key elements are usually involved in the successful operation of a JIT system. These elements include maintaining a limited number of highly qualified suppliers, improving the plant layout, reducing the setup time needed for production runs, striving for zero defects, and developing a flexible workforce.

Limited Number of Suppliers. To successfully operate a JIT system, a company must learn to rely on a few ultrareliable suppliers who are willing to make frequent deliveries in small lots. Rather than deliver a week's (or a month's) parts and materials at one time, suppliers must be willing to make deliveries as often as *several times a day,* and in the exact quantities specified by the buyer. Undependable suppliers who do not meet delivery schedules or who deliver defective units must be weeded out. Dependability is essential, since companies are highly vulnerable to any interruption in supply when JIT is in use. If a single part is unavailable, the entire assembly operation may have to be shut down. Consequently, suppliers are often required to complete a *supplier certification program* that demonstrates their ability to operate successfully in a JIT environment.

Improving Plant Layout. To properly implement JIT, a company typically must improve the manufacturing flow lines in its plant. A **flow line** is the physical path taken by a product as it moves through the manufacturing process from receipt of raw materials to shipment of the completed goods.

Traditionally, companies have designed their plant floors so that similar machines are grouped together. Such a functional layout results in all drill presses in one place, all lathes in another place, and so forth. This approach to plant layout requires that work in process be moved from one group of machines to another—frequently across the plant or even to another building. The result is extensive material-handling costs, large work in process inventories, and unnecessary delays.

In a JIT system, all machines needed to make a particular product are often brought together in one location. This approach to plant layout creates an individual "mini" factory for each separate product, frequently referred to as a **focused factory** or as a "factory within a factory." The flow line for a product can be straight, as shown earlier in Exhibit 1–3, or it can be in a U-shaped configuration as shown in Exhibit 1–4. The key point is that all machines in a product flow line are tightly grouped together so that partially completed units are not shifted from place to place all over the factory. *Manufacturing cells*

---

[5]Richard Kitney, "Production Systems with Pull," *CMA Magazine* (July–August 1994), pp. 21–24.

EXHIBIT 1-4

Plant Layout in a JIT System

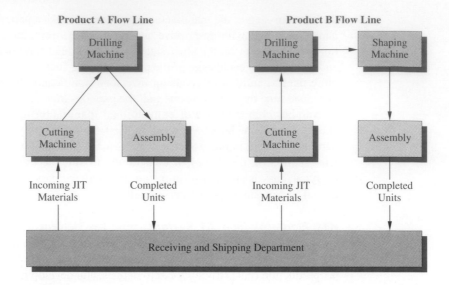

Product A Flow Line

Drilling Machine

Cutting Machine

Assembly

Incoming JIT Materials

Completed Units

Product B Flow Line

Drilling Machine

Shaping Machine

Cutting Machine

Assembly

Incoming JIT Materials

Completed Units

Receiving and Shipping Department

are also often part of a JIT product flow line. In a **cell**, a single worker operates several machines. An example of a cell is illustrated in Exhibit 1–5.

The focused factory approach allows workers to focus all of their efforts on a product from start to finish and minimizes handling and moving. After one large manufacturing company rearranged its plant layout and organized its products into individual flow lines, the company determined that the distance travelled by one product had been decreased from 5 kilometres to slightly more than 90 metres. Apart from reductions in handling, this more compact layout makes it much easier to keep track of where a particular job is in the production process.

As the accompanying focus box illustrates, an improved plant layout can dramatically increase **throughput,** which is the total volume of production through a facility during a period, and it can dramatically reduce **throughput time** (also known as **cycle time**), which is the time required to make a product.

EXHIBIT 1-5

Example of a Manufacturing Cell

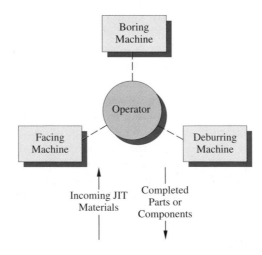

Boring Machine

Operator

Facing Machine

Deburring Machine

Incoming JIT Materials

Completed Parts or Components

American Standard uses cell manufacturing to cut inventories and reduce manufacturing time. At its plant in Leeds, England, it used to take as much as three weeks to manufacture a vacuum pump and another week to process the paperwork for an order. Therefore, customers had to place orders a month in advance. "Today Leeds . . . has switched to manufacturing cells that do everything from lathing to assembly in quick sequence. The result is a breakthrough in speed. Manufacturing a pump now takes just six minutes."[6]

Reduced Setup Time.   **Setups** involve activities—such as moving materials, changing machine settings, setting up equipment, and running tests—that must be performed whenever production is switched over from making one type of item to another. For example, it may not be a simple matter to switch over from making 1/2-inch brass screws to making 3/4-inch brass screws on a typical manually controlled milling machine. Many preparatory steps must be performed, and these steps can take hours. Because of the time and expense involved in such setups, many managers believe setups should be avoided and therefore items should be produced in large batches. For example, one batch of 400 units requires only one setup, whereas four batches of 100 units each would require four setups. The problem with big batches is that they create large amounts of inventory that must wait for days, weeks, or even months before further processing at the next workstation or before they are sold.

One advantage of a dedicated flow line, such as the one illustrated in Exhibit 1–4, is that it requires fewer setups. If equipment is dedicated to a single product or a single product line, then setups are largely eliminated and products can be produced in any batch size desired. Even when dedicated flow lines are not used, it is often possible to slash setup time by using techniques such as *single-minute-exchange-of-dies.* A die is a device used for cutting out, forming, or stamping material. For example, a die is used to produce the stamped metal door panels on an automobile. A die must be changed when it wears out or when production is switched to a different product. This changeover can be time-consuming. The goal with **single-minute-exchange-of-dies** is to reduce the amount of time required to change a die to a minute or less. This can be done by simple techniques such as doing as much of the changeover work in advance as possible rather than waiting until production is shut down.[7] When such techniques are followed, unproductive setup time can be made neglible and batch sizes can be very small.

Smaller batches reduce the level of inventories, make it easier to respond quickly to the market, reduce cycle times, and generally make it much easier to spot manufacturing problems before they result in a large number of defective units.

Zero Defects and JIT.   Defective units create big problems in a JIT environment. If there is a defective unit in a completed order, the company must ship the order with less than the promised quantity or it must restart the whole production process to make just one unit. At minimum, this creates a delay in shipping the order and may generate a ripple effect that delays other orders. For this and other reasons, defects cannot be tolerated in a JIT system. Companies that are deeply involved in JIT tend to become zealously

[6]Shawn Tully, "Raiding a Company's Hidden Cash," *Fortune* (August 22, 1994), pp. 82–87.
[7]Shigeo Shingo and Alan Robinson, *Modern Approaches to Manufacturing Improvement: The Shingo System* (Cambridge, Mass.: Productivity Press, 1990).

committed to a goal of *zero defects*. Even though it may be next to impossible to attain the zero defect goal, companies have found that they can come very close. For example, Motorola now measures its defects in terms of the number of defects per *billion* units of product.

In a traditional company, parts and materials are inspected for defects when they are received from suppliers, and quality inspectors inspect units as they progress along the production line. In a JIT system, the company's suppliers are responsible for the quality of incoming parts and materials. And instead of using quality inspectors, the company's production workers are directly responsible for spotting defective units. This is sometimes referred to as *continuous monitoring*. A worker who discovers a defect is supposed to punch an alarm button that stops the production flow line and sets off flashing lights. Supervisors and other workers then descend on the workstation to determine the cause of the defect and correct it before any further defective units are produced. This procedure ensures that problems are quickly identified and corrected, but it does require that defects are rare—otherwise there would be constant disruptions to the production process.

Flexible Workforce.   Workers on a JIT line must be multiskilled and flexible. Workers assigned to a particular JIT product flow line are often expected to operate all of the equipment on the line. Moreover, workers are expected to perform minor repairs and do maintenance work when they would otherwise be idle. In contrast, on a conventional assembly line a worker performs a single task all the time every day and all maintenance work is done by a specialized maintenance crew.

The Shingo Prize for Excellence in Manufacturing recognizes companies that have demonstrated outstanding achievements in manufacturing processes, quality enhancement, productivity improvement and customer satisfaction. One of the six winners of the 1996 Shingo award is Johnson Controls of Orangeville, Ontario. This company has successfully implemented what is termed "Total Predictive Maintenance" whereby the company is committed to zero down-time. Their success has been measured by the 94% maintenance team time allocated to proactive (as opposed to reactive) projects.[8]

Benefits of a JIT System.   Many companies—large and small—have employed JIT with great success. JIT firms in Canada are represented in a wide variety of industries including aerospace, automotive, electronic, publishing, and tool and die. Some well-known companies using JIT are Ford Motor Company in its St. Thomas, Ontario, plant; Polycom Industries of Guelph, Ontario, a major supplier of Ford bumpers; Magna International; Fred Deeley Imports, the Canadian distributor for Harley Davidson; and Northern Telecom in Calgary, Alberta. The main benefits of JIT are the following:

1. Working capital is bolstered by the recovery of funds that were tied up in inventories.

2. Areas previously used to store inventories are made available for other, more productive uses.

3. Throughput time is reduced, resulting in greater potential output and quicker response to customers.

4. Defect rates are reduced, resulting in less waste and greater customer satisfaction.

[8]David Richey, *Journal for Quality and Participation* (July–August 1996), pp. 28–31.

As a result of benefits such as those cited above, more companies are embracing JIT each year. Most companies find, however, that simply reducing inventories is not enough. To remain competitive in an ever changing and ever more competitive business environment, companies must strive for *continuous improvement.* For example, Magna International has made significant improvements in its Milton plant that are due to a strong commitment to continuous improvement. The Milton plant was experiencing machine down-time in the late 1980s. The plant now runs three shifts a day, six days a week making parts for Chrysler and Ford. Minimal inventory is kept on-site (i.e., one hour's worth) and assembly lines are based on flexible manufacturing.[9]

Total Quality Management (TQM)

OBJECTIVE 4

Describe the total quality management (TQM) approach to continuous improvement.

The most popular approach to continuous improvement is known as *total quality management.* There are two major characteristics of **total quality management (TQM):** (1) a focus on serving customers and (2) systematic problem solving using teams made up of front-line workers. A variety of specific tools are available to aid teams in their problem solving. One of these tools, **benchmarking,** involves studying organizations that are among the best in the world at performing a particular task. For example, when Xerox wanted to improve its procedures for filling customer orders, it studied how mail-order company L. L. Bean processes its customer orders. Another example of benchmarking is provided by Chrysler Canada in Windsor, Ontario. Chrysler's goal is to be the world's "premier" maker of cars and trucks. In essence, Chrysler has set a series of benchmarks to meet. For example, in terms of manufacturing quality Chrysler wants to meet the standard set by Toyota. It wants its engineering to be the calibre displayed by Mercedes-Benz AG. Benchmarking was used by Chrysler when it designed the successful Neon sub-compact a few years ago. Chrysler took a close look at the Honda Civic as the standard it wanted to meet or surpass with the Neon.[10]

The Plan-Do-Check-Act Cycle.   Perhaps the most important and pervasive TQM problem-solving tool is the *plan-do-check-act (PDCA) cycle,* which is also referred to as the Deming Wheel.[11] The **plan-do-check-act cycle** is a systematic, fact-based approach to continuous improvement. The basic elements of the PDCA cycle are illustrated in Exhibit 1–6. Notice that the PDCA cycle basically applies the scientific method to problem solving. In the Plan phase, the problem-solving team analyzes data to identify possible causes for the problem and then proposes a solution. In the Do phase, an experiment is conducted. In the Check phase, the results of the experiment are analyzed. And in the Act phase, if the results of the experiment are favourable, the plan is implemented. If the results of the experiment are not favourable, the team goes back to the original data and starts all over again.

An Example of TQM in Practice.   Sterling Chemicals, Inc., a producer of basic industrial chemicals, provides a good example of the use of TQM.[12] Among many other problems, the company had been plagued by pump failures. In one year, a particular type

---

[9]"Magna's Success More Than the Sum of Its Parts," *The Globe and Mail Metro Edition,* October 21, 1994, pp. B1, B6.

[10]"Chrysler Aims to Be #1 by Turn of Century," *The Financial Post,* February 17/19, 1996, p. A14.

[11]Dr. W. Edwards Deming, a pioneer in TQM, introduced many of the elements of TQM to Japanese industry after World War II. TQM was further refined and developed at Japanese companies such as Toyota.

[12]The information about Sterling Chemicals in this section was taken from Karen Hopper Wruck and Michael C. Jensen, "Science, Specific Knowledge, and Total Quality Management," *Journal of Accounting and Economics* 18 (1994), pp. 247–87. The quotations are from pages 260 and 261 of this article and are used with permission.

EXHIBIT 1-6

The Plan-Do-Check-
Act Cycle

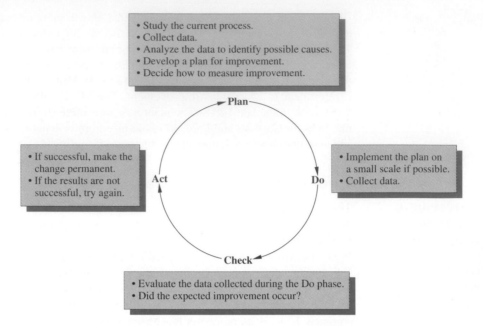

of pump failed 22 times at an average cost of about $10,000 per failure. The company first tried to solve the problem using a traditional, non-TQM approach. A committee of "experts"—in this case engineers and manufacturing supervisors—was appointed to solve the problem. A manager at Sterling Chemicals describes the results:

> This team immediately concluded that each of the 22 pump failures . . . was due to a special or one-of-a-kind cause. There was some finger pointing by team members trying to assign blame. Maintenance engineers claimed that production personnel didn't know how to operate the pumps, and production supervisors blamed maintenance people for poor repair work.

One year later, a TQM team was formed to tackle the same pump failure problem. The team consisted primarily of hourly workers with hands-on experience working with the pumps. A Sterling Chemicals' manager describes what happened:

> Based on their knowledge and the data they had collected, the team brainstormed and listed 57 theories that potentially explained the high pump failure rates. The team reviewed and edited the brainstorming list, testing each theory against the data. Through this process, they reduced the brainstorming list to four potential causes of failure: i) the pump seal installation procedure, ii) pump suction pressure, iii) excessive pump vibration, and iv) missing or broken equipment upstream from the pump.
>
> They then experimented to determine which of these causes were important determinants of pump failure. Testing the pump suction theory rejected it as a cause of failure. The broken or missing equipment theory was eliminated through inspection. Since testing the two remaining theories required making changes and observing the results of those changes over time, the team developed recommendations to address [them] both . . . The recommendations were implemented . . . Since then we have had no pump failures.

Notice how the plan-do-check-act cycle was used to solve this pump failure problem. Instead of bickering over who was responsible for the problem, the team began by collecting data. They then hypothesized a number of possible causes for the problem, and these hypotheses were checked against the data. Perhaps the most important feature of TQM is that "it improves productivity by encouraging the use of science in decision making and discouraging counterproductive defensive behaviour."[13]

TQM Is Widely Used.   Thousands of organizations have been involved in TQM.[14] Some of the more well-known companies are American Express, Bell Canada Enterprises, Corning, Dun & Bradstreet, Ericsson of Sweden, General Electric, Hewlett Packard Canada, Hospital Corporation of America, Hydro Quebec, IBM, Johnson & Johnson, KLM Royal Dutch Airlines, LTV, Milliken & Company, Northern Telecom, Phillips of the Netherlands, 3M, Westinghouse Electric, and Xerox. As this list illustrates, TQM is international in scope and is not confined to manufacturing. Indeed, a survey by the American Hospital Association of 3,300 hospitals found that 69% have launched quality-improvement programs. For example, Intermountain Healthcare's LDS Hospital in Salt Lake City is using total quality management techniques to reduce infection rates among surgery patients and the toxic side effects of chemotherapy.[15]

An important element of TQM is its focus on the customer. The accounting and consulting firm KPMG Peat Marwick periodically surveys its customers' satisfaction with its services. The firm's CEO points out that it costs four times as much to gain a new customer as to keep an old customer, and the most satisfied customers are generally the most profitable customers for the firm. "For each complaint that you hear, there are fifty you don't hear. If you don't monitor clients' satisfaction, you may find out about their dissatisfaction as they walk out the door."[16]

In summary, TQM provides tools and techniques for continuous improvement based on facts and analysis and, if properly implemented, avoids counterproductive organizational infighting.

FOCUS ON CURRENT PRACTICE

TQM is not just a big company phenomenon. Penril DataComm is a Maryland designer and producer of data communications equipment. Before embarking on TQM, defect rates were so high that the company was reworking or scrapping one-third of everything it made. Applying TQM techniques resulted in an 81% decrease in defects, an 83% decrease in failures in the first three months of use, and a 73% decrease in first-year warranty repairs. TQM is credited with taking the company "from the brink of financial disaster" to excellent financial health.[17]

Process Reengineering

OBJECTIVE 5

Explain the basic ideas underlying process reengineering.

Process reengineering is a more radical approach to improvement than TQM. Instead of tweaking the existing system in a series of incremental improvements, in **process reengineering** a *business process* is diagrammed in detail, questioned, and then completely redesigned in order to eliminate unnecessary steps, to reduce opportunities for errors, and

---

[13]Wruck and Jensen, "Science, Specific Knowledge, and Total Quality Management," p. 247.

[14]There are several management programs that are closely related to TQM. One is called *cost management,* which is concerned with the effective use of resources to create, market, and distribute products and services to customers.

[15]Ron Wilson, "Excising Waste: Health-Care Providers Try Industrial Tactics in U.S. to Cut Costs," *The Wall Street Journal Europe,* November 10, 1993, pp. 1, 8.

[16]Jon C. Madonna, "A Service Company Measures, Monitors and Improves Quality," *Leadership and Empowerment for Total Quality,* The Conference Board Report No. 992 (New York, 1992), pp. 9–11.

[17]"Poor Quality Nearly Short Circuits Electronics Company," *Productivity* (February 1993), pp. 1–3.

to reduce costs. A **business process** is any series of steps that are followed in order to carry out some task in a business. For example, the steps followed to make a large pineapple and bacon pizza at Godfather's Pizza are a business process. The steps followed by your bank when you deposit a cheque are a business process. While process reengineering is similar in some respects to TQM, its proponents view it as a more sweeping approach to change. One difference is that while TQM emphasizes a team approach involving people who work directly in the processes, process reengineering is more likely to be imposed from above and to use outside consultants.

Process reengineering focuses on *simplification* and *elimination of wasted effort.* A central idea of process reengineering is that *all activities that do not add value to a product or service should be eliminated.* Activities that do not add value to a product or service are known as **non-value-added activities.** For example, moving large batches of work in process from one workstation to another is a non-value-added activity that can be eliminated by redesigning the factory layout as discussed earlier in the section on JIT. To some degree, JIT involves process reengineering as does TQM. These management approaches often overlap.[18]

Process reengineering has been used by many companies to deal with a wide variety of problems. For example, the EMI Records Group was having difficulty filling orders for its most popular CDs. Retailers and recording stars were rebelling —it took the company as much as 20 days to deliver a big order for a hit CD, and then nearly 20% of the order would be missing. Small, incremental improvements would not be enough, so the company reengineered its entire distribution process with dramatic effects on on-time

---

FOCUS ON
CURRENT PRACTICE

Widespread cost-realignment, downsizing, process reengineering, total quality management initiatives, and other advanced management accounting practices reflect a new emphasis on cost-competitiveness and improving customer service. Referring to the restructuring of Bell Canada into BCE Inc., Canada's largest telco holding company, Mr. Leonard van der Heyden, VP of human resources and corporate services of Bell Canada International has said:

> The biggest challenge within the BCE organization at the time of its creation was that, although we really operated with about 50 people, the organization had a 50,000-employee mentality because it came out of Bell Canada. With the Bell Canada culture came the expectations of processes and procedures that were already in place. In order to deal with the new realities, we had to be able to innovate, to be pro-active in an environment that was changing every day. That's also what is important today. However, today our tactical and operational priorities are on value-added activities and on ensuring that we have a handle on our business strategy and linkages. Our focus is on marketing, quality customer service, cost containment and absolute cost reduction. The people at Bell Canada are no longer prescribing what is good for the customer. They are responding innovatively to the needs of the customer.[19]

---

[18]Activity-based costing and activity-based management, both of which are discussed in Chapter 5, can be helpful in identifying areas in the company that could benefit from process reengineering.
[19] "CMAs in Telecommunications: The Challenge Ahead," *CMA Magazine* (February 1996) pp. 24–26.

delivery and order fill rates.[20] Another example of reengineering is provided by Petro-Canada which is continually improving its refining operations, maintenance procedures and management of supply in its strategy to be a low-cost producer of quality refined petroleum products and services. Petro-Canada's 1996 annual report reveals that the refining segment garnered the full benefit of a reengineering initiative, resulting in estimated annual before-tax expense and cost of sale savings of $58 million.

An Example of Process Reengineering.   Racing Strollers Inc., of Yakima, Washington, provides an interesting illustration of process reengineering at work. The company originated the three-wheeled stroller for joggers in 1984.[21] While the company was still the market leader in 1995, there was growing concern about losing ground to competitors—some of whom were selling strollers for half the price charged by Racing Strollers. Mary Baechler, the president of Racing Strollers, felt that a radical approach such as process reengineering was required to keep Racing Strollers competitive.

Mary Baechler describes the results of using process reengineering on a very simple task—receiving orders over the fax machine:

> Take faxes. Pretty simple, right? Not at our place! We had 15 steps just to get a fax from the fax machine to the computers, where an order would be entered into our accounting program. (Laugh all you want, but you probably do something similar at your place.) A fax would come in. We'd log it into a fax book. (Someone once told us to do that for legal reasons.) A copy of each fax would be saved for me. (Someone once told me I should glance at all faxes.) It all added up to those 15 steps. Only after a lot of work did we reduce the number to 4.
>
> That was just one area, and it's typical of what we found throughout the company. If you were to look at all those steps for a fax, every one originally had a purpose. The process was very much like a tribal superstition, though, since the original reason for each step had disappeared long ago. What was even worse was that no one could remember who started many of the steps. I had no idea why we were doing them, and everybody else thought they were what I wanted done!

Note that Racing Strollers is a comparatively young company. The situation is typically much worse at older companies—a step may have been introduced into a process many decades ago to handle a problem that has long since disappeared and no one can remember.

The Problem of Employee Morale.   A recurrent problem in process reengineering is employee resistance. The cause of much of this resistance is the fear that people may lose their jobs. Workers reason that if process reengineering succeeds in eliminating non-value-added activities, there will be less work to do and management may be tempted to reduce the payroll. Process reengineering, if carried out insensitively and without regard to such fears, can undermine morale and will ultimately fail to improve the bottom line (i.e., profits). As with other improvement projects, employees must be convinced that the end result of the improvement will be more secure, rather than less secure, jobs. Real improvement can have this effect if management uses the improvement to generate more business rather than to cut the workforce. If by improving processes the company is able

---

[20]Glenn Rifkin, "EMI: Technology Brings the Music Giant a Whole New Spin," *Forbes ASAP* (February 27, 1995), pp. 32–38.
[21]The information in this section about Racing Strollers Inc., was taken from an article by Mary Baechler. Reprinted with permission, *Inc.* magazine, May 1995. Copyright 1995 by Goldhirsh Group, Inc., 38 Commercial Wharf, Boston, MA 02110.

to produce a better product at lower cost, the company will have the competitive strength to prosper. A prosperous company is a much more secure employer than a company that is in trouble.

Automation

Another approach to radical improvement is automation. While automation is expensive, there can be substantial benefits in the form of dramatic reductions in setup time, greater flexibility, reductions in defects, and a higher rate of output. Automation commonly involves **numerically controlled (NC) machines.** The functions of NC machines are controlled by a computer that has been programmed to guide the equipment through all the steps necessary to complete some task. With automation, dramatic reductions in setup time are possible because the setup consists mainly of just changing computer programs. Thus, a company can move from production of one product to another very quickly and avoid the necessity of large batches.

Even greater efficiency can be achieved when the NC machines on a production flow line are linked together with an automated material-handling system and the flows between NC machines are controlled by a central computer. Such an arrangement is called a **flexible manufacturing system (FMS).** With FMS, a single flow line becomes capable of quickly producing many different products in batch sizes as small as a single unit. This flexibility can be a powerful competitive advantage.

The Theory of Constraints (TOC)

OBJECTIVE 6
Describe how the theory of constraints (TOC) can be used to focus improvement efforts.

Air Canada is constrained by the number of available gates. Delays tie up gates and result in fewer flights and frustrated customers.

A **constraint** is anything that prevents you from getting more of what you want. Every individual and every organization faces at least one constraint, so it is not difficult to find examples of constraints. You may not have enough time to study thoroughly for every subject *and* go out with your friends on the weekend, so time is your constraint. Air Canada has only a limited number of loading gates available at its busy Toronto hub, so its constraint is loading gates. Vail Resorts has only a limited amount of land to develop as homesites and commercial lots at its ski areas, so its constraint is land.

Since a constraint prevents you from getting more of what you want, the **theory of constraints (TOC)** maintains that effectively managing the constraint is a key to success. For example, Air Canada should concentrate on quickly turning around its aircraft on the ground so that they do not tie up precious gates. Delays on the ground decrease the number of flights that can be flown out of Toronto and therefore result in lost business.

EXHIBIT 1-7

A Flowchart of an
Aluminum Tennis
Racket Production
Line

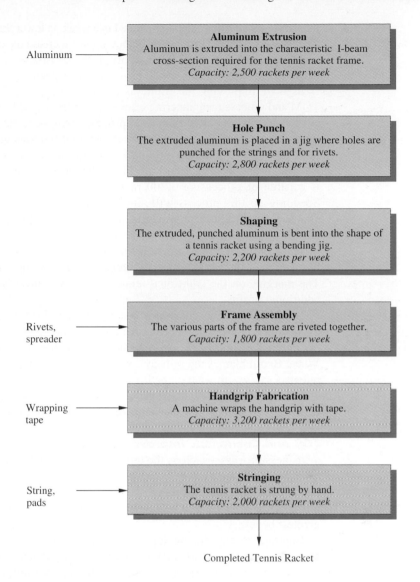

Aluminum Extrusion
Aluminum is extruded into the characteristic I-beam
cross-section required for the tennis racket frame.
Capacity: 2,500 rackets per week

Aluminum →

Hole Punch
The extruded aluminum is placed in a jig where holes are
punched for the strings and for rivets.
Capacity: 2,800 rackets per week

Shaping
The extruded, punched aluminum is bent into the shape of
a tennis racket using a bending jig.
Capacity: 2,200 rackets per week

Frame Assembly
The various parts of the frame are riveted together.
Capacity: 1,800 rackets per week

Rivets,
spreader →

Handgrip Fabrication
A machine wraps the handgrip with tape.
Capacity: 3,200 rackets per week

Wrapping
tape →

Stringing
The tennis racket is strung by hand.
Capacity: 2,000 rackets per week

String,
pads →

Completed Tennis Racket

An Example of TOC. A simple example will be used to illustrate the role of a constraint. ProSport Equipment, Inc., manufactures aluminum tennis rackets on the production flow line that is sketched in Exhibit 1–7. Each workstation has a particular capacity that, in this case, may be stated in terms of the maximum number of rackets processed in a week. For example, the aluminum extruding workstation can extrude enough aluminum each week to build as many as 2,500 tennis rackets.

Suppose the company could sell as many as 1,900 rackets each week. Is there a production constraint, and if so, where is it? Because the frame assembly workstation can only process 1,800 rackets per week and demand is 1,900 rackets, it is the constraint.[22] Frame assembly is the constraint, or *bottleneck,* in this situation, since its capacity, in terms of the

---

[22]If demand was less than 1,800 tennis rackets per week, there would not be a production constraint. However, there would still be a constraint of some type. For example, the company's constraint might be a poor logistical system that limits how many tennis rackets can be distributed in a timely fashion to retailers. All businesses that are organized to make a profit face at least one constraint.

number of rackets that can be processed in a week, is lower than for any other workstation. If the company wants to increase its output, it must increase the capacity of this workstation.

There are several ways the capacity of the constraint can be increased. These will be discussed in Chapter 13. As one example, the capacity of the frame assembly can be increased by improving the frame assembly process so that it requires less time. Thus, TQM and process reengineering efforts can be leveraged by targeting the constraint.

Consider what would happen if process reengineering were used to improve one of the *nonconstraints*. Suppose, for example, that the handgrip fabrication process is improved so that it requires only half as much time. Will this increase profits? The answer is "Probably not." Handgrip fabrication already has plenty of excess capacity —it is capable of processing 3,200 rackets per week, but demand is only 1,900 rackets. Speeding up this process will simply create more excess capacity. Unless resources can now be shifted from handgrip fabrication to the constraint area (frame assembly) or unless spending can be cut in the handgrip fabrication work centre, there will be no increase in profits. In contrast, if the processing time were cut in half in frame assembly, which is the constraint, the company could produce and sell more tennis rackets. The margins on the additional tennis rackets would go straight to the bottom line as additional profits.

Bottlenecks may occur in any business sector. For Western Canadian farmers, for example, the bottleneck has been in the transportation part of their operations, costing farmers millions of dollars of lost revenue plus penalties for shipping delays. The Canadian Wheat Board blames the railways, saying they don't give wheat a high priority while the railways say severe winter weather and other factors have been the problem.[23] In the pulp and paper industry the bottlenecks are usually in the drying operations and the industry is currently researching new drying methods for their production facilities.[24]

TOC and Continuous Improvement.   In TOC, an analogy is often drawn between a business process—such as the tennis racket production line—and a chain. If you want to increase the strength of a chain, what is the most effective way to do this? Should you concentrate your efforts on strengthening the strongest link, the largest link, all the links, or the weakest link? Clearly, focusing effort on the weakest link will bring the greatest benefit.

Continuing with this analogy, the procedure to follow in strengthening the chain is straightforward. First, identify the weakest link, which is the constraint. Second, don't place a greater strain on the system than the weakest link can handle. Third, concentrate improvement efforts on strengthening the weakest link. Fourth, if the improvement efforts are successful, eventually the weakest link will improve to the point where it is no longer the weakest link. At this point, the new weakest link (i.e., the new constraint) must be identified, and improvement efforts must be shifted over to that link. This simple sequential process provides a powerful strategy for continuous improvement. The TOC approach is a perfect complement to TQM and process reengineering—it focuses improvement efforts where they are likely to be most effective.

[23]"Deregulation Answer to Grain Shipment Woes: CPR's Ritchie," *The Financial Post*, February 22/24, 1997.
[24]J. F. Bond, V. G. Gomes, and W. J. Douglas, "Computer Simulation of Drying Paper by Multiple Techniques," *Pulp & Paper Canada* (December 1996) pp. 110–12.

The Lessines plant of Baxter International makes medical products such as sterile bags. The management of the plant is acutely aware of the necessity to actively manage its constraints. For example, when materials are a constraint, management may go to a secondary vendor and purchase materials at a higher cost than normal. When a machine is the constraint, a weekend shift is often added on the machine. If a particular machine is chronically the constraint and management has exhausted the possibilities of using it more effectively, then additional capacity is purchased. For example, when the constraint was the plastic extruding machines, a new extruding machine was ordered. However, even before the machine arrived, management had determined that the constraint would shift to the blenders once the new extruding capacity was added. Therefore, a new blender was already being planned. By thinking ahead and focusing on the constraints, management is able to increase the plant's real capacity at the lowest possible cost.[25]

Due to lower tariffs, improved transportation, and a more sophisticated market, many businesses now compete on an international scale. The manager of a company must be aware of not only local competition but also businesses throughout the world.

INTERNATIONAL COMPETITION

OBJECTIVE 7
Discuss the impact of international competition on businesses and on managerial accounting.

Over the last several decades, competition has become worldwide in many industries. This has been caused by reductions in tariffs, quotas, and other barriers to free trade; improvements in global transportation systems; and increasing sophistication in international markets. These factors work together to reduce the costs of conducting international trade and make it possible for foreign companies to compete on a more equal footing with local firms.

The movement toward freer trade has been most dramatic in the European Community (EC). The EC has grown from a very small free-trade zone involving a few basic commodities such as coal and steel in the late 1950s to a free-trade zone of over a dozen European nations involving almost unlimited movement of goods and services

[25]Eric Noreen, Debra Smith, and James Mackey, *The Theory of Constraints and Its Implications for Management Accounting* (Montvale, N.J.: The IMA Foundation for Applied Research, Inc., 1995), p. 67.

across national borders. This vast, largely unified market has a population of over 370 million, as compared with 261 million in the United States and 125 million in Japan. The new NAFTA trading block, which consists of Canada, the United States, and Mexico, has a combined population in excess of 380 million.

Such reductions in trade barriers have made it easier for agile and aggressive companies to expand outside of their home markets. As a result, very few firms can afford to be complacent. A company may be very successful today in its local market relative to its local competitors, but tomorrow the competition may come from halfway around the globe. As a matter of survival, even firms that are presently doing very well in their home markets must become world-class competitors. On the bright side, the freer international movement of goods and services presents tremendous export opportunities for those companies that can transform themselves into world-class competitors. From the standpoint of consumers, heightened competition promises an even greater variety of goods, at higher quality and lower prices.

What are the implications for managerial accounting of increased global competition? It would be very difficult for a firm to become world class if it plans, directs, and controls its operations and makes decisions using a second-class management accounting system. An excellent management accounting system will not by itself guarantee success, but a poor management accounting system can stymie the best efforts of people in an organization to make the firm truly competitive.

Throughout this text we will highlight the differences between obsolete management accounting systems that get in the way of success and well-designed management accounting systems that can enhance a firm's performance. It is noteworthy that elements of well-designed management accounting systems have originated in many countries. More and more, managerial accounting has become a discipline that is worldwide in scope.

FOCUS ON
CURRENT PRACTICE

Global competition sometimes comes from unexpected sources. Companies in the former Soviet bloc in Central and Eastern Europe are rapidly raising the quality of their products to Western standards and are beginning to provide stiff competition. The Hungarian company Petofi Printing & Packaging Co., a maker of cardboard boxes, wrappers, and other containers, provides a good example. "Only a few years ago, Petofi's employees drank beer at work. Flies buzzing in open windows got stuck in the paint and pressed into the paperboard. Containers were delivered in the wrong colours and sizes." Under the Communist system, the company's customers didn't dare complain, since there was no other source for their packaging needs.

The company was privatized after the fall of the Soviet system, and the company "began overhauling itself, leapfrogging Western companies with state-of-the-art machinery. It whipped its workforce into shape with a combination of inducements and threats." Now, most of its products are exported. PepsiCo, for example, buys Petofi wrappers for Cheetos and Ruffles snacks and claims that Petofi's quality compares very favourably with Western suppliers. PepsiCo's buyer states, "They have filled the gap between competitive quality and best cost."[26]

---

[26]Dana Milbank, "New Competitor: East Europe's Industry Is Raising Its Quality and Taking on West," *The Wall Street Journal,* September 21, 1994, pp. A1, A7.

ORGANIZATIONAL STRUCTURE

Since organizations are made up of people, management must accomplish its objectives by working *through* people. Presidents of companies like Good Vibrations, Inc., could not possibly execute all of their company's strategies alone; they must rely on other people. This is done by creating an organizational structure that permits *decentralization* of management responsibilities.

Decentralization

Decentralization means the delegation of decision-making authority throughout an organization by allowing managers at various operating levels the authority to make decisions relating to their area of responsibility. Some organizations are more decentralized than others. Because of Good Vibrations, Inc.'s geographic dispersion and the peculiarities of local markets, the company is highly decentralized.

Good Vibrations, Inc.'s president (also called chief executive officer or CEO) sets the broad strategy for the company and makes major strategic decisions such as opening stores in new markets, but much of the remaining decision-making authority is delegated to managers on various levels throughout the organization. These levels are as follows: The company has a number of retail stores, each of which has a store manager as well as a separate manager for each section such as international rock and classical/jazz. In addition, the company has a central purchasing department, a treasurer's office, a personnel department, and an accounting department. The organizational structure of the company is depicted in Exhibit 1–8.

The arrangement of boxes shown in Exhibit 1–8 is called an **organization chart.** The purpose of an organization chart is to show how responsibility has been divided among managers and to show formal lines of reporting and communication, or *chain of command.* Each box depicts an area of management responsibility, and the lines between the boxes show the lines of formal authority between managers. The chart tells us, for example, that the store managers are responsible to the operations vice president. In turn, the latter is responsible to the company president, who in turn is responsible to the board of directors. Following the lines of authority and communication on the organization chart, we can see that the manager of the Hong Kong store would ordinarily report to the operations vice president rather than directly to the president of the company.

Informal relationships and channels of communication often develop outside the formal reporting relationships on the organization chart as a result of personal contacts between managers. The informal structure does not appear on the organization chart, but it is often vital to effective operations.

Line and Staff Relationships

An organization chart also depicts *line* and *staff* positions in an organization. A person in a **line** position is *directly* involved in achieving the basic objectives of the organization. A person in a **staff** position, by contrast, is only *indirectly* involved in achieving those basic objectives. Staff positions *support* or provide assistance to line positions or other parts of the organization, but they do not have direct authority over line positions. Refer again to the organization chart in Exhibit 1–8. Since the basic objective of Good Vibrations, Inc., is to sell recorded music at a profit, those managers whose areas of responsibility are directly related to the sales effort occupy line positions. These positions, which are shown in a darker colour in the exhibit, include the managers of the various music departments in each store, the store managers, the operations vice president, and members of top management.

EXHIBIT 1-8   Organizational Chart, Good Vibrations, Inc.

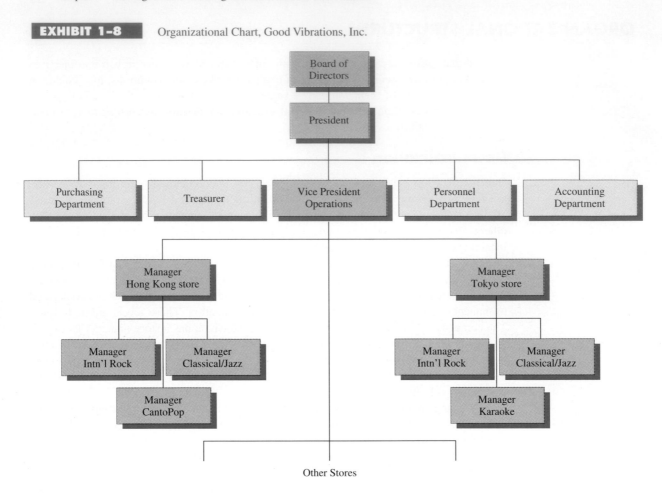

By contrast, the manager of the central purchasing department occupies a staff position, since the only function of the purchasing department is to support and serve the line departments by doing their purchasing for them. Good Vibrations, Inc.'s organization chart shows only four staff departments —one of which is the accounting department.

The Controller

OBJECTIVE 8
Describe the role the controller plays in a decentralized organization.

As previously mentioned, in Canada the manager in charge of the accounting department is usually known as the *controller*. The controller is the member of the top-management team who is given the responsibility of providing relevant and timely data to support planning and control activities and of preparing financial statements for external users.

The organization of a typical controller's office is shown in Exhibit 1–9. From that organization chart we see that the controller's office combines a number of important functions including, quite often, management of the company's computer services. Because of the broad experience gained by the controller in analyzing all parts of a company's operations and by working with managers throughout the company, it is not unusual for the controller's office to be a stepping-stone to the top position in a company.

EXHIBIT 1-9   Organization of the Controller's Office

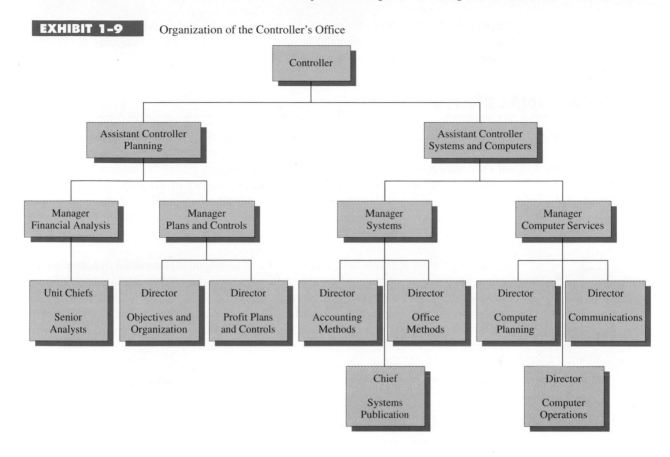

THE PROFESSIONAL MANAGEMENT ACCOUNTANT

Three professional accounting groups in Canada have members who make up the ranks of management acountants. CGAs, CAs, and CMAs represent designations used by professional accountants who belong to provincial societies or associations known as *Certified General Accountants Associations, Institutes (Ordré) of Chartered Accountants,* and *Societies of Management Accountants.* Members of these three associations work in various fields—industry, commerce, government, education, and public practice—after completing their particular programs of study and passing their professional certification examinations. In the United States, both CPAs and CMAs make up the professional management accountants. The CPA designation is used by members of the American Institute of Certified Public Acountants or various state CPA associations. The CMAs are members of the *Institute of Management Accountants.*

Management accounting is not subject to the type of regulation that is evident for financial accounting. However, the Society of Management Accountants of Canada issues *management accounting guidelines* on fundamental areas of practice. Adherence to the guidelines is voluntary, but wide acceptance is expected because of the relevance and expertise used in their preparation. As of the end of 1996, 42 guidelines have been issued on such topics as capital expenditures, internal control, cash management, foreign currency risk management, the annual financial statement audit, managing quality improvements, benchmarking, activity-based costing, incentive plans, value chain analysis, and just-in-time production systems. New topics are continually being presented to the accounting community.

PROFESSIONAL ETHICS

OBJECTIVE 9
Explain the importance of ethical standards in an advanced market economy.

In recent years, many concerns have been raised regarding ethical behaviour in business and in public life. These concerns have resulted from insider trading scandals, violations of environmental standards by manufacturers, fraudulent billing by defence contractors, the BRE-X minerals scandal attempts by securities dealers to illegally control markets, scandal in government departments, and management fraud in the financial institutions. Indeed, allegations of unethical conduct have been directed toward managers in virtually all segments of society, including government, business, charitable organizations, and even religion.

Although these scandals have received a lot of attention, it is doubtful that they represent a wholesale breakdown of the moral fibre of the nation. After all, hundreds of millions of transactions are conducted every day untainted by any scandal. Nevertheless, it is important to have an appreciation of what is and is not acceptable behaviour in business and why. Fortunately, the major accounting bodies in Canada and the United States have developed useful codes of ethics and professional conduct.

Code of Conduct for Management Accountants

In a nutshell, the management accountant has ethical responsibilities in four broad areas: first, to maintain a high level of professional competence; second, to treat sensitive matters with confidentiality; third, to maintain personal integrity; and fourth, to be objective in all disclosures. Professional accounting bodies around the globe incorporate these general guidelines into their codes of professional conduct. For example Exhibit 1–10 illustrates the Standards of Ethical Conduct of the Institute of Management Accountants. Note that this exhibit provides examples of competence, confidentiality, integrity, and objectivity and also provides steps to be taken in the case of ethical conflict.

Ethical standards provide sound, practical advice for the management accountant (or manager for that matter). Most of the rules in the ethical standards are motivated by a very practical consideration—if these rules were not generally followed in business, then the economy would come to a screeching halt. Consider the following specific examples of the consequences of not abiding by the standards:

- Suppose employees could not be trusted with confidential information. Then top managers would be reluctant to distribute confidential information within the company. As a result, operations would deteriorate, since they would be based on incomplete information.
- Suppose employees accepted bribes from suppliers. Then contracts would tend to go to suppliers who pay the highest bribes rather than to the most competent suppliers. Would you like to fly in an aircraft whose wings were made by the subcontractor who was willing to pay the highest bribe to a purchasing agent? What would happen to the airline industry if its safety record deteriorated due to shoddy workmanship on contracted parts and assemblies?

EXHIBIT 1-10

Standards of Ethical
Conduct for
Management
Accountants

Management accountants have an obligation to the organizations they serve, their profession, the public, and themselves to maintain the highest standards of ethical conduct. In recognition of this obligation, the Institute of Management Accountants, formerly the National Association of Accountants, has promulgated the following standards of ethical conduct for management accountants. Adherence to these standards is integral to achieving the *Objectives of Management Accounting.** Management accountants shall not commit acts contrary to these standards nor shall they condone the commission of such acts by others within their organizations.

Competence   Management accountants have a responsibility to:
- Maintain an appropriate level of professional competence by ongoing development of their knowledge and skills.
- Perform their professional duties in accordance with relevant laws, regulations, and technical standards.
- Prepare complete and clear reports and recommendations after appropriate analyses of relevant and reliable information.

Confidentiality   Management accountants have a responsibility to:
- Refrain from disclosing confidential information acquired in the course of their work except when authorized, unless legally obligated to do so.
- Inform subordinates as appropriate regarding the confidentiality of information acquired in the course of their work and monitor their activities to assure the maintenance of that confidentiality.
- Refrain from using or appearing to use confidential information acquired in the course of their work for unethical or illegal advantage either personally or through third parties.

Integrity   Management accountants have a responsibility to:
- Avoid actual or apparent conflicts of interest and advise all appropriate parties of any potential conflict.
- Refrain from engaging in any activity that would prejudice their ability to carry out their duties ethically.
- Refuse any gift, favor, or hospitality that would influence or would appear to influence their actions.
- Refrain from either actively or passively subverting the attainment of the organization's legitimate and ethical objectives.
- Recognize and communicate professional limitations or other constraints that would preclude responsible judgment or successful performance of an activity.
- Communicate unfavorable as well as favorable information and professional judgments or opinions.
- Refrain from engaging in or supporting any activity that would discredit the profession.

Objectivity   Management accountants have a responsibility to:
- Communicate information fairly and objectively.
- Disclose fully all relevant information that could reasonably be expected to influence an intended user's understanding of the reports, comments, and recommendations presented.

RESOLUTION OF ETHICAL CONFLICT

In applying the standards of ethical conduct, management accountants may encounter problems in identifying unethical behavior or in resolving an ethical conflict. When faced with significant ethical issues, management accountants should follow the established policies of the organization bearing on the resolution of such conflict. If these policies do not resolve the ethical conflict, management accountants should consider the following course of action:
- Discuss such problems with the immediate superior except when it appears that the superior is involved, in which case the problem should be presented initially to the next higher managerial level. If satisfactory resolution cannot be achieved when the problem is initially presented, submit the issues to the next higher managerial level.

   If the immediate superior is the chief executive officer, or equivalent, the acceptable reviewing authority may be a group such as the audit committee, executive committee, board of directors, board of trustees, or owners. Contact with levels above the immediate superior should be initiated only with the superior's knowledge, assuming the superior is not involved.
- Clarify relevant concepts by confidential discussion with an objective advisor to obtain an understanding of possible courses of action.
- If the ethical conflict still exists after exhausting all levels of internal review, the management accountant may have no other recourse on significant matters than to resign from the organization and to submit an informative memorandum to an appropriate representative of the organization.

Except where legally prescribed, communication of such problems to authorities or individuals not employed or engaged by the organization is not considered appropriate.

*Institute of Management Accountants, formerly National Association of Accountants, *Statements on Management Accounting: Objectives of Management Accounting,* Statement No. 1B, New York, N.Y., June 17, 1982.

- Suppose the presidents of companies routinely lied in their annual reports to share-holders and grossly distorted financial statements. If the basic integrity of a company's financial statements could not be relied on, investors and creditors would have little basis for making informed decisions. Suspecting the worst, rational investors would pay less for securities issued by companies. As a consequence, less funds would be available for productive investments and many firms might be unable to raise any funds at all. Ultimately, this would lead to slower economic growth, fewer goods and services, and higher prices.

As these examples suggest, if ethical standards were not generally adhered to, there would be undesirable consequences for everyone. Essentially, abandoning ethical standards would lead to a lower standard of living with lower-quality goods and services, less to choose from, and higher prices. In short, following ethical rules is not just a matter of being "nice"; it is absolutely essential for the smooth functioning of an advanced market economy.

Company Codes of Conduct

"Those who engage in unethical behaviour often justify their actions with one or more of the following reasons: (1) the organization expects unethical behaviour, (2) everyone else is unethical, and/or (3) behaving unethically is the only way to get ahead."[27]

To counter the first justification for unethical behaviour, many companies have adopted formal ethical codes of conduct. These codes are generally broad-based statements of a company's responsibilities to its employees, its customers, its suppliers, and the communities in which the company operates. Codes rarely spell out specific do's and don'ts or suggest proper behaviour in a specific situation. Instead, they give broad guidelines. An ethical code can never serve as the final moral authority. Accountants have an obligation to develop moral competence in addition to technical competence. Society should expect accountants to act with the highest standards of integrity and not just conform to written codes of professional conduct.

According to Leonard Brooks of the University of Toronto the majority of large companies in Canada and abroad have issued codes of conduct. Professor Brooks surveyed chief executive officers of many of these companies and found CEOs to be relatively satisfied with their codes of conduct. CEOs did indicate, however, that improvements can and need to be made to improve code effectiveness and compliance. Areas singled out as needing code content improvement include environmental and community responsibilities and training, compliance, evaluation and reporting ethical performance.[28] An example of a corporate code of conduct is illustrated in Exhibit 1–11.

Unfortunately, the single-minded emphasis placed on short-term profits in some companies may make it seem like the only way to get ahead is to act unethically. When top managers say, in effect, that they will only be satisfied with bottom-line results and will accept no excuses, they are asking for trouble. See the accompanying focus box concerning Sears, Roebuck & Company's automobile service centres for a vivid example.

---

[27]Michael K. McCuddy, Karl E. Reichardt, and David Schroeder, "Ethical Pressures: Fact or Fiction?" *Management Accounting* (April 1993), pp. 57–61.

[28]L. Brooks, "A Survey on the Effectiveness/Compliance of Corporate Codes of Conduct in Canada," in *Professional Ethics for Accountants* (New York: West Publishing Company, 1995).

Top managers at Sears, Roebuck & Company created a situation in its automotive service business that led to unethical actions by its front-line employees.[29]

Consumers and attorneys general in more than 40 states had accused the company of misleading customers and selling them unnecessary parts and services, from brake jobs to front-end alignments. It would be a mistake, however, to see this situation . . . in terms of any one individual's moral failings. Nor did management set out to defraud Sears customers . . .

In the face of declining revenues, shrinking market share, and an increasingly competitive market, . . . Sears management attempted to spur performance of its auto centers . . . The company increased minimum work quotas and introduced productivity incentives for mechanics. The automotive service advisers were given product-specific sales quotas—sell so many springs, shock absorbers, alignments, or brake jobs per shift—and paid a commission based on sales. According to advisers, failure to meet quotas could lead to a transfer or a reduction in work hours. Some employees spoke of the "pressure, pressure, pressure" to bring in sales.

This pressure-cooker atmosphere created conditions under which employees felt that the only way to satisfy top management was by selling customers products and services they didn't really need.

Shortly after the allegations against Sears became public, CEO Edward Brennan acknowledged management's responsibility for putting in place compensation and goal-setting systems that "created an environment in which mistakes did occur."

Codes of Conduct on the International Level

The *Guideline on Ethics for Professional Accountants,* issued in July 1990 by the International Federation of Accountants (IFAC), governs the activities of *all* professional accountants throughout the world, regardless of whether they are practising as independent public accountants, employed in government service, or employed as internal accountants.[30] In addition to outlining ethical requirements in matters dealing with competence, objectivity, independence, and confidentiality, the IFAC's code also outlines the accountant's ethical responsibilities in matters relating to taxes, fees and commissions, advertising and solicitation, the handling of monies, and cross-border activities. Where cross-border activities are involved, the IFAC ethical requirements must be followed if these requirements are stricter than the ethical requirements of the country in which the work is being performed.[31]

---

[29]Reprinted by permission of *Harvard Business Review.* Excerpt from Lynn Sharp Paine, "Managing for Organizational Integrity," *Harvard Business Review* (March–April 1994). Copyright © 1994 by the President and Fellows of Harvard College. All rights reserved.

[30]A copy of this code can be obtained by writing to International Federation of Accountants, 540 Madison Avenue, New York, NY 10022.

[31]*Guideline on Ethics for Professional Accountants* (New York: International Federation of Accountants, July 1990), p. 23.

EXHIBIT 1-11

Ethical Guidelines Summary

Many companies have their own codes of business conduct such as the following summarization provided by Petro-Canada

- **Integrity**
  In all our business affairs, the Corporation and each of us individually must behave with integrity; our success and reputation depend on it.

- **Trust**
  Petro-Canada places the highest trust in the honesty, integrity and dedication of its employees; in turn, employees have the right to be treated with honesty, respect and fairness.

- **Customers**
  We will provide value for money and deal fairly and honestly with our customers.

- **Social Responsibility**
  Petro-Canada is committed to workplace safety, valuing workforce diversity, and employee freedom from discrimination and harassment. We will strive to be a positive force in the social and environmental welfare of the communities in which we operate.

- **Illegal or Unethical Actions**
  Petro-Canada does not condone nor permit any employee, partner or supplier to commit an illegal or unethical act on behalf of the Corporation nor to instruct any other person or company to do so.

- **Conflict of Interest**
  There can be no situations where our personal or personal business arrangements conflict with the interests of the Company. Using our position with the Company in an unsanctioned manner for personal gain is unacceptable.

- **Confidential Information**
  We will safeguard competitive and confidential information from disclosure. Information about our competitors will be acquired only through legal means.

- **Insider Trading**
  It is illegal to use knowledge gained through our position with Petro-Canada, that is not public information, to trade in securities of Petro-Canada or another company.

- **Secret Commissions**
  Bribes, payoffs, or kickbacks to business representatives, suppliers, or public officials as payments to obtain business are prohibited both domestically and internationally.

Source: *Code of Business Conduct*, Petro-Canada, p. 3.

SUMMARY

Managerial accounting assists managers in carrying out their responsibilities, which include planning, directing and motivating, and controlling.

Since managerial accounting is geared to the needs of the manager rather than to the needs of outsiders, it differs substantially from financial accounting. Managerial accounting is oriented more toward the future, places less emphasis on precision, emphasizes segments of an organization (rather than the organization as a whole), is not governed by generally accepted accounting principles, and is not mandatory.

The business environment in recent years has been characterized by increasing competition and a relentless drive for continuous improvement. Several approaches have been developed to assist organizations in meeting these challenges—including just-in-time (JIT), total quality management (TQM), process reengineering, automation, and the theory of constraints (TOC).

JIT emphasizes the importance of reducing inventories to the barest minimum possible. This reduces working capital requirements, frees up space, reduces throughput time, reduces defects, and eliminates waste.

TQM involves focusing on the customer, and it employs systematic problem-solving using teams made up of front-line workers. Specific TQM tools include benchmarking and the plan-do-check-act (PDCA) cycle. By emphasizing teamwork, a focus on the customer, and facts, TQM can avoid the organizational infighting that might otherwise block improvement.

Process reengineering involves completely redesigning a business process in order to eliminate non-value-added activities and to reduce opportunities for errors. Process reengineering relies more on outside specialists than TQM and is more likely to be imposed by top management.

The theory of constraints emphasizes the importance of managing the organization's constraints. Since the constraint is whatever is holding back the organization, improvement efforts usually must be focused on the constraint in order to be really effective.

Most organizations are decentralized to some degree. The organization chart depicts who works for whom in the organization and which units perform staff functions rather than line functions. Accountants perform a staff function—they support and provide assistance to others inside the organization.

Ethical standards serve a very important practical function in an advanced market economy. Without widespread adherence to ethical standards, the economy would slow down dramatically. Ethics are the lubrication that keep a market economy functioning smoothly. The Standards of Ethical Conduct for Management Accountants provides sound, practical guidelines for resolving ethical problems that might arise in an organization.

KEY TERMS FOR REVIEW

OBJECTIVE 10
Define or explain the key terms listed at the end of the chapter.

At the end of each chapter, a list of key terms for review is given, along with the definition of each term. (These terms are printed in boldface where they are defined in the chapter.) Carefully study each term to be sure you understand its meaning, since these terms are used repeatedly in the chapters that follow. The list for Chapter 1 follows.

Benchmarking   A study of organizations that are among the best in the world at performing a particular task. (p. 17)

Budget   A detailed plan for the future, usually expressed in formal quantitative terms. (p. 5)

Business process   A series of steps that are followed in order to carry out some task in a business. (p. 20)

Cell   A manufacturing workstation in which a single worker operates several machines. (p. 14)

Constraint   Anything that prevents an organization or individual from getting more of what it wants. (p. 22)

Control   The process of instituting procedures and then obtaining feedback as needed to ensure that all parts of the organization are functioning effectively and moving toward overall company goals. (p. 5)

Controller   The manager in charge of the accounting department in an organization. (p. 5)

Controlling   Ensuring that the plan is actually carried out and is appropriately modified as circumstances change. (p. 4)

Cycle time   See *Throughput time.* (p. 14)

Decentralization   The delegation of decision-making authority throughout an organization by allowing managers at various operating levels to make key decisions relating to their area of responsibility. (p. 27)

Directing and motivating   Mobilizing human and other resources to carry out plans and run routine operations. (p. 4)

Feedback   Accounting and other reports that help managers monitor performance and focus on problems and/or opportunities that might otherwise go unnoticed. (p. 5)

Financial accounting   The phase of accounting concerned with providing information to shareholders, creditors, and others outside the organization. (p. 4)

Finished goods   Units of product that have been completed but have not yet been sold to customers. (p. 11)

Flexible manufacturing system (FMS)   A production flow line in which cells are linked together with an automated material-handling system and that is controlled by a central computer. (p. 22)

Flow line   The physical path taken by a product as it moves through the manufacturing process from receipt of raw materials to shipment of completed units. (p. 13)

Focused factory   A single work centre that contains all of the machines needed to make a particular product. A focused factory is also known as a "factory within a factory." (p. 13)

Just-in-time (JIT)   A production system in which materials are purchased and units are produced only as needed to meet actual customer demand. (p. 11)

Line   A position in an organization that is directly related to the achievement of the organization's basic objectives. (p. 27)

Managerial accounting   The phase of accounting concerned with providing information to managers for use in planning and controlling operations and in decision making. (p. 4)

Non-value-added activity   An activity that consumes resources or takes time but that does not add value for which customers are willing to pay. (p. 20)

Numerically controlled (NC) machine   A machine whose functions are controlled by a computer that has been programmed to guide the equipment through all the steps necessary to complete some task. (p. 22)

Organization chart   A visual diagram of a firm's organizational structure that depicts formal lines of reporting, communication, and responsibility between managers. (p. 27)

Performance report   A detailed report comparing budgeted data to actual data. (p. 6)

Plan-do-check-act (PDCA) cycle   A systematic approach to continuous improvement that applies the scientific method to problem solving. (p. 17)

Planning   Selecting a course of action and specifying how the action will be implemented. (p. 4)

Planning and control cycle   The flow of management activities through planning, directing and motivating, and controlling, and then back to planning again. (p. 7)

Process reengineering   An approach to improvement that involves completely redesigning business processes in order to eliminate unnecessary steps, reduce errors, and reduce costs. (p. 19)

Raw materials   Materials that are used to make a product. (p. 11)

Segment   Any part of an organization that can be evaluated independently of other parts and about which the manager seeks financial data. Examples include a product line, a sales territory, a division, or a department. (p. 9)

Setup   Activities that must be performed whenever production is switched over from making one type of item to another. (p. 15)

Single-minute-exchange-of-dies   Techniques that have the goal of reducing setup time to a minute or less. (p. 15)

Staff   A position in an organization that is only indirectly related to the achievement of the organization's basic objectives. Such positions are supportive in nature in that they provide service or assistance to line positions or to other staff positions. (p. 27)

Theory of constraints (TOC)   A management approach that emphasizes the importance of managing constraints. (p. 22)

Throughput   The total volume of production through a facility during a period. (p. 14)

Throughput time   The time required to make a completed unit of product starting with raw materials. Throughput time is also known as cycle time. (p. 14)

Total quality management (TQM)   An approach to continuous improvement that focuses on customers and using teams of front-line workers to systematically identify and solve problems. (p. 17)

Work in process   Units of product that are only partially completed and will require further work before they are ready for sale to a customer. (p. 11)

QUESTIONS

1–1 What is the basic difference between financial and managerial accounting?

1–2 What are the three major activities of a manager?

1–3 Describe the four steps in the planning and control cycle.

1–4 What function does *feedback* play in the work of the manager?

1–5 Distinguish between line and staff positions in an organization.

1–6 What are the major differences between financial and managerial accounting?

1–7 In a just-in-time system, what is meant by the pull approach to the flow of goods, as compared to the push approach used in conventional systems?

1–8 How does the plant layout differ in a company using JIT as compared to a company that uses a more conventional approach to manufacturing? What benefits accrue from a JIT layout?

1–9 Identify the benefits that can result from reducing the setup time for a product.

1–10 How does a workforce in a JIT facility differ from the workforce in a conventional facility?

1–11 What are the major benefits of a JIT system?

1–12 Explain how the plan-do-check-act cycle applies the scientific method to problem solving.

1–13 Why is process reengineering a more radical approach to improvement than total quality management?

1–14 How can process reengineering undermine employee morale?

1–15 Why does the theory of constraints emphasize managing constraints?

1–16 Why is adherence to ethical standards important for the smooth functioning of an advanced market economy?

EXERCISES

E1–1 Listed below are several terms that relate to organizations, the work of management, and the role of managerial accounting:

Budgets	Controller
Decentralization	Directing and motivating
Feedback	Financial accounting
Line	Managerial accounting
Nonmonetary data	Planning
Performance report	Staff
Precision	

Choose the term or terms above that most appropriately complete the following statements.

1. _____ is concerned with providing information for the use of those who are inside the organization, whereas _____ is concerned with providing information for the use of those who are outside the organization.

2. _____ consists of identifying alternatives, selecting from among the alternatives the one that is best for the organization, and specifying what actions will be taken to implement the chosen alternative.

3. When _____ , managers oversee day-to-day activities and keep the organization functioning smoothly.

4. The accounting and other reports coming to management that are used in controlling the organization are called _____ .

5. The delegation of decision-making authority throughout an organization by allowing managers at various operating levels to make key decisions relating to their area of responsibility is called _____ .

6. A position on the organization chart that is directly related to achieving the basic objectives of an organization is called a _____ position.

7. A _____ position provides service or assistance to other parts of the organization and does not directly achieve the basic objectives of the organization.

8. The manager in charge of the accounting department is generally known as the _____.

9. The plans of management are expressed formally in _____.

10. A detailed report to management comparing budgeted data against actual data for a specific time period is called a _____.

11. Managerial accounting places less emphasis on _____ and more emphasis on _____ than financial accounting.

E1–2 Listed below are several terms that relate to just-in-time, total quality management, process reengineering, automation, and theory of constraints:

Constraint	Flexible manufacturing system
Flow line	Frequent
Just-in-time	Nonconstraint
Non-value-added activities	Plan-do-check-act cycle
Pull	Setup
Business process	

Choose the term or terms above that most appropriately complete the following statements.

1. A production system in which units are produced and materials are purchased only as needed to meet actual customer demand is called _____.

2. The physical path taken by a product as it moves through the manufacturing process from receipt of raw materials to shipment of the completed good is called a _____.

3. In just-in-time, the flow of goods is controlled by what is described as a_____ _____ approach to manufacturing.

4. The activities involved in getting equipment ready to produce a different product are called a _____.

5. To successfully operate a JIT system, a company must learn to rely on a few suppliers who are willing to make _____ deliveries.

6. The _____ is a systematic, fact-based approach to continuous improvement that resembles the scientific method.

7. A _____ is any series of steps that are followed in order to carry out some task in a business.

8. In process reengineering, two objectives are to simplify and to eliminate_____ _____.

9. When the cells on a product flow line are linked together with an automated material-handling system and the flows between cells are controlled by a central computer, a _____ is in operation.

10. The theory of constraints suggests that improvement efforts should be focused on the company's _____.

11. Increasing the rate of output of a _____ as the result of an improvement effort is unlikely to have much effect on profits.

E1–3 The management at Megafilters, Inc., has been discussing the possible implementation of a JIT production system at its Ontario plant, where oil and air filters are manufactured. The metal stamping department at the Ontario plant has already instituted a JIT system for controlling raw materials inventory, but the remainder of the plant is still discussing how to proceed with the implementation of this concept. The metal stamping department implemented JIT with no advance planning, and some of the other department managers have become uneasy about adopting JIT after hearing about the problems that have arisen.

Robert Goertz, manager of the Ontario plant, is a strong proponent of the JIT approach.

He recently made the following statement at a meeting of all departmental managers:

> Just-in-time is often referred to as a management philosophy. We will all have to make many changes in the way we think about our employees, our suppliers, and our customers if we are going to be successful in using JIT procedures. Rather than dwelling on some of the negative things you have heard from the metal stamping department, I want each of you to prepare a list of things we can do to make a smooth transition to the JIT approach for the rest of the plant.

Required

1. The JIT approach has several characteristics that distinguish it from conventional production systems. Describe these characteristics.
2. For the JIT approach to be successful, Megafilters, Inc., must establish appropriate relationships with its suppliers. Describe these relationships under JIT.

(CMA, adapted)

PROBLEMS

P1–4 Preparing an Organization Chart   Bristow University is a large university headed by a president who has five vice presidents reporting to him. These vice presidents are responsible for, respectively, auxiliary services, admissions and records, academics, financial services (controller), and physical plant.

In addition, the university has managers over several areas who report to these vice presidents. These include managers over central purchasing, the university press, and the university bookstore, all of whom report to the vice president for auxiliary services; managers over computer services and over accounting and finance, who report to the vice president for financial services; and managers over grounds and custodial services and over plant and maintenance, who report to the vice president for physical plant.

The university has four faculties—business, humanities, fine arts, and engineering and quantitative methods—and a law school. Each of these units has a dean who is responsible to the academic vice president. Each faculty has several departments.

Required

1. Prepare an organization chart for Bristow University.
2. Which of the positions on your chart would be line positions? Why would they be line positions? Which would be staff positions? Why?
3. Which of the positions on your chart would have need for accounting information? Explain.

P1–5 Ethics   Paul Sarver is the controller of a corporation whose shares are not listed on a national stock exchange. The company has just received a patent on a product that is expected to yield substantial profits in a year or two. At the moment, however, the company is experiencing financial difficulties; and because of inadequate working capital, it is on the verge of defaulting on a note held by its bank.

At the end of the most recent fiscal year, the company's president instructed Sarver not to record several invoices as accounts payable. Sarver objected since the invoices represented bona fide liabilities. However, the president insisted that the invoices not be recorded until after year-end, at which time it was expected that additional financing could be obtained. After several very strenuous objections—expressed to both the president and other members of senior management—Sarver finally complied with the president's instructions.

Required

1. Did Sarver act in an ethical manner? Explain fully.
2. If the new product fails to yield substantial profits and the company becomes insolvent, can Sarver's actions be justified by the fact that he was following orders from a superior? Explain.

P1–6 Line and Staff Positions; Organization Chart   The Association of Medical Personnel (AMP) is a membership/educational organization that serves a wide range of individuals who work for medical institutions including hospitals, clinics, and medical practices. The membership is composed of doctors, nurses, medical assistants, and professional administrators.

EXHIBIT 1–12   Partial Organization Chart for the Association of Medical Personel

```
                              ┌─────────────┐
                              │ Board of    │
                              │ Directors   │
                              └─────────────┘
                                    │
                              ┌─────────────┐
                              │ President   │
                              └─────────────┘
```

Staff Liaison to the Chairperson — Jere Feldon

Meetings Coordinator

Vice President, Research

Vice President, Publications

Vice President, Educational Programs

Vice President, Membership

Vice President, Administration

Editor, *AMP Review*

Director of Continuing Education Programs

Director of Membership Marketing

Director of General Accounting

Editor of Special Publications — Jesse Paige

Director of Seminars and Conferences

Director of Chapter Services

Director of Data Processing

Director of Self-Study Programs — Lana Dickson

Manager of Personnel — George Ackers

The purpose of the organization is to provide individuals in the medical field with a professional organization that offers educational and training opportunities through local chapters, a monthly magazine (*AMP Review*), continuing education programs, seminars, self-study courses, and research publications.

AMP is governed by a board of directors who are members elected to these positions by the membership. The chairperson of the board is the highest-ranking volunteer member and presides over the board; the board establishes policy for the organization. The policies are administered and carried out by AMP's paid professional staff. The president's chief responsibility is to manage the operations of the professional staff. Like any organization, the professional staff of AMP is composed of line and staff positions. A partial organization chart of the AMP professional staff is shown in Exhibit 1–12.

Four of the positions appearing in the organization chart are described below.

Jere Feldon, Staff Liaison to the Chairperson

Feldon is assigned to work with the chairperson of AMP by serving as an intermediary between the chairperson and the professional staff. All correspondence to the chairperson is funneled through Feldon. Feldon also works very closely with the president of AMP, especially on any matters that have to be brought to the attention of the chairperson and the board.

Lana Dickson, Director of Self-Study Programs

Dickson is responsible for developing and marketing the self-study programs offered by AMP. Self-study courses consist of cassette tapes and a workbook. Most of the courses are developed by outside contractors who work under her direction. Dickson relies on the director of membership marketing to assist her in the marketing of these courses.

Jess Paige, Editor of Special Publications

Paige is primarily responsible for the publication and sale of any research monographs that are generated by the research department. In addition, he coordinates the publication of any special projects that may be prepared by any other AMP committees or departments. Paige also works with AMP's Publication Committee which sets policy on the types of publications that AMP should publish.

George Ackers, Manager of Personnel

Ackers works with all of the departments of AMP in the hiring of professional and clerical staff. The individual departments screen and interview prospective employees for professional positions, but Ackers is responsible for advertising open positions. Ackers plays a more active role in the hiring of clerical personnel by screening individuals before they are sent to the departments for interviews. In addition, Ackers coordinates the employee performance evaluation program and administers AMP's salary schedule and fringe benefit program.

Required

1. Distinguish between line positions and staff positions in an organization by defining each. Include in your discussion the role, purpose, and importance of each.
2. Many times, conflicts will arise between line and staff managers in organizations. Discuss the characteristics of line and staff managers that may cause conflicts between the two.
3. For each of the four individuals identified by name in the text,
   a. Identify whether the individual's position is a line or staff position and explain why.
   b. Identify potential problems that could arise in each individual's position, either due to the type of position (i.e., line or staff) or to the location of the individual's position within the organization.

(CMA, adapted)

P1–7 Ethics   Adam Williams was recently hired as assistant controller of GroChem, Inc., which processes chemicals for use in fertilizers. Williams was selected for this position because of his past experience in the chemical processing field. During his first month on the job, Williams made a point of getting to know the people responsible for the plant operations and learning how things are done at GroChem.

During a conversation with the plant supervisor, Williams asked about the company procedures for handling toxic waste materials. The plant supervisor replied that he was not involved with the disposal of wastes and suggested that Williams might be wise to ignore this issue. This response strengthened Williams's determination to probe this area further to be sure that the company was not vulnerable to litigation.

Upon further investigation, Williams discovered evidence that GroChem was using a nearby residential landfill to dump toxic wastes. It appeared that some members of GroChem's management team were aware of this situation and may have been involved in arranging for this dumping; however, Williams was unable to determine whether his superior, the controller, was involved.

Uncertain how he should proceed, Williams began to consider his options by outlining the following three alternative courses of action:

- Seek the advice of his superior, the controller.
- Anonymously release the information to the local newspaper.
- Discuss the situation with an outside member of the board of directors with whom he is acquainted.

Required

1. Discuss why Adam Williams has an ethical responsibility to take some action in the matter of GroChem, Inc., and the dumping of toxic wastes. Refer to the specific ethical standards (competence, confidentiality, integrity, and/or objectivity) in support of your answer.
2. For each of the three alternative courses of action that Adam Williams has outlined, explain whether or not the action is appropriate.
3. Without prejudice to your answer in (2) above, assume that Adam Williams sought the advice of his superior, the controller, and discovered that the controller was involved in the dumping of toxic wastes. Describe the steps that Williams should take to resolve this situation.

(CMA, adapted)

P1–8 JIT; Process Reengineering   Snedden Products manufactures athletic equipment, including footballs. The footballs are manufactured in several steps, which are listed below.

a. Leather and other materials are received at a centrally located dock where the materials are checked to be sure they conform to exacting company standards. Rejected materials are returned to the supplier.
b. Acceptable materials are transported to a stores warehouse pending use in production.
c. A materials requisition form is issued, and materials are transferred from the stores warehouse to the cutting department where all cutting equipment is located.
d. Since the cutting department cuts materials for a variety of products, the leather is placed on large pallets and stationed by the appropriate machines.
e. The leather and other materials are cut to proper shape, with the operator taking care to cut all sections of a football from a single piece of leather. Waste materials are placed in a bin, and at the end of each day the materials are sorted to reclaim the items that can be used in manufacturing other products.
f. Each cut item of material is examined by one of three checkers to ensure uniformity of cut, thickness of the leather, and direction of the grain. Rejected pieces are tossed in the scrap bin.
g. Cut materials are placed on pallets and transferred to the centralized sewing department, where the pallets are placed in a staging area.
h. Materials are taken from the pallets, the company's name and logo are stamped into one section of each set of cut pieces, and the pieces are then sewn together.
i. The sewn pieces are placed in bins, which are then transferred to the staging area of the assembly department.
j. An operator in the assembly department installs a lining in the football, stitches the ball closed with a stitching machine, and then inflates it.
k. The completed footballs are placed on a conveyor belt that passes by another set of checkers. Each ball is checked for uniformity of shape and for other potential defects.
l. Completed footballs are boxed and transferred to the finished goods warehouse.

Required

Assume that the company adopts JIT inventory practices and establishes individual product flow lines. Explain what changes would have to be made in manufacturing procedures and prepare a sketch of how the football product flow line would be arranged.

P1–9 Ethics   Refer to the Focus on Current Practice box concerning Sears, Roebuck & Company's automotive service business on page 33. Suppose all automotive service businesses routinely followed the practice of attempting to sell customers unnecessary parts and services.

Required

1. How would this unethical behaviour affect customers? How might customers attempt to protect themselves against this unethical behaviour?
2. How would this unethical behaviour probably affect profits and employment in the automotive service industry?

GROUP EXERCISES

GE1–10 Rethinking the Corporation   The business world is changing rapidly from what it was just a few short years ago. Businesses now face a world of intense domestic and international competition and widespread uncertainty about the uses of technology. Companies are undergoing a major upheaval in how they are organized and how they conduct business. There will be many new opportunities for innovative businesses that understand the new competitive environment and can evolve rapidly to take advantage of these opportunities. It is important that you know what these trends are and understand how they are affecting business if you are to be successful in your business career.

Required

1. Identify the major forces affecting the business world today.
2. Explain how these forces are bringing about change in the world of business.

GE1–11 The Changing Face of Education   This is a time of extraordinary change for business and education alike. Education will continue to be a critical element in the determination of business competitiveness. Therefore, business schools cannot afford to be complacent and settle for the status quo. Yet, business is telling higher education that there is mismatch between the needs of business and the skills students are receiving. Many of the same trends and market forces that caused business to remake itself in the eighties will reshape business education in the nineties. As a result, business education is undergoing sweeping changes to the basic educational model that has been in place for over 25 years.

Required

1. What skills and capabilities will students need to compete in the business world of the twenty-first century?
2. How must business education change in order to develop the skills and capabilities that will be critical to success?
3. How can the principles of total quality management be applied to reinventing business education?

GE1–12 Why Is It So Difficult to Change?   Critics have identified a variety of economic, institutional, and cultural factors that may help explain the reluctance to adapt to the needs of today's competitive environment, both in business and in academia.

Required

1. Why do you think change is such a challenge?
2. What role will technology play in implementing change in business and education?

GE1–13 One Example of Change   The following often-repeated quotation is indicative of the broad impact that one field, engineering, can have on the rest of a company: "80% of manufacturing costs are committed during the first 20% of the design process." If your school has a faculty of engineering, invite one of its staff who is knowledgeable in product design to speak to your class. If your school does not have a faculty of engineering, contact a company in your area that designs and manufactures its own products. See if you can make arrangements to have one of their design engineers come to speak to your class.

Required

1. What do design engineers do?
2. How does design affect a product's cost?
3. How do product designs affect other parts of a company?
4. What could business students do to make themselves more aware of these issues?
5. How could accounting education change to incorporate awareness of these issues?
6. Would it be helpful for engineering students to take a course like managerial accounting?

PART I THE FOUNDATION:
Cost Terms, Systems Design, and Cost Behaviour

COST TERMS, CONCEPTS, AND CLASSIFICATIONS

LEARNING OBJECTIVES

After studying Chapter 2, you should be able to:

1 Identify and give examples of each of the three basic cost elements involved in the manufacture of a product.

2 Distinguish between period costs and product costs and give examples of each.

3 Explain the difference between the financial statements of a manufacturing company and those of a merchandising company.

4 Prepare a schedule of cost of goods manufactured in good form.

5 Explain the flow of direct materials cost, direct labour cost, and manufacturing overhead cost from the point of incurrence to sale of the completed product.

6 Identify and give examples of variable costs and fixed costs, and explain the difference in their behaviour.

7 Define and give examples of direct and indirect costs.

8 Define and give examples of cost classifications used in making decisions: differential costs, opportunity costs, and sunk costs.

9 Define or explain the key terms listed at the end of the chapter.

10 (Appendix 2A) Properly classify labour costs associated with idle time, overtime, and fringe benefits.

Manufacturing should have a broad interpretation and can include activities that are often considered services. Movie studios, for example, "manufacture" movies, such as Titanic.

A s explained in Chapter 1, the work of management focuses on (1) planning, which includes setting objectives and outlining how to attain these objectives; and (2) control, which includes the steps to take to ensure that objectives are realized. To carry out these planning and control responsibilities, managers need *information* about the organization. From an accounting point of view, this information often relates to the *costs* of the organization.

In managerial accounting, the term *cost* is used in many different ways. The reason is that there are many types of costs, and these costs are classified differently according to the immediate needs of management. For example, managers may want cost data to prepare external financial reports, to prepare planning budgets, or to make decisions. Each different use of cost data demands a different classification and definition of costs. For example, the preparation of external financial reports requires the use of historical cost data, whereas decision making may require current cost data.

In this chapter, we discuss many of the possible uses of cost data and how costs are defined and classified for each use. Our first task is to explain how costs are classified for the purpose of preparing external financial reports—particularly in manufacturing companies. To set the stage for this discussion, we begin the chapter by defining some terms commonly used in manufacturing.

GENERAL COST CLASSIFICATIONS

Costs are associated with all types of organizations—business, nonbusiness, manufacturing, retail, and service. Generally, the kinds of costs that are incurred and the way in which these costs are classified depends on the type of organization involved. Managerial accounting is as applicable to one type of organization as to another. For this reason, we will consider in our discussion the cost characteristics of a variety of organizations—manufacturing, merchandising, and service.

Our initial focus in this chapter is on manufacturing companies, since their basic activities include most of the activities found in other types of business organizations. Manufacturing companies such as Magna Corp. and Molson Breweries are involved in acquiring

All businesses— not just manufacturers— incur costs. Grocery stores are merchandising businesses that have many costs similar to manufacturers: rent, wages and salaries, and packing materials, for example.

raw materials, producing finished goods, marketing, distributing, billing, and almost every other business activity. Therefore, an understanding of costs in a manufacturing company can be very helpful in understanding costs in other types of organizations.

The term *manufacturing* should not be too narrowly defined. In this text, **manufacturing** simply means transforming an input such as a raw material into a form that has greater value to customers. When broadly interpreted, manufacturing includes many activities that are often considered to be services—for example, fast-food outlets such as Kentucky Fried Chicken and Wendy's, movie studios such as Disney and Paramount, and consulting firms such as Andersen Consulting and KPMG. As we proceed, you should keep in mind that the concepts we discuss apply to a broad spectrum of organizations and not just the assembly line or metal fabricating facility usually thought of when manufacturing is mentioned.

In contrast to manufacturing, the simplest businesses are in **merchandising,** which sell finished goods acquired from a manufacturer or other source. Canadian Tire, Zellers, Loblaws, Sears, The Bay, and Coles Books are all examples of merchandising companies.

Manufacturing Costs

OBJECTIVE 1
Identify and give examples of each of the three basic cost elements involved in the manufacture of a product.

Most manufacturing companies divide manufacturing costs into three broad categories: direct materials, direct labour, and manufacturing overhead. A discussion of each of these categories follows.

Direct Materials.   The materials that go into the final product are called **raw materials.** This term is somewhat misleading, since it seems to imply basic, natural resources like wood pulp or iron ore. Actually, raw materials refer to any materials that are used in the final product; and the finished product of one company can become the raw materials of another company. For example, the plastics produced by Du Pont are a raw material used by Apple Computer in its personal computers.

Direct materials are those materials that are an integral part of the finished product and that can be physically and conveniently traced into it. This would include, for example, the seats Bombardier purchases from subcontractors to install in its commercial aircraft. It would also include the tiny electric motor Panasonic uses in its CD players to make the CD spin.

Sometimes it may not be worth the effort to trace the costs of relatively insignificant materials to the end products. Such minor items would include the solder used to make electrical connections in a computer or the glue used to assemble an Ethan Allen chair.

Some products—such as computer chips— that are the finished good of one company become the raw materials for another company.

Materials such as solder and glue are called **indirect materials** and are included as part of manufacturing overhead, which is discussed later in this section.

Direct Labour.   The term **direct labour** is reserved for those labour costs that can be easily (i.e., physically and conveniently) traced to products. Direct labour is sometimes called *touch labour*, since direct labour workers typically touch the product while it is being made. The labour costs of assembly-line workers, for example, would be direct labour costs, as would the labour costs of carpenters, bricklayers, and machine operators.

Labour costs that cannot be physically traced to the creation of products, or that can be traced only at great cost and inconvenience, are termed **indirect labour** and treated as part of manufacturing overhead, along with indirect materials. Indirect labour includes the labour costs of janitors, supervisors, materials handlers, and night security guards. Although the efforts of these workers are essential to production, it would be either impractical or impossible to accurately relate their costs to specific units of product. Hence, such labour costs are treated as indirect labour.

In some industries, major shifts are taking place in the structure of labour costs. Partly as a response to increased competition and partly as a result of changing technology, direct labour is decreasing in importance. Sophisticated automated equipment, run and maintained by skilled indirect workers, is increasingly replacing direct labour. In a few companies, direct labour has become such a minor element of cost that it has disappeared altogether as a separate cost category. More is said in later chapters about this trend and about the impact it is having on cost systems. However, for the present, the vast majority of manufacturing companies throughout the world continue to recognize direct labour as a separate cost category.

An example of companies shifting away from labour costs can be found in the UK where over 3,000 of Gelco Expense Management's customers outsource the time-consuming task of processing and paying employee expenses. Gelco takes care of this otherwise labour-intensive task in an automated fashion freeing up managers' time.[1]

Manufacturing Overhead.   **Manufacturing overhead**, the third element of manufacturing cost, includes all costs of manufacturing except direct materials and direct labour. Included in manufacturing overhead are such items as indirect materials; indirect labour; maintenance and repairs on production equipment; and heat and light, property taxes, depreciation, and insurance on manufacturing facilities. A company also incurs costs for heat and light, property taxes, insurance, depreciation, and so forth, associated with its selling and administrative functions, but these costs are not included as part of manufacturing overhead. Only those costs associated with *operating the factory* are included in the manufacturing overhead category.

---

[1]Anonymous, *Management Accounting London* (January 1996), p. 49.

Various names are used for manufacturing overhead, such as *indirect manufacturing cost, factory overhead,* and *factory burden.* All of these terms are synonymous with *manufacturing overhead.*

Manufacturing overhead combined with direct labour is known as **conversion cost.** This term stems from the fact that direct labour costs and overhead costs are incurred in the conversion of materials into finished products. Direct labour combined with direct materials is known as **prime cost.**

The proportion of labour to overhead varies from company to company and even within companies within the same industry. Some automated companies have a large proportion of overhead compared to direct labour costs. A number even classify all labour as overhead. Others, such as those engaged in meat packing, have a large proportion of direct labour. There are those production companies that buy materials partially assembled while others manufacture their subassembled parts to be used by other departments in the manufacturing process. How organizations determine their proportions of materials, labour and overhead is a significant part of their strategic planning.

Nonmanufacturing Costs

Generally, nonmanufacturing costs are subclassified into two categories:
1.   Marketing or selling costs.
2.   Administrative costs.

Marketing or selling costs include all costs necessary to secure customer orders and get the finished product or service into the hands of the customer. These costs are often called **order-getting and order-filling costs.** Examples of marketing costs include advertising, shipping, sales travel, sales commissions, sales salaries, and costs associated with finished goods warehouses. All businesses have marketing costs, regardless of whether they are in manufacturing or merchandising, or provide an intangible service.

Administrative costs include all executive, organizational, and clerical costs associated with the *general management* of an organization rather than associated with manufacturing, marketing, or selling. Examples of administrative costs include executive compensation, general accounting, secretarial, public relations, and similar costs involved in the overall, general administration of the organization *as a whole.* As with marketing costs, all organizations have administrative costs.

As stated earlier, managerial accounting concepts and techniques apply just as much to nonmanufacturing activities as they do to manufacturing activities, although in the past the central focus has been on the manufacturing environment. Service organizations in particular are making increased use of cost concepts in analyzing and costing their services. For example, banks now use cost analysis in determining the cost of offering such services as chequing accounts, consumer loans, and credit cards; and insurance companies determine costs of servicing customers by geographic location, age, marital status, and occupation. Cost breakdowns of these types provide data for control over selling and administrative functions in the same way that manufacturing cost breakdowns provide data for control over manufacturing functions.

PERIOD COSTS VERSUS PRODUCT COSTS

OBJECTIVE 2
Distinguish between
period costs and
product costs and give
examples of each.

In addition to being placed in manufacturing and nonmanufacturing categories, costs can also be classified as either *period costs* or *product costs*. To understand the difference between period costs and product costs, we must first refresh our understanding of the matching principle.

Recall from your earlier accounting studies that the matching principle was followed in preparing external financial reports. In financial accounting, the matching principle states that *the costs incurred to generate a particular revenue should be recognized as expenses in the same time period that the revenue is recognized.*

This matching principle is the key to distinguishing between period costs and product costs. Some costs are *matched against periods of time* and become expenses immediately, because all the associated revenues are recognized immediately. Other costs, however, are *matched against products* and don't become expenses until the products are sold, which may be in a following time period. This important distinction between the various costs in an organization is discussed further in the following paragraphs.

Period Costs

Period costs are those costs that are matched against revenues on a time period basis. As such, period costs are not included as part of the cost of either purchased or manufactured goods. Sales commissions and office rent are good examples of the kind of costs we are talking about. Neither commissions nor office rent is included as part of the cost of purchased or manufactured goods. Rather, both items are treated as expenses and deducted from revenues in the time period in which they are incurred. Thus, they are said to be period costs.

As suggested above, *all selling and administrative expenses are considered to be period costs.* Therefore, advertising, executive salaries, sales commissions, public relations, and other nonmanufacturing costs discussed earlier would all be period costs. They will appear on the income statement as expenses in the time period in which they are incurred.

Product Costs

Some costs are better matched against products than they are against periods of time. Costs of this type—called **product costs**—consist of the costs involved in the purchase or manufacture of goods. In the case of manufactured goods, these costs consist of direct materials, direct labour, and manufacturing overhead. Product costs are viewed as "attaching" to units of product as the goods are purchased or manufactured, and they remain attached as the goods go into inventory awaiting sale. At the point of sale, the costs are released from inventory as expenses (typically called cost of goods sold) and matched against sales revenue. Since product costs are assigned to inventories, they are also known as **inventoriable costs.**

We must emphasize that unlike period costs, product costs are not necessarily treated as expenses in the time period in which they are incurred. Rather, as explained above, they are treated as expenses in the time period in which the related products *are sold.* This means that a product cost such as direct materials or direct labour might be incurred during one time period but not treated as an expense until a following period when sale of the completed product takes place.

Exhibit 2–1 contains a summary of the cost terms that we have introduced so far.

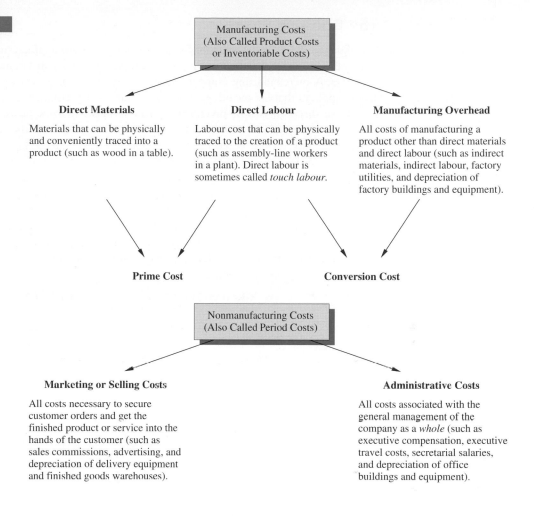

EXHIBIT 2-1

Summary of Cost Terms

Manufacturing Costs
(Also Called Product Costs
or Inventoriable Costs)

Direct Materials

Materials that can be physically
and conveniently traced into a
product (such as wood in a table).

Direct Labour

Labour cost that can be physically
traced to the creation of a product
(such as assembly-line workers
in a plant). Direct labour is
sometimes called *touch labour*.

Manufacturing Overhead

All costs of manufacturing a
product other than direct materials
and direct labour (such as indirect
materials, indirect labour, factory
utilities, and depreciation of
factory buildings and equipment).

Prime Cost

Conversion Cost

Nonmanufacturing Costs
(Also Called Period Costs)

Marketing or Selling Costs

All costs necessary to secure
customer orders and get the
finished product or service into the
hands of the customer (such as
sales commissions, advertising, and
depreciation of delivery equipment
and finished goods warehouses).

Administrative Costs

All costs associated with the
general management of the
company as a *whole* (such as
executive compensation, executive
travel costs, secretarial salaries,
and depreciation of office
buildings and equipment).

COST CLASSIFICATIONS ON FINANCIAL STATEMENTS

OBJECTIVE 3

Explain the difference
between the financial
statements of a
manufacturing
company and those of
a merchandising
company.

In your prior accounting training, you learned that firms prepare periodic financial reports
for creditors, shareholders, and others to show the financial condition of the firm and the
firm's earnings performance over some specified interval. The reports you studied were
probably those of merchandising companies, such as retail stores, which simply purchase
goods from suppliers for resale to customers.

The financial statements prepared by a *manufacturing* company are more complex
than the statements prepared by a merchandising company. As stated earlier, manufacturing companies are more complex organizations than merchandising companies because
the manufacturing company must produce its goods as well as market them. The production process gives rise to many costs that do not exist in a merchandising company, and
somehow these costs must be accounted for on the manufacturing company's financial
statements. In this section, we focus our attention on how this accounting is carried out in
the balance sheet and income statement.

The Balance Sheet

The balance sheet, or statement of financial position, of a manufacturing company is similar to that of a merchandising company. However, there are differences in the inventory accounts. A merchandising company has only one class of inventory—goods purchased from suppliers that are awaiting resale to customers. By contrast, manufacturing companies have three classes of inventories—*raw materials, work in process,* and *finished goods.* As discussed in Chapter 1, *work in process* consists of goods that are only partially completed, and *finished goods* consist of goods that are ready to be sold. The breakdown of the overall inventory figure into these three classes of inventories is usually provided in a footnote to the financial statements.

We will use two companies—Graham Manufacturing and Reston Bookstore—to illustrate the concepts discussed in this section. Graham Manufacturing is located in British Columbia and makes precision brass fittings for yachts. Reston Bookstore is a small bookstore in Halifax, specializing in books about war and peace.

The footnotes to Graham Manufacturing's Annual Report reveal the following information concerning its inventories:

GRAHAM MANUFACTURING CORPORATION
Inventory Accounts

	Beginning Balance	Ending Balance
Raw Materials	$ 60,000	$ 50,000
Work in Process	90,000	60,000
Finished Goods	125,000	175,000
Total inventory accounts	$275,000	$285,000

In the example used in this chapter, Graham Manufacturing creates brass fittings for yachts. Its finished goods include brass locks for cabin doors.

The 3200 Series

Graham Manufacturing's raw materials inventory consists largely of brass rods and brass blocks. The work in process inventory consists of partially completed brass fittings. The finished goods inventory consists of brass fittings that are ready to be sold to customers.

In contrast, the inventory account at Reston Bookstore consists entirely of the costs of books the company has purchased from publishers for resale to the public. In merchandising companies like Reston, these inventories may be called *merchandise inventory*. The beginning and ending balances in this account appear below:

RESTON BOOKSTORE
Inventory Account

	Beginning Balance	Ending Balance
Merchandise Inventory	$100,000	$150,000

The Income Statement

Exhibit 2–2 compares the income statements of Reston Bookstore and Graham Manufacturing. For purposes of illustration, these statements contain more detail about cost of goods sold than you will generally find in published financial statements.

At first glance, the income statements of merchandising and manufacturing firms like Reston Bookstore and Graham Manufacturing are very similar. The only apparent difference is in the labels of some of the entries that go into the computation of the cost of

---

EXHIBIT 2-2   Comparative Income Statements: Merchandising and Manufacturing Companies

MERCHANDISING COMPANY
Reston Bookstore

Sales		$1,000,000
Cost of goods sold:		
Beginning merchandise inventory	$100,000	
Add purchases	650,000	
Goods available for sale	750,000	
Ending merchandise inventory	150,000	600,000
Gross margin		400,000
Less operating expenses:		
Selling expense	100,000	
Administrative expense	200,000	300,000
Net income		$ 100,000

The cost of merchandise inventory purchased from outside suppliers during the period. → Add purchases

MANUFACTURING COMPANY
Graham Manufacturing

Sales		$1,500,000
Cost of goods sold:		
Beginning finished goods inventory	$125,000	
Add cost of goods manufactured	850,000	
Goods available for sale	975,000	
Ending finished goods inventory	175,000	800,000
Gross margin		700,000
Less operating expenses:		
Selling expense	250,000	
Administrative expense	300,000	550,000
Net income		$ 150,000

The manufacturing costs associated with the goods that were finished during the period. (See Exhibits 2–3 and 2–4 for details.) → Add cost of goods manufactured

goods sold figure. In the exhibit, the computation of cost of goods sold relies on the following basic equation for inventory accounts:

Basic Equation for Inventory Accounts

$$\begin{matrix} \text{Beginning} \\ \text{balance} \end{matrix} + \begin{matrix} \text{Additions} \\ \text{to inventory} \end{matrix} = \begin{matrix} \text{Ending} \\ \text{balance} \end{matrix} + \begin{matrix} \text{Withdrawals} \\ \text{from inventory} \end{matrix}$$

For example, cost of goods sold in a merchandising company like Reston Bookstore is determined with the following variation on the basic equation:

Cost of Goods Sold in a Merchandising Company

$$\begin{matrix} \text{Beginning} \\ \text{merchandise} \\ \text{inventory} \end{matrix} + \text{Purchases} = \begin{matrix} \text{Ending} \\ \text{merchandise} \\ \text{inventory} \end{matrix} + \begin{matrix} \text{Cost of} \\ \text{goods sold} \end{matrix}$$

or

$$\begin{matrix} \text{Cost of} \\ \text{goods sold} \end{matrix} = \begin{matrix} \text{Beginning} \\ \text{merchandise} \\ \text{inventory} \end{matrix} + \text{Purchases} - \begin{matrix} \text{Ending} \\ \text{merchandise} \\ \text{inventory} \end{matrix}$$

The cost of goods sold for a manufacturing company like Graham Manufacturing is determined as follows:

Cost of Goods Sold in a Manufacturing Company

$$\begin{matrix} \text{Beginning finished} \\ \text{goods inventory} \end{matrix} + \begin{matrix} \text{Costs of goods} \\ \text{manufactured} \end{matrix} = \begin{matrix} \text{Ending finished} \\ \text{goods inventory} \end{matrix} + \begin{matrix} \text{Costs of} \\ \text{goods sold} \end{matrix}$$

or

$$\begin{matrix} \text{Cost of} \\ \text{goods sold} \end{matrix} = \begin{matrix} \text{Beginning finished} \\ \text{goods inventory} \end{matrix} + \begin{matrix} \text{Costs of goods} \\ \text{manufactured} \end{matrix} - \begin{matrix} \text{Ending finished} \\ \text{goods inventory} \end{matrix}$$

To determine the cost of goods sold in a merchandising company like Reston Bookstore, we only need to know the beginning and ending balances in the Merchandise inventory account and the purchases. Total purchases can be easily determined in a merchandising company by simply adding together all purchases from suppliers.

To determine the cost of goods sold in a manufacturing company like Graham Manufacturing, we need to know the *cost of goods manufactured* and the beginning and ending balances in the Finished Goods inventory account. The **cost of goods manufactured** consists of the manufacturing costs associated with goods that were finished during the period. The cost of goods manufactured figure for Graham Manufacturing is derived in Exhibit 2–3, which contains a *schedule of cost of goods manufactured.*

Schedule of Cost of Goods Manufactured

OBJECTIVE 4

Prepare a schedule of cost of goods manufactured in good form.

At first glance, the **schedule of cost of goods manufactured** in Exhibit 2–3 appears complex and perhaps even intimidating. However, it is all quite logical. Notice that the schedule of cost of goods manufactured contains the three elements of product costs that we discussed earlier—direct materials, direct labour, and manufacturing overhead. The total

EXHIBIT 2-3

Schedule of Cost of
Goods Manufactured

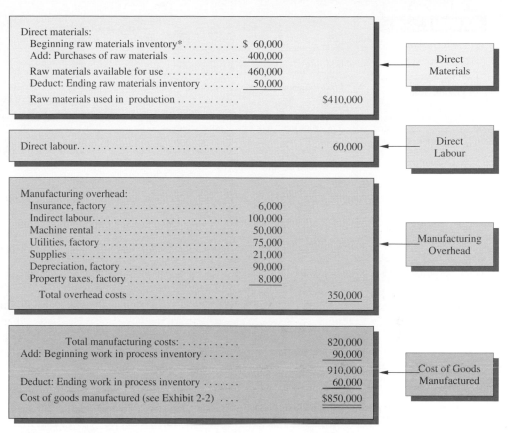

Direct materials:
   Beginning raw materials inventory*. . . . . $ 60,000
   Add: Purchases of raw materials 400,000
   Raw materials available for use 460,000
   Deduct: Ending raw materials inventory 50,000
   Raw materials used in production $410,000

— Direct Materials

Direct labour. 60,000

— Direct Labour

Manufacturing overhead:
   Insurance, factory   6,000
   Indirect labour. 100,000
   Machine rental   50,000
   Utilities, factory   75,000
   Supplies   21,000
   Depreciation, factory   90,000
   Property taxes, factory   8,000
     Total overhead costs   350,000

— Manufacturing Overhead

Total manufacturing costs: 820,000
Add: Beginning work in process inventory 90,000
                               910,000
Deduct: Ending work in process inventory 60,000
Cost of goods manufactured (see Exhibit 2-2) $850,000

— Cost of Goods Manufactured

* We assume in this example that the Raw Materials inventory account contains only direct materials and that indirect materials are carried in a separate Supplies account. Using a Supplies account for indirect materials is a common practice among companies. In Chapter 3, we discuss the procedure to be followed if *both* direct and indirect materials are carried in a single account.

of these three cost elements is *not* the cost of goods manufactured, however. The reason is that some of the materials, labour, and overhead costs incurred during the period relate to goods that are not yet completed. The costs that relate to goods that are not yet completed are shown in the work in process inventory figures at the bottom of the schedule. Note that the beginning work in process inventory must be added to the manufacturing costs of the period, and the ending work in process inventory must be deducted, to arrive at the cost of goods manufactured.

    The logic underlying the schedule of cost of goods manufactured and the computation of cost of goods sold is laid out in a different format in Exhibit 2–4. To compute the cost of goods sold, go to the top of the exhibit and work your way down using the following steps:
1. Compute the raw materials used in production in the top section of the exhibit.
2. Insert the total raw materials used in production ($410,000) into the second section of the exhibit, and compute the total manufacturing cost.
3. Insert the total manufacturing cost ($820,000) into the third section of the exhibit, and compute the cost of goods manufactured.
4. Insert the cost of goods manufactured ($850,000) into the bottom section of the exhibit, and compute the cost of goods sold.

EXHIBIT 2-4

An Alternative
Approach to
Computation of Cost
of Goods Sold

Computation of Raw Materials Used in Production

Beginning raw materials inventory	$ 60,000
+ Purchases of raw materials	400,000
− Ending raw materials inventory	50,000
= Raw materials used in production	$410,000

Computation of Total Manufacturing Cost

Raw materials used in production	$410,000
+ Direct labour	60,000
+ Total manufacturing overhead costs	350,000
= Total manufacturing cost	$820,000

Computation of Cost of Goods Manufactured

Beginning work in process inventory	$ 90,000
+ Total manufacturing cost	820,000
− Ending work in process inventory	60,000
= Cost of goods manufactured	$850,000

Computation of Cost of Goods Sold

Beginning finished goods inventory	$125,000
+ Cost of goods manufactured	850,000
− Ending finished goods inventory	175,000
= Cost of goods sold	$800,000

PRODUCT COSTS—A CLOSER LOOK

OBJECTIVE 5

Explain the flow of
direct materials cost,
direct labour cost, and
manufacturing
overhead cost from the
point of incurrence to
sale of the completed
product.

Earlier in the chapter, we defined product costs as consisting of those costs that are involved in either the purchase or the manufacture of goods. For manufactured goods, we stated that these costs consist of direct materials, direct labour, and manufacturing overhead. To understand product costs more fully, it will be helpful at this point to look briefly at the flow of costs in a manufacturing company. By doing so, we will be able to see how product costs move through the various accounts and affect the balance sheet and the income statement in the course of the manufacture and sale of goods.

Exhibit 2–5 illustrates the flow of costs in a manufacturing company. Raw materials purchases are recorded in the Raw Materials inventory account. When raw materials are used in production, their costs are transferred to the Work in Process inventory account as direct materials. Notice that direct labour cost and manufacturing overhead cost are added directly to Work in Process. Work in Process can be viewed most simply as the assembly line in a manufacturing plant, where workers are stationed and where products slowly take shape as they move from one end of the assembly line to the other. The direct materials, direct labour, and manufacturing overhead costs added to Work in Process in Exhibit 2–5 are the costs needed to complete these products as they move along this assembly line.

As goods are completed, notice from the exhibit that their cost is transferred from Work in Process into Finished Goods. Here the goods await sale to a customer. As goods are sold, their cost is then transferred from Finished Goods into Cost of Goods Sold. It is at this point that the various material, labour, and overhead costs that were involved in the manufacture of the units being sold are finally treated as expenses.

EXHIBIT 2-5

Cost Flows and
Classifications in a
Manufacturing
Company

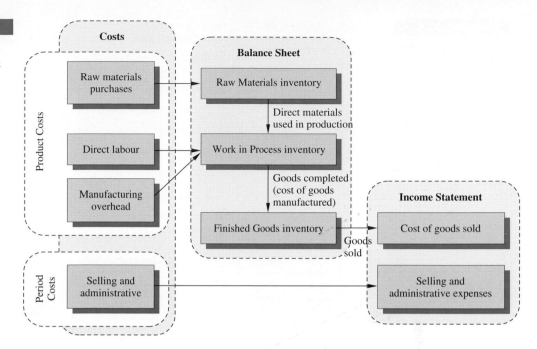

Inventoriable Costs

As stated earlier, product costs are often called inventoriable costs. The reason is that these costs go directly into inventory accounts as they are incurred (first into Work in Process and then into Finished Goods), rather than going into expense accounts. Thus, they are termed *inventoriable costs. This is a key concept in managerial accounting, since such costs can end up on the balance sheet as assets if goods are only partially completed or are unsold at the end of a period.* To illustrate this point, refer again to the data in Exhibit 2–5. The materials, labour, and overhead costs that are associated with the units in the Work in Process and Finished Goods inventory accounts at the end of a period will appear on the balance sheet at that time as part of the company's assets. As explained earlier, these costs will not become expenses until later when the goods are completed and sold.

As shown in Exhibit 2–5, selling and administrative expenses are not involved in the manufacture of a product. For this reason, they are not treated as product costs but rather as period costs that go directly into expense accounts as they are incurred.

An Example of Cost Flows

To provide a numerical example of cost flows in a manufacturing company, assume that a company's annual insurance cost is $2,000. Three-fourths of this amount ($1,500) applies to factory operations, and one-fourth ($500) applies to selling and administrative activities. Therefore, $1,500 of the $2,000 insurance cost would be a product (inventoriable) cost and would be added to the cost of the goods produced during the year. This concept is illustrated in Exhibit 2–6, where $1,500 of insurance cost is added into Work in Process. As shown in the exhibit, this portion of the year's insurance cost will not become an expense until the goods that are produced during the year are sold—which may not

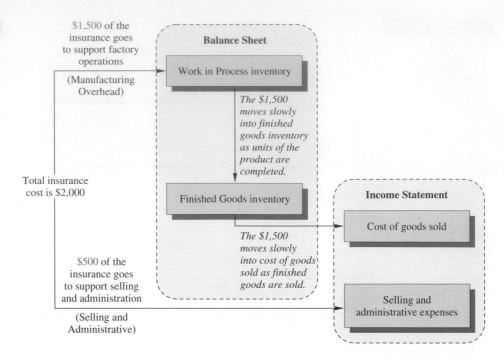

EXHIBIT 2-6

An Example of Cost
Flows in a
Manufacturing
Company

happen until the following year. Until the goods are sold, the $1,500 will remain as part of the asset, inventory (either as part of Work in Process or as part of Finished Goods), along with the other costs of producing the goods.

By contrast, the $500 of insurance cost that applies to the company's selling and administrative activities will go into an expense account immediately as a charge against the period's revenue.

Thus far, our discussion has been mainly concerned with classifications of manufacturing costs for the purpose of determining inventory valuations on the balance sheet and cost of goods sold on the income statement. There are, however, many other purposes for which costs are used, and each purpose requires a different classification of costs. We will consider several different purposes for cost classifications in the remaining sections of this chapter. These purposes and the corresponding cost classifications are summarized in Exhibit 2–7. To maintain focus, we suggest that you refer back to this exhibit frequently as you progress through the rest of this chapter.

COST CLASSIFICATIONS FOR PREDICTING COST BEHAVIOUR

OBJECTIVE 6
Identify and give
examples of variable
costs and fixed costs,
and explain the
difference in their
behaviour.

Quite frequently, it is necessary to predict how a certain cost will behave in response to a change in activity. For example, a manager at Sask Tel may want to estimate the impact a 5% increase in revenue-generating long-distance calls would have on the company's total electric bill or on the total wages the company pays its long-distance operators. **Cost behaviour** means how a cost will react or respond to changes in the level of business activity. As the activity level rises and falls, a particular cost may rise and fall as well—or it may remain constant. For planning purposes, a manager must be able to anticipate which of these will happen; and if a cost can be expected to change, the manager must know by how much it will change. To help make such distinctions, costs are often categorized as variable or fixed.

EXHIBIT 2-7

Summary of Cost
Classifications

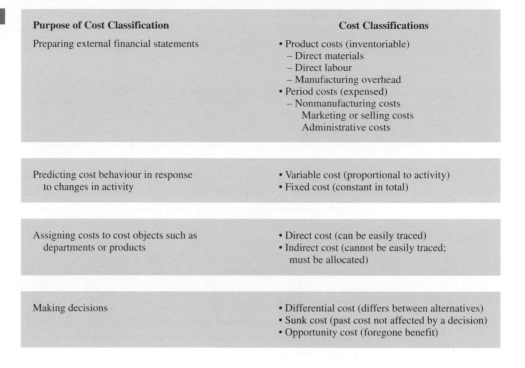

Purpose of Cost Classification	Cost Classifications

Preparing external financial statements	• Product costs (inventoriable)
	 – Direct materials
	 – Direct labour
	 – Manufacturing overhead
	• Period costs (expensed)
	 – Nonmanufacturing costs
	  Marketing or selling costs
	  Administrative costs

Predicting cost behaviour in response to changes in activity	• Variable cost (proportional to activity) • Fixed cost (constant in total)
Assigning costs to cost objects such as departments or products	• Direct cost (can be easily traced) • Indirect cost (cannot be easily traced; must be allocated)
Making decisions	• Differential cost (differs between alternatives) • Sunk cost (past cost not affected by a decision) • Opportunity cost (foregone benefit)

Variable Cost

A **variable cost** is a cost that varies, in total, in direct proportion to changes in the level of activity. The activity can be expressed in many ways, such as units produced, units sold, kilometres driven, beds occupied, lines of print, hours worked, and so forth. A good example of a variable cost is direct materials. The cost of direct materials used during a period will vary, in total, in direct proportion to the number of units that are produced. To illustrate this idea, consider the Canadian-based Nova Bus Corporation. Each bus requires one battery. As the output of buses increases and decreases, the number of batteries used will increase and decrease proportionately. If bus production goes up 10%, then the number of batteries used will also go up 10%. The concept of a variable cost is shown in graphic form in Exhibit 2–8.

EXHIBIT 2-8

Variable and Fixed
Cost Behaviour

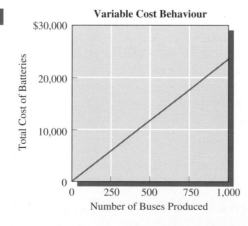

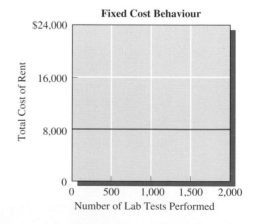

It is important to note that when we speak of a cost as being variable, we do so in terms of its *total dollar amount*—the total cost rises and falls as the activity level rises and falls. This idea is presented below, assuming that a bus battery costs $24:

Number of Buses Produced	Cost per Battery	Total Variable Cost— Batteries
1	$24	$ 24
500	24	12,000
1,000	24	24,000

One interesting aspect of variable cost behaviour is that a variable cost is constant if expressed on a *per unit* basis. Observe from the tabulation above that the per unit cost of batteries remains constant at $24 even though the total amount of cost involved increases and decreases with activity. The reader may be inclined to say, "Wait a minute, how can a variable cost be constant per unit, when quantity discounts are available for bulk purchases? The more I buy, the less I pay per unit." Although quantity discounts do exist for many items, managers typically focus on the price that must be paid within a "normal" range of operating activity. If, for example, an airline normally uses between 20,000 and 32,000 litres of fuel a day, then it would focus on the price to be paid within that *relevant range* of activity. A **relevant range** can be defined as the range of activity within which assumptions relative to variable and fixed cost behaviour are valid. More is said about the relevant range in Chapter 6.

There are many examples of variable costs. In a manufacturing company, they would usually include direct materials, direct labour, some items of manufacturing overhead (such as utilities, supplies, and lubricants), and perhaps shipping costs and sales commissions. In a merchandising company, they would include cost of goods sold, commissions to salespersons, and billing costs.

During the 1980s, steel companies operating in North America lost a substantial portion of their business to foreign producers. Since steel production involves a large amount of fixed cost, the loss of business drove per tonne manufacturing costs upward for North American companies, resulting in huge operating losses. But by modernizing plants and focusing on regaining lost market share, North American companies have now driven per tonne manufacturing costs back downward to the point where only South Korea and Britain produce for less.

The greatest threat now to North American steel companies is a loss of market share to new "minimills" that focus on various market niches. Such a loss of market share would again drive per tonne manufacturing costs upward. The reason is that the level of fixed costs in major steel companies is even higher today than it was 15 years ago due to the large-scale modernization that has taken place.[2]

2"The Big Threat to Big Steel's Future," *Fortune* (July 15, 1991), pp. 106–8.

Fixed Cost

A **fixed cost** is a cost that remains constant, in total, regardless of changes in the level of activity within the relevant range. That is, unlike variable costs, fixed costs are not affected by changes in activity within the relevant range during a period. Consequently, as the activity level rises and falls, the fixed costs remain constant in total amount unless influenced by some outside force, such as price changes. Rent is a good example of a fixed cost. Suppose the Quebec Clinic rents a machine for $8,000 per month that tests blood samples for the presence of leukemia cells. The $8,000 monthly rental cost will be sustained regardless of the number of tests that may be performed during the month. The concept of a fixed cost is shown in graphic form in Exhibit 2–8.

The presence of fixed costs in an organization can create difficulties if it becomes necessary to express the costs on a per unit basis. This is because if fixed costs are expressed on a per unit basis, they will react *inversely* with changes in activity. In the Quebec Clinic example mentioned above, for example, the average cost per test will fall as the number of tests performed increases. This is because the $8,000 rental cost will be spread over more tests. Conversely, as the number of tests performed in the clinic declines, the average cost per test will rise as the $8,000 rental cost is spread over fewer tests. This concept is illustrated in the table below:

Monthly Rental Cost	Number of Tests Performed	Average Cost per Test
$8,000	10	$800
8,000	500	16
8,000	2,000	4

Note that if the Quebec Clinic performs only 10 tests each month, the rental cost of the equipment will average $800 per test. But if 2,000 tests are performed each month, the average cost will drop to only $4 per test. More will be said later about the problems created for both the accountant and the manager by this variation in unit costs.

Examples of fixed costs include straight-line depreciation, insurance, property taxes, rent, supervisory salaries, administrative salaries, and advertising.

A summary of both variable and fixed cost behaviour is presented in Exhibit 2–9 on the following page. Study this exhibit carefully, along with the material in the preceding paragraphs, until you thoroughly understand the concepts.

Medical centres use many expensive pieces of equipment, including dialysis machines and MRI scanners. Often, these machines are rented rather than purchased. The rental cost is classified as a fixed cost.

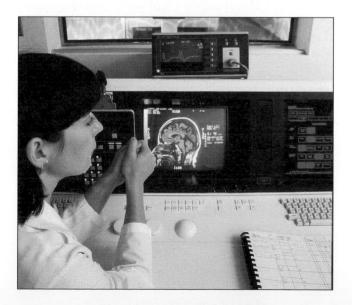

EXHIBIT 2-9

Summary of Variable
and Fixed Cost
Behaviour

Cost	Behaviour of the Cost (within the relevant range)	
	In Total	Per Unit
Variable cost	Total variable cost increases and decreases in proportion to changes in the activity level.	Variable costs remain constant per unit.
Fixed cost	Total fixed cost is not affected by changes in the activity level within the relevant range (i.e., total fixed cost remains constant even if the activity level changes).	Fixed costs decrease per unit as the activity level rises and increase per unit as the activity level falls.

COST CLASSIFICATIONS FOR ASSIGNING COSTS TO COST OBJECTS

OBJECTIVE 7
Define and give
examples of direct and
indirect costs.

Costs are assigned to objects for a variety of purposes including pricing, profitability studies, and control of spending. A **cost object** is anything for which cost data are desired—including products, product lines, customers, jobs, and organizational subunits. For purposes of assigning costs to cost objects, costs are classified as either *direct* or *indirect*.

Direct Cost

A **direct cost** is a cost that can be easily and conveniently traced to the particular cost object under consideration. The concept of direct cost extends beyond just direct materials and direct labour. For example, if Reebok is assigning costs to its various regional and national sales offices, then the salary of the sales manager in its Tokyo office would be a direct cost of that office.

Indirect Cost

An **indirect cost** is a cost that cannot be easily and conveniently traced to the particular cost object under consideration. The factory manager's salary at a Moosehead Breweries plant, for example, would be an indirect cost of a particular brand of beer such as Alpine Light. The reason is that the factory manager's salary is not caused by any one product but rather is incurred as a consequence of running a factory. *To be traced to a cost object such as a particular product, the cost must be caused by the cost object.* Indirect costs are also known as **common costs.**

A particular cost may be direct or indirect, depending upon the cost object. While the Moosehead Breweries factory manager's salary is an *indirect* cost of manufacturing beer, it is a *direct* cost of the manufacturing division. In the first case, the cost object is the beer product. In the second case, the cost object is the entire manufacturing division.

COST CLASSIFICATIONS FOR DECISION MAKING

OBJECTIVE 8
Define and give
examples of cost
classifications used in
making decisions:
differential costs,
opportunity costs, and
sunk costs.

Costs are an important feature of many business decisions. In making decisions, it is essential to have a firm grasp of the concepts *differential cost, opportunity cost,* and *sunk cost.*

Differential Cost and Revenue

Decisions involve choosing between alternatives. In business decisions, each alternative will have certain costs and benefits that must be compared to the costs and benefits of the other available alternatives. A difference in costs between any two alternatives is known as a **differential cost.** A difference in revenues between any two alternatives is known as **differential revenue.**

A differential cost is also known as an **incremental cost,** although technically an incremental cost should refer only to an increase in cost from one alternative to another; decreases in cost should be referred to as *decremental costs.* Differential cost is a broader term, encompassing both cost increases (incremental costs) and cost decreases (decremental costs) between alternatives.

The accountant's differential cost concept can be compared to the economist's marginal cost concept. In speaking of changes in cost and revenue, the economist employs the terms *marginal cost* and *marginal revenue.* The revenue that can be obtained from selling one more unit of product is called marginal revenue, and the cost involved in producing one more unit of product is called marginal cost. The economist's marginal concept is basically the same as the accountant's differential concept.

Differential costs can be either fixed or variable. To illustrate, assume that Nature Way Cosmetics, Inc., is thinking about changing its marketing method from distribution through retailers to distribution by door-to-door direct sale. Present costs and revenues are compared to projected costs and revenues in the following table:

	Retailer Distribution (present)	Direct Sale Distribution (proposed)	Differential Costs and Revenues
Revenues (V)	$700,000	$800,000	$100,000
Cost of goods sold (V)	350,000	400,000	50,000
Advertising (F)	80,000	45,000	(35,000)
Commissions (V)	-0-	40,000	40,000
Warehouse depreciation (F)	50,000	80,000	30,000
Other expenses (F)	60,000	60,000	–0–
Total	540,000	625,000	85,000
Net income	$160,000	$175,000	$ 15,000

V = Variable; F = Fixed.

According to the above analysis, the differential revenue is $100,000, and the differential costs total $85,000, leaving a positive differential net income of $15,000 under the proposed marketing plan.

The decision of whether Nature Way Cosmetics should stay with the present retail distribution or switch to door-to-door direct selling could be made on the basis of the net incomes of the two alternatives. As we see in the above analysis, the net income under the present distribution method is $160,000, whereas the net income under door-to-door direct selling is estimated to be $175,000. Therefore, the door-to-door direct distribution method is preferred, since it would result in $15,000 higher net income. Note that we would have

According to the year ended December 31, 1996, annual report of Island Telephone Company of Prince Edward Island, net income increased to $8.2 million or $2.15 per common share, compared to $7.1 million or $1.90 per common share in 1995.

Island Tel's expenses were $46.9 million in 1996 compared to $42.8 million in 1995. Depreciation expense associated with the Company's expanding telecommunications network accounted for $1.5 million of this increase. The second major cause of expense growth was the *incremental* cost of adding each new customer to Island Tel Mobility's rapidly growing cellular network.

arrived at exactly the same conclusion by simply focusing on the differential revenues, differential costs, and differential net income which also show a $15,000 advantage for the direct selling method.

In general, only the differences between alternatives are relevant in decisions. Those items that are the same under all alternatives and that are not affected by the decision can be ignored. For example, in the Nature Way Cosmetics example above, the "Other expenses" category, which is $60,000 under both alternatives, can be ignored, since it has no effect on the decision. If it were removed from the calculations, the door-to-door direct selling method would still be preferred by $15,000. This is an extremely important principle in management accounting that we will return to in later chapters.

Opportunity Cost

Opportunity cost is the potential benefit that is given up when one alternative is selected over another. To illustrate this important concept, consider the following examples:

Example A

Vicki has a part-time job that pays her $100 per week while attending college. She would like to spend a week at the beach during spring break, and her employer has agreed to give her the time off, but without pay. The $100 in lost wages would be an opportunity cost of taking the week off to be at the beach.

Example B

Suppose that The Bay is considering investing a large sum of money in land that may be a site for a future store. Rather than invest the funds in land, the company could invest the funds in high-grade securities. If the land is acquired, the opportunity cost will be the investment income that could have been realized if the securities had been purchased instead.

Example C

Steve is employed with a company that pays him a salary of $20,000 per year. He is thinking about leaving the company and returning to school. Since returning to school would require that he give up his $20,000 salary, the foregone salary would be an opportunity cost of seeking further education.

Opportunity cost is not usually entered in the accounting records of an organization, but it is a cost that must be explicitly considered in every decision a manager makes.

Virtually every alternative has some opportunity cost attached to it. In example C above, for instance, if Steve decides to stay at his job, there still is an opportunity cost involved: it is the greater income that could be realized in future years as a result of returning to school.

Sunk Cost

A **sunk cost** is a cost *that has already been incurred* and that cannot be changed by any decision made now or in the future. Since sunk costs cannot be changed by any present or future decision, they are not differential costs, and therefore they can, and should, be ignored when analyzing future courses of action.

To illustrate a sunk cost, assume that a firm has paid $50,000 for a special-purpose machine. Since the cost outlay *has been made,* the $50,000 investment in the machine is a sunk cost. Even though by hindsight the purchase may have been unwise, no amount of regret can relieve the company of its decision, nor can any future decision cause the cost to be avoided. In short, the $50,000 is "out the window" from a decision point of view and will have to be reckoned with regardless of what future course of action the company may take. For this reason, such costs are said to be sunk and should be ignored in decisions.

SUMMARY

In this chapter, we have looked at some of the ways in which managers classify costs. How the costs will be used—for preparing external reports, predicting cost behaviour, assigning costs to cost objects, or decision making—will dictate how the costs will be classified.

For purposes of valuing inventories and determining expenses for the balance sheet and income statement, costs are classified as either product costs or period costs. Product costs are assigned to inventories and are considered assets until the products are sold. At the point of sale, product costs become cost of goods sold on the income statement. Period costs, in contrast, are taken directly to the income statement as expenses in the period in which they are incurred.

In a merchandising company, product cost is whatever the company paid for its merchandise. For external financial reports in a manufacturing company, product costs consist of all manufacturing costs. In both kinds of companies, selling and administrative costs are considered to be period costs and are expensed as incurred.

For purposes of predicting cost behaviour—how costs will react to changes in activity—managers commonly classify costs into two categories—variable and fixed. Variable costs, in total, are strictly proportional to activity. Thus, the variable cost per unit is constant. Fixed costs, in total, remain at the same level for changes in activity that occur within the relevant range. Thus, the average fixed cost per unit decreases as the number of units increases.

For purposes of assigning costs to cost objects such as products or departments, costs are classified as direct or indirect. Direct costs can be conveniently traced to the cost objects. Indirect costs cannot be conveniently traced to cost objects.

For purposes of making decisions, the concepts of differential costs and revenue, opportunity cost, and sunk cost are of vital importance. Differential cost and revenue are the cost and revenue items that differ between alternatives. Opportunity cost is the benefit that is foregone when one alternative is selected over another. Sunk cost is a cost that occurred in the past and cannot be altered. Differential cost and opportunity cost should be carefully considered in decisions. Sunk cost is always irrelevant in decisions and should be ignored.

REVIEW PROBLEM 1: COST TERMS

Many new cost terms have been introduced in this chapter. It will take you some time to learn what each term means and how to properly classify costs in an organization. To assist in this learning process, consider the following example: Porter Company manufactures furniture, including tables. Selected costs associated with the manufacture of the tables and the general operation of the company are given below:

1. Wood is used in the manufacture of the tables, at a cost of $100 per table.
2. The tables are assembled by workers, at a wage cost of $40 per table.
3. Workers assembling the tables are supervised by a factory supervisor who is paid $25,000 per year.
4. Electrical costs of $2 per machine-hour are incurred to manufacture the tables. (Four machine-hours are required to produce a table.)
5. The depreciation cost of the machines used to make the tables totals $10,000 per year.
6. The salary of the president of Porter Company is $100,000 per year.
7. Porter Company spends $250,000 per year to advertise its products.
8. Salespersons are paid a commission of $30 for each table sold.
9. Instead of producing the tables, Porter Company could rent its factory space out at a rental income of $50,000 per year.

Required

In the tabulation below, these costs are classified according to various cost terms used in the chapter. *Carefully study the classification of each cost.* If you don't understand why a particular cost is classified the way it is, reread the section of the chapter discussing the particular cost term.

Solution to Review Problem 1

	Variable Cost	Fixed Cost	Period (selling and administrative) Cost	Direct Materials	Direct Labour	Manufacturing Overhead	Direct	Indirect	Sunk Cost	Opportunity Cost
				Product Cost			**To Units of Product**			
1. Wood used in a table (at $100 per table)	X			X			X			
2. Labour cost to assemble a table (at $40 per table) .	X				X		X			
3. Salary of the factory supervisor (at $25,000 per year)		X				X		X		
4. Cost of electricity to produce tables (at $2 per machine-hour) ...	X					X		X		
5. Depreciation of machines used to produce tables (at $10,000 per year)		X				X		X	X*	
6. Salary of the company president (at $100,000 per year)		X	X							
7. Advertising expense (at $250,000 per year)		X	X							
8. Commissions paid to salespersons (at $30 per table sold)	X		X							
9. Rental income foregone on factory space										X†

* This is a sunk cost, since the outlay for the equipment was made in some previous period.

† This is an opportunity cost, since it represents the potential benefit that is lost or sacrificed as a result of using the factory space to produce tables. Opportunity cost is a special category of cost that is not ordinarily recorded in an organization's accounting books. To avoid possible confusion with other costs, we will not attempt to classify this cost in any other way except as an opportunity cost.

REVIEW PROBLEM 2: SCHEDULE OF COST OF GOODS MANUFACTURED AND INCOME STATEMENT

The following was taken from the ledger accounts of Klear-Seal Company for last year:

Selling expenses	$ 140,000
Raw materials inventory, January 1	90,000
Raw materials inventory, December 31	60,000
Utilities, factory	36,000
Direct labour cost	150,000
Depreciation, factory	162,000
Purchases of raw materials	750,000
Sales	2,500,000
Insurance, factory	40,000
Supplies, factory	15,000
Administrative expenses	270,000
Indirect labour	300,000
Maintenance, factory	87,000
Work in process inventory, January 1	180,000
Work in process inventory, December 31	100,000
Finished goods inventory, January 1	260,000
Finished goods inventory, December 31	210,000

Management wants to organize these data into a better format so that financial statements can be prepared for the year.

Required

1. Prepare a schedule of cost of goods manufactured.
2. Compute the cost of goods sold.
3. Using data as needed from (1) and (2) above, prepare an income statement.

Solution to Review Problem 2

1.

KLEAR-SEAL COMPANY
Schedule of Cost of Goods Manufactured
For the Year Ended December 31

Direct materials:		
Raw materials inventory, January 1	$ 90,000	
Add: Purchases of raw materials	750,000	
Raw materials available for use	840,000	
Deduct: Raw materials inventory, December 31	60,000	
Raw materials used in production		$ 780,000
Direct labour		150,000
Manufacturing overhead:		
Utilities, factory	36,000	
Depreciation, factory	162,000	
Insurance, factory	40,000	
Supplies, factory	15,000	
Indirect labour	300,000	
Maintenance, factory	87,000	
Total overhead costs		640,000
Total manufacturing costs		1,570,000
Add: Work in process inventory, January 1		180,000
		1,750,000
Deduct: Work in process inventory, December 31		100,000
Cost of goods manufactured		$1,650,000

2. The cost of goods sold would be computed as follows:

Finished goods inventory, January 1	$ 260,000
Add: Cost of goods manufactured	1,650,000
Goods available for sale	1,910,000
Deduct: Finished goods inventory, December 31	210,000
Cost of goods sold	$1,700,000

3.

KLEAR-SEAL COMPANY
Income Statement
For the Year Ended December 31

Sales		$2,500,000
Less cost of goods sold (above)		1,700,000
Gross margin		800,000
Less selling and administrative expenses:		
Selling expenses	$140,000	
Administrative expenses	270,000	
Total expenses		410,000
Net income		$ 390,000

KEY TERMS FOR REVIEW

OBJECTIVE 9
Define or explain the key terms listed at the end of the chapter.

Administrative costs All executive, organizational, and clerical costs associated with the general management of an organization rather than with manufacturing, marketing, or selling. (p. 51)

Common costs See *Indirect cost.* (p. 64)

Conversion cost Direct labour cost plus manufacturing overhead cost. (p. 51)

Cost behaviour The way in which a cost reacts or responds to changes in the level of business activity. (p. 60)

Cost object Anything for which cost data are desired. Examples of possible cost objects are products, product lines, customers, jobs, and organizational subunits such as departments or divisions of a company. (p. 64)

Cost of goods manufactured The manufacturing costs associated with the goods that were finished during the period. (p. 56)

Differential cost A difference in cost between any two alternatives. Also see *Incremental cost.* (p. 65)

Differential revenue The difference in revenue between any two alternatives. (p. 65)

Direct cost A cost that can be easily and conveniently traced to the particular cost object under consideration. (p. 64)

Direct labour Those factory labour costs that can be easily traced to particular products. Also called *touch labour.* (p.50)

Direct materials Those materials that become an integral part of a finished product and can be conveniently traced into it. (p. 49)

Fixed cost A cost that remains constant, in total, regardless of changes in the level of activity within the relevant range. If a fixed cost is expressed on a per unit basis, it varies inversely with the level of activity. (p. 63)

Incremental cost An increase in cost between two alternatives. Also see *Differential cost.* (p. 65)

Indirect cost A cost that cannot be easily and conveniently traced to the particular cost object under consideration. An indirect cost is also known as a *common cost.* (p. 64)

Indirect labour The labour costs of janitors, supervisors, materials handlers, and other factory workers that cannot be conveniently traced directly to particular products. (p. 50)

Indirect materials Small items of material such as glue and nails. These items may become an integral part of a finished product but are traceable into the product only at great cost or inconvenience. (p. 50)

Inventoriable costs Synonym for *product costs.* (p. 52)

Manufacturing The transformation of an input such as a raw material into a form that has greater value to customers. (p. 49)

Manufacturing overhead All costs associated with manufacturing except direct materials and direct labour. (p. 50)

Marketing or selling costs   All costs necessary to secure customer orders and get the finished product or service into the hands of the customer. This term is synonymous with *order-getting and order-filling costs.* (p. 51)

Merchandising   The sale of products that are in finished form that have been acquired from a manufacturer or other outside source. (p. 49)

Opportunity cost   The potential benefit that is given up when one alternative is selected over another. (p. 66)

Order-getting and order-filling costs   Synonym for *marketing or selling costs.* (p. 51)

Period costs   Those costs that are taken directly to the income statement as expenses in the period in which they are incurred; such costs consist of selling (marketing) and administrative expenses. (p. 52)

Prime cost   Direct materials cost plus direct labour cost. (p. 51)

Product costs   All costs that are involved in the purchase or manufacture of goods. In the case of manufactured goods, these costs consist of direct materials, direct labour, and manufacturing overhead. Also see *Inventoriable costs.* (p. 52)

Raw materials   Any materials that go into the final product. (p. 49)

Relevant range   The range of activity within which assumptions relative to variable and fixed cost behaviour are valid. (p. 62)

Schedule of cost of goods manufactured   A schedule showing the direct materials, direct labour, and manufacturing overhead costs incurred for a period and assigned to Work in Process and completed goods. (p. 56)

Sunk cost   Any cost that has already been incurred and that cannot be changed by any decision made now or in the future. (p. 67)

Variable cost   A cost that varies, in total, in direct proportion to changes in the level of activity. A variable cost is constant per unit. (p. 61)

APPENDIX 2A: FURTHER CLASSIFICATION OF LABOUR COSTS

OBJECTIVE 10
Properly classify labour costs associated with idle time, overtime, and fringe benefits.

Of all the costs of an organization, labour costs often present the most difficult problems of segregation and classification. Although companies vary considerably in how they break down labour costs, the following subdivisions represent the most common approach:

Direct Labour	Indirect Labour (part of manufacturing overhead)	Other Labour Costs
(Discussed earlier)	Janitors Supervisors Materials handlers Night security guards Maintenance workers	Idle time Overtime premium Labour fringe benefits

The costs listed in the Indirect Labour and Other Labour Costs columns should not be viewed as being inclusive but rather as being representative of the kinds of costs that one might expect to find under these classifications. The costs in the Other Labour Costs column require further comment.

Idle Time

Idle time represents the costs of direct labour workers who are unable to perform their assignments due to machine breakdowns, materials shortages, power failures, and the like. Although direct labour workers are involved, the costs of idle time are treated as part of manufacturing overhead cost rather than as part of direct labour cost. The reason is that

Even in small companies such as the one that makes these pirogues (hand-built canoes), the payroll cost is more than just the wages paid to employees.

managers feel that such costs should be spread over *all* the production of a period rather than just over the jobs that happen to be in process when breakdowns and the like occur.

To give an example of how the cost of idle time is computed, assume that a press operator earns $12 per hour. If the press operator is paid for a normal 40-hour workweek but is idle for 3 hours during a given week due to breakdowns, labour cost would be allocated as follows:

Direct labour ($12 × 37 hours)	$444
Manufacturing overhead (idle time: $12 × 3 hours)	36
Total cost for the week	$480

Overtime Premium

The overtime premium paid to *all* factory workers (direct labour as well as indirect labour) is usually considered to be part of manufacturing overhead and not assignable to any particular order or batch of production. At first glance this may seem strange, since overtime is always spent working on some particular order. Why not charge that order for the overtime cost? The reason is that production is usually scheduled on a random basis. If production is randomly scheduled, then it would be unfair to charge an overtime premium against a particular batch of goods simply because the batch *happened* to fall on the tail end of the daily scheduling sheet.

To illustrate, assume that two batches of goods, order A and order B, each takes three hours to complete. The production run on order A is scheduled early in the day, but the production run on order B isn't scheduled until late in the afternoon. By the time the run on order B is completed, two hours of overtime have been logged in. The necessity to work overtime was a result of the fact that *total* production exceeded the regular time available. Order B was no more responsible for the overtime than was order A. Therefore, managers feel that all production should share in the premium charge that resulted. This is considered a more equitable way of handling overtime premium in that it doesn't penalize one run simply because it happens to occur late in the day.

Let us again assume that a press operator in a plant earns $12 per hour. He is paid time and a half for overtime (time in excess of 40 hours a week). During a given week, he works 45 hours and has no idle time. His labour cost for the week would be allocated as follows:

Direct labour ($12 × 45 hours)	$540
Manufacturing overhead (overtime premium: $6 × 5 hours)	30
Total cost for the week	$570

Observe from this computation that only the overtime premium of $6 per hour is charged to the overhead account—*not* the entire $18 earned for each hour of overtime work ($12 regular rate × 1.5 = $18).

Labour Fringe Benefits

The proper classification of labour fringe benefits is not so clearly defined in practice as is idle time or overtime premium. Labour fringe benefits are made up of employment-related costs paid by the employer and include the costs of insurance programs, retirement plans, various supplemental unemployment benefits, and hospitalization plans.

The employer also pays the employer's share of the Canada Pension Plan (CPP), workers' compensation, and employment insurance (EI).

Many firms treat all such costs as indirect labour by adding them in total to manufacturing overhead. Other firms treat the portion of fringe benefits that relates to direct labour as additional direct labour cost. This approach is conceptually superior, since the fringe benefits provided to direct labour workers clearly represent an added cost of their services.

QUESTIONS

2–1 What are the three major elements of product costs in a manufacturing company?

2–2 Distinguish between the following: (a) direct materials, (b) indirect materials, (c) direct labour, (d) indirect labour, and (e) manufacturing overhead.

2–3 Explain the difference between a product cost and a period cost.

2–4 Describe how the income statement of a manufacturing company differs from the income statement of a merchandising company.

2–5 Of what value is the schedule of cost of goods manufactured? How does it tie into the income statement?

2–6 Describe how the inventory accounts of a manufacturing company differ from the inventory account of a merchandising company.

2–7 Why are product costs sometimes called inventoriable costs? Describe the flow of such costs in a manufacturing company from the point of incurrence until they finally become expenses on the income statement.

2–8 Is it possible for costs such as salaries or depreciation to end up as assets on the balance sheet? Explain.

2–9 What is meant by the term *cost behaviour*?

2–10 "A variable cost is a cost that varies per unit of product, whereas a fixed cost is constant per unit of product." Do you agree? Explain.

2–11 How do fixed costs create difficulties in costing units of product?

2–12 Why is manufacturing overhead considered an indirect cost of a unit of product?

2–13 Define the following terms: differential cost, opportunity cost, and sunk cost.

2–14 Only variable costs can be differential costs. Do you agree? Explain.

2–15 (Appendix 2A) Mary Adams is employed by Acme Company. Last week she worked 34 hours assembling one of the company's products and was idle 6 hours due to material shortages. Acme's employees are engaged at their workstations for a normal 40-hour week. Ms. Adams is paid $8 per hour. Allocate her earnings between direct labour cost and manufacturing overhead cost.

2–16 (Appendix 2A) John Olsen operates a stamping machine on the assembly line of Drake Manufacturing Company. Last week Mr. Olsen worked 45 hours. His basic wage rate is $5 per hour, with time and a half for overtime (time worked in excess of 40 hours per week). Allocate Mr. Olsen's wages for the week between direct labour cost and manufacturing overhead cost.

EXERCISES

E2–1 Following are several cost terms introduced in the chapter:

Period cost	Fixed cost
Variable cost	Prime cost
Opportunity cost	Conversion cost
Product cost	Sunk cost

Choose the cost term or terms above that most appropriately describe the costs identified in each of the following situations. A cost term can be used more than once.

1. Crown Books, Inc., prints a small book titled *The Pocket Speller* that is popular with college students. The paper going into the manufacture of the book would be called direct materials and classified as a _____ cost. In terms of cost behaviour, the paper could also be described as a _____ cost.
2. Instead of compiling the words in the book, the author hired by the company could have spent many hours consulting with business organizations. The consulting fees foregone would be called _____ cost.
3. The paper and other materials used in the manufacture of the book, combined with the direct labour cost involved, would be called _____ cost.
4. The salary of Crown Books's president would be classified as a _____ cost, since the salary will appear on the income statement as an expense in the time period in which it is incurred.
5. Depreciation on the equipment used to print the book would be classified by Crown Books as a _____ cost. However, depreciation on any equipment used by the company in selling and administrative activities would be classified as a _____ cost. In terms of cost behaviour, depreciation would probably be classified as a _____ cost.
6. A _____ cost is also known as an inventoriable cost, because such costs go into the Work in Process inventory account and then into the Finished Goods inventory account before appearing on the income statement as part of cost of goods sold.
7. Taken together, the direct labour cost and manufacturing overhead cost involved in the manufacture of the book would be called _____ cost.
8. Crown Books sells the book through agents who are paid a commission on each book sold. The company would classify these commissions as a _____ cost. In terms of cost behaviour, commissions would be classified as a _____ cost.
9. Several hundred copies of the book were left over from the previous edition and are stored in a warehouse. The amount invested in these books would be called a _____ cost.

10. Costs can often be classified in several ways. For example, Crown Books pays $4,000 rent each month on the building that houses its printing press. The rent would be part of manufacturing overhead. In terms of cost behaviour, it would be classified as a _____ cost. The rent can also be classified as a _____ cost and as part of _____ cost.

E2–2 Ryser Company was organized on May 1. On that date the company purchased 35,000 plastic emblems, each with a peel-off adhesive backing. The front of the emblems contained the company's name, accompanied by an attractive logo. Each emblem cost Ryser Company $2.

During May, 31,000 emblems were drawn from the Raw Materials inventory account. Of these, 1,000 were taken by the sales manager to an important sales meeting with prospective customers and handed out as an advertising gimmick. The remaining emblems drawn from inventory were affixed to units of the company's product that were being manufactured during May. Of the units of product having emblems affixed during May, 90% were completed and transferred from Work in Process to Finished Goods. Of the units completed during the month, 75% were sold and shipped to customers.

Required

1. Determine the cost of emblems that would be in each of the following accounts at May 31:
     a. Raw Materials.
     b. Work in Process.
     c. Finished Goods.
     d. Cost of Goods Sold.
     e. Advertising Expense.
2. Specify whether each of the above accounts would appear on the balance sheet or on the income statement at May 31.

E2–3 The following cost and inventory data for last year are taken from the accounting books of Eccles Company:

Costs incurred:

Advertising expense	$100,000
Direct labour cost	90,000
Purchases of raw materials	132,000
Rent, factory building	80,000
Indirect labour	56,300
Sales commissions	35,000
Utilities, factory	9,000
Maintenance, factory equipment	24,000
Supplies, factory	700
Depreciation, office equipment	8,000
Depreciation, factory equipment	40,000

	January 1 (beginning of year)	December 31 (end of year)
Inventories:		
Raw materials	$ 8,000	$10,000
Work in process	5,000	20,000
Finished goods	70,000	25,000

Required

1. Prepare a schedule of cost of goods manufactured in good form.
2. Prepare the cost of goods sold section of Eccles Company's income statement for the year.

E2–4 Suppose that you have been given a summer job at Fairwings Avionics, a company that manufactures sophisticated radar sets for commercial aircraft. The company, which is privately owned, has approached a bank for a loan to help finance its tremendous growth. The bank requires financial statements before approving such a loan. You have been asked to help prepare the financial statements and were given the following list of costs:

1. The cost of the memory chips used in a radar set.
2. Factory heating costs.

3. Factory equipment maintenance costs.
4. Training costs for new administrative employees.
5. The cost of the solder that is used in assembling the radar sets.
6. The travel costs of the company's salespersons.
7. Wages and salaries of factory security personnel.
8. The cost of air-conditioning executive offices.
9. Wages and salaries in the department that handles billing customers.
10. Depreciation on the equipment in the fitness room used by factory workers.
11. Telephone expenses incurred by factory management.
12. The costs of shipping completed radar sets to customers.
13. The wages of the workers who assemble the radar sets.
14. The president's salary.
15. Workers' Compensation insurance premiums for factory personnel.

Required

Classify the above costs as either product (inventoriable) costs or period (noninventoriable) costs for purposes of preparing the financial statements for the bank.

E2–5 Below are a number of costs that might be incurred in a service, merchandising, or manufacturing company. Copy the list of costs onto your answer sheet, and then place an *X* in the appropriate column for each cost to indicate whether the cost involved would be variable or fixed with respect to the goods and services produced by the organization.

		Cost Behaviour	
	Cost	Variable	Fixed
1.	Small glass plates used for lab tests in a hospital		
2.	Straight-line depreciation of a building		
3.	Top-management salaries		
4.	Electrical costs of running machines		
5.	Advertising of products and services		
6.	Batteries used in manufacturing trucks		
7.	Commissions to salespersons		
8.	Insurance on a dentist's office		
9.	Leather used in manufacturing footballs		
10.	Rent on a medical centre		

E2–6 Below are listed various costs that can be found in service, merchandising, and manufacturing companies:
1. The costs of turn signal switches used at the General Motors Windsor, Ontario, plant. These are one of the parts installed in the steering columns assembled at the plant.
2. Interest expense on CBC's long-term debt.
3. Salesperson's commissions at Avon Products, a company that sells cosmetics door to door.
4. Insurance on one of Slocan Forest Products plant buildings.
5. The costs of shipping brass fittings from Graham Manufacturing's plant in Dartmouth to customers in Vancouver.
6. Depreciation on the bookshelves at Waterloo Bookstore.
7. The costs of X-ray film at the Mayo Clinic's radiology lab.
8. The cost of leasing an 800 telephone number at CBC-Toronto's Cross Canada Checkup program. Assume that the monthly charge for the 800 number is independent of the number of calls taken.
9. The depreciation on the playground equipment at a McDonald's outlet in Montreal.
10. The cost of mozzarella cheese used at a Quebec City Pizza Hut outlet.

Required

Classify each cost as either variable or fixed with respect to the volume of goods or services produced by the organization. Also classify each cost as a selling and administrative cost or a product cost. Prepare your answer sheet as shown below:

	Cost Behaviour		Selling and Administrative Cost	Product Cost
Cost Item	Variable	Fixed		

E2–7 (Appendix 2A) Several weeks ago you called Jiffy Plumbing Company to have some routine repair work done on the plumbing system in your home. The plumber came about two weeks later, at four o'clock in the afternoon, and spent two hours completing your repair work. When you received your bill from the company, it contained a $75 charge for labour—$30 for the first hour and $45 for the second.

When questioned about the difference in hourly rates, the company's service manager explained that the higher rate for the second hour contained a charge for an "overtime premium," since the union required that plumbers be paid time and a half for any work in excess of eight hours per day. The service manager further explained that the company was working overtime to "catch up a little" on its backlog of work orders, but still needed to maintain a "decent" profit margin on the plumbers' time.

Required

1. Do you agree with the company's computation of the labour charge on your job?
2. Assume that the company pays its plumbers $20 per hour for the first eight hours worked in a day and $30 per hour for any additional time worked. Prepare computations to show how the cost of the plumber's time for the day (nine hours) should be allocated between direct labour cost and general overhead cost on the company's books.
3. Under what circumstances might the company be justified in charging an overtime premium for repair work on your home?

E2–8 (Appendix 2A) Fred Austin is employed by White Company. He works on the company's assembly line and assembles a component part for one of the company's products. Fred is paid $12 per hour for regular time, and he is paid time and a half for all work in excess of 40 hours per week.

Required

1. Assume that during a given week Fred is idle for two hours due to machine breakdowns and that he is idle for four more hours due to material shortages. No overtime is recorded for the week. Allocate Fred's wages for the week between direct labour cost and manufacturing overhead cost.
2. Assume that during a following week Fred works a total of 50 hours. He has no idle time for the week. Allocate Fred's wages for the week between direct labour cost and manufacturing overhead cost.
3. Fred's company provides an attractive package of fringe benefits for its employees. This package includes a retirement program and a health insurance program. So far as direct labour workers are concerned, explain two ways that the company could handle the costs of fringe benefits in its cost records.

PROBLEMS

P2–9 Ethics and the Manager   The top management of Halifax Electronics, Inc., is well known for "managing by the numbers." With an eye on the company's desired growth in overall net profit, the company's CEO (chief executive officer) sets target profits at the beginning of the year for each of the company's divisions. The CEO has stated her policy as follows: "I won't interfere with operations in the divisions. I am available for advice, but the division vice presidents are free to do anything they want so long as they hit the target profits for the year."

In November, Stan Richart, the vice president in charge of the Cellular Telephone Technologies Division, saw that making the current year's target profit for his division was going to be very difficult. Among other actions, he directed that discretionary expenditures be delayed until the beginning of the new year. On December 30, he was angered to discover that a warehouse clerk had ordered $350,000 of cellular telephone parts earlier in December even though the parts weren't really needed by the assembly department until January or February. Contrary to common accounting practice, the Halifax Electronics, Inc., Accounting Policy Manual states that such parts are to be recorded as an expense when delivered. To avoid recording the expense, Mr. Richart asked that the order be cancelled, but the purchasing department reported that the parts had already been delivered and the supplier would not accept returns. Since the bill had not yet been paid, Mr. Richart asked the accounting department to correct the clerk's mistake by delaying recognition of the delivery until the bill is paid in January.

Required

1. Are Mr. Richart's actions ethical? Explain why they are or are not ethical.
2. Do the general management philosophy and accounting policies at Halifax Electronics encourage or discourage ethical behaviour? Explain.

P2–10 Cost Identification   Several years ago Medex Company purchased a small building adjacent to its manufacturing plant in order to have room for expansion when needed. Since the company had no immediate need for the extra space, the building was rented out to another company for a rental revenue of $40,000 per year. The renter's lease will expire next month, and rather than renewing the lease, Medex Company has decided to use the building itself to manufacture a new product.

Direct materials cost for the new product will total $40 per unit. It will be necessary to hire a supervisor to oversee production. His salary will be $1,500 per month. Workers will be hired to manufacture the new product, with direct labour cost amounting to $18 per unit. Manufacturing operations will occupy all of the building space, so it will be necessary to rent space in a warehouse nearby in order to store finished units of product. The rental cost will be $1,000 per month. In addition, the company will need to rent equipment for use in producing the new product; the rental cost will be $3,000 per month. The company will continue to depreciate the building on a straight-line basis, as in past years. Depreciation on the building is $10,000 per year.

Advertising costs for the new product will total $50,000 per year. Costs of shipping the new product to customers will be $10 per unit. Electrical costs of operating machines will be $2 per unit.

To have funds to purchase materials, meet payrolls, and so forth, the company will have to liquidate some temporary investments. These investments are presently yielding a return of $6,000 per year.

Required

Prepare an answer sheet with the following column headings:

Name of the Cost	Variable Cost	Fixed Cost	Product Cost			Period (selling and administrative) Cost	Opportunity Cost	Sunk Cost
			Direct Materials	Direct Labour	Manufacturing Overhead			

List the different costs associated with the new product decision down the extreme left column (under Name of the Cost). Then place an X under each heading that helps to describe the type of cost involved. There may be X's under several column headings for a single cost. (For example, a cost may be a fixed cost, a period cost, and a sunk cost; you would place an X under each of these column headings opposite the cost.)

P2–11 Incomplete Data   Supply the missing data in the four cases below. Each case is independent of the others.

	Case			
	1	2	3	4
Direct materials	$ 7,000	$ 9,000	$ 6,000	$ 8,000
Direct labour	2,000	4,000	?	3,000
Manufacturing overhead	10,000	?	7,000	21,000
Total manufacturing costs	?	25,000	18,000	?
Beginning work in process inventory	?	1,000	2,000	?
Ending work in process inventory	4,000	3,500	?	2,000
Cost of goods manufactured	$18,000	$?	$16,000	$?
Sales	$25,000	$40,000	$30,000	$50,000
Beginning finished goods inventory	6,000	?	7,000	9,000
Cost of goods manufactured	?	?	?	31,500
Goods available for sale	?	?	?	?
Ending finished goods inventory	9,000	4,000	?	7,000
Cost of goods sold	?	26,500	18,000	?
Gross margin	?	?	?	?
Operating expenses	6,000	?	?	10,000
Net income	$?	$ 5,500	$ 3,000	$?

P2–12 Allocating Labour Costs   (Appendix 2A) Lynn Bjorland is employed by Ottawa Laboratories, Inc., and is directly involved in preparing the company's leading antibiotic drug. Lynn's basic wage rate is $12 per hour. The company pays its employees time and a half for any work in excess of 40 hours per week.

Required

1. Suppose that in a given week Lynn works 45 hours. Compute Lynn's total wages for the week. How much of this cost would the company allocate to direct labour cost? To manufacturing overhead cost?

2. Suppose in another week that Lynn works 50 hours but is idle for 4 hours during the week due to equipment breakdowns. Compute Lynn's total wages for the week. How much of this amount would be allocated to direct labour cost? To manufacturing overhead cost?

3. Ottawa Laboratories has an attractive package of fringe benefits that costs the company $4 for each hour of employee time (either regular time or overtime). During a particular week, Lynn works 48 hours but is idle for 3 hours due to material shortages. Compute Lynn's total wages and fringe benefits for the week. If the company treats all fringe benefits as part of manufacturing overhead cost, how much of Lynn's wages and fringe benefits for the week would be allocated to direct labour cost? To manufacturing overhead cost?

4. Refer to the data in (3) above. If the company treats that part of fringe benefits relating to direct labour as added direct labour cost, how much of Lynn's wages and fringe benefits for the week will be allocated to direct labour cost? To manufacturing overhead cost?

P2–13 Schedule of Cost of Goods Manufactured; Cost Behaviour   Various cost and sales data for Medco, Ltd., are given below for last year:

Purchases of raw materials	$ 90,000
Raw materials inventory, January 1	10,000
Raw materials inventory, December 31	17,000
Depreciation, factory	42,000
Insurance, factory	5,000
Direct labour cost	60,000
Maintenance, factory	30,000
Administrative expenses	70,000
Sales	450,000
Utilities, factory	27,000
Supplies, factory	1,000
Selling expenses	80,000
Indirect labour	65,000
Work in process inventory, January 1	7,000
Work in process inventory, December 31	30,000
Finished goods inventory, January 1	10,000
Finished goods inventory, December 31	40,000

Required

1. Prepare a schedule of cost of goods manufactured.

2. Prepare an income statement.

3. Assume that the company produced the equivalent of 10,000 units of product during the year. What was the unit cost for direct materials? What was the unit cost for factory depreciation?

4. Assume that the company expects to produce 15,000 units of product during the coming year. What per unit cost and what total cost would you expect the company to incur for direct materials at this level of activity? For factory depreciation? (In preparing your answer, assume that direct materials is a variable cost and that depreciation is a fixed cost; also assume that depreciation is computed on a straight-line basis.)

5. As the manager responsible for production costs, explain to the president any difference in unit costs between (3) and (4) above.

P2–14 Cost Identification   Heritage Company manufactures a beautiful bookcase that enjoys widespread popularity. The company has a backlog of orders that is large enough to keep production going indefinitely at the plant's full capacity of 4,000 bookcases per year. Annual cost data at full capacity follow:

Materials used (wood and glass)	$430,000
General office salaries	110,000
Factory supervision	70,000
Sales commissions	60,000
Depreciation, factory building	105,000
Depreciation, office equipment	2,000
Indirect materials, factory	18,000
Factory labour (cutting and assembly)	90,000
Advertising	100,000
Insurance, factory	6,000
General office supplies (billing)	4,000
Property taxes, factory	20,000
Utilities, factory	45,000

Required

1. Prepare an answer sheet with the column headings shown below. Enter each cost item on your answer sheet, placing the dollar amount under the appropriate headings. As examples, this has been done already for the first two items in the list above. Note that each cost item is classified in two ways: first, as being either variable or fixed; and second, as being either a selling and administrative cost or a product cost. (If the item is a product cost, it should be classified as being either direct or indirect as shown.)

	Cost Behaviour		Selling or Administrative	Product Cost	
Cost Item	Variable	Fixed	Cost	Direct	Indirect*
Materials used	$430,000			$430,000	
General office salaries		$110,000	$110,000		

*To units of product.

2. Total the dollar amounts in each of the columns in (1) above. Compute the cost to produce one bookcase.
3. Due to a recession, assume that production drops to only 2,000 bookcases per year. Would you expect the cost per bookcase to increase, decrease, or remain unchanged? Explain. No computations are necessary.
4. Refer to the original data. The president's next-door neighbour has considered making himself a bookcase and has priced the necessary materials at a building supply store. He has asked the president whether he could purchase a bookcase from the Heritage Company "at cost," and the president has agreed to let him do so.
a. Would you expect any disagreement between the two men over the price the neighbour should pay? Explain. What price does the president probably have in mind? The neighbour?
b. Since the company is operating at full capacity, what cost term used in the chapter might be justification for the president to charge the full, regular price to the neighbour and still be selling "at cost"? Explain.

P2–15 Classification of Salary Cost   You have just been hired by EduRom Company, which was organized on January 2 of the current year. The company manufactures and sells a variety of educational CD-ROMs for personal computers. It is your responsibility to supervise the employees who take orders from customers over the phone and to arrange for shipping orders via Canada Post, Purolator, Knight Hawk Airlines, and other freight carriers.

The company is unsure how to classify your $35,000 annual salary in its cost records. The company's cost analyst says that your salary should be classified as a manufacturing (product) cost; the controller says that it should be classified as a selling expense; and the president says that it doesn't matter which way your salary cost is classified.

Required

1. Which viewpoint is correct? Why?
2. From the point of view of the reported net income for the year, is the president correct in saying that it doesn't matter which way your salary cost is classified? Explain.

P2–16 Cost Classification   Listed below are several costs that might typically be found in a service, merchandising, or manufacturing company.
1. Depreciation, executive jet.
2. Costs of shipping finished goods to customers.

3. Wood used in furniture manufacturing.
4. Sales manager's salary.
5. Electricity used in furniture manufacturing.
6. Secretary to the company president.
7. Aerosol attachment placed on a spray can.
8. Billing costs.
9. Packing supplies for shipping products overseas.
10. Sand used in concrete manufacturing.
11. Supervisor's salary, factory.
12. Depreciation of video games in the factory lunchroom.
13. Executive life insurance.
14. Sales commissions.
15. Fringe benefits, assembly-line workers.
16. Advertising costs.
17. Boxes used for packaging breakfast cereal.
18. Property taxes on finished goods warehouses.
19. Security guard, factory.
20. Lubricants for machines.

Required

Prepare an answer sheet with column headings as shown below. For each cost item, indicate whether it would be variable or fixed with respect to the goods and services produced by the firm, and then whether it would be a selling cost, an administrative cost, or a manufacturing cost. If it is a manufacturing cost, indicate whether it would typically be treated as a direct or indirect cost with respect to units of product. Three sample answers are provided for illustration.

				Manufacturing (product) Cost	
Cost Item	Variable or Fixed	Selling Cost	Administrative Cost	Direct	Indirect
Direct labour	V			X	
Executive salaries	F		X		
Factory rent	F				X

P2–17 Cost Identification   Frieda Bronkowski has invented a new type of flyswatter. After giving the matter much thought, Frieda has decided to quit her $3,000 per month job with a computer firm and produce and sell the flyswatters full time. Frieda will rent a garage that will be used as a production plant. The rent will be $150 per month. Frieda will rent production equipment at a cost of $500 per month.

The cost of materials for each flyswatter will be $0.30. Frieda will hire workers to produce the flyswatters. They will be paid $0.50 for each completed unit. Frieda will rent a room in the house next door for use as her sales office. The rent will be $75 per month. She has arranged for the telephone company to attach a recording device to her home phone to get off-hours messages from customers. The device will increase her monthly phone bill by $20. In addition, she will be charged $0.50 for each message recorded on the device.

Frieda has some money in savings that is earning interest of $1,000 per year. These savings will be withdrawn and used for about a year to get the business going. To sell her flyswatters, Frieda will advertise heavily in the local area. Advertising costs will be $400 per month. In addition, Frieda will pay a sales commission of $0.10 for each flyswatter sold.

For the time being, Frieda does not intend to draw any salary from the new company. Frieda will continue to live in the house she bought several years ago for $150,000.

Required

1. Prepare an answer sheet with the following column headings:

Name of the Cost	Variable Cost	Fixed Cost	Product Cost			Period (selling and administrative) Cost	Opportunity Cost	Sunk Cost
			Direct Materials	Direct Labour	Manufacturing Overhead			

List the different costs associated with the company down the extreme left column (Name of the Cost). Place an X under each heading that describes the type of cost involved. There may be X's under several column headings for a single cost. (That is, a cost may be a fixed cost, a period cost, and a sunk cost, etc.)

2. All of the costs you have listed above, except one, would be differential costs between the alternatives of Frieda producing flyswatters or staying with the computer firm. Which cost is *not* differential? Explain.

P2–18 Preparing Manufacturing Statements   Skyler Company was organized on November 1 of the previous year. After seven months of start-up losses, management had expected to earn a profit during June, the most recent month. Management was disappointed, however, when the income statement for June showed that losses were still being realized by the company. June's income statement follows:

SKYLER COMPANY
Income Statement
For the Month Ended June 30

Sales		$600,000
Less operating expenses:		
Selling and administrative salaries	$ 35,000	
Rent on facilities	40,000	
Purchases of raw materials	190,000	
Insurance	8,000	
Depreciation, sales equipment	10,000	
Utilities costs	50,000	
Indirect labour	108,000	
Direct labour	90,000	
Depreciation, factory equipment	12,000	
Maintenance, factory	7,000	
Advertising	80,000	630,000
Net loss		$ (30,000)

After seeing the $30,000 loss for June, Skyler's president stated, "I was sure we'd be profitable within six months, but after eight months we're still spilling red ink. Maybe it's time for us to throw in the towel and accept one of those offers we've had for the company. To make matters worse, I just heard that Linda won't be back from her surgery for at least six more weeks."

Linda is the company's controller; in her absence, the statement above was prepared by a new assistant who has had little experience in manufacturing operations. Additional information about the company follows:

a. Only 80% of the rent on facilities applies to factory operations; the remainder applies to selling and administrative activities.

b. Inventory balances at the beginning and end of the month were as follows:

	June 1	June 30
Raw materials	$17,000	$42,000
Work in process	70,000	85,000
Finished goods	20,000	60,000

c. Some 75% of the insurance and 90% of the utilities cost apply to factory operations; the remaining amounts apply to selling and administrative activities.

The president has asked you to check over the above income statement and make a recommendation as to whether the company should continue operations.

Required

1. As one step in gathering data for a recommendation to the president, prepare a schedule of cost of goods manufactured in good form for June.

2. As a second step, prepare a new income statement for the month.

3. Based on your statements prepared in (1) and (2) above, would you recommend that the company continue operations?

P2–19 Schedule of Cost of Goods Manufactured; Cost Behaviour   The following selected account balances for the year ended December 31 are provided for Valenko Company:

Advertising expense	$215,000
Insurance, factory equipment	8,000
Depreciation, sales equipment	40,000
Rent, factory building	90,000
Utilities, factory	52,000
Sales commissions	35,000
Cleaning supplies, factory	6,000
Depreciation, factory equipment	110,000
Selling and administrative salaries	85,000
Maintenance, factory	74,000
Direct labour	?
Purchases of raw materials	260,000

Inventory balances at the beginning and end of the year were as follows:

	January 1 (beginning of year)	December 31 (end of year)
Raw materials	$50,000	$40,000
Work in process	?	33,000
Finished goods	30,000	?

The total manufacturing costs for the year were $675,000; the goods available for sale totalled $720,000; and the cost of goods sold totalled $635,000.

Required

1. Prepare a schedule of cost of goods manufactured in good form and the cost of goods sold section of the company's income statement for the year.
2. Assume that the dollar amounts given above are for the equivalent of 30,000 units produced during the year. Compute the unit cost for direct materials used, and compute the unit cost for rent on the factory building.
3. Assume that in the following year the company expects to produce 50,000 units. What per unit and total cost would you expect to be incurred for direct materials? For rent on the factory building? (In preparing your answer, you may assume that direct materials is a variable cost and that rent is a fixed cost.)
4. As the manager in charge of production costs, explain to the president the reason for any difference in unit costs between (2) and (3) above.

P2–20 Cost Classification   Various costs associated with manufacturing operations are given below:
1. Plastic washers used in auto production.
2. Production superintendent's salary.
3. Labourers assembling a product.
4. Electricity for operation of machines.
5. Janitorial salaries.
6. Clay used in brick production.
7. Rent on a factory building.
8. Wood used in ski production.
9. Screws used in furniture production.
10. A supervisor's salary.
11. Cloth used in suit production.
12. Depreciation of cafeteria equipment.
13. Glue used in textbook production.
14. Lubricants for machines.
15. Paper used in textbook production.

Required

Classify each cost as being either variable or fixed with respect to volume or level of activity. Also indicate whether each cost would typically be treated as a direct cost or an indirect cost with respect to units of product. Prepare your answer sheet as shown below:

	Cost Behaviour		To Units of Product	
Cost Item	**Variable**	**Fixed**	**Direct**	**Indirect**
Example: Factory insurance		X		X

P2–21 Cost Behaviour; Manufacturing Statement; Unit Costs   Hickey Company, a manufacturing firm, produces a single product. The following information has been taken from the company's production, sales, and cost records for last year:

Production in units	30,000
Sales in units	?
Ending finished goods inventory in units	?
Sales in dollars	$650,000
Costs:	
Advertising	$ 50,000
Direct labour	80,000
Indirect labour	60,000
Raw materials purchased	160,000
Building rent (production uses 80% of the space; administrative and sales offices use the rest)	50,000
Utilities, factory	35,000
Royalty paid for use of production patent, $1 per unit produced	?
Maintenance, factory	25,000
Rent for special production equipment, $6,000 per year plus $0.10 per unit produced	?
Selling and administrative salaries	140,000
Other factory overhead costs	11,000
Other selling and administrative expenses	20,000

	January 1 (beginning of year)	December 31 (end of year)
Inventories:		
Raw materials	$20,000	$10,000
Work in process	30,000	40,000
Finished goods	-0-	?

The finished goods inventory is being carried at the average unit production cost for the year. The selling price of the product is $25 per unit.

Required

1. Prepare a schedule of cost of goods manufactured for the year.
2. Compute the following:
    a. The number of units in the finished goods inventory at December 31.
    b. The cost of the units in the finished goods inventory at December 31.
3. Prepare an income statement for the year.

CASES

C2–22 Inventory Computations from Incomplete Data   While snoozing at the controls of his Pepper Six airplane, Dunse P. Sluggard leaned heavily against the door; suddenly, the door flew open and a startled Dunse tumbled out. As he parachuted to the ground, Dunse watch helplessly as the empty plane smashed into Operex Products's plant and administrative offices.

"The insurance company will never believe this," cried Mercedes Juliet, the company's controller, as she watched the ensuing fire burn the building to the ground. "The entire company is wiped out!"

"There's no reason to even contact the insurance agent," replied Ford Romero, the company's operations manager. "We can't file a claim without records, and all we have left is this copy of last year's annual report. It shows that raw materials at the beginning of this year

(January 1) totalled $30,000, work in process totalled $50,000, and finished goods totalled $90,000. But what we need is a record of these inventories as of today, and our records are up in smoke."

"All except this summary page I was working on when the plane hit the building," said Mercedes. "It shows that our sales to date this year have totalled $1,350,000 and that manufacturing overhead cost has totalled $520,000."

"Hey! This annual report is more helpful than I thought," exclaimed Ford. "I can see that our gross margin rate has been 40% of sales for years. I can also see that direct labour cost is one-quarter of the manufacturing overhead cost."

"We may have a chance after all," cried Mercedes. "My summary sheet lists the sum of direct labour and direct materials at $510,000 for the year, and it says that our goods available for sale to customers this year has totalled $960,000 at cost. Now if we just knew the amount of raw materials purchased so far this year."

"I know that figure," yelled Ford. "It's $420,000! The purchasing agent gave it to me in our planning meeting yesterday."

"Fantastic," shouted Mercedes. "We'll have our claim ready before the day is over!"

To file a claim with the insurance company, Operex Products must determine the amount of cost in its inventories as of October 15, the date of the accident. You may assume that all of the materials used in production during the year were direct materials.

Required   Determine the amount of cost in the raw materials, work in process, and finished goods inventories as of the date of the accident. (Hint: One way to proceed would be to reconstruct the various schedules and statements that would have been affected by the company's inventories during the year.)

C2–23 Missing Data; Statements; Inventory Computation   "I know I'm a pretty good scientist, but I guess I still have some things to learn about running a business," said Staci Morales, founder and president of Medical Technology, LTEE. "Demand has been so strong for our heart monitor that I was sure we'd be profitable immediately, but just look at the gusher of red ink for the first quarter." The data to which Staci was referring are shown below:

MEDICAL TECHNOLOGY, LTEE.
Income Statement
For the Quarter Ended June 30

Sales (16,000 monitors)		$ 975,000
Less operating expenses:		
Selling and administrative salaries	$ 90,000	
Advertising	200,000	
Cleaning supplies, production	6,000	
Indirect labour cost	135,000	
Depreciation, office equipment	18,000	
Direct labour cost	80,000	
Raw materials purchased	310,000	
Maintenance, production	47,000	
Rental cost, facilities	65,000	
Insurance, production	9,000	
Utilities	40,000	
Depreciation, production equipment	75,000	
Travel, salespersons	60,000	
Total operating expenses		1,135,000
Net loss		$ (160,000)

"At this rate we'll be out of business in a year," said Guy Louganis, the company's accountant. "But I've double-checked these figures, so I know they're right."

Medical Technology was organized on April 1 of the current year to produce and market a revolutionary new heart monitor. The company's accounting system was set up by Pierre Le-Braun, an experienced accountant who recently left the company. The statement above was prepared by Louganis, his assistant.

"We may not last a year if the insurance company doesn't pay the $227,000 it owes us for the 4,000 monitors lost in the truck accident last week," said Staci. "The agent says our claim is inflated, but that's a lot of baloney."

Just after the end of the quarter, a truck carrying 4,000 monitors wrecked and burned, destroying the entire load. The monitors were a part of the 20,000 units completed during the quarter ended June 30. They were in a warehouse awaiting sale at quarter-end and were sold and shipped on July 3 (this sale is *not* included on the income statement above). The trucking company's insurer is liable for the cost of the goods lost. Louganis has determined this cost as follows:

$$\frac{\text{Total costs for the quarter, } \$1,135,000}{\text{Monitors produced during the quarter, } 20,000} = \$56.75 \text{ per unit}$$

$$4,000 \text{ monitors} \times \$56.75 = \$227,000$$

The following additional information is available on the company's activities during the quarter ended June 30:

a.   Inventories at the beginning and end of the quarter were as follows:

	April 1	June 30
Raw materials	-0-	$40,000
Work in process	-0-	30,000
Finished goods	-0-	?

b.   80% of the rental cost for facilities and 90% of the utilities cost relate to manufacturing operations. The remaining amounts relate to selling and administrative activities.

Required

1.   What conceptual errors, if any, were made in preparing the income statement above?
2.   Prepare a schedule of cost of goods manufactured for the quarter.
3.   Prepare a corrected income statement for the quarter. Your statement should show in detail how the cost of goods sold is computed.
4.   Do you agree that the insurance company owes Medical Technology, Inc., $227,000? Explain your answer.

GROUP EXERCISES

GE2–24 So This Is Why They're Organized This Way   Management accounting systems tend to parallel the manufacturing systems they support and control. Traditional manufacturing systems emphasized productivity (average output per hour or per employee) and cost. This was the result of a competitive philosophy that was based on mass producing a few standard products and "meeting or beating competitors on price." If a firm is going to compete on price, it had better be a low-cost producer.

Firms achieved low unit cost for a fixed set of resources by maximizing the utilization of those resources. That is, traditional production strategies were based on the economies of mass production and maximizing output for a given productive capacity. North American has experienced over 100 years of unprecedented economic prosperity in large part because innovators like Henry Ford applied these economic principles with a vengeance.

Competitors, never being completely satisfied with their present condition, were always looking for ways to lower the cost of a product or service even further in order to gain some temporary cost advantage. Additional productivity gains were achieved by standardizing work procedures, specializing work, and using machines to enhance the productivity of individual workers.

Required

1.   Henry Ford made a now-famous statement that the Model T "could be had in any colour, as long as it was black." Explain what he meant by this statement.

2. How would Henry Ford or any other manufacturer with a narrow product line gain even further efficiencies based on the traditional production model described above?

3. Are there any limits to lowering the cost of black Model Ts, black Bic pens, or any high-volume, commodity product? Explain.

4. Once understood, the economies of mass production were applied to most sectors of the economy. Universities, hospitals, and airlines are prime examples. Describe how the concepts of mass production, standardization, and specialization have been applied to lower the costs of a university education. Of a stay in the hospital.

5. As you study additional chapters in this text, refer back to the basic principles described here. An understanding of these concepts will go a long way toward helping you understand why traditional management accounting systems are designed with an emphasis on cost.

GE2–25 If Big Is Good, Bigger Must Be Better   The Focus on Current Practice on page 62 stated that steel production involved a large amount of fixed costs. Since competition was defined primarily in terms of price, SteelCo and other steel manufacturers (and many of their manufacturing and service industry counterparts) tried to gain a competitive advantage by using economies of scale and investment in technology to increase productivity and drive unit costs lower. Their substantial fixed costs are the result of their size.

Required

1. How are fixed costs and variable costs normally defined?

2. Give examples of fixed costs and variable costs for a steel company. What is the relevant measure of production activity?

3. Give examples of fixed and variable costs for a hospital, university, and auto manufacturer. What is the relevant measure of production or service activity for each of these organizations?

4. Using the examples of fixed and variable costs for steel companies from (2), explain the relationship between production output at a steel company and each of the following: total fixed costs, fixed cost per unit, total variable costs, variable cost per unit, total costs, and average unit cost.

5. With an X axis (horizontal axis) of tonnes produced and a Y axis (vertical axis) of total costs, graph total fixed costs, total variable costs, and total costs against tonnes produced.

6. With an X axis of tonnes produced and a Y axis of unit costs, graph fixed cost per unit, variable cost per unit, and total (or average) cost per unit against tonnes produced.

7. Explain how costs (total and per unit) behave with changes in demand once capacity has been set.

GE2–26 Overhead Is a Real Burden   "Excessive overheads are why you're now seeing so much cutting of white-collar workforces and delayering of management," says Dexter F. Baker, head of Air Products & Chemicals, Inc. and chairman of the National Association of Manufacturers. Source: Thane Peterson, "Can Corporate America Get Out from under Its Overhead?" *Business Week* (May 18, 1992), p. 102.

A 1990 Boston University study found that overhead of U.S. manufacturers was nearly 50% greater than typical Japanese firms and almost 20% greater than West European companies. With such high levels of overhead, U.S. firms will not be able to compete over the long term.

Required

1. What is the makeup of overhead? If necessary, speak with several experienced business people to find out what overhead is (i.e., the different categories of overhead) and what activities these overhead resources perform.

2. Why would overhead of U.S. firms be so much greater than their international rivals?

3. If we assume that overhead must be reduced to be more competitive, what (or who) gets cut? Again, you may want to speak with several businesspeople to find out how businesses are actually reducing their overhead costs.

4. If we assume that people whose jobs are eliminated to reduce overhead were busy performing some useful business-related activity, who is going to perform this work when their positions are eliminated?

5. What is the downside to such cuts?

GE2–27 Let's Take a Closer Look at the Impact of Technology on Work   A technological revolution is occurring throughout business. Technology is a major force behind the way work is being transformed. Microprocessor-controlled manufacturing technology is changing the nature of blue-collar work on the shop floor, and, more recently, advanced information technology has begun to change white-collar work.

Required

1. How is technology transforming your intended profession, be it accounting, engineering, finance, management, marketing, or some other profession?
2. How is this changing the way work is done in your intended profession?
3. What impact is technology having on the following industries: automobile parts manufacturers like Magna, large comprehensive hospitals like the Toronto General Hospital, financial institutions like the Bank of Montreal, retail firms like Eatons, airlines like Canadian Airlines, and universities like the University of Toronto?
4. How is this affecting costs and the mix of costs between fixed and variable costs?

SYSTEMS DESIGN: JOB-ORDER COSTING

LEARNING OBJECTIVES

After studying Chapter 3, you should be able to:

1 Distinguish between process costing and job-order costing, and identify companies that would use each costing method.

2 Identify the documents used to control the flow of costs in a job-order costing system.

3 Compute predetermined overhead rates and explain why estimated overhead costs (rather than actual overhead costs) are used in the costing process.

4 Prepare journal entries to record the flow of direct materials cost, direct labour cost, and manufacturing overhead cost in a job-order costing system.

5 Apply overhead cost to Work in Process by use of a predetermined overhead rate.

6 Prepare T-accounts to show the flow of costs in a job-order costing system and prepare schedules of cost of goods manufactured and cost of goods sold.

7 Compute any balance of under- or overapplied overhead cost for a period and prepare the journal entry needed to close the balance into the appropriate accounts.

8 Explain why multiple overhead rates are needed in many organizations.

9 Define or explain the key terms listed at the end of the chapter.

10 (Appendix 3A) Prepare journal entries to record the flow of costs in a just-in-time (JIT) inventory system.

11 (Appendix 3B) Account for scrap and rework of unacceptable production.

The Hibernia production platform, located in the offshore oil field off Newfoundland's coast, is comprised of five supermodules, each representing a large job order inside the overall job and each containing many smaller job orders.

A s discussed in Chapter 2, product costing is the process of assigning manufacturing costs to manufactured goods. An understanding of this process is vital to any manager, because the way in which a product is costed can have a substantial impact on reported net income, as well as on the current assets section of the balance sheet.

In this chapter and in Chapter 4, we look at product costing from the **absorption cost** approach. The approach is so named because it provides for the absorption of all manufacturing costs, fixed and variable, into units of product. It is also known as the **full cost** approach, although technically the term *full cost* of an object is the sum of its direct costs plus a fair share of applicable indirect costs.[1] Further discussions of the implications of this definition are undertaken in Chapter 8. In Chapter 8 we also look at product costing from another point of view (called *variable costing*) and discuss the strengths and weaknesses of the two approaches.

While studying product costing, we must keep clearly in mind that *the essential purpose of any costing system is to accumulate costs for managerial use.* A costing system is not an end in itself. Rather, it is a managerial tool in that it exists to provide managers with the cost data needed to direct the affairs of organizations. Nevertheless, external reporting to shareholders and regulators together with income tax reporting do influence how costs are accumulated and summarized.

THE NEED FOR UNIT COST DATA

Managers need unit cost data for a variety of reasons. First, unit costs are needed to cost inventories on financial statements and to determine a period's net income. If unit costs are incorrectly computed, then both assets and net income will be equally incorrect, as well es the reported profitability of individual product lines.

Second, unit costs are needed to assist management in planning and control of operations. Budgets must be prepared on expected costs at various operation levels, and reports must be generated to provide feedback on where operations can be improved. The usefulness of these budgets and reports will depend in large part on the accuracy of unit cost data.

Finally, managers need unit cost data to assist them in a broad range of decision-making situations. Without unit cost data, management may find it very difficult to set selling prices for output.[2] A knowledge of unit costs is also vital in a number of special decision areas, such as whether to add or drop product lines, whether to make or buy production components, whether to expand or contract operations, and whether to accept special orders at special prices. Unit cost information can improve the manager's ability to interpret cost information in strategic discussions, marketing decisions, personnel decisions, and a wide variety of operational decisions. For example, the production cost of $2,385 for a given set of products might be compared to $2,465 that was incurred last period if the number of units were exactly the same. However, if this period's production involved 10 units while last period involved 12 of the same units, the manager could interpret performance better using unit costs of $238.50 versus $205.42.

---

[1] Institute of Management Accountants, "Allocation of Service and Administrative Costs," *Statement on Management Accounting Number 4B* (New York, June 13, 1985), p. 2.

[2] We should note here that unit cost represents only one of many factors involved in pricing decisions. Pricing is discussed in depth in an appendix at the end of the text.

Because particular unit costs differ in terms of their relevance to the various decision-making situations, we need to learn not only how to derive unit costs but also how to differentiate between those costs that are relevant and those that are not. The matter of relevant costs is reserved until Chapter 13. For the moment, we are concerned with gaining an understanding of the concept of unit cost in its broadest sense.

A doctor's office illustrates job-order costing in a service environment. Each patient is a different "job" incurring different costs. The physician will bill the government based on the specific treatment given to that patient.

TYPES OF COSTING SYSTEMS

OBJECTIVE 1
Distinguish between process costing and job-order costing, and identify companies that would use each costing method.

In computing unit costs, managers are faced with a difficult problem. Many costs (such as rent) are incurred uniformly from month to month, whereas production levels may change frequently. In addition to variations in the level of production, several different types of goods may be produced in a given period. Under these conditions, how is it possible to determine accurate unit costs? The answer is that the computation of unit costs must involve an *averaging* of some type. The way in which this averaging is carried out depends heavily on the manufacturing process involved. Two costing systems have emerged in response to variations in the manufacturing process; these two systems are commonly known as *process costing* and *job-order costing*. Each has its own unique way of averaging costs and thus providing management with unit cost data.

Process Costing

A **process costing system** is employed in those situations where manufacturing involves a single, homogeneous product that is produced for long periods at a time. Examples that use process costing include cement produced by La Farge, flour by Dover Mills, steel by Dofasco, and various utilities (e.g., water by the Halifax Regional Water Commission, electricity by Nova Scotia Power). All of these industries are characterized by a basically homogeneous product that flows evenly through the production process on a continuous basis.

The basic approach to process costing is to accumulate costs in a particular operation or department for an entire period (month, quarter, year) and then to divide this total by the number of units produced during the period. The basic formula for process costing would be:

$$\frac{\text{Total costs of manufacturing}}{\text{Total units produced (litres, kilograms, bottles)}} = \text{Unit cost (per litre, kilogram, bottle)}$$

Since one unit of product (litre, kilogram, bottle) is completely indistinguishable from any other unit of product, each unit bears the same average cost as any other unit produced during the period. This costing technique results in a broad, average unit cost figure that applies to many thousands of like units flowing in an almost endless stream off the assembly or processing line.

Job-Order Costing

A **job-order costing system** is used in those manufacturing situations where many *different* products, jobs, or batches of production are produced each period. Examples that would typically use job-order costing include large-scale construction such as the Hibernia oil platform, special-order printing, furniture manufacturing, shipbuilding, and equipment manufacturing.

Job-order costing is also used extensively in the service industries. Hospitals, law firms, movie studios, accounting firms, advertising agencies, and repair shops, for example, all use job-order costing to accumulate costs for accounting and billing purposes. For example, the production of a sports broadcast of international cricket by the Asian Television Network Ltd. of Newmarket, Ontario, is an assignment suitable for job costing. Although the detailed example of job-order costing provided in the following section deals with a manufacturing firm, the same basic concepts and procedures are used by many service organizations. More is said on this point later in the chapter.

Because the output of firms involved in the industries mentioned tends to be heterogeneous, managers need a costing system in which costs can be accumulated *by job (or by client or customer)* and in which distinct unit costs can be determined for each job completed. Job-order costing provides such a system. However, it is a more complex system than that required by process costing. Under job-order costing, rather than dividing total costs by many thousands of like units, one must somehow divide total costs by a few, basically unlike units. Thus, job-order costing involves certain problems of recordkeeping and cost assignment that are not found in a process costing system.

Summary of Costing Methods

To summarize this brief introduction to process and job-order costing, regardless of which system one is dealing with, the problem of determining unit costs involves a need for averaging of some type. If the activity or production is homogeneous, then the activity divided into the total costs produces a meaningful unit cost. If the activity or product is heterogeneous, the costs have to be broken down into groupings that allow them to be appropriate for the homogeneous sets of units contained in the job. Only then can meaningful unit costs be computed.

For example, if you were costing the preparation of income tax returns at H&R Block, each return involves different levels of complexity so each return could be a job. On the other hand, if you were producing bricks, the homogeneity of the batch of bricks would permit a meaningful unit cost per brick by dividing the producing costs by the number of bricks. The essential difference between the process and job-order methods is the way in which this averaging is carried out.

In this chapter, we focus on the design of a job-order costing system. In the following chapter, we focus on process costing and also look more closely at the similarities and differences between the two costing methods.

JOB-ORDER COSTING—AN OVERVIEW

OBJECTIVE 2
Identify the documents used to control the flow of costs in a job-order costing system.

To introduce job-order costing, we will follow a specific job as it progresses through the manufacturing process. This job consists of two experimental couplings that Yost Precision Machining has agreed to produce for Loops Unlimited, a manufacturer of roller coasters. Before we begin our discussion, recall from Chapter 2 that companies generally classify manufacturing costs into three broad categories: (1) direct materials, (2) direct labour, and (3) manufacturing overhead. As we study the operation of a job-order costing system, we will see how each of these costs is recorded and accumulated.

Yost Precision Machining will use job-order costing when making the experimental couplings that Loops Unlimited is considering for its roller coasters.

▼   ▼   ▼   ▼   ▼

MANAGERIAL ACCOUNTING IN ACTION—THE ISSUE

The top managers of Yost Precision Machining were gathered in the company's conference room for the daily 8:00 AM planning meeting. The company's president, Jean Yost, opened the meeting:

"The production schedule indicates we'll be starting job 2B47 today. Isn't that the special order for experimental couplings, Roger?"

Roger Johnson, the marketing manager, responded: "That's right, Jean. That's the order from Loops Unlimited for two couplings for their new roller coaster ride for Magic Mountain."

A bit puzzled, the production manager Debbie Turner piped in: "Why only two couplings? Don't they need a coupling for every car?"

Roger replied: "Yes, they do. But this is a completely new roller coaster. The cars will go faster and will be subjected to more twists, turns, drops, and loops than on any other existing roller coaster. To hold up under these stresses, Loops Unlimited's engineers had to completely redesign the cars and couplings. They want to thoroughly test the design before proceeding to large-scale production. So they want us to make just two of these new couplings for testing purposes. If the design works, then we can bid on the order to supply couplings for the whole ride."

Turning to Mark White, the company's controller, Jean Yost asked: "We agreed to take on this initial order at our cost just to get our foot in the door. Will there be any problem documenting our cost?"

Mark quickly responded: "No problem. The contract with Loops stipulates that they will pay us an amount equal to our cost of goods sold. With our job-order costing system, I can tell you what the cost of goods sold will be on the day the job is completed."

Jean closed the discussion by saying: "Is there anything else we should discuss about this job at this time? No? Good. Let's move on to the next item of business."

▼   ▼   ▼   ▼   ▼

Measuring Direct Materials Cost

The classic production process begins with the transfer of raw materials from the storeroom to the production line. The bulk of these raw materials are traceable directly to the goods being produced and are therefore termed *direct materials*. Other materials, generally termed *indirect materials*, are not charged to a specific job but rather are included within the general category of manufacturing overhead. As discussed in Chapter 2, indirect materials would include costs of glue, nails, and miscellaneous supplies.

To make the two experimental couplings, Yost Precision Machining will require four G7 connectors and two M46 housings. If this were a standard product, there would be a *bill of materials* for the product. A **bill of materials** is a document that lists the type and quantity of each item of materials needed to complete a unit of product. In this case, there is no established bill of materials, so Yost's production staff determined the

EXHIBIT 3–1

Materials Requisition Form

Materials Requisition Number ___14873___   Date ___March 2___
Job Number to Be Charged ___2B47___
Department ___Milling___

Description	Quantity	Unit Cost	Total Cost
M46 Housing	2	$124	$248
G7 Connector	4	103	412
			$660

Authorized
Signature ___Bill White___

materials requirements from the blueprints submitted by the customer. Each coupling requires two connectors and one housing, so to make two couplings, four connectors and two housings are required.

Raw materials needed to complete the jobs are drawn from the storeroom on presentation of a **materials requisition form** similar to the form in Exhibit 3–1.

This form shows that the company's milling department has requisitioned two M46 Housings and four G7 Connectors to be used in completing job 2B47. Thus, the requisition form is a detailed source document that (1) specifies the type and quantity of materials to be drawn from the storeroom and (2) identifies the job to which the materials are to be charged. It therefore serves as a means for controlling the flow of materials into production and also for making entries in the accounting records.

The use of computer programs to prepare many of the job cost forms has resulted in numerous peculiarities in their design. Most commercial programs have a prespecified format for the forms the program is asked to generate. Companies such as Nebs Business Forms Ltd. provide forms designed to suit the more popular software packages. To permit you to focus on the key aspects of the form rather than the peculiarities for specific software programs, the forms displayed in the following pages are generic in nature.

The Job Cost Sheet

The cost of direct materials is entered on a job cost sheet similar to the one presented in Exhibit 3–2. A **job cost sheet** is a form prepared for each separate job initiated into production. It serves (1) as a means for accumulating materials, labour, and overhead costs chargeable to a job, and (2) as a means for computing unit costs. Normally, the job cost sheet is not prepared until the accounting department has received notification from the production department that a production order has been issued for a particular job. In turn, a production order is not issued until a definite agreement has been reached with the customer in terms of quantities, prices, and shipment dates.

As direct materials are issued, the accounting department makes entries directly on the job cost sheet, thereby charging the specific job noted on the sheet with the cost of

EXHIBIT 3-2

Job Cost Sheet

JOB COST SHEET

Job Number _____ 2B47 _____

Date Initiated _____ March 2, 19x2 _____

Date Completed _____

Department _____ Milling _____

Units Completed _____

Item _____ Special order coupling _____

For Stock _____

Direct Materials		Direct Labour			Manufacturing Overhead		
Req. No.	Amount	Ticket	Hours	Amount	Hours	Rate	Amount
14873	$ 660	843	5	$ 45			

Cost Summary		Units Shipped		
Direct Materials	$	Date	Number	Balance
Direct Labour	$			
Manufacturing Overhead	$			
Total Cost	$			
Unit Cost	$			

materials used in production. Note from Exhibit 3–2, for example, that the $660 cost for direct materials shown earlier on the materials requisition form is charged to job 2B47 on its job cost sheet. The requisition number 14873 is also recorded on the job cost sheet to make it easier to identify the source document for the direct materials charge. When the job is completed, the total cost of materials used can be summarized in the cost summary section as one element involved in determining the total unit cost of the order.

In addition to serving as a means for charging costs to jobs, the job cost sheet also serves as a key part of a firm's accounting records. The job cost sheets relating to all jobs in process at a given point in time form a *subsidiary ledger* to the Work in Process account. Thus, to determine the dollar amount of Work in Process at any point, the manager simply totals the costs appearing on the job cost sheets for all jobs still in production at that moment.

EXHIBIT 3-3

Employee Time
Ticket

Time Ticket No. 843			Date __March 3, 19x2__		
Employee __Mary Holden__			Station __4__		

Started	Ended	Time Completed	Rate	Amount	Job Number
7:00	12:00	5.0	$9	$45	2B47
12:30	2:30	2.0	9	18	2B50
2:30	3:30	1.0	9	9	Maintenance
Totals		8.0		$72	

Supervisor __R. W. Pace__

Measuring Direct Labour Cost

Direct labour cost is accumulated and measured in much the same way as direct materials cost. Direct labour includes those labour charges directly traceable to a particular job in process. By contrast, those labour charges that cannot be traced directly to a particular job, or that can be traced only with the expenditure of great effort, are treated as part of manufacturing overhead. As discussed in Chapter 2, this latter category of labour costs is termed *indirect labour* and would include such tasks as maintenance, supervision, and cleanup.

Labour costs are generally accumulated by means of some type of work record prepared each day by each employee. These work records, often termed **time tickets,** constitute an hour-by-hour summary of the activities completed during the day by the employee. An example of an employee time ticket is shown in Exhibit 3–3. When working on a specific job, the employee enters the job number on the time ticket and notes the number of hours spent on the particular task involved. When not assigned to a particular job, the employee enters the type of indirect labour tasks to which he or she was assigned (such as cleanup and maintenance) and the number of hours spent on each separate task.

At the end of the day, the time tickets are gathered and the accounting department carefully analyzes each in terms of the number of hours assignable as direct labour to specific jobs and the number of hours assignable to manufacturing overhead as indirect labour. Those hours assignable as direct labour are entered on individual job cost sheets (such as the one shown in Exhibit 3–2), along with the appropriate charges involved. When all direct labour charges associated with a particular job have been accumulated on the job cost sheet, the total can be summarized in the cost summary section. The daily time tickets, in essence, constitute basic source documents used as a basis for labour cost entries into the accounting records.

The system we have just described is a manual system for recording and posting labour costs. Many companies no longer record labour time manually; rather, they do this recording automatically with the aid of technology such as bar coding. Each employee and each job has a unique bar code. When an employee begins work on a job, he or she scans three bar codes—the bar code on his or her identity badge, another bar code signaling that work is beginning on a job, and the bar code attached to the job itself. This information is fed automatically by means of an electronic network to a computer where it is recorded. When the employee's work on the job is completed, he or she again scans three bar codes—the bar code on his or her identity badge, another bar code indicating that work is finished on the job, and the bar code attached to the job. This information is again relayed to the computer, and a time ticket is automatically prepared. Since all of the source data is already in computer files, the labour costs are automatically posted to job cost sheets (or their electronic equivalents). Computers, coupled with technology such as bar codes, can eliminate much of the drudgery involved in routine bookkeeping activities while at the same time increasing timeliness and accuracy.

Advanced technology for recording data is even found in strawberry fields where the pay of workers is traditionally based on the amount of berries they pick. The Bob Jones Ranch in Oxnard, California, is using dime-sized metal buttons to record how many boxes of fruit each worker picks. The buttons, which are stuffed with microelectronics, are carried by the field workers. The buttons can be read in the field with a wand-like probe that immediately downloads data to a laptop computer. The information picked up by the probe includes the name of the worker; the type and quality of the crop; and the time, date, and location of the field being picked. Not only does the system supply the data needed to pay over 700 field workers but it also provides farm managers with information about which fields are most productive. Previously, two people were required every night to process the time tickets for the field workers.[3]

Application of Manufacturing Overhead

OBJECTIVE 3
Compute predetermined overhead rates and explain why estimated overhead costs (rather than actual overhead costs) are used in the costing process.

Manufacturing overhead must be considered along with direct materials and direct labour in determining unit costs of production. However, the assignment of manufacturing overhead to units of product is often a difficult task. There are several reasons why this is so.

First, as explained in Chapter 2, manufacturing overhead is an *indirect* cost to units of product and therefore cannot be traced directly to a particular product or job. Second, manufacturing overhead consists of many unlike items, involving both variable and fixed costs. It ranges from the grease used in machines to the annual salary of the production superintendent. Finally, firms with large seasonal variations in production often find that even though output is fluctuating, manufacturing overhead costs tend to remain relatively constant. The reason is that fixed costs generally constitute a large part of manufacturing overhead.

Given these problems, about the only acceptable way to assign overhead costs to units of product is to do so through an allocation process. This allocation of overhead costs to products is accomplished by having the manager select an *activity base* common to all products that the company manufactures or to all services that the company renders. Then by means of this base, an appropriate amount of overhead cost is assigned to each product or service. The trick, of course, is to choose the right base so that the overhead application will be equitable among jobs.

[3]Mark Boslet, "Metal Buttons Carried by Crop Pickers Serve as Mini Databases for Farmers," *The Wall Street Journal,* May 31, 1994, p. A11A.

The most widely used activity bases have been direct labour-hours (DLH) and direct labour cost, with machine-hours (MH) and even units of product (where a company has only a single product) also used to some extent.

Once an activity base has been chosen, it is divided into the estimated total manufacturing overhead cost of the period to obtain a **predetermined overhead rate.** The rate is called predetermined because it is computed before the period begins and because it is based entirely on estimated data. After the predetermined overhead rate has been computed, it is then used to apply overhead cost to jobs. In summary, the formula for computing the predetermined overhead rate is:

$$\frac{\text{Estimated total manufacturing overhead costs}}{\text{Estimated total units in the base (MH, DLH, etc.)}} = \text{Predetermined overhead rate}$$

Instead of using the term *estimated* in this formula, some companies prefer to use the terms *forecasted* or *budgeted.*

Using the Predetermined Overhead Rate.   The assigning of overhead cost to jobs (and thereby to units of product) is called **overhead application.** To illustrate the steps involved, assume that a firm has estimated its total manufacturing overhead costs for the year to be $320,000 and has estimated 40,000 total direct labour-hours for the year. Its predetermined overhead rate for the year would be $8 per direct labour-hour, shown as follows:

$$\frac{\$320,000}{40,000 \text{ direct labour-hours}} = \$8 \text{ per direct labour-hour}$$

The job cost sheet in Exhibit 3–4 indicates that a total of 27 direct labour-hours was charged to job 2B47. Therefore, a total of $216 of overhead cost was assigned to the job:

$$\begin{array}{ccc} \text{Predetermined} & \times\ \text{Actual direct} & =\ \text{Applied} \\ \text{overhead rate} & \text{labour-hours} & \text{overhead} \end{array}$$

($8/DLH)   (for job 2B47)   =   (to job 2B47)

($8/DLH) × 27 Direct labour-hours = $216 of overhead applied to job 2B47

This overhead application is shown on the job cost sheet in Exhibit 3–4. When a company applies overhead cost to jobs as we have done—that is, by multiplying actual activity times the predetermined overhead rate—it is using a **normal cost system.**

Whether the overhead application in Exhibit 3–4 is made slowly as the job is worked on during the period, or in a single application at the time of completion, is a matter of choice and convenience to the company involved. If a job is not completed at year-end, however, overhead should be applied to value properly the work in process inventory.

Although estimates are involved in the computation of predetermined overhead rates, managers typically become very skilled at making these estimates. As a result, predetermined overhead rates are generally quite accurate, and any difference between the amount of overhead cost that is actually incurred during a period and the amount that is applied to products is usually quite small. This point is discussed later in this chapter.

The Need for a Predetermined Rate.   Instead of using a predetermined rate, a company could wait until the end of the accounting period to compute an actual overhead rate based on the *actual* total manufacturing costs and the *actual* total units in the activity

EXHIBIT 3-4

A Completed Job
Cost Sheet

JOB COST SHEET

Job Number __2B47__   Date Initiated __March 2, 19x2__
                                           Date Completed __March 8, 19x2__

Department __Milling__   Units Completed __2__
Item __Special order coupling__
For Stock _____

Direct Materials		Direct Labour			Manufacturing Overhead		
Req. No.	Amount	Ticket	Hours	Amount	Hours	Rate	Amount
14873	$ 660	843	5	$ 45	27	$8/DLH	$216
14875	506	846	8	60			
14912	238	850	4	21			
	$1,404	851	10	54			
			27	$180			

Cost Summary		Units Shipped		
		Date	Number	Balance
Direct Materials	$1,404			
Direct Labour	$ 180	March 8, 19x2	—	2
Manufacturing Overhead	$ 216			
Total Cost	$1,800			
Unit Cost*	$ 900			

*$1,800 ÷ 2 units = $900 per unit.

base for the period. However, managers cite several reasons for using predetermined overhead rates instead of actual overhead rates:

1. Before the end of the accounting period, managers would like to know the accounting system's valuation of completed jobs. Suppose, for example, that Yost Precision Machining waits until the end of the year to compute its overhead rate. Then there would be no way for managers to know the cost of goods sold for job 2B47 until the close of the year, even though the job was completed and shipped to the customer in March. The seriousness of this problem can be reduced to some extent by computing the actual overhead more frequently, but that immediately leads to another problem as discussed below.

2. If actual overhead rates are computed frequently, seasonal factors in overhead costs or in the activity base can produce fluctuations in the overhead rates. Managers generally feel that such fluctuations in overhead rates serve no useful purpose and are misleading.

3. The use of a predetermined overhead rate simplifies record keeping. To determine the overhead cost to apply to a job, the accounting staff at Yost Precision Machining simply multiplies the direct labour-hours recorded for the job by the predetermined overhead rate of $8 per direct labour-hour.

For these reasons, most companies use predetermined overhead rates rather than actual overhead rates in their cost accounting systems.

Choice of an Activity Base

An activity base should be used that acts as a *cost driver* in the incurrence of overhead cost. A **cost driver** is a factor, such as machine-hours, beds occupied, computer time, or flight-hours, that causes overhead costs. If a base is used to compute overhead rates that does not "drive" overhead costs, then the result will be inaccurate overhead rates and distorted product costs. For example, if direct labour-hours is used to allocate overhead, but in reality overhead has little to do with direct labour-hours, then products with high direct labour-hour requirements will shoulder an unrealistic burden of overhead and will be overcosted.

Most companies use direct labour-hours or direct labour cost as the activity base for manufacturing overhead. However, as discussed in earlier chapters, major shifts are taking place in the structure of costs in many industries. In the past, direct labour accounted for up to 60% of the cost of many products, with overhead cost making up only a portion of the remainder. This situation has been changing for two reasons. First, sophisticated automated equipment has taken over functions that used to be performed by direct labour workers. Since the costs of acquiring and maintaining such equipment are classified as overhead, this increases overhead while decreasing direct labour. Second, products are themselves becoming more sophisticated and complex and change more frequently. This increases the need for highly skilled indirect workers such as engineers. As a result of these two trends, direct labour is becoming less of a factor and overhead is becoming more of a factor in the cost of products in many industries.

In companies where direct labour and overhead costs have been moving in opposite directions, it would be difficult to argue that direct labour "drives" overhead costs. Accordingly, in recent years, managers in some companies have used *activity-based costing* principles to redesign their cost accounting systems. Activity-based costing is a costing technique that is designed to more accurately reflect the demands that products, customers, and other cost objects make on overhead resources. The activity-based approach is discussed in more detail in Chapter 5.

We hasten to add that although direct labour may not be an appropriate allocation basis in some industries, in others it continues to be a significant driver of manufacturing overhead.[4] The key point is that the allocation base used by the company should really drive, or cause, overhead costs, and direct labour is not always an appropriate activity base.

---

[4] George Foster and Mahendra Gupta, "Manufacturing Overhead Cost Drive Analysis," *Journal of Accounting and Economics* (January 1990), pp. 309–37.

Computation of Unit Costs

With the application of Yost Precision Machining's $216 manufacturing overhead to the job cost sheet in Exhibit 3–4, the job cost sheet is almost complete. There are two final steps. First, the totals for direct materials, direct labour, and manufacturing overhead are transferred to the Cost Summary section of the job cost sheet and added together to obtain the total cost for the job. Then the total cost ($1,800) is divided by the number of units (2) to obtain the unit cost ($900). As indicated earlier, *this unit cost is an average cost and should not be interpreted as the cost that would actually be incurred if another unit were produced.* Much of the actual overhead would not change at all if another unit were produced, so the incremental cost of an additional unit is something less than the average unit cost of $900.

The completed job cost sheet is now ready to be transferred to the Finished Goods inventory account, where it will serve as the basis for valuing unsold units in ending inventory and determining cost of goods sold.

Despite the decreasing importance of direct labour in many industries, it is still widely used as a base in assigning overhead cost to products and services. A recent survey of 244 companies found that direct labour is used more often than any other base, and that this holds true regardless of the size of the company or the type of operation involved. (The survey covered companies in traditional manufacturing, high-tech operations, and service activities.) Results of the survey were (in terms of the *primary* base used):[5]

	Percent of Companies Using the Base
Direct labour (either hours or cost)	62
Machine-hours	12
Production volume	5
Direct material (either weight or cost)	8
Revenue	3
Other (primarily combinations of more than one base)	10
Total	100

Although direct labour is still widely used as an allocation base, evidence from other studies suggests that the trend is downward and that over time its use may be slowly decreasing.[6]

---

[5]Jeffrey R. Cohen and Laurence Paquette, "Management Accounting Practices: Perceptions of Controllers," *Journal of Cost Management* (Fall 1991), p. 75.

[6]See Henry R. Schwarzbach, "The Impact of Automation on Accounting for Indirect Costs," *Management Accounting* (December 1985); and James R. Emore and Joseph A. Ness, "The Slow Pace of Meaningful Change in Cost Systems," *Journal of Cost Management* (Winter 1991). In his 1985 study, Schwarzbach surveyed 112 companies and found that nearly 94% used direct labour to some extent (either as the primary or secondary base) in overhead costing. In their 1991 study, Emore and Ness surveyed 70 midwestern manufacturers and found that only 74% used direct labour (either as the primary or secondary base) in overhead costing.

Japanese companies, like companies in the United States, most frequently use direct labour-hours as a basis for allocating manufacturing overhead. One survey of over 250 manufacturing companies in Japan found the following breakdown:[7]

Basis for Allocation of Manufacturing Overhead	Percent
Direct labour-hours only	41.7
Machine-hours only	6.4
Both direct labour-hours and machine-hours	43.6
Other allocation bases	8.3
Total	100.0

▼   ▼   ▼   ▼   ▼

MANAGERIAL ACCOUNTING IN ACTION—WRAP-UP

In the 8:00 AM management meeting on March 9, Jean Yost, the president of Yost Precision Machining, drew attention once again to job 2B47:

"I see job 2B47 is completed. Let's get those couplings shipped immediately to Loops Unlimited so they can get their testing program under way. How much are we going to bill Loops for those two units?"

The controller, Mark White, consulted the job cost sheets for the week and said: "Under the agreement with Loops Unlimited to sell the experimental units at cost, we will charge them just $900 a unit."

"Fine. Let's hope the couplings work out and we make some money on the big order later."

▼   ▼   ▼   ▼   ▼

Summary of Document Flows

The sequence of events just discussed is summarized in Exhibit 3–5 on the following page. A careful study of the flow of documents in this exhibit will provide a visual overview of the overall operation of a job-order costing system.

---

[7]Michiharu Sakurai, "The Influence of Factory Automation on Management Accounting Practices," in Robert Kaplan, ed., *Measures for Manufacturing Excellence* (Cambridge, Mass.: Harvard Press, 1990), p. 43.

EXHIBIT 3-5

The Flow of
Documents in a Job-
Order Costing
System

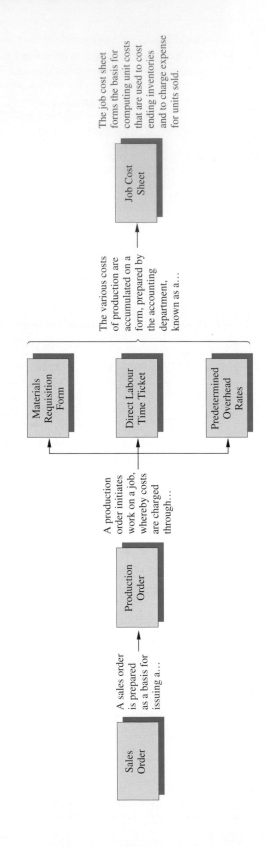

A sales order is prepared as a basis for issuing a…

Sales Order

A production order initiates work on a job, whereby costs are charged through…

Production Order

Materials Requisition Form

Direct Labour Time Ticket

Predetermined Overhead Rates

The various costs of production are accumulated on a form, prepared by the accounting department, known as a…

Job Cost Sheet

The job cost sheet forms the basis for computing unit costs that are used to cost ending inventories and to charge expense for units sold.

JOB-ORDER COSTING—THE FLOW OF COSTS

OBJECTIVE 4
Prepare journal entries to record the flow of direct materials cost, direct labour cost, and manufacturing overhead cost in a job-order costing system.

Having obtained a broad, conceptual perspective of the operation of a job-order costing system, we are now prepared to take a look at the flow of actual costs through the system itself. We consider a single month's activity for a hypothetical company, presenting all data in summary form. As a basis for discussion, let us assume that Rand Company has two jobs in process during April, the first month of its fiscal year. Job A, the production of 30,000 special medals to commemorate the opening of the Confederation Bridge to PEI, was started during March and had $30,000 in manufacturing costs (materials, labour, and overhead) already accumulated on April 1. Job B, 14,000 medals to denote the 500-year anniversary of the landing of John Cabot in Newfoundland, was started during April.

The Purchase and Issue of Materials

On April 1, Rand Company had $7,000 in raw materials on hand. During April, Rand Company purchased $60,000 in raw materials for use in production. The purchase is recorded in Entry 1 as follows:

(1)

Raw Materials	60,000	
Accounts Payable		60,000

As explained in Chapter 2, Raw Materials is an inventory account. Thus, any materials remaining in the account at the end of a period will appear on the balance sheet under an inventory (an asset) classification.

Issue of Direct and Indirect Materials. During April, $52,000 in raw materials were requisitioned from the storeroom for use in production. Entry 2 records the issue of the materials to the production departments.

(2)

Work in Process	50,000	
Manufacturing Overhead	2,000	
Raw Materials		52,000

The materials charged to Work in Process represent direct materials assignable to specific jobs on the production line. As these materials are entered into the Work in Process account, they are also recorded on the separate job cost sheets to which they relate. This point is illustrated in Exhibit 3–6, where $28,000 of the $50,000 in direct materials is charged to job A's cost sheet and the remaining $22,000 is charged to job B's cost sheet.

The $2,000 charged to Manufacturing Overhead in Entry 2 represents indirect materials used in production during April. Observe that the Manufacturing Overhead account is separate from the Work in Process account. The purpose of the Manufacturing Overhead account is to accumulate all manufacturing overhead costs as they are incurred during a period.

Before leaving Exhibit 3–6 we need to point out one additional thing. Notice from the exhibit that the job cost sheet for job A contains a beginning balance of $30,000. We stated earlier that this balance represents the cost of work done during March that has been carried forward to April. Also note that the Work in Process account contains the same $30,000 balance. *The reason the $30,000 appears in both places is that the Work in Process account is a control account and the job costs sheets form a subsidiary ledger. Thus, the Work in Process account contains a summarized total of all costs appearing on the individual job cost sheets for all jobs in process at any given point in time.* (Since

EXHIBIT 3-6

Raw Materials Cost
Flows

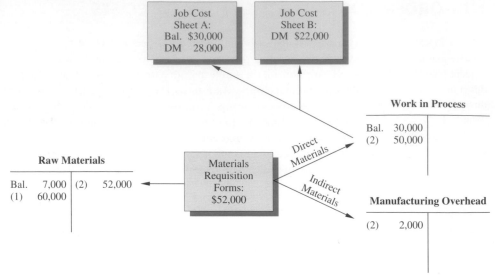

DM = Direct materials.

Rand Company had only job A in process at the beginning of April, job A's $30,000 balance on that date is equal to the balance in the Work in Process account.)

Issue of Direct Materials Only. Sometimes the materials drawn from the Raw Materials inventory account are all direct materials. In this case, the entry to record the issue of the materials into production would be:

Work in Process	XXX	
Raw Materials		XXX

Labour Cost

As work is performed in various departments of Rand Company from day to day, employee time tickets are generated, collected, and forwarded to the accounting department. There the tickets are costed according to the various rates paid to the employees, and the resulting costs are classified as either direct or indirect labour. This costing and classification for April resulted in the following entry:

(3)

Work in Process	60,000	
Manufacturing Overhead	15,000	
Salaries and Wages Payable		75,000

Only that portion of labour cost that represents direct labour is added to the Work in Process account. For the Rand Company, this amounted to $60,000 for April.

At the same time that direct labour costs are added to Work in Process they are also added to the individual job cost sheets, as shown in Exhibit 3–7. During April, $40,000 of direct labour cost was chargeable to job A and the remaining $20,000 was chargeable to job B.

The labour costs charged to Manufacturing Overhead represent the indirect labour costs of the period, such as supervision, janitorial work, and maintenance.

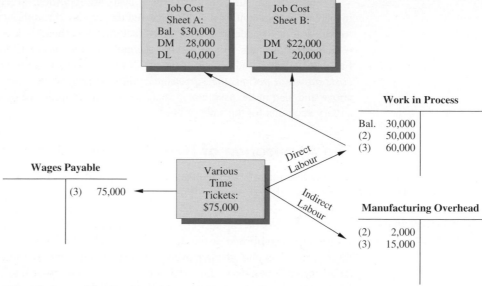

EXHIBIT 3-7

Labour Cost Flows

DM = Direct materials; DL = Direct labour.

Manufacturing Overhead Costs

As we learned in Chapter 2, all costs of operating the factory other than direct materials and direct labour are classified as manufacturing overhead costs. These costs are entered directly into the Manufacturing Overhead account as they are incurred. To illustrate, assume that the Rand Company incurred the following general factory costs during the month of April:

Utilities (heat, water, and power)	$21,000
Rent on equipment	16,000
Miscellaneous factory costs	3,000
Total	$40,000

The entry to record the incurrence of these costs would be:

(4)

Manufacturing Overhead	40,000	
Accounts Payable		40,000

In addition, let us assume that during April the Rand Company recognized $13,000 in accrued property taxes and $7,000 in insurance expired on factory buildings and equipment. The entry to record these items would be:

(5)

Manufacturing Overhead	20,000	
Property Taxes Payable		13,000
Prepaid Insurance		7,000

Finally let us further assume that the company recognized $18,000 in depreciation on factory equipment during April. The entry to record the accrual of depreciation would be:

(6)

Manufacturing Overhead	18,000	
Accumulated Depreciation		18,000

In short, *all* manufacturing overhead costs are recorded directly into the Manufacturing Overhead account as they are incurred day by day throughout a period. It is important for the reader to understand that Manufacturing Overhead is a control account for many —perhaps thousands—of subsidiary accounts such as Indirect Materials, Indirect Labour, Factory Utilities, and so forth. *As the Manufacturing Overhead account is debited for costs during a period, the various subsidiary accounts are also debited.* In the example above and also in the assignment material for this chapter, we omit the entries to the subsidiary accounts for the sake of brevity.

The Application of Manufacturing Overhead

OBJECTIVE 5

Apply overhead cost to Work in Process by use of a predetermined overhead rate.

Since actual manufacturing costs are charged to the Manufacturing Overhead control account rather than to Work in Process, how are manufacturing overhead costs assigned to Work in Process? The answer is, by means of the predetermined overhead rate. Recall from our discussion earlier in the chapter that for costing purposes a predetermined overhead rate is established at the beginning of each year. The rate is calculated by dividing the estimated manufacturing overhead cost for the year by the estimated activity (measured in machine-hours, direct labour-hours, or some other base). For example, if direct labour-hours is the base, overhead cost is applied to each job by multiplying the number of direct labour-hours charged to the job by the predetermined overhead rate.

To illustrate the cost flows involved, assume that the Rand Company has used machine-hours in computing its predetermined overhead rate and that this rate is $6 per machine-hour. Also assume that during April, 10,000 machine-hours were worked on job A and 5,000 machine-hours were worked on job B (a total of 15,000 machine-hours). Thus, $90,000 in overhead cost (15,000 machine-hours × $6 = $90,000) would be applied to Work in Process. The entry to record the application would be:

(7)

Work in Process	90,000	
Manufacturing Overhead		90,000

The flow of costs through the Manufacturing Overhead account is shown in T-account format in Exhibit 3–8.

The actual overhead costs in the Manufacturing Overhead account in Exhibit 3–8 are the costs that were added to the account in Entries 2 to 6. Observe that the incurrence of these actual overhead costs (Entries 2 to 6) and the application of overhead to Work in Process (Entry 7) represent two separate and distinct processes.[8]

The Concept of a Clearing Account. The Manufacturing Overhead account operates as a clearing account. As we have noted, actual factory overhead costs are charged to it as they are incurred day by day throughout the year. At certain intervals during the year, usually when a job is completed, overhead cost is released from the Manufacturing Overhead account and is applied to the Work in Process account by means of the predetermined overhead rate. This sequence of events is illustrated as:

Manufacturing Overhead
(a Clearing Account)

Actual overhead costs are charged to the account as these costs are incurred day by day throughout the period.	→	→	Overhead is applied to Work in Process on a periodic basis by means of the predetermined overhead rate.

---

[8]If an actual cost system were used, the actual overhead costs could be applied in the same procedural manner as the predetermined overhead.

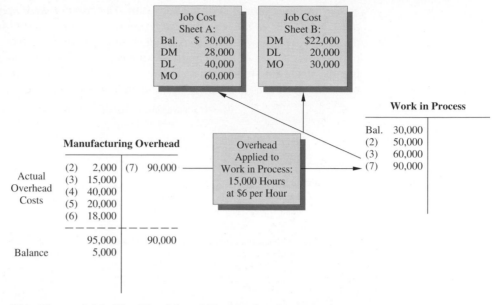

EXHIBIT 3–8

The Flow of Costs in
Overhead Application

DM = Direct materials; DL = Direct labour; MO = Manufacturing overhead.

The actual overhead costs incurred and shown as debits in the manufacturing account are a result of many different types of overhead costs. A brief list of some of the different types is presented in the journal entries, numbers 5 and 6, or in the schedule of cost of goods manufactured, shown in Exhibit 3–11 or previously in Exhibit 2–3. The clearing account concept actually represents a general ledger control account for a subsidiary ledger that contains the detailed information on each type of overhead cost.

As we emphasized earlier, the predetermined overhead rate is based entirely on estimates of what overhead costs are *expected* to be, and it is established before the year begins. As a result, the overhead cost applied during a year may turn out to be more or less than the overhead cost that is actually incurred. For example, notice from Exhibit 3–8 that the Rand Company's actual overhead costs for the period are $5,000 greater than the overhead cost that has been applied to Work in Process, resulting in a $5,000 debit balance in the Manufacturing Overhead account. We reserve discussion of what to do with this $5,000 balance until a later section, "Problems of Overhead Application."

For the moment, we can conclude by noting from Exhibit 3–8 that the cost of a completed job consists of the actual materials cost of the job, the actual labour cost of the job, and an *applied* amount of overhead cost to the job. The fact that it is applied overhead cost (not actual overhead cost) that goes into the Work in Process account and onto the job cost sheets is a subtle point that is easy to miss. Thus, this section of the chapter requires special study and consideration.

Nonmanufacturing Costs

In addition to manufacturing costs such as salaries, utilities, and insurance as part of the operation, production firms also incur these same kinds of costs in relation to other parts of their operations. For example, there are costs arising from activities in the front office where secretaries, top management, and others work. There are identical kinds of costs arising from the operation of the sales staff. *The costs of these nonmanufacturing operations should not go into the Manufacturing Overhead account because the incurrence of these costs is not related to the manufacture of products.* Rather, these costs should be treated as expenses of the period, as explained in Chapter 2, and charged directly to the income statement. To illustrate, assume that the Rand Company incurred selling and administrative costs as follows during the month of April:

Top-management salaries	$21,000
Other office salaries	9,000
Total salaries	$30,000

The entry to record these salaries would be:

(8)

Salaries Expense	30,000	
Salaries and Wages Payable		30,000

Assume that depreciation on administrative office equipment during the month of April was $7,000. The entry would be:

(9)

Depreciation Expense	7,000	
Accumulated Depreciation		7,000

Pay particular attention to the difference between this entry and Entry 6, where we recorded depreciation on factory equipment.

Finally, assume that advertising was $42,000 and that other selling and administrative expenses totalled $8,000 for the month. The entry to record these items would be:

(10)

Advertising Expense	42,000	
Other Selling and Administrative Expense	8,000	
Accounts Payable		50,000

Because the amounts in Entries 8 through 10 all go directly into expense accounts, they have no effect on the costing of Rand Company's production for the month. The same is true of all other selling and administrative expenses incurred during the month, including sales commissions, depreciation on sales equipment, rent on office facilities, insurance on office facilities, and related costs.

The distinction between manufacturing overhead costs and nonmanufacturing costs such as selling and administrative expenses is sometimes difficult because the type of cost, for example depreciation or salaries, is the same but the classification is different. In practice the classification has to be based on what the firm does to incur the costs. If it sells or markets then this is not production and the distinction is clear. If, however, it administers then the distinction depends on what is administered and how important it is to separate production administration from overall administration. For example, if all the company does is produce the Hibernia oil platform, then administration is production (manufacturing) overhead. However, if the company is administering many jobs and marketing new jobs at the same time, it may not be able to distinguish overhead from administrative time on the part of the senior management. Thus unless costs are needed for a cost recovery billing, administration salaries expense may be the expeditious way to treat the salaries.

Cost of Goods Manufactured

When a job has been completed, the finished output is transferred from the production departments to the finished goods warehouse. By this time, the accounting department has charged the job with direct materials and direct labour cost, and the job has absorbed a portion of manufacturing overhead through the application process discussed earlier. A transfer of these costs must be made within the costing system that *parallels* the physical transfer of the goods to the finished goods warehouse. The transfer within the costing system is to move the costs of the completed job out of the Work in Process account and into the Finished Goods account. The sum of all amounts transferred between these two accounts represents the cost of goods manufactured for the period. (This point was illustrated earlier in Exhibit 2–5 in Chapter 2. The reader may wish to go back to Exhibit 2–5 and refresh this point before reading on.)

In the case of the Rand Company, let us assume that job A was completed during April. The entry to transfer the cost of job A from Work in Process to Finished Goods would be:

(11)

Finished Goods	158,000	
Work in Process		158,000

The $158,000 represents the completed cost of job A, as shown on the job cost sheet in Exhibit 3–8. Because job A was the only job completed during April, the $158,000 also represents the cost of goods manufactured for the month.

Job B was not completed by month-end, so its cost remains in the Work in Process account and carries over to the next month. If a balance sheet is prepared at the end of April, the cost accumulated thus far on job B appears under the caption "work in process inventory" in the assets section.

Cost of Goods Sold

As units of product in finished goods are shipped to fill customers' orders, the unit cost appearing on the job cost sheets is used as a basis for transferring the cost of the sold items from the Finished Goods account into the Cost of Goods Sold account. If a complete job is shipped, as in the case where a job has been done to a customer's specifications, then it is a simple matter to transfer the entire cost appearing on the job cost sheet into the Cost of Goods Sold account. In most cases, however, only a portion of the units involved in a particular job are sold. In these situations, the unit cost is particularly important in knowing how much product cost should be removed from Finished Goods and charged into Cost of Goods Sold.

For the Rand Company, we assume that three-fourths of the units in job A were shipped to customers by month-end. The total selling price of these units was $225,000. The entries needed to record the sale would be (all sales are on account):

(12)

Accounts Receivable	225,000	
Sales		225,000

(13)

Cost of Goods Sold	118,500	
Finished Goods		118,500
($158,000 total cost × ¾ = $118,500)		

With Entry 13, the flow of costs through our job-order costing system is completed. Each of entries (1) to (13) is posted to its respective T-account as shown in Exhibit 3–9. To pull the entire Rand Company example together, journal entries (1) to (13) are repeated in Exhibit 3–10.

EXHIBIT 3-9   A Summary of Cost Flows—The Rand Company

Accounts Receivable			Accounts Payable			Capital Stock	
XX				XX			XX

Prepaid Insurance						Retained Earnings	
XX							XX

Raw Materials			Salaries and Wages Payable			Sales	
Bal. 7,000				XX			

Work in Process			Property Taxes Payable			Cost of Goods Sold	
Bal. 30,000				XX			

Salaries Expense

Finished Goods	
Bal. 10,000	

Depreciation Expense

Advertising Expense

Accumulated Depreciation	
	XX

Other Selling and Administrative Expense

Manufacturing Overhead

Note: XX = Normal balance in the account (for example, Accounts Receivable normally carries a debit balance).

A Summary of Cost Flows

EXHIBIT 3-10

Summary of Rand
Company Journal
Entries

(1)		
Raw Materials	60,000	
Accounts Payable		60,000
(2)		
Work in Process	50,000	
Manufacturing Overhead	2,000	
Raw Materials		52,000
(3)		
Work in Process	60,000	
Manufacturing Overhead	15,000	
Salaries and Wages Payable		75,000
(4)		
Manufacturing Overhead	40,000	
Accounts Payable		40,000
(5)		
Manufacturing Overhead	20,000	
Property Taxes Payable		13,000
Prepaid Insurance		7,000
(6)		
Manufacturing Overhead	18,000	
Accumulated Depreciation		18,000
(7)		
Work in Process	90,000	
Manufacturing Overhead		90,000
(8)		
Salaries Expense	30,000	
Salaries and Wages Payable		30,000
(9)		
Depreciation Expense	7,000	
Accumulated Depreciation		7,000
(10)		
Advertising Expense	42,000	
Other Selling and Administrative Expense	8,000	
Accounts Payable		50,000
(11)		
Finished Goods	158,000	
Work in Process		158,000
(12)		
Accounts Receivable	225,000	
Sales		225,000
(13)		
Cost of Goods Sold	118,500	
Finished Goods		118,500

OBJECTIVE 6

Prepare T-accounts to
show the flow of costs
in a job-order costing
system and prepare
schedules of cost of
goods manufactured
and cost of goods sold.

Exhibit 3–11 presents a schedule of cost of goods manufactured and a schedule of cost of goods sold for the Rand Company. Note particularly from Exhibit 3–11 that the cost of goods manufactured for the month ($158,000) agrees with the amount transferred from Work in Process to Finished Goods for the month as recorded earlier in Entry 11. Careful thought is needed here because the previous example adopts a perpetual inventory approach to cost accumulation and journal entry presentation. This approach is a reasonably

EXHIBIT 3–11

Schedules of Cost of
Goods Manufactured
and Cost of Goods
Sold

Cost of Goods Manufactured

Direct materials:		
Raw materials inventory, April 1	$ 7,000	
Add: Purchases of raw materials	60,000	
Total raw materials available	67,000	
Deduct: Raw materials inventory, April 30	15,000	
Raw materials used in production	52,000	
Deduct: Indirect materials (below)	2,000	
Direct materials used in production		$ 50,000
Direct labour		60,000
Manufacturing overhead:		
Indirect materials	2,000	
Indirect labour	15,000	
Utilities	21,000	
Rent	16,000	
Miscellaneous factory costs	3,000	
Property taxes	13,000	
Insurance	7,000	
Depreciation	18,000	
Actual overhead costs	95,000	
Deduct: Underapplied overhead	5,000*	
Overhead applied to work in process		90,000
Total manufacturing costs		200,000
Add: Beginning work in process inventory		30,000
		230,000
Deduct: Ending work in process inventory		72,000
Cost of goods manufactured		$158,000

Cost of Goods Sold

Opening finished goods inventory	$ 10,000
Add: Cost of goods manufactured	158,000
Goods available for sale	168,000
Ending finished goods inventory	49,500
Cost of goods sold	118,500
Add: Underapplied overhead	5,000
Adjusted cost of goods sold	$123,500

*Note that underapplied overhead must be deducted from actual overhead costs and only the difference ($90,000) is added to direct materials and direct labour. The reason is that the schedule of cost of goods manufactured represents a summary of costs flowing through the Work in Process account during a period and therefore must exclude any overhead costs that were incurred but never applied to production. If a reverse situation had existed and overhead had been overapplied during the period, then the amount of overapplied overhead would have been added to actual overhead costs on the schedule. This would have brought the actual overhead costs up to the amount that had been applied to production.

common one where inventory details are required. The alternate periodic inventory approach to all the previous transactions can be used and results in some alterations in how entries are sequenced and presented. Nevertheless, the end results from these entries for the income statement and balance sheet are very similar, if not identical. It is the processing sequence that would change under the periodic inventory system. Appendix A will explain some of the specific issues accompanying alternative systems to the perpetual one.

An income statement for April is presented in Exhibit 3–12. Observe that the cost of goods sold figure on this statement ($123,500) is carried down from Exhibit 3–11.

EXHIBIT 3-12

Income Statement

RAND COMPANY

Income Statement For the Month Ending April 30, 19xx

Sales		$225,000
Deduct cost of goods sold ($118,500 + $5,000)		123,500
Gross margin		101,500
Deduct selling and administrative expenses:		
Salaries expense	$30,000	
Depreciation expense	7,000	
Advertising expense	42,000	
Other expense	8,000	87,000
Net income		$ 14,500

PROBLEMS OF OVERHEAD APPLICATION

OBJECTIVE 7

Compute any balance of under- or overapplied overhead cost for a period and prepare the journal entry needed to close the balance into the appropriate accounts.

We need to briefly consider three problem areas relating to overhead application. These are (1) the computation of underapplied and overapplied overhead; (2) the disposition of any balance remaining in the Manufacturing Overhead account at the end of a period; and (3) the use of multiple overhead rates by some companies.

Underapplied and Overapplied Overhead

Because the predetermined overhead rate is established before a period begins and because it is based entirely on estimated data, generally there is a difference between the amount of overhead cost that is applied to the Work in Process account and the actual overhead costs that materialize during the period. In the case of Rand Company, for example, the predetermined overhead rate of $6 per hour resulted in $90,000 of overhead cost being applied to Work in Process, whereas actual overhead costs proved to be $95,000 for the month (see Exhibit 3–8). The difference between the overhead cost applied to Work in Process and the actual overhead costs of a period is termed either **underapplied** or **overapplied overhead.** For the Rand Company, overhead was underapplied because the applied cost ($90,000) was $5,000 less than the actual cost ($95,000). If the tables had been reversed and the company had applied $95,000 in overhead cost to Work in Process while incurring actual overhead costs of only $90,000, then a situation of overapplied overhead would have existed.

Exhibit 3–11 presents a somewhat confusing treatment of overhead on the schedule of cost of goods manufactured. This peculiarity involves the $5,000 deducted from the actual overhead costs of $95,000.

To understand this peculiarity, it is necessary to note that $158,000, cost of goods manufactured, equals the credit to work in process in Exhibit 3–9. This total is the manufacturing cost of the units completed in the period. The total is composed of the direct materials used of $50,000, the direct labour used of $60,000, and the manufacturing overhead applied of $90,000. The total of these three costs is adjusted for the beginning and ending work in process inventories to yield the cost of completed units, $158,000.

If the schedule of cost of goods manufactured did not disclose the details of the overhead costs, then only the overhead applied, $90,000, would appear on the schedule. In this case, the confusion would disappear. However, because users of the schedule of cost of goods manufactured might wish to know the components of the overhead incurred, the $95,000, this total has to be adjusted to the applied amount of overhead. Thus, the required amount for the total manufacturing costs is the $90,000 applied overhead.

The underapplied overhead in the cost of goods sold is the usual adjustment needed to reflect the amount of underapplied (or overapplied) overhead at the end of the accounting period. It serves a completely different purpose from the amount on the cost of goods manufactured schedule.

Any difference between applied overhead cost and actual overhead cost must be traceable to the estimates going into the overhead rate computation, because the amount of overhead applied to Work in Process is dependent on the predetermined overhead rate. Generally, the cause can be traced to one of two factors. First, the cost of inputs (lubricants, utilities, and so forth) may change from what was estimated at the beginning of the period because of external market forces. Second, the actual level of activity may be different from what was estimated at the beginning of the period because of either greater or less demand for the company's goods and services. To illustrate, refer again to the formula used in computing the predetermined overhead rate:

$$\frac{\text{Estimated total manufacturing overhead costs}}{\substack{\text{Estimated total units in the base} \\ \text{(machine-hours, etc.)}}} = \substack{\text{Predetermined} \\ \text{overhead rate}}$$

If either the estimated cost or the estimated level of activity used in this formula differs from the actual cost or the actual level of activity for a period, then the predetermined overhead rate proves to be inaccurate. The result is either under- or overapplied overhead for the period. Assume, for example, that two companies have prepared the following estimated data for the year 19x1:

	CoSteel	Acadia Roofers
Predetermined overhead rate based on	Machine-hours	Direct labour cost
Estimated manufacturing overhead for 19x1	$100,000 (a)	$120,000 (a)
Estimated machine-hours for 19x1	50,000 (b)	—
Estimated direct labour cost for 19x1	—	$ 80,000 (b)
Predetermined overhead rate, (a) ÷ (b)	$2 per machine-hour	150% of direct labour cost

Now assume that the *actual* overhead cost and the *actual* level of activity for 19x1 for each company are shown as follows:

	CoSteel	Acadia Roofers
Actual manufacturing overhead costs	$99,000	$128,000
Actual machine-hours	48,000	—
Actual direct labour cost	—	$ 88,000

For each company, notice that the actual cost and activity data differ from the estimates used in computing the predetermined overhead rate. The computation of the resulting under- or overapplied overhead for each company is:

	CoSteel	Acadia Roofers
Actual manufacturing overhead costs	$99,000	$128,000
Manufacturing overhead cost applied to Work in Process during 19x1:		
48,000 *actual* machine-hours × $2	96,000	
$88,000 *actual* direct labour cost × 150%		132,000
Underapplied (overapplied) overhead	$ 3,000	$ (4,000)

For CoSteel, notice that the amount of overhead cost that has been applied to Work in Process ($96,000) is less than the actual overhead cost for the year ($99,000). Therefore, overhead is underapplied. Also notice that the original estimate of overhead in CoSteel ($100,000) is not directly involved in this computation. Its impact is felt only through the $2 predetermined overhead rate that is used.

EXHIBIT 3-13

Summary of
Overhead Concepts

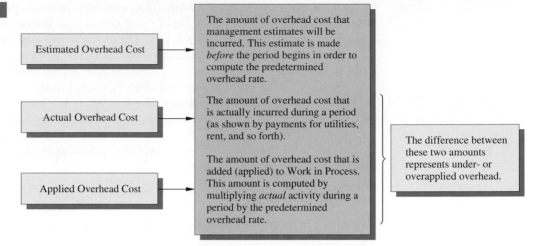

Estimated Overhead Cost → The amount of overhead cost that management estimates will be incurred. This estimate is made *before* the period begins in order to compute the predetermined overhead rate.

Actual Overhead Cost → The amount of overhead cost that is actually incurred during a period (as shown by payments for utilities, rent, and so forth).

Applied Overhead Cost → The amount of overhead cost that is added (applied) to Work in Process. This amount is computed by multiplying *actual* activity during a period by the predetermined overhead rate.

The difference between these two amounts represents under- or overapplied overhead.

For Acadia Roofers, the amount of overhead cost that has been applied to Work in Process ($132,000) is greater than the actual overhead cost for the year ($128,000), and so a situation of overapplied overhead exists.

A summary of the concepts discussed in this section is presented in Exhibit 3–13.

Disposition of Under- or Overapplied Overhead Balances

What disposition should be made of any under- or overapplied balance remaining in the manufacturing overhead account at the end of a period? Generally, any balance in the account is treated in one of three ways:

1. Closed out to Cost of Goods Sold.
2. Allocated between Work in Process, Finished Goods, and Cost of Goods Sold in a proportion based on balances in these accounts.[9]
3. Carried forward to the next period.

Closed Out to Cost of Goods Sold. Most firms close out any under- or overapplied overhead to Cost of Goods Sold, because this approach is simpler than allocation. Returning to the example of the Rand Company, the entry to close the underapplied overhead to Cost of Goods sold would be (see Exhibit 3–12 for the $5,000 cost figure):

(14)

Cost of Goods Sold	5,000	
Manufacturing Overhead		5,000

With this entry, the cost of goods sold for the month increases to $123,500, as shown earlier:

Cost of goods sold (from Exhibit 3–9)	$118,500
Add underapplied overhead [Entry 14]	5,000
Adjusted cost of goods sold	$123,500

An income statement for the Rand Company for April would therefore appear as shown in Exhibit 3–12.

---

[9]Some firms prefer to make the allocation on a basis of the amount of *overhead cost* in the preceding accounts at the end of a period. This approach to allocation yields more accurate results in those situations where the amount of overhead cost differs substantially between jobs. For purposes of consistency, when we allocate in this book it is always based on the total manufacturing costs in the balances in the preceding accounts.

Allocated among Accounts. Allocation of under- or overapplied overhead among Work in Process, Finished Goods, and Cost of Goods Sold is more accurate than closing the entire balance into Cost of Goods Sold. The reason is that allocation assigns overhead costs to where they would have gone in the first place had it not been for the errors in the estimates going into the predetermined overhead rate. Although allocation is more accurate than direct write-off, it is used less often in actual practice because of the time and difficulty involved in the allocation process. Most firms feel that the greater accuracy simply is not worth the extra effort that allocation requires, particularly when the dollar amounts are small.

Had we chosen to allocate the underapplied overhead in the Rand Company example, the computations and entry would have been:

Work in process inventory, April 30		$ 72,000	36.00%
Finished goods inventory, April 30		49,500	24.75
Cost of goods sold	$118,500		
Less: Work in Process inventory, April 1	30,000		
Finished goods inventory, April 1	10,000	78,500	39.25
Total		$200,000	100.00%

Work in Process (36.0% × $5,000)	1,800	
Finished Goods (24.75% × $5,000)	1,237	
Cost of Goods Sold (39.25% × $5,000)	1,963	
Manufacturing Overhead		5,000

If overhead had been overapplied, the preceding entry would have been just the reverse, because a credit balance would have existed in the Manufacturing Overhead account.

The rationale for deducting the beginning work in process and finished goods inventories from the cost of goods sold is to permit the allocation to be based on costs from the current period. By doing so, the 39.25% in the Rand Company example reflects only costs from April and thus corresponds to the period in which the underapplied overhead occurred. Without this adjustment, cost of goods sold would be assigned the overhead difference based on costs carried over from March and thus bear a disproportionate amount of the under- or overapplied overhead.

Carry the Balance Forward. Recall the section earlier in this chapter entitled "Application of Manufacturing Overhead." Notice that some firms have large seasonal variations in output while being faced with relatively constant overhead costs. Predetermined overhead was used to even out fluctuations in the cost of overhead caused by seasonal variations in output and seasonal variations in costs (e.g., heating costs). The predetermined overhead rate is computed using estimated total manufacturing costs for a year divided by estimated total units in the base. The result is an average rate. When the average predetermined rate is applied to actual production for the period, the applied overhead is determined. The under- or overapplied overhead is a result of two factors, an actual base that is different from one-twelfth of the annual estimated base and actual overhead costs that do not equal one-twelfth of the total estimated overhead costs. Therefore, for any given month, an under- or overapplied overhead amount would be expected. In some months, it would be positive; in other months, it would be negative. Over the year these amounts may largely cancel out. If this is the situation, then significant debits and credits could be carried forward to the year-end so that a final disposition can be made either by adjusting Cost of Goods Sold or allocating (sometimes termed *prorating*) the amount to the inventories and Cost of Goods Sold.

The Rand Company example would be treated as follows:

Underapplied Overhead [a deferred debit balance on the balance sheet] 5,000
    Manufacturing Overhead   5,000

Multiple Predetermined Overhead Rates

OBJECTIVE 8

Explain why multiple overhead rates are needed in many organizations.

Our discussion in this chapter has assumed that a single overhead rate was being used throughout an entire factory operation. In small companies, and even in some medium-sized companies, a single overhead rate (called a **plantwide overhead rate**) is used and is entirely adequate as a means of allocating overhead costs to production jobs. But in larger companies, **multiple predetermined overhead rates** are common for the reason that a single rate may not be capable of equitably handling the overhead costs of all departments. One department may be labour intensive, for example, and rely almost solely on the efforts of workers in performing needed functions. Allocation of overhead costs in such a department could, perhaps, be done most equitably on a basis of labour-hours or labour cost. Another department in the same factory may be machine intensive, requiring little in the way of worker effort. Allocation of overhead costs in this department could, perhaps, be done most equitably on a basis of machine-hours.

In short, larger organizations often have many predetermined overhead rates—perhaps a different one for each department. As a unit of product moves along the production line, overhead is applied in each department, according to the various overhead rates that have been set. The accumulation of all of these overhead applications represents the total overhead cost of the job.

A General Model of Product Cost Flows

The flow of costs in a product costing system can be presented in general model form, as shown in Exhibit 3–14. This model applies as much to a process costing system as it does to a job-order costing system. Visual inspection of the model can be very helpful in gaining a perspective as to how costs enter a system, flow through it, and finally end up as cost of goods sold on the income statement. A modern computer system would contain various databases comparable to elements of the system described. Even small business computer accounting packages contain the cost elements as part of their job costing structures.

JOB-ORDER COSTING IN SERVICE COMPANIES

We stated earlier in the chapter that job-order costing is used extensively in service organizations such as law firms, movie studios, hospitals, and repair shops, as well as in manufacturing firms. In a law firm, for example, each client represents a job, and the costs of that job are accumulated day by day on a job cost sheet as the client's case is handled by the firm. Paper supplies and similar inputs represent the direct materials for the job, the time expended by lawyers represents the direct labour, and the costs of secretaries, clerks, rent, depreciation, and so forth, represent the overhead.

In a movie studio, each picture produced by the studio is a job, and costs for direct materials (costumes, props, and film) and direct labour (actors, directors, and extras) are carefully accounted for and charged to each picture's job cost sheet. A proportionate share of the studio's overhead costs, such as utilities, depreciation of equipment, salaries

EXHIBIT 3-14   A General Model of Cost Flows

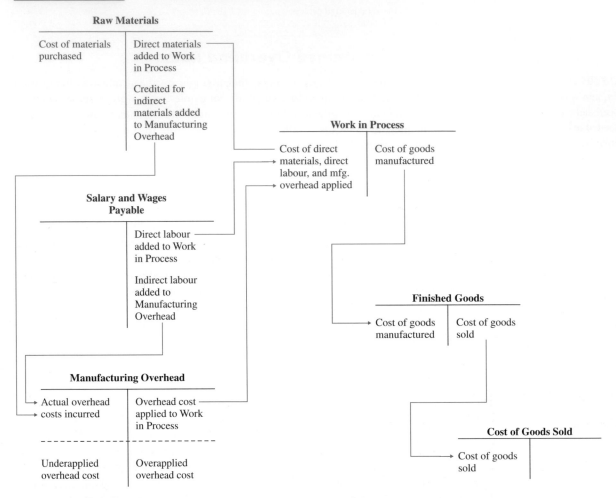

Jobs come in many forms and often from government sources. The list of government contract spending in Ottawa provides examples of many types of job cost situations.

Here are 10 of 20 categories where the largest amount of money was spent in the fiscal year of 1992–1993 with comparable figures for 1984–1985 in parentheses:

Unspecified business services:
$498.5 million ($207.3 million)
Unspecified professional services:
$413.4 million ($158.9 million)
Unspecified engineering services:
$248.6 million ($89 million)
Aircraft repair and maintenance:
$332.7 million ($178.9 million)
Purchase of services for development assistance:
$331.4 million ($152.7 million)

Office building repair:
$193.6 million ($89.7 million)
Management consulting:
$181.9 million ($56.4 million)
Computer services:
$151.7 million ($78.9 million)
EDP consultants:
$139.3 million ($40.07 million)
Dental services:
$131.3 million ($38.3 million)[10]

[10]Gord McIntosh, "Ottawa Spends $5b on Outsourcing Contracts," *The Mail Star,* May 5, 1994, p. B10. © *The Canadian Press.*

of maintenance workers, and so forth, is also charged to each picture. In a movie studio, overhead would typically be applied to jobs on a basis of camera time, or space and time occupied in a studio, rather than applied on a basis of actors' time or cost. On the other hand, in a law firm a lawyer's time may be the most appropriate basis for recognizing overhead cost when determining the cost of a case and billing a client.

In summary, the reader should be aware that job-order costing is a versatile and widely used costing method, and that he or she can expect to encounter it in virtually any organization where the output differs between products, patients, clients, or customers.

USE OF BAR CODE TECHNOLOGY

Earlier in the chapter we discussed the use of bar code technology in recording labour time. Some companies are going beyond just labour in the use of bar codes and are extending bar code technology to include all steps in the manufacturing process. Since bar code languages (called symbologies) are typically numeric, they allow people who speak different human languages to identify items, amounts, locations, work steps, and so forth, and also to communicate this information to others throughout the world. Thus, bar codes are becoming an international link that allows direct communication between a company, its customers, and its suppliers regardless of where they may be located.

Bar codes are often used in conjunction with electronic data interchange (EDI), which involves a networking of computers between organizations. The EDI network

Bar code technology is improving all steps of manufacturing. Bar codes are especially useful for tracking inventory and costs.

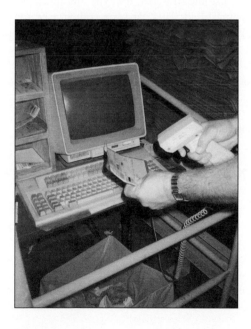

allows an electronic exchange of business documents and other information that extends into all areas of business activity from the order of raw materials to the shipment of completed goods.

J. M. Schneider, Inc., and Erb Transport Limited are two Canadian companies who use EDI to handle transportation transactions for J. M. Schneider's shipments to customers on Erb Transport's truck fleet. The EDI technology is used to handle freight charges and transmit customer invoices to Erb's loading docks for 2,000 to 3,000 deliveries per week. These companies have used EDI since March 1991 to reduce data entry time and errors and to smooth delivery schedules.[11]

In a company with a well-developed bar code system, the manufacturing cycle begins with the receipt of a customer's order via EDI. The raw materials to produce the goods come from suppliers who have bar coded the materials according to the company's preset specifications. When materials arrive at the company's plant, the bar codes are scanned to update inventory records. The bar codes are scanned again when the materials are requisitioned for use in production to relieve inventory of the amount and type of goods involved, and to charge the Work in Process account.

When materials are put into process, bar codes are attached and scanned as the goods move along the production line. These bar codes indicate the manufacturing steps to be performed, and they also update Work in Process records for labour and other costs incurred in the manufacturing process. When goods are completed, another scan is performed that transfers both the cost and quantity of goods from the Work in Process inventory account to the Finished Goods inventory account, or charges Cost of Goods Sold for goods ready to be shipped.

Goods ready to be shipped are packed into containers, which are bar coded with information that includes the customer number, the type and quantity of goods being shipped, and the order number being filled. This bar code is then used for preparing billing information and for tracking the packed goods until they are placed on a carrier for shipment to the customer. Some customers require that the packed goods be bar coded with point-of-sale labels that can be scanned at retail checkout counters. These scans allow the retailer to update inventory records, verify price, and generate a customer receipt.

In short, bar code technology is being integrated into all areas of business activity. Use of this technology undoubtedly will continue to spread until it has penetrated all levels of manufacturing, distribution, and retail sales worldwide.

INTERNATIONAL JOB COSTING

Studies of the international accounting scene suggest that the general principles of product costing are universally applicable.[12] Nevertheless, differences do exist from country to country in how specific costs are classified. For example, a study of Russian operational accounting and statistical recordkeeping, the equivalent of product costing, suggests that the required reporting structure in Russia would assign some cost elements we might classify as selling or administrative to inventory. Other costs such as the rent on plant facilities would be classified outside of the usual overhead category.[13] If a company were executing

---

[11]"Implementing Electronic Data Interchange," *Management Accounting Guideline* 24 (Hamilton, Ont.: Society of Management Accountants of Canada, 1994).

[12]Dhia D. AlHashin and Jeffrey S. Arpan, *International Dimensions of Accounting,* 2nd ed. (Boston, Mass.: PWS-Kent, 1988), p. 180.

[13]Adolf J. H. Enthoven, "Accounting in Russia: From Perestroika to Profits," *Management Accounting* (October 1992), pp. 22–31.

a contract with a foreign government, the differences in what is or is not permitted as contract costs would be particularly important. Similarly, what Supply and Services Canada will allow as contract costs is described by the word "prudent" and elaborated in a specific list of costs excluded from product costs.[14] For example, these requirements would permit certain general and selling costs to be included if a prudent person would incur such costs as part of the contract. Thus, while the general principles may be similar, the specifics can vary as a result of government regulations.

SUMMARY

Unit cost of production is one of the most useful items of cost data to a manager. Two methods for determining unit costs are in widespread use; these two methods are known as job-order costing and process costing, respectively. Job-order costing is used in those manufacturing situations where products differ from each other, such as in furniture manufacture and shipbuilding. Process costing is used in those situations where units of product are homogeneous, such as in the manufacture of flour or cement. We have also noted that job-order costing is used extensively in the service industries.

Materials requisition forms and labour time tickets control the assignment of direct materials and direct labour cost to production. Indirect manufacturing costs are assigned to production through use of a predetermined overhead rate, which is developed by estimating the level of manufacturing overhead to be incurred during a period and by dividing this estimate by a base common to all the jobs to be worked on during the period. The most frequently used bases are machine-hours and direct labour-hours or costs.

Because the predetermined overhead rate is based on estimates, the actual overhead cost incurred during a period may be somewhat more or somewhat less than the amount of overhead cost applied to production. Such a difference is referred to as under- or overapplied overhead. The under- or overapplied overhead for a period can be (1) closed out to Cost of Goods Sold, (2) allocated between Work in Process, Finished Goods, and Cost of Goods Sold, or (3) carried forward to deferred debit or deferred credit accounts on the balance sheet of an interim period.

Bar code technology is now being used in all steps of the manufacturing process. Bar codes are attached to materials to control their purchase and use, and bar codes are attached to goods in process to control the steps in their manufacture. When goods are completed, they are packed into containers that are bar coded with information that includes the customer number, the quantity of goods being shipped, and the order number being filled. In addition, bar codes can be used to bill customers and prepare point-of-sale labels that can be scanned at retail checkout counters.

General principles of product costing seem to be applicable universally on the international scene. However, specific differences in cost classification exist from country to country.

---

[14]Section 3, General Conditions, DSS–MAS 1031–2, "Contract Cost Principles," *Standard Acquisition Clauses and Conditions Manual*, Public Works and Government Services Canada, 1997.

REVIEW PROBLEM: JOB-ORDER COSTING

Hogle Company is a manufacturing firm that uses job-order costing. On January 1, 19x5, the company's inventory balances were as follows:

Raw materials	$20,000
Work in process	15,000
Finished goods	30,000

The company applies overhead cost to jobs on the basis of machine-hours worked. For 19x5, the company estimated that it would work 75,000 machine-hours and incur $450,000 in manufacturing overhead cost. The following transactions were recorded for the year:

a.   Raw materials were purchased on account, $410,000.

b.   Raw materials were requisitioned for use in production, $380,000 ($360,000 direct and $20,000 indirect).

c.   The following costs were incurred for employee services: direct labour, $75,000; indirect labour, $110,000; sales commissions, $90,000; and administrative salaries, $200,000.

d.   Sales travel costs were incurred, $17,000.

e.   Utility costs were incurred in the factory, $43,000.

f.   Advertising costs were incurred, $180,000.

g.   Depreciation was recorded for the year, $350,000 (80% relates to factory operations, and 20% relates to selling and administrative activities).

h.   Insurance expired during the year, $10,000 (70% relates to factory operations, and the remaining 30% relates to selling and administrative activities).

i.   Manufacturing overhead was applied to production. Due to greater than expected demand for its products, the company worked 80,000 machine-hours during the year.

j.   Goods costing $900,000 to manufacture were completed during the year.

k.   Goods were sold on account to customers during the year at a total selling price of $1,500,000. The goods cost $870,000 to manufacture.

Required

1.   Prepare journal entries to record the transactions above.

2.   Post the entries in (1) to T-accounts (don't forget to enter the opening balances in the inventory accounts).

3.   Is Manufacturing Overhead underapplied or overapplied for the year? Prepare a journal entry to close any balance in the Manufacturing Overhead account to Cost of Goods Sold.

4.   Prepare an income statement for the year. Include a schedule of costs of goods manufactured and costs of goods sold.

Solution to Review Problem

1. a. Raw materials 410,000

    Accounts Payable 410,000

    b. Work in Process 360,000

    Manufacturing Overhead 20,000

    Raw Materials 380,000

    c. Work in Process 75,000

    Manufacturing Overhead 110,000

    Sales Commissions Expense 90,000

    Administrative Salaries Expense 200,000

    Salaries and Wages Payable 475,000

    d. Sales Travel Expense 17,000

    Accounts Payable 17,000

    e. Manufacturing Overhead 43,000

    Accounts Payable 43,000

    f. Advertising Expense 180,000

    Accounts Payable 180,000

    g. Manufacturing Overhead 280,000

    Depreciation Expense 70,000

    Accumulated Depreciation 350,000

    h. Manufacturing Overhead 7,000

    Insurance Expense 3,000

    Prepaid Insurance 10,000

    i. The predetermined overhead rate for the year would be computed as follows:

$$\frac{\text{Estimated manufacturing overhead, } \$450,000}{\text{Estimated machine-hours, } 75,000} = \$6 \text{ per machine-hour}$$

Based on the 80,000 machine-hours actually worked during the year, the company would have applied $480,000 in overhead cost to production: 80,000 machine-hours × $6 = $480,000. The entry to record this application of overhead cost would be:

Work in Process 480,000

Manufacturing Overhead 480,000

    j. Finished Goods 900,000

    Work in Process 900,000

    k. Accounts Receivable 1,500,000

    Sales 1,500,000

    Cost of Goods Sold 870,000

    Finished Goods 870,000

2.

Accounts Receivable		
(k)	1,500,000	

Manufacturing Overhead			
(b)	20,000	(i)	480,000
(c)	110,000		
(e)	43,000		
(g)	280,000		
(h)	7,000		
	460,000		480,000
		Bal.	20,000

Sales		
		(k)	1,500,000

Cost of Goods Sold		
(k)	870,000	

Prepaid Insurance		
		(h)	10,000

Accumulated Depreciation		
		(g)	350,000

Commissions Expense		
(c)	90,000	

Administrative Salary Expense		
(c)	200,000	

Raw Materials			
Bal	20,000	(b)	380,000
(a)	410,000		
Bal	50,000		

Accounts Payable			
		(a)	410,000
		(d)	17,000
		(e)	43,000
		(f)	180,000

Sales Travel Expense		
(d)	17,000	

Advertising Expense		
(f)	180,000	

Work in Process			
Bal.	15,000	(j)	900,000
(b)	360,000		
(c)	75,000		
(i)	480,000		
Bal.	30,000		

Salaries and Wages Payable		
		(c)	475,000

Depreciation Expense		
(g)	70,000	

Insurance Expense		
(h)	3,000	

Finished Goods			
Bal.	30,000	(k)	870,000
(j)	900,000		
Bal.	60,000		

3. Manufacturing overhead is overapplied for the year. The entry to close it out to Cost of Goods Sold would be:

Manufacturing Overhead	20,000	
Cost of Goods Sold		20,000

4.

HOGLE COMPANY

Income Statement
For the Year Ended December 31, 19x5

Sales	$1,500,000
Less: Cost of goods sold ($870,000 – $20,000)	850,000
Gross margin	650,000

Less: Selling and administrative expenses:

Commissions expense	$ 90,000	
Administrative salaries expense	200,000	
Sales travel expense	17,000	
Advertising expense	180,000	
Depreciation expense	70,000	
Insurance expense	3,000	560,000
Net income		$ 90,000

HOGLE COMPANY

Schedule of Cost of Goods Manufactured and
Cost of Goods Sold

Direct Materials:

Raw materials inventory, January 1	$ 20,000	
Add: Purchases of raw materials	410,000	
Total raw materials available	430,000	
Deduct: Raw materials inventory, December 31	50,000	
Raw materials used in production	380,000	
Less: Indirect materials (below)	20,000	
Direct materials used in production		$ 360,000
Direct Labour		75,000

Manufacturing overhead:

Indirect materials	20,000	
Indirect labour	110,000	
Utilities	43,000	
Depreciation	280,000	
Insurance	7,000	
Actual overhead costs	460,000	
Add: Overapplied overhead	20,000	
Overhead applied to work in process		480,000
Total manufacturing costs		915,000
Add: Beginning work in process inventory		15,000
		930,000
Deduct: Ending work in process inventory		30,000
Cost of goods manufactured		900,000
Add: Finished goods inventory, January 1		30,000
Goods available for sale		930,000
Deduct: Finished goods inventory, December 31		60,000
Cost of Goods Sold		870,000
Deduct: overapplied overhead		20,000
Adjusted cost of goods sold		$ 850,000

KEY TERMS FOR REVIEW

Absorption cost   A costing method that includes all manufacturing costs—direct materials, direct labour, and both variable and fixed overhead—as part of the cost of a finished unit of product. This term is synonymous with *full cost*. (p. 92)

Bill of materials   A control sheet that shows the type and quantity of each item of material going into a completed unit of product. (p. 96)

Cost driver   Machine-hours, direct labour-hours, or a similar base that is a causal factor in the incurrence of overhead cost, or is closely correlated with its incurrence. (p. 103)

Full cost   The sum of all direct costs and a fair share of the applicable indirect costs of a cost object. (p.92)

Job cost sheet   A form prepared for each job initiated into production that serves as a means for accumulating the materials, labour, and overhead costs chargeable to the job and as a means for computing unit costs. (p. 97)

Job-order costing system   A costing system used in those manufacturing situations where many different products, jobs, or batches of production are being produced each period. (p. 94)

Materials requisition form   A detailed source document that specifies the type and quantity of materials that are to be drawn from the storeroom and identifies the job to which the materials are to be charged. (p. 97)

Multiple predetermined overhead rates   The setting of a different predetermined overhead rate for each department, rather than having a single predetermined overhead rate for the entire company. (p. 121)

Normal cost system   Applying overhead cost to jobs by multiplying activity times the predetermined overhead rate. (p. 101)

Overapplied overhead   A credit balance in the Manufacturing Overhead account that arises when the amount of overhead cost applied to Work in Process is greater than the amount of overhead cost actually incurred during a period. (p. 117)

Overhead application   The charging of manufacturing overhead cost to the job cost sheets and to the Work in Process account. (p. 101)

Plantwide overhead rate   A single predetermined overhead rate that is used in all departments of a company, rather than each department having its own separate predetermined overhead rate. (p. 121)

Predetermined overhead rate   A rate used to charge overhead cost to jobs in production; the rate is established in advance for each period by use of estimates of manufacturing overhead cost and production activity for the period. (p. 101)

Process costing system   A costing system used in those manufacturing situations where a single, homogeneous product (such as cement or flour) is produced for relatively long periods of time. (p. 94)

Time ticket   A detailed source document used to record an employee's hour-by-hour activities during a day. (p. 99)

Underapplied overhead   A debit balance in the Manufacturing Overhead account that arises when the amount of overhead cost actually incurred is greater than the amount of overhead cost applied to Work in Process during a period. (p. 117)

APPENDIX 3A: COST FLOWS IN A JIT SYSTEM

When a company utilizes JIT inventory methods, its cost flows are greatly simplified from those we have discussed on preceding pages. Typically, when JIT is in use, only two inventory accounts are utilized. One is a new account, Raw and In-Process Inventory, and the other is the same Finished Goods inventory account with which we are already familiar. Cost flows in a JIT system, as compared to cost flows in a conventional job-order system, are illustrated in Exhibit 3–15.

EXHIBIT 3-15   Cost Flows in a JIT System

Transaction	Entries—Conventional System		Entries—JIT System	

1. Purchase of direct materials on account, $400,000 (of which $50,000 is planned for inventory).	Raw Materials 400,000
	    Accounts Payable ....
		400,000	Raw and In-Process Inventory ... 350,000
			    Accounts Payable ....
				350,000

2. Issue of direct materials to production, $350,000.	Work in Process .... 350,000 Raw Materials	350,000	—	
3. Incurrence of direct labour cost, $40,000.	Work in Process .... 40,000 Factory Wages Payable	40,000	—	

4. Incurrence of manufacturing overhead cost, $160,000.	Manufacturing Overhead 160,000
	    Accounts Payable ....
		160,000	Manufacturing Overhead 200,000
			    Factory Wages Payable ......
			    Accounts Payable ....
				40,000
				160,000

5. Application of manufacturing overhead cost to products, $170,000.	Work in Process .... 170,000 Manufacturing Overhead ...	170,000	—	

6. Completion of products, $560,000 total cost.	Finished Goods 560,000
	    Work in Process ....
		560,000	Finished Goods 560,000
			    Raw and In-Process Inventory .
			    Manufacturing Overhead .....
				350,000
				210,000*

*Under JIT, the overhead applied consists of:

Direct labour cost added to overhead	$ 40,000
Other overhead costs applied, per transaction 5	170,000
Total overhead cost applied	$210,000

Under both systems, note that overhead costs were overapplied by $10,000 for the period (conventional system: $160,000 incurred − $170,000 applied = $10,000 overapplied; JIT system: $200,000 incurred − $210,000 applied = $10,000 overapplied). This $10,000 would be closed out to Cost of Goods Sold at the end of the period.

In the following paragraphs we discuss Exhibit 3–15 transaction by transaction as we trace the cost flows under JIT. The numbers below relate to the transaction numbers in the exhibit.

As stated in Chapter 1, the JIT philosophy focuses on simplicity and on the elimination of any activity that does not add value to products. This philosophy is clearly evident in the operation of a JIT system, as described in the preceding paragraphs.

We must emphasize, however, that backflush costing is appropriate *only* in those situations where a *true* JIT system is in operation. If either raw materials or work in process inventories exist at the end of a period, then backflush costing is not appropriate and will be costly to operate. The reason is that when inventories are present, frequent and expensive physical counts of inventory will be necessary to determine the amount of materials and the amount of partially completed goods still on hand. Moreover, with no requisition slips or work orders available, it will be difficult to identify how much cost should be applied to raw materials and work in process inventories and how much should be applied to completed output. Thus, in the absence of a *true* JIT system, backflush costing may result in less timely, less accurate, and more expensive data than a conventional costing system.

Transaction	Comments
1	Under JIT, materials are purchased *only* as needed for production. Thus, only $350,000 in materials would be purchased under JIT ($400,000 – $50,000 = $350,000), as compared to the entire $400,000 under a conventional system. (The extra $50,000 under the conventional system would remain in inventory.) The materials purchased under JIT would go directly into a **Raw and In-Process Inventory** account, which is a combination of the Raw Materials and Work in Process inventory accounts found in job-order costing.
2	Purchase of materials and issue of materials into production occur simultaneously in a JIT environment. Therefore, the entry for transaction 1 under JIT encompasses the entries for both transactions 1 and 2 in a conventional system. This greatly simplifies the recordkeeping process, since under JIT there are no inventory records to maintain, no requisition forms, no issue slips, and so forth, to be concerned with. Also note the absence of a separate Work in Process account under JIT.
3	Direct labour is not treated as a separate cost item in a JIT system. Rather, *it is added to manufacturing overhead* (see the entry for transaction 4 under JIT in the exhibit). There are two reasons for this treatment of direct labour. First, it simplifies the costing process. Second, direct labour cost is too small to be dealt with separately in a highly automated, FMS setting where JIT is typically used. Note particularly from the exhibit how few entries are made in a JIT system. When companies adopt JIT, they typically report that *thousands* of journal entries are eliminated each month.
4	Transaction 4, which deals with the incurrence of manufacturing overhead costs, differs in two ways in a JIT system. First, direct labour costs are included, as discussed above. Second, costs are accumulated by *activity* rather than in a single pool for the entire company. The concept of activity-based costing was discussed in the main body of the chapter.
5	Under JIT, overhead cost is applied to products only at the time of completion.
6	Material and conversion costs in a JIT system are not added to products until the products are completed and ready for shipment. This eliminates the need to track costs and the need for job cost sheets. When products are completed under JIT, costs are moved from the Raw and In-Process Inventory account and from the Manufacturing Overhead account into Finished Goods. The transfer of costs to Finished Goods under JIT is sometimes referred to as **backflush costing,** since costs are "flushed" out of the system *after* products are completed.

Small businesses with a need for job costs but with small amounts of work in process and finished goods could use a variation of the backflush procedures, namely, the periodic inventory system. Such a system is usually described in a merchandising context, but small businesses such as construction contractors could effectively use the periodic approach. Thus, jobs would be costed but inventories would only be costed if and when they are needed. If desired, a perpetual raw materials system could be used with periodic work in process and finished goods systems. Costs and benefits should dictate the approach adopted for accounting purposes, not a rigid adherence to a particular style.

KEY TERMS FOR REVIEW (APPENDIX 3A)

Backflush costing A term used under JIT that refers to flushing costs out of the system after goods are completed and the charging of these costs directly to the Finished Goods inventory account. (p. 132)

Raw and In-Process Inventory An account used in a JIT system that is a combination of the Raw Materials and Work in Process inventory accounts found in a job-order costing system. (p. 132)

APPENDIX 3B: SCRAP AND REWORK

OBJECTIVE 11

Account for scrap and rework of unacceptable production.

Businesses are interested in quality because it tends to enhance profitability. A survey of 340 Canadian businesses reported 80 percent had a strong commitment to a quality-oriented strategy.[15] Lack of quality costs the company in the form of scrap, rework,

---

[15]Douglas Snetsinger, "Why Quality Must Pay—or Pay the Price," *The Globe and Mail,* June 23, 1992, p. 322.

delays in production, inventories, warranty cost, and poor customer relations. Estimates of these costs are 25 to 35% of total product cost.[16]

Total quality control systems are being designed to provide organizations with a systematic approach to quality management. Prevention of quality failures by design, material procurement, and conversion procedures represents one aspect. Inspection appraisals to assess production results to ensure they meet the standards desired is another. The costs of prevention and inspection appraisals represent discretionary costs that are based on management policy. Failures both as part of production and while the product is in the hands of the customer are nondiscretionary. A study of Canadian practice suggests a 40/30/30 rule for the causes of quality defects. Design problems account for 40% of the defects. Production errors and defective materials cause the other 60% of quality difficulties.[17]

Prevention costs include training and planning costs. Inspection costs include the salaries and overhead necessary to carry out the quality inspection. Failures occurring as part of production have costs associated with scrap, rework, discounts, inspection, and interruptions. External failures have costs associated with returns and allowances, warranty corrections, and future lost sales.

A total quality control philosophy was articulated to Japanese industry after World War II by the late W. Edwards Deming, a true pioneer in quality control practices.[18] Some of his suggested charting systems and ratios developed to assist management in monitoring quality will be presented in later chapters.

To illustrate the accounting for unacceptable units of production, two alternatives are examined, one where no recovery occurs and one where there is a recovery.

1. No Recovery

Assume a situation where 2,000 units are started but only 1,900 are finished with an acceptable level of quality. The material, labour, and overhead applied to the job totals $4,800. Treatment alternatives:

a. If all good units are charged with the losses, the unit cost of $1,900 units would be $4,800 ÷ 1,900 or $2.53 per unit.

b. If the rejections are charged to overhead so that they can, in turn, be charged to all jobs, the following would occur:

Manufacturing Overhead	240	
Work in Process Inventory		240

Calculations:
$4,800 ÷ 2,000 = $2.40 per unit.
   100 units × $2.40 = $240.
Net cost of 1,900 good units ($4,800 – $240 = $4,560) or $2.40 per unit.

Notice carefully the fact that treatment method *b* has a circular property: $2.40 contains overhead applied to the job. When a total of $240 for the 100 units is charged to manufacturing overhead, part of the amount is overhead applied. Thus, overhead applied becomes manufacturing overhead, which in turn determines overhead applied because it is part of the estimate used in the calculation of the predetermined overhead rate for next

---

[16]Robert A. Howell, "World-Class Manufacturing Controls: Management Accounting for the Factory of the Future" in *Cost Accounting, Robotics, and the New Manufacturing Environment,* ed. Robert Cappettini and Donald K. Clancy (Sarasota, Fla.: American Accounting Association, 1987), p. 2.3.

[17]"Implementing Just-in-Time Production Systems," *Management Accounting Guideline* 19 (Hamilton, Ont.: Society of Management Accountants of Canada, 1993), p. 25.

[18]An obituary for the late Dr. W. Edwards Deming was reported by Associated Press, "Quality-Control Expert Helped Japan," *The Globe and Mail,* December 21, 1993, p. A16.

year (and probably this year). If the amounts are small, no harm is done. If the amounts are significant, then one should remove only the direct materials and direct labour to avoid the duplication of overhead.

2. A Recovery

Situations:

a. No rework is undertaken; items are sold for scrap. The scrap recovery could be credited to the job or to manufacturing overhead depending on the method of original treatment of the rejects.

b. Rework or repair is undertaken. The materials and labour involved in the rework could be charged to the job. As an alternative, these costs could be charged to manufacturing overhead so they can be spread over all jobs.

A careful reading of the previous procedures points out that a number of the suggested costs of poor quality are not recognized as part of the transactions. Delays in production and poor customer relations are not transactions thus do not trigger entries. Extra inventories would be required to provide the materials for rework, and extra production is necessary to allow for the scrap so that a complete job is accomplished. The cost of delays is an example of an opportunity cost and can be recognized only by special analysis of the situations.

Many industrial processes produce by-products that are environmentally hazardous. Some of these by-products can be recycled, some are sent to a disposal incinerator, and others are sent to a landfill. New systems for monitoring the disposal costs of these hazardous by-products are needed. Costs of equipment and ongoing accounting for hazardous waste together with the losses from environmental cleanups net of any insurance recoveries represent accounting areas concerned with environmental protection. In turn, these ongoing costs have to be allocated to the products of the production process. Accounting for and costing of waste represents a means of providing management with the economic information associated with scrap and waste from the production process.

QUESTIONS

3–1 State the purposes for which it is necessary or desirable to compute unit costs.

3–2 Distinguish between job-order costing and process costing.

3–3 What is the essential purpose of any costing system?

3–4 What is the purpose of the job cost sheet in a job-order costing system?

3–5 What is a predetermined overhead rate, and how is it computed?

3–6 Explain how a sales order, a production order, a materials requisition form, and a labour time ticket are involved in the production and costing of products.

3–7 Explain why some production costs must be assigned to products through an allocation process. Name several such costs. Would such costs be classified as *direct* or as *indirect* costs?

3–8 Why do firms use predetermined overhead rates rather than actual manufacturing overhead costs in applying overhead to units of product?

3–9 What factors should be considered in selecting a base to be used in computing the predetermined overhead rate?

3–10 What is meant by the statement that overhead is "absorbed" into units of product? If a company fully absorbs its overhead costs, does this guarantee that a profit will be earned for the period?

3–11 What account is credited when overhead cost is applied to Work in Process? Would you expect the amount applied for a period to equal the actual overhead costs of the period? Why or why not?

3–12 What is underapplied overhead? Overapplied overhead? What disposition is made of these amounts at period end?

3–13 Enumerate several reasons why overhead might be underapplied in a given year.

3–14 What adjustment is made for underapplied overhead on the schedule of cost of goods manufactured, and why is this adjustment necessary? What adjustment is made on the schedule of cost of goods sold?

3–15 What adjustment is made for overapplied overhead on the schedule of cost of goods manufactured, and why is this adjustment necessary? What adjustment is made on the schedule of cost of goods sold?

3–16 Sigma Company applies overhead cost to jobs on a basis of direct labour cost. Job A, which was started and completed during the current period, shows charges of $5,000 for direct materials, $8,000 for direct labour, and $6,000 for overhead on its job cost sheet. Job B, which is still in process at year-end, shows charges of $2,500 for direct materials and $4,000 for direct labour. Should any overhead cost be added to job B at year-end? Explain.

3–17 What happens to overhead rates based on direct labour when automated equipment replaces direct labour?

3–18 A company assigns overhead cost to completed jobs on a basis of 125% of direct labour cost. The job cost sheet for job 313 shows that $10,000 in direct materials has been used on the job and that $12,000 in direct labour cost has been incurred. If 1,000 units were produced in job 313, what is the cost per unit?

3–19 What is a plantwide overhead rate? Why are multiple overhead rates, rather than a plantwide rate, used in some companies?

3–20 Predetermined overhead rates smooth product costs. Do you agree? Why?

3–21 Explain clearly the rationale for why under- and overapplied overhead for an interim period should be carried to the balance sheet. What conceptual factor is assumed in the argument?

3–22 Why does the calculation of the percentages for prorating the under- or overapplied overhead reduce the costs of goods sold by the opening inventories? What would happen if such a deduction were not made?

3–23 (Appendix 3A) How is the purchase of materials and the issue of materials to production handled in a JIT system? In what way does this approach to the handling of materials save money? What happens to the Work in Process account in a JIT system?

3–24 (Appendix 3A) In what way is direct labour cost handled differently in a JIT system than in a conventional system? What are the reasons for this difference in treatment?

3–25 (Appendix 3A) At what point are materials and overhead costs added to products in a JIT system? Why is this approach to the adding of costs to products sometimes called *backflush costing?*

3–26 (Appendix 3B) Rework and scrap can cause a circular treatment of overhead. Explain how this could happen.

3–27 (Appendix 3B) Why is the cost of customer dissatisfaction with poor quality products not recognized in the accounts? How can the cost be determined?

EXERCISES

E3–1 Which would be more appropriate in each of the following situations—job-order costing or process costing?
a. A custom yacht builder.
b. A golf course designer.
c. A potato chip manufacturer.
d. A business consultant.
e. A plywood manufacturer.
f. A soft-drink bottler.
g. A film studio.
h. A firm that supervises bridge construction projects.
i. A manufacturer of fine custom jewelry.
j. A made-to-order garment factory.
k. A factory making one personal computer model.
l. A fertilizer factory.

E3–2 Javadi Company manufactures a product that is subject to wide seasonal variations in demand. Unit costs are computed on a quarterly basis by dividing each quarter's manufacturing costs (materials, labour, and overhead) by the quarter's production in units. The company's estimated costs, by quarter, for the coming year are given below:

	Quarter			
	First	**Second**	**Third**	**Fourth**
Direct materials	$240,000	$120,000	$ 60,000	$180,000
Direct labour	96,000	48,000	24,000	72,000
Manufacturing overhead	228,000	204,000	192,000	216,000
Total manufacturing costs	$564,000	$372,000	$276,000	$468,000
Number of units to be produced	80,000	40,000	20,000	60,000
Estimated cost per unit	$7.05	$9.30	$13.80	$7.80

Management finds the variation in unit costs to be confusing and difficult to work with. It has been suggested that the problem lies with manufacturing overhead, since it is the largest element of cost. Accordingly, you have been asked to find a more suitable way of assigning manufacturing overhead cost to units of product. After some analysis, you have determined that the company's overhead costs are mostly fixed and therefore show little sensitivity to changes in the level of production.

Required

1. The company uses a job-order costing system. How would you recommend that manufacturing overhead cost be assigned to production? Be specific, and show computations.
2. Recompute the company's unit costs in accordance with your recommendations in (1) above.

E3–3 Foley Company uses a job-order costing system. The following data relate to the month of October, the first month of the company's fiscal year:
a. Raw materials purchased on account, $210,000.
b. Raw materials issued to production, $190,000 (80% direct and 20% indirect).
c. Direct labour cost incurred, $49,000; and indirect labour cost incurred, $21,000.
d. Depreciation recorded on factory equipment, $105,000.
e. Other manufacturing overhead costs incurred during October, $130,000 (credit Accounts Payable).
f. The company applies manufacturing overhead cost to production on a basis of $4 per machine-hour. There were 75,000 machine-hours recorded for October.
g. Production orders costing $510,000 were completed during October and transferred to Finished Goods.

h.   Production orders that had cost $450,000 to complete were shipped to customers during the month. These goods were invoiced at 50% above cost to manufacture. The goods were sold on account.

Required

1.   Prepare journal entries to record the information given above.
2.   Prepare T-accounts for Manufacturing Overhead and Work in Process. Post the relevant information above to each account. Compute the ending balance in each account, assuming that Work in Process has a beginning balance of $35,000.

E3–4 Estimated cost and operating data for three companies for the current year are given below:

	Company		
	A	B	C
Direct labour-hours	60,000	30,000	40,000
Machine-hours	25,000	90,000	18,000
Raw materials cost	$300,000	$160,000	$240,000
Manufacturing overhead cost	432,000	270,000	384,000

Predetermined overhead rates are computed using the following bases in the three companies:

Company	Overhead Rate Based on—
A	Direct labour-hours
B	Machine-hours
C	Raw materials cost

Required

1.   Compute the predetermined overhead rate to be used in each company.
2.   Assume that three jobs are worked on during the year in Company A. Direct labour-hours recorded by job are: job 308, 7,000 hours; job 309, 30,000 hours; and job 310, 21,000 hours. How much overhead cost will the company apply to Work in Process for the year? If actual costs are $420,000 for the year, will overhead be underapplied or overapplied? By how much?

E3–5 Medusa Products is a manufacturing company that operates a job-order costing system. Overhead costs are charged to production on the basis of machine-hours. At the beginning of the year, management estimated that the company would incur $170,000 in manufacturing overhead costs for the year and work 85,000 machine-hours.

Required

1.   Compute the company's predetermined overhead rate.
2.   Assume that during the year the company actually works only 80,000 machine-hours and incurs the following costs in the Manufacturing Overhead and Work in Process accounts:

Manufacturing Overhead			Work in Process	
(Utilities)	14,000	?	(Direct materials)	530,000
(Insurance)	9,000		(Direct labour)	85,000
(Maintenance)	33,000		(Overhead)	?
(Indirect materials)	7,000			
(Indirect labour)	65,000			
(Depreciation)	40,000			

Copy the data in the T-accounts above onto your answer sheet. Compute the amount of overhead cost that should be applied to Work in Process for the year, and make the entry in your T-accounts.
3.   Compute the amount of under- or overapplied overhead for the year, and show the balance in your Manufacturing Overhead T-account. Prepare the journal entry that most companies would make to close out the balance in this account.

E3–6 Diewold Company has two departments, milling and assembly. The company uses a job-order cost system and computes a predetermined overhead rate in each department. The milling department bases its rate on machine-hours, and the assembly department bases its rate on direct labour cost. At the beginning of the year, the company made the following estimates:

	Department	
	Milling	**Assembly**
Direct labour-hours	8,000	75,000
Machine-hours	60,000	3,000
Manufacturing overhead cost	$510,000	$800,000
Direct labour cost	72,000	640,000

Required

1. Compute the predetermined overhead rate to be used in each department.
2. Assume that the overhead rates you computed in (1) above are in effect. The job cost sheet for job 407, which was started and completed during the year, showed the following:

	Department	
	Milling	**Assembly**
Direct labour-hours	5	20
Machine-hours	90	4
Materials requisitioned	$800	$370
Direct labour cost	45	160

   Compute the total overhead cost of job 407.
3. Would you expect substantially different amounts of overhead cost to be charged to some jobs if the company used a plantwide overhead rate based on direct labour cost instead of using departmental rates? Explain. No computations are necessary.

E3–7 The following cost data relate to the manufacturing activities of Black Company:

Manufacturing overhead costs incurred during the year:
Property taxes	$ 3,000
Utilities, factory	5,000
Indirect labour	10,000
Depreciation, factory	24,000
Insurance, factory	6,000
Total actual costs	$48,000

Other costs incurred during the year:
Purchases of raw materials	$32,000
Direct labour cost	40,000

Inventories:
Raw materials, January 1	8,000
Raw materials, December 31	7,000
Work in process, January 1	6,000
Work in process, December 31	7,500

The company uses a predetermined overhead rate to charge overhead cost to production. The rate for the year was $5 per machine-hour; a total of 10,000 machine-hours was recorded for the year.

Required

1. Compute the amount of under- or overapplied overhead cost for the year.
2. Prepare a schedule of cost of goods manufactured for the year.

E3–8 The following information is taken from the end-of-year account balances of FasGrow Company:

	Manufacturing Overhead				Work in Process		
(a)	380,000	410,000	(b)	Bal.	105,000	760,000	(c)
					210,000		
		30,000	Bal.		115,000		
				(b)	410,000		
				Bal.	80,000		

	Finished Goods				Cost of Goods Sold		
Bal.	160,000	820,000	(d)	(d)	820,000		
(c)	760,000						
Bal.	100,000						

Required

1. Identify the reasons for entries (a) through (d).
2. Assume that the company closes any balance in the Manufacturing Overhead account directly to Cost of Goods Sold. Prepare the necessary journal entry.
3. Assume instead that the company allocates any balance in the Manufacturing Overhead account to the other accounts. Prepare the necessary journal entry, with supporting computations.

E3–9 Custom Metal Works produces castings and other metal parts to customer specifications. The company uses a job-order costing system. For the current year, the company estimated that it would work 576,000 machine-hours and incur $4,320,000 in manufacturing overhead cost.

The company had no work in process at the beginning of the year. The entire month of January was spent on job 382, which was an order for 8,000 machine parts. Cost data for January follow:

a. Raw materials purchased on account, $315,000.
b. Raw materials requisitioned for production, $270,000 (80% direct and 20% indirect).
c. Labour cost incurred in the factory, $190,000, of which $80,000 was direct labour and $110,000 was indirect labour.
d. Depreciation recorded on factory equipment, $63,000.
e. Other manufacturing overhead costs incurred, $85,000 (credit Accounts Payable).
f. Manufacturing overhead cost was applied to production on a basis of 40,000 machine-hours worked during January.
g. The completed job was moved into the finished goods warehouse on January 31 to await delivery to the customer. (In computing the dollar amount for this entry, remember that the cost of a completed job consists of direct materials, direct labour, and *applied* overhead.)

Required

1. Prepare journal entries to record items (a) through (f) above. Ignore item (g) for the moment.
2. Prepare T-accounts for Manufacturing Overhead and Work in Process. Post the relevant items from your journal entries to these T-accounts.
3. Prepare a journal entry for item (g) above, and then compute the unit cost that will appear on the job cost sheet for job 382.

E3–10 Munster, Inc., uses a job-order costing system. The following table provides selected data on the three jobs worked on during last month:

	Job Number		
	101	102	103
Units of product in the job	400	200	150
Machine-hours worked	200	80	120
Direct materials cost	$4,800	$1,800	$3,600
Direct labour cost	2,400	1,000	1,500

Actual overhead costs totalling $16,000 were incurred during the month. Manufacturing overhead cost is applied to production on the basis of machine-hours at a predetermined rate of $45 per machine-hour. Jobs 101 and 102 were completed during the month; job 103 was not completed. There were no other jobs in process during the month.

Required

1. Compute the amount of manufacturing overhead costs that would have been charged to each job during the month.
2. Compute the unit costs for jobs 101 and 102.
3. Prepare a journal entry showing the transfer of completed jobs into the finished goods warehouse.
4. What is the balance in the Work in Process account at the end of the month?
5. What is the balance in the Manufacturing Overhead account at the end of the month? What is this balance called?

E3–11 Toronto Company began operations on January 2. The following activity was recorded in the company's Work in Process account for the first month of operations:

Work in Process

Direct materials	200,000	To finished goods	570,000
Direct labour	90,000		
Manufacturing overhead	320,000		

Toronto Company uses a job-order costing system and applies manufacturing overhead cost to Work in Process on the basis of direct materials cost. At the end of January, only one job was still in process. This job (job 15) had been charged with $13,500 in direct materials.

Required

1. Compute the predetermined overhead rate that was in use during January.
2. Complete the following job cost sheet for the partially completed job 15:

Job Cost Sheet—Job 15
As of January 31

Direct materials	$	?
Direct labour		?
Manufacturing overhead		?
Total cost to January 31 ...	$	?

PROBLEMS

P3–12 Straightforward Journal Entries; Partial T-Accounts; Income Statement   Ravsten Company is a manufacturing firm that uses a job-order cost system. On January 1, the beginning of the current year, the company's inventory balances were as follows:

Raw materials	$16,000
Work in process	10,000
Finished goods	30,000

The company applies overhead cost to jobs on the basis of machine-hours. For the current year, the company estimated that it would work 36,000 machine-hours and incur $153,000 in manufacturing overhead cost. The following transactions were recorded for the year:

a. Raw materials purchased on account, $200,000.

b. Raw materials requisitioned for use in production, $190,000 (80% direct and 20% indirect).

c. The following costs were incurred for employee services:

Direct labour	$160,000
Indirect labour	27,000
Sales commissions	36,000
Administrative salaries	80,000

d. Heat, power, and water costs incurred in the factory, $42,000.

e. Prepaid insurance expired during the year, $10,000 (90% relates to factory operations, and 10% relates to selling and administrative activities).

f. Advertising costs incurred, $50,000.

g. Depreciation recorded for the year, $60,000 (85% relates to factory operations, and 15% relates to selling and administrative activities).

h. Manufacturing overhead cost was applied to production. The company recorded 40,000 machine-hours for the year.

i. Goods costing $480,000 to manufacture were completed during the year.

j. Goods were sold on account to customers during the year at a total selling price of $700,000. These goods cost $475,000 to manufacture.

Required

1. Prepare journal entries to record the transactions given above.

2. Prepare T-accounts for inventories, Manufacturing Overhead, and Cost of Goods Sold. Post relevant data from your journal entries to these T-accounts (don't forget to enter the opening balances in your inventory accounts). Compute an ending balance in each account.

3. Is Manufacturing Overhead underapplied or overapplied for the year? Prepare a journal entry to close any balance in the Manufacturing Overhead account to Cost of Goods Sold.

4. Prepare an income statement for the year. (Do not prepare a schedule of cost of goods manufactured; all of the information needed for the income statement is available in the journal entries and T-accounts you have prepared.)

P3–13 Entries Directly into T-Accounts; Income Statement   Durham Company's trial balance as of January 1, the beginning of the current year, is given below:

Cash	$ 8,000	
Accounts Receivable	13,000	
Raw Materials	7,000	
Work in Process	18,000	
Finished Goods	20,000	
Prepaid Insurance	4,000	
Plant and Equipment	230,000	
Accumulated Depreciation		$ 42,000
Accounts Payable		30,000
Capital Stock		150,000
Retained Earnings		78,000
Total	$300,000	$300,000

Durham Company manufactures items to customers' specifications and employs a job-order cost system. During the year, the following transactions took place:

a. Raw materials purchased on account, $45,000.

b. Raw materials requisitioned for use in production, $40,000 (80% direct and 20% indirect).

c. Factory utility costs incurred, $14,600.

d. Depreciation recorded on plant and equipment, $28,000. Three-fourths of the depreciation relates to factory equipment, and the remainder relates to selling and administrative equipment.

e. Costs for salaries and wages were incurred as follows:

Direct labour	$40,000
Indirect labour	18,000
Sales commissions	10,400
Administrative salaries	25,000

f. Prepaid insurance expired during the year, $3,000 (80% relates to factory operations, and 20% relates to selling and administrative activities).

g. Miscellaneous selling and administrative expenses incurred, $18,000.

h. Manufacturing overhead was applied to production. The company applies overhead on the basis of 150% of direct labour cost.

i. Goods costing $130,000 to manufacture were transferred to the finished goods warehouse.

j. Goods that had cost $120,000 to manufacture were sold on account for $200,000.

k. Collections from customers during the year totalled $197,000.

l. Payments to suppliers on account during the year, $100,000; and payments to employees for salaries and wages, $90,000.

Required

1. Prepare a T-account for each account in the company's trial balance, and enter the opening balances shown above.

2. Record the transactions above directly into the T-accounts. Prepare new T-accounts as needed. Key your entries to the letters (a) through (l) above. Find the ending balance in each account.

3. Is manufacturing overhead under- or overapplied for the year? Make an entry in the T-accounts to close any balance in the Manufacturing Overhead account to Cost of Goods Sold.

4. Prepare an income statement for the year. (Do not prepare a schedule of cost of goods manufactured; all of the information needed for the income statement is available in the journal entries and T-accounts you have prepared.)

P3–14 Movie Prop Producer; Entries Directly into T-Accounts; Income Statement   Fantastic Props, Inc., designs and fabricates movie props such as mock-ups of starfighters and cybernetic robots. The company's balance sheet as of January 1, the beginning of the current year, appears below:

FANTASTIC PROPS, INC.
Balance Sheet
January 1

Assets

Current assets:		
Cash		$ 15,000
Accounts receivable		40,000
Inventories:		
Raw materials	$ 25,000	
Work in process	30,000	
Finished goods (Props awaiting shipment)	45,000	100,000
Prepaid insurance		5,000
Total current assets		160,000
Buildings and equipment	500,000	
Less accumulated depreciation	210,000	290,000
Total assets		$450,000

Liabilities and Shareholders' Equity

Accounts payable		$ 75,000
Capital stock	$250,000	
Retained earnings	125,000	375,000
Total liabilities and shareholders' equity		$450,000

Since each prop is a unique design and may require anything from a few hours to a month or more to complete, Fantastic Props uses a job-order costing system. Overhead in the fabrication shop is charged to props on the basis of direct labour cost. The company estimated that it would incur $80,000 in manufacturing overhead and $100,000 in direct labour cost during the year. The following transactions were recorded during the year:

a. Raw materials, such as wood, paints, and metal sheeting, were purchased on account, $80,000.
b. Raw materials were issued to production, $90,000; $5,000 of this amount was for indirect materials.
c. Payroll costs incurred and paid: direct labour, $120,000; indirect labour, $30,000; and selling and administrative salaries, $75,000.
d. Fabrication shop utilities costs incurred, $12,000.
e. Depreciation recorded for the year, $30,000 ($5,000 on selling and administrative assets; $25,000 on fabrication shop assets).
f. Prepaid insurance expired, $4,800 ($4,000 related to fabrication shop operations, and $800 related to selling and administrative activities).
g. Shipping expenses incurred, $40,000.
h. Other manufacturing overhead costs incurred, $17,000 (credit Accounts Payable).
i. Manufacturing overhead was applied to production. Overhead is applied on a basis of direct labour cost.
j. Movie props costing $310,000 to fabricate were completed during the year.
k. Props that had cost $300,000 to fabricate were delivered to customers who were then billed for $450,000.
l. Collections on account from customers, $445,000.
m. Payments on account to suppliers, $150,000.

Required

1. Prepare a T-account for each account on the company's balance sheet, and enter the opening balances above.
2. Make entries directly into the T-accounts for the transactions given above. Create new T-accounts as needed. Determine an ending balance for each T-account.
3. Was manufacturing overhead underapplied or overapplied for the year? Assume that the company allocates any overhead balance between the Work in Process, Finished Goods, and Cost of Goods Sold accounts. Prepare a journal entry to show the allocation. (Round allocation percentages to one decimal place.)
4. Prepare an income statement for the year. (Do not prepare a schedule of cost of goods manufactured; all of the information needed for the income statement is available in the T-accounts.)

P3–15 Straightforward Journal Entries; Partial T-Accounts; Income Statement   Sovereign Millwork, Ltd., produces reproductions of antique residential moldings at a plant located in Manchester, England. Since there are hundreds of products, some of which are made only to order, the company uses a job-order costing system. On July 1, the start of the company's fiscal year, inventory account balances were as follows:

Raw Materials	£10,000
Work in Process	4,000
Finished Goods	8,000
Total	£22,000

The company applies overhead cost to jobs on the basis of machine-hours using the same principles followed by companies in the United States and elsewhere. For the fiscal year starting July 1, it was estimated that the plant would operate 45,000 machine-hours and incur £99,000 in manufacturing overhead cost. During the year, the following transactions were completed:

a. Raw materials purchased on account, £160,000.
b. Raw materials requisitioned for use in production, £140,000 (materials costing £120,000 were chargeable directly to jobs; the remaining materials were indirect).
c. Costs for employee services were incurred as follows:

Direct labour	£90,000
Indirect labour	60,000
Sales commissions	20,000
Administrative salaries	50,000

d. Prepaid insurance expired during the year, £18,000 (£13,000 of this amount related to factory operations, and the remainder related to selling and administrative activities).

e. Utility costs incurred in the factory, £10,000.

f. Advertising costs incurred, £15,000.

g. Depreciation recorded on equipment, £25,000. (£20,000 of this amount was on equipment used in factory operations; the remaining £5,000 was on equipment used in selling and administrative activities.)

h. Manufacturing overhead cost was applied to production, £ ___?___. (The company recorded 50,000 machine-hours of operating time during the year.)

i. Goods costing £310,000 to manufacture were transferred into the finished goods warehouse.

j. Sales (all on account) to customers during the year totalled £498,000. These goods had cost £308,000 to manufacture.

Required

1. Prepare journal entries to record the transactions for the year.

2. Prepare T-accounts for inventories, Manufacturing Overhead, and Cost of Goods Sold. Post relevant data from your journal entries to these T-accounts (don't forget to enter the opening balances in your inventory accounts). Compute an ending balance in each account.

3. Is Manufacturing Overhead underapplied or overapplied for the year? Prepare a journal entry to close any balance in the Manufacturing Overhead account to Cost of Goods Sold.

4. Prepare an income statement for the year. (Do not prepare a schedule of cost of goods manufactured; all of the information needed for the income statement is available in the journal entries and T-accounts you have prepared.)

P3–16 Schedule of Cost of Goods Manufactured; Pricing; Work in Process Analysis The Pacific Manufacturing Company operates a job-order cost system and applies overhead cost to jobs on the basis of direct labour cost. In computing an overhead rate for the year, the company's estimates were: manufacturing overhead cost, $126,000; and direct labour cost, $84,000. The company's inventory accounts at the beginning and end of the year were as follows:

	January 1, (beginning of year)	December 31, (end of year)
Raw Materials	$21,000	$16,000
Work in Process	44,000	40,000
Finished Goods	68,000	60,000

The following actual costs were incurred during the year:

Purchase of raw materials (all direct)	$133,000
Direct labour cost	80,000
Manufacturing overhead costs:	
Insurance, factory	7,000
Depreciation of equipment	18,000
Indirect labour	42,000
Property taxes	9,000
Maintenance	11,000
Rent, building	36,000

Required

1. a. Compute the predetermined overhead rate for the year.
   b. Compute the amount of under- or overapplied overhead for the year.

2. Prepare a schedule of cost of goods manufactured for the year.

3. Compute the cost of goods sold for the year. (Do not include any under- or overapplied overhead in your cost of goods sold figure.) What options are available for disposing of under- or overapplied overhead?

4. Job 137 was started and completed during the year. What price would have been charged to the customer if the job required $3,200 in materials and $4,200 in direct labour cost, and the company priced its jobs at 40% above cost to manufacture?

5. Direct labour made up $8,000 of the $40,000 ending Work in Process inventory balance. Supply the information missing below:

Direct materials	$?
Direct labour	8,000
Manufacturing overhead	?
Work in process inventory	$40,000

P3–17 Multiple Departments; Overhead Rates; Costing Units of Product

Clark Technology, Inc., employs a job-order costing system. The company uses predetermined overhead rates to apply manufacturing overhead cost to individual jobs. The predetermined overhead rate in department A is based on machine-hours, and the rate in department B is based on direct materials cost. At the beginning of the year, the company's management made the following estimates for the year:

	Department	
	A	B
Machine-hours	80,000	21,000
Direct labour-hours	35,000	65,000
Direct materials cost	$190,000	$400,000
Direct labour cost	280,000	530,000
Manufacturing overhead cost	416,000	720,000

Job 127 was initiated into production on April 1 and completed on May 12. The company's cost records show the following information on the job:

	Department	
	A	B
Machine-hours	350	70
Direct labour-hours	80	130
Direct materials cost	$940	$1,200
Direct labour cost	710	980

Required

1. Compute the predetermined overhead rate that should be used during the year in department A. Compute the rate that should be used in department B.
2. Compute the total overhead cost applied to job 127.
3. What would be the total cost of job 127? If the job contained 25 units, what would be the cost per unit?
4. At the end of the year, the records of Clark Technology, Inc., revealed the following *actual* cost and operating data for all jobs worked on during the year:

	Department	
	A	B
Machine-hours	73,000	24,000
Direct labour-hours	30,000	68,000
Direct materials cost	$165,000	$420,000
Manufacturing overhead cost . . .	390,000	740,000

What was the amount of underapplied or overapplied overhead in each department at the end of the year?

P3–18 Job Cost Sheets; Overhead Rates; Journal Entries   Kenworth Company employs a job-order costing system. Only three jobs—job 105, job 106, and job 107—were worked on during November and December. Job 105 was completed on December 10; the other two jobs were still in production on December 31, the end of the company's operating year. Job cost sheets on the three jobs are given below:

Job Cost Sheet

	Job 105	Job 106	Job 107
November costs incurred:			
Direct materials	$16,500	$ 9,300	$ —
Direct labour	13,000	7,000	—
Manufacturing overhead	20,800	11,200	—
December costs incurred:			
Direct materials	—	8,200	21,300
Direct labour	4,000	6,000	10,000
Manufacturing overhead	?	?	?

The following additional information is available:
a. Manufacturing overhead is assigned to jobs on the basis of direct labour cost.
b. Balances in the inventory accounts at November 30 were as follows:

Raw Materials	$40,000
Work in Process....	?
Finished Goods	85,000

Required

1. Prepare T-accounts for Raw Materials, Work in Process, Finished Goods, and Manufacturing Overhead. Enter the November 30 inventory balances given above; in the case of Work in Process, compute the November 30 balance and enter it into the Work in Process T-account.
2. Prepare journal entries for *December* as follows:
    a. Prepare an entry to record the issue of materials into production, and post the entry to appropriate T- accounts. (In the case of direct materials, it is not necessary to make a separate entry for each job.) Indirect materials used during December totalled $4,000.
    b. Prepare an entry to record the incurrence of labour cost, and post the entry to appropriate T-accounts. (In the case of direct labour cost, it is not necessary to make a separate entry for each job.) Indirect labour cost totalled $8,000 for December.
    c. Prepare an entry to record the incurrence of $19,000 in various actual manufacturing overhead costs for December (credit Accounts Payable).
3. What apparent predetermined overhead rate does the company use to assign overhead cost to jobs? Using this rate, prepare a journal entry to record the application of overhead cost to jobs for December (it is not necessary to make a separate entry for each job). Post this entry to appropriate T-accounts.
4. As stated earlier, job 105 was completed during December. Prepare a journal entry to show the transfer of this job off of the production line and into the finished goods warehouse. Post the entry to appropriate T-accounts.
5. Determine the balance at December 31 in the Work in Process inventory account. How much of this balance consists of costs of job 106? Job 107?

P3–19 Fireworks Fabrication; Job-Order Cost Journal Entries; T-Accounts; Income Statement   Celestial Displays, Inc., puts together large-scale fireworks displays —primarily for First of July celebrations sponsored by corporations and municipalities. The company assembles and orchestrates complex displays using pyrotechnic components purchased from suppliers throughout the world. The company has built a reputation for safety and for the awesome power and brilliance of its computer-controlled shows. Celestial Displays builds its own launch platforms and its own electronic controls. Because of the company's reputation, customers order shows up to a year in advance. Since each show is different in terms of duration and components used, Celestial Displays uses a job-order costing system.

Celestial Displays' trial balance as of January 1, the beginning of the current year, is given below:

Cash	$ 9,000	
Accounts Receivable	30,000	
Raw Materials	16,000	
Work in Process	21,000	
Finished Goods	38,000	
Prepaid Insurance	7,000	
Buildings and Equipment	300,000	
Accumulated Depreciation		$128,000
Accounts Payable		60,000
Salaries and Wages Payable		3,000
Capital Stock		200,000
Retained Earnings		30,000
Total	$421,000	$421,000

The company charges manufacturing overhead costs to jobs on the basis of direct labour-hours. (Each customer order for a complete fireworks display is a separate job.) Management estimated that the company would incur $135,000 in manufacturing overhead costs in the fabrication and electronics shops and would work 18,000 direct labour-hours during the year. The following transactions occurred during the year:

a. Raw materials, consisting mostly of skyrockets, mortar bombs, flares, wiring, and electronic components, were purchased on account, $820,000.

b. Raw materials were issued to production, $830,000 ($13,000 of this amount was for indirect materials, and the remainder was for direct materials).

c. Fabrication and electronics shop payrolls were accrued, $200,000 (70% direct labour and 30% indirect labour). A total of 20,800 direct labour-hours were worked during the year.

d. Sales and administrative salaries were accrued, $150,000.

e. The company prepaid additional insurance premiums of $38,000 during the year. Prepaid insurance expiring during the year was $40,000 (only $600 relates to selling and administrative; the other $39,400 relates to the fabrication and electronics shops because of the safety hazards involved in handling fireworks).

f. Marketing cost incurred, $100,000.

g. Depreciation charges for the year, $40,000 (70% relates to fabrication and electronics shop assets, and 30% relates to selling and administrative assets).

h. Property taxes accrued on the shop buildings, $12,600 (credit Accounts Payable).

i. Manufacturing overhead cost was applied to jobs.

j. Jobs completed during the year had a total production cost of $1,106,000 according to their job cost sheets.

k. Revenue (all on account), $1,420,000. Cost of Goods Sold (before any adjustment for underapplied or overapplied overhead), $1,120,000.

l. Cash collections on account from customers, $1,415,000.

m. Cash payments on accounts payable, $970,000. Cash payments to employees for salaries and wages, $348,000.

Required

1. Prepare journal entries for the year's transactions.

2. Prepare a T-account for each account in the company's trial balance, and enter the opening balances given above. Post your journal entries to the T-accounts. Prepare new T-accounts as needed. Compute the ending balance in each account.

3. Is manufacturing overhead under- or overapplied for the year? Prepare the necessary journal entry to close the balance in the Manufacturing Overhead account to Cost of Goods Sold.

4. Prepare an income statement for the year. (Do not prepare a statement of cost of goods manufactured; all of the information needed for the income statement is available in the T-accounts.)

P3–20 Law Firm: Multiple Departments; Overhead Rates   Winkle, Kotter, and Zale is a small law firm that contains 10 partners and 10 support persons. The firm employs a job-order costing system to accumulate costs chargeable to each client, and it is organized into two departments—the research and documents department and the litigation department. The firm uses predetermined overhead rates to charge the costs of these departments to its clients. At the beginning of the current year, the firm's management made the following estimates for the year:

	Department	
	Research and Documents	Litigation
Research-hours	20,000	—
Direct lawyer-hours	9,000	16,000
Materials and supplies	$ 18,000	$ 5,000
Direct lawyer cost	430,000	800,000
Departmental overhead cost	700,000	320,000

The predetermined overhead rate in the research and documents department is based on research-hours, and the rate in the litigation department is based on direct lawyer cost.

The costs chargeable to each client are made up of three elements: materials and supplies used, direct lawyer costs incurred, and an applied amount of overhead from each department in which work is performed on the case.

Case 618-3 was initiated on February 10 and completed on June 30. During this period, the following costs and time were recorded on the case:

	Department	
	Research and Documents	Litigation
Research-hours	18	—
Direct lawyer-hours	9	42
Materials and supplies	$ 50	$ 30
Direct lawyer cost	410	2,100

Required

1. Compute the predetermined overhead rate that should be used during the year in the research and documents department. Compute the rate that should be used in the litigation department.
2. Using the rates you computed in (1) above, compute the total overhead cost applied to case 618-3.
3. What would be the total cost charged to case 618-3? Show computations by department and in total for the case.
4. At the end of the year, the firm's records revealed the following *actual* cost and operating data for all cases handled during the year:

	Department	
	Research and Documents	Litigation
Research-hours	23,000	—
Direct lawyer-hours	8,000	15,000
Materials and supplies	$ 19,000	$ 6,000
Direct lawyer cost	400,000	725,000
Departmental overhead cost	770,000	300,000

Determine the amount of underapplied or overapplied overhead cost in each department for the year.

P3–21 T-Account Analysis of Cost Flows Selected ledger accounts for Rolm Company are given below for the current year:

Raw Materials

Bal. 1/1	30,000	Credits	?
Debits	420,000		
Bal. 12/31	60,000		

Manufacturing Overhead

Debits	385,000	Credits	?

Work in Process

Bal. 1/1	70,000	Credits	810,000
Direct materials	320,000		
Direct labour	110,000		
Overhead	400,000		
Bal. 12/31	?		

Factory Wages Payable

Debits	179,000	Bal. 1/1	10,000
		Credits	175,000
		Bal. 12/31	6,000

Finished Goods

Bal. 1/1	40,000	Credits	?
Debits	?		
Bal. 12/31	130,000		

Cost of Goods Sold

Debits	?	

Required

1. What was the cost of raw materials put into production during the year?
2. How much of the materials in (1) above consisted of indirect materials?
3. How much of the factory labour cost for the year consisted of indirect labour?
4. What was the cost of goods manufactured for the year?
5. What was the cost of goods sold for the year (before considering under- or overapplied overhead)?
6. If overhead is applied to production on the basis of direct materials cost, what rate was in effect during the year?
7. Was manufacturing overhead under- or overapplied? By how much?
8. Compute the ending balance in the Work in Process inventory account. Assume that this balance consists entirely of goods started during the year. If $32,000 of this balance is direct materials cost, how much of it is direct labour cost? Manufacturing overhead cost?

P3–22 Disposition of Under-or Overapplied Overhead Savallas Company is highly automated and uses computers to control manufacturing operations. The company has a job-order costing system in use and applies manufacturing overhead cost to products on the basis of computer-hours of activity. The following estimates were used in preparing a predetermined overhead rate for the current year:

> Computer-hours   85,000
> Manufacturing overhead cost $1,530,000

During the year, a severe economic recession caused a curtailment of production and a buildup of inventory in Savallas Company's warehouses. The company's cost records revealed the following actual cost and operating data for the year:

> Computer-hours   60,000
> Manufacturing overhead cost $1,350,000
>
> Inventories at year-end:
>   Raw materials   400,000
>   Work in process   160,000
>   Finished goods   1,040,000
>   Cost of goods sold   2,800,000

Required

1. Compute the company's predetermined overhead rate for the year.
2. Compute the under- or overapplied overhead for the year.
3. Assume the company closes any under- or overapplied overhead directly to Cost of Goods Sold. Prepare the appropriate entry.
4. Assume that the company allocates any under- or overapplied overhead to Work in Process, Finished Goods, and Cost of Goods Sold. Prepare the journal entry to show the allocation. (You may assume that no inventories existed at the beginning of the year.)
5. How much higher or lower will net income be for the year if the under- or overapplied overhead is allocated rather than closed directly to Cost of Goods Sold?

P3–23 Comprehensive Problem: Journal Entries; T-Accounts; Statements; Pricing   Southworth Company uses a job-order cost system and applies manufacturing overhead cost to jobs on the basis of the cost of direct materials used in production. At the beginning of the current year, the following estimates were made as a basis for computing a predetermined overhead rate for the year: manufacturing overhead cost, $248,000; and direct materials cost, $155,000. The following transactions took place during the year (all purchases and services were acquired on account):

a. Raw materials purchased, $142,000.
b. Raw materials requisitioned for use in production (all direct materials), $150,000.
c. Utility bills incurred in the factory, $21,000.
d. Costs for salaries and wages were incurred as follows:

> Direct labour $216,000
> Indirect labour   90,000
> Selling and administrative salaries . . . 145,000

e. Maintenance costs incurred in the factory, $15,000.
f. Advertising costs incurred, $130,000.
g. Depreciation recorded for the year, $50,000 (90% relates to factory assets, and the remainder relates to selling and administrative assets).
h. Rental cost incurred on buildings, $90,000 (80% of the space is occupied by the factory, and 20% is occupied by sales and administration).
i. Miscellaneous selling and administrative costs incurred, $17,000.
j. Manufacturing overhead cost was applied to jobs, $_____?_____.
k. Cost of goods manufactured for the year, $590,000.
l. Sales for the year (all on account) totalled $1,000,000. These goods cost $600,000 to manufacture.

The balances in the inventory accounts at the beginning of the year were as follows:

> Raw Materials $18,000
> Work in Process   24,000
> Finished Goods   35,000

Required

1. Prepare journal entries to record the above data.
2. Post your entries to T-accounts. (Don't forget to enter the opening inventory balances above.) Determine the ending balances in the inventory accounts and in the Manufacturing Overhead account.
3. Prepare a schedule of cost of goods manufactured.
4. Prepare a journal entry to close any balance in the Manufacturing Overhead account to Cost of Goods Sold. Prepare a schedule of cost of goods sold.
5. Prepare an income statement for the year. Ignore income taxes.
6. Job 218 was one of the many jobs started and completed during the year. The job required $3,600 in materials and 400 hours of direct labour time at a rate of $11 per hour. If the job contained 500 units and the company billed at 75% above the cost to manufacture, what price per unit would have been charged to the customer?

P3–24 Comprehensive Problem: T-Accounts; Job-Order Cost Flows; Statements; Pricing Top-Products, Inc., produces goods to customers' orders and uses a job-order costing system. A trial balance for the company as of January 1, the beginning of the current year, is given below:

Cash	$ 18,000	
Accounts Receivable	40,000	
Raw Materials	25,000	
Work in Process	32,000	
Finished Goods	60,000	
Prepaid Insurance	5,000	
Plant and Equipment	400,000	
Accumulated Depreciation		$148,000
Accounts Payable		90,000
Salaries and Wages Payable		3,000
Capital Stock		250,000
Retained Earnings		89,000
Total	$580,000	$580,000

The company applies manufacturing overhead cost to jobs on the basis of direct labour cost. The following estimates were made at the beginning of the year for purposes of computing a predetermined overhead rate for the year: manufacturing overhead cost, $228,000; and direct labour cost, $190,000. Summarized transactions of the company for the year are given below:

a. Raw materials purchased on account, $180,000.
b. Raw materials requisitioned for use in production, $190,000 (all direct materials).
c. Utility costs incurred in the factory, $57,000.
d. Salary and wage costs were incurred as follows:

Direct labour	$200,000
Indirect labour	90,000
Selling and administrative salaries	120,000

e. Prepaid insurance expired during the year, $4,000 (75% related to factory operations, and 25% related to selling and administrative activities).
f. Property taxes incurred on the factory building, $16,000.
g. Advertising costs incurred, $150,000.
h. Depreciation recorded for the year, $50,000 (80% related to factory assets, and the remainder related to selling and administrative assets).
i. Other costs were incurred (credit Accounts Payable): for factory overhead, $30,000; and for miscellaneous selling and administrative expenses, $18,000.
j. Manufacturing overhead cost applied to jobs, $___?___.
k. Cost of goods manufactured for the year, $635,000.
l. Sales for the year totalled $1,000,000 (all on account); the cost of goods sold was $___?___. (The ending balance in the Finished Goods inventory account was $45,000.)
m. Cash collections from customers during the year, $950,000.
n. Cash payments during the year: to employees, $412,000; on accounts payable, $478,000.

Required

1. Enter the company's transactions for the year directly into T-accounts. (Don't forget to enter the opening balances into the T-accounts.) Key your entries to the letters (a) through (n) above. Create new T-accounts as needed. Find the ending balance in each account.
2. Prepare a schedule of cost of goods manufactured.
3. Prepare a journal entry to close any balance in the Manufacturing Overhead account to Cost of Goods Sold. Prepare a schedule of cost of goods sold.
4. Prepare an income statement for the year. Ignore income taxes.
5. Job 316 was one of the many jobs started and completed during the year. The job required $2,400 in materials and $3,000 in direct labour cost. If the job contained 300 units and the company billed the job at 140% of the cost to manufacture, what price per unit would have been charged to the customer?

P3–25 Plantwide versus Departmental Overhead Rates "Don't tell me we've lost another bid!" exclaimed Sandy Kovallas, president of Lenko Products, Inc. "I'm afraid so," replied Doug Martin, the operations vice president. "One of our competitors underbid us by about $10,000 on the Hastings job." "I just can't figure it out," said Kovallas. "It seems we're either too high to get the job or too low to make any money on half the jobs we bid any more. What's happened?"

Lenko Products manufactures specialized goods to customers' specifications and operates a job-order costing system. Manufacturing overhead cost is applied to jobs on the basis of direct labour cost. The following estimates were made at the beginning of the current year:

	Department			
	Cutting	Machining	Assembly	Total Plant
Direct labour	$300,000	$200,000	$400,000	$ 900,000
Manufacturing overhead	540,000	800,000	100,000	1,440,000

Jobs require varying amounts of work in the three departments. The Hastings job, for example, would have required manufacturing costs in the three departments as follows:

	Department			
	Cutting	Machining	Assembly	Total Plant
Direct materials	$12,000	$ 900	$ 5,600	$18,500
Direct labour	6,500	1,700	13,000	21,200
Manufacturing overhead	?	?	?	?

The company uses a plantwide overhead rate to apply manufacturing overhead cost to jobs.

Required

1. Assuming use of a plantwide overhead rate:
   a. Compute the rate for the current year.
   b. Determine the amount of manufacturing overhead cost that would have been applied to the Hastings job.
2. Suppose that instead of using a plantwide overhead rate, the company had used a separate predetermined overhead rate in each department. Under these conditions:
   a. Compute the rate for each department for the current year.
   b. Determine the amount of manufacturing overhead cost that would have been applied to the Hastings job.
3. Assume that it is customary in the industry to bid jobs at 150% of total manufacturing cost (direct materials, direct labour, and applied overhead). What was the company's bid price on the Hastings job? What would the bid price have been if departmental overhead rates had been used to apply overhead cost?
4. At the end of the current year, the company assembled the following *actual* cost data relating to all jobs worked on during the year:

	Department			
	Cutting	Machining	Assembly	Total Plant
Direct materials	$760,000	$ 90,000	$410,000	$1,260,000
Direct labour	320,000	210,000	340,000	870,000
Manufacturing overhead	560,000	830,000	92,000	1,482,000

Compute the under- or overapplied overhead for the year (a) assuming that a plantwide overhead rate is used and (b) assuming that departmental overhead rates are used.

P3–26 Backflush Costing and Rework (Appendix 3A) Norman Company Ltd. is a construction company using two cells, one for new home construction and one for renovations/repairs. In either case, the company buys what it needs for each job and does not keep an inventory of materials. Norman Company implemented backflush costing to simplify its bookkeeping. Labour costs are treated as part of overhead and no finished goods inventory is needed.

Overhead is charged to jobs based on the number of hours worked. Estimates used to set the overhead rates for each cell are as follows:

	Cell C	Cell R
Direct labour	$300,000	$200,000
Direct overhead	90,000	70,000
	$390,000	$270,000
Hours available	15,000	10,000

During the current year, Norman had the following activities:

	Cell C	Cell R
Materials purchased	$150,000	$ 75,000
Direct labour costs	290,000	210,000
Direct overhead	88,000	76,000
Hours worked	14,800	10,900

At the year end, all jobs were finished.

Required

Record the transactions for the year using backflush procedures.

P3–27 **Backflush Costing and Periodic Inventory Method**   (Appendix 3A) Able Service Centre Ltd. conducts auto repairs on demand by customers. Because of the cost, Able uses a JIT purchasing system to avoid the need for inventories. Able's accountant, Jane Kosh, is interested in experimenting with the entry process for backflush costing and comparing it to the old periodic system she had studied in university. The following are the costs for May:

Materials purchased	$13,000
Labour—mechanics	3,500
Overhead costs—rent, depreciation, supervision, etc.	18,000
Overhead applied to material costs and labour costs on jobs— (Labour and material costs are charged separately)	20,000

No beginning inventories existed at May 1. One job was unfinished at the end of May because the customer was not anxious for his vehicle. Costs were: Materials, $200; Labour, $180; Overhead applied, $490.

Required

1. Prepare the general ledger entries for the month of May using the perpetual inventory system.
2. Prepare the general ledger entries for the month of May using backflush accounting.
3. Prepare the general ledger entries for the month of May using the periodic inventory system.

P3–28 **Job Costing and Rework**   (Appendix 3B) Terry Construction Ltd. is a mid-sized contractor engaged in both home renovations and new home construction. It employs a job costing system so it can have a record of costs for various types of jobs and to maintain a test of bidding accuracy.

The following information relates to its activities for the last month of its fiscal year. This month began with the following balances:

Cash	$ 2,000
Accounts receivable	5,000
Inventory—raw materials	1,000
Inventory—work in process	3,000 (job 1107)
Inventory—finished jobs	800 (job 1105)
Prepaid insurance	1,000
Property and equipment	100,000
Accumulated depreciation	(40,000)
Vehicles	30,000
Accumulated depreciation	(7,000)
Total assets	$ 95,800
Accounts payable	$ 6,000
Bank loan	45,000
Common stock	5,000
Retained earnings	39,800
Total liabilities and shareholders' equity	$ 95,800

The following activities occurred during the current month:
a. Purchased raw materials for $6,000 on credit.
b. Used $6,500 of raw materials for the following jobs: 1201, $800; 1202, $700; 1203, $3,000; and 1204, $2,000.
c. Wages paid to employees: $6,500 for the following jobs: 1107, $300; 1201, $700; 1202, $2,000; 1203, $2,500; 1204, $1,000.
d. Supervision salaries paid in cash $2,000.
e. Depreciation for property and equipment $2,000, vehicles $1,000.
f. Insurance expired, $150.
g. Maintenance for equipment, $500, paid in cash.
h. Overhead applied totalled $5,850: Job 1107, $270; Job 1201, $630; Job 1202, $1,800; Job 1203, $2,250; Job 1204, $900.
i. Bidding expenses paid in cash, $800.
j. Administrative salary, $2,500.
k. Revenues billed: Job 1105, $2,000; Job 1107, $5,000; Job 1201, $2,500; Job 1202, $4,200; Job 1203, $10,000.
l. Cash collected on receivables, $23,000.
m. Cash paid on accounts payable $8,000, interest $500.
n. Job 1204 remained unfinished at the end of the month.

   Job 1204 was unfinished at the end of the period in part because of some damage resulting from a late storm that removed some shingles that did not have time to stick. Materials amounting to $200 and labour in the amount of $90 were needed to correct the problem. Terry expects some further work will be needed early in the new year before the contract will be completed.

Required

1. Record the activities for the final month of the current fiscal year.
2. Prepare income results for jobs 1107, 1203, and 1105.
3. Compute the inventory evaluation for Job 1204 at the end of the fiscal year.

CASES

C3–29 Ethics and the Manager   Terri Ronsin had recently been transferred to the Home Security Systems Division of National Home Products. Shortly after taking over her new position as divisional controller, she was asked to develop the division's predetermined overhead rate for the upcoming year. The accuracy of the rate is of some importance, since it is used throughout the year and any overapplied or underapplied overhead is closed out to Cost of Goods Sold only at the end of the year. National Home Products uses direct labour-hours in all of its divisions as the allocation base for manufacturing overhead.

To compute the predetermined overhead rate, Terri divided her estimate of the total manufacturing overhead for the coming year by the production manager's estimate of the total direct labour-hours for the coming year. She took her computations to the division's general manager for approval, but was quite surprised when he suggested a modification in the base. Her conversation with the general manager, Harry Irving, went like this:

RONSIN: Here are my calculations for next year's predetermined overhead rate. If you approve, we can enter the rate into the computer on January 1 and be up and running in the job-order costing system right away this year.

IRVING: Thanks for coming up with the calculations so quickly, and they look just fine. There is, however, one slight modification I would like to see. Your estimate of the total direct labour-hours for the year is 440,000 hours. How about cutting that to about 420,000 hours?

RONSIN: I don't know if I can do that. The production manager says she will need about 440,000 direct labour-hours to meet the sales projections for the year. Besides, there are going to be over 430,000 direct labour-hours during the current year and sales are projected to be higher next year.

IRVING: Terri, I know all of that. I would still like to reduce the direct labour-hours in the base to something like 420,000 hours. You probably don't know that I had an agreement with your predecessor as divisional controller to shave 5% or so off the estimated direct labour-hours every year. That way, we kept a reserve that usually resulted in a big boost to net income at the end of the fiscal year in December. We called it our Christmas bonus. Corporate headquarters always seemed as pleased as punch that we could pull off such a miracle at the end of the year. This system has worked well for many years, and I don't want to change it now.

Required

1. Explain how shaving 5% off the estimated direct labour-hours in the base for the predetermined overhead rate usually results in a big boost in net income at the end of the fiscal year.
2. Should Terri Ronsin go along with the general manager's request to reduce the direct labour-hours in the predetermined overhead rate computation to 420,000 direct labour-hours?

C3–30 Incomplete Data; Review of Cost Flows   After a dispute concerning wages, Orville Arson tossed an incendiary device into the Sparkle Company's record vault. Within moments, only a few charred fragments were readable from the company's factory ledger, as shown below:

Raw Materials			Manufacturing Overhead		
Bal. 4/1	12,000		Actual costs for April	14,800	

Work in Process			Accounts Payable		
Bal. 4/1	4,500				
			Bal. 4/30		8,000

Finished Goods			Cost of Goods Sold		
Bal. 4/30	16,000				

Sifting through ashes and interviewing selected employees has turned up the following additional information:

a. The controller remembers clearly that the predetermined overhead rate was based on an estimated 60,000 direct labour-hours to be worked over the year and an estimated $180,000 in manufacturing overhead costs.

b. The production superintendent's cost sheets showed only one job in process on April 30. Materials of $2,600 had been added to the job, and 300 direct labour-hours had been expended at $6 per hour.

c. The accounts payable are for raw material purchases only, according to the accounts payable clerk. He clearly remembers that the balance in the account was $6,000 on April 1. An analysis of cancelled cheques (kept in the treasurer's office) shows that payments of $40,000 were made to suppliers during April. (All materials used during April were direct materials.)

d. A charred piece of the payroll ledger shows that 5,200 direct labour-hours were recorded for the month. The employment department has verified that there were no variations in pay rates among employees. (This infuriated Orville, who felt that his services were underpaid.)

e. Records maintained in the finished goods warehouse indicate that the finished goods inventory totalled $11,000 on April 1.

f. From another charred piece in the vault, you are able to discern that the cost of goods manufactured for April was $89,000.

Required

Determine the following amounts:

1. Work in process inventory, April 30.
2. Raw materials purchased during April.
3. Overhead applied to work in process.
4. Cost of goods sold for April.
5. Over- or underapplied overhead for April.
6. Raw materials usage during April.
7. Raw materials inventory, April 30.

(Hint: A good way to proceed is to bring the fragmented T-accounts up-to-date through April 30 by posting whatever entries can be developed from the information provided.)

C3–31 Critical Thinking; Interpretation of Manufacturing Overhead Rates
Sharpton Fabricators Company manufactures a variety of parts for the automotive industry. The company uses a job-order costing system with a plantwide predetermined overhead rate based on direct labour-hours. On December 10, 19x5, the company's controller made a preliminary estimate of the predetermined overhead rate for 19x6. The new rate was based on the estimated total manufacturing overhead cost of $2,475,000 and the estimated 52,000 total direct labour-hours for 19x6:

$$\text{Predetermined overhead rate} = \frac{\$2,475,000}{52,000 \text{ hours}}$$

$$= \$47.60 \text{ per direct labour-hour}$$

This new predetermined overhead rate was communicated to top managers in a meeting on December 11. The rate did not cause any comment because it was within a few pennies of the overhead rate that had been used during 19x5. One of the subjects discussed at the meeting was a proposal by the production manager to purchase an automated milling machine centre built by Central Robotics. The president of Sharpton Fabricators, Kevin Reynolds, agreed to meet with the regional sales representative from Central Robotics to discuss the proposal.

On the day following the meeting, Mr. Reynolds met with Jay Warner, Central Robotics's sales representative. The following discussion took place:

REYNOLDS: Larry Winter, our production manager, asked me to meet with you since he is interested in installing an automated milling machine centre. Frankly, I am skeptical.

You're going to have to show me this isn't just another expensive toy for Larry's people to play with.

WARNER: That shouldn't be too difficult, Mr. Reynolds. The automated milling machine centre has three major advantages. First, it is much faster than the manual methods you are using. It can process about twice as many parts per hour as your present milling machines. Second, it is much more flexible. There are some up-front programming costs, but once those have been incurred, there is almost no setup required on the machines for standard operations. You just punch in the code of the standard operation, load the machine's hopper with raw material, and the machine does the rest.

REYNOLDS: Yeah, but what about cost? Having twice the capacity in the milling machine area won't do us much good. That centre is idle much of the time anyway.

WARNER: I was getting there. The third advantage of the automated milling machine centre is lower cost. Larry Winters and I looked over your present operations, and we estimated that the automated equipment would eliminate the need for about 6,000 direct labour-hours a year. What is your direct labour cost per hour?

REYNOLDS: The wage rate in the milling area averages about $21 per hour. Fringe benefits raise that figure to about $30 per hour.

WARNER: Don't forget your overhead.

REYNOLDS: Next year the overhead rate will be about $48 per hour.

WARNER: So including fringe benefits and overhead, the cost per direct labour-hour is about $78.

REYNOLDS: That's right.

WARNER: Since you can save 6,000 direct labour-hours per year, the cost savings would amount to about $468,000 a year.

REYNOLDS: That's pretty impressive, but you aren't giving away this equipment are you?

WARNER: Several options are available, including leasing and out-right purchase. Just for comparison purposes, our 60-month lease plan would require payments of only $300,000 per year.

REYNOLDS: Sold! When can you install the equipment?

Shortly after this meeting, Mr. Reynolds informed the company's controller of the decision to lease the new equipment, which would be installed over the Christmas vacation period. The controller realized that this decision would require a recomputation of the predetermined overhead rate for 19x6 since the decision would affect both the manufacturing overhead and the direct labour-hours for the year. After discussing these issues with both the production manager and the sales representative from Central Robotics, the controller issued the following revised predetermined overhead rate for the plant for 19x6:

$$\text{Predetermined overhead rate} = \frac{\$2,820,000}{46,000 \text{ hours}}$$

$$= \$61.30 \text{ per direct labour-hour}$$

(Note: In addition to the lease cost, a skilled technician/programmer must be hired to maintain and program the equipment at a cost of about $45,000 per year. This cost would be classified as part of manufacturing overhead.)

When this revised predetermined overhead rate for 19x6 was circulated among the company's top managers, there was considerable consternation. The costs of all of the company's products would be considerably higher in 19x6 than they were in 19x5.

Required

1. Explain why the revised predetermined overhead rate is higher than the original estimate. What effect would this new rate have on the cost of jobs that do not use the new automated milling machine centre?

2. After seeing the new predetermined overhead rate, the production manager argued that he probably wouldn't be able to eliminate all of the 6,000 direct labour-hours after all.

Due to labour contracts, he would be unable to lay off several of the older workers. As a result, the real labour cost savings in the milling area would be only about half the 6,000-hour figure. In the light of this additional information, evaluate the original decision to acquire the automated milling machine centre from Central Robotics.

C3–32 Overhead Treatment   Camco Ltd. is a large manufacturing concern that produces only one product and applies factory overhead as a fixed percentage, based on direct labour-hours. In the two preceding years, this method has produced very small variances between the actual and applied overhead.

During the current year, the company received from the federal government a large nonrecurring order which has taken up all of the factory's idle time. As a result of this full capacity for most of the year the company has an overabsorption of factory overhead amounting to $300,000. All of the goods manufactured for the government were shipped and billed prior to the year-end.

The company intends to defer the overabsorption until next year when, in the opinion of management, it will be absorbed because of a larger-than-normal reduction in plant operating capacity.

Required   Comment on each of the following proposed accounting treatments for the overabsorbed factory overhead:
1. The method now suggested by Camco Ltd.
2. Prorating the overabsorbed overhead Cost of Sales, Work in Process, and Finished Goods.
3. Applying the overabsorption to Cost of Sales.

(CICA, adapted)

GROUP EXERCISES

GE3–33 What Do Traditional Product Cost Systems Look Like?   To understand some of the criticisms levelled at conventional cost systems, it helps to have a clear understanding of how these cost systems are designed and used. The following series of questions will help you learn more about product costing practices and their limitations when applied to diverse product lines and complex production environments.

Required
1. What is the primary purpose served by traditional cost accounting systems? Why did the field of manufacturing cost accounting originate?
2. Identify as many other uses of product cost numbers as you can.
3. How are research and development costs (upstream costs) and sales, marketing, distribution, administrative, and product support costs (downstream costs) accounted for? Why are SG&A costs accounted for in this manner?
4. In a 1988 study of product costing practices, 30% of the responding firms used plantwide overhead rates to allocate manufacturing overhead to jobs. Plantwide cost pools accumulate all the different heterogeneous overhead costs into a single cost pool. Under what circumstances would the use of a plantwide overhead cost rate be acceptable? Be potentially unacceptable or misleading?
5. As of 1988, the majority of firms used departmental cost pools and a two-stage process for allocating overhead costs to jobs. Describe the two-stage process for assigning manufacturing overhead costs to products. Under what circumstances would the use of departmental overhead cost rates be acceptable? Be potentially unacceptable or misleading?
6. Several studies have determined that direct labour cost or direct labour-hours (and to a much lesser degree, machine-hours) are the primary allocation bases for overhead costs. In today's job manufacturing environment, what is the relationship between changes in direct labour-hours or direct labour cost and manufacturing overhead costs? Explain. Does it seem that increases and decreases in direct labour cause increases and decreases in manufacturing overhead?

GE3–34 The Plant Layout Case   Now that students have a background in job costing, Rantoul Tool is an excellent instructional case illustrating the impact that different manufacturing environments have on product costing procedures. The case includes a narrative description of three manufacturing processes (traditional functional process, cellular process or "factory within a factory," and a flexible manufacturing system) and diagrams of the plant layout for each manufacturing system. The objective of the case is to challenge students to develop a narrative description and evaluation of each production system. It provides students with further insight into different product costing environments and other important issues. With some preliminary explanation as to why factories are organized the way they are, students find the case very interesting. Refer to Wayne J. Morse, "Instructional Case: Rantoul Tool, Inc.," *Issues in Accounting Education* (Spring 1990), pp. 78–83.

GE3–35 We're Doing Well but We Don't Know Why   "Many U.S. companies don't know where they are making money and where they are losing (money)," says Robert S. Kaplan, a Harvard University accounting professor. Kaplan was aiming his criticism directly at traditional cost accounting systems and, in particular, at the methods used to allocate overhead costs among the many different products produced by job shops, batch manufacturers, and assemblers. Source: Ford S. Worthy, "Accounting Bores You? Wake Up," *Fortune* (October 12, 1987), pp. 43, 44, 48–50.

PART I: Standard Products   Firms that sell a complete line of products usually have their bread-and-butter products. These high-volume standard or commodity products, while few in number (e.g., 20%–25% of the product line), may account for as much as 70%–80% of the business or sales volume of their firms.

Required

1. Looking at firms that manufacture a wide range of products, high-volume standard products tend to get systematically overcosted under conventional product costing systems. Describe these products along the following dimensions: competitive environment, how prices are set, stage of life cycle, market acceptance, profit margins (price less cost), general age of technology used to produce these products, degree of labour intensity in the manufacturing process, complexity of product, and batch size when manufactured.
2. Assuming the allocation of manufacturing overhead is based on direct labour cost, explain how these products get overcosted.
3. Since high-volume standard products face fierce price competition, what implications does overcosting have for reported product profitability, product emphasis, market share, future allocations of resources to support the product, and potential product discontinuance?

PART II: Specialty Products   Firms that sell a complete line of products will likely have a product line dominated by a large number of low-volume specialty or custom products. While the firm may produce a large number of specialty products (e.g., 70%–80% of the product line), the cumulative sales of low-volume custom products may amount to no more than 25%–30% of sales revenues.

Required

1. Low-volume specialty or custom products tend to get systematically undercosted under conventional product costing systems. These products meet the unique needs of a particular customer and, therefore, the level of sales of any one custom product is usually relatively low when compared to the sales volume of standard products. Describe these products along the following dimensions: competitive environment, how prices are set, stage of life cycle, market acceptance, profit margins (price less cost), general age of technology used to produce these products, degree of labour intensity in the manufacturing process, complexity of product, and batch size when manufactured.
2. Assuming the allocation of manufacturing overhead is based on direct labour cost, explain how these products get undercosted.
3. As a rule, low-volume specialty products don't face the kind of direct head-to-head price competition that high-volume products confront. Instead, they compete on their unique features or performance more so than price. What implications does undercosting have for reported product profitability, product emphasis, market share, future allocations of resources to support the product, and managements' perception of the future role to be played by specialty products?

SYSTEMS DESIGN: PROCESS COSTING

LEARNING OBJECTIVES

After studying Chapter 4, you should be able to:

1 Enumerate the major similarities and differences between job-order and process costing.

2 Prepare journal entries to record the flow of materials, labour, and overhead through a process costing system.

3 Compute the equivalent units of production by the weighted-average method.

4 Prepare a quantity schedule for a period by the weighted-average method.

5 Compute the total and unit costs for a period by the weighted-average method.

6 Prepare a cost reconciliation for a period by the weighted-average method.

7 Combine the quantity schedule and equivalent units, the total and unit costs, and the cost reconciliation into a production report.

8 State the conditions under which operation costing is useful to management, and explain the impact of a flexible manufacturing system on job-order and process costing.

9 Define or explain the key terms listed at the end of the chapter.

10 (Appendix 4A) Compute the equivalent units of production by the FIFO method.

11 (Appendix 4A) Prepare a quantity schedule for a period by the FIFO method.

12 (Appendix 4A) Compute the unit costs for a period by the FIFO method.

13 (Appendix 4A) Prepare a cost reconciliation for a period by the FIFO method.

14 (Appendix 4B) Compute the cost of lost units or shrinkage.

Process costing is used when the product is homogeneous in nature. A bakery, which makes many loaves of the same type of bread every day, will use process costing.

As explained in the preceding chapter, there are two basic costing systems in use: job-order costing and process costing. A job-order costing system is used in those situations where many different jobs or batches of production are worked on each period. Examples of industries that would typically use job-order costing include furniture manufacture, special-order printing, shipbuilding, and many types of service organizations.

By contrast, **process costing** is used in industries that produce homogenous (i.e., uniform) products on a continuous basis, such as bricks, corn flakes, or paper. Process costing is particularly used in industries that convert basic raw materials into homogeneous products, such as Alcan (aluminum ingots), Scott Paper (toilet paper), Dover Mills (flour), Imperial Oil (gasoline and lubricating oils), and Christie's (crackers). In addition, process costing is often employed in companies that use a form of process costing in their assembly operations, such as Panasonic (video monitors), Compaq (personal computers), General Electric (refrigerators), Toyota (automobiles), Maytag (washing machines), and Sony (CD players). A form of process costing may also be used in utilities that produce gas, water, and electricity. As suggested by the length of this list, process costing is in very wide use.

Process costing is usually associated with heavy industry, such as oil refining. Process costing, however, can be applied to service companies such as McDonald's; one type of hamburger is made continuously and is homogeneous.

Careful study of the nature of process costing will provide an indication that homogeneity of units of product is not the limiting factor in deciding what situation can use process costing. Homogeneity of conversion activity of different raw materials can be adapted to process costing by treating raw materials as a job and conversion as a process. Such hybrid costing systems take advantage of the flexibility of job costing and the simplicity of process costing. The section on operation costing later in this chapter will describe some of these applications, the nature of which should be easier to understand once the pure form of process costing is studied.

Our purpose in this chapter is to extend the discussion of product costing started in the preceding chapter to include a process costing system.

COMPARISON OF JOB-ORDER AND PROCESS COSTING

In some ways process costing is very similar to job-order costing, and in some ways it is very different. In the following two sections, we focus on these similarities and differences to provide a foundation for the detailed discussion of process costing that follows.

Similarities between Job-Order and Process Costing

OBJECTIVE 1

Enumerate the major similarities and differences between job-order and process costing.

Much of what was learned in the preceding chapter about costing and about cost flows applies equally well to process costing in this chapter. That is, we are not throwing out all that we have learned about costing and starting from scratch with a whole new system. The similarities between job-order and process costing can be summarized as follows:
1. The same basic purposes exist in both systems, (a) to assign material, labour, and overhead costs to products; (b) to provide a mechanism for computing unit costs; and (c) to provide data essential for planning, control, and decision making.
2. Both systems maintain and use the same basic manufacturing accounts, including Manufacturing Overhead, Raw Materials, Work in Process, and Finished Goods.
3. Cost flows through the manufacturing accounts just mentioned move in basically the same way in both systems.

As can be seen from this comparison, much of the knowledge that we have already acquired about costing is applicable to a process costing system. Our task now is simply to refine and extend this knowledge to meet special process costing needs.

Differences between Job-Order and Process Costing

The differences between job-order and process costing arise from two factors. (1) The flow of units in a process costing system is more or less continuous, and (2) these units are indistinguishable from one another. Under process costing, it makes no sense to try to identify materials, labour, and overhead costs with a particular order from a customer (as we did with job-order costing), because each order is just one of many that are filled from a continuous flow of units from the production line. Instead of accumulating costs by order, we accumulate costs *by department* and assign these costs equally to all units that pass through the department during a period.

A further difference between the two cost systems is that because process costing is department oriented rather than job oriented, the job cost sheet is of no value in a process costing system. In a process costing system, instead of using job cost sheets, a document known as a **production report** is prepared for each department. The production report

Job-Order Costing	Process Costing
1. Many different jobs are worked on during each period, with each job having different production requirements.	1. A single product is produced either on a continuous basis or for long periods of time. All units of product are identical or at least what is done is identical.
2. Costs are accumulated by individual job.	2. Costs are accumulated by department.
3. The *job cost sheet* is the key document controlling the accumulation of costs by a job.	3. The *department production report* is the key document showing the accumulation and disposition of costs by a department.
4. Unit costs are computed *by job* on the job cost sheet.	4. Unit costs are computed *by department* on the department production report.

serves three functions. It provides a summary of the number of units moving through a department during a period, and it also provides a computation of unit costs. In addition, it shows what costs were charged to a department during a period and what disposition was made of these costs, a process we will term a *cost reconciliation*. As these comments suggest, the department production report is a key document in a process costing system. The major differences between job-order and process costing are summarized in Exhibit 4–1.

A PERSPECTIVE OF PROCESS COST FLOWS

Before presenting a detailed example of process costing, it is helpful to gain a visual perspective of how manufacturing costs flow through a process costing system.

Processing Departments

A **processing department** is any location in the factory where work is performed on a product and where materials, labour, or overhead costs are added to the product. For example, a potato chip factory operated by Hostess might have three processing departments— one for preparing potatoes, one for cooking, and one for inspecting and packaging. A brick factory might have two processing departments—one for mixing and molding clay into brick form and one for firing the molded brick. A company can have as many or as few processing departments as are needed to complete the manufacture of a product. Some products may go through several processing departments, while others may go through only one or two. Regardless of the number of departments involved, all processing departments have two essential features. First, the activity performed in the processing department must be performed uniformly on all of the units passing through it. Second, the output of the processing department must be homogeneous.

The processing departments involved in the manufacture of a product such as bricks would probably be organized in a *sequential* pattern. By **sequential processing,** we mean that units flow in sequence from one department to another. An example of processing departments arranged in a sequential pattern is given in Exhibit 4–2.

A different type of processing pattern, known as *parallel processing,* is required in the manufacture of some products. **Parallel processing** is used in those situations where after a certain point, some units may go through different processing departments than others. For example, Petro Canada in their petroleum refining operations input crude oil into one processing department and then use the refined output for further processing into several end products. Each end product may undergo several steps of further processing after the

A beer brewery will have several processing departments— fermenting, filtering, and bottling— that follow a sequential pattern.

Sequential Processing Departments: e.g., Potato Chip Factory

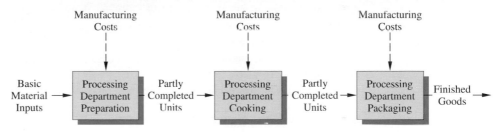

initial refining, some of which may be shared with other end products and some of which may not. Exhibit 4–3 illustrates one type of parallel processing. The number of possible variations in parallel processing patterns is virtually limitless. The example given in Exhibit 4–3 is intended as just one sample of the many processing patterns in use today.

The Flow of Materials, Labour, and Overhead Costs

Cost accumulation is simpler in a process costing system than in a job-order costing system. The reason is that costs need to be identified only by processing department—not by separate job. Thus, in a process costing system, instead of having to trace costs to hundreds of different jobs, costs are traced to only a few processing departments. This means that costs can be accumulated for longer periods of time and that just one allocation is needed at the end of a period (week, month, and so forth) to assign the accumulated costs to the period's output.

A T-account model of materials, labour, and overhead cost flows in a process costing system is given in Exhibit 4–4. Several key points should be noted from this exhibit. First, note that a separate Work in Process account is maintained for *each processing*

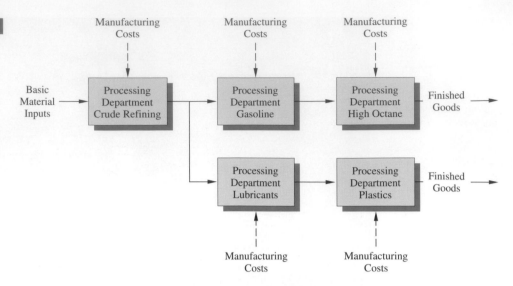

EXHIBIT 4–3

Parallel Processing Departments: e.g., Refining Crude Oil

department, rather than having only a single Work in Process account for the entire company. Second, note that the completed production of the first processing department (department A in the exhibit) is transferred into the Work in Process account of the second processing department (department B), where it undergoes further work. After this further work, the completed units are then transferred into Finished Goods. (In Exhibit 4–4, we show only two processing departments; there may be several such departments in some companies.)

Finally, note that materials, labour, and overhead costs can be entered directly into *any* processing department—not just the first. Costs in department B's Work in Process account would therefore consist of the materials, labour, and overhead costs entered directly into the account plus the costs attached to partially completed units transferred in from department A (called **transferred-in costs**).

Materials, Labour, and Overhead Cost Entries

OBJECTIVE 2

Prepare journal entries to record the flow of materials, labour, and overhead through a process costing system.

To complete our discussion of cost flows in a process costing system, in the following sections we show journal entries relating to materials, labour, and overhead costs and also make brief, further comments relating to each of these cost categories.

Materials Costs.   As in a perpetual inventory job-order costing system, materials are drawn from the storeroom by use of a materials requisition form. Charging these materials to departments, rather than to jobs, generally reduces the amount of requisitioning needed, because large amounts of materials can be drawn and put into production at a time. As stated earlier, materials can be added in any processing department, although it is not unusual for materials to be added only in the first processing department, with subsequent departments adding only labour and overhead costs as the partially completed units move along toward completion.

Assuming that the first processing department in a company is department A, the journal entry for placing materials into process would be:

Work in Process—Department A.   XXX
    Raw Materials   XXX

EXHIBIT 4–4

A T-Account Model
of Process Costing
Flows

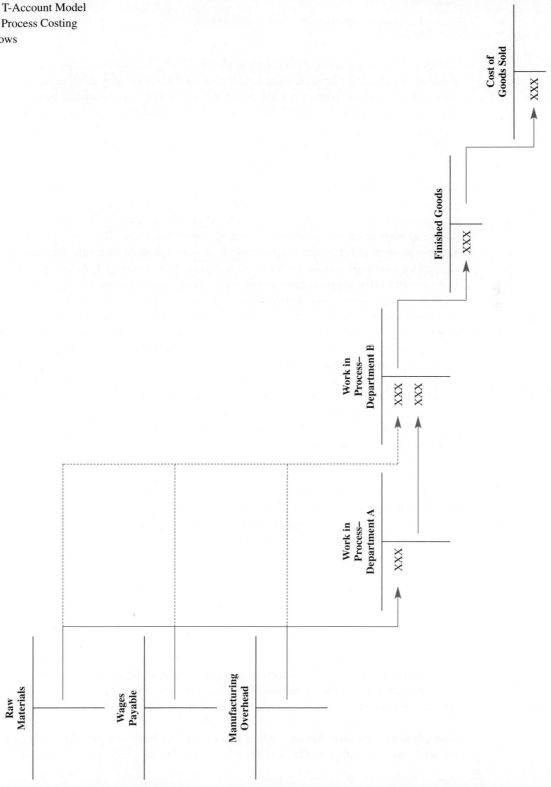

If other materials are subsequently added in another processing department, the entry would be:

Work in Process—Department B.   XXX
　　Raw Materials   XXX

Labour Costs.   As it is not necessary to identify costs with specific jobs, a time clock is generally adequate for accumulating labour costs and for allocating them to the proper department in a process costing system. Assuming again that a company has two processing departments, A and B, the journal entry to record labour costs for a period would be:

Work in Process—Department A.   XXX
Work in Process—Department B.   XXX
　　Salaries and Wages Payable.   XXX

Overhead Costs.   The simplest method of handling overhead costs in a process costing system is to charge products with the actual overhead costs of the period rather than with applied overhead costs. Under this approach, no predetermined overhead rate is computed; overhead costs in each department are simply added directly to that department's Work in Process account either as the costs are incurred or at specified intervals. Because there is no applied overhead cost in the sense we talked about in Chapter 3, there is no under- or overapplied overhead balance remaining at the end of a period when this approach is used.

Why is it possible to use actual overhead costs in a process costing system while normal overhead costing is preferable under job-order costing? The answer lies in the nature of the work flowing through the two systems. Under job-order costing, jobs tend to be heterogeneous, requiring different inputs and different times to complete. Also, several jobs are in process at a given time, each having different output requirements. Thus, the overhead cost chargeable to a job has to be estimated. Under process costing, homogeneous units flow continuously through a department, thus making it possible to charge units with the department's actual overhead costs as the costs are incurred. This approach works well, however, only if production is quite stable from period to period and only if overhead costs are incurred uniformly over the year.

If production levels fluctuate or if overhead costs are not incurred uniformly, then predetermined overhead rates should be used to charge overhead cost to products, the same as in job-order costing. When predetermined overhead rates are used, each department has its own separate rate with the rates being computed in the same way as was discussed in Chapter 3. Overhead cost is then applied to units of product as the units move through the various departments. As predetermined overhead rates are widely used in process costing, we assume their use throughout the remainder of this chapter.

If a company has two processing departments, A and B, the journal entry to apply overhead cost to products would be:

Work in Process—Department A.   XXX
Work in Process—Department B.   XXX
　　Manufacturing Overhead.   XXX

As we stated in Chapter 2, direct labour cost combined with manufacturing overhead cost is often referred to as **conversion cost,** as these cost inputs are necessary to covert raw materials into finished products. The term *conversion cost* is widely used in process costing in the preparation of department production reports.

Completing the Cost Flows.   Once processing has been completed in a department, the units are transferred to the next department for further processing, as was illustrated in the T-accounts in Exhibit 4–4. The entry to transfer partially completed units from department A into department B would be:

Work in Process—Department B.	XXX	
Work in Process—Department A.		XXX

The journal entry transferring costs of materials, labour, and overhead from department A to department B assumes the process is organized sequentially such as that illustrated in Exhibit 4–2 or as shown in Exhibit 4–3 for departments Gasoline and High Octane or Lubricants and Plastics. A parallel system would result in the costs being kept separate by department until they reach their final destination, for example finished goods, as we illustrate next.

After processing has been completed in department B, the completed units are then transferred into the Finished Goods inventory account:

Finished Goods	XXX	
Work in Process—Department B.		XXX

Finally, when a customer's order is filled and units are sold, the cost of the units is transferred into Cost of Goods Sold:

Cost of Goods Sold	XXX	
Finished Goods		XXX

To summarize, we stated earlier that the cost flows between accounts are basically the same in a process costing system as they are in a job-order costing system. As shown by the preceding entries, this is indeed correct. The only differences are that in a process costing system (a) a separate Work in Process account is maintained for each department, and (b) each department can be charged directly for manufacturing costs in addition to those transferred in from the preceding department.

▼　▼　▼　▼　▼

MANAGERIAL ACCOUNTING IN ACTION—THE ISSUE

Samantha Trivers, president of Double Diamond Skis, was worried about the future of the company. After a rocky start, the company had come out with a completely re-designed ski called The Ultimate. It was made of exotic materials and featured flashy graphics. Exhibit 4–5 illustrates how this ski is manufactured. The ski was a run-away best seller—particularly among younger skiers—and had provided the company with much-needed cash for two years. However, last year a dismal snowfall in the Rocky Mountains had depressed sales, and Double Diamond was once again strapped for cash. Samantha was worried that another bad ski season would force Double Diamond into bankruptcy.

Just before starting production of next year's model of The Ultimate, Samantha called Jerry Madison, the company controller, into her office to discuss the reports she would need in the coming year.

SAMANTHA: Jerry, I am going to need more frequent production information this year. I really have to stay on top of things—particularly our costs.
JERRY: What do you have in mind?

(continued)

EXHIBIT 4–5

The Production
Process at Double
Diamond Skis*

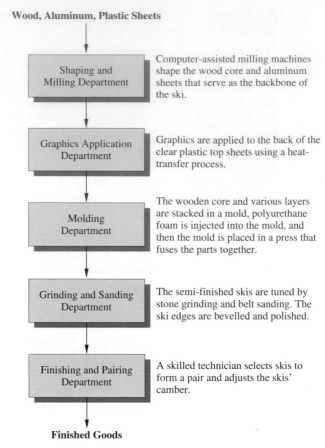

Wood, Aluminum, Plastic Sheets

Shaping and Milling Department — Computer-assisted milling machines shape the wood core and aluminum sheets that serve as the backbone of the ski.

Graphics Application Department — Graphics are applied to the back of the clear plastic top sheets using a heat-transfer process.

Molding Department — The wooden core and various layers are stacked in a mold, polyurethane foam is injected into the mold, and then the mold is placed in a press that fuses the parts together.

Grinding and Sanding Department — The semi-finished skis are tuned by stone grinding and belt sanding. The ski edges are bevelled and polished.

Finishing and Pairing Department — A skilled technician selects skis to form a pair and adjusts the skis' camber.

Finished Goods

*Adapted from Bill Gout, Jesse James Doquilo, and Studio M D, "Capped Crusaders," *Skiing,* October 1993, pp. 138–44.

SAMANTHA: I'd like reports at least once a month that detail how many skis have been produced and how much they cost to produce, and I need this for each department.

Jerry: That shouldn't be much of a problem. We already compile almost all of the necessary data for the annual report. The only complication is our work in process inventories. They haven't been a problem in our annual reports, since our fiscal year ends at a time when we have finished producing skis for the last model year and haven't yet started producing for the new model year. Consequently, there aren't any work in process inventories to value for the annual report. But that won't be true for monthly reports.

SAMANTHA: I'm not sure why that is a problem, Jerry. But I'm sure you can figure out how to solve it.

JERRY: You can count on me.

(continued)

The output of Double Diamond Skis is used for recreation by everyday consumers. Process costing is used to determine the unit costs as well as the equivalent units of the skis the company produces.

▼   ▼   ▼   ▼   ▼

EQUIVALENT UNITS OF PRODUCTION

Jerry, the controller of Double Diamond Skis, was concerned with the following problem: After materials, labour, and overhead costs have been accumulated in a department, the department's output must be determined so that unit costs can be computed. The difficulty is that a department usually has some partially completed units in its ending inventory. It does not seem reasonable to count these partially completed units as equivalent to fully completed units when counting the department's output. Therefore, what Jerry will do, and what is done routinely in process costing, is to convert those partially completed units into fully completed *equivalent units*. **Equivalent units** are defined as the equivalent, in terms of completed units, of partially completed units. They are the number of complete whole units one could obtain from the materials and effort contained in partially completed units.

For example, suppose the molding department at Double Diamond has 500 units in its ending work in process inventory that are 60% complete. These 500 partially complete units are equivalent to 300 fully complete units (500 × 60% = 300). Therefore, the ending work in process inventory would be said to contain 300 equivalent units. These equivalent units would be added to any fully completed units to determine the period's output for the department—called the *equivalent units of production.*

There are two different ways of computing the equivalent units of production for a period. In this chapter, we discuss the *weighted-average method.* In Appendix 4A, the *FIFO method* is discussed. The **FIFO method** of process costing is a method in which equivalent units and unit costs relate only to work done during the current period. In contrast, the **weighted-average method** blends together units and costs from the current period with units and costs from the prior period. In the weighted-average method, the equivalent units of production for a department are the number of units transferred to the next department (or to finished goods) plus the equivalent units in the department's ending work in process inventory.

Weighted-Average Method

Under the weighted-average method, a department's equivalent units are computed just as described above: Equivalent units of production = Units transferred to the next department (or to finished goods) + Equivalent units in ending work in process inventory. We do not have to make an equivalent units calculation for units transferred to the next department, since we can assume that they would not have been transferred unless they were 100% complete with respect to the work performed in the transferring department.

Consider the shaping and milling department at Double Diamond. This department uses computerized milling machines to precisely shape the wooden core and metal sheets that will be used to form the backbone of the ski. The following activity took place in the department in May, several months into the production of the new model of The Ultimate ski:

| | Units | Percent Completed | |
		Materials	Conversion
Work in process, May 1	200	50	30
Units started into production during May	5,000		
Units completed during May and transferred to the next department	4,800		
Work in process, May 31	400	40	25

Note the use of the term *conversion* in the above table. Conversion cost, as defined in Chapter 2, is direct labour cost plus manufacturing overhead cost. In process costing, conversion cost is often—but not always—treated as a single element of product cost.

Also note that the May 1 beginning work in process was 50% complete with respect to materials costs and 30% complete with respect to conversion costs. This means that 50% of the materials costs required to complete the units had already been incurred. Likewise, 30% of the conversion costs required to complete the units had already been incurred.

Since Double Diamond's work in process inventories are at different stages of completion in terms of the amounts of materials cost and conversion cost that have been added, two equivalent unit figures must be computed. The equivalent units computations are given in Exhibit 4–6.

Note from the computations in Exhibit 4–6 that units in the beginning work in process inventory are ignored and that an adjustment is made only for partially completed units in the ending inventory. The weighted-average method is concerned only with the fact that there are 4,900 equivalent units for conversion cost in ending inventories and in units transferred to the next department—the method is not concerned with the additional fact that some of this work was accomplished in prior periods. This is a key point in the weighted-average method that is easy to overlook.

The weighted-average method blends together the work that was accomplished in prior periods with the work that was accomplished in the current period. In the FIFO method, the units and costs of prior periods are cleanly separated from the units and costs of the current period. Some managers believe the FIFO method is more accurate for this reason. However, the FIFO method is more complex than the weighted-average method and for that reason is covered in Appendix 4A.

EXHIBIT 4-6

Equivalent Units of
Production:
Weighted-Average
Method

	Materials	Conversion
Units transferred to the next department	4,800	4,800
Work in process, May 31:		
400 units × 40%	160	
400 units × 25%		100
Equivalent units of production	4,960	4,900

Averages, in general, hide the details of the elements that make up the average. For example, the average of 2 + 4 is 3. The average of 1 + 5 is 3. If the manager is uninterested in the details of the elements, then the average provides all the information needed. If costs from one period to the next are approximately equal (for example, 3 + 3) the average is also a reasonable representation of the results. A third explanation for the use of the average approach is the relative size of the beginning inventory of work in process compared to the current production. For example, if the beginning inventory is only one-tenth the current production, the average (weighted) of $\frac{1}{10}(1) + \frac{9}{10}(5) = 4.60$ is very accurate and very close to a FIFO result.

Thus, besides the ease of calculation, the weighted average may be very accurate where costs from one period to the next are stable, or where the size of current production dwarfs the beginning inventory.

A visual perspective of the computation of equivalent units of production is provided in Exhibit 4–7. The data are for conversion costs in the shaping and milling department of Double Diamond Skis. Study this exhibit carefully before going on.

EXHIBIT 4-7

Visual Perspective of
Equivalent Units of
Production

DOUBLE DIAMOND SKIS
Shaping and Milling Department
Conversion Costs
(weighted-average method)

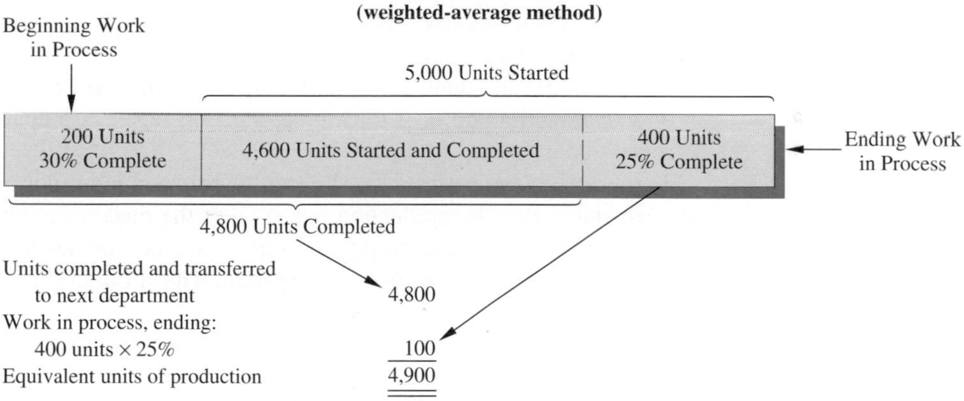

The sequential processing illustrated with the journal entries results in an additional column in the equivalent units calculation and the cost calculations that will occur when the unit costs are derived. For example, assume that we were calculating the equivalent units for Double Diamond, but for the graphics application department instead of shaping and milling. The following data are for graphics application, the second department in the sequence:

	Units	Percentage Completed		
		Transferred In	Materials	Conversion
Work in process beginning..............	100	100%	100%	40%
Units started into production during the month........................	4,800			
Units completed during the month and transferred to molding	4,600			
Work in process, ending................	200	100	100	60

The equivalent units for graphics application would be calculated as follows:

	Transferred In	Materials	Conversion
Units transferred to molding	4,600	4,600	4,600
Work in process, ending:			
200 units × 100%..............................	200		
200 units × 100%..............................		200	
200 units × 60%..............................			120
Equivalent units of production........................	4,800	4,800	4,720

When reviewing the above, note the units started into production during the month equals the units completed in the shaping and milling department. The equivalent units amount for these transferred-in elements is computed the same way as was done for materials added to production at the start of processing in the example provided above for graphics application.

PRODUCTION REPORT—WEIGHTED-AVERAGE METHOD

The production report contains the information requested by the president of Double Diamond Skis. The purpose of the production report is to summarize for the manager all of the activity that takes place in a department's Work in Process account for a period. This activity includes the units that flow through the Work in Process account as well as the costs that flow through it. A separate production report is prepared for each department, as illustrated in Exhibit 4–8.

Earlier, when we outlined the differences between job-order costing and process costing, we stated that the production report takes the place of a job cost sheet in a process costing system. Thus, the production report is a key document for the manager and is vital to the proper operation of the system. The production report has three separate (though highly interrelated) parts:

1. A quantity schedule, which shows the flow of units through the department, and a computation of equivalent units.
2. A computation of total and unit costs.
3. A reconciliation of all cost flows into and out of the department during the period.

We will use the data below for the May operations of the shaping and milling department of Double Diamond Skis to illustrate the production report. Keep in mind that this report is only one of the five reports that would be prepared for the company, since the company has five processing departments.

Work in process, beginning:	
Units in process	200
Stage of completion with respect to materials	50%
Stage of completion with respect to conversion	30%
Costs in the beginning inventory:	
Materials cost................................	$3,000
Conversion cost	1,000
Total cost in process.........................	$4,000
Units started into production during May	5,000
Units completed and transferred out	4,800
Costs added to production during May:	
Materials cost................................	$ 74,000
Conversion cost	70,000
Total cost added in the department	$144,000
Work in process, ending:	
Units in process	400
Stage of completion with respect to materials	40%
Stage of completion with respect to conversion	25%

In this section, we show how a production report is prepared when the weighted-average method is used to compute equivalent units and unit costs. The preparation of a production report under the FIFO method is illustrated in Appendix 4A at the end of this chapter.

EXHIBIT 4-8   The Position of the Production Report in the Flow of Costs

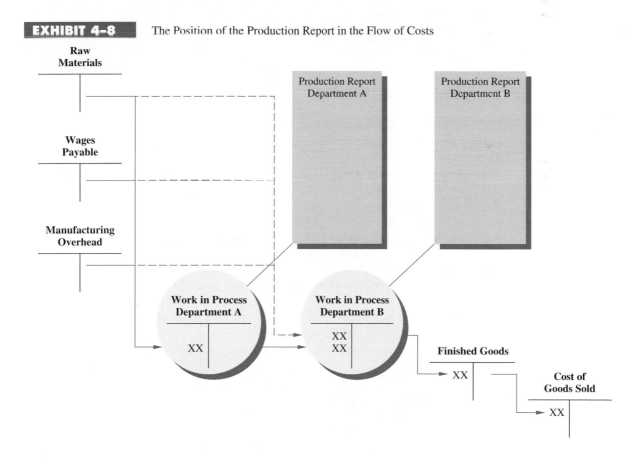

Step 1: Prepare a Quantity Schedule and Compute the Equivalent Units

OBJECTIVE 4
Prepare a quantity schedule for a period by the weighted-average method.

The first part of a production report consists of a **quantity schedule,** which accounts for the physical flow of units through a department, and a computation of the equivalent units for the period. The equivalent units are computed in this part of the production report, since the quantity schedule provides the data from which these figures are derived. To illustrate, a quantity schedule combined with a computation of equivalent units is given below for the shaping and milling department of Double Diamond Skis.

	Quantity Schedule	Equivalent Units	
		Materials	Conversion
Units to be accounted for:			
Work in process, May 1 (50% materials; 30% conversion added last month)	200		
Started into production	5,000		
Total units	5,200		
Units accounted for as follows:			
Transferred to the next department	4,800	4,800	4,800
Work in process, May 31 (40% materials; 25% conversion added this month)	400	160*	100†
Total units	5,200	4,960	4,900

*40% × 400 units = 160 equivalent units.

The quantity schedule permits the manager to see at a glance how many units moved through the department during a period as well as to see the stage of completion of any in-process units. In addition to providing this information, the quantity schedule serves as an essential guide in preparing and tying together the remaining parts of a production report. The equivalent units, for example, are easily computed by simply following the data provided in the quantity schedule, as shown above.

Step 2: Compute the Total and Unit Costs

OBJECTIVE 5
Compute the total and unit costs for a period by the weighted-average method.

As stated earlier, the weighted-average method blends together the work that was accomplished in the prior period with the work that was accomplished in the current period. That is why it is called the weighted-average method; it averages together units and costs from both the prior and current periods. Thus, the cost in the beginning work in process inventory is added to the current period costs to determine both the total and unit costs. These computations are shown below for the shaping and milling department for May:

	Total Cost	Materials	Conversion	Whole Unit
Cost to be accounted for:				
Work in process, May 1	$ 4,000	$ 3,000	$ 1,000	
Cost added in the shaping and milling department	144,000	74,000	70,000	
Total cost (a)	$148,000	$77,000	$71,000	
Equivalent units (above) (b)		4,960	4,900	
Unit cost, (a) ÷ (b)		$15.524 +	$14.490 =	$30.014

The total unit cost that we have computed for the shaping and milling department will be used to apply cost to units that are transferred to the next department, graphics application, and will also be used to compute the cost in the ending work in process inventory. For example, each unit transferred out of the shaping and milling department to the graphics application department will carry with it a cost of $30.014. Since the costs are passed on from department to department, the unit cost of the last department, finishing and pairing, will represent the final manufacturing cost of a completed unit of product.

Step 3: Prepare a Cost Reconciliation

OBJECTIVE 6

Prepare a cost reconciliation for a period by the weighted-average method.

The purpose of a **cost reconciliation** is to show how the costs that have been charged to a department during a period are accounted for. Typically, the costs charged to a department will consist of the following:
1. Cost in the beginning work in process inventory.
2. Materials, labour, and overhead costs added during the period.
3. Cost (if any) transferred in from the preceding department.

In a production report, these costs are generally titled "Cost to be accounted for." They are so titled in step 2 above where we summarized the costs chargeable to the shaping and milling department. These costs are accounted for in a production report by computing the following amounts:
1. Cost transferred out to the next department (or to Finished Goods).
2. Cost remaining in the ending work in process inventory.

In short, when a cost reconciliation is prepared, the "Cost to be accounted for" from step 2 is reconciled with the sum of the cost transferred out during the period plus the cost in the ending work in process inventory. This concept is shown graphically in Exhibit 4–9. Study this exhibit carefully before going on to the cost reconciliation for the shaping and milling department.

EXHIBIT 4-9

Graphic Illustration of the Cost Reconciliation Part of a Production Report

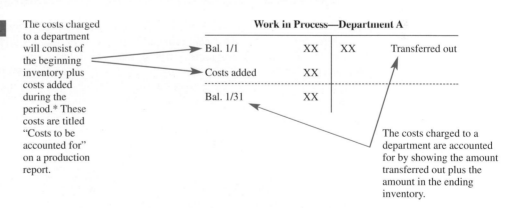

The costs charged to a department will consist of the beginning inventory plus costs added during the period.* These costs are titled "Costs to be accounted for" on a production report.

Work in Process—Department A

Bal. 1/1	XX	XX	Transferred out
Costs added	XX		
Bal. 1/31	XX		

The costs charged to a department are accounted for by showing the amount transferred out plus the amount in the ending inventory.

*Departments that follow department A (department B and so forth) will need to show the amount of cost transferred in from the preceding department.

OBJECTIVE 7

Combine the quantity schedule and equivalent units, the total and unit costs, and the cost reconciliation into a production report.

Example of a Cost Reconciliation.   The cost reconciliation depends heavily on the quantity schedule that was developed earlier. In fact, *the simplest way to prepare a cost reconciliation is to follow the quantity schedule line for line and show the cost associated with each group of units.* This is done in Exhibit 4–10, where we present a completed production report for the shaping and milling department.

The quantity schedule in the exhibit shows that **200** units were in process on May 1 and that an additional **5,000** units were started into production during the month. Looking at the "Cost to be accounted for" in the middle part of the exhibit, notice that the units in process on May 1 had $4,000 in cost attached to them and that the shaping and milling department added another $144,000 in cost to production during the month. Thus, the department has **$148,000** ($4,000 + $144,000) in cost to be accounted for.

This cost is accounted for in two ways. As shown on the quantity schedule, **4,800** units were transferred to the graphics application department, the next department in the production process. Another **400** units were still in process in the shaping and milling department at the end of the month. Thus, part of the $148,000 "Cost to be accounted for" goes with the 4,800 units to the graphics application department, and part of it remains with the 400 units in the ending work in process inventory in the shaping and milling department.

Each of the **4,800** units transferred to the graphics application department is assigned **$30.014** in cost, for a total **$144,067.** The 400 units still in process at the end of the month are assigned cost according to their stage of completion. To determine the stage of completion, we refer to the equivalent units computation and bring the equivalent units figures down to the cost reconciliation part of the report. We then assign cost to these units, using the unit cost figures already computed.

After cost has been assigned to the ending work in process inventory, the total cost that we have accounted for ($148,000) agrees with the amount that we had to account for ($148,000). Thus, the cost reconciliation is complete.

▼   ▼   ▼   ▼   ▼

MANAGERIAL ACCOUNTING IN ACTION—WRAP-UP

JERRY: Here's an example of the kind of report I can put together for you every month. This particular report is for the shaping and milling department. It follows a fairly standard format for industries like ours and is called a production report. I hope this is what you have in mind.

SAMANTHA: The quantity schedule makes sense to me. I can see we had a total of 5,200 units to account for in the department, and 4,800 of those were transferred to the next department while 400 were still in process at the end of the month. What are these "equivalent units"?

JERRY: That's the problem I mentioned earlier. While there are 400 units still in process, they are far from complete. When we compute the unit costs, it wouldn't make sense to count them as whole units.

SAMANTHA: I suppose not. I see what you are driving at. Since those 400 units are only 25% complete with respect to our conversion costs, they should only be counted as 100 units when we compute the unit costs for conversion.

JERRY: That's right. Is the rest of the report clear?

SAMANTHA: Yes, it does seem pretty clear, although I want to work the numbers through on my own to make sure I thoroughly understand the report.

JERRY: Does this report give you the information you wanted?

SAMANTHA: Yes, it does. I can tell how many units are in process, how complete they are, what happened to them, and their costs. While I know the unit costs are averages and are heavily influenced by our volume, they still can give me some idea of how well we are doing on the cost side. Thanks, Jerry.

▼   ▼   ▼   ▼   ▼

EXHIBIT 4-10   Production Report—Weighted-Average Method

DOUBLE DIAMOND SKIS
Shaping and Milling Department Production Report
(weighted-average method)

Quantity Schedule and Equivalent Units

	Quantity Schedule
Units to be accounted for:	
Work in process, May 1 (50% materials; 30% conversion added last month)	200
Started into production	5,000
Total units	5,200

	Quantity Schedule	Equivalent Units — Materials	Equivalent Units — Conversion
Units accounted for as follows:			
Transferred to the next department	4,800	4,800	4,800
Work in process, May 31 (40% materials; 25% conversion added this month)	400	160*	100†
Total units	5,200	4,960	4,900

Total and Unit Costs

	Total Cost	Materials	Conversion	Whole Unit
Cost to be accounted for:				
Work in process, May 1	$ 4,000	$ 3,000	$ 1,000	
Cost added in the shaping and milling department	144,000	74,000	70,000	
Total cost (a)	$148,000	$77,000	$71,000	
Equivalent units (above) (b)		4,960	4,900	
Unit cost, (a) ÷ (b)		$15.524 +	$14.490 =	$30.014

Cost Reconciliation

	Total Cost	Equivalent Units (above) — Materials	Equivalent Units (above) — Conversion
Cost accounted for as follows:			
Transferred to next department:			
4,800 units × $30.014 each	$144,067	4,800	4,800
Work in process, May 31:			
Materials, at $15.524 per EU	2,484	160	
Conversion, at $14.490 per EU	1,449		100
Total work in process, May 31	3,933		
Total cost	$148,000		

*40% × 400 units = 160 equivalent units.
†25% × 400 units = 100 equivalent units.
EU = Equivalent unit.

A Comment about Rounding Errors

If you use a calculator or microcomputer spreadsheet and do not round off the unit costs, there shouldn't be any discrepancy between the "Costs to be accounted for" and the "Costs accounted for" in the cost reconciliation. However, if you round off unit costs, the two figures will not always exactly agree. For the report in Exhibit 4–10, the two figures do agree, but this will not always happen. In all of the homework assignments and other materials, we follow two rules: (1) all unit costs are rounded off to three decimal places as in Exhibit 4–10, and (2) any adjustment needed to reconcile the "Costs accounted for" with the "Costs to be accounted for" is made to the cost "transferred" amount rather than to the ending inventory.

INNOVATIONS IN COSTING SYSTEMS

OBJECTIVE 8
State the conditions under which operation costing is useful to management, and explain the impact of a flexible manufacturing system on job-order and process costing.

The costing systems discussed in Chapters 3 and 4 represent the two ends of a continuum. On one end we have job-order costing, which is used by companies that produce many different items—generally to customers' specifications. On the other end we have process costing, which is used by companies that produce basically homogeneous products in large quantities. Between these two extremes there are many hybrid systems that include characteristics of both job-order and process costing. One of these hybrids—called **operation costing**—is widely used in actual practice. Also, the ends of the job-order/process continuum are moving closer together as a result of the use of flexible manufacturing systems (FMS) in various industries. Both operation costing and the impact of FMS on job-order and process costing are discussed in following sections.

Operation Costing

Many companies have products that possess some common characteristics and some individual characteristics. Shoes, for example, have certain common characteristics in that all styles involve cutting and sewing that can be done on a repetitive basis, using the same equipment and following the same basic procedures. These same shoes, however, can also have some individual characteristics in that some may be made of expensive leather

Shoes are a good example of operation costing. Several steps are the same for all shoes, while different styles of shoes will have individual characteristics and, therefore, need different or additional steps.

and others may be made of inexpensive vinyl. When products have some common characteristics and some individual characteristics, such as in the case of shoes, a system known as *operation costing* is often used to determine unit costs for management.

As mentioned above, operation costing is a hybrid system in that it employs certain aspects of both job-order and process costing. Products are typically handled in batches when operation costing is in use, with each batch charged for the specific materials used in its production. In this sense, operation costing is similar to job-order costing. Labour and overhead costs are accumulated by operation or by department, however, and these costs are assigned to batches on an average per unit basis, as done in process costing. If shoes are being produced, for example, each style is charged the same per unit conversion cost, regardless of the style involved, but charged with its specific materials cost. Thus, the company is able to distinguish between batches in terms of materials, but it is able to employ the simplicity of a process costing system for labour and overhead costs.

Examples of other products for which operation costing is frequently used include electronic equipment (such as semiconductors), textiles, clothing, and jewellery (such as rings, bracelets, and medallions). Products of this type are typically produced in batches, but they can vary considerably from model to model or from style to style in terms of the cost of raw material inputs. Therefore, an operation costing system is well suited for providing necessary cost information for management.

Flexible Manufacturing Systems

In the two preceding chapters, we discussed the use of the FMS concept, in which plants are heavily automated and the activities are organized around cells, or islands, of automated equipment. The FMS concept is having a major impact on costing in several ways. One of these is through allowing companies to switch their systems from the more costly job-order approach to the less costly process or operation approaches. This switching is made possible through the fact that FMS is proving to be highly efficient in reducing the setup time required between products and jobs. With setup time only a small fraction of previous levels, companies are able to move between products and jobs with about the same speed as if they were working in a continuous, process-type environment. The result is that these companies are able to employ process costing techniques in situations that previously required job-order costing. As the use of FMS grows (and becomes even more efficient), some managers predict that job-order costing will slowly disappear except in a few, selected industries.

A further impact of FMS is through its focus on cells rather than on departments. Although production reports are still prepared in FMS settings, these reports are either much broader to include the entire production process (many cells) or much narrower to include only a single cell or workstation. As stated earlier, if JIT is practised, then the production report becomes greatly simplified, regardless of the level at which it is prepared.

SUMMARY

Process costing is used in those manufacturing situations where homogeneous products are produced on a continuous basis. A process costing system is similar to a job-order costing system in that (1) both systems have the same basic purpose of providing data for the manager, (2) both systems use the same manufacturing accounts, and (3) costs flow through the manufacturing accounts in basically the same way in both systems. A process costing system differs from a job-order system in that (1) a single product is involved, (2) costs are accumulated by department (rather than by job), (3) the department production report replaces the job cost sheet, and (4) unit costs are computed by department (rather than by job).

To compute unit costs in a department, the department's equivalent units must be determined. Equivalent units can be computed in two ways—by the weighted-average method and by the FIFO method. The weighted-average method treats partially completed units in the beginning work in process inventory as if they were started and completed during the current period. The FIFO method distinguishes between work completed in the prior period and work completed currently, so that equivalent units represent only work completed during the current period.

The activity in a department is summarized on a production report. There are three separate (though highly interrelated) parts to a production report. The first part is a quantity schedule, which shows the flow of units through a department during a period and a computation of the equivalent units. The second part consists of a computation of unit costs, with unit costs being provided individually for materials, labour, and overhead as well as in total for the period. The third part consists of a cost reconciliation, which summarizes all cost flows through a department for a period.

Hybrid combinations of job costing and process costing are illustrated by the concept of operation costing. The homogeneity of the conversion process permits process costing to be applied to unique raw materials. Flexible manufacturing systems are also providing the opportunity to use process costing because of the ease of changing from one type of product to another.

REVIEW PROBLEM: PROCESS COST FLOWS AND REPORTS

Wicker Company manufactures a single product and uses a process costing system. The product goes through two sequential departments, A and B. Information relating to the company's operations for April 19x1 is given below.

a. Raw materials were issued for use in production: department A, $851,000; and department B, $629,000.
b. Direct labour costs were incurred: department A, $330,000; and department B, $270,000.
c. Manufacturing overhead cost was applied to products: department A, $665,000; and department B, $405,000.
d. Products that were complete as to processing in department A were transferred to department B, $1,850,000.
e. Products that were complete as to processing in department B were transferred to Finished Goods, $3,200,000.

Required

1. Prepare journal entries to record items (a) through (e) above.
2. Post the journal entries from (1) to T-accounts. The balance in department A's Work in Process account on April 1 was $150,000; the balance in department B's Work in Process account was $70,000. After posting entries to the T-accounts, find the ending balance in each department's Work in Process account.
3. Prepare a production report for department A for April. The following additional information is available regarding production in department A during the month:

Production data:

Units in process, April 1: 100% complete as to

materials, 60% complete as to labour and overhead   30,000

Units started into production during April   420,000

Units completed and transferred to department B.   370,000

Units in process, April 30: 50% complete as to

materials, 25% complete as to labour and overhead   80,000

Cost data:

Work in process inventory, April 1:

Materials . . . . $ 92,000

Labour   21,000

Overhead   37,000

Total cost $150,000

Cost added during April [see the entries in (1)]:

Materials $851,000

Labour   330,000

Overhead   665,000

Solution to Review Problem

1. a.   Work in Process—Department A   851,000

Work in Process—Department B   629,000

Raw Materials   1,480,000

b.   Work in Process—Department A   330,000

Work in Process—Department B   270,000

Salaries and Wages Payable   600,000

c.   Work in Process—Department A   665,000

Manufacturing Overhead—Department A   665,000

Work in Process—Department B   405,000

Manufacturing Overhead—Department B   405,000

d.   Work in Process—Department B   1,850,000

Work in Process—Department A   1,850,000

e.   Finished Goods   3,200,000

Work in Process—Department B   3,200,000

2.

Raw Materials					Salaries and Wages Payable		
Bal.	XXX	(a)	1,480,000			(b)	600,000

Work in Process—Department A					Manufacturing Overhead—Department A		
Bal.	150,000	(d)	1,850,000	(Various actual costs)		(c)	665,000
(a)	851,000						
(b)	330,000						
(c)	665,000						
Bal.	146,000						

					Manufacturing Overhead—Department B		
				(Various actual costs)		(c)	405,000

Work in Process—Department B					Finished Goods		
Bal.	70,000	(e)	3,200,000	Bal.	XXX		
(a)	629,000			(e)	3,200,000		
(b)	270,000						
(c)	405,000						
(d)	1,850,000						
Bal.	24,000						

3.

WICKER COMPANY
Production Report—Department A
For the Month Ended April 30, 19x1

Quantity Schedule and Equivalent Units

	Quantity Schedule	Equivalent Units		
		Materials	Labour	Overhead
Units to be accounted for:				
Work in process, April 1 (all materials, 60% labour and overhead added last month)	30,000	(Work done last month)		
Started into production	420,000			
Total units	450,000			
Units accounted for as follows:				
Transferred to department B	370,000	370,000	370,000	370,000
Work in process, April 30 (50% materials, 25% labour and overhead added this month)	80,000	40,000*	20,000*	20,000*
Total units	450,000	410,000	390,000	390,000

Total and Unit Costs

	Total Cost	Materials	Labour	Overhead
Cost to be accounted for:				
Work in process, April 1	$ 150,000	$ 92,000	$ 21,000	$ 37,000
Cost added by the department	1,846,000	851,000	330,000	665,000
Total cost (a)	$1,996,000	$943,000	$351,000	$702,000
Equivalent units (b)	—	410,000	390,000	390,000
Unit cost, (a) ÷ (b)	$ 5.00 =	$2.30 +	$0.90 +	$1.80

Cost Reconciliation

	Total Cost	Equivalent Units (above)		
		Materials	Labour	Overhead
Cost accounted for as follows:				
Transferred to department B:				
370,000 units × $5.00	$1,850,000	370,000	370,000	370,000
Work in process, April 30:				
Materials, at $2.30 per EU	92,000	40,000		
Labour, at $0.90 per EU	18,000		20,000	
Overhead, at $1.80 per EU	36,000			20,000
Total work in process	146,000			
Total cost	$1,996.000			

*Materials: 80,000 units × 50% = 40,000 equivalent units; labour and overhead: 80,000 units × 25% = 20,000 equivalent units.
EU = Equivalent unit.

KEY TERMS FOR REVIEW

OBJECTIVE 9
Define or explain the key terms listed at the end of the chapter.

Conversion cost   Direct labour cost combined with manufacturing overhead cost. (p. 168)

Cost reconciliation   The part of a production report that shows what costs a department has to account for during a period and how those costs are accounted for. (p. 177)

Equivalent units   The number of units that would have been produced during a period if all of a department's efforts had resulted in completed units of product. (p. 171)

FIFO method   A method of accounting for cost flows in a process costing system in which equivalent units and unit costs relate only to work done during the current period. (p. 171)

Operation costing   A costing system used when products are manufactured in batches and when the products have some common characteristics and some individual characteristics. This system handles materials the same as in job-order costing and labour and overhead the same as in process costing. (p. 180)

Parallel processing   A method of arranging processing departments in which, after a certain point, the units are split to go through different processing departments. (p. 164)

Process costing   A costing method used in those industries that produce homogeneous products on a continuous basis. (p. 162)

Processing department   Any location in a factory where work is performed on a product and where materials, labour, or overhead costs are added to the product. (p. 164)

Production report   A report that summarizes all activity in a department's Work in Process account during a period and that contains three sections: a quantity schedule and a computation of equivalent units, unit costs, and a cost reconciliation. (p. 163)

Quantity schedule   The part of a production report that shows the flow of units through a department during a period. (p. 176)

Sequential processing   A method of arranging processing departments in which all units flow in sequence from one department to another. (p. 164)

Transferred-in cost   The amount of cost attached to units of product that have been received from a prior processing department. (p. 166)

Weighted-average method   A method of accounting for cost flows in a process costing system in which units in the beginning work in process inventory are treated as if they were started and completed during the current period. (p. 171)

APPENDIX 4A: FIFO METHOD

The FIFO method of process costing differs from the weighted-average method in two basic ways: (1) the computation of equivalent units, and (2) the way in which costs of beginning inventory are treated in the cost reconciliation report. The FIFO method is generally considered more accurate than the weighted-average method, but it is more complex. The complexity is not a problem for computers, but the FIFO method is a little more difficult to understand and to learn than the weighted-average method.

Equivalent Units—FIFO Method

OBJECTIVE 10
Compute the equivalent units of production by the FIFO method.

The computation of equivalent units under the FIFO method differs from the computation under the weighted-average method in two ways.

First, the "units transferred out" figure is divided into two parts. One part consists of the units from the beginning inventory that were completed and transferred out, and the other part consists of the units that were both *started* and *completed* during the current period.

Second, full consideration is given to the amount of work expended during the current period on units in the *beginning* work in process inventory as well as on units in the ending inventory. Thus, under the FIFO method, it is necessary to convert both inventories to an equivalent units basis. For the beginning inventory, the equivalent units represent the work done *to complete* the units; for the ending inventory, the equivalent units represent the work done to bring the units to a stage of partial completion at the end of the period (the same as with the weighted-average method).

EXHIBIT 4–11

Equivalent Units
of Production:
FIFO Method

	Materials	Conversion
Work in process, May 1:		
200 units × (100% – 50%)*	100	
200 units × (100% – 30%)*		140
Units started and completed in May	4,600†	4,600†
Work in process, May 31:		
400 units × 40%	160	
400 units × 25%		100
Equivalent units of production	4,860	4,840

*This is the work needed *to complete* the units in beginning inventory.
†4,800 units transferred out to the next department – 200 units in beginning inventory. The FIFO method assumes that the units in beginning inventory are finished first.

In summary, the equivalent units figure under the FIFO method consists of three amounts:

1. The work needed *to complete* the units in the beginning inventory.
2. The work expended on the units *started* and *completed* during the period.
3. The work expended on partially completed units in the ending inventory.

To illustrate, refer again to the data for the shaping and milling department at Double Diamond Skis. The department completed and transferred 4,800 units to the next department, the graphics application department, during May. Since 200 of these units came from the beginning inventory, the shaping and milling department must have started and completed 4,600 units during May. The 200 units in the beginning inventory were 50% complete with respect to materials and only 30% complete with respect to conversion costs when the month started. Thus, to complete these units the department must have added another 50% of materials costs and another 70% of conversion costs (100% – 30% = 70%). Following this line of reasoning, the equivalent units for the department for May would be computed as shown in Exhibit 4–11.

Comparison of Equivalent Units of Production under the Weighted-Average and FIFO Methods

Stop at this point and compare the data in Exhibit 4–11 with the data in Exhibit 4–6 in the chapter, which shows the computation of equivalent units under the weighted-average method. Also refer to Exhibit 4–12, which provides a visual comparison of the two methods.

The essential difference between the two methods is that the weighted-average method blends work and costs from the prior period with work and costs in the current period, whereas the FIFO method cleanly separates the two periods. To see this more clearly, consider the following comparison of the two calculations of equivalent units:

	Materials	Conversion
Equivalent units—weighted-average method	4,960	4,900
Less equivalent units in beginning inventory:		
200 units × 50%	100	
200 units × 30%		60
Equivalent units of production—FIFO method	4,860	4,840

From the above, it is evident that the FIFO method removes the equivalent units that were already in beginning inventory from the equivalent units as defined using the weighted-average method. Thus, the FIFO method isolates the equivalent units due to

EXHIBIT 4-12

Visual Perspective of
Equivalent Units of
Production

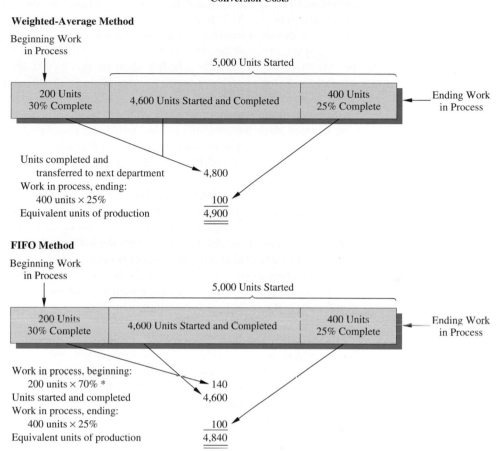

DOUBLE DIAMOND SKIS
Shaping and Milling Department
Conversion Costs

Weighted-Average Method

Beginning Work
in Process

5,000 Units Started

| 200 Units 30% Complete | 4,600 Units Started and Completed | 400 Units 25% Complete |

Ending Work
in Process

Units completed and transferred to next department	4,800
Work in process, ending:	
400 units × 25%	100
Equivalent units of production	4,900

FIFO Method

Beginning Work
in Process

5,000 Units Started

| 200 Units 30% Complete | 4,600 Units Started and Completed | 400 Units 25% Complete |

Ending Work
in Process

Work in process, beginning:	
200 units × 70% *	140
Units started and completed	4,600
Work in process, ending:	
400 units × 25%	100
Equivalent units of production	4,840

* 100% – 30% = 70%. This 70% represents the work needed to complete the units in the beginning inventory.

work performed during the current period. The weighted-average method blends together the equivalent units already in beginning inventory with the equivalent units due to work performed in the current period.

Since the weighted-average method blends together units and costs from different periods, it can be argued that the FIFO method is more accurate. While the FIFO method is more complex and difficult to learn, computers can handle the additional complexity without any problem once they have been programmed.

Production Report—FIFO Method

When the FIFO method is used to account for cost flows in a process costing system, the steps followed in preparing a production report are the same as those discussed earlier for the weighted-average method. However, since the FIFO method makes a distinction between units in the opening inventory and units started during the year, the cost reconciliation portion of the report is more complex under the FIFO method than it is under the weighted-average method. To illustrate the FIFO method, we will again use the data for Double Diamond Skis found on page 172.

OBJECTIVE 11
Prepare a quantity
schedule for a period
by the FIFO method.

Step 1: Prepare a Quantity Schedule and Compute the Equivalent Units.

There is only one difference between a quantity schedule prepared under the FIFO method and one prepared under the weighted-average method. This difference relates to units transferred out. As explained earlier in our discussion of equivalent units, the FIFO method divides units transferred out into two parts. One part consists of the units in the opening inventory, and the other part consists of the units started and completed during the current period. A quantity schedule showing this format for units transferred out is presented in Exhibit 4–13, along with a computation of equivalent units for the month.

We explained earlier that in computing equivalent units under the FIFO method, we must first show the amount of work required *to complete* the units in the beginning inventory. We then show the number of units started and completed during the period, and finally we show the amount of work *completed* on the units still in process at the end of the period. Carefully trace through these computations in Exhibit 4–13.

OBJECTIVE 12
Compute the unit costs
for a period by the
FIFO method.

Step 2: Compute the Total and Unit Costs.

In computing unit costs under the FIFO method, we use only those costs that were incurred during the current period, and we ignore any costs in the beginning work in process inventory. The reason we ignore costs in the beginning inventory is that under the FIFO method, *unit costs are intended to relate only to work done during the current period.*

The unit costs computed in Exhibit 4–13 are used to cost units of product transferred to the next department; in addition, they are used to show the cost attached to partially completed units in the ending work in process inventory.

OBJECTIVE 13
Prepare a cost
reconciliation for a
period by the FIFO
method.

Step 3: Prepare a Cost Reconciliation.

In the main body of the chapter we learned that the purpose of cost reconciliation is to show how the costs charged to a department during a period are accounted for. We also learned that the best way to prepare a cost reconciliation is to follow the quantity schedule line for line and show the costs associated with each group of units.

When the FIFO method is used, two cost elements are associated with the units in the beginning work in process inventory. The first element is the cost carried over from the prior period. The second element is the cost needed *to complete* these units. For the shaping and milling department, $4,000 in cost was carried over from last month. In the cost reconciliation in Exhibit 4–13 we add to thms figure the $1,523 in materials cost and $2,025 in conversion cost needed to complete these units. Note from the exhibit that these materials and conversion cost figures are computed by multiplying the unit costs for materials and conversion times the equivalent units of work needed *to complete* the items that were in the beginning inventory. (The equivalent units figures used in this computation are brought down from the "Equivalent units" portion of the production report.)

For units started and completed during the month, we simply multiply the number of units started and completed by the total cost per unit to determine the amount transferred out. This would be $136,570 (4,600 units × $29.689 = $136,570) for the department.

Finally, the amount of cost attached to the ending work in process inventory is computed by multiplying the unit cost figures for the month times the equivalent units for materials and conversion costs in the ending inventory. Once again, the equivalent units needed for this computation are brought down from the "Equivalent units" portion of the production report.

Exhibit 4–14 summarizes the major similarities and differences between production reports prepared under the weighted-average and FIFO methods.

EXHIBIT 4-13

Production Report—
FIFO Method

DOUBLE DIAMOND SKIS
Shaping and Milling Department Production Report
(FIFO method)

Quantity Schedule and Equivalent Units

	Quantity Schedule
Units to be accounted for:	
Work in process, May 1 (50% materials; 30% conversion added last month)	200
Started into production	5,000
Total units	5,200

	Quantity Schedule	Equivalent Units Materials	Equivalent Units Conversion
Units accounted for as follows:			
Transferred to next department:			
From the beginning inventory*	200	100	140
Started and completed this month†	4,600	4,600	4,600
Work in process, May 31 (40% materials; 25% conversion added this month)‡	400	160	100
Total units	5,200	4,860	4,840

Total and Unit Costs

	Total Cost	Materials	Conversion	Whole Unit
Cost to be accounted for:				
Work in process, May 1	$ 4,000			
Cost added in the department (a)	144,000	$74,000	$70,000	
Total cost	$148,000			
Equivalent units (above) (b)		4,860	4,840	
Unit cost, (a) ÷ (b)		$15.226 +	$14.463 =	$29.689

Cost Reconciliation

	Total Cost	Equivalent Units (above) Materials	Equivalent Units (above) Conversion
Cost accounted for as follows:			
Transferred to next department:			
From the beginning inventory:			
Cost in the beginning inventory	$ 4,000		
Cost to complete these units:			
Materials, at $15.226 per EU	1,523	100*	
Conversion, at $14.463 per EU	2,025		140*
Total cost	7,548		
Units started and completed this month, at $29.689 per unit	136,570	4,600†	4,600†
Total cost transferred	144,118		
Work in process, May 31:			
Materials, at $15.226 per EU	2,436	160‡	
Conversion, at $14.463 per EU	1,446		100‡
Total work in process, May 31	3,882		
Total cost	$148,000		

*Materials: 200 × (100% − 50%) = 100 equivalent units. Conversion: 200 × (100% − 30%) = 140 equivalent units.
†4,800 units started − 200 units in beginning inventory = 4,600 units started and completed.
‡Materials: 400 × (40%) = 160 equivalent units. Conversion: 400 × (25%) = 100 equivalent units.
EU = Equivalent units.

EXHIBIT 4-14

A Comparison of
Production Report
Content

Weighted-Average Method	FIFO Method
Quantity Schedule and Equivalent Units	
1. The quantity schedule includes all units transferred out in a single figure.	1. The quantity schedule divides the units transferred out into two parts. One part consists of units in the beginning inventory, and the other part consists of units started and completed during the current period.
2. In computing equivalent units, the units in the beginning inventory are treated as if they were started and completed during the current period.	2. Only work needed to *complete* units in the beginning inventory is included in the computation of equivalent units. Units started and completed during the current period are shown as a separate figure.
Total and Unit Costs	
1. The "Cost to be accounted for" part of the report is the same for both metlods.	1. The "Cost to be accounted for" part of the report is the same for both methods.
2. Costs in the beginning inventory are added in with costs of the current period in unit cost computations.	2. Only costs of the current period are included in unit cost computations.
3. Unit costs will contain some element of cost from the prior period.	3. Unit costs will contain only elements of cost from the current period.
Cost Reconciliation	
1. All units transferred out are treated the same, regardless of whether they were part of the beginning inventory or started and completed during the period.	1. Units transferred out are divided into two groups: (a) units in the beginning inventory and (b) units started and completed during the period.
2. Units in the ending inventory have cost applied to them in the same way under both methods.	2. Units in the ending inventory have cost applied to them in the same way under both methods.

A Comparison of Costing Methods

In most situations, the weighted-average and FIFO methods will produce unit costs that are nearly the same. Either erratic prices or erratic production levels would be required to generate much of a real difference in unit costs under the two methods. This is because the weighted-average method will blend the unit costs from the prior period with the unit costs of the current period. Unless these unit costs differ greatly, the blending will not make much difference.

Nevertheless, from the standpoint of cost control, the FIFO method is clearly superior to the weighted-average method. The reason is that current performance should be measured in relation to costs of the current period only, and the weighted-average method mixes these costs with costs of the prior period. Thus, under the weighted-average method, the manager's apparent performance is influenced by what happened in the prior period. This problem does not arise under the FIFO method, since it makes a clear distinction between costs of prior periods and costs incurred during the current period.

On the other hand, some managers feel that the weighted-average method is simpler to apply than the FIFO method. Although this may have been true in the past when much accounting work was done by hand, due to the advent of the computer it is doubtful whether it is still true today. The computer can handle either method with ease. The FIFO method would require a more complex programming effort when a process costing system is first set up, but after that there should be little difference between the two methods so far as difficulty in operating the system is concerned.

JIT and Process Costing

JIT impacts on process costing in two ways. First, it largely eliminates the differences in unit costs between the FIFO and weighted-average methods; and second, it allows companies that previously used job-order costing to use process costing instead.

JIT Impact on Unit Costs.   The use of JIT has resulted in a significant narrowing of the difference in unit costs between the FIFO and weighted-average methods, and in some cases this difference has disappeared entirely. The reason is as follows: Recall that under the JIT concept, raw materials are received *just in time* to go into production and parts are completed *just in time* to be assembled into products. As a result, under JIT the raw materials and work in process inventories are either eliminated or reduced to nominal levels. Since the difference between the FIFO and weighted-average methods centres on how the costs of work in process inventories are handled, *the elimination of these inventories through JIT automatically eliminates the distinction between the two costing methods.*

APPENDIX 4B: SHRINKAGE AND LOST UNITS

OBJECTIVE 14

Compute the cost of lost units or shrinkage.

The illustrations presented in Chapter 4 assume units that are in process are either completed or still awaiting completion at the end of each period. In reality, units can disappear because of evaporation, losses, or rejection. Such missing units can be considered a normal part of the processing or may be deemed abnormal. Abnormal losses can be thought of as costs akin to unusual losses studied in financial accounting. Normal losses would be normal costs of operating the process department.

Two accounting treatments are prevalent for normal losses. One, the amount of the loss can be charged to a specific loss account which could be charged to manufacturing overhead. Two, the amount of the loss could be spread over all the good units of work done during the period.

If significant in amount and truly abnormal, abnormal losses should always be assigned to the unusual section of the income statement where they can be offset by any recoveries from insurance or other means.

The following illustrates the two alternative treatments of normal losses. The weighted-average method is used for illustration.

Case 1: Normal Loss Charged to Manufacturing Overhead

Assume Stabler Chemical had a machine breakdown causing a loss of 10,000 units that were 100 percent complete as to materials and 60% complete for labour and overhead. Exhibit 4–15 presents the cost of production report for Stabler Chemical after the assumption is included in the data for the problem. The lost units are included in the units accounted for and the equivalent units lost become a separate line in the equivalent units calculation. When costs are accounted for, the lost units, whether normal (as they are in this case) or abnormal, are costed according to their equivalent units completed. The journal entry for normal losses would be:

Manufacturing Overhead	11,272	
Work in Process		11,272

The total number of units lost, both normal and abnormal, can be determined from the quantity schedule. Units accounted for have to be transferred out, in Work in Process at the end of the period, or lost. Thus, even when lost units cannot be physically counted, they can be mathematically calculated by knowing the total units to account for. What is more difficult is to distinguish normal from abnormal losses. A common approach is to use a percentage to express what is normal. Usually this percentage is expressed in terms of the number of units that pass a prespecified inspection point. Thus, in Exhibit 4–15, the inspection point could be at 60% of the total production conversion process. If, for example, 5% of good output is considered to be normal losses, then 8,000 (0.05 × 160,000) units would be normal losses and 2,000 abnormal. Notice the ending Work in Process is only 40% complete so it has not reached the inspection point. Thus, the 5% figure would not be applied to the 30,000 units in the ending Work in Process.

An assumption is needed here to avoid a significant complexity. The preceding entry assumes predetermined overhead is used so that $11,272 is an actual overhead cost that was previously estimated when the overhead rate was calculated. As mentioned in Appendix B of Chapter 3, because the $11,272 includes $4,632 for overhead, overhead is being charged to overhead resulting in some cost duplication, but the amount of error introduced is assumed to be minor.

If the losses were considered to be abnormal, the entry to record the loss would be:

Unusual Loss—Machine Breakdown.	11,272	
Work in Process		11,272

Case 2: Normal Loss Charged to All Good Output

Assume Stabler Chemical had normal evaporation of liquid evenly through the process. The illustrated solution is presented in Exhibit 4–16. Notice first that the amount of loss is not given in units. The units lost have to be determined from the quantity schedule by computing the difference between the total units to be accounted for and what is known to have been completed or is still in process.

The number of units lost is assigned a 0 equivalent units amount. The resulting smaller number of units is used to determine the unit costs. When costs are accounted for, the unit costs are greater because they include the costs of the evaporation or normal losses. Thus, no entry is required to record the normal loss.

Careful thinking about these two cases presents a number of theoretical issues as to where to charge losses and whether or not it is fair to charge Work in Process with losses if the units in this ending inventory have not been inspected at their stage of completion.

Exhibit 4–15 provides an opportunity to look at one type of complication. Normal losses have to be calculated and separated from abnormal losses where both types of losses are present. In Exhibit 4–15, 10,000 units of normal losses represent all of the units lost. In addition, these units were lost at the 60% stage of production. If, however, the ending work in process had reached or passed the 60% stage, then normal losses could be separated from the known total losses by applying the normal loss percentage to both the completed units and the ending work in process.

For example, if 10,000 were the total lost units and the ending work in process was 70% complete instead of the assumed 40%, then a normal loss percentage of, say, 5% would be applied as follows to separate normal and abnormal:

$$5\% \times 160,000 \;=\; 8,000 \text{ (from completed items)}$$
$$5\% \times 30,000 \;=\; \underline{1,500} \text{ (from ending work in process)}$$

Total normal losses	9,500
Abnormal	500 (balance of losses)
Total losses	10,000

EXHIBIT 4-15   Production Report—Weighted-Average Method

Quantity Schedule and Equivalent Units

	Quantity Schedule
Units to be accounted for:	
Work in process, beginning (all materials, 30% labour and overhead added last month)...	20,000
Started into production	180,000
Total units to be accounted for	200,000

		Equivalent Units (EU)		
		Materials	Labour	Overhead
Units accounted for as follows:				
Transferred out	160,000	160,000	160,000	160,000
Units lost, normal (100% of materials, 60% labour and overhead)	10,000	10,000	6,000	6,000
Work in process, ending (all materials, 40% labour and overhead added this month)	30,000	30,000	12,000*	12,000*
Total units accounted for...	200,000	200,000	178,000	178,000

Unit Costs

	Total	Materials	Labour	Overhead
Work in process, beginning..	$ 17,000	$ 8,000	$ 3,600	$ 5,400
Cost added by the department......................................	283,000	63,000	88,000	132,000
Total cost (a)	$300,000	$ 71,000	$ 91,600	$137,400
Equivalent units (b)..		200,000	178,000	178,000
Unit cost, (a) ÷ (b)...	$1.642	= $0.355	+ $0.515	+ $0.772

Cost Reconciliation

	Costs
Cost to be accounted for	
Work in process, beginning.......................................	$ 17,000
Cost added by the department......................................	283,000
Total cost to be accounted for	$300,000

		Equivalent Units (EU)		
Cost accounted for as follows:				
Transferred to cooking: 160,000 × $1.642	$262,720	160,000	160,000	160,000
Normal losses				
Materials (at $0.355 × 10,000)	3,550	10,000		
Labour (at $0.515 × 6,000)	3,090		6,000	
Overhead (at $0.772 × 6,000)	4,632			6,000
Total normal losses	11,272			
Work in process, ending:				
Materials (at $0.355 × 30,000)	10,650	30,000		
Labour (at $0.515 × 12,000)	6,180		12,000	
Overhead (at $0.772 × 12,000)	9,264			12,000
Total work in process, ending	26,094			
Total cost accounted for	300,086			
Less: Rounding	86			
Total cost accounted for	$300,000			

* 40% × 30,000 units = 12,000 equivalent units.
EU = Equivalent unit.

EXHIBIT 4-16 Production Report—Weighted-Average Method

Quantity Schedule

	Quantity Schedule
Units to be accounted for:	
Work in process, beginning (all materials, 30% labour and overhead added last month).	20,000
Started into production	180,000
Total units to be accounted for	200,000

		Equivalent Units (EU)		
		Materials	Labour	Overhead
Units accounted for as follows:				
Transferred out	160,000	160,000	160,000	160,000
Units lost—normal	10,000*	–0–	–0–	–0–
Work in process, ending (all materials, 40% labour and overhead added this month)	30,000	30,000	12,000†	12,000†
Total units accounted for.	200,000	190,000	172,000	172,000

Unit Costs

	Total	Materials	Labour	Overhead
Work in process, beginning.	$ 17,000	$ 8,000	$ 3,600	$ 5,400
Cost added by the department.	283,000	63,000	88,000	132,000
Total cost (a)	$300,000	$71,000	$91,600	$137,400
Equivalent units (b).		190,000	172,000	172,000
Unit cost, (a) ÷ (b).	$1.706	= $0.374	+ $0.533	+ $0.799

Cost Reconciliation

	Costs
Cost to be accounted for:	
Work in process, beginning.	$ 17,000
Cost added by the department.	283,000
Total cost to be accounted for	$300,000

		Equivalent Units (EU)		
Cost accounted for as follows:				
Transferred to cooking: (160,000 × $1.706)	$272,960	160,000	160,000	160,000
Work in process, ending:				
Materials (at $0.374 × 30,000)	11,220	30,000		
Labour (at $0.533 × 12,000)	6,396		12,000	
Overhead (at $0.799 × 12,000)	9,588			12,000
Total work in process, ending	27,204			
Total cost accounted for	300,164			
Less: Rounding	164			
Total cost accounted for	$300,000			

* Total units to be accounted for 200,000 – units transferred 160,000 – units in process, ending 30,000 = 10,000 units lost.

† 40% × 30,000 units = 12,000 EU.

EU = Equivalent unit.

QUESTIONS

4–1 Under what conditions would it be appropriate to use a process costing system?

4–2 What similarities exist between job-order and process costing?

4–3 Costs are accumulated by job in a job-order costing system; how are costs accumulated in a process costing system?

4–4 What two essential features characterize any processing department?

4–5 Distinguish between departments arranged in a sequential pattern and departments arranged in a parallel pattern.

4–6 Why is cost accumulation easier under a process costing system than it is under a job-order costing system?

4–7 How many Work in Process accounts are maintained in a company using process costing?

4–8 Assume that a company has two processing departments, mixing and firing. Prepare a journal entry to show a transfer of partially completed units from the mixing department to the firing department.

4–9 Assume again that a company has two processing departments, mixing and firing. Explain which costs might be added to the firing department's Work in Process account during a period.

4–10 What is mean by the term *equivalent units of production?*

4–11 Under the weighted-average method, what assumption is made relative to units in the beginning work in process inventory when equivalent units and unit costs are computed?

4–12 (Appendix 4A) How does the computation of equivalent units under the FIFO method differ from the computation of equivalent units under the weighted-average method?

4–13 What is a quantity schedule, and what purpose does it serve?

4–14 (Appendix 4A) On the cost reconciliation part of the production report, the weighted-average method treats all units transferred out in the same way. How does this differ from the FIFO method of handling units transferred out?

4–15 Under process costing, it is often suggested that a product is like a rolling snowball as it moves from department to department. Why is this an apt comparison?

4–16 (Appendix 4A) From the standpoint of cost control, why is the FIFO method superior to the weighted-average method?

4–17 Is homogeneity of products necessary for process costing to be an effective costing system?

4–18 (Appendix 4A) If you were asked to determine whether or not costs this period were in line with those of last period, would you prefer a FIFO or weighted-average costing method? Would the size and stability of the amount of work in process alter your conclusion?

4–19 Why is homogeneous treatment of products by a department necessary for it to use process costing? *Hint:* Consider carefully the law of mathematics $ax + ay = a(x + y)$.

4–20 Why is a single unit cost permitted for units started and completed, while unit costs for each cost component have to be used for ending work in process?

4–21 (Appendix 4B) Describe two methods of dealing with normal losses in a process.

4–22 (Appendix 4B) Which of the two methods of dealing with normal losses would you prefer from a management control viewpoint? Why?

4–23 Watkins Trophies, Inc., produces thousands of medallions made of bronze, silver, and gold. The medallions are identical except for the materials used in their manufacture. What costing system would you advise the company to use?

4–24   Give examples of companies that might use operation costing.

4–25   Job-order costing is likely to increase in importance as a result of the widespread use of flexible manufacturing systems? Do you agree? Explain.

4–26   (Appendix 4A) How does the use of JIT reduce or eliminate the difference in unit costs between the FIFO and weighted-average methods?

EXERCISES

E4–1   Lindex Company manufactures a product that goes through three departments, A, B, and C. Information relating to activity in department A during October is given below:

		Percent Completed	
	Units	Materials	Conversion
Work in process, October 1	50,000	90	60
Started into production	390,000		
Completed and transferred to department B	410,000		
Work in process, October 31	30,000	70	50

Required

Compute the equivalent units for October, assuming that the company uses the weighted-average method of accounting for units and costs.

E4–2   (Appendix 4A) Refer to the data for Lindex Company in E4–1.

Required

Compute the equivalent units of production for October, assuming that the company uses the FIFO method of accounting for units and costs.

E4–3   Societe Clemeau, a company located in Lyons, France, manufactures cement for the construction industry in the immediate area. Data relating to the kilograms of cement processed through the mixing department, the first department in the production process, are provided below for May:

		Percent Completed	
	Kilograms of Cement	Materials	
Conversion			
Work in process, May 1	80,000	80	20
Started into production during May	300,000	—	—

Required

1. Compute the number of kilograms of cement completed and transferred out of the mixing department during May.
2. Prepare a quantity schedule for the mixing department for May, assuming that the company uses the weighted-average method.

E4–4   (Appendix 4A) Refer to the data for Societe Clemeau in E4–3.

Required

1. Compute the number of kilograms of cement completed and transferred out of the mixing department during May.
2. Prepare a quantity schedule for the mixing department for May, assuming that the company uses the FIFO method.

E4–5   Gulf Fisheries, Inc., processes tuna for various distributors. Two departments are involved, department 1 and department 2. Data relating to kilograms of tuna processed in department 1 during May are given below:

	Kilograms of Tuna	Percent Completed*
Work in process, May 1	30,000	55
Started into processing during May	480,000	—
Work in process, May 31	20,000	90

*Labour and overhead only.

All materials are added at the beginning of processing in department 1. Labour and overhead costs are incurred uniformly throughout processing.

Required

Prepare a quantity schedule and a computation of equivalent units for May, assuming that the company uses the weighted-average method of accounting for units.

E4–6 (Appendix 4A) Refer to the data for Gulf Fisheries, Inc., in E4–5.

Required

Prepare a quantity schedule and a computation of equivalent units for May, assuming that the company uses the FIFO method of accounting for units.

E4–7 Schneider Brot is a bread-baking company located in Aachen, Germany, near the Dutch border. The company uses a process costing system for its single product—a popular pumpernickel bread. Schneider Brot has two processing departments—mixing and baking. The T-accounts below show the flow of costs through the two departments in April (all amounts are in German marks):

Work in Process—Mixing

Bal. 4/1	10,000	760,000	Transferred out
Direct materials	330,000		
Direct labour	260,000		
Overhead	190,000		

Work in Process—Baking

Bal. 4/1	20,000	980,000	Transferred out
Transferred in	760,000		
Direct labour	120,000		
Overhead	90,000		

Required

Prepare journal entries showing the flow of costs through the two processing departments during April.

E4–8 Kalox, Inc., manufactures an antacid product that passes through two departments. Data for May for the first department follow:

	Litres	Materials	Labour	Overhead
Work in process, May 1.....................	80,000	$ 69,300	$ 28,000	$ 45,000
Litres started in process....................	760,000			
Litres transferred out.......................	790,000			
Work in process, May 31....................	50,000			
Cost added during May.....................	—	907,200	370,000	592,000

The beginning work in process inventory was 80% complete as to materials and 75% complete as to processing. The ending work in process inventory was 60% complete as to materials and 20% complete as to processing.

Required

1. Assume that the company uses the weighted-average method of accounting for units and costs. Prepare a quantity schedule and a computation of equivalent units for May's activity.
2. Determine the total and unit costs for May.

E4–9 (Appendix 4A) Refer to the data for Kalox, Inc., in E4–8.

Required

1. Assume that the company uses the FIFO method of accounting for units and costs. Prepare a quantity schedule and a computation of equivalent units for May's activity.
2. Determine the total and unit costs for May.

E4–10 Solex Company produces a high-quality insulation material that passes through two production processes. A quantity schedule for June for the first process follows:

	Quantity Schedule
Units to be accounted for:	
Work in process, June 1 (75% materials,	
40% conversion cost added last month)	60,000
Started into production	280,000
Total units to be accounted for	340,000

	Quantity Schedule	Equivalent Units Materials	Equivalent Units Conversion
Units accounted for as follows:			
Transferred to the next process.	300,000	?	?
Work in process, June 30 (50% materials,			
25% conversion cost added this month)	40,000	?	?
Total units accounted for.	340,000	?	?

Costs in the beginning work in process inventory were: materials, $57,000; and conversion cost, $16,000. Costs added during June were: materials, $385,000; and conversion cost, $214,500.

Required

1. Assume that the company uses the weighted-average method of accounting for units and costs. Determine the equivalent units for June.
2. Compute the total and unit costs for June.

E4–11 (This exercise should be assigned only if E4–10 is also assigned.) Refer to the data in E4–10 and to the equivalent units and unit costs you have computed there.

Required

Complete the following cost reconciliation for the first process:

	Total Cost	Equivalent Units Materials	Equivalent Units Conversion
Cost accounted for as follows:			
Transferred to the next process:			
_____ units × _____ each	$?		
Work in process, June 30:			
Materials, at _____ per EU	?	?	
Conversion, at _____ per EU	?		?
Total work in process, June 30	?		
Total cost accounted for	$?		

E4–12 (Appendix 4A) Refer to the data for Solex Company in E4–10. Assume that the company uses the FIFO cost method.

Required

1. Prepare a quantity schedule and a computation of equivalent units for June.
2. Compute the total and unit costs for June.

E4–13 (Appendix 4A) (This exercise should be assigned only if E4–12 is also assigned.) Refer to the data in E4–10 for Solex Company and to the equivalent units and unit costs that you computed in E4–12.

Required

Complete the following cost reconciliation for the first process:

	Total Cost	Equivalent Units	
		Materials	Conversion
Cost accounted for as follows:			
Transferred to the next process:			
From the beginning inventory:			
Cost in the beginning inventory	$?		
Cost to complete these units:			
Materials, at _____ per EU	?	?	
Conversion, at _____ per EU	?		?
Total cost	?		
Units started and completed this month:			
_____ units × _____ each	?	?	?
Total cost transferred	?		
Work in process, June 30:			
Materials, at _____ per EU	?	?	
Conversion, at _____ per EU	?		?
Total work in process, June 30	?		
Total cost accounted for	?		

PROBLEMS

P4–14 Partial Production Report   Rolex Company uses a process costing system and manufactures a single product. Activity for July has just been completed. A partially completed production report using the weighted-average method for July for the first processing department follows:

ROLEX COMPANY
Production Report
For the Month Ending July 31

Quantity Schedule and Equivalent Units

	Quantity Schedule
Units to be accounted for:	
Work in process, July 1 (all materials, 80% labour and overhead added last month)	10,000
Started into production	100,000
Total units to account for	110,000

		Equivalent Units		
		Materials	Labour	Overhead
Units accounted for as follows:				
Transferred to the next department	95,000	?	?	?
Work in process, July 31 (60% materials, 20% labour and overhead added this month)	15,000	?	?	?
Total units accounted for	110,000	?	?	?

Total and Unit Costs

	Total	Materials	Labour	Overhead	Whole Unit
Work in process, July 1	$ 8,700	$ 1,500	$ 1,800	$ 5,400	
Cost added by the department	245,300	154,500	22,700	68,100	
Total cost (a)	$254,000	$156,000	$24,500	$73,500	
Equivalent units (b)	—	104,000	98,000	98,000	
Unit cost, (a) ÷ (b)		$1.50 +	$0.25 +	$0.75 =	$2.50

Cost Reconciliation

Cost accounted for as follows:
?

Required

1. Prepare a schedule showing how the equivalent units were computed.
2. Complete the "Cost reconciliation" part of the production report.

P4–15 Step-by-Step Production Report   The PVC Company manufactures a high-quality plastic pipe in two departments, cooking and molding. Materials are introduced at various points during work in the cooking department. After the cooking is completed, the materials are transferred into the molding department, in which pipe is formed. Materials are accounted for in the cooking department on a kilograms basis. Conversion costs are incurred evenly during the cooking process.

Selected data relating to the cooking department during May are given below:

Production data:
Kilograms in process, May 1: 100% complete as to materials,
90% complete as to conversion costs.................... 70,000
Kilograms started into production during May.............. 350,000
Kilograms completed and transferred to molding............   ?
Kilograms in process, May 31: 75% complete as to materials,
25% complete as to conversion costs.................... 40,000

Cost data:
Work in process inventory, May 1:
Materials cost...................................... $ 86,000
Conversion cost 36,000
Cost added during May:
Materials cost...................................... 447,000
Conversion cost 198,000

The company uses the weighted-average method to account for units and costs.

Required

Prepare a production report for the cooking department. Use the following three steps as a guide in preparing your report:

1. Prepare a quantity schedule and compute the equivalent units.
2. Compute the total and unit costs for May.
3. Using the data from (1) and (2) above, prepare a cost reconciliation.

P4–16 Step-by-Step Production Report; FIFO Method   (Appendix 4A) Reutter Company manufactures a single product and uses a process costing system. The company's product goes through two processes, etching and wiring. The following activity was recorded in the etching department during July:

Production data:
Units in process, July 1: 60% complete as to materials,
and 30% complete as to conversion costs 60,000
Units started into production 510,000
Units completed and transferred to wiring ....   ?
Units in process, July 31: 80% complete as to materials,
and 40% complete as to conversion costs 70,000

Cost data:
Work in process inventory, July 1:
Materials cost....................................... $ 27,000
Conversion cost .... 13,000 $ 40,000

Cost added during July:
Materials cost....................................... 468,000
Conversion cost 357,000   825,000
Total cost $865,000

Materials are added at several stages during the etching process. Conversion costs are incurred uniformly as the etching takes place. The company uses the FIFO cost method.

Required

Prepare a production report for the etching department for July. Use the following three steps as a guide in preparing your report:

1. Prepare a quantity schedule and compute the equivalent units.
2. Compute the total and unit costs for July.
3. Using the data from (1) and (2) above, prepare a cost reconciliation.

P4–17 Basic Production Report   Honeybutter, Inc., manufactures a product that goes through two departments prior to completion. The following information is available on work in the mixing department during June.

| | Units | Amount Completed | |
		Materials	Conversion
Work in process, June 1	70,000	5/7	3/7
Started into production.	460,000		
Completed and transferred out.	450,000		
Work in process, June 30	80,000	3/4	5/8

Cost in the beginning work in process inventory and cost added during June were as follows:

	Materials	Conversion
Work in process, June 1.	$ 35,000	$ 17,000
Cost added during June.	391,000	282,000

The company uses the weighted-average method to compute unit costs. The mixing department is the first department in the production process; after mixing has been completed, the units are transferred to the bottling department.

Required   Prepare a production report for the mixing department for June.

P4–18 Basic Production Report; FIFO Method   (Appendix 4A) Refer to the data for Honeybutter, Inc., in P4–17. Assume that the company uses the FIFO method to compute unit costs rather than the weighted-average method.

Required   Prepare a production report for the mixing department for June.

P4–19 Analysis of Work in Process T-Account   Brady Products manufactures a silicone paste wax that goes through three processing departments—cracking, blending, and packing. All of the raw materials are introduced at the start of work in the cracking department, with conversion costs being incurred uniformly as cracking takes place. The Work in Process T-account for the cracking department for May follows:

Work in Process—Cracking Department

Inventory, May 1 (35,000 kg, 4/5 processed)	63,700	Completed and transferred to blending (? kg)	?
May costs added:			
Raw materials (280,000 kg)	397,600		
Labour and overhead	189,700		
Inventory, May 31 (45,000 kg, 2/3 processed)	?		

The May 1 work in process inventory consists of $43,400 in materials cost and $20,300 in labour and overhead cost. The company uses the weighted-average method to account for units and costs.

Required
1. Prepare a production report for the cracking department for May.
2. What criticism can be made of the unit costs that you have computed on your production report?

P4–20 Analysis of Work in Process T-Account; FIFO Method   (Appendix 4A) Hiko, Inc., manufactures a high-quality pressboard out of wood scraps and sawmill waste. The pressboard goes through two processing departments, shredding and forming. Activity in the shredding department during July is summarized in the department's Work in Process account below:

Work in Process—Shredding Department

Inventory, July 1 (10,000 kg, 30% processed)	13,400	Completed and transferred to forming (_?_ kg)	_?_
July costs added:			
Wood materials (170,000 kg)	139,400		
Labour and overhead	244,200		
Inventory, July 31 (20,000 kg, 40% processed)	_?_		

The wood materials are entered into production at the beginning of work in the shredding department. Labour and overhead costs are incurred uniformly throughout the shredding process. The company uses the FIFO cost method.

Required   Prepare a production report for the shredding department for July.

P4–21 Interpreting a Production Report   Bell Computers, Ltd., located in Liverpool, England, assembles a standardized personal computer from parts it purchases from various suppliers. The production process consists of several steps, starting with assembly of the "mother" circuit board, which contains the central processing unit. This assembly takes place in the CPU assembly department. The company recently hired a new accountant who prepared the following partial production report for this department for May using the weighted-average method:

Quantity Schedule

Units to be accounted for:	
Work in process, May 1 (90% materials; 80% conversion cost added last month)	5,000
Started into production	29,000
Total units 34,000	
Units accounted for as follows:	
Transferred to next department	30,000
Work in process, May 31 (75% materials; 50% conversion cost added this month)	4,000
Total units 34,000	

Total Cost

Cost to be accounted for:	
Work in process, May 1	£ 13,400
Cost added in the department	87,800
Total cost. £101,200	

Cost Reconciliation

Cost accounted for as follows:	
Transferred to next department	£ 93,000
Work in process, May 31	8,200

The company's management would like some additional information about May's operation in the CPU assembly department.

Required
1. How many units were started and completed during May?
2. What were the equivalent units for May for materials and conversion costs?

3. What were the unit costs for May? The following additional data are available concerning the department's costs:

	Total	Materials	Conversion
Work in process, May 1	£13,400	£ 9,000	£ 4,400
Costs added during May.	87,800	57,000	30,800

4. Verify the accountant's ending work in process inventory figure (£8,200) given in the report.
5. The new manager in the CPU assembly department was asked to estimate the incremental cost of processing an additional 1,000 units through the department. He took the unit cost for an equivalent whole unit you computed in (3) above and multiplied this figure by 1,000. Will this method yield a valid estimate of incremental cost? Explain.

P4–22 Journal Entries; T-Accounts; Production Report   Nature's Way, Inc., keeps one of its production facilities busy making a perfume called Essence de la Vache. The perfume goes through two processing departments: blending and bottling.

The following incomplete Work in Process account is provided for the blending department for March:

Work in Process—Blending

March 1 bal. (40,000 millilitres; 100% complete as to materials; 80% complete as to labour and overhead)	32,800	Completed and transferred to bottling (760,000 millilitres)	?
Raw materials	147,600		
Direct labour	73,200		
Overhead	481,000		
March 31 bal. (30,000 millilitres; 60% complete as to materials; 40% complete as to labour and overhead)	?		

The $32,800 figure for the beginning inventory in the blending department consisted of the following cost elements: raw materials, $8,000; direct labour, $4,000; and overhead applied, $20,800.

Costs incurred during March in the bottling department were: materials used, $45,000; direct labour, $17,000; and overhead cost applied to production, $108,000.

The company accounts for units and costs by the weighted-average method.

Required

1. Prepare journal entries to record the cost incurred in both the blending and bottling departments during March. Key your entries to the items (a) through (g) below:
   a. Raw materials were issued for use in production.
   b. Direct labour costs were incurred.
   c. Manufacturing overhead costs for the entire factory were incurred, $596,000. (Credit Accounts Payable and use a single Manufacturing Overhead control account for the entire factory.)
   d. Manufacturing overhead was applied to production based on a predetermined overhead rate.
   e. Products that were complete as to processing in the blending department were transferred to the bottling department, $722,000.
   f. Products that were complete as to processing in the bottling department were transferred to Finished Goods, $920,000.
   g. Completed products were sold on account for $1,400,000. The cost of goods sold was $890,000.

2. Post the journal entries from (1) above to T-accounts. The following account balances existed at the beginning of March. (The beginning balance in the blending department's Work in Process account is given above.)

Raw Materials	$198,600
Work in Process—Bottling Department.	49,000
Finished Goods.	20,000

After posting the entries to the T-accounts, find the ending balance in the inventory accounts and the manufacturing overhead account.

3. Prepare a production report for the blending department for March.

P4–23 Equivalent Units; Costing of Inventories   Zap Rap, Inc., is a manufacturer of audio CDs. The company's chief financial officer is trying to verify the accuracy of the December 31 work in process and finished goods inventories prior to closing books for the year. He strongly suspects that the year-end dollar balances are incorrect, but he believes that all the other data are accurate. The year-end balances shown on Zap Rap's books are as follows:

	Units	Costs
Work in process, Dec. 31 (100% complete as to materials;		
50% as to conversion)	30,000	$ 95,000
Finished goods, Dec. 31	50,000	201,000

There were no finished goods inventories at the beginning of the year. The company uses the weighted-average method of process costing. There is only one processing department.

A review of the company's inventory and cost records has disclosed the following data, all of which are accurate:

		Costs	
	Units	Materials	Conversion
Work in process, Jan. 1 (100% complete			
as to materials; 80% as to conversion)	20,000	$ 22,000	$ 48,000
Started into production	800,000		
Costs added during the year		880,000	2,367,000
Units completed during the year	790,000		

Required

1. Determine the equivalent units and the unit costs for materials and conversion for the year.
2. Determine the amount of cost that should be assigned to the ending work in process and finished goods inventories.
3. Prepare the necessary correcting journal entry to adjust the work in process and finished goods inventories to the correct balances as of December 31.
4. Determine the cost of goods sold for the year, assuming that there is no under- or over applied overhead.

(CPA, adapted)

P4–24 Journal Entries: T-Accounts; Production Report   Security Systems, Inc., makes a device that alerts a central dispatching office when activated and emits a radio signal that police can home in on. The device goes through two processing departments—the assembly department and the testing and packaging department. The company has recently hired a new assistant accountant, who has prepared the following summary of activity in the assembly department for May using the weighted-average method.

Assembly department costs:
  Work in process inventory, May 1: 8,000 units;
    70% complete as to materials; 20% complete
    as to labour and overhead . . . . $ 49,000*
  Materials cost added during May   422,000
  Labour cost added during May   316,500
  Overhead cost applied during May   200,000
      Total departmental cost $987,500

Assembly department costs assigned to:
  Units completed and transferred to the testing
    and packaging department:
    42,000 units at __?__ per unit . . . . $?
  Work in process inventory, May 31:
    5,000 units; 60% complete as to materials;
      20% complete as to labour and overhead . . . . $?
      Total departmental costs assigned . . . . $?

*Consists of materials, $28,000; labour, $6,000; and overhead, $15,000.

The new assistant accountant has calculated the cost per unit transferred to the testing and packaging department to be $23.512, as follows:

$$\frac{\text{Total assembly department costs, \$987,500}}{\text{Units completed and transferred, 42,000}} = \$23.512$$

However, the assistant accountant is unsure whether he should use this unit cost figure to assign cost to the ending work in process inventory. In addition, the company's general ledger shows only $945,000 transferred to the testing and packaging department, which does not agree with the $987,500 figure above.

The general ledger also shows the following costs incurred in the testing and packaging department during May: materials used, $23,000; direct labour cost incurred, $57,000; and overhead cost applied, $42,000.

Required

1. Prepare journal entries as follows to record activity in the company during May. Key your entries to the letters (a) through (g) below.
   a. Raw materials were issued to the two departments for use in production.
   b. Direct labour costs were incurred in the two departments.
   c. Manufacturing overhead costs were incurred, $254,000. (Credit Accounts Payable.) The company maintains a single Manufacturing Overhead control account for both departments.
   d. Manufacturing overhead cost was applied to production in each department using predetermined overhead rates.
   e. Units completed with respect to processing in the assembly department were transferred to the testing and packaging department, $945,000.
   f. Units completed in the testing and packaging department were transferred to finished goods, $1,080,000.
   g. Units were sold on account for $1,630,000. The cost of goods sold was $1,070,000.

2. Post the journal entries from (1) to T-accounts. Balances in selected accounts on May 1 are given below:

   Raw Materials $460,000
   Work in Process—Testing and Packaging
     Department.   43,000
   Finished Goods   30,000

   After posting the entries to the T-accounts, find the ending balance in the inventory accounts and the Manufacturing Overhead account.

3. Prepare a production report for the assembly department for May.

CASES

C4–25 Analysis of Data; Production Report; Second Department   Durall Company manufactures a plastic gasket that is used in automobile engines. The gaskets go through three processing departments: mixing, forming, and stamping. The company's accountant (who is very inexperienced) has prepared a summary of production and costs for the forming department as follows for October:

Forming department costs:	
Work in process inventory, October 1, 8,000 units; all materials added; ⅝ complete as to conversion costs............	$ 22,420*
Costs transferred in from the mixing department.................	81,480
Material added during October (added when processing is 50% complete in the forming department)...................	27,600
Conversion costs added during October.......................	96,900
Total departmental costs.....................................	$228,400

Forming department costs assigned to:	
Units completed and transferred to the stamping department, 100,000 units at $2.284 each	$228,400
Work in process inventory, October 31, 5,000 units, ⅖ complete as to conversion costs	—
Total departmental costs assigned	$228,400

*Consists of cost transferred in, $8,820; materials cost, $3,400; and conversion costs, $10,200

After mulling over the data above, Durall's president commented, "I can't understand what's happening here. Despite a concentrated effort at cost reduction, our unit cost actually went up in the forming department last month. With that kind of performance, year-end bonuses are out of the question for the people in that department."

The company uses the weighted-average method to account for units and costs.

Required

1. Prepare a revised production report for the forming department for October.
2. Explain to the president why the unit cost figure appearing on the report prepared by the accountant is so high.

C4–26 Analysis of Data; Production Report; Second Department; FIFO Method   (Appendix 4A) Refer to the data for Durall Company in the preceding case. Assume that the company uses the FIFO method to account for units and costs.

Required

1. Prepare a production report for the forming department for October.
2. Assume that in order to remain competitive, the company undertook a major cost-cutting program during October. Would the effects of this cost-cutting program tend to show up more under the weighted-average method or under the FIFO method? Explain your answer.

C4–27 Ethics and the Manager   Gary Stevens and Mary James are production managers in the Consumer Electronics Division of General Electronics Company, which has several dozen plants scattered in locations throughout the world. Mary manages the plant located in Regina, Saskatchewan, while Gary manages the plant in Calgary, Alberta. Production managers are paid a salary and get an additional bonus equal to 5% of their base salary if the entire division meets or exceeds its target profits for the year. The bonus is determined in March after the company's annual report has been prepared and issued to shareholders.

Shortly after the beginning of the new year, Mary received a phone call from Gary that went like this:

GARY: How's it going, Mary?

MARY: Fine, Gary. How's it going with you?

GARY: Great! I just got the preliminary profit figures for the division for last year and we are within $50,000 of making the year's target profits. All we have to do is to pull a few strings, and we'll be over the top!

MARY: What do you mean?

GARY: Well, one thing that would be easy to change is your estimate of the percentage completion of your ending work in process inventories.

MARY: I don't know if I can do that, Gary. Those percentage completion figures are supplied by Tom Winthrop, my lead supervisor, who I have always trusted to provide us with good estimates. Besides, I have already sent the percentage completion figures to the corporate headquarters.

GARY: You can always tell them there was a mistake. Think about it, Mary. All of us managers are doing as much as we can to pull this bonus out of the hat. You may not want the bonus cheque, but the rest of us sure could use it.

Required

1. Explain why changing the estimate of the percentage completion of ending work in process inventories would affect the profits reported by the division. To increase reported profits, would Gary Stevens want the estimate of percentage completion to be increased or decreased?

2. Do you think Mary James should go along with the request to alter the estimates of percentage completion? Why or why not?

C4–28 Process III and Spoilage   (Appendix 4B) Fish Processing Ltd. produces several lines of artificial food substitutes. Chickenlike, its most successful product, is mass-produced in a continuous processing environment. In its production, Chickenlike passes through four processes: a mixing, a blending, and a molding process before being packed in process IV. In the past, most of the spoiled product has been isolated in processes I and II, so inspection has been concentrated there. A number of customer complaints have been registered, however, which has led the product line manager to suspect additional spoilage in processes III and IV.

An engineering quality study of processes III and IV has revealed that there is a potential 1% normal spoilage of the good product that passes the final inspection in each of the two processes. Any spoilage in excess of the 1% expected in each process is considered to be abnormal.

The inspection was set up in process III (the molding process). The inspection was done when the product was 70% of the way through the process, immediately preceding the addition of material to the partially molded product units.

Shown below is the cost and production data for process III for the month of November: The company uses FIFO process costing for process III.

	Units	Cost
November 1, work in process (60% complete)	10,000 kg	$ 60,000
Transferred in from process II in November	100,000 kg	$325,000
Transferred to process IV in November	102,000 kg	
November 30, work in process (80% complete)	6,000 kg	
Cost of materials used in November		97,560
Cost of conversion in November		291,612
Total cost added in November		$714,172

Required

1. Determine the following amounts:
   a. Cost of ending work in process, November 30.
   b. Cost of abnormal spoilage for November.
   c. Cost of goods completed and transferred in November.
2. Prepare the journal entry(ies) to record the transactions in the accounts for process III for November.

(SMAC, adapted)

C4–29 Process Costing—Second Department: Spoilage (Appendix 4B) The Matheson Mfg. Co. Ltd. operates under a weighted-average process cost system. It has two departments, 1 and 2. In department 2, materials are added at the end of the process, following inspection. Normal spoilage is considered to be 10% of good output. Labour and overhead costs are assumed to apply evenly throughout the process.

Inventory at the beginning of the period was one-half complete; ending inventory is two-thirds complete.

Following are the costs and unit production statistics for the period:

Beginning inventory, ...	2,000 units
Received from department 1	8,000 units
Completed and transferred to finished goods storeroom	7,000 units
Ending inventory	1,500 units

Costs	Transferred from Department 1	Materials	Labour	Overhead
Beginning inventory	$ 6,100	—	$ 1,400	$ 550
Current costs	23,900	$7,000	12,000	5,050

Required

Prepare a cost of production report for department 2, including the amount to be charged to finished goods, the value of the ending inventory, and the disposition of the cost of spoiled units.

(CGA-Canada, adapted)

GROUP EXERCISES

GE4–30 Productivity in a Process Industry Large integrated steel companies like Dofasco Steel are highly capital-intensive process businesses. Their product line is narrower, their production volume is greater, and their equipment is much more specialized (i.e., dedicated to a single activity or group of related activities) than that normally found in job or batch manufacturing environments.

Required

1. What are the critical factors on which firms in process industries normally compete?
2. From your microeconomics class, how do capital-derived scale effects benefit a firm?
3. What risks does such a strategy entail?
4. Describe the mix of fixed and variable costs in the cost structure of capital-intensive industries such as steel. Give several examples of the major fixed and variable costs for a steel firm.
5. Why do process firms keep their product line narrow or more focused?
6. Summarize your responses to (1) to (5) above into a cohesive strategy for competing in a process industry.

GE4–31 There Has to Be an Easier Way to Make Money Airline travel serves as a good example of process costing within a service industry. The work in process inventory in this case consists of the passengers flying a particular route, say from Toronto to Quebec City. Each passenger must make a reservation, receive a ticket, check baggage, be assigned a seat, board the plane, fly, eat (peanuts and a drink), deboard, and pick up baggage.

Required

1. What has been the competitive environment in the airline industry throughout the nineties?
2. What is the cost structure of an airline?
3. Over the last 15 years, the airlines have consolidated. But the fears of higher fares resulting from an industry controlled by a few airlines (the classic oligopoly) never materialized. According to microeconomics, an oligopolist's pricing power comes from his ability to restrict supply, for example, reduce the number of seats available on a flight or reduce the number of flights.

    a. Why isn't it likely that airlines will restrict the number of seats on a flight?

    b. Why isn't it likely that airlines will reduce the number of flights?

4. What can an airline do to maximize the profit (or minimize the loss) of a scheduled flight?

5. What can an airline do to maximize the profit (or minimize the loss) of its entire fleet of airplanes?

6. What is an airline's primary avenue of cost reduction?

7. There has been a proliferation of flights over the last 15 years just as there has been a proliferation of products coming out of manufacturers' plants.

    a. Why has there been a proliferation of flights?

    b. Has this proliferation of flights led to the same faulty costs that a proliferation of products led to? Explain.

GE4–32 Paper Is Public Enemy No. 1   Businesses can be viewed as a series of functions and processes. Business processes, such as the procurement or the materials acquisition process, built up around functions, such as requisitioning, purchasing, receiving, accounts payable, and treasury. Firms organized around functions in order to standardize work, allow worker specialization, and decouple the work of each individual from other individuals, thus allowing the worker to maximize output.

    Let's use the typical accounts payable application as an example. Each day hundreds if not thousands of sales invoices can arrive from suppliers. Each invoice must be matched against the original purchase order and the receiving report prepared when a shipment was received from the supplier. Checks must be made of items ordered and received, quantities, pricing terms, payment terms, and other conditions of purchase. If "exceptions" (price or quantity discrepancies, lost paperwork, invoices not paid, etc.) occur, additional time is required to identify and rectify the reason for the discrepancy. "Exceptions" can occur on up to 40% or more of the purchases. Aside from the "exceptions," there is a mass of paper flowing around among requisitioner, purchasing, suppliers, receiving, accounts payable, and treasury (payment). It is not uncommon for a vendor to wait two months or longer for payment.

    A large company could easily process over 1 million invoices per year. Some invoices for parts or components could run into the thousands of dollars. Other invoices for office supplies (e.g., a ribbon cartridge for a computer) might cost less than $25.

Required   Redesign the accounts payable function so that it reduces costs, improves customer satisfaction (i.e., the vendor), corrects quality problems, and speeds up the entire process. (Hint: It might help to diagram the existing process so that you have some point of departure for discussing what is wrong.)

SYSTEMS DESIGN: ACTIVITY-BASED COSTING AND QUALITY MANAGEMENT

LEARNING OBJECTIVES

After studying Chapter 5, you should be able to:

1 Explain why overhead costing methods based on volume measures such as direct labour-hours are no longer adequate for costing products and services in some companies.

2 Describe activity-based costing and explain how it differs from more conventional costing methods.

3 Identify the four steps involved in the design of an activity-based costing system.

4 Compute the cost of a unit of product using activity-based costing.

5 Enumerate the benefits and limitations of activity-based costing.

6 Distinguish between grade, quality of design, and quality of conformance.

7 Identify the four types of quality costs.

8 Be familiar with the organization, content, and uses of a quality cost report.

9 Define or explain the key terms listed at the end of the chapter.

10 (Appendix 5A) Record the flow of costs in an activity-based costing system.

Historically, overhead costs, such as administration and clerical work, were allocated by a plantwide overhead rate. Under activity-based costing, these costs are allocated by activity.

In response to increased costs, reduced profits, and intensifying worldwide competition, companies have searched for ways to strengthen their operations and gather more accurate data for decision-making purposes. The result of this search has been the development of several powerful new management tools, including *activity-based costing (ABC)* and *total quality management (TQM)*. ABC helps managers identify more clearly the costs involved in manufacturing a product or providing a service, and thereby provides more accurate unit cost information on which to base pricing and other decisions. TQM helps managers maintain quality standards and thus guard against an eroding market share. It assists in identifying costs associated with quality assurance, provides a method of reporting such costs to management, and guides management in the use of quality cost information.

THE CONCEPT OF ACTIVITY-BASED COSTING

OBJECTIVE 1
Explain why overhead costing methods based on volume measures such as direct labour-hours are no longer adequate for costing products and services in some companies.

The most difficult task in computing accurate unit costs lies in determining the proper amount of overhead cost to assign to each job, unit of product, or service activity. Three different approaches are available to help the manager in the task of overhead assignment. These approaches differ in terms of level of complexity, ranging from what we term Level One, the least complex, to Level Three, the most complex. Level Three, which deals with activity-based costing, is widely viewed as the most accurate of the three approaches to overhead cost assignment.

Level One: Plantwide Overhead Rate

Our discussion in the two preceding chapters assumed that a single overhead rate was being used throughout an entire factory operation. We explained in Chapter 3 that such a rate is called a *plantwide overhead rate*. Historically, such rates have dominated industry practice, but their accuracy is now being called into question because they tend to rely solely on direct labour as an allocation base, which in turn can lead to distorted unit costs.

Direct Labour as a Base.   In the early part of the twentieth century, when cost systems first began to be developed, direct labour constituted a significant part of total product cost. Data relating to direct labour were readily available and highly convenient to use, and accountants believed there was a high correlation between direct labour and the incurrence of overhead cost. Therefore, direct labour made a useful allocation base.

Even today, direct labour remains a viable base for applying overhead cost in some companies, both in this country and abroad. In Japan, for example, which has become a world leader in manufacturing technology, direct labour-hours are still widely used as a base in overhead application.[1] Recent studies also reveal high correlations between direct labour and the incurrence of overhead costs in some industries.[2] The circumstances under which direct labour may be appropriate as a base for assigning overhead cost to products include the following:

1. Direct labour is a significant element of total product cost.
2. The amount of direct labour input and the amount of machine input do not differ greatly between products.

---

[1]Callie Berliner and James A. Brimson, eds., *Cost Management for Today's Advanced Manufacturing* (Boston, Mass.: Harvard Business School Press, 1988), p. 232.
[2]George Foster and Mahendra Gupta, "Manufacturing Overhead Cost Driver Analysis," *Journal of Accounting and Economics* (1990), pp. 309–37.

3. Products do not differ greatly in terms of volume, individual lot size, or complexity of manufacturing.
4. A high statistical correlation can be established between direct labour and the incurrence of overhead costs (i.e., direct labour acts as a cost driver for overhead).

Changing Manufacturing Environment.   So long as the above circumstances exist, reasonably accurate unit costs can be obtained using direct labour as an allocation base. However, events of the past two decades have made drastic changes in these circumstances in some industries. First, automation has greatly decreased the amount of direct labour required in the manufacture of many products. Second, **product diversity** has increased in that companies are manufacturing a wider range of products, and these products differ substantially in volume, lot size, and complexity of design. And third, total overhead cost has increased to the point in some companies that a correlation no longer exists between it and direct labour.

Where these changes have prevailed, companies that have continued to use plantwide overhead rates and direct labour as a basis for overhead cost assignment have experienced major distortions in unit costs. To overcome these distortions, managers have turned to other overhead assignment methods.

Level Two: Departmental Overhead Rates

Rather than use a plantwide overhead rate, some companies use a "two-stage" allocation process. In the first stage, overhead costs are assigned to cost pools, such as individual departments or operations. In the second stage, costs are applied from the cost pools (departments) to individual jobs. These second-stage applications are made on various bases according to the nature of the work performed in the department, as explained in Chapter 3. The two-stage allocation process is illustrated in Exhibit 5–1.

EXHIBIT 5–1

Two-Stage Overhead Costing

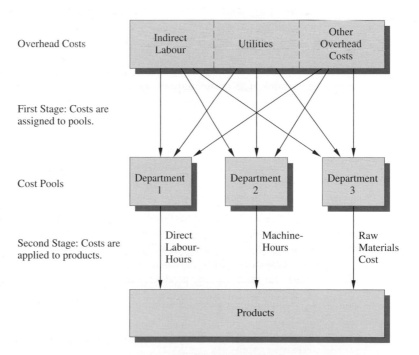

Overhead Costs | Indirect Labour | Utilities | Other Overhead Costs

First Stage: Costs are assigned to pools.

Cost Pools | Department 1 | Department 2 | Department 3

Second Stage: Costs are applied to products.

Direct Labour-Hours | Machine-Hours | Raw Materials Cost

Products

Unfortunately, even departmental overhead rates will not correctly assign overhead costs in situations where a company has a range of products that differ in volume, lot size, or complexity of production. The reason is that the departmental approach relies solely on *volume* as the key factor in allocating overhead cost to products. Where diversity exists among products (i.e., where products differ in terms of number of units produced, lot size, or complexity of production), overhead cost assignments based on volume will not provide accurate product costs. Studies show that overhead cost assignments based on volume systematically overcost high-volume products and undercost low-volume products. Moreover, this is true regardless of whether volume is stated in terms of direct labour, machine time, or quantity of materials used.[3] In situations where product diversity exists, to obtain more accurate unit costs, *activity-based costing* should be used.

Level Three: Activity-Based Costing

OBJECTIVE 2

Describe activity-based costing and explain how it differs from more conventional costing methods.

Activity-based costing (ABC) involves a two-stage allocation process, as described earlier, with the first stage again assigning overhead costs to cost pools. However, more pools are used under this approach, and they are defined differently. Rather than being defined as departments, the pools represent *activities,* such as setups, purchase orders, and inspections. In the second stage, costs are assigned to jobs according to the number of these activities required in their completion.

An **activity** is any event or transaction that is a cost driver—that is, it causes the incurrence of cost in an organization. Examples of activities that act as cost drivers include the following:

1. Machine setups.
2. Purchase orders.
3. Quality inspections.
4. Production orders (scheduling).
5. Engineering change orders.
6. Machine time.
7. Power consumed.
8. Kilometres driven.
9. Shipments.
10. Material receipts.
11. Inventory movements.
12. Maintenance requests.
13. Scrap/rework orders.
14. Computer-hours logged.
15. Beds occupied.
16. Flight-hours logged.

The number of the cost drivers in an organization is a function of the complexity of operations. The more complex a company's operations, the more cost-driving activities it is likely to have. As companies have moved from the simple, direct labour-based operations of 60 years ago to the complex, highly automated operations of today, the number of cost-driving activities has increased manyfold. Managers have discovered, however, that not all products and services share equally in these activities.

One product in a company, for example, may be a low-volume item that requires frequent machine setups, has many intricate parts requiring numerous purchase orders, and requires constant inspections to maintain quality. Another product in the same company may be a high-volume item that requires few machine setups, few purchase orders, and no quality inspections at all. If management ignores the impact of these two products on the company's cost-driving activities and simply assigns overhead costs to the products on a basis of volume (such as labour-hours, machine-hours, or quantity of materials used), the high-volume product will bear the lion's share of the overhead cost pool. The result will be a serious distortion in unit costs for *both* products.

---

[3]See Robin Cooper and Robert S. Kaplan, "How Cost Accounting Distorts Product Costs," *Management Accounting* (April 1988), pp. 20–27.

EXHIBIT 5-2

Activity-Based
Costing Model

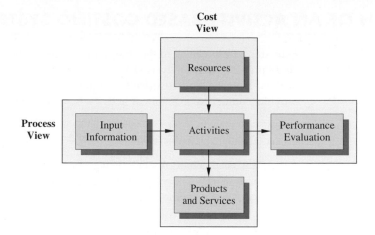

As stated earlier, activity-based costing reduces the problem of cost distortion. This is accomplished by creating a cost pool for *each* activity or transaction that can be identified as a cost driver, and by assigning overhead cost to products or jobs on the basis of the number of separate activities they require in their completion. Thus, in the situation above, the low-volume product would be assigned the bulk of the costs for machine setups, purchase orders, and quality inspections, thereby showing it to have high unit costs as compared to the other product.

Activity-based costing is sometimes referred to as **transactions costing.** Its major advantage over other costing methods is that *it improves the traceability of overhead costs* and thus results in more accurate unit cost data for management.

Activity-Based Costing Model.   Exhibit 5–2 provides a model depicting the flow of information in an activity-based costing system.[4] Note that information in such a system can be viewed from two perspectives. The *cost view* in the model shows the flow of costs. This flow is from resources to activities, and from activities to products and services. For example, assume that one of the activities in a company is material handling. The resources consumed by moving materials around the plant will be traced to particular products based on some observed activity, such as the number of times an item is moved. This cost view in the model summarizes the key concept underlying activity-based costing: *resources are consumed by activities, and activities are caused by products and services.*

The *process view* in the model shows the flow of input information, which would be the observed transactions associated with an activity. In the case of material handling, information is gathered on the number of times an item of material is moved to determine the extent of activity during a period. This information provides the "activity" data needed to complete the costing of products, and it also provides the data needed for performance evaluation, as depicted by the horizontal flow in the model.

In this chapter, we focus our attention on the product costing portion of the model. Discussion of performance evaluation is reserved until Chapter 10, where both the traditional and activity-based approaches to performance evaluation are discussed.

---

[4]Adapted from Norm Raffish, "How Much Does That Product Really Cost?" *Management Accounting* (March 1991), p. 38. Used by permission.

DESIGN OF AN ACTIVITY-BASED COSTING SYSTEM

OBJECTIVE 3
Identify the four steps involved in the design of an activity-based costing system.

Four steps are involved in the design of an activity-based costing system. These steps include process value analysis (PVA), identifying activity centres, tracing costs to activity centres, and selecting cost drivers. After discussing these steps in this section, we then provide a numerical example of activity-based costing.

Process Value Analysis (PVA)

A well-designed activity-based costing system starts with *process value analysis*. **Process value analysis (PVA)** consists of systematically analyzing the activities required to make a product or perform a service. It identifies all resource-consuming activities involved in manufacturing a product or providing a service and labels these activities as being either value-added or non-value-added in nature. As stated in Chapter 1, only the actual processing of goods is a value-added activity; all other steps in the manufacturing process, including moving goods from station to station, inspection, and waiting for processing, are non-value-added activities in that they consume resources without adding value to the product. In completing a PVA, the manager should proceed as follows:

First, prepare a flowchart detailing each step in the manufacturing process from the receiving of materials to the final inspection of the completed product. This requires walking through each operation and documenting *every* activity observed. The time involved in each activity should be recorded on the flowchart, since time can be a good indicator of the amount of resources being consumed by a product.

Second, analyze each activity documented on the flowchart and determine whether it is value-added or non-value-added in nature. Exhibit 5–3 contains the results of an actual PVA performed on a product manufactured by a large company. The PVA showed that 20 days were required from receipt of materials to shipment of goods to the customer, and that most of this time was non-value-added in nature.[5]

Third, identify ways to either reduce or eliminate the non-value-added activities documented on the flowchart. The company in Exhibit 5–3, for example, was able to cut its manufacturing time in half through elimination of various non-value-added activities, resulting in a more efficient product flow and an annual savings of a half million dollars in manufacturing costs.

PVA has been so successful in helping companies manage their activities that the original term *activity-based costing* is giving way to a broader concept called *activity-based management* (or *activity-based cost management*). In addition to linking costs to activities, **activity-based management** helps managers focus on *continuous improvement* of operations and processes.

Identifying Activity Centres

After a PVA has been completed, the activities involved with the production of each product will be clearly documented on a process flowchart. Since there may be dozens of activities identified, a decision must be made at this point as to how many of these activities to treat as separate *activity centres*. An **activity centre** can be defined as a part of the production process for which management wants a separate reporting of the cost of the activity involved.

---

[5]Adapted from Mark E. Beischel, "Improving Production with Process Value Analysis," *Journal of Accountancy* (September 1990), p. 55.

EXHIBIT 5–3   Process Value Analysis: Value-Added and Non-Value-Added Activities

Present—20 Days

Receiv-ing	Store Raw Materials	Move and Wait	Oper-ation No. 1	Move and Wait	Oper-ation No. 2	Store Finished Goods	Pack and Ship
NVA	NVA	NVA	VA	NVA	VA	NVA	VA
1	5	1	1	2	1	8	1

Total Time Required: VA   3
NVA 17
Total 20

Goal—10 Days

Receiv-ing	Store Raw Materials	Oper-ation No. 1	Move and Wait	Oper-ation No. 2	Store Finished Goods	Pack and Ship
NVA	NVA	VA	NVA	VA	NVA	VA
1	2	1	1	1	3	1

Total Time Required: VA   3
NVA   7
Total 10

VA = Value-added activity; NVA = Non-value-added activity.

For most companies, it would not be economically feasible to treat every single activity as a separate activity centre. Rather, companies frequently combine several related activities into one centre to reduce the amount of detail and record-keeping cost. For example, several actions may be involved in the handling and movement of raw materials, but these are typically combined into a single activity centre titled *material handling.*

Perhaps the greatest accuracy in costing is achieved by recognizing four general levels of activities, with these levels then subdivided into specific activity centres. These four general levels can be described as follows:[6]

1. *Unit-level activities,* which are performed each time a unit is produced;
2. *Batch-level activities,* which are performed each time a batch of goods is handled or processed;
3. *Product-level activities,* which are performed as needed to support the production of each different type of product; and
4. *Facility-level activities,* which simply sustain a facility's general manufacturing process.

Unit-level activities are those that arise as a result of the total volume of production going through a facility. The consumption of power, for example, is a function of the number of hours of machine time required to complete *all* units of product and would therefore be considered a unit-level activity. In like manner, maintenance performed, indirect labour support required, and factory supplies consumed are typically regarded as unit-level activities, because they are dependent on the volume of output. Some compa-

---

[6]Robin Cooper, "Cost Classification in Unit-Based and Activity-Based Manufacturing Cost Systems," *Journal of Cost Management* (Fall 1990), p. 6.

Some business observers suggest that activity-based costing systems should be kept "off line" and not integrated into the general ledger. These observers suggest that companies should retain and continue to use their traditional cost accounting systems for reporting purposes, and use the activity-based costing data only for special studies. Evidence is mounting that for some companies at least, this is *not* sound advice. A growing number of companies are reporting that they have successfully integrated activity-based costing into the general ledger, and these companies report that doing so has facilitated both its implementation and use.[7]

The major problem with keeping activity-based costing "off line" is that management will not be inclined to pay attention to the data it generates, particularly if that data conflicts with what is being reported through the general ledger via the traditional costing system. As one pair of writers have stated, "Until management integrates activity-based costing into the company's formal system of reporting, ABC is in danger of remaining a sideshow exercise, championed by staff groups and consultants but of little real meaning to the day-to-day operations of the company."[8]

nies combine activities at the unit level into a single activity centre, while others recognize at least two unit-level activity centres—one related to machine activity and the other related to labour activity.

Batch-level activities include tasks such as the placement of purchase orders, setups of equipment, shipments to customers, and receipts of material. Costs at the batch level are generated *according to the number of batches processed* rather than according to the number of units produced, the number of units sold, or other measures of volume. In addition, costs at the batch level are generally independent of the size of the batch. The cost of placing a purchase order, for example, is the same regardless of whether one unit or 5,000 units of an item are ordered. Thus, the total cost generated by a batch-level activity such as purchasing will be a function of the *number* of orders placed and not a function of the size of these orders. The batch concept is recognized under activity-based costing by the creation of a separate activity centre for each batch-level activity that can be identified.

Product-level activities (sometimes called *product-sustaining activities*) are those that relate to specific products manufactured by a company. These activities are performed as needed to support production of each different type of product; thus, product-level activities will relate to some products but not to others. Product-level activities include maintaining parts inventories, issuing engineering change notices (the modifying of a product to meet a customer's specifications), and developing special test routines. Typically, a separate activity centre is needed for each product-level activity that can be identified.

Facility-level activities (sometimes called *facility-sustaining activities*) are typically combined into a single activity centre, since they relate to overall production and not to any specific batch or product. Facility-level costs include such items as factory management, insurance, property taxes, and worker recreational facilities.

---

[7]See Frances Gammell and C. J. McNair, "Jumping the Growth Threshold through Activity-Based Cost Management," *Management Accounting* (September 1994), pp. 37–46; William O. Stratton, "ABC: An All-Purpose Solution for Financial Reporting," *Management Accounting* (May 1993), pp. 44–49; Hal Thilmony, "Product Costing: One Set of Books or Two?" *Journal of Cost Management* (Winter 1993), pp. 37–44; and C. Mike Merz and Arlene Hardy, "ABC Puts Accountants on Design Team at HP," *Management Accounting* (September 1993), pp. 22–27.

[8]Daniel P. Keegan and Robert G. Eiler, "Let's Reengineer Cost Accounting," *Management Accounting* (August 1994), p. 27.

Theoretically, facility-level costs should not be added to products, because doing so involves the use of arbitrary, volume-based measures such as direct labour-hours or machine-hours. However, virtually all companies *do* add facility-level costs to products. Some of these companies use activity-based costing as their primary costing system and therefore must generate full product costs for external reporting purposes (to be in compliance with generally accepted accounting principles). Other companies, which do not use activity-based costing as their primary costing system, probably allocate facility-level costs to products simply because they have always done so under their old, volume-based systems.

If a company uses activity-based costing only as a secondary costing system—that is, only to provide data internally for management—*then facility-level costs should not be added to products.* Adding such costs to products can result in misleading data and unwise decisions on the part of management. This point is considered further in Chapter 13, where we deal with relevant costs in decision making. In the present chapter, to be comprehensive in our coverage, we assume that activity-based costing is being used as the primary costing system.

Exhibit 5–4 contains examples of activity centres found at each of the four levels discussed above. The exhibit also contains examples of cost drivers used at each of these levels and examples of the costs involved.

Assigning Costs to Activity Centres

We stated earlier that activity-based costing utilizes a two-stage costing process. In the first stage, costs are assigned to the activity centres where they are accumulated while waiting to be applied to products. Costs can either be assigned *directly* to activity centres in this first stage or they can be assigned by use of first-stage cost drivers.

Where possible, companies prefer to assign costs directly to activity centres in order to avoid any distortion in costing. If a company has an activity centre titled *material handling,* for example, then the company would identify all costs directly associated with material handling and assign the costs to that centre as they are incurred. Such costs may include salaries, depreciation, and the use of various supplies. Other costs associated with material handling might arise from some resource that is shared by two or more activity centres; these costs would need to be assigned to the centres according to some first-stage cost driver that controls utilization of the costs involved. Plant space, for example, might be shared by several activity centres, including material handling. The costs associated with plant space would be assigned to the centres according to the amount of space occupied by each. The identification and use of first-stage cost drivers is discussed in detail in Chapter 16.

Selecting Cost Drivers

The second stage of the two-stage costing process involves assigning costs from the activity centres to products. This is accomplished through the selection and use of second-stage cost drivers. Two factors must be considered when selecting a cost driver for use in this second stage:[9]

1. The ease of obtaining data relating to the cost driver.
2. The degree to which the cost driver measures actual consumption by products of the activity involved.

---

[9]For a more detailed discussion, see Robin Cooper, "Elements of Activity-Based Costing," in Barry J. Brinker, ed., *Emerging Practices in Cost Management* (Boston, Mass.: Warren, Gorham & LaMont, 1990), p. 16.

EXHIBIT 5–4

Examples of Activity
Centres, Cost
Drivers, and

Unit-Level Activities

Examples of activity centres:
  Machine-related activities, such as
    milling, cutting, and maintenance
  Labour-related activities, including
    fringe benefits

Examples of cost drivers:
  Machine-hours
  Labour-hours
  Number of units of output

Examples of traceable costs:
  Power costs
  Maintenance costs
  Labour costs
  Factory supplies
  Depreciation of general-use machines
    and equipment
  Depreciation of maintenance
    equipment

Product-Level Activities

Examples of activity centres:
  Product testing
  Parts inventory management
  Product design

Examples of cost drivers:
  Number of tests
  Hours of testing time
  Number of part types
  Hours of design time
  Number of engineering change orders

Examples of traceable costs:
  Testing facility costs
  Parts administration costs
  Parts carrying costs
  Product engineering costs
  Design costs

Batch-Level Activities

Examples of activity centres:
  Purchase order processing
  Production order processing
  Equipment setups
  Material handling
  Quality inspection

Examples of cost drivers:
  Number of orders processed
  Number of material receipts
  Kilograms of material handled
  Number of setups
  Hours of setup time
  Number of inspections
  Hours of inspection time

Examples of traceable costs:
  Clerical costs
  Supplies consumed
  Labour setup costs
  Labour cost to handle material
  Depreciation of office, setup, and
    material-handling equipment
  Quality control costs

Facility-Level Activities

Examples of activity centres:
  General factory
  Plant occupancy
  Personnel administration and training*

Examples of cost drivers:
  Machine-hours
  Labour-hours
  Number of employees (head count)
  Hours of training time

Examples of traceable costs:
  Plant management salaries
  Plant depreciation
  Property taxes and insurance
  Personnel administration costs
  Employee training costs
  Worker recreational facilities

*The costs of some of these activities may be traceable in part to the facility level and in part to *other* activity centres
at the unit level, product level, and batch level. Personnel administration and training may be such an activity.
Activities of this type, which provide essential, companywide services, are discussed in depth in Chapter 16.

The ease of obtaining data strikes at the very heart of activity-based costing, since detailed information relating to a particular cost driver may be difficult to find. Assume again that a company wants to establish an activity centre titled *material handling*. After careful analysis, management has determined that *number of times handled* would be the appropriate cost driver to use in assigning material-handling cost to products. But then management discovers that no cost-effective means is available for recording how many times a particular item of material is handled during a period, thereby making use of the new activity centre economically unfeasible.

The matter of economic feasibility is a major barrier to the use of activity-based costing, and it is the factor most often mentioned by companies that have decided *not* to adopt the activity approach. To make activity-based costing workable, managers have found that either they must devise new methods of gathering data relating to cost drivers or they must use drivers for which data are readily available.

In choosing a cost driver for an activity centre, managers must be sure that the cost driver that is selected accurately measures the actual consumption of the activity by the company's various products. If a high degree of correlation does not exist between the cost driver and actual consumption, then inaccurate costing will result.

Graphic Example of Activity-Based Costing

Once the design decisions relating to PVA, identifying activity centres, tracing costs to activity centres, and selecting cost drivers have been made, the structure of a company's activity-based costing system will be evident. This structure will differ from company to company depending on the number and type of activity centres maintained. For some companies, the structure will be simple with only one or two activity centres at the unit, batch, or product level. For other companies, the structure will be complex with many such centres.

Exhibit 5–5 provides a graphic example of an activity-based costing system of medium complexity. The purpose of this exhibit is to tie together the concepts discussed on preceding pages and also to present a bird's-eye view of what an activity-based costing system looks like. In addition to manufacturing overhead costs, the exhibit shows that

▼   ▼   ▼   ▼   ▼

MANAGERIAL ACCOUNTING IN ACTION—THE ISSUE

Comtek Sound, Inc., makes two products, a radio with a built-in tape player (called a tape unit) and a radio with a built-in compact disc player (called a CD unit), which are sold to automobile manufacturers for installation in new vehicles. The president of the company, Sarah Kastler, recently returned from a management conference at which activity-based costing was discussed. Following the conference, she called a meeting of the top managers in the company to discuss what she had learned. Attending the meeting were the production manager Frank Hines, the marketing manager Nicole Sermone, and the accounting manager Tom Frazier.

SARAH: I'm glad we could all get together this morning. The conference I just attended dealt with some issues that I think have direct application to our company.

FRANK: Did anyone at the conference explain why my equipment always breaks down at the worst possible moment?

SARAH: Sorry, Frank, I guess it must be bad karma or something.

Continued

EXHIBIT 5-5

Graphic Example of
Activity-Based
Costing

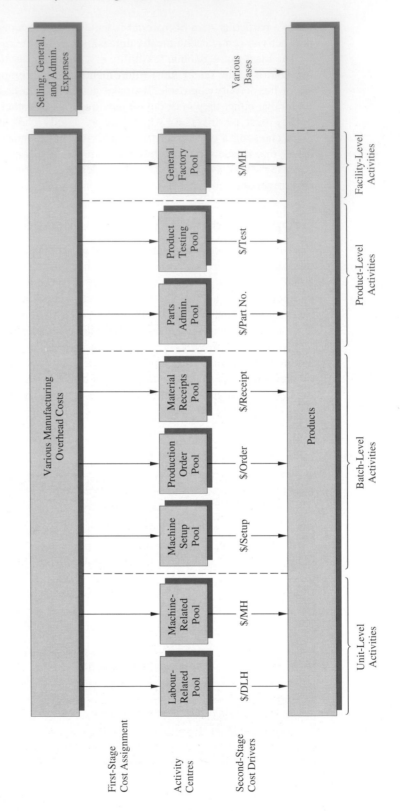

NICOLE: Did the conference tell you why we've been losing all those bids lately on our bread-and-butter tape units and winning every bid on our specialty CD units?

SARAH: Nicole, you probably weren't expecting this answer, but, yes, there may be a simple reason why we're losing bids on our high-volume bread-and-butter business but winning bids on low-volume specialty business.

NICOLE: Let me guess. The competition doesn't want to produce the more complex CD units, so they've decided to concentrate on the simpler tape units.

SARAH: Yes, the competition has a lot to do with it. But Nicole, we may have been shooting ourselves in the foot.

NICOLE: How so? I don't know about anyone else, but we marketing types have been hustling like crazy to get more business for the company.

FRANK: Wait a minute, Nicole, my production people have been turning in tremendous improvements in defect rates, on-time delivery, you name it.

SARAH: Whoa, everybody. Calm down. I don't think anyone is to blame for us losing so many bids on our high-volume bread-and-butter product. Nicole, when you talk with our customers, what reasons do they give for taking their tape unit business to our competitors? Is it a problem with the quality of our unit or our on-time delivery?

NICOLE: No, they don't have any problem with our product or our service—our customers readily admit that we're among the best in the business.

FRANK: Darn right!

SARAH: Then what's the problem?

NICOLE: Price. The competition is undercutting our price on the tape units and then bidding unreasonably high prices on the CD units. As a result, they're stealing away our more profitable tape business and leaving us with just the low-volume CD business.

SARAH: Why is our price so high for the tape units that the competition is able to undercut us?

NICOLE: Our price isn't too high. Theirs is too low. Our competitors must be pricing below their costs on the tape units.

SARAH: Why do you think that?

NICOLE: Well, if we charged the prices for our tape units that our competitors are quoting, we'd be pricing below *our* cost when you consider both manufacturing cost and selling and administrative expenses, and I know we're just as efficient as any competitor.

FRANK: Nicole, why would our competitors price below their cost?

NICOLE: They're out to grab market share.

FRANK: Does that make any sense? What good does more market share do them if they're pricing below their cost?

SARAH: I think Frank has a point, Nicole. Tom, you're the expert with the numbers. Can you suggest another explanation?

TOM: I was hoping you'd ask that. Those product cost figures my department reports to you are primarily intended to be used to value inventories and determine cost of goods sold for our external financial statements. I am awfully uncomfortable about using them for bidding. In fact, I have mentioned this several times, but no one was interested.

SARAH: Now I'm interested. Tom, are you telling us that the product cost figures we have been using for bidding may be wrong? Are you suggesting that we really don't know what the manufacturing cost is for either the tape units or the CD units?

TOM: Yes, that could be the problem. Our cost system isn't designed to recognize that our two products place different demands on our resources. The tape units are simple to manufacture, and the CD units are more complex. For example, both products take the same amount of labour time for assembly, but the more complex CD units take a disproportionate amount of machine and testing time. We need a cost system that recognizes this difference in demand on resources.

Continued

> **Sarah:** That's exactly what was being talked about at my conference. The conference speakers suggested we go home and recost our products using something called activity-based costing. Tom, can you help us give it a try?
>
> **Tom:** You bet! But we need to do it as a team. Can each person in the room appoint one of their top people to work with me?
>
> **Sarah:** Let's do it! I'd like the special team to report back to this group as soon as possible. If there's a problem with our costs, we need to know it before the competition plows us under.

selling, general, and administrative expenses are also charged to products in an activity-based costing system. Our focus in this chapter, however, is only on the manufacturing overhead cost portion of the exhibit. Later, in Chapter 12, we broaden our focus and show how selling, general, and administrative expenses can be charged to products and services when activity-based costing is used.

NUMERICAL EXAMPLE OF ACTIVITY-BASED COSTING

OBJECTIVE 4

Compute the cost of a unit of product using activity-based costing.

The real key to understanding the need for activity-based costing in some companies is to recognize that different products can place different demands on resources. This difference in demand on resources—which is *not* recognized by traditional costing systems—can be readily illustrated by looking at some cost data for a multi-product company.

Comtek Sound, Inc.'s Basic Data

Tom Frazier and the special team immediately set about to gather basic information relating to the company's two products. As a basis for its study, the team decided to use the cost and other data planned for the current year. A summary of some of this information follows:

For the current year, the company has budgeted to sell 50,000 CD units and 200,000 tape units. Both products require two direct labour-hours to complete. Therefore, the company plans to work 500,000 direct labour-hours during the current year, computed as follows:

	Hours
CD units: 50,000 units × 2 hours	100,000
Tape units: 200,000 units × 2 hours	400,000
Total hours	500,000

Costs for materials and labour for one unit of each product are given below:

	CD Units	Tape Units
Direct materials	$90	$50
Direct labour (at $10 per hour)	20	20

The company's estimated manufacturing overhead costs for the current year total $10,000,000. The special team discovered that although the same amount of direct labour time is required for each product, the more complex CD units require more machine time, more machine setups, and more testing than the tape units. Also, the team found that it is necessary to manufacture the CD units in smaller lots, so they require a relatively large number of production orders as compared to the tape units.

The company has always used direct labour-hours as the base for assigning overhead cost to its products.

With this information in hand, the special team decided to assign overhead cost to the company's products using two different approaches. First, the team decided it would use direct labour-hours as the overhead assignment base (which the company has been doing for many years), and second, the team decided it would use activities as the overhead assignment base.

Direct Labour-Hours as a Base

With Tom Frazier's help, the special team found that the company's predetermined overhead rate is $20 per hour if direct labour-hours are used as the base for assigning overhead cost to products. This rate is computed as follows:

$$\frac{\text{Manufacturing overhead costs, } \$10,000,000}{\text{Direct labour-hours, } 500,000} = \$20 \text{ per direct labour-hour}$$

Using this rate, the special team then computed the unit product costs as given below:

	CD Units	Tape Units
Direct materials (above)	$ 90	$ 50
Direct labour (above)	20	20
Manufacturing overhead (2 hours × $20) ...	40	40
Total unit product cost	$150	$110

Tom Frazier explained to the special team that the problem with this costing approach is that it relies entirely on labour time in assigning overhead cost to products and does not consider the impact of other factors—such as setups required or testing performed—on the overhead costs of the company. Therefore, since these other factors are being ignored, and since the two products require equal amounts of labour time, they are assigned equal amounts of overhead cost.

Tom explained that while this method of computing costs is fast and simple, it is accurate only in those situations where other factors affecting overhead costs are not significant. Tom stated that he believed these other factors *are* significant in the case of Comtek Sound, Inc., and he was anxious for the team to analyze the various activities of the company to see what impact these activities have on costs.

Activities as a Base

The special team then analyzed Comtek Sound, Inc.'s operations and identified eight activity centres in the factory, along with their associated cost drivers. (These eight activity centres are identical to the ones illustrated earlier in Exhibit 5–5.) Cost and other data relating to the activity centres are presented in Exhibit 5–6.

As shown in the Basic Data at the top of the exhibit, the special team estimated the amount of overhead cost for each activity centre, along with the expected activity for the current year. The machine setups activity centre, for example, has $1,600,000 in overhead cost, and it is expected to complete 4,000 setups during the year, of which 3,000 will be due to the CD units and 1,000 will be due to the tape units. Data for other activity centres are as shown in the exhibit.

Using the appropriate cost drivers as a base, the special team then computed a predetermined overhead rate for *each activity centre*. These rates in turn were used to assign the activity centre costs to the two products. (See the middle and bottom portions of Exhibit 5–6.)

EXHIBIT 5-6

Overhead Costing by
an Activity Approach

Basic Data

Activity Centre (and Cost Driver)	Estimated Overhead Costs	Expected Activity—Cost Driver		
		Total	CD Units	Tape Units
Labour related (labour-hours)	$ 800,000	500,000	100,000	400,000
Machine related (machine-hours)	2,100,000	1,000,000	300,000	700,000
Machine setups (setups)	1,600,000	4,000	3,000	1,000
Production orders (orders)	450,000	1,200	400	800
Material receipts (receipts)	1,000,000	5,000	1,800	3,200
Parts administration (part types)	350,000	700	400	300
Product testing (tests)	1,700,000	20,000	16,000	4,000
General factory (machine-hours)	2,000,000	1,000,000	300,000	700,000
	$10,000,000			

Overhead Rates by Activity Centre

Activity Centre	(a) Estimated Overhead Costs	(b) Total Expected Activity	(a) ÷ (b) Predetermined Overhead Rate
Labour related	$ 800,000	500,000	$1.60/DLH
Machine related	2,100,000	1,000,000	$2.10/MH
Machine setups	1,600,000	4,000	$400/setup
Production orders	450,000	1,200	$375/order
Material receipts	1,000,000	5,000	$200/receipt
Parts administration	350,000	700	$500/part type
Product testing	1,700,000	20,000	$85/test
General factory	2,000,000	1,000,000	$2/MH

Overhead Cost per Unit of Product

	CD Units		Tape Units	
	Expected Activity	Amount	Expected Activity	Amount
Labour related, at $1.60/DLH	100,000	$ 160,000	400,000	$ 640,000
Machine related, at $2.10/MH	300,000	630,000	700,000	1,470,000
Machine setups, at $400/setup	3,000	1,200,000	1,000	400,000
Production orders, at $375/order	400	150,000	800	300,000
Materials receipts, at $200/receipt	1,800	360,000	3,200	640,000
Parts administration, at $500/part type ...	400	200,000	300	150,000
Product testing, at $85/test	16,000	1,360,000	4,000	340,000
General factory, at $2/MH	300,000	600,000	700,000	1,400,000
Total overhead costs assigned (a)		$4,660,000		$5,340,000
Number of units produced (b)		50,000		200,000
Overhead cost per unit (a) ÷ (b)		$93.20		$26.70

Note from the exhibit that the use of an activity approach has resulted in $93.20 in overhead cost being assigned to each CD unit and $26.70 in overhead cost being assigned to each tape unit. The special team then used these amounts to determine the unit product cost of each product under activity-based costing, as presented in the table at the top of page 227. For comparison, the table also presents the unit costs derived earlier when direct labour was used as the base for assigning overhead cost to the products.

	Activity-Based Costing		Direct-Labour-Based Costing	
	CD Units	Tape Units	CD Units	Tape Units
Direct materials	$ 90.00	$50.00	$ 90.00	$ 50.00
Direct labour	20.00	20.00	20.00	20.00
Manufacturing overhead	93.20	26.70	40.00	40.00
Total unit product cost	$203.20	$96.70	$150.00	$110.00

The special team members were shocked by their findings, which Tom Frazier summarized as follows in the team's report:

> In the past, the company has been charging $40.00 in overhead cost to a unit of either product, whereas it should have been charging $93.20 in overhead cost to each CD unit and only $26.70 to each tape unit. Thus, as a result of using direct labour as the base for overhead costing, in the past too little overhead cost has been charged to the CD units and too much has been charged to the tape units. Consequently, unit costs have been badly distorted. Depending on selling prices, the company may even have been suffering a loss on the CD units without knowing it because the cost of these units has been so vastly understated. Through activity-based costing, we have been able to better identify the overhead costs of each product and thus derive more accurate cost data.

The pattern of cost distortion shown by the special team's findings is quite common. Such distortion can happen in any company that relies solely on direct labour in assigning overhead cost to products and ignores other significant factors affecting overhead cost incurrence.

▼   ▼   ▼   ▼   ▼

MANAGERIAL ACCOUNTING IN ACTION—WRAP-UP

The special team member, Tom Frazier, presented the results of their work in a meeting attended by all of the top managers of Comtek Sound, Inc., including the president Sarah Kastler, the production manager Frank Hines, and the marketing manager Nicole Sermone. After the formal presentation, the following discussion took place:

SARAH: I would like to personally thank the special team for all the work they have done and for an extremely interesting and informative presentation. I am now beginning to wonder about some of the decisions we have made in the past using our old cost accounting system.

TOM: I hope I don't have to remind anyone that I have been warning people about this problem for quite some time.

SARAH: No, you don't have to remind us, Tom. I guess we just didn't understand the problem before.

NICOLE: It's obvious from this activity-based costing information that we had everything backwards. We thought the competition was pricing below cost on the tape units, but in fact *we* were overcharging for these units because our costs were overstated. And we thought the competition was bidding unreasonably high prices on the CD units, but in fact *our* bid prices were way too low because our costs for these units were understated. I'll bet the competition has really been laughing behind our backs!

SARAH: You can bet they won't be laughing when they see our next bids. Now that we have a better understanding of what drives our costs we're going to be the terror of the industry!

▼   ▼   ▼   ▼   ▼

FOCUS ON
CURRENT PRACTICE

Activity-based costing can have dramatic effects on pricing decisions, as Hewlett-Packard experienced when it switched to ABC.

The shift in overhead cost between products can be very great when activity-based costing is introduced. For many years, Hewlett-Packard assigned overhead cost to products on the basis of material cost. When the company introduced activity-based costing, one circuit board that would have been assigned about $5 in overhead cost under the old system was assigned about $25 in overhead cost when activity-based costing was used, which is a 400% increase. Another circuit board that would have been assigned $123 in overhead cost under the old system was assigned only $45 under the activity-based costing system.[10]

This shift in overhead cost between products can also have a significant companywide impact. Two observers of the Hewlett-Packard experience report the following: "During a recent six-month forecast and budget cycle, the ABC system resulted in shifting millions of dollars of cost between customers and products and thus had a dramatic impact on pricing and product design decisions."[11]

Shifting of Overhead Cost.   When a company installs an activity-based costing system, overhead cost is often shifted from the high-volume products to the low-volume products, with a higher unit cost resulting for the low-volume products. We saw this happen in our example above, where overhead cost was shifted to the CD units—the low-volume product—and their unit cost increased from $150 to $203.20 per unit. Why does this shifting of cost take place? It is the result of two related factors.

First, rather than treating overhead cost as a lump amount and spreading it uniformly over all products, activity-based costing attempts to more accurately assign costs to specific products. Since low-volume products often require special equipment, special handling, and so forth, they typically are responsible for the incurrence of a disproportionately large amount of overhead cost. When these costs are assigned to the low-volume products, it drives their unit costs upward.

Second, many overhead costs are incurred at the batch level. Since low-volume products typically have fewer units processed per batch than high-volume products, their average processing cost per unit is higher. For example, consider the cost of issuing production orders, which is a batch activity, for Comtek Sound, Inc. As shown in Exhibit 5–6, the average cost to Comtek Sound to issue a single production order is $375. However, fewer CD units (the low-volume product) are processed per production order than tape units:

	CD Units	Tape Units
Number of units produced per year (a)	50,000	200,000
Number of production orders issued per year (b)	400	800
Number of units processed per production order (a) ÷ (b)	125	250

[10]C. Mike Merz and Arlene Hardy, "ABC Puts Accountants on Design Team at HP," *Management Accounting* (September, 1993), p. 24.

[11]Ibid., p. 25.

If we now spread the $375 cost to issue a production order over the number of units processed per order, we get the following:

	CD Units	Tape Units
Cost to issue a production order (a)	$375	$375
Number of units processed per production order (above) (b)	125	250
Production order cost per unit (a) ÷ (b)	$3.00	$1.50

Thus, the production order cost for a CD unit (the low-volume product) is $3, which is *double* the $1.50 cost for a tape unit. This subtle (but real) difference in cost is ignored when direct labour is used to assign overhead cost to products, since the direct labour approach spreads the cost of *all* production orders evenly over the two products. As a result, the tape units are forced to subsidize the CD units, the low-volume product. When this subsidy is taken away through activity-based costing, the unit cost of the low-volume product is driven upward.

Cost Flows under Activity-Based Costing.   The flow of costs through Raw Materials, Work in Process, Finished Goods, and other accounts is the same under activity-based costing as was illustrated in Chapter 3. Since the flow of costs is the same, the journal entries to record this flow are also the same. The only difference is that a company will have *several* predetermined overhead rates—as we saw in Exhibit 5–6—rather than just one. A specific example to show the flow of costs in an activity-based costing system is provided in Appendix 5A at the end of this chapter.

BENEFITS AND LIMITATIONS OF ACTIVITY-BASED COSTING

OBJECTIVE 5
Enumerate the benefits and limitations of activity-based costing.

At first glance, activity-based costing might seem to be the answer to all of a manager's costing problems. Although certain benefits can be identified, activity-based costing also has several limitations. These benefits and limitations are discussed in this section.

Benefits of Activity-Based Costing

Activity-based costing improves the costing systems of organizations in the following ways, thereby leading to more accurate product costs:

First, activity-based costing *increases the number of cost pools used to accumulate overhead costs.* Rather than accumulating all overhead costs in a single, companywide pool, or accumulating them in departmental pools, costs are accumulated by activity. As a result, many pools are created according to the number of cost-driving activities that can be identified.

Second, activity-based costing *changes the base used to assign overhead costs to products.* Rather than assigning costs on a basis of direct labour or some other measure of volume, costs are assigned on a basis of the portion of cost-driving activities that can be traced to the product or service involved.

Third, activity-based costing *changes a manager's perception of many overhead costs* in that costs that were formerly thought to be indirect (such as power, inspection, and machine setup) are identified with specific activities and thereby are recognized as being traceable to individual products.

As a result of having more accurate product costs, managers are in a position to make better decisions relating to product retention, marketing strategy, product profitability, and so forth. Moreover, activity-based costing leads to better cost control, because managers can see that the best way to control costs is to control the activities that generate the costs in the first place.

Siemens Electric Motor Works has found that by adding only two batch-level activity centres to its costing system, it has been able to achieve significantly more accurate unit costs. The amount of overhead cost traceable to these two activity centres represents only 9% of the total overhead cost of the company. The remaining 91% continues to be allocated to products on a volume basis (principally machine-hours, direct labour-hours, and material cost).[12]

Limitations of Activity-Based Costing

The benefits above are offset somewhat by two limitations that surround activity-based costing. These limitations are (1) the necessity to still make some arbitrary allocations and (2) the high measurement costs associated with multiple activity centres and cost drivers.

The Need for Arbitrary Allocations.   Critics of activity-based costing point out that even though some overhead costs can be traced directly to products through the use of activity centres, the portion that relates to facility-level activities must still be allocated to products by means of some arbitrary base such as machine-hours or labour-hours. It is argued that facility-level activities account for the bulk of overhead cost in many companies, thereby rendering any attempt to gain more accurate product costs through the use of activity-based costing largely meaningless.

Proponents of activity-based costing reply that it is not necessary to have the majority of overhead cost traceable to unit-level, batch-level, or product-level activity centres in order to have activity-based costing yield more accurate unit cost data. For some companies, only a small amount of overhead cost traceable to activity centres at these levels is adequate to improve the costing process.

Moreover, proponents of activity-based costing state that *any* amount of overhead cost traceable directly to products through activity centres is preferable to just assigning all costs arbitrarily by some volume measure. In short, proponents say that it is better to have product costs approximately right than precisely wrong.

High Measurement Costs.   Another significant limitation of activity-based costing is the high measurement costs that are required for its operation. As shown earlier in Exhibit 5–6, even a moderately complex system requires a great amount of detail and many separate computations in order to determine the cost of a unit of product. In Exhibit 5–6, we had only two products; the complexities involved are multiplied manyfold for companies that have hundreds or thousands of products. In short, the implementation of activity-based costing can present a formidable challenge, and management may decide that the measurement costs are too great to justify the expected benefits. Companies that have some of the following characteristics are most likely to benefit from activity-based costing:

1. Products differ substantially in volume, lot size, or complexity of manufacture.
2. Products differ substantially in their need for various activities such as setups, inspections, and so forth, involved in the manufacturing process.
3. The variety of products being manufactured has increased significantly since the existing cost system was established.

---

[12]Robin Cooper, "Cost Classifications in Unit-Based and Activity-Based Manufacturing Cost Systems," *Journal of Cost Management* (Fall 1990), p. 11.

4. Overhead costs are high and increasing.
5. Top management and marketing people largely ignore the cost data provided by the existing system when setting prices or making other product decisions.
6. Manufacturing technology has changed significantly since the existing cost system was established. For example, the factory has been automated or product flow lines have been redesigned.

Volkswagen Canada of Barrie, Ontario, found itself in the 1990s subject to technological change and competition, the same as other automotive manufacturers and suppliers. Activity-based costing was introduced in the early 1990s to help provide clear information needed to be competitive while earning a return on investment demanded by head office. For example, in one area, 80% of the products were losing money or contributing little to the overall profits of the area. Volkswagen is extending ABC to activity-based management and is using the information to support the total quality management activities.[13]

Some companies that use activity-based costing limit their systems to one or two activity centres because of the measurement problems involved. When a company has only one or two activity centres, it is said to have a *partial* activity-based costing system. As such a company grows, it can expand its costing system step by step until activity-based costing is in full use.

Activity-Based Costing and Service Industries

Although initially conceived as a tool for manufacturing companies, activity-based costing is also being used in service industries. Successful implementation of an activity-based costing system depends on identifying the key activities that generate costs and being able to keep track of how many of those activities are performed for each service that is provided.

Two common problems exist in service firms that sometimes make implementation of activity-based costing relatively difficult. One problem is that a larger proportion of costs in service industries tend to be facility-level costs that cannot be traced to any particular billable service provided by the firm. Another problem is that it is more difficult to capture activity data in service companies, because so many of the activities tend to involve nonrepetitive human tasks that cannot be easily recorded.[14] Nevertheless, activity-based costing systems have been implemented in a number of service firms, including railroads, hospitals, banks, and data services companies.

Our discussion in this chapter has focused on the use of activity-based costing in manufacturing companies. We will defer further discussion of its use in service-type operations to Chapter 16, where we discuss its specific application in greater depth.

---

[13]Jim Gurowka, "ABC, ABM, and the Volkswagen Saga," *CMA Magazine* (May 1996), pp. 30–33.
[14]William Rotch, "Activity-Based Costing in Service Industries," *Journal of Cost Management* (Summer 1990), p. 8.

FOCUS ON CURRENT PRACTICE

A 1992 survey of 352 large Canadian companies states that 67% had not considered activity-based costing (ABC) while 14% had implemented or were implementing ABC and 15% were currently assessing the methodology; 4% had considered ABC and decided not to implement it. The development of ABC in Canada appears to be behind that in the United States. Given that 9% of U.K. companies had considered ABC and rejected it, acceptance in Canada appears to be higher than in the U.K. The manufacturing sector shows the highest rate of development, while resource, retail, and communications sectors are further behind.[15]

INTERNATIONAL USE OF ACTIVITY-BASED COSTING

Activity-based costing was pioneered in the United States, although several of the early field studies were performed by American researchers on German companies. The concept is relatively new, with the term *activity-based costing* having been coined by the management of John Deere Company within the last 15 years.

To date, activity-based costing has not spread as rapidly throughout the world as has JIT and TQM. Perhaps the reason is traceable to the costs of implementation and to the fact that it is sometimes difficult to collect the data needed to operate the system. In Japan, activity-based costing is rarely used. Instead, Japanese managers seem to prefer volume measures such as direct labour-hours to assign overhead cost to products. This preference, according to Japanese researchers, can be explained by the fact that Japanese managers are "convinced that reducing direct labour is essential for ongoing cost improvement."[16] It is argued that by using direct labour as an overhead allocation base, managers are forced to watch direct labour more closely and to seek ways to reduce it. In short, Japanese managers tend to be more concerned about cost reduction and working toward specific long-term company goals than they are about obtaining more accurate product costs.

The most extensive application of activity-based costing has been in the United States, with some applications having been made in Europe, particularly in Germany and Northern Europe.

QUALITY MANAGEMENT

OBJECTIVE 6
Distinguish between grade, quality of design, and quality of conformance.

In recent years, international competition has become an increasingly important factor in many industries. One result of this increased competition has been the development of activity-based costing, which we have seen helps managers in their pricing and other decisions by giving them new insights into their costs. Another result has been increased emphasis on the importance of maintaining quality in products and services. Managers have learned that market share can be eroded just as fast by poor-quality products as it can by inappropriate selling prices.

---

[15]"Activity-Based Costing," *Management Accounting Issues Paper 3* (Hamilton, Ont.: Society of Management Accountants of Canada, 1993), pp. 9–13.

[16]Toshiro Hiromoto, "Another Hidden Edge—Japanese Management Accounting," *Harvard Business Review* (July–August 1988), p. 23.

A common rule of thumb illustrates the importance companies attach to quality control. The idea is that it costs 10 times more to win a client than to keep one. A happy customer tells 5 others at no cost to the company. On the other hand, an unhappy customer talks to 10 other people about the problem.

Appendixes to Chapters 3 and 4 explained specific accounting practices for scrap, rework, and lost units. In this section, our focus is on identifying additional costs associated with quality assurance and methods of reporting such costs to management. In addition, we allude to methods for timely reporting needed by operating personnel to monitor quality on an ongoing basis.

The demand by customers for ever-higher quality in products and services has led companies to introduce *total quality management* and to make huge investments in various quality control programs. Of course, these programs involve costs, and management must have methods available to measure these costs in terms of both amount and effectiveness. We now turn our attention to identifying the costs associated with quality assurance and to methods of reporting these costs to management.

The word *quality* has various meanings, but for our purposes **quality** can be defined as conformance to customer expectations in terms of features and performance of the product or service involved.[17] Thus, quality is achieved when a product or service contains all of the features that a customer would expect and when the product or service performs in such a way that the customer is satisfied. In this context, three factors underlie the overall quality of a product or service. These factors are *grade, quality of design,* and *quality of conformance.*

Grade

Grade relates to differences in degree, worth, or ranking between products or services that have the same functional use. For example, a 24-pin dot matrix printer and a laser printer have the same functional use in that both are designed to handle the output of a computer. But the laser printer is viewed as being higher in grade than the dot matrix printer because of its clearer print and its greater speed. In like manner, a laser printer that can handle output in colour is viewed as being higher in grade than one that can print only in black.

Companies provide products and services that differ in grade because of differences in needs and purchasing power among customers. As needs increase and as customers become more affluent, they purchase the higher-grade products because of the features that these products contain. The laser printer is purchased, for example, because of a need for clearer reports, a need for faster output, or a need to print in colour. Since higher-grade products fill more needs and thus render greater satisfaction, they are viewed as being higher in quality than lower-grade products. Thus, grade and quality go hand in hand in the eyes of the customer. The higher the grade of a product, the greater is its expected quality.

Quality of Design

To compete in a particular product market, a company must do three things. First, it must determine customers' expectations relating to features and performance for the various grades of the product that could be offered. Second, the company must identify the grade

---

[17]Wayne J. Morse, Harold P. Roth, and Kay M. Poston, *Measuring, Planning, and Controlling Quality Costs* (Montvale, N.J.: National Association of Accountants, 1987), p. 8. Much of the material in this section is based on this excellent study.

"Quality" can have many different meanings. Grade is one factor used in defining quality. A Mercedes automobile, for example, is of a much higher grade than a low-end automobile.

level(s) at which it wishes to compete. And third, it must develop product specifications that are appropriate for the grade level(s) chosen.

If a company wants to compete in the top-of-the-line laser printer market, for example, it must determine the features that customers would expect to find in a printer sold in that market and then proceed to develop a printer that contains these features. **Quality of design** is the degree to which a company's design specifications for a product or service meet customers' expectations *for the grade level chosen.*[18] That is, a product or service has a high quality of design if—for the grade level chosen—it contains all the features and operates in the way that customers would expect it to operate. Thus, a laser printer competing in the top-grade colour market that is capable of printing in sharp, clear colours would have a high quality of design, whereas another printer competing in the same market that is capable of printing only ill-defined and blotchy colours would have a low quality of design.

The costs associated with quality of design are opportunity costs and come in the form of lost sales. Over time, customers will gravitate toward those products that consistently deliver the features they want. These features can be very subtle in nature and can include how a product looks, sounds, and feels.

In summary, quality of design is a key consideration in measuring the overall quality of a product. If a product's design is such that its features and performance fail to meet customers' expectations for the grade level chosen, then the customers will simply turn elsewhere.

Quality of Conformance

A product can be high in grade and have a high quality of design, but it can still be low in overall quality if defects or other problems cause it to fall short of what the designers intended.

---

[18]Ibid., p. 10.

Nissan Motor Company has hired anthropologists to probe into what makes people buy a car and to determine those small touches in design that can make a car more "user friendly." Honda Motor Company has designed its door locks, stereo buttons, and turn signals to require exactly the same pressure to operate, which gives its cars a more "comfortable" feel. This attention to quality of design avoids reactions such as that of one car owner who wrote to the manufacturer and complained that working his turn signal was "akin to breaking a chicken's leg."[19]

Quality of conformance is the degree to which the actual product that is manufactured or the actual service that is rendered meets its design specifications and is free of defects or problems that might affect appearance or performance.[20] For example, a colour laser printer might be well designed as shown by the clear, even output provided by design prototypes. It would have a low quality of conformance, however, if units manufactured and shipped to customers are assembled in a sloppy manner, resulting in frequent breakdowns or blotchy, uneven output. Thus, for a product or service to have a high quality of conformance, it must function in the way the designer intended and be free of defects, breakdowns, and related problems.

To summarize the key definitions covered in this section, the relationship among grade, quality of design, and quality of conformance is shown in graphic form in Exhibit 5–7.

EXHIBIT 5–7   Relationship among Grade, Quality of Design and Quality of Conformance

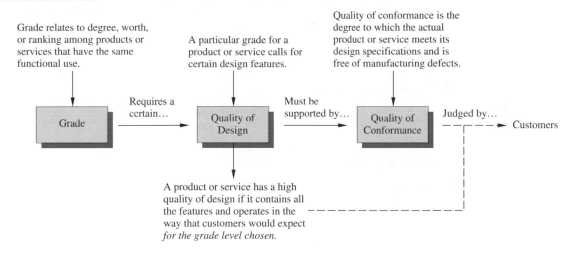

QUALITY OF CONFORMANCE—A CLOSER LOOK

OBJECTIVE 7
Identify the four types of quality costs.

The bulk of all quality costs are usually associated with the quality of conformance. These costs can be broken down into four broad groups. Two of these groups—known as *prevention costs* and *appraisal costs*—are incurred in an effort to keep poor quality of conformance from occurring. The other two groups of costs—known as *internal failure costs* and

---

[19]"A New Era for Auto Quality," *Business Week* (October 22, 1990), p. 85.
[20]Morse et al., "Measuring, Planning, and Controlling Quality Costs," p. 11.

Prevention Costs

Systems development
Quality engineering
Quality training
Quality circles
Statistical process control activities
Supervision of prevention activities
Quality data gathering, analysis, and reporting
Quality improvement projects
Technical support provided to suppliers
Audits of the effectiveness of the quality
    system

Appraisal Costs

Test and inspection of incoming materials
Test and inspection of in-process goods
Final product testing and inspection
Supplies used in testing and inspection
Supervision of testing and inspection
    activities
Depreciation of test equipment
Maintenance of test equipment
Plant utilities in the inspection area
Field testing and appraisal at customer site

Internal Failure Costs

Net cost of scrap
Net cost of spoilage
Rework labour and overhead
Reinspection of reworked products
Retesting of reworked products
Downtime caused by quality problems
Disposal of defective products
Analysis of the cause of defects in production
Re-entering data because of keying errors
Debugging of software errors

External Failure Costs

Cost of field servicing and handling complaints
Warranty repairs and replacements
Repairs and replacements beyond the warranty
    period
Product recalls
Liability arising from defective products
Returns and allowances arising from quality
    problems
Lost sales arising from a reputation for poor
    quality

external failure costs—are incurred because poor quality of conformance has occurred. Examples of the kinds of costs involved in each of these four groups are given in Exhibit 5–8.

Several things should be noted about the quality costs shown in the exhibit. First, note that quality costs don't relate to just manufacturing; rather, they relate to all activities in a company from initial research and development (R&D) through customer servicing. Second, note that the number of costs associated with quality is very large; therefore, total quality cost is likely to be quite high unless management gives this area special attention. Finally, note how different the costs are in the four groupings. We will now look at each of these groupings more closely.

Prevention Costs

The most effective way to minimize quality costs while maintaining high-quality output is to avoid having quality problems arise in the first place. This is the purpose of **prevention**

A member of top management from Hewlett-Packard has stated that "the earlier you detect and prevent a defect, the more you can save. If you throw away a defective 2-cent resistor before you use it, you lose 2 cents. If you don't find it until it has been soldered into a computer component, it may cost $10 to repair the part. If you don't catch the defect until it is in the computer user's hands, the repair will cost hundreds of dollars. Indeed, if a $5,000 computer must be repaired in the field, the expense may exceed the manufacturing cost."[21]

[21]David A. Garvin, "Product Quality: Profitable at Any Cost," *The New York Times,* March 3, 1985, p. F3. Copyright © 1985 by The New York Times Company. Reprinted by permission.

costs; such costs relate to any activity that reduces the number of defects in products or services. Companies have learned that it is much less costly to prevent a problem from ever happening than it is to find and correct the problem after it has occurred.

Note from Exhibit 5–8 that prevention costs include those activities relating to quality circles and statistical process control. **Quality circles** consist of small groups of employees that meet on a regular basis to discuss ways to improve the quality of output. Both management and workers are included in these circles. Quality circles are widely used and can be found in the utility, telecommunications, health, and finance industries as well as in manufacturing. **Statistical process control (SPC)** is a technique whereby workers use charts to monitor the quality of the parts or components that pass through their workstations. By using SPC, companies are able to involve workers directly in quality control, and to take a piece-by-piece and step-by-step approach to maintaining the overall quality of their products. Note also from the list of prevention costs in Exhibit 5–8 that companies provide technical support to their suppliers as a method of preventing defects. In our discussion of JIT systems in Chapter 1, we learned that such support to suppliers is vital and that suppliers in turn must certify that they will deliver materials that are free of defects.

Professor John K. Shank of Dartmouth College has aptly stated, "The old-style approach was to say, 'We've got great quality. We have 40 quality control inspectors in the factory.' Then somebody realized that if you need 40 inspectors, it must be a lousy factory. So now the trick is to run a factory without any quality control inspectors; each employee is his or her own quality control person."[22]

Appraisal Costs

If defective parts and products can't be prevented, then the next best thing is to catch them as early as possible. **Appraisal costs,** which are sometimes called *inspection costs,* are incurred to identify defective products *before* the products are shipped to customers. Unfortunately, performing appraisal activities doesn't keep defects from happening again in a company, and most managers now realize that maintaining an army of inspectors is a costly (and ineffective) approach to quality control.

In our discussion of JIT in Chapter 1, we found that employees in modern factories are, indeed, responsible for their own quality control. This approach to appraisal, along with high quality of design, allows quality to be *manufactured* into products rather than *inspected* into products.

Internal Failure Costs

If a product fails to conform to its design specifications, then failure costs are incurred. Failure costs can be either internal or external. **Internal failure costs** result from identification of defects during the appraisal process. Such costs include scrap, rejected products, reworking

---

[22]Robert W. Casey, "The Changing World of the CEO," *PPM World* (1990), p. 31.

of defective units, and downtime caused by quality problems. It is crucial that any failure in product conformance be discovered during production or before a product is shipped, or else defective items will be placed in the hands of customers. Of course, the more effective a company's appraisal activities, the greater the chance of catching defects internally and the greater the level of internal failure costs (as compared to external failure costs). Unfortunately, appraisal activities focus on symptoms rather than on causes and they do nothing to reduce the number of defective items. Appraisal activities do bring defects to the attention of management, however, so that steps can be taken to improve the quality of conformance.

Maytag has staked its reputation on few or no external failure costs. The famous "Lonely Maytag Repairman" ads reinforce Maytag's commitment to quality.

[23]Howard Schultz, "Washing Away the Sin of Overpayment," *The Wall Street Journal,* August 9, 1993, p. A12.

EXHIBIT 5-9

Effect of Quality
Costs on Quality of
Conformance

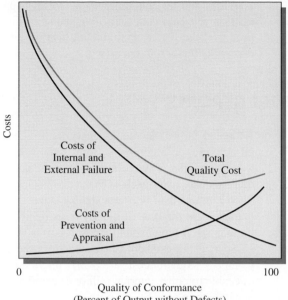

External Failure Costs

When a product that is defective in some way is delivered to a customer, then **external failure costs** result. As shown in Exhibit 5–8, external failure costs include warranty repairs and replacements, product recalls, liability arising from legal action against a company, and lost sales arising from a reputation for poor quality. Such costs can be devastating to a company and, if left unchecked, can decimate profits.

In the past, some companies have taken the attitude, "Let's go ahead and ship everything to customers, and we'll take care of any problems under the warranty." This attitude generally results in high external failure costs, increasing customer ill will, and declining market share.

Distribution of Quality Costs

We stated earlier that a company's total quality cost is likely to be very high unless management gives this area special attention. Indeed, studies show that quality costs for North American companies range between 10% and 20% of total sales, whereas experts say that these costs should be more in the 2% to 4% range. How does a company reduce its total quality cost but still maintain a high quality of conformance? The answer lies in a *redistribution* of the quality costs that the company incurs. Refer to the graph in Exhibit 5–9.

The graph shows that when the quality of conformance is low, total quality cost is high and that most of this cost consists of costs of internal and external failure. However, as a company spends more and more on costs of prevention and appraisal, total quality cost drops rapidly; the graph shows that this drop is due to a sharp reduction in the costs of internal and external failure. Thus, a company can reduce its total quality cost by focusing its efforts on prevention and appraisal so that failures are minimized and any defects are detected before delivery of products to customers.

As a company's quality program becomes more refined and as its failure costs begin to fall, efforts toward further reduction of these costs should focus more on prevention activities and less on appraisal activities. Appraisal can only *find* defects, whereas prevention can *eliminate* them. We stated earlier that quality should be manufactured into products; the way to manufacture quality into products is to take those steps needed to *prevent* defects from occurring.

QUALITY COST REPORTS

OBJECTIVE 8
Be familiar with the organization, content, and uses of a quality cost report.

We noted earlier that quality costs don't relate to just manufacturing; rather, they relate to all activities in a company from initial research and development (R&D) through customer servicing. Therefore, as part of the quality cost system, companies must extract the quality costs from each activity and accumulate these costs on a **quality cost report.** Such a report then becomes the backbone of the quality cost system in that it will show management the type of quality costs being incurred, as well as the amount and trend of these costs. A typical quality cost report is shown in Exhibit 5–10.

Several things should be noted from the data in the exhibit. First, note that Ventura Company's quality costs are poorly distributed in both years, with most of the costs being traceable to either internal failure or external failure. The external failure costs are particularly high in year 1 in comparison to other costs.

Second, note that the company increased its spending on prevention and appraisal activities in year 2. As a result, internal failure costs go up in that year (from $2 million in year 1 to $3 million in year 2), but external failure costs drop sharply (from $5.15 million in year 1 to only $2 million in year 2). The reason internal failure costs go up is that through increased appraisal activity, defects are being caught and corrected before products are shipped to customers. Thus, the company is incurring more cost for scrap, rework, and so forth, but it is saving huge amounts in warranty repairs, warranty replacements, and other external failure costs.

Third, note that as a result of greater emphasis on prevention and appraisal, *total* quality cost has decreased in year 2. As continued emphasis is placed on prevention and appraisal in future years, total quality cost should continue to decrease in the same manner that we see in the exhibit. That is, future increases in prevention and appraisal costs should be more than offset by decreases in failure costs. Thus, total quality cost should continue to fall. Finally, note that total quality cost equals 18% of sales in year 1 and 15% of sales in year 2. Through the JIT concept of continuous improvement, the company should strive to reduce this figure to the range of 2% to 4% of sales. Experience shows that such a reduction is possible through a concerted effort toward *prevention* of defects.

Quality Cost Reports in Graphic Form

As a supplement to the quality cost report shown in Exhibit 5–10, companies frequently prepare quality cost information in graphic form. Graphic presentations include pie charts, bar graphs, trend lines, and so forth. The data for Ventura Company from Exhibit 5–10 is presented in bar graph form in Exhibit 5–11.

The first bar graph in Exhibit 5–11 is scaled in terms of dollars of quality cost, and the second is scaled in terms of quality cost as a percentage of sales. The reader should note that in both graphs the data are "stacked" upward. That is, appraisal costs are stacked on top of prevention costs, internal failure costs are stacked on top of the sum of prevention costs plus appraisal costs, and so forth, until total quality costs are represented in the graphs. The percentage figures in the second graph show that total quality cost equals 18% of sales in year 1 and 15% of sales in year 2, the same as reported in Exhibit 5–10.

EXHIBIT 5–10

Quality Cost Report

VENTURA COMPANY
Quality Cost Report For Years 1 and 2

	Year 2		Year 1	
	Amount	Percent*	Amount	Percent*
Prevention costs:				
Systems development	$ 400,000	0.80	$ 270,000	0.54
Quality training	210,000	0.42	130,000	0.26
Supervision of prevention activities	70,000	0.14	40,000	0.08
Quality improvement projects	320,000	0.64	210,000	0.42
Total	1,000,000	2.00	650,000	1.30
Appraisal costs:				
Inspection	600,000	1.20	560,000	1.12
Reliability testing	580,000	1.16	420,000	0.84
Supervision of testing and inspection ..	120,000	0.24	80,000	0.16
Depreciation of test equipment	200,000	0.40	140,000	0.28
Total	1,500,000	3.00	1,200,000	2.40
Internal failure costs:				
Net cost of scrap	900,000	1.80	750,000	1.50
Rework labour and overhead	1,430,000	2.86	810,000	1.62
Downtime due to defects in quality	170,000	0.34	100,000	0.20
Disposal of defective products	500,000	1.00	340,000	0.68
Total	3,000,000	6.00	2,000,000	4.00
External failure costs:				
Warranty repairs	400,000	0.80	900,000	1.80
Warranty replacements	870,000	1.74	2,300,000	4.60
Allowances	130,000	0.26	630,000	1.26
Cost of field servicing	600,000	1.20	1,320,000	2.64
Total	2,000,000	4.00	5,150,000	10.30
Total quality cost	$7,500,000	15.00	$9,000,000	18.00

*As a percentage of total sales. We assume that in each year sales totalled $50,000,000.

Data in graphic form help managers to see trends more clearly and to see the magnitude of the various costs in relation to each other. Such graphs are easily prepared using computer graphics packages.

Uses of Quality Cost Information

The information provided by a quality cost system is used by managers in several ways. First, quality cost information helps managers see the financial significance of quality. Studies have shown that managers usually are not aware of the magnitude of their quality costs because, as we have noted, these costs cut across departmental lines and are not normally tracked and accumulated by the cost system. Thus, when first presented with a quality cost report, managers often are surprised when they see the amount of cost involved.

Second, quality cost information helps managers identify the relative importance of the quality problems faced by the firm. For example, the quality cost report may show that scrap is a major quality problem or that the company is incurring huge warranty costs. With this information, management can see where to focus its efforts.

Third, quality cost information helps managers see whether their quality costs are poorly distributed, and when needed, it helps them work toward a better distribution of

EXHIBIT 5-11

Quality Cost Reports
in Graphic Form

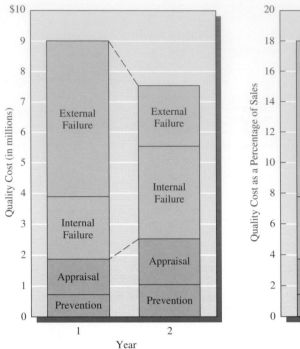

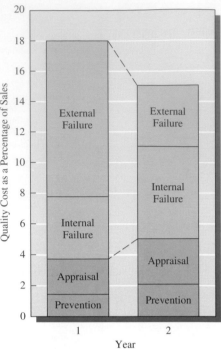

costs. We learned earlier that quality costs should be distributed more toward prevention and appraisal activities and less toward failures of various types.

Fourth, quality cost information provides a basis for establishing budgets for quality costs as management seeks to reduce the total cost involved. The budgets, in turn, provide a basis for performance evaluation from year to year.

Counterbalancing these uses, we must recognize three limitations of quality cost information. First, simply measuring and reporting quality costs does not solve quality problems. Problems can be solved only by action on the part of management. Second, a lag will usually exist between when quality improvement programs are put into effect and when the results are seen. Initially, total quality cost may even increase as quality control systems are designed and installed. Decreases in these costs may not begin to occur until the quality program has been in effect for a year or more. And third, some important quality costs are typically omitted from the quality cost report. These costs include the opportunity cost of lost sales arising from poor product design or customer ill will, and the cost of top management time in designing and administering the quality program. The reason these costs are omitted from cost reports is that they are difficult to quantify.

Service and merchandising organizations are also concerned with quality. For example, supermarkets want detailed information about cashier accuracy, stock-outs, waiting time for checkouts, and so on. While management may wish to have reports such as those in Exhibits 5–10 and 5–11 tailored to a supermarket chain, operating personnel who must implement quality need timely reports on their specific aspects of the operations. Produce managers need details on spoilage, for example, while meat managers need details about cutting yields. Cashiers want specifics about cash differences on a daily basis. Timely, accurate, and understandable reports of this sort are necessary where operating personnel are expected to monitor performances. In such cases, operating personnel can correct certain quality problems as they occur rather than sometime in the future when financial reports appear.

INTERNATIONAL ASPECTS OF QUALITY

A realization that quality must be manufactured (rather than inspected) into products came many years earlier in European and Japanese companies than in North American companies. In the 1950s, Japanese companies started developing methods of quality control that focused on prevention activities and in which quality was the responsibility of *every* employee—not just those in the quality control department. Quality circles had their origin in Japan in 1962, and this control tool still has its widest use in that country. Also, heavy responsibility has been placed on suppliers in Japan for many years to deliver "zero defects" material to manufacturers.

In the 1960s, both European and Japanese companies began to make large investments in quality training programs, and in the 1970s, they began to make investments in automated facilities. The training programs consisted of on-going, *companywide* training—not just one-day quality control seminars for selected managers that have been so popular in this country. As a result of their early start and huge investment in quality control techniques, by the 1980s the European and Japanese companies were setting the world standard for quality products. This emphasis on quality has not diminished, and managers can expect to find well-developed quality control programs in most European companies and in virtually any Japanese company with which they may do business.

The ISO 9000 Standards

The level of quality in products is now often monitored by a set of quality control guidelines issued in 1987 by the International Standards Organization (ISO), which is based in Geneva, Switzerland. These quality guidelines, known as the **ISO 9000 standards,** provide a way for companies to certify to their customers that:

1. They have a quality control system in use, and the system clearly defines an expected level of quality.
2. The system is fully operational and is backed up with detailed documentation of quality control procedures.
3. The intended level of quality is being achieved on a sustained, consistent basis.

The key to receiving certification under the ISO 9000 standards is documentation. It's one thing for a company to say that it has a quality control system in operation, but it's quite a different thing to be able to document the steps in that system. This documentation must be so detailed and precise under ISO 9000 that if all the employees in a company were suddenly replaced, the new employees could use the documentation to manufacture the product exactly as the old employees had been doing. Even companies with good quality control systems find that it takes up to two years of painstaking work to develop documentation of this type. But these companies often find that in addition to providing the data needed to pass an ISO 9000 certification audit, the documentation results in improvements to their quality systems.

The ISO 9000 standards form a series, which consists of five separate standards. The first standard—which gives the series its name—is ISO 9000. This standard provides basic definitions and acts as a road map for using the other standards. With ISO 9000 available as a map on how to proceed, a company can choose to be certified under either ISO 9001, ISO 9002, ISO 9003, or ISO 9004.

ISO 9001 provides the broadest certification and is used by companies involved in the whole range of activities from design and development through production, installation, and servicing. This would include engineering, construction, and manufacturing firms that design, produce, install, and service their products. The next standard, ISO 9002, covers companies whose products must adhere to already existing requirements and specifications. Such companies would include those in the chemical, food, and pharmaceutical industries. The third standard, ISO 9003, relates only to final inspection and testing of products that have been manufactured by someone else. Companies receiving certification under this standard would include equipment distributors who inspect and test the products they receive from a supplier before delivering the products to their own customers. The final standard, ISO 9004, provides specific guidelines for developing and implementing a quality system.

Any drive through an industrial area in Canada will provide a composite picture about the popularity of ISO standards and how businesses pride themselves on achieving these standards of practice. Signs dot the outsides of buildings and are portrayed in advertisements. One example is Northern Telecom, a leader in ISO 9000 registration and efforts, who entered the process because it was demanded by its customers and because management perceived operational benefits from these standards.[24]

The ISO 9000 standards have become an international measure of quality. Although these standards were developed to control the quality of goods sold in European countries, they have become so widely accepted that no company can ignore them—even if it isn't selling directly in Europe. NATO, for example, has adopted the ISO 9000 standards, and the U.S. Department of Defense will soon require adherence by all of its suppliers. Moreover, large companies such as Du Pont and IBM are likely to put pressure on their own suppliers to comply with the ISO 9000 standards, since these large companies must document the quality of the materials going into their products as part of their own ISO 9000 certification. In short, the ISO 9000 standards are here to stay, and any company—regardless of where it may be doing business—can ignore them only at its own peril.

SUMMARY

Activity-based costing has been developed in response to the manager's need for more accurate product costs. Four steps are involved in the design of an activity-based costing system. These include PVA (process value analysis), which helps the manager identify and eliminate non-value-added activities in the company; identifying activity centres, which are the "pools" used to accumulate overhead costs; tracing costs to the activity centres; and selecting cost drivers, which are the tools used to charge costs from the activity centres to the products.

Activity-based costing provides several benefits to the manager, including more accurate product costs, better data for decision making, and tighter cost control. Activity-based

---

[24]"Becoming ISO 9000 Registered," *Management Accounting Guideline 25* (Hamilton, Ontario: The Society of Management Accountants of Canada, March 1994).

costing also has several limitations, the chief of which is the difficulty involved with gathering data relating to activity centres and cost drivers.

Three factors underlie the quality of a product or service. These factors are grade, quality of design, and quality of conformance. The bulk of all quality costs are associated with quality of conformance, and these costs can be broken down into four broad groups. Two of these groups, prevention costs and appraisal costs, are incurred in an effort to keep poor quality of conformance from occurring. The other two groups, known as internal failure costs and external failure costs, are incurred because poor quality of conformance has taken place. A company can reduce its total quality costs by focusing its efforts on prevention and appraisal. By this means, failures are minimized and any defects are detected before delivery of products to customers.

Quality costs are summarized on a quality cost report. Such a report is the backbone of a quality cost system in that it shows management the type of quality costs being incurred, as well as the amount and trend of these costs. The availability of quality cost information helps managers (1) see the financial significance of quality, (2) identify quality problems facing the company, (3) see whether the company's quality costs are poorly distributed, and (4) establish budgets in an effort to reduce total quality costs.

REVIEW PROBLEM: ACTIVITY-BASED COSTING

Aerodec, Inc., manufactures and sells two products, X and Y. Annual sales in units, labour time per unit, and total manufacturing time per year are provided below:

	Total Hours
Product X: 2,000 units × 5 hours	10,000
Product Y: 10,000 units × 4 hours	40,000
Total hours	50,000

Costs for materials and labour for one unit of each product are given below:

	Product	
	X	Y
Direct materials	$25	$17
Direct labour (at $6 per hour)	30	24

Manufacturing overhead costs total $800,000 each year. The breakdown of these costs between the company's six activity centres is given below. The cost driver for each activity centre is shown in parentheses.

Activity Centre (and Cost Driver)	Estimated Overhead Costs	Expected Activity—Cost Driver		
		Total	Product X	Product Y
Labour related (direct labour-hours)	$ 80,000	50,000	10,000	40,000
Machine setups (number of setups)	150,000	5,000	3,000	2,000
Product testing (number of tests)	160,000	8,000	5,000	3,000
Production orders (number of orders)	70,000	400	100	300
Material receipts (number of receipts)	90,000	750	150	600
General factory (machine-hours)	250,000	40,000	12,000	28,000

$800,000

Required

1. Aerodec, Inc., has six activity centres. Refer to the data in Exhibit 5–4 and classify the activity in each of Aerodec's activity centres as either a unit-level, batch-level, product-level, or facility-level activity.
2. Assume that the company applies overhead cost to products on a basis of direct labour-hours.
   a. Compute the predetermined overhead rate that would be used.
   b. Determine the unit product cost of each product, using the predetermined overhead rate computed in (2)(a) above.
3. Assume that the company uses activity-based costing to compute overhead rates.
   a. Compute the predetermined overhead rate for each of the six activity centres listed above.
   b. Using the rates developed in (3)(a) above, determine the amount of overhead cost that should be assigned to a unit of each product.
   c. Determine the unit product cost of each product and compare this cost to the cost computed in (2)(b) above.

Solution to Review Problem

1.

Activity Centre	Type of Activity
Labour related	Unit level
Machine setups	Batch level
Product testing	Product level
Production orders.	Batch level
Material receipts	Batch level
General factory	Facility level

2. a.

$$\frac{\text{Manufacturing overhead costs, \$800,000}}{\text{Direct labour-hours, 50,000}} = \$16 \text{ per direct labour-hour}$$

b.

	Product	
	X	Y
Direct materials	$ 25	$17
Direct labour	30	24
Manufacturing overhead applied:		
Product X: 5 hours × $16	80	
Product Y: 4 hours × $16.		64
Total unit product cost.	$135	$105

3. a.

Activity Centre	(a) Estimated Overhead Costs	(b) Total Expected Activity	(a) ÷ (b) Predetermined Overhead Rate
Labour related	$ 80,000	50,000	$1.60/DLH
Machine setups	150,000	5,000	$30/setup
Product testing	160,000	8,000	$20/test
Production orders.	70,000	400	$175/order
Material receipts	90,000	750	$120/receipt
General factory	250,000	40,000	$6.25/MH

b.

	Product X		Product Y	
	Expected Activity	Amount	Expected Activity	Amount
Labour related, at $1.60/DLH	10,000	$ 16,000	40,000	$ 64,000
Machine setups, at $30/setup	3,000	90,000	2,000	60,000
Product testing, at $20/test	5,000	100,000	3,000	60,000
Production orders, at $175/order	100	17,500	300	52,500
Material receipts, at $120/receipt	150	18,000	600	72,000
General factory, at $6.25/MH	12,000	75,000	28,000	175,000
Total overhead cost assigned (a)		$316,500		$483,500
Number of units produced (b)		2,000		10,000
Overhead cost per unit, (a) ÷ (b)		$ 158.25		$ 48.35

c.

	Product	
	X	Y
Direct materials	$ 25.00	$17.00
Direct labour.........................	30.00	24.00
Manufacturing overhead (see above)........	158.25	48.35
Total unit product cost	$213.25	$89.35

Note that the unit product cost of product X is much greater than the cost computed in (2)(b) above, and the unit product cost of product Y is much less. Using volume (direct labour-hours) in (2)(b) as a basis for applying overhead cost to products has resulted in too little overhead cost being applied to product X (the low-volume product) and too much overhead cost being applied to product Y (the high-volume product).

KEY TERMS FOR REVIEW

OBJECTIVE 9
Define or explain the key terms listed at the end of the chapter.

Activity Any event or transaction that is a cost driver—that is, it causes the incurrence of cost in an organization. (p. 214)

Activity-based costing (ABC) A two-stage costing method that creates a cost pool for each major activity in an organization (such as setups required, purchase orders issued, or number of inspections completed). Overhead costs are assigned to products and services on the basis of the number of these activities involved in manufacturing the product or providing the service. (p. 214)

Activity-based management The use of activity-based costing to help managers focus on continuous improvement of operations and processes. (p. 216)

Activity centre A part of the production process for which management wants a separate reporting of the cost of the activity involved. (p. 216)

Appraisal costs Costs that are incurred to identify defective products before the products are shipped to customers. (p. 237)

Batch-level activities Activities that are performed each time a batch of goods is handled or processed. Such activities would include purchase orders, setups of equipment, and shipments to customers. (p. 218)

External failure costs Costs that are incurred when a product or service that is defective in some way is delivered to a customer. (p. 239)

Facility-level activities Activities that relate to overall production and therefore can't be traced to specific products. Costs associated with these activities pertain to a plant's general manufacturing process. (p. 218)

Grade   Differences in degree, worth, or ranking between products or services that have the same functional use. (p. 233)

Internal failure costs   Costs that are incurred as a result of identification of defective products during the appraisal process. (p. 237)

ISO 9000 standards   Quality control requirements issued by the International Standards Organization that relate to products sold in European countries. (p. 243)

Prevention costs   Costs that are incurred to prevent quality problems from arising in the first place. (pp. 236–37)

Process value analysis (PVA)   A systematic approach to gaining an understanding of the activities required to make a product or perform a service. PVA identifies all resource-consuming activities involved in the manufacturing or service process and labels these activities as being either value-added or non-value-added in nature. (p. 216)

Product diversity   A range of products that differ substantially in volume, lot size, or complexity of design. (p. 213)

Product-level activities   Activities that relate to specific products; such activities—for example, maintaining parts inventories—are performed on behalf of specific products as needed to support production. (p. 218)

Quality   The conformance of a product or service to customer expectations in terms of features and performance. (p. 233)

Quality circles   Small groups of employees that meet on a regular basis to discuss ways to improve the quality of output. (p. 237)

Quality cost report   A report that extracts the quality costs from each activity along the value chain and accumulates the costs in such a way that management can see the kinds of quality costs being incurred, as well as their magnitude and trend. (p. 240)

Quality of conformance   The degree to which the actual product manufactured or the actual service rendered meets its design specifications and is free of defects or other problems that might affect appearance or performance. (p. 235)

Quality of design   The degree to which a company's design specifications for a product or service meets customers' expectations for the grade level chosen. (p. 234)

Statistical process control (SPC)   A technique whereby workers use charts to monitor the quality of the parts or components that pass through their workstations. (p. 237)

Transactions costing   See *Activity-based costing*. (p. 215)

Unit-level activities   Activities that arise as a result of the total volume of production going through a facility, and that are performed each time a unit is produced. (p. 217)

APPENDIX 5A: COST FLOWS IN AN ACTIVITY-BASED COSTING SYSTEM

OBJECTIVE 10
Record the flow of costs in an activity-based costing system.

As stated in the main body of the chapter, the flow of costs through Raw Materials, Work in Process, and other accounts is the same under activity-based costing as was illustrated in Chapter 3. Although the flow of costs is the same, a company must compute several predetermined overhead rates when activity-based costing is being used and that complicates the journal entries and T-accounts somewhat. Our purpose in this appendix is to provide a detailed example of cost flows in an activity-based costing system.

An Example of Cost Flows

Note that the company in the following example has five activity centres and therefore must compute five predetermined overhead rates. Also note from the example how underapplied and overapplied overhead costs are computed when activity-based costing is being used.

Basic Data.   Sarvik Company installed an activity-based costing system several years ago. The company has five activity centres for costing purposes. These activity centres are listed below, along with the estimated overhead cost and the expected level of activity in each centre for the coming year.

Activity Centre	Cost Driver	Estimated Overhead Cost	Expected Activity
Machine related	CPU hours	$175,000	5,000 CPU hours
Purchase orders	Number of orders	63,000	700 orders
Machine setups.....................	Number of setups	92,000	460 setups
Product testing	Number of tests	160,000	200 tests
General factory.....................	Machine-hours	300,000	25,000 machine-hours

At the beginning of the year, the company had inventory balances as follows:

Raw materials	$3,000
Work in process.........	4,000
Finished goods	–0–

Selected transactions recorded by the company during the year are given below:

a.   Raw materials were purchased on account, $915,000.

b.   Raw materials were requisitioned for use in production, $900,000 ($810,000 direct and $90,000 indirect). The indirect materials were traceable to the activity centres as follows:

Machine related	$16,000
Purchase orders.........	3,000
Machine setups.........	8,000
Product testing	21,000
General factory.........	42,000
Total	$90,000

c.   Labour costs were incurred in the factory, $370,000 ($95,000 direct labour and $275,000 indirect labour). The indirect labour costs were traceable to the activity centres as follows:

Machine related	$ 30,000
Purchase orders........	40,000
Machine setups........	25,000
Product testing	60,000
General factory........	120,000
Total	$275,000

d.   Depreciation was recorded on factory assets, $180,000. This depreciation was traceable to the activity centres as follows:

Machine related	$ 72,000
Purchase orders........	9,000
Machine setups........	16,000
Product testing	48,000
General factory........	35,000
Total	$180,000

e.   Miscellaneous manufacturing overhead costs were incurred, $230,000. These overhead costs were traceable to the activity centres as follows:

Machine related	$ 50,000
Purchase orders........	18,000
Machine setups........	45,000
Product testing	27,000
General factory........	90,000
Total	$230,000

f. Manufacturing overhead cost was applied to production. *Actual* activity in the various activity centres during the year was as follows:

Machine related . . . . 4,600 CPU hours
Purchase orders . . . . 800 orders issued
Machine setups. . . . . 500 setups completed
Product testing . . . . 190 tests completed
General factory. . . . . 23,000 machine-hours worked

g. Goods costing $1,650,000 to manufacture were completed during the year.

Required

1. Compute the predetermined overhead rate for each activity centre.
2. Prepare journal entries to record transactions (a) through (g) above. When applying overhead cost to production in entry (f), note that you have five predetermined overhead rates, rather than just one.
3. Post the entries in (2) above to T-accounts. As part of this posting, *create a T-account for each activity centre and treat these accounts as subsidiary accounts to Manufacturing Overhead.*
4. Compute the underapplied or overapplied overhead cost in the Manufacturing Overhead account and in each activity centre.

Solution

1. Predetermined overhead rates for the activity centres:

Activity Centre	(1) Estimated Overhead Cost	(2) Expected Activity	(1) ÷ (2) Predetermined Overhead Rate
Machine related	$175,000	5,000 CPU hours	$35/CPU hour
Purchase orders	63,000	700 orders	$90/order
Machine setups	92,000	460 setups	$200/setup
Product testing	160,000	200 tests	$800/test
General factory	300,000	25,000 machine-hours	$12/machine-hour

2. a. Raw Materials 915,000
         Accounts Payable.   915,000

    b. Work in Process 810,000
        Manufacturing Overhead 90,000
         Raw Materials   900,000

    c. Work in Process 95,000
        Manufacturing Overhead 275,000
         Salaries and Wages Payable.   370,000

    d. Manufacturing Overhead 180,000
        Accumulated Depreciation.   180,000

    e. Manufacturing Overhead 230,000
        Accounts Payable.   230,000

f. Recall from Chapter 3 that the formula for computing applied overhead cost is as follows:

Predetermined overhead rate × Actual activity = Applied overhead cost

Since we have *five* activity centres and *five* predetermined overhead rates, we must determine the amount of applied overhead cost for *each* activity centre. The computations are as follows:

Activity Centre	(1) Predetermined Overhead Rate	(2) Actual Activity	(1) × (2) Applied Overhead Cost
Machine related	$35/CPU hour	4,600 CPU hours	$161,000
Purchase orders	$90/order	800 orders issued	72,000
Machine setups.	$200/setup	500 setups completed	100,000
Product testing	$800/test	190 tests completed	152,000
General factory.	$12/machine-hour	23,000 machine-hours	276,000
Total			$761,000

By totalling these five applied overhead cost figures, we find that the company applied $761,000 in overhead cost to products during the year. The following entry records this application of overhead cost:

```
Work in Process ..........................................  761,000
        Manufacturing Overhead ...............................          761,000

g.  Finished Goods...........................................  1,650,000
        Work in Process ......................................          1,650,000
```

3. See the T-accounts in Exhibit 5–12 on the following page. Note from these T-accounts that when amounts are posted to Manufacturing Overhead, the amounts must also be posted to the activity centre accounts to which they relate.

4. The underapplied or overapplied overhead cost is computed in the T-accounts in Exhibit 5–12 for Manufacturing Overhead and for each of the activity centre accounts. These computations can be summarized as follows:

		Activity Centre				
	Total	Machine Related	Purchase Orders	Machine Setups	Product Testing	General Factory
Actual overhead cost	$775,000	$168,000	$70,000	$94,000	$156,000	$287,000
Applied overhead cost	761,000	161,000	72,000	100,000	152,000	276,000
Underapplied or (overapplied) overhead cost	$ 14,000	$ 7,000	$(2,000)	$(6,000)	$ 4,000	$ 11,000

Note from the computations above that the $14,000 total underapplied overhead cost is equal to the sum of the underapplied and overapplied amounts from the five activity centres.

QUESTIONS

5–1   What three levels of overhead cost application are available to a company?

5–2   Why are new approaches to overhead cost application, such as activity-based costing, needed in many companies today?

5–3   Why are departmental overhead rates sometimes not accurate in assigning overhead cost to products?

5–4   When designing an activity-based costing system, why should PVA (process value analysis) always be the starting point?

5–5   What four general levels of activity can be identified in a company?

5–6   Why is activity-based costing described as a "two-stage" costing method?

5–7   When activity-based costing is used, why are overhead costs often shifted from high-volume products to low-volume products?

5–8   In what three ways does activity-based costing improve the costing system of an organization?

5–9   What are the two chief limitations of activity-based costing?

5–10   Can activity-based costing be used in service organizations?

5–11   Distinguish between grade, quality of design, and quality of conformance.

EXHIBIT 5-12

T-Accounts Showing
Activity Centres

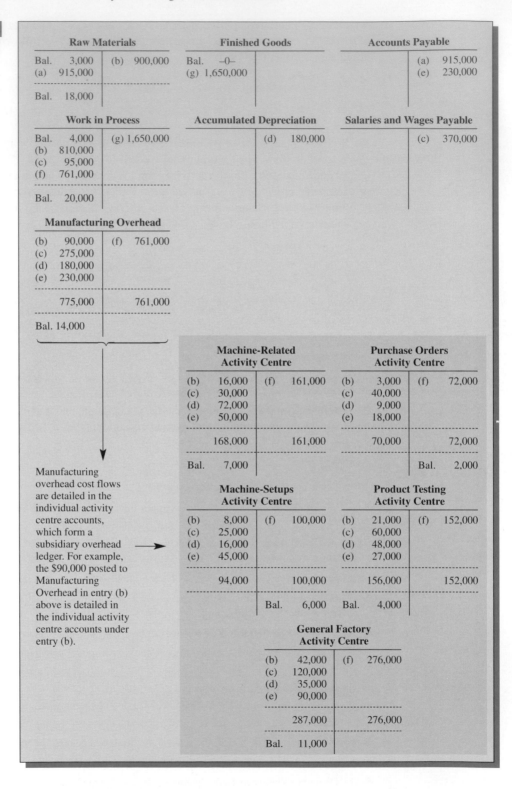

	Raw Materials		
Bal.	3,000	(b)	900,000
(a)	915,000		
Bal.	18,000		

	Finished Goods		
Bal.	–0–		
(g)	1,650,000		

	Accounts Payable		
		(a)	915,000
		(e)	230,000

	Work in Process		
Bal.	4,000	(g)	1,650,000
(b)	810,000		
(c)	95,000		
(f)	761,000		
Bal.	20,000		

	Accumulated Depreciation		
		(d)	180,000

	Salaries and Wages Payable		
		(c)	370,000

	Manufacturing Overhead		
(b)	90,000	(f)	761,000
(c)	275,000		
(d)	180,000		
(e)	230,000		
	775,000		761,000
Bal. 14,000			

Manufacturing overhead cost flows are detailed in the individual activity centre accounts, which form a subsidiary overhead ledger. For example, the $90,000 posted to Manufacturing Overhead in entry (b) above is detailed in the individual activity centre accounts under entry (b).

	Machine-Related Activity Centre		
(b)	16,000	(f)	161,000
(c)	30,000		
(d)	72,000		
(e)	50,000		
	168,000		161,000
Bal.	7,000		

	Purchase Orders Activity Centre		
(b)	3,000	(f)	72,000
(c)	40,000		
(d)	9,000		
(e)	18,000		
	70,000		72,000
		Bal.	2,000

	Machine-Setups Activity Centre		
(b)	8,000	(f)	100,000
(c)	25,000		
(d)	16,000		
(e)	45,000		
	94,000		100,000
		Bal.	6,000

	Product Testing Activity Centre		
(b)	21,000	(f)	152,000
(c)	60,000		
(d)	48,000		
(e)	27,000		
	156,000		152,000
Bal.	4,000		

	General Factory Activity Centre		
(b)	42,000	(f)	276,000
(c)	120,000		
(d)	35,000		
(e)	90,000		
	287,000		276,000
Bal.	11,000		

5–12   Costs associated with the quality of conformance can be broken down into what four broad groups? How do these groups differ?

5–13   What is meant when a company is said to have a poor distribution of quality costs?

5–14   What is the most effective way to reduce total quality cost in a company?

5–15   What are the ISO 9000 standards?

EXERCISES

E5–1 Listed below are several activities that you have observed in Meredith Company. The company manufactures a number of products.
  a. Issue of purchase orders.
  b. Design work for new products.
  c. Management of parts inventories.
  d. Rough milling work that is done on all products.
  e. Hiring new employees through a company personnel office.
  f. Receipts of material in the company's receiving department.
  g. Maintenance of general-use equipment by maintenance workers.
  h. Occupancy of the general plant building.

Required

  1. Classify each of the activities above as either a unit-level, batch-level, product-level, or facility-level activity.
  2. For each activity above, name one or more cost drivers that might be used to assign the costs generated by the activity to products.

E5–2 Listed below are various activities observed in Morales Company. Each activity has been classified as unit level, batch level, product level, or facility level in nature.

Activity	Activity Classification	Examples of Traceable Costs	Examples of Cost Drivers
a. Materials are moved from the receiving dock to product flow lines by a material-handling crew	Batch level		
b. Direct labour workers assemble various products	Unit level		
c. Ongoing training is provided to all employees in the company.................	Facility level		
d. A product is designed by a specialized design team	Product level		
e. Equipment setups are performed on a regular basis...........................	Batch level		
f. Numerical control (NC) machines are used to cut and shape materials	Unit level		

Required

Complete the table above by listing examples of traceable costs and examples of cost drivers for each activity.

E5–3 Erte, Inc., manufactures two models of high-pressure steam valves, the XR7 model and the ZD5 model. Data regarding the two products follow:

Product	Direct Labour-Hours per Unit	Annual Production	Total Direct Labour-Hours
XR7 .... 0.2		20,000 units	4,000
ZD5 .... 0.4		40,000 units	16,000
			20,000

Additional information about the company follows:
  a. Product XR7 requires $35 in direct materials per unit, and product ZD5 requires $25.
  b. The direct labour rate is $20 per hour.

c. The company has always used direct labour-hours as the base for applying manufacturing overhead cost to products. Manufacturing overhead totals $1,480,000 per year.

d. Product XR7 is more complex to manufacture than product ZD5 and requires the use of a special milling machine.

e. Because of the special work required in (d) above, the company is considering the use of activity-based costing to apply overhead cost to products. Three activity centres have been identified as follows:

Activity Centre	Cost Driver	Estimated Overhead Cost	Expected Activity— Cost Driver		
			Total	XR7	ZD5
Machine setups	Number of setups	$ 180,000	250	150	100
Special milling.......	Machine-hours	300,000	1,000	1,000	—
General factory	Direct labour-hours	1,000,000	20,000	4,000	16,000
		$1,480,000			

Required

1. Assume that the company continues to use direct labour-hours as the base for applying overhead cost to products.
   a. Compute the predetermined overhead rate.
   b. Determine the unit product cost of each product.
2. Assume that the company decides to use activity-based costing to apply overhead cost to products.
   a. Compute the overhead rate for each activity centre. Also compute the amount of overhead cost that would be applied to each product.
   b. Determine the unit product cost of each product.
3. Explain why overhead cost shifted from the high-volume product to the low-volume product under activity-based costing.

E5–4 Below are listed several activities that are part of a company's quality control system:
a. Repairs of goods still under warranty.
b. Customer returns due to defects.
c. Statistical process control.
d. Disposal of spoiled goods.
e. Maintaining testing equipment.
f. Inspecting finished goods.
g. Downtime caused by quality problems.
h. Debugging errors in software.
i. Recalls of defective products.
j. Training quality engineers.
k. Re-entering data due to typing errors.
l. Inspecting materials received from suppliers.
m. Audits of the quality system.
n. Supervision of testing personnel.
o. Rework labour.

Required

1. Classify the costs associated with each of these activities into one of the following categories: prevention cost, appraisal cost, internal failure cost, or external failure cost.
2. Which of the four types of costs listed in (1) above are incurred to keep poor quality of conformance from occurring? Which of the four types of costs are incurred because poor quality of conformance has occurred?

E5–5 Listed below are several terms relating to activity-based costing that are used or introduced in the chapter:

Process value analysis	Plantwide overhead rate
Facility level	Low volume
High volume	Batch level
Activity centres	Two stage
Product level	Unit level
Volume	Stage

Required   Choose the term or terms above that most appropriately complete the following statements. The terms can be used more than once. (Note that a blank can hold more than one word.)

1. A single overhead rate used throughout an entire plant operation is known as a _____.

2. The major problem with using direct labour-hours or machine-hours as the basis for assigning overhead cost to products is that these bases rely on _____ as the sole factor in overhead cost assignment.

3. Activity-based costing involves a _____ allocation process, in which the first _____ assigns overhead costs to activity centres and the second _____ assigns overhead costs from activity centres to products and services.

4. _____, which involves a systematic analysis of the activities required to make a product or perform a service, is the beginning point in activity-based costing.

5. _____ activities, such as the consumption of power, are performed each time a unit is produced and arise as a result of the total volume of production going through a facility.

6. _____ activities, which are performed each time a batch of goods is handled or processed, include tasks such as the placement of a purchase order.

7. _____ activities, which are performed as needed to support the production of a particular product, include tasks such as maintaining parts inventories.

8. _____ activities just sustain a facility's general manufacturing process and include items such as insurance or general factory management.

9. The use of activity-based costing often causes a shift in overhead costs from _____ products to _____ products, thereby causing the unit cost of the _____ products to sharply increase.

10. One of the benefits of activity-based costing is that it increases the number of cost pools, or _____, used to accumulate and assign overhead costs to products and services.

E5–6 Listed below are activity centres that might be found in a company using activity-based costing.

a. Product prototype testing.
b. Equipment setups.
c. General factory.
d. Machine related.
e. Parts inventory management.
f. Personnel administration.

g. Purchase orders.
h. Product design.
i. Labour related.
j. Quality inspections.
k. Production orders.

Required   Prepare an answer sheet with column headings as follows:

Activity Centre	Unit-Level Activities	Batch-Level Activities	Product-Level Activities	Facility-Level Activities
a.				
b.				
c.				

For each activity centre, place an *X* under the proper heading to indicate whether the activity centre would be unit level, batch level, product level, or facility level.

E5–7 Listed below are several terms relating to quality management that are used or introduced in the chapter:

Appraisal costs
Quality cost report
Grade
Quality of design
Internal failure costs

Quality circles
Prevention costs
Quality
External failure costs
Quality of conformance

Required   Choose the term or terms that most appropriately complete the following statements. The terms can be used more than once. (Note that a blank can hold more than one word.)

1. When a product or service does not conform to customer expectations in terms of features or performance, it is viewed as being poor in _____.
2. The Lexus and Tercel automobiles are generally regarded as being high in quality and having the same functional use, but they differ in _____ because of their difference in worth or ranking in the eyes of customers.
3. A product has a high _____ if for the grade level chosen, it contains all the features and operates in the way that customers would expect it to operate.
4. A product or service may have a high _____, but it will have a low _____ if it does not function the way its designers intended, or if it has many defects as a result of sloppy manufacture.
5. A company incurs _____ and _____ in an effort to keep poor quality of conformance from occurring.
6. A company incurs _____ and _____ because poor quality of conformance has occurred.
7. Of the four groups of costs associated with quality of conformance, _____ are generally the most damaging to a company.
8. Inspection, testing, and other costs incurred to keep defective products from being shipped to customers are known as _____.
9. _____ are incurred in an effort to eliminate poor product design, defective manufacturing practices, and the providing of substandard service.
10. The costs relating to defects, rejected products, and downtime caused by quality problems are known as _____.
11. When a product that is defective in some way is delivered to a customer, then _____ are incurred.
12. Over time a company's total quality costs should decrease if it redistributes its quality costs by placing its greatest emphasis on _____ and _____.
13. In many companies, small groups of employees, known as _____, meet on a regular basis to discuss ways to improve the quality of output.
14. The way to ensure that management is aware of the costs associated with quality is to summarize such costs on a _____.

E5–8 (Appendix 5A) Sultan Company manufactures four products and employs activity-based costing. The company has five activity centres, as shown below.

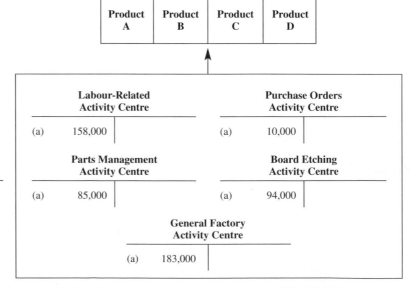

The company has completed part of its entries to the Manufacturing Overhead account for the current year as shown by entry (a) above.

Required

1. In a general sense, what cost would be represented by entry (a)?
2. At the beginning of the year, the company made the following estimates of cost and activity in the five activity centres in order to compute predetermined overhead rates:

Activity Centre	Cost Driver	Estimated Overhead Cost	Expected Activity
Labour related..............	Direct labour-hours	$156,000	26,000 direct labour-hours
Purchase orders............	Number of orders	11,000	220 orders
Parts management..........	Number of part types	80,000	100 part types
Board etching	Number of boards	90,000	2,000 boards
General factory	Machine-hours	180,000	20,000 machine-hours

Compute the predetermined overhead rate for each activity centre.

3. During the year, activity was recorded in the various activity centres as follows:

Activity Centre	Actual Activity
Labour related	25,000 direct labour-hours
Purchase orders	200 orders
Parts management	110 part types
Board etching	1,800 boards
General factory	22,000 machine-hours

Determine the amount of manufacturing overhead cost applied to production for the year, and determine the amount of underapplied or overapplied overhead cost for each activity centre and for Manufacturing Overhead.

E5–9 (Appendix 5A) (This exercise is a continuation of E5–8; it should be assigned *only* if E5–8 is also assigned.) Refer to the data in E5–8. During the year, the activities in the five activity centres were traceable to Sultan Company's products as follows:

Activity Centre		Actual Activity			
	Total	Product A	Product B	Product C	Product D
Labour related	25,000 DLH	6,000	10,000	4,000	5,000
Purchase orders	200 orders	60	30	20	90
Parts managment	110 part types	30	25	40	15
Board etching	1,800 boards	500	900	400	—
General factory.........	22,000 MH	3,000	8,000	5,000	6,000

Required

1. Compute the amount of overhead cost charged to each product during the year.
2. How do the dollar amounts charged to products in (1) above relate to the activity centre accounts and to the Manufacturing Overhead account in E5–8?

PROBLEMS

P5–10 Classifying Activities under Activity-Based Costing   Himmer A/S of Denmark manufactures a variety of products in a single facility. Management has just completed a process value analysis and has identified the following basic activities:
   a. Parts inventories are maintained for products.
   b. Quality inspections are carried out on batches.
   c. General-purpose equipment is maintained by the maintenance crew.
   d. Machine setups are performed for various products.
   e. Employees are trained by the company's training staff.
   f. Prototypes of new products are tested in the company's testing centre.
   g. Material is received on the receiving dock and moved about the plant.
   h. Recreational facilities are available to all employees.
   i. Purchase orders are issued for materials.
   j. The personnel department hires new employees.

k. Equipment is used for grinding parts used in various products.
l. Occupancy for all of the company's operations is provided in one building.
m. Production orders are issued.

Required

1. Classify each of the activities above as either a unit-level, batch-level, product-level, or facility-level activity.
2. Identify one or more traceable costs for each activity listed above.
3. For each activity above, name one or more cost drivers that might be used to charge the costs of the activity to products.

P5–11 Activity-Based Costing   Rehm Company manufactures a product that is available in both a deluxe model and a regular model. The company has manufactured the regular model for years. The deluxe model was introduced several years ago to tap a new segment of the market. Since introduction of the deluxe model, the company's profits have steadily declined, and management has become concerned about the accuracy of its costing system. Sales of the deluxe model have been increasing rapidly.

Overhead is assigned to the products on the basis of direct labour-hours. For the current year, the company has estimated that it will incur $6,000,000 in overhead cost and produce 15,000 units of the deluxe model and 120,000 units of the regular model. The deluxe model requires 1.6 hours of direct labour time per unit, and the regular model requires 0.8 hour. Materials and labour costs per unit are as follows:

	Model	
	Deluxe	**Regular**
Direct materials	$154	$112
Direct labour	16	8

Required

1. Using direct labour-hours as the base for assigning overhead cost to products, compute the predetermined overhead rate. Using this rate and other data from the problem, determine the unit product cost of each model.
2. Assume that the company's overhead costs can be traced to four activity centres. These activity centres, their cost drivers, and estimated cost and activity data for each centre are given below. Determine the overhead rate for each of the four activity centres.

Activity Centre (and Cost Driver)	Estimated Overhead Costs	Expected Activity—Cost Driver		
		Total	**Deluxe**	**Regular**
Purchase orders (number of orders).	$ 252,000	1,200	400	800
Scrap/rework orders (number of orders)	648,000	900	500	400
Product testing (number of tests).	1,350,000	15,000	6,000	9,000
Machine related (machine-hours)	3,750,000	50,000	20,000	30,000
Total overhead cost	$6,000,000			

3. Using activity-based costing and the data from (2) above, do the following:
    a. Determine the total amount of overhead cost assignable to each model. After these totals have been computed, determine the amount of overhead cost per unit for each model.
    b. Compute the unit product cost of each model (materials, labour, and overhead).
4. From the data you have developed in (1) through (3) above, identify factors that may account for the company's declining profits.
5. Is the controller ethical if direct labour-hours are used to allocate overhead when the results of parts 2 and 3 are known?

P5–12 Quality Cost Report   Yedder Enterprises was a pioneer in designing and producing precision surgical lasers. Yedder's product was brilliantly designed, but the manufacturing process was neglected by management with a consequence that quality problems have been chronic. When customers complained about defective units, Yedder would simply send out a repairperson or replace the defective unit with a new one. Recently, several competitors came out with similar products without Yedder's quality problems, and as a consequence Yedder's sales have declined.

To rescue the situation, Yedder embarked on an intensive campaign to strengthen its quality control at the beginning of 19x6. These efforts met with some success—the downward slide in sales was reversed, and sales grew from $95 million in 19x5 to $100 million in 19x6. To help monitor the company's progress, costs relating to quality and quality control were compiled for the previous year (19x5) and for the first full year of the quality campaign (19x6). The costs, which do not include the lost sales due to a reputation for poor quality, appear below:

	For the Year (in thousands)	
	19x6	**19x5**
Product recalls......................	$ 600	$3,500
Systems development	680	120
Inspection	2,770	1,700
Net cost of scrap	1,300	800
Supplies used in testing...............	40	30
Warranty repairs	2,800	3,300
Rework labour......................	1,600	1,400
Statistical process control	270	—
Customer returns of defective goods	200	3,200
Cost of testing equipment	390	270
Quality engineering..................	1,650	1,080
Downtime due to quality problems......	1,100	600

Required

1. Prepare a quality cost report for both 19x5 and 19x6. Prepare the report in the format illustrated in Exhibit 5–10. Carry percentage computations to two decimal places.
2. Prepare a bar graph showing the distribution of the various quality costs by category.
3. Prepare a written evaluation to accompany the reports you have prepared in (1) and (2) above. This evaluation should discuss the distribution of quality costs in the company, changes in the distribution over the last year, and any other information you believe would be useful to management.

P5–13 Activity-Based Costing   For many years, Gorski Company manufactured a single product called a mono-circuit. Then, three years ago, the company automated a portion of its plant and at the same time introduced a second product called a bi-circuit. The bi-circuit has become increasingly popular, and the company is now producing 10,000 units of it each year as compared to 40,000 units of the mono-circuit. Because the gross margin is greater on the bi-circuit than on the mono-circuit, the company views it as the more profitable product.

Although the bi-circuit is more profitable, it is also more complex to produce than the mono-circuit. It requires two hours of direct labour time per unit to manufacture, and it requires extensive machining in the automated portion of the plant. In addition, it requires numerous inspections to ensure that high quality is maintained. By contrast, the mono-circuit requires only one hour of direct labour time per unit, only a small amount of machining, and few quality control checks. Overhead costs are assigned to the products on the basis of direct labour-hours.

Despite the increasing popularity of the company's new bi-circuit, profits have declined steadily over the last three years since it was introduced. Management is beginning to believe that a problem may exist with the company's costing system. Unit costs for materials and labour for the two products follow:

	Mono-Circuit	**Bi-Circuit**
Direct materials..........................	$40	$80
Direct labour: $10 × 1 hour and 2 hours	10	20

For the current year, the company estimates that it will incur $3,000,000 in manufacturing overhead costs.

Required

1. Compute the predetermined overhead rate assuming that the company continues to apply overhead cost to products on the basis of direct labour-hours. Using this rate and other data from the problem, determine the unit product cost of each product.
2. Assume that the company's overhead costs can be traced to four activity centres. These activity centres, their cost drivers, and estimated data relating to each centre for the year are given below:

Activity Centre (and Cost Driver)	Estimated Overhead Costs	Expected Activity—Cost Driver		
		Total	Mono-Circuit	Bi-Circuit
Parts inventory (number of part types)	$ 360,000	900	300	600
Purchase orders (number of orders)...........	540,000	3,000	2,000	1,000
Quality control (number of tests)............	600,000	8,000	2,000	6,000
Machine related (machine-hours)	1,500,000	50,000	20,000	30,000

Total overhead cost ....
$3,000,000

Determine the overhead rate for each of the four activity centres.
3. Using activity-based costing and the data from (2) above, do the following:
   a. Determine the total amount of overhead cost assignable to each product for the year. After these totals have been computed, determine the amount of overhead cost per unit of each product.
   b. Compute the unit product cost of each product.
4. Look at the data you have computed in (3) above. In terms of overhead cost, what factors make the bi-circuit more costly to produce than the mono-circuit? Is the bi-circuit as profitable as the company thinks it is? Explain.

P5–14 Quality Cost Report Carrie Lee, the president of Lee Enterprises, was concerned about the results of her company's new quality control efforts. "Maybe the emphasis we've placed on upgrading our quality control system will pay off in the long run, but it doesn't seem to be helping us much right now. I thought improved quality would give a real boost to sales, but sales have remained flat at about $10,000,000 for the last two years."

Lee Enterprises has seen its market share decline in recent years due to increased foreign competition. An intensive effort to strengthen the quality control system was initiated a year ago (on January 1, 19x6) in the hope that better quality would strengthen the company's competitive position and also reduce warranty and servicing costs. Costs relating to quality and quality control over the last two years are given in the next table.

	For the Year	
	19x6	19x5
Warranty repairs	$140,000	$420,000
Rework labour.......................	200,000	140,000
Supplies used in testing...............	6,000	4,000
Depreciation of testing equipment	34,000	22,000
Warranty replacements	18,000	60,000
Field servicing......................	120,000	180,000
Inspection	120,000	76,000
Systems development	106,000	64,000
Disposal of defective products	76,000	54,000
Net cost of scrap	124,000	86,000
Product recalls......................	82,000	340,000
Product testing	160,000	98,000
Statistical process control	74,000	—
Quality engineering..................	80,000	56,000

Required

1. Prepare a quality cost report that contains data for both 19x5 and 19x6. Prepare the report in the format illustrated in Exhibit 5–10. Carry percentage computations to two decimal places.
2. Prepare a bar graph showing the distribution of the various quality costs by category.
3. Prepare a written evaluation to accompany the reports you have prepared in (1) and (2) above. This evaluation should discuss the distribution of quality costs in the company, changes in this distribution that you detect have taken place over the last year, and any other information you believe would be useful to management.

P5–15 Cost Flows under Activity-Based Costing; Partial T-Accounts (Appendix 5A) Nicolai Products, Inc., installed an activity-based costing system several years ago. The company manufactures four products in a single facility and has identified five major activity centres relating to manufacturing overhead.

As shown in the following T-accounts, direct materials and direct labour costs for the current year have been added to Work in Process. However, no entries have been made for either actual or applied manufacturing overhead cost.

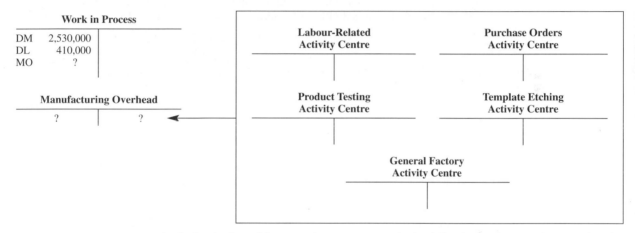

At the beginning of the year, the company made the following estimates of cost and activity in the five activity centres for the purpose of computing predetermined overhead rates:

Activity Centre	Cost Driver	Estimated Overhead Cost	Expected Activity
Labour related	Direct labour-hours	$280,000	40,000 direct labour-hours
Purchase orders	Number of orders	96,000	1,200 orders
Product testing	Number of tests	420,000	3,500 tests
Template etching	Number of templates	315,000	10,500 templates
General factory	Machine-hours	810,000	90,000 machine-hours

Required

1. Compute the predetermined overhead rate for each activity centre for the year.
2. During the year, actual manufacturing overhead cost and actual activity were recorded in the five activity centres as follows:

Activity Centre	Actual Overhead Cost	Actual Activity
Labour related	$ 272,000	37,000 direct labour-hours
Purchase orders	98,000	1,250 orders
Product testing	415,000	3,400 tests
Template etching	330,000	11,500 templates
General factory	801,000	87,000 machine-hours
Total overhead cost	$1,916,000	

a. Prepare a journal entry to record the incurrence of the total actual manufacturing overhead cost for the year (credit Accounts Payable).

b. Prepare T-accounts for Manufacturing Overhead and for each of the activity centres, and post the entry in (2)(a) above to these accounts. Label this as entry (a).

3. Refer again to the "actual activity" data in (2) above.

a. Determine the amount of overhead cost applied to production for the year. In determining this amount, remember that you have five predetermined overhead rates, rather than just one.

b. Prepare a journal entry to record the amount of applied overhead cost for the year. Label this as entry (b), and post the entry to the Manufacturing Overhead and activity centre T-accounts.

4. Determine the amount of underapplied or overapplied manufacturing overhead cost for the year for each activity centre and for Manufacturing Overhead.

P5–16 Activity-Based Costing: Assigning Overhead to Products (Appendix 5A) (This problem is a continuation of P5–15; it should be assigned *only* if P5–15 is also assigned.) Refer to the "actual activity" data you have just used in requirements (2) and (3) in P5–15. Assume that these activities are traceable to Nikolai Products Inc.'s four products as follows:

Activity Centre	Total	Product A	Product B	Product C	Product D
Labour related	37,000 DLH	7,000	8,500	11,000	10,500
Purchase orders	1,250 orders	250	300	500	200
Product testing	3,400 tests	600	700	1,200	900
Template etching	11,500 templates	—	4,500	—	7,000
General factory	87,000 MH	15,000	21,000	35,000	16,000

Actual Activity

Required

1. Using the appropriate predetermined overhead rates from P5–15, determine the amount of overhead cost for the year chargeable to each product. Total the amount of overhead cost for each product, and also show the total amount of overhead cost for the four products combined.

2. Refer to the journal entries and T-accounts you have prepared for P5–15. Does the total overhead cost figure for the four products that you have computed in (1) above "tie in" to these journal entries and T- accounts in any way? Explain.

P5–17 Cost Flows under Activity-Based Costing; Partial T-Accounts (Appendix 5A) Krongstad Company manufactures four products and uses activity-based costing. The company has five activity centres, as shown in the boxed T-accounts on the next page. Direct materials and direct labour costs for the current year were recorded in the Work in Process T-account. However, no entries have been made for either actual or applied manufacturing overhead cost.

At the beginning of the year, the company made the following estimates of cost and activity in the five activity centres in order to compute predetermined overhead rates:

Activity Centre	Cost Driver	Estimated Overhead Cost	Expected Activity
Labour related	Direct labour-hours	$220,000	20,000 direct labour-hours
Production orders	Number of orders	40,000	500 orders
Material handling	Number of loads	126,000	1,800 loads
Testing	Number of tests	160,000	4,000 tests
General factory	Machine-hours	550,000	25,000 machine-hours

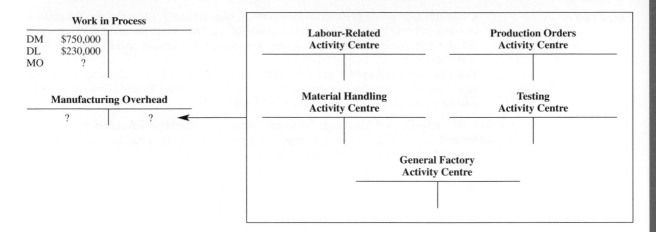

Required

1. Compute the predetermined overhead rate for each activity centre for the year.
2. During the year, actual manufacturing overhead cost and actual activity were recorded in the various activity centres as follows:

Activity Centre	Actual Overhead Cost	Actual Activity
Labour related	$ 225,000	21,000 direct-labour hours
Production orders.............................	39,000	550 orders
Material handling.............................	124,000	1,850 loads
Testing	165,000	4,100 tests
General factory................................	552,000	25,500 machine-hours
Total manufacturing overhead..................	$1,105,000	

a. Prepare a journal entry to record the incurrence of the total actual manufacturing overhead cost for the year (credit Accounts Payable).
b. Prepare T-accounts for Manufacturing Overhead and for each of the activity centres, and post the entry in (2)(a) above to these accounts. Label this as entry (a).
3. Refer to the "actual activity" data in (2) above.
a. Determine the amount of overhead cost applied to production for the year. In determining this amount, remember that you have five predetermined overhead rates, rather than just one.
b. Prepare a journal entry to record the amount of applied overhead cost for the year. Label this as entry (b), and then post the entry to the Manufacturing Overhead and activity centre T-accounts.
4. Determine the amount of underapplied or overapplied manufacturing overhead cost for each activity centre and for Manufacturing Overhead.

P5–18 Activity-Based Costing: Assigning Overhead to Products (Appendix 5A) (This problem is a continuation of P5–17; it should be assigned *only* if P5–17 is also assigned.) Refer to the "actual activity" data you have just used in requirements (2) and (3) in P5–17. Assume that these activities are traceable to Krongstad Company's four products as follows:

Activity Centre	Total	Actual Activity			
		Product A	Product B	Product C	Product D
Labour related	21,000 DLH	5,000	6,000	2,000	8,000
Production orders.......	550 orders	100	150	120	180
Material handling.......	1,850 loads	250	500	350	750
Testing	4,100 tests	1,300	1,700	—	1,100
General factory.........	25,500 MH	5,000	8,000	2,500	10,000

Required

1. Using the appropriate predetermined overhead rates from P5–17, determine the amount of overhead cost chargeable to each product for the year. Total the amount of overhead cost for each product, and also show the total amount of overhead cost for the four products combined.

2. Refer to the journal entries and T-accounts you prepared for P5–17. Does the total overhead cost figure for the four products that you computed in (1) above "tie in" to these journal entries and T-accounts in any way? Explain.

P5–19 Activity-Based Costing: Journal Entries; Complete T-Accounts; Income Statement   (Appendix 5A) Jarvis Company is a manufacturing firm that has just installed an activity-based costing system. The company has identified the five activity centres that are listed below, along with the estimated overhead cost and expected level of activity in each centre for the coming year.

Activity Centre	Cost Driver	Estimated Overhead Cost	Expected Activity
Machining.	Computer-hours	$250,000	10,000 computer-hours
Purchase orders.	Number of orders	120,000	2,000 orders
Parts management.	Number of part types	40,000	500 part types
Testing.	Number of tests	125,000	5,000 tests
General factory	Machine-hours	350,000	50,000 machine-hours

At the beginning of the year, the company had inventory balances as follows:

Raw materials.	$25,000
Work in process	70,000
Finished goods	45,000

The following transactions were recorded during the year:

a. Raw materials were purchased on account, $375,000.

b. Raw materials were requisitioned for use in production, $390,000 ($340,000 direct and $50,000 indirect). The indirect materials were traceable to activity centres as follows:

Machining	$30,000
Purchase orders	8,000
Testing	12,000
Total	$50,000

c. The following costs were incurred for employee services: direct labour, $110,000; indirect labour, $280,000; sales commissions, $90,000; and administrative salaries, $240,000. The indirect labour costs were traceable to the activity centres as follows:

Purchase orders	$ 80,000
Parts management	25,000
Testing	65,000
General factory.	110,000
Total	$280,000

d. Sales travel costs were incurred, $42,000.

e. Miscellaneous manufacturing overhead costs were incurred, $68,000. These overhead costs were traceable to activity centres as follows:

Machining	$19,000
Purchase orders	11,000
Parts management	2,000
Testing	7,000
General factory.	29,000
Total	$68,000

f. Advertising costs were incurred, $165,000.

g. Depreciation was recorded for the year, $320,000 ($270,000 related to factory operations and $50,000 related to selling and administrative activities). The depreciation related to factory operations was traceable to activity centres as follows:

Machining	$130,000
Parts management	4,000
Testing	28,000
General factory.	108,000
Total	$270,000

h. Miscellaneous manufacturing overhead costs were incurred, $220,000. These overhead costs were traceable to activity centres as follows:

Machining	$ 70,000
Purchase orders	21,000
Parts management	12,000
Testing	15,000
General factory.	102,000
Total	$220,000

i. Manufacturing overhead cost was applied to production. *Actual* activity in the various activity centres during the year was as follows:

Machining	10,200 computer-hours
Purchase orders	2,050 orders issued
Parts management	475 part types held in stock
Testing	4,880 tests completed
General factory	51,000 machine-hours worked

j. Goods costing $1,365,000 to manufacture were completed during the year.

k. Goods were sold on account to customers during the year at a total selling price of $1,975,000. The goods cost $1,360,000 to manufacture.

Required

1. Compute the predetermined overhead rate for each activity centre.
2. Prepare journal entries to record transactions (a) through (k) above. When applying overhead cost to production in entry (i), note that you have five predetermined overhead rates, rather than just one.
3. Post the entries in (2) above to T-accounts. As part of this posting, *create a T-account for each activity centre and treat these accounts as subsidiary accounts to Manufacturing Overhead.*
4. Compute the underapplied or overapplied overhead cost in Manufacturing Overhead and in each activity centre for the year. Prepare a journal entry to close any balance in the Manufacturing Overhead account to Cost of Goods Sold.
5. Prepare an income statement for the year.

P5–20 Analyzing a Quality Cost Report   Bergen, Inc., produces telephone equipment at its Ottawa plant. In recent years, the company's market share has been eroded by stiff competition from Asian and European competitors. Price and product quality are the two key areas in which companies compete in this market.

Two years ago, Jerry Holman, Bergen's president, decided to devote more resources to the improvement of product quality after learning that his company's products had been ranked fourth in product quality in a 1996 survey of telephone equipment users. He believed that Bergen could no longer afford to ignore the importance of product quality. Holman set up a task force that he headed to implement a formal quality improvement program. Included on this task force were representatives from engineering, sales, customer service, production, and accounting. This broad representation was needed because Holman believed that this was a companywide program, and that all employees should share the responsibility for its success.

After the first meeting of the task force, Sheila Haynes, manager of sales, asked Tony Reese, production manager, what he thought of the proposed program. Reese replied, "I have reservations. Quality is too abstract to be attaching costs to it and then to be holding you and me responsible for cost improvements. I like to work with goals that I can see and count! I'm nervous about having my annual bonus based on a decrease in quality costs; there are too many variables that we have no control over."

Bergen's quality improvement program has now been in operation for two years. The company's most recent quality cost report is shown below.

BERGEN, INC.
Quality Cost Report
(in thousands)

	12/31/97	12/31/98
Prevention costs:		
Machine maintenance	$ 215	$ 160
Training suppliers	5	15
Design reviews	20	95
Total	240	270
Appraisal costs:		
Incoming inspection	45	22
Final testing	160	94
Total	205	116
Internal failure costs:		
Rework	120	62
Scrap..................	68	40
Total	188	102
External failure costs:		
Warranty repairs	69	23
Customer returns..........	262	80
Total	331	103
Total quality cost...........	$ 964	$ 591
Total production cost	$4,120	$4,510

As they were reviewing the report, Haynes asked Reese what he now thought of the quality improvement program. "The work is really moving through the production department," Reese replied. "We used to spend time helping the customer service department solve their problems, but they are leaving us alone these days. I have no complaints so far, and I'm relieved to see that the new quality improvement hasn't adversely affected our bonuses. I'm anxious to see if it increases our bonuses in the future."

Required

1. By analyzing the company's quality cost report, determine if Bergen, Inc.'s quality improvement program has been successful. *List specific evidence to support your answer.* Show percentage figures in two ways: first, as a percentage of total production cost; and second, as a percentage of total quality cost. Carry all computations to one decimal place.

2. Discuss why Tony Reese's current reaction to the quality improvement program is more favourable than his initial reaction.

3. Jerry Holman believed that the quality improvement program was essential and that Bergen, Inc., could no longer afford to ignore the importance of product quality. Discuss how Bergen, Inc., could measure the opportunity cost of not implementing the quality improvement program.

(CMA, adapted)

CASES

C5–21 Activity-Based Costing and Pricing   Coffee Bean Inc. (CBI) is a processor and distributor of a variety of blends of coffee. The company buys coffee beans from around the world and roasts, blends, and packages them for resale. CBI currently has 40 different coffees that it offers to gourmet shops in 300-gram bags. The major cost of the coffee is raw materials. However, there is a substantial amount of manufacturing overhead in the company's predominantly automated roasting, blending, and packing process. The company uses relatively little direct labour.

Some of the coffees are very popular and sell in large volumes, while a few of the newer blends have very low volumes. CBI prices its coffee at manufacturing cost plus a markup of

30%. If CBI's prices for certain coffees are significantly higher than market, adjustments are made to bring CBI's prices more into alignment with the market. The company competes primarily on the quality of its products, but customers are price conscious as well.

For the coming year, CBI's budget includes estimated manufacturing overhead cost of $3,000,000. CBI assigns manufacturing overhead to products on the basis of direct labour-hours. The expected direct labour cost totals $600,000, which represents 50,000 hours of direct labour time. Based on the sales budget and expected raw materials costs, the company will purchase and use $6,000,000 of raw materials (mostly coffee beans) during the year.

The expected costs for direct materials and direct labour for 300-g bags of two of the company's coffee products appear below.

	Mona Loa	Malaysian
Direct materials	$4.20	$3.20
Direct labour (0.025 hours per bag).............	0.30	0.30

CBI's controller believes that the company's traditional costing system may be providing misleading cost information. To determine whether or not this is correct, the controller has prepared an analysis of the year's expected manufacturing overhead costs, as shown in the following table:

Activity Centre	Cost Driver	Expected Activity	Expected Cost
Purchasing...................	Purchase orders	1,710 orders	$ 513,000
Material handling	Number of setups	1,800 setups	720,000
Quality control	Number of batches	600 batches	144,000
Roasting	Roasting hours	96,100 hours	961,000
Blending	Blending hours	33,500 hours	402,000
Packaging	Packaging hours	26,000 hours	260,000

Total manufacturing overhead cost $3,000,000

Data regarding the expected production of Mona Loa and Malaysian coffee are presented below. There will be no raw materials inventory for either of these coffees at the beginning of the year.

	Mona Loa	Malaysian
Expected sales	100,000 bags	2,000 bags
Batch size...............	10,000 bags	500 bags
Setups..................	3 per batch	3 per batch
Purchase order size	20,000 bags	500 bags
Roasting time.............	1 hr./100 bags	1 hr./100 bags
Blending time.............	0.5 hr./100 bags	0.5 hr./100 bags
Packaging time...........	0.1 hr./100 bags	0.1 hr./100 bags

Required

1. Using direct labour-hours as the base for assigning manufacturing overhead cost to products, do the following:
   a. Determine the predetermined overhead rate that will be used during the year.
   b. Determine the unit product cost of one bag of the Mona Loa coffee and one bag of the Malaysian coffee.
   c. Determine the selling price of one bag of the Mona Loa coffee and one bag of the Malaysian coffee using the company's 30% markup.
2. Using activity-based costing as the basis for assigning manufacturing overhead cost to products, do the following:
   a. Determine the total amount of manufacturing overhead cost assignable to the Mona Loa coffee and to the Malaysian coffee for the year. Show all computations in good form.
   b. Using the data developed in (2)(a) above, determine the amount of manufacturing overhead cost per bag of the Mona Loa coffee and the Malaysian coffee. Carry all computations to three decimal places.
   c. Determine the unit product cost of one bag of the Mona Loa coffee and one bag of the Malaysian coffee.

3. Write a brief memo to the president of CBI explaining what you have found in (1) and (2) above, and discussing the implications to the company of using direct labour as the base for assigning manufacturing overhead cost to products.

(CMA, adapted)

C5–22 Activity-Based Costing; Product Decision   "Wow! Is that B-10 model ever a loser! I say the time has come to cut back its production and shift our resources toward the new C-20 model," said Rory Moncur, executive vice president of Hammer Products, Inc. "Just look at this statement I've received from accounting. The C-20 is generating twice as much in profits as the B-10, and it has only about one-fifth as much in sales. I'm convinced that our future depends on the C-20." The year-end statement to which Rory was referring follows:

HAMMER PRODUCTS, INC.
Income Statement

	Total	Product Model	
		B-10	C-20
Sales...........................	$14,500,000	$12,000,000	$2,500,000
Cost of goods sold	9,000,000	7,200,000	1,800,000
Gross margin	5,500,000	4,800,000	700,000
Less selling and administrative expenses..........	4,900,000	4,600,000	300,000
Net income.....................	$ 600,000	$ 200,000	$ 400,000
Number of units produced and sold	—	60,000	10,000
Net income per unit	—	$3.33	$40.00

"The numbers sure look that way," replied Connie Collins, the company's sales manager. "But why isn't the competition more excited about the C-20? I know we've only been producing the model for three years, but I'm surprised that more of our competitors haven't recognized what a cash cow it is."

"I think it's our new automated plant," replied Rory. "Now it takes only one direct labour-hour to produce a unit of the B-10 and one-and-a-half direct labour-hours to produce a unit of the C-20. That's considerably less than it used to take us."

"I agree that automation is wonderful," replied Connie. "I suppose that's how we're able to hold down the price of the C-20. Borst Company in Germany tried to bring out a C-20 but discovered they couldn't touch our price. But Borst is killing us on the B-10 by undercutting our price with some of our best customers. I suppose they'll pick up all of our B-10 business if we move out of that market. But who cares? We don't even have to advertise the C-20; it just seems to sell itself."

"My only concern about automation is how our manufacturing overhead rate has shot up," said Rory. "Our total manufacturing overhead cost is $3,600,000. That comes out to be a hefty amount per direct labour-hour, but Fred down in accounting has been using labour-hours as the base for computing overhead rates for years and doesn't want to change. I don't suppose it matters so long as costs get assigned to products."

"I've never understood that debit and credit stuff," replied Connie. "But I think you've got a problem in production. I had lunch with Joanne yesterday and she complained about how complex the C-20 is to produce. Apparently they have to do a lot of setups, special soldering, and other work on the C-20 just to keep production moving. And they have to inspect every single unit."

"It'll have to wait," said Rory. "I'm writing a proposal to the board of directors to phase out the B-10. We've got to bring our bottom line up or we'll all be looking for jobs."

Required

1. Compute the predetermined overhead rate that the company used during the year. (You may assume that there was no under- or overapplied overhead for the year.)
2. Materials and labour costs per unit for the two products are as follows:

	B-10	C-20
Direct materials	$60	$90
Direct labour	12	18

Using these data and the rate computed in (1) above, determine the unit product cost of each product.

3. Assume that the company's $3,600,000 in manufacturing overhead cost is traceable to six activity centres, as follows:

Activity Centre (and Cost Driver)	Estimated Overhead Costs	Expected Activity—Cost Driver		
		Total	B-10	C-20
Machine setups (number of setups).......	$ 416,000	3,200	2,000	1,200
Quality control (number of inspections) ...	720,000	18,000	8,000	10,000
Purchase orders (number of orders).......	180,000	2,400	1,680	720
Soldering (number of solder joints).......	900,000	400,000	120,000	280,000
Shipments (number of shipments)........	264,000	1,200	800	400
Machine related (machine-hours)	1,120,000	140,000	60,000	80,000
	$3,600,000			

Given these data, would you support a recommendation to expand sales of the C-20? Explain your position, and show unit costs, an income statement, and other data to help the board of directors make a decision.

4. From the data you have prepared in (3) above, why do you suppose the C-20 "just seems to sell itself"?

5. If you were president of Hammer Products, Inc., what strategy would you follow from this point forward to improve the company's overall profits?

6. Examine the costs in (3) above. Which of these costs might be reduced (or even eliminated) if the company adopted the philosophy of continuous improvement?

7. Is there any justification for using the overhead rate from part (1), given the technology that exists today?

C5–23 Activity-Based Costing; Product Retention Decision   (Adapted from a case written by Professors Harold P. Roth and Imogene Posey for the Institute of Management Accountants.[25])

"Two dollars of gross margin per briefcase? That's ridiculous!" roared Caspar Thurmond, president of FirstLine Cases, Inc. "Why do we go on producing those standard briefcases when we're able to make over $11 per unit on our specialty items? Maybe it's time to get out of the standard line and focus the whole plant on specialty work."

Mr. Thurmond is referring to a summary of unit costs and revenues that he had just received from the company's accounting department:

	Standard Briefcases	Specialty Briefcases
Selling price per unit..............	$26.25	$42.50
Unit manufacturing cost............	24.25	31.40
Gross margin per unit.............	$ 2.00	$11.10

FirstLine Cases produces briefcases from leather, fabric, and synthetic materials in a single plant. The basic product is a standard briefcase that is made from leather lined with fabric. The standard briefcase is a high-quality item and has sold well for many years.

Last year, the company decided to expand its product line and produce specialty briefcases for special orders. These briefcases differ from the standard in that they vary in size, they contain the finest leather and synthetic materials, and they are imprinted with the buyer's name. To reduce the labour costs on the specialty briefcases, most of the cutting and stitching is done by automated machines. These machines are used to a much lesser degree in the production of standard briefcases.

"I agree that the specialty business is looking better and better," replied Beth Mersey, the company's marketing manager. "And there seems to be plenty of specialty work out there, particularly since the competition hasn't been able to touch our price. Did you know that Velsun Company, our biggest competitor, charges over $50 a unit for its specialty items? Now that's what I call gouging the customer!"

[25]Harold P. Roth and Imogene Posey, "Management Accounting Case Study: CarryAll Company," *Management Accounting Campus Report,* Institute of Management Accountants (Fall 1991), p. 9. Used by permission.

A breakdown of the manufacturing cost for each of FirstLine Cases' product lines is given below:

		Standard Briefcases		Specialty Briefcases
Units produced each month		10,000		2,500
Direct materials:				
Leather		$ 8.00		$12.00
Fabric		2.00		1.00
Synthetic.................				7.00
Total materials..........		10.00		20.00
Direct labour...............	0.5 hr. @ $12.00	6.00	0.4 hr. @ $12.00	4.80
Manufacturing overhead.......	0.5 hr. @ $16.50	8.25	0.4 hr. @ $16.50	6.60
Total cost per unit		$24.25		$31.40

Manufacturing overhead is applied to products on the basis of direct labour-hours. The rate of $16.50 per hour is determined by dividing the total manufacturing overhead cost for a month by the direct labour-hours:

$$\frac{\text{Manufacturing overhead cost, } \$99,000}{\text{Direct labour-hours, } 6,000} = \$16.50 \text{ per direct labour-hour}$$

The following additional information is available about the company and its products:

a. Standard briefcases are produced in batches of 1,000 units, and specialty briefcases are produced in batches of 100 units. Thus, the company does 10 setups for the standard items each month and 25 setups for the specialty items. A setup for the standard items requires one hour of time, whereas a setup for the specialty items requires two hours of time.

b. All briefcases are inspected to ensure that quality standards are met. A total of 200 hours of inspection time is spent on the standard briefcases and 400 hours of inspection time is spent on the specialty briefcases each month.

c. A standard briefcase requires 0.5 hour of machine time, and a specialty briefcase requires 1.2 hours of machine time.

Required

1. The company's $99,000 in monthly overhead cost is traceable to six activities, as follows:

		Expected Activity—Cost Driver		
Activity (and Cost Driver)	Estimated Overhead Costs	Total	Standard Briefcases	Specialty Briefcases
Purchasing (number of orders).........	$15,000			
Leather		60	50	10
Fabric		90	70	20
Synthetic material		150	—	150
Material handling (number of receipts)...	16,000			
Leather		80	70	10
Fabric		105	85	20
Synthetic material		215	—	215
Production orders and equipment setup (setup hours)...................	6,000	?	?	?
Inspection (inspection hours)...........	18,000	600	200	400
Frame assembly (assembly-hours).......	12,000	1,500	700	800
Machine related (machine-hours)	32,000	?	?	?
	$99,000			

Using activity-based costing, determine the amount of manufacturing overhead cost that should be applied to each standard briefcase and each specialty briefcase.

2. Using the data computed in (1) above and other data from the case as needed, determine the unit product cost of each product line from the perspective of activity-based costing.

3. Evaluate the president's concern about the profitability of the two product lines. From the data you have computed, would you recommend that the company shift its resources entirely to the production of specialty briefcases? Explain.

4. Beth Mersey stated that "the competition hasn't been able to touch our price" on specialty business. Why do you suppose the competition hasn't been able to touch FirstLine Cases' price?

GROUP EXERCISES

GE5–24 Traditional Product Cost Systems Are Out-of-Date   Many firms realize that there are fundamental problems with the methods they use to cost their products or services. But should they change from traditional product costing methods to activity-based costing (ABC) methods? It is important first of all to understand the limitations of existing product costing systems in today's competitive environment typified by a diverse product line populated by many low-volume complex products.

Required

1. What's wrong with traditional product costing systems that they no longer meet the needs of today's managers?
2. How does the cost structure of most manufacturing firms today differ from their cost structure of 20 years ago?
3. What caused this change in cost structure?
4. Why can't traditional product costing systems account for costs of product diversity? Volume diversity? Product complexity?

GE5–25 The ABCs of ABC   While a form of ABC was being used by General Electric back in the sixties, widespread use of ABC didn't begin in the United States until the late eighties. The early focus on ABC was on developing more reliable product cost numbers to improve firms' product-related strategies (e.g., pricing, product profitability, product emphasis). But more recently, companies have found activity-based management to be of even greater benefit.

Required

1. Why change to ABC? What is different about the competitive, product, and process environment today that would cause a company to consider implementing an ABC system?
2. What are the objectives of using ABC?
3. Why is ABC important, that is, what are the benefits of an ABC system?
4. Give examples of how an ABC system can result in more reliable product costs than conventional labour-based product costing systems.
5. Why did the use of ABC change from a focus on generating more accurate product cost numbers to a greater emphasis on its use for cost planning and cost reduction?

GE5–26 ABC's Impact on Decisions   ABC can have an enormous impact across an organization. How could each of the following specific areas benefit from using ABC information: Cost estimating, sales/marketing, product engineering, manufacturing engineering, manufacturing, manufacturing development, and make versus buy group?

GE5–27 TQM and COQ   Total quality management, or TQM, is to North American companies competing in the nineties what it was for Japanese firms throughout the seventies and eighties. The concept of cost of quality (COQ) gives quality a bottom-line discipline that is at the core of many well-managed quality improvement programs (QIP). With a focus on satisfying the customer, those who view quality as a marathon race stand a greater chance of improving market share than do those who view quality as the latest project with a start date and a completion date.

Required

1. Surveys have shown that when financial managers are asked to estimate the total cost of quality (prior to implementing a QIP), half or more estimate that COQ is less than 5% of sales revenue. The reality is that actual COQ is typically 10% to 20% of sales, and in some cases it has exceeded 60% of sales. Why do you think there is such a large gap between the perception and the reality of the quality problem?
2. Why do you think the cost of poor quality reached such an epidemic level before companies were motivated to do something about the problem?
3. What function(s) does COQ reporting play in a quality improvement program?
4. For most companies starting a QIP, investments in prevention and appraisal usually result in major cost savings in other areas. Explain this phenomenon.
5. The traditional view of quality is that the total costs of prevention and appraisal plus internal and external failure costs are minimized at a point before zero defects are reached. Additional investments in prevention beyond this point would result in savings that are less than the additional investment in prevention. An alternative view of quality is that the total costs of the four categories of quality are minimized at zero defects. Additional investments in prevention will always result in larger reductions in appraisal and failure costs. With the zero defects model, the search for quality improvements is continuous. Explain these two viewpoints.

COST BEHAVIOUR: ANALYSIS AND USE

LEARNING OBJECTIVES

After studying Chapter 6 you should be able to:

1 Identify examples of variable costs, and explain the effect of a change in activity on both total variable costs and per unit variable costs.

2 Define the relevant range, and explain its significance in cost behaviour analysis.

3 Identify examples of fixed costs, and explain the effect of a change in activity on both total fixed costs and fixed costs expressed on a per unit basis.

4 Distinguish between committed and discretionary fixed costs.

5 Use a cost formula to predict costs at a new level of activity.

6 Analyze a mixed cost using the high-low method.

7 Analyze a mixed cost using the scattergraph method.

8 Explain the least-squares regression method for analyzing a mixed cost.

9 Prepare an income statement using the contribution format.

10 Define or explain the key terms listed at the end of the chapter.

11 (Appendix 6A) Analyze a mixed cost using the least-squares regression method.

Many manufacturing and service companies use highly skilled workers who receive long and complicated training to operate sophisticated programs. With such a large investment, employers are reluctant to lay off these workers when business is slack. In such instances, some portion of direct labour may be considered a fixed cost.

In our discussion of cost terms and concepts in Chapter 2, we stated that one way in which costs can be classified is by behaviour. We defined cost behaviour as meaning how a cost will react or change as changes take place in the level of business activity. An understanding of cost behaviour is the key to many decisions in an organization. Managers who understand how costs behave are better able to predict what costs will be under various operating circumstances. Experience has shown that attempts at decision making without a thorough understanding of the costs involved—and how these costs may change with the activity level—can lead to disaster. For example, a decision to double production of a particular product line might result in the incurrence of far greater costs than could be generated in additional revenues. To avoid such problems, a manager must be able to accurately predict what costs will be at various activity levels. In this chapter, we shall find that the key to effective cost prediction lies in an understanding of cost behaviour patterns.

We briefly review in this chapter the definitions of variable costs and fixed costs and then discuss the behaviour of these costs in greater depth than we were able to do in Chapter 2. After this review and discussion, we turn our attention to the analysis of mixed costs. We conclude the chapter by introducing a new income statement format—called the contribution format—in which costs are organized by behaviour rather than by the traditional functions of production, sales, and administration.

TYPES OF COST BEHAVIOUR PATTERNS

In our brief discussion of cost behaviour in Chapter 2, we mentioned only variable and fixed costs. There is a third behaviour pattern, generally known as a *mixed* or *semivariable* cost. All three cost behaviour patterns—variable, fixed, and mixed—are found in most organizations. The relative proportion of each type of cost present in a firm is known as the firm's **cost structure.** For example, a firm might have many fixed costs but few variable costs or mixed costs. Alternatively, it might have many variable costs but few fixed or mixed costs. A firm's cost structure can have a significant impact on decisions. We must reserve a detailed discussion of cost structure until the next chapter, however, and concentrate for the moment on gaining a fuller understanding of the behaviour of each type of cost.

Nooksack Expeditions is a service company that provides whitewater rafting trips. Nooksack's costs are both variable (such as meals for guests) and fixed (rent for storage). Understanding how the behaviour of these costs relates to changes in volume is one key to a manager's success in operating the business.

Variable Costs

OBJECTIVE 1

Identify examples of variable costs, and explain the effect of a change in activity on both total variable costs and per unit variable costs.

We found in Chapter 2 that a variable cost is so named because its total dollar amount varies in direct proportion to changes in the activity level. If the activity level doubles, the total dollar amount of the variable costs also doubles. If the activity level increases by only 10%, then the total dollar amount of the variable costs increases by 10% as well.

We also found in Chapter 2 that a variable cost remains constant if expressed on a *per unit* basis. To provide an example, consider Nooksack Expeditions, a small company that provides daylong whitewater rafting excursions on rivers in Northern B.C. The company provides all of the necessary equipment and experienced guides, and it serves gourmet meals to its guests. The meals are purchased from an exclusive caterer for $30 a person for a daylong excursion. If we look at the cost of the meals on a *per person* basis, the cost remains constant at $30. This $30 cost per person will not change, regardless of how many people participate in a daylong excursion. The behaviour of a variable cost, on both a per unit and a total basis, is tabulated below:

Number of Guests	Cost of Meals Per Guest	Total Cost of Meals
250	$30	$ 7,500
500	30	15,000
750	30	22,500
1,000	30	30,000

The idea that a variable cost is constant per unit but varies in total with the activity level is crucial to an understanding of cost behaviour patterns. We shall rely on this concept again and again in this chapter and in chapters ahead.

Exhibit 6–1 provides a graphic illustration of variable cost behaviour. The exhibit contains three cost lines—one at $30 per guest, and two others showing what would happen to the slope of the line if the of meals increased to $40 per guest or dropped to $20 per guest. Note that as the variable cost per unit increases, the cost line becomes steeper.

EXHIBIT 6–1

Variable Cost Behaviour

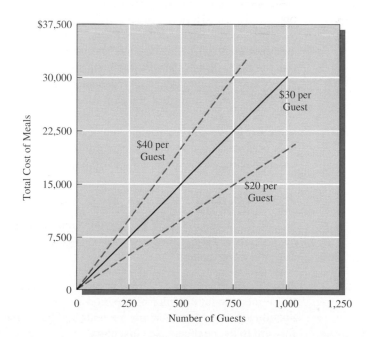

The Activity Base.   For a cost to be variable, it must be variable *with respect to something*. That "something" is its *activity base*. An **activity base** is a measure of whatever causes the incurrence of variable cost. In Chapter 3, we mentioned that an activity base is sometimes referred to as a *cost driver*. Some of the most common activity bases are machine-hours, units produced, and units sold. Other activity bases (cost drivers) might include the number of kilometres driven by salespersons, the number of kilograms of laundry processed by a hotel, the number of letters typed by a secretary, the number of hours of labour time logged, and the number of occupied beds in a hospital.

To plan and control variable costs, a manager must be well acquainted with the various activity bases within the firm. People sometimes get the notion that if a cost doesn't vary with production or with sales, then it is not really a variable cost. This is not correct. As suggested by the range of bases listed above, costs are caused by many different activities within an organization. Whether a cost is considered to be variable depends on whether it is caused by the activity under consideration. For example, if a manager is analyzing the cost of service calls under a product warranty, the relevant activity measure will be the number of service calls made. Those costs that vary in total with the number of service calls made are the variable costs of making service calls.

Extent of Variable Costs.   The number and type of variable costs present in an organization will depend in large part on the organization's structure and purpose. A public utility like Nova Scotia Power, with large investments in equipment, will tend to have few variable costs. The bulk of its costs will be associated with its plant, and these costs will tend to be quite insensitive to changes in levels of service provided. A manufacturing company like Rocky Mountain Bicycle of British Columbia, by contrast, will often have many variable costs; these costs will be associated with both the manufacture and distribution of its products to customers.

A merchandising company like Canadian Tire will usually have a high proportion of variable costs in its cost structure. In most merchandising companies, the cost of merchandise purchased for resale, a variable cost, constitutes a very large component of total cost. Service companies, by contrast, have diverse cost structures. For example, fast-food outlets like Tim Hortons Donuts, with their food costs and hourly employees, have high variable cost components. On the other hand, service companies involved in consulting, auditing, engineering, dental, medical, and architectural activities have very large fixed costs in the form of expensive facilities and highly trained salaried employees.

Some of the more frequently encountered variable costs are listed in Exhibit 6–2. This exhibit is not a complete listing of all costs that can be considered variable. Moreover, some of the costs listed in the exhibit may behave more like fixed than variable costs in some firms. We will see some examples of this later in the chapter. Nevertheless, Exhibit 6–2 provides a useful listing of many of the costs that normally would be considered variable with respect to the volume of output.

True Variable versus Step-Variable Costs

Not all variable costs have exactly the same behaviour pattern. Some variable costs behave in a *true variable* or *proportionately variable* pattern. Other variable costs behave in a *step-variable* pattern.

True Variable Costs.   Direct materials is a true or proportionately variable cost because the amount used during a period will vary in direct proportion to the level of production activity. Moreover, any amounts purchased but not used can be stored and carried forward to the next period as inventory.

EXHIBIT 6-2

Examples of Costs
that Are Normally
Variable with
Respect to Volume

Type of Organization	Variable Costs
Merchandising company	Cost of goods (merchandise) sold
Manufacturing company	Manufacturing costs: 　Prime costs: 　　Direct materials 　　Direct labour 　Variable portion of manufacturing overhead: 　　Indirect materials 　　Lubricants 　　Supplies 　　Power
Both merchandising and manufacturing companies	Selling, general, and administrative costs: 　Commissions 　Clerical costs, such as invoicing 　Shipping costs
Service organizations	Supplies, travel, clerical

Step-Variable Costs.   The wages of maintenance workers are often considered to be a variable cost, but this labour cost doesn't behave in quite the same way as the cost of direct materials. Unlike direct materials, the time of maintenance workers is obtainable only in large chunks. Moreover, any maintenance time not utilized cannot be stored as inventory and carried forward to the next period. Either the time is used effectively as it expires hour by hour, or it is gone forever. Furthermore, a maintenance crew can work at a fairly leisurely pace if pressures are light but intensify its efforts if pressures build up. For this reason, somewhat small changes in the level of production may have no effect on the number of maintenance people needed to properly carry on maintenance work.

A cost that is obtainable only in large chunks (such as the labour cost of maintenance workers) and that increases or decreases only in response to fairly wide changes in the activity level is known as a **step-variable cost.** The behaviour of a step-variable cost, contrasted with the behaviour of a true variable cost, is illustrated in Exhibit 6–3.

Notice that the need for maintenance help changes only with fairly wide changes in volume and that when additional maintenance time is obtained, it comes in large, indivisible chunks. The strategy of management in dealing with step-variable costs must be to obtain the fullest use of services possible for each separate step. Great care must be taken

EXHIBIT 6-3

True Variable versus
Step-Variable Costs

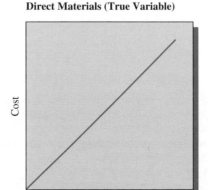

Direct Materials (True Variable)

Cost

Volume

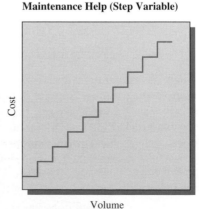

Maintenance Help (Step Variable)

Cost

Volume

Curvilinear Costs
and the Relevant
Range

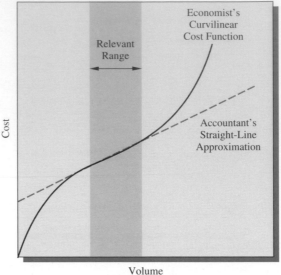

in working with these kinds of costs to prevent "fat" from building up in an organization. There is a tendency to employ additional help more quickly than might be needed, and there is generally a natural reluctance to lay people off when volume declines.

The Linearity Assumption and the Relevant Range

OBJECTIVE 2

Define the relevant range, and explain its significance in cost behaviour analysis.

In dealing with variable costs, we have assumed a strictly linear relationship between cost and volume, except in the case of step-variable costs. Economists correctly point out that many costs that the accountant classifies as variable actually behave in a *curvilinear* fashion. The behaviour of a **curvilinear cost** is shown in Exhibit 6–4.

Although many costs are not strictly linear when plotted as a function of volume, a curvilinear cost can be satisfactorily approximated with a straight line within a narrow band of activity known as the *relevant range*. The **relevant range** is that range of activity within which the assumptions made about cost behaviour by the manager are valid. For example, note that the dashed line in Exhibit 6–4 can be used as an approximation to the curvilinear cost with very little loss of accuracy within the shaded relevant range. However, outside of the relevant range the straight line is a poor approximation to the curvilinear cost relationship. Managers should always keep in mind that a particular assumption made about cost behaviour may be very inappropriate if activity falls outside of the relevant range.

Fixed Costs

OBJECTIVE 3

Identify examples of fixed costs, and explain the effect of a change in activity on both total fixed costs and fixed costs expressed on a per unit basis.

In our discussion of cost behaviour patterns in Chapter 2, we stated that fixed costs remain constant in total dollar amount despite changes in the level of activity. To continue the Nooksack Expeditions example, assume the company decides to rent a building for $500 per month to store its equipment. The *total* amount of rent paid is the same regardless of the number of guests the company takes on its expeditions during any given month. This concept is shown graphically in Exhibit 6–5.

Since fixed costs remain constant in total, the amount of fixed cost computed on a *per unit* basis becomes progressively smaller as the level of activity increases. If Nooksack Expeditions has only 250 guests in a month, the $500 fixed rental cost would amount to

Convention centres have large fixed costs —for example, heating and air conditioning, interest payments, and electricity—that must be covered whether or not the facilities are in use.

$2 per guest. If there are 1,000 guests, the fixed rental cost would amount to only 50 cents per guest. This aspect of the behaviour of fixed costs is also displayed in Exhibit 6–5. Note that as the number of guests increases, the average unit cost drops, but it drops at a decreasing rate. The first guests have the biggest impact on unit costs.

As we noted in Chapter 2, this aspect of fixed costs can be confusing, although it is necessary in some contexts to express fixed costs on an average per unit basis. We found in Chapter 3, for example, that a broad unit cost figure containing both variable and fixed cost elements is used in *external* financial statements. For *internal* uses, however,

EXHIBIT 6-5   Fixed Cost Behaviour

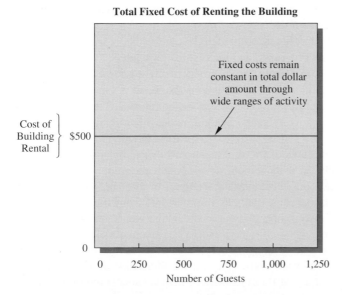

Total Fixed Cost of Renting the Building

Fixed costs remain constant in total dollar amount through wide ranges of activity

Cost of Building Rental $500

Number of Guests

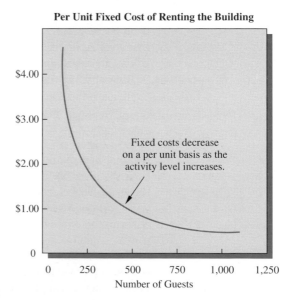

Per Unit Fixed Cost of Renting the Building

Fixed costs decrease on a per unit basis as the activity level increases.

Number of Guests

fixed costs should not be expressed on a per unit basis because of the potential confusion involved. Experience has shown that for internal uses, fixed costs are most easily (and most safely) dealt with on a total basis rather than on a per unit basis.

Types of Fixed Costs

OBJECTIVE 4

Distinguish between committed and discretionary fixed costs.

Fixed costs are sometimes referred to as capacity costs, because they result from outlays made for plant facilities, equipment, and other items needed to provide the basic capacity for sustained operations. For planning purposes, fixed costs can be viewed as being either *committed* or *discretionary*.

Committed Fixed Costs.   **Committed fixed costs** relate to the investment in facilities, equipment, and the basic organizational structure of a firm. Examples of such costs include depreciation of buildings and equipment, taxes on real estate, insurance, and salaries of top management and operating personnel.

The two key factors about committed fixed costs are that (1) they are long term in nature and (2) they can't be reduced to zero even for short periods of time without seriously impairing the profitability or long-run goals of a firm. Even if operations are interrupted or cut back, the committed fixed costs will still continue largely unchanged. During a period of economic recession, for example, a firm won't usually discharge key executives or sell off key facilities. The basic organizational structure and facilities ordinarily must be kept intact. In terms of long-run goals, the costs of any other course of action are likely to be far greater than any short-run savings that might be realized.

Because it is difficult to change a committed fixed cost once the commitment has been made, management should approach these decisions with particular care. Decisions to acquire major equipment or to take on other committed fixed costs involve a long planning horizon. Management should make such commitments only after careful analysis of long-run trends and the available alternatives. Once a decision is made to build a certain size facility, a firm becomes locked into that decision for many years to come.

While not much can be done about committed fixed costs in the short run, management is generally very concerned about how these resources are *utilized*. The strategy of management must be to utilize the capacity of the organization as effectively as possible.

Discretionary Fixed Costs.   **Discretionary fixed costs** (often referred to as *managed* fixed costs) usually arise from *annual* decisions by management to spend in certain fixed cost areas. Examples of discretionary fixed costs include advertising, research, public relations, management development programs, and internships for students.

Basically, two key differences exist between discretionary fixed costs and committed fixed costs. First, the planning horizon for a discretionary fixed cost is fairly short term—usually a single year. By contrast, as we indicated earlier, committed fixed costs have a planning horizon that encompasses many years. Second, under dire circumstances it may be possible to cut back certain discretionary fixed costs for short periods of time with minimal damage to the long-run goals of the organization. For example, a firm that has been spending $50,000 annually on management development programs may be forced because of poor economic conditions to reduce its spending in that area during a given year. Although some unfavourable consequences might result from the cutback, it is doubtful that these consequences would be as great as those that would result if the company decided to economize during the year by laying off key personnel.

The most important characteristic of discretionary fixed costs is that management is not locked into a decision regarding such costs. They can be adjusted from year to year or even perhaps during the course of a year if circumstances demand such a modification.

Top-Management Philosophy.   In our discussion of fixed costs, we have drawn a sharp line between committed fixed costs and discretionary fixed costs. As a practical matter, the line between these two classes of costs is somewhat flexible. Whether a cost is committed or discretionary will depend in large part on the philosophy of top management.

Some management groups prefer to exercise discretion as often as possible on as many costs as possible. They prefer to review and adjust costs frequently as conditions warrant. Managers who are inclined in this direction tend to view fixed costs as being largely discretionary. Other management groups are slow to make adjustments in costs (especially adjustments downward) as conditions change. They prefer to maintain the status quo and to leave programs and personnel largely undisturbed, even though changing conditions might suggest the desirability of adjustments. Managers who are inclined in this direction tend to view virtually all fixed costs as being committed.

To cite an example, during recessionary periods when the level of home building is down, many construction companies lay off their workers and virtually disband operations for a period of time. Other construction companies continue large numbers of employees on the payroll, even though the workers have little or no work to do. In the first instance, management views its fixed costs as largely discretionary in nature. In the second instance, management views its fixed costs as largely committed. The approach of most management groups will fall somewhere between these two extremes.

The Trend toward Fixed Costs

The trend in many companies is toward greater fixed costs relative to variable costs. At least two factors are responsible for this trend.

First, automation is becoming increasingly important in all types of organizations—including those involved in services and merchandising. Increased automation results in increased investment in equipment, with the attendant fixed depreciation or lease charges.

Second, companies have become much more reluctant to adjust the workforce on a short-term basis. Labour unions have successfully fought for stabilized employment, but even without that pressure, most companies realize that their employees are a very valuable asset. More and more, highly skilled and trained employees are required to operate sophisticated equipment, and these workers are not easy to replace. Layoffs undermine morale and result in a loss of trained workers who may never return. Nevertheless, many larger companies have undergone waves of "downsizing" in recent years in which large

Some large Japanese companies are reconsidering their commitments to lifetime employment due to the lack of flexibility these commitments impose during economic downturns. For example, Toyota Motor Corp. has created a new category of temporary professional workers. Among these workers are automotive designers, who the company is hiring under one-year contracts. To compensate for the lack of lifelong job security, the company is paying such workers a high annual salary based on individual merit rather than the customary method of linking increases in pay to seniority and overall company performance.[1]

---

[1]Michael Williams, "Toyota Creates Work Contracts Challenging Lifetime-Job System," *The Wall Street Journal,* January 24, 1994, p. A10.

This textile mill uses automation in its processes. Automation requires large investments in equipment, which become part of fixed costs through depreciation or rental charges.

numbers of employees—particularly middle managers—have lost their jobs. This downsizing has been the result of attempts to reengineer business processes to make them more efficient rather than a response to a decline in sales activity. A good example of this trend is the banking industry. The Royal Bank cut 3,500 jobs and the Bank of Montreal cut 2,000 jobs in September 1995. In early 1996 the CIBC announced it was merging back-end processing operations with the Bank of Nova Scotia, a move affecting about 4,800 employees from the CIBC and 1,800 from ScotiaBank.[2]

In addition, managers do not want to be caught with a bloated payroll in an economic downturn and be faced with the unpleasant prospect of layoffs. Therefore, there is an increased reluctance to add workers when sales activity picks up. Consequently, at least in the short run, wages and salaries in many companies tend to act more like fixed costs than variable costs.

The shift away from variable costs toward fixed costs has been so significant in some firms that they have become largely "fixed cost" organizations. The textile industry, for example, can be cited as one in which most firms have moved heavily toward automation, with basically inflexible fixed costs replacing flexible, more responsive variable costs. These shifts are very significant. For example, planning becomes much more crucial when one is dealing with large amounts of committed fixed costs. The reason is that when dealing with committed fixed costs, the manager is much more "locked in" and generally has fewer options available in day-to-day decisions.

Fixed Costs and the Relevant Range

The concept of the relevant range, which was introduced in our discussion of variable costs, also has application in dealing with fixed costs, particularly those of a discretionary

---

[2]"Is There a Job in Your Future? Have We Finally Reached the Point Where Computers, Software and Telecommunications Can Do Your Job Cheaper and Faster Than You?" *BC Business Magazine* (November 1996), pp. 54–56.

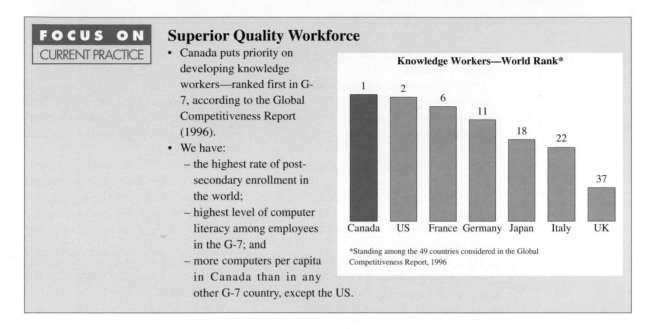

FOCUS ON
CURRENT PRACTICE

Superior Quality Workforce

- Canada puts priority on developing knowledge workers—ranked first in G-7, according to the Global Competitiveness Report (1996).
- We have:
  - the highest rate of post-secondary enrollment in the world;
  - highest level of computer literacy among employees in the G-7; and
  - more computers per capita in Canada than in any other G-7 country, except the US.

Knowledge Workers—World Rank*

Canada	US	France	Germany	Japan	Italy	UK
1	2	6	11	18	22	37

*Standing among the 49 countries considered in the Global Competitiveness Report, 1996

nature. At the beginning of a period, programs are set and budgets established. The level of discretionary fixed costs will depend on the support needs of the programs that have been planned, which in turn will depend at least in part on the level of activity envisioned in the overall organization. At very high levels of activity, programs are usually broadened or expanded. For example, the advertising needs of a company striving to increase sales by 25% would probably be much greater than if no sales increase was planned. Thus, fixed costs often move upward in steps as the activity level increases. This concept is illustrated in Exhibit 6–6, which depicts fixed costs and the relevant range.

Although discretionary fixed costs are more susceptible to adjustment than committed fixed costs, the step pattern depicted in Exhibit 6–6 also has application to committed

EXHIBIT 6–6

Fixed Costs and the Relevant Range

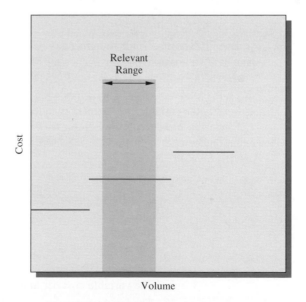

fixed costs. As a company expands its level of activity, it may outgrow its present facilities, or the key management team may need to be expanded. The result, of course, will be increased committed fixed costs as larger facilities are built and as new management positions are created.

One reaction to the step pattern depicted in Exhibit 6–6 is to say that discretionary and committed fixed costs are really just step-variable costs. To some extent this is true, since virtually *all* costs vary in the long run. There are two major differences, however, between the step-variable costs depicted earlier in Exhibit 6–3 and the fixed costs depicted in Exhibit 6–6.

The first difference is that the step-variable costs can often be adjusted quickly as conditions change, whereas once fixed costs have been set, they often can't be changed easily. A step-variable cost such as maintenance labour, for example, can be adjusted upward or downward by hiring and laying off maintenance workers. By contrast, once a company has signed a lease for a building, it is locked into that level of lease cost for the life of the contract.

The second difference is that the *width of the steps* depicted for step-variable costs is much narrower than the width of the steps depicted for the fixed costs in Exhibit 6–6. The width of the steps relates to volume or level of activity. For step-variable costs, the width of a step may be 40 hours of activity or less if one is dealing, for example, with maintenance labour cost. For fixed costs, however, the width of a step may be *thousands* or even *tens of thousands* of hours of activity. In essence, the width of the steps for step-variable costs is generally so narrow that these costs can be treated essentially as variable costs for most purposes. The width of the steps for fixed costs, on the other hand, is so wide that these costs must generally be treated as being entirely fixed within the relevant range.

Mixed Costs

A **mixed cost** is one that contains both variable and fixed cost elements. Mixed costs are also known as **semivariable costs.** To continue the Nooksack Expeditions example, the company must pay a licence fee of $25,000 per year plus $3 per rafting party to the province's Department of Natural Resources. If the company runs 1,000 rafting parties this year, then the total fees paid to the province would be $28,000, made up of $25,000 in fixed cost plus $3,000 in variable cost. The behaviour of this mixed cost is shown graphically in Exhibit 6–7.

Even if Nooksack fails to attract any customers and there are no rafting parties, the company will still have to pay the licence fee of $25,000. This is why the cost line in Exhibit 6–7 intersects the vertical cost axis at the $25,000 point. For each rafting party the company organizes, the total cost of provincial fees will increase by $3. Therefore, the total cost line slopes upward as the variable cost element is added to the fixed cost element.

Since the mixed cost in Exhibit 6–7 is represented by a straight line, the following equation for a straight line can be used to express the relationship between mixed cost and the level of activity:

$$Y = a + bX$$

In this equation,

Y = The total mixed cost
a = The total fixed cost (the vertical intercept of the line)
b = The variable cost per unit of activity (the slope of the line)
X = The level of activity

EXHIBIT 6-7

Mixed Cost
Behaviour

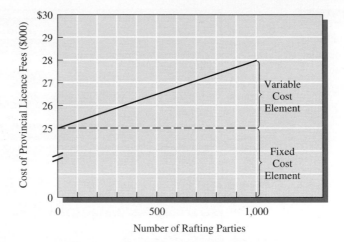

FOCUS ON
CURRENT PRACTICE

A total of 257 American and 40 Japanese manufacturing firms responded to a questionnaire concerning their management accounting practices.[3] Among other things, the firms were asked whether they classified certain costs as variable, semivariable, or fixed. Some of the results are summarized in Exhibit 6–8. Note that firms do not all classify costs in the same way. For example, roughly 45% of the U.S. firms classify material-handling labour costs as variable, 35% as semivariable, and 20% as fixed. Also note that the Japanese firms are much more likely than U.S. firms to classify labour costs as fixed. This is a consequence of the lifetime employment policies followed by many Japanese firms. These policies make it very difficult and expensive for Japanese firms to adjust their labour force in response to changes in activity.

In the case of the provincial fees paid by Nooksack Expeditions, the equation is written as follows:

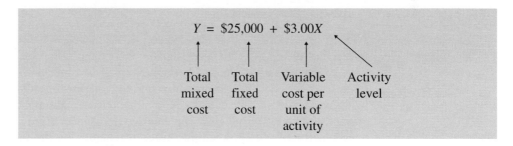

$$Y = \$25,000 + \$3.00X$$

Total mixed cost	Total fixed cost	Variable cost per unit of activity	Activity level

OBJECTIVE 5

Use a cost formula to predict costs at a new level of activity.

This equation makes it very easy to calculate what the total mixed cost would be for any level of activity within the relevant range. For example, suppose that the company expects to organize 800 rafting parties in the next year. Then the total provincial fees would be $27,400 calculated as follows:

$$Y = \$25,000 + (\$3.00 \times 800 \text{ rafting parties})$$
$$= \$27,400$$

---

[3]NAA Tokyo Affiliate, "Management Accounting in the Advanced Management Surrounding—Comparative Study on Survey in Japan and U.S.A.," October 1988.

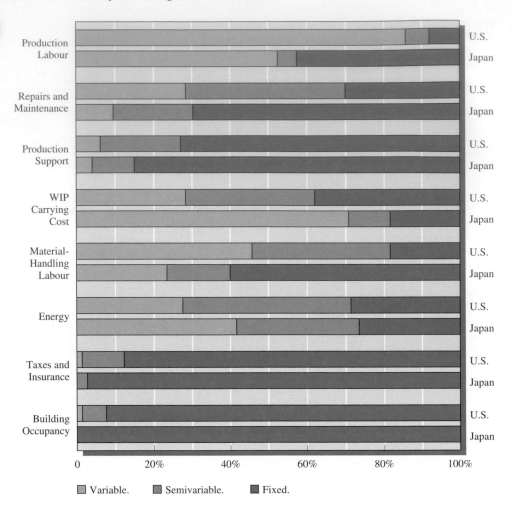

Percentages of Firms
Classifying Specific
Costs as Variable,
Semivariable, or
Fixed

THE ANALYSIS OF MIXED COSTS

In practice, mixed costs are very common. For example, the cost of providing X-ray services to patients at the Queen Elizabeth Hospital is a mixed cost. There are substantial fixed costs for equipment depreciation and for salaries for radiologists and technicians, but there are also variable costs for X-ray film, power, and supplies. At Air Canada, maintenance costs are a mixed cost. The company must incur fixed costs for renting maintenance facilities and for keeping skilled mechanics on the payroll, but the costs of replacement parts, lubricating oils, tires, and so forth, are variable with respect to how often and how far the company's aircraft are flown.

The fixed portion of a mixed cost represents the basic, minimum cost of just having a service *ready and available* for use. The variable portion represents the cost incurred for *actual consumption* of the service. The variable element varies in proportion to the amount of service that is consumed.

How does management go about actually estimating the fixed and variable components of a mixed cost? The ideal approach would be to take each invoice as it comes in and break it down into its fixed and variable elements. As a practical matter, even if it

X-ray services at a hospital are a good example of mixed costs. Salaries and equipment depreciation are fixed, but film and other supplies vary with the number of X rays taken.

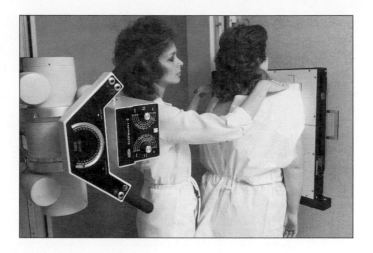

were possible to make this type of detailed breakdown, the cost of doing so would probably be prohibitive. Instead, analysis of mixed costs can be done on an aggregate basis, concentrating on the past behaviour of a cost at various levels of activity. If this analysis is done carefully, good approximations of the fixed and variable elements of a cost can be obtained with a minimum of effort.

▼   ▼   ▼   ▼   ▼

MANAGERIAL ACCOUNTING IN ACTION—THE ISSUE

D r. Derek Chalmers, the chief executive officer of Brentline Hospital, motioned Kinh Nguyen, the chief financial officer of the hospital, into his office.

DEREK: Kinh, come on in.

KINH: What can I do for you?

DEREK: Well for one, could you get the government to rescind the bookcase full of regulations against the wall over there?

KINH: Sorry, that's a bit beyond my authority.

DEREK: Just wishing, Kinh. Actually, believe it or not, I wanted to talk to you about our maintenance expenses. I didn't used to have to pay attention to such things, but these expenses seem to be bouncing around a lot. Over the last half year or so they have been as low as $7,400 and as high as $9,800 per month.

KINH: Actually, that's pretty normal variation in those expenses.

DEREK: Well, we budgeted a constant $8,400 a month. Can't we do a better job of predicting what these costs are going to be? And how do we know when we've spent too much in a month? Shouldn't there be some explanation for these variations?

KINH: Now that you mention it, we are in the process right now of tightening up our budgeting process. Our first step is to break all of our costs down into fixed and variable components.

DEREK: How will that help?

Continued

KINH: Well, that will permit us to predict what the level of costs will be. Some costs are fixed and shouldn't change much. Other costs go up and down as our activity goes up and down. The trick is to figure out what is driving the variable component of the costs.

DEREK: What about the maintenance costs?

KINH: My guess is that the variations in maintenance costs are being driven by our overall level of activity. When we treat more patients, our equipment is used more intensively which leads to more maintenance expense.

DEREK: How would you measure the level of overall activity? Would you use patient-days?

KINH: I think so. Each day a patient is in the hospital counts as one patient-day. The greater the number of patient-days in a month, the busier we are. Besides, our budgeting is all based on projected patient-days.

DEREK: Okay, so suppose you are able to break the maintenance costs down into fixed and variable components. What will that do for us?

KINH: Basically, I will be able to predict what maintenance costs should be as a function of the number of patient-days.

DEREK: I can see where that would be useful. We could use it to predict costs for budgeting purposes.

KINH: We could also use it as a benchmark. Based on the actual number of patient-days for a period, I can predict what the maintenance costs should have been. We can compare this to the actual spending on maintenance.

DEREK: Sounds good to me. Let me know when you get the results.

OBJECTIVE 6

Analyze a mixed cost using the high-low method.

We will examine three methods that Kinh Nguyen might use to break down mixed costs into their fixed and variable elements—the *high-low method,* the *scattergraph method,* and the *least-squares regression method.*

The High-Low Method

The **high-low method** of analyzing mixed costs is based on costs observed at both the high and low levels of activity within the relevant range. The difference in cost observed at the two extremes is divided by the change in activity between the extremes in order to determine the amount of variable cost involved.

The following records for Brentline Hospital will be used to analyze their maintenance costs within the relevant range of 5,000 to 8,000 patient-days:

Month	Activity Level: Patient-Days	Maintenance Cost Incurred
January	5,600	$7,900
February	7,100	8,500
March	5,000	7,400
April	6,500	8,200
May	7,300	9,100
June	8,000	9,800
July	6,200	7,800

Since total maintenance cost appears to generally increase as the activity level increases, it is likely that some variable cost element is present. Using the high-low method, we first identify the periods with the highest and lowest *activity*—in this case, June and March. We then use the activity and cost data from these two periods to estimate the variable cost component as follows:

	Patient-Days	Maintenance Cost Incurred
High activity level (June)	8,000	$9,800
Low activity level (March)	5,000	7,400
Change observed	3,000	$2,400

$$\text{Variable cost } = \frac{\text{Change in cost}}{\text{Change is activity}} = \frac{\$2,400}{3,000} = \$0.80 \text{ per patient-day}$$

Having determined that the variable rate for maintenance cost is 80 cents per patient-day, we can now determine the amount of fixed cost. This is done by taking total cost at *either* the high or the low activity level and deducting the variable cost element. In the computation below, total cost at the high activity level is used in computing the fixed cost element:

$$\begin{aligned} \text{Fixed cost element} &= \text{Total cost} - \text{Variable cost element} \\ &= \$9,800 - (\$0.80 \text{ per patient-day} \times 8,000 \text{ patient-days}) \\ &= \$3,400 \end{aligned}$$

Both the variable and fixed cost elements have now been isolated. The cost of maintenance within the relevant range analyzed can be expressed as $3,400 plus 80 cents per patient-day. This is sometimes referred to as a **cost formula.**

$$\left.\begin{array}{c} \text{Cost formula for maintenance cost} \\ \text{over the relevant range of 5,000} \\ \text{to 8,000 patient-days} \end{array}\right\} = \begin{array}{l} \$3,400 \text{ fixed cost plus} \\ \$0.80 \text{ per patient-day} \end{array}$$

This cost formula can also be expressed in terms of the equation for a straight line as follows:

$$Y = \$3,400 + \$0.80X$$

$$\underset{\substack{\uparrow \\ \text{Maintenance} \\ \text{cost}}}{} \qquad\qquad \underset{\substack{\uparrow \\ \text{Patient-days}}}{}$$

The data used in this illustration are shown graphically in Exhibit 6–9. Three things should be noted in relation to this exhibit:

1. Notice that cost, Y, is plotted on the vertical axis. Cost is known as the **dependent variable,** since the amount of cost incurred during a period will be dependent on the level of activity for the period. (That is, as the level of activity increases, total cost will also increase.)
2. Notice that activity, X (patient-days in this case), is plotted on the horizontal axis. Activity is known as the **independent variable,** since it controls the amount of cost that will be incurred during a period.
3. Notice that the relevant range is highlighted on the exhibit. In using a cost formula, the manager must remember that the formula may not be valid outside the relevant range from which the underlying data have been drawn.

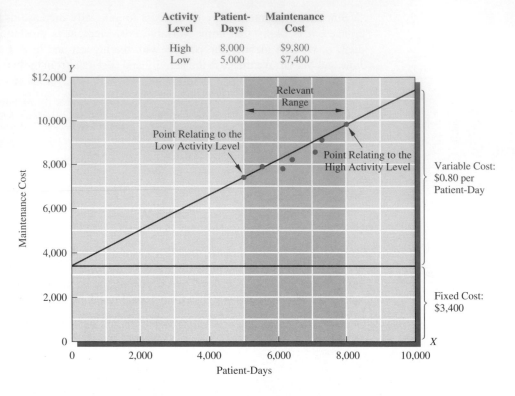

EXHIBIT 6-9

High-Low Method of
Cost Analysis

Activity Level	Patient-Days	Maintenance Cost
High	8,000	$9,800
Low	5,000	$7,400

Sometimes the high and low levels of activity don't coincide with the high and low amounts of cost. For example, the period that has the highest level of activity may not have the highest amount of cost. Nevertheless, the highest and lowest levels of *activity* are always used to analyze a mixed cost. The reason is that the activity presumably causes costs, so the analyst would like to use data that reflects the greatest possible variation in activity.

The high-low method is very simple to apply, but it suffers from a major (and sometimes critical) defect in that it utilizes only two data points. Generally, two points are not enough to produce accurate results in cost analysis work. Additionally, periods in which the activity level is unusually low or unusually high will tend to produce inaccurate results. A cost formula that is estimated solely using data from these unusual periods may seriously misrepresent the true cost relationship that holds during normal periods. Such a distortion is evident in Exhibit 6–9. The straight line should probably be shifted down somewhat so that it is closer to more of the data points. For these reasons, other methods of cost analysis that utilize a greater number of points will generally be more accurate than the high-low method. If a manager chooses to use the high-low method, he or she should do so with a full awareness of the method's limitations.

The Scattergraph Method

OBJECTIVE 7

Analyze a mixed cost
using the scattergraph
method.

A more accurate way of analyzing mixed costs is to use the **scattergraph method,** which takes into account all of the cost data. A graph like the one that we used in Exhibit 6–9 is constructed in which cost is shown on the vertical axis and the level of activity is shown on the horizontal axis. Costs observed at various levels of activity are then plotted on the graph, and a line is fitted to the plotted points. However, rather than just fitting the line to

EXHIBIT 6-10

Scattergraph Method
of Cost Analysis

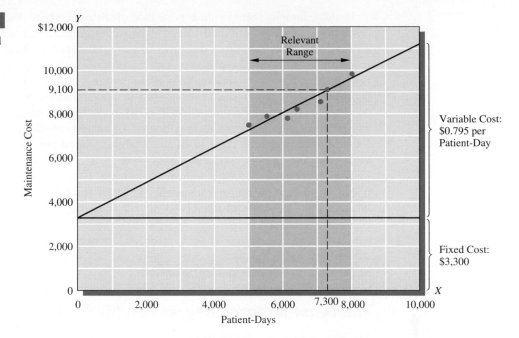

the high and low points, *all points* are considered when the line is drawn. This is done through simple visual inspection of the data, with the analyst taking care that the placement of the line is representative of all points, not just the high and low ones. Typically, the line is placed so that approximately equal numbers of points fall above and below it.

A graph of this type is known as a *scattergraph,* and the line fitted to the plotted points is known as a **regression line.** The regression line, in effect, is a line of averages, with the average variable cost per unit of activity represented by the slope of the line and the average total fixed cost represented by the point where the regression line intersects the cost axis.

The scattergraph approach using the Brentline Hospital maintenance data is illustrated in Exhibit 6–10. Note that the regression line has been placed in such a way that approximately equal numbers of points fall above and below it. Also note that the line has been drawn so that it goes through one of the points. This is not absolutely necessary, but it makes subsequent calculations a little easier.

Since the regression line strikes the vertical cost axis at $3,300, that amount represents the fixed cost element. The variable cost element can be computed by subtracting the fixed cost of $3,300 from the total cost for any point lying on the regression line. Since the point representing 7,300 patient-days lies on the regression line, we can use it. The variable cost (to the nearest tenth of a cent) would be 79.5 cents per patient-day, computed as follows:

Total cost for 7,300 patient-days
    (a point falling on the regression line) $9,100
Less fixed cost element   3,300
Variable cost element $5,800

$5,800 ÷ 7,300 patient-days = $0.795 per patient-day

Thus, the cost formula using the regression line in Exhibit 6–10 would be $3,300 per month plus 79.5 cents per patient-day.

In this example, there is not a great deal of difference between the cost formula derived using the high-low method and the cost formula derived using the scattergraph method. However, sometimes there *will* be a big difference. In those situations, more reliance should ordinarily be placed on the results of the scattergraph approach.

A scattergraph can be an extremely useful tool in the hands of an experienced analyst. Quirks in cost behaviour due to strikes, bad weather, breakdowns, and so on, become immediately apparent to the trained observer, who can make appropriate adjustments to the data when fitting the regression line. Some cost analysts would argue that a scattergraph should be the beginning point in all cost analyses, due to the benefits to be gained from having the data visually available in graph form.

The scattergraph method is sometimes criticized because it is subjective. No two analysts who look at the same scattergraph are likely to draw exactly the same regression line. Also, the estimates of fixed costs are not as precise as they are with other methods because it is difficult to precisely measure the dollar amount where the regression line intersects the vertical cost axis. Some managers are uncomfortable with these elements of subjectivity and imprecision and desire a method that will yield a precise answer that will be the same no matter who does the analysis.

The Least-Squares Regression Method

OBJECTIVE 8

Explain the least-squares regression method for analyzing a mixed cost.

The **least-squares regression method** is a more objective and precise approach to estimating the regression line than the scattergraph method. Rather than fitting a regression line through the scattergraph data by visual inspection, the least-squares regression method uses mathematical formulas to fit the regression line. Also, unlike the high-low method, the least-squares regression method takes all of the data into account when estimating the cost formula.

The basic idea underlying the least-squares regression method is illustrated in Exhibit 6–11 using hypothetical data points. Notice from the exhibit that the deviations from the plotted points to the regression line are measured vertically on the graph. These vertical deviations are called the regression errors and are the key to understanding what least-squares regression does.

EXHIBIT 6–11

The Concept of Least-Squares Regression

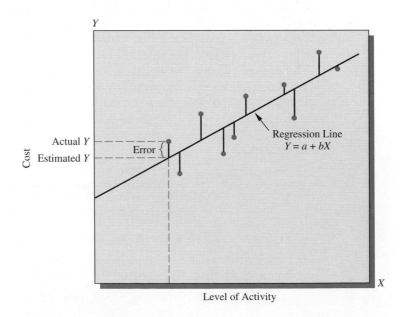

There is nothing mysterious about the least-squares regression method. It simply computes the regression line that minimizes the sum of these squared errors. The formulas that accomplish this are fairly complex and involve numerous calculations, but the principle is very simple.

Fortunately, computers are adept at carrying out the computations required by the least-squares regression formulas. The data—the observed values of X and Y—are entered into the computer, and software does the rest. In the case of the Brentline Hospital maintenance cost data, we used a statistical software package on a personal computer to calculate the following least-squares regression estimates of the total fixed cost (a) and the variable cost per unit of activity (b):

$$a = \$3,431$$
$$b = \$0.759$$

Therefore, using the least-squares regression method, the fixed element of the maintenance cost is \$3,431 per month and the variable portion is 75.9 cents per patient-day.

In terms of the linear equation $Y = a + bX$, the cost formula can be written as

$$Y = \$3,431 + \$0.759X$$

where activity (X) is expressed in patient-days.

While we used a personal computer to calculate the values of a and b in this example, they can also be calculated by hand. In Appendix 6A to this chapter, we show how this is done.

▼ ▼ ▼ ▼ ▼

MANAGERIAL ACCOUNTING IN ACTION—WRAP-UP

Affter completing the analysis of maintenance costs, Kinh Nguyen met with Dr. Derek Chalmers to discuss the results.

KINH: We used least-squares regression analysis to estimate the fixed and variable components of maintenance costs. According to the results, the fixed cost per month is \$3,431 and the variable cost per patient-day is 75.9 cents.

DEREK: Okay, so if we plan for 7,800 patient-days next month, what is your estimate of the maintenance costs?

KINH: That will take just a few seconds to figure out. Here it is. [And Kinh wrote the following calculations on a pad of paper.]

Fixed costs	\$3,431
Variable costs:	
7,800 patient-days × \$0.759 per patient-day	5,920
Total expected maintenance costs	\$9,351

DEREK: Nine thousand three hundred and fifty *one* dollars; isn't that a bit *too* precise?

KINH: Sure. I don't really believe the maintenance costs will be exactly this figure. However, based on the information we have, this is the best estimate we can come up with.

DEREK: Don't let me give you a hard time. Even though it is an estimate, it will be a lot better than just guessing like we have done in the past. Thanks. I hope to see more of this kind of analysis.

▼ ▼ ▼ ▼ ▼

The Use of Judgment in Cost Analysis

Although a cost formula has the appearance of exactness, the breakdown of a mixed cost by any of the three techniques that we have discussed involves a substantial amount of estimating. The breakdowns represent *approximations* of the fixed and variable cost elements involved; they should not be construed as being precisely accurate. Managers must be ready to step in at any point in their analysis of a cost and adjust their computations for judgment factors that in their view are critical to a proper understanding of the mixed cost involved. However, the fact that computations are not exact and involve estimates and judgment does not prevent data from being useful and meaningful in decision making. Managers who wait to make a decision until they have perfect data will rarely have an opportunity to demonstrate their decision-making ability.

Multiple Regression Analysis

In the discussion thus far, we have assumed that a single factor such as patient-days drives the variable cost component of mixed costs. This assumption is acceptable for many mixed costs, but in some situations there may be more than one causal factor driving the variable cost element. For example, shipping costs may depend on both the number of units shipped *and* the weight of the units. In a situation such as this, *multiple regression* is necessary. **Multiple regression** is an analytical method that is used when the dependent variable (i.e., cost) is caused by more than one factor. In this situation the equation for a simple regression would be expanded to include the additional variable:

$$Y = a + bX + cW$$

Where a = the estimated fixed shipping cost, b = the variable cost per unit of X, c = the variable cost per unit weight W, and Y denotes the expected shipping cost. Although adding more factors, or variables, makes the computations more complex, the principles involved are the same as in the simple least-squares regressions discussed above. Because of the complexity of the calculations, multiple regression is nearly always done with a computer.

Determining the Fit of the Regression Line.   The fit of the regression line to the observations is often assessed by what is denoted as R^2 (pronounced R Squared). R^2 has a range of 0 to 1. It denotes the percentage of the variation in the dependent variable, the Ys, that is explained by changes in the independent variable and their effect on the regression line prediction. A perfect fit would yield an R^2, also termed a **coefficient of determination,** of 1. The R^2 would be in 0 in a situation where no fit was achieved by the regression line. The appropriate level of an R^2 requires a knowledge of the type of fit expected in the situation where the regression is used.

Engineering Approach to Cost Study

Some firms use the engineering approach to analyze cost behaviour. Essentially, this approach involves a detailed analysis of what cost behaviour should be, based on an industrial engineer's evaluation of the production methods to be used, the materials specifications, labour requirements, equipment usage, efficiency of production, power consumption, and so on. The engineering approach must be used in those situations where no past experience is available concerning activity and costs. In addition, it is often used in tandem with the methods we have discussed above in order to sharpen the accuracy of cost analysis.

THE CONTRIBUTION FORMAT

OBJECTIVE 9

Prepare an income statement using the contribution format.

Once the manager has separated costs into fixed and variable elements, what does he or she do with the data? We have already answered this question somewhat by showing how a cost formula can be used to predict costs. To answer this question more fully will require most of the remainder of this text, since much of what the manager does rests in some way on an understanding of cost behaviour. One immediate and very significant application of the ideas we have developed, however, is found in a new income statement format known as the **contribution approach.** The unique thing about the contribution approach is that it provides the manager with an income statement geared directly to cost behaviour.

Why a New Income Statement Format?

The **traditional approach** to the income statement, as illustrated in Chapter 2, is not organized in terms of cost behaviour. Rather, it is organized in a "functional" format—emphasizing the functions of production, administration, and sales in the classification and presentation of cost data. No attempt is made to distinguish between the behaviour of costs included under each functional heading. Under the heading "Administrative expense," for example, one can expect to find both variable and fixed costs lumped together.

Although an income statement prepared in the functional format may be useful for external reporting purposes, it has serious limitations when used for internal purposes. Internally, the manager needs cost data organized in a format that will facilitate carrying out planning, control, and decision-making responsibilities. As we shall see in chapters ahead, these tasks are much easier when cost data are available in a fixed and variable format. The contribution approach to the income statement has been developed in response to this need.

The Contribution Approach

Exhibit 6–12 illustrates the contribution approach to the income statement, along with the traditional approach discussed in Chapter 2.

EXHIBIT 6–12 Comparison of the Contribution Income Statement with the Traditional Income Statement

Traditional Approach (costs organized by function)			Contribution Approach (costs organized by behaviour)		
Sales		$12,000	Sales		$12,000
Less cost of goods sold		6,000*	Less variable expenses:		
Gross margin		6,000	Variable production	$2,000	
Less operating expenses:			Variable selling	600	
Selling	$3,100*		Variable administrative	400	3,000
Administrative	1,900*	5,000	Contribution margin		9,000
Net income		$1,000	Less fixed expenses:		
			Fixed production	4,000	
			Fixed selling	2,500	
			Fixed administrative	1,500	8,000
			Net income		$ 1,000

*Contains both variable and fixed expenses. This is the income statement for a *manufacturing* company; thus, when the income statement is placed in the contribution format, the "cost of goods sold" figure is divided between variable production costs and fixed production costs. If this were the income statement for a *merchandising* company (which simply purchases completed goods from a supplier), then the "cost of goods sold" would *all* be variable.

Notice that the contribution approach separates costs into fixed and variable categories, first deducting variable expenses from sales to obtain what is known as the *contribution margin*. The **contribution margin** is the amount remaining from sales revenues after variable expenses have been deducted. This amount *contributes* toward the covering of fixed expenses and then toward profits for the period.

The contribution approach to the income statement is used as an internal planning and decision-making tool. Its emphasis on costs by behaviour facilitates cost-volume-profit analysis, such as we shall be doing in the next chapter. The approach is also very useful in appraising management performance, in segmented reporting of profit data, and in budgeting. Moreover, the contribution approach helps managers organize data pertinent to all kinds of special decisions such as product-line analysis, pricing, use of scarce resources, and make or buy analysis. All of these topics are covered in later chapters.

SUMMARY

Managers analyze cost behaviour to have a basis for predicting how costs will respond to changes in activity levels. We have looked at three types of cost behaviour—variable, fixed, and mixed. In the case of mixed costs, we have studied three methods of breaking a mixed cost into its basic variable and fixed elements. The high-low method is the simplest of the three, having as its underlying assumption that the variable element of a mixed cost can be determined by analyzing the change in cost between two extreme points. In most situations, however, two points are not enough to produce accurate results, and the manager should therefore use either the scattergraph method or the least-squares regression method to derive a cost formula. Both of these methods require the construction of a regression line, the slope of which represents the average rate of variability in the mixed cost being analyzed. The least-squares regression method is the more precise and objective of the two in that it uses mathematical formulas to fit a regression line to an array of data.

Managers use costs organized by behaviour as a basis for many decisions. To facilitate this use, the income statement can be prepared in a contribution format. The contribution format classifies costs on the income statement by cost behaviour rather than by the functions of production, administration, and sales.

REVIEW PROBLEM 1: COST BEHAVIOUR

Neptune Rentals offers a boat rental service. Consider the following costs of the company over a relevant range of 5,000 to 20,000 hours of operating time for its boats:

	\multicolumn{4}{c}{Hours of Operating Time}			
	5,000	**10,000**	**15,000**	**20,000**
Total costs:				
Variable costs	$ 20,000	$?	$?	$?
Fixed costs	180,000	?	?	?
Total costs	$200,000	$?	$?	$?
Cost per hour:				
Variable cost	$?	$?	$?	$?
Fixed cost	?	?	?	?
Total cost per hour	$?	$?	$?	$?

Required

Compute the missing amounts, assuming that implied cost behaviour patterns remain unchanged over the relevant range of 5,000 to 20,000 hours.

Solution to Review Problem 1

The variable cost per hour of operating time can be computed as follows:

$$\$20,000 \div 5,000 \text{ hours} = \$4 \text{ per hour}$$

Therefore, in accordance with the behaviour of variable and fixed costs, the missing amounts are as follows:

	Hours of Operating Time			
	5,000	**10,000**	**15,000**	**20,000**
Total costs:				
Variable costs	$ 20,000	$ 40,000	$ 60,000	$ 80,000
Fixed costs	180,000	180,000	180,000	180,000
Total costs	$200,000	$220,000	$240,000	$260,000
Cost per hour:				
Variable cost	$ 4	$ 4	$ 4	$ 4
Fixed cost	36	18	12	9
Total cost per hour	$ 40	$ 22	$ 16	$ 13

Observe that the variable costs increase, in total, proportionately with increases in the number of hours of operating time, but that these costs remain constant at $4 if expressed on a per hour basis.

In contrast, the fixed costs by definition do not change in total with changes in the level of activity. They remain constant at $180,000. With increases in activity, however, the fixed costs decrease on a per hour basis, dropping from $36 per hour when the boats are operated 5,000 hours a period to only $9 per hour when the boats are operated 20,000 hours a period. *Because of this troublesome aspect of fixed costs, they are most easily (and most safely) dealt with on a total basis, rather than on a unit basis, in cost analysis work.*

REVIEW PROBLEM 2: HIGH-LOW METHOD

The administrator of Azalea Hills Hospital would like a cost formula linking the costs involved in admitting patients to the number of patients admitted during a month. The admitting department's costs and the number of patients admitted during the immediately preceding eight months are given in the following table:

Month	Number of Patients Admitted	Admitting Department Costs
May	1,800	$14,700
June	1,900	15,200
July	1,700	13,700
August	1,600	14,000
September	1,500	14,300
October	1,300	13,100
November	1,100	12,800
December	1,500	14,600

Required

1. Use the high-low method to estimate the fixed and variable components of admitting costs.
2. Express the fixed and variable components of admitting costs as a cost formula in the linear equation form $Y = a + bX$.

**Solution to
Review Problem 2**

1. The first step in the high-low method is to identify the periods of the lowest and highest activity. Those periods are November (1,100 patients admitted) and June (1,900 patients admitted).

   The second step is to compute the variable cost per unit using those two points:

Month	Number of Patients Admitted	Admitting Department Costs
High activity level (June)	1,900	$15,200
Low activity level (November)	1,100	12,800
Change observed	800	$ 2,400

$$\text{Variable cost} = \frac{\text{Change in cost}}{\text{Change in activity}} = \frac{\$2,400}{800} = \$3 \text{ per patient admitted}$$

   The third step is to compute the fixed cost element by deducting the variable cost element from the total cost at either the high or low activity. In the computation below, the high point of activity is used:

$$\text{Fixed cost element} = \text{Total cost} - \text{Variable cost element}$$
$$= \$15,200 - (\$3 \times 1,900 \text{ patients admitted})$$
$$= \$9,500$$

2. The cost formula expressed in the linear equation form is $Y = \$9,500 + \$3X$.

KEY TERMS FOR REVIEW

OBJECTIVE 10
Define or explain the key terms listed at the end of the chapter.

Activity base   A measure of whatever causes the incurrence of a variable cost. For example, the total cost of X-ray film in a hospital will increase as the number of X rays taken increases. Therefore, the number of X rays is an activity base for explaining the total cost of X-ray film. (p. 276)

Coefficient of determination   A measure of regression line fit that indicates the percentage variation in the dependent variable that is explained by changes in the independent variable. (p. 294)

Committed fixed costs   Those fixed costs that are difficult to adjust and that relate to the investment in facilities, equipment, and the basic organizational structure of a firm. (p. 280)

Contribution approach   An income statement format that is geared to cost behaviour in that costs are separated into variable and fixed categories rather than being separated according to the functions of production, sales, and administration. (p. 295)

Contribution margin   The amount remaining from sales revenues after all variable expenses have been deducted. (p. 296)

Cost formula   A formula relating cost to activity. This expression is generally in the form of the linear equation $Y = a + bX$, where Y is the total cost, a is the total fixed cost, b is the variable cost rate, and X is the activity. (p. 289)

Cost structure   The relative proportion of fixed, variable, and mixed costs found within an organization. (p. 274)

Curvilinear costs   A relationship between cost and activity that is a curve rather than a straight line. (p. 278)

Dependent variable   A variable that reacts or responds to some causal factor; total cost is the dependent variable, as represented by the letter Y, in the equation $Y = a + bX$. (p. 289)

Discretionary fixed costs   Those fixed costs that arise from annual decisions by management to spend in certain fixed cost areas, such as advertising and research. (p. 280)

High-low method   A method of separating a mixed cost into its fixed and variable elements by analyzing the change in cost between the high and low levels of activity. (p. 288)

Independent variable   A variable that acts as a causal factor; activity is the independent variable, as represented by the letter X, in the equation $Y = a + bX$. (p. 289)

Least-squares regression method   A method of separating a mixed cost into its fixed and variable elements by fitting a regression line that minimizes the sum of the squared errors. (p. 292)

Mixed cost   A cost that contains both variable and fixed cost elements. Also see *Semivariable cost*. (p. 284)

Multiple regression   An analytical method required in those situations where variations in a dependent variable are caused by more than one factor. (p. 294)

Regression line   A line fitted to an array of plotted points. The slope of the line, denoted by the letter b in the linear equation $Y = a + bX$, represents the average variable cost per unit of activity. The point where the line intersects the cost axis, denoted by the letter a in the above equation, represents the average total fixed cost. (p. 291)

Relevant range   The range of activity within which assumptions relative to variable and fixed cost behaviour are valid. (p. 278)

Scattergraph method   A method of separating a mixed cost into its fixed and variable elements. Under this method, a regression line is fitted to an array of plotted points by simple, visual inspection. (p. 290)

Semivariable cost   A cost that contains both variable and fixed cost elements. Also see *Mixed cost*. (p. 284)

Step-variable cost   A cost (such as the cost of a maintenance worker) that is obtainable only in large pieces and that increases and decreases only in response to fairly wide changes in the activity level. (p. 277)

Traditional approach   An income statement format in which costs are organized and presented according to the functions of production, administration, and sales. (p. 295)

APPENDIX 6A: LEAST-SQUARES REGRESSION CALCULATIONS

OBJECTIVE 11

Analyze a mixed cost using the least-squares regression method.

The least-squares regression method for estimating a linear relationship is based on the equation for a straight line:

$$Y = a + bX$$

The following formulas are used to calculate the values of the vertical intercept (a) and the slope (b) that minimize the sum of the squared errors:[4]

$$b = \frac{n(\Sigma\,XY) - (\Sigma\,X)(\Sigma\,Y)}{n(\Sigma\,X^2) - (\Sigma\,X)^2}$$

$$a = \frac{(\Sigma\,Y) - b(\Sigma\,X)}{n}$$

---

[4]See a calculus or statistics book for details concerning how these formulas are derived.

where:

X = The level of activity (independent variable)

Y = The total mixed cost (dependent variable)

a = The total fixed cost (the vertical intercept of the line)

b = The variable cost per unit of activity (the slope of the line)

n = Number of observations

Σ = Sum across all n observations

To illustrate how these calculations are accomplished, we will use the Brentline Hospital data from page 288.

Step 1. Compute ΣX, ΣY, ΣXY, ΣX^2, and n.

Month	Patient-Days X	Maintenance Costs Y	XY	X²
January	5,600	$ 7,900	$ 44,240,000	31,360,000
February	7,100	8,500	60,350,000	50,410,000
March	5,000	7,400	37,000,000	25,000,000
April	6,500	8,200	53,300,000	42,250,000
May	7,300	9,100	66,430,000	53,290,000
June	8,000	9,800	78,400,000	64,000,000
July	6,200	7,800	48,360,000	38,440,000
Totals Σ	45,700	$58,700	$388,080,000	304,750,000

From this table:

$$\Sigma X = 45,700$$

$$\Sigma Y = \$58,700$$

$$\Sigma XY = \$388,080,000$$

$$\Sigma X^2 = 304,750,000$$

$$n = 7$$

Step 2. Insert the values computed in step 1 into the formula for the slope (b).

$$b = \frac{n\left(\Sigma\, XY\right) - \left(\Sigma\, X\right)\left(\Sigma\, Y\right)}{n\left(\Sigma\, X^2\right) - \left(\Sigma\, X\right)^2}$$

$$b = \frac{7(388,080,000) - (45,700)(58,700)}{7(304,750,000) - (45,700)^2}$$

$$b = \$0.759$$

Therefore, the maintenance cost is 75.9 cents per patient-day.

Step 3. Insert the values computed in step 1 and the value of b computed in step 2 into the formula for the intercept (a).

$$a = \frac{\left(\Sigma\, Y\right) - b\left(\Sigma\, X\right)}{n}$$

$$a = \frac{(\$58,700) - \$0.759(45,700)}{7}$$

$$a = \$3,431$$

Therefore, the fixed maintenance cost is $3,431 per month. The cost formula for maintenance cost is as follows:

$$Y = a + bX$$
$$Y = \$3,431 + \$0.759X$$

QUESTIONS

6–1 Distinguish between (a) a variable cost, (b) a fixed cost, and (c) a mixed cost.

6–2 What effect does an increase in volume have on—
  a. Unit fixed costs?
  b. Unit variable costs?
  c. Total fixed costs?
  d. Total variable costs?

6–3 Define the following terms: (a) cost behaviour and (b) relevant range.

6–4 What is meant by an *activity base* when dealing with variable costs? Give several examples of activity bases.

6–5 Distinguish between (a) a variable cost, (b) a mixed cost, and (c) a step-variable cost. Chart the three costs on a graph, with activity plotted horizontally and cost plotted vertically.

6–6 The accountant often assumes a strictly linear relationship between cost and volume. How can this practice be defended in light of the fact that many variable costs are curvilinear in form?

6–7 Distinguish between discretionary fixed costs and committed fixed costs.

6–8 Classify the following fixed costs as normally being either committed or discretionary:
  a. Depreciation on buildings.
  b. Advertising.
  c. Research.
  d. Long-term equipment leases.
  e. Pension payments to the firm's retirees.
  f. Management development and training.

6–9 What factors are contributing to the trend toward increasing fixed costs, and why is this trend significant from a managerial accounting point of view?

6–10 Does the concept of the relevant range have application to fixed costs? Explain.

6–11 What is the major disadvantage of the high-low method?

6–12 What methods are available for separating a mixed cost into its fixed and variable elements? Which method is most accurate? Why?

6–13 What is meant by a regression line? Give the general formula for a regression line. Which term represents the variable cost? The fixed cost?

6–14 Once a regression line has been drawn, how does one determine the fixed cost element? The variable cost element?

6–15 What is meant by the term *least squares?*

6–16 What is the difference between single regression analysis and multiple regression analysis?

6–17 What is the meaning of R^2?

6–18 What is the difference between the contribution approach to the income statement and the traditional approach to the income statement?

6–19 What is meant by contribution margin? How is it computed?

EXERCISES

E6–1 The number of X rays taken and X-ray costs over the last nine months in Beverly Hospital are given below:

Month	X Rays Taken	X-Ray Costs
January	6,250	$28,000
February	7,000	29,000
March	5,000	23,000
April	4,250	20,000
May	4,500	22,000
June	3,000	17,000
July	3,750	18,000
August	5,500	24,000
September	5,750	26,000

Required

1. Using the high-low method, determine the cost formula for X-ray costs.
2. Using the cost formula you derived above, what X-ray costs would you expect to be incurred during a month in which 4,600 X rays are taken?

E6–2 Refer to the data in E6–1.

Required

1. Prepare a scattergraph using the data from E6–1. Plot cost on the vertical axis and activity on the horizontal axis. Fit a regression line to your plotted points by visual inspection.
2. What is the approximate monthly fixed cost for X rays? The approximate variable cost per X ray taken?
3. Scrutinize the points on your graph, and explain why the high-low method would or would not yield an accurate cost formula in this situation.

E6–3 Zerbel Company has noticed considerable fluctuation in its shipping expense from month to month, as shown below:

Month	Units Shipped	Total Shipping Expense
January	4	$22
February	7	31
March	5	26
April	2	15
May	3	22
June	6	30
July	8	36

Required

1. Using the high-low method, determine the cost formula for shipping expense.
2. The president has no confidence in the high-low method and would like you to "check out" your results using the scattergraph method. Do the following:
   a. Prepare a scattergraph, using the data given above. Plot cost on the vertical axis and activity on the horizontal axis. Fit a regression line to your plotted points by visual inspection.
   b. Using your scattergraph, determine the approximate variable cost per unit shipped and the approximate fixed cost per month.

E6–4 (Appendix 6A) Refer to the data for Zerbel Company in E6–3.

Required

1. Using the least-squares regression method, determine the cost formula for shipping expense.
2. If you also completed E6–3, prepare a simple table comparing the variable and fixed cost elements of shipping expense as computed under the high-low method, the scattergraph method, and the least-squares regression method.

E6–5 Resort Inns, Inc., has a total of 2,000 rooms in its nationwide chain of motels. On the average, 70% of the rooms are occupied each day. The company's operating costs are $21 per occupied room per day at this occupancy level, assuming a 30-day month. This $21 figure contains both variable and fixed cost elements. During October, the occupancy rate dropped to only 45%. A total of $792,000 in operating cost was incurred during October.

Required

1. Determine the variable cost per occupied room per day.
2. Determine the total fixed operating costs per month.
3. Assume that the occupancy rate increases to 60% during November. What total operating costs would you expect the company to incur during October?

E6–6 Parker Company manufactures and sells a single product. The company typically operates within a relevant range of 60,000 to 100,000 units produced and sold each year. A partially completed schedule of the company's total and per unit costs over this range is given below:

	Units Produced and Sold		
	60,000	**80,000**	**100,000**
Total costs:			
Variable costs.........	$150,000	?	?
Fixed costs..........	360,000	?	?
Total costs	$510,000	?	?
Cost per unit:			
Variable cost	?	?	?
Fixed cost	?	?	?
Total cost per unit ...	?	?	?

Required

1. Complete the schedule of the company's total and unit costs above.
2. Assume that the company produces and sells 90,000 units during a year. The selling price is $7.50 per unit. Prepare an income statement in the contribution format for the year.

E6–7 The data below have been taken from the cost records of the Atlantic Processing Company. The data relate to the cost of operating one of the company's processing facilities at various levels of activity:

Month	Units Processed	Total Cost
January	8,000	$14,000
February	4,500	10,000
March	7,000	12,500
April	9,000	15,500
May	3,750	10,000
June	6,000	12,500
July	3,000	8,500
August	5,000	11,500

Required

1. Prepare a scattergraph by plotting the above data on a graph. Plot cost on the vertical axis and activity on the horizontal axis. Fit a regression line to your plotted points by visual inspection.
2. What is the approximate monthly fixed cost? The approximate variable cost per unit processed? Show your computations.

E6–8 (Appendix 6A) One of Varic Company's products goes through a glazing process. The company has observed glazing costs as follows over the last six quarters (the numbers have been simplified for ease of computation):

Quarter	Units Produced	Total Glazing Cost
1	8	$27
2	5	20
3	10	31
4	4	19
5	6	24
6	9	29

For planning purposes, the company's management must know the amount of variable glazing cost per unit and the total fixed glazing cost per quarter.

Required

1. Using the least-squares regression method, determine the variable and fixed elements of the glazing cost.
2. Express the cost data in (1) above in the form $Y = a + bX$.
3. If the company processes seven units next quarter, what would be the expected total glazing cost?

E6–9 Speedy Parcel Service operates a fleet of delivery trucks in a large metropolitan area. A careful study by the company's cost analyst has determined that if a truck is driven 120,000 kilometres during a year, the average operating cost is 11.6 cents per kilometre. If a truck is driven only 80,000 kilometres during a year, the average operating cost increases to 13.6 cents per kilometre.

Required

1. Using the high-low method, determine the variable and fixed cost elements of the annual cost of truck operation.
2. Express the variable and fixed costs in the form $Y = a + bX$.
3. If a truck were driven 100,000 kilometres during a year, what total cost would you expect to be incurred?

E6–10 Haaki Shop, Ltd., is a large retailer of water sports equipment. An income statement for the company's surfboard department for the most recent quarter is presented below:

THE HAAKI SHOP, LTD.
Income Statement—Surfboard Department
For the Quarter Ended May 31

Sales		$800,000
Less cost of goods sold		300,000
Gross margin		500,000
Less operating expenses:		
Selling expenses	$250,000	
Administrative expenses	160,000	410,000
Net income		$ 90,000

The surfboards sell, on the average, for $400 each. The department's variable selling expenses are $50 per surfboard sold. The remaining selling expenses are fixed. The administrative expenses are 25% variable and 75% fixed. The company purchases its surfboards from a supplier at a cost of $150 per surfboard.

Required

1. Prepare an income statement for the quarter using the contribution approach.
2. What was the contribution toward fixed expenses and profits from each surfboard sold during the quarter? (State this figure in a single dollar amount per surfboard.)

PROBLEMS

P6–11 High-Low Method; Contribution Income Statement Frankel Company, a British merchandising firm, is the exclusive distributor of a product that is gaining rapid market acceptance. The company's revenues and expenses (in British pounds) for the last three months are given below:

FRANKEL COMPANY
Comparative Income Statement
For the Three Months Ended June 30

	April	May	June
Sales in units	3,000	3,750	4,500
Sales revenue	£420,000	£525,000	£630,000
Less cost of goods sold	168,000	210,000	252,000
Gross margin	252,000	315,000	378,000

	April	May	June
Less operating expenses:			
Shipping expense	£ 44,000	£ 50,000	£ 56,000
Advertising expense	70,000	70,000	70,000
Salaries and commissions	107,000	125,000	143,000
Insurance expense	9,000	9,000	9,000
Depreciation expense	42,000	42,000	42,000
Total operating expenses	272,000	296,000	320,000
Net income (loss)	£(20,000)	£ 19,000	£ 58,000

Required

1. Identify each of the company's expenses (including cost of goods sold) as being either variable, fixed, or mixed.
2. By use of the high-low method, separate each mixed expense into variable and fixed elements. State the cost formula for each mixed expense.
3. Redo the company's income statement at the 4,500-unit level of activity using the contribution format.

P6–12 High-Low Method of Cost Analysis   Golden Company's total overhead costs at various levels of activity are presented below:

Month	Machine-Hours	Total Overhead Costs
March	50,000	$194,000
April	40,000	170,200
May	60,000	217,800
June	70,000	241,600

Assume that the overhead costs above consist of utilities, supervisory salaries, and maintenance. The breakdown of these costs at the 40,000 machine-hour level of activity is as follows:

Utilities (V)	$ 52,000
Supervisory salaries (F)	60,000
Maintenance (M)	58,200
Total overhead costs	$170,200

V = variable; F = fixed; M = mixed.

The company wants to break down the maintenance cost into its basic variable and fixed cost elements.

Required

1. As shown above, overhead costs in June amounted to $241,600. Determine how much of this consisted of maintenance cost. (Hint: To do this, it may be helpful to first determine how much of the $241,600 consisted of utilities and supervisory salaries. Think about the behaviour of variable and fixed costs within the relevant range!)
2. By means of the high-low method, determine the cost formula for maintenance.
3. Express the company's total overhead costs in the linear equation form $Y = a + bX$.
4. What total overhead costs would you expect to be incurred at an operating activity level of 45,000 machine-hours?

P6–13 Least-Squares Regression Method of Cost Analysis; Graphing   (Appendix 6A) Amanda King has just been appointed director of recreation programs for Highland Park, a rapidly growing community in Alberta. In the past, the city has sponsored a number of softball leagues in the summer months. From the city's cost records, Amanda has found the following total costs associated with the softball leagues over the last several years:

Year	Number of Leagues	Total Cost
19x1	5	$13,000
19x2	2	7,000
19x3	4	10,500
19x4	6	14,000
19x5	3	10,000

Each league requires its own paid supervisor and paid umpires as well as printed schedules and other copy work. Therefore, Amanda knows that some variable costs are associated with the leagues. She would like to know the amount of variable cost per league and the total fixed cost per year associated with the softball program. This information would help her for planning purposes.

Required

1. Using the least-squares regression method, compute the variable cost per league and the total fixed cost per year for the softball program.
2. Express the cost data derived in (1) above in the linear equation form $Y = a + bX$.
3. Assume that Amanda would like to expand the softball program during the coming year to involve a total of seven leagues. Compute the expected total cost for the softball program. Can you see any problem with using the cost formula from (2) above to derive this total cost figure?
4. Prepare a scattergraph, and fit a regression line to the plotted points using the cost formula expressed in (2) above.

P6–14 Contribution versus Traditional Income Statement   House of Organs, Inc., purchases organs from a well-known manufacturer and sells them at the retail level. The organs sell, on the average, for $2,500 each. The average cost of an organ from the manufacturer is $1,500.

House of Organs, Inc., has always kept careful records of its costs. The costs that the company incurs in a typical month are presented below:

Costs	Cost Formula
Selling:	
Advertising	$950 per month
Delivery of organs	$60 per organ sold
Sales salaries and commissions	$4,800 per month, plus 4% of sales
Utilities	$650 per month
Depreciation of sales facilities	$5,000 per month
Administrative:	
Executive salaries	$13,500 per month
Depreciation of office equipment	$900 per month
Clerical	$2,500 per month, plus $40 per organ sold
Insurance	$700 per month

During November, the company sold and delivered 60 organs.

Required

1. Prepare an income statement for November using the traditional format with costs organized by function.
2. Redo (1) above, this time using the contribution format with costs organized by behaviour. Show costs and revenues on both a total and a per unit basis down through contribution margin.
3. Refer to the income statement you prepared in (2) above. Why might it be misleading to show the fixed costs on a per unit basis?

P6–15 High-Low Method of Cost Analysis   Echeverria SA is an Argentinian manufacturing company whose total factory overhead costs fluctuate somewhat from year to year according to the number of machine-hours worked in its production facility. These costs (in Argentinian pesos) at high and at low levels of activity over recent years are given below:

	Level of Activity	
	Low	High
Machine-hours	60,000	80,000
Total factory overhead costs	274,000 pesos	312,000 pesos

The factory overhead costs above consist of indirect materials, rent, and maintenance. The company has analyzed these costs at the 60,000 machine-hours level of activity as follows:

Indirect materials (V)	90,000	pesos
Rent (F)	130,000	
Maintenance (M)	54,000	
Total factory overhead costs	274,000	pesos

V = variable; F = fixed; M = mixed.

For planning purposes, the company wants to break down the maintenance cost into its variable and fixed cost elements.

Required

1. Determine how much of the factory overhead cost of 312,000 pesos at the high level of activity above consists of maintenance cost. (Hint: To do this, it may be helpful to first determine how much of the 312,000 pesos cost consists of indirect materials and rent. Think about the behaviour of variable and fixed costs within the relevant range!)
2. By means of the high-low method of cost analysis, determine the cost formula for maintenance.
3. What *total* overhead costs would you expect the company to incur at an operating level of 65,000 machine-hours?

P6–16 Identifying Cost Patterns   Below are a number of cost behaviour patterns that might be found in a company's cost structure. The vertical axis on each graph represents total cost, and the horizontal axis on each graph represents level of activity (volume).

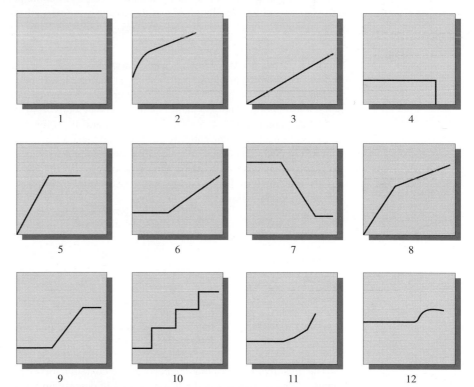

Required

1. For each of the following situations, identify the graph that illustrates the cost pattern involved. Any graph may be used more than once.
    a. Electricity bill—a flat fixed charge, plus a variable cost after a certain number of kilowatt-hours are used.
    b. City water bill, which is computed as follows:

First 1,000,000 litres or less ..... $1,000 flat fee
Next 10,000 litres .... 0.003 per litre used
Next 10,000 litres .... 0.006 per litre used
Next 10,000 litres .... 0.009 per litre used
Etc. .... Etc.

c. Depreciation of equipment, where the amount is computed by the straight-line method. When the depreciation rate was established, it was anticipated that the obsolescence factor would be greater than the wear and tear factor.
d. Rent on a factory building donated by the city, where the agreement calls for a fixed fee payment unless 200,000 labour-hours or more are worked, in which case no rent need be paid.
e. Cost of raw materials, where the cost decreases by 5 cents per unit for each of the first 100 units purchased, after which it remains constant at $2.50 per unit.
f. Salaries of maintenance workers, where one maintenance worker is needed for every 1,000 hours of machine-hours or less (that is, 0 to 1,000 hours requires one maintenance worker, 1,001 to 2,000 hours requires two maintenance workers, etc.)
g. Cost of raw material used.
h. Rent on a factory building donated by the county, where the agreement calls for rent of $100,000 less $1 for each direct labour-hour worked in excess of 200,000 hours, but a minimum rental payment of $20,000 must be paid.
i. Use of a machine under a lease, where a minimum charge of $1,000 is paid for up to 400 hours of machine time. After 400 hours of machine time, an additional charge of $2 per hour is paid up to a maximum charge of $2,000 per period.

2. How would a knowledge of cost behaviour patterns such as those above be of help to a manager in analyzing the cost structure of his or her firm?

(CPA, adapted)

P6–17 Scattergraph Method of Cost Analysis

In the past, Big Piney Resort has had great difficulty in predicting its costs at various levels of activity through the year. The reason is that the company has never attempted to study its cost structure by analyzing cost behaviour patterns. The president has now become convinced that such an analysis is necessary if the company is to maintain its profits and its competitive position. Accordingly, an analysis of cost behaviour patterns has been undertaken.

The company has managed to identify variable and fixed costs in all areas of its operation except for food services. Costs in this area do not seem to exhibit either a strictly variable or a strictly fixed pattern. Food costs over the past several months, along with the number of meals served, are given below:

Month	Number of Meals Served (000)	Total Food Cost
January	4	$18,000
February	5	21,000
March	6	24,000
April	10	33,000
May	12	35,000
June	11	33,000
July	9	30,000
August	8	27,000
September	7	26,000

The president believes that the costs above contain a mixture of variable and fixed cost elements. He has assigned you the responsibility of determining whether this is correct.

Required

1. Prepare a scattergraph using the data given above. Place cost on the vertical axis and activity (meals served) on the horizontal axis. Fit a regression line to the plotted points by simple visual inspection.
2. Is the president correct in assuming that food costs contain both variable and fixed cost elements? If so, what is the approximate total fixed cost and the approximate variable cost per meal served?

P6–18 Least-Squares Regression Method of Cost Analysis (Appendix 6A)
Refer to the data for Big Piney Resort in P6–17.

Required

1. By use of the least-squares regression method, determine the variable and fixed cost elements in total food cost. (Since "Number of meals served" is in thousands of meals, the variable rate you compute will also be in thousands of meals. It can be left in this form, or you can convert your variable rate to a per meal basis by dividing it by 1,000.)
2. From the data determined in (1) above, express the cost formula for food in linear equation form.

P6–19 High-Low and Scattergraph Method of Cost Analysis   Sebolt Wire
Company heats copper ingots to very high temperatures by placing the ingots in a large heat coil. The heated ingots are then run through a shaping machine that shapes the soft ingot into wire. Due to the long heat-up time involved, the coil is never turned off. When an ingot is placed in the coil, the temperature is raised to an even higher level, and then the coil is allowed to drop to the "waiting" temperature between ingots. Management needs to know the variable cost of power involved in heating an ingot and to know the fixed cost of power during "waiting" periods. The following data on ingots processed and power costs are available:

Month	Ingots	Power Cost
January	110	$5,500
February	90	4,500
March	80	4,400
April	100	5,000
May	130	6,000
June	120	5,600
July	70	4,000
August	60	3,200
September	50	3,400
October	40	2,400

Required

1. Using the high-low method, calculate the cost formula for power cost. Express the formula in the form $Y = a + bX$.
2. Prepare a scattergraph by plotting ingots processed and power cost on a graph. Fit a regression line to the plotted points by visual inspection, and determine the cost formula for power cost.

P6–20 Least-Squares Regression Method of Cost Analysis (Appendix 6A)
Refer to the data for Sebolt Wire Company in P6–19.

Required

1. Using the least-squares regression method, calculate the cost formula for power cost. Again express the formula in the form $Y = a + bX$. (Round the variable rate to two decimal places and the fixed rate to the nearest whole dollar.)
2. Prepare a simple table showing the total fixed cost per month and the variable rate per ingot under each of the three methods used in P6–19 and P6–20. Then comment on the accuracy and usefulness of the data derived by each method.

P6–21 Manufacturing Statements; High-Low Method of Analysis   NuWay,
Inc., manufactures a single product. Selected data from the company's cost records for two recent months are given below:

	Level of Activity	
	July–Low	**October–High**
Equivalent number of units produced	9,000	12,000
Cost of goods manufactured	$285,000	$390,000
Work in process inventory, beginning	14,000	22,000
Work in process inventory, ending	25,000	15,000
Direct materials cost per unit	15	15
Direct labour cost per unit	6	6
Manufacturing overhead cost, total	?	?

The company's manufacturing overhead cost consists of both variable and fixed cost elements. In order to have data available for planning, management wants to determine how much of the overhead cost is variable with units produced and how much of it is fixed per year.

Required

1. For both July and October, determine the amount of manufacturing overhead cost added to production. The company had no under- or overapplied overhead in either month. (Hint: A useful way to proceed might be to construct a schedule of cost of goods manufactured.)

2. By means of the high-low method of cost analysis, determine the cost formula for manufacturing overhead. Express the variable portion of the formula in terms of a variable rate per unit of product.

3. If 9,500 units are produced during a month, what would be the cost of goods manufactured? (Assume that the company's beginning work in process inventory for the month is $16,000 and that its ending work in process inventory is $19,000. Also assume that there is no under- or overapplied overhead cost for the month.)

P6–22 Least-Squares Regression Analysis; Contribution Income Statement (Appendix 6A) Alden Company has decided to use the contribution approach to the income statement internally for planning purposes. The company has analyzed its expenses and developed the following cost formulas:

Cost	Cost Formula
Cost of good sold	$20 per unit sold
Advertising expense	$170,000 per quarter
Sales commissions	5% of sales
Administrative salaries	$80,000 per quarter
Shipping expense	?
Depreciation expense	$50,000 per quarter

Management has concluded that shipping expense is a mixed cost, containing both variable and fixed cost elements. Units sold and the related shipping expense over the last eight quarters are given below:

Quarter	Units Sold (000)	Shipping Expense
19x1:		
First	16	$160,000
Second	18	175,000
Third	23	210,000
Fourth	19	180,000
19x2:		
First	17	170,000
Second	20	190,000
Third	25	230,000
Fourth	22	205,000

Management would like a cost formula derived for shipping expense so that a budgeted income statement using the contribution approach can be prepared for the next quarter.

Required

1. Using the least-squares regression method, derive a cost formula for shipping expense. (Since the Units Sold above are in thousands of units, the variable rate you compute will also be in thousands of units. It can be left in this form, or you can convert your variable rate to a per unit basis by dividing it by 1,000.)

2. In the first quarter, 19x3, the company plans to sell 21,000 units at a selling price of $50 per unit. Prepare an income statement for the quarter using the contribution format.

CASES

C6–23 Least-Squares Regression Method; Graphing; Comparison of Cost Bases (Appendix 6A) The Hard Rock Mining Company is developing cost formulas to have data available for management planning and decision-making purposes. The company's cost analyst has concluded that utilities cost is a mixed cost, and he is attempting to find a base with which the cost might be closely correlated. The controller has suggested that tonnes mined might be a good base to use in developing a cost formula. The production superintendent disagrees; she thinks that direct labour-hours would be a better base. The cost analyst has decided to try both bases and has assembled the following information:

Quarter	Tonnes Mined (000)	Direct Labour-Hours (000)	Utilities Cost
19x4:			
First	15	5	$ 50,000
Second	11	3	45,000
Third	21	4	60,000
Fourth	12	6	75,000
19x5:			
First	18	10	100,000
Second	25	9	105,000
Third	30	8	85,000
Fourth	28	11	120,000

Required

1. Using tonnes mined as the independent (X) variable:
   a. Determine a cost formula for utilities cost using the least-squares regression method. (The variable rate you compute will be in thousands of tonnes. It can be left in this form, or you can convert your variable rate to a per tonne basis by dividing it by 1,000.)
   b. Prepare a scattergraph and plot the observed points of tonnes mined and utilities cost. (Place cost on the vertical axis and tonnes mined on the horizontal axis.) Fit a regression line to the plotted points using the cost formula determined in (a) above.
   c. Scrutinize the data on the scattergraph. Is there a high or a low correlation between utilities cost and tonnes mined?
2. Using direct labour-hours as the independent (X) variable, repeat the computations in (a), (b), and (c) above.
3. Would you recommend that the company use tonnes mined or direct labour-hours as a base for planning utilities cost?

C6–24 Scattergraph Analysis of Mixed Costs; Selection of an Activity Base Mapleleaf Sweepers of Toronto manufactures replacement rotary sweeper brooms for the large sweeper trucks that clear leaves and snow from city streets. The business is to some degree seasonal, with the largest demand during and just preceding the fall and winter months. Since there are so many different kinds of sweeper brooms used by its customers, Mapleleaf Sweepers makes all of its brooms to order.

The company has been analyzing its overhead accounts to determine fixed and variable components for planning purposes. Below are data for the company's janitorial labour costs over the last nine months. (Cost data are in Canadian dollars.)

	Number of Units Produced	Number of Janitorial Workdays	Janitorial Labour Cost
January	115	21	$3,840
February	109	19	3,648
March	102	23	4,128
April	76	20	3,456
May	69	23	4,320
June	108	22	4,032
July	77	16	2,784
August	71	14	2,688
September	127	21	3,840

The number of workdays varies from month to month due to the number of weekdays, holidays, days of vacation, and sick leave taken in the month. The number of units produced in a month varies depending on demand and the number of workdays in the month.

There are two janitors who each work an eight-hour shift each workday. They each can take up to 10 days of paid sick leave each year. Their wages on days they call in sick and their wages during paid vacations are charged to miscellaneous overhead rather than to the janitorial labour cost account.

Required

1. Prepare a scattergraph and plot the janitorial labour cost and units produced. (Place cost on the vertical axis and units produced on the horizontal axis.) Fit a regression line to the plotted points by visual inspection. Express the resulting cost formula in the form $Y = a + bX$.
2. Prepare a scattergraph and plot the janitorial labour cost and number of workdays. (Place cost on the vertical axis and the number of workdays on the horizontal axis.) Fit a regression line to the plotted points by visual inspection. Express the resulting cost formula in the form $Y = a + bX$.
3. Which cost formula should the company use for planning purposes, the cost formula based on units produced from (1) above or the cost formula based on the number of working days in a month from (2) above? Fully explain your answer.

C6–25 Evaluation of Forecasts   Northern Baths Ltd. manufactures and sells bathroom fixtures (tubs, sinks, showers, hardware). It is a well-established firm with a reputation for high-quality products.

Located in Owen Sound, Ontario (175 kilometres from Toronto), it distributes its products nationally through a series of warehouses and sales offices. The largest warehouse is in Toronto.

Northern's fast sales growth over recent years has made it the envy of the industry, especially considering the recently depressed housing market.

Rich Munroe, Northern's controller, is reviewing the information which follows, as he ponders the question put to him by the firm's president: "Should we close the Toronto warehouse?"

Toronto Market

The Toronto market is considered the most competitive market in Canada. Northern currently has a 7.8 percent share of this market. Northern sells to three major types of customers.

1. *Dealers* are individual outlets and regional chains of building material suppliers who sell to small contractors (builders) and consumers (do-it-yourselfers). These buyers want quality products and a good price. The contractors also want reasonable credit terms. Some dealers have recently formed buying groups to obtain volume discounts from Northern. Dealers represent about 10 percent of Northern's sales.
2. *Custom Builders* are those who build a home to the specifications of the purchaser. These are primarily expensive homes where the main concern for the builders and their customers is quality, with price being less important. Most custom builders are small firms and thus selling direct to them is costly. Custom builders who purchase from Northern are highly satisfied. This class of customer represents the vast majority of Northern's customers.
3. *Larger "Spec" Builders* are those who buy and subdivide, install sewers and roads, and build entire subdivisions, speculating that they will be able to sell the homes as they are constructed. Spec builders take large risks and typically are large companies that demand volume discounts. They also prefer to buy from the manufacturer to obtain the lowest possible price. Delivery timing is also important to the Spec builders. Northern does not have a low-priced, low-quality line in which large builders are interested.

Forecasting Model

The industry assumes a relationship between housing starts in Ontario and the Ontario fixtures industry sales. Historical, economic, and demographic data are then used to estimate the number of single, semidetached, and row housing units. Row housing includes condominiums and townhouses.

By multiplying the unit sales price by the estimated number of the type of unit to be built, the total market potential is derived. The Toronto market forecasts are shown in Exhibit 6–13.

The relationship between housing starts (x) and industry sales (y) in Ontario for the last 10 years is as follows:

$$\text{The linear regression model is } y = 7{,}422 + 2.53x$$

EXHIBIT 6–13   Northern Bath's Toronto Market Projections

| | 19x5 | | | 19x6 | | | 19x7 | | |
	Housing Starts	Unit Sales Value	Total (000s)	Housing Starts	Unit Sales Value	Total (000s)	Housing Starts	Unit Sales Value	Total (000s)
Single	6,020	$2,136	$12,859	5,980	$2,285	$13,664	6,010	$2,445	$14,694
Semidetached	2,960	1,543	4,567	2,980	1,651	4,920	3,020	1,766	5,333
Row	4,810	1,071	5,152	4,790	1,146	5,489	4,700	1,226	5,762
Total projected market sales			$22,578			$24,073			$25,789

Based on this model, current and forecasted Toronto housing starts for the next three years would be:

| | Housing Units | | |
	Single	Semidetached	Row
19x4 (current)	6,170	2,850	4,740
19x5	6,020	2,960	4,810
19x6	5,980	2,980	4,790
19x7	6,010	3,020	4,700

Actual (current year) and estimated sales unit prices are shown in the following table.

| | Dollar Value of Bathroom Fixtures per Housing Unit | | |
	Single	Semidetached	Row
19x4 (current)	$1,996	$1,422	$1,001
19x5	$2,136	$1,543	$1,071
19x6	$2,285	$1,651	$1,146
19x7	$2,445	$1,766	$1,226

EXHIBIT 6-14

Northern Bath's
Current Expenses for
the Toronto
Warehouse

Operating Statement
(000s)
Current Year

	$	
Sales		$1,647
Cost of goods sold*		999
Gross profit		648
Operating expenses		
Warehouse labour		77
Supervisors		40
Rent		32
Property tax		4
Property insurance		5
Heat and light		15
Maintenance		12
Selling expenses†		115
Depreciation—equipment		16
Head office charges		10
Total expenses		326
Net income before taxes		322
Estimated income taxes		149
Net income after taxes		$ 173

	$	% Sales
Cost summary: Cost of goods sold	$ 999	60.7
Operating expenses	326	19.8
Total	$1,325	80.5

*Transferred to warehouse at full manufacturing cost plus freight (delivery to branch) cost. Freight cost makes up approximately 6 percent of cost of goods sold.

†Selling expenses are primarily made up of salespersons' commissions, which are 7 percent of sales.

The Toronto warehouse is considered on a cost minimization basis. Current year costs to operate the facility are shown in Exhibit 6–14. Munroe believes that closing the warehouse could result in a sales decline of $300,000 to $600,000 from the company's current sales volume in Toronto. To accommodate the Toronto market, inventory carrying costs will probably increase by $8,000 to $10,000 at the Owen Sound plant. As well, Northern is currently able to take advantage of carload and half-carload freight costs. This cost is included in the cost of goods sold by the warehouse. Closure of the warehouse may result in increased freight costs of 20 to 40% depending on required delivery response time from Owen Sound. The warehouse equipment will be moved back to the plant. Munroe also believes that if the warehouse closes, sales in Toronto will be 60% to dealers and 40% to builders within the next two years.

Required

Prepare a report to the president of Northern Baths recommending whether or not to close the Toronto warehouse. Fully substantiate your recommendations. Include in your analysis an evaluation of the forecasting model.

(SMAC, adapted)

GROUP EXERCISES

GE6–26 Economies or Diseconomies of Scale?   Increased efficiency and lower costs result from economies of scale. An increase in scale or size (i.e., capacity) seldom requires a proportional increase in investment, research and development, sales and marketing, or administration. Therefore, high-volume, large-scale facilities create the potential for lower unit cost. It has been estimated that scale-related costs decrease as volume increases, usually falling by 15%–25% per unit each time volume doubles.

Many industries including steel, autos, electric power, and universities have used scale-based economies to lower the cost of their product or service. Throughout the 1980s, North American steel companies invested enormous sums to modernize their plants, lower their costs, and rise from the huge losses inflicted by foreign competition. But now, "minimills," smaller, more specialized plants, are a new threat that could cause the large North American steel companies' profits to come crashing down if they are unable to fully realize the benefits of their size.

Required

1. Explain what impact steel company investments in modernizing their plants had on total fixed costs, fixed cost per unit, total variable costs, variable cost per unit, total costs, and average unit cost. Place this information on two graphs. On both graphs, label the *X* axis *Production Volume.* The *Y* axis on one graph should be labeled *Total Costs,* and on the other graph label the *Y* axis *Unit Cost.*
2. Which fixed costs are increasing rapidly, committed fixed costs (the costs related to the facilities and equipment) or discretionary fixed costs (the costs related to people who support production and sales)? Develop a specific scenario explaining how a particular fixed cost could increase over time.
3. What could cause fixed costs to increase so rapidly in your scenario?
4. Explain how gains and losses of market share can have such a huge impact on operating profits and losses of North American steel companies.

GE6–27 Product Proliferation Is the Real Cause of Costs   In 1963, Peter F. Drucker, in a now-classic article, wrote about what has only recently been recognized as one of the basic problems of U.S. competitive strength in the world economy—product clutter. "We fritter away our competitive advantage in the volume products by subsidizing an enormous array of 'specialties,' of which only a few recover their true cost." That article is still relevant for both Canada and the U.S. because the problem of product clutter is even more pronounced today than it was in 1963. Source: Peter F. Drucker, "Managing for Business Effectiveness," *Harvard Business Review,* May–June 1963.

Required

1. Read the original Drucker article.
2. What is the first duty and continuing responsibility of a business manager?
3. What is the manager's job?
4. What is the major problem in that job? (Hint: What is the difference between efficiency and effectiveness?)
5. What is the principle for defining and analyzing this problem?
6. One reason managers do not understand this problem is that they mistakenly identify accounting data and analysis with economic data and analysis. Explain this statement.

PART II THE CENTRAL THEME:
Planning and Control

COST-VOLUME-PROFIT RELATIONSHIPS

LEARNING OBJECTIVES

After studying Chapter 7, you should be able to:

1 Explain how changes in activity affect contribution margin and net income.

2 Compute the contribution margin ratio (CM ratio) and use it to compute changes in contribution margin and net income.

3 Show the effects on contribution margin of changes in variable costs, fixed costs, selling price, and volume.

4 Compute the break-even point by both the equation method and the contribution margin method.

5 Prepare a cost-volume-profit (CVP) graph, and explain the significance of each of its components.

6 Use the CVP formulas to determine the activity level needed to achieve a desired target net profit figure.

7 Compute the margin of safety and explain its significance.

8 Compute the degree of operating leverage at a particular level of sales, and explain how the degree of operating leverage can be used to predict changes in net income.

9 Compute the break-even point for a multiple product company, and explain the effects of shifts in the sales mix on contribution margin and the break-even point.

10 Define or explain the key terms listed at the end of the chapter.

11 Understand cost-volume-profit with uncertainty.

Canada Post Corporation has fixed costs, such as salaries for postal carriers, that do not change with the volume of mail delivered. However, revenue increases during December, when more letters and parcels are mailed.

Cost-volume-profit (CVP) analysis is one of the most powerful tools that managers have at their command. It helps them understand the interrelationship among cost, volume, and profit in an organization by focusing on interactions among the following five elements:

1. Prices of products.
2. Volume or level of activity.
3. Per unit variable costs.
4. Total fixed costs.
5. Mix of products sold.

Because CVP analysis helps managers understand the interrelationship among cost, volume, and profit, it is a vital tool in many business decisions. These decisions include, for example, what products to manufacture or sell, what pricing policy to follow, what marketing strategy to employ, and what type of productive facilities to acquire.

▼   ▼   ▼   ▼   ▼

MANAGERIAL ACCOUNTING IN ACTION—THE ISSUE

Acoustic Concepts, Ltd., was founded by Prem Narayan, a graduate student in engineering, to market a radical new speaker he had designed for automobile sound systems. The speaker, called the Sonic Blaster, uses an advanced microprocessor chip to boost amplification to awesome levels. Prem contracted with a Taiwanese electronics manufacturer to produce the speaker. With seed money provided by his family, Prem placed an order with the manufacturer for completed units and ran advertisements in auto magazines.

The Sonic Blaster was an almost immediate success, and sales grew to the point that Prem moved the company's headquarters out of his apartment and into rented quarters in a neighbouring industrial park. He also hired a receptionist, an accountant, a sales manager, and a small sales staff to sell the speakers to retail stores. The accountant, Bob Luchinni, had worked for several small companies where he had acted as a business advisor as well as accountant and bookkeeper. The following discussion occurred soon after Bob was hired:

PREM: Bob, I've got a lot of questions about the company's finances that I hope you can help answer.

BOB: We're in great shape. The loan from your family will be paid off within a few months.

PREM: I know, but I am worried about the risks I've taken on by expanding operations. What would happen if a competitor entered the market and our sales slipped? How far could sales drop for our Sonic Blaster without putting us into the red? Another question I've been trying to resolve is how much our sales would have to increase in order to justify the big marketing campaign the sales staff is pushing for.

BOB: Marketing always wants more money for advertising.

PREM: And they are always pushing me to drop the selling price on the speaker. I agree with them that a lower price will boost our volume, but I'm not sure the increased volume will offset the loss in revenue from the lower price.

BOB: It sounds like these questions all are related in some way to the relationships between our selling prices, our costs, and our volume. We shouldn't have a problem coming up with some answers. I'll need a day or two, though, to gather some data.

PREM: Why don't we set up a meeting for three days from now? That would be Thursday.

BOB: That'll be fine. I'll have some preliminary answers for you as well as a model you can use for answering similar questions in the future.

PREM: Good. I'll be looking forward to seeing what you come up with.

▼   ▼   ▼   ▼   ▼

With an accurate CVP analysis, managers can make the best decisions concerning where to focus limited resources, which products to manufacture, and what facilities to acquire. CVP analysis can also affect marketing and pricing strategies.

THE BASICS OF COST-VOLUME-PROFIT (CVP) ANALYSIS

Bob Luchinni's preparation for the Thursday meeting begins where our study of cost behaviour in the preceding chapter left off—with the contribution income statement. The contribution income statement emphasizes the behaviour of costs and therefore is extremely helpful to a manager in judging the impact on profits of changes in selling price, cost, or volume. Bob will base his analysis on the following contribution income statement he prepared last month:

ACOUSTIC CONCEPTS, LTD.
Contribution Income Statement
For the Month of June

	Total	Per Unit
Sales (400 speakers)	$100,000	$250
Less variable expenses	60,000	150
Contribution margin	40,000	$100
Less fixed expenses	35,000	
Net income	$ 5,000	

Notice that sales, variable expenses, and contribution margin are expressed on a per unit basis as well as in total. This is commonly done on income statements prepared for management's own use, because, as we shall see, it facilitates profitability analysis.

Contribution Margin

OBJECTIVE 1

Explain how changes
in activity affect
contribution margin
and net income.

As explained in Chapter 5, contribution margin is the amount remaining from sales revenue after variable expenses have been deducted. Thus, it is the amount available to cover fixed expenses and then to provide profits for the period. Notice the sequence here—contribution margin is used *first* to cover the fixed expenses, and then whatever remains goes toward profits. If the contribution margin is not sufficient to cover the fixed expenses, then a loss occurs for the period. To illustrate with an extreme example, assume that by the middle of a particular month Acoustic Concepts has been able to sell only one speaker. At that point, the company's income statement will appear as follows:

	Total	Per Unit
Sales (1 speaker)	$ 250	$250
Less variable expenses	150	150
Contribution margin	100	$100
Less fixed expenses	35,000	
Net loss	$ (34,900)	

For each additional speaker that the company is able to sell during the month, $100 more in contribution margin will become available to help cover the fixed expenses. If a second speaker is sold, for example, then the total contribution margin will increase by $100 (to a total of $200) and the company's loss will decrease by $100, to $34,800:

	Total	Per Unit
Sales (2 speakers)	$ 500	$250
Less variable expenses	300	150
Contribution margin	200	$100
Less fixed expenses	35,000	
Net loss	$(34,800)	

If enough speakers can be sold to generate $35,000 in contribution margin, then all of the fixed costs will be covered and the company will have managed to at least *break even* for the month—that is, to show neither profit nor loss but just cover all of its costs. To reach this break-even point, the company will have to sell 350 speakers in a month, because each speaker sold yields $100 in contribution margin:

	Total	Per Unit
Sales (350 speakers)	$ 87,500	$250
Less variable expenses	52,500	150
Contribution margin	35,000	$100
Less fixed expenses	35,000	
Net income	$ –0–	

Computation of the break-even point is discussed in detail later in the chapter; for the moment, note that the **break-even point** can be defined either as the point where total sales revenue equals total expenses, variable and fixed, or as the point where total contribution margin equals total fixed expenses.

Once the break-even point has been reached, net income will increase by the unit contribution margin for each additional unit sold. If 351 speakers are sold in a month, for example, then we can expect that the net income for the month will be $100, because the company will have sold 1 speaker more than the number needed to break even:

	Total	Per Unit
Sales (351 speakers)	$ 87,750	$250
Less variable expenses	52,650	150
Contribution margin	35,100	$100
Less fixed expenses	35,000	
Net income	$ 100	

If 352 speakers are sold (2 speakers above the break-even point), then we can expect that the net income for the month will be $200, and so forth. To know what the profits will be at various levels of activity, therefore, it is not necessary for a manager to prepare a whole series of income statements. The manager can simply take the number of units to be sold over the break-even point and multiply that number by the unit contribution margin. The result will represent the anticipated profits for the period. Or, if an increase in

Elgin Sweeper Company, the leading manufacturer of street sweepers in North America, manufactures five distinct sweeper models in a single facility. Historically, the company has used the traditional format for the income statement, which shows cost of goods sold, gross margin, and so forth. In 1986, the company abandoned this format for internal use and adopted the contribution approach. By using the contribution approach, management has discovered that key differences exist between the five sweeper models. CM ratios differ by model due to differences in variable inputs. Also, due to differences in volume, the five models differ substantially in terms of the total amount of contribution margin generated each year. Income statements in the contribution format—with breakdowns of sales, contribution margin, and CM ratios by sweeper model—now serve as the basis for internal decision making by management.[1]

sales is planned and the manager wants to know what the impact of that increase will be on profits, he or she can simply multiply the increase in units sold by the unit contribution margin. The result will be the expected increase in profits. To illustrate, if Acoustic Concepts is selling 400 speakers per month and plans to increase sales to 425 speakers per month, the following impact on profits will occur:

Increased number of speakers to be sold	25
Contribution margin per speaker	× $100
Increase in net income	$2,500

These calculations can be verified as follows:

	Sales Volume			
	400 Speakers	425 Speakers	Difference 25 Speakers	Per Unit
Sales	$100,000	$106,250	$6,250	$250
Less variable expenses	60,000	63,750	3,750	150
Contribution margin	40,000	42,500	2,500	$100
Less fixed expenses	35,000	35,000	–0–	
Net income	$ 5,000	$ 7,500	$2,500	

[1]John P. Callan, Wesley N. Tredup, and Randy S. Wissinger, "Elgin Sweeper Company's Journey toward Cost Management," *Management Accounting* (July 1991), p. 27; and telephone interviews with management.

To summarize the series of examples given above, if there were no sales, the company's loss would equal its fixed expenses. Each unit that is sold reduces the loss by the amount of the unit contribution margin. Once the break-even point has been reached, each additional unit sold increases the company's profit by the amount of the unit contribution margin.

Contribution Margin Ratio (CM Ratio)

OBJECTIVE 2
Compute the contribution margin ratio (CM ratio) and use it to compute changes in contribution margin and net income.

In addition to being expressed on a per unit basis, revenues, variable expenses, and contribution margin for Acoustic Concepts can also be expressed on a percentage basis:

	Total	Per Unit	Percent
Sales (400 speakers)	$100,000	$250	100
Less variable expenses	60,000	150	60
Contribution margin	40,000	$100	40
Less fixed expenses	35,000		
Net income	$ 5,000		

The percentage of contribution margin to total sales is referred to as the **contribution margin ratio (CM ratio).** This ratio is computed as follows:

$$\frac{\text{Contribution margin}}{\text{Sales}} = \text{CM ratio}$$

For Acoustic Concepts, the computations are as follows:

$$\frac{\text{Total contribution margin, } \$40,000}{\text{Total sales, } \$100,000} = 40\% \quad \text{or} \quad \frac{\text{Per unit contribution margin, } \$100}{\text{Per unit sales, } \$250} = 40\%$$

The CM ratio is extremely useful in that it shows how the contribution margin will be affected by a given dollar change in total sales. To illustrate, notice that Acoustic Concepts has a CM ratio of 40%. This means that for each dollar increase in sales, total contribution margin will increase by 40 cents ($1 sales × CM ratio of 40%). Net income will also increase by 40 cents, assuming that there are no changes in fixed costs.

As this illustration suggests, *the impact on net income of any given dollar change in total sales can be computed in seconds by simply applying the CM ratio to the dollar change.* If Acoustic Concepts plans a $30,000 increase in sales during the coming month, for example, management can expect contribution margin to increase by $12,000 ($30,000 increased sales × CM ratio of 40%). As we noted above, net income will also increase by $12,000 if the fixed costs do not change.

This is verified by the following table:

	Sales Volume			
	Present	**Expected**	**Increase**	**Percent**
Sales	$100,000	$130,000	$30,000	100
Less variable expenses	60,000	78,000*	18,000	60
Contribution margin	40,000	52,000	12,000	40
Less fixed expenses	35,000	35,000	–0–	
Net income	$ 5,000	$ 17,000	$12,000	

*$130,000 expected sales × 60% variable expense ratio = $78,000.

Some managers prefer to work with the CM ratio rather than the unit contribution margin figure. The CM ratio is particularly valuable in those situations where the manager must make trade-offs between more dollar sales of one product versus more dollar sales of another. Generally speaking, when trying to increase sales, the manager will want to emphasize those products that yield the greatest amount of contribution margin per dollar of sales.

FOCUS ON
CURRENT PRACTICE

Ultramar initiated its Value Plus ad campaign in mid-1996, which promised the lowest gasoline prices in the market. The result of the campaign was a price war which lasted about six weeks. During this time, prices fell as low as 19.9 cents just outside Montreal. Petro-Canada broke the costly war, elevating their prices to 58 cents per litre—still below the break-even point of 62 cents.

Some Applications of CVP Concepts

OBJECTIVE 3
Show the effects on contribution margin of changes in variable costs, fixed costs, selling price, and volume.

Bob Luchinni, the accountant at Acoustic Concepts, wanted to demonstrate to the company's president Prem Narayan how the concepts developed on the preceding pages can be used in planning and decision making. Bob gathered together the following basic data:

	Per Unit	Percent
Sales price	$250	100
Less variable expenses	150	60
Contribution margin	$100	40

Recall that fixed expenses are $35,000 per month. Bob Luchinni will use these data to show the effects of changes in variable costs, fixed costs, sales price, and sales volume on the company's profitability.

Change in Fixed Costs and Sales Volume. Acoustic Concepts is currently selling 400 speakers per month (monthly sales of $100,000). The sales manager feels that a $10,000 increase in the monthly advertising budget would increase monthly sales by $30,000. Should the advertising budget be increased?

Solution

Expected total contribution margin:	
$130,000 × 40% CM ratio	$52,000
Present total contribution margin:	
$100,000 × 40% CM ratio	40,000
Incremental contribution margin	12,000
Change in fixed costs:	
Less incremental advertising expense	10,000
Increased net income	$ 2,000

Yes, based on the information above and assuming that other factors in the company don't change, the advertising budget should be increased.

Since in this case only the fixed costs and the sales volume change, the solution can be presented in an even shorter format, as follows:

Alternative Solution

Incremental contribution margin:
$30,000 × 40% CM ratio	$12,000
Less incremental advertising expense	10,000
Increased net income	$ 2,000

Notice that this approach does not depend on a knowledge of what sales were previously. Also notice that it is unnecessary under either approach to prepare an income statement. Both of the solutions above involve an **incremental analysis** in that they consider only those items of revenue, cost, and volume that will change if the new program is implemented. Although in each case a new income statement could have been prepared, most managers would prefer the incremental approach. The reason is that it is simpler and more direct, and it permits the decision maker to focus attention on the specific items involved in the decision.

Change in Variable Costs and Sales Volume.   Refer to the original data. Recall that Acoustic Concepts is currently selling 400 speakers per month. Management is contemplating the use of higher-quality components, which would increase variable costs (and thereby reduce the contribution margin) by $10 per speaker. However, the sales manager predicts that the higher overall quality would increase sales to 480 speakers per month. Should the higher-quality components be used?

Solution

The $10 increase in variable costs will cause the unit contribution margin to decrease from $100 to $90.

Expected total contribution margin:
480 speakers × $90	$43,200
Present total contribution margin:	
400 speakers × $100	40,000
Increase in total contribution margin	$ 3,200

Yes, based on the information above, the higher-quality components should be used. Since the fixed costs will not change, net income will increase by the $3,200 increase in contribution margin shown above.

Change in Fixed Cost, Sales Price, and Sales Volume.   Refer to the original data and recall again that the company is currently selling 400 speakers per month. To increase sales, the sales manager would like to cut the selling price by $20 per speaker and increase the advertising budget by $15,000 per month. The sales manager argues that if these two steps are taken, unit sales will increase by 50%. Should the changes be made?

Solution

A decrease of $20 per speaker in the selling price will cause the unit contribution margin to decrease from $100 to $80.

Expected total contribution margin:
400 speakers × 150% × $80	$48,000
Present total contribution margin:	
400 speakers × $100	40,000
Incremental contribution margin	8,000
Change in fixed costs:	
Less incremental advertising expense	15,000
Reduction in net income	$ (7,000)

No, based on the information above, the changes should not be made. The same solution can be obtained by preparing comparative income statements:

	Present 400 Speakers per Month		Expected 600 Speakers per Month		
	Total	Per Unit	Total	Per Unit	Difference
Sales	$100,000	$250	$138,000	$230	$38,000
Less variable expenses	60,000	150	90,000	150	30,000
Contribution margin	40,000	$100	48,000	$ 80	8,000
Less fixed expenses	35,000		50,000*		15,000
Net income (loss)	$ 5,000		$ (2,000)		$(7,000)

*$35,000 + $15,000 = $50,000.

Notice that the answer is the same as that obtained by the incremental analysis above.

Change in Variable Cost, Fixed Cost, and Sales Volume.   Refer to the original data. As before, the company is currently selling 400 speakers per month. The sales manager would like to place the sales staff on a commission basis of $15 per speaker sold, rather than on flat salaries that now total $6,000 per month. The sales manager is confident that the change will increase monthly sales by 15%. Should the change be made?

Solution

Changing the sales staff from a salaried basis to a commission basis will affect both fixed and variable costs. Fixed costs will decrease by $6,000, from $35,000 to $29,000. Variable costs will increase by $15, from $150 to $165, and the unit contribution margin will decrease from $100 to $85.

Expected total contribution margin:		
400 speakers × 115% × $85		$39,100
Present total contribution margin:		
400 speakers × $100		40,000
Decrease in total contribution margin		(900)
Change in fixed costs:		
Add salaries avoided if a commission is paid		6,000
Increase in net income		$ 5,100

Yes, based on the information above, the changes should be made. Again, the same answer can be obtained by preparing comparative income statements:

	Present 400 Speakers per Month		Expected 460 Speakers per Month		Difference: Increase or (Decrease) in Net Income
	Total	Per Unit	Total	Per Unit	
Sales	$100,000	$250	$115,000*	$250	$15,000
Less variable expenses	60,000	150	75,900	165	(15,900)
Contribution margin	40,000	$100	39,100	$ 85	(900)
Less fixed expenses	35,000		29,000		6,000
Net income	$ 5,000		$ 10,100		$ 5,100

*400 speakers × 115% = 460 speakers.
 460 speakers × $250 = $115,000.

Change in Regular Sales Price.   Refer to the original data where Acoustic Concepts is currently selling 400 speakers per month. The company has an opportunity to make a bulk sale of 150 speakers to a wholesaler if an acceptable price can be worked out. This sale would not disturb the company's regular sales. What price per speaker should be quoted to the wholesaler if Acoustic Concepts wants to increase its monthly profits by $3,000?

Solution

Variable cost per speaker	$150
Desired profit per speaker:	
$3,000 ÷ 150 speakers	20
Quoted price per speaker	$170

Notice that no element of fixed cost is included in the computation. This is because fixed costs are not affected by the bulk sale, so all of the additional revenue that is in excess of variable costs goes to increasing the profits of the company.

If Acoustic Concepts had been operating at a loss rather than at a profit, many managers would look at the situation somewhat differently. Instead of a modest profit of $3,000, many managers would attempt to reverse all or part of the company's overall loss by quoting a higher price. To illustrate this point, assume that Acoustic Concepts presently has a loss of $6,000 this month and that the company would like to make enough money on the bulk sale of speakers to turn this loss into a profit of $3,000. Under these circumstances, the quoted price on the 150 new speakers would be computed as shown below.

Variable cost per speaker	$150
Present net loss:	
$6,000 ÷ 150 speakers	40
Desired profit:	
$3,000 ÷ 150 speakers	20
Quoted price per speaker	$210

The $210 price we have computed represents a substantial discount from the $250 regular selling price per speaker. Thus, both the wholesaler and the company would benefit from the bulk order at this price. This will not always happen, however. By attempting to cover all of the company's losses on one special order, a manager may quote such a high price that the order is lost. Any price greater than $150 will help to reduce the company's loss. A manager must always keep such market considerations in mind when deciding on prices.

FOCUS ON
CURRENT PRACTICE

A group of investors are planning to open Canada's first used-car superstores in the spring of 1998. Two pieces of property that could hold as many as 900 vehicles each are under investigation in the Toronto area. The stores will be located near suburban highways to draw traffic, and include a small cafeteria and a children's play area and the indoor showroom will likely hold as many as 80 cars. According to the investors' business plan, the used-car superstore would break even selling 1,000 vehicles a month—three times what the average Canadian new-car dealer sells in a year. The plan calls for an average selling price of $16,000, including a 10% mark-up. The mark-up may be a little unrealistic considering Statistics Canada finds that the average dealer achieved pre-tax profit margins of only 1.1 percent in the third quarter of 1996. Nevertheless, the investors expect to make a profit by the end of its second year.[2]

---

[2]Ian Jack, "Used-Car Superstores Planned for Next Spring," *The Financial Post Daily,* April 4, 1997, p. 9.

Importance of the Contribution Margin

As stated in the introduction to the chapter, CVP analysis seeks the most profitable combination of variable costs, fixed costs, selling price, and sales volume. The above examples show that the effect on the contribution margin is a major consideration in deciding on the most profitable combination of these factors. We have seen that profits can sometimes be improved by reducing the contribution margin if fixed costs can be reduced by a greater amount. More commonly, however, we have seen that the way to improve profits is to increase the total contribution margin figure. Sometimes this can be done by reducing the selling price and thereby increasing volume; sometimes it can be done by increasing the fixed costs (such as advertising) and thereby increasing volume; and sometimes it can be done by trading off variable and fixed costs with appropriate changes in volume. Many other combinations of factors are possible.

The size of the unit contribution margin figure (and the size of the CM ratio) will have a heavy influence on what steps a company is willing to take to improve profits. For example, the greater the unit contribution margin for a product, the greater is the amount that a company will be willing to spend in order to increase unit sales of the product by a given percentage. This explains in part why companies with high unit contribution margins (such as auto manufacturers) advertise so heavily, while companies with low unit contribution margins (such as dishware manufacturers) tend to spend much less for advertising.

In short, the effect on the contribution margin holds the key to many decisions in a company.

BREAK-EVEN ANALYSIS

CVP analysis is sometimes referred to simply as break-even analysis. This is unfortunate because break-even analysis is only one element of CVP analysis—although an important element. Break-even analysis is designed to answer questions such as those asked by Prem Narayan concerning how far sales could drop before the company begins to lose money.

Break-Even Computations

OBJECTIVE 4
Compute the break-even point by both the equation method and the contribution margin method.

Earlier in the chapter, we stated that the break-even point can be defined equally well as the point where total sales revenue equals total expenses, variable and fixed, or as the point where total contribution margin equals total fixed expenses. As suggested by these two definitions of the break-even point, break-even analysis can be approached in two ways—first, by the *equation method;* and second, by the *contribution margin method.*

The Equation Method.   The **equation method** centres on the contribution approach to the income statement illustrated earlier in the chapter. The format of this statement can be expressed in equation form as follows:

Sales – (Variable expenses + Fixed expenses) = Profits

Rearranging this equation slightly yields the following equation, which is widely used in CVP analysis:

Sales = Variable expenses + Fixed expenses + Profits

At the break-even point, profits will be zero. Therefore, the break-even point can be computed by finding that point where sales just equal the total of the variable expenses plus the fixed expenses. For Acoustic Concepts, this would be as follows:

$$\text{Sales} = \text{Variable expenses} + \text{Fixed expenses} + \text{Profits}$$

$$\$250X = \$150X + \$35,000 + \$0$$
$$\$100X = \$35,000$$
$$X = \$35,000 \div \$100$$
$$X = 350 \text{ speakers}$$

where:

$$X = \text{Number of speakers sold}$$
$$\$250 = \text{Unit sales price}$$
$$\$150 = \text{Unit variable expenses}$$
$$\$35,000 = \text{Total fixed expenses}$$

After the break-even point in units sold has been computed, the break-even point in sales dollars can be computed by multiplying the break-even level of units by the sales price per unit:

$$350 \text{ speakers} \times \$250 = \$87,500$$

FOCUS ON
CURRENT PRACTICE

Why did Volkswagen have difficulty operating at a profit in the early 1990s despite manufacturing high-quality vehicles and achieving record sales?

In the early 1990s, after a string of very bad years, Volkswagen AG of Germany had a record year in terms of number of vehicles sold. However, instead of experiencing record profits, the company's profits plunged. The reason is that the company had allowed itself to get into a position where its break-even point was above 90% of capacity. As a result, there was a very narrow band of volume within which the company could operate profitably. The record car sales were made possible only by running its factories overtime using expensive overtime labour. In contrast, some of the stronger European auto companies have break-even points below 70% of their capacity.[3]

---

[3]Timothy Aeppel, "VW Chief Declares a Crisis and Prescribes Bold Action," *The Wall Street Journal,* April 1, 1993, p. B4.

At times, the *dollar* relationship between variable expenses and sales may not be known. In these cases, if one knows the *percentage* relationship between variable expenses and sales, then the break-even point can still be computed as follows:

$$\text{Sales} = \text{Variable expenses} + \text{Fixed expenses} + \text{Profits}$$

$$X = 0.60X + \$35{,}000 + \$0$$
$$0.40X = \$35{,}000$$
$$X = \$35{,}000 \div 0.40X$$
$$= \$87{,}500$$

where:

$$X = \text{Total sales dollars}$$
$$0.60 = \text{Variable expenses as a percentage of sales}$$
$$\$35{,}000 = \text{Total fixed expenses}$$

Firms often have data available only in percentage form, and the approach we have just illustrated must then be used to find the break-even point. Notice that use of percentages in the equation yields a break-even point in sales dollars rather than in units sold. The break-even point in units sold is the following:

$$\$87{,}500 \div \$250 = 350 \text{ speakers}$$

The Contribution Margin Method.   The **contribution margin method** is actually just a variation of the equation method already described. The approach centres on the idea discussed earlier that each unit sold provides a certain amount of contribution margin that goes toward the covering of fixed costs. To find how many units must be sold to break even, one must divide the total fixed costs by the contribution margin being generated by each unit sold:

$$\frac{\text{Fixed expenses}}{\text{Unit contribution margin}} = \text{Break-even point in units sold}$$

In 1986, USX Corporation closed its Geneva Steel facility, which consisted of an antiquated plant located in Utah that was losing millions each year. A year later the Geneva Steel facility was purchased by two lawyers who managed to negotiate a purchase price of $40 million for a plant that had cost $47 million to build in the 1940s. The lawyers, along with a newly assembled staff of managers and accountants, immediately set about to slash operating costs. Lower cost contracts were negotiated for *all* of the plant's variable costs, including iron ore, electricity, labour, and transportation. In addition, fixed costs were driven sharply downward through a reduction in the number of white-collar and other support workers.

With lower variable costs, the contribution margin per ton of steel rose sharply. This factor, combined with lower fixed costs, drove the plant's break-even point downward to a level where the company made a profit in the first year of its operation. Moreover, this profit was achieved in a year in which the steel industry was in a slump and competitors were struggling. By continuing to pay careful attention to CVP factors, the company has been earning as much as $53 per ton for steel shipped, which is three times as much as its "big steel" competitors.[4]

---

[4]"Miracle Mill: Utah's Geneva Steel, Once Called Hopeless, Is Racking Up Profits," *The Wall Street Journal*, November 20, 1991, p. 1.

Each speaker that Acoustic Concepts sells generates a contribution margin of $100 ($250 selling price, less $150 variable expenses). Since the total fixed expenses are $35,000, the break-even point is as follows:

$$\frac{\text{Fixed expenses}}{\text{Unit contribution margin}} = \frac{\$35,000}{\$100} = 350 \text{ speakers}$$

There is a variation of this method that uses the CM ratio instead of the unit contribution margin. The result is the break-even in total sales dollars rather than in total units sold.

$$\frac{\text{Fixed expenses}}{\text{CM ratio}} = \text{Break-even point in total sales dollars}$$

In the Acoustic Concepts example, the calculations are as follows:

$$\frac{\text{Fixed expenses}}{\text{CM ratio}} = \frac{\$35,000}{40\%} = \$87,500$$

This approach to break-even analysis is particularly useful in those situations where a company has multiple product lines and wishes to compute a single break-even point for the company as a whole. More is said on this point in a later section titled The Concept of Sales Mix.

CVP Relationships in Graphic Form

OBJECTIVE 5
Prepare a cost-volume-profit (CVP) graph, and explain the significance of each of its components.

The relationships among revenue, cost, profit, and volume can be expressed graphically by preparing a **cost-volume-profit (CVP) graph.** A CVP graph highlights CVP relationships over wide ranges of activity and can give managers a perspective that can be obtained in no other way. To help explain his analysis to Prem Narayan, Bob Luchinni decided to prepare a CVP graph for Acoustic Concepts.

Preparing the CVP Graph.   Preparing a CVP graph (sometimes called a *break-even chart*) involves three steps. These steps are keyed to the graph in Exhibit 7–1:

1. Draw a line parallel to the volume axis to represent total fixed expenses. For Acoustic Concepts, total fixed expenses are $35,000.
2. Choose some volume of sales, and plot the point representing total expenses (fixed and variable) at the activity level you have selected. In Exhibit 7–1, Bob Luchinni chose a volume of 600 speakers. Total expenses at that activity level would be as follows:

Fixed expenses	$ 35,000
Variable expenses (600 speakers × $150)	90,000
Total expenses	$125,000

After the point has been plotted, draw a line through it back to the point where the fixed expenses line intersects the dollars axis.
3. Again choose some volume of sales, and plot the point representing total sales dollars at the activity level you have selected. In Exhibit 7–1, Bob Luchinni again chose a volume of 600 speakers. Sales at that activity level total $150,000 (600 speakers × $250). Draw a line through this point back to the origin.

EXHIBIT 7-1

Preparing the CVP
Graph

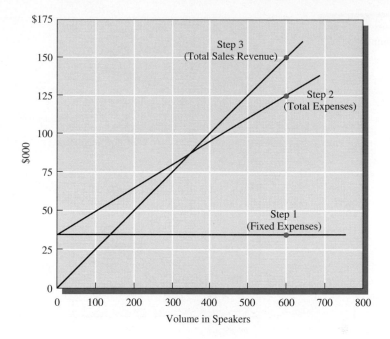

The interpretation of the completed CVP graph is given in Exhibit 7–2. The antici-pated profit or loss at any given level of sales is measured by the vertical distance be-tween the total revenue line (sales) and the total expenses line (variable expenses plus fixed expenses).

The break-even point is where the total revenue and total expenses lines cross. The break-even point of 350 speakers in Exhibit 7–2 agrees with the break-even point ob-tained for Acoustic Concepts in earlier computations.

An Alternative Format.   Some managers prefer an alternative format to the CVP graph, as illustrated in Exhibit 7–3.

Note that the total revenue and total expenses lines are the same as in Exhibit 7–2. However, the new format in Exhibit 7–3 places the fixed expenses above the variable ex-penses. This change allows the contribution margin to be depicted on the graph. Other-wise, the graphs in the two exhibits are the same.

The Profitgraph.   Another approach to the CVP graph is presented in Exhibit 7–4 on page 336. This approach, called a **profitgraph,** is preferred by some managers because it focuses more directly on how profits change with changes in volume. It has the added advantage of being easier to interpret than the more traditional approaches illustrated in Exhibits 7–2 and 7–3. It has the disadvantage, however, of not showing as clearly how costs are affected by changes in the level of sales.

The profitgraph is constructed in two steps. These steps are illustrated in Exhibit 7–4 (page 336).

1.   Locate total fixed expenses on the vertical axis, assuming zero level of activity. This point will be in the "loss area."

EXHIBIT 7-2

The Completed CVP Graph

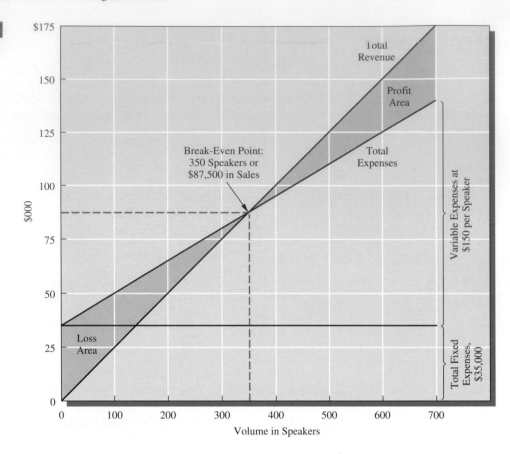

2. Plot a point representing expected profit or loss at any chosen level of sales. In Exhibit 7–4, Bob Luchinni at Acoustic Concepts chose to plot the point representing expected profits at a sales volume of 600 speakers. At this activity level, expected profits are as follows:

Sales (600 speakers × $250)	$150,000
Less variable expenses (600 speakers × $150)	90,000
Contribution margin	60,000
Less fixed expenses	35,000
Net income	$ 25,000

After this point is plotted, draw a line through it back to the point on the vertical axis representing total fixed expenses. The interpretation of the completed profitgraph is given in Exhibit 7–5 on page 337. The break-even point is where the profit line crosses the break-even line.

The vertical distance between the two lines represents the expected profit or loss at any given level of sales volume. This vertical distance can be translated directly into dollars by referring to the profit and loss figures on the vertical axis.

EXHIBIT 7-3

Alternative Format to
the CVP Graph

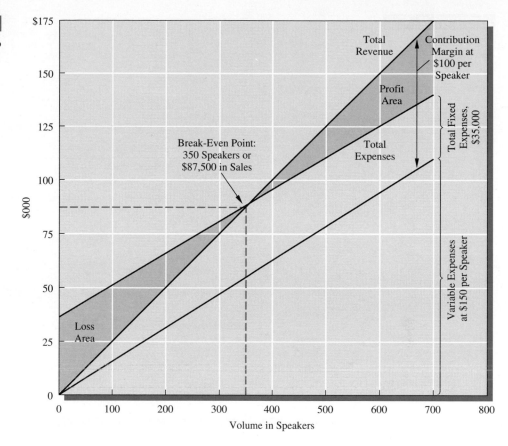

Target Net Profit Analysis

OBJECTIVE 6
Use the CVP formulas
to determine the
activity level needed to
achieve a desired
target net profit figure.

CVP formulas can be used to determine the sales volume needed to achieve a target net profit figure. Suppose that Prem Narayan of Acoustic Concepts would like to earn a target net profit of $40,000 per month. How many speakers would have to be sold?

The CVP Equation.   One approach is to use the equation method discussed on page 329. Instead of solving for the unit sales where profits are zero, you solve for the unit sales where profits are $40,000.

$$\text{Sales} = \text{Variable expenses} + \text{Fixed expenses} / \text{Profits}$$

$$\$250X = \$150X + \$35,000 + \$40,000$$
$$\$100X = \$75,000$$
$$X = \$75,000 \div \$100$$
$$X = 750 \text{ speakers}$$

where:

$$X = \text{Number of speakers sold}$$
$$\$250 = \text{Unit sales price}$$
$$\$150 = \text{Unit variable expenses}$$
$$\$35,000 = \text{Total fixed expenses}$$
$$\$40,000 = \text{Target net profit}$$

Thus, the target net profit can be achieved by selling 750 speakers per month, which represents $187,500 in total sales ($250 × 750 speakers).

EXHIBIT 7-4

Preparing the
Profitgraph

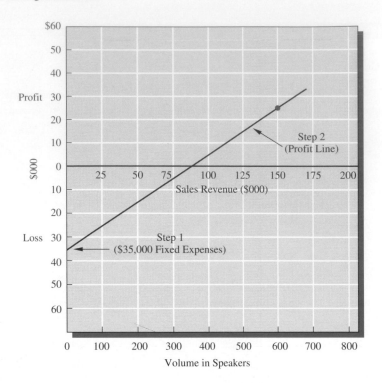

The Contribution Margin Approach. A second approach would be to expand the contribution margin formula to include the target net profit requirement:

$$\frac{\text{Fixed expenses} + \text{Target profit}}{\text{Unit contribution margin}} = \text{Units sold to attain the target profit}$$

$$\frac{\$35,000 \text{ fixed expenses} + \$40,000 \text{ target net profit}}{\$100 \text{ contribution margin per speaker}} = 750 \text{ speakers}$$

This approach is simpler and more direct than using the CVP equation. In addition, it shows clearly that once the fixed costs are covered, the unit contribution margin is fully available for meeting profit requirements.

After-Tax Analysis

Net profit in the preceding analysis has ignored income taxes and is actually income before taxes. In general, income after tax can be computed as a fixed percentage of income before taxes (B). To calculate the income taxes, we simply multiple the tax rate (t) by the before-tax profit (B). After-tax profit is equal to before-tax profit times 1 minus the tax rate and is derived as follows:

$$\text{Income after taxes} = \text{Before-tax profit} - \text{Taxes}$$
$$= B - t(B)$$
$$= B(1-t)$$

EXHIBIT 7-5

The Completed
Profitgraph

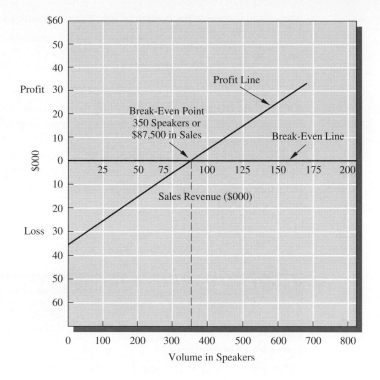

Dividing both sides by 1 – t, income before taxes is equal to income after taxes divided by 1 minus the tax rate (1 – t).

$$B = \frac{\text{Income after taxes}}{(1-t)}$$

Using the previous example, assume that the tax rate is 40% and the target profit is $48,000 after taxes. The target profit can be achieved by selling 1,150 speakers. The appropriate formula to use would be:

$$\frac{\text{Fixed expenses } + \left[\left(\text{Target after-tax profit}\right)/\left(1 - \text{tax rate}\right)\right]}{\text{Contribution margin per unit}}$$

$$\frac{\$35,000 + \left[\$48,000/(1 - .4)\right]}{\$100} = 1,150 \text{ speakers}$$

The Margin of Safety

OBJECTIVE 7

Compute the margin of safety and explain its significance.

The **margin of safety** is the excess of budgeted (or actual) sales over the break-even volume of sales. It states the amount by which sales can drop before losses begin to be incurred. The formula for its calculation is as follows:

Total sales – Break-even sales = Margin of safety

The margin of safety can also be expressed in percentage form. This percentage is obtained by dividing the margin of safety in dollar terms by total sales:

$$\frac{\text{Margain of safety in dollars}}{\text{Total sales}} = \text{Margin of safety percentage}$$

The calculations for the margin of safety for Acoustic Concepts are as follows:

Sales (at the current volume of 400 speakers) (a)	$100,000
Break-even sales (at 350 speakers)	87,500
Margin of safety (in dollars) (b)	$ 12,500
Margin of safety as a percentage of sales (b) ÷ (a)	12.5%

This margin of safety means that at the current level of sales and with the company's current prices and cost structure, a reduction in sales of $12,500, or 12.5%, would result in just breaking even.

In a single-product firm like Acoustic Concepts, the margin of safety can also be expressed in terms of the number of units sold by dividing the margin of safety in dollars by the selling price per unit. In this case, the margin of safety is 50 units ($12,500 ÷ $250 per unit = 50 units).

▼ ▼ ▼ ▼ ▼

MANAGERIAL ACCOUNTING IN ACTION—WRAP-UP

It is Thursday morning, and Prem Narayan and Bob Luchinni are discussing the results of Bob's analysis.

PREM: Bob, everything you have shown me is pretty clear. I can see what impact some of the sales manager's suggestions would have on our profits. Some of those suggestions are quite good and some are not so good. I also understand that our break-even is 350 speakers, so we have to make sure we don't slip below that level of sales. What really bothers me is that we are only selling 400 speakers a month now. What did you call the 50-speaker cushion?

BOB: That's the margin of safety.

PREM: Such a small cushion makes me very nervous. What can we do to increase the margin of safety?

BOB: We have to increase total sales or decrease the break-even point or both.

PREM: And to decrease the break-even point, we have to either decrease our fixed expenses or increase our unit contribution margin.

BOB: Exactly.

PREM: And to increase our unit contribution margin, we have to either increase our selling price or decrease the variable cost per unit.

BOB: Correct.

PREM: So what do you suggest?

BOB: Well, the analysis doesn't tell us which of these to do, but it does indicate we have a potential problem here.

PREM: If you don't have any immediate suggestions, I would like to call a general meeting next week to discuss ways we can work on increasing the margin of safety. I think everyone will be concerned about how vulnerable we are to even small downturns in sales.

BOB: I agree. This is something everyone will want to work on.

▼ ▼ ▼ ▼ ▼

CVP CONSIDERATIONS IN CHOOSING A COST STRUCTURE

We stated in the preceding chapter that *cost structure* refers to the relative proportion of fixed and variable costs in an organization. We also stated that an organization often has some latitude in trading off between fixed and variable costs. Such a trade-off is possible, for example, by automating facilities rather than using direct labour workers.

In this section, we discuss various considerations involved in choosing a cost structure. We look first at the matter of cost structure and profit stability, and then we discuss the effect of cost structure on an important concept known as *operating leverage*. Finally, we conclude the section by comparing capital-intensive (automated) and labour-intensive companies in terms of the potential risks and rewards that are inherent in the cost structures these companies have chosen.

Cost Structure and Profit Stability

When a manager has some latitude in trading off between fixed and variable costs, which cost structure is better—high variable costs and low fixed costs, or the opposite? No categorical answer to this question is possible; we can simply note that there may be advantages either way, depending on the specific circumstances involved. To show what we mean by this statement, refer to the income statements given below for two blueberry farms. Bogside Farm depends on migrant workers to pick its berries by hand, whereas Sterling Farm has invested in expensive berry-picking machines. Consequently, Bogside Farm has higher variable costs, whereas Sterling Farm has higher fixed costs as a result of its investment in machines to pick its berries.

Sterling Farm invested in machinery to harvest its crop of blueberries; Bogside Farm uses manual labour. The consequent differing cost structures will affect income statements in several ways. Is one method— high fixed costs— better than the other— higher variable costs? That depends on other factors, such as sales and the amount of berries harvested year to year.

	Bogside Farm		Sterling Farm	
	Amount	Percent	Amount	Percent
Sales	$100,000	100	$100,000	100
Less variable expenses	60,000	60	30,000	30
Contribution margin	40,000	40	70,000	70
Less fixed expenses	30,000		60,000	
Net income	$ 10,000		$ 10,000	

The question as to which farm has the better cost structure depends on many factors, including the long-run trend in sales, year-to-year fluctuations in the level of sales, and the attitude of the owners toward risk. If sales are expected to trend above $100,000 in the future, then Sterling Farm probably has the better cost structure. The reason is that its CM ratio is higher, and its profits will therefore increase more rapidly as sales increase. To illustrate, assume that each farm experiences a 10% increase in sales. The new income statements will be as follows:

	Bogside Farm		Sterling Farm	
	Amount	Percent	Amount	Percent
Sales	$110,000	100	$110,000	100
Less variable expenses	66,000	60	33,000	30
Contribution margin	44,000	40	77,000	70
Less fixed expenses	30,000		60,000	
Net income	$ 14,000		$ 17,000	

As we would expect, for the same dollar increase in sales, Sterling Farm has experienced a greater increase in net income due to its higher CM ratio.

What if sales can be expected to drop below $100,000 from time to time? What are the break-even points of the two farms? What are their margins of safety? The computations needed to answer these questions are carried out below using the contribution margin method:

	Bogside Farm	Sterling Farm
Fixed expenses	$ 30,000	$ 60,000
Contribution margin ratio	÷40%	÷70%
Break-even in total sales dollars	$ 75,000	$ 85,714
Total current sales (a)	$100,000	$100,000
Break-even sales	75,000	85,714
Margin of safety in sales dollars (b)	$ 25,000	$ 14,286
Margin of safety as a percentage of sales (b) ÷ (a)	25.0%	14.3%

This analysis makes it clear that Bogside Farm is less vulnerable to downturns than Sterling Farm. We can identify two reasons why it is less vulnerable. First, due to its lower fixed expenses, Bogside Farm has a lower break-even point and a higher margin of safety, as shown by the computations above. Therefore, it will not incur losses as quickly as Sterling Farm in periods of sharply declining sales. Second, due to its lower CM ratio, Bogside Farm will not lose contribution margin as rapidly as Sterling Farm when sales fall off. Thus, Bogside Farm's income will be less volatile. We saw earlier that this is a drawback when sales increase, but it provides more protection when sales drop.

To summarize, without knowing the future, it is not obvious which cost structure is better. Both have advantages and disadvantages. Sterling Farm, with its higher fixed costs and lower variable costs, will experience wider swings in net income as changes take place in sales, with greater profits in good years and greater losses in bad years. Bogside Farm, with its lower fixed costs and higher variable costs, will enjoy greater stability in net income and will be more protected from losses during bad years, but at the cost of lower net income in good years.

Entourage Technology Solutions Inc. posted a 33% higher than expected growth rate for 1996. One of the factors accounting for the company's growth is their contract to supply inside wiring services to all of Bell Canada's residential customers. Also, Entourage's workforce, which consists of many former Bell employees, took an $8 an hour pay cut to $17 per hour. Jacque Leveque, president of Entourage, commented on the pay cut, "That was a critical agreement. An open market wouldn't be able to sustain $25." Entourage's lower cost structure allows it to charge $55 per hour for its services versus Bell's rate of $72 per hour.

Operating Leverage

OBJECTIVE 8

Compute the degree of operating leverage at a particular level of sales, and explain how the degree of operating leverage can be used to predict changes in net income.

To the scientist, leverage explains how one is able to move a large object with a small force. To the manager, leverage explains how one is able to achieve a large increase in profits with only a small increase in sales and/or assets. One type of leverage that the manager uses to do this is known as *operating leverage*.[5]

Operating leverage is a measure of the extent to which fixed costs are being used in an organization. It is greatest in companies that have a high proportion of fixed costs in relation to variable costs. Conversely, operating leverage is lowest in companies that have a low proportion of fixed costs in relation to variable costs. If a company has high operating leverage (that is, a high proportion of fixed costs in relation to variable costs), then profits will be very sensitive to changes in sales. Just a small percentage increase (or decrease) in sales can yield a large percentage increase (or decrease) in profits.

Operating leverage can be illustrated by returning to the data given above for the two blueberry farms. Sterling Farm has a higher proportion of fixed costs in relation to its variable costs than does Bogside Farm, although *total* costs are the same in the two farms at a $100,000 sales level. We previously showed that with a 10% increase in sales (from $100,000 to $110,000 in each farm), the net income of Sterling Farm increases by 70% (from $10,000 to $17,000), whereas the net income of Bogside Farm increases by only 40% (from $10,000 to $14,000). Thus, for a 10% increase in sales, Sterling Farm experiences a much greater percentage increase in profits than does Bogside Farm. The reason is that Sterling Farm has greater operating leverage as a result of the greater amount of fixed cost in its cost structure.

The **degree of operating leverage** at a given level of sales is computed by the following formula:

$$\frac{\text{Contribution margin}}{\text{Net income}} = \text{Degree of operating leverage}$$

[5]There are two types of leverage—operating and financial. Financial leverage is discussed in Chapter 17.

The degree of operating leverage is a measure, at a given level of sales, of how a percentage change in sales volume will affect profits. To illustrate, the degree of operating leverage for the two farms at a $100,000 sales level would be as follows:

$$\text{Bogside Farm:} \quad \frac{\$40,000}{\$10,000} = 4$$

$$\text{Sterling Farm:} \quad \frac{\$70,000}{\$10,000} = 7$$

These figures tell us that *for a given percentage change in sales* we can expect a change four times as great in the net income of Bogside Farm and a change seven times as great in the net income of Sterling Farm. Thus, if sales increase by 10%, then we can expect the net income of Bogside Farm to increase by four times this amount, or by 40%, and the net income of Sterling Farm to increase by seven times this amount, or by 70%.

	(1) Percent Increase in Sales	(2) Degree of Operating Leverage	(3) Percent Increase in Net Income (1) × (2)
Bogside Farm	10	4	40
Sterling Farm	10	7	70

These computations explain why the 10% increase in sales mentioned earlier caused Bogside Farm's net income to increase from $10,000 to $14,000 (an increase of 40%) and Sterling Farm's net income to increase from $10,000 to $17,000 (an increase of 70%).

The degree of operating leverage is greatest at sales levels near the break-even point and decreases as sales and profits rise. This can be seen from the tabulation below, which shows the degree of operating leverage for Bogside Farm at various sales levels. (Data used earlier for Bogside Farm are shown in colour.)

Sales	$75,000	$80,000	$100,000	$150,000	$225,000
Less variable expenses	45,000	48,000	60,000	90,000	135,000
Contribution margin (a)	30,000	32,000	40,000	60,000	90,000
Less fixed expenses	30,000	30,000	30,000	30,000	30,000
Net income (b)	$ –0–	$ 2,000	$ 10,000	$ 30,000	$ 60,000
Degree of operating leverage, (a) ÷ (b) ...	∞	16	4	2	1.5

Thus, a 10% increase in sales would increase profits by only 15% (10% × 1.5) if the company were operating at a $225,000 sales level, as compared to the 40% increase we computed earlier at the $100,000 sales level. The degree of operating leverage will continue to decrease the farther the company moves from its break-even point. At the break-even point, the degree of operating leverage will be infinitely large ($30,000 contribution margin ÷ $0 net income = ∞).

A manager can use the degree of operating leverage to quickly estimate what impact various percentage changes in sales will have on profits, without the necessity of preparing detailed income statements. As shown by our examples, the effects of operating leverage can be dramatic. If a company is fairly near its break-even point, then even small increases in sales can yield large increases in profits. *This explains why management will often work very hard for only a small increase in sales volume.* If the degree of operating leverage is 5, then a 6% increase in sales would translate into a 30% increase in profits.

CanWest is a broadcasting company that owns seven television stations in Canada plus the Global Television Network in Ontario. It has economic interests in several international networks as well. For the first six months of fiscal 1996, revenues were up 14%, net earnings were up 31%, and operating profit was up 37%. One of the reasons for CanWest's improvement was due to a recovery in advertising markets in Canada. CanWest's results illustrate the concept of operating leverage. An increase in revenue caused a much larger increase in profit. This is due to the fact that broadcasters have high fixed operating costs. When advertising revenues drop below their break-even points, they suffer. When ad revenues recover and climb above break-even, cash tends to drop directly to the bottom line since fixed costs have already been covered and variable costs are low.[6]

Automation: Risks and Rewards from a CVP Perspective

We have noted in preceding chapters that several factors, including the move toward flexible manufacturing systems and other uses of automation, have resulted in a shift toward greater fixed costs and less variable costs in organizations. In turn, this shift in cost structure has had an impact on product CM ratios, on the break-even point, and on other CVP factors in automated companies. Some of this impact has been favourable and some has not, as shown in Exhibit 7–6.

Many benefits can accrue from automation, but as shown in the exhibit, certain risks are introduced when a company moves toward greater amounts of fixed costs. These risks suggest that management must be careful as it automates to ensure that investment decisions are made in accordance with a carefully devised long-run operating strategy. This point is discussed further in Chapter 14 where we deal with investment decisions in an automated environment.

STRUCTURING SALES COMMISSIONS

Companies generally compensate salespeople by paying them either a commission based on sales or a salary plus a sales commission. Commissions based on sales dollars can lead to lower profits in a company. To illustrate, consider Pipeline Unlimited, a producer of surfing equipment. Salespeople for the company sell the company's product to retail sporting goods stores throughout North America and the Pacific Basin. Data for two of the company's surfboards, the XR7 and Turbo models, appear below:

	Model	
	XR7	**Turbo**
Selling price	$100	$150
Less variable expenses	75	132
Contribution margin	$ 25	$ 18

---

[6]"CanWest Shares Beaming Again," *The Financial Post Daily,* April 9, 1996, p. 21.

EXHIBIT 7-6   CVP Comparison of Capital-Intensive (automated) and Labour-Intensive Companies

The comparison below is between two companies in the same industry that produce identical products for the same market. One of the companies has chosen to automate its facilities (capital-intensive) and the other has chosen to rely heavily on direct labour inputs (labour-intensive).

Item	Capital-Intensive (automated) Company	Labour-Intensive Company	Comments
The CM ratio for a given product will tend to be relatively . . .	High	Low	Variable costs in an automated company will tend to be lower than in a labour-intensive company, thereby causing the CM ratio for a given product to be higher.
Operating leverage will tend to be . . .	High	Low	Since operating leverage is a measure of the use of fixed costs in an organization, it will typically be higher in an automated company than in a company that relies on direct labour input.
In periods of increasing sales, net income will tend to increase . . .	Rapidly	Slowly	Since both operating leverage and product CM ratios tend to be high in automated companies, net income will increase rapidly after the break-even point has been reached.
In periods of decreasing sales, net income will tend to decrease . . .	Rapidly	Slowly	Just as net income increases rapidly in an automated company after the break-even point has been reached, so will net income decrease rapidly as sales decrease.
The volatility of net income with changes in sales will tend to be . . .	Greater	Less	Due to its higher operating leverage, the net income in an automated company will tend to be much more sensitive to changes in sales than in a labour-intensive company.
The break-even point will tend to be . . .	Higher	Lower	The break-even point in an automated company will tend to be higher because of its greater fixed costs.
The margin of safety at a given level of sales will tend to be . . .	Lower	Higher	The margin of safety in an automated company will tend to be lower because of its higher break-even point.
The latitude available to management in times of economic stress will tend to be . . .	Less	Greater	With high committed fixed costs in an automated company, management is more "locked in" and has fewer options when dealing with changing economic conditions.

Which model will salespeople push hardest if they are paid a commission of 10% of sales revenue? The answer is the Turbo, since it has the higher selling price. On the other hand, from the standpoint of the company (assuming other factors are equal), will profits be greater if salespeople steer customers toward the XR7 or Turbo model? The answer this time is the XR7 model, because it has the higher contribution margin.

To eliminate such conflicts, some companies base salespersons' commissions on contribution margin generated rather than on sales generated. The reasoning goes like this: Since contribution margin represents the amount of sales revenue available to cover fixed expenses and profits, a firm's well-being will be maximized when contribution margin is maximized. By tying salespersons' commissions to contribution margin, the salespersons are automatically encouraged to concentrate on the element that is of most importance to the firm. There is no need to worry about what mix of products the salespersons sell because they will *automatically* sell the mix of products that will maximize the base on which their commissions are to be paid. That is, if salespersons are aware that their commissions will

FOCUS ON
CURRENT PRACTICE

The method of compensating salespersons must be chosen with a great deal of care. Digital Equipment Corporation's founder believed that salespersons should never sell customers something they don't need, and accordingly Digital paid them salaries rather than sales commissions. This approach worked fine for many years because "Digital's products were the hottest alternatives to expensive mainframe computers, and because they were cheaper, they almost sold themselves. But when competition arrived, the Digital sales staff was hopelessly outclassed." When commissions were introduced in an attempt to stem the tide, the new system backfired. "Some salesmen sold product at little, or no profit to pump up volume—and their compensation."[7]

depend on the amount of contribution margin that they are able to generate, then they will use all of the experience, skill, and expertise at their command to sell the mix of products that will maximize the contribution margin base. In effect, by maximizing their own well-being, they automatically maximize the well-being of the firm.

As a further step, some firms deduct from the total contribution margin generated by salespersons the amount of the travelling, entertainment, and other expenses that they incur. This encourages the salespersons to be sensitive to their own costs in the process of making sales.

THE CONCEPT OF SALES MIX

OBJECTIVE 9
Compute the break-even point for a multiple product company, and explain the effects of shifts in the sales mix on contribution margin and the break-even point.

The preceding sections have given us some insights into the principles involved in CVP analysis, as well as some selected examples of how these principles are used by the manager. Before concluding our discussion, it will be helpful to consider one additional application of the ideas that we have developed—the use of CVP concepts in analyzing sales mix.

The Definition of Sales Mix

The term **sales mix** means the relative combination in which a company's products are sold. Managers try to achieve the combination, or mix, that will yield the greatest amount of profits. Most companies have several products, and often these products are not equally profitable. Where this is true, profits will depend to some extent on the sales mix that the company is able to achieve. Profits will be greater if high-margin items make up a relatively large proportion of total sales than if sales consist mostly of low-margin items.

Changes in the sales mix can cause interesting (and sometimes confusing) variations in a company's profits. A shift in the sales mix from high-margin items to low-margin items can cause total profits to decrease even though total sales may increase. Conversely, a shift in the sales mix from low-margin items to high-margin items can cause the reverse effect—total profits may increase even though total sales decrease. In the competitive brewing industry, for example, Heineken, the Dutch brewing giant has been able to increase profits due to a favourable shift in its own sales mix toward premium beers.

---

[7]John R. Wilke, "At Digital Equipment, a Resignation Reveals Key Problem: Selling," *The Wall Street Journal*, April 26, 1994, pp. A1, A11.

Given the possibility of these types of variations in profits, one measure of the effectiveness of a company's sales force is the sales mix that it is able to generate. It is one thing to achieve a particular sales volume; it is quite a different thing to sell the most profitable mix of products.

Sales Mix and Break-Even Analysis

If a company sells more than one product, break-even analysis is somewhat more complex than discussed earlier in the chapter. The reason is that different products will have different selling prices, different costs, and different contribution margins. Consequently, the break-even point will depend on the mix in which the various products are sold. To illustrate, consider Sound Unlimited, a small company that imports CD-ROMs from France for use in personal computers. Presently, the company is distributing two CD-ROMs to retail computer stores—Le Louvre and Le Vin. The Le Louvre CD is a multimedia free-form tour of the famous art museum in Paris. The Le Vin CD features the wines and wine-growing regions of France. Both multimedia products have sound, photos, and sophisticated software. The company's sales, expenses, and break-even point are shown in Exhibit 7–7 for the month of September.

As shown in the exhibit, the break-even point is $60,000 in sales. This is computed by dividing the fixed costs by the company's *overall* CM ratio of 45%. But $60,000 in sales represents the break-even point for the company only so long as the sales mix does not change. *If the sales mix changes, then the break-even point will also change.* This is illustrated by the results for October in which the sales mix shifted away from the more profitable Le Vin CD (which has a 50% CM ratio) toward the less profitable Le Louvre CD (which has only a 25% CM ratio). These results appear in Exhibit 7–8.

Although sales have remained unchanged at $100,000, the sales mix is exactly the reverse of what it was in Exhibit 7–7, with the bulk of the sales now coming from the Le Louvre CD rather than from the Le Vin CD. Notice that this shift in the sales mix has caused both the overall CM ratio and total profits to drop sharply from the prior month—the overall CM ratio has dropped from 45% in September to only 30% in October, and

EXHIBIT 7–7

Multiple-Product
Break-Even Analysis

	SOUND UNLIMITED Contribution Income Statement For the Month of September					
	Le Louvre CD		Le Vin CD		Total	
	Amount	Percent	Amount	Percent	Amount	Percent
Sales	$20,000	100	$80,000	100	$100,000	100
Less variable expenses	15,000	75	40,000	50	55,000	55
Contribution margin	$ 5,000	25	$40,000	50	45,000	45*
Less fixed expenses					27,000	
Net income					$ 18,000	

Computation of the break-even point:

$$\frac{\text{Fixed expenses, } \$27,000}{\text{Overall CM ratio, } 45\%} = \$60,000$$

*$45,000 ÷ $100,000 = 45%.

EXHIBIT 7-8

Multiple-Product
Break-Even
Analysis: A Shift in
Sales Mix (see
Exhibit 7–7)

SOUND UNLIMITED
Contribution Income Statement
For the Month of October

	Le Louvre CD		Le Vin CD		Total	
	Amount	Percent	Amount	Percent	Amount	Percent
Sales	$80,000	100	$20,000	100	$100,000	100
Less variable expenses	60,000	75	10,000	50	70,000	70
Contribution margin	$20,000	25	$10,000	50	30,000	30*
Less fixed expenses					27,000	
Net income					$ 3,000	

Computation of the break-even point:

$$\frac{\text{Fixed expenses, } \$27,000}{\text{Overall CM ratio, } 30\%} = \$90,000$$

*$30,000 ÷ $100,000 = 30%.

net income has dropped from $18,000 to only $3,000. In addition, with the drop in the overall CM ratio, the company's break-even point is no longer $60,000 in sales. Because the company is now realizing less average contribution margin per dollar of sales, it takes more sales to cover the same amount of fixed costs. Thus, the break-even point has increased from $60,000 to $90,000 in sales per year.

In preparing a break-even analysis, some assumption must be made concerning the sales mix. Usually the assumption is that it will not change. At times managers may find it necessary to change prices of individual products in response to varying market conditions. These pricing decisions may result in a new product mix and, consequently, a new break-even point. In such cases it seems advisable for managers to do calculations assuming alternative sales mixes or at least use an expected sales mix to take uncertainty into account. By performing sensitivity analysis on the impact of changes in product mix, the management accountant can provide a means of evaluating a firm's capacity constraints and the feasibility of taking on various contracts. Otherwise, the manager may be making decisions on the basis of outmoded or faulty data.

Sales Mix and per Unit Contribution Margin

Sometimes the sales mix is measured in terms of the average per unit contribution margin. To illustrate, we have added unit sales information concerning Sound Unlimited's products in Exhibit 7–9.

Two things should be noted about the data in this exhibit. First, note that the sales mix in September was 500 units of the Le Louvre CD and 2,000 units of the Le Vin CD. This sales mix yielded an average per unit contribution margin of $18.

Second, note that the sales mix in October shifted to 2,000 units of the Le Louvre CD and 500 units of the Le Vin CD, although total sales remained constant at 2,500 units. This sales mix yielded an average per unit contribution margin of $12, a decrease of $6 from September.

What caused the decrease in average per unit contribution margin between the two months? The answer is the shift in sales mix toward the less profitable product. Although the total number of units sold did not change, the total and per unit average contribution margins changed simply because of the change in sales mix.

EXHIBIT 7-9

Sales Mix and per
Unit Contribution
Margin Analysis

	Total Units Sold		**Contribution Margin per Unit**	**Total Contribution Margin**	
	September	October		September	October
Le Louvre CD	500	2,000	$10	$ 5,000	$20,000
Le Vin CD	2,000	500	20	40,000	10,000
	2,500	2,500		$45,000	$30,000

SOUND UNLIMITED
Per Unit Contribution Margin Analysis
For the Months of September and October

Average per unit contribution margin:
September ($45,000 ÷ 2,500 units) $18
October ($30,000 ÷ 2,500 units) $12

ASSUMPTIONS OF CVP ANALYSIS

There are several assumptions underlying the simplest form of CVP analysis—such as the break-even formulas. The major assumptions are as follows:

1. Selling price is constant throughout the entire relevant range. The price of a product or service will not change as volume changes.
2. Costs are linear throughout the entire relevant range, and they can be accurately divided into variable and fixed elements. The variable element is constant per unit, and the fixed element is constant in total over the entire relevant range.
3. In multiproduct companies, the sales mix is constant.
4. In manufacturing companies, inventories do not change. The number of units produced equals the number of units sold (this assumption is considered further in the next chapter).

While some of these assumptions may be technically violated, the violations are usually not serious enough to call into question the basic validity of CVP analysis. For example, in most multiproduct companies the sales mix is not exactly constant from one period to the next. However, the sales mix is constant enough so that the results of CVP analysis are reasonably valid.

Perhaps the greatest danger lies in relying on simple CVP analysis when a manager is contemplating a large change in volume that lies outside of the relevant range. For example, a manager might be contemplating increasing the level of sales far beyond what the company has ever experienced before. However, even in these situations a manager can adjust the model as we have done in this chapter to take into account anticipated changes in selling prices, fixed costs, and the sales mix that would otherwise violate the assumptions. For example, in a decision that would affect fixed costs, the change in fixed costs can be explicitly taken into account as illustrated earlier in the chapter in the Acoustic Concepts example on page 338.

SUMMARY

The analysis of CVP relationships is one of management's most significant responsibilities. Basically, it involves finding the most favourable combination of variable costs, fixed costs, selling price, sales volume, and mix of products sold. We have found that trade-offs are possible between types of costs, as well as between costs and selling price, and between selling price and sales volume. Sometimes these trade-offs are desirable, and sometimes they are not. CVP analysis provides the manager with a powerful tool for identifying those courses of action that will improve profitability.

The concepts developed in this chapter represent a *way of thinking* rather than a mechanical set of procedures. That is, to put together the optimum combination of costs, selling price, and sales volume, the manager must be trained to think in terms of the unit contribution margin, the break-even point, the CM ratio, the sales mix, and the other concepts developed in this chapter. These concepts are dynamic in that a change in one will trigger changes in others—changes that may not be obvious on the surface. Only by learning to *think* in CVP terms can the manager move with assurance toward the firm's profit objectives.

REVIEW PROBLEM: CVP RELATIONSHIPS

Voltar Company manufactures and sells a telephone answering machine. The company's income statement for the most recent year is given below:

	Total	Per Unit	Percent
Sales (20,000 units).............	$1,200,000	$60	100
Less variable expenses	900,000	45	?
Contribution margin	300,000	$15	?
Less fixed expenses	240,000		
Net income	$ 60,000		

Management is anxious to improve the company's profit performance and has asked for several items of information.

Required

1. Compute the company's CM ratio and variable expense ratio.
2. Compute the company's break-even point in both units and sales dollars. Use the equation method.
3. Assume that sales increase by $400,000 next year. If cost behaviour patterns remain unchanged, by how much will the company's net income increase? Use the CM ratio to determine your answer.
4. Refer to the original data. Assume that next year management wants the company to earn a minimum profit of $90,000. How many units will have to be sold to meet this target profit figure?
5. Refer to the original data. Compute the company's margin of safety in both dollar and percentage form.
6. a. Compute the company's degree of operating leverage at the present level of sales.
   b. Assume that through a more intense effort by the sales staff the company's sales increase by 8% next year. By what percentage would you expect net income to increase? Use the operating leverage concept to obtain your answer.
   c. Verify your answer to (b) by preparing a new income statement showing an 8% increase in sales.

7. In an effort to increase sales and profits, management is considering the use of a higher-quality speaker in the answering machine. The higher-quality speaker would increase variable costs by $3 per unit, but management could eliminate one quality inspector who is paid a salary of $30,000 per year. The sales manager estimates that the higher-quality speaker would increase annual sales by at least 20%.

   a. Assuming that changes are made as described above, prepare a projected income statement for next year. Show data on a total, per unit, and percentage basis.
   b. Compute the company's new break-even point in both units and dollars of sales. Use the contribution margin method.
   c. Would you recommend that the changes be made?

Solution to Review Problem

1. CM ratio: Variable expense ratio:

$$\frac{\text{Contribution margin, }\$15}{\text{Selling price, }\$60} = 25\% \qquad \frac{\text{Variable expense, }\$45}{\text{Selling price, }\$60} = 75\%$$

2.   Sales = Variable expenses + Fixed expenses + Profits

$$\$60X = \$45X + \$240,000 + \$0$$
$$\$15X = \$240,000$$
$$X = \$240,000 \div \$15$$
$$X = 16,000 \text{ units; or at \$60 per unit, \$960,000}$$

Alternative solution:

$$X = 0.75X + \$240,000 + \$0$$
$$0.25X = \$240,000$$
$$X = \$240,000 \div 0.25$$
$$X = \$960,000; \text{ or at \$60 per unit, 16,000 units}$$

3.

Increase in sales	$400,000
Multiply by the CM ratio	× 25%
Expected increase in contribution margin	$100,000

Since the fixed expenses are not expected to change, net income will increase by the entire $100,000 increase in contribution margin computed above.

4. Equation method:

Sales = Variable expenses + Fixed expenses + Profits

$$\$60X = \$45X + \$240,000 + \$90,000$$
$$\$15X = \$330,000$$
$$X = \$330,000 \div \$15$$
$$X = 22,000 \text{ units}$$

Contribution margin method:

$$\frac{\text{Fixed expenses + Target profit}}{\text{Contribution margin per unit}} = \frac{\$240,000 + \$90,000}{\$15} = 22,000 \text{ units}$$

5.   Total sales – Break-even sales = Margin of safety in dollars
$$\$1,200,000 - \$960,000 = \$240,000$$

$$\frac{\text{Margin of safety in dollars, }\$240,000}{\text{Total sales, }\$1,200,000} = 20\%$$

6. a.
$$\frac{\text{Contribution margin, \$300,000}}{\text{Net income, \$60,000}} = 5 \text{ (degree of operating leverage)}$$

b.

Expected increase in sales.................	8%
Degree of operating leverage	× 5
Expected increase in net income...........	40%

c. If sales increase by 8%, then 21,600 units (20,000 × 1.08 = 21,600) will be sold next year. The new income statement will be as follows:

	Total	Per Unit	Percent
Sales (21,600 units)	$1,296,000	$60	100
Less variable expenses.....	972,000	45	75
Contribution margin.......	324,000	$15	25
Less fixed expenses	240,000		
Net income.............	$ 84,000		

Thus, the $84,000 expected net income for next year represents a 40% increase over the $60,000 net income earned during the current year:

$$\frac{\$84,000 - \$60,000}{\$60,000} = 40\% \text{ increase}$$

Note from the income statement above that the increase in sales from 20,000 to 21,600 units has resulted in increases in *both* total sales and total variable expenses. It is a common error to overlook the increase in variable expenses when preparing a projected income statement such as this one!

7. a. A 20% increase in sales would result in 24,000 units being sold next year: 20,000 units × 1.20 = 24,000 units.

	Total	Per Unit	Percent
Sales (24,000 units)	$1,440,000	$60	100
Less variable expenses.....	1,152,000	48*	80*
Contribution margin....... 288,000.............$12	20		
Less fixed expenses	210,000†		
Net income	$ 78,000		

*$45 + $3 = $48; $48 ÷ $60 = 80%.

Note that the change in per unit variable expenses results in a change in both the per unit contribution margin and the CM ratio.

b.
$$\frac{\text{Fixed expenses, \$210,000}}{\text{Contribution margin per unit, \$12}} = 17,500 \text{ units}$$

$$\frac{\text{Fixed expenses, \$210,000}}{\text{CM ratio, 20\%}} = \$1,050,000 \text{ break-even sales}$$

c. Yes, based on these data the changes should be made. The changes will increase the company's net income from the present $60,000 to $78,000 per year. Although the changes will also result in a higher break-even point (17,500 units as compared to the present 16,000 units), the company's margin of safety will actually be wider than before:

Total sales – Break-even sales = Margin of safety in dollars
$1,400,000 – $1,050,000 = $350,000

As shown in (5) above, the company's present margin of safety is only $240,000. Thus, several benefits will accrue from the proposed changes.

KEY TERMS FOR REVIEW

OBJECTIVE 10
Define or explain the key terms listed at the end of the chapter.

Break-even point   The level of activity at which an organization neither earns a profit nor incurs a loss. The break-even point can also be defined as the point where total revenue equals total costs and as the point where total contribution margin equals total fixed costs. (p. 322)

Contribution margin method   A method of computing the break-even point in which the fixed costs are divided by the contribution margin per unit. (p. 331)

Contribution margin ratio (CM ratio)   The contribution margin as a percentage of total sales. (p. 324)

Cost-volume-profit (CVP) graph   The relationship between revenues, costs, and level of activity in an organization presented in graphic form. (p. 332)

Degree of operating leverage   A measure, at a given level of sales, of how a percentage change in sales volume will affect profits. The degree of operating leverage is computed by dividing contribution margin by net income. (p. 341)

Equation method   A method of computing the break-even point that relies on the equation Sales = Variable expenses + Fixed expenses + Profits. (p. 329)

Incremental analysis   An analytical approach that focuses only on those items of revenue, cost, and volume that will change as a result of a decision in an organization. (p. 326)

Margin of safety   The excess of budgeted (or actual) sales over the break-even volume of sales. (p. 337)

Operating leverage   A measure of the extent to which fixed costs are being used in an organization. The greater the fixed costs, the greater is the operating leverage available and the greater is the sensitivity of net income to changes in sales. (p. 341)

Profitgraph   An alternative form of the CVP graph that focuses more directly on how profits change with changes in volume. (p. 333)

Sales mix   The relative combination in which a company's products are sold. Sales mix is computed by expressing the sales of each product as a percentage of total sales. (p. 345)

APPENDIX 7A: COST-VOLUME-PROFIT WITH UNCERTAINTY

OBJECTIVE 11
Understand cost-volume-profit with uncertainty.

CVP analysis is often employed to assess what future prospects might be under various arrangements. Given the compactness of the analysis, the CVP formula is a convenient approach to conducting such assessments. Consider the following example:

Novelties Ltd. produces and sells highly faddish products directed toward the teenage market. A new product has come onto the market that the company is anxious to produce and sell. Enough capacity exists in the company's plant to product 15,000 units each month. Variable costs to manufacture and sell one unit would be $1.60, and fixed costs would total $16,000 per month.

Management of Novelties wants to assess the implications of various alternatives. As part of the investigation, management wants an analysis of the profits before income taxes if various alternative sales volumes, selling prices, and variable expenses occur. Sales volumes would be 13,500 units or 15,000 units. Selling prices would be $3.50 or $4.00. Variable expenses were estimated as being $1.28 or $1.60 depending on a series of outcomes. First consider the eight ($2 \times 2 \times 2$) possible outcomes:

Alternatives	Variable Expenses	Selling Prices	Sales Volumes	Fixed Expenses	Profits before Taxes
1	$1.28	$3.50	13,500	$16,000	$13,970
2	1.28	3.50	15,000	16,000	17,300
3	1.28	4.00	13,500	16,000	20,720
4	1.28	4.00	15,000	16,000	24,800
5	1.60	3.50	13,500	16,000	9,650
6	1.60	3.50	15,000	16,000	12,500
7	1.60	4.00	13,500	16,000	16,400
8	1.60	4.00	15,000	16,000	20,000

EXHIBIT 7-10

A Decision Tree

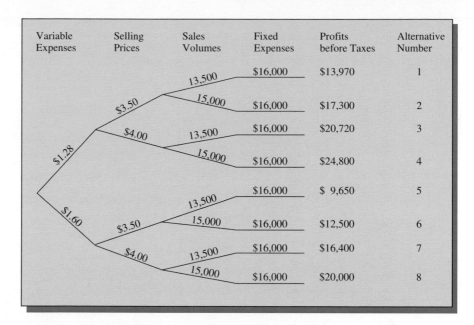

Variable Expenses	Selling Prices	Sales Volumes	Fixed Expenses	Profits before Taxes	Alternative Number
		13,500	$16,000	$13,970	1
	$3.50	15,000	$16,000	$17,300	2
	$4.00	13,500	$16,000	$20,720	3
$1.28		15,000	$16,000	$24,800	4
		13,500	$16,000	$ 9,650	5
$1.60	$3.50	15,000	$16,000	$12,500	6
	$4.00	13,500	$16,000	$16,400	7
		15,000	$16,000	$20,000	8

By noticing the repetitions of variable expenses and selling prices, the preceding table can be represented in the form of a tree, commonly termed a *decision tree,* as shown in Exhibit 7–10.

As a manager, one would like alternative 4 with a profit of $24,800. If a manager can force the future components of a profit to be the following—variable expenses, $1.28; selling price, $4.00; and sales volume, 15,000 units—a profit of $24,800 before taxes can be achieved. Unfortunately, managers do not have such a luxury.

Assume the best the manager can do is assess the chances of each alternative occurring. These chances are commonly termed *subjective probabilities* and can represent what the manager believes will occur. Each of the possible chances can also be placed on the tree as shown in Exhibit 7–11.

Close observation reveals several important and general results to the manager of Novelties. First, the chances for each uncertain factor are expressed in decimal form and sum to one. Second, the chances are multiplied on the tree in the same sequence as the CVP elements. Third, no chance was assigned to fixed expenses because they are known in every case.

The manager notes that if the subjective probabilities are correct, there is only a 2% chance, or 2 chances in 100, of having a profit of $24,800.

To ascertain what Novelties might expect future profits to be, the expected value (often termed a *mean*) is computed as follows:

Alternatives	Profits	Chances	Products	
1	$13,970	.38	$ 5,308.60	($13,970 × .38)
2	17,300	.04	692.00	($17,300 × .04)
3	20,720	.16	3,315.20	
4	24,800	.02	496.00	
5	9,650	.25	2,412.50	
6	12,500	.03	375.00	
7	16,400	.11	1,804.00	
8	20,000	.01	200.00	
		1.00		
Total expected value			$14,603.30	

EXHIBIT 7-11

A Decision Tree

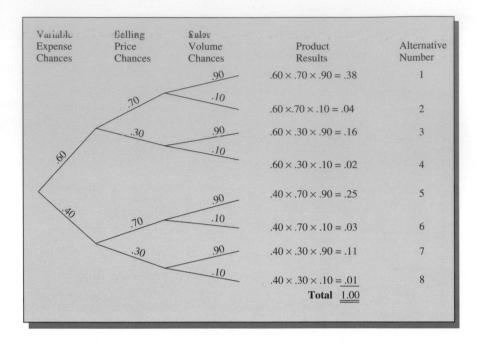

Variable Expense Chances	Selling Price Chances	Sales Volume Chances	Product Results	Alternative Number
		.90	.60 × .70 × .90 = .38	1
	.70	.10	.60 × .70 × .10 = .04	2
	.30	.90	.60 × .30 × .90 = .16	3
.60		.10	.60 × .30 × .10 = .02	4
		.90	.40 × .70 × .90 = .25	5
	.70	.10	.40 × .70 × .10 = .03	6
.40	.30	.90	.40 × .30 × .90 = .11	7
		.10	.40 × .30 × .10 = .01	8
			Total 1.00	

The expected value, $14,603.30, is a reasonable estimate of what the profit of Novelties might be for next period given the data and the chances supplied to the analysis.

The decision tree analysis is very powerful. A computer can facilitate the tedious calculations. However, it is important to note that the number of calculations increases dramatically with both the number of alternatives (e.g., 1.28 or 1.60 for variable expenses) considered (e.g., $3 \times 3 \times 3 = 27$, $4 \times 4 \times 4 = 64$) and the number of factors (e.g., selling prices, sales volumes, etc.) considered in the CVP formulation (e.g., $2 \times 2 \times 2 \times 2 = 16$, $2 \times 2 \times 2 \times 2 = 32$). Even a computer can be taxed very quickly.

QUESTIONS

7–1   What is meant by a product's CM ratio? How is this ratio useful in the planning of business operations?

7–2   Often the most direct route to a business decision is to make an incremental analysis based on the information available. What is meant by an *incremental analysis*?

7–3   Company A's cost structure includes costs that are mostly variable, whereas Company B's cost structure includes costs that are mostly fixed. In a time of increasing sales, which company will tend to realize the most rapid increase in profits? Explain.

7–4   What is meant by the term *operating leverage*?

7–5   A 10% decrease in the selling price of a product will have the same impact on net income as a 10% increase in the variable expenses. Do you agree? Why or why not?

7–6   What is meant by the term *break-even point*?

7–7   Name three approaches to break-even analysis. Briefly explain how each approach works.

7–8   In response to a request from your immediate supervisor, you have prepared a CVP graph portraying the cost and revenue characteristics of your company's product and operations.

Explain how the lines on the graph and the break-even point would change if (a) the selling price per unit decreased, (b) fixed costs increased throughout the entire range of activity portrayed on the graph, and (c) variable costs per unit increased.

7–9   Using the following notations, write out the correct formula for computing the break-even level of sales in units: S = sales in units, SP = selling price per unit, FC = total fixed costs, and VC = variable cost per unit.

7–10   Al's Auto Wash charges $4 to wash a car. The variable costs of washing a car are 15% of sales. Fixed costs total $1,700 monthly. How many cars must be washed each month for Al to break even?

7–11   What is meant by the margin of safety?

7–12   Companies X and Y are in the same industry. Company X is highly automated, whereas Company Y relies primarily on labour in the manufacture of its products. If sales in the two companies are about the same, which would you expect to have the lower margin of safety? Why?

7–13   What is meant by the term *sales mix*? CVP analysis includes some inherent, simplifying assumptions. What assumption is usually made concerning sales mix?

7–14   Explain how a shift in the sales mix could result in both a higher break-even point and a lower net income.

7–15   Why do accountants commonly use linear CVP analysis rather than the curvilinear form?

7–16   What effect would a 30% income tax rate have on the CVP formula?

7–17   Why must inventories be assumed to be constant in the CVP formula?

7–18   What would happen to CVP analysis if worker productivity increased as the top of the relevant range was reached?

7–19   Describe how uncertainty can be explicitly considered in CVP analysis.

7–20   Does the concept of relevant range imply more than one break-even point? Explain.

EXERCISES

E7–1   Pringle Company manufactures and sells a single product. The company's sales and expenses for a recent month follow:

	Total	Per Unit
Sales	$600,000	$40
Less variable expenses	420,000	28
Contribution margin	180,000	$12
Less fixed expenses	150,000	
Net income	$ 30,000	

Required

1.   What is the monthly break-even point in units sold and in sales dollars?
2.   Without resorting to computations, what is the total contribution margin at the break-even point?
3.   How many units would have to be sold each month to earn a minimum target net income of $18,000? Use the contribution margin method. Verify your answer by preparing a contribution income statement at the target level of sales.
4.   Refer to the original data. Compute the company's margin of safety in both dollar and percentage terms.
5.   What is the company's CM ratio? If monthly sales increase by $80,000 and there is no change in fixed costs, by how much would you expect monthly net income to increase?

E7–2 Super Sales Company is the exclusive distributor for a new product. The product sells for $60 per unit and has a CM ratio of 40%. The company's fixed expenses are $360,000 per year.

Required

1. What are the variable expenses per unit?
2. Using the equation method:
   a. What is the break-even point in units and in sales dollars?
   b. What sales level in units and in sales dollars is required to earn an annual profit of $90,000?
   c. Assume that through negotiation with the manufacturer the Super Sales Company is able to reduce its variable expenses by $3 per unit. What is the company's new break-even point in units and in sales dollars?
3. Repeat (2) above using the contribution margin method.

E7–3 Chi Omega Sorority is planning its annual Riverboat Extravaganza. The Extravaganza committee has assembled the following expected costs for the event:

Dinner (per person)	$ 7
Favours and program (per person)	3
Band	1,500
Tickets and advertising	700
Riverboat rental	4,800
Floorshow and strolling entertainers	1,000

The committee members would like to charge $30 per person for the evening's activities.

Required

1. Compute the break-even point for the Extravaganza (in terms of the number of persons that must attend).
2. Assume that only 250 persons attended the Extravaganza last year. If the same number attend this year, what price per ticket must be charged to break even?
3. Refer to the original data ($30 ticket price per person). Prepare a CVP graph for the Extravaganza from a zero level of activity up to 800 tickets sold. Number of persons should be placed on the horizontal (X) axis, and dollars should be placed on the vertical (Y) axis. (Note: E7–4 has further requirements for the data in this exercise.)

E7–4 (This exercise is a continuation of E7–3.) Refer to the data in E7–3.

Required

1. Prepare a profitgraph for the Riverboat Extravaganza.
2. The extravaganza committee has just learned that Brute Springstern, a widely regarded alumnus of the university, will make an appearance during the evening. Accordingly, the committee has decided to raise the ticket price to $35 per person. Will this cause the slope of the profit line to be steeper or flatter on the graph? Explain.

E7–5 Superior Door Company manufactures and sells prehung doors to home builders. The doors are sold for $60 each. Variable costs are $42 per door, and fixed costs total $450,000 per year. The company is currently selling 30,000 doors per year.

Required

1. Compute the degree of operating leverage at the present level of sales.
2. Management is confident that the company can sell 37,500 doors next year (an increase of 7,500 doors, or 25%, over current sales). Compute the following:
   a. The expected percentage increase in net income for next year.
   b. The expected total dollar net income for next year.

E7–6 Fill in the missing amounts in each of the eight case situations below. Each case is independent of the others. (Hint: One way to find the missing amounts would be to prepare a contribution income statement for each case, enter the known data, and then compute the missing items.)

a.   Assume that only one product is being sold in each of the four following case situations:

Case	Units Sold	Sales	Variable Expenses	Contribution Margin per Unit	Fixed Expenses	Net Income (Loss)
1	9,000	$270,000	$162,000	$?	$ 90,000	$?
2	?	350,000	?	15	170,000	40,000
3	20,000	?	280,000	6	?	35,000
4	5,000	160,000	?	?	82,000	(12,000)

b.   Assume that more than one product is being sold in each of the four following case situations:

Case	Sales	Variable Expenses	Average Contribution Margin (percent)	Fixed Expenses	Net Income (Loss)
1	$450,000	$?	40	$?	$65,000
2	200,000	130,000	?	60,000	?
3	?	?	80	470,000	90,000
4	300,000	90,000	?	?	(15,000)

E7–7 Porter Company's most recent income statement is shown below:

	Total	Per Unit
Sales (30,000 units)	$150,000	$5
Less variable expenses	90,000	3
Contribution margin	60,000	$2
Less fixed expenses	50,000	
Net income	$10,000	

Required

Prepare a new income statement under each of the following conditions (consider each case independently):

1.   The sales volume increases by 15%.
2.   The selling price decreases by 50 cents per unit, and the sales volume increases by 20%.
3.   The selling price increases by 50 cents per unit, fixed expenses increase by $10,000, and the sales volume decreases by 5%.
4.   Variable expenses increase by 20 cents per unit, the selling price increases by 12%, and the sales volume decreases by 10%.

E7–8 Reveen Products manufactures and sells camping equipment. One of the company's products, a camp lantern, sells for $90 per unit. Variable expenses are $63 per lantern, and fixed expenses associated with the lantern total $135,000 per month.

Required

1.   Compute the company's break-even point in number of lanterns and in total sales dollars.
2.   If the variable expenses per lantern increase as a percentage of the selling price, will it result in a higher or a lower break-even point? Why? (Assume that the fixed expenses remain unchanged.)
3.   At present, the company is selling 8,000 lanterns per month. The sales manager is convinced that a 10% reduction in the selling price will result in a 25% increase in the number of lanterns sold each month. Prepare two contribution income statements, one under present operating conditions, and one as operations would appear after the proposed changes. Show both total and per unit data on your statements.
4.   Refer to the data in (3) above. How many lanterns would have to be sold at the new selling price to yield a minimum net income of $72,000 per month?

E7–9 Okabee Enterprises sells two products, A and B. Monthly sales and the contribution margin ratios for the two products follow:

	Product		
	A	**B**	**Total**
Sales	$700,000	$300,000	$1,000,000
Contribution margin ratio	60%	70%	?

The company's fixed expenses total $598,500 per month.

Required

1. Prepare an income statement for the company as a whole. Use the format shown in Exhibit 7–7.
2. Compute the break-even point for the company based on the current sales mix.

PROBLEMS

P7–10 Basics of CVP Analysis   Stratford Company makes a product that sells for $15 per unit. Variable costs are $6 per unit, and fixed costs total $180,000 annually.

Required

Answer the following independent questions:

1. What is the product's CM ratio?
2. Use the CM ratio to determine the break-even point in sales dollars.
3. The company estimates that sales will increase by $45,000 during the coming year due to increased demand. By how much should net income increase?
4. Assume that the operating results for last year were as follows:

Sales	$360,000
Less variable expenses	144,000
Contribution margin	216,000
Less fixed expenses	180,000
Net income	$ 36,000

   a. Compute the degree of operating leverage at the current level of sales.
   b. The president expects sales to increase by 15% next year. By how much should net income increase?
5. Refer to the original data. Assume that the company sold 28,000 units last year. The sales manager is convinced that a 10% reduction in the selling price, combined with a $70,000 increase in advertising expenditures, would cause annual sales in units to increase by 50%. Prepare two contribution income statements, one showing the results of last year's operations and one showing what the results of operations would be if these changes were made. Would you recommend that the company do as the sales manager suggests?
6. Refer to the original data. Assume again that the company sold 28,000 units last year. The president feels that it would be unwise to change the selling price. Instead, he wants to increase the sales commission by $2 per unit. He thinks that this move, combined with some increase in advertising, would cause annual sales to double. By how much could advertising be increased with profits remaining unchanged? Do not prepare an income statement; use the incremental analysis approach.

P7–11 Basic CVP Analysis, with Graphing   Shirts Unlimited operates a chain of shirt stores around the country. The stores carry many styles of shirts that are all sold at the same price. To encourage sales personnel to be aggressive in their sales efforts, the company pays a substantial sales commission on each shirt sold. Sales personnel also receive a small basic salary.

The following cost and revenue data relate to Store 36 and are typical of one of the company's many outlets:

	Per Shirt
Sales price	$40
Variable expenses:	
Invoice cost	$18
Sales commission	7
Total variable expenses	$25

	Per Year
Fixed expenses:	
Rent	$ 80,000
Advertising	150,000
Salaries	70,000
Total fixed expenses	$300,000

Shirts Unlimited is a fairly new organization. The company has asked you, as a member of its planning group, to assist in some basic analysis of its stores and company policies.

Required

1. Calculate the annual break-even point in dollar sales and in unit sales for Store 36.
2. Prepare a CVP graph showing cost and revenue data for Store 36 from a zero level of activity up to 45,000 shirts sold each year. Clearly indicate the break-even point on the graph.
3. If 19,000 shirts are sold in a year, what would be Store 36's net income or loss?
4. The company is considering paying the store manager of Store 36 an incentive commission of $3 per shirt (in addition to the salespersons' commissions). If this change is made, what will be the new break-even point in dollar sales and in unit sales?
5. Refer to the original data. As an alternative to (4) above, the company is considering paying the store manager a $3 commission on each shirt sold in excess of the break-even point. If this change is made, what will be the store's net income or loss if 23,500 shirts are sold in a year?
6. Refer to the original data. The company is considering eliminating sales commissions entirely in its stores and increasing fixed salaries by $107,000 annually.
   a. If this change is made, what will be the new break-even point in dollar sales and in unit sales in Store 36?
   b. Would you recommend that the change be made? Explain.

P7–12 Basics of CVP Analysis; Cost Structure   Memofax, Inc., produces a single product. Sales have been very erratic, with some months showing a profit and some months showing a loss. The company's income statement for the most recent month is given below:

Sales (13,500 units at $20)	$270,000
Less variable expenses	189,000
Contribution margin	81,000
Less fixed expenses	90,000
Net loss	$ (9,000)

Required

1. Compute the company's CM ratio and its break-even point in both units and dollars.
2. The sales manager feels that an $8,000 increase in the monthly advertising budget, combined with an intensified effort by the sales staff, will result in a $70,000 increase in monthly sales. If the sales manager is right, what will be the effect on the company's monthly net income or loss? (Use the incremental approach in preparing your answer.)
3. The president is convinced that a 10% reduction in the selling price, combined with an increase of $35,000 in the monthly advertising budget, will cause unit sales to double. What will the new income statement look like if these changes are adopted?
4. Refer to the original data. The company's advertising agency thinks that a new package for the company's product would help sales. The new package being proposed would increase packaging costs by $0.60 per unit. Assuming no other changes in cost behaviour, how many units would have to be sold each month to earn a profit of $4,500?

5. Refer to the original data. By automating certain operations, the company could slash its variable expenses in half. However, fixed costs would increase by $118,000 per month.
    a. Compute the new CM ratio and the new break-even point in both units and dollars.
    b. Assume that the company expects to sell 20,000 units next month. Prepare two income statements, one assuming that operations are not automated and one assuming that they are.
    c. Would you recommend that the company automate its operations? Explain.

P7–13 Sales Mix Assumptions; Break-Even Analysis   Marlin Company has been operating for only a few months. The company sells three products—A, B, and C. Budgeted sales by product and in total for the coming month are shown below:

	Product							
	A		**B**		**C**		**Total**	
Percentage of total sales	48%		20%		32%		100%	
Sales	$240,000	100%	$100,000	100%	$160,000	100%	$500,000	100%
Less variable expenses	72,000	30%	80,000	80%	88,000	55%	240,000	48%
Contribution margin	$168,000	70%	$ 20,000	20%	$ 72,000	45%	260,000	52%
Less fixed expenses........							223,600	
Net income							$ 36,400	

$$\text{Break-even sales: } \frac{\text{Fixed expenses, } \$223{,}600}{\text{CM ratio, } 0.52} = \$430{,}000$$

As shown by these data, net income is budgeted at $36,400 for the month, and break-even sales at $430,000.

Assume that actual sales for the month total $500,000 as planned. Actual sales by product are: A, $160,000; B, $200,000; and C, $140,000.

Required

1. Prepare a contribution income statement for the month based on actual sales data. Present the income statement in the format shown above.
2. Compute the break-even sales for the month, based on your actual data.
3. Considering the fact that the company met its $500,000 sales budget for the month, the president is shocked at the results shown on your income statement in (1) above. Prepare a brief memo for the president explaining why both the operating results and break-even sales are different from what was budgeted.

P7–14 The Case of the Deceptive Fixed Costs   The Marbury Stein Shop sells steins from all parts of the world. The owner of the shop, Clint Marbury, is thinking of expanding his operations by hiring local university students, on a commission basis, to sell steins at the local university. The steins will bear the school emblem.

These steins must be ordered from the manufacturer three months in advance, and because of the unique emblem of each university, they cannot be returned. The steins would cost Mr. Marbury $15 each with a minimum order of 200 steins. Any additional steins would have to be ordered in increments of 50.

Since Mr. Marbury's plan would not require any additional facilities, the only costs associated with the project would be the cost of the steins and the cost of the sales commissions. The selling price of the steins would be $30 each. Mr. Marbury would pay the students a commission of $6 for each stein sold.

Required

1. To make the project worthwhile in terms of his own time, Mr. Marbury would require a $7,200 profit for the first six months of the venture. What level of sales in units and dollars would be required to meet this target net income figure? Show all computations.
2. Assume that the venture is undertaken and an order is placed for 200 steins. What would be Mr. Marbury's break-even point in units and in sales dollars? Show computations, and explain the reasoning behind your answer.

P7–15 Sales Mix; Break-Even Analysis; Margin of Safety   Puleva Milenario SA, a company located in Toledo, Spain, manufactures and sells two models of luxuriously finished cutlery—Alvaro and Bazan. Present revenue, cost, and sales data on the two products appear below. All currency amounts are stated in terms of Spanish pesetas (e.g., 400 ptas represents 400 Spanish pesetas).

	Alvaro	Bazan
Selling price per unit	400 ptas	600 ptas
Variable expenses per unit	240 ptas	120 ptas
Number of units sold monthly	200 units	80 units

Fixed expenses are 66,000 ptas per month.

Required

1. Assuming the sales mix above, do the following:
   a. Prepare a contribution income statement showing both Peseta and Percent columns for each product and for the company as a whole.
   b. Compute the break-even point in pesetas for the company as a whole and the margin of safety in both pesetas and percent of sales.
2. The company has developed another product, Cano, that the company plans to sell for 800 ptas each. At this price, the company expects to sell 40 units per month of the product. The variable expenses would be 600 ptas per unit. The company's fixed expenses would not change.
   a. Prepare another contribution income statement, including the Cano product (sales of the other two products would not change).
   b. Compute the company's new break-even point in pesetas for the company as a whole and the new margin of safety in both pesetas and percent of sales.
3. The president of the company was puzzled by your analysis. He did not understand why the break-even point has gone up even though there has been no increase in fixed costs and the addition of the new product has increased the total contribution margin. Explain to the president what has happened.

P7–16 Interpretive Questions on the CVP Graph   A CVP graph, as illustrated below, is a useful technique for showing relationships among costs, volume, and profits in an organization.

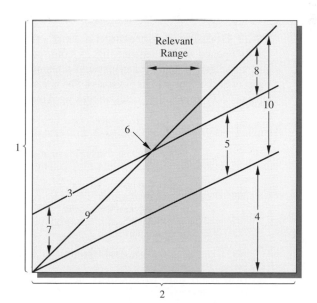

Required

1. Identify the numbered components in the CVP graph.
2. State the effect of each of the following actions on line 3, line 9, and the break-even point. For line 3 and line 9, state whether the action will cause the line to:

> Remain unchanged.
> Shift upward.
> Shift downward.
> Have a steeper slope (i.e., rotate upward).
> Have a flatter slope (i.e., rotate downward).
> Shift upward *and* have a steeper slope.
> Shift upward *and* have a flatter slope.
> Shift downward *and* have a steeper slope.
> Shift downward *and* have a flatter slope.

In the case of the break-even point, state whether the action will cause the break-even point to:

> Remain unchanged.
> Increase.
> Decrease.
> Probably change, but the direction is uncertain.

Treat each case independently

x. *Example.* Fixed costs are increased by $20,000 each period.
    Answer (see choices above): Line 3: Shift upward.
    Line 9: Remain unchanged.
    Break-even point: Increase.

a. The unit selling price is decreased from $30 to $27.
b. The per unit variable costs are increased from $12 to $15.
c. The total fixed costs are reduced by $40,000.
d. Five thousand fewer units are sold during the period than were budgeted.
e. Due to purchasing a robot to perform a task that was previously done by workers, fixed costs are increased by $25,000 per period, and variable costs are reduced by $8 per unit.
f. As a result of a decrease in the cost of materials, both unit variable costs and the selling price are decreased by $3.
g. Advertising costs are increased by $50,000 per period, resulting in a 10% increase in the number of units sold.
h. Due to paying salespersons a commission rather than a flat salary, fixed costs are reduced by $21,000 per period, and unit variable costs are increased by $6.

P7–17 Graphing; Incremental Analysis; Operating Leverage   Teri Hall has recently opened Sheer Elegance, Inc., a store specializing in fashionable stockings. Ms. Hall has just completed a course in managerial accounting, and she believes that she can apply certain aspects of the course to her business. She is particularly interested in adopting the cost-volume-profit (CVP) approach to decision making. Thus, she has prepared the following analysis:

Sales price per pair of stockings	$2.00
Variable expense per pair of stockings	0.80
Contribution margin per pair of stockings	$1.20

Fixed expenses per year:

Building rental	$12,000
Equipment depreciation	3,000
Selling	30,000
Administrative	15,000
Total fixed expenses	$60,000

Required

1. How many pairs of stockings must be sold to break even? What does this represent in total dollar sales?
2. Prepare a CVP graph for the store from a zero level of activity up to 90,000 pairs of stockings sold each year. Indicate the break-even point on the graph.

3. How many pairs of stockings must be sold to earn a $9,000 target net income for the first year?

4. Ms. Hall now has one full-time and one part-time salesperson working in the store. It will cost her an additional $8,000 per year to convert the part-time position to a full-time position. Ms. Hall believes that the change would bring in an additional $20,000 in sales each year. Should she convert the position? Use the incremental approach (do not prepare an income statement).

5. Refer to the original data. Actual operating results for the first year are as follows:

Sales	$125,000
Less variable expenses	50,000
Contribution margin	75,000
Less fixed expenses	60,000
Net income	$ 15,000

a. What is the store's degree of operating leverage?

b. Ms. Hall is confident that with some effort she can increase sales by 20% next year. What would be the expected percentage increase in net income? Use the operating leverage concept to compute your answer.

P7–18 Various CVP Questions: Break-Even Point; Cost Structure; Target Sales   Tyrene Products manufactures recreational equipment. One of the company's products, a skateboard, sells for $37.50. The skateboards are manufactured in an antiquated plant that relies heavily on direct labour workers. Thus, variable costs are high, totalling $22.50 per skateboard.

Over the past year the company sold 40,000 skateboards, with the following operating results:

Sales (40,000 skateboards)	$1,500,000
Less variable expenses	900,000
Contribution margin	600,000
Less fixed expenses	480,000
Net income	$ 120,000

Management is anxious to maintain and perhaps even improve its present level of income from the skateboards.

Required

1. Compute (a) the CM ratio and the break-even point in skateboards, and (b) the degree of operating leverage at last year's level of sales.

2. Due to an increase in labour rates, the company estimates that variable costs will increase by $3 per skateboard next year. If this change takes place and the selling price per skateboard remains constant at $37.50, what will be the new CM ratio and the new break-even point in skateboards?

3. Refer to the data in (2) above. If the expected change in variable costs takes place, how many skateboards will have to be sold next year to earn the same net income ($120,000) as last year?

4. Refer again to the data in (2) above. The president has decided that the company may have to raise the selling price on the skateboards. If Tyrene Products wants to maintain *the same CM ratio as last year,* what selling price per skateboard must it charge next year to cover the increased labour costs?

5. Refer to the original data. The company is considering the construction of a new, automated plant to manufacture the skateboards. The new plant would slash variable costs by 40%, but it would cause fixed costs to increase by 90%. If the new plant is built, what would be the company's new CM ratio and new break-even point in skateboards?

6. Refer to the data in (5) above.
   a. If the new plant is built, how many skateboards will have to be sold next year to earn the same net income ($120,000) as last year?

b. Assume that the new plant is constructed and that next year the company manufactures and sells 40,000 skateboards (the same number as sold last year). Prepare a contribution income statement, and compute the degree of operating leverage.

c. Explain why the operating leverage figure you have just computed is so much higher than the operating leverage figure computed in (1) above. Given the data in (1)–(6), if you were a member of top management, would you have voted in favour of constructing the new plant? Explain.

P7–19 Sales Mix; Break-Even Analysis   Topper Sports, Inc., produces high-quality sports equipment. The company's Racket Division manufactures three tennis rackets—the Standard, the Deluxe, and the Pro—that are widely used in amateur play. Selected information on the rackets is given below:

	Standard	Deluxe	Pro
Selling price per racket	$40.00	$60.00	$90.00
Variable expenses per racket:			
Production	22.00	27.00	31.50
Selling (5% of selling price)	2.00	3.00	4.50

All sales are made through the company's own retail outlets. The Racket Division has the following fixed costs:

	Per Month
Fixed production costs	$120,000
Advertising expense	100,000
Administrative salaries	50,000
Total.	$270,000

Sales, in units, over the past two months have been as follows:

	Standard	Deluxe	Pro	Total
April	2,000	1,000	5,000	8,000
May.	8,000	1,000	3,000	12,000

Required

1. Using the contribution approach, prepare an income statement for April and an income statement for May, with the following headings:

Standard		Deluxe		Pro		Total	
Amount	Percent	Amount	Percent	Amount	Percent	Amount	Percent

Sales . . .
Etc. . . . .

Place the fixed expenses only in the Total column. Carry percentage computations to one decimal place. Do not show percentages for the fixed expenses.

2. Upon seeing the income statements in (1) above, the president stated, "I can't believe this! We sold 50% more rackets in May than in April, yet profits went down. It's obvious that costs are out of control in that division." What other explanation can you give for the drop in net income?

3. Compute the Racket Division's break-even point in dollars for April.

4. Has May's break-even point in dollars gone up or down from April's break-even point? Explain without computing a break-even point for May.

5. Assume that sales of the Standard racket increase by $20,000. What would be the effect on net income? What would be the effect if Pro racket sales increased by $20,000? Do not prepare income statements; use the incremental analysis approach in determining your answer.

P7–20 Sensitivity Analysis of Net Income; Changes in Volume   Detmer Holdings AG of Zurich, Switzerland, has just introduced a new fashion watch for which the company is trying to find an optimal selling price. Marketing studies suggest that the company can increase sales by 5,000 units for each SFr2 per unit reduction in the selling price. (SFr2 denotes

2 Swiss francs.) The company's present selling price is SFr90 per unit, and variable expenses are SFr60 per unit. Fixed expenses are SFr840,000 per year. The present annual sales volume (at the SFr90 selling price) is 25,000 units.

Required

1. What is the present yearly net income or loss?
2. What is the present break-even point in units and in Swiss franc sales?
3. Assuming that the marketing studies are correct, what is the maximum profit that the company can earn yearly? At how many units and at what selling price per unit would the company generate this profit?
4. What would be the break-even point in units and in Swiss franc sales using the selling price you determined in (3) above (e.g., the selling price at the level of maximum profits)? Why is this break-even point different from the break-even point you computed in (1) above?

P7–21 Changing Levels of Fixed and Variable Costs   Novelties, Inc., produces and sells highly faddish products directed toward the preteen market. A new product has come onto the market that the company is anxious to produce and sell. Enough capacity exists in the company's plant to produce 30,000 units each month. Variable costs to manufacture and sell one unit would be $1.60, and fixed costs would total $40,000 per month.

The marketing department predicts that demand for the product will exceed the 30,000 units that the company is able to produce. Additional production capacity can be rented from another company at a fixed cost of $2,000 per month. Variable costs in the rented facility would total $1.75 per unit, due to somewhat less efficient operations than in the main plant. The product would sell for $2.50 per unit.

Required

1. Compute the monthly break-even point for the new product in units and in total dollar sales. Show all computations in good form.
2. How many units must be sold each month to make a monthly profit of $9,000?
3. If the sales manager receives a bonus of 15 cents for each unit sold in excess of the break-even point, how many units must be sold each month to earn a return of 25% on the monthly investment in fixed costs?

P7–22 Changes in Cost Structure   Frieden Company's income statement for the most recent month is given below:

Sales (40,000 units)	$800,000
Less variable expenses.	560,000
Contribution margin.	240,000
Less fixed expenses	192,000
Net income.	$ 48,000

The industry in which Frieden Company operates is quite sensitive to cyclical movements in the economy. Thus, profits vary considerably from year to year according to general economic conditions. The company has a large amount of unused capacity and is studying ways of improving profits.

Required

1. New equipment has come on the market that would allow Frieden company to automate a portion of its operations. Variable costs would be reduced by $6 per unit. However, fixed costs would increase to a total of $432,000 each month. Prepare two contribution-type income statements, one showing present operations and one showing how operations would appear if the new equipment is purchased. Show an Amount column, a Per Unit column, and a Percent column on each statement. Do not show percentages for the fixed costs.
2. Refer to the income statements in (1) above. For both present operations and the proposed new operations, compute (a) the degree of operating leverage, (b) the break-even point in dollars, and (c) the margin of safety in both dollar and percentage terms.
3. Refer again to the data in (1) above. As a manager, what factor would be paramount in your mind in deciding whether to purchase the new equipment? (You may assume that ample funds are available to make the purchase.)

4. Refer to the original data. Rather than purchase new equipment, the president is thinking about changing the company's marketing method. Under the new method, the president estimates that sales would increase by 50% each month and that net income would increase by two-thirds. Fixed costs would be slashed to only $160,000 per month. Using the president's estimates, compute the break-even point in dollars for the company after the change in marketing method. What risks can you see in the president's proposal?

P7–23 Missing Data; Integration of CVP Factors   After being fired for padding his travel expense reports, a disgruntled employee of Putrex Company hacked into the company's computer system and proceeded to alter or destroy several important files. Among the files was a report containing an analysis of one of the company's products that you had just completed and sent via e-mail to your supervisor. This report is needed for a meeting of the company's planning committee later in the day. The report contained the following *projected* income statement for next month on the product (the question marks indicate obliterated data):

PUTREX COMPANY
Projected Income Statement
For the Month Ended August 31

	Total	Per Unit	Percent
Sales (90,000 units)	$?	$?	?
Less variable expenses	?	?	?
Contribution margin	?	$?	?
Less fixed expenses	?		
Net income	$243,000		

The report also contained results of actual sales and expenses for the product for the month just completed, as well as certain analytical data that you had prepared. These data are given below:

PUTREX COMPANY
Actual Income Statement
For the Month Ended July 31

	Total	Per Unit	Percent
Sales (? units)	$?	$?	100
Less variable expenses	?	?	?
Contribution margin	?	$?	?
Less fixed expenses.	?		
Net income	$?		

Degree of operating leverage	?
Break-even point:	
In units	? units
In dollars	$1,012,500
Margin of safety:	
In dollars	$?
In percentage	25%

The supervisor has just requested that you "work up" the missing information and have the completed report back within the hour. You are spurred on by the realization that the fired employee's position will need to be filled quickly, and a sterling effort on your part could make you a leading candidate for the job.

You recall from your prior work on the report that the net income for July on the product was $135,000. You also remember that sales for August are projected to be 20% higher than July's sales. Finally, you remember that your supervisor likes to use the degree of operating leverage as a predictive tool.

Total fixed expenses, the unit selling price, and the unit variable expenses are planned to be the same in August as they were in July.

Required

1. For the July actual data, do the following:
   a. Complete the July income statement (all three columns).
   b. Compute the break-even point in units, and verify the break-even point in dollars. Use the contribution margin method.
   c. Compute the margin of safety in dollars, and verify the margin of safety percentage.
   d. Compute the degree of operating leverage as of July 31.
2. For the August data, do the following:
   a. Complete the August projected income statement (all three columns).
   b. Compute the margin of safety in dollars and percent, and compute the degree of operating leverage. Why has the margin of safety gone up and the degree of operating leverage gone down?
3. Excited over the fact that you were able to complete (1) and (2) above so quickly, you decide to "lock up" the new job by providing your supervisor with some valuable additional information. You have just learned from the purchasing agent that the cost of direct materials may increase by $0.90 per unit next year. Assuming that this cost increase takes place and that selling price and other cost factors remain unchanged, how many units will the company have to sell in a month to earn a net income equal to 15% of sales?

P7–24 Break-Even Analysis and Sensitivity   Prince Company produces a single product. It sold 25,000 units last year with the following results.

Sales		$625,000
Variable costs	$375,000	
Fixed costs.	150,000	525,000
Net income before taxes		100,000
Income taxes (45%)		45,000
Net income		$ 55,000

In an attempt to improve its product in the coming year, Prince is considering replacing a component in its product that has a cost of $2.50, with a new and better part costing $4.50 per unit. A new machine will also be needed to increase plant capacity. The machine would cost $18,000 with a useful life of six years and no salvage value. The company uses straight-line depreciation on all plant assets for both financial statements and tax purposes.

Required

1. What was Prince Company's break-even point in number of units last year?
2. How many units of product would Prince Company have had to sell in the last year to earn $77,000 in net income after taxes?
3. If Prince Company holds the sales price constant and makes the suggested changes, how many units of product must be sold in the coming year to break even?
4. If Prince Company holds the sales price constant and makes the suggested changes, how many units of product will the company have to sell to make the same net income after taxes as last year?
5. If Prince Company wishes to maintain the same contribution margin ratio after implementing the changes, what selling price per unit of product must it charge next year to cover the increased material costs?

(CGA-Canada, adapted)

P7–25 CVP under Uncertainty   (Appendix 7A)   The marketing manager for Forestem Inc. wants to decide which of two market strategies to adopt in marketing a new product. He has assessed three levels of potential buyers: a small, moderate, or large number. The problem is to decide which strategy to choose based on estimates of profits associated with the two strategies for each level of potential buyers. The payoffs in net profits and the probabilities for the three levels are:

Number of Potential Buyers	Probability	Profits for Marketing Strategy ($000)	
		A	B
Small	0.3	$ 50	$ 10
Moderate	0.5	100	75
Large	0.2	400	250

Required

1. Construct the decision tree for this problem.
2. Calculate the expected profits for the two strategies. What decision should the marketing manager take?

(CGA-Canada, adapted)

P7–26 CVP under Uncertainty (Appendix 7A)   A firm producing stereo amplifiers can manufacture a subassembly or purchase it from another company. Anticipated profits for each alternative, make or buy, and for three levels of demand for the stereo amplifier, are given in the following table:

Demand	Probability of Demand	Profits ($000)	
		Make	Buy
High	0.40	$50.0	$35.0
Medium	0.30	30.0	30.0
Low	0.30	–10.0	5.0

Required

1. Draw and label the decision tree for this problem.
2. Which action—make or buy—should the firm take to maximize profits?

(CGA-Canada, adapted)

P7–27 CVP, Uncertainty, and Bidding (Appendix 7A)   The city has just announced plans to build a library and arts centre complex. To encourage development of creative design concepts, the city has indicated its intention to hold a design competition. The best entry will win the architectural contract which will generate a revenue of $200,000 before the design costs.

A local firm of architects is considering submitting a proposal. They know that a well-thought-out design would greatly enhance their chance of winning. However, such a design is costly. On the other hand, a less costly design proposal has a limited chance of winning.

The architectural firm has two proposals under consideration. Each proposal has the following cost and probabilities associated with it:

	Cost of Design Proposal	Probability of Winning Contract
Proposal A	$60,000	.50
Proposal B	$20,000	.30

Design costs are assumed to be incurred at the beginning of the current year. Income taxes are 40 percent.

Required

Which proposal would you recommend the architectural firm submit to the design competition? Show all calculations.

(SMAC, adapted)

P7–28 CVP under Uncertainty (Appendix 7A)   Far East Inc. is a manufacturer of several clothing lines based on Oriental motifs. Aggressive advertising and sales campaigns have resulted in rapid growth up to existing capacity and the owner, Patrick Cheng, is now considering the purchase of additional production equipment to start up a new dress line.

Cheng's purchasing manager has selected a machine with the following characteristics:

Initial cost per machine	$100,000
Estimated salvage in 5 years	$ 5,000
Capacity per year	500 units
Capital cost allowance, class 8	20%

In an effort to improve its own sagging fortunes, the company selling the machine has offered to sell Cheng a second or any subsequent machine required at a 20 percent discount from the normal single unit cost.

Market research has indicated that annual demand for the new dress line can be established and stabilized at a static figure for a period of five years.

The production manager has estimated that the manufacturing cost for the new dress will be as follows:

Direct materials:	$35 per unit
Direct labour:	6 hours at $5 per hour
Variable overhead:	20 percent of direct labour cost

Required

1. The sales manager had estimated the probability distribution for annual demand based on a price of $165 as follows:

Demand Level	Probability
800	.20
1,000	.30
1,200	.40
1,400	.10

Determine the expected contribution before taxes.

2. Not satisfied with the uncertainty of this distribution, the sales manager hired an industrial specialist who has prior information regarding the fashion market. Using his prior information, the specialist predicted the following table of conditional probabilities:

Demand Level	Conditional Probabilities
800	.1250
1,000	.1875
1,200	.2500
1,400	.4375

Determine the expected contribution after receipt of this new information.

(SMAC, adapted)

CASES

C7–29 Cost Structure; Break-Even Point; Target Profits Marston Corporation manufactures disposable thermometers that are sold to hospitals through a network of independent sales agents located in the United States and Canada. These sales agents sell a variety of products to hospitals in addition to Marston's disposable thermometer. The sales agents are currently paid an 18% commission on sales, and this commission rate was used when Marston's management prepared the following budgeted income statement for the upcoming year.

MARSTON CORPORATION
Budgeted Income Statement

Sales.		$30,000,000
Cost of goods sold:		
Variable	$17,400,000	
Fixed	2,800,000	20,200,000
Gross profit		9,800,000
Selling and administrative expenses:		
Commissions.	5,400,000	
Fixed advertising expense	800,000	
Fixed administrative expense	3,200,000	9,400,000
Net income.		$ 400,000

Since the completion of the above statement, Marston's management has learned that the independent sales agents are demanding an increase in the commission rate to 20% of sales for the upcoming year. This would be the third increase in commissions demanded by the independent sales agents in five years. As a result, Marston's management has decided to investigate the possibility of hiring its own sales staff to replace the independent sales agents.

Marston's controller estimates that the company will have to hire eight salespeople to cover the current market area, and the total annual payroll cost of these employees will be about $700,000, including fringe benefits. The salespeople will also be paid commissions of 10% of sales. Travel and entertainment expenses are expected to total about $400,000 for the year. The company will also have to hire a sales manager and support staff whose salaries and fringe benefits will come to $200,000 per year. To make up for the promotions that the independent sales agents had been running on behalf of Marston, management believes that the company's budget for fixed advertising expenses should be increased by $500,000.

Required

1. Assuming sales of $30,000,000, construct a budgeted contribution format income statement for the upcoming year for each of the following alternatives:
   a. The independent sales agents' commission rate remains unchanged at 18%.
   b. The independent sales agents' commission rate increases to 20%.
   c. The company employs its own sales force.
2. Calculate Marston Corporation's break-even point in sales dollars for the upcoming year assuming the following:
   a. The independent sales agents' commission rate remains unchanged at 18%.
   b. The independent sales agents' commission rate increases to 20%.
   c. The company employs its own sales force.
3. Refer to your answer to (1)(b) above. If the company employs its own sales force, what volume of sales would be necessary to generate the net income the company would realize if sales are $30,000,000 and the company continues to sell through agents (at a 20% commission rate).
4. Determine the volume of sales at which net income would be equal regardless of whether Marston Corporation sells through agents (at a 20% commission rate) or employs its own sales force.
5. Prepare a profitgraph on which you plot the profit lines for both of the following alternatives:
   a. The independent sales agents' commission rate increases to 20%.
   b. The company employs its own sales force.
   On the profitgraph, use total sales revenue as the measure of activity.
6. Write a memo to the president of Marston Corporation in which you make a recommendation as to whether the company should continue to use independent sales agents (at a 20% commission rate) or employ its own sales force. Fully explain the reasons for your recommendation in the memo.

(CMA, adapted)

C7–30 Detailed Income Statement; CVP Analysis   Alpine, Inc., has been experiencing losses for some time, as shown by its most recent income statement.

All variable expenses in the company vary in terms of units sold, except for sales commissions, which are based on sales dollars. Variable manufacturing overhead is 50 cents per unit. There were no beginning or ending inventories. The company's plant has a capacity of 70,000 units.

Management is particularly disappointed with 1996's operating results. Several possible courses of action are being studied to determine what should be done to make 1997 profitable.

Required

1. Redo Alpine, Inc.'s 1996 income statement in the contribution format. Show both a Total column and a Per Unit column on your statement. Leave enough space to the right of your numbers to enter the solution to both parts of (2) below.
2. In an effort to make 1997 profitable, the president is considering two proposals prepared by members of her staff:

ALPINE, INC.
Income Statement
For the Year Ended June 30, 1996

Sales (40,000 units at $12).		$480,000
Less cost of goods sold:		
Direct materials	$120,000	
Direct labour	65,600	
Manufacturing overhead	90,000	275,600
Gross margin		204,400
Less operating expenses:		
Selling expenses:		
Variable:		
Sales commission.	$38,400	
Shipping.	14,000	52,400
Fixed (advertising, salaries).	110,000	
Administrative expenses:		
Variable (billing, other)	3,200	
Fixed (salaries, other).	85,000	250,600
Net loss.		$ (46,200)

a. The sales manager would like to reduce the unit selling price by 25%. He is certain that this would fill the plant to capacity.

b. The executive vice president would like to increase the unit selling price by 25%, increase the sales commissions to 12% of sales, and increase advertising by $90,000. Based on experience in another company, he is confident this would trigger a 50% increase in unit sales.

Prepare two contribution income statements, one showing what profits would be under the sales manager's proposal and one showing what profits would be under the vice president's proposal. On each statement, include both Total and Per Unit columns (do not show per unit data for the fixed costs).

3. Refer to the original data. The president thinks it would be unwise to change the selling price. Instead, she wants to use less costly materials in manufacturing units of product, thereby reducing costs by $1.73 per unit. How many units would have to be sold during 1997 to earn a target profit of $59,000 for the year?

4. Refer to the original data. Alpine, Inc.'s advertising agency thinks that the problem lies in inadequate promotion. By how much can advertising be increased and still allow the company to earn a target return of 4.5% on sales of 60,000 units?

5. Refer to the original data. The company has been approached by an overseas distributor who wants to purchase 15,000 units on a special price basis. There would be no sales commission on these units. However, shipping costs would be increased by 80%, and variable administrative costs would be reduced by 50%. Alpine, Inc., would have to pay a foreign import duty of $3,150 on behalf of the overseas distributor in order to get the goods into the country. Given these data, what unit price would have to be quoted on the 15,000 units by Alpine, Inc., to allow the company to earn a profit of $18,000 on total operations? Regular business would not be disturbed by this special order.

C7–31 **CVP and Regression** T Manufacturing Ltd. produces several products and sells them directly to consumers under its own T brand name. One product, Troys, is sold at $16 per unit. Although the company has operated at a profitable level for the past several years, a decline in sales activity in 19x0 has resulted in the company experiencing its first operating loss. During 19x0, sales of Troys averaged 4,000 units per month, which represents one-third of the firm's normal productive capacity for this product.

Sam K, the president, received an offer from a chain store for 5,000 Troys per month beginning in January and ending in December 19x1. The units would carry the chain label and would be packed and shipped at the chain's expense. The chain offered $6.80 per unit on the basis of a one-year contract. The management of the company anticipates an upturn in their consumer sales beginning in 19x2 but forecast 19x1 sales at 4,000 units per month. They do not believe the chain store offer would replace the existing volume of sales, nor would the offer increase selling or administrative expenses. If the offer is acceptable, T Manufacturing Ltd. would only enter into such an arrangement for the one-year period.

Sam K called his managers together to discuss the offer. The comptroller presented the following 19x0 budgeted figures on manufacturing, selling, and administrative expenses for Troys at two production levels, 4,000 and 8,000 units, per month. The comptroller stated that the budgeted figures were based on the existing cost structure and, apart from the need for a second supervisor at the 6,000 unit level, there would not be any incremental fixed costs in moving from 4,000 units to capacity of 12,000 units per month, and the marginal manufacturing cost per unit would be the same per unit production above the 8,000 units production level as for units in the 4,000 to 8,000 production range. The production manager noted that minor design modifications for this order would involve $20,000 for special tooling. His review of 19x0 cost data indicated that irrespective of acceptance of the proposed contract there would not be any cost change for 19x1, with the exception of a direct labour increase of 10%, an increase in property taxes of 15%, and a decrease in direct material costs of 4% over or under 19x0 budgeted levels.

K has another problem he would like resolved. In developing the budget for 19x1, he would like an estimate of the costs involved to ship another product, Retros, which the company manufactures. K has not had any training in statistics but understands that quantitative techniques can be used to help management to predict and control costs.

T MANUFACTURING LTD.
Comparative 19x0 Budgeted Monthly Costs for Troys

Monthly Production	4,000 units	8,000 units
Manufacturing costs:		
Direct labour	$ 6,800	$13,600
Salary—supervisors	750	1,500
Power	400	700
Direct materials	12,000	24,000
Depreciation of building	1,916	1,916
Maintenance	1,050	2,450
Property taxes	1,530	1,530
Heat and light	2,365	3,465
Depreciation of equipment	3,460	3,460
Indirect labour	3,116	4,816
Miscellaneous supplies	700	1,200
Employee benefits	310	590
Total manufacturing costs	$34,397	$59,227
Per unit	$8.60	$7.40
Selling expenses:		
Manager's salary	$ 1,250	$ 1,500
Salespeople's compensation	5,650	12,740
Travel	740	830
Advertising	980	1,600
Clerical salaries	400	400
Packing and shipping	2,300	3,200
Miscellaneous	1,650	2,280
Total selling expenses	$12,970	$22,550
Per unit	$3.24	$2.82
Administrative and general expenses:		
Officers' salaries	$ 4,530	$ 4,530
Office salaries	1,980	1,980
Telephone	1,300	1,400
Supplies	480	625
Bad debts	625	865
Miscellaneous	415	760
Total administrative and general expenses	$ 9,330	$10,160
Per unit		

Required

1. What effect would acceptance of the offer from the chain store have on income before income taxes of T Manufacturing Ltd. for the year 19x1? Submit the necessary calculations and schedules to support your conclusion.
2. Explain what regression analysis is and how K might use it to forecast the 19x1 shipping costs for Retros.

(CICA, adapted)

C7–32 CVP under Uncertainty (Appendix 7A) Brunswick Limited (BL) is a manufacturer of small household appliances. The company has only one manufacturing facility which services all of Canada. BL is well established and sells its products directly to department stores.

BL wishes to begin manufacturing and marketing its newly developed cordless steam iron. In order to evaluate properly the performance of this new product, management has decided to create a new division for its production and distribution.

Two of BL's competitors have recently introduced their own brands of cordless steam irons at a price of $28 each. BL's usual pricing strategy for new products is full absorption cost plus a 100% markup. For the new iron, at a production and sales volume of 350,000 units per year, this strategy would imply a price of $31.50. BL's president, Mr. T. C. Edward, is not sure whether this pricing strategy would be appropriate for the new iron and is considering other proposals as follows:

a. Variable product cost plus a 200% markup.
b. A price of $27 to undercut the competition.

Mr. Edward has hired a market research firm to study the likely demand for BL's cordless steam iron at the three proposed prices. The research firm conducted an extensive market test resulting in projected annual sales volumes over the next five years at these prices. These sales projections are summarized in Exhibit 7–12. The research firm, however, made it clear that there were no guarantees that the market would respond according to the projections.

Mr. Edward was not happy with the probabilities that the market research firm assigned to the various price/volume levels. He therefore used his own knowledge and past experience to assign different probabilities (see Exhibit 7–13). Mr. Edward then called on Joan Help, the chief financial officer, to analyze the situation and recommend a five-year pricing strategy for the new cordless steam iron. As a first step, Joan assembled some relevant data which are presented in Exhibit 7–14.

Required

As Joan Help, comply with Mr. Edward's request. Include in your analysis consideration of both quantitative and qualitative factors in determining a five-year pricing strategy for the new iron.

(SMAC, adapted)

EXHIBIT 7-12

Market Research Data for BL's Cordless Steam Iron

Selling Price	Volume	Probability
$24.00	500,000	20%
	400,000	50
	300,000	30
27.00	400,000	25
	350,000	45
	250,000	30
31.50	300,000	30
	250,000	50
	200,000	20

EXHIBIT 7-13

President's
Probability Data for
BL's Cordless Steam
Iron

Selling Price	Volume	Probability
$24.00	500,000	10%
	400,000	50
	300,000	40
27.00	400,000	20
	350,000	40
	250,000	40
31.50	300,000	40
	250,000	50
	200,000	10

EXHIBIT 7-14

Other Relevant Data
for BL's Cordless
Steam Iron

Expected Costs Based on Annual Production of 350,000 Units

Total variable costs	$2,800,000
Total fixed overhead	$2,712,500

Plant and Equipment

No additional machinery or plant space will be required to produce the cordless steam iron. The plant has capacity available to produce 500,000 units per year.

Inventory Levels

Just-in-time inventory management will result in virtually no inventory being stored at any particular time.

GROUP EXERCISES

GE7–33 When Will All This Bad News Stop?   Let's start with the premise that you have to be a low-cost producer to be successful over the long term. Almost without exception, daily news releases continue to bring announcements of yet another sale of a division, plant closing, or elimination of an unprofitable product line. The hourly and salaried workforce has shrunk dramatically—in some cases by as much as 40%. There have been bitter fights with unions to gain wage concessions and slow down the rate of future wage and benefit increases. Firms have adopted Japanese lean inventory management techniques and become more effective at collecting receivables on time. It used to be that firms resorted to such measures only during recessions. But companies continue to impose fiscal discipline even as earnings surge.

Required

1. Many industries have undergone major restructurings in the past decade. Can you identify some of the more notable restructurings? Why do you think firms in these industries needed to restructure?
2. What impact has this had on the cost-volume-profit structure of these firms? Explain.
3. What effect has this had on the operating leverage of firms? Explain this in terms of changes in demand, earnings growth, and earnings decline.
4. What are the risks of excessive cost cutting?
5. While many firms have been successful in cutting their operating leverage, they are now adding to their short-term debt to cover the cost of restocking inventories to meet rising demand and adding to their long-term debt to bring out new products or expand into new markets. What implications does this increasing financial leverage have for firms?

GE7–34 Cost Structure of Airlines   The cost structure of the airline industry can serve as the basis for a discussion of a number of different cost concepts. Airlines also provide an excellent illustration of the concept of operating leverage, the sensitivity of a firm's operating profits to changes in demand, and the opportunities and risks presented by such a cost structure. Airline profits and stock prices are among some of the most volatile on the stock exchanges. A recent study of the U.S. airline industry disclosed the following operating cost categories and their percentage of total operating cost:[8]

Uniform System of Accounts Required by the Department of Transportation	Mean Percentage of Operating Cost, 1981–85
Fuel and oil	24.27%
Flying operations labour (flight crews—pilots, copilots, navigators, and flight engineers)	8.57
Passenger service labour (flight attendants)	4.60
Aircraft traffic and servicing labour (personnel servicing aircraft and handling passengers at gates, baggage, and cargo)	8.86
Promotions and sales labour (reservations and sales agents, advertising and publicity)	9.03
Maintenance labour (maintenance of flight equipment and ground property and equipment)	6.95
Maintenance materials and overhead	2.06
Ground property and equipment (landing fees, and rental expenses and depreciation for ground property and equipment)	12.52
Flight equipment (rental expenses and depreciation on aircraft frames and engines)	8.42
General overhead (administrative personnel, utilities, insurance, communications, etc.)	14.62
Total	100.00%

Required

1. What should be the objectives of airline cost accounting systems?
2. Before a flight is scheduled, what are the variable and fixed costs and their percentages?
3. Before a flight is scheduled, what are the direct and indirect costs and their percentages?
4. Once a flight is scheduled, what are the variable and fixed costs and their percentages?
5. Once a flight is scheduled, what are the direct and indirect costs and their percentages?
6. How is knowledge of variable and fixed costs useful? How is knowledge of direct and indirect costs useful?
7. Once a flight is scheduled, what is the cost of carrying extra passengers?
8. Why are profits more sensitive (more variable) to changes in demand when the cost structure contains a high proportion of fixed costs?

GE7–35 Vertical Integration   It used to be accepted practice that a high level of vertical integration was the better way to do business. Vertical integration is the combination of two or more stages of production that are usually separate. In automobile manufacturing, there are three distinct steps: component manufacturing, subassembly, and assembly. As of the early eighties, it was estimated that GM was by far the most vertically integrated of the Big Three. At that time, GM made 80%–85% of its parts. Today, however, through a process known as deintegration, GM has cut that percentage to 47%, while Ford and Chrysler make just 38% and 34% of their components, respectively. For 1994, Chrysler was the low-cost producer and made the highest profit per vehicle in the industry. Toyota never was very vertically integrated and still makes only 25% of its parts.

The problem for GM and firms in other industries, where vertical integration has been a major source of competitive advantage, is to strike the right balance between investing in vertical integration and encouraging suppliers to invest in the necessary engineering and technology to make components.

---

[8]R. D. Banker and H. H. Johnson, "An Empirical Study of Cost Drivers in the U.S. Airline Industry," *The Accounting Review* (July 1993), pp. 576–601.

Required

1. Vertical integration has only recently fallen into disfavour, so there must have been clear advantages to committing resources to vertically integrate. What are the benefits of vertical integration?
2. At least in the auto industry, the dynamics of the business apparently dictate that deintegration (greater dependence on suppliers) is the wave of the (foreseeable) future. What are the disadvantages of vertical integration?
3. How would the deintegration of GM affect its cost-volume-profit structure, break-even point, operating leverage, and operating risk?

It might prove helpful to read T. Kumpe and P. T. Bolwijn, "Manufacturing: The New Case for Vertical Integration," *Harvard Business Review* (March–April 1988), pp. 75–81.

GE7–36 Is the Past Prologue?   The "baby bust" of the 1960s and early 1970s resulted in the number of university-age 18- and 19-year-olds contrasting sharply from 1980 to 1993. The number of graduating high school seniors peaked in 1979 and declined to a low of 6.9 million in 1992, a drop of nearly 40%. Throughout the eighties, tuition at universities rose at an average of 9% per year, a figure far above the rise in household family incomes. Now, the demographics are about to reverse themselves: the number of 18- and 19-year-olds will begin to increase in 1996 and will continue until they peak in 2010 at about 9.3 million for nearly a 33% increase in the university-eligible population. By 1994, tuition costs for four years at a U.S. private university had jumped to an average of $44,000 from around $13,000 in 1980. With room and board added on, the cost is at least $20,000 higher.

Required

1. If tuition increases revert to the 9% increases of the 1980s, what will four years' tuition at a university cost by the year 2010? How affordable will a college education be at this level?
2. What scenario do you envision for university tuition costs between now and the year 2010? Why?
3. What is the cost of adding an extra student to a typical classroom? Explain this in terms of the cost structure of a university.
4. After two decades of almost uninterrupted expansion, the "baby bust" enrollment drop left many universities with considerable underutilized capacity. What impact will increasing enrollment and economies of scale have on costs and tuition?
5. Which universities do you expect will be helped the most—public or private?
6. Given that severe student shortages will still exist for many years to come, what strategies would you suggest to university administrators for achieving a better balance between costs and tuition revenues?

VARIABLE COSTING:
A TOOL FOR MANAGEMENT

LEARNING OBJECTIVES

After studying Chapter 8, you should be able to:

1 Explain how variable costing differs from absorption costing, and compute the unit product cost under each method.

2 Describe how fixed manufacturing overhead costs are deferred in inventory and released from inventory under absorption costing.

3 Prepare income statements using both variable and absorption costing, and reconcile the two net income figures.

4 Explain the effect of changes in production on the net income reported under both variable and absorption costing.

5 Explain the advantages and limitations of both the variable and absorption costing methods.

6 Explain how the use of JIT inventory methods decreases or eliminates the difference in net income reported under the variable and absorption costing methods.

7 Define or explain the key terms listed at the end of the chapter.

Emerald Isle Knitters, Ltd., of Ireland manufactures traditional wool fisherman's sweaters that it sells wholesale to retail outlets. Emerald Isle can use different rules for generating accounting information, depending on the purpose of the information and whether it is for internal or external users.

One aspect of the accountant's work centres on the problem of assigning costs to various parts of an organization. Cost assignment is necessary to provide useful and relevant data for three purposes:

1. For product costing and for pricing.
2. For appraisal of managerial performance.
3. For making special decisions.

In assigning costs for these purposes, the accountant can use either of two approaches. One approach, known as *absorption costing,* was discussed at length in Chapter 3. The other approach, called *variable costing,* is preferred by some companies and must be used when an income statement is prepared in the contribution format. In this chapter, we learn how to compute the cost of products and services using variable costing. As we study variable costing, we will learn that a difference in net income can result from using it as compared to absorption costing, and we will learn the reasons for this difference. During our discussion, we consider the arguments for and against each costing method, and we will show how management decisions can be affected by the costing method chosen.

OVERVIEW OF ABSORPTION AND VARIABLE COSTING

OBJECTIVE 1

Explain how variable costing differs from absorption costing, and compute the unit product cost under each method.

As discussed in Chapter 3, absorption costing allocates a portion of fixed manufacturing overhead to each unit produced during a period, along with variable manufacturing costs. Since absorption costing mingles variable and fixed costs together, units of product costed by that method are not well suited for inclusion in a contribution-type income statement. This has led to the development of variable costing, which focuses on *cost behaviour* in computing unit costs. One of the strengths of variable costing is that it harmonizes fully with both the contribution approach and the CVP concepts discussed in the preceding chapter.

Absorption Costing

In Chapter 3, we learned that **absorption costing** treats *all* costs of production as product costs, regardless of whether they are variable or fixed in nature. Thus, absorption costing allocates a portion of fixed manufacturing overhead cost to each unit of product, along with the variable manufacturing costs. The cost of a unit of product under the absorption costing method therefore consists of direct materials, direct labour, and *both* variable and fixed overhead. Because absorption costing includes all costs of production as product costs, it is frequently referred to as the **full cost method.**

Variable Costing

Under **variable costing,** only those costs of production that vary with activity are treated as product costs. This would include direct materials, direct labour, and the variable portion of manufacturing overhead. Fixed manufacturing overhead is not treated as a product cost under this method. Rather, fixed manufacturing overhead is treated as a period cost and, like selling and administrative expenses, it is charged off in its entirety against revenue each period. Consequently, the inventory cost of a unit of product under the variable costing method contains no element of fixed overhead cost.

EXHIBIT 8-1

Cost Classifications
—Absorption versus
Variable Costing

	Absorption Costing		Variable Costing
Product costs	{ Direct materials, Direct labour, Variable manufacturing overhead	}	Product Costs
	Fixed manufacturing overhead	}	Period costs
Period costs	{ Selling and administrative expenses		

Variable costing is sometimes referred to as **direct costing** or **marginal costing.** The term *direct costing* was popular for many years, but it is slowly disappearing from day-to-day use. This is fortunate because the term *variable costing* is more descriptive of the way in which product costs are computed when a contribution income statement is prepared.

To complete this summary comparison of absorption and variable costing, we need to consider briefly the handling of selling and administrative expenses. These expenses are never treated as product costs, regardless of the costing method in use. Thus, under either absorption or variable costing, selling and administrative expenses are always treated as period costs and deducted from revenues as incurred.

The concepts discussed so far in this section are illustrated in Exhibit 8–1, which shows the classification of costs under both absorption and variable costing.

Unit Cost Computations

To illustrate the computation of unit costs under both absorption and variable costing, assume the following data:

Boley Company produces a single product. The cost characteristics of the product and of the manufacturing plant are given below:

Number of units produced each year	6,000
Variable costs per unit:	
Direct materials	$ 2
Direct labour	4
Variable manufacturing overhead	1
Variable selling and administrative expenses	3
Fixed costs per year:	
Manufacturing overhead	30,000
Selling and administrative expenses	10,000

Required

1. Compute the cost of a unit of product under absorption costing.
2. Compute the cost of a unit of product under variable costing.

Solution

Absorption Costing

Direct materials	$ 2
Direct labour	4
Variable overhead	1
Total variable production cost	7
Fixed overhead ($30,000 ÷ 6,000 units of product)	5
Total cost per unit	$12

Variable Costing

Direct materials	$ 2
Direct labour	4
Variable overhead	1

(The $30,000 fixed overhead will be charged off in total against revenue as a period expense along with the fixed selling and administrative expenses.)

Under the absorption costing method, notice that *all* production costs, variable and fixed, have been added when determining the cost of a unit of product. Thus, if the company sells a unit of product and absorption costing is being used, then $12 (consisting of $7 variable cost and $5 fixed cost) will be deducted on the income statement as cost of goods sold. Similarly, any unsold units will be carried as inventory on the balance sheet at $12 each.

Under the variable costing method, notice that only the variable production costs have been added when determining the cost of a unit of product. Thus, if the company sells a unit of product, only $7 will be deducted as cost of goods sold, and unsold units will be carried in the balance sheet inventory account at only $7 each.

The Controversy over Fixed Overhead Cost

Probably no subject in all of managerial accounting has created as much controversy among accountants as variable costing. The controversy isn't over whether costs should be separated as between variable and fixed in matters relating to planning and control. Rather, the controversy is over the theoretical justification for excluding fixed overhead costs from the cost of units produced and therefore from inventory.

Advocates of variable costing argue that fixed overhead costs relate to the *capacity* to produce rather than to the actual production of units of product in a given year. That is, they argue that costs for facilities and equipment, insurance, supervisory salaries, and the like, represent costs of being *ready* to produce and therefore will be incurred regardless of whether any actual production takes place during the year. For this reason, advocates of variable costing believe that such costs should be charged against the period rather than against the product.

Advocates of absorption costing argue, on the other hand, that so far as product costing is concerned, it makes no difference whether a manufacturing cost is variable or fixed. They argue that fixed overhead costs such as depreciation and insurance are just as essential to the production process as are the variable costs, and therefore cannot be ignored in costing units of product. They argue that to be fully costed, each unit of product must bear an equitable portion of *all* manufacturing costs.

Although this difference in the handling of fixed overhead might seem slight, it can have a substantial impact on both the clarity and the usefulness of statement data, as we shall see in this chapter.

INCOME COMPARISON OF ABSORPTION AND VARIABLE COSTING

OBJECTIVE 2
Describe how fixed manufacturing overhead costs are deferred in inventory and released from inventory under absorption costing.

Income statements prepared under the absorption and variable costing approaches are shown in Exhibit 8–2. In preparing these statements, we use the data for Boley Company presented earlier, along with other information about the company as given below:

Beginning inventory in units	–0–
Units produced	6,000
Units sold	5,000
Ending inventory in units	1,000
Selling price per unit	$ 20
Selling and administrative expenses:	
Variable per unit	3
Fixed per year	$10,000

EXHIBIT 8-2   Comparison of Absorption and Variable Costing—Boley Company

Absorption Costing

Sales (5,000 units × $20)		$100,000
Cost of goods sold:		
Beginning inventory	$ –0–	
Cost of goods manufactured (6,000 units × $12)	72,000	
Goods available for sale	72,000	
Less ending inventory (1,000 units × $12)	12,000	
Cost of goods sold		60,000
Gross margin		40,000
Less selling and administrative expenses		
($15,000 total variable plus $10,000 fixed)		25,000
Net income		$ 15,000

Note the difference in ending inventories. Fixed overhead cost at $5 per unit is included under the absorption approach. This explains the difference in ending inventory and in net income (1,000 units × $5 = $5,000).

Variable Costing

Sales (5,000 units × $20)		$100,000
Less variable expenses:		
Variable cost of goods sold:		
Beginning inventory	$ –0–	
Variable manufacturing costs (6,000 units × $7)	42,000	
Goods available for sale	42,000	
Less ending inventory (1,000 units × $7)	7,000	
Variable cost of goods sold	35,000	
Variable selling and administrative expenses (5,000 units × $3)	15,000	50,000
Contribution margin		50,000
Less fixed expenses:		
Fixed overhead costs	30,000	
Fixed selling and administrative expenses	10,000	40,000
Net income		$ 10,000

	Absorption Costing	Variable Costing
Unit product cost:		
Direct materials	$ 2	$2
Direct labour	4	4
Variable overhead	1	1
Fixed overhead ($30,000 ÷ 6,000 units)	5	—
Total cost per unit	$12	$7

Several points can be made from the statements in Exhibit 8–2:

1.   Under the absorption costing method, it is possible to defer a portion of the fixed overhead costs of the current period to future periods through the inventory account. Such a deferral is known as **fixed overhead cost deferred in inventory.** The process involved can be explained by referring to the data for Boley Company. During the current period, Boley Company produced 6,000 units but sold only 5,000 units, thus leaving 1,000 units in the ending inventory. Under the absorption costing method, each unit produced was assigned $5 in fixed overhead cost (see the unit cost computations above). Therefore, each of the 1,000 units going into inventory at the end of the period has $5 in fixed overhead cost attached to it, or a total of $5,000 to the 1,000 units involved. *This amount of fixed overhead cost of the current period has thereby been deferred in inventory to the next period when, we may hope, these units will be taken out of inventory and sold.* The deferral

of fixed overhead cost we are talking about can be seen clearly by analyzing the $12,000 ending inventory figure under the absorption costing method:

Variable manufacturing costs: 1,000 units × $7	$ 7,000
Fixed overhead costs: 1,000 units × $5	5,000
Total inventory value	$12,000

In summary, of the $30,000 in fixed overhead cost incurred during the period, only $25,000 (5,000 units sold × $5) has been included in cost of goods sold. The remaining $5,000 (1,000 units *not* sold × $5) has been deferred in inventory to the next period.

2.   Under the variable costing method, the entire $30,000 in fixed overhead cost has been treated as an expense of the current period (see the bottom portion of the variable costing income statement).

3.   The ending inventory figure under the variable costing method is $5,000 lower than it is under the absorption costing method. The reason is that under variable costing, only the variable manufacturing costs have been added to units of product and therefore included in inventory:

Variable manufacturing costs: 1,000 units × $7	$ 7,000

The $5,000 difference in ending inventories explains the difference in net income reported between the two costing methods. Net income is $5,000 *higher* under absorption costing because, as explained above, $5,000 of fixed overhead cost has been deferred in inventory to the next period under that costing method.

4.   The absorption costing income statement makes no distinction between fixed and variable costs; therefore, it is not well suited for CVP computations, which we have emphasized as being important to good planning and control. To generate data for CVP analysis, it would be necessary to spend considerable time reworking and reclassifying the absorption statement.

[1]William P. Cress and James B. Pettijohn, "A Survey of Budget-Related Planning and Control Policies and Procedures," *Journal of Accounting Education* (Fall 1985), p. 73. For a lively discussion of super variable costing, see Eliyahu M. Goldratt and Jeff Cox, *The Goal,* 2nd ed. (Croton-on-Hudson, N.Y.: North River Press, 1992). For super absorption costing, see Robert S. Kaplan, "Management Accounting for Advanced Technological Environments," *Science* (August 25, 1989), p. 822.

5.   The variable costing approach to costing units of product blends very well with the contribution approach to the income statement, since both concepts are based on the idea of classifying costs by behaviour. The variable costing data in Exhibit 8–2 could be used immediately in CVP computations.

The Definition of an Asset

Essentially, the difference between the absorption costing method and the variable costing method centres on the matter of timing. Advocates of variable costing say that fixed manufacturing costs should be released against revenues immediately in total, whereas advocates of absorption costing say that fixed manufacturing costs should be released against revenues bit by bit as units of product are sold. Any units of product not sold under absorption costing result in fixed costs being inventoried and carried forward *as assets* to the next period. The solution to the controversy about which costing method is "right" should therefore rest, in large part, on whether fixed costs added to inventory fall within the definition of an asset as this concept is generally viewed in accounting theory.

What Is an Asset?   A cost is normally viewed as being an asset if it can be shown that it has revenue-producing powers, or if it can be shown that it will be beneficial in some way to operations in future periods. In short, a cost is an asset if it can be shown that it has *future service potential* that can be identified. For example, insurance prepayments are viewed as being assets, since they have future service potential. The prepayments acquire protection that can be used in future periods to guard against losses that might otherwise hinder operations. If fixed production costs added to inventory under absorption costing are indeed properly called assets, then they too must meet this test of service potential.

The Absorption Costing View.   Advocates of absorption costing argue that fixed production costs added to inventory do, indeed, have future service potential. They take the position that if production exceeds sales, then a benefit to future periods is created in the form of inventory that can be carried forward and sold, resulting in a future inflow of revenue. They argue that *all costs* involved in the creation of inventory should be carried forward as assets—not just the variable costs. The fixed costs of depreciation, taxes, insurance, supervisory salaries, and so on, are just as essential to the creation of units of product as are the variable costs. It would be just as impossible to create units of product in the absence of equipment as it would be to create them in the absence of raw materials or in the absence of workers to operate the machines.

In summary, proponents of absorption costing argue that until the fixed production costs have been recognized and attached, units of product have not been fully costed. Both variable and fixed costs become inseparably attached as units are produced and *remain* inseparably attached regardless of whether the units are sold immediately or carried forward as inventory to generate revenue in future periods.

The Variable Costing View.   Advocates of variable costing argue that a cost has service potential and is therefore an asset *only if its incurrence now will make it unnecessary to incur the same cost again in the future.* Service potential is therefore said to hinge on the matter of *future cost avoidance.* If the incurrence of a cost now will have no effect on whether or not the same cost will be incurred again in the future, then that cost is viewed as having no relevance to future events. It is argued that such a cost can in no way represent a future benefit or service.

For example, the prepayment of insurance is viewed as being an asset because the cash outlays made when the insurance is acquired make it unnecessary to sustain the same outlays again in the future periods for which insurance protection has been purchased. In short, by making insurance payments now, a company *avoids* having to make payments in the future. Since prepayments of insurance result in *future cost avoidance,* the prepayments qualify as assets.

This type of cost avoidance does not exist in the case of fixed production costs. The incurrence of fixed production costs in one year in no way reduces the necessity to incur the same costs again in the following year. Since the incurrence of fixed production costs does not result in *future cost avoidance,* the costs of one year can have no relevance to future events and therefore cannot possibly represent a future benefit or service. Variable costing advocates argue, therefore, that no part of the fixed production costs of one year should ever be carried forward as an asset to the following year. Such costs do not result in future cost avoidance—the key test for any asset.

EXTENDED COMPARISON OF INCOME DATA

▼   ▼   ▼   ▼   ▼

MANAGERIAL ACCOUNTING IN ACTION—THE ISSUE

Mary O'Meara is the owner and manager of Emerald Isle Knitters, Ltd., of Galway, Republic of Ireland. The company is very small, with only 10 employees. Mary started the company three years ago with cash loaned to her by a local bank. The company manufactures a traditional wool fisherman's sweater from a pattern Mary learned from her grandmother. Like most apparel manufacturers, Emerald Isle Knitters sells its product to department stores and clothing store chains rather than to retail customers.

The sweater was an immediate success, and all of the first year's production was sold out. However, in the second year of operations, one of the company's major customers cancelled its order due to bankruptcy, and the company ended the year with large stocks of unsold sweaters. The third year of operations was a great year in contrast to that disastrous second year. Sales rebounded dramatically, and all of the unsold production carried over from the second year was sold by the end of the third year.

Shortly after the close of the third year, Mary met with her accountant Sean MacLafferty to discuss the results for the year. (Note: In Ireland, the unit of currency is the pound, which is denoted by the symbol £.)

MARY: Sean, the results for this year look a lot better than for last year, but I am frankly puzzled why this year's results aren't even better than this income statement shows.

SEAN: I know what you mean. The net income for this year is just £90,000. Last year it was £30,000. That is a huge improvement, but it seems that profits this year should have been even higher and profits last year should have been much less. We were in big trouble last year. I was afraid we might not even break even—yet we showed a healthy £30,000 profit. Somehow it doesn't seem quite right.

MARY: I wondered about that £30,000 profit last year, but I didn't question it since it was the only good news I had gotten for quite some time.

SEAN: In case you're wondering, I didn't invent that profit last year just to make you feel better. Our auditor required that I follow certain accounting rules in preparing those reports for the bank. This may sound heretical, but we *could* use different rules for our own internal reports.

MARY: Wait a minute, rules are rules—especially in accounting.

SEAN: Yes and no. For our internal reports, it might be better to use different rules than we use in the reports we send to the bank.

MARY: As I said, rules are rules. Still, I'm willing to listen if you want to show me what you have in mind.

SEAN: It's a deal.

▼   ▼   ▼   ▼   ▼

OBJECTIVE 3

Prepare income statements using both variable and absorption costing, and reconcile the two net income figures.

Immediately after the meeting with Mary, Sean put together the data and financial reports that appear in Exhibit 8–3. To make the principles clearer, Sean simplified the data so that the illustrations all use round figures.

The basic data appears at the top of Exhibit 8–3, and the absorption costing income statements as reported to the bank for the last three years appear immediately below the basic data. Sean decided to try using the variable costing approach to see what effect that might have on net income. The variable costing income statements for the last three years appear at the bottom of Exhibit 8–3.

Note that the company maintained a steady rate of production of 25,000 sweaters per year. In year 1, production and sales were equal. In year 2, production exceeded sales and there was a buildup in inventories due to the cancelled order. Mn year 3, sales exceeded production and the company ended the year with no inventories.

The data in Exhibit 8–3 illustrate the general conclusions that are summarized in Exhibit 8–4. These conclusions are discussed below:

1.   When production and sales are equal, as in year 1 for Emerald Isle Knitters, net income will generally be the same regardless of whether absorption or variable costing is used. The reason is as follows: The *only* difference that can exist between absorption and variable costing net income is the amount of fixed manufacturing overhead recognized as expense on the income statement. When everything that is produced in the year is sold, all of the fixed manufacturing overhead assigned to units of product under absorption

---

EXHIBIT 8–3   Absorption and Variable Costing Statements—Emerald Isle Knitters, Ltd.

Basic Data

Selling price per unit sold . . . . £	20
Variable manufacturing cost per unit produced.	7
Fixed manufacturing overhead costs per year.	150,000
Variable selling and administrative expenses per unit sold.	1
Fixed selling and administrative expenses per year	90,000

	Year 1	Year 2	Year 3	Three Years Together
Units in beginning inventory	–0–	–0–	5,000	–0–
Units produced.	25,000	25,000	25,000	75,000
Units sold.	25,000	20,000	30,000	75,000
Units in ending inventory.	–0–	5,000	–0–	–0–

Unit Product Costs

	Year 1	Year 2	Year 3
Under variable costing (variable manufacturing costs only)	£ 7	£ 7	£ 7
Under absorption costing:			
Variable manufacturing costs.	£ 7	£ 7	£ 7
Fixed manufacturing overhead costs (£150,000 spread over the number of units produced in each year).	6	6	6
Total absorption cost per unit.	£13	£13	£13

(continued)

EXHIBIT 8-3   *(concluded)*

	Year 1	Year 2	Year 3	Three Years Together
Absorption Costing				
Sales	£500,000	£ 400,000	£ 600,000	£1,500,000
Less cost of goods sold:				
Beginning inventory	–0–	–0–	65,000	–0–
Add cost of goods manufactured (25,000 units × £13).	325,000	325,000	325,000	975,000
Goods available for sale	325,000	325,000	390,000	975,000
Less ending inventory (5,000 units × £13)	–0–	65,000	–0–	–0–
Cost of goods sold.	325,000	260,000	390,000	975,000
Gross margin.	175,000	140,000	210,000	525,000
Less selling and administrative expenses	115,000*	110,000*	120,000*	345,000
Net income	£ 60,000	£ 30,000	£ 90,000	£ 180,000

*The selling and administrative expenses are computed as follows:
Year 1: 25,000 units × £1 variable plus £90,000 fixed = £115,000.
Year 2: 20,000 units × £1 variable plus £90,000 fixed = £110,000.
Year 3: 30,000 units × £1 variable plus £90,000 fixed = £120,000.

Variable Costing				
Sales	£500,000	£400,000	£600,000	£1,500,000
Less variable expenses:				
Variable cost of good sold:				
Beginning inventory	–0–	–0–	35,000	–0–
Variable manufacturing costs (25,000 units × £7)	175,000	175,000	175,000	525,000
Goods available for sale	175,000	175,000	210,000	525,000
Less ending inventory (5,000 units × £7)	–0–	35,000	–0–	–0–
Variable cost of goods sold	175,000*	140,000*	210,000*	525,000
Variable selling and administrative expenses (£1 per unit sold) . .	25,000	20,000	30,000	75,000
Total variable expenses	200,000	160,000	240,000	600,000
Contribution margin	300,000	240,000	360,000	900,000
Less fixed expenses:				
Fixed manufacturing overhead	150,000	150,000	150,000	450,000
Fixed selling administrative expenses	90,000	90,000	90,000	270,000
Total fixed expenses	240,000	240,000	240,000	720,000
Net income	£ 60,000	£ –0–	£120,000	£ 180,000

*The variable cost of goods sold could have been computed more simply as follows:
Year 1: 25,000 units sold × £7 = £175,000.
Year 2: 20,000 units sold × £7 = £140,000.
Year 3: 30,000 units sold × £7 = £210,000.

costing become part of the year's cost of goods sold. Under variable costing, the total fixed manufacturing overhead flows directly to the income statement as an expense. So under either method, when production equals sales, all the fixed manufacturing overhead incurred during the year flows through to the income statement as expense. Therefore, the net income under the two methods is the same.

2.   When production exceeds sales, the net income reported under absorption costing will generally be greater than the net income reported under variable costing (see year 2

EXHIBIT 8-4

Comparative Income Effects—Absorption and Variable Costing

Relation between Production and Sales for the Period	Effect on Inventories	Relation between Absorption and Variable Costing Net Incomes
Production = Sales	No change in inventories	Absorption costing net income = Variable costing net income
Production > Sales	Inventories increase	Absorption costing net income > Variable costing net income*
Production < Sales	Inventories decrease	Absorption costing net income < Variable costing net income†

*Net income is higher under absorption costing, because fixed manufacturing overhead cost is *deferred* in inventory under absorption costing as inventories increase.

†Net income is lower under absorption costing, because fixed manufacturing overhead cost is *released* from inventory under absorption costing as inventories decrease.

in Exhibit 8–3). The reason is that when more is produced than is sold, part of the fixed manufacturing overhead costs of the current period are deferred in inventory to the next period under absorption costing, as discussed earlier. In year 2, for example, £30,000 of fixed manufacturing overhead cost (5,000 units × £6 per unit) has been deferred in inventory to year 3 under the absorption approach. Only that portion of the fixed manufacturing overhead costs of year 2 under absorption costing that is associated with *units sold* is charged against income for that year.

Under variable costing, however, *all* of the fixed manufacturing overhead costs of year 2 have been charged immediately against income as a period cost. As a result, the net income for year 2 under variable costing is £30,000 *lower* than it is under absorption costing. Exhibit 8–5 contains a reconciliation of the variable costing and absorption costing net income figures.

3. When production is less than sales, the net income reported under the absorption costing approach will generally be less than the net income reported under the variable costing approach (see year 3 in Exhibit 8–3). The reason is that when more is sold than is produced, inventories are drawn down and fixed manufacturing overhead costs that were previously deferred in inventory under absorption costing are released and charged against income (known as **fixed manufacturing overhead cost released from inventory**). In

EXHIBIT 8-5

Reconciliation of Variable Costing and Absorption Costing —Net Income Data from Exhibit 8–3

	Year 1	Year 2	Year 3
Variable costing net income	£60,000	£ –0–	£120,000
Add fixed manufacturing overhead costs deferred in inventory under absorption costing (5,000 units × £6 per unit)	–0–	30,000	–0–
Deduct fixed manufacturing overhead costs released from inventory under absorption costing (5,000 units × £6 per unit)	–0–	–0–	(30,000)
Absorption costing net income	£60,000	£30,000	£ 90,000

year 3, for example, the £30,000 in fixed manufacturing overhead cost deferred in inventory under the absorption approach from year 2 to year 3 is released from inventory through the sales process and charged against income. As a result, the cost of goods sold for year 3 contains not only all of the fixed manufacturing overhead costs for year 3 (since all that was produced in year 3 was sold in year 3) but £30,000 of fixed manufacturing overhead cost from year 2 as well.

By contrast, under variable costing only the fixed manufacturing overhead costs of year 3 have been charged against year 3. The result is that net income under variable costing is £30,000 *higher* than it is under absorption costing. Exhibit 8–5 contains a reconciliation of the variable costing and absorption costing net income figures.

4.   Over an *extended* period of time, the net income figures reported under absorption costing and variable costing will tend to be the same. The reason is that over the long run sales can't exceed production, nor can production much exceed sales. The shorter the time period, the more the net income figures will tend to differ.

EFFECT OF CHANGES IN PRODUCTION ON NET INCOME

OBJECTIVE 4

Explain the effect of changes in production on the net income reported under both variable and absorption costing.

In the Emerald Isle Knitters example in the preceding section, production was constant and sales fluctuated over the three-year period. Since sales fluctuated, the data Sean MacLafferty presented in Exhibit 8–3 allowed us to see the effect of changes in sales on net income under both variable and absorption costing.

To further investigate the differences between variable and absorption costing, Sean next put together the hypothetical example in Exhibit 8–6. In this hypothetical example, sales are constant and production fluctuates (the opposite of Exhibit 8–3). The purpose of Exhibit 8–6 is to illustrate for Mary O'Meara the effect of changes in *production* on net income under both variable and absorption costing.

Variable Costing

Net income is *not* affected by changes in production under variable costing. Notice from Exhibit 8–6 that net income is the same for all three years under the variable costing approach, although production exceeds sales in one year and is less than sales in another year. In short, a change in production has no impact on net income when variable costing is in use.

Absorption Costing

Net income *is* affected by changes in production when absorption costing is in use, however. As shown in Exhibit 8–6, net income under the absorption approach goes up in year 2, in response to the increase in production for that year, and then goes down in year 3, in response to the drop in production for that year. Note particularly that net income goes up and down between these two years *even though the same number of units is sold in each year*. The reason for this effect can be traced to the shifting of fixed manufacturing overhead cost between periods under the absorption costing method.

Since this shifting of fixed manufacturing overhead cost has already been discussed in preceding sections, at this point all we need to consider is how it affects the data in Exhibit 8–6. As shown in the exhibit, production exceeds sales in year 2, thereby causing 10,000 units to be carried forward as inventory to year 3. Each unit produced during year 2 has £6 in

EXHIBIT 8–6   Sensitivity of Costing Methods to Changes in Production—Hypothetical Data

Basic Data

Selling price per unit sold	£ 25
Variable manufacturing cost per unit produced.....................................	10
Fixed manufacturing overhead costs per year.......................................	300,000
Variable selling and administrative expenses per unit sold......................	1
Fixed selling and administrative expenses per year	200,000

	Year 1	Year 2	Year 3
Units in beginning inventory	–0–	–0–	10,000
Units produced	40,000	50,000	30,000
Units sold	40,000	40,000	40,000
Units in ending inventory	–0–	10,000	–0–

Unit Product Costs

	Year 1	Year 2	Year 3
Under variable costing (variable manufacturing costs only)	£10.00	£10.00	£10.00
Under absorption costing:			
Variable manufacturing costs	£10.00	£10.00	£10.00
Fixed manufacturing overhead costs (£300,000 total spread			
over the number of units produced in each year)	7.50	6.00	10.00
Total absorption cost per unit	£17.50	£16.00	£20.00

Absorption Costing

	Year 1	Year 2	Year 3
Sales (40,000 units)...	£1,000,000	£1,000,000	£1,000,000
Less cost of goods sold:			
Beginning inventory	–0–	–0–	160,000
Add cost of goods manufactured	700,000*	800,000*	600,000*
Goods available for sale	700,000	800,000	760,000
Less ending inventory....................................	–0–	160,000†	–0–
Cost of goods sold......................................	700,000	640,000	760,000
Gross margin...	300,000	360,000	240,000
Less selling and administrative expenses (40,000 units × £1 plus £200,000)...........	240,000	240,000	240,000
Net income	£ 60,000	£ 120,000	£ –0–

*Cost of goods manufactured:
Year 1: 40,000 units × £17.50 = £700,000.
Year 2: 50,000 units × £16.00 = £800,000.
Year 3: 30,000 units × £20.00 = £600,000.

†Observe that 50,000 units are produced in year 2, but only 40,000 units are sold. The 10,000 units in the ending inventory have the following costs attached to them:

	Absorption Costing	Variable Costing
Variable manufacturing costs: 10,000 units × £10	£100,000	£100,000
Fixed manufacturing overhead costs: 10,000 units × £6	60,000	–0–
Total inventory cost	£160,000	£100,000

(continued)

EXHIBIT 8–6   *(concluded)*

Variable Costing	Year 1	Year 2	Year 3
Sales (40,000 units)...	£1,000,000	£1,000,000	£1,000,000
Less variable expenses:			
Variable cost of goods sold:			
Beginning inventory..	–0–	–0–	100,000
Variable manufacturing costs, at £10 per unit produced......................	400,000	500,000	300,000
Goods available for sale....................................	400,000	500,000	400,000
Less ending inventory.....................................	–0–	100,000*	–0–
Variable cost of goods sold.................................	400,000	400,000	400,000
Variable selling and administrative expenses........................	40,000	40,000	40,000
Total variable expenses...................................	440,000	440,000	440,000
Contribution margin...	560,000	560,000	560,000
Less fixed expenses:			
Fixed manufacturing overhead................................	300,000	300,000	300,000
Fixed selling and administrative expenses........................	200,000	200,000	200,000
Total fixed expenses.....................................	500,000	500,000	500,000
Net income..	£ 60,000	£ 60,000	£ 60,000

*See the inventory computations in the second footnote above under the absorption costing example.

fixed manufacturing overhead cost attached to it (see the unit cost computations at the top of Exhibit 8–6). Therefore, £60,000 (10,000 units × £6) of the fixed manufacturing overhead costs of year 2 are not charged against that year but rather are added to the inventory account (along with the variable manufacturing costs). As a result, the net income of year 2 rises sharply, even though the same number of units is sold in year 2 as in the other years.

The reverse effect occurs in year 3. Because sales exceed production in year 3, that year is forced to cover all of its own fixed manufacturing overhead costs as well as the fixed manufacturing overhead costs carried forward in inventory from year 2. The result is a substantial drop in net income during year 3, although, as we have noted, the same number of units is sold in that year as in the other years.

▼   ▼   ▼   ▼   ▼

MANAGERIAL ACCOUNTING IN ACTION—WRAP-UP

After checking all of his work, Sean took the exhibits he had prepared to Mary's office where the following conversation took place:

SEAN: I have some calculations I would like to show you.

MARY: Will this take long? I only have a few minutes before I have to meet with the buyer from The Bay.

SEAN: Well, we can at least get started. These exhibits should help explain why our net income didn't increase this year as much as you thought it should have.

MARY: This first exhibit (i.e., Exhibit 8–3) looks like it just summarizes our income statements for the last three years.

Continued

SEAN: Not exactly. There are actually two sets of income statements on this exhibit. The absorption costing income statements are the ones I originally prepared and we submitted to the bank. Below the absorption costing income statements are another set of income statements.

MARY: Those are the ones labelled variable costing.

SEAN: That's right. You can see that the net incomes are the same for the two sets of income statements in our first year of operations, but they differ for the other two years.

MARY: I'll say! The variable costing statements indicate that we just broke even in the second year instead of earning a £30,000 profit. The increase in net income between the second and third years is £120,000 instead of just £60,000. I don't know how you come up with two different net income figures, but the variable costing net income seems to be much closer to the truth. The second year was almost a disaster. We barely sold enough sweaters to cover all of our fixed costs.

SEAN: You and I both know that, but the accounting rules view the situation a little differently. If we produce more than we sell, the accounting rules require that we take some of the fixed cost and assign it to the units that end up in inventories at year-end.

MARY: You mean that instead of appearing on the income statement as an expense, some of the fixed costs wind up on the balance sheet as inventories?

SEAN: Precisely.

MARY: I thought accountants were conservative. Since when was it conservative to call an expense an asset?

SEAN: We accountants have been debating whether fixed production costs are an asset or an expense for over 50 years.

MARY: It must have been a *fascinating* debate.

SEAN: I have to admit that it ranks right up there with watching grass grow in terms of excitement level.

MARY: I don't know what the arguments are, but I can tell you for sure that we don't make any money by just producing sweaters. If I understand what you have shown me, I can increase my net income under absorption costing by simply making more sweaters—we don't have to sell them.

SEAN: Correct.

MARY: So all I have to do to enjoy the lifestyle of the rich and famous is to hire every unemployed knitter in Ireland to make sweaters I can't sell.

SEAN: We would have a major cash flow problem, but our net income would certainly go up.

MARY: Well, if the banks want us to use absorption costing so be it. I don't know why they would want us to report that way, but if that's what they want, that's what they'll get. Is there any reason why we can't use this variable costing method ourselves? The statements are easier to understand, and the net income figures make more sense to me. Can't we do both?

SEAN: I don't see why not. Making the adjustment from one method to the other is very simple.

MARY: Good. Let's talk about this some more after I get back from the meeting with The Bay.

The Impact on the Manager

Like Mary O'Meara, opponents of absorption costing argue that shifting fixed manufacturing overhead cost between periods can be confusing and can lead to misinterpretations and even to faulty decisions. Look again at the data in Exhibit 8–6; a manager might wonder why net income went up substantially in year 2 under absorption costing, when sales remained the same as in the prior year. Was it a result of lower selling costs, more

While managers can artificially increase net income under absorption costing by producing more than is really necessary and building up inventories, a few unscrupulous managers have stepped over the line into the area of outright fraud. By claiming inventories that don't exist, an unethical manager can produce instant profits and dress up the balance sheet. Since the value of ending inventories is subtracted from the cost of goods available for sale in order to arrive at the cost of goods sold, phantom inventories directly reduce cost of goods sold. Phantom inventories also beef up the balance sheet by increasing assets.

Auditors attempt to uncover such fraud by physically verifying the existence of inventory reported on the balance sheet. This is done by counting random samples of perhaps 5% to 10% of reported inventory items. However, this audit approach isn't always effective. For example, the auditors of Windsor Packing Company were found guilty of professional negligence by the Supreme Court of Ontario when they failed to confirm a sizable inventory that was stored off the premises. The inventory was overstated by $300,000. This item combined with other errors resulted in approximately a $4.5 million damage claim against the auditors in favour of the Federal Business Development Bank and the Guarantee Company of North America who had loaned money based on the financial statements.[2]

efficient operations, or was some other factor involved? The manager is unable to tell, looking simply at the absorption costing income statement. Then in year 3, net income drops sharply, even though again the same number of units is sold as in the other two years. Why would income rise in one year and then drop in the next? The figures seem erratic and contradictory and can lead to confusion and a loss of confidence in the integrity of the statement data.

By contrast, the variable costing income statements in Exhibit 8–6 are clear and easy to read. Sales remain constant over the three-year period covered in the exhibit, so both contribution margin and net income also remain constant. The statements are consistent with what the manager would expect to happen under the circumstances, so they tend to generate confidence rather than confusion.

To avoid mistakes when absorption costing is used, the manager must be alert to any changes that may take place during a period in inventory levels or in unit costs. By this means, he or she should be able to properly interpret any erratic movement in net income that may occur under the absorption costing method.

One way to overcome problems such as those discussed above is to use *normalized overhead rates*. A **normalized overhead rate** is a rate based on the *average* activity of many periods—past and present—rather than based only on the expected activity of the current period. Thus, unit product costs are stable from year to year. Even if normalized overhead rates are used, however, net income can still be erratic if the under- or overapplied overhead that results from an imbalance between production and sales is taken to cost of goods sold. The only way to avoid the problems entirely is to use normalized overhead rates and to place any under- or overapplied overhead in a balance sheet clearing account of some type. However, this is rarely done in practice.

OTHER FACTORS IN CHOOSING A COSTING METHOD

OBJECTIVE 5
Explain the advantages and limitations of both the variable and absorption costing methods.

In choosing between variable and absorption costing, several additional factors should be considered by the manager. These factors are discussed in this section.

[2]*The Bottom Line* (March 1998), p. 9.

CVP Analysis and Absorption Costing

Absorption costing is widely used for both internal and external reports. Many firms use the absorption approach exclusively because of its focus on "full" costing of units of product. A weakness of the method, however, is its inability to dovetail well with CVP analysis.

To illustrate, refer again to Exhibit 8–3. Let us compute the break-even point for Emerald Isle Knitters. To obtain the break-even point, we divide total fixed costs by the contribution margin per unit:

Selling price per unit	£20
Variable costs per unit (f7 + f1)	8
Contribution margin per unit	£12
Fixed manufacturing overhead costs	£150,000
Fixed selling and administrative costs	90,000
Total fixed costs	£240,000

$$\frac{\text{Total fixed costs}}{\text{Contribution margin per unit}} = \frac{£240,000}{£12} = 20,000 \text{ units}$$

The break-even point is 20,000 units. Notice from Exhibit 8–3 that in year 2 the firm sold exactly 20,000 units, the break-even volume. Under the contribution approach, using variable costing, the firm does break even in year 2, showing zero net income. *Under absorption costing, however, the firm shows a positive net income of £30,000 for year 2.* How can this be? How can absorption costing produce a positive net income when the firm sold exactly the break-even volume of units?

The answer lies in the fact that £30,000 in fixed manufacturing overhead costs were deferred in inventory during year 2 under absorption costing and therefore did not appear as charges against income. By deferring these fixed manufacturing overhead costs in inventory, the income statement shows a profit even though the company sold exactly the break-even volume of units. Absorption costing runs into similar kinds of difficulty in other areas of CVP analysis, and absorption costing data often require considerable manipulation before the data are usable for decision-making purposes.

Pricing Decisions

In addition to the points mentioned above regarding CVP analysis, advocates of variable costing argue that it provides more useful cost information for pricing decisions than does absorption costing. Since variable costing focuses on cost behaviour and permits the use of a contribution income statement, it is argued that management is able to see the effects of changes in volume on costs more readily than when absorption costing is in use. With better information available on the relationship between volume and cost, it is argued that management is in a better position to make effective pricing decisions.

Furthermore, it is argued that when absorption costing is in use, there is a tendency to reject any price that is less than full cost. We saw in the preceding chapter, however, that under some conditions a price less than full cost can be advantageous to a firm. Management may be able to see such conditions more readily when variable costing is in use, and thereby they may be able to set prices in such a way as to improve profits for the firm. Pricing decisions are discussed more fully in the Appendix at the end of the text.

External Reporting and Income Taxes

Practically speaking, absorption costing is required for external reports in the United States. A company that attempts to use variable costing on its external financial reports runs the risk that its auditors may not accept the financial statements as conforming to generally accepted accounting principles (GAAP).[3]

In Canada, accounting standards for external reporting require a company to assign to work in process and finished goods the laid down cost of materials plus the cost of direct labour and the applicable share of overhead expenses properly chargeable to production.[4] This implies that both variable and absorption costing are possible in Canada. For income tax purposes in Canada, *Interpretation Bulletin 473,* permits both variable and absorption costing for the purpose of determining taxable income.[5]

Even if a company must use absorption costing for its external reports, a manager can, as Mary O'Meara suggests, use variable costing statements for internal reports. No particular accounting problems are created by using *both* costing methods—the variable costing method for internal reports and the absorption costing method for external reports. As we demonstrated earlier in Exhibit 8–5, the adjustment from variable costing net income to absorption costing net income is a simple one that can be easily made at year-end.

We must note, however, that using two sets of accounting data can create a problem for the top executives of publicly held corporations. The problem is that these executives are usually evaluated based on the external reports prepared for shareholders. It is difficult for managers to make decisions based on one set of accounting statements when they will be evaluated with a different set of accounting statements. Nevertheless, one study found that about half of the companies surveyed use variable costing as either the primary or as a supplementary format in reports prepared for top management.[6]

Advantages of the Contribution Approach

As stated above, many managers feel that there are certain advantages to be gained from using the contribution approach (with variable costing) internally, even if the absorption approach is used externally for reporting purposes. These advantages can be summarized as follows:

1. CVP relationship data needed for profit planning purposes are readily obtained from the regular accounting statements.
2. The profit for a period is not affected by changes in absorption of fixed manufacturing overhead costs resulting from building or reducing inventory. Other things remaining equal (for example, selling prices, costs, sales mix), profits move in the same direction as sales when variable costing is in use.

---

[3]The situation is actually slightly ambiguous concerning whether absorption costing is strictly required. Michael Schiff, "Variable Costing: A Closer Look," *Management Accounting* (February 1987), pp. 36–39, and Eric W. Noreen and Robert M. Bowen, "Tax Incentives and the Decision to Capitalize or Expense Manufacturing Overhead," *Accounting Horizons* (March 1989), pp. 29–42, argue that official pronouncements do not actually prohibit variable costing. Both articles provide examples of companies that expense significant elements of their fixed manufacturing costs on their external reports. Nevertheless, the reality is that most accountants believe that absorption costing is required for external reporting and a manager who argues otherwise is likely to be unsuccessful.
[4]*Canadian Institute of Chartered Accountants' Handbook,* Section 3030, "Inventories," para. 06.
[5]Robert E. Beam and Stanley N. Laiken, *Introduction to Federal Income Taxation in Canada,* 17 ed. (North York, Ont. CCH Canadian Limited, 1996), p. 149.
[6]William P. Cress and James B. Pettijohn, "Survey of Budget-Related Planning and Control Policies and Procedures," *Journal of Accounting Education* (Fall 1985), p. 73.

3. Manufacturing cost and income statements in the variable cost form follow management's thinking more closely than does the absorption cost form for these statements. For this reason, management finds it easier to understand and to use variable cost reports.

4. The impact of fixed costs on profits is emphasized under the variable costing and contribution approach. The total amount of fixed costs appears explicitly on the income statement rather than being buried in inventory accounts and in cost of goods sold.

5. Variable costing data facilitate relative appraisal of products, territories, classes of customers, and other segments of the business without having the results obscured by arbitrary allocations of fixed costs. These issues will be further discussed in Chapter 12.

6. Variable costing ties in with cost control methods such as standard costs and flexible budgets. Standard costs and flexible budgets are discussed in Chapters 10 and 11.

7. Variable costing net income is closer to net cash flow than absorption costing net income. This is particularly important for companies that may be experiencing difficulties with their cash flows.

While experiments and alterations exist in practice to adjust from absorption costing to various forms of variable costing, proposals also exist to increase costs to include more than materials, labour and overhead so that decisions consider the full cost of activities.

One such proposal is to charge the economic, social and environmental impacts of company activities to the extent these factors can be estimated. Costs such as the effect on human health, crops and structures represent potentially measurable costs of operating for electric utilities such as Ontario Hydro. Inclusion of such environmental costs in income determination is suggested as a way in which such costs can become an important factor in business decisions.[7]

Variable Costing and the Theory of Constraints

Largely because of the advantages cited above, a form of variable costing is used in the theory of constraints (TOC) management approach that was discussed in Chapter 1. The major difference between the variable costing approach illustrated in this chapter and the TOC approach is that direct labour is generally considered to be a fixed cost in TOC. As discussed in earlier chapters, as a matter of policy in many companies, direct labour is not adjusted to the activity level during a particular period. While direct labour workers may be paid on an hourly basis, in many companies there is a commitment—sometimes enforced in labour contracts—to guarantee workers a minimum number of paid hours. In TOC companies, there are two additional reasons to consider direct labour to be a fixed cost.

First, direct labour is not usually the constraint. In the simplest cases, the constraint is a machine. In more complex cases, the constraint is a policy (such as a poorly designed compensation scheme for salespersons) that prevents the company from using its resources more

[7]Corinne Boone and Daniel Blake Rubinstein, "Natural Solution," *CA Magazine* (May 1997), pp. 18–22.

effectively. If direct labour is not the constraint, there is no reason to increase it. Hiring more direct labour would increase costs without increasing the output of salable products and services.

Second, TOC emphasizes continuous improvement to maintain competitiveness. Without committed and enthusiastic employees, sustained continuous improvement is virtually impossible. Because layoffs often have devastating effects on employee morale, managers involved in TOC are extremely reluctant to lay off employees.

For these reasons, most managers in TOC companies believe that direct labour in their companies behaves much more like a committed fixed cost than a variable cost. Hence, in the modified form of variable costing used in TOC companies, direct labour is not included as a part of product costs.

IMPACT OF JIT INVENTORY METHODS

OBJECTIVE 6

Explain how the use of JIT inventory methods decreases or eliminates the difference in net income reported under the variable and absorption costing methods.

We have learned in this chapter that variable and absorption costing will provide different net income figures whenever the number of units produced is different from the number of units sold. We have also learned that the absorption costing net income figure can be erratic, sometimes moving in a direction that is different from the movement in sales.

When companies employ JIT inventory methods, these problems are either eliminated or become insignificant. The reason is as follows: The erratic movement of net income under absorption costing and the differences in net income between absorption and variable costing arise *because of changing levels of inventory.* Under JIT, goods are produced to customers' orders. As a result, there are few goods in process at year-end, and no finished goods in warehouses waiting for orders from customers. Thus, with production geared strictly to sales, inventories are largely (or entirely) eliminated, thereby eliminating also any opportunity for significant amounts of fixed manufacturing overhead costs to be shifted between periods under absorption costing. When JIT is in operation, therefore, both variable and absorption costing will show basically the same net income figure, and the net income under absorption costing will move in the same direction as movements in sales.

Northern Telecom, a large technologically focused company, has modified its income statement to better able its managers to make decisions and manage costs. Previously Northern Telecom used full absorption costing to determine inventories and cost of goods sold.

Under the proposed system direct material costs were the only cost to be included in inventory and cost of goods sold. Labour and overhead were treated as a period expense to determine internal net profit numbers. Activity based costing was used to link physical activities with dollar costs to help operating personnel control costs.

The concern held by Northern Telecom that the income number was not consistent with their desired external reporting requirements was alleviated by a special adjustment to transform inventories and net income to the desired required absorption cost approach.[8]

---

[8]Paul Sharman, "Time to Re-examine the P&L," *CMA Magazine* (September 1991), pp. 22–25.

Of course, the cost of a unit of product will still be different between variable and absorption costing, as explained earlier in the chapter. But the differences in net income will largely disappear when JIT is used, thereby making it easier for management to interpret the data produced on an absorption costing income statement.

SUMMARY

In costing products and services, companies can use either variable or absorption costing. Under variable costing, only those production costs that vary with output are treated as product costs. This includes direct materials, direct labour, and variable overhead. Fixed manufacturing overhead is treated as a period cost and charged off against revenue as it is incurred, the same as selling and administrative expenses. By contrast, absorption costing treats fixed manufacturing overhead as a product cost, along with direct materials, direct labour, and variable overhead.

Because absorption costing treats fixed manufacturing overhead as a product cost, a portion of fixed manufacturing overhead is assigned to each unit as it is produced. If units of product are unsold at the end of a period, then the fixed manufacturing overhead cost attached to the units is carried with them into the inventory account and deferred to the next period. When these units are sold during the next period, the fixed manufacturing overhead cost attached to them is released from the inventory account and charged against revenues as part of cost of goods sold. Thus, under absorption costing, it is possible to defer a portion of the fixed manufacturing overhead cost of one period to the next period through the inventory account.

Unfortunately, this shifting of fixed manufacturing overhead cost between periods can cause net income to move in an erratic manner and can result in confusion and unwise decisions on the part of management. To guard against mistakes when they interpret income statement data, managers must be alert to any changes that may have taken place in inventory levels or in unit product costs during the period.

Variable costing may not be used externally for either financial reporting or income tax purposes in some jurisdictions. However, it is often used internally for planning purposes. The variable costing approach dovetails well with CVP concepts that are often indispensable in profit planning and decision making.

REVIEW PROBLEM

Dexter Company produces and sells a single product. Selected cost and operating data relating to the product for a recent year are given below:

Units in beginning inventory	–0–
Units produced during the year	10,000
Units sold during the year	8,000
Units in ending inventory	2,000
Selling price per unit	$ 50
Manufacturing costs:	
Variable per unit:	
Direct materials	11
Direct labour	6
Variable overhead	3
Fixed per year	100,000
Selling and administrative costs:	
Variable per unit	5
Fixed per year	70,000

Required

1. Assume that the company uses absorption costing.
   a. Compute the unit product cost.
   b. Prepare an income statement for the year.
2. Assume that the company uses variable costing.
   a. Compute the unit product cost.
   b. Prepare an income statement for the year.
3. Reconcile the variable costing and absorption costing net income figures.

Solution to Review Problem

1. a. Under absorption costing, all manufacturing costs, variable and fixed, are included in unit product costs:

Direct materials	$11
Direct labour	6
Variable manufacturing overhead	3
Fixed manufacturing overhead ($100,000 ÷ 10,000 units)	10
Unit product cost	$30

   b. The absorption costing income statement follows:

Sales (8,000 units × $50)		$400,000
Cost of goods sold:		
Beginning inventory	$ –0–	
Add cost of goods manufactured		
(10,000 units × $30)	300,000	
Goods available for sale	300,000	
Less ending inventory (2,000 units × $30)	60,000	240,000
Gross margin		160,000
Less selling and administrative expenses		110,000*
Net income		$ 50,000

*Variable (8,000 units × $5)	$ 40,000	
Fixed per year	70,000	
Total	$110,000	

2. a. Under variable costing, only the variable manufacturing costs are included in unit product costs:

Direct materials	$11
Direct labour	6
Variable manufacturing overhead	3
Unit product cost	$20

   b. The variable costing income statement follows. Notice that the variable cost of goods sold is computed in a simpler, more direct manner than in the examples provided earlier. On a variable costing income statement, either approach is acceptable.

Sales (8,000 units × $50)		$400,000
Less variable expenses:		
Variable cost of goods sold		
(8,000 units × $20)	$160,000	
Variable selling and administrative		
expenses (8,000 units × $5)	40,000	200,000
Contribution margin		200,000
Less fixed expenses:		
Fixed manufacturing overhead	100,000	
Fixed selling and administrative expenses	70,000	170,000
Net income		$ 30,000

3. The reconciliation of the variable and absorption costing net income figures follows:

Variable costing net income	$30,000
Add fixed manufacturing overhead costs deferred in inventory under absorption costing (2,000 units × $10)	20,000
Absorption costing net income	$50,000

KEY TERMS FOR REVIEW

Absorption costing   A costing method that includes all manufacturing costs—direct materials, direct labour, and both variable and fixed manufacturing overhead—in the cost of a unit of product. Absorption costing is also referred to as the *full cost* method. (p. 380)

Direct costing   Another term for variable cost. See *Variable costing*. (p. 381)

Fixed overhead cost deferred in inventory   The portion of the fixed manufacturing overhead cost of a period that goes into inventory under the absorption costing method as a result of production exceeding sales. (p. 383)

Fixed manufacturing overhead cost released from inventory   The portion of the fixed manufacturing overhead cost of a *prior* period that becomes an expense of the current period under the absorption costing method as a result of sales exceeding production. (pp. 389–400)

Full cost method   See *Absorption costing*. (p. 380)

Marginal costing   Another term for variable costing. See *Variable costing*. (p. 381)

Normalized overhead rate   A rate based on the average activity of many periods—past and present—rather than based only on the expected activity of the current period. (p. 394)

Variable costing   A costing method that includes only variable manufacturing costs—direct materials, direct labour, and variable manufacturing overhead—in the cost of a unit of product. Also see *Marginal costing or Direct costing*. (p. 380)

QUESTIONS

8–1   What is the basic difference between absorption costing and variable costing?

8–2   Are selling and administrative expenses treated as product costs or as period costs under variable costing?

8–3   Explain how fixed manufacturing overhead costs are shifted from one period to another under absorption costing.

8–4   What arguments can be advanced in favour of treating fixed overhead costs as product costs?

8–5   What arguments can be advanced in favour of treating fixed overhead costs as period costs?

8–6   If production and sales are equal, which method would you expect to show the higher net income, variable costing or absorption costing? Why?

8–7   If production exceeds sales, which method would you expect to show the higher net income, variable costing or absorption costing? Why?

8–8   If fixed overhead costs are released from inventory under absorption costing, what does this tell you about the level of production in relation to the level of sales?

8–9   During 19x3, Parker Company had $5,000,000 in sales and reported a $300,000 loss in its annual report to shareholders. According to a CVP analysis prepared for management's use, $5,000,000 in sales is the break-even point for the company. Did the company's inventory level for the year increase, decrease, or remain unchanged? Explain.

8–10   Under absorption costing, how is it possible to increase net income without increasing sales?

8–11   What limitations are there to the use of variable costing?

8–12   Develop a reason from financial accounting theory which would support a recommendation of absorption costing for financial accounting purposes.

8–13   How does the use of JIT inventory methods reduce or eliminate the difference in reported net income between absorption and variable costing?

EXERCISES

E8–1 CompuDesk, Inc., makes an oak desk specially designed for personal computers. The desk sells for $200. Data for last year's operations follow:

Units in beginning inventory	–0–
Units produced	10,000
Units sold	9,000
Units in ending inventory	1,000

Variable costs per unit:

Direct materials	$	60
Direct labour		30
Variable manufacturing overhead		10
Variable selling and administrative		20
Total variable cost per unit	$	120

Fixed costs:

Fixed manufacturing overhead	$300,000
Fixed selling and administrative	450,000
Total fixed costs	$750,000

Required

1. Assume that the company uses variable costing. Compute the unit product cost for one computer desk.
2. Assume that the company uses variable costing. Prepare an income statement for the year in good form using the contribution format.
3. What is the company's break-even point in terms of units sold?

E8–2 Refer to the data in E8–1 for CompuDesk. Assume in this exercise that the company uses absorption costing.

Required

1. Compute the unit product cost for one computer desk.
2. Prepare an income statement for the year in good form.

E8–3 Shastri Bicycle of Bombay, India, produces an inexpensive, yet rugged, bicycle for use on the city's crowded streets that it sells for 500 rupees. (Indian currency is denominated in rupees, denoted by R.) Selected data for the company's operations last year follow:

Units in beginning inventory	–0–
Units produced	10,000
Units sold	8,000
Units in ending inventory	2,000

Variable costs per unit:

Direct materials	R120
Direct labour	140
Variable manufacturing overhead	50
Variable selling and administrative	20

Fixed costs:

Fixed manufacturing overhead	R600,000
Fixed selling and administrative	400,000

Required

1. Assume that the company uses absorption costing. Compute the unit product cost for one bicycle.
2. Assume that the company uses variable costing. Compute the unit product cost for one bicycle.

E8–4 Refer to the data in E8–3 for Shastri Bicycle. An income statement prepared under the absorption costing method by the company's accountant appears below:

Sales (8,000 units × R500)		R4,000,000
Costs of goods sold:		
Beginning inventory	R –0–	
Cost of goods manufactured (10,000 units × R _?_)	3,700,000	
Goods available for sale	3,700,000	
Less ending inventory (2,000 units × R _?_)	740,000	2,960,000
Gross margin		1,040,000
Less selling and administrative expenses:		
Variable selling and administrative	160,000	
Fixed selling and administrative	400,000	560,000
Net income		R 480,000

Required

1. Determine how much of the ending inventory of R740,000 above consists of fixed manufacturing overhead cost deferred in inventory to the next period.
2. Prepare an income statement for the year using the variable costing method. Explain the difference in net income between the two costing methods.

E8–5 Amcor, Inc., produces and sells a single product. The following costs relate to its production and sale:

Variable costs per unit:	
Direct materials	$10
Direct labour	5
Variable manufacturing overhead	2
Variable selling and administrative expenses	4
Fixed costs per year:	
Fixed manufacturing overhead	$ 90,000
Fixed selling and administrative expenses	300,000

During the last year, 30,000 units were produced and 25,000 units were sold. The Finished Goods inventory account at the end of the year shows a balance of $85,000 for the 5,000 unsold units.

Required

1. Is the company using absorption costing or variable costing to cost units in the Finished Goods inventory account? Show computations to support your answer.
2. Assume that the company wishes to prepare financial statements for the year to issue to its shareholders.
   a. Is the $85,000 figure for Finished Goods inventory the correct figure to use on these statements for external reporting purposes? Explain.
   b. At what dollar amount *should* the 5,000 units be carried in inventory for external reporting purposes?

E8–6 Morey Company was organized just one year ago. The results of the company's first year of operations are shown below (absorption costing basis):

MOREY COMPANY
Income Statement

Sales (40,000 units at $33.75)		$1,350,000
Less cost of goods sold:		
Beginning inventory	$ –0–	
Cost of goods manufactured (50,000 units at $21)	1,050,000	
Goods available for sale	1,050,000	
Ending inventory (10,000 units at $21)	210,000	840,000
Gross margin		510,000
Less selling and administrative expenses		420,000
Net income		$ 90,000

The company's selling and administrative expenses consist of $300,000 per year in fixed expenses and $3 per unit sold in variable expenses. The company's $21 unit product cost given above is computed as follows:

Direct materials	$10
Direct labour	4
Variable manufacturing overhead	2
Fixed manufacturing overhead ($250,000 ÷ 50,000 units)	5
Unit product cost	$21

Required

1. Redo the company's income statement in the contribution format, using variable costing.
2. Reconcile any difference between the net income figure on your variable costing income statement and the net income figure on the absorption costing income statement above.

E8–7 Maxwell Company manufactures and sells a single product. The following costs were incurred during the company's first year of operations:

Variable costs per unit:	
Production:	
Direct materials	$18
Direct labour	7
Variable manufacturing overhead	2
Variable selling and administrative	5
Fixed costs per year:	
Fixed manufacturing overhead	$160,000
Fixed selling and administrative expenses	110,000

During the year, the company produced 20,000 units and sold 16,000 units. The selling price of the company's product is $50 per unit.

Required

1. Assume that the company uses the absorption costing method:
   a. Compute the unit product cost.
   b. Prepare an income statement for the year.
2. Assume that the company uses the variable costing method:
   a. Compute the unit product cost.
   b. Prepare an income statement for the year.

PROBLEMS

P8–8   Straightforward Variable Costing Statements   During Denton Company's first two years of operations, the company reported net income as follows (absorption costing basis):

	Year 1	Year 2
Sales (at $50)	$1,000,000	$1,500,000
Less cost of goods sold:		
Beginning inventory	–0–	170,000
Add cost of goods manufactured (at $34)	850,000	850,000
Goods available for sale	850,000	1,020,000
Less ending inventory (at $34)	170,000	–0–
Cost of goods sold	680,000	1,020,000
Gross margin	320,000	480,000
Less selling and administrative expenses*	310,000	340,000
Net income	$ 10,000	$ 140,000

*$3 per unit variable; $250,000 fixed each year.

The company's $34 unit product cost is computed as follows:

Direct materials	$ 8
Direct labour	10
Variable manufacturing overhead	2
Fixed manufacturing overhead ($350,000 ÷ 25,000 units)	14
Unit product cost	$34

Production and cost data for the two years are given below:

	Year 1	Year 2
Units produced	25,000	25,000
Units sold	20,000	30,000

Required

1. Prepare an income statement for each year in the contribution format using variable costing.
2. Reconcile the absorption costing and variable costing net income figures for each year.

P8–9 Straightforward Comparison of Costing Methods   Wiengot Antennas, Inc., produces and sells a unique type of TV antenna. The company has just opened a new plant to manufacture the antenna, and the following cost and revenue data have been reported for the first month of the plant's operation:

Beginning inventory	–0–
Units produced	40,000
Units sold	35,000
Selling price per unit	$ 60
Selling and administrative expenses:	
Variable per unit	$ 2
Fixed (total)	560,000
Manufacturing costs:	
Direct materials cost per unit	15
Direct labour cost per unit	7
Variable manufacturing overhead cost per unit	2
Fixed manufacturing overhead cost (total)	640,000

Since the new antenna is unique in design, management is anxious to see how profitable it will be and has asked that an income statement be prepared for the month.

Required

1. Assume that the company uses absorption costing.
   a. Determine the unit product cost.
   b. Prepare an income statement for the month.
2. Assume that the company uses the contribution approach with variable costing.
   a. Determine the unit product cost.
   b. Prepare an income statement for the month.

3. Explain the reason for any difference in the ending inventory under the two costing methods and the impact of this difference on reported net income.

P8–10   A Comparison of Costing Methods   Advance Products, Inc., has just organized a new division to manufacture and sell specially designed tables for mounting and using personal computers. The company's new plant is highly automated and thus requires high monthly fixed costs, as shown in the schedule below:

Manufacturing costs:
Variable costs per unit:
Direct materials . . . . $ 50
Direct labour   36
Variable manufacturing overhead   4
Fixed manufacturing overhead costs (total)   240,000

Selling and administrative costs:
Variable . . . .   15% of sales
Fixed (total) $160,000

During the first month of operations, the following activity was recorded:

Units produced   4,000
Units sold   3,200
Selling price per unit $250

Required

1. Compute the unit product cost under:
    a. Absorption costing.
    b. Variable costing.
2. Prepare an income statement for the month using absorption costing.
3. Prepare an income statement for the month using variable costing.
4. Assume that in order to continue operations, the company must obtain additional financing. As a member of top management, which of the statements that you have prepared in (2) and (3) above would you prefer to take with you as you negotiate with the bank?
5. Reconcile the absorption costing and variable costing net income figures in (2) and (3) above for the month.

P8–11   Absorption and Variable Costing; Production Constant, Sales Fluctuate   Sandi Scott obtained a patent on a small electronic device and organized Scott Products, Inc., in order to produce and sell the device. During the first month of operations, the device was very well received on the market, so Ms. Scott looked forward to a healthy profit from sales. For this reason, she was surprised to see a loss for the month on her income statement. This statement was prepared by her accounting service, which takes great pride in providing its clients with timely financial data. The statement follows:

SCOTT PRODUCTS, INC.
Income Statement

Sales (40,000 units)		$200,000
Less variable expenses:		
Variable cost of goods sold*	$80,000	
Selling and administrative expenses	30,000	110,000
Contribution margin		90,000
Less fixed expenses:		
Fixed manufacturing overhead	$75,000	
Selling and administrative expenses	20,000	$ 95,000
Net loss		$ (5,000)

*Consists of direct materials, direct labour, and variable manufacturing overhead.

Ms. Scott is discouraged over the loss shown for the month, particularly since she had planned to use the statement to encourage investors to purchase shares in the new company. A friend, who is a CA, insists that the company should be using absorption costing rather than variable costing. He argues that if absorption costing had been used, the company would probably have reported a nice profit for the month.

Selected cost data relating to the product and to the first month of operations follow:

Units produced	50,000
Units sold	40,000

Variable costs per unit:

Direct materials	$1.00
Direct labour	0.80
Variable manufacturing overhead	0.20
Variable selling and administrative expenses	0.75

Required

1. Complete the following:
   a. Compute the unit product cost under absorption costing.
   b. Redo the company's income statement for the month using absorption costing.
   c. Reconcile the variable and absorption costing net income figures.
2. Was the CA correct in suggesting that the company really earned a "profit" for the month? Explain.
3. During the second month of operations, the company again produced 50,000 units but sold 60,000 units. (Assume no change in total fixed costs.)
   a. Prepare an income statement for the month using variable costing.
   b. Prepare an income statement for the month using absorption costing.
   c. Reconcile the variable costing and absorption costing net income figures.

P8–12   Preparation and Reconciliation of Variable Costing Statements

Linden Company manufactures and sells a single product. Cost data for the product follow:

Variable costs per unit:

Direct materials	$ 6
Direct labour	12
Variable factory overhead	4
Variable selling and administrative	3
Total variable costs per unit	$25

Fixed costs per month:

Factory overhead	$240,000
Selling and administrative	180,000
Total fixed costs per month	$420,000

The product sells for $40 per unit. Production and sales data for May and June, the first two months of operations, are as follows:

	Units Produced	Units Sold
May	30,000	26,000
June	30,000	34,000

Income statements prepared by the accounting department, using absorption costing, are presented below:

	May	June
Sales	$1,040,000	$1,360,000
Less cost of goods sold:		
Beginning inventory	–0–	120,000
Cost of goods manufactured	900,000	900,000
Goods available for sale	900,000	1,020,000
Less ending inventory	120,000	–0–
Cost of goods sold	780,000	1,020,000
Gross margin	260,000	340,000
Less selling and administrative expenses	258,000	282,000
Net income	$ 2,000	$ 58,000

Required

1. Determine the unit product cost under:
   a. Absorption costing.
   b. Variable costing.
2. Prepare income statements for May and June using the contribution approach with variable costing.
3. Reconcile the variable costing and absorption costing net income figures.
4. The company's accounting department has determined the break-even point to be 28,000 units per month, computed as follows:

$$\frac{\text{Fixed cost per month}}{\text{Unit contribution margin}} = \frac{\$420,000}{\$15} = 28,000 \text{ units}$$

Upon receiving this figure, the president commented, "There's something peculiar here. The controller says that the break-even point is 28,000 units per month. Yet we sold only 26,000 units in May, and the income statement we received showed a $2,000 profit. Which figure do we believe?" Prepare a brief explanation of what happened on the May income statement.

P8–13   Prepare and Interpret Statements; Changes in Both Sales and Production; Automation; JIT   Memotec, Inc., was organized on January 2, 19x1, to manufacture and sell a unique electronic part. Operating results for the first three years of activity were as follows (absorption costing basis):

	19x1	19x2	19x3
Sales	$1,000,000	$800,000	$1,000,000
Cost of goods sold:			
Beginning inventory.................	–0–	–0–	280,000
Cost of goods manufactured...........	800,000	840,000	760,000
Goods available for sale.............. 800,000 840,000	1,040,000		
Less ending inventory................	–0–	280,000	190,000
Cost of goods sold 800,000 560,000	850,000		
Gross margin....................... 200,000 240,000	150,000		
Less selling and administrative			
expenses	170,000	150,000	170,000

Sales dropped by 20% during 19x2 due to the entry of several foreign competitors into the market. Memotec had expected sales to remain constant at 50,000 units for the year; production was set at 60,000 units in order to build a buffer of protection against unexpected spurts in demand. By the start of 19x3, management could see that spurts in demand were unlikely and that the inventory was excessive. To work off the excessive inventories, Memotec cut back production during 19x3, as shown below:

	19x1	19x2	19x3
Production in units	50,000	60,000	40,000
Sales in units	50,000	40,000	50,000

Additional information about the company follows:
a. The company's plant is highly automated. Variable manufacturing costs (direct materials, direct labour, and variable manufacturing overhead) total only $4 per unit, and fixed manufacturing costs total $600,000 per year.
b. Fixed manufacturing costs are applied to units of product on the basis of each year's production. (That is, a new fixed overhead rate is computed each year, as in Exhibit 8–6.)
c. Variable selling and administrative expenses are $2 per unit sold. Fixed selling and administrative expenses total $70,000 per year.
d. The company uses a FIFO inventory flow.

Memotec's management can't understand why profits tripled during 19x2 when sales dropped by 20%, and why a loss was incurred during 19x3 when sales recovered to previous levels.

Required

1. Prepare a new income statement for each year using the contribution approach with variable costing.
2. Refer to the absorption costing income statements above.
   a. Compute the unit product cost in each year under absorption costing. (Show how much of this cost is variable and how much is fixed.)
   b. Reconcile the variable costing and absorption costing net income figures for each year.
3. Refer again to the absorption costing income statements. Explain why net income was higher in 19x2 than it was in 19x1 under the absorption approach, in light of the fact that fewer units were sold in 19x2 than in 19x1.
4. Refer again to the absorption costing income statements. Explain why the company suffered a loss in 19x3 but reported a profit in 19x1, although the same number of units was sold in each year.
5. a. Explain how operations would have differed in 19x2 and 19x3 if the company had been using JIT inventory methods.
   b. If JIT had been in use during 19x2 and 19x3, what would the company's net income (or loss) have been in each year under absorption costing? Explain the reason for any differences between these income figures and the figures reported by the company in the statements above.

CASES

C8–14 Ethics and the Manager; Absorption Costing Income Statements

Michael Lee was hired as chief executive officer (CEO) in late November by the board of directors of Hunter Electronics, a company that produces a state-of-the-art CD-ROM drive for personal computers. The previous CEO had been fired by the board due to a series of questionable business practices including prematurely recording revenues on products that had not yet been shipped to customers.

Michael felt that his first priority on the job was to restore employee morale—which had suffered during the previous CEO's reign. He was particularly anxious to build a sense of trust between himself and the company's employees. His second priority was to prepare the budget for the coming year, which the board of directors wanted to review in their December 15 meeting.

After hammering out the details in meetings with key managers, Michael was able to put together a budget that he felt the company could realistically meet during the coming year. That budget appears below:

Basic Budget Data

Units in beginning inventory	–0–
Units produced	200,000
Units sold	200,000
Units in ending inventory	–0–
Variable costs per unit:	
Direct materials	$ 50
Direct labour	40
Variable manufacturing overhead	20
Variable selling and administrative	10
Total variable cost per unit	$120
Fixed costs:	
Fixed manufacturing overhead	$ 8,400,000
Fixed selling and administrative	3,600,000
Total fixed costs	$12,000,000

HUNTER ELECTRONICS
Budget Income Statement
(absorption method)

Sales (200,000 units)		$40,000,000
Cost of goods sold:		
Beginning inventory	$ –0–	
Cost of goods manufactured (200,000 units × $152)	30,400,000	
Goods available for sale	30,400,000	
Less ending inventory	–0–	30,400,000
Gross margin		9,600,000
Less selling and administrative expenses:		
Variable selling and administrative	2,000,000	
Fixed selling and administrative	3,600,000	5,600,000
Net income		$ 4,000,000

While the board of directors did not oppose the budget, they made it clear that the budget was not as ambitious as they had hoped. The most influential member of the board stated that "our top managers should have to really stretch to meet profit goals." After some discussion, the board decided to set a profit goal of $4,800,000 for the coming year. To provide strong incentives and a win-win situation, the board agreed to pay out bonuses to top managers of $200,000 if this profit goal were met. Michael's share of the bonus pool would be $50,000. The bonus would be all-or-nothing. If actual net income turned out to be $4,800,000 or more, the bonus would be paid. Otherwise, no bonus would be allowed.

Required

1. Assuming that the company does not build up its inventory (i.e., production equals sales) and its selling price and cost structure remain the same, how many units of the CD-ROM drive would have to be sold to meet the target net income of $4,800,000?

2. Verify your answer to (1) above by constructing a revised budget and budgeted income statement that yields a net income of $4,800,000. Use the absorption costing method.

3. Unfortunately, by October of the next year it had become clear that the company would not be able to make the $4,800,000 target profit. In fact, it looked like the company would wind up the year as originally planned, with sales of 200,000 units, no ending inventories, and a profit of $4,000,000.

    Several managers who were reluctant to lose their year-end bonuses approached Michael and suggested that the company could still show a profit of $4,800,000. The managers argued that at the present rate of sales, there was enough capacity by working overtime to produce tens of thousands of additional CD-ROM drives for the warehouse. Overtime cost might have to be incurred, but all of this additional cost would be assigned to the CD-ROM drives in ending inventory.

    If sales are 200,000 units for the year and the selling price and cost structure remain the same, how many units would have to be produced to show a profit of at least $4,800,000 under absorption costing? (Round your answer up to the nearest whole unit.)

4. Verify your answer to (3) above by constructing an income statement. Use the absorption costing method.

5. Do you think Michael Lee should approve the plan to build ending inventories in order to attain the target profit?

6. What advice would you give to the board of directors concerning how they determine bonuses in the future?

C8–15   Absorption and Variable Costing; Uneven Production; Break-Even Analysis; Automation; JIT Impact   "I thought that new, automated plant was supposed to make us more efficient and therefore more profitable," exclaimed Marla Warner, president of Visic Company. "Just look at these monthly income statements for the second quarter. Sales have risen steadily month by month, but income is going in the opposite direction, and we even show a loss for June! Can someone explain what's happening?"

The statements to which Ms. Warner was referring are given below:

VISIC COMPANY
Monthly Income Statement
For the Second Quarter

	April	May	June
Sales (at $25)	$1,500,000	$1,625,000	$1,750,000
Less cost of goods sold:			
Beginning inventory.........................	70,000	280,000	350,000
Cost applied to production:			
Variable manufacturing costs (at $6)	450,000	420,000	300,000
Fixed manufacturing overhead..............	600,000	560,000	400,000
Cost of goods manufactured................	1,050,000	980,000	700,000
Goods available for sale	1,120,000	1,260,000	1,050,000
Less ending inventory........................	280,000	350,000	70,000
Cost of goods sold	840,000	910,000	980,000
Underapplied or (overapplied) overhead cost......	(40,000)	—	160,000
Adjusted cost of goods sold	800,000	910,000	1,140,000
Gross margin................................	700,000	715,000	610,000
Less selling and administrative expenses...........	620,000	665,000	710,000
Net income (loss)	$ 80,000	$ 50,000	$(100,000)

"Fixed costs associated with the new plant are very high," replied Brian Hauber, the controller. "We're just following good absorption costing, as we have for years."

"Maybe the costing method *is* the problem," responded Teri Carlyle, the financial vice president. "A management development seminar I just attended suggested that the contribution approach, with variable costing, is the best way to report profit data to management. The contribution approach is particularly good when production is erratic, as ours has been lately."

Production and sales data for the second quarter follow:

	April	May	June
Production in units...........	75,000	70,000	50,000
Sales in units	60,000	65,000	70,000

Additional information about the company's operations is given below:

a. Five thousand units were in inventory on April 1.

b. Fixed manufacturing overhead costs total $1,680,000 per quarter and are incurred evenly throughout the quarter. This fixed manufacturing overhead cost is applied to units of product on the basis of a budgeted production volume of 70,000 units per month.

c. Variable selling and administrative expenses are $9 per unit sold. The remainder of the selling and administrative expenses on the statements above are fixed.

d. The company uses a FIFO inventory flow. Work in process inventories are insignificant and can be ignored.

"We had to build inventory early in the year in anticipation of a strike in June," said Mr. Hauber. "Since the union settled without a strike, we then had to cut back production in June in order to work off the excess inventories. The income statements you have are completely accurate."

Required

1. Prepare an income statement for each month using the contribution approach with variable costing.
2. Compute the monthly break-even point in units under variable costing.
3. Explain to Ms. Warner why profits have moved erratically over the three-month period shown in the absorption costing income statements above and why profits have not been more closely correlated with changes in sales volume.
4. Reconcile the variable costing and absorption costing net income (loss) figures for each month. Show all computations, and show how you derive each figure used in your reconciliation.

5. Assume that the company had decided to introduce JIT inventory methods at the beginning of June. (Sales and production during April and May were as shown above.)

   a. How many units would have been produced during June under JIT?

   b. Starting with the next quarter (July, August, and September), would you expect any difference between the income reported under absorption costing and under variable costing? Explain why there would or would not be any difference.

   c. Refer to your computations in (2) above. How would JIT help break-even analysis "make sense" under absorption costing?

C8–16 The Case of the Perplexed President; Automation; JIT Impact   John Ovard, president of Mylar, Inc., was looking forward to receiving the company's second quarter income statement. He knew that the sales budget of 20,000 units sold had been met during the second quarter and that this represented a 25% increase in sales over the first quarter. He was especially happy about the increase in sales, since Mylar was about to approach its bank for additional loan money for expansion purposes. He anticipated that the strong second-quarter results would be a real plus in persuading the bank to extend the additional credit.

For this reason Mr. Ovard was shocked when he received the second-quarter income statement below, which showed a substantial drop in net income from the first quarter.

MYLAR, INC.
Income Statements
For the First Two Quarters

	First Quarter		Second Quarter	
Sales		$1,600,000		$2,000,000
Less cost of goods sold:				
Beginning inventory	$ 210,000		$ 490,000	
Cost of goods manufactured	1,400,000		980,000	
Goods available for sale	1,610,000		1,470,000	
Less ending inventory..................	490,000		70,000	
Cost of goods sold....................	1,120,000		1,400,000	
Add underapplied overhead	–0–	1,120,000	240,000	1,640,000
Gross margin...........................		480,000		360,000
Less selling and administrative expenses		310,000		330,000
Net income		$ 170,000		$ 30,000

Mr. Ovard was certain there had to be an error somewhere and immediately called the controller into his office to find the problem. The controller stated, "That net income figure is correct, John. I agree that sales went up during the second quarter, but the problem is in production. You see, we budgeted to produce 20,000 units each quarter, but a strike in one of our supplier's plants forced us to cut production back to only 14,000 units in the second quarter. That's what caused the drop in net income."

Mr. Ovard was angered by the controller's explanation. "I call you in here to find out why income dropped when sales went up, and you talk about production! So what if production was off? What does that have to do with the sales that we made? If sales go up, then income ought to go up. If your statements can't show a simple thing like that, then we're due for some changes in your area!"

Budgeted production and sales for the year, along with actual production and sales for the first two quarters, are given below:

	Quarter			
	First	**Second**	**Third**	**Fourth**
Budgeted sales (units)......................	16,000	20,000	20,000	24,000
Actual sales (units)	16,000	20,000	—	—
Budgeted production (units)	20,000	20,000	20,000	20,000
Actual production (units)	20,000	14,000	—	—

The company's plant is heavily automated, so fixed manufacturing overhead costs total $800,000 per quarter. Variable manufacturing costs are $30 per unit. The fixed manufacturing overhead cost is applied to units of product at the rate of $40 per unit (based on the budgeted production shown above). Any under- or overapplied overhead is taken directly to cost of goods sold for the quarter.

The company had 3,000 units in inventory to start the first quarter and uses the FIFO inventory method. Variable selling and administrative expenses are $5 per unit sold.

Required

1. What characteristic of absorption costing caused the drop in net income for the second quarter and what could the controller have said to explain the problem more fully?
2. Prepare income statements for each quarter using the contribution approach, with variable costing.
3. Reconcile the absorption costing and the variable costing net income figures for each quarter.
4. Identify and discuss the advantages and disadvantages of using the variable costing method for internal reporting purposes.
5. Assume that the company had introduced JIT inventory methods at the beginning of the second quarter. (Sales and production during the first quarter were as shown above.)
   a. How many units would have been produced during the second quarter under JIT?
   b. Starting with the third quarter, would you expect any difference between the net income reported under absorption costing and under variable costing? Explain why there would or would not be any difference.

C8–17 Multiple Inventories; Prepare and Reconcile Variable Costing Statement
Magna Computers Ltd. specializes in manufacturing computers used in medical practices. Since the specifications for the computers are determined by the customer and vary considerably, the company uses a job-order costing system. Factory overhead is applied to jobs on the basis of direct labour-hours, utilizing the absorption cost method. Magna's predetermined overhead rates for 19x1 and 19x2 were based on the following estimated data:

	19x1	19x2
Direct labour-hours....................	32,500	44,000
Variable factory overhead..............	$162,500	$198,000
Fixed factory overhead................	130,000	176,000

Jim Hacking, Magna's controller, would like to use a special variable costing for internal reporting purposes since he believes statements prepared using the proposed costing are more appropriate.

a. Magna's comparative income statement for 19x1–x2 follows:

	19x1	19x2
Sales.......................................	$1,140,000	$1,520,000
Cost of goods sold:		
Finished goods inventory, January 1	16,000	25,000
Add cost of goods manufactured	720,000	976,000
Goods available for sale.........................	736,000	1,001,000
Finished goods inventory, December 31	25,000	14,000
Cost of goods sold	711,000	987,000
Add underapplied overhead	12,000	7,000
Adjusted cost of goods sold	723,000	994,000
Gross margin	417,000	526,000
Less operating expenses:		
Selling expense................................	150,000	190,000
Administrative expense	160,000	187,000
Total operating expenses	310,000	377,000
Net income......................................	$ 107,000	$ 149,000

b. The company's cost of goods manufactured for 19x2 is based on the following statement:

Dirtect materials used........................		$ 210,000
Direct labour cost............................		435,000
Manufacturing overhead cost:		
Actual manufacturing overhead cost	$364,000	
Less underapplied overhead..................	7,000	
Overhead applied to work in process...........		357,000
Total manufacturing costs		1,002,000
Add work in process, January 1.................		34,000
		1,036,000
Deduct work in process, December 31		60,000
Cost of goods manufactured....................		$ 976,000

The $364,000 actual overhead cost above consists of $189,000 in actual variable overhead cost and $175,000 in actual fixed overhead cost incurred during 19x2.

c. The company's inventories at the beginning and end of the year 19x2 contained the following cost elements:

	January 1, 19x2		December 31, 19x2	
Work in process:				
Direct material		$ 7,500		$12,000
Direct labour.........................		13,900		26,750
Manufacturing overhead:				
Variable overhead.....................	$?		$?	
Fixed overhead	?	12,600	?	21,250
Total cost inventory $34,000		$60,000		
Direct labour-hours expended...............		1,400		2,500
Finished goods:				
Direct material		$ 5,000		$ 3,000
Direct labour.........................		10,280		6,325
Manufacturing overhead:				
Variable overhead.....................	$?		$?	
Fixed overhead	?	9,720	?	4,675
Total cost in inventory $25,000		$14,000		

d. All administrative expenses in the company are fixed. The only variable selling expense is an 8% commission on sales.

e. As shown on the statements above, the company closes any under- or overapplied overhead to cost of goods sold.

f. Jim Hacking wants only materials charged to inventories. Direct labour and overhead are to be treated as period expenses. As part of his analysis, Jim determined the material and direct labour costs for 19x1 ending inventories and those for 19x2. Units on hand and in process at January 1, 19x2, were 75, each, half done as to materials and one-third done as to labour and overhead. At December 31, 19x2, work in process consisted of 50 units, half done as to materials and one-quarter done as to conversion. Finished goods January 1, 19x2, was composed of 25 units and 13 units on December 31, 19x2.

Required

1. Prepare an income statement for the company for 19x2 using the typical variable costing approach proposed. Show *all* supporting computations in good form.

2. Prepare a reconciliation of the variable costing and absorption costing net income figures for 19x2.

3. Prepare an income statement for 19x2 using the approach suggested by Jim Hacking in part f.

(CMA, heavily adapted)

C8–18 Segment Costing   The Grand Bank, one of Canada's newest Canadian-owned banks, opened three years ago. There is only one large office, as the bank has not grown enough to expand. It offers most of the services offered by the larger banks in Canada.

As a management accountant, you have been asked to undertake an examination of the cost of providing various services to customers. The reason for this examination is the president's concern about recent criticism about service charges the bank is charging to its customers. You have had time to review many of its methods and some of the data you collected follow.

Average balances for the past year were:

Current accounts	$2,000,000	Demand loans	$5,000,000
Savings accounts	8,000,000	Term loans	6,000,000
Chequing-savings accounts	4,000,000	Personal loans	5,000,000
Term deposit accounts	6,000,000	Mortgage loans	2,000,000
		Reserves Bank of Canada	2,000,000

Notes regarding the preceding accounts include:

a. No interest is paid on current accounts, as half the balances are left on deposit by customers, who prefer to leave a balance on hand to offset their other costs. For example, some customers keep a required minimum balance of $300 to receive free chequing. The remaining half of the current account balances is to cover cheques in process that have been deposited by the recipients but have not yet been posted off the issuers' accounts.

b. Savings accounts are paid interest of 5% during the year.

c. Chequing-savings are paid 4% interest, and customers are not required to pay for the processing of their cheques.

d. Average interest on term deposit accounts is 10%, with deposits made for terms of one to five years.

e. Demand loans earn 11% interest, and may be recovered with short notice, although this option is rarely used.

f. Term loans are made for various fixed terms and earn 12% during the year.

g. Mortgages earn 12% and personal loans earn 14%.

h. The government requires that Grand Bank, like all other banks, keep a reserve amounting to 10% of total deposits. This reserve does not earn interest.

There are other items on the balance sheet, but you have set them aside for future investigation. Your current investigation has focused on the deposits department of the bank, and you have extracted the following information by observation, inquiry, and time studies.

Interest rates are set by a combination of (1) government policy, (2) the weekly setting of the bank rate, and (3) rates offered by competing banks. The Grand Bank is not large enough to be a rate leader. As the funds are received by the deposits department, they are turned over to the loans department at a transfer rate of 9%. This transfer rate was agreed to by the two department managers at the beginning of the year, and each manager is expected to show a profit for the department using that rate.

The distribution of costs in the Grand Bank is:

50%	direct salaries
12	indirect salaries of which one-half are classed as fixed
18	premises costs
10	other variable costs
10	other fixed costs
100%	total

As salaries are such a large component of costs, standard measured times are used to estimate staff requirements:

Staffing is a problem as it is difficult to anticipate what customers' needs will be, and very little preliminary work can be done. Some of the standard times are as follows:

Minutes	By	Item
7	Clerk	Sell a Canada Savings Bond (CSB)
3	Clerk	Sell a money order
4	Sr. Clerk	Sell a term deposit
10	Manager	Open a savings account
60	Manager	Complete a personal loan request form
180	Manager	Complete a mortgage request form

These data are for the fiscal year ending October 31, 19x8; November has passed and it is now December. Your present investigation is for the month of November.

Further investigation has revealed the following information:

a. During November, the deposits counter was quite busy and the manager felt they had accomplished a great deal, but they would like to know how well things have gone. November was the month that many customers exchanged Canada Savings Bonds for new issues, and he had noticed that due to the new forms required by the government, and greater choices available, it took nine minutes to sell a bond. During the month, the deposits department had worked 640 hours at the counter, made up of 450 clerical, 160 senior clerical, and 30 manager hours.

   The manager of the department had been called to assist with some customers who preferred his advice as the choice of bonds was no longer a simple one. The normal workweek is 40 hours with pay grades of $288 per week for clerks, $480 for senior clerks, and $576 for the manager. When the plans were made up, the expected rates had been $264 for clerks, $480 for senior clerks, and $600 for the manager. The average bond size sold was $1,200 per transaction, with a commission of $1/8\%$.

   Volume of sales handled during the month was as follows:

	Sales	
	Actual	Planned
Canada Savings Bonds.	4,000	3,000
Money orders.	300	400
Term deposits.	2,000	4,500
New accounts opened	30	40

b. The deposits manager expressed his concern about the new Canada Savings Bond form. It was taking nine minutes to complete each sale and he wondered if it was really profitable and, if so, by how much.

Required

Prepare the report to the president analyzing the activity associated with CSBs. Include also an analysis of actual costs, planned costs, and incurred costs for the deposits department.

(SMAC, aadapted)

GROUP EXERCISES

GE8–19   One Size Fits All?   Nearly 70 years ago, eminent economist J. Maurice Clarke stated that "accountants use different costs because of their differing objectives." The business world has certainly become a lot more complicated since Professor Clarke's time. Yet students and managers often cling to the myth of a single, unique unit cost.

Required

1. How is accounting information used? That is, for what purposes, functions, or roles is cost information used?
2. Once you've identified the uses for cost information, how would you determine the makeup of the unit cost for each use? For example, one of the uses you should have identified is the need for a unit cost to value inventory and determine incomes for external financial reporting purposes. What do generally accepted accounting principles (GAAP) have to say about what is an inventoriable cost for financial reporting purposes?

GE8–20   Who Needs Customers? I Can Make Money without Them
Tough times always seem to bring out the worst in people. When companies are desperate to stay in business or to report more favourable earnings to Bay Street, some managers just can't seem to resist the temptation to manipulate reporting profits. Unfortunately, inventory is sometimes a tempting source of such manipulations. Understanding how such earning's distortions can occur, whether they result from intentional actions or innocent miscalculations, is

an important part of your learning. (Authors' Note: By assigning this exercise, the instructor is not trying to teach you how to perpetrate a fraud. Rather, the instructor is aware of how easy it is to commit such financial shenanigans if auditors and others are naive, negligent, or incompetent. For example, a standing joke at one company was that the next outside auditor "would be fresh out of high school." Someone so inexperienced is very vulnerable.)

Required

1. What unit cost concept is the basis for inventory valuation and cost of goods sold determination for external financial reporting purposes?
2. Explain the concept of "phantom" or "illusory" profits. Excluding inflation and changes in the selling prices of products, how could a firm with the same sales as last year report significantly higher profits? Could a firm with sales below the break-even point report profits? Explain.
3. Are all such "fictitious" profits an attempt to distort profits and mislead investors and creditors? If not, under what economic conditions would this most likely occur?
4. Could the reverse situation occur? That is, could lower accounting profits be reported even though the firm is not economically worse off? Under what economic conditions would this most likely occur? (Authors' Note: While usually not flagrant, such manipulations can have the effect of smoothing out earnings. And if capital markets prefer more predictable earnings and overreact when confronted with earnings surprises, then some managers may be tempted to give Bay Street what it wants without much regard for how they do it. In their mind, the end may justify the means.)
5. A far more serious indiscretion is inventory fraud by reporting fictitious inventories. Explain how this could result in a serious overstatement of earnings and assets.

GE8–21   Changing Cost Structures and Product Costing   As firms automate their operations with advanced manufacturing technology and information technology, cost structures are becoming more fixed and more indirect.

Required

1. What implications does this trend hold for arguments favouring full absorption cost? What implications does this trend hold for arguments favouring variable costing?
2. If full absorption costing continues to be used for external financial reporting, what impact will inventory buildups or inventory liquidations have on future reported earnings compared with the effect of inventory fluctuations on past reported earnings?
3. Most firms evaluate and compensate top management, in part, on the basis of reported income. Given changes in cost structures and implementation of JIT inventory techniques, would top management have a preference for variable costing or full absorption costing? Explain.

GE8–22   What's the Relationship between Costs and Prices?   Assume you have two restaurants in the same general area of town. One restaurant is an up-scale dining establishment offering a wide variety of appetizers, soups, entrees, and desserts. The other restaurant is a franchise of a national fast-food chain.

Required

1. What role do costs play in arriving at prices?
2. What are the variable and fixed costs?
3. How are prices determined at these two different establishments?
4. Are the products of both restaurants quality products?
5. What is the product at each restaurant?

PROFIT PLANNING

LEARNING OBJECTIVES

After studying Chapter 9, you should be able to:

1 Define budgeting and explain the difference between planning and control.

2 Enumerate the principal advantages of budgeting.

3 Diagram and explain the master budget interrelationships.

4 Prepare a sales budget, including a computation of expected cash receipts.

5 Prepare a production budget.

6 Prepare a direct materials budget, including a computation of expected cash disbursements for purchases of materials.

7 Prepare a manufacturing overhead budget and a selling and administrative expense budget.

8 Prepare a cash budget.

9 Prepare a budgeted income statement and a budgeted balance sheet.

10 Describe JIT purchasing and explain how it differs from JIT production.

11 Describe budgeting in the context of not-for-profit entities.

12 Define or explain the key terms listed at the end of the chapter.

When creating a budget—and therefore planning a profit structure—a large department store chain must plan for more than just its total sales. The chain must set budgets for each store and region. Based on targets set by corporate headquarters, the manager of an individual store will create profit plans for each department: men's wear, furniture, housewares, and so forth.

T he overall plan for a company is presented in the form of a business plan. A business plan is a description of all aspects of the business. It consists of information about the company's basic product or service and about the steps to be taken to reach its potential market. The business plan includes information about production methods, the competition, the management team, and details on how the business will be financed.

THE BUSINESS PLAN

The business plan is a key document for the internal management of the organization. It provides the basis for evaluation and control of the enterprise. It is also valuable for external use in attracting resources from potential creditors and investors. The answers to many of the questions raised by providers of funds can be found in the business plan.

Exhibit 9–1 shows a flowchart of the steps taken in a typical business plan. The 16-week time span is for illustrative purposes only. The actual length of the business plan varies with the nature and complexity of the venture and could span anywhere from a few weeks to several months. Note from the flowchart that it is essential that certain steps be completed before others are begun. It makes no sense, for example, to talk about forecasting sales (step 5) until a product or service has been picked (step 3) and the market has been researched (step 4).

EXHIBIT 9-1

Flowchart of the Steps in Developing a Business Plan.[1]

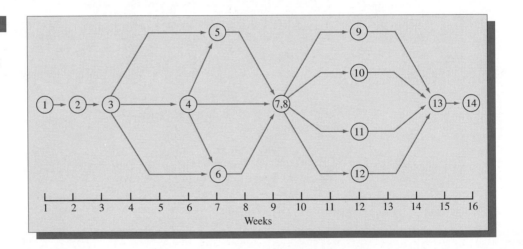

Key:
1. Decide to go into business.
2. Analyze yourself.
3. Pick product or service.
4. Research market.
5. Forecast sales revenues.
6. Pick site.
7. Develop production plan.
8. Develop marketing plan.
9. Develop personnel plan.
10. Decide whether to incorporate.
11. Explain need for records.
12. Develop insurance plan.
13. Develop financial plan.
14. Write summary overview.

---

[1]Adapted from Nicholas C. Siropolis, *Small Business Management: A Guide to Entrepreneurship,* 2nd ed. (Boston: Houghton Mifflin, 1982), pp. 138–41.

In the remainder of this chapter we turn our attention to the financial aspects of the business plan and to the steps taken by business organizations to achieve certain desired levels of profits—a process that is generally called **profit planning,** step 13 in the sequence presented in Exhibit 9–1. Keep in mind as you work your way through the chapter that the process you see occurs after numerous steps involving strategy selection, market research, site and production design and personnel planning along with various legal and systems decisions. Only then can details of the profit plan be constructed.

In our study, we shall see that profit planning is accomplished through the preparation of a number of budgets, which, when brought together, form an integrated part of a business plan known as the *master budget.* We shall find that the data going into the preparation of the master budget focus heavily on the future, rather than on the past.

THE BASIC FRAMEWORK OF BUDGETING

Definition of Budgeting

OBJECTIVE 1

Define budgeting and explain the difference between planning and control.

A **budget** is a detailed plan outlining the acquisition and use of financial and other resources over a given time period. It represents a plan for the future expressed in formal quantitative terms. The act of preparing a budget is called *budgeting.* The use of budgets to control a firm's activities is known as *budgetary control.*

The **master budget** is a summary of all phases of a company's plans and goals for the future. It sets specific targets for sales, production, distribution, and financing activities, and it generally culminates in a projected statement of net income and a projected statement of cash flows. In short, it represents a comprehensive expression of management's plans for the future and how these plans are to be accomplished.

Personal Budgets

Nearly everyone budgets to some extent, even though many of the people who prepare and use budgets do not recognize what they are doing as budgeting. For example, most people make estimates of the income to be realized over some future time period and plan expenditures for food, clothing, housing, and so on, accordingly. As a result of this planning, spending will usually be restricted by limiting it to some predetermined, allowable amount. In taking these steps, the individual clearly goes through a budget process in that he or she (1) makes an estimate of income, (2) plans expenditures, and (3) restricts spending in accordance with the plan. In other situations, individuals use estimates of income and expenditures to predict what their financial condition will be in the future. The budgets involved here may exist only in the mind of the individual, but they are budgets nonetheless in that they involve plans of how resources will be acquired and used over some specific time period.

The budgets of a business firm serve much the same functions as the budgets prepared informally by individuals. Business budgets tend to be more detailed and to involve more work in preparation (mostly because they are formal rather than informal), but they are similar to the budgets prepared by individuals in most other respects. Like personal budgets, they assist in planning and controlling expenditures; they also assist in predicting operating results and financial condition in future periods.

Budgets are for everyone—from large multinational firms such as Bombardier or McDonald's to households planning for a mortgage, school tuition and retirement.

Difference between Planning and Control

The terms *planning* and *control* are often confused, and occasionally these terms are used in such a way as to suggest that they mean the same thing. Actually, planning and control are two quite distinct concepts. **Planning** involves the development of future objectives and the preparation of various budgets to achieve these objectives. **Control** involves the steps taken by management to ensure that the objectives set down at the planning stage are attained, and to ensure that all parts of the organization function in a manner consistent with organizational policies. To be completely effective, a good budgeting system must provide for *both* planning and control. Good planning without effective control is time wasted. On the other hand, unless plans are laid down in advance, there are no objectives toward which control can be directed.

Advantages of Budgeting

OBJECTIVE 2
Enumerate the principal advantages of budgeting.

There is an old saying to the effect that "a man is usually down on what he isn't up on." Managers who have never tried budgeting or attempted to find out what benefits might be available through the budget process are usually quick to state that budgeting is a waste of time. These managers may argue that even though budgeting may work well in *some* situations, it would never work well in their companies because operations are too complex or because there are too many uncertainties involved. In reality, however, managers who argue this way usually will be deeply involved in planning (albeit on an informal basis). These managers will have clearly defined thoughts about what they want to accomplish and when they want it accomplished. The difficulty is that unless they have some way of communicating their thoughts and plans to others, the only way their companies will ever attain the desired objectives will be through accident. In short, even though companies may attain a certain degree of success without budgets, they never attain the heights that could have been reached had a coordinated system of budgets been in operation.

Companies realize many benefits from a budgeting program. Among these benefits are the following:

1. Budgets provide a means of *communicating* management's plans throughout the organization.

2. Budgets force managers to *think about* and plan for the future. In the absence of the necessity to prepare a budget, too many managers would spend all of their time dealing with daily emergencies.
3. The budgeting process provides a means of *allocating resources* to those parts of the organization where they can be used most effectively.
4. The budgeting process can uncover potential *bottlenecks* before they occur.
5. Budgets *coordinate* the activities of the entire organization by *integrating* the plans of the various parts. Budgeting helps to ensure that everyone in the organization is pulling in the same direction.
6. Budgets define goals and objectives that can serve as *benchmarks* for evaluating subsequent performance.

In the past, some managers have not initiated a budgeting program because of the time and cost involved in the budgeting process. It can be argued that budgeting is actually "free" in that the time and cost involved are more than offset by greater efficiency and profits. Moreover, with the advent of computer spreadsheet programs *any* company—large or small—can implement and maintain a budgeting program at minimal cost. Budgeting lends itself well to spreadsheet programs, and such programs are readily available for any microcomputer.

Responsibility Accounting

Most of what we say in the remainder of this chapter and in Chapters 10, 11, and 12 centres on the concept of *responsibility accounting*. The basic idea behind **responsibility accounting** is that each manager's performance should be judged by how well he or she manages those items directly under his or her control. To judge a manager's performance in this way, the costs (and revenues) of an organization must be carefully scrutinized and classified according to the various levels of management under whose control the cost rests. Each level of management is then charged with those costs under its care, and the managers at each level are held responsible for variations between budgeted goals and actual results. In effect, responsibility accounting *personalizes* accounting information by looking at costs from a *personal control* standpoint, rather than from an *institutional* standpoint. This concept is central to any effective profit planning and control system.

We will look at responsibility accounting in more detail in Chapters 10, 11, and 12. For the moment, we can summarize the overall idea by noting that it rests on three basic premises. The first premise is that costs can be organized in terms of levels of management responsibility. The second premise is that the costs charged to a particular level are controllable at that level by its managers. And the third premise is that effective budget data can be generated as a basis for evaluating actual performance. This chapter on profit planning is concerned with the third of these premises, in that the purpose of the chapter is to show the steps involved in budget preparation.

Choosing a Budget Period

Budgets covering acquisition of land, buildings, and other items of capital equipment (often called **capital budgets**) generally have quite long time horizons and may extend 30 years or more into the future. The later years covered by such budgets may be quite indefinite, but the lengthy time horizon is needed to assist management in its planning and to ensure that funds will be available when purchases of equipment become necessary. As time passes, capital equipment plans that were once somewhat indefinite come more sharply into focus, and the capital budget is updated accordingly. Without such long-term planning, an organization can suddenly come to the realization that substantial purchases of capital equipment are needed, but find that no funds are available to make the purchases.

Operating budgets are ordinarily set to cover a one-year period. The one-year period should correspond to the company's fiscal year so that the budget figures can be compared with the actual results. Many companies divide their budget year into four quarters. The first quarter is then subdivided into months, and monthly budget figures are established. These near-term figures can usually be established with considerable accuracy. The last three quarters are carried in the budget at quarterly totals only. As the year progresses, the figures for the second quarter are broken down into monthly amounts, then the third quarter figures are broken down, and so forth. This approach has the advantage of requiring a constant review and reappraisal of budget data.

Continuous or *perpetual budgets* are becoming quite popular. A **continuous** or **perpetual budget** is one that covers a 12-month period but which is constantly adding a new month or quarter on the end as the current month or quarter is completed. Advocates of continuous budgets state that this approach to budgeting is superior to other approaches in that it keeps management thinking and planning a full 12 months ahead. Thus, it stabilizes the planning horizon. Under the other budget approaches, the planning horizon becomes shorter as the year progresses.

The Self-Imposed Budget

The success of a budget program will be determined in large part by the way in which the budget itself is developed. Generally, the most successful budget programs are those that permit managers with responsibility over cost control to prepare their own budget estimates, as illustrated in Exhibit 9–2. This approach to preparing budget data is particularly important if the budget is to be used in controlling a manager's activities after it has been developed. If a budget is forced on a manager from above, it will probably generate resentment and ill will rather than cooperation and increased productivity.

EXHIBIT 9–2

The Initial Flow of Budget Data

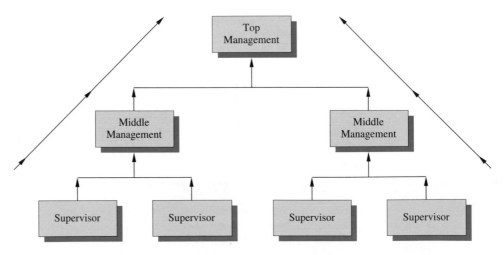

The initial flow of budget data is from lower levels of responsibility to higher levels of responsibility. Each person with responsibility for cost control will prepare his or her own budget estimates and submit them to the superior. These estimates are consolidated as they move upward in the organization.

When managers prepare their own budget figures, the budgets that they prepare become *self-imposed*. Certain distinct advantages arise from the **self-imposed budget** (also called a **participative budget**):

1. Individuals at all levels of the organization are recognized as members of the team, whose views and judgments are valued by top management.
2. The person in direct contact with an activity is in the best position to make budget estimates. Therefore, budget estimates prepared by such persons tend to be more accurate and reliable.
3. People are more likely to work at fulfilling a budget that they have participated in setting than they are to work at fulfilling a budget that is imposed from above.
4. A self-imposed budget contains its own unique system of control in that if people are not able to meet budget specifications, they have only themselves to blame. On the other hand, if a budget is imposed on them from above, they can always say that the budget was unreasonable or unrealistic to start with, and therefore was impossible to meet.

Once self-imposed budgets are prepared, are they subject to any kind of review? The answer is yes. Even though individual preparation of budget estimates is usually critical to a successful budgeting program, such budget estimates cannot necessarily be accepted without question by higher levels of management. If no system of checks and balances is present, the danger exists that self-imposed budgets will be too loose and allow too much freedom in activities. The result will be inefficiency and waste. Therefore, before budgets are accepted, they must be carefully reviewed by immediate superiors. If changes from the original budget seem desirable, the items in question are discussed, and compromises are reached that are acceptable to all concerned.

In essence, all levels of an organization should work together to produce the budget. Since top management is generally unfamiliar with detailed, day-to-day cost matters, it should rely on subordinates to provide detailed budget information. On the other hand, top management has a perspective on the company as a whole that is vital in making broad policy decisions in budget preparation. Each level of responsibility in an organization contributes in the way that it best can in a *cooperative* effort to develop an integrated budget document.

An interesting, but unresolved, problem for management accountants is how to design incentives to encourage subordinates to communicate accurate budget detail to top management. Subordinates can often control their own performance results by the nature of the budget information they feed through the system. This can be a problem for profit enterprises, not-for-profit enterprises, and government entities alike. Budgets can be used to set targets or quotas that in turn influence how top management allocates bonuses to managers and additional resources to the various units within the enterprise. Fundamentally, to provide incentives for a reward scheme, a designer needs to know what the alternative rewards will be from truthful forecasting rather than biased forecasting.[2] Unfortunately these alternatives cannot be known beforehand, which is when the incentive scheme has to be set. Thus, to be effective, organizations must rely on a cooperative atmosphere among subordinates, not a competitive or self-serving one, and on the ability of top management to assess the reasonableness of forecasts obtained from subordinates.

---

[2]Anthony A. Atkinson, "Truth-Inducing Schemes in Budgeting and Resource Allocation," *Cost and Management* (May–June, 1985), pp. 38–42.

The Matter of Human Relations

Whether or not a budget program is accepted by lower management personnel will reflect (1) the degree to which top management accepts the budget program as a vital part of the company's activities, and (2) the way in which top management uses budgeted data.

If a budget program is to be successful, it must have the complete acceptance and support of the persons who occupy key management positions. If lower or middle management personnel sense that top management is lukewarm about budgeting, or if they sense that top management simply tolerates budgeting as a necessary evil, then their own attitudes will reflect a similar lack of enthusiasm. Budgeting is hard work, and if top management is not enthusiastic about and committed to the budget program, then it is unlikely that anyone else in the organization will be either.

In administering the budget program, it is particularly important that top management not use the budget as a "club" to pressure employees or as a way to find someone to "blame" for a particular problem. This negative emphasis will simply breed hostility, tension, and mistrust rather than greater cooperation and productivity. Unfortunately, research suggests that the budget is often used as a pressure device and that great emphasis is placed on "meeting the budget" under all circumstances.[3]

Rather than as a pressure device, the budget should be used as a positive instrument to assist in establishing goals, in measuring operating results, and in isolating areas that are in need of extra effort or attention. Any misgivings that employees have about a budget program can be overcome by meaningful involvement at all levels and by proper use of the program over a period of time. Administration of a budget program requires a great deal of insight and sensitivity on the part of management. The ultimate objective must be to develop the realization that the budget is designed to be a positive aid in achieving both individual and company goals.

Management must keep clearly in mind that the human dimension in budgeting is of key importance. It is easy for the manager to become preoccupied with the technical aspects of the budget program to the exclusion of the human aspects. Accountants are particularly open to criticism in this regard. Indeed, the study cited earlier found that use of budget data in a rigid and inflexible manner was the greatest single complaint of persons whose performance is being evaluated through the budget process.[4] In light of these facts, management should remember that the purposes of the budget are to motivate employees and to coordinate efforts. Preoccupation with the dollars and cents in the budget, or being rigid and inflexible in budget administration, can only lead to frustration of these purposes.

The Budget Committee

A standing **budget committee** will usually be responsible for overall policy matters relating to the budget program and for coordinating the preparation of the budget itself. This committee generally consists of the president; vice presidents in charge of various functions such as sales, production, and purchasing; and the controller. Difficulties and disputes between segments of the organization in matters relating to the budget are resolved by the budget committee. In addition, the budget committee approves the final budget and receives periodic reports on the progress of the company in attaining budgeted goals.

---

[3]Paul J. Carruth, Thurrell O. McClendon, and Milton R. Ballard, "What Supervisors Don't Like about Budget Evaluations," *Management Accounting* (February 1983), p. 42.
[4]Ibid.

In establishing a budget, how challenging should budget targets be? In practice, companies typically set their budgets either at a "stretch" level or a "highly achievable" level. A stretch-level budget is one that has only a small chance of being met and in fact may be met less than half the time by even the most capable managers. A highly achievable budget is one that is challenging, but which can be met through hard work. Research shows that managers prefer highly achievable budgets.[5] Such budgets are generally coupled with bonuses that are given when budget targets are met, along with added bonuses when these targets are exceeded. Highly achievable budgets are believed to build a manager's confidence and to generate greater commitment to the budget program.

Disputes can (and do) erupt over budget matters. Because budgets allocate resources, the budgeting process to a large extent determines which departments get more resources and which get relatively less. Also, the budget sets the benchmarks by which managers and their departments will be evaluated. Therefore, it should not be surprising that managers take the budgeting process very seriously and invest considerable energy and even emotion in ensuring that their interests, and those of their departments, are protected. Because of this, the budgeting process can easily degenerate into an interoffice brawl in which the ultimate goal of working together toward common goals is forgotten.

Running a successful budgeting program that avoids interoffice battles requires considerable interpersonal skills in addition to purely technical skills. But even the best interpersonal skills will fail if, as discussed earlier, top management uses the budget process inappropriately as a club or as a way to find blame.

Budgeting is often an intensely political process in which managers jockey for resources and relaxed goals for the upcoming year. One group of consultants describes the process in this way: Annual budgets "have a particular urgency in that they provide the standard and most public framework against which managers are assessed and judged. It is, therefore, not surprising that budget-setting is taken seriously . . . Often budgets are a means for managers getting what they want. A relaxed budget will secure a relatively easy twelve months, a tight one means that their names will constantly be coming up in the monthly management review meeting. Far better to shift the burden of cost control and financial discipline to someone else. Budgeting is an intensely political exercise conducted with all the sharper managerial skills not taught at business school, such as lobbying and flattering superiors, forced haste, regretted delay, hidden truth, half-truths, and lies."[6]

---

[5]See Kenneth A. Merchant, *Rewarding Results: Motivating Profit Center Managers* (Boston, Mass.: Harvard Business School Press, 1989). For further discussion of budget targets, see Kenneth A. Merchant, "How Challenging Should Profit Budget Targets Be?" *Management Accounting* (November 1990), pp. 46–48.
[6]Michael Morrow, ed., *Activity-Based Management* (New York: Woodhead-Faulkner, 1992), p. 91.

The Master Budget—A Network of Interrelationships

OBJECTIVE 3

Diagram and explain
the master budget
interrelationships.

The master budget is a network consisting of many separate budgets that are interdependent. This network is illustrated in Exhibit 9–3.

The Sales Budget.   A **sales budget** is a detailed schedule showing the expected sales for coming periods; typically, it is expressed in both dollars and units of product. Much time and effort are put into preparing an accurate sales budget because it is the key to the entire budgeting process. The reason it is the key is that all other parts of the master budget are dependent on the sales budget in some way, as illustrated in Exhibit 9–3. Thus, if the sales budget is sloppily done, then the rest of the budgeting process is largely a waste of time.

After the sales budget has been set, a decision can be made on the level of production that will be needed for the period to support sales, and the production budget can be set as well. The production budget then becomes a key factor in the determination of other budgets, including the direct materials budget, the direct labour budget, and the manufacturing overhead budget. These budgets, in turn, are needed to assist in formulating a cash budget for the budget period. In essence, the sales budget triggers a chain reaction that leads to the development of many other budget figures in an organization.

As shown in Exhibit 9–3, the selling and administrative expense budget is both dependent on and a determinant of the sales budget. This reciprocal relationship arises from the fact that sales will in part be determined by the funds available for advertising and sales promotion.

EXHIBIT 9–3

The Master Budget
Interrelationships

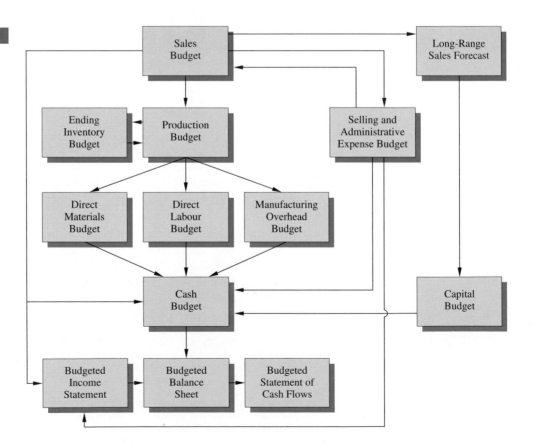

The Cash Budget.   Once the operating budgets (sales, production, and so on) have been established, the cash budget and other financial budgets can be prepared. A **cash budget** is a detailed plan showing how cash resources will be acquired and used over some specified time period. Observe from Exhibit 9–3 that all of the operating budgets, including the sales budget, have an impact of some type on the cash budget. In the case of the sales budget, the impact comes from the planned cash receipts to be received on sales. In the case of the other budgets, the impact comes from the planned cash expenditures within the budgets themselves. Remember that profit and cash are not the same thing. Sales growth tends to increase inventory and accounts receivable. Often overhead expenses will have to be incurred ahead of planned sales increases. An investment in capital assets may require cash immediately but the effect on profits could be realized over the long-run.

Sales Forecasting—A Critical Step

The sales budget is usually based on a *sales forecast.* A **sales forecast** is broader than a sales budget, generally encompassing potential sales for the entire industry, as well as potential sales for the firm preparing the forecast. Factors that are considered in making a sales forecast include the following:

1. Past experience in terms of sales volume.
2. Prospective pricing policy.
3. Unfilled order backlogs.
4. Market research studies.
5. General economic conditions.
6. Industry economic conditions.
7. Movements of economic indicators such as gross national product, employment, prices, and personal income.
8. Advertising and product promotion.
9. Industry competition.
10. Market share.

Sales results from prior years are used as a starting point in preparing a sales forecast. Forecasters examine sales data in relation to various factors, including prices, competitive conditions, availability of supplies, and general economic conditions. Projections are then made into the future, based on those factors that the forecasters feel will be significant over the budget period. In-depth discussions generally characterize the gathering and interpretation of all data going into the sales forecast. These discussions, held at all levels of the organization, develop perspective and assist in assessing the significance and usefulness of data.

Computer spreadsheets and other software are a common aid to forecasting, allowing the forecaster to play "what if" games with pricing and product mixes. Quaker Oats Co. of Canada, for example, a $285-million-a-year food-processing giant, makes heavy use of spreadsheets to analyze data on North American spending habits, inflation rates, population growth, age groups, attitudes, and other demographic data. Trends are identified and used to estimate short-term sales targets, production schedules, and budgets for the company's cereal, snack, and baking-product markets.

Statistical tools such as regression analysis, trend and cycle projection, and correlation analysis are used in sales forecasting. In addition, some firms have found it useful to build econometric models of their industry or of the nation to assist in forecasting problems. Such models hold great promise for improving the overall quality of budget data.

Spreadsheets and other software enable managers to spot trends as they happen—lending real substance to strategic planning.

More managers are turning to spreadsheets, forecasting programs and even artificial intelligence software to help sort through the numbers and predict where their businesses are going.

Electronic spreadsheets are still the workhorses of forecasting and simpler to use than most other forecasting software. There are dozens of ready-made templates on the market. Professional forecasters suggest, however, that you not only have to pick the right software, but know how to use it. Techniques used include moving average forecasting and linear regression models; both tend to work best in stable sales environments.

There are problems associated with forecasting, however, because many other factors such as labour disputes and in-store promotions can influence product sales. Few managers ever verify spreadsheet results to see if they are really correct. Computer forecasts should be checked against a known outcome for validity before being utilized as models.

Visual modelling tends to be more effective than numerical results because the changes are more obvious at a glance; however, graphs are more useful for the overall picture. Fuzzy logic programs are useful when managers cannot commit to a single number for each cell. They are able to accept a range instead, yet produce a result of one specific number.[7]

PREPARING THE MASTER BUDGET

▼ ▼ ▼ ▼ ▼

MANAGERIAL ACCOUNTING IN ACTION—THE ISSUE

Tom Wills is the majority shareholder and chief executive officer of Hampton Freeze, Inc., a company he started in 1996. The company makes premium popsicles using only natural ingredients and featuring exotic flavours such as tangy tangerine and minty mango. The company's business is highly seasonal, with most of the sales occurring in spring and summer.

In 1997, the company's second year of operations, there was a major cash crunch in the first and second quarters that almost forced the company into bankruptcy. In spite of this cash crunch, 1997 turned out to be overall a very successful year in terms of both cash flow and net income. Partly as a result of that harrowing experience, Tom decided toward the end of 1997 to hire a professional financial manager. Tom interviewed several promising candidates for the job and settled on Larry Green, who had considerable experience in the packaged foods industry. In the job interview, Tom questioned Larry about the steps he would take to prevent a recurrence of the 1997 cash crunch:

TOM: As I indicated to you earlier, we are going to wind up 1997 with a very nice profit. What you may not know is that we had some very big financial problems this year.

LARRY: Let me guess. You ran out of cash sometime in the first or second quarter.

Continued

[7]M. Crawford, "The Future at Your Fingertips," *Canadian Business,* Special Issue (Spring 1994), pp. 10–18.

Tom: How did you know?

Larry: Most of your sales are in the second and third quarter, right?

Tom: Sure, everyone wants to buy popsicles in the spring and summer, but nobody wants them when the weather turns cold.

Larry: So you don't have many sales in the first quarter?

Tom: Right.

Larry: And in the second quarter, which is the spring, you are producing like crazy to fill orders?

Tom: Sure.

Larry: Do your customers, the grocery stores, pay you the day you make your deliveries?

Tom: Are you kidding? Of course not.

Larry: So in the first quarter, you don't have many sales. In the second quarter, you are producing like crazy, which eats up cash, but you aren't paid by your customers until long after you have paid your employees and suppliers. No wonder you had a cash problem. I see this pattern all the time in food processing because of the seasonality of the business.

Tom: So what can we do about it?

Larry: The first step is to predict the magnitude of the problem before it occurs. If we can predict early in the year what the cash shortfall is going to be, we can go to the bank and arrange for credit before we really need it. Bankers tend to be leery of panicky people who show up begging for emergency loans. They are much more likely to make the loan if you look like you know what you are doing, you have done your homework, and you are in control of the situation.

Tom: How can we predict the cash shortfall?

Larry: You can put together a cash budget. While you're at it, you might as well do a master budget. You'll find it is well worth the effort.

Tom: I don't like budgets. They are too confining. My wife budgets everything at home, and I can't spend what I want.

Larry: Can I ask a personal question?

Tom: What?

Larry: Where did you get the money to start this business?

Tom: Mainly from our family's savings. I get your point. We wouldn't have had the money to start the business if my wife hadn't been forcing us to save every month.

Larry: Exactly. I suggest you use the same discipline in your business. It is even more important here because you can't expect your employees to spend your money as carefully as you would.

Tom: I'm sold. And by the way, when can you start working here?

With the full backing of Tom Wills, Larry Green set out to create a master budget for the company for 1998. In his planning for the budgeting process, Larry drew up the following list of documents that would be a part of the master budget:

1. A sales budget, including a computation of expected cash receipts.
2. A production budget (or merchandise purchases budget for a merchandising company).
3. A direct materials budget, including a computation of expected cash payments for raw materials.
4. A direct labour budget.
5. A manufacturing overhead budget.
6. An ending finished goods inventory budget.

Hampton Freeze makes popsicles; most of its sales occur in the second and third quarters. How can better planning and budgeting improve their cash flow?

7. A selling and administrative expense budget.
8. A cash budget.
9. A budgeted income statement.
10. A budgeted balance sheet.

Larry felt it was important to get everyone's cooperation in the budgeting process, so he asked Tom to call a companywide meeting in which the budgeting process would be explained. At the meeting there was initially some grumbling, but Tom was able to convince nearly everyone of the necessity for planning and getting better control over spending. It helped that the cash crisis earlier in the year was still fresh in everyone's minds. As much as some people disliked the idea of budgets, they liked their jobs even more.

The budget documents that were prepared subsequent to that meeting are illustrated in Schedules 1 through 10 that appear in this section.

The Sales Budget

OBJECTIVE 4

Prepare a sales budget, including a computation of expected cash receipts.

The sales budget is the starting point in preparing the master budget. As shown earlier in Exhibit 9–2, nearly all other items in the master budget, including production, purchases, inventories, and expenses, depend on it in some way.

The sales budget is constructed by multiplying the expected sales in units by the selling price. Schedule 1 on page 433 contains the sales budget for Hampton Freeze for 1998, by quarters. Notice from the schedule that the company plans to sell 100,000 cases of popsicles during the year, with sales peaking in the third quarter.

The sales budget is followed by preparation of a Schedule of Expected Cash Collections such as the one that appears in Schedule 1 for Hampton Freeze. This schedule is needed to prepare the cash budget. Expected cash receipts are composed of collections on sales to customers in prior periods plus collections on sales made in the current budget period. At Hampton Freeze, experience has shown that 70% of sales are collected in the quarter in which the sale is made and the remaining 30% are collected in the following quarter.

The Production Budget

OBJECTIVE 5

Prepare a production budget.

After the sales budget has been prepared, the production requirements for the forthcoming budget period can be determined and organized in the form of a **production budget.** Sufficient goods will have to be available to meet sales needs and provide for the desired ending inventory. A portion of these goods will already exist in the form of a beginning inventory. The remainder will have to be produced. Therefore, production needs can be determined as follows:

Budgeted sales in units	XXXX
Add desired ending inventory	XXXX
Total needs	XXXX
Less beginning inventory	XXXX
Required production	XXXX

Schedule 2 on page 434 contains the production budget for Hampton Freeze.

Note that production requirements for a quarter are influenced by the desired level of the ending inventory. Inventories should be carefully planned. Excessive inventories tie up funds and create storage problems. Insufficient inventories can lead to lost sales or crash production efforts in the following period. At Hampton Freeze, management believes that an ending inventory equal to 20% of the next quarter's sales strikes the appropriate balance between inventory carrying costs and the costs of not carrying sufficient inventories.

SCHEDULE 1

HAMPTON FREEZE COMPANY
Sales Budget
For the Year Ended December 31, 1998

	Quarter				
	1	2	3	4	Year
Expected sales in units	10,000	30,000	40,000	20,000	100,000
Selling price per unit	× $20	× $20	× $20	× $20	× $20
Total sales	$200,000	$600,000	$800,000	$400,000	$2,000,000

Schedule of Expected Cash Collections

	1	2	3	4	Year
Accounts receivable, 12/31/97	$ 90,000*				$ 90,000
First-quarter sales ($200,000 × 70%, 30%)†	140,000	$ 60,000			200,000
Second-quarter sales ($600,000 × 70%, 30%)		420,000	$180,000		600,000
Third-quarter sales ($800,000 × 70%, 30%)			560,000	$240,000	800,000
Fourth-quarter sales ($400,000 × 70%)‡				280,000	280,000
Total cash collections	$230,000	$480,000	$740,000	$520,000	$1,970,000

*Cash collections from last year's fourth-quarter sales. See the beginning-of-year balance sheet on page 442.

†Cash collections from sales are as follows: 70% collected in the quarter of sale, and the remaining 30% collected in the quarter following.

‡Uncollected fourth-quarter sales appear as accounts receivable on the company's end-of-year balance sheet (see Schedule 10 on page 445).

SCHEDULE 2

HAMPTON FREEZE COMPANY
Production Budget
For the Year Ended December 31, 1998
(in units)

	Quarter				
	1	2	3	4	Year
Expected sales (Schedule 1)	10,000	30,000	40,000	20,000	100,000
Add desired ending inventory of finished goods*	6,000	8,000	4,000	3,000†	3,000
Total needs	16,000	38,000	44,000	23,000	103,000
Less beginning inventory of finished goods‡	2,000	6,000	8,000	4,000	2,000
Units to be produced	14,000	32,000	36,000	19,000	101,000

*20% of the next quarter's sales.

†Estimated.

‡The same as the prior quarter's *ending* inventory.

Inventory Purchases—Merchandising Firm

Hampton Freeze Company prepares a production budget because it is a *manufacturing* firm. If it were a *merchandising* firm, then instead of a production budget it would prepare a **merchandise purchases budget** showing the amount of goods to be purchased from its suppliers during the period. The merchandise purchases budget is in the same basic format as the production budget, except that it shows goods to be purchased rather than goods to be produced, as shown below:

Budgeted cost of goods sold (in units or in dollars)	XXXXX
Add desired ending merchandise inventory ...	XXXXX
Total needs	XXXXX
Less beginning merchandise inventory	XXXXX
Required purchases (in units or in dollars)	XXXXX

The merchandising firm would prepare an inventory purchases budget such as this one for each item carried in stock. Some large retail organizations make such computations on a frequent basis (particularly at peak seasons) to ensure that adequate stocks are on hand to meet customer needs.

The Direct Materials Budget

OBJECTIVE 6

Prepare a direct materials budget, including a computation of expected cash disbursements for purchases of materials.

Returning to the Hampton Freeze Company example, after production needs have been computed, a **direct materials budget** should be prepared to show the materials that will be required in the production process. Sufficient raw materials will have to be available to meet production needs, and to provide for the desired ending raw materials inventory for the budget period. Part of this raw materials requirement will already exist in the form of a beginning raw materials inventory. The remainder will have to be purchased from suppliers. In summary the format for computing raw materials needs is:

SCHEDULE 3

HAMPTON FREEZE
Direct Materials Budget
For the Year Ended December 31, 1998

	Quarter				
	1	2	3	4	Year
Units to be produced (Schedule 2)	14,000	32,000	36,000	19,000	101,000
Raw materials needed per unit (kilograms)	× 5	× 5	× 5	× 5	× 5
Production needs (kilograms)	70,000	160,000	180,000	95,000	505,000
Add desired ending inventory of raw materials (kilograms)*	16,000	18,000	9,500	7,500	7,500
Total needs (kilograms)	86,000	178,000	189,500	102,500	512,500
Less beginning inventory of raw materials (kilograms)	7,000	16,000	18,000	9,500	7,000
Raw materials to be purchased (kilograms)	79,000	162,000	171,500	93,000	505,500
Cost of raw materials to be purchased at $0.60 per kilogram	$47,400	$ 97,200	$102,900	$ 55,800	$303,300

*10% of the next quarter's production needs. For example, the second-quarter production needs are 160,000 kilograms. Therefore, the desired ending inventory for the first quarter would be 10% × 160,000 kilograms = 16,000 kilograms. The ending inventory of 7,500 kilograms for the fourth quarter is estimated.

Schedule of Expected Cash Disbursements

Accounts payable, 12/31/97	$25,800*				$ 25,800
First-quarter purchases ($47,400 × 50%, 50%)†	23,700	$ 23,700			47,400
Second-quarter purchases ($97,200 × 50%, 50%)		48,600	$ 48,600		97,200
Third-quarter purchases ($102,900 × 50%, 50%)			51,450	$ 51,450	102,900
Fourth-quarter purchases ($55,800 × 50%)‡				27,900	27,900
Total cash disbursements	$49,500	$ 72,300	$100,050	$ 79,350	$301,200

*Cash payments for last year's fourth-quarter material purchases. See the beginning-of-year balance sheet on page 442.

†Cash payments for purchases are as follows: 50% paid for in the quarter of purchase, and the remaining 50% paid for in the quarter following.

‡Unpaid fourth-quarter purchases appear as accounts payable on the company's end-of-year balance sheet (see Schedule 10 on page 445).

Raw materials needed to meet the production schedule	XXXXX
Add desired ending inventory of raw materials	XXXXX
Total raw materials needs	XXXXX
Less beginning inventory of raw materials	XXXXX
Raw materials to be purchased	XXXXX

Schedule 3 contains a direct materials purchases budget for Hampton Freeze Company. Notice that materials requirements are first determined in units (kilograms, litres, and so on) and then translated into dollars by multiplying by the appropriate unit cost.

The direct materials budget is usually accompanied by a computation of expected cash disbursements for raw materials. This computation is needed to assist in developing a cash budget. Disbursements for raw materials consist of payments for prior periods, plus payments for purchases for the current budget period. Schedule 3 contains a computation of expected cash disbursements for Hampton Freeze Company. Typically, materials are direct materials but they could include indirect material as defined in Chapter 2. The assumption here is that all materials are direct materials.

Preparing a budget of this kind is one step in a company's overall **material requirements planning (MRP).** MRP is an operations management tool that employs the computer to assist the manager in overall materials and inventory planning. Exhibit 9–4 presents an overview of an MRP computer system. The objective of MRP is to ensure that the right materials are on hand, in the right quantities, and at the right time to support the production process. Each item being produced is supported by a formal set of plans including a bill of materials, time-phased requirements, suppliers, routing, and other details necessary to assure the correct available inputs at the correct time to avoid excess inventory or waste in the production process. The computer program combines the schedule of production plans with the bill of materials, the schedule of inventory information on what is available and when to order with a time schedule of when materials and completed items called *subassemblies* must be present to satisfy the needs of production. Information about exceptions to production plans such as late orders, excessive scrap, and errors are generated by the system to assist management. Computer simulations of what-if questions also provide information about alternative schedules. Extensions of the basic MRP approach have been made to incorporate financial as well as marketing expertise with the production and procurement decisions. The detailed operation of MRP is covered in most operations research textbooks: for this reason, it will not be considered further here, other than to point out that the concepts we are discussing are an important part of the overall MRP technique.

| **EXHIBIT 9–4** | Overview of MRP[8] |

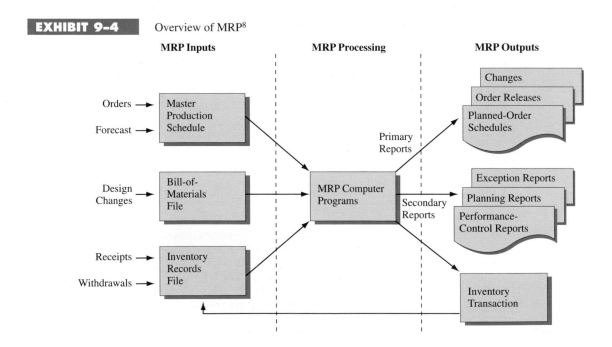

[8]William J. Stevenson, *Production/Operations Management* (Homewood, Ill.: Richard D. Irwin, 1990), p. 585.

SCHEDULE 4

HAMPTON FREEZE COMPANY					
Direct Labour Budget					
For the Year Ended December 31, 1998					
			Quarter		
	1	**2**	**3**	**4**	**Year**
Units to be produced (Schedule 2)	14,000	32,000	36,000	19,000	101,000
Direct labour time per unit (hours)	× 0.8	× 0.8	× 0.8	× 0.8	× 0.8
Total hours of direct labour time needed	11,200	25,600	28,800	15,200	80,800
Direct labour cost per hour	× $7.50	× $7.50	× $7.50	× $7.50	× $7.50
Total direct labour cost	$84,000	$192,000	$216,000	$114,000	$606,000

The Direct Labour Budget

The **direct labour budget** is also developed from the production budget. Direct labour requirements must be computed so that the company will know whether sufficient labour time is available to meet production needs. By knowing in advance just what will be needed in the way of labour time throughout the budget year, the company can develop plans to adjust the labour force as the situation may require. Firms that neglect to budget run the risk of facing labour shortages or having to hire and lay off at awkward times. Erratic labour policies lead to insecurity and inefficiency on the part of employees.

To compute direct labour requirements, the number of units of finished product to be produced each period (month, quarter, and so on) is multiplied by the number of direct labour-hours required to produce a single unit. Many different types of labour may be involved. If so, then computations should be by type of labour needed. The direct labour requirements can then be translated into expected direct labour costs. How this is done will depend on the labour policy of the firm. In Schedule 4, we assume that the direct labour force can be adjusted as the work requirements change from quarter to quarter. In that case, the total direct labour cost is computed by simply multiplying the direct labour-hour requirements by the direct labour rate per hour as was done in Schedule 4.

However, many companies have employment policies or contracts that prevent them from laying off and rehiring workers as needed. Suppose, for example, that Hampton Freeze Company has 50 workers who are classified as direct labour and each of them is guaranteed at least 480 hours of pay each quarter at a rate of $7.50 per hour. In that case, the minimum direct labour cost for a quarter would be:

$$50 \text{ workers} \times 480 \text{ hours} \times \$7.50 = \$180,000$$

Note that in Schedule 4 the direct labour costs for the first and fourth quarters would have to be increased to a $180,000 level if Hampton Freeze Company's labour policy did not allow it to adjust the workforce at will. Such a "no layoff" policy would have a dramatic impact on Hampton Freeze Company's cash flows and profitability.

The Manufacturing Overhead Budget

OBJECTIVE 7

Prepare a manufacturing overhead budget and a selling and administrative expense budget.

The **manufacturing overhead budget** should provide a schedule of all costs of production other than direct materials and direct labour. These costs should be broken down by cost behaviour for budgeting purposes, and a predetermined overhead rate developed. This rate will be used to apply manufacturing overhead to units of product throughout the budget period.

SCHEDULE 5

HAMPTON FREEZE COMPANY
Manufacturing Overhead Budget
For the Year Ended December 31, 1998

	Quarter				
	1	2	3	4	Year
Budgeted direct labour-hours	11,200	25,600	28,800	15,200	80,800
Variable overhead rate	× $2	× $2	× $2	× $2	× $2
Budgeted variable overhead	$22,400	$ 51,200	$ 57,600	$30,400	$161,600
Budgeted fixed overhead	60,600	60,600	60,600	60,600	242,400
Total budgeted overhead	83,000	111,800	118,200	91,000	404,000
Less depreciation	15,000	15,000	15,000	15,000	60,000
Cash disbursements for overhead	$68,000	$ 96,800	$103,200	$76,000	$344,000

A computation showing budgeted cash disbursements for manufacturing overhead should be made for use in developing the cash budget. The critical thing to remember in making this computation is that *depreciation is a noncash charge*. Therefore, any depreciation charges included in manufacturing overhead must be deducted from the total in computing expected cash payments.

At Hampton Freeze the variable overhead is $2 per direct labour-hour and fixed overhead costs are budgeted at $60,600 per quarter, of which $15,000 represents depreciation. All overhead costs involving cash disbursements are paid for in the quarter incurred. The manufacturing overhead budget, by quarters, and the expected cash disbursements, by quarters, are both shown in Schedule 5.

The Ending Finished Goods Inventory Budget

After completing Schedules 1–5, Larry Green has all of the data needed to compute the cost of a unit of finished product. This computation was needed for two reasons: first, to know how much to charge as cost of goods sold on the budgeted income statement; and second, to know what amount to place on the balance sheet for unsold units. The dollar value of the unsold units planned to be on hand is computed in the **ending finished goods inventory budget.**

Although Larry Green considered using variable costing in preparing Hampton Freeze's budget statements, he decided to use absorption costing instead, because the bank would very likely require that absorption costing be used. He also knew that it would be easy to convert the absorption costing financial statements to a variable costing basis later. At this point, the primary concern was to determine what financing, if any, would be required in 1998 and then to arrange for that financing from the bank.

The unit product cost computations are shown in Schedule 6. For Hampton Freeze, the absorption costing unit product cost is $13 per case of popsicles—consisting of $3 of direct materials, $6 of direct labour, and $4 of manufacturing overhead. For convenience, the manufacturing overhead is applied to units of product on the basis of direct labour-hours. The budgeted carrying cost of the expected ending inventory is $39,000.

The Selling and Administrative Expense Budget

The **selling and administrative expense budget** contains a list of anticipated expenses for the budget period that will be incurred in areas other than manufacturing. The budget will be

SCHEDULE 6

HAMPTON FREEZE COMPANY
Ending Finished Goods Inventory Budget
For the Year Ended December 31, 1998

Item	Quantity	Cost	Total
Production cost per unit:			
Direct materials	5.0 kilograms	$0.60 per kilogram	$ 3
Direct labour	0.8 hours	7.50 per hour	6
Manufacturing overhead	0.8 hours	5.00 per hour*	4
			$13
Budgeted finished goods inventory:			
Ending finished goods inventory in units (Schedule 2)			3,000
Total production cost per unit (see above)			× $13
Ending finished goods inventory in dollars			$39,000

*$404,000 ÷ 80,800 hours = $5.

made up of many smaller, individual budgets submitted by various persons having responsibility for cost control in selling and administrative matters. If the number of expense items is very large, separate budgets may be needed for the selling and administrative functions.

Schedule 7 contains the selling and administrative expense budget for Hampton Freeze Company for 1998. The total insurance costs for the year are $39,650, of which $1,900 is paid in quarter 2 and $37,750 is paid in quarter 3. The total cost is divided equally among the quarters. Property tax is estimated at $18,150 to be paid in the fourth quarter. This cost is also prorated to each quarter according to normal accrual accounting practice.

SCHEDULE 7

HAMPTON FREEZE COMPANY
Selling and Administrative Expense Budget
For the Year Ended December 31, 1998

	Quarter				
	1	2	3	4	Year
Budgeted sales in units	10,000	30,000	40,000	20,000	100,000
Variable selling and administrative expense per unit*	× $1.80	× $1.80	× $1.80	× $1.80	× $1.80
Budgeted variable expense	$ 18,000	$ 54,000	$ 72,000	$ 36,000	$180,000
Fixed selling and administrative expense:					
Advertising	40,000	40,000	40,000	40,000	160,000
Executive salaries	35,000	35,000	35,000	35,000	140,000
Insurance	9,912	9,913	9,912	9,913	39,650
Property taxes	4,538	4,537	4,538	4,537	18,150
Total budgeted selling and administrative expenses	$107,450	$143,450	$161,450	$125,450	$537,800

*Commissions, clerical, and freight-out.

The Cash Budget

OBJECTIVE 8

Prepare a cash budget.

The cash budget pulls together much of the data developed in the preceding steps, as illustrated earlier in Exhibit 9–3. The reader should restudy this exhibit before reading on. Note that in contrast to Schedule 7 accrual accounting practices do not apply to the preparation of the cash budget.

The cash budget is composed of four major sections:

1. The receipts section.
2. The disbursements section.
3. The cash excess or deficiency section.
4. The financing section.

The receipts section consists of the opening cash balance added to whatever is expected in the way of cash receipts during the budget period. Generally, the major source of receipts will be from sales, as discussed earlier.

The disbursements section consists of all cash payments that are planned for the budget period. These payments will include raw materials purchases, direct labour payments, manufacturing overhead costs, and so on, as contained in their respective budgets. In addition, other cash disbursements such as income taxes, capital equipment purchases, and dividend payments will also be included.

The cash excess or deficiency section consists of the difference between the cash receipts section totals and the cash disbursements section totals. If a deficiency exists, the company will need to arrange to borrow funds from its bank. If an excess exists, funds borrowed in previous periods can be repaid or the idle funds can be placed in short-term investments.

The financing section provides a detailed account of the borrowings and repayments projected to take place during the budget period. It also includes a detail of interest payments that will be due on money borrowed. Banks are becoming increasingly insistent that firms in need of borrowed money give long advance notice of the amounts and times that funds will be needed. This permits the banks to plan and helps to assure that funds will be ready when needed. Moreover, careful planning of cash needs via the budgeting process avoids unpleasant surprises for companies as well. Few things are more disquieting to an organization than to run into unexpected difficulties in the Cash account. A well-coordinated budgeting program eliminates uncertainty as to what the cash situation will be in two months, six months, or a year from now.

The cash budget should be broken down into time periods that are as short as feasible. Many firms budget cash on a weekly basis, and some larger firms go so far as to plan daily cash needs. The more common planning horizons are geared to monthly or quarterly figures. Larry Green has prepared a quarterly cash budget for Hampton Freeze in Schedule 8. Larry has assumed in the budget that an open line of credit can be arranged with the bank that can be used as needed to bolster the cash position. Interest on loans is 10% per annum. He assumed that all borrowings and repayments must be in round $1,000 amounts and that all borrowings take place at the beginning of a quarter and that all repayments are made at the end of a quarter.

In the case of Hampton Freeze Company, all loans have been repaid by year-end. If all loans are not repaid and a budgeted income statement or balance sheet is being prepared, then interest must be accrued on the unpaid loans. This interest will *not* appear on the cash budget (since it has not yet been paid), but it will appear as part of interest expense on the budgeted income statement and as a liability on the budgeted balance sheet.

SCHEDULE 8

HAMPTON FREEZE COMPANY
Cash Budget
For the Year Ended December 31, 1998

	Schedule	Quarter 1	Quarter 2	Quarter 3	Quarter 4	Year
Cash balance, beginning		$ 42,500	$ 40,000	$ 40,000	$ 40,500	$ 42,500
Add receipts:						
Collections from customers	1	230,000	480,000	740,000	520,000	1,970,000
Total cash available before current financing		272,500	520,000	780,000	560,500	2,012,500
Less disbursements:						
Direct materials	3	49,500	72,300	100,050	79,350	301,200
Direct labour	4	84,000	192,000	216,000	114,000	606,000
Manufacturing overhead	5	68,000	96,800	103,200	76,000	344,000
Selling and administrative**	7	93,000	130,900	184,750	129,150	537,800
Income taxes	9	18,000	18,000	18,000	18,000	72,000
Equipment purchases		30,000	20,000	—	—	50,000
Dividends		10,000	10,000	10,000	10,000	40,000
Total disbursements		352,500	540,000	632,000	426,500	1,951,000
Excess (deficiency) of cash available over disbursements		(80,000)	(20,000)	148,000	134,000	61,500
Financing:						
Borrowings (at beginning)		120,000*	60,000	—	—	180,000
Repayments (at ending)		—	—	(100,000)	(80,000)	(180,000)
Interest (at 10% per annum)		—	—	(7,500)†	(6,500)†	(14,000)
Total financing		120,000	60,000	(107,500)	(86,500)	(14,000)
Cash balance, ending		$ 40,000	$ 40,000	$ 40,500	$ 47,500	$ 47,500

*The company requires a minimum cash balance of $40,000. Therefore, borrowing must be sufficient to cover the cash deficiency of $80,000 and to provide for the minimum cash balance of $40,000. All borrowings and all repayments of principal are in round $1,000 amounts.

†The interest payments relate only to the principal being repaid at the time it is repaid. For example, the interest in quarter 3 relates only to the interest due on the $100,000 principal being repaid from quarter 1 borrowing, as follows: $100,000 × 10% × 3/4 = $7,500. The interest paid in quarter 4 is computed as follows:

$20,000 × 10% × 1 year $2,000
$60,000 × 10% × 3/4 4,500
Total interest paid $6,500

**$107,450 − $9,912 − $4,538 = $93,000; $143,450 − $9,913 − $4,537 + $1,900 = $130,900; $161,450 − $9,912 − $4,538 = $37,750 = $184,750; $125,450 − $9,913 − $4,537 + $18,150 = $129,150

OBJECTIVE 9

Prepare a budgeted income statement and a budgeted balance sheet.

The Budgeted Income Statement

A budgeted income statement can be prepared from the data developed in Schedules 1–8. *The budgeted income statement is one of the key schedules in the budget process.* It is the document that tells how profitable operations are anticipated to be in the forthcoming period. After it has been developed, it stands as a benchmark against which subsequent company performance can be measured.

Schedule 9 contains a budgeted income statement for Hampton Freeze Company for 1998.

The Budgeted Balance Sheet

The budgeted balance sheet is developed by beginning with the current balance sheet and adjusting it for the data contained in the other budgets. A Hampton Freeze Company

HAMPTON FREEZE COMPANY
Balance Sheet
December 31, 1997

Assets

Current assets:

Cash	$ 42,500	
Accounts receivable	90,000	
Raw materials inventory (7,000 kilograms)	4,200	
Finished goods inventory (2,000 units)	26,000	
Total current assets		$162,700

Capital assets:

Land	80,000	
Buildings and equipment	700,000	
Accumulated depreciation	(292,000)	
Plant and equipment, net		488,000
Total assets		$650,700

Liabilities and Shareholders' Equity

Current liabilities:

Accounts payable (raw materials)		$ 25,800
Shareholders' equity:		
Common stock, no par	$ 175,000	
Retained earnings	449,900	
Total shareholders' equity		624,900
Total liabilities and shareholders' equity		$650,700

budgeted balance sheet for 1998 is presented in Schedule 10 (page 445). The company's beginning-of-year balance sheet, from which the budgeted balance sheet in Schedule 10 has been derived in part, is presented above.

The balance sheet reflects the assets, liabilities, and shareholders' equity balances at the end of the budget period. The required amounts come from the prepared budget schedules.

The ending cash balance, for example, is the ending cash balance of the cash budget (Schedule 8). Accounts receivable represents the uncollected sales in the sales budget. Schedule 1 suggests that 30% of the fourth-quarter sales will be collected in the next quarter. This leaves $120,000 for accounts receivable to be reported on the balance sheet. Inventories of materials and finished goods represent the ending quarterly dollar costs from the materials purchases schedule (Schedule 3), and the direct material, direct labour, and manufacturing overhead budgeted costs applied to the desired ending finished goods inventory level in the production budget (Schedule 2). The calculation is shown on Schedule 6.

Capital asset balances are determined by starting with the beginning balances and adjusting for any new purchases or disposals. Accumulated depreciation is determined from the beginning balance sheet, adding the current period's depreciation relating to both manufacturing and nonmanufacturing activities less any depreciation accumulated on capital assets that have been disposed of during the period.

Liability amounts are the unpaid amounts relating to borrowings and acquisitions as of the end of the year.

Shareholders' equity consists of common shares and retained earnings. The common shares amount is unchanged because no new issues or retirements of common shares occurred during the budget period. Retained earnings is updated from last period's balance by adding net income and deducting dividends declared.

Expanding the Budgeted Income Statement

The master budget income statement in Schedule 9 focuses on a single level of activity and has been prepared using absorption costing. Some managers prefer an alternate format

▼   ▼   ▼   ▼   ▼

MANAGERIAL ACCOUNTING IN ACTION—WRAP-UP

After completing the master budget, Larry Green took the documents to Tom Wills, chief executive officer of Hampton Freeze, for his review. The following conversation took place:

LARRY: Here's the budget. Overall, the net income is excellent, and the net cash flow for the entire year is positive.

TOM: Yes, but I see on this cash budget that we have the same problem with negative cash flows in the first and second quarters that we had last year.

LARRY: That's true. I don't see any way around that problem. However, there is no doubt in my mind that if you take this budget to the bank today, they'll approve an open line of credit that will allow you to borrow enough to make it through the first two quarters without any problem.

TOM: Are you sure? They didn't seem very happy to see me last year when I came in for an emergency loan.

LARRY: Did you repay the loan on time?

TOM: Sure.

LARRY: I don't see any problem. You won't be asking for an emergency loan this time. The bank will have plenty of warning. And with this budget, you have a solid plan that shows when and how you are going to pay off the loan. Trust me, they'll go for it.

TOM: Fantastic! It would sure make life a lot easier this year.

▼   ▼   ▼   ▼   ▼

that focuses on a *range* of activity and that is prepared using the contribution approach. An example of a master budget income statement using this alternative format is presented in Exhibit 9–5 (page 444).

A statement such as that in Exhibit 9–5 is *flexible* in its use since it is geared to more than one level of activity. If, for example, the company planned to sell 2,000 units during a period but actually sold only 1,400 units, then the budget figures at the 1,400-unit level would be used to compare against actual costs and revenues. Other columns could be added to the budget as needed by simply applying the budget formulas provided.

SCHEDULE 9

HAMPTON FREEZE COMPANY
Budgeted Income Statement
For the Year Ended December 31, 1998

	Schedule	
Sales (100,000 units at $20)	1	$2,000,000
Less cost of goods sold (100,000 units at $13)	6	1,300,000
Gross margin		700,000
Less selling and administrative expenses	7	537,800
Net operating income		162,200
Less interest expense	8	14,000
Income before taxes		148,200
Less income taxes	*	72,000
Net income		$ 76,200

*Estimated

EXHIBIT 9–5

Alternate Master
Budget Income
Statement

EXAMPLE COMPANY
Master Budget Income Statement

	Budget Formula (per unit)	Sales in Units			
		800	1,400	2,000	2,800
Sales	$75.00	$ 60,000	$105,000	$150,000	$210,000
Less variable expenses:					
Direct materials	12.00	9,600	16,800	24,000	33,600
Direct labour	31.00	24,800	43,400	62,000	86,800
Variable overhead	7.50	6,000	10,500	15,000	21,000
Variable selling and other	4.00	3,200	5,600	8,000	11,200
Total variable expenses	54.50	43,600	76,300	109,000	152,600
Contribution margin	$20.50	16,400	28,700	41,000	57,400
Less fixed expenses:					
Manufacturing overhead		18,000	18,000	18,000	18,000
Selling and administrative		9,000	9,000	9,000	9,000
Total fixed expenses		27,000	27,000	27,000	27,000
Net income (loss)		$ (10,600)	$ 1,700	$ 14,000	$ 30,400

FOCUS ON
CURRENT PRACTICE

Springfield Remanufacturing Corporation (SRC) rebuilds used engines. SRC was a failing division of International Harvester when it was purchased by Jack Stack and a group of employees. Mr. Stack, the CEO of the company, likens a successful business to a winning team on the playing field. He argues that in order to win,

- All team players must know the rules of the game.
- All team players must follow the action and know how to keep score.
- All team players must have a stake in the outcome.

At SRC, every employee is required to receive formal training in understanding the company's income statement, balance sheet, and statement of cash flows. Each Wednesday all managers attend "The Great Huddle" in which a projected income statement for the current month is filled in on a blank form. Managers report and discuss the numbers for which they are responsible. The managers then return to their departments and hold a series of "huddles" with employees in which the projected income statement is discussed and actions (called new plays) are planned. Employees are given a stake in the outcome by receiving bonuses if certain overall financial goals are met. In addition, an employee stock ownership program (ESOP) encourages employees to take a direct financial stake in the company.

The company has been very successful. Over the six years since leaving International Harvester, shares in the company that were originally worth $63 have grown in value to $26,250.[9]

In short, a master budget income statement in this expanded format can be very useful to the manager in the planning and control of operations. The concepts underlying a flexible approach to budgeting are covered in the following two chapters.

---

[9]Olen L. Greer, Stevan K. Olson, and Mary Callison, "The Key to Real Teamwork: Understanding the Numbers," *Management Accounting* (May 1992), pp. 39–44.

SCHEDULE 10

HAMPTON FREEZE COMPANY
Budgeted Balance Sheet
December 31, 1998

Assets

Current assets:

Cash	$ 47,500	(a)
Accounts receivable	120,000	(b)
Raw materials inventory	4,500	(c)
Finished goods inventory	39,000	(d)
Total current assets		$211,000

Capital assets:

Land	80,000	(e)
Buildings and equipment	750,000	(f)
Accumulated depreciation	(352,000)	(g)
Capital Assets, net		478,000
Total assets		$689,000

Liabilities and Shareholders' Equity

Current liabilities:

Accounts payable (raw materials)	$27,900	(h)

Shareholders' equity:

Common shares, no par	$175,000	(i)
Retained earnings	486,100	(j)
Total shareholders' equity		661,100
Total liabilities and shareholders' equity		$689,000

Explanation of December 31, 1998, balance sheet figures:

a. The ending cash balance, as projected by the cash budget in Schedule 8.
b. 30% of fourth-quarter sales, from Schedule 1 ($400,000 × 30% = $120,000).
c. From Schedule 3, the ending raw materials inventory will be 7,500 kilograms. This material costs $0.60 per kilogram. Therefore, the ending inventory in dollars will be 7,500 kilograms × $0.60 = $4,500.
d. From Schedule 6.
e. From the December 31, 1997, balance sheet (no change).
f. The December 31, 1997, balance sheet indicated a balance of $700,000. During 1998, $50,000 additional equipment will be purchased (see Schedule 8), bringing the December 31, 1998, balance to $750,000.
g. The December 31, 1997, balance sheet indicated a balance of $292,000. During 1998, $60,000 of depreciation will be taken (see Schedule 5), bringing the December 31, 1998, balance to $352,000.
h. One-half of the fourth-quarter raw materials purchases, from Schedule 3.
i. From the December 31, 1997, balance sheet (no change).
j. December 31, 1997, balance $449,900
   Add net income, from Schedule 9 76,200

   526,100
   Deduct dividends paid, from Schedule 8 40,000

   December 31, 1998, balance $486,100

JIT PURCHASING

OBJECTIVE 10
Describe JIT purchasing and explain how it differs from JIT production.

It is important that we distinguish between JIT production and JIT purchasing. JIT *production* can be used only by manufacturing companies, since it focuses on the manufacture of goods. We have learned that it is based on a demand-pull concept, where inventories are largely (or entirely) eliminated and where all production activities respond to the "pull" exerted by the final assembly stage. JIT *purchasing*, on the other hand, can be used by *any* organization—retail, wholesale, distribution, service, or manufacturing. It focuses on the *acquisition* of goods. These goods might either be resold to customers (such as in a retail store) or be used as raw materials in the production process.

Under JIT purchasing:

1. *Goods are delivered immediately before demand or use.* Companies that have adopted JIT purchasing require an increase in the number of deliveries, accompanied by a decrease in the number of items per delivery. A manufacturing company might receive several deliveries of a particular raw material each day. This concept of daily (or at least frequent) delivery also has application at the retail level. For many years, retail food stores have received daily deliveries of milk and bread. Various other retail organizations are now moving toward this concept for their goods as well. Food outlets are guaranteeing that baked goods are no more than a few *hours* old, which means that output must be geared to anticipated demand at various times of the day. Even in those manufacturing or retailing situations where some inventories must be maintained, the level of these inventories under JIT purchasing can be reduced to only a fraction of previous amounts.

2. *The number of suppliers is greatly decreased.* All purchases are concentrated on a few, highly dependable suppliers who can meet stringent delivery requirements. IBM, for example, eliminated 95% of the suppliers from one of its plants, reducing the number from 640 to only 32.[10] With this decrease in suppliers comes a corresponding decrease in the amount of resources needed for purchase negotiations and for processing of purchasing data.

3. *Long-term agreements are signed with suppliers; these agreements stipulate the delivery schedule, the quality of the goods, and the price to be paid.* Long-term agreements make it unnecessary to separately negotiate each purchase and eliminate much of the paperwork ordinarily associated with purchase transactions. Delivery schedules are set far in advance, and these schedules must be strictly adhered to by suppliers. Since there are virtually no materials inventories that can be drawn upon in the event that defects are found, the materials must be defect-free when delivered. Therefore, in a JIT system, suppliers must certify that the materials they deliver are defect-free. In the absence of an absolute standard for high quality, it is not possible to use JIT successfully.

4. *Incoming goods are not inspected.* As stated above, suppliers are obligated to deliver defect-free goods under a JIT purchasing agreement. Therefore, there is no need to inspect incoming goods. In addition, some companies require suppliers to deliver goods in "shop-ready" containers that contain exactly the number and types of items required to carry out an assembly operation. Such containers eliminate many non-value-added activities such as unpacking, sorting, and then repacking materials.

5. *Payments are not made for each individual shipment; rather, payments are "batched" for each supplier.* A supplier may make dozens or even hundreds of shipments each month. Rather than paying for each individual shipment, the invoices are batched into a single monthly payment to the supplier. Computers are used to track shipments, match invoices to the goods received, and determine the amounts due.

Companies that adopt JIT purchasing often realize substantial savings from streamlined operations. Note particularly that the adoption of purchasing practices such as those outlined above does not require that a company eliminate *all* inventories. Indeed, retail organizations must maintain *some* inventories or they couldn't operate. But the amount of time a good spends on the shelf or in the warehouse can be greatly reduced even in a retail organization through the JIT approach.

---

[10]George Foster and Charles T. Horngren, "JIT: Cost Accounting and Cost Management Issues," *Management Accounting* (June 1987), p. 20.

 Improved budgeting can result from directing the right questions to clients. Many NFP entities are finding that customer service surveys are a useful starting point for launching total quality management programs and reducing budget costs. The Student Federation at the University of Ottawa conducted a student survey that generated comments and data on customer satisfaction. Computers were placed in high-traffic areas around the campus, and students keyed in their responses to on-screen questions. Through employee participation and by focusing on what the students really wanted the federation was able to reduce its budget for orientation by 50% ($130,000) while doubling student satisfaction.[11]

BUDGETING FOR NOT-FOR-PROFIT ENTITIES

OBJECTIVE 11
Describe budgeting in the context of not-for-profit entities.

Up to this point we have discussed budgeting in the context of profit-seeking enterprises. The sales estimate is the critical ingredient around which the rest of the master budget depends. Inaccurate sales estimates create additional inaccuracies in all other budgets. With profit-oriented bodies there is an intricate relationship between expenses and revenues. With not-for-profit (NFP) entities there is often no relationship between revenue sources expected to be received and expenditures expected to be incurred. Examples of NFP entities include municipal, provincial, and federal governmental units as well as hospitals, universities, voluntary associations, professional associations, and many others. The profit motive is replaced with a service orientation in NFP organizations. Budget information is gathered to assist in decisions regarding what programs and expenditures the entity will undertake. Subsequently the NFP entity estimates what revenues are needed to support these programs and anticipated expenditures. Revenue sources may be in the form of grants, donations, or special tax or membership levies. The very survival of NFP organizations such as art galleries depends on their ability to attract donors. In 1991, for example, Alcan Aluminum Ltd., Levalin Inc., and others slashed their budgets for sponsoring art exhibitions. Cutbacks and closures of art galleries were seen throughout the province of Quebec.

Accountability is of critical importance to most NFP entities. To ensure continued support from contributors it is advantageous to have a budgeting process in place to assist in planning how resources are effectively and efficiently used. Budgets of NFP entities should be formally approved by the entity's governing body. A formally approved budget sends a signal to employees and volunteers alike that the governing body is committed to meeting revenue and expenditure goals.

A budget can be prepared either on an expenditure basis or on a program basis. An expenditure-based budget simply lists the total expected costs of such items as rent, insurance, salaries, and depreciation but does not detail how much of these various expenses relate to particular programs. For many NFP organizations there is a need to report information on the basis of programs rather than line-item expenses. Preparation of the budget on the basis of programs facilitates performance evaluation and allows for the comparison of budgeted with actual revenues and expenses of each program. This should aid decision making about resource allocation among various programs. Budgeting by program also facilitates a stewardship objective by providing information in a format permitting determination of whether designated funds are being spent as intended.

---

[11]*The Globe and Mail Metro Edition*, October 26, 1993, p. 828.

ZERO-BASE BUDGETING

Zero-base budgeting has received considerable attention as an approach to preparing budget data, particularly for use in not-for-profit, governmental, and service-type organizations. The type of budget prepared under this approach—called a **zero-base budget**—is so named because managers are required to start at zero budget levels every year and justify all costs as if the programs involved were being initiated for the first time. By "justify," we mean that no costs are viewed as being ongoing in nature; the manager must start at the ground level each year and present justification for all costs in the proposed budget, regardless of the type of cost involved. This is done in a series of "decision packages" in which the manager ranks all of the activities in the department according to relative importance, going from those that he or she considers essential to those that he or she considers of least importance. Presumably, this allows top management to evaluate each decision package independently and to pare back in those areas that appear less critical or that do not appear to be justified in terms of cost.

This process differs from traditional budgeting, in which budgets are generally initiated on an incremental basis; that is, the manager starts with last year's budget and simply adds to it (or subtracts from it) according to anticipated needs. The manager doesn't have to start at the ground each year and justify ongoing costs (such as salaries) for existing programs.

In a broader sense, zero-base budgeting isn't really a new concept at all. Managers have always advocated in-depth review of departmental costs. The only difference is the frequency with which this review is carried out. Zero-base budgeting says that it should be done annually; critics of the zero-base idea say that it is too often and that such reviews should only be made every five years or so. These critics say that annual in-depth reviews are too time-consuming and too costly to be really feasible, and that in the long run such reviews probably cannot be justified in terms of the cost savings involved. In addition, it is argued that annual reviews soon become mechanical and that the whole purpose of the zero-base idea is then lost.

The question of frequency of zero-base reviews must be left to the judgment of the individual manager. In some situations, annual zero-base reviews may be justified; in other situations, they may not because of the time and cost involved. Whatever the time period chosen, however, most managers would agree that zero-base reviews can be helpful and should be an integral part of the overall budgeting process.

INTERNATIONAL ASPECTS OF BUDGETING

A multinational company (MNC) faces special problems in preparing a budget. These problems arise because of two major factors that can impact a company operating in international markets. These factors are foreign currency exchange rates and inflation.

Foreign currency exchange rates are important in the budgeting process because such rates control the exchange of monetary units between countries, and these rates fluctuate on a daily basis. A common approach to the exchange rate problem is to use a single exchange rate throughout the budget period and then attempt to compensate for rate changes through hedging operations.

When an MNC uses hedging operations, the costs of the hedging activities must be budgeted along with other expense items.

How foreign currency exchange rates can complicate budget preparation is illustrated by the experience of a famous enterprise that must operate across borders and attempts to protect itself through hedging.

[In] 1985 the Toronto Blue Jays budgeted a loss for the season despite the fact that the team had the best win-loss record in the major leagues. The majority of team expenses were paid in U.S. dollars in contrast to their revenue, which was earned in Canadian dollars. To protect themselves against adverse changes in the exchange rate, the Blue Jays made forward purchases of U.S. dollars in late 1984 at 75 cents per Canadian dollar to cover a large portion of their budgeted 1985 U.S. dollar denominated expenses. In 1985, the Blue Jays profited on their hedged position when the Canadian dollar depreciated, which helped to offset losses on unhedged U.S. dollar denominated expenses during the same period.[12]

Sometimes an MNC will have operations in a country with a high inflation rate and this creates additional difficulties in the budgeting process. The inflation rate in some countries may exceed 100% annually. Such high inflation rates—called *hyper-inflation*—require that the lead time for preparing a budget be reduced to minimize inflationary effects. Even when budget lead times are reduced, it is generally necessary to revise the budget just before implementation to adjust for the inflation that has taken place since the budget process started. Then, at the end of the budget period, it is necessary to adjust data for the actual inflation experienced during the year. Only after such inflation adjustments have been made can the manager determine the variations between budgeted and actual revenues and expenses.

In addition to problems with exchange rates and inflation, MNCs must be sensitive to government policies in the countries in which they operate that might affect labour costs, equipment purchases, cash management, or other budget items.

ACTIVITY-BASED BUDGETING

In Chapter 5 we saw that activity-based costing has been developed to help provide the manager with more accurate product or service costs. More accurate costs should translate into better decision making and tighter control over costs. Activity-based costing principles can also be applied to budgeting. With **activity-based budgeting** the emphasis is on budgeting the costs of the activities needed to produce and market the firm's goods and services.

Activity-based budgeting involves several stages. First, the budgeted cost of accomplishing each unit of activity is determined. Recall that an activity is a cost driver such as machine setup, a purchase order, a quality inspection, or a maintenance request. Next, sales and production targets are used to estimate the demand for these activities. The unit cost of each activity is then multiplied by the expected demand to determine the total cost of each activity. The result is a budget based on activities that drive costs rather than the traditional budget based on business functions and expense classifications.

---

[12]Paul V. Mannino and Ken Milani, "Budgeting for an International Business," *Management Accounting* (February 1992), p. 37. Used by permission.

THE NEED FOR FURTHER BUDGETING MATERIAL

The material covered in this chapter represents no more than an introduction into the vast area of budgeting and profit planning. Our purpose has been to present an overview of the budgeting process and to show how the various operating budgets build on each other in guiding a firm toward its profit objectives. However, the matter of budgeting and profit planning is so critical to the intelligent management of a firm in today's business environment that we can't stop with simply an overview of the budgeting process. We need to look more closely at budgeting to see how it helps managers in the day-to-day conduct of business affairs. We will do this by studying standard costs and flexible budgets in the following two chapters and by introducing the concept of performance reporting. In Chapter 12, we will expand on these ideas by looking at budgeting and profit planning as tools for control of decentralized operations and as facilitating factors in judging managerial performance.

In summary, the materials in the following three chapters build on the budgeting and profit planning foundation that has been laid in this chapter by expanding on certain concepts that have been introduced and by refining others. The essential thing to keep in mind at this point is that the material covered in this chapter does not conclude our study of budgeting and profit planning, but rather just introduces the ideas.

REVIEW PROBLEM: BUDGET SCHEDULES

Mylar Company manufactures and sells a product that has a highly seasonal variation in demand, with peak sales coming in the third quarter. The following information is available concerning expected sales and other operating data operations for 19x2—the coming year —and for the first two quarters of 19x3:

a. The company's single product sells for $8 per unit. Budgeted sales in units for the next six quarters are as follows:

	19x2 Quarter				19x3 Quarter	
	1	2	3	4	1	2
Budgeted sales in units . . .	40,000	60,000	100,000	50,000	70,000	80,000

b. Sales are collected in the following pattern: 75% in the quarter the sales are made, and the remaining 25% in the following quarter. On January 1, 19x2, the company's balance sheet showed $65,000 in accounts receivable, all of which will be collected in the first quarter of the year. Bad debts are negligible and can be ignored.

c. The company requires an ending inventory of finished units on hand at the end of each quarter equal to 30% of the budgeted sales for the next quarter. This requirement was met on December 31, 19x1, in that the company had 12,000 units on hand to start the new year.

d. Five kilograms of raw materials are required to complete one unit of product. The company requires an ending inventory of raw materials on hand at the end of each quarter equal to 10% of the production needs of the following quarter. This requirement was met on December 31, 19x1, in that the company had 23,000 kilograms of raw materials on hand to start the new year.

e. The raw material costs $0.80 per kilogram. Purchases of raw material are paid for in the following pattern: 60% paid in the quarter the purchases are made, and the remaining 40% paid in the following quarter. On January 1, 19x2, the company's balance sheet showed $81,500 in accounts payable for raw material purchases, all of which will be paid for in the first quarter of the year.

Required

Prepare the following budgets and schedules for the year, showing both quarterly and total figures:

1. A sales budget and a schedule of expected cash collections.
2. A production budget.
3. A direct materials purchases budget and a schedule of expected cash payments for material purchases.

Solution to Review Problem

1. The sales budget would be prepared as follows:

	19x2 Quarter				
	1	2	3	4	Year
Budgeted sales in units	40,000	60,000	100,000	50,000	250,000
Selling price per unit	× $8	× $8	× $8	× $8	× $8
Budgeted sales	$320,000	$480,000	$800,000	$400,000	$2,000,000

Based on the budgeted sales above, the schedule of expected cash collections would be prepared as follows:

	19x2 Quarter				
	1	2	3	4	Year
Accounts receivable, 12/31/x1	$ 65,000				$ 65,000
First-quarter sales: $320,000 × 75%, 25%	240,000	$ 80,000			320,000
Second-quarter sales: $480,000 × 75%, 25%		360,000	$120,000		480,000
Third-quarter sales: $800,000 × 75%, 25%			600,000	$200,000	800,000
Fourth-quarter sales: $400,000 × 75%				300,000	300,000
Total cash collections	$305,000	$440,000	$720,000	$500,000	$1,965,000

2. Based on the sales budget in units, the production budget would be prepared as follows:

	19x2 Quarter					19x3 Quarter	
	1	2	3	4	Year	1	2
Budgeted sales in units	40,000	60,000	100,000	50,000	250,000	70,000	80,000
Add desired ending inventory*	18,000	30,000	15,000	21,000†	21,000	24,000	
Total needs	58,000	90,000	115,000	71,000	271,000	94,000	
Less beginning inventory	12,000	18,000	30,000	15,000	12,000	21,000	
Units to be produced	46,000	72,000	85,000	56,000	259,000	73,000	

*30% of the following quarter's budgeted sales in units.

†30% of the budgeted 19x3 first-quarter sales.

3. Based on the production budget figures, raw materials will need to be purchased as follows during the year:

	19x2 Quarter					19x3 Quarter
	1	2	3	4	Year	1
Units to be produced	46,000	72,000	85,000	56,000	259,000	73,000
Raw materials needed per unit (kilograms)	× 5	× 5	× 5	× 5	× 5	× 5
Production needs (kilograms)	230,000	360,000	425,000	280,000	1,295,000	365,000
Add desired ending inventory (kilograms)*	36,000	42,500	28,000	36,500†	36,500	
Total needs (kilograms)	266,000	402,500	453,000	316,500	1,331,500	
Less beginning inventory (kilograms)	23,000	36,000	42,500	28,000	23,000	
Raw materials to be purchased (kilograms)	243,000	366,500	410,500	288,500	1,308,500	

*10% of the following quarter's production needs in kilograms.

†10% of the 19x3 first-quarter production needs in kilograms.

Based on the raw material purchases above, expected cash payments would be computed as follows.

	19x2 Quarter				
	1	2	3	4	Year
Cost of raw materials to be purchased at $0.80 per kilogram	$194,400	$293,200	$328,400	$230,800	$1,046,800
Accounts payable, 12/31/x1	$ 81,500				$ 81,500
First-quarter purchases: $194,400 × 60%, 40%	116,640	$ 77,760			194,400
Second-quarter purchases: $293,200 × 60%, 40%		175,920	$117,280		293,200
Third-quarter purchases: $328,400 × 60%, 40%			197,040	$131,360	328,400
Fourth-quarter purchases: $230,800 × 60%				138,480	138,480
Total cash payments	$198,140	$253,680	$314,320	$269,840	$1,035,980

KEY TERMS FOR REVIEW

OBJECTIVE 12
Define or explain the key terms listed at the end of the chapter.

Activity-based budgeting   A budgeting system aimed at determining the costs of activities or cost drivers that are necessary to produce and market goods and services. (p. 449)

Budget   A detailed plan for the acquisition and use of financial and other resources over a specified time period. (p. 421)

Budget committee   A group of key management persons who are responsible for overall policy matters relating to the budget program and for coordinating the preparation of the budget itself. (p. 426)

Capital budget   A budget covering the acquisition of land, building, and items of capital equipment; such a budget may have a time horizon extending 30 years or more into the future. (p. 423)

Cash budget   A detailed plan showing how cash resources will be acquired and used over some specific time period. (p. 429)

Continuous or perpetual budget   A 12-month budget that covers a 12-month period but is constantly adding a new month on the end as the current month is completed. (p. 424)

Control   Those steps taken by management to ensure that the objectives set down at the planning stage are attained and to ensure that all parts of the organization function in a manner consistent with organizational policies. (p. 422)

Direct labour budget   A detailed plan showing labour requirements over some specific time period. (p. 437)

Direct materials budget   A detailed plan showing the amount of raw materials that must be purchased during a period to meet both production and inventory needs. (p. 434)

Ending finished goods inventory budget   A budget showing the dollar amount of cost expected to appear on the balance sheet for unsold units at the end of a period. (p. 438)

Manufacturing overhead budget   A detailed plan showing the production costs, other than direct materials and direct labour, that will be incurred in attaining the output budgeted for a period. (p. 437)

Master budget   A summary of all phases of a company's plans and goals for the future, in which specific targets are set for sales, production, and financing activities, and which generally culminates in a projected statement of net income and a projected statement of cash flows. (p. 421)

Material requirements planning (MRP)   An operations management tool that employs the computer to assist the manager in overall materials and inventory planning. (p. 436)

Merchandise purchases budget   A budget used by a merchandising company that shows the amount of goods that must be purchased from suppliers during the period. (p. 434)

Participative budget   See *Self-imposed budget*. (p. 425)

Planning   The development of objectives in an organization and the preparation of various budgets to achieve these objectives. (p. 422)

Production budget A detailed plan showing the number of units that must be produced during a period in order to meet both sales and inventory needs. (p. 433)

Profit planning Steps taken by a business organization to achieve certain desired levels of profits. (p. 421)

Responsibility accounting A system of accounting in which costs are assigned to various managerial levels according to where control of the costs is deemed to rest, with the managers then held responsible for differences between budgeted and actual results. (p. 423)

Sales budget A detailed schedule showing the expected sales for coming periods; these sales are typically expressed in both dollars and units. (p. 428)

Sales forecast A schedule of expected sales for an entire industry. (p. 429)

Self-imposed budget A method of budget preparation in which managers with responsibilities over cost control prepare their own budget figures; these budget figures are reviewed by the managers' supervisors, and any questions are then resolved in face-to-face meetings. A self-imposed budget is also called a *participative budget.* (p. 425)

Selling and administrative expense budget A detailed schedule of planned expenses that will be incurred in areas other than manufacturing during a budget period. (p. 438)

Zero-based budget A method of budgeting in which managers are required to start at zero budget levels every year and to justify all costs as if the programs involved were being initiated for the first time. (p. 448)

QUESTIONS

9–1 What is a budget? What is budgetary control?

9–2 Discuss some of the major benefits to be gained from budgeting.

9–3 What is meant by the term *responsibility accounting?*

9–4 "Budgeting is designed primarily for organizations that have few complexities and uncertainties in their day-to-day operations." Do you agree? Why or why not?

9–5 What is a master budget? Briefly describe its contents.

9–6 Which is a better basis for judging actual results, budgeted performance or past performance? Why?

9–7 Why is the sales forecast the starting point in budgeting?

9–8 Is there any difference between a sales forecast and a sales budget? Explain.

9–9 "As a practical matter, planning and control mean exactly the same thing." Do you agree? Explain.

9–10 Describe the flow of budget data in an organization. Who are the participants in the budgeting process, and how do they participate?

9–11 "To a large extent, the success of a budget program hinges on education and good salesmanship." Do you agree? Explain.

9–12 What is a self-imposed budget? What are the major advantages of self-imposed budgets? What caution must be exercised in their use?

9–13 How can budgeting assist a firm in its employment policies?

9–14 "The principal purpose of the cash budget is to see how much cash the company will have in the bank at the end of the year." Do you agree? Explain.

9–15 How does JIT purchasing differ from JIT production?

9–16 What are the five key ideas associated with JIT purchasing?

9–17 Does a company have to eliminate all inventories in order to adopt JIT purchasing?

9–18 How does zero-base budgeting differ from traditional budgeting?

9–19 "With profit, not-for-profit, and government entities there is generally a direct relationship between revenues and expenditures." Do you agree with this statement? Why or why not?

EXERCISES

E9–1 Peak sales for Manitoba Products, Inc., occur in August. The company's sales budget for the third quarter showing these peak sales is given below:

	July	August	September	Total
Budgeted sales	$600,000	$900,000	$500,000	$2,000,000

From past experience, the company has learned that 20% of a month's sales is collected in the month of sale, that another 70% is collected in the month following sale, and that the remaining 10% is collected in the second month following sale. Bad debts are negligible and can be ignored. May sales totalled $430,000, and June sales totalled $540,000.

Required

1. Prepare a schedule of budgeted cash collections from sales, by month and in total, for the third quarter.
2. Assume that the company will prepare a budgeted balance sheet as of September 30. Compute the accounts receivable as of that date.

E9–2 Warner Company has budgeted the sales of its product over the next four months as follows:

	Sales in Units
July	30,000
August	45,000
September	60,000
October	50,000

The company is now in the process of preparing a production budget for the third quarter. Past experience has shown that end-of-month inventories of finished goods must equal 10% of the next month's sales. The inventory at the end of June was 3,000 units.

Required

Prepare a production budget for the third quarter showing the number of units to be produced each month and for the quarter in total.

E9–3 Micro Products, Inc., has developed a very powerful electronic calculator. Each calculator requires three small "chips" in its manufacture. The chips cost $2 each and are purchased from an overseas supplier. Micro Products has prepared a production budget for the calculator by quarters for 19x5 and for the first quarter of 19x6, as shown below:

	19x5				19x6
	First	Second	Third	Fourth	First
Budgeted production, in calculators	60,000	90,000	150,000	100,000	80,000

The chip used in production of the calculator is sometimes hard to get, so it is necessary to carry large inventories as a precaution against stockouts. For this reason, the inventory of chips at the end of a quarter must be equal to 20% of the following quarter's production needs. Some 36,000 chips will be on hand to start the first quarter of 19x5.

Required

Prepare a materials purchases budget for chips, by quarter and in total, for 19x5. At the bottom of your budget, show the dollar amount of purchases for each quarter and for the year in total.

E9–4 Calgon Products needs a cash budget for September. The following information is available:

a. The cash balance at the beginning of September is $9,000.

b. Actual sales for July and August and expected sales for September are as follows:

	July	August	September
Cash sales	$ 6,500	$ 5,250	$ 7,400
Sales on account	20,000	30,000	40,000
Total sales	$26,500	$35,250	$47,400

Sales on account are collected over a three-month period in the following ratio: 10% collected in the month of sale, 70% collected in the month following sale, and 18% collected in the second month following sale. The remaining 2% is uncollectible.

c. Purchases of inventory will total $25,000 for September. Twenty percent of a month's inventory purchases are paid for during the month of purchase. The accounts payable remaining from August's inventory purchases total $16,000, all of which will be paid in September.

d. Selling and administrative expenses are budgeted at $13,000 for September. Of this amount, $4,000 is for depreciation.

e. Equipment costing $18,000 will be purchased for cash during September, and dividends totaling $3,000 will be paid during the month.

f. The company must maintain a minimum cash balance of $5,000. An open line of credit is available from the company's bank to bolster the cash position as needed.

Required

1. Prepare a schedule of expected cash collections for September.
2. Prepare a schedule of expected cash payments to suppliers during September for inventory purchases.
3. Prepare a cash budget for September. Indicate in the financing section any borrowing that will be needed during September.

E9–5 A cash budget, by quarters, is given below (000 omitted). The company requires a minimum cash balance of $5,000 to start each quarter.

	Quarter				
	1	2	3	4	Year
Cash balance, beginning	$ 9	$?	$?	$?	$?
Add collections from customers	?	?	125	?	391
Total cash available	85	?	?	?	?
Less disbursements:					
Purchase of inventory	40	58	?	32	?
Operating expenses	?	42	54	?	180
Equipment purchases	10	8	8	?	36
Dividends	2	2	2	2	?
Total disbursements	?	110	?	?	?
Excess (deficiency) of cash					
available over disbursements	(3)	?	30	?	?
Financing:					
Borrowings	?	20	—	—	?
Repayments (including interest)*	—	—	(?)	(7)	(?)
Total financing	?	?	?	?	?
Cash balance, ending	$?	$?	$?	$?	$?

*Interest will total $4,000 for the year.

Required

Fill in the missing amounts in the table above.

E9–6 Joe Abel recently received his electrician's papers from the province. After apprenticing with a local electrician, he felt he wanted to start his own business. Using his savings of $12,000, he believed he could buy what he needed to begin.

After consulting his solicitor, he decided to incorporate and transfer his $12,000 to the business to exchange for shares. The business name was Joe's Electric Limited.

Joe used the corporate account to purchase a used truck for $9,000 and tools for $1,500. He rented storage space in a local U-Haul storage yard and placed an ad in the local paper.

Joe decided, on advice from his banker, to prepare a budget for the next year. He estimated his service revenue at $32,000 which he expected he would fully collect. Wages for an assistant he expected to be $8,500 with benefits at $175. Supplies should cost $9,500; gas and oil for the truck, $1,200; insurance, $700; rent, $500; telephone, $825; sundry including advertising, $600. Uncollected service revenue at year-end he estimated to be $3,000. Income taxes due six months after the year were assessed at 30%. Depreciation on capital assets should amount to $1,200.

Required

Prepare a budgeted income statement for the first year of operations.

E9–7 Greenup, Inc., manufactures a product that has peak sales in March of each year. The company's budgeted sales for the first quarter of 19x6 are given below:

	January	February	March	April
Budgeted sales	$500,000	$700,000	$1,800,000	$3,000,000

The company is in the process of preparing a cash budget for the first quarter and must determine the expected cash collections by month. To this end, the following information has been assembled:

Collections on sales:	60%	in month of sale
	30%	in month following sale
	8%	in second month following sale
	2%	uncollectible

The company gives a 2% cash discount for payments made by customers during the month of sale. The accounts receivable balance to start the year is $220,000, of which $40,000 represents uncollected November 19x5 sales and $180,000 represents uncollected December 19x5 sales.

Required

1. What were the total sales for November 19x5? For December 19x5?
2. Prepare a schedule showing the budgeted cash collections from sales, by month, and in total, for the first quarter of 19x6.

E9–8 The following data relate to the operations of the Fred Company Ltd., a retail store:

Sales Forecast—19x9

April	$ 70,000
May	60,000
June	80,000
July	100,000
August	120,000

a. Cost of sales is 40% of sales. Other variable costs are 20% of sales.
b. Inventory is maintained at twice the budgeted sales requirements for the following month.
c. Fixed costs are $20,000 per month.
d. The income tax rate is estimated to be 40%.

Required

1. Prepare a purchases budget in dollars for June 19x9.
2. Prepare a budgeted income statement for June 19x9.

(CGA-Canada, adapted)

PROBLEMS

P9–9   Production and Purchases Budgets   Tonga Toys manufactures and distributes a number of products to retailers. One of these products, Playclay, requires three kilograms of material A in the manufacture of each unit. The company is now planning raw materials needs for the third quarter—July, August, and September. Peak sales of Playclay occur in the third quarter of each year. To keep production and shipments moving smoothly, the company has the following inventory requirements:

a. The finished goods inventory on hand at the end of each month must be equal to 5,000 units plus 30% of the next month's sales. The finished goods inventory on June 30 is budgeted to be 17,000 units.
b. The raw materials inventory on hand at the end of each month must be equal to one-half of the following month's production needs for raw materials. The raw materials inventory on June 30 for material A is budgeted to be 64,500 kilograms.
c. The company maintains no work in process inventories.

A sales budget for Playclay for the last six months of the year is given below:

	Budgeted Sales in Units
July	40,000
August	50,000
September	70,000
October	35,000
November	20,000
December	10,000

Required

1. Prepare a production budget for Playclay for the months July–October.
2. Examine the production budget that you have prepared. Why will the company produce more units than it sells in July and August and less units than it sells in September and October?
3. Prepare a budget showing the quantity of material A to be purchased for July, August, and September and for the quarter in total.

P9–10 Cash Budget   Jodi Horton, president of Crestline Products, has just approached the company's bank with a request for a $30,000, 90-day loan. The purpose of the loan is to assist the company in building inventories in support of peak April sales. Since the company has had some difficulty in paying off its loans in the past, the loan officer has asked for a cash budget to help determine whether the loan should be made. The following data are available for the months April–June, during which the loan will be used:

a. On April 1, the start of the loan period, the cash balance will be $26,000. Accounts receivable on April 1 will total $151,500, of which $141,000 will be collected during April and $7,200 will be collected during May. The remainder will be uncollectible.

b. Past experience shows that 20% of a month's sales are collected in the month of sale, 75% in the month following sale, and 4% in the second month following sale. The other 1% represents bad debts that are never collected. Budgeted sales and expenses for the period follow:

	April	May	June
Sales	$200,000	$300,000	$250,000
Merchandise purchases	120,000	180,000	150,000
Payroll	9,000	9,000	8,000
Lease payments	15,000	15,000	15,000
Advertising	70,000	80,000	60,000
Equipment purchases	8,000	—	—
Depreciation	10,000	10,000	10,000

c. Merchandise purchases are paid in full during the month following purchase. Accounts payable for merchandise purchases on March 31, which will be paid during April, total $108,000.

d. In preparing the cash budget, assume that the $30,000 loan will be made in April and repaid in June. Interest on the loan will total $1,200.

Required

1. Prepare a schedule of budgeted cash collections for April, May, and June and for the three months in total.
2. Prepare a cash budget, by month and in total, for the three-month period.
3. If the company needs a minimum cash balance of $20,000 to start each month, can the loan be repaid as planned? Explain.

P9–11 Master Budget Preparation   The balance sheet of Phototec, Inc., as of May 31 is given below:

PHOTOTEC, INC.

Balance Sheet

May 31

Assets

Cash	$ 8,000
Accounts receivable	72,000
Inventory	30,000
Plant and equipment, net of depreciation	500,000
Total assets	$610,000

Liabilities and Shareholders' Equity

Accounts payable, suppliers	$ 90,000
Note payable	15,000
Capital stock, no par	420,000
Retained earnings	85,000
Total liabilities and shareholders' equity	$610,000

Phototec, Inc., has not budgeted previously, and for this reason it is limiting its master budget planning horizon to just one month ahead—namely, June. The company has assembled the following budgeted data relating to June:

a. Sales are budgeted at $250,000. Of these sales, $60,000 will be for cash; the remainder will be credit sales. One-half of a month's credit sales are collected in the month the sales are made, and the remainder is collected in the month following. All of the May 31 accounts receivable will be collected in June.

b. Purchases of inventory are expected to total $200,000 during June. These purchases will all be on account. Forty percent of all inventory purchases are paid for in the month of purchase; the remainder is paid in the following month. All of the May 31 accounts payable to suppliers will be paid during June.

c. The June 30 inventory balance is budgeted at $40,000.

d. Operating expenses for June are budgeted at $51,000, exclusive of depreciation. These expenses will all be paid in cash. Depreciation is budgeted at $2,000 for the month.

e. The note payable on the May 31 balance sheet will be paid during June. The company's interest expense for June (on all borrowing) will be $500, which will be paid in cash.

f. New equipment costing $9,000 will be purchased for cash during June.

g. During June, the company will borrow $18,000 from its bank by giving a new note payable to the bank for that amount. The new note will be due in one year.

Required

1. Prepare a cash budget for June. Support your budget with schedules showing budgeted cash receipts from sales and budgeted cash payments for inventory purchases.

2. Prepare a budgeted income statement for June. Use the traditional income statement format, as shown in Schedule 9.

3. Prepare a budgeted balance sheet as of June 30.

P9–12 Cash Budget   Prince George Co.'s fiscal year begins on April 1. The following is an extract from a trial balance at May 31, 1997:

	DR	CR
Cash	3,500	
Accounts receivable	27,200	
Allowance for doubtful accounts		2,240
Inventory—merchandise	16,000	
Accounts payable, merchandise		7,000

Data concerning the company's purchases of merchandise inventory:

Purchase price per unit—$8
75% of any month's purchases are payable in the month of purchase while the rest is due and paid for in the following month. At the end of each month the company's policy is to have an inventory equal to 50% of the following month's unit sales.

Sales data:

Selling price per unit	$	16
April actual sales revenue		32,000
May actual sales revenue		48,000
June estimated sales revenue		64,000
July estimated sales revenue		56,000
Total sales expected in fiscal year		$800,000

50% of billings are collected during the month of sale, 40% in the following calendar month, 7% in the next following calendar month, and 3% is uncollectible. Customers are allowed a 2% cash discount if payment is made by the end of the calendar month in which the sale took place.

Selling and administrative expenses (exclusive of bad debts expense):

Total selling and administrative expenses for fiscal year	$108,000
Total fixed selling and administrative expenses for fiscal year (included in total)—incurred evenly throughout the year	24,000
Annual depreciation expense (included in fixed selling and administrative expense)	6,000
Variable selling and administrative expenses vary with sales revenue.	
Selling and administrative expenses are paid as incurred.	

Required

Prepare a case budget for Prince George Co. for June 1997.

(CGA-Canada, adapted)

P9–13   Behavioural Aspects of Budgeting   Five years ago, Jack Cadence left his position at a large company to start Advanced Technologies Co. (ATC), a software design company. ATC's first product was a unique software package that seamlessly integrates networked PCs. Robust sales of this initial product permitted the company to begin development of other software products and to hire additional personnel. The staff at ATC quickly grew from 3 people working out of Cadence's basement to over 70 individuals working in leased spaces at an industrial park. Continued growth led Cadence to hire seasoned marketing, distribution, and production managers and an experienced accountant, Bill Cross.

Recently, Cadence decided that the company had become too large to run on an informal basis and that a formalized planning and control program centred around a budget was necessary. Cadence asked the accountant, Bill Cross, to work with him in developing the initial budget for ATC.

Cadence forecasted sales revenues based on his projections for both the market growth for the initial software and successful completion of new products. Cross used this data to construct the master budget for the company, which he then broke down into departmental budgets. Cadence and Cross met a number of times over a three-week period to hammer out the details of the budgets.

When Cadence and Cross were satisfied with their work, the various departmental budgets were distributed to the department managers with a covering letter explaining ATC's new budgeting system. The letter requested everyone's assistance in working together to achieve the budget objectives.

Several of the department managers were displeased with how the budgeting process was undertaken. In discussing the situation among themselves, they felt that some of the budget projections were overly optimistic and not realistically attainable.

Required

1. How does the budgeting process Cadence and Cross used at ATC differ from recommended practice?
2. What are the behavioural implications of the way Cadence and Cross went about preparing the master budget?

(CMA, adapted)

P9–14   Ethics and the Manager   Granger Stokes, managing partner of the venture capital firm of Halston and Stokes, was dissatisfied with the top management of PrimeDrive, a manufacturer of computer disk drives. Halston and Stokes had invested $20 million in PrimeDrive, and the return on their investment had been below par for several years. In a tense meeting of the board of directors of PrimeDrive, Stokes exercised his firm's rights as the major equity investor in PrimeDrive and fired PrimeDrive's chief executive officer (CEO). He then quickly moved to have the board of directors of PrimeDrive appoint himself as the new CEO.

Stokes prided himself on his hard-driving management style. At the first management meeting, he asked two of the managers to stand and fired them on the spot, just to show everyone who was in control of the company. At the budget review meeting that followed, he ripped up the departmental budgets that had been submitted for his review and yelled at the managers for their "wimpy, do nothing targets." He then ordered everyone to submit new budgets calling for at least a 40% increase in sales volume and announced that he would not accept excuses for results that fell below budget.

Keri Kalani, an accountant working for the production manager at PrimeDrive, discovered toward the end of the year that her boss had not been scrapping defective disk drives that had been returned by customers. Instead, he had been shipping them in new cartons to customers in order to avoid booking losses. Quality control had deteriorated during the year as a result of the drive for increased volume, and returns of defective TRX drives were running as high as 15% of the new drives shipped. When she confronted her boss with her discovery, he told her to mind her own business. And then, in the way of a justification for his actions, he said, "All of us managers are finding ways to hit Stokes's targets."

Required

1. Is Granger Stokes using budgets as a planning and control tool?
2. What are the behavioural consequences of the way budgets are being used at PrimeDrive?
3. What, if anything, do you think Keri Kalani should do?

P9–15   Integration of Sales, Production, and Purchases Budgets   Crydon, Inc., manufactures a single product whose peak sales occur in August. Management is now preparing detailed budgets for the third quarter, July through September, and has assembled the following information to assist in the budget preparation:

a. The marketing department has estimated sales as follows for the remainder of the year (in units):

July	6,000	October	4,000
August	7,000	November	3,000
September	5,000	December	3,000

The selling price of the company's product is $50 per unit.

b. All sales are on account. Based on past experience, sales are expected to be collected in the following pattern:

40% in the month of sale
50% in the month following sale
10% uncollectible

The beginning accounts receivable balance (excluding uncollectible amounts) on July 1 will be $130,000.

c. The company maintains finished goods inventories equal to 10% of the following month's sales. The inventory of finished goods on July 1 will be 600 units.

d. Each finished unit of product requires 2 kilograms of geico compound. To prevent shortages, the company would like the inventory of geico compound on hand at the end of each month to be equal to 20% of the following month's production needs. The inventory of geico compound on hand on July 1 will be 2,440 kilograms.

e. Geico compound costs $2.50 per kilogram. Crydon pays for 60% of its purchases in the month of purchase; the remainder is paid for in the following month. The accounts payable balance for geico compound purchases will be $11,400 on July 1.

Required

1. Prepare a sales budget, by month and in total, for the third quarter. (Show your budget in both units and dollars.) Also prepare a schedule of expected cash collections, by month and in total, for the third quarter.
2. Prepare a production budget for each of the months July through October.
3. Prepare a materials purchases budget for geico compound, by month and in total, for the third quarter. Also prepare a schedule of expected cash payments for geico compound, by month and in total, for the third quarter.

P9–16   Planning Bank Financing by Means of a Cash Budget   The president of Univax, Inc., has just approached the company's bank seeking short-term financing for the coming year, 19x2. The bank has stated that the loan request must be accompanied by a detailed cash budget that shows the quarters in which financing will be needed, as well as the amounts that will be needed and the quarters in which repayments can be made.

To provide this information for the bank, the president has directed that the following data be gathered from which a cash budget can be prepared:

a. Budgeted sales and merchandise purchases for 19x2, as well as actual sales and purchases for the last quarter of 19x1, are as follows:

	Sales	Merchandise Purchases
19x1:		
Fourth quarter actual	$300,000	$180,000
19x2:		
First quarter budgeted	400,000	260,000
Second quarter budgeted	500,000	310,000
Third quarter budgeted	600,000	370,000
Fourth quarter budgeted	480,000	240,000

b. The company typically collects 33% of a quarter's sales before the quarter ends and another 65% in the following quarter. The remainder is uncollectible. This pattern of collections is now being experienced in the actual data for the 19x1 fourth quarter.

c. Some 20% of a quarter's merchandise purchases are paid for within the quarter. The remainder is paid in the quarter following.

d. Operating expenses for 19x2 are budgeted quarterly at $90,000 plus 12% of sales. Of the fixed amount, $20,000 each quarter is depreciation.

e. The company will pay $10,000 in cash dividends each quarter.

f. Equipment purchases will be made as follows during the year: $80,000 in the second quarter and $48,500 in the third quarter.

g. The Cash account contained $20,000 at the end of 19x1. The company must maintain a minimum cash balance of at least $18,000.

h. Any borrowing will take place at the beginning of a quarter, and any repayments will be made at the end of a quarter at an annual interest rate of 10%. Interest is paid only when principal is repaid. All borrowings and all repayments of principal must be in round $1,000 amounts. Interest payments can be in any amount.

i. At present, the company has no loans outstanding.

Required

1. Prepare the following, by quarter and in total, for the year 19x2:
   a. A schedule of budgeted cash collections on sales.
   b. A schedule of budgeted cash payments for merchandise purchases.
2. Compute the expected cash payments for operating expenses, by quarter and in total, for the year 19x2.
3. Using the data from (1) and (2) above and other data as needed, prepare a cash budget for 19x2, by quarter and in total for the year. Show clearly on your budget the quarter(s) in which borrowing will be needed and the quarter(s) in which repayments can be made, as requested by the company's bank.

P9–17 Cash Budget with Supporting Schedules Janus Products, Inc., is a merchandising company that sells binders, paper, and other school supplies. The company is planning its cash needs for the third quarter. In the past, Janus Products has had to borrow money during the third quarter to support peak sales of back-to-school materials, which occur during August. The following information has been assembled to assist in preparing a cash budget for the quarter:

a. Budgeted monthly income statements for July–October are as follows:

	July	August	September	October
Sales	$40,000	$70,000	$50,000	$45,000
Cost of goods sold	24,000	42,000	30,000	27,000
Gross margin	16,000	28,000	20,000	18,000
Less operating expenses:				
Selling expense	7,200	11,700	8,500	7,300
Administrative expense*	5,600	7,200	6,100	5,900
Total operating expenses	12,800	18,900	14,600	13,200
Net income	$ 3,200	$ 9,100	$ 5,400	$ 4,800

*Includes $2,000 depreciation each month.

b. Sales are 20% for cash and 80% on credit.

c. Credit sales are collected over a three-month period in the ratio of 10% in the month of sale, 70% in the month following sale, and 20% in the second month following sale. May sales totalled $30,000, and June sales totalled $36,000.

d. Inventory purchases are paid for within 15 days. Therefore, 50% of a month's inventory purchases are paid for in the month of purchase. The remaining 50% is paid in the following month. Accounts payable for inventory purchases at June 30 total $11,700.

e. The company maintains its ending inventory levels at 75% of the cost of the merchandise to be sold in the following month. The merchandise inventory at June 30 is $18,000.

f. Equipment costing $4,500 will be purchased in July.

g. Dividends of $1,000 will be declared and paid in September.

h. The cash balance on June 30 is $8,000; the company must maintain a cash balance of at least this amount at all times.

i. The company can borrow from its bank as needed to bolster the Cash account. Borrowings and repayments must be in multiples of $1,000. All borrowings take place at the beginning of a month, and all repayments are made at the end of a month. The annual interest rate is 12%. Compute interest on whole months ($\frac{1}{12}, \frac{2}{12}$, and so on).

Required

1. Prepare a schedule of budgeted cash collections from sales for each of the months July, August, and September and for the quarter in total.

2. Prepare the following for merchandise inventory:
    a. An inventory purchases budget for each of the months July, August, and September.
    b. A schedule of expected cash disbursements for inventory for each of the months July, August, and September and for the quarter in total.

3. Prepare a cash budget for the third quarter, by month as well as for the quarter in total. Show borrowings from the company's bank and repayments to the bank as needed to maintain the minimum cash balance.

P9–18   Master Budget Preparation   Nordic Company, a merchandising company, prepares its master budget on a quarterly basis. The following data have been assembled to assist in preparation of the master budget for the second quarter.

a. As of March 31 (the end of the prior quarter), the company's balance sheet showed the following account balances:

Cash	$ 9,000	
Accounts Receivable	48,000	
Inventory	12,600	
Plant and Equipment (net)	214,100	
Accounts Payable		$ 18,300
Capital Stock		190,000
Retained Earnings		75,400
	$283,700	$283,700

b. Actual sales for March and budgeted sales for April–July are as follows:

March (actual)	$60,000
April	70,000
May	85,000
June	90,000
July	50,000

c. Sales are 20% for cash and 80% on credit. All payments on credit sales are collected in the month following sale. The accounts receivable at March 31 are a result of March credit sales.

d. The company's gross profit rate is 40% of sales.

e. Monthly expenses are budgeted as follows: salaries and wages, $7,500 per month; shipping, 6% of sales; advertising, $6,000 per month; depreciation, $2,000 per month; other expense, 4% of sales.

f. At the end of each month, inventory is to be on hand equal to 30% of the following month's sales needs, stated at cost.

g. Half of a month's inventory purchases are paid for in the month of purchase and half in the following month.

h. Equipment purchases during the quarter will be as follows: April, $11,500; and May, $3,000.

i. Dividends totalling $3,500 will be declared and paid in June.

j. The company must maintain a minimum cash balance of $8,000. An open line of credit is available at a local bank. All borrowing is done at the beginning of a month, and all repayments are made at the end of a month. Borrowings and repayments of principal must be in multiples of $1,000. Interest is paid only at the time of repayment of principal. The annual interest rate is 12%. (Figure interest on whole months, e.g., $\frac{1}{12}$, $\frac{2}{12}$.)

Required

Using the data above, complete the following statements and schedules for the second quarter:

1. Schedule of expected cash collections:

	April	May	June	Total
Cash sales	$14,000			
Credit sales	48,000			
Total collections	$62,000			

2. a. Inventory purchases budget:

	April	May	June	Total
Budgeted cost of goods sold	$42,000*	$51,000		
Add: Desired ending inventory	15,300†			
Total needs	57,300			
Deduct: Opening inventory	12,600			
Required purchases	$44,700			

*For April sales: $70,000 sales × 60% cost ratio = $42,000.

†$51,000 × 30% = $15,300.

b. Schedule of cash disbursements for purchases:

	April	May	June	Total
For March purchases	$18,300			$18,300
For April purchases	22,350	$22,350		44,700
For May purchases				
For June purchases				
Total cash disbursements	$40,650			

3. Schedule of cash disbursements for expenses:

	April	May	June	Total
Salaries and wages	$ 7,500			
Shipping	4,200			
Advertising	6,000			
Other expenses	2,800			
Total cash disbursements	$20,500			

4. Cash budget:

	April	May	June	Total
Cash balance, beginning	$ 9,000			
Add cash collections	62,000			
Total cash available	71,000			
Less disbursements:				
For inventory purchases	40,650			
For operating expenses	20,500			
For equipment purchases	11,500			
For dividends	—			
Total disbursements	72,650			
Excess (deficiency) of cash	(1,650)			
Financing				
Etc.				

5. Prepare an income statement for the quarter ending June 30. (Use the functional format in preparing your income statement, as shown in Schedule 9 in the chapter.)
6. Prepare a balance sheet as of June 30.

P9–19 Budgeted Income Statement and Balance Sheet   Chen Company is a retail book store that sells both to nonbusiness and other retail stores. Su Chen, the manager, is interested in preparing a budget balance sheet and income statement for the upcoming year.

Su prepared the following estimates for the upcoming year: Sales, $100,000, one-half made on credit; depreciation expense, $20,000; capital asset additions, $10,000; $1,500 in unpaid income taxes at the year-end, and no payments for the long-term note. Interest, however, will be paid. Dividends should be $12,000. Receivables and inventory were expected to be in the same proportion as the current year. Similarly, accounts payable, income taxes, and gross margin should continue as before.

The financial statements for Chen Company for 19x were:

Income Statement

Sales	$ 95,000
Cost of goods sold	46,000
Gross Margin	49,000
Expenses (including depreciation $18,000 and $3,000 interest)	33,000
Pretax income	16,000
Income tax (22%)	3,520
Net income	$ 12,480

Balance Sheet

Assets

Cash	$ 20,000
Accounts receivable	30,000
Inventory	40,000
Capital asset (net)	100,000
Total assets	$190,000

Liabilities

Accounts payable	$ 50,000
Income taxes payable	1,000
Notes payable, long-term	25,000
	76,000

Shareholders' Equity

Capital stock (8,000 no par shares)	80,000
Retained earnings	34,000
	114,000
Total liabilities and shareholders' equity	$190,000

Required   Prepare a budgeted income statement and balance sheet for 19y.

P9–20 Not-for-Profit Cash Collections   Jane Conrad, city manager for the Halifax Regional Municipality, is engaged in some preliminary analysis of the city's revenues for the upcoming year. Revenue estimation is an important aspect of budgeting for the city because it helps to determine what revenues will be available for program expenditures set by city council.

City revenues are a function of property tax assessments, the tax rate, and new construction as well as various fines and fees. Fines and fees are in turn related to population growth. Government grants from the province are a particularly difficult matter because they are unknown until the province sets its budget, usually after the city has set a tax rate. Thus grant projections are typically estimated based on the rate of inflation and last year's amount. If errors do occur in the estimate they can be offset by program expenditure adjustments later in the year.

Jane uses the following formulae to estimate the revenue components:

$$Pt_t = rA_t \text{ where}$$

Pt_t is the property tax revenue for year t
r is the tax rate per \$1,000 of assessment
A_t is the assessment in \$1,000 units for year t

$A_t = 1.05\, A_{t-1} + .5\, S$ where this regression formula relates last year's assessment A_{t-1} and new construction S and includes the fact that all new construction does not happen at the beginning of the year.

Fines and fees (Ff) relate to population by the following formula:

$$Ff_t = [(1 + G)\, P_{t-1}]*\$5$$

where

G is the population growth percentage
P_{t-1} is the population for last year, t–1.

Government grants (Gg) from the province are set as follows:

$$Gg_t = (1 + I)\, Gg_{t-1}$$

where

I is the inflation rate for the current year.

Collection of tax revenue and fines and fees is scattered throughout the year. Monthly revenues are an important factor in minimizing financial borrowing. Government grants are paid to the city twice per year, September and January so these require little estimation of collection dates. However, the tax revenue is typically collected according to the following pattern:

April	2%	October	25%
May	30%	November	3%
June	18%	December	3%
July	2%	January	2%
August	1%	February	1%
September	10%	March	1%
			98%

2% of revenue is lost from bad debts.

Fines and fees are collected in a relatively even pattern throughout the year, April to March.

The following data were collected by Jane to assist with the calculations.

$$A_{t-1} = \$8,000,000 \text{ in 1,000 units}$$
$$r = \$65 \text{ per } \$1,000 \text{ assessed value}$$
$$S = \$100,000 \text{ in 1,000 units}$$
$$P_{t-1} = 375,000 \text{ people}$$
$$G = 12\%$$
$$I = 3\%$$
$$Gg_{t-1} = \$10,000,000$$

Required

Estimate the monthly collections for Halifax Regional Municipality.

P9–21 Cash Budget for One Month   The treasurer of Household Company, Ltd., states, "Our monthly financial budget shows me our cash surplus or deficiency and assures me that an unexpected cash shortage will not occur."

A cash budget is now being prepared for May. The following information has been gathered to assist in preparing the budget:

a. Budgeted sales and production requirements are as follows:

Budgeted sales $650,000

Production requirements:
Raw materials to be used 301,000
Direct labour cost 85,000

The raw materials inventory is budgeted to increase by $6,000 during the month; other inventories will not change.

b. Customers are allowed a 2% cash discount on accounts paid within 10 days after the end of the month of sale. Only 50% of the payments made in the month following sale fall within the discount period.

c. Accounts receivable outstanding at April 30 were as follows:

Month	Sales	Accounts Receivable at April 30	Percentage of Sales Uncollected at April 30	Percentage to Be Collected in May
January	$340,000	$ 8,500	2½	?
February	530,000	31,800	6	?
March	470,000	47,000	10	?
April	550,000	$550,000	100	?

Bad debts are negligible. All January receivables outstanding will have been collected by the end of May, and the collection pattern since the time of sale will be the same in May as in previous months.

d. Raw materials purchases are paid in the month following purchase, and $320,000 in accounts payable for purchases was outstanding at the end of April.

e. Accrued wages on April 30 were $11,000. All May payroll amounts will be paid within the month of May.

f. Budgeted operating expenses and overhead costs for May are as follows:

Overhead and other charges:
Indirect labour $34,000
Real estate taxes 1,500
Depreciation 25,000
Utilities 1,500
Wage benefits 9,000
Fire insurance 1,500
Amortization of patents 5,000
Spoilage of materials in the warehouse 1,500 $79,000
Sales salaries 45,000
Administrative salaries 15,000

g. Real estate taxes are paid in August each year.

h. Utilities are billed and paid within the month.

i. The $9,000 monthly charge above for "Wage benefits" includes the following:

Employment insurance (payable monthly) $1,350
Canada pension plan (payable monthly) 820
Holiday pay, which represents ½ of the annual cost
  (May holidays will require $2,040) 1,100
Company pension fund, including ½ of a $10,800
  adjustment that was paid in January 5,000
Group insurance (payable quarterly, with the last
  payment having been made in February) 730

j. Fire insurance premiums were paid in January, in advance.

k. Shipping costs for May will be $1,000, all payable during the month.

l. The cash balance on April 30 was $5,750.

Required

1. Prepare a schedule showing expected cash collections for May.
2. Prepare a cash budget for May in good form.
3. Comment briefly on the treasurer's statement quoted at the beginning of the problem.

(SMA, adapted)

P9-22   Integrated Operating Budgets   The East Division of Kensic Company manufactures a vital component that is used in one of Kensic's major product lines. The East Division has been experiencing some difficulty in coordinating activities between its various departments, which has resulted in some shortages of the component at critical times. To overcome the shortages, the manager of East Division has decided to initiate a monthly budgeting system that is integrated between departments.

The first budget is to be for the second quarter of the current year. To assist in developing the budget figures, the divisional controller has accumulated the following information:

Sales.   Sales through the first three months of the current year were 30,000 units. Actual sales in units for January, February, and March, and planned sales in units over the next five months, are given below:

January (actual)	6,000
February (actual)	10,000
March (actual)	14,000
April (planned)	20,000
May (planned)	35,000
June (planned)	50,000
July (planned)	45,000
August (planned)	30,000

In total, the East Division expects to produce and sell 250,000 units during the current year.

Direct Material.   Two different materials are used in the production of the component. Data regarding these materials are given below:

Direct Material	Units of Direct Materials per Finished Component	Cost per Unit	Inventory at March 31
No. 208	4 kilograms	$5.00	46,000 kilograms
No. 311	9 metres	2.00	69,000 metres

Material No. 208 is sometimes in short supply. Therefore, the East Division requires that enough of the material be on hand at the end of each month to provide for 50% of the following month's production needs. Material No. 311 is easier to get, so only one-third of the following month's production needs must be on hand at the end of each month.

Direct Labour.   The East Division has three departments through which the components must pass before they are completed. Information relating to direct labour in these departments is given below:

Department	Direct Labour-Hours per Finished Component	Cost per Direct Labour-Hour
Shaping	0.75	$6.00
Assembly	2.80	4.00
Finishing	0.25	8.00

Direct labour is adjusted to the workload each month.

Manufacturing Overhead.   East Division manufactured 32,000 components during the first three months of the current year. The actual variable overhead costs incurred during this three-month period are shown below. East Division's controller believes that the variable overhead costs incurred during the last nine months of the year will be at the same rate per component as experienced during the first three months.

Utilities	$ 57,000
Indirect labour	31,000
Supplies	16,000
Other	8,000
Total variable overhead	$112,000

The actual fixed manufacturing overhead costs incurred during the first three months amounted to $1,170,000. The East Division has planned fixed manufacturing overhead costs for the entire year as follows:

Supervision	$ 872,000
Property taxes	143,000
Depreciation	2,910,000
Insurance	631,000
Other	72,000
Total fixed manufacturing overhead	$4,628,000

Finished Goods Inventory.   The desired monthly ending inventory of completed components is 20% of the next month's estimated sales. The East Division has 4,000 units in the finished goods inventory on March 31.

Required

1. Prepare a production budget for the East Division for the second quarter ending June 30. Show computations by month and in total for the quarter.
2. Prepare a direct materials purchases budget in units and in dollars for each type of material for the second quarter ending June 30. Again show computations by month and in total for the quarter.
3. Prepare a direct labour budget in hours and in dollars for the second quarter ending June 30. This time it is *not* necessary to show monthly figures; show quarterly totals only.
4. Assume that the company plans to manufacture a total of 250,000 units for the year. Prepare a manufacturing overhead budget for the nine-month period ending December 31. Again, it is *not* necessary to show monthly figures.

CASES

C9–23 Spreadsheet Budget   The Ray Company Ltd. is a small retail store located in Dartmouth. Its sales budget for the first three months of 19x8 is shown below.

January	$40,000
February	50,000
March	60,000

Sales consist of 60% cash and 40% credit. According to the experience of 19x7, half of the credit sales are collected in the month of sale, and the rest are collected in the month following the sale. Bad debts are minimal and can be ignored. Total sales in December 19x7 were $70,000.

The following spreadsheet contains some information about the budgeted cash collections from sales for the first quarter of 19x8.

	A	B	C	D	E	F	G
				RAY COMPANY			
1							
2							
3			**Budgeted Cash Collections from Sales**				
4			**For the First Quarter, 19x8**				
5							
6				**January**	**February**	**March**	**Quarter**
7	Total sales			$40,000	$50,000	$60,000	
8	Less credit sales			16,000			
9							
10	Cash sales			$24,000			
11	Add collections on						
12	credit sales from						
13	previous month						
14	Add collections on						
15	credit sales from						
16	current month						
17							
18							
19							
20							

Required

1. What formulas, values, or labels must the following cells contain to facilitate the completion of this budget? List the cell reference on the left with the formula, value, or label on the right.

Cell Reference	Answer	Cell Reference	Answer
A18		F10	
D13		F13	
D16		F16	
D18		F18	
E8		G7	
E10		G8	
E13		G10	
E16		G13	
E18		G16	
F8		G18	

2. Suppose that the total budgeted sales for January were $80,000. Recalculate the value of cell D18.

(CGA-Canada, adapted)

C9–24   Budget Theory   Abel Systems Ltd. (ASL) is a company that manufactures three product lines and has attained a sales level of $10 million in 19x8. Each year, a budget is developed on a product line basis for the next fiscal year in total and by quarter. In the budget, expenses are broken down into functional categories (i.e., selling, production, research and development, finance, and administration) and, for each function, estimated fixed and variable portions are identified.

Until his sudden death in 19x7, the executive vice president, one of the founders of ASL, directed the preparation of the annual budget. His procedure was as follows:

1. Sales forecasts and budgets by product line were prepared in conjunction with the president and the sales manager.
2. Inventory and production plans were prepared by product line for each of the four plant departments. These plans were based on the sales budget and were prepared with the plant manager.
3. For each functional area, tentative total cost budgets were prepared. These costs were established with the managers of the functional areas.

The total budget was usually revised several times before it was finalized. The chief accountant produced the final budget from the information supplied by the executive vice president.

At the end of each quarter, an income statement by product line was produced in the same format as the budget. Corporate performance was judged by comparing the income statement to the corresponding budget component. No other control reports were prepared. The executive vice president worked very closely with the individual managers to ensure that they conformed to the budget. Over the years, ASL has earned a reputation for both quality of product and profitability of operations.

After the death of the executive vice president, the president and the sales manager met to initiate preparation of the 19x8 budget. They decided that a 10% increase in sales volume over the 19x7 budget should be the 19x8 target. The president directed the chief accountant to develop the budget based on a 10% increase in sales and only a 5% increase in costs. Individual managers were directed to conform to this budget. The president decided not to replace the executive vice president until he felt enough confidence in one of his managers to promote him or her to this position.

The 19x8 first quarter results were disappointing and returns became more so with each succeeding quarter, despite the president's demands for higher volume and lower costs. The actual profit for 19x8 was only 60% of the budgeted profit.

In 19x8, the president hired a bright young CMA to prepare the 19x9 budget under his supervision. The president believed that in order for ASL to maintain its usual market position, sales would have to increase by 15% over the 19x8 budget, profit would have to be at least 16% of sales, and research and development would require a 20% increase in budget. As a result, the production and selling costs would have to be held at the 19x8 budgeted level. The budget was prepared accordingly.

After completing the 19x9 budget, the CMA prepared a proposal for a new comprehensive planning and control program which she claimed would more clearly reflect the decision-making structure of the organization's operations and would emphasize greater participation in the process by all managers. The president objected to the formalized nature of the proposed system and was absolutely opposed to a process that would be so demanding of management time. He noted that ASL had done very well with a simple system in the past, and would do so again when the current downturn reversed itself. The president's negative response to the CMA's proposal prompted her decision to resign from ASL.

Quarterly results progressively grew worse. In the third quarter of 19x9, the president felt compelled to order the managers of all functional areas, without exception, to cut expenses by 15% to avoid a disastrous loss for the year.

Before preparing the 19x0 budget, the president attended a seminar on zero-base budgeting. After the seminar, he was convinced that such a system might be just what was needed at ASL. He felt that this system would not be so formalized and demanding of management time as the system proposed by the CMA.

Required

1. Identify three of the president's actions that likely contributed to the failure of ASL to meet its budgets in 19x8 and 19x9. Explain why each action may have contributed to this failure.
2. Would the president's idea to house a zero-based budgeting system be appropriate for ASL? Explain.

(SMAC, adapted)

C9–25   Master Budget with Supporting Budgets   You have just been hired as a management trainee by Cravat Sales Company, a nationwide distributor of a designer's silk ties. The company has an exclusive franchise on distribution of the ties, and sales have grown so rapidly over the last few years that it has become necessary to add new members to the management team. You have been given direct responsibility for all planning and budgeting. Your first assignment is to prepare a master budget for the next three months, starting April 1. You are anxious to make a favourable impression on the president and have assembled the information below.

The company desires a minimum ending cash balance each month of $10,000. The ties are sold to retailers for $8 each. Recent and forecast sales in units are as follows:

January (actual)	20,000	June	60,000
February (actual)	24,000	July	40,000
March (actual)	28,000	August	36,000
April	35,000	September	32,000
May	45,000		

The large buildup in sales before and during June is due to Father's Day. Ending inventories are supposed to equal 90% of the next month's sales in units. The ties cost the company $5 each.

Purchases are paid for as follows: 50% in the month of purchase and the remaining 50% in the following month. All sales are on credit, with no discount, and payable within 15 days. The company has found, however, that only 25% of a month's sales are collected by month-end. An additional 50% is collected in the month following, and the remaining 25% is collected in the second month following. Bad debts have been negligible.

The company's monthly operating expenses are given below:

Variable:	
Sales commissions	$1 per tie

Fixed:	
Wages and salaries	$22,000
Utilities	14,000
Insurance expired	1,200
Depreciation	1,500
Miscellaneous	3,000

All operating expenses are paid during the month, in cash, with the exception of depreciation and insurance expired. New fixed assets will be purchased during May for $25,000 cash. The company declares dividends of $12,000 each quarter, payable in the first month of the following quarter. The company's balance sheet at March 31 is given below:

Assets

Cash	$ 14,000
Accounts receivable ($48,000 February sales; $168,000 March sales)	216,000
Inventory (31,500 units)	157,500
Unexpired insurance	14,400
Fixed assets, net of depreciation	172,700
Total assets	$574,600

Liabilities and Shareholders' Equity

Accounts payable, purchases	$ 85,750
Dividends payable	12,000
Capital stock, no par	300,000
Retained earnings	176,850
Total liabilities and shareholders' equity	$574,600

The company can borrow money from its bank at 12% annual interest. All borrowing must be done at the beginning of a month, and repayments must be made at the end of a month. Repayments of principal must be in round $1,000 amounts. Borrowing (and payments of interest) can be in any amount.

Interest is computed and paid at the end of each quarter on all loans outstanding during the quarter. Round all interest payments to the nearest whole dollar. Compute interest on whole months ($\frac{1}{12}$, $\frac{2}{12}$, and so forth). The company wishes to use any excess cash to pay loans off as rapidly as possible.

Required

Prepare a master budget for the three-month period ending June 30. Include the following detailed budgets:
1. a.   A sales budget by month and in total.
    b.   A schedule of budgeted cash collections from sales and accounts receivable, by month and in total.
    c.   A purchases budget in units and in dollars. Show the budget by month and in total.
    d.   A schedule of budgeted cash payments for purchases, by month and in total.
2. A cash budget. Show the budget by month and in total.
3. A budgeted income statement for the three-month period ending June 30. Use the contribution approach.
4. A budgeted balance sheet as of June 30.

C9–26   Evaluating a Company's Budget Procedures   Tom Emory and Jim Morris strolled back to their plant from the administrative offices of Ferguson & Son Mfg. Company. Tom was manager of the machine shop in the company's factory; Jim was manager of the equipment maintenance department.

The men had just attended the monthly performance evaluation meeting for plant department heads. These meetings had been held on the third Tuesday of each month since Robert Ferguson, Jr., the president's son, had become plant manager a year earlier.

As they were walking, Tom Emory spoke: "Boy, I hate those meetings! I never know whether my department's accounting reports will show good or bad performance. I'm beginning to expect the worst. If the accountants say I saved the company a dollar, I'm called 'Sir,' but if I spend even a little too much—boy, do I get in trouble. I don't know if I can hold on until I retire."

Tom had just been given the worst evaluation he had ever received in his long career with Ferguson & Son. He was the most respected of the experienced machinists in the company. He had been with Ferguson & Son for many years and was promoted to supervisor of the machine shop when the company expanded and moved to its present location. The president (Robert Ferguson, Sr.) had often stated that the company's success was due to the high quality of the work of machinists like Tom. As supervisor, Tom stressed the importance of craftsmanship and told his workers that he wanted no sloppy work coming from his department.

When Robert Ferguson, Jr., became the plant manager, he directed that monthly performance comparisons be made between actual and budgeted costs for each department. The departmental budgets were intended to encourage the supervisors to reduce inefficiencies and to seek cost reduction opportunities. The company controller was instructed to have his staff "tighten" the budget slightly whenever a department attained its budget in a given month; this was done to reinforce the plant supervisor's desire to reduce costs. The young plant manager often stressed the importance of continued progress toward attaining the budget; he also made it known that he kept a file of these performance reports for future reference when he succeeded his father.

Tom Emory's conversation with Jim Morris continued as follows:

EMORY: I really don't understand. We've worked so hard to get up to budget, and the minute we make it they tighten the budget on us. We can't work any faster and still maintain quality. I think my men are ready to quit trying. Besides, those reports don't tell the whole story. We always seem to be interrupting the big jobs for all those small rush orders. All that setup and machine adjustment time is killing us. And quite frankly, Jim, you were no help. When our hydraulic press broke down last month, your people were nowhere to be found. We had to take it apart ourselves and got stuck with all that idle time.

MORRIS: I'm sorry about that, Tom, but you know my department has had trouble making budget, too. We were running well behind at the time of that problem, and if we'd spent a day on that old machine, we would never have made it up. Instead we made the scheduled inspections of the forklift trucks because we knew we could do those in less than the budgeted time.

EMORY: Well, Jim, at least you have some options. I'm locked into what the scheduling department assigns to me and you know they're being harassed by sales for those special orders. Incidentally, why didn't your report show all the supplies you guys wasted last month when you were working in Bill's department?

MORRIS: We're not out of the woods on that deal yet. We charged the maximum we could to our other work and haven't even reported some of it yet.

EMORY: Well, I'm glad you have a way of getting out of the pressure. The accountants seem to know everything that's happening in my department, sometimes even before I do. I thought all that budget and accounting stuff was supposed to help, but it just gets me into trouble. It's all a big pain. I'm trying to put out quality work; they're trying to save pennies.

Required

1. Identify the problems that appear to exist in Ferguson & Son Mfg. Company's budgetary control system and explain how the problems are likely to reduce the effectiveness of the system.

2. Explain how Ferguson & Son Mfg. Company's budgetary control system could be revised to improve its effectiveness.

(CMA, adapted)

C9–27 Cash Budget for a Growing Company   Roller, Ltd., of Melbourne, Australia, is the exclusive distributor in Australia and the South Pacific of a popular brand of in-line skates manufactured in Mexico. The company is in the process of putting together its cash budget for the second quarter—April, May, and June—of next year. The president of the company suspects that some financing will be required in the second quarter because sales are expanding and the company intends to make several major equipment purchases in that quarter. The president is confident that the company will be able to meet or exceed the following budgeted sales figures (all in Australian dollars) next year:

January	$158,000	July	$190,000
February	160,000	August	192,000
March	164,000	September	210,000
April	172,000	October	230,000
May	176,000	November	260,000
June	184,000	December	180,000

The following additional information will be used in formulating the cash budget:

a. All of the company's sales are on credit terms. The company collects 30% of its billings in the month after the sale and the remaining 70% in the second month after the sale. Uncollectible amounts are negligible.

b. The cost of sales is 75% of sales. Because of the shipping time from Mexico, the company orders skates from the manufacturer one month in advance of their expected sale. The company desires to maintain little or no inventory.

c. The company orders the skates on credit terms from the manufacturer. The company pays half of the bill in the month after it orders the skates and the other half in the second month after it places the order.

d. Operating expenses, other than cost of sales, are budgeted to be $178,800 for the year. The composition of these expenses is given below. All of these expenses are incurred evenly throughout the year except for the property taxes. Property taxes are paid in four equal installments in the last month of each quarter.

Salaries and wages	$120,000
Advertising and promotion . . .	12,000
Property taxes	18,000
Insurance	4,800
Utilities	6,000
Depreciation	18,000
Total operating expenses . . .	$178,800

e. Income tax payments are made by the company in the first month of each quarter based on the taxable income for the prior quarter. The income tax payment due in April is $16,000.

f. Because of expanding sales, the company plans to make equipment purchases of $22,300 in April and $29,000 in May.

g. The company has a policy of maintaining an end-of-month cash balance of $20,000. Cash is borrowed or invested monthly, as needed, to maintain this balance. All borrowing is done at the beginning of the month, and all investments and repayments are made at the end of the month. As of March 31, there are no investments of excess cash and no outstanding loans.

h. The annual interest rate on loans from the bank is 12%. Compute interest on whole months ($\frac{1}{12}$, $\frac{2}{12}$, and so forth). The company will pay off any loans, including accumulated interest, at the end of the second quarter if sufficient cash is available.

Required

1. Prepare a cash budget for Roller, Ltd., by month and in total for the second quarter.

2. Discuss why cash budgeting is particularly important for an expanding company like Roller, Ltd.

C9–28   Budgeting   Local Electronics Limited is a Canadian public corporation that manufactures special electronic steering systems for various types of vehicles. Local's sales have grown steadily since it was incorporated. The draft financial statements for 19x8, however, show a net income of $1,685,600, which is a decrease in profits for the first time (see Exhibit 9–6).

Recently, Local was awarded a large contract with DOT Company, a large North American pleasure boat manufacturer. The contract is for 100,000 electronic steering systems, 40% to be delivered uniformly throughout 19x9 and 60% to be delivered uniformly throughout 19x0. In order to accommodate this contract, Local is required to make a capital investment of $5,000,000 for specialized manufacturing equipment. After two years, this equipment can be adapted to the regular production process. Value analysis indicates that investment in this equipment is worthwhile. However, Local has insufficient cash to pay for the equipment and, since it cannot lease the equipment and DOT is not prepared to advance any funds, Local's president decided to meet with the bank manager to arrange the necessary financing.

PRESIDENT: As you know, four years ago you helped to finance a replacement of all of Local's manufacturing equipment. Now, we've won a large contract with DOT, a large boat manufacturer, but, to fill the order, we need to buy some special equipment. Will the bank finance the $5,000,000 we need for the special equipment?

EXHIBIT 9-6

Draft (Summarized)
19x8 Financial
Statements

LOCAL ELECTRONICS LIMITED
Balance Sheet
As at December 31, 19x8

Assets

Current assets:

Cash	$ 200,000	
Accounts receivable	10,000,000	
Inventory	10,000,000	20,200,000

Fixed assets:

Machinery and equipment	70,000,000	
Less accumulated depreciation	(28,000,000)	42,000,000
Total assets		$62,200,000

Liabilities and Shareholders' Equity

Current liabilities:

Accounts payable			$ 2,736,000

Long-term liabilities

Bank loan payable (Note 1)			30,000,000

Shareholders' equity:

Common shares		$12,500,000	
Retained earnings			
—Opening balance	$15,778,400		
—1988 net income	1,685,600		
—1988 dividends	(500,000)	16,964,000	29,464,000
Total liabilities and shareholders' equity			$62,200,000

Note:

1. In January 19x5, the bank loaned Local $50,000,000 to help finance replacement of its equipment. The terms of the loan stipulated that a payment of $5,000,000 plus interest be made at the end of each year for 10 years. The annual interest rate was set at 12%.

BANK MANAGER: I've seen your 19x8 draft financial statements, which indicate that profits are down. Also, your cash position could be better. What are your total sales expectations for 19x9?

PRESIDENT: The DOT contract is for $25,000,000 over two years, which is a good start. Other than that, I'm not sure since sales depend on what other contracts we win. Some new foreign competition has invaded the market by undercutting domestic manufacturers. We've had to cut our bids to a minimum in order to compete. That's why our profits dropped for 19x8. This new competition is making it increasingly difficult to predict sales. There's simply no way to anticipate which contracts we'll win. All we can do is adjust our bidding policy to try to maximize capacity utilization.

BANK MANAGER: Well, the bank will need a cash budget for at least 19x9 before it will consider lending Local any more money.

PRESIDENT: The last time we prepared any kind of budget for you was four years ago. You saw how useless that was. Sales turned out to be lower and expenses higher than the budget. That's why we don't have any cash now to finance the new equipment. We even had to reduce dividends to $500,000 in 19x8 in order to maintain our $200,000 minimum cash balance.

BANK MANAGER: You'll just have to do your best to estimate sales. Are there any other major factors which would affect cash flow over the next few years?

PRESIDENT: Only a reasonable increase in fixed costs. Under the circumstances, we will continue to pay dividends of $500,000 annually until cash flow has improved. It is doubtful that sales will increase sufficiently to necessitate further capital expenditure other than the $5,000,000 which we need now.

EXHIBIT 9–6

(continued)

LOCAL ELECTRONICS LIMITED
Operating Statement
For the Year Ended December 31, 19x8

Sales		$60,000,000
Manufacturing cost of goods sold:		
Variable manufacturing cost	$30,000,000	
Machinery and equipment depreciation	7,000,000	
Fixed manufacturing overhead	8,000,000	45,000,000
Gross margin		15,000,000
Expenses:		
Variable selling and administration expenses	4,200,000	
Interest expense (Note 1)	4,200,000	
Fixed selling and administration expenses	4,500,000	12,900,000
Income before taxes		2,100,000
Income taxes (Note 2)		414,400
Net income		$ 1,685,600

Note:

1. In January 19x5, the bank loaned Local $50,000,000 to help finance replacement of its equipment. The terms of the loan stipulated that a payment of $5,000,000 plus interest be made at the end of each year for 10 years. The annual interest rate was set at 12%.

2. Income taxes were calculated as 40% times taxable income as follows:

Income before taxes	$2,100,000
Plus depreciation	7,000,000
Less CCA (UCC of $40,320,000 × 20%)	(8,064,000)
Taxable income	1,036,000
Times tax rate	× 0.40
Income taxes	$ 414,400

BANK MANAGER: If the loan is approved, the bank would prefer that it be repaid within two years at an interest rate of 12% per year payable at the end of each year. Next Monday, I'll expect to see a cash budget to support your loan request.

The next day, the president asked Local's newly appointed controller for his advice on how best to finance the required equipment purchase. After being briefed on the president's meeting with the bank manager, the controller indicated that he would conduct a quick initial analysis and present his preliminary findings within 24 hours.

Back in his office, the controller decided that his initial analysis should consist of the following:

a. Preparation of a draft cash budget for 19x9.
b. Consideration of alternative sources of financing.
c. Analysis of Local's general financial planning and control system, and identification of alternatives for improvement.

The controller then gathered some data on which to base his cash budget (see Exhibit 9–7 on page 476).

Required

As Local's newly appointed controller, complete the initial analysis as outlined above.

(SMAC, adapted)

GROUP EXERCISES

GE9–29   Budgets Strike Fear into the Hearts of Workers and Managers Alike "The term 'budget' tends to conjure up in the minds of many managers images of inaccurate estimates, produced in tedious detail, which are never exactly achieved but whose

EXHIBIT 9-7

Underlying Data for
19x9 Cash Budget

Sales

DOT contract, 19x9, 40,000 units at $250/unit = $10,000,000.

Other sales: The president estimated that sales for 19x9, other than the DOT contract, would be as follows:

Low	$40,000,000	(25% probability)
Most likely	$50,000,000	(50% probability)
High	$60,000,000	(25% probability)

Manufacturing Cost of Goods Sold

For all sales, including the DOT contract, the relationship of variable manufacturing cost of goods sold dollars to sales dollars is expected to be the same as for 19x8.

If the new equipment is purchased, related fixed manufacturing overhead of $750,000 will be required in 19x9. Fixed manufacturing overhead related to current operations for 19x9 is expected to be 5% greater than for 19x8.

Both the existing machinery and equipment and the new special equipment have useful lives of 10 years and are depreciated on a straight-line basis. The net disposal costs are expected to be zero. The CCA rate for all machinery and equipment owned by Local, including the new special equipment, is 20%.

Selling and Administration Expenses

For all sales, including the DOT contract, the relationship of variable selling and administration expenses dollars to sales dollars is expected to be the same as for 19x8.

If the DOT contract is accepted, related fixed selling and administration expensed of $300,000 will be required in 19x9. Fixed selling and administrative expenses related to current operations for 19x9 are expected to be 5% greater than for 19x8.

Working Capital

Sales are made uniformly over the year and all customers, including DOT, pay 60 days after delivery. Local's policy is to maintain a minimum cash balance of $200,000, and inventory levels are expected to be maintained at the $10,000,000 level.

The average accounts payable balance will be maintained at 8% of the total variable costs (i.e., variable manufacturing, selling, and administration costs) incurred during the year.

All fixed costs are paid in the year they are incurred.

shortfalls or overruns require explanation." (Source: Neil Churchill, "Budget Choice: Planning vs. Control," *Harvard Business Review* (July–August 1984), p. 150.) In some companies, the term *budgeting* is about as popular as the term *layoff*. It's hard to argue that budgets are misunderstood, since they seem to have earned a well-deserved reputation at many organizations. But it is true that they are often viewed too narrowly.

In most companies, budgets serve a variety of roles, each of which must be balanced in order to achieve the overall objectives of the organization. Some of these roles are more important than others, but budgets must to some degree address each of the following purposes: planning, motivation, coordination, evaluation, communication, and education.

Required

1. Briefly define or describe each of these roles. What is the major objective of each role?
2. It is inevitable that the objectives and requirements of one role (e.g., planning) may come into conflict with the objectives and requirements of another role (e.g., evaluation). Describe some of the behavioural implications or potential conflicts that can arise between planning and motivation, between motivation and evaluation, and between planning and evaluation.
3. What suggestions would you have for managers who must resolve or at least reduce some of these conflicts?
4. What factors determine whether budgets are viewed in a negative way, such as the view described by Churchill above, or in a more positive light?

It may prove helpful to read M. Edgar Barrett and LeRoy Fraser III, "Conflicting Roles in Budgeting for Operations," *Harvard Business Review (*July–August 1977), pp. 137–45.

GE9–30   Financial Pressures Hit Higher Education   In the late eighties and early nineties, universities found that they were no longer immune to the financial stress faced by other institutions and business. Budget cuts were in the air across the land. When the budget axe hit, the cuts often came without warning and their size was sometimes staggering. Support for some institutions dropped by 40% or more. Most university administrators had only managed through budget increases, never having faced budget cuts. Also, the budget setbacks usually occurred at the most inopportune time—during the school year when contractual commitments with faculty and staff had been signed, programs had been planned, and students were enrolled and taking classes.

Required

1. Should the administration be "fair" to all affected and institute a round of across-the-board cuts whenever the province announces another subsidy reduction?
2. If not across-the-board cutbacks in programs, then would you recommend more focused reductions, and if so, what priorities would you establish for bringing spending in line with revenues?
3. Since these usually are not one-time-only cutbacks, how would you manage continuous, long-term reductions in budgets extending over a period of years?
4. Should the decision-making process be top-down (centralized with top administrators) or bottom-up (participative)? Why?
5. How should such issues as malaise among faculty and staff, faculty and staff with a protect-their-turf mentality, resistance to change, and consensus building be dealt with?
6. Since no university can afford a reputation of "going downhill," what innovative ideas or initiatives would you recommend that would return a university to a more stable, predictable environment?

Adapted from Sherry Penny, "What a University Has Learned from 4 Years of Financial Stress," *The Chronicle of Higher Education* (May 5, 1993), pp. B1–B3.

GE9–31   JIT Isn't So Simple   JIT extols the virtues of simplicity. But JIT writers, in their exuberance to tout the benefits of JIT, do not always communicate the challenges confronting any JIT practitioner. In the early years, many large JIT purchasers told their suppliers that they were expected to supply the large customer on a JIT basis beginning on a certain date. Of course the result was, as you might imagine, near total disarray on the part of the supplier. Assuming all parties want JIT to be a success, what responsibilities seem reasonable for both supplier and customer to ensure the greatest likelihood that the vendor will be able to supply the customer on a JIT basis?

GE9–32   University Budgeting 101   Who better to tell new students about the ins and outs of budgeting for university than those who have recently lived the experience—you. Suppose you are advising incoming freshmen, or those living off campus for the first time, on money matters and how to live within a budget.

Required

1. Provide a list of typical expenses for a new university student living on campus. What is different about a student who is living off campus?
2. What advice should parents give to new students before sending them off to live on their own for the first time?
3. Which expenses should be split between parents and students? How will they be divided?
4. Which expenses can be reduced? How?
5. What role should work play?
6. What are the advantages and disadvantages of credit cards?
7. How would you suggest handling a situation where a student has spent more than his or her budget? Should parents bail the student out?
8. If the student were living off campus with several other roommates, what options do they have for handling expenses such as utilities, rent, and food? How would you advise them?
9. What should a student do if one or more of his or her roommates are not financially responsible and do not pay their fair share of expenses?
10. What do you do with a roommate who eats or drinks more than his or her share?

Adapted from Deborah Lohse, "Students Can Learn a Lesson on Budgeting," *The Wall Street Journal,* August 23, 1995, p. C1; and Bill Lubinger, "College Tests Your Money Handling Skills," *The Plain Dealer,* September 2, 1995, p. 3–E.

STANDARD COSTS AND OPERATING PERFORMANCE MEASURES

LEARNING OBJECTIVES

After studying Chapter 10, you should be able to:

1 Distinguish between ideal standards and practical standards.

2 Explain how direct materials standards and direct labour standards are set.

3 Enumerate the advantages and disadvantages of using standard costs.

4 Compute the direct materials price and quantity variances and explain their significance.

5 Compute mix and yield variances for materials and explain their significance.

6 Compute the direct labour rate and efficiency variances and explain their significance.

7 Compute the variable overhead spending and efficiency variances.

8 Explain how the manager would determine whether a variance constituted an "exception" that would require his or her attention.

9 Enumerate the operating performance measures and explain how they are used.

10 Compute the delivery cycle time, the throughput time, and the manufacturing cycle efficiency (MCE).

11 Define or explain the key terms listed at the end of the chapter.

12 (Appendix 10A) Prepare journal entries to record standard costs and variances.

13 (Appendix 10B) Explain the concept of learning curves.

Nova Pewter Company makes pewter bookends. How much raw material (pewter ingots) is required to make one set of bookends, assuming the material is an acceptable grade and the workers are sufficiently trained? The answer to this question can have a profound effect on costs and profits.

I n attempting to control costs and to optimize output, managers have many decisions to make. Some of these decisions relate to the inputs of the firm in terms of prices paid and quantities used. As managers acquire inputs, they are expected to pay the lowest possible prices that are consistent with the quality of output desired. They are also expected to consume the minimum quantity of whatever inputs they have at their command, again consistent with the quality of output desired. Breakdowns in control over either price or quantity will lead to excessive costs and to deteriorating profit margins.

How do managers control prices paid and quantities used? They could examine every transaction that takes place, but this obviously would be an inefficient use of management time. For many companies, the answer to the control problem lies in *standard costs*. For other companies, standard costs are supplemented by various other methods of control, many of which are nonfinancial in nature. In this chapter, we focus first on the development and use of standard costs. We then turn to the other methods of control that are gaining popularity, particularly with companies that operate in an automated environment.

STANDARD COSTS—MANAGEMENT BY EXCEPTION

A *standard* can be defined as a benchmark or "norm" for measuring performance. Standards are found in many facets of day-to-day life. Students who wish to enter a community college or university are often required to perform at a certain level on school examinations as a condition for admittance; the autos we drive are built under exacting engineering standards; and the food we eat is prepared under standards of cleanliness and nutritional content. Standards are also widely used in managerial accounting. Here the standards relate to the *quantity* and *cost* of inputs used in manufacturing goods or providing services.

Quantity and cost standards are set by managers for the three elements of cost input—materials, labour, and overhead—that we have discussed in preceding chapters. *Quantity standards* indicate how much of a cost element, such as labour time or raw materials, should be used in manufacturing a unit of product or in providing a unit of service. *Cost standards* indicate what the cost of the time or the materials should be. Actual quantities and actual costs of inputs are measured against these standards to see whether operations are proceeding within the limits that management has set. If either the quantity or the cost of inputs exceeds the bounds that management has set, attention is directed to the difference, thereby permitting the manager to focus his or her efforts where they will do the most good. This process is called **management by exception.**

Firestone runs a chain of auto service centres that uses standard costs for specific jobs. For example, installing a muffler may be standardized at 1.5 hours. Actual performance is then measured against this standard.

Who Uses Standard Costs?

Manufacturing, service, food, and not-for-profit organizations all make use of standards (in terms of either costs or quantities) to some extent. Auto service centres, for example, often set specific labour time standards for the completion of certain work tasks, such as installing a carburetor or doing a valve job, and then measure actual performance against these standards. Fast-food outlets such as McDonald's have exacting standards as to the quantity of meat going into a sandwich, as well as standards for the cost of the meat. Hospitals have standard costs (for food, laundry, and other items) for each occupied bed per day, as well as standard time allowances for the performing of certain routine activities, such as laboratory tests. In short, the business student is likely to run into standard cost concepts in virtually any line of business that she or he may enter.

The broadest application of the standard cost idea is probably found in manufacturing companies, where standards relating to materials, labour, and overhead are developed in detail for each separate product line. These standards are then organized into a **standard cost card** that tells the manager what the final, manufactured cost should be for a single unit of product. In the following section, we provide a detailed example of the setting of standard costs and the preparation of a standard cost card.

SETTING STANDARD COSTS

The setting of standard costs is more an art than a science. It requires the combined thinking and expertise of all persons who have responsibility over prices and quantities of inputs. In a manufacturing setting, this would include the managerial accountant, the purchasing agent, the industrial engineer, production supervisors, line managers, and the production workers themselves.

The beginning point in setting standard costs is a rigorous look at past experience. The managerial accountant can be of great help in this task by preparing data on the cost characteristics of prior years' activities at various levels of operations. A standard for the future must be more than simply a projection of the past, however. Data must be adjusted for

Standard costs can be applied in many areas, including raising cattle. In this instance, setting standard costs requires more expertise and judgment in the field than merely "running the numbers" back in the office. But standards can be developed; for example, it may require ½ hectare of pasture to feed one steer for one week.

changing economic patterns, changing demand and supply characteristics, and changing technology. Past experience in certain costs may be distorted as a consequence of inefficiencies. To the extent that such inefficiencies can be identified, the data must be appropriately adjusted. The manager must realize that the past is of value only insofar as it helps to predict the future. In short, standards must be reflective of efficient *future* operations, not inefficient *past* operations.

Ideal versus Practical Standards

OBJECTIVE 1
Distinguish between ideal standards and practical standards.

Should standards be attainable all of the time, should they be attainable only part of the time, or should they be so tight that they become, in effect, "the impossible dream"? Opinions among managers vary, but standards tend to fall into one of two categories—either ideal or practical.

Ideal standards are those that can be attained only under the best circumstances. They allow for no machine breakdowns or other work interruptions, and they call for a level of effort that can be attained only by the most skilled and efficient employees working at peak effort 100% of the time. Some managers feel that such standards have a motivational value. These managers argue that even though employees know they will never stay within the standard set, it is a constant reminder of the need for ever-increasing efficiency and effort. Few firms use ideal standards. Most managers are of the opinion that ideal standards tend to discourage even the most diligent workers. Moreover, when ideal standards are used, variances from standards have little meaning. The reason is that the variances contain elements of "normal" inefficiencies, not just the abnormal inefficiencies that managers would like to have isolated and brought to their attention.

Practical standards can be defined as standards that are "tight but attainable." They allow for normal machine downtime and employee rest periods, and are such that they can be attained through reasonable, though highly efficient, efforts by the average worker at a task. Variances from such a standard are very useful to management in that they represent deviations that fall outside of normal, recurring inefficiencies and signal a need for management attention. Furthermore, practical standards can serve multiple purposes. In addition to signaling abnormal deviations in costs, they can also be used in forecasting cash flows and in planning inventory. By contrast, ideal standards cannot be used in forecasting and planning; they do not allow for normal inefficiencies, and therefore they result in unrealistic planning and forecasting figures.

Throughout the remainder of this chapter, we will assume the use of practical rather than ideal standards.

▼   ▼   ▼   ▼   ▼

MANAGERIAL ACCOUNTING IN ACTION—THE ISSUE

The Nova Pewter Company was organized a year ago. The company's only product at present is a reproduction of an eighteenth century pewter bookend. The bookend is made largely by hand, using traditional metal-working tools. Consequently, the manufacturing process is labour intensive and requires a high level of skill.

Nova Pewter has recently expanded its workforce to take advantage of unexpected demand for the bookends as gifts. The company started with a small cadre of experienced pewter workers but has had to hire less experienced workers as a result of the expansion. The president of the

Continued

company. J. D. Wriston, has called a meeting to discuss production problems. Attending the meeting are Tom Kuchel, the production manager; Janet Warner, the purchasing manager; and Terry Sherman, the corporate controller.

J. D.: I've got a feeling that we aren't getting the production we should out of our new people.

Tom: Give us a chance. Some of the new people have been on board for less than a month.

Janet: Let me add that production seems to be wasting an awful lot of material—particularly pewter. That stuff is very expensive.

Tom: What about the shipment of defective pewter you bought a couple of months ago—the one with the iron contamination? That caused us major problems.

Janet: That's ancient history. How was I to know it was off-grade? Besides, it was a great deal.

J. D.: Calm down everybody. Let's get the facts before we start sinking our fangs into each other.

Tom: I agree. The more facts the better.

J. D.: Okay, Terry, it's your turn. Facts are the controller's department.

Terry: I'm afraid I can't provide the answers off the top of my head, but it won't take me too long to set up a system that can routinely answer questions relating to worker productivity, material waste, and input prices.

J. D.: How long is "not too long"?

Terry: I will need all of your cooperation, but how about a week from today?

J. D.: That's okay with me. What about everyone else?

Tom: Sure.

Janet: Fine with me.

J. D.: Let's mark it on our calendars.

▼   ▼   ▼   ▼   ▼

Setting Direct Materials Standards

OBJECTIVE 2

Explain how direct materials standards and direct labour standards are set.

Terry Sherman's first task was to prepare price and quantity standards for the company's only significant raw material, pewter ingots. The **standard price per unit** for any direct materials purchased by a company should reflect the final, delivered cost of the materials, net of any discounts taken. After consulting with purchasing manager Janet Warner, Terry prepared the following documentation for the standard price of a kilogram of pewter in ingot form:

Purchase price, top-grade pewter ingots, in 15-kilogram ingots	$ 3.60
Freight, by truck, from the supplier's warehouse	0.44
Receiving and handling.	0.05
Less purchase discount	(0.09)
Standard price per kilogram	$ 4.00

Notice that the standard price reflects a particular grade of material (top grade), purchased in particular lot sizes (15 kilogram ingots), and delivered by a particular type of carrier (truck). Allowances have also been made for handling and discounts. If everything proceeds according to these expectations, the net standard price of a kilogram of pewter should therefore be $4.

The **standard quantity per unit** for direct materials should reflect the amount of material going into each unit of finished product, as well as an allowance for unavoidable waste, spoilage, and other normal inefficiencies. After consulting with the production manager, Tom Kuchel, Terry Sherman prepared the following documentation for the standard quantity of pewter going into a pair of bookends:

Material requirements as specified in the bill of materials for
a pair of bookends, in kilograms 2.7
Allowance for waste and spoilage, in kilograms 0.2
Allowance for rejects, in kilograms . . . .   <u>0.1</u>

Standard quantity per pair of bookends, in kilograms . . . .   <u>3.0</u>

A **bill of materials** is simply a list that shows the type and quantity of each item of material going into a unit of finished product. It is a handy source for determining the basic material input per unit, but it should be adjusted for waste and other factors, as shown above, when determining the standard quantity per unit of product. "Waste and spoilage" in the table above refers to materials that are wasted as a normal part of the production process or that spoil before they are used. "Rejects" refers to the direct material contained in units that are defective and must be scrapped.

After many years of operating a standard cost system, a major wood products company reviewed the materials standards for its products by breaking each standard down into its basic elements. In doing so, the company discovered that there was a 20% waste factor built into the standard cost for every product. This discovery completely surprised management, and they were dismayed to learn that the dollar amount of "allowable" waste was very large. Because the quantity standards had not been scrutinized for many years, management was unaware of the existence of this significant cost improvement potential in the company.[1]

Although it is common to recognize allowances for waste, spoilage, and rejects when setting standard costs, this practice is now coming into question. Those involved in TQM (total quality management) and similar management approaches argue that no amount of waste or defects should be tolerated. If allowances for waste, spoilage, and rejects are built into the standard cost, the levels of those allowances should be periodically reviewed and reduced over time to reflect improved processes, better training, and better equipment.

Once the price and quantity standards have been set, the standard cost of material per unit of finished product can be computed as follows:

$$3.0 \text{ kilograms per unit} \times \$4 \text{ per kilogram} = \$12 \text{ per unit}$$

This $12 cost figure will appear as one item on the standard cost card of the product.

Setting Direct Labour Standards

Direct labour price and quantity standards are usually expressed in terms of a labour rate and labour-hours. The **standard rate per hour** for direct labour would include not only

---

[1]James M. Reeve, "The Impact of Variation on Operating System Performance," *Performance Excellence* (Sarasota, Fla: American Accounting Association, 1990), p. 77.

wages earned but also an allowance for fringe benefits and other labour-related costs. The computation might be as follows:

Basic wage rate per hour	$10
Employment taxes at 10% of the basic rate	1
Fringe benefits at 30% of the basic rate	3
Standard rate per direct labour-hour	$14

Many companies prepare a single standard rate for all employees in a department that reflects an expected "mix" of workers, even though the actual wage rates may vary somewhat because of skills or seniority. This simplifies the use of standard costs and also permits the manager to monitor the use of employees within departments. More is said on this point a little later. If all proceeds according to plan, the direct labour rate for Nova Pewter should average $14 per hour.

The standard direct labour time required to complete a unit of product (generally called the **standard hours per unit**) is perhaps the single most difficult standard to determine. One approach is to divide each operation performed on the product into elemental body movements (such as reaching, pushing, and turning over). Published tables of standard times for such movements are available. These times can be applied to the movements and then added together to determine the total standard time allowed per operation. Another approach is for an industrial engineer to do a time and motion study, actually clocking the time required for certain tasks. As stated earlier, the standard time developed must include allowances for coffee breaks, personal needs of employees, cleanup, and machine downtime. After consulting with the production manager, Terry prepared the following documentation for the standard hours per unit:

Basic labour time per unit, in hours	1.9
Allowance for breaks and personal needs	0.1
Allowance for cleanup and machine downtime	0.3
Allowance for rejects	0.2
Standard hours per unit of product	2.5

Once the rate and time standards have been set, the standard labour cost per unit of product can be computed as follows:

$$2.5 \text{ hours per unit} \times \$14 = \$35 \text{ per unit}$$

This $35 cost figure appears along with direct materials as one item on the standard cost card of the product under consideration.

Standard labour-hours have declined in relative importance for some organizations. This is particularly true in highly automated manufacturing firms. Service organizations and numerous other construction and processing organizations, however, still retain a major interest in labour and want to know how it performs. Standard labour-hours inform workers and managers what is expected and how labour should be used. Standard labour-hours assist in formulating, testing, and revising the plans of the organization. More specifically, standards and the resulting comparisons to actual labour-hours may serve to motivate workers and managers. Labour standards can influence individuals in setting their own goals. If standards are perceived as realistic and if the variances from these standards are used fairly and constructively, then employees will generally be motivated to work for the organizational objectives conveyed by the standards. Feelings of success or failure impact on performance, but pressure can invigorate or intimidate employees. Erosion of effort and performance levels can result when standards are set inappropriately and used incorrectly.

Standard Cost Card—
Variable Production
Cost

Inputs	(1) Standard Quantity or Hours	(2) Standard Price or Rate	(3) Standard Cost (1) × (2)
Direct materials	3.0 kilograms	$ 4.00	$12.00
Direct labour	2.5 hours	14.00	35.00
Variable manufacturing overhead	2.5 hours	3.00	7.50
Total standard cost per unit			$54.50

Setting Variable Overhead Standards

As with direct labour, the price and quantity standards for variable overhead are generally expressed in terms of rate and hours. The rate represents *the variable portion of the predetermined overhead rate* discussed in Chapter 3; the hours represent whatever hours base is used to apply overhead to units of product (often machine-hours, computer time, or direct labour-hours, as we learned in Chapter 3). At Nova Pewter the variable portion of the predetermined overhead rate is $3 per direct labour-hour. Therefore, the standard variable overhead cost per unit of product would be:

2.5 hours per unit × $3.00 = $7.50 per unit

A more detailed look at the setting of overhead standards is reserved until Chapter 11.

To summarize our example on the setting of standard costs, the completed standard cost card for one unit of product is presented in Exhibit 10–1. Observe that the **standard cost per unit** is computed by multiplying the standard quantity or hours by the standard price or rate.

Advantages of Standard Costs

OBJECTIVE 3
Enumerate the advantages and disadvantages of using standard costs.

A number of distinct advantages can be cited in favour of using standard costs in an organization.

1. As stated earlier, the use of standard costs makes possible the concept of management by exception. So long as costs remain within the standards set, no attention by management is needed. When costs fall outside the standards set, then the matter is brought to the attention of management at once as an "exception." Management by exception makes possible more productive use of management time.
2. Standard costs facilitate cash planning and inventory planning.
3. If standards are set on a "practical" basis, they promote economy and efficiency in that employees normally become very cost and time conscious. In addition, wage incentive systems can be tied to a system of standard costs once the standards have been set.
4. In income determination, a system of standard costs may be more economical and simpler to operate than a historical cost system. Standard cost cards can be kept for each product or operation, and costs for material, labour, and manufacturing overhead charged out according to the standards set. This greatly simplifies the bookkeeping process.
5. Standard costs can assist in the implementation of "responsibility accounting," in which responsibility over cost control is assigned, and the extent to which that responsibility has been discharged can be evaluated through performance reports.

Disadvantages of Standard Costs

Although the advantages of using standard costs are significant, we must recognize that certain difficulties can be encountered by the manager in applying the standard cost idea. Moreover, improper use of standard costs and the management by exception principle can lead to adverse behavioural problems in an organization. Managers cite the following as being either problems or potential problems in using standard costs:

1. Difficulty may be experienced in determining which variances are "material" or significant in amount. (Ways to address this problem are discussed later in the chapter.)
2. By focusing only on variances above a certain level (that is, on variances that are considered to be material in amount), other useful information, such as trends, may not be noticed at an early stage.
3. If management performance evaluation is tied to the exception principle, subordinates may be tempted to cover up negative exceptions or not report them at all. In addition, subordinates may not receive reinforcement for the positive things they do, such as controlling or reducing costs charged to their areas of responsibility, but may only receive reprimands for those items that exceed the acceptable cost standards. Thus, subordinate morale may suffer because of the lack of positive reinforcement for work well done.
4. The management by exception technique may also affect supervisory employees in an unsatisfactory manner. Supervisors may feel that they are not getting a complete review of operations because they are always just keying in on problems. In addition, supervisors may feel that they are constantly being critical of their subordinates, that is, always "running them down." This may have a negative impact on supervisory morale.

These potential problems suggest that considerable care must be exercised by the manager in organizing and administering a standard cost system. It is particularly important that the manager focus on the positive, rather than on the negative, and that work that is well done be appropriately recognized.

A GENERAL MODEL FOR VARIANCE ANALYSIS

One reason for separating standards into two categories—price and quantity—is that control decisions relating to price paid and quantity used will generally fall at different points in time. In the case of raw materials, for example, control over price paid comes at the time of purchase. By contrast, control over quantity used does not come until the raw materials are used in production, which may be many weeks or months after the purchase date. In addition, control over price paid and quantity used will generally be the responsibility of two different managers and will therefore need to be assessed independently. As we have stressed earlier, no manager should be held responsible for a cost over which he or she has no control. It is important, therefore, that we separate price considerations from quantity considerations in our approach to the control of costs.

Price and Quantity Variances

The manager separates price considerations from quantity considerations in the control of costs through the use of a general model that distinguishes between these two cost elements and that provides a base for *variance* analysis. A **variance** is the difference

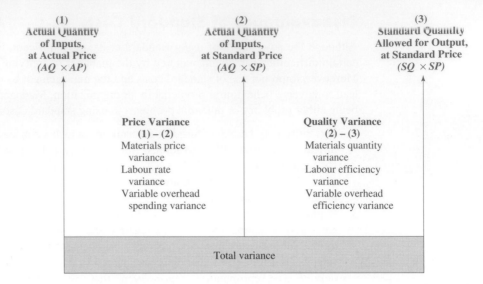

EXHIBIT 10–2

A General Model for
Variance Analysis—
Variable Production
Costs

between *standard* prices and quantities and *actual* prices and quantities. This model, which deals with variable costs, isolates price variances from quantity variances and shows how each of these variances is computed.[2] The model is presented in Exhibit 10–2.

Three things should be noted from Exhibit 10–2. First, note that a price variance and a quantity variance can be computed for all three variable cost elements—direct materials, direct labour, and variable manufacturing overhead—even though the variance is not called by the same name in all cases. For example, a price variance is called a *materials price variance* in the case of direct materials but a *labour rate variance* in the case of direct labour and an *overhead spending variance* in the case of variable manufacturing overhead.

Second, note that even though a price variance may be called by different names, it is computed in exactly the same way regardless of whether one is dealing with direct materials, direct labour, or variable manufacturing overhead. The same is true with the quantity variance.

Third, note that variance analysis is actually a matter of input-output analysis. The inputs represent the actual quantity of direct materials, direct labour, and variable manufacturing overhead used; the output represents the good production of the period, expressed in terms of the *standard quantity (or the standard hours) allowed* in its manufacture (see column 3 in Exhibit 10–2). By **standard quantity allowed** or **standard hours allowed,** we mean the amount of direct materials, direct labour, or variable manufacturing overhead *that should have been used* to produce what was produced during the period. This might be more or less than what was *actually* used, depending on the efficiency or inefficiency of operations. The standard quantity allowed is computed by multiplying the actual output in units by the standard input allowed per unit.

With this general model as a foundation, we will now examine the price and quantity variances in more detail.

---

[2]Variance analysis of fixed costs is reserved until Chapter 11.

USING STANDARD COSTS—DIRECT MATERIALS VARIANCES

After determining Nova Pewter Company's standard costs for direct materials, direct labour, and variable manufacturing overhead, Terry Sherman's next step was to compute the company's variances for June, the most recent month. As discussed in the preceding section, variances are computed by comparing standard costs against actual costs. To facilitate this comparison, Terry referred to the standard cost data contained in Exhibit 10–1. This exhibit shows that the standard cost of direct materials per unit of product is as follows:

$$3.0 \text{ kilograms per unit} \times \$4 \text{ per kilogram} = \$12 \text{ per unit}$$

Nova Pewter's purchasing records for June showed that 6,500 kilograms of pewter were purchased at a cost of $3.80 per kilogram. This cost figure included freight and handling and was net of the quantity discount. All of the material purchased was used during June to manufacture 2,000 pairs of pewter bookends. Using these data and the standard costs from Exhibit 10–1, Terry computed the price and quantity variances shown in Exhibit 10–3.

A variance is labelled unfavourable (commonly denoted by U) if the actual price or quantity exceeds the standard price or quantity; a variance is favourable (commonly denoted by F) if the actual price or quantity is less than the standard.

The data in Exhibit 10–3 assumes that all of the material purchased was used in production during the period. How are the variances computed if a different amount of material is purchased from what is used? To illustrate, assume that during June the company purchased 6,500 kilograms of material, as before, but that it used only 5,000 kilograms of material during the month and produced only 1,600 units. In this case, the variances would be as shown in Exhibit 10–4.

Note from the exhibit that the price variance is computed on the entire amount of material purchased (6,500 kilograms), as before, whereas the quantity variance is computed only on the portion of this material used in production during the month (5,000 kilograms). A quantity variance on the 1,500 kilograms of material that was purchased during the month but *not* used in production (6,500 kilograms purchased – 5,000 kilograms used = 1,500 kilograms unused) will be computed in a future period when these materials are

EXHIBIT 10-3

Variance Analysis— Direct Materials

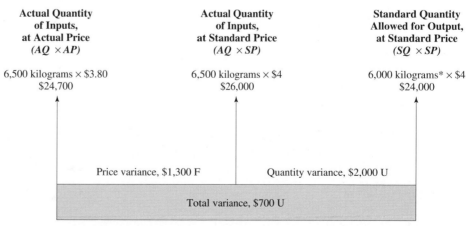

Actual Quantity of Inputs, at Actual Price $(AQ \times AP)$	Actual Quantity of Inputs, at Standard Price $(AQ \times SP)$	Standard Quantity Allowed for Output, at Standard Price $(SQ \times SP)$
6,500 kilograms × $3.80 $24,700	6,500 kilograms × $4 $26,000	6,000 kilograms* × $4 $24,000

Price variance, $1,300 F   Quantity variance, $2,000 U

Total variance, $700 U

*2,000 units × 3.0 kilograms per unit = 6,000 kilograms.
F = Favourable; U = Unfavourable.

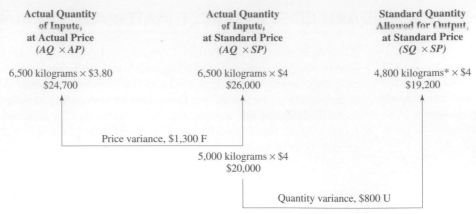

EXHIBIT 10-4

Variance Analysis—Direct Materials, When the Amount Purchased Differs from the Amount Used

Actual Quantity of Inputs, at Actual Price (AQ × AP)	Actual Quantity of Inputs, at Standard Price (AQ × SP)	Standard Quantity Allowed for Output, at Standard Price (SQ × SP)
6,500 kilograms × $3.80 $24,700	6,500 kilograms × $4 $26,000	4,800 kilograms* × $4 $19,200

Price variance, $1,300 F

5,000 kilograms × $4
$20,000

Quantity variance, $800 U

A total variance can't be computed in this situation, since the amount of materials purchased (6,500 kilograms) differs from the amount used in production (5,000 kilograms).

*1,600 units × 3.0 kilograms per unit = 4,800 kilograms.

drawn out of inventory and used in production. The situation illustrated in Exhibit 10–4 is common for companies that purchase materials several weeks (or months) in advance of use and store the materials in warehouses while awaiting the production process.

Materials Price Variance—A Closer Look

A **materials price variance** measures the difference between what is paid for a given quantity of materials and what should have been paid according to the standard that has been set. From Exhibit 10–3, this difference can be expressed by the following formula:

$$(AQ \times AP) - (AQ \times SP) = \text{Materials price variance}$$

The formula can be factored into simpler form as:

$$AQ(AP - SP) = \text{Materials price variance}$$

Some managers prefer this simpler formula, since it permits variance computations to be made very quickly. Using the data from Exhibit 10–3 in this formula, we have:

$$6,500 \text{ kilograms } (\$3.80 - \$4.00) = \$1,300 \text{ F}$$

Notice that the answer is the same as that yielded in Exhibit 10–3. If the company wanted to put these data into a performance report, the data would appear as follows:

NOVA PEWTER COMPANY
Performance Report—Purchasing Department

Item Purchased	(1) Quantity Purchased	(2) Actual Price	(3) Standard Price	(4) Difference in Price (2) – (3)	(5) Total Price Variance (1) × (4)	Explanation
Material A	6,500 kilograms	$3.80	$4.00	$0.20	$1,300 F	Bargained for an especially favourable price

F = Favourable; U = Unfavourable.

Isolation of Variances.   At what point should variances be isolated and brought to the attention of management? The answer is, the earlier the better. One of the basic reasons for utilizing standard costs is to facilitate cost control. Therefore, the sooner deviations from standard are brought to the attention of management, the sooner problems can be evaluated and corrected. If long periods are allowed to elapse before variances are computed, costs that could otherwise have been controlled may accumulate to the point of doing significant damage to profits. Most firms compute the materials price variance, for example, when materials *are purchased* rather than when the materials are placed into production. This permits earlier isolation of the variance, since materials may remain in the warehouse before being used in production. Isolating the price variance when materials are purchased also permits the company to carry its raw materials in the inventory accounts at standard cost. This greatly simplifies the selection of the proper cost figure to use when raw materials are later placed into production.[3]

Once a performance report has been prepared, what does management do with the price variance data? The variances should be viewed as "red flags," calling attention to the fact that an exception has occurred that will require some follow-up effort. Normally, the performance report itself will contain some explanation of the reason for the variance, as shown above. In the case of Nova Pewter Company, the purchasing manager, Janet Warner, said that the favourable price variance was due to bargaining for an especially favourable price.

FOCUS ON
CURRENT PRACTICE

A study of large manufacturing companies found that about 60% prepare variance reports on a monthly basis, another 13% prepare reports on a weekly basis, and nearly 22% prepare reports on a daily basis. The number of companies preparing daily reports has more than doubled over the past five years.[4] A second study reported essentially the same results, with only slightly fewer companies preparing monthly reports and only slightly more preparing weekly or daily reports.[5]

Responsibility for the Variance.   Who is responsible for the materials price variance? Generally speaking, the purchasing manager has control over the price to be paid for goods and is therefore responsible for any price variances. Many factors influence the price paid for goods, including size of lots purchased, delivery method used, quantity discounts available, rush orders, and the quality of materials purchased. To the extent that the purchasing agent can control these factors, he or she is responsible for seeing that they are kept in agreement with the factors anticipated when the standard costs were initially set. A deviation in any factor from what was intended in the initial setting of a standard cost can result in a price variance. For example, purchase of second-grade materials rather than top-grade materials would result in a

---

[3]See Appendix A at the end of the chapter for an illustration of journal entries in a standard cost system.
[4]Bruce R. Gaumnitz and Felix P. Kollaritsch, "Manufacturing Cost Variances: Current Practice and Trends," *Journal of Cost Management* (Spring 1991), p. 60.
[5]Jeffrey R. Cohen and Laurence Paquette, "Management Accounting Practices: Perceptions of Controllers," *Journal of Cost Management* (Fall 1991), p. 77.

favourable price variance, since the lower-grade materials would generally be less costly (but perhaps less suitable for production).

There may be times, however, when someone other than the purchasing agent is responsible for a materials price variance. Production may be scheduled in such a way, for example, that the purchasing agent is required to obtain delivery by airfreight, rather than by truck, or he or she may be forced to buy in uneconomical quantities. In these cases, the production manager would bear responsibility for the price variances that develop.

A word of caution is in order. Variance analysis should not be used as an excuse to conduct witch hunts or as a means of beating line managers and workers over the head. The emphasis must be on the control function in the sense of *supporting* the line managers and *assisting* them in meeting the goals that they have participated in setting for the company. In short, the emphasis should be positive rather than negative. Excessive dwelling on what has already happened, particularly in terms of trying to find someone to "blame," can often be destructive to the functioning of an organization.

Materials Quantity Variance—A Closer Look

The **materials quantity variance** measures the difference between the quantity of materials used in production and the quantity that should have been used according to the standard that has been set. Although the variance is concerned with the physical usage of materials, it is generally stated in dollar terms, as shown in Exhibit 10–3. The formula for the materials quantity variance is:

$$(AQ \times SP) - (SQ \times SP) = \text{Materials quantity variance}$$

Again, the formula can be factored into simpler terms:

$$SP(AQ - SQ) = \text{Materials quantity variance}$$

Using the data from Exhibit 10–3 in the formula, we have:

$$\$4(6{,}500 \text{ kilograms} - 6{,}000 \text{ kilograms*}) = \$2{,}000 \text{ U}$$

*2,000 units × 3.0 kilograms per unit = 6,000 kilograms.

The answer, of course, is the same as that yielded in Exhibit 10–3. The data would appear as follows if a formal performance report were prepared:

NOVA PEWTER COMPANY
Performance Report—Production Department

Item Purchased	(1) Standard Price	(2) Actual Quantity	(3) Standard Quantity Allowed	(4) Difference in Quantity (2) – (3)	(5) Total Quantity Variance (1) × (4)	Explanation
Material A	$4	6,500 kilograms	6,000 kilograms	500 kilograms	$2,000 U	Second-grade materials unsuitable for production

F = Favourable; U = Unfavourable.

The materials quantity variance is best isolated at the time that materials are placed into production.[6] Materials are drawn for the number of units to be produced, according to the

---

[6]If a company uses process costing, then it may be necessary in some situations to compute the materials quantity variance on a periodic basis as production is *completed*. This is because under process costing it is sometimes difficult to know in advance what the output will be for a period. We assume the use of a job-order costing system throughout this chapter (including all assignment materials).

standard bill of materials for each unit. Any additional materials are usually drawn on an excess materials requisition slip, which is different in colour from the normal requisition slips. This procedure calls attention to the excessive usage of materials *while production is still in process* and provides an opportunity for early control of any developing problem.

Excessive usage of materials can result from many factors, including faulty machines, inferior quality of materials, untrained workers, and poor supervision. Generally speaking, it is the responsibility of the production department to see that material usage is kept in line with standards. There may be times, however, when the *purchasing* department may be responsible for an unfavourable materials quantity variance. If the purchasing department obtains materials of inferior quality in an effort to economize on price, the materials may prove to be unsuitable for use on the production line and may result in excessive waste. Thus, purchasing rather than production would be responsible for the quantity variance.

FURTHER ANALYSIS OF MATERIAL VARIANCES

OBJECTIVE 5
Compute mix and yield variances for materials and explain their significance.

A survey of the cost accounting practices of the 1,000 largest U.S. industrial companies[7] found that two other types of standard cost variances are frequently computed.[8] These are subcomponents of the material usage variance: a *material mix* and *material yield variance*. A representation of these variances is presented in Exhibit 10–5.

The production of most goods generally requires input from more than one material. Chemical firms, for example, may use varying proportions of interchangeable materials. The same is true with food processing companies. For example, a company that produces flour with a mixture of red and white wheat may, on occasion, substitute one kind of wheat for the other. When legally permitted, a manufacturer of canned fruit may substitute peaches for pears and a manufacturer of sausages may substitute pork for beef. The calculation of mix and yield variances is appropriate only if different types of material can be substituted for one another. A **mix variance** results if the actual mix of materials differs from the budgeted mix of materials. The budgeted mix reflects a proportional mix of materials that is expected to be used to produce a given

EXHIBIT 10-5

Extended Model for Variance Analysis—Materials

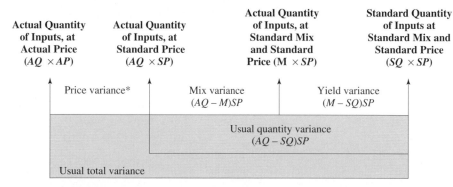

* Same as previous analysis, e.g., Exhibit 10-2.

[7]Max Laudeman and F. W. Schaeberle, "The Cost Accounting Practices of Firms Using Standard Costs," *Cost and Management* (July–August 1985), pp. 21–25.
[8]Ibid.

product. A mix variance is calculated to determine the effects of a change in the material mix on the total material cost. Where a manager has control over the composition of the mix, the mix variance can be a useful measure of the manager's performance.

The amount of quantity variance remaining after deducting the mix variance from the total quantity variance is the **yield variance.** A yield variance occurs when the actual combination of inputs generates a different rate of output from what would have been produced by the input mix used in setting the standards. In other words, the actual yield differs from the standard yield expected from a given mix of inputs.

To illustrate the calculation of the mix and yield variances assume that Cape Breton Chemical Company combines secret ingredients A and B to make a product known as super cleaner Bjax. The standard composition calls for a mix of 2 kilograms of A and 3 kilograms of B to produce one unit of Bjax. The standard mix for A and B is therefore $\frac{2}{5}$ and $\frac{3}{5}$ respectively. Assume that 150 units were produced using 350 kilograms of A and 450 kilograms of B. Material A has a standard unit price of $1.50 and material B has a standard price of $2.50 per unit.

For a given input, the mix variance can be calculated in two steps. First, multiply the budgeted mix percentage by the actual *total* input and subtract the actual quantity. This is the mix variance expressed in physical terms. Second, multiply your answer from step one by the standard cost of the input.

$$\frac{\text{Mix}}{\text{variance}} = \left[\frac{\text{Actual}}{\text{quantity}} - \left(\frac{\text{Budgeted}}{\%} \times \frac{\text{Total}}{\text{input}} \right) \right] \times \frac{\text{Standard}}{\text{price}}$$

For material A this would be:

$$[350 - \tfrac{2}{5}(350 + 450)] \times \$1.50 = \$45 \text{ U}$$

Similarly, for material B the mix variance is

$$[450 - \tfrac{3}{5}(350 + 450)] \times \$2.50 = \$75 \text{ F}$$

The budgeted percent times the total input of material A is 320 $[\frac{2}{5}(350 + 450)]$ kilograms. This is the amount of material A that would have been used if the budget had been adhered to. Since the amount of material used, 350 kilograms, exceeds the budgeted amount, the mix variance is unfavourable. If the budget had been adhered to in the case of material B, 480 $[\frac{3}{5}(350 + 450)]$ kilograms would have been used. Since the actual usage of material B was only 450 kilograms, the material mix variance of material B is favourable.

The variances can also be calculated using the following notation. For material A:

$$\text{Mix variance} = (AQ_A - M_A)SP_A$$
$$= [350 - \tfrac{2}{5}(350 + 450)]\$1.50 = \$45U$$
$$\text{Yield variance} = (M_A - SQ_A)SP_A$$
$$= [\tfrac{2}{5}(350 + 450) - 150(2)]\$1.50 = \$30U$$
$$\frac{\text{Total material}}{\text{quantity variance}} = (AQ_A - SQ_A)SP_A$$

$$= (350 - 150(2))\$1.50 = \$75U$$
$$\text{or mix variance + yield variance}$$
$$\$45U + \$30U = \$75U$$

where
AQ_A is the actual quantity used of material A.
M_A is the standard mix of material A actually used.
SQ_A is the standard quantity of material A.

For material B:

$$\text{Mix variance} = \left[450 - \tfrac{3}{5}(350 + 450)\right]\$2.50 = -\$75 \text{ F}$$
$$\text{Yield variance} = \left[\tfrac{3}{5}(350 + 450) - 3(150)\right]\$2.50 = \$75 \text{ U}$$
$$\text{Total material quantity variance} = \left[450 - 3(150)\right]\$2.50 = \$0.0$$

or

$$\$75 \text{ F} - \$75 \text{ U} = \$0.0$$

Labour efficiency variances, described in the section to follow, can be analyzed in a similar manner if the composition of a work group is provided in the standard. For example, if all junior staff are assigned to other jobs a public accounting firm might assign senior staff to a job that would normally be done by more junior personnel. The standard mix of employees can be applied to the total hours worked in the group to determine the standard mix for each employee group.

The calculation of mix and yield variances provides a means of separating the quantity variance into a set of constituents. This breakdown can be meaningful where managers are able to change the mix in production, thereby affecting the quantities of each type of material used. If the standard mix is the ideal, then departures from this mix should be made evident to statement users.

Managers, however, should carefully examine the effect of mix and yield variances to see how other costs such as labour and overhead are affected by the change in mix and its effect on yield. Often there are interrelationships among the mix, yield, and material price variances. For example, a production manager may respond to changes in relative prices of inputs by changing the mix. The new mix may, in turn, affect the yield. If examined in isolation, the appropriateness of the decision to change the mix could not be properly assessed. This raises performance evaluation issues. The budgeted mix is no longer optimal and, therefore, cannot be used as a valid benchmark for evaluating the manager's performance.

One problem of mix and yield variances stems from its use of standard prices. When prices differ from standard, it is the change in actual relative prices within the materials composition which may make changes in the mix and yield worthwhile. The fact that these price changes are held constant when calculating the mix and usage variances makes it difficult to interpret the effectiveness of managerial decisions to make changes in the mix of inputs. Conceptually, these variances can be left in physical units. Multiplying by standard prices is to facilitate aggregation by providing a common denominator.

USING STANDARD COSTS — DIRECT LABOUR VARIANCES

OBJECTIVE 6
Compute the direct labour rate and efficiency variances and explain their significance.

Terry's next step in determining Nova Pewter's variances for June was to compute the direct labour variances for the month. Recall from Exhibit 10–1 that the standard direct labour cost per unit of product is $35, computed as follows:

$$2.5 \text{ hours per unit} \times \$14 \text{ per hour} = \$35 \text{ per unit}$$

During June, the company paid its direct labour workers $74,250, including employment taxes and fringe benefits, for 5,400 hours of work. This was an average of $13.75 per

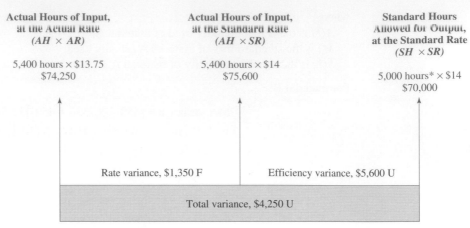

EXHIBIT 10–6

Variance Analysis—
Direct Labour

Actual Hours of Input, at the Actual Rate ($AH \times AR$)	Actual Hours of Input, at the Standard Rate ($AH \times SR$)	Standard Hours Allowed for Output, at the Standard Rate ($SH \times SR$)
5,400 hours × $13.75 $74,250	5,400 hours × $14 $75,600	5,000 hours* × $14 $70,000

Rate variance, $1,350 F   Efficiency variance, $5,600 U

Total variance, $4,250 U

*2,000 units × 2.5 hours per unit = 5,000 hours.
F = Favourable; U = Unfavourable.

hour. Using these data and the standard costs from Exhibit 10–1, Terry computed the direct labour rate and efficiency variances that appear in Exhibit 10–6.

Notice that the column headings in Exhibit 10–6 are the same as those used in the materials exhibits, except that in Exhibit 10–6 the terms *hours* and *rate* are used in place of the terms *quantity* and *price*.

Labour Rate Variance—A Closer Look

As explained earlier, the price variance for direct labour is commonly termed a **labour rate variance.** This variance measures any deviation from standard in the average hourly rate paid to direct labour workers. From Exhibit 10–6, the formula for the labour rate variance would be expressed as follows:

$$(AH \times AR) - (AH \times SR) = \text{Labour rate variance}$$

The formula can be factored into simpler form as:

$$AH(AR - SR) = \text{Labour rate variance}$$

Using the data from Exhibit 10–6 in the formula, we have:

$$5,400 \text{ hours } (\$13.75 - \$14.00) = \$1,350 \text{ F}$$

In most firms, the rates paid to workers are set by union contract; therefore, rate variances, in terms of amounts paid to workers, tend to be almost nonexistent. Rate variances can arise, though, through the way labour is used. Skilled workers with high hourly rates of pay can be given duties that require little skill and call for low hourly rates of pay. This type of misallocation of the workforce will result in unfavourable labour rate variances, because the actual hourly rate of pay will exceed the standard rate authorized for the particular task being performed. A reverse situation exists when unskilled or untrained workers are assigned to jobs that require some skill or training. The lower pay scale for these workers will result in favourable rate variances, although the workers may be highly inefficient in terms of output. Finally, unfavourable rate variances can arise from overtime work at premium rates if any portion of the overtime premium is added to the direct labour account.

Who is responsible for controlling the labour rate variance? Because rate variances generally arise as a result of how labour is used, those supervisors in charge of effective utilization of labour time bear responsibility for seeing that labour rate variances are kept under control.

Labour Efficiency Variance—A Closer Look

The quantity variance for direct labour, more commonly called the **labour efficiency variance,** measures the productivity of labour time. No variance is more closely watched by management, since increasing productivity of labour time is a vital key to reducing unit costs of production. From Exhibit 10–6, the formula for the labour efficiency variance would be expressed as follows:

$$(AH \times SR) - (SH \times SR) = \text{Labour efficiency variance}$$

Factored into simpler terms, the formula is:

$$SR(AH - SH) = \text{Labour efficiency variance}$$

Using the data from Exhibit 10–6 in the formula, we have:

$$\$14(5,400 \text{ hours} - 5,000 \text{ hours*}) = \$5,600 \text{ U}$$

*2,000 units $\times$ 2.5 hours per unit = 5,000 hours.

Causes of the labour efficiency variance include poorly trained workers; poor quality materials, requiring more labour time in processing; faulty equipment, causing breakdowns and work interruptions; and poor supervision of workers. The managers in charge of production would generally be responsible for control of the labour efficiency variance. However, the variance might be chargeable to purchasing if the acquisition of poor materials resulted in excessive labour processing time.

When the labour force is essentially fixed in the short term, another important cause of an unfavourable labour efficiency variance is insufficient demand for the output of the factory. In some firms, the actual labour-hours worked is basically fixed—particularly in the short term. Managers in these firms argue that it is difficult, and perhaps even unwise, to constantly adjust the workforce in response to changes in the workload. Therefore, the only way a work centre manager can avoid an unfavourable labour efficiency variance in such firms is by keeping everyone busy all of the time. The option of reducing the number of workers on hand is not available.

Thus, if there are insufficient orders from customers to keep the workers busy, the work centre manager has two options—either accept an unfavourable labour efficiency variance or build inventory.[9] A central lesson of JIT is that building inventory is a bad idea. Inventory—particularly work in process inventory—leads to high defect rates, obsolete goods, and generally inefficient operations. As a consequence, when the workforce is basically fixed in the short term, managers must be cautious about how labour efficiency variances are used. Some managers advocate dispensing with labour efficiency variances entirely in such situations—at least for the purposes of motivating and controlling workers on the shop floor.

USING STANDARD COSTS—VARIABLE OVERHEAD VARIANCES

OBJECTIVE 7
Compute the variable overhead spending and efficiency variances.

The final step in Terry's analysis of Nova Pewter's variances for June was to compute the variable manufacturing overhead variances. The variable portion of manufacturing overhead can be analyzed using the same basic formulas that are used to analyze direct materials

---

[9]For further discussion, see Eliyahu M. Goldratt and Jeff Cox, *The Goal,* 2nd rev. ed. (Croton-on-Hudson, N.Y.: North River Press, 1992).

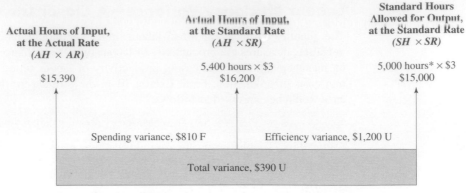

EXHIBIT 10-7

Variance Analysis—
Variable Overhead

Actual Hours of Input, at the Actual Rate (AH × AR)	Actual Hours of Input, at the Standard Rate (AH × SR)	Standard Hours Allowed for Output, at the Standard Rate (SH × SR)
$15,390	5,400 hours × $3 $16,200	5,000 hours* × $3 $15,000

Spending variance, $810 F   Efficiency variance, $1,200 U

Total variance, $390 U

*2,000 units × 2.5 hours per unit = 5,000 hours.
F = Favourable; U = Unfavourable.

and direct labour. Recall from Exhibit 10–1 that the standard variable manufacturing overhead is $7.50 per unit of product, computed as follows:

$$2.5 \text{ hours per unit} \times \$3 \text{ per hour} = \$7.50 \text{ per unit}$$

Nova Pewter's cost records showed that the total actual variable manufacturing overhead cost for June was $15,390. Recall from the earlier discussion of the direct labour variances that 5,400 hours of direct labour time were recorded during the month and that the company produced 2,000 pairs of bookends. Terry's analysis of this overhead data appears in Exhibit 10–7 above.

Notice the similarities between Exhibits 10–6 and 10–7. These similarities arise from the fact that direct labour-hours are being used as a base for allocating overhead cost to units of product; thus, the same hourly figures appear in Exhibit 10–7 for variable overhead as in Exhibit 10–6 for direct labour. The main difference between the two exhibits is in the standard hourly rate being used, which is much lower for variable overhead.

Overhead Variances—A Closer Look

As its name implies, the **variable overhead spending variance** measures deviations in amounts spent for overhead inputs such as lubricants and utilities. The formula for the variance can be expressed as:

$$(AH \times AR) - (AH \times SR) = \text{Variable overhead spending variance}$$

Or, factored into simpler terms:

$$AH(AR - SR) = \text{Variable overhead spending variance}$$

Using the data from Exhibit 10–7 in the formula, we have:

$$5,400 \text{ hours}(\$2.85^* - \$3.00) = \$810 \text{ F}$$

*$15,390 ÷ 5,400 hours = $2.85

The **variable overhead efficiency variance** is a measure of the difference between the actual activity of a period and the standard activity allowed, multiplied by the variable part of the predetermined overhead rate. The formula for the variance can be expressed as:

$$(AH \times SR) - (SH \times SR) = \text{Variable overhead efficiency variance}$$

Or, factored into simpler terms:

$$SR(AH - SH) = \text{Variable overhead efficiency variance}$$

Again using the data from Exhibit 10–7, the computation of the variance would be:

$$\$3(5,400 \text{ hours} - 5,000 \text{ hours*}) = \$1,200 \text{ U}$$

*2,000 units × 2.5 hours per unit = 5,000 hours.

We will reserve further discussion of the variable overhead spending and efficiency variances until Chapter 11, where overhead analysis is discussed in depth.

Before proceeding further, it will be helpful for the reader to pause at this point and go back and review the data contained in Exhibits 10–1 through 10–7. These exhibits and the accompanying text discussion represent a comprehensive, integrated illustration of standard setting and variance analysis.

▼   ▼   ▼   ▼   ▼

MANAGERIAL ACCOUNTING IN ACTION—WRAP-UP

In preparation for the scheduled meeting to discuss Terry's analysis of Nova Pewter's standard costs and variances, Terry distributed Exhibits 10–1 through 10–7 (except 10–5), with supporting explanations, to the management group of Nova Pewter. This included J. D. Wriston, the president of the company; Tom Kuchel, the production manager; and Janet Warner, the purchasing manager. J. D. Wriston opened the meeting with the following question:

J. D.: Terry, I think I understand the report you distributed, but just to make sure, would you mind summarizing the highlights of what you found?

TERRY: As you can see, the biggest problems are the unfavourable materials quantity variance of $2,000 and the unfavourable labour efficiency variance of $5,600.

J. D.: Tom, you're the production boss. What do you think is responsible for the unfavourable labour efficiency variance?

TOM: It pretty much has to be the new production workers. Our experienced workers shouldn't have much problem meeting the standard of 2.5 hours per unit. We all knew that there would be some inefficiency for a while as we brought new people on board.

J. D.: No one is disputing that, Tom. However, $5,600 is a lot of money. Is this problem likely to go away very soon?

TOM: I hope so. If we were to contrast the last two weeks of June with the first two weeks, I'm sure we would see some improvement.

J. D.: I don't want to beat up on you, Tom, but this is a significant problem. Can you do something to accelerate the training process?

TOM: Sure. I could pair up each of the new guys with one of our old-timers and have them work together for a while. It would slow down our older guys a bit, but I'll bet the new workers would learn a lot.

J. D.: Let's try it. Now, what about that $2,000 unfavourable materials quantity variance?

TOM: Are you asking me?

J. D.: Well, I would like someone to explain it.

TOM: Don't look at me. It's that iron-contaminated pewter that Janet bought on her "special deal."

JANET: We got rid of that stuff months ago.

J. D.: Hold your horses. We're not trying to figure out who to blame here. I just want to understand what happened. If we can understand what happened, maybe we can fix it.

Continued

> **TERRY:** Tom, are the new workers generating a lot of scrap?
>
> **TOM:** Yeah, I guess so.
>
> **J. D.:** I think that could be part of the problem. Can you do anything about it?
>
> **TOM:** I can watch the scrap real closely for a few days to see where it's being generated. If it is the new workers, I can have the old-timers work with them on the problem when I team them up.
>
> **J. D.:** Good. Let's reconvene in a few weeks and see what has happened. Hopefully, we can get those unfavourable variances under control.

STRUCTURE OF PERFORMANCE REPORTS

On preceding pages we have learned that performance reports are used in a standard cost system to communicate variance data to management. Exhibit 10–8 provides an overview of how these reports can be integrated to form a responsibility reporting system.

Note from the exhibit that the performance reports *start at the bottom and build upward,* with managers at each level receiving information on their own performance as well as information on the performance of each manager under them in the chain of responsibility. This variance information flows upward from level to level in a pyramid fashion, with the president finally receiving a summary of all activities in the organization. If the manager at a particular level (such as the production superintendent) wants to know the reasons behind a variance, he or she can ask for the detailed performance reports prepared by the various operations or departments.

In the following section, we turn our attention to the question of how a manager can determine which variances on these reports are significant enough to warrant further attention.

VARIANCE ANALYSIS AND MANAGEMENT BY EXCEPTION

OBJECTIVE 8
Explain how the manager would determine whether a variance constituted an "exception" that would require his or her attention.

Variance analysis and performance reports provide a vehicle for implementing the concept of *management by exception.* Simply put, management by exception means that the manager's attention must be directed toward those parts of the organization where things are not proceeding according to plan. Since a manager's time is limited, every hour must be used as effectively as possible, and time and effort must not be wasted looking after those parts of the organization where things are going smoothly.

The budgets and standards discussed in this chapter and in the preceding chapter represent the "plans" of management. If all goes smoothly, then costs would be expected to fall within the budgets and standards that have been set. To the extent that this happens, the manager is free to spend time elsewhere, with the assurance that at least in the budgeted areas all is proceeding according to expectations. To the extent that actual costs and revenues do not conform to the budget, however, a signal comes to the manager that an "exception" has occurred. This exception comes in the form of a variance from the budget or standard that was originally set.

The words *favourable* and *unfavourable* convey a message to a reader. If only unfavourable variances get attention, a manager may feel a sense of failure. This may encourage managers to reduce their efforts and to adopt "play-it-safe" strategies. It is important also to see the interconnectedness of the variances. For example, viewing material with

EXHIBIT 10-8   Upward Flow of Performance Reports

President's Report

The president's performance report summarizes all company data. Since variances are given, the president can trace the variances downward through the company as needed to determine where top management time should be spent.

	Budget	Actual	Variance
Responsibility centre:			
Sales manager	X	X	X
Production superintendent	$26,000	$29,000	$3,000 U
Engineering head	X	X	X
Personnel supervisor	X	X	X
Controller	X	X	X
	$54,000	$61,000	$7,000 U

Production Superintendent

The performance of each department head is summarized for the production superintendent. The totals on the superintendent's performance report are then passed upward to the next level of responsibility.

	Budget	Actual	Variance
Responsibility centre:			
Cutting department	X	X	X
Machining department	X	X	X
Finishing department	$11,000	$12,500	$1,500 U
Packaging department	X	X	X
	$26,000	$29,000	$3,000 U

Finishing Department Head

The performance report of each supervisor is summarized on the performance report of the department head. The department totals are then summarized upward to the production superintendent.

	Budget	Actual	Variance
Responsibility centre:			
Sanding operation	X	X	X
Wiring operation	$5,000	$5,800	$800 U
Assembly operation	X	X	X
	$11,000	$12,500	$1,500 U

Wiring Operation Supervisor

The supervisor of each operation receives a performance report on his or her centre of responsibility. The totals on these reports are then communicated upward to the next higher level of responsibility.

	Budget	Actual	Variance
Variable costs:			
Direct materials	X	X	X
Direct labour	X	X	X
Manufacturing overhead	X	X	X
	$5,000	$5,800	$800 U

labour or labour with overhead or price with quantity may enlighten the firm to a completely opposite view from that conveyed by a single variance in isolation. A favourable material price variance may be attributable to the use of lower quality materials. It may take a longer time to convert lower quality materials to a finished product. The aggregate effect of the favourable material price variance and the unfavourable labour efficiency variance may indeed be negative. Certainly, favourable variances do not necessarily deserve praise and an unfavourable variance, may, in fact, net out to be a good thing.

The major question at this point is: "Are *all* variances to be considered exceptions that will require the attention of management?" The answer is no. If every variance was considered an exception, then management would get little else done other than chasing down nickel-and-dime differences. It is probably safe to say that only by the rarest of coincidences will actual costs and revenues ever conform exactly to the budgeted pattern. The reason is that actual costs are subject to large numbers of random and unpredictable influences. Workers seldom work at exactly the pace set in the standard, and their efficiency may be influenced by random factors such as the weather. Prices of some raw materials can change suddenly and without warning. Because of these unpredictable random factors, one can expect that in every period virtually every cost category will produce a variance of some kind.

Care is needed here to avoid the impression that an exception is a deviation from the status quo. Maintaining the status quo may mean losing out to the competition. This implies that over time, standards can and must change if the company expects to prosper. If standards truly reflect what is expected, exceptions are deviations from what is expected, not deviations from the status quo. In this way, exceptions are interpreted as deviations from what is anticipated at a particular evolutionary point for the organization.

Criteria for Determining Exceptions

As implied in the previous section, even though budgets may be prepared with the greatest of care, it is never possible to develop budgeted data that contain the precise allowances necessary for each of the multitude of variables that can affect actual costs and revenues. For this reason, one can expect that in every period virtually every budgeted figure produces a variance of some type when compared to actual cost data. How do managers decide which of these variances are worthy of their attention? We can identify at least four criteria used in actual practice: materiality, consistency of occurrence, ability to control, and nature of the item.

Materiality.   Ordinarily, management is interested only in those variances that are material in amount. To separate material variances from immaterial variances, firms often set guidelines, such as stating that any variance that differs from the budget by 5% or more is considered a material variance. Notice that we say differs from the budget, not exceeds the budget. We say differs because management is just as interested in those variances that are *under* the budget as it is in those that exceed it. This is because a level of spending under the budget can be just as critical to profitability as a level of spending that exceeds the budget. For example, if advertising is budgeted to be $100,000 during a period and only $80,000 is spent, this favourable spending variance could be damaging to profits because of insufficient promotion of the firm's products.

Generally, a guideline such as a 5% deviation from budget is not sufficient to judge whether a variance is material. The reason is that a 2% variance in some costs could be far more critical to profits than a 10% variance in other costs. Therefore, a firm often supplements the percentage guideline with some minimum absolute dollar figure, stating that even if a variance does not exceed the percentage guideline, it is still considered material if it exceeds the minimum dollar figure. To illustrate, a firm might state that any variance is considered material if it differs from the budget by 5% or more, or by $1,000.

Consistency of Occurrence.   Even if a variance never exceeds the minimum stated percentage or the minimum dollar amount, many firms want it brought to the attention of management if it comes *close* to these limits period after period. The thinking here is that the budget or standard may be out of date, and that adjustment to more current levels might improve overall profit planning. Alternatively, some laxness in cost control may be present, warranting an occasional check by the relevant supervisor.

Ability to Control.   Some costs are largely beyond the control of management. When such costs are present in a company, no follow-up action on management's part is necessary even though variances may occur that are material in amount. For example, utility rates and local tax rates are generally not controllable internally, and large variances resulting from rate increases therefore require little or no follow-up effort on management's part. However, such variances are frequently presented on variance reports for information purposes.

Nature of the Item.   By their very nature, some costs are much more critical to long-run profitability than others. One such cost is advertising. As mentioned earlier, underutilization of the advertising budget can have an adverse impact on sales, with a resulting loss of revenue that greatly outweighs any saving in advertising dollars. Another such cost is maintenance. Although inadequate maintenance may produce short-run savings in costs, these savings are probably more than offset by future breakdowns, repairs, and loss of revenue from reduced productivity and efficiency.

Because of the critical nature of such costs as advertising and maintenance, the guidelines for determining whether a variance is material are usually much more stringent for these costs than for other costs. That is, variances in these areas are generally watched more closely by management than variances in other, less critical, areas. It may be that management may want to see *any* variance in certain key areas such as advertising and promotion. In addition, the normal guidelines may be reduced by half in other key areas such as maintenance and certain critical component parts.

Statistical Analysis of Random Variances

The purpose of establishing criteria for separating material from immaterial variances is to isolate those variances that are *not* due to random causes, and that can and should be

When applying standards in a business, care must be taken that the standards are still appropriate. For example, the great number of computers found in most offices of the 1990s means that the standards set for the office environment of the 1950s or 1960s are no longer accurate.

controlled by the company. The "5% of budget, or $1,000" approach described in the preceding section is a somewhat crude way of accomplishing this objective, although it is widely used. The approach is crude because it is based on rough guessing and on rules of thumb rather than on precise analysis.

A much more dependable way of separating random variances from variances that are uncontrollable can be found in statistical analysis. This approach to segregating random variances has its basis in the idea that a budget or standard represents a *range* of acceptability, rather than a single point. Any variance falling within this range is considered to be due solely to random causes that either are not within the ability of management to control or that would be impractical to control. Grant and Leavenworth put the idea this way:

> Measured quality of manufactured product is always subject to a certain amount of variation as a result of chance. Some stable "system of chance uses" is inherent in any particular scheme of production and inspection. Variation within this stable pattern is inevitable. The reasons for variation outside this stable pattern [should] be discovered and corrected.[10]

How does a firm isolate the range within which variances from budget are due to chance or random causes? This is done by means of statistical sampling of the population represented by the budgeted data. Random samples of the population are drawn, and the amounts found in these samples are plotted on a *control chart* such as that illustrated in Exhibit 10–9. In effect, the upper and lower limits on the chart represent results taken from the normal distribution (bell-shaped curve), with the upper and lower limits generally being at least one standard deviation (the square root of the statistical variance) from the grand mean. Any amounts falling within the upper and lower control limits are due simply to chance occurrences and, therefore, either are not within the ability of management to control or are not large enough to warrant management time. Any amounts falling outside these limits are not due to random or chance causes and are considered exceptions toward which management attention needs to be directed.

The value of a budgeting system is greatly increased if amounts are analyzed by a statistical approach such as that just described rather than by the "5%, or $1,000" approach described earlier. The reason, of course, is that the statistical approach eliminates guesswork and zeroes management in on those cost variations that are indeed within its ability to control.

Statistical control charts were developed for use in repetitive operations such as stamping machines and the like. The control limits can be obtained from a sample of 25 to 50 previous results. Then repeated observations can be compared to the limits set from the control chart. Actual application of the technique to standard cost variances can present some difficulties. If the standard cost variance is generated monthly, then two to four years of observations are needed to set the control limits. The problem presented is that standards reflect changing operations and the control limits are likely to be based on operations that are outdated by the time the control limits can be set. Although some efficiencies have been attempted in constructing control charts, the problem of an insufficient number of observations still remains in practice.

The second problem with the use, in practice, of control charts comes from the fact that they are based on limits of random performance of a process that is running correctly. Another set of limits would exist for a process that is not running correctly. Observations from the two situations overlap; that is, performance from the correct process falls in the same area as those from the incorrect one. Thus, a single observation could be within the control limits shown in Exhibit 10–9, yet be from a process that is out of control. Also, an observation outside the control limits could actually be one from the in-control process or

---

[10]Eugene L. Grant and Richard L. Leavenworth, *Statistical Quality Control,* 4th ed. (New York: McGraw-Hill, 1972), p. 3.

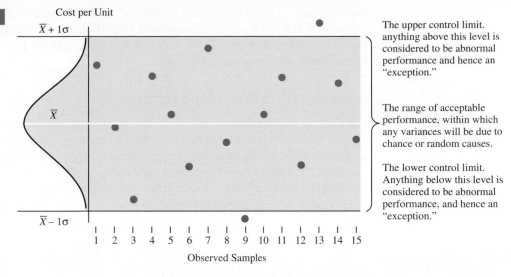

EXHIBIT 10-9

A Statistical Control Chart

The upper control limit. anything above this level is considered to be abnormal performance and hence an "exception."

The range of acceptable performance, within which any variances will be due to chance or random causes.

The lower control limit. Anything below this level is considered to be abnormal performance, and hence an "exception."

maybe from the out-of-control process. Thus, it is possible to make an error in the conclusion about the nature of an observation (in statistics these errors are called *type I* or *type II* errors, respectively). The key issue is to consider which error is more important, investigating a variance when the process is in control, a type I error, or *not* investigating a variance when the process is out of control, a type II error. Usually the second is considered the more serious case, but notice that the control chart concentrates on the first type of error because it is drawn from an in-control process. Experience and adaptations of the control chart can help, but the problem remains and is even more serious when only a few observations are available to construct the control chart.

The practical solution to the question of which variance to investigate is still an unresolved issue. However, control charts do help to clarify the thinking of managers when they have to judge which variances should be investigated.

OPERATING PERFORMANCE MEASURES

As stated earlier, standard costs are widely used in manufacturing, service, food, and not-for-profit organizations. Indeed, the list of companies that employ standards as a method for controlling costs and for measuring performance continues to grow. In the new competitive environment that has developed in recent years, however, managers have found it necessary to supplement their standard costs with several new operating performance measures. For some companies, these new operating performance measures have even replaced standard cost systems altogether.

Standard Costs and the New Competitive Environment

There are several reasons why traditional standards may be inappropriate for companies operating in the new competitive environment. First, for companies that have invested heavily in automation, labour is less significant and tends to be more fixed. Thus, the traditional labour variances are of little value to management. Second, whenever labour is essentially fixed, a focus on the labour efficiency variance may prompt production of needless inventories. Third, some managers argue that preoccupation with standard cost variances may result in low-quality output and poor delivery performance. Finally, managers involved in total quality management (TQM), theory of constraints (TOC), just-in-time (JIT), and similar management approaches argue that the goal should be continual improvement, not just meeting standards.

New Performance Measures

OBJECTIVE 9
Enumerate the operating performance measures and explain how they are used.

Many new performance measures are emerging as managers seek to streamline their operations, to improve quality and service, and to employ sophisticated new concepts such as JIT and FMS. These new performance measures can be classified into five general groupings consisting of quality control, material control, inventory control, machine performance, and delivery performance. These groupings, along with specific measures that they encompass, are provided in Exhibit 10–10.

EXHIBIT 10-10

Operating Performance Measures

Measures	Desired Change
Quality Control Measures	
Warranty claims as a percentage of units sold	Decrease
Customer complaints as a percentage of units sold	Decrease
Defects as a percentage of units produced	Decrease
First-time pass rate	Increase
Field failure rate	Decrease
Total quality cost	Decrease
Material Control Measures	
Material as a percentage of total cost	Decrease
Lead time	Decrease
Scrap as a percentage of good pieces	Decrease
Scrap as a percentage of total cost	Decrease
Actual scrap loss	Decrease
Inventory Control Measures	
Inventory turnover:	
Raw materials (by type)	Increase
Finished goods (by product)	Increase
Number of inventoried items	Decrease
Machine Performance Measures	
Percentage of machine availability	Increase
Percentage of machine downtime	Decrease
Setup time	
Machine stops (breakdowns)	
Preventive maintenance	
Use as a percentage of availability	Increase
Setup time	Decrease
Delivery Performance Measures	
Percentage of on-time deliveries	Increase
Delivery cycle time	Decrease
Throughput time, or velocity*	Decrease
Manufacturing cycle efficiency (MCE)	Increase
Order backlog	Decrease
Total throughput, or output rate	Increase

*Sometimes referred to as *manufacturing cycle time.*

In an article about the big three auto makers in North America, *The Wall Street Journal* reported the following:

> General Motors is wrestling with how to change a way of life in a sprawling, hidebound bureaucracy . . . That's why GM has spent more than a year overhauling how it measures success.

> "Traditionally, we measured labor efficiency in the plants," Mr. Hoglund [a GM executive vice president] says, to elicit greater output per unit of labor. "Then we found out it drove all the wrong behaviors—people got rewarded for higher and higher volumes, but there was no incentive for quality." Moreover, all the comparisons were internal. Now, he says, the key measures are customer satisfaction and how various processes stack up against the best of the competition.[11]

The new performance measures listed in the exhibit tend to be nonfinancial in nature and some are more subjective than traditional standard costs. Also, their computation and use differ in several ways from standard costs. First, these new measures are often computed on an *on-line* basis so that management and workers are able to monitor activities continually. On-line access to data allows problems to be identified and corrected "on the factory floor" as the problems occur, rather than waiting several days for a report to be generated. This approach to the control process is easy when managers routinely use personal computers in their work, as is true in many companies today. Second, many of the measures are computed at the *plant* level in order to emphasize the concept of an integrated, interdependent operation. Although performance is also measured at the cell level, plantwide performance is emphasized. And third, in using the measures, managers focus more directly on *trends* over time than on any particular change during the current period. The key objectives are *progress* and *improvement,* rather than meeting any specific standards.

In the discussion that follows, we look at each of the groupings in Exhibit 10–10 in more detail. The reader should be aware that the measures included in these groupings are representative and not exhaustive of the possibilities. Many other measures are possible, depending on individual company needs.

Quality Control Measures

We have stated several times in preceding chapters that high quality is a major objective in the new competitive environment. To monitor quality, managers look at measures such as warranty claims, customer complaints, and defects in units. Although such items have always been watched by management, the difference today is *speed.* Immediate steps are taken to correct design defects that may result in claims, and immediate steps are taken to resolve complaints. Managers have learned that insensitivity to such matters can be disastrous in markets that have become worldwide in scope.

Managers also pay close attention to the first-time pass rate in each process and in the company as a whole, which indicates whether products are being built to specifications

[11]"Tooling Along: With Auto Profits Up, Big Three Again Get a Major Opportunity," *The Wall Street Journal,* May 4, 1994, pp. A1, A11.

FOCUS ON
CURRENT PRACTICE

An AT&T facility located in Dallas, Texas, that manufactures electronic transformers has devised the following measures to monitor performance on its production line:[12]

Measurement	Typical Monthly Results*	Goal
Number of defective items	300 PPM†	0 PPM
First pass quality percent yield	97%	100%
On-time percent shipped	94%	100%
Manufacturing cycle time	8 hours	5 hours
Shop WIP inventory	$19,000	$8,000
WIP turnover	87 turns/yr.	160 turns/yr.
Finished goods inventory	$16,000	$0
WIP & FG turnover	47.1 turns/yr.	100 turns/yr.
Cost of scrap	$2,400	$1,500
Scrap as a percent of output	2.2%	1%
Number of line disruptions	29	0
Percent of workers cross trained	70%	100%
Percent completion JIT/TQC checklist	65%	100%

*Hypothetical figures are used (actual figures proprietary).
†PPM = Parts per million.

without rework. In addition to being a measure of quality, a high first-time pass rate means less rework and less output going into the scrap bin. To get a fuller picture of the costs associated with quality assurance, some companies prepare a quality cost report as discussed in Chapter 5. Such a report crosses the lines between departments and accumulates all costs traceable to the quality program. By means of this report, management can monitor both the magnitude and trend of total quality cost in a company.

Material Control Measures

We stated earlier that traditional standard costing seeks to control material cost through the materials price variance. In many companies today, the focus is in a different direction—it is toward higher quality, shorter lead time, and greater control over scrap.

Lead time is defined as the interval between when an order is placed and when the order is finally received from the supplier. Where JIT is in use, the goal is to reduce the lead time to only a few hours so that materials are available immediately as needed on the production line. Lead time is computed by supplier as well as by type of material so that undependable and slow suppliers can be identified.

A major difference between traditional standard costing and the new performance measures is the focus of the latter on the cost of scrap. Under standard costing, the cost of scrap is included as part of the materials quantity variance. But this variance doesn't include *all* the cost of scrap, because some "acceptable" level is built right into the standard itself. Under the new performance measures, scrap is treated as a separate item and there is no "acceptable" level. *Any* amount of scrap is viewed as a loss that must be eliminated. As shown in Exhibit 10–10, managers can monitor progress toward achieving zero scrap by computing the dollar amounts and the ratio of scrapped parts to good parts.

---

[12]F. B. Green, Felix Amenkhienan, and George Johnson, "Performance Measures and JIT," *Management Accounting* (February 1991), p. 53.

Inventory Control Measures

Historically, companies have operated under the assumption that some level of inventory was needed to act as a buffer against stock-outs. Now managers are recognizing that the cost of carrying inventory is much greater than was previously supposed. As a result, orders are placed more frequently and in smaller amounts. To monitor progress toward the goal of zero inventories, companies compute inventory turnover by type of material and also by individual product. Broadly defined, **inventory turnover** means how many times the average inventory balance has been used (and thereby replaced) during the period. The smaller the inventory balance, the greater the number of times that turnover will occur. Therefore, an increase in the turnover rate is a positive indicator of progress toward reducing the amount of inventory on hand.

The use of operating performance measures is by no means limited to manufacturing operations. Every month Hershey Foods Corporation mails a one-page survey to a sample of its customers (i.e., food distributors, wholesalers, and grocery chains). The survey asks customers to rate Hershey on a number of characteristics including the following:

- Courtesy, speed, and accuracy of customer service personnel.
- Quality of Hershey's carriers.
- Delivery dependability.
- Completeness of shipments.
- Condition of products when delivered.
- Speed and accuracy of Hershey's invoicing.

Customers are asked to rate Hershey in comparison with their very best suppliers, not just Hershey's direct competitors. "Whenever we see a 'poorer than' rating, the customer gets a follow-up phone call from the manager of the customer service center. This call probes for more information about the problem. Once the manager has additional information, he or she involves others in the company who can help rectify the situation. We then thank the customer for the information, explain how we will correct it, and ask them to let us know if things change."[13]

Machine Performance Measures

One of the most significant trends in the new competitive environment is toward greater use of automation. With greater automation comes a massive, fixed investment in equipment that requires considerably more attention from management than is needed in a nonautomated setting. Several measures have been developed to determine the availability and use of equipment, as shown in Exhibit 10–10.

The first two of these measures, which focus on machine availability and machine downtime, are the inverse of each other. That is, if a machine isn't available, then it's down for some reason; the reasons for being down are given in the exhibit. The goal, of course, is to minimize the amount of downtime so that machines are available as much as possible.

---

[13]Randy O. Main, "Creating Customer Satisfaction," *Sustaining Total Quality,* The Conference Board Report Number 1025 (New York, 1993), pp. 34–35.

The third measure, "Use as a percentage of available capacity," is designed primarily for control of bottleneck operations. The goal in a bottleneck operation is to keep machine use at 100% of available capacity so that maximum output can be achieved. This measure has less significance in a *non*bottleneck operation, since the goal there should be to use the equipment *only* as needed to support overall production. Trying to achieve 100% use in a nonbottleneck operation might result in producing more than is required to maintain a smooth flow, and thereby precipitate a needless buildup of inventory.

Reducing setup time is very important—particularly at bottlenecks. Setup time is non-value-added time that wastes productive capacity. When a machine is being set up, it cannot be used to produce output. Consequently, as discussed in Chapter 1, managers are devoting considerable resources and ingenuity to reducing setup times through the use of flexible manufacturing systems and techniques such as single-minute-exchange-of-dies. The success of such setup reduction efforts should be reflected in lower setup times. The improvements are often dramatic—setup time can often be cut from hours to minutes.

Delivery Performance Measures

OBJECTIVE 10

Compute the delivery cycle time, the throughput time, and the manufacturing cycle efficiency (MCE).

The purpose of production is to get a high-quality product into the hands of a customer as quickly as possible. If a customer has to wait months for a delivery and a competitor can provide the needed item in a few weeks, then the competitor probably will get the business. Thus, in the new competitive environment, speed has become as important as quality in gaining (or retaining) customers in some industries.

There are several key measures of delivery performance. As shown in Exhibit 10–10, the first of these is the percentage of on-time deliveries. Companies strive for 100% on-time deliveries, but whether or not this goal is achieved depends on several other factors. One of these is the **delivery cycle time,** which represents the amount of time required from receipt of an order from a customer to shipment of the completed goods.[14] Another factor is the **throughput time,** which measures the amount of time required to turn raw materials into completed products. Throughput time is also known as the **manufacturing cycle time** or **velocity** of production. The relationship between the delivery cycle time and the throughput (manufacturing cycle) time is illustrated in Exhibit 10–11.

Throughput (Manufacturing Cycle) Time.   As shown in Exhibit 10–11, the throughput time, or manufacturing cycle time, is made up of process time, inspection time, move time, and queue time. *Process time* is the amount of time in which work is actually done on the product. *Inspection time* is the amount of time spent ensuring that the product is not defective. *Move time* is the time required to move materials or partially completed products from workstation to workstation. *Queue time* is the amount of time a product spends waiting to be worked on, to be moved, to be inspected, or in storage waiting to be shipped.

As shown at the bottom of Exhibit 10–11, the only one of these four activities that adds value to the product is process time. The other three activities—inspecting, moving, and queueing—add no value and should be eliminated as much as possible.

Manufacturing Cycle Efficiency (MCE).   Through concerted efforts to eliminate the *non-value-added* activities of inspecting, moving, and queueing, some companies have reduced their throughput time to only a fraction of previous levels. In turn, this has

---

[14]Sometimes the delivery cycle time is improperly referred to as the lead time. The term *lead time* should be used only in conjunction with the purchase of raw materials.

EXHIBIT 10-11

Delivery Cycle Time
and Throughput
(Manufacturing
Cycle) Time

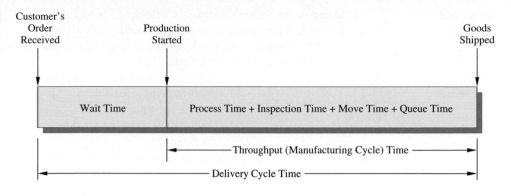

Value-Added Time	Non-Value-Added Time
Process Time	Wait Time
	Inspection Time
	Move Time
	Queue Time

helped to reduce the delivery cycle time from months to only weeks or hours. The throughput time, which is considered to be a key measure in delivery performance, can be put into better perspective by computing the **manufacturing cycle efficiency (MCE).** The MCE is computed by relating the value-added time to the throughout time. The formula is as follows:

$$MCE = \frac{\text{Value added time}}{\text{Throughput (manufacturing cycle) time}}$$

If the MCE is less than 1, then non-value-added time is present in the production process. An MCE of 0.5, for example, would mean that half of the total production time consisted of inspection, moving, and similar non-value-added activities. In many manufacturing companies, the MCE is less than 0.1 (10%), which means that 90% of the time a unit is in process is spent on activities that do not add value to the product.[15] By monitoring the MCE, companies are able to pare away non-value-added activities and thus get products into the hands of customers more quickly.

To provide a numeric example of these measures, assume the following data for Novex Company:

Novex Company keeps careful track of the time relating to orders and their production. During the most recent quarter, the following average times were recorded for each unit or order:

	Days
Wait time	17.0
Inspection time	0.4
Process time	2.0
Move time	0.6
Queue time	5.0

Goods are shipped as soon as production is completed.

---

[15]Callie Berlinger and James A. Brimson, eds., *Cost Management for Today's Advanced Manufacturing* (Boston, Mass.: Harvard Business School Press, 1988), p. 4.

Required

1. Compute the throughput time, or velocity of production.
2. Compute the manufacturing cycle efficiency (MCE).
3. What percentage of the production time is spent in non-value-added activities?
4. Compute the delivery cycle time.

Solution

1. Throughput time = Process time + Inspection time + Move time
$$+ \text{ Queue time}$$
$$= 2.0 \text{ days} + 0.4 \text{ days} + 0.6 \text{ days} + 5.0 \text{ days}$$
$$= 8.0 \text{ days}$$

2. Only process time represents value-added time; therefore, the computation of the MCE would be as follows:

$$\text{MCE} = \frac{\text{Value-added time, } 2.0 \text{ days}}{\text{Throughput time, } 8.0 \text{ days}}$$
$$= 0.25$$

Thus, once put into production, a typical unit is actually being worked on only 25% of the time.

3. Since the MCE is 25%, the complement of this figure, or 75% of the total production time, is spent in non-value-added activities.

4. Delivery cycle time = Wait time + Throughput time
$$= 17.0 \text{ days} + 8.0 \text{ days}$$
$$= 25.0 \text{ days}$$

FOCUS ON CURRENT PRACTICE

One of the most effective ways for companies to reduce their costs is to decrease the throughput time (and thus increase the MCE) of their plants. For example, by paring out non-value-added activities, a Canadian manufacturer of metal products was able to reduce the throughput time from 22 days to just 7 days, thus dramatically increasing its MCE and slashing its total costs. Moreover, since part of the reduction in throughput time was in the form of more rapid processing, the company effectively increased its manufacturing capacity. These results were achieved in just one year's time.[16]

Standard Costs and Operating Performance Measures

As mentioned previously, the new operating performance measures are often used side by side with the standard costs developed earlier in the chapter. The new performance measures complement standard costs, since they focus on many key areas (such as warranty claims, on-time deliveries, and delivery cycle time) that traditional cost standards do not cover. In addition, companies report that as they embrace new management approaches such as total quality management (TQM) and just-in-time (JIT), important changes take place in the way that standard costs are used.

---

[16]Patrick Northey, "Cut Total Costs with Cycle Time Reduction," *CMA Magazine* (February 1991), p. 22.

First, standard costs are used less frequently to measure performance. Instead, they are used primarily to value inventory and to determine cost of goods sold for financial reporting purposes.

Second, when standard costs *are* used to measure performance, engineered standards may be replaced either by a rolling average of actual costs or by very challenging target costs. The reason for this change is the necessity to encourage continual improvement rather than simply meeting a static standard.

Third, variances may be computed on a more frequent basis to provide more immediate feedback. In some companies, variances are computed and reported daily.

Fourth, there is more emphasis on the *trends* of the variances. If a continuous improvement program is working, key variances should improve over time.

Fifth, direct labour may be included as part of overhead rather than accounted for separately.

Sixth, particularly when JIT purchasing is used, materials price variances may not be computed. Under JIT purchasing, price variances for materials tend to be small or nonexistent due to long-term contracts with suppliers.

In summary, standard costs are still found in all types of companies, but in some settings their use is more limited and focuses on dynamic standards, long-term trends in variances, inventory valuation, and efficiency in record keeping.

INTERNATIONAL USES OF STANDARD COSTS

Standard costs are used by companies worldwide. A comparative study of cost accounting practices in four countries—the United States, the United Kingdom, Canada, and Japan—found that three-fourths of the companies surveyed in the United Kingdom, two-thirds of the companies surveyed in Canada, and 40% of the companies surveyed in Japan used standard cost systems.[17]

Standard costs were first introduced in Japan after World War II, with Nippon Electronics Company (NEC) being one of the first Japanese companies to adopt standard costs for all of its products. Many other Japanese companies followed NEC's lead and developed standard cost systems. The ways in which these standard costs are used in Japan—and also in the other three countries cited above—are shown in Exhibit 10–12.

EXHIBIT 10–12

Uses of Standard Costs in Four Countries[18]

	United States	United Kingdom	Canada	Japan
Cost management..................	1*	2	2	1
Budgetary planning and control†........	2	3	1	3
Pricing decisions	3	1	3	2
Financial statement preparation	4	4	4	4

*The numbers 1 through 4 denote importance of use, from greatest to least.
†Includes management planning.

[17]Shin'ichi Inoue, "Comparative Studies of Recent Development of Cost Management Problems in U.S.A., U.K., Canada, and Japan," Research Paper No. 29, Kagawa University (March 1988), p. 17.

[18]Compiled from the data in ibid., p.20. The study included 95 United States companies, 52 United Kingdom companies, 82 Canadian companies, and 646 Japanese companies.

Over time, the pattern of use shown in Exhibit 10–12 may change, but at present managers can expect to encounter standard costs in most industrialized nations. Moreover, unless a company is automated, these standards are likely to be used primarily for either cost management or budgetary planning purposes.

SUMMARY

A standard is a benchmark or "norm" for measuring performance. In business organizations, standards are set for both the cost and the quantity of inputs needed to manufacture goods or to provide services. Quantity standards indicate how much of a cost element, such as labour time or raw materials, should be used in manufacturing a unit of product or in providing a unit of service. Cost standards indicate what the cost of the time or the materials should be.

Standards are normally "practical" in nature, meaning that they can be attained by reasonable, though highly efficient, efforts. Such standards are generally felt to have a favourable motivational impact on employees.

When standards are compared against actual performance, the difference is referred to as a *variance*. Variances are computed and reported to management on a regular basis for both the price and the quantity elements of materials, labour, and overhead. Specific formulas are available to assist in these computations.

Not all variances are considered to be "exceptions" that require management time or attention. If a variance falls outside the permissible limits set by management, it is then considered to be an exception toward which management time and attention must be directed.

The traditional standard cost variance reports should often be supplemented with other performance measures. The most important reason for this is that standard costs do not cover critical areas such as product quality and on-time delivery. While different companies use different operating performance measures, most of the measures fall into five general groupings: quality control, material control, inventory control, machine performance, and delivery performance. These operating performance measures are reported frequently, and managers are generally most interested in their trends over time.

REVIEW PROBLEM: STANDARD COSTS

Xavier Company produces a single product. The standard costs for one unit of product are:

Direct material: 6 grams at $0.50 per gram	$3
Direct labour: 1.8 hours at $10 per hour	18
Variable overhead: 1.8 hours at $5 per hour	9
Total standard variable cost per unit	$30

During June, 2,000 units were produced. The costs associated with June were:

Material purchased: 18,000 grams at $0.60	$10,800
Material used in production: 14,000 grams	—
Direct labour: 4,000 hours at $9.75	39,000
Variable overhead costs incurred	20,800

Materials Variances

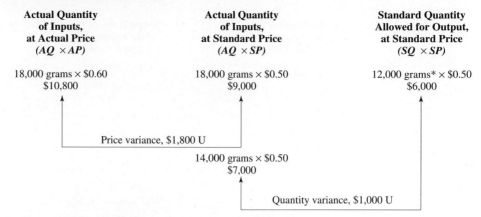

Actual Quantity of Inputs, at Actual Price $(AQ \times AP)$	Actual Quantity of Inputs, at Standard Price $(AQ \times SP)$	Standard Quantity Allowed for Output, at Standard Price $(SQ \times SP)$
18,000 grams × $0.60 $10,800	18,000 grams × $0.50 $9,000	12,000 grams* × $0.50 $6,000

Price variance, $1,800 U

14,000 grams × $0.50
$7,000

Quantity variance, $1,000 U

A total variance can't be computed in this situation, because the amount of materials purchased (18,000 grams) differs from the amount used in production (14,000 grams).

*2,000 units × 6 grams = 12,000 grams.

The same variances in shortcut format would be:

$$AQ(AP - SP) = \text{Materials price variance}$$
$$18,000 \text{ grams } (\$0.60 - \$0.50) = \$1,800 \text{ U}$$
$$SP(AQ - SQ) = \text{Materials quantity variance}$$
$$\$0.50(14,000 \text{ grams} - 12,000 \text{ grams}) = \$1,000 \text{ U}$$

Labour Variances

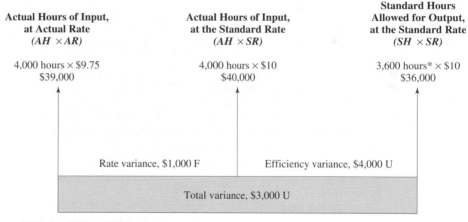

Actual Hours of Input, at Actual Rate $(AH \times AR)$	Actual Hours of Input, at the Standard Rate $(AH \times SR)$	Standard Hours Allowed for Output, at the Standard Rate $(SH \times SR)$
4,000 hours × $9.75 $39,000	4,000 hours × $10 $40,000	3,600 hours* × $10 $36,000

Rate variance, $1,000 F   Efficiency variance, $4,000 U

Total variance, $3,000 U

*2,000 units × 1.8 hours = 3,600 hours.

The same variances in shortcut format would be:

$$AH(AR - SR) = \text{Labour rate variance}$$
$$4,000 \text{ hours}(\$9.75 - \$10) = \$1,000 \text{ F}$$
$$SR(AH - SH) = \text{Labour efficiency variance}$$
$$\$10(4,000 \text{ hours} - 3,600 \text{ hours}) = \$4,000 \text{ U}$$

Variable Overhead Variances

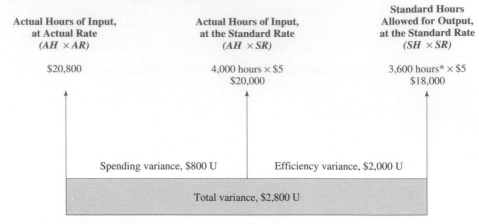

Actual Hours of Input, at Actual Rate ($AH \times AR$)	Actual Hours of Input, at the Standard Rate ($AH \times SR$)	Standard Hours Allowed for Output, at the Standard Rate ($SH \times SR$)
$20,800	4,000 hours × $5 $20,000	3,600 hours* × $5 $18,000

Spending variance, $800 U   Efficiency variance, $2,000 U

Total variance, $2,800 U

*2,000 units × 1.8 hours = 3,600 hours.

The same variances in shortcut form would be:

$$AH(AR - SR) = \text{Variable overhead spending variance}$$
$$4,000 \text{ hours}(\$5.20^* - \$5.00) = \$800 \text{ U}$$

$$^*\$20,800 \div 4,000 \text{ hours} = \$5.20$$

$$SR(AH - SH) = \text{Variable overhead efficiency variance}$$
$$\$5(4,000 \text{ hours} - 3,600 \text{ hours}) = \$2,000 \text{ U}$$

KEY TERMS FOR REVIEW

Bill of materials   A listing of the type and quantity of each item of material required in the manufacture of product. (p. 484)

Delivery cycle time   The amount of time required from receipt of an order from a customer to shipment of the completed goods. (p. 510)

Ideal standards   Standards that allow for no machine breakdowns or other work interruptions and that require peak efficiency at all times. (p. 482)

Inventory turnover   The number of times the average inventory balance has been used (and thereby replaced) during the period. (p. 509)

Labour efficiency variance   A measure of the difference between the actual hours required to complete a task and the standard hours allowed, multiplied by the standard hourly rate. (p. 497)

Labour rate variance   A measure of the difference between the actual hourly labour rate and the standard rate allowed, multiplied by the number of hours worked during the period. (p. 496)

Management by exception   A system of management in which standards are set for various operating activities, with actual results then compared against these standards. Any differences that are deemed significant are brought to the attention of management as "exceptions." (p. 480)

Manufacturing cycle efficiency (MCE)   Process (value-added) time as a percentage of throughput time. (p. 511)

Manufacturing cycle time   See *Throughput time*. (p. 510)

Materials price variance   A measure of the difference between the actual unit price paid for an item and the standard price that should have been paid, multiplied by the quantity purchased. (p. 490)

Materials quantity variance   A measure of the difference between the actual quantity of materials used in production and the standard quantity allowed, multiplied by the standard price per unit of materials. (p. 492)

Mixed variance   The dollar effect of a difference between the actual mix of materials and the budgeted mix of materials on total material cost. (p. 493)

Practical standards   Standards that allow for normal machine downtime and other work interruptions and that can be attained through reasonable, though highly efficient, efforts by the average worker at a task. (p. 482)

Standard cost card   A detailed listing of the standard amounts of materials, labour, and overhead that should go into a unit of product, multiplied by the standard price or rate that has been set. (p. 481)

Standard cost per unit   The expected cost of a unit of product as shown on the standard cost card; it is computed by multiplying the standard quantity or hours by the standard price or rate. (p. 486)

Standard hours allowed   The time that should have been taken to complete the period's output as computed by multiplying the number of units produced by the standard hours per unit. (p. 488)

Standard hours per unit   The amount of labour time that should be required to complete a single unit of product, including allowances for breaks, machine downtime, cleanup, rejects, and other normal inefficiencies. (p. 485)

Standard price per unit   The price that should be paid for a single unit of materials, including allowances for quality, quantity purchased, freight-in, receiving, and other such costs, net of any discounts allowed. (p. 483)

Standard quantity allowed   The amount of materials that should have been used to complete the period's output as computed by multiplying the number of units produced by the standard quantity per unit. (p. 488)

Standard quantity per unit   The amount of materials that should be required to complete a single unit of product, including allowances for normal waste, spoilage, rejects, and similar inefficiencies. (p. 483)

Standard rate per hour   The labour rate that should be incurred per hour of labour time, including allowances for employment taxes, fringe benefits, and other such labour costs. (p. 484)

Throughput time   The time required to turn raw materials into completed products. Also called *manufacturing cycle time* or *velocity* of production. (p. 510)

Variable overhead efficiency variance   A measure of the difference between the actual activity (direct labour-hours, machine-hours, or some other base) of a period and the standard activity allowed, multiplied by the variable part of the predetermined overhead rate. (p. 498)

Variable overhead spending variance   A measure of the difference between the actual variable overhead cost incurred during a period and the standard cost that should have been incurred, based on the actual activity of the period. (p. 498)

Variance   The difference between standard prices and quantities and actual prices and quantities (p. 487)

Velocity   A measure of the speed with which goods move through the production process. See *Throughput time.* (p. 510)

Yield variance   The portion of the quantity variance which is not the mix variance. It occurs when the actual yield differs from the standard yield expected from a given mix of inputs. (p. 494)

APPENDIX 10A: GENERAL LEDGER ENTRIES TO RECORD VARIANCES

OBJECTIVE 12

Prepare journal entries to record standard costs and variances.

Although standard costs and variances can be computed and used by management without being formally entered into the accounting records, most organizations prefer to make formal entries for three reasons. First, entry into the accounting records encourages early recognition of variances. As mentioned in the main body of the chapter, the earlier that variances can be recognized, the greater is their value to management in the control of costs. Second, formal entry tends to give variances a greater emphasis than is generally possible through informal, out-of-record computations. This emphasis gives a clear signal of management's desire to keep costs within the limits that have been set. Third, formal use of standard costs simplifies the bookkeeping process. By using standard costs within the accounting system itself, management eliminates the need to keep track of troublesome variations in actual costs and quantities, thereby providing for a flow of costs that is smoother, simpler, and more easily accounted for.

Direct Materials Variances

To illustrate the general ledger entries needed to record standard cost variances, we will return to the data contained in the review problem at the end of the chapter. The entry to record the purchase of direct materials would be:

Raw Materials (18,000 grams at $0.50)	9,000	
Materials Price Variance (18,000 grams at $0.10 U)	1,800	
Accounts Payable (18,000 grams at $0.60)		10,800

Notice that the price variance is recognized when purchases are made, rather than when materials are actually used in production. This permits the price variance to be isolated early, and it also permits the materials to be carried in the inventory account at standard cost. As direct materials are later drawn from inventory and used in production, the quantity variance is isolated as follows:

Work in Process (12,000 grams at $0.50)	6,000	
Materials Quantity Variance (2,000 grams U at $0.50)	1,000	
Raw Materials (14,000 grams at $0.50)		7,000

Thus, direct materials enter into the Work in Process account at standard cost, in terms of both price and quantity.

Notice that both the price variance and the quantity variance above are unfavourable, thereby showing up as debit (or additional cost) balances. If these variances had been favourable, they would have appeared as credit (or reduction in cost) balances, as in the case of the direct labour rate variance below.

Direct Labour Variances

Referring again to the cost data in the review problem at the end of the chapter, the general ledger entry to record the incurrence of direct labour cost would be:

Work in Process (3,600 hours at $10)	36,000	
Labour Efficiency Variance (400 hours U at $10)	4,000	
Labour Rate Variance (4,000 hours at $0.25 F)		1,000
Wages Payable (4,000 hours at $9.75)		39,000

Thus, as with direct materials, direct labour costs enter into the Work in Process account at standard, both in terms of the rate and in terms of the hours allowed for the production of the period.

Variable Overhead Variances

Variable overhead variances generally are not recorded in the accounts separately but rather are determined as part of the general analysis of overhead, which is discussed in Chapter 11.

APPENDIX 10B: LEARNING CURVES

OBJECTIVE 13

Explain the concept of learning curves.

Most workers become more proficient at their tasks the more they do them. Learning takes place especially through the early stages of a job. For example, contractors constructing a high-rise apartment building find the 20th story goes on faster than the 8th story. This effect means break-even analysis would have multiple break-even points when learning occurs because the assumption of constant worker and machine productivity stated in Chapter 7 would be violated.[19] Studies of the learning of workers suggests the pattern illustrated in Exhibit 10–13.

The learning curve represents the fact that the time spent per unit declines by a constant percentage as the number of units produced doubles. This phenomenon has been observed where new long-term production activities are undertaken or where a long production cycle is conducted, such as building construction projects, airplane manufacture, and shipbuilding. Selling prices and workforce needs, as well as standards for time, can be assessed from such an analysis. Care is needed, however, because management practices, design, production technology, and quality requirements can interfere with the actual time spent by employees. Behaviour considerations can also affect learning. Factors such as peer pressure, union imposed constraints, and the state of management-worker relationships can affect productivity and limit learning.

The functional form of the pattern in Exhibit 10–13 can be expressed as follows:

$$y = aQ^b$$

where

Q is the cumulative production in units.
b is a number representing the learning rate and expressed as follows:
   log (learning rate)/log 2
a is the hours required to produce the first unit.
y is the average time required to produce one unit.

If the learning rate is, say, 80%, then $b = \log.80/\log 2 = -.09691/.30103 = -.32193$. The pattern of an 80% learning curve is as shown in the table below. Note that every time experience doubles, the average hours to complete each unit drops to 80% of the preceding level. In other words, an 80% learning curve means that as cumulative production quantities double, the average time per unit falls by 20%.

Cumulative Quantity	Average Hours per Unit	Total Hours to Produce Cumulative Quantity
1	2	2
2	1.6(2 hours × .80)	3.2(2 × 1.6 hours)
4	1.3(1.6 hours × .80)	5.2(4 × 1.3 hours)
8	1.0(1.3 hours × .80)	8.0(8 × 1.0 hour)
16	0.8(1.0 hours × .80)	12.8(16 × 0.8 hour)
32	0.6(0.8 hour × .80)	19.2(32 × 0.6 hour)

With a computer, functional forms are often more convenient than tables. The total number of hours needed to produce Q units would be:

$$T = Qy = QaQ^b = aQ^{b+1}$$

---

[19]Woody M. Liao, "The Effects of Learning on Cost-Volume-Profit Analysis," *Cost and Management* (November–December 1983), pp. 38–40, illustrates this issue.

EXHIBIT 10–13

Learning Curve

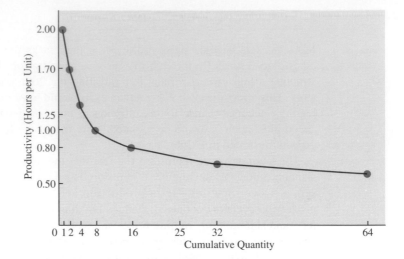

For a situation where T hours are available, the possible quantity of units that can be produced (Q) would be:

$$Q = (T/a)^x$$

where

$$x = 1/(b + 1)$$

Care is needed when using this formula. Assume, for example, a firm has produced 16 units already and wants to know the time required for another 16 units. By examining the earlier example, you can see the type of calculation required. Total time to produce 32 units is 19.2 hours. Total time to produce 16 units is 12.8 hours. Therefore, the last 16 units would take (19.2 – 12.8) or 6.4 hours; that is, 0.4 hours per unit. Mathematically, the exact answer can be determined by the following difference:

$$IT = a(Q_2)^{b+1} - a(Q_1)^{b+1}$$

where IT is the incremental time required, the 6.4 hours.

Interestingly, regression analysis, as described in Chapter 6, can be used to derive the parameters of a learning curve of the past history of an operation.

$$T = aQ^{b+1}$$

is the same as:

$$\log(T) = \log(a) + (b+1)\log(Q)$$

If each T value and each Q amount is logged, a regression result can be calculated for the slope ($b+1$) and the intercept, log a. The regression value for log a can be converted to a by the following calculation, $10^{(\log a)}$, the y^x calculation on most standard hand calculators. The purpose of the log function is to convert the curved line displayed in Exhibit 10–13 into a straight line so that the linear regression gives an accurate result.

Learning curves can serve as a method of setting and revising standard labour hours in a repetitive task environment. The use of the approach would be most appropriate where many workers are learning a task over a reasonably extended period of time. Short-run learning effects can be dealt with within a single accounting period using an average performance rate. Single employees can have labour efficiency variances occurring during their learning periods without serious inaccuracies being introduced to the standard cost variances. However, large groups functioning at the same stage, particularly early in a production sequence when the effects of learning are pronounced, need evaluation relative to their projected learning curve. Incorporating the learning curve times into the standard times should help avoid misleading standard cost variances.

It should be borne in mind that learning curve phenomena are applicable for labour-intensive manufacturing. Learning curve effects were originally studied in connection with aircraft manufacture in World War II. The learning curve has typically been employed in industries such as construction, shipbuilding, and electronics. In the new manufacturing environment, learning curves have less relevance. Automated manufacturing is unlikely to have much variation or to display a regular learning curve. In less-automated processes, however, where learning curves do occur, it is important to take the resulting decline in labour hours and costs into account in setting standards, determining prices, planning production, or setting up work schedules.

QUESTIONS

10–1   What types of organizations make use of standard costs?

10–2   What is a quantity standard? What is a price standard?

10–3   What is the beginning point in setting a standard? Where should final responsibility for standard setting fall?

10–4   Why must a standard for the future be more than simply a projection of the past?

10–5   Distinguish between ideal and practical standards.

10–6   If employees are unable to meet a standard, what effect would you expect this to have on their productivity?

10–7   What is meant by the term *variance?*

10–8   What is meant by the term *management by exception?*

10–9   Why are variances generally segregated in terms of a price variance and a quantity variance?

10–10 Who is generally responsible for the materials price variance? The materials quantity variance? The labour efficiency variance?

10–11 The materials price variance can be computed at what two different points in time? Which point is better? Why?

10–12 An examination of the cost records of the Chittenden Furniture Company reveals that the materials price variance is favourable but that the materials quantity variance is unfavourable by a substantial amount. What might this indicate?

10–13 What dangers lie in using standards as punitive tools?

10–14 "Our workers are all under labour contracts; therefore, our labour rate variance is bound to be zero." Discuss.

10–15 What effect, if any, would you expect poor quality materials to have on direct labour variances?

10–16 If variable manufacturing overhead is applied to production on a basis of direct labour-hours and the direct labour efficiency variance is unfavourable, will the variable overhead efficiency variance be favourable or unfavourable, or could it be either? Explain.

10–17 What is a statistical control chart, and how is it used?

10–18 How does the nature, computation, and use of performance measures in an automated environment differ from the nature, computation, and use of standard costs?

10–19 Into what five general groupings can the operating performance measures be placed?

10–20 What danger is there in trying to keep the use of equipment at 100% of available capacity in all operations?

10–21 What is the difference between the delivery cycle time and the throughput time? What four elements make up the throughput time? Into what two classes can these four elements be placed?

10–22 If a company has an MCE of less than 1, what does it mean? How would you interpret an MCE of 0.40?

10–23 (Appendix 10A) What advantages can be cited in favour of making formal journal entries in the accounting records for variances?

10–24 What is a mix variance?

10–25 Can standard costs be used for financial accounting purposes? Explain.

10–26 (Appendix 10B) What is a learning curve?

10–27 (Appendix 10B) If production workers perform according to a 70% learning curve, what pattern of labour times does this suggest?

10–28 (Appendix 10B) The cost function for Lapp Co. reflects a 75% learning curve. The average time to complete a task with 50 units is 6 minutes. What is the projected time to complete the next 100 units?

EXERCISES

E10–1 Sonne Company produces a perfume called Whim. The direct materials and direct labour standards for one bottle of Whim are given below:

	Standard Quantity or Hours	Standard Price or Rate	Standard Cost
Direct materials	7.2 millilitres	$2.50 per millilitre	$18
Direct labour	0.4 hours	$10 per hour	4

During the most recent month, the following activity was recorded:
a. Twenty litres of material were purchased at a cost of $2.40 per mL.
b. All of the material was used to produce 2,500 bottles of Whim.
c. Nine hundred hours of direct labour time were recorded at a total labour cost of $10,800.

Required
1. Compute the direct materials price and quantity variances for the month.
2. Compute the direct labour rate and efficiency variances for the month.

E10–2 Refer to the data in E10–1. Assume that instead of producing 2,500 bottles of Whim during the month, the company produced only 2,000 bottles using 16,000 litres of material in the production process. (The rest of the material purchased remained in inventory.)

Required
Compute the direct materials price and quantity variances for the month.

E10–3 Topper Toys has developed a new toy called the Brainbuster. The company has a standard cost system to help control costs and has established the following standards for the Brainbuster toy:

> Direct materials: 8 diodes per toy at $0.30 per diode
> Direct labour: 1.2 hours per toy at $7 per hour

During August, the company produced 5,000 Brainbuster toys. Production data on the toy for August follow:

Direct materials: 70,000 diodes were purchased for use in production at a cost of $0.28 per diode. Some 20,000 of these diodes were still in inventory at the end of the month.
Direct labour: 6,400 direct labour-hours were worked at a cost of $48,000.

Required
1. Compute the following variances for August:
    a. Direct materials price and quantity variances.
    b. Direct labour rate and efficiency variances.
2. Prepare a brief explanation of the significance and possible causes of each variance.

E10–4 As business organizations grow in size and complexity, cost control becomes more difficult. A system to provide information and assist in cost control is imperative for effective management. Management by exception is one technique that is often used to foster cost control.

Required

1. Describe how a standard cost system helps to make management by exception possible.
2. Discuss the potential benefits of management by exception to an organization.
3. Identify and discuss the behavioural problems that might occur in an organization using standard costs and management by exception.

(CMA, adapted)

E10–5 Harmon Household Products, Inc., manufactures a number of consumer items for general household use. One of these products, a chopping board, requires an expensive hardwood in its manufacture. During a recent month, the company manufactured 4,000 chopping boards using 11,000 board feet of hardwood in the process. The hardwood cost the company $18,700.

The company's standards for one chopping board are 2.5 board feet of hardwood, at a cost of $1.80 per board foot.

Required

1. What cost for wood should have been incurred in the manufacture of the 4,000 chopping blocks? How much greater or less is this than the cost that was incurred?
2. Break down the difference computed in (1) above in terms of a materials price variance and a materials quantity variance.

E10–6 Hollowell Audio, Inc., manufactures compact discs. The company uses standards to control its costs. The labour standards that have been set for one disc are as follows:

Standard Hours	Standard Rate per Hour	Standard Cost
24 minutes	$6.00	$2.40

During July, 8,500 hours of direct labour time were recorded in the manufacture of 20,000 discs. The direct labour cost totalled $49,300 for the month.

Required

1. What direct labour cost should have been incurred in the manufacture of the 20,000 discs? By how much does this differ from the cost that was incurred?
2. Break down the difference in cost from (1) above into a labour rate variance and a labour efficiency variance.
3. The budgeted variable manufacturing overhead rate is $4 per direct labour-hour. During July, the company incurred $39,100 in variable manufacturing overhead cost. Compute the variable overhead spending and efficiency variances for the month.

E10–7 Svenska Pharmicia, a Swedish pharmaceutical company, makes an anticoagulant drug. The main ingredient in the drug is a raw material called Alpha SR40. Information concerning the purchase and use of Alpha SR40 follows:

Purchase of Alpha SR40: The raw material Alpha SR40 is purchased in 2-kilogram containers at a cost of 3,000 Kr per kilogram. (The Swedish currency is the krona, which is abbreviated as Kr.) Discount terms of 2/10, n/30 are offered by the supplier, and Svenska Pharmicia takes all discounts. Shipping costs, which Svenska Pharmicia must pay, amount to 1,000 Kr for an average shipment of ten 2-kilogram containers.

Use of Alpha SR40: The bill of materials calls for 6 grams of Alpha SR40 per capsule of the anticoagulant drug. About 4% of all Alpha SR40 purchased is rejected as unsuitable before being used to make the anticoagulant drug. In addition, after the addition of Alpha SR40, about 1 out of every 26 capsules is rejected at final inspection, due to defects of one sort or another in the capsule.

Required

1. Compute the standard purchase price for one gram of Alpha SR40.
2. Compute the standard quantity of Alpha SR40 (in grams) per capsule that passes final inspection. (Carry computations to two decimal places.)
3. Using the data from (1) and (2) above, prepare a standard cost card showing the standard cost of Alpha SR40 per capsule of the anticoagulant drug.

E10–8 The Worldwide Credit Card, Inc., uses standards to control the labour time involved in opening mail from card holders and recording the enclosed remittances. Incoming mail is gathered into batches, and a standard time is set for opening and recording each batch. The labour standards relating to one batch are given below:

	Standard Hours	Standard Rate	Standard Cost
Per batch............	2.5	$6	$15

The record showing the time spent last week in opening batches of mail has been misplaced. However, the batch supervisor recalls that 168 batches were received and opened during the week, and the controller recalls the following variance data relating to these batches:

Total labour variance..........	$330 U
Labour rate variance	150 F

Required

1. Determine the number of actual labour-hours spent opening batches during the week.
2. Determine the actual hourly rate paid to employees for opening batches last week.

(Hint: A useful way to proceed would be to work from known to unknown data either by using the variance formulas or by using the columnar format shown in Exhibit 10–6.)

E10–9 Lipex, Inc., is interested in cutting the amount of time between when a customer places an order and when the order is completed. For the first quarter of the year, the following data were reported:

Inspection time.............	0.5 days
Process time...............	2.8 days
Wait time	16.0 days
Queue time................	4.0 days
Move time	0.7 days

Management is unsure how to use these data to measure performance and control operations.

Required

1. Compute the throughput time, or velocity of production.
2. Compute the manufacturing cycle efficiency (MCE) for the quarter. How do you interpret the MCE?
3. What percentage of the throughput time was spent in non-value-added activities?
4. Compute the delivery cycle time.
5. If by use of JIT all queue time can be eliminated in production, what would be the new MCE?

E10–10 (Appendix 10A) Aspen Products, Inc., began production of product A on April 1. The company uses a standard cost system and has established the following standards for one unit of product A:

	Standard Quantity	Standard Price or Rate	Standard Cost
Direct materials...........	3.5 metres	$6 per m	$21
Direct labour	0.4 hours	$10 per hour	4

During April, the following activity was recorded relative to product A:
a. Purchased 7,000 metres of material at a cost of $5.75 per m.
b. Used 6,000 metres of material to produce 1,500 units of product A.
c. Worked 725 direct labour-hours on product A at a cost of $8,120.

Required

1. For materials:
   a. Compute the direct materials price and quantity variances.
   b. Prepare journal entries to record the purchase of materials and the use of materials in production.
2. For direct labour:
   a. Compute the direct labour rate and efficiency variances.
   b. Prepare journal entries to record the incurrence of direct labour cost for the month.

3. Post the entries you have prepared to the T-accounts below:

Raw Materials		Accounts Payable	
?	?		40,250
Bal. ?			

Materials Price Variance		Wages Payable	
			8,120

Materials Quantity Variance		Labour Rate Variance	

Work in Process—Product A		Labour Efficiency Variance	
Materials used ?			
Labour cost ?			

PROBLEMS

P10–11   Straightforward Variance Analysis   Barberry, Inc., manufactures a product called Fruta. The company uses a standard cost system and has established the following standards for one unit of Fruta:

	Standard Quantity	Standard Price or Rate	Standard Cost
Direct materials	1.5 kilograms	$6 per kilogram	$9.00
Direct labour	0.6 hours	$12 per hour	7.20
Variable manufacturing overhead	0.6 hours	$2.50 per hour	1.50
			$17.70

During June, the company recorded this activity relative to production of Fruta:
a.   The company produced 3,000 units during June.
b.   A total of 8,000 kilograms of material were purchased at a cost of $46,000.
c.   There was no beginning inventory of materials on hand to start the month; at the end of the month, 2,000 kilograms of material remained in the warehouse unused.
d.   The company employs 10 persons to work on the production of Fruta. During June, each worked an average of 160 hours at an average rate of $12.50 per hour.
e.   Variable manufacturing overhead is assigned to Fruta on the basis of direct labour-hours. Variable manufacturing overhead costs during June totalled $3,600.

The company's management is anxious to determine the efficiency of the activities surrounding the production of Fruta.

Required

1.   For materials used in the production of Fruta:
  a.   Compute the price and quantity variances.
  b.   The materials were purchased from a new supplier who is anxious to enter into a long-term purchase contract. Would you recommend that the company sign the contract? Explain.

2. For labour employed in the production of Fruta:
   a. Compute the rate and efficiency variances.
   b. In the past, the 10 persons employed in the production of Fruta consisted of 4 senior workers and 6 assistants. During June, the company experimented with 5 senior workers and 5 assistants. Would you recommend that the new labour mix be continued? Explain.
3. Compute the variable overhead spending and efficiency variances. What relationship can you see between this efficiency variance and the labour efficiency variance?

P10–12   Hospital; Basic Variance Analysis   "What's going on in that lab?" asked Derek Warren, chief administrator for Cottonwood Hospital, as he studied the prior month's reports. "Every month the lab teeters between a profit and a loss. Are we going to have to increase our lab fees again?"

"We can't," replied Lois Ankers, the controller. "We're getting *lots* of complaints about the last increase, particularly from the insurance companies and governmental health units. They're now paying only about 80% of what we bill. I'm beginning to think the problem is on the cost side."

To determine if lab costs are in line with other hospitals, Mr. Warren has asked you to evaluate the costs for the past month. Ms. Ankers has provided you with the following information:

a. Two basic types of tests are performed in the lab—smears and blood tests. During the past month, 2,700 smears and 900 blood tests were performed in the lab.
b. Small glass plates are used in both types of tests. During the past month, the hospital purchased 16,000 plates at a cost of $38,400. This cost is net of a 4% quantity discount. A total of 2,000 of these plates were still on hand unused at the end of the month; there were no plates on hand at the beginning of the month.
c. During the past month, 1,800 hours of labour time were used in performing smears and blood tests. The cost of this labour time was $18,450.
d. Variable overhead cost last month in the lab for utilities and supplies totalled $11,700.

Cottonwood Hospital has never used standard costs. By searching industry literature, however, you have determined the following nationwide averages for hospital labs:

Plates: Three plates are required per lab test. These plates cost $2.50 each and are disposed of after the test is completed.
Labour: Each smear should require 0.3 hours to complete, and each blood test should require 0.6 hours to complete. The average cost of this lab time is $12 per hour.
Overhead: Overhead cost is based on direct labour-hours. The average rate of variable overhead is $6 per hour.

Mr. Warren would like a complete analysis of the cost of plates, labour, and variable overhead in the lab for the last month so that he can determine if costs in the lab are indeed out of line.

Required

1. Compute the materials price variance for the plates purchased last month, and compute a materials quantity variance for the plates used last month.
2. For labour cost in the lab:
   a. Compute a labour rate variance and a labour efficiency variance.
   b. In most hospitals, three-fourths of the workers in the lab are certified technicians and one-fourth are assistants. In an effort to reduce costs, Cottonwood Hospital employs only one-half certified technicians and one-half assistants. Would you recommend that this policy be continued? Explain.
3. Compute the variable overhead spending and efficiency variances. Is there any relationship between the variable overhead efficiency variance and the labour efficiency variance? Explain.

P10–13 Basic Variance Analysis   Sault Company's Ironton Plant produces precast ingots for industrial use. Carlos Santiago, who was recently appointed general manager of the Ironton Plant, has just been handed the plant's income statement for October. The statement is shown below:

	Budgeted	Actual
Sales (5,000 ingots)	$250,000	$250,000
Less variable expenses:		
Variable cost of goods sold*	80,000	96,390
Variable selling expenses	20,000	20,000
Total variable expenses	100,000	116,390
Contribution margin	150,000	133,610
Less fixed expenses:		
Manufacturing overhead	60,000	60,000
Selling and administrative	75,000	75,000
Total fixed expenses	135,000	135,000
Net income (loss)	$15,000	$ (1,390)

*Contains direct materials, direct labour, and variable manufacturing overhead.

Mr. Santiago was shocked to see the loss for the month, particularly since sales were exactly as budgeted. He stated, "I sure hope the plant has a standard cost system in operation. If it doesn't, I won't have the slightest idea of where to start looking for the problem."

The plant does use a standard cost system, with the following standard variable cost per ingot:

	Standard Quantity or Hours	Standard Price or Rate	Standard Cost
Direct materials	4.0 kilograms	$2.50 per kilogram	$10.00
Direct labour	0.6 hours	$9.00 per hour	5.40
Variable manufacturing overhead	0.3 hours*	$2.00 per hour	0.60
Total standard variable cost................			$16.00

*Based on machine-hours.

Mr. Santiago has determined that during October the plant produced 5,000 ingots and incurred the following costs:

a. Purchased 25,000 kilograms of materials at a cost of $2.95 per kilogram. There were no raw materials in inventory at the beginning of the month.
b. Used 19,800 kilograms of materials in production. (Finished goods and work in process inventories are insignificant and can be ignored.)
c. Worked 3,600 direct labour-hours at a cost of $8.70 per hour.
d. Incurred a total variable manufacturing overhead cost of $4,320 for the month. A total of 1,800 machine-hours was recorded.

It is the company's policy to close all variances to cost of goods sold on a monthly basis.

Required

1. Compute the following variances for October:
    a. Direct materials price and quantity variances.
    b. Direct labour rate and efficiency variances.
    c. Variable manufacturing overhead spending and efficiency variances.
2. Summarize the variances that you computed in (1) above by showing the net overall favourable or unfavourable variance for October. What impact did this figure have on the company's income statement?
3. Pick out the two most significant variances that you computed in (1) above. Explain to Mr. Santiago the possible causes of these variances so that he will know where to concentrate his and his subordinates' time.

P10-14 Variances; Unit Costs; Journal Entries (Appendix 10A) Truro Mills, Inc., is a large producer of men's and women's clothing. The company uses standard costs for all of its products. The standard costs and actual costs for a recent period are given below for one of the company's product lines (per unit of product):

	Standard Cost	Actual Cost
Direct materials:		
Standard: 4.0 metres at $3.60 per m	$14.40	
Actual:4.4 metres at $3.35 per m		$14.74
Direct labour:		
Standard: 1.6 hours at $4.50 per hour	7.20	
Actual: 1.4 hours at $4.85 per hour		6.79
Variable manufacturing overhead:		
Standard: 1.6 hours at $1.80 per hour	$ 2.88	
Actual: 1.4 hours at $2.15 per hour		$ 3.01
Total cost per unit	$24.48	$24.54

During this period, the company produced 4,800 units of product. A comparison of standard and actual costs for the period on a total cost basis is given below:

Actual costs: 4,800 units at $24.54	$117,792
Standard costs: 4,800 units at $24.48	117,504
Difference in cost—unfavourable	$ 288

There was no inventory of materials on hand to start the period. During the period, 21,120 metres of materials were purchased, all of which were used in production.

Required

1. For direct materials:
   a. Compute the price and quantity variances for the period.
   b. Prepare journal entries to record all activity relating to direct materials for the period.
2. For direct labour:
   a. Compute the rate and efficiency variances.
   b. Prepare a journal entry to record the incurrence of direct labour cost for the period.
3. Compute the variable manufacturing overhead spending and efficiency variances.
4. On seeing the $288 total cost variance, the company's president stated, "This variance of $288 is only 0.2% of the $117,504 standard cost for the period. It's obvious that our costs are well under control." Do you agree? Explain.
5. State possible causes of each variance that you have computed.

P10-15 Operating Performance Measures MacIntyre Fabrications, Ltd., of Aberdeen Scotland has recently begun a continuous improvement campaign in conjunction with a move toward JIT production and purchasing. Management has developed new performance measures as part of this campaign. The following operating data have been gathered over the last four months:

	Month			
	1	2	3	4
Quality control measures:				
Customer complaints as a percentage of units sold	1.8%	1.6%	1.5%	1.4%
Warranty claims as a percentage of units sold	3.6%	3.1%	2.9%	2.8%
Defects as percentage of units produced	2.1%	1.7%	1.6%	1.4%
Material control measures:				
Purchase order lead time (days)	10	7	4	2
Scrap as a percentage of total cost	1.2%	1.0%	0.9%	0.7%
Inventory control measures:				
Raw materials turnover (times)	10	11	14	18
Finished goods turnover (times)	9	8	9	8

	Month			
	1	**2**	**3**	**4**
Machine performance measures:				
Percentage of machine downtime........................	22%	18%	14%	13%
Use as a percentage of availability.......................	65%	62%	59%	58%
Average setup time (hours)............................	5.4	5.2	3.5	3.1
Delivery performance measures:				
Throughput time, or velocity	?	?	?	?
Manufacturing cycle efficiency	?	?	?	?
Delivery cycle time	?	?	?	?
Percentage of on-time deliveries	72%	73%	78%	85%
Total throughput (units)	10,540	10,570	10,550	10,490

Management would like to know the company's throughput time, manufacturing cycle efficiency, and delivery cycle time. The data to compute these measures have been gathered and appear below:

	Month			
	1	**2**	**3**	**4**
Move time per unit, in days..............	0.5	0.5	0.4	0.5
Process time per unit, in days	0.6	0.5	0.5	0.4
Wait time per order before start				
of production, in days	9.6	8.7	5.3	4.7
Queue time per unit, in days	3.6	3.6	2.6	1.7
Inspection time per unit, in days	0.7	0.7	0.4	0.3

As part of its continuous improvement program, the company is planning to move toward a JIT purchasing and production system.

Required

1. For each month, compute the following operating performance measures:
   a. The throughput time, or velocity of production.
   b. The manufacturing cycle efficiency (MCE).
   c. The delivery cycle time.
2. Using the performance measures given in the problem and those you computed in (1) above, identify whether the trend over the four months is generally favourable, generally unfavourable, or mixed. What areas apparently require improvement and how might they be improved?
3. Refer to the move time, process time, and so forth, given above for month 4.
   a. Assume that in month 5 the move time, process time, and so forth, are the same as for month 4, except that through the implementation of JIT, the company is able to completely eliminate the queue time during production. Compute the new throughput time and MCE.
   b. Assume that in month 6 the move time, process time, and so forth, are the same as for month 4, except that the company is able to completely eliminate both the queue time during production and the inspection time. Compute the new throughput time and MCE.

P10–16 Computations from Incomplete Data Topaz Company produces a single product. The company has set standards as follows for materials and labour:

	Direct Materials	Direct Labour
Standard quantity or hours per unit	? kilograms	2.5 hours
Standard price or rate......................	? per kilogram	$9 per hour
Standard cost per unit......................	?	$22.50

During the past month, the company purchased 6,000 kilograms of direct materials at a cost of $16,500. All of this material was used in the production of 1,400 units of product. Direct labour cost totalled $28,500 for the month. The following variances have been computed:

Materials quantity variance	$1,200 U
Total materials variance	300 F
Labour efficiency variance...........	4,500 F

Required

1. For direct materials:
   a. Compute the standard price per kilogram for materials.
   b. Compute the standard quantity allowed for materials for the month's production.
   c. Compute the standard quantity of materials allowed per unit of product.
2. For direct labour:
   a. Compute the actual direct labour cost per hour for the month.
   b. Compute the labour rate variance.

(Hint: In completing the problem, it may be helpful to move from known to unknown data either by using the variance formulas or by using the columnar format shown in Exhibits 10–4 and 10–6.)

P10–17 Standards and Variances from Incomplete Data   Vitalite, Inc., produces a number of products, including a body-wrap kit. Standard variable costs relating to a single kit are given below:

	Standard Quantity or Hours	Standard Price or Rate	Standard Cost
Direct materials............................	?	$6 per metre	$?
Direct labour..............................	?	?	?
Variable manufacturing overhead..............	?	$2 per hour	?
Total standard cost per kit..................			$42

During August, 500 kits were manufactured and sold. Selected information relating to the month's production is given below:

	Materials Used	Direct Labour	Variable Manufacturing Overhead
Total standard cost*	$?	$8,000	$1,600
Actual costs incurred	10,000	?	1,620
Materials price variance	? U		
Materials quantity variance	600 U		
Labour rate variance		?	
Labour efficiency variance		?	
Overhead spending variance			?
Overhead efficiency variance			?

*For the month's production.

The following additional information is available for August production of kits:

Actual direct labour-hours	900
Overhead is based on	Direct labour-hours
Difference between standard and actual cost per kit produced during August	$0.14 U

Required

1. What was the total standard cost of the materials used during August?
2. How many metres of material are required at standard per kit?
3. What was the materials price variance for August?
4. What is the standard direct labour rate per hour?
5. What was the labour rate variance for August? The labour efficiency variance?
6. What was the overhead spending variance for August? The overhead efficiency variance?
7. Complete the standard cost card for one kit shown at the beginning of the problem.

P10–18 Developing Standard Costs   L'Essence is a small cosmetics company located in the perfume centre of Grasse in southern France. The company plans to introduce a new body oil, called Energique, for which it needs to develop a standard product cost. The following information is available on the production of Energique:

a. The Energique base is made by mixing select lanolin and alcohol. Some loss in volume occurs for both the lanolin and the alcohol during the mixing process. As a result, each 100-litre batch of Energique base requires 100 litres of lanolin and 8 litres of alcohol.

b. After the base has been prepared, a highly concentrated lilac powder is added to impart a pleasing scent. Only 200 grams of the powder is added to each 100-litre batch. The addition of the lilac powder does not affect the total liquid volume.

c. Both the lanolin and the lilac powder are subject to some contamination from naturally occurring materials. For example, the lilac powder often contains some traces of insects that are not detected and removed when the lilac petals are processed. Occasionally such contaminants interact in ways that result in an unacceptable product with an unpleasant odor. About one 100-litre batch in twenty-one is rejected as unsuitable for sale for this reason and is thrown away.

d. It takes a worker two hours to process one 100-litre batch of Energique. Employees work an eight-hour day, including two hours per day for lunch, rest breaks, and cleanup.

Required

1. Determine the standard quantity for each of the raw materials needed to produce an acceptable 100-litre batch of Energique.

2. Determine the standard labour time to produce an acceptable 100-litre batch of Energique.

3. The standard prices for the materials and the labour in French francs (FF) appear below:

Lanolin	80 FF per litre
Alcohol	10 FF per litre
Lilac powder	5 FF per gram
Direct labour cost	60 FF per hour

Prepare a standard cost card for materials and labour for one acceptable 100-litre batch of Energique.

(CMA, adapted)

P10–19 Operating Performance Measures Exeter Corporation has recently begun a continuous improvement campaign. As a consequence, there have been many changes in operating procedures. Progress has been slow, particularly in trying to develop new performance measures for the factory.

Management has been gathering the following data over the past four months:

	Month			
	1	**2**	**3**	**4**
Quality control measures:				
Customer complaints as a percentage of units sold	1.4%	1.3%	1.1%	1.0%
Warranty claims as a percentage of units sold	2.3%	2.1%	2.0%	1.8%
Defects as a percentage of units produced	4.6%	4.2%	3.7%	3.4%
Material control measures:				
Scrap as a percentage of total cost	3.2%	2.9%	3.0%	2.7%
Inventory control measures:				
Raw materials turnover (times)	1.5	1.6	1.5	1.5
Finished goods turnover (times)	1.4	1.3	1.3	1.2
Machine performance measures:				
Percentage of machine availability	80%	82%	81%	79%
Use as a percentage of availability	75%	73%	71%	70%
Average setup time (hours)	2.7	2.5	2.5	2.6
Delivery performance measures:				
Throughput time, or velocity	?	?	?	?
Manufacturing cycle efficiency	?	?	?	?
Delivery cycle time	?	?	?	?
Percentage of on-time deliveries	84%	87%	91%	95%

The president has attended conferences at which the importance of throughput time, manufacturing cycle efficiency, and delivery cycle time were stressed, but no one at the company is sure how they are computed. The data to compute these measures have been gathered and appear below:

	Month			
	1	2	3	4
Wait time per order before start of production, in days	16.7	15.2	12.3	9.6
Inspection time per unit, in days	0.1	0.3	0.6	0.8
Process time per unit, in days	0.6	0.6	0.6	0.6
Queue time per unit, in days	5.6	5.7	5.6	5.7
Move time per unit, in days	1.4	1.3	1.3	1.4

As part of its continuous improvement program, the company is planning to move toward a JIT purchasing and production system.

Required

1. For each month, compute the following operating performance measures:
   a. The throughput time, or velocity of production.
   b. The manufacturing cycle efficiency (MCE).
   c. The delivery cycle time.
2. Using the performance measures given in the problem and those you computed in (1) above, do the following:
   a. Identify the areas where the company seems to be improving.
   b. Identify the areas where the company seems to be deteriorating or stagnating.
   c. Explain why you think some specific areas are improving while others are not.
3. Refer to the move time, process time, and so forth, given above for month 4.
   a. Assume that in month 5 the move time, process time, and so forth, are the same as for month 4, except that through the implementation of JIT, the company is able to completely eliminate the queue time during production. Compute the new throughput time and MCE.
   b. Assume that in month 6 the move time, process time, and so forth, are the same as for month 4, except that the company is able to completely eliminate both the queue time during production and the inspection time. Compute the new throughput time and MCE.

P10–20 Operating Measures and Standard Costs   PC Deco is a small company that makes an attractive and popular solid wood computer desk. Based on the recommendations of the plant manager and the purchasing agent, the president of the company, Tom Hanson, had approved changing over to a JIT production and purchasing system. He was, however, very unhappy with the latest monthly standard cost variance report for the plant.

Tom opened the first management meeting of the month with the following challenge: "I thought JIT was supposed to make us more efficient, but just look at last month's efficiency report. The labour efficiency variance was $50,000 unfavourable. That's nearly five times higher than it's ever been before! If you add on the $29,000 unfavourable material price variance, that's over $79,000 down the drain in a single month! What's going on here?"

"We knew when we adopted JIT that our material costs would go up somewhat," replied Beth Chin, the company's purchasing agent. "But we've negotiated long-term contracts with our very best suppliers, and they're making defect-free deliveries three times a day. In a few months we'll be able to offset all of our higher purchasing costs by completely vacating the warehouse we had been renting."

"And I know our labour efficiency variance looks bad," responded Jose Martin, the plant manager, "but it doesn't tell the whole story. We eliminated the inspection and maintenance positions and turned them all into direct labour workers. And with JIT flow lines and our new equipment, we've never been more efficient in the plant."

"How can you say you're efficient when you took 35,000 direct labour-hours to produce just 20,000 desks last month?" asked Tom Hanson. "That works out to be 1.75 hours per desk, but according to the standard cost card, you should be able to produce a desk in just 1.5 hours. Do you call that efficient?"

"There are several reasons for that," answered Jose, "but the biggest reason is that we don't want to make desks just to keep everyone busy. Under the JIT approach, we start production only when we have an order."

"Well, you've got an order now!" roared Tom Hanson, "I've been looking at these reports for nearly 20 years, and I know inefficiency when I see it. Let's get things back under control!"

After leaving Tom Hanson's office, Jose has approached you for help in explaining to the president why the efficiency report is at odds with the actual progress in the plant. Working with Jose, you have gathered the following information:

a.   The standard cost card for the desks is given below:

	Standard Quantity or Hours	Standard Price or Rate	Standard Cost
Direct materials	15 board feet	$ 2.00 per board foot	$30.00
Direct labour	1.5 hours	10.00 per hour	15.00
Variable manufacturing overhead	1.5 hours	4.00 per hour	6.00
Total standard cost			$51.00

b.   During June, the most recent month, the company purchased 290,000 board feet of material at a cost of $2.10 per board foot. All of this material was used in the production of 20,000 desks during the month.

c.   The company maintains a stable workforce. Persons who previously were inspectors and on the maintenance crew have been reassigned as direct labour workers. During June, 35,000 hours were logged by direct labour workers. The average pay rate was $9.80 per hour.

d.   Variable manufacturing overhead cost is applied on the basis of direct labour-hours. During June, the company incurred $118,000 in variable manufacturing overhead costs.

e.   The following operating data has been gathered:

Processing: As workers have become more familiar with the new equipment and procedures, average processing time per unit has declined over the last three months from 1.6 hours in April, to 1.5 hours in May, to 1.3 hours in June.

Inspection: Workers are now directly responsible for quality control, which accounts for the following changes in inspection time per unit over the last three months: April, 0.3 hours; May, 0.2 hours; and June, 0.1 hours.

Movement of goods: With the change to JIT flow lines, goods now move shorter distances between workstations. Move time per unit over the past three months has been: April, 3.2 hours; May, 2.7 hours; and June, 1.2 hours.

Queue time: Better coordination of production with demand has resulted in less queue time as goods move along the production line. The average queue time per unit for the last three months has been: April, 14.9 hours; May, 10.6 hours; and June, 3.9 hours.

Required

1.   Compute the materials price and quantity variances using traditional variance analysis. Is the decrease in waste apparent in this computation? Explain. If the company wants to compute the materials price variance, what should be done to make this computation more appropriate?

2.   Compute the direct labour rate and efficiency variances using traditional variance analysis. Do you agree with Tom Hanson that the efficiency variance is still appropriate as a measure of performance for the company? Explain why you do or do not agree.

3.   Compute the variable manufacturing overhead spending and efficiency variances using traditional variance analysis. Would you expect that a correlation still exists between direct labour and the incurrence of variable manufacturing overhead cost in the company? Explain, using data from your variance computations to support your position.

4.   Compute the following for April, May, and June:
   a.   The throughput time per unit.
   b.   The manufacturing cycle efficiency (MCE).

5.   Which performance measure do you think is more appropriate in this situation—the labour efficiency variance or the throughput time per unit and manufacturing cycle efficiency?

P10–21 Variance Analysis: Multiple Lots   Ricardo Shirts, Inc., manufactures short-
and long-sleeved men's shirts for large stores. Ricardo produces a single-quality shirt in lots to
each customer's order and attaches the store's label to each shirt. The standard direct costs for
a dozen long-sleeved shirts include:

Direct materials:	24 metres at $0.65	$15.60
Direct labour:	3 hours at $7.25	21.75

During April, Ricardo worked on three orders for long-sleeved shirts. Job cost records for
the month disclose the following:

Lot	Units in Lot (dozens)	Materials Used (metres)	Hours Worked
30.	1,000	24,100	2,980
31.	1,700	40,440	5,130
32.	1,200	28,825	2,890

The following additional information is available:
a. Ricardo purchased 95,000 metres of material during April at a cost of $66,500.
b. Direct labour cost incurred amounted to $80,740 during April.
c. There was no work in process at April 1. During April, lots 30 and 31 were completed. At
April 30, lot 32 was 100% complete as to materials but only 80% complete as to labour.

Required

1. Compute the materials price variance for April, and show whether the variance was
favourable or unfavourable.
2. Determine the materials quantity variance for April in both metres and dollars:
a. For the company in total.
b. For each lot worked on during the month.
3. Compute the labour rate variance for April, and show whether the variance was
favourable or unfavourable.
4. Determine the labour efficiency variance for April in both hours and dollars:
a. For the company in total.
b. For each lot worked on during the month.
5. In what situations might it be better to express variances in units (hours, metres, and so
on) rather than in dollars? In dollars rather than in units?

(CPA, adapted)

P10–22 Variance Analysis; Incomplete Data; Journal Entries   (Appendix
10A) Topline Surf Boards manufactures a single product. The standard cost of one unit of this
product is as follows:

Direct materials: 6 board feet at $1.	$6.00
Direct labour: 1 hour at $4.50.	4.50
Variable manufacturing overhead: 1 hour at $3	3.00
Total standard variable cost per unit	$13.50

During October, 6,000 units were produced. Selected cost data relating to the month's production follow:

Material purchased: 60,000 board feet at $0.95	$57,000
Material used in production: 38,000 board feet	—
Direct labour: _?_ hours at $ _?_ per hour	27,950
Variable manufacturing overhead cost incurred	20,475
Variable manufacturing overhead efficiency variance	1,500 U

There was no beginning inventory of raw materials. The variable manufacturing overhead rate
is based on direct labour-hours.

Required

1. For direct materials:
a. Compute the price and quantity variances for October.
b. Prepare journal entries to record activity for October.

2. For direct labour:
    a. Compute the rate and efficiency variances for October.
    b. Prepare a journal entry to record labour activity for October.
3. For variable manufacturing overhead:
    a. Compute the spending variance for October, and verify the efficiency variance given above.
    b. If manufacturing overhead is applied to production on the basis of direct labour-hours, is it possible to have a favourable direct labour efficiency variance and an unfavourable variable overhead efficiency variance? Explain.
4. State possible causes of each variance that you have computed.

P10–23 Developing Standard Costs   Le Forestier, S.A., is a small company that processes wild mushrooms found in the forests of central France. For many years, Le Forestier's products have had strong sales in France. However, companies from other countries in the European common market such as Italy and Spain have begun marketing similar products in France, and price competition has become increasingly important. Jean Leveque, the company's controller, is planning to implement a standard cost system for Le Forestier and has gathered considerable information from the purchasing and production managers concerning production and material requirements for Le Forestier's products. Leveque believes that the use of standard costing will allow Le Forestier to improve cost control and thereby better compete with the new entrants into the French market.

Le Forestier's most popular product is dried chanterelle mushrooms, which are sold in small vacuum-packed jars. Each jar contains 15 grams of dried mushrooms. Fresh mushrooms are purchased for 300 FF per kilogram in bulk from individuals who gather them from local forests. (FF stands for French francs) Because of imperfections in the mushrooms and normal spoilage, one-quarter of the fresh mushrooms are discarded. Fifteen minutes is the direct labour time required for inspecting and sorting per kilogram of fresh mushrooms. After sorting and inspecting, the acceptable mushrooms are flash-dried, which requires 10 minutes of direct labour time per kilogram of acceptable, sorted, and inspected fresh mushrooms. The flash-drying removes most of the moisture content of the mushrooms and therefore drastically reduces their weight. A kilogram of acceptable fresh mushrooms yields only about 200 grams of dried mushrooms. After drying, the mushrooms are vacuum-packed in small jars and labels are applied.

Direct labour is paid at the rate of 60 FF per hour. The cost of the glass jars, lids, and labels is 50 FF per 100 jars. The labour time required to pack 100 jars is 10 minutes.

Required

1. Develop the standard cost for the direct labour and materials cost components of a single jar of dried chanterelle mushrooms, including the costs of the mushrooms, inspecting and sorting, drying, and packing.
2. Jean Leveque wonders who should be held responsible—the purchasing manager or the production manager—for the material variances for the chanterelle mushrooms.
    a. Who should be held responsible for the material price variances for the chanterelle mushrooms? Explain.
    b. Who should be held responsible for the material quantity variances for the chanterelle mushrooms? Explain.

P10–24 Determining Standard Costs; Variance Analysis   Helix Company produces several products in its factory, including a karate robe. The company uses a standard cost system to assist in the control of costs. According to the standards that have been set for the robes, the factory should work 780 direct labour-hours each month and produce 1,950 robes. The standard costs associated with this level of production activity are as follows:

	Total	Per Unit of Product
Direct materials	$35,490	$18.20
Direct labour	7,020	3.60
Variable manufacturing overhead (based on direct labour-hours)	2,340	1.20
		$23.00

During April, the factory worked only 760 direct labour-hours and produced 2,000 robes. The following actual costs were recorded during the month.

	Total	Per Unit of Product
Direct materials (6,000 metres)	$36,000	$18.00
Direct labour..........................	7,600	3.80
Variable manufacturing overhead	3,800	1.90
		$23.70

At standard, each robe should require 2.8 metres of material. All of the materials purchased during the month were used in production.

Required

Compute the following variances for April:
1. The materials price and quantity variances.
2. The labour rate and efficiency variances.
3. The variable manufacturing overhead spending and efficiency variances.

P10–25   Mix and Yield Variances
The Sticky Division manufactures and sells two special purpose adhesives, Yum and Zob. The two products emerge from the same production process, which requires three input materials: Amak, Brill, and Comad. The division developed standard costs for these two adhesives as follows:

Joint Processing Costs

Materials—Amak.........	6 kilograms at $2.40 per kilogram	$ 14.40
—Brill...........	4 kilograms at 4.20 per kilogram	16.80
—Comad........	1 kilogram at 5.15 per kilogram	5.15
Total materials input.......	11 kilograms	36.35
Labour (applied at $5.60 per kilogram × 11 kilograms)		61.60
Overhead—Variable (applied at $2.80 per kilogram × 11 kilograms)		30.80
—Fixed (applied at $5.00 per kilogram × 11 kilograms)		55.00
Joint costs to produce 10 kilograms of good output		$183.75

Costs Assigned to the Two Joint Products

Product	Good Output	Market Value Per Kilogram	Total	Joint* Costs	Standard Cost per Kilogram
Yum........	7 kilograms	$20	$140	$105.00	$15.00
Zob	3 kilograms	35	105	78.75	26.25
	10 kilograms		$245	$183.75	

*Joint costs are allocated to the products on the basis of market value.

Normal monthly volume is 11,000 kilograms of input materials processed or 10,000 kilograms of good output. Some variations of input quantities are permissible without affecting the quality of the finished products.

Materials are purchased from another division and are readily available; therefore, very little raw materials stock is kept by Sticky Division. Material prices are negotiated annually between the divisions. All production is furnished daily; therefore, there are no work in process inventories.

Actual production of good output amounted to 11,400 kilograms. The production costs were calculated as follows:

Materials input —Amak............	7,500 kilograms at $2.40 per kilogram	$18,000
—Brill.............	4,050 kilograms at 4.20 per kilogram	17,010
—Comad...........	1,100 kilograms at 5.15 per kilogram	5,665
Total input......................	12,650 kilograms	40,675
Labour for 12,650 kilograms processed .		$70,840
Good input: Yum 7,900 kilograms		
Zob 3,500 kilograms		

Required

Calculate the material and labour cost variances in as much detail as the data permit for the Sticky Division for the month of April. Comment on the performance of the production function of the Sticky Division during April by explaining the significance of the variances you calculated.

(SMAC, adapted)

P10–26 Mix and Yield Variances Lawrence Division uses three materials, Alpha, Beta, and Gamma, to produce its product Omega. The materials are mixed in the following standard proportions to yield 100 litres of Omega:

Material	Quantity (Litres)	Cost per Litre
Alpha............	80	$2.00
Beta.............	40	4.00
Gamma	30	10.00

It requires 50 hours of direct labour at $15.00 per hour to produce 100 litres of Omega.

On average, the division can produce and sell 200,000 litres of Omega per month. In a recent month, the division used the following amounts of materials and labour to produce 175,000 litres of Omega:

Material	Quantity (Litres)	Total Actual Cost
Alpha...........	159,000	$ 323,565
Beta............	72,000	290,102
Gamma	44,000	435,000
	275,000	$1,048,667
Direct labour	91,000 hours	$1,380,000

Required

1. Calculate the following materials variances for Omega:
   a. Price.
   b. Usage.
   c. Mix.
   d. Yield.
2. The supervisor on the Omega produce line argued that the workers were operating at standard, if not better, despite a large unfavourable labour efficiency variance of $52,500. Is the supervisor correct? Why or why not?

(SMAC, adapted)

P10–27 Process and Standard Costs The Audel Inc. uses a standard cost system in its single manufacturing department and has developed the following standard costs:

Materials	6 sheets × $0.50	$3.00
Direct labour	1 hour × $6.00	6.00
Variable overhead.........	1 hour × $4.00	4.00
Fixed overhead...........	1 hour × $2.00	2.00
		$15.00

Denominator activity is 35,000 units per month. All material is added at the beginning of the process. Conversion costs are added uniformly throughout the process. Inspection takes place when the units are 90% complete. The process is designed so that defective units equal 5% of the number of units which pass inspection.

Actual data for the month of September:

a. Beginning inventory, 10,000 units, 60% complete.
b. Units started during the month, 32,300.
c. Material purchased, 200,000 sheets at $0.48.
d. Material used, 195,000 sheets.
e. Direct labour payroll, $234,000 (36,000 hours).

f. Variable overhead, $140,000.
g. Fixed overhead, $71,000.
h. Abnormal spoilage, 300 units.
i. Ending inventory, 15,000 units, 95% complete.

Required

1. Equivalent production.
2. Cost of abnormal spoilage.
3. Cost of ending inventory of work in process.
4. Materials price and quantity variances.
5. Variable overhead spending and efficiency variances.

(CGA–Canada, adapted)

P10–28 Process and Standard Costs   The Centennial Co. Ltd. uses a standard process costing system in accounting for its one product, which is produced in one department. Materials are all added at the beginning of the process. Inspection takes place at the end of the process. Normal spoilage is expected to be 3% of good output.

Standard Cost per Unit

Materials...............	3 square metres at $1.20	$3.60
Direct labour............	½ hour at $7.00	3.50
Variable overhead........	½ hour at $2.00	1.00
Fixed overhead..........	½ hour at $2.80	1.40
		$9.50

Denominator activity	17,500 hours

Actual data for January 19x8:
a. Beginning inventory, 5,000 units (40 percent complete)
b. Started during January, 30,000 units
c. Spoiled during January, 1,000 units
d. Ending inventory, 2,000 units (80 percent complete)
e. Actual costs:

Materials purchased	100,000	square metres at $1.19
Materials used.....................	92,000	square metres
Direct labour.....................	16,000	hours at $7.35
Variable overhead..................	$34,000	
Fixed overhead....................	$50,000	

Required

1. Compute equivalent production for materials and conversion costs.
2. Compute two variances for materials, labour, and variable overhead manufacturing cost.

(CGA–Canada, adapted)

P10–29 Standard Cost and Learning   (Appendix 10B) The Roune Co. Ltd. is concerned with its cost to produce a subassembly. The standard cost of material for the subassembly is $20 per unit. Budgeted setup activity costs are $50 per setup. Labour is a standard rate of $9 per hour and variable overhead is a standard predetermined rate of 140% of direct labour costs.

The subassembly production is a repetitive process that requires practice to reach usual productivity levels. Standards reflect a 90% learning rate. The initial subassembly requires five hours to produce.

Required

1. Determine the average unit cost of eight units.
2. If the subassembly can be purchased for $120, how many units should be in the lot size to enable Roune Co. to save by producing internally?

P10–30 Learning Curves   (Appendix 10B) Halifax Instruments has just completed the assembly of some 400 sonic buoys for the Canadian Forces; these buoys are especially equipped to detect undersea vessels. The company is now being asked to submit an estimate of the cost of an additional 800 units. Its management has noted that the direct labour-hours (DLH) on each item seem to be declining. For the first 200 units produced, the average hours per unit were 2.1. For the assembly of the 400 units, however, the average hours per unit dropped to 1.68.

Required

1. Using these values, calculate the total labour hours required to assemble 1,600 units.
2. Suppose incremental costs (labour plus variable overhead costs) are $15 per direct labour-hour. What would be the incremental assembly costs for a new order of 800 units?
3. Using the following data, determine the formula for total hours for various cumulative units produced using the high-low approach.

	Labour-Hours	
Cumulative units Produced	**Average per Unit**	**Total**
200	2.100	420.0
400	1.680	672.0
800	1.344	1,075.2

4. Halifax fills the order for the additional 800 units, and produces another 100 units for a second customer. Its cumulative experience with producing these 100 buoys shows 90 total direct labour-hours or an average of 0.90 DLH per buoy. Is this consistent with the learning curve you estimated? If not, suggest an explanation for the deviation.

P10–31 Variances and Standards   (Appendix 10B) Residents in a municipally funded home for the aged in the province of Ontario are classified as Level 1 residents if they require less than 1.5 hours of direct nursing or medical care per day and as Level 2 residents if the direct nursing or medical care requirement lies between 1.5 and 2.5 hours per day.

An analyst from the municipal board of management for a newly constructed home for the aged obtained the following data for last year's financial results from several other similar homes in the province:

Home	Total Nursing Hours	X_1—Level 1 Resident Days	X_2—Level 2 Resident Days
1.	205,210	75,190	56,210
2.	47,122	24,455	8,030
3.	162,798	72,270	37,230
4.	23,952	13,505	3,650
5.	28,954	16,425	4,380
6.	91,602	44,165	19,710
7.	59,200	24,820	13,505
8.	120,027	55,115	25,550

The analyst completed a two-variable regression using total nursing hours as the dependent variable, Level 1 resident days as the first independent variable, and Level 2 resident days as the second independent variable. The results were:

Individual Analysis of Variables	Coefficient
Level 1 Resident Days (X_1)	1.179
Level 2 Resident Days (X_2)	2.059
Constant	1,025

Required

1. On the basis of the preceding analysis, give the predictive equation relating Level 1 and Level 2 resident days to the total number of nursing care hours required.
2. Because the home is still new and the finishing touches are still being put on the construction, residential care admissions are not yet completed. It is expected that the home will begin with 55 Level 1 residents and admit an additional Level 1 resident every 25 days until the maximum allowable number of 58 Level 1 residents is achieved. Level 2 residents will total 26 at the start of the year and will remain at that Level throughout the year. Using the predictive equation developed in item 1, calculate the expected number of total nursing care hours required in the first year. (Assume 365 days per year.)

3. A time-and-motion study in the home subsequently determined that actual resident/nursing direct contact time amounts to only 1.12 hours per day for Level 1 residents and 1.85 hours per day for Level 2 residents. This included, for example, feeding, bathing, examination, administration of medications, and direct medical treatment.

In an accounting sense, what might you call the difference between coefficients 1 and 2 as calculated in item 1 and the figures from the time and motion study? In the real world, what reasons might a director of nursing give to account for such a difference?

(SMAC, adapted)

CASES

C10–32 Ethics and the Manager   Stacy Cummins, the newly hired controller at Merced Home Products, Inc., was disturbed by what she had discovered about the standard costs at the Home Security Division. In looking over the past several years of quarterly earnings reports at the Home Security Division, she noticed that the first-quarter earnings were always poor, the second-quarter earnings were slightly better, the third-quarter earnings were again slightly better, and then the fourth quarter and the year always ended with a spectacular performance in which the Home Security Division always managed to meet or exceed its target profit for the year. She also was concerned to find letters from the company's external auditors to top management warning about an unusual use of standard costs at the Home Security Division.

When Ms. Cummins ran across these letters, she asked the assistant controller, Gary Farber, if he knew what was going on at the Home Security Division. Gary said that it was common knowledge in the company that the vice president in charge of the Home Security Division, Preston Lansing, had rigged the standards at the Home Security Division in order to produce the same quarterly earnings pattern every year. According to company policy, variances are taken directly to the income statement as an adjustment to cost of goods sold.

Favourable variances have the effect of increasing net income, and unfavourable variances have the effect of decreasing net income. Lansing had rigged the standards so that there were always large favourable variances. Company policy was a little vague about when these variances have to be reported on the divisional income statements. While the intent was clearly to recognize variances on the income statement in the period in which they arise, nothing in the company's accounting manuals actually explicitly required this. So for many years Lansing had followed a practice of saving up the favourable variances and using them to create a nice smooth pattern of earnings growth in the first three quarters, followed by a big "Christmas present" of an extremely good fourth quarter. (Financial reporting regulations clearly forbade carrying variances forward from one year to the next on the annual audited financial statements, so all of the variances had to appear on the divisional income statement by the end of the year.)

Ms. Cummins was concerned about these revelations and attempted to bring up the subject with the president of Merced Home Products but was told that "we all know what Lansing's doing, but as long as he continues to turn in such good reports, don't bother him." When Ms. Cummins asked if the board of directors was aware of the situation, the president somewhat testily replied, "Of course they are aware."

Required

1. How did Preston Lansing probably "rig" the standard costs—are the standards set too high or too low? Explain.
2. Should Preston Lansing be permitted to continue his practice of managing reported earnings?
3. What should Stacy Cummins do in this situation?

C10–33 Fragmentary Data; Journal Entries; Unit Costs   (Appendix 10A) You have just been hired by Esprix Company, which manufactures cough syrup. The syrup requires two materials, A and B, in its manufacture, and it is produced in batches. The company uses a standard cost system, with the controller preparing variances on a weekly basis. These variances are discussed at a meeting attended by all relevant managers. The meeting to discuss last week's variances is tomorrow. Since you will be working initially in the planning and control area, the president thinks that this would be a good chance for you to get acquainted with the company's control system and has asked that you attend and be prepared to participate fully in the discussion. Accordingly, you have taken home the controller's figure sheet containing last week's variances, as well as the ledger pages from which these variances were derived. You are sure that with a little study you will be able to make a sterling impression and be launched into a bright and successful career.

After completing your study that night, the weather being warm and humid, you leave your windows open upon retiring, only to arise the next morning horrified to discover that a sudden shower has obliterated most of the controller's figures (left lying on a table by an open window). Only the following fragments are readable:

Raw Materials—A				Wages Payable	
Bal. 6/1	720				1,725
Bal. 6/7	1,500				

Raw Materials—B				Material A—Price Variance	
Bal. 6/1	–0–	600		220	
Bal. 6/7	200				

Work in Process				Material B—Quantity Variance	
Bal. 6/1	–0–				40
Material A	2,400				
Bal. 6/7	–0–				

Accounts Payable				Labour Efficiency Variance	
	4,240			240	

Not wanting to admit your carelessness to either the president or the controller, you have decided that your only alternative is to reproduce the obliterated data. From your study last night, you recall the following:

a. The wages payable are only for direct labour.
b. The accounts payable are for purchases of both material A and material B.
c. The standard cost of material A is $6 per litre, and the standard quantity is 25 litres per batch of syrup.
d. Purchases last week were: material A, 2,750 litres; and material B, 96 kilograms.
e. The standard rate for direct labour is $8 per hour; a total of 230 actual hours were worked last week.

Required

1. How many batches of syrup were produced last week? (Double-check this figure before going on!)
2. For material A:
   a. How many litres were used in production last week?
   b. What was the quantity variance?
   c. What was the cost of material A purchased during the week?
   d. Prepare journal entries to record all activity relating to material A during the week.

3. For material B:
   a. What is the standard cost per kilogram of material B?
   b. How many kilograms of material B were used in production last week? How many kilograms should have been used at standard?
   c. What is the standard quantity of material B per batch?
   d. What was the price variance for material B?
   e. Prepare journal entries to record all activity relating to material B during the week.
4. For direct labour:
   a. What were the standard hours allowed for last week's production?
   b. What are the standard hours per batch?
   c. What was the direct labour rate variance?
   d. Prepare a journal entry to record all activity relating to direct labour during the week.
5. In terms of materials and labour, compute the standard cost of one batch of syrup.

C10–34 Operating Performance Measures; Missing Data   Jardine Products, Inc., recently embarked on a campaign to switch over to JIT production and purchasing. The program is in its initial stages, having been started just four months ago in April. The president of the company, K. J. Harani, is unsure about the progress of the campaign and has asked your assistance in analyzing recent performance data. Unfortunately, some of the data in the report given to you are illegible and the person who prepared the report has gone on vacation. Your copy of the report appears below:

Production and Cycle Times
April–July

	April	May	June	July
Average time required per unit, in days:				
Process time	1.5	?	?	?
Inspection time	0.8	0.7	0.3	0.2
Move time	0.6	0.5	0.4	?
Queue time	4.0	3.8	3.5	3.2
Wait time from order to start of production	9.6	8.7	5.3	4.7

General Performance Measures
April–July

	April	May	June	July
Quality control measures:				
Warranty claims as a percentage of units sold	2.5%	2.7%	3.2%	3.3%
Customer complaints as a percentage of units sold	1.1%	1.1%	1.5%	1.8%
Number of defects as a percentage of units produced	4.8%	4.7%	3.2%	2.1%
Material control measures:				
Purchase order lead time (days)	13	13	11	8
Scrap as a percentage of total cost	3.1%	3.8%	2.4%	1.9%
Inventory control measures:				
Raw material turnover (times)	5	6	9	11
Finished goods turnover (times)	4	4	6	7
Machine performance measures:				
Percentage of machine availability	87%	88%	91%	92%
Use as a percentage of availability	76%	74%	75%	78%
Setup time (hours)	2.3	2.2	1.1	0.5
Delivery performance measures:				
Throughput time, or velocity (days)	?	6.3	?	?
Manufacturing cycle efficiency (MCE)	?	?	?	24.0%
Delivery cycle time (days)	?	?	10.8	9.7
Percentage of on-time deliveries	74%	73%	64%	63%

Required

1. For each month, determine the following items:
   a. The throughput time (velocity) per unit, including all elements that make up throughput time.
   b. The MCE (manufacturing cycle efficiency), including all elements from which MCE is computed.
   c. The delivery cycle time, including all elements that make up the delivery time.

2. Refer to the General Performance Measures given above. Indicate for each item whether the trend is generally favourable, generally unfavourable, or mixed. What advice would you give the president on the basis of this analysis?

3. Refer to the Production and Cycle Times given above for July.

   a. Assume in August that these times are the same as for July, except that through further improvements in JIT production the company is able to completely eliminate the queue time during production. Compute the new throughput time and MCE.

   b. Assume in September that the Production and Cycle Times again are the same as in July, except that the company is able to eliminate both the queue time during production and the move time. Compute the new throughput time and MCE.

C10–35 Behavioural Impact of Standard Costs and Variances Terry Travers is the manufacturing supervisor of Aurora Manufacturing Company, which produces a variety of plastic products. Some of these products are standard items that are listed in the company's catalogue, while others are made to customer specifications. Each month, Travers receives a performance report showing the budget for the month, the actual activity, and the variance between budget and actual. Part of Travers' annual performance evaluation is based on his department's performance against budget. Aurora's purchasing manager, Sally Christensen, also receives monthly performance reports and she, too, is evaluated in part on the basis of these reports.

The monthly reports for June had just been distributed when Travers met Christensen in the hallway outside their offices. Scowling, Travers began the conversation, "I see we have another set of monthly performance reports hand-delivered by that not very nice junior employee in the budget office. He seemed pleased to tell me that I'm in trouble with my performance again."

CHRISTENSEN: I got the same treatment. All I ever hear about are the things I haven't done right. Now I'll have to spend a lot of time reviewing the report and preparing explanations. The worst part is that it's now the 21st of July so the information is almost a month old, and we have to spend all this time on history.

TRAVERS: My biggest gripe is that our production activity varies a lot from month to month, but we're given an annual budget that's written in stone. Last month we were shut down for three days when a strike delayed delivery of the basic ingredient used in our plastic formulation, and we had already exhausted our inventory. You know about that problem, though, because we asked you to call all over the country to find an alternate source of supply. When we got what we needed on a rush basis, we had to pay more than we normally do.

CHRISTENSEN: I expect problems like that to pop up from time to time—that's part of my job —but now we'll both have to take a careful look at our reports to see where the charges are reflected for that rush order. Every month I spend more time making sure I should be charged for each item reported than I do making plans for my department's daily work. It's really frustrating to see charges for things I have no control over.

TRAVERS: The way we get information doesn't help, either. I don't get copies of the reports you get, yet a lot of what I do is affected by your department, and by most of the other departments we have. Why do the budget and accounting people assume that I should only be told about my operations even though the president regularly gives us pep talks about how we all need to work together, as a team?

CHRISTENSEN: I seem to get more reports than I need, and I am never asked to comment on them until top management calls me on the carpet about my department's shortcomings. Do you ever hear comments when your department shines?

TRAVERS: I guess they don't have time to review the good news. One of my problems is that all the reports are in dollars and cents. I work with people, machines, and materials. I need information to help me *this* month to solve *this* month's problems—not another report of the dollars expended *last* month or the month before.

Required

1. Based on the conversation between Terry Travers and Sally Christensen, describe the likely motivation and behaviour of these two employees resulting from Aurora Manufacturing Company's standard cost and variance reporting system.
2. When properly implemented, both employees and companies should benefit from a system involving standard costs and variances.
   a. Describe the benefits that can be realized from a standard cost system.
   b. Based on the situation presented above, recommend ways for Aurora Manufacturing Company to improve its standard cost and variance reporting system so as to increase employee motivation.

(CMA, adapted)

GROUP EXERCISES

GE10–36 Conventional Purchasing Practices   Traditionally, firms have defined competitiveness as the ability to beat competitors on price. Even today, many products have become standardized or commodity-like and face unrelenting price wars. To continually beat competitors on price, firms have to be "efficient, low-cost producers." These firms are under a constant cost squeeze. Historically, material costs amounted to approximately 50% of total manufacturing costs. Clearly, without strict control of material cost per unit, it is unlikely that a firm's products would be cost competitive. Since manufacturing was striving to achieve low material cost per unit, cost accounting measures were developed to measure and evaluate the performance of purchasing department personnel.

Required

1. Traditionally, what performance measure(s) was (were) used to measure and evaluate the performance of purchasing department personnel?
2. How did plant management view quality in this environment, and what role did quality play in the decisions of purchasing agents?
3. Given that everyone from the head of the purchasing department on down wants to perform well, with what incentives did these performance measures provide purchasing personnel when dealing with their suppliers?
4. What impact did these performance measures have on the purchasing department itself?
5. What potential results did these purchasing practices have for raw materials inventory and the raw materials inventory warehouse?
6. Today, purchasing management is not only under pressure to contain (if not reduce) costs but customers are also demanding (and getting) increasing quality and a wider choice of products and services. How would purchasing management likely respond to demands for higher-quality materials and a wider variety of finished products while still functioning under traditional purchasing systems and practices?

GE10–37 Modern Purchasing Practices   Just-in-time (JIT) purchasing techniques are based on an entirely different philosophy and approach to dealing with vendors than that traditionally practised.

Required

1. What is the JIT philosophy?
2. What concepts or aspects of the JIT philosophy are pivotal to its success?
3. What are the characteristics of JIT systems?
4. What factors are important to the purchasing function?
5. What is the motivation for a change to JIT purchasing?
6. What are the key factors in organizing a world-class purchasing function today?
7. How does JIT purchasing differ from the traditional way manufacturers managed and controlled the purchase of materials in the pre-JIT era?
8. How does the performance measurement system differ under JIT purchasing from that under traditional purchasing systems? Give specific examples of JIT performance measures.

9. How is the cost accounting system affected by a change to JIT purchasing?
10. Today, purchasing management is not only under pressure to contain (if not reduce) costs but customers are also demanding (and getting) increasing quality and a wider choice of products and services. How do you reconcile the seemingly conflicting demands for greater quality and variety on one hand and lower costs on the other?
11. Do you see any limitations of the practice of JIT purchasing?

GE10–38 Conventional Production Practices

Traditional manufacturing systems were based on the economies of mass production and, therefore, focused primarily on productivity (average output per shift or per employee) and unit cost. Work processes were standardized, and production volume was maximized by increasing investments in economies of scale. Historically, direct labour costs amounted to approximately 30% to 40% of total manufacturing costs. To control high labour costs, North American plant managers were constantly exhorted to increase output, produce at or below standard unit costs, and minimize unfavourable cost variances.

Required

1. Can you cite service industries that have used the same mass production and economies of scale philosophy to prosper?
2. Describe the traditional manufacturing environment and how North American companies manage costs by maximizing production volume.
3. Traditionally, what performance measures were used to measure and evaluate the performance of direct labour and shop floor personnel?
4. Given that everyone from the plant manager on down wants to perform well, what incentives did these performance measures provide factory workers and shop floor supervisors?
5. What potential results did these performance incentives have?
6. Cycle time or throughput time, the time it takes to complete a job once it is started, is very important to customers. What impact did the combination of production factors—the factory layout, increasing volume, and decreasing unit cost—have on cycle times?
7. Today, production management is not only under pressure to contain (if not reduce) costs but customers are also demanding (and getting) increasing quality and a wider choice of products and services. How would production managers likely respond to demands for higher-quality parts and a wider variety of finished products while still functioning under traditional mass-production systems?

GE10–39 Lean (i.e., JIT) Production Systems

Lean production systems are one of the most important productivity-increasing innovations of this century. Toyota Motor Company deserves much credit for developing many of the key features of modern-day lean production systems. Lean production is delivering materials to the shop floor just in time for use and producing just in time to meet present demand. Successful implementations of lean production techniques eliminate a lot of the waste, excess, delay, and uncertainty associated with traditional manufacturing systems.

Required

1. What is lean (i.e., JIT) production?
2. Describe the JIT manufacturing environment and how companies manage costs by producing just in time.
3. If properly implemented, how does lean production benefit the firm? How does JIT manufacturing affect traditional performance measures such as direct labour efficiency, direct labour utilization, and machine utilization? What sort of performance measures must be implemented in order to achieve rather than defeat the objectives of JIT manufacturing?
4. How does the performance measurement system differ under JIT production from that under traditional production systems? Give specific examples of JIT performance measures.
5. How is the cost accounting system affected by a change to lean production?
6. Today, production managers are not only under pressure to reduce costs but to increase quality and shorten lead times. How do lean production systems manage to improve these three seemingly conflicting demands?
7. Do you see any limitations of the practice of lean production?

GE10–40 Integrated Performance Measurement Systems Operational control and performance measurement systems have narrowly focused their efforts on the productivity and efficiency of direct labour. This is now viewed by many as wrongheaded for a variety of reasons. Modern global markets are complex and highly competitive. Firms will have to take a much broader view of competition if they are to succeed and gain some competitive advantage. Such a broad outlook no longer revolves around products, processes, and competitors but, instead, places satisfying the customer at the centre of its manufacturing strategy.

Required

1. Customer satisfaction is good strategy, but we need to define what we mean by satisfying the customer. What are the key success factors (KSFs) behind customer satisfaction?
2. Translate these KSFs by operationalizing them. What performance measures would you use to evaluate progress toward achieving these key success factors?
3. Are these all financial-based performance measures or have you included appropriate non-financial or operational measures of performance?
4. Are the financial and nonfinancial measures of performance overlapping or do they serve different roles?
   a. What are some of the benefits and limitations of using financial measures of performance?
   b. What are some of the benefits and limitations of using nonfinancial or operational measures of performance?
5. Are all the performance measures internal in nature (e.g., manufacturing cycle time) or have you included appropriate external performance measures also?

11

FLEXIBLE BUDGETS AND OVERHEAD ANALYSIS

LEARNING OBJECTIVES

After studying Chapter 11, you should be able to:

1 Prepare a flexible budget, and explain the advantages of the flexible budget approach over the static budget approach.

2 Use the flexible budget to prepare a variable overhead performance report containing only a spending variance.

3 Use the flexible budget to prepare a variable overhead performance report containing both a spending and an efficiency variance.

4 Explain how flexible budgets are used in a company that employs activity-based costing.

5 Explain the significance of the denominator activity figure in determining the standard cost of a unit of product.

6 Properly apply overhead cost to units of product in a standard cost system.

7 Compute and properly interpret the fixed overhead budget and volume variances.

8 Show how variances can be presented on the income statement for management's use.

9 Define or explain the key terms listed at the end of the chapter.

Rocco Company, which manufactures sweatshirts such as those being worn by the students here, can use a static budget or a flexible budget. Which type of budget will more accurately reflect variances in cost and production?

I n Chapter 9, we introduced the master budget and discussed how its preparation is the first step in the planning and control process. Then, in Chapter 10, we introduced standard costs and demonstrated how they can be used by service and manufacturing firms to plan and control material and labour inputs. In the present chapter we take these concepts one step further by showing how budgets can be prepared on a *flexible basis* for better planning and control. We also complete the study of overhead variances that we started in Chapter 10.

Overhead cost control involves four problems. First, manufacturing overhead is usually made up of many separate costs. Second, these separate costs are often very small in dollar amount, making it highly impractical to control them in the same way that direct materials and direct labour costs are controlled. Third, these small, separate costs are often the responsibility of different managers. And fourth, manufacturing overhead costs vary in behaviour, some being variable, some fixed, and some mixed.

Most of these problems can be overcome by use of a *flexible budget*. Flexible budgets were touched on briefly in Chapter 9. In this chapter, we study flexible budgets in greater detail and learn how they are used to control costs. We also expand the study of overhead variances that we started in Chapter 10.

FLEXIBLE BUDGETS

OBJECTIVE 1

Prepare a flexible budget, and explain the advantages of the flexible budget approach over the static budget approach.

Characteristics of a Flexible Budget

The master budget presented in Chapter 9 was essentially a **static budget** in nature. A static budget has two characteristics:

1. It is geared toward only one level of activity.
2. Actual results are always compared against budgeted costs at the original budget activity level.

A **flexible budget** differs from a static budget on both of these points. First, it does not confine itself to only one level of activity, but rather is geared toward a *range* of activity. Second, actual results do not have to be compared against budgeted costs at the original budget activity level. Since the flexible budget covers a *range* of activity, if actual costs are incurred at a different activity level from what was originally planned, then the manager is able to construct a new budget, as needed, to compare against actual results—hence, the term *flexible budget*. In summary, the characteristics of a flexible budget are:

1. It is geared toward *all* levels of activity within the relevant range, rather than toward only one level of activity.
2. It is *dynamic* in nature rather than static. A budget can be tailored for any level of activity within the relevant range, even after the period is over. That is, a manager can look at the activity level *attained* during a period and then turn to the flexible budget to determine what costs *should have been* at that activity level.

▼   ▼   ▼   ▼   ▼

MANAGERIAL ACCOUNTING IN ACTION

Mable Rocco, the president of Rocco Company, just received the income statement for the sweatshirt operations for the year. Given the success of last year's operations and the budgeted income of $110,000 she was concerned as to why income results declined to $30,000 for the current year. She dialed her controller, Jack Rocco, to meet her in an hour to go over the variation from budget.

MABLE: Jack, have you had an opportunity to analyze the reasons for our drop in income? I had expected from the budget a much better result to take to our shareholders.

JACK: I have not had an opportunity to review the difference but it looks as though part of the problem was the loss of the 5,000 unit sale to Eatons. However, I will conduct an analysis and get back to you tomorrow. I need to look at the budget when 20,000 units are sold. This will permit a look at what our budget would have been without the sale to Eatons.

▼   ▼   ▼   ▼   ▼

Deficiencies of the Static Budget

To analyze the difference between a static master budget and a flexible budget, Jack determined that in preparing its master budget for 19x1, Rocco Company budgeted to produce and sell 25,000 units for the year. However, the company was not able to meet this goal; actual production and sales for the year totalled only 20,000 units. *With a statistic budget approach,* the company's overall performance for the year appears as shown in Exhibit 11–1.

What is wrong with the income statement in Exhibit 11–1 for performance evaluation? The static budget approach used to prepare the statement has a major deficiency in that it fails to distinguish between the *activity control* and the *cost control* dimensions of a manager's responsibility. Activity control is involved with seeing that sales and production goals are met. Cost control is involved with seeing that sales are made and that output is produced at the least possible cost, consistent with quality standards. These are different responsibilities, and they must be kept separate in attempting to assess how well a manager is doing his or her job.

Of these two responsibilities, the static budget does a good job of determining whether or not activity control is being maintained. Look again at the data in Exhibit 11–1. The data on the top line relate to the sales activity for the year. These data properly reflect the fact that activity control was not maintained, and that the company failed to meet its production sales by 5,000 units.

The remainder of the data in the statement deal with cost control. These data are of little value in that they compare apples to oranges. Note, for example, that all of the variances associated with the variable expenses are favourable. Does this mean that the company maintained good cost control over variable expenses for the year? Not necessarily. The reason the variances are favourable is that the master budget is based on an activity level of 25,000 units whereas the actual costs were incurred at an activity level substantially below this (only 20,000 units). From a cost-control point of view, it is total nonsense to try to compare costs at one activity level with costs at a different activity level. Such comparisons always make a manager look good as long as actual activity is less than budgeted activity.

EXHIBIT 11-1

ROCCO COMPANY
Static Budget Income Statement
For the Year Ended March 31, 19x1

	Actual	Master Budget	Variance
Number of units	20,000	25,000	5,000 U
Sales	$500,000	$625,000	$125,000 U
Less variable expenses:			
Direct materials	153,500	175,000	21,500 F
Direct labour	57,000	75,000	18,000 F
Variable overhead	71,000	75,000	4,000 F
Selling and administrative	20,000	25,000	5,000 F
Total variable expenses	301,500	350,000	48,500 F
Contribution margin	198,500	275,000	76,500 U
Less fixed expenses:			
Manufacturing overhead	93,500	90,000	3,500 U
Selling and administrative	75,000	75,000	—
Total fixed expenses	168,500	165,000	3,500 U
Net income	$30,000	110,000	80,000 U

How the Flexible Budget Works

The basic idea of the flexible budget approach is that through a study of cost behaviour patterns, a budget can be prepared that is geared to a *range* of activity, rather than to a single level. The basic steps in preparing a flexible budget are:

1. Determine the relevant range over which activity is expected to fluctuate during the coming period.
2. Analyze costs that will be incurred over the relevant range to ascertain their cost behaviour patterns (variable, fixed, mixed).
3. Separate costs by behaviour, determining the formula for variable and mixed costs, as discussed in Chapter 6.
4. Using the formula for the variable portion of the costs, prepare a budget showing which costs will be incurred at various points throughout the relevant range.

To investigate the differences in income, Jack determined that Rocco Company's sales normally fluctuate between 15,000 and 30,000 units each year. A study of cost behaviour patterns over this relevant range has revealed the following formulas for variable costs:

Cost	Variable Cost Formula (per unit)
Direct materials	$7
Direct labour	3
Variable overhead	3
Selling and administrative	1

Based on these cost formulas, a flexible budget for Rocco Company would appear as shown in Exhibit 11–2.

Using the Flexible Budget. Once prepared, the flexible budget has several uses in his analysis. At the beginning of a period, it is used as a basis for determining the expected

EXHIBIT 11-2

	ROCCO COMPANY Flexible Budget Budget Formula (per Unit)	Sales in Units			
		15,000	20,000	25,000	30,000
Sales	$25	$375,000	$500,000	$625,000	$750,000
Less variable expenses					
Direct materials	7	105,000	140,000	175,000	210,000
Direct labour	3	45,000	60,000	75,000	90,000
Variable overhead	3	45,000	60,000	75,000	90,000
Selling and administrative	1	15,000	20,000	25,000	30,000
Total variable expenses	14	210,000	280,000	350,000	420,000
Contribution margin	$11	165,000	220,000	275,000	330,000
Less fixed expenses:					
Manufacturing overhead		90,000	90,000	90,000	90,000
Selling and administrative		75,000	75,000	75,000	75,000
Total fixed expenses		165,000	165,000	165,000	165,000
Net income		$ –0–	$ 55,000	$110,000	$165,000

revenues, costs, and net income at the budgeted activity level. In the case of Rocco Company, for example, 25,000 units were budgeted to be sold during 19x1. By use of the flexible budget, Mable can easily determine expected revenues and expected costs for the year at this activity level.

At the end of a period, Mable can readily compare actual results against appropriate budget figures anywhere within the relevant range. Since the budget is *flexible,* is does not matter at which level these actual sales occur. Rocco Company actually produced and sold only 20,000 units during 19x1. Under the flexible budget approach, the company's performance would appear as shown in Exhibit 11–3.

In contrast to the statement prepared earlier under the static budget approach (Exhibit 11–1), this statement in Exhibit 11–3 clearly distinguishes between activity control and cost control. The sales data at the top of the statement indicate that the sales goal for the year was not met. The cost data within the statement tell how well costs were controlled for the 20,000 units that were sold during the year. Note that most of these variances are very different from the variances obtained earlier under the static budget approach. The reason is that by means of the flexible budget approach we are able to compare budgeted and actual costs *at the same activity level.*

What if actual sales had been some odd figure, such as 19,800 units, rather than 20,000 units? The manager would have used the flexible budget formulas to develop budget figures for the 19,800-unit level of activity to compare against actual results. Herein lies the strength and dynamism of the flexible budget approach. By simply applying the budget formulas, it is possible to develop a budget at any time for any activity level within the relevant range.

Reconciliation of Income Figures

To summarize the analysis, Jack prepared the reconciliation of net income figures shown on page 554 from Exhibits 11–2 and 11–3.

EXHIBIT 11–3

Overall Performance Report

ROCCO COMPANY
Income Statement
For the Year Ended March 31, 19x1

Budgeted sales in units 25,000
Actual sales in units. 20,000

	Actual 20,000 Units	Budget Based on 20,000 Units	Variance
Sales...	$500,000	$500,000	$ —
Less variable expenses:			
Direct materials	153,500	140,000	13,500 U
Direct labour	57,000	60,000	3,000 F
Variable overhead	71,000	60,000	11,000 U
Selling and administrative	20,000	20,000	—
Total variable expenses	301,500	280,000	21,500 U
Conribution margin	198,500	220,000	21,500 U
Less fixed expenses:			
Manufacturing overhead	93,500	90,000	3,500 U
Selling and administrative	75,000	75,000	— U
Total fixed expenses.........................	168,500	165,000	3,500 U
Net income....................................	$ 30,000	$ 55,000	$ 25,000 U

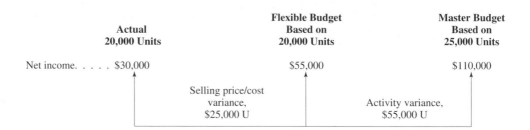

	Actual 20,000 Units	Flexible Budget Based on 20,000 Units	Master Budget Based on 25,000 Units
Net income.	$30,000	$55,000	$110,000

Selling price/cost variance, $25,000 U

Activity variance, $55,000 U

The **activity variance** represents the net income lost through failure to achieve the budgeted sales in units for the period. This variance is also known as the *sales variance* or the *sales volume variance*. It is computed by multiplying the difference between budgeted sales and actual sales (in units) by the budgeted contribution margin per unit. For Rocco Company, the computation would be:

$$(25,000 \text{ units} - 20,000 \text{ units}) \times \$11^* = \$55,000$$

*\$25 – \$14 = \$11; see Exhibit 11–2

In short, the company lost 55,000 in contribution margin (and net income) by its failure to achieve the budgeted sales level in units for the year.

The **selling price/cost variance** measures the net income lost through failure to maintain control over selling price and over various costs that a company incurred. The selling price element is computed by multiplying any difference between budgeted selling price and actual selling price per unit by the number of units sold. Because Rocco Company maintained its selling price at $25 per unit during 19x1, it shows no variance for selling price in Exhibit 11–3. The cost element consists of the total amount of all cost variances on a company's income statement; for 19x1, this amounted to $25,000 for Rocco Company (see Exhibit 11–3).

For each period, the manager analyzes these individual cost variances in detail to determine their cause. In Chapter 10 we showed how direct materials and direct labour variances can be analyzed; we now focus our attention on a detailed analysis of overhead variances.

The Measure of Activity

Sales units serve to measure activity for the flexible budget for income. Production activity, however, drives the overhead flexible budget. As shown in Exhibit 11–4, Rocco Company's flexible budget for income is based on units of product sold whereas the company's overhead flexible budget is based on machine-hours. Thus care is necessary

EXHIBIT 11-4   Relationship between the Flexible Income Budget and the Overhead Flexible Budget

ROCCO COMPANY
Flexible Income Budget

	Budget Formula (per Unit)	Sales in Units			
		15,000	20,000	25,000	30,000
Sales.	$25	$375,000	$500,000	$625,000	$750,000
Less variable expenses					
Direct materials	7	105,000	140,000	175,000	210,000
Direct labour	3	45,000	60,000	75,000	90,000
Variable overhead . . .	3	45,000	60,000	75,000	90,000
Selling and administrative. . .	1	15,000	20,000	25,000	30,000
Total variable expenses . . .	14	210,000	280,000	350,000	420,000
Contribution margin . . .	11	165,000	220,000	275,000	330,000
Less variable expenses:					
Manufacturing overhead . . .		90,000	90,000	90,000	90,000
Selling and administrative. . .		75,000	75,000	75,000	75,000
Total fixed expenses . . .		165,000	165,000	165,000	165,000
Net income (loss). . . .		$ –0–	$ 55,000	$110,000	$165,000

Overhead Flexible Budget

Overhead Cost	Cost Formula (per Hour)	Machine-Hours*			
		30,000	40,000	50,000	60,000
Variable costs:					
Indirect labour	$0.80	$ 24,000	$ 32,000	$ 40,000	$ 48,000
Lubricants.	0.30	9,000	12,000	15,000	18,000
Power	0.40	12,000	16,000	20,000	24,000
Total variable cost. . .	$1.50	45,000	60,000	75,000	90,000
Fixed costs:					
Depreciation.		40,000	40,000	40,000	40,000
Supervisory sales . . .		40,000	40,000	40,000	40,000
Insurance		10,000	10,000	10,000	10,000
Total fixed costs . . .		90,000	90,000	90,000	90,000
Total overhead costs. . .		$135,000	$150,000	$165,000	$180,000

*Two machine-hours are required to complete production of one unit of product.

with flexible budgets to define which activity drives the budget. If a company has only one product, then units can be used in the overall flexible budget as well as in the income flexible budget. But most companies find it more practical to use some input measure, such as machine-hours or labour-hours, to plan and control overhead costs. This is especially true when more than one product is manufactured.

At least three factors should be considered in selecting an activity base for an overhead flexible budget:

1. The existence of a causal relationship between the activity base and overhead costs.
2. The avoidance of dollars in the activity base itself.
3. The selection of an activity base that is simple and easily understood.

Causal Relationship.   There should be a direct causal relationship between the activity base and a company's variable overhead costs. That is, the variable overhead costs should vary as a result of changes in the activity base. In a machine shop, for example, one would expect power usage and other variable overhead cost to vary in relationship to the number of machine-hours worked. Machine-hours would therefore be the proper base to use in a flexible budget. As explained in Chapter 3, an activity base is frequently referred to as a *cost driver*, because it is the controlling factor in the incurrence of cost.

Other common activity bases (cost drivers) include direct labour-hours, kilometres driven by salespersons, contacts made by salespersons, number of invoices processed, number of occupied beds in a hospital, and number of X rays given. Any one of these could be used as the base for preparing a flexible budget in the proper situation.

Do Not Use Dollars.   Whenever possible, the activity base should be expressed in units rather than in dollars. If dollars are used, they should be standard dollars rather than actual dollars.

The problem with dollars is that they are subject to price-level changes, which can cause a distortion in the activity base if it is expressed in dollar terms. A similar problem arises when wage-rate changes take place if direct labour cost is being used as the activity base in a flexible budget. The change in wage rates causes the activity base to change, even though a proportionate change may not take place in the overhead costs themselves. These types of fluctuations generally make dollars difficult to work with, and they argue strongly for units rather than dollars in the activity base. The use of *standard* dollar costs rather than *actual* dollar costs overcomes the problem to some degree, but standard costs still have to be adjusted from time to time as changes in actual costs take place. On the other hand, *units* as a measure of activity (beds, hours, kilometres, etc.) are subject to few distorting influences and are less likely to cause problems in preparing and using a flexible budget.

Keep the Base Simple.   The activity base should be simple and easily understood. A base that is not easily understood by the manager who works with it day by day will probably cause confusion and misunderstanding rather than serve as a positive means of cost control.

VARIABLE OVERHEAD PERFORMANCE REPORT

We stated earlier that the overhead flexible budget is used to plan and control overhead costs in much the same way that the flexible income budget is used to plan and control activities for the company as a whole. This similarity led Jack to analyze the overhead of Rocco Company by using the overhead flexible budget to prepare an overhead performance report.

Recall that Rocco Company budgeted to produce and sell 25,000 units during 19x1; this would be equivalent to 50,000 machine-hours of activity (as stated in Exhibit 11–4, two machine-hours are required to produce one unit of product). Also recall that the company actually produced and sold only 20,000 units during the year. Thus, the standard hours allowed for the years' output would be 40,000 machine-hours (20,000 units × 2 hours = 40,000 hours). Jack ascertained that 42,000 machine-hours were actually required for the production of the 20,000 units. A summary of the year's activities follows:

Budgeted machine-hours	50,000
Actual machine-hours	42,000
Standard machine-hours allowed.	40,000
Actual variable overhead costs:	
Indirect labour	$36,000
Lubricants	11,000
Power	24,000
Total actual costs	$71,000

In preparing a variable overhead performance report, Jack had to decide what activity base Rocco Company should use in computing budget allowances to compare against actual results. There are two possibilities. The company could use:

1. The 42,000 machine-hours actually worked.
2. The 40,000 standard machine-hours allowed for the year's output.

Which base is chosen depends on how much detailed variance information it wants. As we learned in the preceding chapter, variable overhead can be analyzed in terms of a *spending* variance and an *efficiency* variance. The two bases provide different variance output.

Spending Variance Alone

OBJECTIVE 2

Use the flexible budget to prepare a variable overhead performance report containing only a spending variance.

If Rocco Company chooses alternative 1 and bases its performance report on the 42,000 machine-hours actually worked during the year, then the performance report shows only a spending variance for variable overhead. A performance report prepared in this way is shown in Exhibit 11–5.

The formula behind the spending variance was introduced in the preceding chapter. For review, that formula is:

$$(AH \times AR) - (AH \times SR) = \text{Variable overhead spending variance}$$

Or, in factored form:

$$AH(AR - SR) = \text{Variable overhead spending variance}$$

The report in Exhibit 11–5 is prepared around the first, or unfactored, format.

Interpreting the Spending Variance.   The overhead spending variance is affected by two things. First, a spending variance may occur simply because of price increases over what is shown in the flexible budget. For Rocco Company, this means that prices paid for overhead items may have gone up during the year, resulting in unfavourable spending variances. This portion of the overhead spending variance is just like the price variance for raw materials.

Second, the overhead spending variance is affected by waste or excessive usage of overhead materials. A first reaction is to say that waste or excessive usage of materials ought to show up as part of the efficiency variance. But this is not true as far as overhead is concerned. Waste or excessive usage shows up as part of the spending variance. The

EXHIBIT 11-5

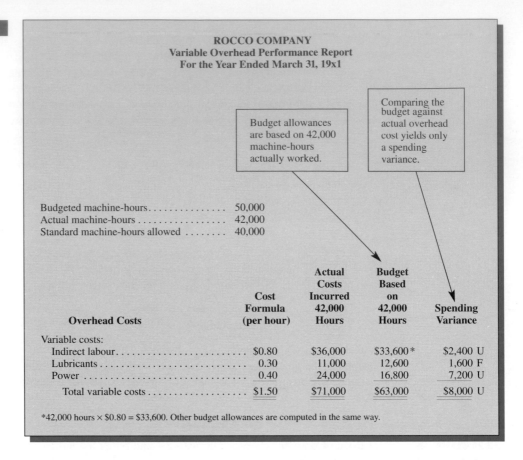

ROCCO COMPANY
Variable Overhead Performance Report
For the Year Ended March 31, 19x1

Budget allowances are based on 42,000 machine-hours actually worked.

Comparing the budget against actual overhead cost yields only a spending variance.

Budgeted machine-hours............... 50,000
Actual machine-hours 42,000
Standard machine-hours allowed 40,000

Overhead Costs	Cost Formula (per hour)	Actual Costs Incurred 42,000 Hours	Budget Based on 42,000 Hours	Spending Variance
Variable costs:				
Indirect labour.......................	$0.80	$36,000	$33,600*	$2,400 U
Lubricants	0.30	11,000	12,600	1,600 F
Power	0.40	24,000	16,800	7,200 U
Total variable costs	$1.50	$71,000	$63,000	$8,000 U

*42,000 hours × $0.80 = $33,600. Other budget allowances are computed in the same way.

reason is that the Manufacturing Overhead account is charged with *all* overhead costs incurred during a period, including those costs that arise as a result of waste. Because the spending variance represents any difference between the standard rate per hour and the actual hours of base and the actual costs incurred, waste automatically shows up as part of this variance, along with any excessive prices paid for variable overhead items.

In summary, many overhead spending variances contain both price and quantity (waste) elements. These two elements could be broken out and shown separately on the performance report, but this is rarely done in actual practice.

Usefulness of the Spending Variance.   Most firms consider the overhead spending variance to be highly useful. Generally, the price element in this variance is small, so the variance permits a focusing of attention on what the supervisor can control—the use of overhead in production. In many cases, firms limit their overhead analysis to the spending variance alone, feeling that the information it yields is sufficient for overhead cost control.

OBJECTIVE 3
Use the flexible budget to prepare a variable overhead performance report containing both a spending and an efficiency variance.

Both Spending and Efficiency Variances

If Rocco Company wants both a spending and an efficiency variance for overhead, then it should compute budget allowances for *both* the 40,000 machine-hour and the 42,000 machine-hour levels of activity. Jack prepared a performance report in this way as shown in Exhibit 11–6.

EXHIBIT 11-6

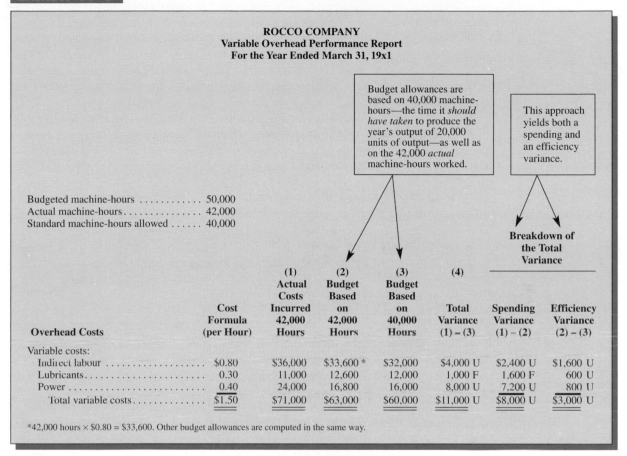

ROCCO COMPANY
Variable Overhead Performance Report
For the Year Ended March 31, 19x1

Budget allowances are based on 40,000 machine-hours—the time it *should have taken* to produce the year's output of 20,000 units of output—as well as on the 42,000 *actual* machine-hours worked.

This approach yields both a spending and an efficiency variance.

Budgeted machine-hours 50,000
Actual machine-hours 42,000
Standard machine-hours allowed 40,000

Breakdown of the Total Variance

Overhead Costs	Cost Formula (per Hour)	(1) Actual Costs Incurred 42,000 Hours	(2) Budget Based on 42,000 Hours	(3) Budget Based on 40,000 Hours	(4) Total Variance (1) – (3)	Spending Variance (1) – (2)	Efficiency Variance (2) – (3)
Variable costs:							
Indirect labour	$0.80	$36,000	$33,600 *	$32,000	$4,000 U	$2,400 U	$1,600 U
Lubricants	0.30	11,000	12,600	12,000	1,000 F	1,600 F	600 U
Power	0.40	24,000	16,800	16,000	8,000 U	7,200 U	800 U
Total variable costs	$1.50	$71,000	$63,000	$60,000	$11,000 U	$8,000 U	$3,000 U

*42,000 hours × $0.80 = $33,600. Other budget allowances are computed in the same way.

Note from Exhibit 11–6 that the spending variance is the same as the spending variance shown in Exhibit 11–5. The performance report in Exhibit 11–6 has simply been expanded to include an efficiency variance as well. Together, the spending and efficiency variances make up the total variance, as explained in the preceding chapter. The reader should trace the total variance ($11,000) back into the overall performance report for the company in Exhibit 11–3.

Interpreting the Efficiency Variance.   The term *overhead efficiency variance* is a misnomer, since this variance has nothing to do with efficiency in the use of overhead. What the variance really measures is how efficiently the *base* underlying the flexible budget has been utilized in production. Recall from the preceding chapter that the variable overhead efficiency variance is a function of the difference between the actual hours utilized in production and the hours that should have been taken to produce the period's output:

$$(AH \times SR) - (SH \times SR) = \text{Variable overhead efficiency variance}$$

Or, in factored form:

$$SR(AH - SH) = \text{Variable overhead efficiency variance}$$

If more hours are worked than are allowed at standard, then the overhead efficiency variance is unfavourable to reflect this inefficiency. As a practical matter, however, the inefficiency is not in the use of overhead *but rather in the use of the base itself.*

This point can be illustrated by looking again at Exhibit 11–6. Two thousand more machine-hours were used during the period than should have been used to produce the period's output. Each of these hours required the incurrence of $1.50 of variable overhead cost, resulting in an unfavourable variance of $3,000 (2,000 hours × $1.50 = $3,000). Although this $3,000 variance is called an *overhead efficiency variance,* it could better be called a *machine-hours efficiency variance,* because it measures the efficiency of utilization of machine time. However, the term *overhead efficiency variance* is so firmly ingrained in day-to-day use that a change is unlikely. Even so, the user must be careful to interpret the variance with a clear understanding of what it really measures.

Control of the Efficiency Variance. Who is responsible for control of the overhead efficiency variance? As the variance really measures efficiency in the utilization of the base underlying the flexible budget, whoever is responsible for control of this base is responsible for control of the variance. If the base is direct labour-hours, then the supervisor responsible for the use of labour time chargeable is for any overhead efficiency variance.

FIXED COSTS AND THE FLEXIBLE BUDGET

Should the flexible budget contain fixed costs as well as variable costs? The term *flexible budget* implies variable costs only, because just the variable costs change with changes in activity. As a practical matter, however, most firms also include fixed overhead costs in their flexible budgets (as we have done for Rocco Company).

Fixed costs are often included in the flexible budget for at least two reasons. First, to the extent that a fixed cost is controllable by a manager, it should be included in the evaluation of his or her performance. Such costs should be placed on the manager's performance report, along with the variable costs for which he or she is responsible. And second, fixed costs are needed in the flexible budget for product costing purposes. Recall from Chapter 3 that overhead costs are added to units of product by means of the predetermined overhead rate. *The flexible budget provides the manager with the information needed to compute this rate, and thereby it assists in the costing of products.* Later in the chapter we illustrate the use of the flexible budget in computing overhead rates and in product costing.

Activity-Based Costing and the Flexible Budget

OBJECTIVE 4
Explain how flexible budgets can be used in a company that employs activity-based costing.

If a company has an activity-based costing system in use, does it have any need for a flexible budget? The answer is an emphatic yes. In fact, the use of flexible budgeting actually enhances a company's ability to construct and operate an activity-based costing system. The key difference between a company that employs activity-based costing and one that employs a more traditional costing system lies in the *number* of flexible budgets that are used.

We learned in Chapter 5 that when a company employs activity-based costing, it identifies various activity centres associated with the manufacture of its products and then traces its overhead costs to these centres. In Exhibit 5–10 (page 241), for example, we identified eight activity centres for the company involved, and in Exhibit 5–11 (page 245) we showed the amount of overhead cost traceable to each. If the company in these exhibits uses flexible budgeting, it will construct a flexible budget *for each activity centre.* Thus, rather than having a single flexible budget for the entire company, it will have *eight* flexible budgets. The flexible budget for each activity centre will be geared to the activity

EXHIBIT 11-7

Multiple-Flexible
Budgets and
Activity-Based
Costing

Flexible Budget
Activity Centre—Machine Setups

Cost Driver: Setups Completed

Overhead Costs	Cost Formula (per setup)	Number of Setups			
		1,500	2,000	2,500	3,000
Variable costs: (detailed)	$80	$120,000	$160,000	$200,000	$240,000
Fixed costs: (detailed)		70,000	70,000	70,000	70,000
Total overhead costs..............		$190,000	$230,000	$270,000	$310,000

Flexible Budget
Activity Centre—Production Orders

Cost Driver: Orders Issued

Overhead Costs	Cost Formula (per setup)	Number of Orders			
		400	500	600	700
Variable costs: (detailed)	$130	$ 52,000	$ 65,000	$ 78,000	$ 91,000
Fixed costs: (detailed)		9,000	9,000	9,000	9,000
Total overhead costs..............		$ 61,000	$ 74,000	$ 87,000	$100,000

Flexible Budget
Activity Centre—Material Receipts

Cost Driver: Deliveries Received

Overhead Costs	Cost Formula (per setup)	Number of Deliveries			
		2,000	3,000	4,000	5,000
Variable costs: (detailed)	$40	$ 80,000	$120,000	$160,000	$200,000
Fixed costs: (detailed)		30,000	30,000	30,000	30,000
Total overhead costs..............		$110,000	$150,000	$190,000	$230,000

measure (cost driver) that controls the incurrence of overhead cost in that centre. The concept of multiple flexible budgets is illustrated in Exhibit 11–7.

In summary, the concept of a flexible budget is not unique to a company that uses a single, plantwide overhead rate to cost its products. Flexible budgets can be (and are) used to develop multiple overhead rates in a company, with the company having as many flexible budgets and overhead rates as it has activity centres.

The use of multiple flexible budgets actually enhances the accuracy of a company's costing system. This is because multiple budgets provide a closer correlation between overhead costs and the base on which these costs are applied to products. In addition to more accurate costing, multiple budgets also result in more usable variance data, since the costs on which the variances are computed relate to a single activity centre.[1]

---

[1]For further discussion of these points, see Robert E. Malcom, "Overhead Control Implications of Activity Costing," *Accounting Horizons* (December 1991), pp. 69–77. This is an excellent paper that raises several stimulating questions regarding traditional variance analysis.

Caterpillar, Inc., a manufacturer of heavy equipment and a pioneering company in the development and use of activity-based costing, divides its overhead costs into three large pools—the logistics cost pool, the manufacturing cost pool, and the general cost pool. In turn, these three cost pools are subdivided into scores of activity centres, with each centre having its own flexible budget from which variable and fixed overhead rates are developed. In an article describing the company's cost system, the systems manager stated that "the many manufacturing cost centre rates are the unique elements that set Caterpillar's system apart from simple cost systems."[2]

FIXED OVERHEAD ANALYSIS

The analysis of fixed overhead differs considerably from the analysis of variable overhead, simply because of the difference in the nature of the costs involved. To provide a background for our discussion, we will first review briefly the need for, and computation of, predetermined overhead rates. This review is helpful as the predetermined overhead rate plays a role in fixed overhead analysis. We then show how fixed overhead variances are computed and make certain observations as to their usefulness to the manager.

Flexible Budgets and Overhead Rates

OBJECTIVE 5
Explain the significance of the denominator activity figure in determining the standard cost of a unit of product.

Fixed costs come in large, indivisible pieces that by definition do not change with changes in the level of activity. As shown in Chapter 3, this creates a problem in product costing, since a given level of fixed overhead cost spread over a small number of units will result in a higher cost per unit than if the same amount of cost is spread over a large number of units. Consider the data in the following table:

Month	(1) Fixed Overhead Cost	(2) Number of Units Produced	(3) Unit Cost (1) ÷ (2)
January	$6,000	1,000	$6.00
February	6,000	1,500	4.00
March	6,000	800	7.50

Notice that the large number of units produced in February results in a low unit cost ($4), whereas the small number of units produced in March results in a high unit cost ($7.50). This problem arises only in connection with the fixed portion of overhead, because by definition the variable portion of overhead remains constant on a per unit basis, rising and falling in total proportionately with changes in the activity level. For product costing purposes, managers need to stabilize the fixed portion of unit cost so that a single unit-cost figure can be used throughout the year without regard to month-by-month changes in activity levels. As demonstrated in Chapter 3, this stability can be accomplished through use of the predetermined overhead rate.

[2]Lou F. Jones, "Product Costing at Caterpillar," *Management Accounting* (February 1991), p. 39.

Denominator Activity. The formula that we used in Chapter 3 to compute the predetermined overhead rate follows, with one added feature. We have titled the estimated activity portion of the formula as being the **denominator activity:**

$$\frac{\text{Estimated total manufacturing overhead costs}}{\substack{\text{Estimated total units in the base (MH, DLH, etc.)} \\ \text{(denominator activity)}}} = \substack{\text{Predetermined} \\ \text{overhead rate}}$$

Recall from our discussion in Chapter 3 that once an estimated activity level (denominator activity) has been chosen, it remains unchanged throughout the year, even if actual activity later proves the estimate (denominator) to be somewhat different. The reason for not changing the denominator, of course, is to maintain stability in the amount of overhead applied to each unit of product regardless of when it is produced during the year.

Computing the Overhead Rate. When we discussed predetermined overhead rates in Chapter 3, we did so without elabouration as to the source of the estimated data going into the formula. These data are normally derived from the overhead flexible budget. To illustrate, refer to Rocco Company's overhead flexible budget in Exhibit 11–4. The company planned to produce 25,000 units during 19x1, which would require 50,000 machine-hours of time. The 50,000 machine-hours become the denominator activity in the predetermined overhead rate formula, and the overhead cost at this activity level from the overhead flexible budget becomes the estimated cost in the formula ($375,000 from Exhibit 11–4). In summary, Jack determined the 19x1 predetermined overhead rate for Rocco Company to be:

$$\frac{\$165,000}{50,000 \text{ MH}} = \$3.30 \text{ per machine-hour}$$

Alternatively, Jack broke down the predetermined overhead rate into variable and fixed elements rather than using a single combined figure:

$$\text{Variable element} \frac{\$75,000}{50,000 \text{ MH}} = \$1.50 \text{ per machine-hour}$$

$$\text{Fixed element} \frac{\$90,000}{50,000 \text{ MH}} = \$1.80 \text{ per machine-hour}$$

For every standard machine-hour of operation, Work in Process is charged with $3.30 of overhead, of which $1.50 is variable overhead and $1.80 is fixed overhead. If a unit of product takes two machine-hours to complete, then its cost includes $3 variable overhead and $3.60 fixed overhead, as shown on the following standard cost card:

Standard Cost Card—Per Unit

Direct materials (Exhibit 11–4).	$ 7
Direct labour (Exhibit 11–4)	3
Variable overhead (2 machine-hours at $1.50)	3
Fixed overhead (2 machine-hours at $1.80)	3.60
Total standard cost per unit	$16.60

In summary, the overhead flexible budget provides the manager with both the overhead cost figure and the denominator activity figure needed in computing the predetermined overhead rate; thus, the overhead flexible budget plays a key role in determining the amount of fixed and variable overhead cost that will be charged to units of product.

Overhead Application in a Standard Cost System

To understand the fixed overhead variances, it is necessary first to understand how overhead is applied to work in process in a standard cost system. In Chapter 3, recall that we applied overhead to work in process on the basis of actual hours of activity (multiplied by the predetermined overhead rate). This procedure was correct, because at the time we were dealing with an actual cost system. However, we are now dealing with a standard cost system; and when standards are in operation, overhead is applied to work in process on a basis of the *standard hours allowed for the output of the period* rather than on a basis of the actual number of hours worked. This point is illustrated in Exhibit 11–8.

The reason for using standard hours to apply overhead to production in a standard cost system is to assure that every unit of product moving along the production line bears the same amount of overhead cost, regardless of any time variations that may be involved in its manufacture.

The Fixed Overhead Variances

To analyze the fixed overhead variances, Jack referred again to the overhead flexible budget data for Rocco Company contained in Exhibit 11–4 (p. 555).

Denominator activity in machine-hours	50,000
Budgeted fixed overhead costs	$90,000
Fixed portion of the predetermined overhead rate (computed earlier)	$1.80

The following actual operating results were recorded for the year:

Actual machine-hours	42,000
Standard machine-hours allowed*	40,000
Actual fixed overhead costs:	
Depreciation	$40,000
Supervisory salaries	44,500
Insurance	9,000
Total actual costs	$93,500

*For the actual production of the year.

EXHIBIT 11–8

Applied Overhead Costs: Normal Cost System* versus Standard Cost System

Normal Cost System Manufacturing Overhead		Standard Cost System Manufacturing Overhead	
Actual overhead costs incurred	Applied overhead costs: Actual hours × Predetermined overhead rate	Actual overhead costs incurred	Applied overhead costs: Standard hours allowed for output × Predetermined overhead rate
Under- or overapplied overhead		Under- or overapplied overhead	

*Also termed an actual cost system.

EXHIBIT 11-9

Computation of the
Fixed Overhead
Variances

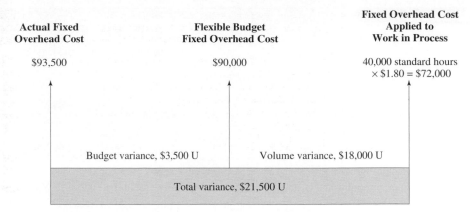

Actual Fixed Overhead Cost	Flexible Budget Fixed Overhead Cost	Fixed Overhead Cost Applied to Work in Process
$93,500	$90,000	40,000 standard hours × $1.80 = $72,000

Budget variance, $3,500 U   Volume variance, $18,000 U

Total variance, $21,500 U

*As originally budgeted (see Exhibit 11–4). This figure can also be expressed as 50,000 denominator hours × $1.80 = $90,000

From these data, two variances can be computed for fixed overhead—a budget variance and a *volume variance*. The variances are shown in Exhibit 11–9.

Notice from the exhibit that overhead has been applied to work in process on the basis of 40,000 standard hours allowed for the output of the year rather than on the basis of 42,000 actual hours worked. As stated earlier, this keeps unit costs from being affected by any efficiency variations.

The Budget Variance—A Closer Look

The **budget variance** represents the difference between actual fixed overhead costs incurred during the period and budgeted fixed overhead costs as contained in the flexible budget. The variance can also be presented in the following format:

Actual fixed overhead cost $93,500
Budgeted fixed overhead costs (from the
   flexible budget in Exhibit 11–4)   90,000
Budget variance . . . . $ 3,500 U

The reader should trace the $3,500 budget variance back into the company's overall performance report in Exhibit 11–3 (page 554).

Although the budget variance is somewhat similar to the variable overhead spending variance, care must be exercised in how it is used. Keep in mind that fixed costs are often beyond immediate managerial control. Therefore, rather than serving as a measure of managerial performance, in many cases the budget variance is computed simply for information purposes to call management's attention to changes in price factors.

Jack decided to combine the fixed overhead costs and variances with those for the variable overhead. To show how this is done, an overhead performance report for Rocco Company containing the fixed overhead budget variance is found in Exhibit 11–10. (The variable overhead cost data in the exhibit are taken from Exhibit 11–5.)

The Volume Variance—A Closer Look

The **volume variance** is a measure of utilization of plant facilities. It is computed in a number of ways:

Budgeted fixed overhead – Applied fixed overhead = Volume variance

EXHIBIT 11-10

Fixed Overhead
Costs on the
Overhead
Performance Report

ROCCO COMPANY
Overhead Performance Report
For the Year Ended March 31, 19x1

Budgeted machine-hours   50,000
Actual machine-hours   42,000
Standard machine-hours allowed   40,000

Overhead Costs	Cost Formula (per hour)	Actual Costs 42,000 Hours	Budget Based on 42,000 Hours	Spending or Budget Variance
Variable costs:				
Indirect labour	$0.80	$36,000	$33,600*	$2,400 U
Lubricants	0.30	11,000	12,600	1,600 F
Power	0.40	24,000	16,800	7,200 U
Total variable costs	$1.50	$71,000	$63,000	$8,000 U
Fixed costs:				
Depreciation		40,000	40,000	—
Supervisory salaries		44,500	40,000	4,500 U
Insurance		9,000	10,000	1,000 F
Total fixed costs		93,500	90,000	3,500 U
Total overhead costs		$164,500	$153,000	$11,500 U

Alternatively:

$$\text{Fixed portion of the predetermined overhead rate} \times \left\{ \begin{array}{c} \text{Denominator hours} \end{array} - \begin{array}{c} \text{Standard hours allowed} \end{array} \right\} = \text{Volume variance}$$

Applying the latter formula to Rocco Company, the volume variance would be:

$$\$1.80 \ (50,000 \ MH - 40,000 \ MH) = \$18,000 \ \text{unfavourable}$$

The two calculations are equivalent because:

$$\text{Fixed portion of the predetermined overhead rate} \times \text{Denominator hours} = \text{Budget fixed overhead}$$

$$\text{Fixed portion of the predetermined overhead rate} \times \text{Standard hours allowed} = \text{Applied fixed overhead}$$

Note that this computation agrees with the volume variance as shown in Exhibit 11–9. At this point we should ask, What caused a volume variance to arise in Rocco Company, and what does the variance mean? The cause of the variance can be explained as follows: If the company's activity level for the period had been 50,000 standard hours as planned, then work in process would have been charged with the full $90,000 in fixed costs contained in the overhead flexible budget; that is,

$$50,000 \ \text{machine-hours} \times \$1.80 = \$90,000$$

But the activity level for the period (at standard) was only 40,000 machine-hours, *so even though the full $90,000 in fixed costs would have been incurred, less than this amount would have been charged to work in process; namely:*

$$40,000 \ \text{machine-hours} \times \$1.80 = \$72,000$$

The difference between these two figures is the volume variance:

$$\$90,000 - \$72,000 = \$18,000$$

As stated earlier, the volume variance is a measure of available facilities. An unfavourable variance, as just shown, means that the company operated at an activity level *below* that planned for the period; a favourable variance would mean that the company operated at an activity level *greater* than that planned for the period. The volume variance does not measure over- or underspending. A company normally would incur the same dollar amount of fixed overhead cost regardless of whether the period's activity was above or below the planned (denominator) level. In short, the volume variance is an activity-related variance in that it is explainable only by activity and is controllable only through activity. Activity variances result from numerous factors: economic recession, government sales tax increase, strikes, shortages, and so on. Responsibility for activity variances is difficult to fix on any area, because of these various possible causes.

To summarize:

1. If the denominator activity and the standard hours allowed for the output of the period are the same, then there is no volume variance.
2. If the denominator activity is greater than the standard hours allowed for the output of the period, then the volume variance is unfavourable, signifying an underutilization of available facilities.
3. If the denominator activity is less than the standard hours allowed for the output of the period, then the volume variance is favourable, signifying a utilization of available facilities.

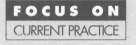

Experimentation is being proposed to permit a more elaborate view of variances for fixed overhead. Capacity related variances are decomposed to budgeted unused capacity cost and capacity utilization variances from the original volume variance. Such suggestions are consistent with the need to manage capacity in terms of the objectives of the organization.[3]

Graphic Analysis of Fixed Overhead Variances

Some insights into the budget and volume variances can be gained through graphic analysis. The needed graph is presented in Exhibit 11–11.

As shown in the graph, fixed overhead cost is applied to work in process at the predetermined rate of $1.80 for each standard hour of activity. (The applied-cost line is the upward-sloping line on the graph.) Since a denominator level of 50,000 machine-hours was used in computing the $1.80 rate, the applied-cost line crosses the budget-cost line at exactly the 50,000 machine-hour point. Thus, if the denominator hours and the standard hours allowed for output are the same, there can be no volume variance, since the applied-cost line and the budget-cost line exactly meet on the graph. It is only when the standard hours differ from the denominator hours that a volume variance can arise.

---

[3]Y. T. Mak and Melvin L. Roush, "Managing Activity Costs with Flexible Budgeting and Variance Analysis," *Accounting Horizons* (September 1996), pp. 141–46.

Graphic Analysis of
Fixed Overhead
Variances

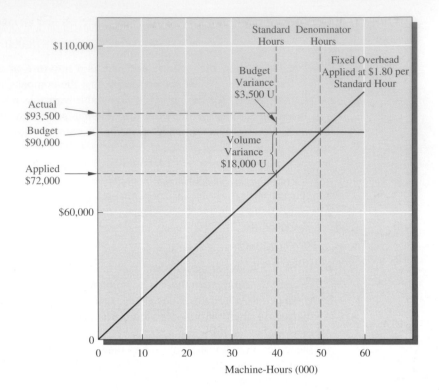

In the case at hand, the standard hours allowed for output (40,000 machine-hours) are less than the denominator hours (50,000 hours); the result is an unfavourable volume variance, as less cost was applied to production than was originally budgeted. If the standard hours allowed for output had exceeded the denominator hours, the volume variance on the graph would have been favourable.

Cautions in Fixed Overhead Analysis

There can be no volume variance for variable overhead because applied costs and budgeted costs are both dependent on activity and thus will always move together. The reason we get a volume variance for fixed overhead is that the incurrence of the fixed costs does not depend on activity; yet when applying the costs to work in process, we act *as if* the costs were variable and depended on activity. This point can be seen from the graph in Exhibit 11–11. Notice from the graph that the fixed overhead costs are applied to work in process at a rate of $1.80 per hour *as if* they were indeed variable. Treating these costs as if they were variable is necessary for product costing purposes, but there are some real dangers here. The manager can easily become misled and start thinking of the fixed costs as if they were *in fact* variable.

The manager must keep clearly in mind that fixed overhead costs come in large, indivisible pieces. Any breakdown of such costs, though necessary for product costing purposes, is artificial in nature and has no significance in matters relating either to actual cost behaviour or to cost control. This is why the volume variance, which arises as a result of treating fixed costs as if they were variable, is not a controllable variance from a spending point of view. The fixed overhead rate used to compute the variance is simply a derived figure needed for product costing purposes; it has no significance in cost control.

Because of these factors, some companies present the volume variance in physical units (hours) rather than in dollars. These companies feel that stating the variance in physical units gives management a clearer signal as to the cause of the variance and how it can be controlled.

Petro-Canada states in its *1996 Annual Report* that its average refinery utilization last year was 99%, up from 93% the previous two years. The report suggests that increasing utilization of refineries permits fixed costs to be spread over a larger volume, thus reducing cost per unit processed. Debottlenecking facilities combined with improved reliability and planned idle time were part of the reasons for the increase.[4]

Managing Capacity

To set standard rates for fixed overhead, it is important to define clearly what is meant by *capacity*. Denominator level of activity is the base used to determine the fixed overhead rate. Yet this activity level is a level of capacity. In practice, various capacity definitions are suggested: theoretical, practical, normal, annual and actual. Theoretical capacity represents an ideal, namely a 24-hour, 7-day operation with zero waste. Practical capacity represents an attainable level of operations which permits unavoidable nonproductive time. Normal capacity is an average capacity utilization which averages expected operations for a defined future period, typically three to five years. Annual is the planned utilization for the next year. Actual capacity represents what is actually used for the period.

[4]Petro-Canada, *1996 Annual Report*, p. 17.

Capacity management attempts to have the organization reduce nonproductive capacity, namely capacity not purposely idle such as unscheduled use for JIT purposes or for other strategic reasons. Set-ups, rework or maintenance all represent unproductive time that could be used or at least kept to a minimum. Design of production systems usually provides for reserve capacity that might be needed if demand exceeds the expected level. However, this unused capacity can be a burden because productive activities must bear the cost. Too much cost associated with reserved capacity can make the firm noncompetitive. Too little reserved capacity can mean that volume additions cannot be met. Management must be aware of the balancing of too much and too little and keep unproductive capacity to a minimum so that idle capacity is at least a choice that management strategically makes. A recent *Management Accounting Guideline* provides a lengthy discussion of various approaches to managing capacity and the associated costs.[5]

PRESENTATION OF VARIANCES ON THE ABSORPTION COSTING INCOME STATEMENT

OBJECTIVE 8

Show how variances can be presented on the income statement for management's use.

We have already shown in Exhibit 11–3 how variances are presented on the contribution income statement. To complete the analysis, Jack presented the variances on an absorption costing basis so that Mable would have results consistent with the income statement presented to the shareholders.

The following variances were computed for Rocco Company:

Direct materials (Exhibit 11–3)		$13,500 U
Direct labour (Exhibit 11–3).		3,000 F
Variable overhead (Exhibit 11–3):		
Spending variance (p. 558).	$8,000 U	
Efficiency variance (p. 559)	3,000 U	11,000 U
Fixed overhead:		
Budget variance (Exhibit 11–3 and p. 565)		3,500 U
Variances from flexible budget.		25,000 U
Volume variance (p. 567)*		18,000 U
Total variances		$43,000 U

*Note that the volume does not appear on the contribution income statement in Exhibit 11–3, but that it is part of the $43,000 total variance on the absorption costing income statement in Exhibit 11–12. The reason it appears only on the absorption costing statement is that the volume variance represents the difference between the budgeted fixed overhead costs for a period and the amount applied to products. Under the contribution approach, there can be no volume variance since fixed overhead costs are not applied to products but rather are deducted in total on the income statement as period costs.

An absorption costing income statement for Rocco Company containing the effects of these variances is presented in Exhibit 11–12. Note that the actual cost of goods sold exceeds the budgeted amount by $18,000, which agrees with the total of the variances from the flexible budget summarized earlier. This type of presentation provides management with a clear picture of the impact of the variance on profits—a picture that could not be obtained by looking at cost performance reports. In the case at hand, Rocco Company's profits have been dramatically reduced by the variances that developed during the period.

The budgeted income statement presented in Exhibit 11–12 contains a $18,000 volume variance for fixed overhead. The difference between the actual and flexible budgeted income

---

[5]"Management and the Cost of Capacity," *Management Accounting Guidelines* (Hamilton, Ont.: The Society of Management Accountants of Canada, May 1996).

EXHIBIT 11–12

ROCCO COMPANY
Absorption Costing Income Statement
For the Year Ended March 31, 19x1

	20,000 Units		
	Actual	**Budgeted**	**Variance**
Sales	$500,000	$500,000	—
Less cost of goods sold at standard cost of $16.60 per			
unit	332,000	332,000	–0–
Variances from standard cost	43,000	18,000	$25,000 U
Total	375,000	350,000	25,000 U
Gross margin	125,000	150,000	25,000 U
Less selling and administrative expense ($20,000			
variable and 75,000 fixed)	95,000	95,000	—
Net income	$ 30,000	$ 55,000	$25,000 U

statements includes only the variances for materials, direct labour, variable overhead, and fixed overhead budget variance. A $18,000 volume variance appears in the budgeted income statements as a result of the fact that the budget is based on the actual sales volume (the same as it was for direct costing in Exhibit 11–3) and actual production volume. Actual production volume was not important for direct costing, but it does affect the volume variance for fixed overhead when absorption costing is used. Rocco had anticipated producing 25,000 units at two machine-hours per unit (p. 563). However, it produced only 20,000 units at a standard of two machine-hours per unit. The budget presented in Exhibit 11–12 is based, as all flexible budgets are, on actual volumes. Therefore, the budgeted income results should include a volume variance of 5,000 units × 2 machine-hours × $1.80 per machine-hour as a fixed overhead volume variance. This volume variance represents one of the activity variances between the master budget and the flexible one just presented. The remainder of the activity variance would result from sales, namely, 5,000 units × ($25 – $7 – $3 – $3 – $3.60 – $1), or 37,000 U. The standard costs of $7, $3, $3 and $3.60 are taken from the standard cost card on page 563 and represent the standard unit costs for direct materials, direct labour, variable overhead, and fixed overhead. The $1 is the variable selling and administrative expense given on page 552. Thus, two volume effects make up the activity variance under absorption costing, namely, sales volume and production volume. The effect on profits resulting from each constitutes the profit effects of the activity changes from the master budget.

In summary, the activity variances constitute the difference between the master budget (p. 552) and the flexible budget in Exhibit 11–12. The composition of the activity variances is as follows:

Master budget net income (p. 552)	$110,000
Flexible budget net income (Exhibit 11–12).	55,000
Total activity variances	$ 55,00
Composition	
Production volume variance (p. 566)	$ 18,000
Sales volume variance (5,000 units × $7.40	
budgeted income per unit, calculated above.	37,000
Total flexible budget variance from master budget	$ 55,00

The remaining variances from the actual net income results are composed of the direct materials, direct labour, variable overhead, and the fixed overhead budget variance shown on page 565.

Using modern technology and giving greater responsibility to production personnel allow variances to be captured in real time permitting faster problem resolution.

A division of Avcorp Industries Inc. based in Laval, Quebec, that manufactures aircraft parts took the company from an $800,000 loss to a small profit within six months. A new "red flag" system had been put into place. Workers raise red flags and alarms when they meet a production snag or a technology-related issue that could hinder a delivery commitment. An alarm sounds for 30-second intervals until a supervisor comes to assist. A report is prepared immediately and logged into a computer system so that those most likely to come up with the solution are notified at once, and the customer also is notified. The result has been lowered costs, an improved flow of production, and better relationships with customers.[6]

MANAGERIAL ACCOUNTING IN ACTION—WRAP-UP

JACK: Mable, I have analyzed the drop in net income and I believe I have a partial explanation for you.

MABLE: Good, give me the details.

JACK: To begin, the large portion of the difference in actual from budget occurred because of the 5,000 units we were unable to sell. Even though we did not produce these units, we were unable to make the income from them.

Once we take the effect of the 5,000 units into account, the remaining cost overruns were for direct materials and variable overhead. These two areas amounted to a total of $24,500. We will need some adjustments in these areas in the future.

MABLE: I will study these items now that you have isolated the main differences. Thank you, Jack, for clearing up the confusion.

Disposition of Variances

Variances from standard costs relating to materials, labour, and overhead typically represent deviations from what is expected, the normal. As such the represent legitimate charges or credits to the income statement of the period, as shown in the previous section. If they are immaterial in amount, then disclosure on the income statement is generally thought to be a reasonable way to dispose of these end-of-period variances. Such an approach is consistent with conventional accounting treatment of deviations from reasonably specified accounting estimates of what is expected.

Occasionally, standards do not reflect expected or normal costs. Outdated standards or ideal standards are the most obvious example. Inaccurate monthly fixed overhead budgets would be another example of a factor causing variances for a specific period. Unless

---

[6]Based on Robert Melnbardis, "A Factory Takes Off," *Canadian Productivity, Canadian Business* supplementary issue, September 1994, p. 45.

fixed overhead budgets reflect the expected monthly costs and standard fixed overhead rates represent a monthly predetermined rate, then volume variants for fixed overhead would be likely.

When variances result from budgets and standards that do not represent expected normal costs, then an argument can be made to follow the procedures discussed in Chapter 3 for disposing of under- or overapplied overhead, namely, apportioning the variance over the associated inventories and cost of goods sold, or assigning the variance to the balance sheet to be carried forward to future periods. The balance sheet treatment is more logical where future offsetting variances are expected, such as would occur for monthly overhead results. Apportioning or prorating is justifiable where costs including the variance represent a more accurate result than those using the standard alone. Most variances would be apportioned to work in process, finished goods, and cost of goods sold based on the amount of material, labour, and overhead costs included for the period. The material price variance, however, is an exception in that it is apportioned to raw materials inventory in addition to the locations used for the other cost elements.

REVIEW PROBLEM: OVERHEAD ANALYSIS

(This problem provides a review of overhead flexible budgets, cost flows in a standard cost system, and the computation of overhead variances.)

An overhead flexible budget for Aspen Company is as follows:

Overhead Costs	Cost Formula (per DLH)	Direct-Labour-Hours		
		4,000	6,000	8,000
Variable costs:				
Supplies....................	$0.20	$ 800	$ 1,200	$ 1,600
Indirect labour...............	0.30	1,200	1,800	2,400
Total variable costs	$0.50	2,000	3,000	4,000
Fixed costs:				
Depreciation		4,000	4,000	4,000
Supervision		5,000	5,000	5,000
Total fixed costs		9,000	9,000	9,000
Total overhead costs		$11,000	$12,000	$13,000

Five hours of machine time are required per unit of product. The company has set denominator activity for the coming period at 6,000 hours (or 1,200 units). The computation of the predetermined overhead rate would be:

$$\text{Total} \frac{\$12,000}{6,000 \text{ DLH}} = \$2 \text{ per DLH}$$

$$\text{Variable element} \frac{\$3,000}{6,000 \text{ DLH}} = \$0.50 \text{ per DLH}$$

$$\text{Fixed element} \frac{\$9,000}{6,000 \text{ DLH}} = \$1.50 \text{ per DLH}$$

Assume the following actual results for the period:

Number of units produced.........................	1,300
Actual direct labour-hours.........................	6,800
Standard direct labour-hours allowed*...............	6,500
Actual variable overhead cost......................	$4,200
Actual fixed overhead cost	9,400

*For 1,300 units of product.

Therefore, the company's manufacturing overhead account would appear as follows at the end of the period:

Manufacturing Overhead

Actual overhead costs	13,600*	13,000†	Overhead costs applied
Underapplied overhead	600		

*\$4,200 variable + \$9,400 fixed = \$13,600.
†6,500 standard hours × \$2 = \$13,000.

Required

Analyze the \$600 underapplied overhead in terms of:

1. A variable overhead spending variance.
2. A variable overhead efficiency variance.
3. A fixed overhead budget variance.
4. A fixed overhead volume variance.

Solution to Review Problem

Variable Overhead Variances

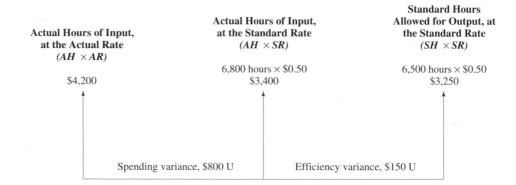

Actual Hours of Input, at the Actual Rate *(AH × AR)*	Actual Hours of Input, at the Standard Rate *(AH × SR)*	Standard Hours Allowed for Output, at the Standard Rate *(SH × SR)*
	6,800 hours × \$0.50	6,500 hours × \$0.50
\$4,200	\$3,400	\$3,250

Spending variance, \$800 U   Efficiency variance, \$150 U

These same variances in the alternative format would be:
Variable overhead spending variance

Actual variable overhead cost......................	\$4,200
Actual inputs at the standard rate: 6,800 hours × \$0.50	3,400
Spending variance.............................	\$800 U

Variable overhead efficiency variance:

$$SR(AH - SH) = \text{Efficiency variance}$$
$$\$0.50\,(6,800 \text{ hours} - 6,500 \text{ hours}) = \$150 \text{ U}$$

Fixed Overhead Variances

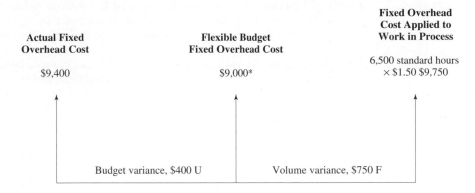

Actual Fixed Overhead Cost	Flexible Budget Fixed Overhead Cost	Fixed Overhead Cost Applied to Work in Process
		6,500 standard hours × $1.50 $9,750
$9,400	$9,000*	

Budget variance, $400 U   Volume variance, $750 F

*Can be expressed as: 6,000 denominator hours × $1.50 = $9,000.

These same variances in the alternative format would be:
Fixed overhead budget variance

Actual fixed overhead cost $9,400
Budgeted fixed overhead 9,000
Budget variance .... $400 U

Fixed overhead volume variance

$$\text{Fixed portion of the predetermined overhead rate} \times \left\{ \frac{\text{Denominator}}{\text{hours}} - \frac{\text{Standard}}{\text{hours}} \right\} = \frac{\text{Volume}}{\text{variance}}$$

$$\$1.50 \ (6,000 \text{ hours} - 6,500 \text{ hours}) = -\$750 \text{ F}$$

Summary of Variances

A summary of the four overhead variances is given below:

Variable overhead:	
Spending variance..........................	$800 U
Efficiency variance..........................	150 U
Fixed overhead:	
Budget variance	400 U
Volume variance...........................	750 F
Underapplied overhead........................	$600 U

Notice that the $600 summary variance figure agrees with the underapplied balance in the company's Manufacturing Overhead account. This agreement stands as proof of the accuracy of our variance analysis. *Each period* the under- or overapplied overhead balance should be analyzed as we have done. These variances will help the manager to see where his or her time of the subordinates should be directed for better control of costs and operations.

KEY TERMS FOR REVIEW

OBJECTIVE 9

Define or explain the key terms listed at the end of the chapter.

Activity variance   The net income gained or lost through failure to achieve the budgeted sales in units for the period. This variance is computed by multiplying the difference between budgeted sales and actual sales by the budgeted contribution margin per unit. (p. 554)

Budget variance   A measure of the difference between the budgeted fixed overhead costs (as contained in the overhead flexible budget) and the actual fixed overhead costs incurred during a period. (p. 565)

Denominator activity   The estimated activity figure used to compute the predetermined overhead rate. (p. 563)

Flexible budget   A budget that is designed to cover a range of activity rather than a single point. It can be used to develop budgeted revenues and/or costs anywhere within that range to compare against actual results. (p. 550)

Selling price/cost variance   A measure of the net income gained or lost through failure to maintain control over selling price and over the various costs that a company may incur. (p. 554)

Static budget   A budget designed to cover only one level of activity and in which actual costs are always compared against budgeted costs at this one activity level. (p. 550)

Volume variance   A measure of the difference between the amount of fixed overhead cost contained in the overhead flexible budget and the amount of fixed overhead cost applied to work in process during a period. (p. 565)

QUESTIONS

11–1   What is a static budget?

11–2   What is a flexible budget, and how does it differ from a static budget? What is the main deficiency of the static budget?

11–3   What are the two prime responsibilities of the production manager? How do these two responsibilities differ?

11–4   What does the activity variance measure, and how is it computed?

11–5   Name three criteria that should be considered in choosing an activity base on which to construct an overhead flexible budget.

11–6   In comparing budgeted data with actual data in a performance report for variable manufacturing overhead, what variance(s) is produced if the budgeted data are based on actual hours worked? On both actual hours worked and standard hours allowed?

11–7   How does the variable manufacturing overhead spending variance differ from the materials price variance?

11–8   Why is the term *overhead efficiency variance* a misnomer?

11–9   "Fixed costs have no place in a flexible budget." Discuss.

11–10   In which way is the overhead flexible budget involved in product costing?

11–11   What costing problem is created by the fact that fixed overhead costs come in large, indivisible chunks?

11–12   What is meant by the term *denominator level of activity?*

11–13   Why do we apply overhead to work in process on a basis of standard hours allowed in Chapter 11 when we applied it on a basis of actual hours in Chapter 3? What is the difference in costing systems between the two chapters?

11–14   In a standard cost system, what two variances can be computed for fixed overhead?

11–15   What does the fixed overhead budget variance measure? Is the variance controllable by management? Explain.

11–16   Under what circumstances would you expect the volume variance to be favourable? Unfavourable? Does the variance measure deviations in spending for fixed overhead items? Explain.

11–17 How might the volume variance be measured, other than in dollars?

11–18 What dangers are there in expressing fixed costs on a per unit basis?

11–19 In Chapter 3, you became acquainted with the concept of under- or overapplied overhead. What four variances can be computed from the under- or overapplied overhead total?

11–20 If factory overhead is overapplied for the month of August, would you expect the total of the overhead variances to be favourable or unfavourable? Why?

11–21 Why would using a master budget contain a standard cost variance?

11–22 Using a direct costing income statement format, what would constitute the difference in income between the master budget and the flexible budget results for a period?

11–23 Why do spending and efficiency variances appear as differences between flexible budget income results and the actual income statement results?

11–24 If standard cost variances are prepared only after a month-end, why would management be interested in full income statement variance analysis?

11–25 If a company operates using a modern high-tech manufacturing process with no significant direct labour and materials purchased on a long-term fixed pricing contract, of what use are standard costs and the resulting variances?

11–26 Explain clearly the rationale for disposing of standard cost variances at the end of an accounting period.

EXERCISES

E11–1 An incomplete flexible budget for overhead is given below:

Overhead Costs	Cost Formula (per Hour)	Machine-Hours			
		6,000	8,000	10,000	12,000
Variable costs:					
Indirect materials			$ 6,000		
Maintenance			4,800		
Utilities			1,200		
Total variable costs					
Fixed costs:					
Rent.			10,000		
Supervisory salaries			20,000		
Insurance.			8,000		
Total fixed costs					
Total overhead costs					

Required

Provide the missing information in the budget.

E11–2 The cost formulas for Swan Company's overhead costs are given below. The costs cover a range of 8,000 to 10,000 machine-hours.

Overhead Costs	Cost Formula
Supplies.	$0.20 per machine-hour
Indirect labour.	$10,000 plus $0.25 per machine-hour
Utilities	$0.15 per machine-hour
Maintenance	$7,000 plus $0.10 per machine-hour
Depreciation	$8,000

Required

Prepare a flexible budget in increments of 1,000 machine-hours. Include the fixed costs in your flexible budget.

E11–3 The variable portion of Whaley Company's flexible budget for overhead is given below:

Overhead Costs	Cost Formula (per Hour)	Machine-Hours 10,000	18,000	24,000
Utilities....................	$1.20	$12,000	$21,600	$28,800
Supplies	0.30	3,000	5,400	7,200
Maintenance..................	2.40	24,000	43,200	57,600
Rework time.................	0.60	6,000	10,800	14,400
Total variable costs	$4.50	$45,000	$81,000	$108,000

During a recent period, the company recorded 16,000 machine-hours of activity. The variable overhead costs incurred were as follows:

Utilities	$20,000
Supplies	4,700
Maintenance.........	35,100
Rework time	12,300

The budgeted activity for the period had been 18,000 machine-hours.

Required

1. Prepare a variable overhead performance report for the period. Indicate whether variances are favourable (F) or unfavourable (U). Show only a spending variance on your report.
2. Discuss the significance of the variances. Might some variances be the result of others? Explain.

E11–4 Operating at a normal level of 24,000 direct labour-hours, Trone Company produces 8,000 units of product. The direct labour wage rate is $6.30 per hour. Two kilograms of raw materials go into each unit of product at a cost of $4.20 per kilogram. A flexible budget is used to plan and control overhead costs:

Flexible Budget Data

Overhead Costs	Cost Formula (per Hour)	Direct Labour-Hours 20,000	22,000	24,000
Variable costs	$1.60	$ 32,000	$ 35,200	$ 38,400
Fixed costs		84,000	84,000	84,000
Total overhead costs		$116,000	$119,200	$122,400

Required

1. Using 24,000 direct labour-hours as the denominator activity, compute the predetermined overhead rate and break it down into fixed and variable elements.
2. Complete the standard cost card below for one unit of product:

Direct materials, 2 kg at $4.20	$8.40
Direct labour, ?......................	?
Variable overhead, ?......................	?
Fixed overhead, ?......................	?
Total standard cost per unit...............	$?

E11–5 Selected operating information on three different companies is given below:

	Company		
	X	Y	Z
Full-capacity direct labour-hours	20,000	9,000	10,000
Budgeted direct labour-hours*	19,000	8,500	8,000
Actual direct labour-hours....................	19,500	8,000	9,000
Standard direct labour-hours allowed for actual output.........................	18,500	8,250	9,500

*Denominator activity for computing the predetermined overhead rate.

Required

For each company, state whether the volume variance would be favourable or unfavourable; also, explain in each case *why* the volume variance would be favourable or unfavourable.

E11–6 Kohler Company's flexible budget for overhead (in condensed form) is given below:

Overhead Costs	Cost Formula (per Hour)	Machine-Hours 12,000	15,000	18,000
Variable costs..............	$1.80	$21,600	$27,000	$32,400
Fixed costs................		60,000	60,000	60,000
Total overhead costs.........		$81,600	$87,000	$92,400

The following information is available for a recent period:
a. The company chose 15,000 machine-hours as the denominator level of activity for computing the predetermined overhead rate.
b. The company produced 9,500 units of product and worked 14,000 actual hours. The standard machine time per unit is 1.5 hours.
c. Actual overhead costs incurred were: variable overhead, $26,000; and fixed overhead, $60,450.

Required

1. Compute the predetermined overhead rate. Divide it into fixed and variable elements.
2. Compute the standard hours allowed for the output of the year.
3. Compute the fixed overhead budget and volume variances.

E11–7 Weller Company's flexible budget for overhead (in condensed form) follows:

Overhead Costs	Cost Formula (per Hour)	Machine-Hours 8,000	9,000	10,000
Variable costs..............	$1.05	$ 8,400	$ 9,450	$10,500
Fixed costs................		24,800	24,800	24,800
Total overhead costs.........		$33,200	$34,250	$35,300

The following information is available for a recent period:
a. A denominator activity of 8,000 machine-hours was chosen to compute the predetermined overhead rate.
b. At the 8,000 standard machine-hours level of activity, the company should produce 3,200 units of product.
c. The company's actual operating results were as follows:

Number of units produced.............	3,500
Actual machine-hours	8,500
Actual variable overhead costs	$ 9,860
Actual fixed overhead costs............	25,100

Required

1. Compute the predetermined overhead rate, and break it down into variable and fixed cost elements.
2. What were the standard hours allowed for the year's output?
3. Compute the variable overhead spending and efficiency variances and the fixed overhead budget and volume variances.

E11–8 Selected information relating to the fixed overhead costs of Westwood Company for a recent period is given below:

Activity:
Number of units produced	9,500
Standard hours allowed per unit.................	2
Denominator activity (machine-hours)...........	20,000

Costs:
Actual fixed overhead costs incurred	$79,000
Budget variance	1,000 F

Overhead cost is applied to products on a basis of machine-hours.

Required

1. What was the fixed portion of the predetermined overhead rate?
2. What were the standard hours allowed for the period's production?
3. What was the volume variance?

E11–9 The standard cost card for the single product manufactured by Prince Company is given below:

Standard Cost Card—Per Unit

Direct materials, 1 metre at $14.....................	$14.00
Direct labour, 0.8 hours at $9.......................	7.20
Variable overhead, 0.8 hours at $2.50	2.00
Fixed overhead, 0.8 hours at $6.....................	4.80
Total standard cost per unit	$28.00

Last year, the company produced 10,000 units of product and worked 8,200 actual direct labour-hours. Overhead cost is applied to production on a basis of direct labour-hours. Selected data relating to the company's fixed overhead cost for the year are shown below:

Actual Fixed Overhead Cost	Flexible Budget Fixed Overhead Cost	Fixed Overhead Cost Applied to Work in Process
$45,600	?	___?___ hrs. × 6 = $ _?_

Budget variance, $ __?__   Volume variance, $3,000 F

Required

1. What were the standard hours allowed for the year's production?
2. What was the amount of fixed overhead cost contained in the flexible budget for the year?
3. What was the budget variance for the year?
4. What denominator activity level did the company use in setting the predetermined overhead rate for the year?

PROBLEMS

P11–10   Standard Cost Card; Materials, Labour, and Overhead Variances

Dresser Company uses a standard cost system and sets predetermined overhead rates on the basis of direct labour-hours. The following data are taken from the company's flexible budget for the current year:

Denominator activity (direct labour-hours).....................	9,000
Variable overhead cost at 9,000 direct labour-hours	$34,200
Fixed overhead cost.......................................	63,000

A standard cost card showing the standard cost to produce one unit of the company's product is given below:

Direct materials, 4 kilograms at $2.60	$10.40
Direct labour, 2 hours at $9...................	18.00
Overhead, 120% of direct labour cost...........	21.60
Standard cost per unit	$50.00

During the year, the company produced 4,800 units of product and incurred the following costs:

Materials purchased, 30 metric tonnes at $2.50 per kg	$75,000
Materials used in production (tonnes)	20,000
Direct labour cost incurred, 10,000 hours at $8.60	$86,000
Variable overhead cost incurred	35,900
Fixed overhead cost incurred	64,800

Required

1. Redo the standard cost card in a clearer, more usable format by detailing the variable and fixed overhead cost elements.
2. Prepare an analysis of the variances for materials and labour for the year.
3. Prepare an analysis of the variances for variable and fixed overhead for the year.
4. What effect, if any, does the choice of a denominator activity level have on standard unit costs? Is the volume variance a controllable variance from a spending point of view? Explain.

P11–11 Absorption Costing Statement; Integration of Materials, Labour, and Overhead Variances "It certainly is nice to see that small variance on the income statement after all the trouble we've had lately in controlling manufacturing costs," said Linda White, vice president of Molina Company. "The $2,250 variance reported last period is well below the 3% limit we have set for variances. We need to congratulate everybody on a job well done." The income statement to which Ms. White was referring is shown below:

	20,000 Units		
	Actual	**Budgeted**	**Variance**
Sales	$1,200,000	$1,200,000	$ —
Less cost of goods sold (standard cost, $38 per unit)	762,250	760,000	2,250
Gross margin	437,750	440,000	(2,250)
Less operating expenses:			
Selling expenses	200,000	200,000	—
Administrative expenses	150,000	150,000	—
Total operating expenses	350,000	350,000	—
Net income	$ 87,750	$ 90,000	$(2,250)

The company produces and sells a single product. The standard cost card for the product follows:

Standard Cost Card—Per Unit

Direct materials, 4 metres at $3.50	$14
Direct labour, 1.5 hours at $8	12
Variable overhead, 1.5 hours at $2	3
Fixed overhead, 1.5 hours at $6	9
Standard cost per unitt	$38

The following additional information is available for the year just completed:
a. The company manufactured and sold 20,000 units of product during the year.
b. A total of 78,000 metres of material were purchased during the year at a cost of $3.75 per metre. All of this material was used to manufacture the 20,000 units. There were no beginning or ending inventories for the year.
c. The company worked 32,500 direct labour-hours during the year at a cost of $7.80 per hour.
d. Overhead cost is applied to products on the basis of direct labour-hours. Data relating to overhead costs follow:

Denominator activity level (direct labour-hours)	25,000
Budgeted fixed overhead costs (from the flexible budget)	$150,000
Actual fixed overhead costs	148,000
Actual variable overhead costs	68,250

e. All variances are closed to cost of goods sold at the end of each year.

Required

1. Compute the direct materials price and quantity variances for the year.
2. Compute the direct labour rate and efficiency variances for the year.
3. For manufacturing overhead, compute the following:
    a. The variable overhead spending and efficiency variances for the year.
    b. The fixed overhead budget and volume variances for the year.
4. Total the variances you have computed, and compare the net amount with the $2,250 variance on the income statement. Do you agree that everyone should be congratulated for a job well done? Explain.

P11–12 Basic Overhead Analysis Highland Shortbread, Ltd., of Aberdeen, Scotland, produces a single product and uses a standard cost system to help in the control of costs. Overhead is applied to production on a basis of machine-hours. According to the company's flexible budget, the following overhead costs should be incurred at an activity level of 18,000 machine-hours (the denominator activity level chosen for the year):

Variable overhead costs	£ 31,500
Fixed overhead costs	72,000
Total overhead costs	£103,500

During the year, the following operating results were recorded:

Actual machine-hours worked	15,000
Standard machine-hours allowed	16,000
Actual variable overhead cost	
incurred	£26,500
Actual fixed overhead cost incurred	£70,000

At the end of the year, the company's Manufacturing Overhead account contained the following data:

Manufacturing Overhead

Actual costs	96,500	92,000	Applied costs
	4,500		

Management would like to determine the cause of the £4,500 underapplied overhead before closing the amount to cost of goods sold.

Required

1. Compute the predetermined overhead rate for the year. Break it down into variable and fixed cost elements.
2. Show how the £92,000 "Applied costs" figure in the Manufacturing Overhead account was computed.
3. Analyze the £4,500 underapplied overhead figure in terms of the variable overhead spending and efficiency variances and the fixed overhead budget and volume variances.
4. Explain the meaning of each variance that you computed in (3) above, and indicate how each variance is controlled.

P11–13 Preparing a Revised Overhead Performance Report Shipley Company has had a comprehensive budgeting system in operation for several years. Feelings vary among the managers as to the value and benefit of the system. The line supervisors are very happy with the reports being prepared on their performance, but upper management often expresses dissatisfaction over the reports being prepared on various phases of the company's operations. A typical overhead performance report for a recent period is shown below:

SHIPLEY COMPANY
Overhead Performance Report—Milling Department
For the Quarter Ended June 30

	Actual	Budgeted	Variance
Machine-hours	25,000	30,000	
Variable overhead:			
Indirect labour	$ 20,000	$ 22,500	$2,500 F
Supplies	5,400	6,000	600 F
Utilities	27,000	30,000	3,000 F
Rework time	14,000	15,000	1,000 F
Total variable costs	66,400	73,500	7,100 F
Fixed overhead:			
Maintenance	61,900	60,000	1,900 U
Inspection	90,000	90,000	— U
Total fixed costs	151,900	150,000	1,900 U
Total overhead costs	$218,300	$223,500	$5,200 F

After receiving a copy of this performance report, the supervisor of the milling department stated, "No one can complain about my department; our variances have been favourable for over a year now. We've saved the company thousands of dollars by our excellent cost control."

The "budget" data above are taken from the department's flexible budget and represent the original planned level of activity for the quarter.

Required

1. The production superintendent is uneasy about the performance reports being prepared and would like you to evaluate their usefulness to the company.
2. What changes, if any, would you recommend be made in the overhead performance report above in order to give the production superintendent better insight into how well the supervisor is doing his job?
3. Prepare a new overhead performance report for the quarter, incorporating any changes you suggested in (2) above.

P11–14 Standard Cost Card and Overhead Analysis   Wymont Company produces a single product that requires a large amount of labour time. Therefore, overhead cost is applied on the basis of direct labour-hours. The company's condensed flexible budget for overhead is given below:

Overhead Costs	Cost Formula (per Hour)	Direct Labour-Hours		
		24,000	30,000	36,000
Variable costs	$2	$ 48,000	$ 60,000	$ 72,000
Fixed costs		180,000	180,000	180,000
Total overhead costs		$228,000	$240,000	$252,000

The company's product requires 4 metres of direct material that has a standard cost of $3 per metre. The product requires 1.5 hours of direct labour time. The standard labour rate is $7 per hour.

During the year, the company had planned to operate at a denominator activity level of 30,000 direct labour-hours and to produce 20,000 units of product. Actual activity and costs for the year were as follows:

Number of units produced	22,000
Actual direct labour-hours worked	35,000
Actual variable overhead cost incurred	$ 63,000
Actual fixed overhead cost incurred	181,000

Required

1. Compute the predetermined overhead rate for the year. Break the rate down into variable and fixed elements.
2. Prepare a standard cost card for the company's product; show the details for all manufacturing costs on your standard cost card.

3. a. Compute the standard hours allowed for the year's production.
    b. Complete the following Manufacturing Overhead T-account for the year:

Manufacturing Overhead

?	?
?	?

4. Determine the reason for the under- or overapplied overhead from (3) above by computing the variable overhead spending and efficiency variances and the fixed overhead budget and volume variances.
5. Suppose the company had chosen 36,000 direct labour-hours as the denominator activity rather than 30,000 hours. State which, if any, of the variances computed in (4) above would have changed, and explain how the variance(s) would have changed. No computations are necessary.

P11–15 Flexible Budgets and Overhead Analysis   Rowe Company manufactures a variety of products in several departments. Budgeted costs for the company's finishing department have been set as follows:

Variable costs:	
Direct materials....................	$ 600,000
Direct labour......................	450,000
Indirect labour.....................	30,000
Utilities..........................	50,000
Maintenance	20,000
Total variable costs...............	1,150,000
Fixed costs:	
Supervisory salaries	60,000
Insurance.........................	5,000
Depreciation	190,000
Equipment rental..................	45,000
Total fixed costs	300,000
Total budgeted costs	$1,450,000
Budgeted direct labour-hours	50,000

After careful study, the company has determined that operating activity in the finishing department is best measured in direct labour-hours. The cost formulas used to develop the budgeted costs above are valid over a relevant range of 40,000 to 60,000 direct labour-hours per year.

Required

1. Prepare an overhead flexible budget in good form for the finishing department. Make your budget in increments of 10,000 hours. (The company does not include direct materials and direct labour costs in the flexible budget.)
2. Assume that the company computes predetermined overhead rates by department. Compute the rates, variable and fixed, that will be used by the finishing department to apply overhead costs to production.
3. Suppose that during the year the following actual activity and costs are recorded in the finishing department:

Actual direct labour-hours worked..................	46,000
Standard direct labour-hours allowed	
for the output of the year	45,000
Actual variable overhead cost incurred	$ 89,700
Actual fixed overhead cost incurred................	296,000

    a. A T-account for manufacturing overhead costs in the finishing department is given below. Determine the amount of applied overhead cost for the year, and compute the under- or overapplied overhead.

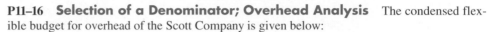

Manufacturing Overhead

Actual costs 385,700	

b.   Analyze the under- or overapplied overhead figure in terms of the variable overhead spending and efficiency variances and the fixed overhead budget and volume variances.

P11–16   Selection of a Denominator; Overhead Analysis   The condensed flexible budget for overhead of the Scott Company is given below:

Overhead Costs	Cost Formula (per hour)	Direct Labour-Hours		
		30,000	**40,000**	**50,000**
Variable costs................	$2.50	$ 75,000	$100,000	$125,000
Fixed costs..................		320,000	320,000	320,000
Total overhead costs.........		$395,000	$420,000	$445,000

The company produces a single product that requires 2.5 direct labour-hours to complete. The direct labour wage rate is $7.50 per hour. Three metres of raw material are required for each unit of product, at a cost of $5 per metre.

Demand for the company's product differs widely from year to year. Expected actual activity for this year is 50,000 direct labour-hours; long-run normal activity is 40,000 direct labour-hours per year.

Required

1.   Assume that the company chooses 40,000 direct labour-hours as the denominator level of activity. Compute the predetermined overhead rate, breaking it down into fixed and variable cost elements.
2.   Assume that the company chooses 50,000 direct labour-hours as the denominator level of activity. Repeat the computations in (1) above.
3.   Complete two standard cost cards as outlined below. Each card should relate to a single unit of product.

Denominator Activity: 40,000 DLH

Direct materials, 3 metres at $5..........	$15.00	
Direct labour, ?.................	?	
Variable overhead, ?.................	?	
Fixed overhead, ?.................	?	
Total standard cost per unit...........	$?	

Denominator Activity: 50,000 DLH

Direct materials, 3 metres at $5..........	$15.00	
Direct labour, ?.................	?	
Variable overhead, ?.................	?	
Fixed overhead, ?.................	?	
Total standard cost per unit...........	$?	

4.   Assume that 48,000 actual hours are worked during the year, and that 18,500 units are produced. Actual overhead costs for the year are as follows:

Variable costs	$124,800
Fixed costs	321,700
Total overhead costs	$446,500

a.   Compute the standard hours allowed for the year's production.
b.   Compute the missing items from the Manufacturing Overhead account below. Assume that the company uses 40,000 direct labour-hours (long-run normal activity) as the denominator activity figure in computing overhead rates, as you have used in (1) above.

Manufacturing Overhead

Actual costs	446,500	?
?		?

c.   Analyze your under- or overapplied overhead balance in terms of variable overhead spending and efficiency variances and fixed overhead budget and volume variances.

5.   Looking at the variances that you have computed, what appears to be the major disadvantage of using long-run normal activity rather than expected actual activity as a denominator in computing the predetermined overhead rate? What advantages can you see to offset this disadvantage?

P11–17   Standard Cost Card; Fixed Overhead Analysis; Graphing   For the current year, Eastwood Company chose a denominator activity level of 15,000 direct labour-hours. According to the company's flexible budget, the following overhead costs should be incurred at this activity level:

> Variable overhead costs. . . . . $ 18,000
> Fixed overhead costs   135,000

The company manufactures a single product that requires 2.5 hours to complete. The direct labour rate is $7 per hour. The product requires 4 kilograms of raw materials; this material has a standard cost of $8 per kg. Overhead is applied to production on the basis of direct labour-hours.

Required

1.   Compute the predetermined overhead rate for the year. Break the rate down into variable and fixed cost elements.

2.   Prepare a standard cost card for one unit of product using the following format:

> Direct materials, 4 kg at $8.00 . . . . $32.00
> Direct labour,   ? . . . .   ?
> Variable overhead, ? . . . .   ?
> Fixed overhead,   ? . . . .   ?
>
> Total standard cost per unit . . . . $?

3.   Prepare a graph with cost on the vertical (Y) axis and direct labour-hours on the horizontal (X) axis. Plot a line on your graph from a zero level of activity to 20,000 direct labour-hours for each of the following costs:
  a.   Budgeted fixed overhead cost (in total).
  b.   Applied fixed overhead cost applied at the hourly rate computed in (1) above.

4.   Assume that during the year the company's actual activity is as follows:

> Number of units produced   5,600
> Actual direct labour-hours worked.   14,500
> Actual fixed overhead cost incurred. $137,400

  a.   Compute the fixed overhead budget and volume variances for the year.
  b.   Show the volume variance on the graph you prepared in (3) above.

5.   Disregard the data in (4) above. Assume instead that the company's actual activity for the year is as follows:

> Number of units produced   6,200
> Actual direct labour-hours worked.   15,800
> Actual fixed overhead cost incurred. $137,400

  a.   Compute the fixed overhead budget and volume variances for the year.
  b.   Show the volume variance on the graph you prepared in (3) above.

P11–18   Detailed Overhead Performance Report   Ronson Products, Ltd., an Australian company, has the following cost formulas (expressed in Australian dollars) for variable overhead costs in one of its machine shops:

Variable Overhead Cost	Cost Formula (per machine-hour)
Supplies.....................	$0.70
Power	1.20
Lubrication	0.50
Wearing tools	3.10
Total	$5.50

During July, the machine shop was scheduled to work 3,200 machine-hours and to produce 16,000 units of product. The standard machine time per unit of product is 0.2 hour. A severe storm during the month forced the company to close for several days, which reduced the level of output for the month. Actual results for July were as follows:

Actual machine-hours worked..............	2,700
Actual number of units produced	14,000

Actual costs for July were as follows:

	Total Actual Cost	Per Machine-Hour
Supplies.................	$ 1,836	$0.68
Power	3,348	1.24
Lubrication	1,485	0.55
Wearing tools	8,154	3.02
Total	$14,823	$5.49

Required

Prepare an overhead performance report for the machine shop for July. Use column headings in your report as shown below:

Overhead Item	Cost Formula	Actual Costs Incurred, 2,700 Hours	Budget Based on ? Hours	Budget Based on ? Hours	Total Variance	Breakdown of the Total Variance	
						Spending Variance	Efficiency Variance

P11–19 Flexible Budget and Overhead Performance Report

Durrant Company has had great difficulty in controlling manufacturing overhead costs. At a recent convention, the president heard about a control device for overhead costs known as a flexible budget, and he has hired you to implement this budgeting program in Durrant Company. After some effort, you have developed the following cost formulas for the company's machining department. These costs are based on a normal operating range of 10,000 to 20,000 machine-hours per month:

Cost	Cost Formula
Utilities	$0.70 per machine-hour
Lubricants	$1.00 per machine-hour plus $8,000 per month
Machine setup	$0.20 per machine-hour
Indirect labour	$0.60 per machine-hour plus $120,000 per month
Depreciation	$32,000 per month

During March, the first month after your preparation of the above data, the machining department worked 18,000 machine-hours and produced 9,000 units of product. The actual costs of this production were as follows:

Utilities	$ 12,000
Lubricants	24,500
Machine setup...........	4,800
Indirect labour...........	132,500
Depreciation	32,000
Total costs	$205,800

There were no variances in the fixed costs. The department had originally been budgeted to work 20,000 machine-hours during March.

Required

1. Prepare a flexible budget for the machining department in increments of 5,000 hours. Include both variable and fixed costs in your budget.
2. Prepare an overhead performance report for the machining department for the month of March. Include both variable and fixed costs in the report (in separate sections). Show only a spending variance on the report.
3. What additional information would you need to compute an overhead efficiency variance for the department?
4. Explain to the president how the flexible budget might be used for product costing purposes as well as for cost control purposes.

P11–20   Spending and Efficiency Variances; Evaluating an Overhead Performance Report   Ronald Davis, superintendent of Mason Company's milling department, is very happy with his performance report for the past month. The report follows:

MASON COMPANY
Overhead Performance Report—Milling Department

	Actual	Budgeted	Variance
Machine-hours	30,000	35,000	
Variable overhead:			
Indirect labour	$ 19,700	$ 21,000	$ 1,300 F
Utilities...........................	50,800	59,500	8,700 F
Supplies	12,600	14,000	1,400 F
Maintenance.......................	24,900	28,000	3,100 F
Total variable costs................	108,000	122,500	14,500 F
Fixed overhead:			
Maintenance......................	52,000	52,000	—
Supervision.......................	110,000	110,000	—
Depreciation......................	80,000	80,000	—
Total fixed costs..................	242,000	242,000	—
Total overhead costs..................	$350,000	$364,500	$14,500 F

Upon receiving a copy of this report, John Arnold, the production manager, commented, "I've been getting these reports for months now, and I still can't see how they help me assess efficiency and cost control in that department. I agree that the budget for the month was 35,000 machine-hours, but that represents 17,500 units of product, since it should take two hours to produce one unit. The department produced only 14,000 units during the month, and took 30,000 machine-hours of time to do it. Why do all the variances turn up favourable?"

Required

1. In answer to Mr. Arnold's question, why do all the variances turn up favourable? Evaluate the performance report.
2. Prepare a new overhead performance report that will help Mr. Arnold assess efficiency and cost control in the milling department. (Hint: Exhibit 11–7 may be helpful in structuring your report; include both variable and fixed costs in the report.)

P11–21   Comprehensive Problem: Flexible Budget; Overhead Performance Report   Elgin Company has recently introduced budgeting as an integral part of its corporate planning process. An inexperienced member of the accounting staff was given the assignment of constructing a flexible budget for overhead costs and prepared it in the format shown below:

Percentage of Capacity	80%	100%
Machine-hours	40,000	50,000
Utilities.........................	$ 41,000	$ 49,000
Supplies	4,000	5,000
Indirect labour	8,000	10,000
Maintenance.....................	37,000	41,000
Supervision	10,000	10,000
Total overhead costs.............	$100,000	$115,000

The company assigns overhead costs to production on a basis of machine-hours. The cost formulas used to prepare the budgeted figures above are relevant over a range of 80% to 100% of capacity and relate to monthly usage of overhead cost items. The managers who will be working under these budgets have control over both fixed and variable overhead costs.

Required

1. Redo the company's flexible budget, presenting it in better format as illustrated in Exhibit 11–8. Show the budgeted costs at 80%, 90%, and 100% levels of capacity. (Use the high-low method to separate fixed and variable costs.)
2. Express the flexible budget prepared in (1) above in cost formula form using a single cost formula to express all overhead costs.
3. During May, the company operated at 86% of capacity in terms of actual machine-hours recorded in the factory. Actual overhead costs incurred during the month were as follows:

Utilities	$ 42,540
Supplies.	6,450
Indirect labour	9,890
Maintenance	35,190
Supervision	10,000
Total actual costs.	$104,070

There were no variances in the fixed costs. Prepare a performance report for May. Include both fixed and variable costs in your report (in separate sections). Structure your report so that it shows only a spending variance for overhead. The company originally budgeted to work 40,000 machine-hours during the month; standard hours allowed for the month's production totalled 41,000 machine-hours.

4. Explain the possible causes of the spending variance for supplies.
5. Compute an efficiency variance for *total* variable overhead cost, and explain the nature of the variance.

P11–22 Standard Cost Variances   The Evans Co. Ltd. is a manufacturing company which has established the following standard cost per unit:

Materials	5 pieces at $4.00 =	$20.00
Direct Labour	2 hours at $8.00 =	16.00
Variable overhead	2 hours at $3.00 =	6.00
Fixed overhead	2 hours at $5.00 =	10.00
		$52.00

Normal activity of 60,000 hours was used as the denominator. Other possible denominators were:

> Expected annual activity, 55,000 hours
> Practical capacity, 75,000 hours

Actual activity during 19x1 included the following:

> Beginning inventory, 0
> Units produced, 28,000
> Materials used, $570,000
> Direct labour, $450,000
> Variable overhead, $170,000
> Fixed overhead, $305,000
> Ending inventory, 7,000 units

Required

Compute the cost of goods sold under each of the following sets of alternatives:

1. Absorption costing.
   Actual materials and labour and predetermined overhead
   Normal activity used as denominator.
2. Variable costing.
   Standard costs.
3. Absorption costing.
   Standard costs.
   Practical activity used as denominator.

(CGA-Canada, adapted)

P11–23 Full Variance Analysis; Direct Costing Shamrock Enterprises Limited manufactures and distributes integrated circuits for electronics firms. In December 19x7, Shamrock required a bank loan and the bank manager insisted that Paddy O'Toole, Shamrock's president, prepare a budget for 19x8. In January 19x9, Shamrock needed an additional loan and O'Toole asked her accountant to prepare a budget for 19x9 to show the bank manager. O'Toole was concerned because Shamrock's profit for 19x8 was considerably less than the 19x8 budget figure given the bank and she knew that the bank manager would want to know why. As a first step in analyzing the differences, O'Toole copied the 19x8 actual figures onto a 19x8 bank budget form shown in Exhibit 11–13.

EXHIBIT 11–13

SHAMROCK ENTERPRISES LIMITED
19x8 Budget Prepared for Bank Loan

Dollars (in 000s)

	Budget	Actual	Variance
Sales—units	110,000	105,000	5,000 U
Sales—dollars	$2,750	$2,520	$230 U
Cost of sales:			
Material	440	421	19 F
Labour	880	845	35 F
Overhead	220	205	15 F
Fixed factory overhead	300	303	3 U
	1,840	1,774	66 F
Operating profit	910	746	164 U
Selling prices:			
Variable	220	209	11 F
Fixed	100	102	2 U
Administration—fixed	200	197	3 F
	520	508	12 F
Profit before income tax	390	238	152 U
Income tax	156	95	61 F
Net Earnings	$ 234	$ 143	$ 91 U

Standard Costs on Which Budget Is Based

	Standard per Unit
Sales price	$25
Direct: Material	$4
Labour, ½ hour at $16 per hour	8
Overhead, ½ hour at $4 per hour	2
Fixed factory overhead:	
Depreciation	$200,000
Other	100,000
	$300,000
Standard output 100,000 units at ½ hour = 50,000 direct labour hours ($300,000 ÷ 50,000) × ½ hour	3
Selling expenses:	
Variable	2
Fixed $100,000 ÷ 100,000 units	1
Administration: Fixed:	
$200,000 ÷ 100,000 units	2
	$22

Standard costs were used for preparing bids whereas the cost accounting system recorded actual costs.

Required

1. Redraft Exhibit 11–13 to show the 19x8 budget, flexible budget, actual, and variances from the flexible budget, with contribution margins separately identified.
2. Present quantitative analysis to demonstrate to management the main causes for the variance from the flexible budget, as a basis for both taking corrective action and explaining the variance from budget to the bank manager.

P11–24   Variance Analysis   The Ripe Company uses a standard cost system in accounting for its production of chairs. Company policy is to isolate all variances as soon as possible. They began the year 19x9 with the following standards based on an expected volume of 60,000 chairs for the year:

	Per Unit
Direct materials (3 metres at $10 per metre)............	$30
Direct labour, type A (4 hours at $8 per hour)..........	32
Direct labour, type B (6 hours at $15 per hour)........	90
Variable overhead (10 hours at $2 per hour)...........	20
Fixed overhead (10 hours at $4 per hour).............	40
Total manufacturing costs	$212

Other expected revenues and expenses:

Selling price	$400	per unit
Variable selling and administration..............	$50	per unit
Fixed selling and administration...............	$20,000	per month
Expected total industry demand	25,000	units per month

Actual results for the month of February 19x9 were as follows:

a.   The company actually produced and sold 5,500 chairs at an average selling price of $390 per chair, and actual total industry sales totalled 30,000 units for the month.
b.   Direct material purchases for the month totalled 15,000 metres at an average cost of $11 per metre. Production in the month used a total of 17,200 metres.
c.   Due to the difference in labour rates for the two different classes of labour, the production foreperson decided to employ more of the type A workers and less of the type B workers. Actual results for the month were:

> Type A—40,000 hours at a total cost of $324,000.
> Type B—29,000 hours at a total cost of $435,000.

d.   Actual overhead results for the month were:

> Variable overhead........ $130,000
> Fixed overhead $210,000

e.   All other revenues and expenses behaved as expected.

Required

1. Calculate all the appropriate variances for the manufacturing costs.
2. Evaluate the decision of the production foreperson to change the composition of the direct labour force.
3. At the end of the month, the vice president of marketing made the following statement:

> I feel the sales force deserves a bonus for the month as they were able to exceed budgeted sales for the month by 10% (500 units). I don't know the total increase in company profits as I have no control over the production costs, but I'm sure it's enough to justify a $50,000 bonus.

Calculate all appropriate variances and evaluate the vice president's statement.

(SMAC, adapted)

CASES

C11–25 Incomplete Data Each of the cases below is independent. You may assume that each company uses a standard cost system and that each company's flexible budget for overhead is based on standard machine-hours.

		Company:	
	Item	**X**	**Y**
1.	Denominator activity in hours	18,000	?
2.	Standard hours allowed for units produced	?	28,000
3.	Actual hours worked................................	?	27,500
4.	Flexible budget variable overhead per machine-hour......	$ 1.60	$?
5.	Flexible budget fixed overhead (total)	?	?
6.	Actual variable overhead cost.......................	30,000	55,275
7.	Actual fixed overhead cost	72,500	134,600
8.	Variable overhead cost applied to production*....................................	31,200	?
9.	Fixed overhead cost applied to production*....................................	?	126,000
10.	Variable overhead spending variance	?	?
11.	Variable overhead efficiency variance	800U	1,000
12.	Fixed overhead budget variance	500U	?
13.	Fixed overhead volume variance	?	9,000
14.	Variable portion of the predetermined overhead rate....................................	?	?
15.	Fixed portion of the predetermined overhead rate....................................	?	?
16.	Underapplied or (overapplied) overhead	?	?

*Based on standard hours allowed for units produced.

Required

Compute the unknown amounts. (Hint: One way to proceed would be to use the format for variance analysis found in Exhibit 10–5 for variable overhead and in Exhibit 11–11 for fixed overhead.)

C11–26 Ethics and the Manager Tom Kemper is the controller of the London manufacturing facility of Prudhom Enterprises, Incorporated. Among the many reports that must be filed with corporate headquarters is the annual overhead performance report. The report covers an entire fiscal year, which ends on December 31, and is due at corporate headquarters shortly after the beginning of the New Year. Kemper does not like putting work off to the last minute, so just before Christmas he put together a preliminary draft of the overhead performance report. Some adjustments would be required for transactions that occur between Christmas and New Year's Day, but there are generally very few of these. A copy of the preliminary draft report, which Kemper completed on December 21, appears below:

LONDON MANUFACTURING FACILITY
Overhead Performance Report
December 21 Preliminary Draft

Budgeted machine-hours............ 200,000
Actual machine-hours.............. 180,000

Overhead Costs	**Cost Formulas (per hour)**	**Actual Costs 180,000 Hours**	**Budget Based on 180,000 Hours**	**Spending or Budget Variance**
Variable costs:				
Power	$0.10	$ 19,750	$ 18,000	$1,750 U
Supplies...................	0.25	47,000	45,000	2,000 U
Abrasives..................	0.30	58,000	54,000	4,000 U
Total variable costs	$0.65	124,750	117,000	7,750 U

Fixed costs:				
Depreciation	345,000	332,000	13,000	U
Supervisory salaries	273,000	275,000	2,000	F
Insurance.	37,000	37,000	—	
Industrial engineering	189,000	210,000	21,000	F
Factory building lease.	60,000	60,000	—	
Total fixed costs	904,000	914,000	10,000	F
Total overhead costs	$1,028,750	$1,031,000	$2,250	F

Melissa Ilianovitch, the general manager at the London facility, asked to see a copy of the preliminary draft report at 4:45 PM on December 23. Kemper carried a copy of the report to her office where the following discussion took place:

ILIANOVITCH: Ouch! Almost all of the variances on the report are unfavourable. The only thing that looks good at all are the favourable variances for supervisory salaries and for industrial engineering. How did we have an unfavourable variance for depreciation?

KEMPER: Do you remember that milling machine that broke down because the wrong lubricant was used by the machine operator?

ILIANOVITCH: Only vaguely.

KEMPER: It turned out we couldn't fix it. We had to scrap the machine and buy a new one.

ILIANOVITCH: This report doesn't look good. I was raked over the coals last year when we had just a few unfavourable variances.

KEMPER: I'm afraid the final report is going to look even worse.

ILIANOVITCH: Oh?

KEMPER: The line item for industrial engineering on the report is for the work we hired Ferguson Engineering to do for us on a contract basis. The original contract was for $210,000, but we asked them to do some additional work that was not in the contract. Under the terms of the contract, we have to reimburse Ferguson Engineering for the costs of the additional work. The $189,000 in actual costs that appear on the preliminary draft report reflects only their billings up through December 21. The last bill they had sent us was on November 28, and they completed the project just last week. Yesterday I got a call from Laura Sunder over at Ferguson and she said they would be sending us a final bill for the project before the end of this year. The total bill, including the reimbursements for the additional work, is going to be . . .

ILIANOVITCH: I am not sure I want to hear this.

KEMPER: $225,000.

ILIANOVITCH: Ouch! Ouch! Ouch!

KEMPER: The additional work we asked them to do added $15,000 to the cost of the project.

ILIANOVITCH: There is no way I can turn in a performance report with an overall unfavourable variance. They'll kill me at corporate headquarters. Call up Laura at Ferguson and ask her not to send the bill until after the first of the year. We have to have that $21,000 favourable variance for industrial engineering on the performance report.

Required

What should Tom Kemper do? Explain.

C11–27 Selling Expense Flexible Budget Mark Fletcher, president of SoftGro Inc., was looking forward to seeing the performance reports for November because he knew the company's sales for the month had exceeded budget by a considerable margin. SoftGro, a distributor of educational software packages, had been growing steadily for approximately two years. Fletcher's biggest challenge at this point was to ensure that the company did not lose control of expenses during this growth period. When Fletcher received the November reports, he was dismayed to see the large unfavourable variance in the company's monthly selling expense report that is presented on the next page.

SOFTGRO INC.
Monthly Selling Expense Report
November

	Annual Budget	November Budget	Actual	Variance
Unit sales	2,000,000	280,000	310,000	30,000 F
Dollar sales	$80,000,000	$11,200,000	$12,400,000	$1,200,000 F
Orders processed	54,000	6,500	5,800	700 U
Salespersons per month	90	90	96	6 U
Expenses:				
Advertising	$19,800,000	$ 1,650,000	$ 1,660,000	$ 10,000 U
Staff salaries	1,500,000	125,000	125,000	— U
Sales salaries	1,296,000	108,000	115,400	7,400 U
Commissions	3,200,000	448,000	496,000	48,000 U
Per diem expense	1,782,000	148,500	162,600	14,100 U
Office expense	4,080,000	340,000	358,400	18,400 U
Shipping expense	6,750,000	902,500	976,500	74,000 U
Total expenses	$38,408,000	$ 3,722,000	$ 3,893,900	$ 171,900 U

Fletcher called in the company's new controller, Susan Porter, to discuss the implications of the variances reported for November and to plan a strategy for improving performance. Porter suggested that the reporting format that the company had been using might not be giving Fletcher a true picture of the company's operations and proposed that SoftGro implement flexible budgeting for reporting purposes. Porter offered to redo the monthly selling expense report for November using flexible budgeting so that Fletcher could compare the two reports and see the advantages of flexible budgeting.

After some analysis, Porter has determined the following data about the company's selling expenses:

a. The total compensation paid to the sales force consists of both a monthly base salary and a commission. The commission varies with sales dollars.

b. Sales office expense is a mixed cost with the variable portion related to the number of orders processed. The fixed portion of office expense is $3,000,000 annually and is incurred uniformly throughout the year.

c. Subsequent to the adoption of the annual budget for the current year, SoftGro decided to open a new sales territory. As a consequence, approval was given to hire six additional salespersons effective November 1. Porter decided that these additional six people should be recognized in her revised report.

d. Per diem reimbursement to the sales force, while a fixed stipend per day, is variable with the number of salespersons and the number of days spent travelling. SoftGro's original budget was based on an average sales force of 90 persons throughout the year with each salesperson travelling 15 days per month.

e. The company's shipping expense is a mixed cost with the variable portion, $3 per unit, dependent on the number of units sold. The fixed portion is incurred uniformly throughout the year.

Using the data above, Porter believed she would be able to redo the November report and present it to Fletcher for his review.

Required

1. Describe the benefits of flexible budgeting, and explain why Susan Porter would propose that SoftGro use flexible budgeting in this situation.

2. Prepare a revised monthly selling expense report for November that would permit Mark Fletcher to more clearly evaluate SoftGro's control over selling expenses. The report should have a line for *each* selling expense item showing the appropriate budgeted amount, the actual selling expense, and the variance for November.

(CMA, adapted)

C11–28 Integrative Case; Working Backwards from Variance Data   You have recently accepted a position with Bork Company, the manufacturer of an unusual product that is popular with some people. As part of your duties, you review the variances that are reported for each period and make a presentation on the variances to the company's executive committee.

Earlier this morning you received the variances for the most recent period. After reviewing the variances and organizing the data for your presentation, you accidently placed the material on top of some papers that were going to the shredder. In the middle of lunch you suddenly realized your mistake and dashed from the executive lunchroom to the shredding room. There you found the operator busily feeding your pages through the machine. You managed to pull only part of one page from the feeding chute, which contains the following information:

Standard Cost Card—Per Unit

Direct materials, 2 metres at $16	$32.00
Direct labour, 3 hours at $5	15.00
Variable overhead, 3 hours at $3	9.00
Fixed overhead, 3 hours at $8	24.00
Standard cost per unit	$80.00

	Total Standard Cost*	Variances Reported			
		Price or Rate	Spending or Budget	Quantity or Efficiency	Volume
Direct materials	$608,000	$11,600 F		$32,000 U	
Direct labour	285,000	8,540 U		20,000 U	
Variable overhead	171,000		$3,700 F	?†	
Fixed overhead	456,000		1,500 F		$24,000 U

*Applied to Work in Process during the period.

†Figure obliterated by the shredder.

You recall that overhead cost is applied to production on the basis of direct labour-hours and that all of the materials purchased during the period were used in production. Since the company uses JIT to control work flows, work in process inventories are insignificant and can be ignored.

At lunch your supervisor said how pleased she was with your work and that she was looking forward to your presentation that afternoon. You realize that to avoid looking like a bungling fool you must somehow generate the necessary "backup" data for the variances before the executive committee meeting starts in one hour.

Required

1. How many units were produced last period? (You'll have to think a bit to derive this figure from the data.)
2. How many metres of direct materials were purchased and used in production?
3. What was the actual cost per metre of material?
4. How many actual direct labour-hours were worked during the period?
5. What was the actual rate per direct labour-hour?
6. How much actual variable overhead cost was incurred during the period?
7. What is the total fixed overhead cost in the company's flexible budget?
8. What were the denominator hours for last period?

C11–29 Absorption Costing Variance Report   The following data relates to Susan Company for the 19x7.

	Master Budget	**Actual**
Sales volume......................	100,000 units	120,000 units
Selling price	$18 per unit	$17.50 per unit
Production volume	90,000 units	110,000 units
Direct materials:		
Quantity......................	1.0 kilogram per unit	1.1 kilogram per unit
Price	$2.00 per kilogram	$1.90 per kilogram
Direct labour:		
Time	0.5 hour per unit	0.4 hours per unit
Rate..........................	$6.00 per hour	$6.20 per hour
Variable overhead	$1.50 per direct labour-hour	$1.60 per direct labour-hour
Fixed overhead	$45,000 (therefore standard cost rate = $1.00 per direct labour-hour)	$42,000
Work in process inventory:		
Beginning	10,000 equivalent units	10,000 equivalent units
Ending..........................	5,000 equivalent units	5,000 equivalent units
Finished goods inventory:		
Beginning	8,000 units	8,000 units
Ending..........................	3,000 units	3,000 units
Selling and administrative expenses:		
Variable.........................	$3.00 per unit sold	$2.80 per unit sold
Fixed	$140,000	$150,000

Required

Prepare an absorption costing variance analysis report showing both activity and other spending, efficiency, and price variances.

C11–30 Budgets and Standards   You are the recently hired manager of the Food Section of the Bedford Foundation. The Foundation was established as a not-for-profit organization to provide various services (food, clothing, shelter, and medical care) to the needy. The Food Section receives funding from the Foundation and from various departments of the government based on the number of meals it is able to provide each year. All funding is established at the beginning of the year (based on meals provided in the previous year) and all expenditures are controlled through a "line-item" budget. The objectives of your division are to provide daily meals to as many needy people as possible (the government makes the decision as to which people qualify as needy and informs you of this decision).

On your first day of work, you met with Mr. Health, the president of the Foundation, who welcomed you to your new position with the following statement:

I see you have a strong background in various industries as a management accountant. Unfortunately, I don't think you will have a chance to implement much of your knowledge here since we are a not-for-profit organization which operates considerably differently from the industries you are acquainted with. Budgeting in this organization consists of a line-item budget that we establish at the beginning of each year. Your evaluation will be based on your ability to keep expenditures within the limit for each item and serve the maximum number of meals. The Foundation does not prepare a master budget or any cash budgets since all cash levels are predetermined at the beginning of the year, and it is impossible to predict accurately what the demand will be. Any budget that might be prepared would not be accurate, so what purpose would it serve?

I understand that in industry, you made much use of flexible budgets, which seem to me to be a complete waste of time. Flexible budgets are prepared after the fact, so of course they are accurate. Anyone can do an accurate budget if they wait until after the event before predicting what will happen. Obviously, the flexible budget will be equal to the actual results, so what purpose does it serve?

If you have any intentions of instituting a standard cost system, you had better forget about that as well. That would work in an industrial setting only. I've heard some mention of program budgeting from various people in the government; I don't know what it is, but I'm sure it is something that might apply to various government departments, but would not have any applications in an organization such as ours.

Required   Write a report to the president of the Foundation responding to his comments. Make specific reference to the budget system currently in use and the applicability to the Foundation of the various management systems mentioned.

(SMAC, adapted)

C11–31 Budgets and Standards   In early 19x0, the president of the Windsor Jacket Co. (WJ) was reviewing the 19x9 operating results and variance report (see Exhibits 11–14 and 11–15). He was pleased to see that sales and net income were higher than the budget, but was not sure how to interpret the variance report that was prepared by the newly hired controller.

WJ produces and sells two lines of jackets: nylon and leather. The market for nylon jackets is large and competitive, but the leather jacket market has traditionally been small, with only a few competing manufacturers. During 19x9, fashion trendsetters highlighted leather jackets, creating a 10-fold increase in the market's demand for leather jackets. Unfortunately, WJ did not foresee this trend and had planned sales of only 5,000 leather jackets in the 19x9 budget (see Exhibit 11–14).

EXHIBIT 11–14

WINDSOR JACKET CO. INC.
19X9 Operating Budget

	Nylon Jackets	Leather Jackets	Total
Sales volume	95,000	5,000	100,000
Sales revenue	$3,325,000	$750,000	$4,075,000
Direct materials	665,000	250,000	915,000
Direct labour	760,000	200,000	960,000
Variable overhead	570,000	30,000	600,000
Variable selling and administration	166,250	37,500	203,750
Total variable costs	2,161,250	517,500	2,678,750
Contribution margin	$1,163,750	$232,500	1,396,250
Fixed overhead			900,000
Fixed selling and admin			250,000
Net income			$ 246,250

WINDSOR JACKET CO. INC.
19x9 Actual Operating Results

	Nylon Jackets	Leather Jackets	Total
Sales volume	93,500	16,500	110,000
Sales revenue	$3,272,500	$2,475,000	$5,747,500
Direct materials	654,500	935,550	1,590,050
Direct labour	748,000	726,000	1,474,000
Variable overhead	561,000	115,500	676,500
Variable selling and administration	149,600	140,250	289,850
Total variable costs	2,113,100	1,917,300	4,030,400
Contribution margin	$1,159,400	$ 557,700	1,717,100
Fixed overhead			1,000,000
Fixed selling and admin			300,000
Net income			$ 417,100

While the increased demand for the leather jackets created a windfall gain in sales for WJ, it created great turmoil in the production plant. Supply of direct materials had been contracted at the beginning of the year based on the budgeted requirements. WJ's buyers had to purchase the increased requirements for leather from various new sources, some of which proved to be unreliable. Workers skilled in cutting and sewing leather were scarce, and the production manager had to hire and train inexperienced workers. Also, three new special sewing machines had to be purchased.

In late December 19x9, the production manager reported to the president that, despite the many necessary adjustments that were made during the year, he managed to fill all orders for both lines of jackets. He was proud of his department's performance and requested that sizeable bonuses be awarded to all production workers and staff.

Hearing about the production manager's request, the marketing manager asked to speak with the president.

MARKETING MANAGER: I hear that the production manager has been boasting about his department's performance this year. Sure, he filled all the orders, but deliveries were usually two to four weeks late and 8% of the leather jackets were sent back for replacement because of flaws, sizing errors, and inferior quality of leather. We've built our reputation on good service and quality products. We've never been late on deliveries before and returns have always been less than 1%. I'm afraid we're going to lose some of our long-standing customers if we don't get our service and quality back to our usual standards.

EXHIBIT 11-15

WINDSOR JACKET CO. INC.
19x9 Detailed Variance Report

	Nylon Jackets	Leather Jackets	Total
Sales price	–0–	–0–	–0–
Sales volume:*			
Mix	$134,750 U	$ 511,500 F	$ 376,750 F
Quantity	116,375 F	23,20 F	139,625 F
Total sales volume	$ 18,375 U	$ 534,750 F	$ 516,375 F
Direct materials:			
Price	–0–	$ 44,550 U	$ 44,550 U
Usage	–0–	66,000 U	66,000 U
Total direct materials	–0–	$ 110,550 U	$ 110,550 U
Direct labour:			
Rate	–0–	$ 99,000 F	$ 99,000 F
Usage	–0–	165,000 U	165,000 U
Total direct labour	–0–	$ 66,000 U	$ 66,000 U
Variable overhead	–0–	$ 16,500 U	$ 16,500 U
Variable selling and administration	$ 14,025 F	$ 16,500 U	$ 2,475 U
Fixed overhead			$ 100,000 U
Fixed selling and admin			$ 50,000 U
Total variance from budget			$ 170,850 F

*Also can be split into market share and industry volume variances.

Market share variance	$104,125 F	$1,557,750 U	$1,453,625 U
Industry volume variance	122,500 U	2,092,500 F	1,970,000 F
Sales volume variance	$ 18,375 U	$ 534,750 F	$ 516,375 F

PRESIDENT: The production manager admitted to having quality control problems because the inexperienced leather workers did not have the time to adequately train and supervise the new inexperienced workers that were hired. However, he assured me that the new workers need only another month or two to perfect their skills and get up to speed.

MARKETING MANAGER: Well, I hope so. The fashion trend for leather jackets is expected to surpass last year and, if we can deliver good quality jackets on time, I think we can sell up to 30,000 leather jackets in 19x0.

After his meeting with the marketing manager, the president met with the new controller. The president described his conversations with both the production and marketing managers and then requested the following information from the controller:

1. A written explanation of the significance of the variances in the 19x9 detailed variance report.
2. A supported opinion on the performance of the marketing and production departments and whether either department should be awarded bonuses.
3. A draft operating budget for 19x0.

The controller immediately collected data from the marketing and production managers on which to base the 19x0 budget (see Exhibit 11–16).

Required   As the controller for WJ, prepare the information requested by the president.

EXHIBIT 11–16

Marketing and Production Data

	Nylon Jackets	Leather Jackets
Market size (units):		
19x9 budget	475,000	12,500
19x9 actual	425,000	125,000
19x0 estimate	400,000	150,000
Expected market share for 19x0	25%	20%
Estimated sales price for 19x0	$37.00	$160.00
19x9 production standards:		
Direct material quantity	2.8 metres	2.5 metres
Standard price/metre	$2.50	$20.00
Direct labour-hours	1 hour	2 hours
Standard rate/hr	$8.00	$20.00
Standard variable overhead cost	$6.00	$6.00
Variable selling and admin	$1.75	$7.50

Unit variable costs for nylon jackets and all fixed costs are expected to increase by 5% over the 19x9 actual costs because of inflation. For leather jackets, variable cost and usage standards were revised as follows to more closely reflect expected conditions:

	19x9 Actual	Revised 19x0 Standard
Direct material quantity	2.7 metres	2.6 metres
Direct material price/metre	$21.00	$23.00
Direct labour-hours	2.5 hours	2.2 hours
Direct labour rate/hour	$17.60	$20.00
Variable overhead	$7.00	$7.25
Variable selling and administration	$8.50	$9.00

(SMAC, adapted)

GROUP EXERCISES

GE11–32 Managing by the Numbers Budgeting is an annual ritual that few managers look forward to. But there are more deep-seated concerns about the impact that budgets have on organizations and the behaviour of their employees than a textbook could ever illustrate.

Required

Below is a list of statements or situations that sooner or later almost everyone confronts. For each statement or situation, give a real-life example of the situation, identify what the problem is, why it is a problem, and what recommendations you would make to resolve the problem. You may want to consult friends, relatives, or others who may be able to help you with real-life experiences that they have had to deal with. Or, if they are the ones making statements similar to these, ask them to explain their side of the story.

1. You have a bright new idea and take it to your boss. She says, "I like it, but it's not in the budget."
2. Budgets—and incentive pay tied to budgets—may cause managers to do incredibly stupid things. (This statement knows no professional boundaries; see if you can provide examples in each of the following areas: engineering, manufacturing, marketing, and finance.)
3. "A penny saved is a penny lost from next year's budget."
4. "It's not my fault."
5. The worst budgets set cost targets only.
6. The worst failure of budgets is what they don't measure.

(Adapted from Thomas Stewart, "Why Budgets Are Bad for Business," *Fortune,* June 4, 1990, pp. 179, 182, 186, 190.)

GE11–33 Overhead Control For years, U.S. manufacturers followed a strategy of low-cost mass production to gain competitive advantage by pursuing economies of scale—maximizing production of a single product in a single facility. In order to leverage economies of scale into further reductions in unit cost, firms built bigger factories and filled those plants with bigger, faster, and more specialized machines. With total overhead costs increasing, plant managers ran larger lots and pushed costs lower by maximizing the volume of throughput in each department and at each workstation.

Of necessity, the variety of products made had to increase in order to gain the volume necessary to fully utilize the ever-larger and more costly facilities and machinery. As the variety of parts and products produced in any single plant increased, the need for support staff to manage and control production through the plant increased. In time, overhead costs had increased to 30%–40% of total manufacturing costs, while direct labour decreased to 10%–15% of total manufacturing costs and is still dropping.

Required

1. How did plant management control machine-related costs? Traditionally, what performance measures were used to measure and evaluate the performance of machinery?
2. What incentives did these machine-based performance measures provide plant management and shop floor supervisors? What potential results did these performance incentives have?
3. What is production support? Describe how and why production support increased over time.
4. How did plant management attempt to control this increasing category of production support overhead?
5. What is the overhead absorption variance? How was underapplied overhead interpreted?
6. Because of the increasing complexity of the plant, quality problems became an ever-present problem in the operations of a factory. How did plant management view quality in this environment, and what role did quality play in the day-to-day operations of the factory? What is the concept of an acceptable quality level (AQL)?
7. How did cost accounting account for scrap, spoilage, and rework?

8. Who was responsible for quality? How was their performance measured? What implications did this have for understanding and controlling the costs of poor quality?

9. Traditional cost accounting systems encourage some highly questionable behaviour. Can you identify any other questionable actions not already identified above?

GE11–34 Cost Control and Company Size Suppose two factories are located side by side. One plant is extremely large and complex with more than 4,000 employees; 40 production departments; 25 production support departments (e.g., production scheduling); three eight-hour shifts; and an annual budget in excess of $250 million. This plant, one of 20 American Motors assembly plants, makes AM's Great Iroquois sport-utility vehicle.

The other factory is much smaller and is managed by its owner. This plant employs 105 workers, has two 10-hour shifts, and has a budget of $4.5 million annually. Although machines of a similar type are grouped together in the plant, the facility is not large enough to be divided into different production departments. In addition to the owner, there is an engineer who designs the products on a computer-aided design system, an accountant, a secretary, and two shift forepersons. This job shop makes molds that are used to produce a variety of products. For example, one recent job was for a mold that would produce the front panel of the disk drive on an MBI Activa personal computer.

Required

1. What are the primary concerns or issues for each plant?
2. What should the objectives of each plant's cost system be?
3. Given these objectives, what kind of accounting reports and performance measures would be appropriate for managing each factory? Be sure to explain your reasoning for using the reports and performance measures that you recommend.
4. To report timely and relevant information, how often would you issue such reports and measures of performance?

GE11–35 Setting Standards; Behaviour Canadian Widget, Inc., makes a number of high-volume standard products that face highly competitive markets. As a result, its cost system stresses cost control. Canadian uses a standard cost system and updates standards on a regular and timely basis. Until recently, expected annual capacity was the basis for determining predetermined factory overhead rates. This rate was used for internal planning and reporting and performance evaluation purposes, as well as for inventory valuation.

Recently, John Phillips, controller, has proposed changing the basis for internal planning and reporting from expected annual capacity to practical capacity. Since practical capacity remains relatively constant unless there is a plant expansion or purchase of new manufacturing machinery, Phillips believes this change would facilitate planning and budgeting.

Phillips has held one meeting with department managers and presented them with their new annual budgets prepared on the basis of the new, proposed practical capacity standard. There was little discussion. Later, a member of the cost accounting staff pointed out that the new standard for determining predetermined overhead rates would be tighter than the old standard.

Required

1. If the new annual budgets for Canadian Widget reflect the implementation of tighter standards based on practical capacity:
    a. What negative behavioural implications for employees and department managers could occur as a result of this change?
    b. What could Canadian Widget management do to mitigate the negative behavioural effects?
2. Explain how tight cost standards within an organization could have positive behavioural effects.
3. Identify the individuals who should participate in setting standards and describe the benefits to an organization of their participation in the standard setting process.

(CMA, adapted)

12

SEGMENT REPORTING, PROFITABILITY ANALYSIS AND DECENTRALIZATION

LEARNING OBJECTIVES

After studying Chapter 12, you should be able to:

1 Identify three business practices that hinder proper cost assignment.

2 Prepare a segmented income statement using the contribution format, and explain the difference between traceable fixed costs and common fixed costs.

3 Explain how to determine customer profitability.

4 Analyze variances from revenue targets.

5 Analyze marketing expenses using cost drivers.

6 Explain the importance of decentralization in a responsibility accounting system.

7 Differentiate between cost centres, profit centres, and investment centres, and explain how performance is measured in each.

8 Compute the return on investment (ROI) by means of the ROI formula.

9 Show how changes in sales, expenses, and assets affect an organization's ROI.

10 Compute the residual income and enumerate the strengths and weaknesses of this method of measuring performance.

11 Define or explain the key terms listed at the end of the chapter.

12 (Appendix 12A) Identify three ways that transfer prices can be set.

13 (Appendix 12A) Use the transfer pricing formula to compute an appropriate transfer price between segments, assuming the selling division (a) is operating at full capacity and (b) has idle capacity.

Nova Chemicals, part of Nova Corporation announced its plans to double its earnings over the next five to seven years using a strategy of "playing where we can win," thus focusing on those limited product areas where they have a significant cost advantage. One key aspect is the implementation of a new integrated information system to provide faster access to sales data, inventory and margin analysis.[1]

[1]Nova Corporation, *1996 Annual Report*, pp. 18–19.

Managers of organizations determine the direction they wish the organization to take. Strategic planning as described in Chapter 1 is the term applied to this planning process. Budgeting is the financial expression of the plans. The short-term version of budgeting was presented in Chapter 9 while Chapter 15 describes long-term capital budgets. Planning, however, is only part of the management process. Managers through a combination of feedback of actual results, comparisons to budgets, comparisons to results of previous periods, and even comparisons to other organizations attempt to assure that the organization moves in the planned direction.

Managers control the organization using a variety of approaches. Accounting reports of financial results represent one important approach to controlling operations because such reports provide a means of obtaining comparisons to budgets, to previous results, and to the results of other organizations as well as a knowledge of actual results. Such financial comparisons also serve as a base for reward schemes used to motivate managers to work toward the achievement of planned goals and objectives.

These financial performance reports can be constructed in various ways so that they better serve the specific control functions that management desires. As this chapter illustrates, segment reporting, profitability analysis, and investment performance are three commonly used reporting structures that provide somewhat different types of information. For each it is important to understand what purpose is served by the report. Each presents information in a manner that permits a different view of the organization and a different aspect of organizational control. Understanding how the aspects change and why managers would want these changes will permit you to integrate the concepts of control with reports about standard cost variances, cost of production, and flexible budget analyses described in earlier chapters.

The new manufacturing environment has promoted the need for flexibility in management to accompany flexibility in production. Flexibility in management requires timely and accurate decisions by members of the organization ranging from top management to the production worker. Timely and accurate decisions require timely and accurate control information appropriate to this wide range of organizational personnel. Extensions of control information to operating or production workers so they can control their operations has posed an interesting challenge for accountants. Traditional reports have been too aggregated for operating workers. Accounting formats often represent approaches that are not well understood by production workers. Monthly, reports, the common management accounting reporting period, are not timely enough to provide a review of operations that must change daily. Some accounting conventions such as expensing items that some view as assets can distort realities or misdirect attention so that incorrect control decisions can occur.

Study is ongoing to rectify some of the deficiencies. Focused indicators of performance such as scrap levels, rework efforts, market share, employee morale, pollutant discharges, and customer profitability are some of the approaches being used or refined. Some measures are financial; some are physical. Aggregations of physical results is the focus of intense study because of the difficulty of having a meaningful total when financial numbers are not used.[2]

This chapter provides an explanation of common financial performance indicators. Such reports represent the cornerstone of performance measurements to managers. Inte-

---

[2]"Developing Comprehensive Performance Indicators," *Management Accounting Guideline* 31 (Hamilton, Ont.: The Society of Management Accountants of Canada, 1994).

grating material on performance from previous chapters with discussions in this and later chapters will provide you with a foundation for understanding developments in performance assessment.

SEGMENT REPORTING

To operate effectively, managers need more information at their disposal than is available in a single, companywide income statement. A companywide income statement provides only a summary of overall operations; as such, it typically does not contain enough detail to allow the manager to detect opportunities and problems that may exist in the organization. For example, some product lines may be profitable while others may be unprofitable; some sales offices may be more effective than others; or some factories may be ineffectively using their capacity and/or resources. To uncover problems such as these, the manager needs not just one but several income statements, and these statements must be designed to focus on various *segments* of the company. The preparation of income statements of this type is known as **segment reporting.**

A **segment** can be defined as any part or activity of an organization about which a manager seeks cost (expense), revenue, or investment data. Examples of segments include sales territories, individual stores, service centres, manufacturing divisions or plants, sales departments, and product lines. Blockbuster Video might segment their businesses by region, while The Bay might segment its business by sales departments.

In this section, we learn how to construct income statements that show the results of segment activities. We also learn how to analyze the profitability of segments and how to measure the performance of segment managers. In addition, as we study these topics, we will learn how to use segment data to extend the concept of responsibility accounting to the company as a whole.

A company like Blockbuster Video may segment its sales and cost reports in many ways, including by specific video title, by video category, by store, and by region.

EXHIBIT 12-1

Business Functions
Making Up the Value
Chain

Research and Development	Product Design	Manufacturing	Marketing	Distribution	Customer Service

Hindrances to Proper Cost Assignment

OBJECTIVE 1

Identify three business
practices that hinder
proper cost
assignment.

For segment reporting to accomplish its intended purposes, costs must be analyzed and properly assigned to the segments to which they relate. If the purpose of a segmented statement is to determine the profitability of a customer, then all of the costs attributable to that customer—and only those costs—should be assigned to the customer. If the purpose is to determine the rate of return being generated by a particular division, then all of the costs attributable to that division—and only those costs—should be assigned to it. Unfortunately, three business practices are in use that greatly hinder proper cost assignment. These three practices are (1) omission of some costs in the assignment process, (2) the use of inappropriate methods for allocating costs among segments of a company, and (3) assignment of costs to segments that are really common costs of the entire organization.

Omission of Costs

The costs assigned to a segment should include all costs attributable to that segment from the company's entire *value chain*. The **value chain,** which is illustrated in Exhibit 12–1, consists of the major business functions that add value to a company's products and services. All of these functions, from research and development, through product design, manufacturing, marketing, distribution, and customer service, are required to bring a product or service to the customer and generate revenues.

However, under commonly used accounting practices, only manufacturing costs are included in product costs for financial reporting purposes. Consequently, when trying to determine product profitability for internal decision-making purposes, some companies deduct only manufacturing costs from product revenues. As a result, such companies omit from their profitability analysis part or all of the "upstream" costs in the value chain, which consist of research and product design, or the "downstream" costs, which consist of marketing, distribution, and customer service.[3] Yet these nonmanufacturing costs are just as essential in determining product profitability as are the manufacturing costs. These upstream and downstream costs, which are usually grouped under the title *Selling, general, and administrative (SG&A)* on the income statement, can represent half or more of the total expenses of an organization. If either the upstream or downstream costs are omitted in profitability analysis, then the product is undercosted and management may unwittingly develop and maintain products that in the long run result in losses rather than profits for the company. For this and other reasons, it is important to properly assign these SG&A expenses to the various products or other segments to which they relate.

Partly to avoid omitting costs that are an essential part of profitability analysis, some firms are turning to a concept known as *life cycle costing.* Essentially, **life cycle costing** focuses on all costs along the value chain that will be generated throughout the *entire* life of a product. This approach to costing helps to ensure that no costs are omitted in profitability analysis.

---

[3]The common accounting practice in Canada is to treat development costs meeting certain criteria as manufacturing (inventoriable) costs while research is expensed. Practices in the United States treat both as period expenses.

Inappropriate Methods for Allocating Costs among Segments

Cross-subsidization, or cost distortion, occurs when costs are improperly assigned among a company's segments. Cross-subsidization can occur in two ways: first, when companies fail to trace costs directly to segments in those situations where it is feasible to do so; and second, when companies use inappropriate bases to allocate costs.

Failure to Trace Costs Directly.   Costs that can be traced directly to a specific segment of a company should not be charged against other segments through some averaging process. Rather, such costs should be charged directly to the responsible segment. For example, the rent for a branch office should be charged directly against the branch to which it relates rather than included in a companywide overhead pool and then spread throughout the company.

FOCUS ON
CURRENT PRACTICE

Inappropriate allocation of costs can affect the profitability of company branches, which in turn can affect promotions, raises, and job security.

E & A Company (the name has been changed to conceal the company's true identity) provides a wide range of engineering and architectural consulting services to both government and industry. For many years, the company pooled all operating costs and allocated them to its three branch offices on the basis of labour cost. When it abandoned this practice and started tracing costs such as rent directly to the offices, while at the same time assigning other costs on a more appropriate basis, the reported profits of one branch office doubled, the reported profits of another branch office changed from a loss to a profit, and the reported profits of the third branch office changed from a profit to a loss.[4]

Inappropriate Allocation Base.   When costs cannot be easily traced to segments, some companies allocate these costs to segments using arbitrary bases such as sales dollars or cost of goods sold. For example, under the sales dollars approach, costs are allocated to the various segments according to the percentage of company sales generated by each segment. Thus, if a segment generates 20 percent of total company sales, it would be allocated 20 percent of the company's SG&A expenses as its "fair share." This same basic procedure is followed if cost of goods sold or some other such measure is used as the allocation base.

The problem with this approach is that frequently no real cause-and-effect relationship exists between the costs being assigned and the allocation base being used. This approach

---

[4]Beth M. Chaffman and John Talbott, "Activity-Based Costing in a Service Organization," *CMA Magazine* (December/January 1991), p. 18.

assumes, in effect, that a dollar of sales for any product generates the same amount of SG&A expense. Such an assumption is rarely valid. Some products are much more costly to market and distribute than others, and some products require much greater customer service. Thus, use of an inappropriate assignment base such as sales dollars, *which ignores the actual consumption of resources,* will result in cross-subsidization of costs.

Arbitrarily Dividing Common Costs among Segments

The third business practice that results in distortion of segment costs is the practice of assigning costs to segments even when the costs are not in any way caused by the segments. For example, some companies allocate the costs of the corporate headquarters building to products, although these costs would be unaffected even if an entire product line was eliminated. Costs such as those associated with the corporate headquarters building are sometimes called *common costs,* since they relate to overall operating activities rather than to particular segments.

Common costs are necessary, of course, to have a functioning organization. Although such costs cannot be significantly reduced even by eliminating whole segments such as product lines, some firms allocate them to segments anyway. This practice is often justified on the grounds that "someone" has to "cover the common costs." While it is undeniably true that the common costs must be covered, arbitrarily allocating common costs to segments does not ensure that this will happen. In fact, adding a share of common costs to the real costs of a segment may make an otherwise profitable segment atpear to be unprofitable. If a manager then erroneously eliminates the segment, the net effect will be to *reduce* the profits of the company as a whole and make it even more difficult to "cover the common costs."

In summary, the way many companies handle segment reporting results in cost distortion. We have noted in our discussion that this distortion results from three practices—the failure to trace costs directly to a specific segment when it is feasible to do so, the use of inappropriate bases for allocating costs, and the allocation of common costs to segments. These practices are widespread. One study found that 60% of the companies surveyed made no attempt to assign SG&A costs to segments on a cause-and-effect basis.[5]

▼ ▼ ▼ ▼ ▼

MANAGERIAL ACCOUNTING IN ACTION—THE ISSUE

SoftSolutions, Inc., is a rapidly growing computer software company founded by Lori Saffer, who had previously worked in a large software company, and Marjorie Matsuo, who had previously worked in the hotel industry as a general manager. They formed the company to develop and market sophisticated, user-friendly accounting and operations software designed specifically for hotels. They quit their jobs, pooled their savings, hired several programmers, and got down to work. Unfortunately, it took far longer to develop the software than they had anticipated, and the firm almost went under in its first year. However, by borrowing from friends and relatives, they were able to keep the firm's creditors at bay.

Continued

---

[5]James R. Emore and Joseph A. Ness, "The Slow Pace of Meaningful Change in Cost Systems," *Journal of Cost Management* (Winter 1991), p. 39.

The first sale was by far the most difficult. No hotel wanted to be the first to use an untested product from an unknown company. After overcoming this obstacle with persistence, good luck, and a very low introductory price, the company's sales burgeoned due to the excellence of its product and the company's dedication to customer service.

The company quickly developed similar business software for other specialized markets and then acquired an even smaller software company involved in consumer products—mainly clip art and computer games. Within four years of its founding, the organization had grown to the point where Saffer and Matsuo were no longer able to personally direct all of the company's activities. Decentralization had become a necessity.

Accordingly, the company was split into two divisions—Business Products and Consumer Products. By mutual consent, Matsuo took the title president and Saffer took the title vice president of the Business Products Division. Chris Worden, the former president of the computer games company, was designated vice president of the Consumer Products Division.

Almost immediately, the issue arose of how best to evaluate the performance of the divisions. Matsuo called a meeting to consider this issue and asked Saffer, Worden, and the controller, Bill Carson, to attend. The following discussion took place at that meeting:

MARJORIE MATSUO: We need to find a better way to measure the performance of the divisions.

CHRIS WORDEN: I agree. Consumer Products has been setting the pace in this company for the last two years, and we should be getting more recognition.

LORI SAFFER: Chris, both Marjorie and I are delighted with the success of the Consumer Products Division.

CHRIS WORDEN: I know. But it is hard to figure out just how successful we are with the present accounting reports. All we have are sales and cost of goods sold figures for the division.

BILL CARSON: What's the matter with those figures?

CHRIS WORDEN: The sales figures are fine. However, cost of goods sold includes some costs that wouldn't go away even if you decided to sell off the Consumer Products Division.

MARJORIE MATSUO: Just a minute, Chris, who is talking about selling your division?

CHRIS WORDEN: That's just a hypothetical to make a point. Let me explain. To take a simple example, our Christmas clip art product consists of a shrink-wrapped printed box that contains a CD-ROM, a manual, a registration card, and a small pamphlet advertising our other products. After these items are packed in the box, but before it is shrink wrapped, a unique identifying bar code is applied to the box.

LORI SAFFER: We know. Every item that is shipped must have a unique identifying bar code attached. That's true for items from the Business Products Division as well as for items from the Consumer Products Division.

CHRIS WORDEN: That's precisely the point. Whether an item comes from the Business Products Division or the Consumer Products Division, it must pass through the automatic bar-coding machine after the software has been packaged. How much of the cost of the automatic bar coder would be saved if we didn't have any consumer products?

MARJORIE MATSUO: Since there is only one automatic bar coder and we would need it anyway to code the business products, I guess none of the cost would be saved.

CHRIS WORDEN: That's right. And since none of the cost could be avoided even if the entire Consumer Products Division were eliminated, how can we logically say that some of the cost of the automatic bar coder is really a cost of the Consumer Products Division?

MARJORIE MATSUO: I see your point, but I don't see how we can have sensible performance reports without making someone responsible for costs like the cost of the automatic bar coder. Bill, as our accounting expert, what do you think?

BILL CARSON: I have some ideas for handling issues like the automatic bar coder. The best approach would probably be for me to put together a draft performance report. We can discuss it at the next meeting when everyone has something concrete to look at.

MARJORIE MATSUO: Let's see what you come up with.

How *should* costs be assigned to segments? On the following pages we present an approach to segment reporting and cost assignment that provides useful data to managers in making a variety of decisions. This approach clearly segregates costs that are attributable to the segments from those that are not and also highlights the behaviour of costs.

SEGMENT REPORTING AND PROFITABILITY ANALYSIS

OBJECTIVE 2

Prepare a segmented income statement using the contribution format, and explain the difference between traceable fixed costs and common fixed costs.

Bill Carson's approach to segment reporting presented here uses the contribution format to the income statement discussed in earlier chapters. Recall that when the contribution format is used, (1) the cost of goods sold consists only of the variable manufacturing costs, (2) the variable and fixed expenses are listed in separate sections, and (3) a contribution margin is computed. In this section, we will learn that when such a statement is segmented, a further breakdown is made of the fixed costs. This breakdown allows a *segment margin* to be computed for each segment of the company.

Levels of Segmented Statements

A portion of the segmented report Bill Carson prepared is shown in Exhibit 12–2. SoftSolutions, Inc., is first segmented in terms of divisions. This is the portion of the report that was specifically requested by the company's divisional managers. However, segmented income statements can be prepared for activities at many levels in a company. To provide even more information to the company's divisional managers, Bill Carson has further segmented the divisions according to their major product lines. In the case of the Consumer Products Division, the product lines are clip art and computer games. In turn, Bill Carson has segmented the product lines according to how they are sold—in retail computer stores or by catalogue sales. In Exhibit 12–2, this further segmentation is illustrated for the computer games product line. Notice that as we go from one segmented statement to another, we are looking at smaller and smaller pieces of the company. While not shown in Exhibit 12–2, Bill Carson also prepared segmented income statements for the major product lines in the Business Products Division.

There are substantial benefits from a series of statements such as those contained in Exhibit 12–2. By carefully examining trends and results in each segment, a manager is able to gain considerable insight into the company's operations viewed from many different angles.

Assigning Costs to Segments

Note particularly how the fixed costs are handled in Exhibit 12–2. Fixed costs are divided into two parts. One part is labelled *traceable,* and the other part is labeled *common.* Only those fixed costs labelled *traceable* are charged to the various segments. If a cost is not traceable to some segment, then it is treated as a common cost and kept separate from the segments themselves. Thus, under the approach illustrated here, a cost should never be averaged, allocated, or otherwise assigned to segments in an *arbitrary* manner.

Two guidelines are followed in assigning costs to the various segments of a company when the contribution format is used:
*   First, according to cost behaviour patterns (that is, variable and fixed).
*   Second, according to whether the costs are *directly traceable* to the segments involved.

We will now consider various parts of Exhibit 12–2 in greater depth.

EXHIBIT 12–2

SoftSolutions, Inc.—
Segmented Income Statements in the Contribution Format

Segments Defined as Divisions

	Total Company	Business Products Division	Consumer Products Division
Sales	$500,000	$300,000	$200,000
Less variable expenses:			
Variable cost of goods sold	180,000	120,000	60,000
Other variable expenses	50,000	30,000	20,000
Total variable expenses	230,000	150,000	80,000
Contribution margin	270,000	150,000	120,000
Less traceable fixed expenses	170,000	90,000	80,000 *
Divisional segment margin	100,000	$ 60,000	$ 40,000
Less common fixed expenses	85,000		
Net income	$ 15,000		

Segments Defined as Product Lines of the Consumer Products Division

	Consumer Products Division	Clip Art	Computer Games
Sales	$200,000	$ 75,000	$125,000
Less variable expenses:			
Variable cost of goods sold	60,000	20,000	40,000
Other variable expenses	20,000	5,000	15,000
Total variable expenses	80,000	25,000	55,000
Contribution margin	120,000	50,000	70,000
Less traceable fixed expenses	70,000	30,000	40,000
Product-line segment margin	50,000	$ 20,000	$ 30,000
Less common fixed expenses	10,000		
Divisional segment margin	$ 40,000		

Segments Defined as Sales Channels for One Product Line, Computer Games, of the Consumer Products Division

	Computer Games	Retail Stores	Catalogue Sales
Sales	$125,000	$100,000	$ 25,000
Less variable expenses:			
Variable cost of goods sold	40,000	32,000	8,000
Other variable expenses	15,000	5,000	10,000
Total variable expenses	55,000	37,000	18,000
Contribution margin	70,000	63,000	7,000
Less traceable fixed expenses	25,000	15,000	10,000
Territorial segment margin	45,000	$ 48,000	$ (3,000)
Less common fixed expenses	15,000		
Divisional segment margin	$ 30,000		

*Notice that this $80,000 in traceable fixed expense is divided into two parts—$70,000 traceable and $10,000 common—when the Consumer Products Division is broken down into product lines. The reasons for this are discussed later under Traceable Costs Can Become Common Costs.

Sales and Contribution Margin

To prepare segmented statements, it is necessary to keep records of sales by individual segment, as well as in total for the organization. After deducting related variable expenses, a contribution margin figure can then be computed for each segment and for the total company, as illustrated in Exhibit 12–2.

It is important to keep in mind that the contribution margin tells us what happens to profits as volume changes—*holding a segment's capacity and fixed costs constant.* As such, the contribution margin is especially valuable in short-run decisions concerning temporary uses of capacity such as special orders. Decisions concerning the most effective uses of existing capacity often involve only variable costs and revenues, which of course are the very elements involved in contribution margin. By carefully monitoring segment contribution margins, the manager will be in a position to make those short-run decisions that will most effectively utilize each segment's capacity and thereby maximize profits. Such decisions will be discussed in greater detail in Chapter 14.

Traceable and Common Fixed Costs

Traceable fixed costs can be defined as those fixed costs that arise because of the existence of a particular segment and therefore can be identified with that segment. A **common fixed cost** is a fixed cost that cannot be identified with a particular segment but rather arises because of overall operations. To be assigned to segments, a common fixed cost would have to be allocated on some highly arbitrary basis having little to do with cause and effect, such as sales dollars.[6]

Examples of traceable fixed costs would include advertising outlays made on behalf of a particular segment, the salary of a segment manager (such as a product-line supervisor), and depreciation of buildings and equipment devoted to the manufacture of a specific product. Examples of common fixed costs would include corporate image advertising (from which many segments benefit), salaries of top administrative officers, depreciation of corporate administrative facilities, and the automatic bar coder at SoftSolutions.

Identifying Traceable Fixed Costs.   The distinction between traceable and common fixed costs is crucial in segment reporting, because traceable fixed costs are charged to the segments, whereas common fixed costs are not. In an actual situation, it is sometimes hard to determine whether a cost should be classified as traceable or common. Two approaches are available to help make this classification. One approach is to use broad, general guidelines in deciding which costs are traceable, and the other approach is to use activity-based costing.

General Guidelines.   The useful guideline or rule of thumb is to treat as traceable costs *only those costs that would disappear over time if the segment itself disappeared.* For example, if the Consumer Products Division in Exhibit 12–2 were discontinued, it would no longer be necessary to pay a salary for a division manager. Therefore the division manager's salary should be classified as a traceable fixed cost of the division. On the other hand, the president of the company undoubtedly would continue to be paid even if the Consumer Products Division were dropped. In fact, he or she might even be paid more if dropping the division was a good idea. Therefore, the president's salary is common to both

---

[6]It can be argued that *all* cost allocations are arbitrary. The use of the term *arbitrary* in this book is intended to convey the thought that a cost is being charged to a segment on something other than a cause-and-effect basis.

divisions. The same idea can be expressed in another way: *treat as traceable costs only those costs that are added as a result of the creation of a segment.*

Activity-Based Costing.   Some costs, such as advertising of a specific product, are easy to identify as traceable costs. A more difficult situation arises when a building or other resource is shared by two or more segments. For example, assume that a multiproduct company leases warehouse space that is used in the distribution of two of its products. Would the lease cost of the warehouse be a traceable or a common cost? Managers familiar with modern profitability analysis would argue that if a cost driver can be identified and consumption measured, then the lease cost is traceable and should be assigned to the two products according to their use of the resource involved. In like manner, these managers would argue that order processing costs, sales support costs, and other SG&A expenses should be charged to segments *according to the segments' use of the services involved,* as determined by an activity approach.

To illustrate, assume that Holt Company has three products—A, B, and C. Warehouse space is leased on a yearly basis as needed and used in the distribution of products A and B. The lease cost of this space is $12 per square metre per year. Product A occupies 1,000 square metres of space, and product B occupies 2,334 square metres. The company also has an order processing department that incurred $150,000 in order processing costs last year. In the judgment of management, order processing costs are driven by the number of orders placed. Last year 2,500 orders were placed, of which 1,200 were for product A, 800 were for product B, and 500 were for product C. Given these data, the following costs would be assigned to each product:

Warehouse space cost:
  Product A: $12 × 1,000 square metres . . . . $ 12,000
  Product B: $12 × 2,334 square metres 28,000
      Total cost assigned . . . . $ 40,000

Order processing costs:
  $150,000 ÷ 2,500 orders = $60 per order
  Product A: $60 × 1,200 orders . . . . $ 72,000
  Product B: $60 × 800 orders. 48,000
  Product C: $60 × 500 orders. 30,000
      Total cost assigned $150,000

This method of assigning costs combines the strength of activity-based costing with the power of the contribution approach and greatly enhances the manager's ability to measure the profitability of segments. However, managers must still ask themselves if the costs would in fact disappear over time if the segment itself disappeared. For example, if elimination of product A would not eventually result in a reduction in warehousing costs of approximately $12,000, then those costs should not be assigned to product A.

In assigning costs to segments, the key point is to resist the temptation to allocate costs (such as depreciation of corporate facilities) that are clearly common. *Any allocation of common costs to segments will reduce the value of the segment margin as a guide to long-run segment profitability.*

Traceable Costs Can Become Common

Fixed costs that are traceable on one segmented statement can become common if the company is divided into smaller segments. This is because there are limits to how finely some costs can be separated without resorting to arbitrary allocation. The more finely segments are defined, the more costs there are that become common.

EXHIBIT 12–3

Reclassification of
Traceable Fixed
Expenses from
Exhibit 12–2

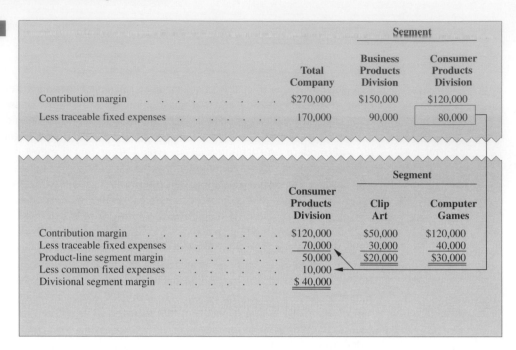

	Total Company	Segment	
		Business Products Division	Consumer Products Division
Contribution margin	$270,000	$150,000	$120,000
Less traceable fixed expenses	170,000	90,000	80,000

	Consumer Products Division	Segment	
		Clip Art	Computer Games
Contribution margin	$120,000	$50,000	$120,000
Less traceable fixed expenses	70,000	30,000	40,000
Product-line segment margin	50,000	$20,000	$30,000
Less common fixed expenses	10,000		
Divisional segment margin	$ 40,000		

This concept can be seen from the diagram in Exhibit 12–3. Notice from the diagram that when segments are defined as divisions, the Consumer Products Division has $80,000 in traceable fixed expenses. Only $70,000 of this amount remains traceable, however, when we narrow our definition of a segment from divisions to that of the product lines of the Consumer Products Division. Notice that the other $10,000 then becomes a common cost of these product lines.

Why would $10,000 of traceable fixed cost become a common cost when the division is divided into product lines? The $10,000 could be the monthly salary of the manager of the Consumer Products Division. This salary would be a traceable cost when we are speaking of the division as a whole, but it would be *common* to the product lines manufactured and sold by the division. Any allocation of this salary cost between the two product lines would have to be on some arbitrary basis. To avoid this, the salary cost of the division manager's salary should be treated as a common cost when the division is segmented into product lines.

The $70,000 that remains a traceable fixed cost even after the Consumer Products Division is segmented into product lines consists of costs that can be identified directly with the product lines on a nonarbitrary (that is, cause-and-effect) basis. The $70,000 might consist of advertising, for example, expended for product-line promotion, of which $30,000 was expended for promotion of the deluxe model and $40,000 was expended for promotion of the regular model. Product-line advertising would be a traceable fixed cost of the product lines, because it could be assigned to the lines without having to make an arbitrary allocation.

Segment Margin

Observe from Exhibit 12–2 that the **segment margin** is obtained by deducting the traceable fixed costs of a segment from the segment's contribution margin. It represents the margin available after a segment has covered all of its own costs. *The segment margin is the best gauge of the long-run profitability of a segment,* since only those costs that are caused by the segment are used in its computation. If in the long run a segment can't cover its own costs, then that segment probably should not be retained (unless it has important side effects on other segments). Notice from Exhibit 12–2, for example, that Catalog Sales has a negative segment margin. This means that the segment is not covering its own costs; it is generating more costs than it collects in revenue.[7]

From a decision-making point of view, the segment margin is most useful in long-run decisions such as capacity changes, long-run pricing, and outsourcing of production. By contrast, as we noted earlier, the contribution margin is most useful in decisions relating to short-run changes in volume, such as pricing of special orders and utilization of existing capacity.

Contribution margin provides an approximation of the incremental or differential profits of the segment. The revenue reflects the incremental revenue of the segment for the period specified. The variable costs reflect the incremental costs of the segment for the same period. If sufficient time is permitted managers can alter the traceable fixed costs, which means segment margin also reflects the incremental profits of the segment. The difference between the two incremental results, contribution margin and segment margin, is based solely on the length of the time horizon rather than on a conceptual difference. Both are incremental profits but each reflects a different time horizon over which managers can make decisions to influence the results.

▼   ▼   ▼   ▼   ▼

MANAGERIAL ACCOUNTING IN ACTION—WRAP-UP

Shortly after Bill Carson, the SoftSolutions, Inc., controller, completed the draft segmented income statement, he sent copies around to the other managers and scheduled a meeting in which the report could be explained. The meeting was held on the Monday following the first meeting; and Marjorie Matsuo, Lori Saffer, and Chris Worden were all in attendance.

LORI SAFFER: I think these segmented income statements are fairly self-explanatory. However, there is one thing I wonder about.

BILL CARSON: What's that?

LORI SAFFER: What is this common fixed expense of $85,000 listed under the total company? And who is going to be responsible for it if neither Chris nor I have responsibility?

BILL CARSON: The $85,000 of common fixed expenses represents expenses like general administrative salaries and the costs of common production equipment such as the automatic barcoding machine. Marjorie, do you want to respond to the question about responsibility for these expenses?

MARJORIE MATSUO: Sure. Since I'm the president of the company, I'm responsible for those costs. Some things can be delegated, others cannot be. It wouldn't make any sense for either you or Chris to make decisions about the bar coder since it affects both of you. That's an important part of my job—making decisions about resources that affect all parts of the organization. This report makes it much clearer who is responsible for what. I like it.

CHRIS WORDEN: So do I—my division's segment margin is higher than the net income for the entire company.

Continued

---

[7]Retention or elimination of product lines and other segments is covered in more depth in Chapter 13.

MARJORIE MATSUO: Don't get carried away, Chris. Let's not misinterpret what this report means. The segment margins *have* to be big to cover the common costs of the company. We can't let the big segment margins lull us into a sense of complacency. If we use these reports, we all have to agree that our objective is to increase all of the segment margins over time.

LORI SAFFER: I'm willing to give it a try.

CHRIS WORDEN: The reports make sense to me.

MARJORIE MATSUO: So be it. Then the first item of business would appear to be a review of catalogue sales of computer games, where we appear to be losing money. Chris, could you brief us on this at our next meeting?

CHRIS WORDEN: I'd be happy to. I have been suspecting for some time that our catalogue sales strategy could be improved.

MARJORIE MATSUO: We look forward to hearing your analysis. Meeting's adjourned.

Varying Breakdowns of Total Sales

SoftSolutions segmented its sales by division, by product line within each division, and by sales channel. There are many other possible ways of presenting segmented data. For example, consider the Windsor Motor Company in Exhibit 12–4 on the following page. This company shows its sales segmented in two ways: first, segmented according to sales territories; and second, segmented according to divisions. Note in the exhibit that these two major segments are then broken down into smaller segments, and that the sum of the sales by these smaller segments will add up to total company sales. Segment breakdowns such as those shown in this exhibit give a company's managers the ability to look at the company from many different directions. With the availability of computers and database software, detailed breakdowns of a company's segments are easy to do.

CUSTOMER PROFITABILITY ANALYSIS

OBJECTIVE 3
Explain how to determine customer profitability.

In prior sections, we have noted that companies analyze profitability in many ways, including by product, by market segment, and by channel of distribution. One frequently overlooked way to analyze profitability is by customer. Although managers generally assume that a dollar of sales to one customer is just as profitable as a dollar of sales to any other customer, this assumption may not be correct. The reason is that customers have varying demands for resource-consuming activities, just as products, markets, or other segments of a company have varying demands. For example, some customers order in smaller lots and more frequently than other customers, requiring more paperwork and materials handling. Some customers order nonstandard parts that require special engineering work, special machinery setups, and perhaps special packaging and handling. Other customers always seem to be in a hurry and want special expediting and delivery services. Customers who demand high levels of these resource-consuming activities should not be cross-subsidized by customers who demand little in the way of

EXHIBIT 12-4   Graphic Presentation of Segment Reporting—Windsor Motor Company

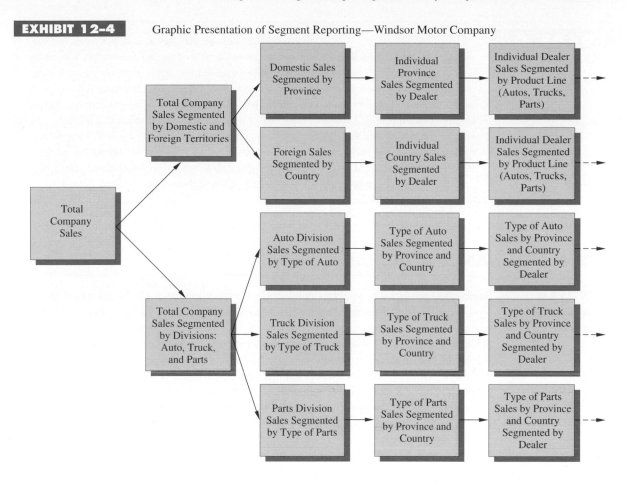

customized services, special packaging, and so forth. However, unless the activities that are provided for customer support are traced to the company's various customers, cross-subsidization almost certainly will occur.

After the various customer-support activities in a company have been identified, the costs of providing these activities should be charged to the customers who require them. Thus, a customer who requires special accounts receivable terms, many small orders and deliveries, the packing of goods in shop-ready containers, and specialized field service should be quoted a price that reflects these costly activities. This is why we stated in earlier chapters that suppliers who make deliveries to customers in a JIT environment frequently quote prices that are somewhat higher than prices charged by other suppliers. The higher prices are needed to compensate these suppliers for the special activities required on their part to support JIT customers.

Businesses that have analyzed customer profitability have been surprised to find that a fairly small number of customers are apparently responsible for most of their profits. It is also common to find that a small number of customers consume far more resources than are warranted by their revenues.

"A small machine shop . . . was operating three shifts per day, seven days per week, but was making very little profit. The major customer provided 50% of the machine shop's volume. A careful examination of customer-driven activities revealed the major customer ordered high-precision machined parts in low lot sizes. The jobs for this customer, therefore, required long setups, intense engineering support, intense NC [numerical control] programming support, intense sales support, high order activity, higher scrapped units, high inspection intensity, and high inventory for this firm. Rather than assigning these incremental costs to the products manufactured for the major customer, however, these costs were spread across the machine shop's complete product line. As a result, this major customer enjoyed subsidized pricing; the machine shop's number-one customer was actually its number-one loser."[8]

REVENUE VARIANCE ANALYSIS

OBJECTIVE 4

Analyze variances from revenue targets.

Segmented profitability analysis combined with the variance analysis discussed in Chapter 11, can be used to generate a series of performance reports so that price and volumes (quantities) can be compared to targets set by the budgeting process. The interaction of price and quantity represents important information for businesses to analyze to determine why the strategic goals and specific budgeted targets were not achieved. Managers want to know the effects of market volume changes, market penetration or share changes, sales mix changes, and price changes. Each of these elements can be isolated but the true test of management is to reconstitute the combination needed for a new marketing strategy. Variances from previous results can provide a valuable start for this process.

The ability to have segment revenue data for analysis depends on the coding attached to the revenue information. Geographic, product line, customer, and sales personnel are common classifications. Managers, with the assistance of the accountant, must decide what they wish to know and what classifications can be realistically structured given the degree of substitutes and complements that exist, the number of products that exist, and the nature of meaningful groupings.

To illustrate the nature of the variance reporting in the revenue area, consider the following example for Ace Video Company.

Budget sales in units:
Deluxe video game   10,000
Standard video game   5,000

Budget price:
Deluxe $20
Standard. $10

Market volume expected:
Deluxe   70,000
Standard.   90,000

Budget variable expense:
Deluxe $8
Standard. $5

The sales price for the deluxe video game was reduced to $18 from the anticipated $20. This resulted in a $16,000 increase in revenue. The standard video game price was increased by $1 per unit resulting in a revenue decrease of $6,000. The reasoning behind

---

[8]Peter B. B. Turney and James M. Reeve, "The Impact of Continuous Improvement on the Design of Activity-Based Cost Systems," *Journal of Cost Management* (Summer 1990), p. 49.

the price and revenue changes is something marketing management should explain so that a new pricing strategy can be considered.

Actual results for the period were:

Unit sales:		
Deluxe		12,000
Standard		4,000
Sales prices:		
Deluxe		$18
Standard		$11
Market volume:		
Deluxe		75,000
Standard		85,000

Exhibit 12–5 presents a summary of the relations among budgeted and actual results.

Analysis of revenue variances can proceed as follows:

$$\text{Sales price variance} = \left(\text{Actual sales price} - \text{Budgeted sales price} \right) \times \text{Actual sales volume}$$

Deluxe	($18 − $20) × 12,000 units =	$24,000 U
Standard	($11 − $10) × 4,000 units =	4,000 F
	Total sales price variance =	$20,000 U

EXHIBIT 12-5

Actual and Budgeted Results

	Actual Results		Flexible Budget		Master Budget	
Revenue:						
Deluxe (12,000 × $18)	$216,000		(12,000 × $20)	$240,000	(10,000 × $20)	$200,000
Standard (4,000 × $11)	44,000		(4,000 × $10)	40,000	(5,000 × $10)	50,000
	260,000			280,000		250,000
Variable expenses:						
Deluxe (12,000 × $8)	96,000		(12,000 × $8)	96,000	(10,000 × $8)	80,000
Standard (4,000 × $5)	20,000		(4,000 × $5)	20,000	(5,000 × $5)	25,000
	116,000			116,000		105,000
Contribution margin	$144,000			$164,000		$145,000

	Sales Price Variance	Sales Quantity Variance
Total variances	$20,000 U	$19,000 F

$$\text{Market volume variance} = \left[\left(\text{Actual market volume} - \text{Budget market volume} \right) \times \text{Anticipated market share percentage} \times \text{Budgeted contribution margin per unit} \right]$$

Deluxe	(75,000 − 70,000) × (10,000/70,000) × ($20 − $8) =	$8,571 F
Standard	(85,000 − 90,000) × (5,000/90,000) × ($10 − $5) =	$1,389 U
Total		$7,182 F

$$\text{Market share variance} = \left[\text{Actual sales quantity} - \left(\text{Actual market volume} \times \text{Anticipated market share} \right) \right] \times \text{Budgeted contribution margin per unit}$$

Deluxe   {12,000 − [75,000 × (10,000/70,000)]} × ($20 − $8) = $15,432 F
Standard   {4,000 − [85,000 × (5,000/90,000)]} × ($10 − $5) =   3,610 U

Total $11,822 F

The market volume analysis and market share variances were calculated using the budget contribution margin. The use of the budget contribution numbers permits the isolation of volume effects from price effects at least for purposes of presentation. Ultimately managers may wish to consider the elasticity of the market in setting their future strategies.

The market volume variance used contribution margins. This is a common approach so that the profit effect of volume changes can be viewed. Alternative valuations could be used such as budgeted sales prices or budgeted gross margins if managers find these values more relevant.

The total market volume variance and market share variance help to analyze why sales quantities were 12,000 deluxe and 4,000 standard instead of the anticipated 10,000 deluxe and 5,000 standard. These quantity shifts resulted in a change in budgeted contribution as follows:

Deluxe   (12,000 − 10,000) × ($20 − $8) = $24,000 F
Standard   (4,000 − 5,000) × ($10 − $5) =   5,000 U

Total $19,000 F

Composition: Market volume   = $7,182 F
              Market share   =   11,822 F

                                             $19,004 F*

*$4 due to rounding

An alternative view of sales quantity variances can be generated by examining sales mix and sales quantity variances in terms of their relationship to the budgeted contribution margin. To be meaningful, management must be in a position to control the mix of products it sells in the market. While alternative formulations are possible using gross margins, sales prices, or weighted average contribution margins, the straightforward use of contributions will be employed in the illustration that follows so the principle can be understood.

$$\text{Sales mix variance} = \left(\text{Actual sales quantity} - \text{Actual sales quantity at anticipated sales mix} \right) \times \text{Budgeted contribution margin per unit}$$

Deluxe   [12,000 − 16,000 × (10/15)] × ($20 − $8) = $15,996 F
Standard   [4,000 − 16,000 × (5/15)] × ($10 − $5) =   6,665 U

Total sales mix variance   = $ 9,331 F

where 16,000 units = (12,000 + 4,000) and 10/15 is the anticipated proportion of deluxe sales while 5/15 is the anticipated standard mix proportion.

$$\text{Sales quantity variance} = \left[\left(\text{Actual sales quantity at anticipated sales mix} \right) - \text{Anticipated sales quantity} \right] \times \text{Budgeted contribution margin per unit}$$

Deluxe   {[16,000 × (10/15)] − 10,000} × ($20 − $8) = $8,004 F
Standard {[16,000 × (5/15)] − 5,000} × ($10 − $5) =   1,665 F

Total sales quantity variance $9,669 F

The total sales quantity variance was $19,000, composed of the following:

Sales mix	$ 9,331 F
Sales quantity	9,669 F
Total	$19,000 F

Incentives

Sales personnel are often rewarded with incentives based on their sales performance. Two bases are used to calculate the commissions. One is to base commissions on sales revenue generated; the other uses contribution margin. Consider the following example from Hall Company.

Product	Sales Revenue	Contribution Margin
X	$40,000	$4,000
Y	20,000	3,000

If Joan Davidson receives 1% of total sales, her commission based on our example would be 1% × ($40,000 + $20,000) or $600. Joan, if she was expected to promote one or the other product, would not care which she sold because she receives the same for each. On the other hand, assume Joan receives 8.6% of the contribution margin. Joan's total commission would be .086 × ($4,000 + $3,000) or $602. However, if Joan was expected to trade off units of X for units of Y in her sales effort, she would be more inclined to sell Y than she would X because she receives .086 × $3,000/$20,000 or 1.29% per sales dollar for Y compared to .086 × 4,000/40,000 or .86% per sales dollar for product X. By determining incentives using contributions, Joan would be consistent in her objectives with the objectives of Hall company because Hall receives 15% per sales dollar for Y compared to 10% for produce X.

Corel Corp. is attempting to gain market share from Microsoft with its Wordperfect Suite. Using both advertising and a very competitive cost of production Corel hopes to obtain better than 50% of the market. Costs to manufacture are quoted as $5 per unit of Office Suite. Retail prices are in the order of $350 U.S. Costs are kept low by using a CD-Roms instead of 30 to 40 diskettes. CD Roms cost less than $1 U.S. to manufacture, $2 to $3 for the manuals and $1 to $2 for packaging used in house production. Marketing and research, however, are added, 23% of sales for research and 50% for advertising, selling and administrative.[9]

MARKETING EXPENSE

OBJECTIVE 5
Analyze marketing expenses using cost drivers.

Knowledge of the nature and behaviour of marketing expenses provides managers with information about the costs of their marketing endeavours. Such information represents a significant aspect of marketing efforts, one that is needed to complement the pricing strategy previously discussed. Transport, warehousing, selling, advertising, and credit are some of the key factors managers need to consider in their marketing strategy. Accurate cost behaviour and allocation by the accounting function can assist marketing decision makers.

Accountants typically decompose marketing expense into two general categories, order getting and order filling. Order getting costs are the pure marketing costs such as advertising, selling commissions, and travel. Order filling includes the costs of warehousing, transportation, packing, and credit. Order getting costs tend to be somewhat

---

[9]Donald Rumball, "The Perfect Pitch," *The Financial Post Magazine* (December 1996), pp. 24–34.

more discretionary than order filling because order filling occurs after the sale rather than to obtain the sale. Nevertheless, marketing managers need to understand the cost behaviour associated with both sets of costs so that analysis can be conducted to decide on what should be done and how. The simplified fixed variable analysis using sales dollars or sales units is too crude to provide suitable answers for many situations.

Consider the following illustration:

Driver Analysis	Total for Period
Transport (kilometres to customer).	390 km
Jones Ltd.—30 km	
Smith Ltd.—60 km	
Selling (hours spent to call on per period)	500 hours
Jones Ltd.—200 hours	
Smith Ltd.—300 hours	
Advertising (relative cost of medium per period).	—
Jones Ltd.—3 weight	
Smith Ltd.—1 weight	
Warehousing (weight of product per unit)	13,000 kg
Product A—500 kg	
Product B—800 kg	
Credit/Collection (invoice ratio per shipment—Jones requires more time to pay and	
line item invoicing):	
Jones Ltd. 2 invoices per shipment, 10 units per invoice (4 of A, 6 of B)	5 shipments
Smith Ltd. 1 invoice per shipment, 10 units per invoice (6 of A, 4 of B).	5 shipments

	Costs for Period	
	Total	Unit
Transport	$ 1,950	$5 per km
Selling	7,500	$15 per hr
Advertising.	4,000	—
Warehousing	6,500	$0.50 per kg
Credit/Collection	750	$50 per invoice
Total	$20,700	

	Costs to Customer		
	Jones Ltd.	Smith Ltd.	Total
Transport:			
$5/km × 5 × 30	$ 750		
$5/km × 4 × 6		$1,200	$ 1,950
Selling:			
$15/hr × 200 hours	3,000		
$15/hr × 300 hours		4,500	7,500
Advertising:			
3/4 × $4,000.	3,000		
1/4 × $4,000.		1,000	4,000
Warehousing:			
$.50/kg × [(4 × 500) + (6 × 800)]	3,400		
$.50/kg × [(6 × 500) + (4 × 800)]		3,100	6,500
Credit/Collection:			
$50/invoice × 2 × 5.	500		
$50/invoice × 1 × 5		250	750
	$ 10,650	$10,050	$ 20,700

When costs for a period are associated with their drivers and drivers can be associated with customers, marketing costs demonstrate the costs associated with particular customers.

	Costs to Products		
	Product A	**Product B**	**Total**
Transport—common	—	—	$ 1,950
Selling—common	—	—	7,500
Advertising—common	—	—	4,000
Warehousing:			
10 × 500 kg × $.50	$2,500		
10 × 800 kg × $.50		$4,000	$ 6,500
Credit/Collection—common.	—	—	750
	$2,500	$4,000	$20,700

Because transport, selling, and advertising are independent of the type of product, they are treated as common costs for the product breakdown above. A similar situation exists for credit/collection since invoicing and collection costs are irrespective of the type of product. Only warehousing is a function of the product type and thus can be broken down by product type as well as customer.

Marketing expense analysis uses the concepts of drivers to provide alternative views of the relationship of marketing costs to sales. The complexity of the analysis depends on the ability to define appropriate cost drivers for the marketing costs in a manner similar to the approach used with overhead costs as explained in Chapter 8. To avoid unnecessarily arbitrary allocations, expenses that do not have suitable drivers should be treated as common costs that are not incremental for the particular categories of the breakdown attempted. Management may decide that further analysis of these common costs can result in refined driver definitions, which in turn will permit cause/effect allocations of common marketing costs.

RESPONSIBILITY ACCOUNTING

Segment reporting is just an extension of the responsibility accounting concept that was introduced in Chapter 9. By assigning costs and revenues to segments, top management is able to see where responsibility lies for control purposes and is able to measure the performance of segment managers.

In this section, we discuss the various levels of responsibility into which companies typically classify their segments. Before discussing these levels of responsibility, however, we must first explain why a *decentralized* approach to decision making is imperative if segment reporting is to achieve the purposes for which it is intended.

Decentralization and Segment Reporting

OBJECTIVE 6
Explain the importance of decentralization in a responsibility accounting system.

Managers have found that segment reporting is of greatest value in organizations that are decentralized. A **decentralized organization** is one in which decision making is not confined to a few top executives but rather is spread throughout the organization, with managers at various levels making key operating decisions relating to their sphere of responsibility. Decentralization must be viewed in terms of degree, since all organizations are decentralized to some extent out of economic necessity. At one extreme, a strongly decentralized organization is one in which there are few, if any, constraints on the freedom of a segment manager to make a decision, even at the lowest levels. At the other extreme, a strongly centralized organization is one in which little freedom exists to make a decision other than at top levels of management. Although most firms fall somewhere between these two extremes, there is a pronounced tendency today toward the decentralized end of the spectrum.

Many benefits result from decentralization. These benefits include the following:

1. By spreading the burden of decision making among many levels of management, top management is relieved of much day-to-day problem solving and is left free to concentrate on long-range planning and on coordination of efforts.
2. Allowing managers greater decision-making control over their segments provides excellent training as these managers rise in the organization. In the absence of such training, managers may be ill-prepared to function in a decision-making capacity as they are given greater responsibility.
3. Added responsibility and decision-making authority often result in increased job satisfaction and provide greater incentive for the segment manager to put forth his or her best efforts.
4. Decisions are best made at that level in an organization where problems and opportunities arise. Top management can't be intimately acquainted with local conditions in all of a company's segments.
5. Decentralization provides a more effective basis for measuring a manager's performance, since through decentralization he or she has power to control segment results.

FOCUS ON
CURRENT PRACTICE

Competition among managers can be counterproductive in the long run, eventually undermining the performance of the company.

Competition among managers within an organization can be taken too far. Alfie Kohn writes: "The surest way to destroy cooperation and therefore, organizational excellence, is to force people to compete for rewards or recognition or to rank themselves against each other. For each person who wins, there are many others who carry with them the feeling of having lost . . . [W]hen employees compete for a limited number of incentives, they will most likely begin to see each other as obstacles to their own success." Moreover, Kohn argues that pay-for-performance can be counterproductive. "Tell people that their income will depend on their productivity or performance rating, and they will focus on the numbers. Sometimes they will manipulate the schedule for completing tasks or even engage in patently unethical and illegal behaviour."[10]

[10]Reprinted by permission of *Harvard Business Review.* Excerpt from Alfie Kohn, "Why Incentive Plans Cannot Work," *Harvard Business Review,* September–October 1993. Copyright © 1993 by the President and Fellows of Harvard College. All rights reserved.

EXHIBIT 12-6   Segments Classified as Cost, Profit, and Investment Centres

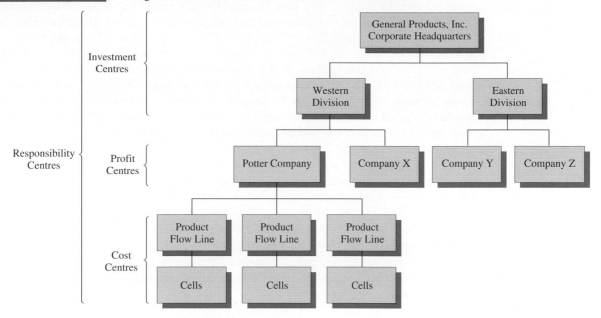

Cost, Profit, and Investment Centres

OBJECTIVE 7

Differentiate among cost centres, profit centres, and investment centres, and explain how performance is measured in each.

Decentralized companies typically divide their segments into three levels of responsibility. These levels consist of cost centres, profit centres, and investment centres, such as illustrated in Exhibit 12–6 for General Products, Inc. The level (or degree) of responsibility ranks from lowest in a cost centre to highest in an investment centre, as explained below.[11]

Cost Centre.   A segment that has control over the incurrence of cost is known as a *cost centre*. A distinguishing feature of a **cost centre** is that it has no control over either the generating of revenue or the use of investment funds. For example, the cells making up the product flow line of Potter Company in Exhibit 12–5 would likely be cost centres.

Profit Centre.   By contrast to a cost centre, a **profit centre** is any segment that has control over both cost and revenue. The Potter Company in Exhibit 12–6, for example, would be a profit centre in the General Products, Inc., organization, since it would be concerned with marketing its goods as well as producing them. Like a cost centre, however, a profit centre generally does not have control over how investment funds are used.

Investment Centre.   An **investment centre** is any segment of an organization that has control over cost and revenue and also over the use of investment funds. The corporate headquarters of General Products, Inc., would clearly be an example of an investment cen-

---

[11]Some organizations also identify *revenue centres,* which are responsible for sales activities only (products are shipped directly from the plant or from a warehouse as orders are submitted). An example of such a revenue centre would be a surplus store. Other companies would consider this to be just another type of profit centre, since costs of some kind (salaries, rent, utilities) are usually present.

tre. Corporate officers have ultimate responsibility for seeing that production and marketing goals are met. In addition, they have responsibility for seeing that adequate facilities are available to carry out the production and marketing functions, and for seeing that adequate working capital is available for operating needs. Whenever a segment of an organization has control over investment in such areas as physical plant and equipment, receivables, inventory, and entry into new markets, then it is termed an *investment centre*. The Potter Company in Exhibit 12–6 could be an investment centre if it were given control over investment funds for some of these purposes. In the more usual situation, however, Potter Company would be a profit centre within the larger organization, with most (or all) investment decisions being made at the divisional or central headquarters levels.

The reader should be cautioned that in everyday business practice the distinction between a profit centre and an investment centre is sometimes blurred, and the term *profit centre* is often used to refer to either one. Thus, a company may refer to one of its segments as being a profit centre when in fact the manager has full control over investment decisions in the segment. For purposes of our discussion, we will continue to maintain a distinction between the two, as made above.

Note from Exhibit 12–6 that cost centres, profit centres, and investment centres are *all* identified as responsibility centres. **Responsibility centre** is a broad term, meaning any point in an organization that has control over the incurrence of cost, the generating of revenue, or the use of investment funds.

Measuring Management Performance

These concepts of responsibility accounting are very important, since they assist in defining a manager's sphere of responsibility and also in determining how performance will be evaluated.

Cost centres are evaluated by means of performance reports, either in terms of meeting cost standards that have been set or in terms of activity-based measures that focus on continuous improvement. Profit centres are evaluated by means of contribution income statements, in terms of meeting sales and cost objectives. Investment centres are also evaluated by means of contribution income statements, but normally in terms of the *rate of return* that they are able to generate on *invested funds*. In the following section, we discuss rate of return as a tool for measuring managerial performance in a segment that operates as an investment centre.

RATE OF RETURN FOR MEASURING MANAGERIAL PERFORMANCE

OBJECTIVE 8
Compute the return on investment (ROI) by means of the ROI formula.

When a company is truly decentralized, segment managers are given a great deal of autonomy in directing the affairs in their particular areas of responsibility. So great is this autonomy that the various profit and investment centres are often viewed as being virtually independent businesses, with their managers having about the same control over decisions as if they were in fact running their own independent firms. With this autonomy, fierce competition often develops among managers, with each striving to make his or her segment the "best" in the company.

Competition among investment centres is particularly keen when it comes to passing out funds for expansion of product lines, or for introduction of new product lines. How do top managers in corporate headquarters go about deciding who gets new investment funds as they become available, and how do these managers decide which investment centres are most profitably using the funds that have already been entrusted to their care? One of the most popular ways of making these judgments is to measure the rate of return that investment centre managers are able to generate on their assets. This can be done through the *return on investment (ROI)* formula.

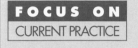

A recent review of successful Canadian companies suggests these companies have decentralized operational matters rather than strategy. Rules, budgets, performance standards, cultural norms, and leadership practices constrained the amount of discretion employees were permitted in these companies. Information technology provided more timely and useful information to employees while at the same time permitting better monitoring by top managers.[12]

The Return on Investment (ROI) Formula

To understand the elements behind the ROI formula, refer to Exhibit 12–7. As shown in the exhibit, **return on investment (ROI)** is the product of an investment centre's *margin* multiplied by its *turnover.* The **margin** portion of the ROI formula is a measure of management's ability to control operating expenses in relation to sales. The lower the operating expenses per dollar of sales, the higher the margin earned. The **turnover** portion of the ROI formula is a measure of the amount of sales that can be generated in an investment centre for each dollar invested in operating assets. In summary, the ROI formula can be expressed as follows:

$$\text{Margin} \times \text{Turnover} = \text{ROI}$$

$$\text{Margin} = \frac{\text{Net operating income}}{\text{Sales}} \qquad \text{Turnover} = \frac{\text{Sales}}{\text{Average operating assets}}$$

Therefore,

$$\frac{\text{Net operating income}}{\text{Sales}} \times \frac{\text{Sales}}{\text{Average operating assets}} = \text{ROI}$$

In the past, managers have tended to focus only on the margin earned and have ignored the turnover of assets. To some degree at least, the margin earned can be a valuable measure of a manager's performance. Standing alone, however, it overlooks one very crucial area of a manager's responsibility—the control of investment in operating assets. Excessive funds tied up in operating assets can be just as much of a drag on profitability as excessive operating expenses. One of the real advantages of the ROI formula is that it forces the manager to control his or her investment in operating assets as well as to control expenses and the margin earned.

---

[12]"Management Control Systems in Excellent Canadian Companies: A Study of Management Control in Ten Canadian Companies," *Management Accounting Issues Paper,* 5 (Hamilton, Ont.: The Society of Management Accountants of Canada, 1994).

EXHIBIT 12-7

Elements of Return
on Investment (ROI)

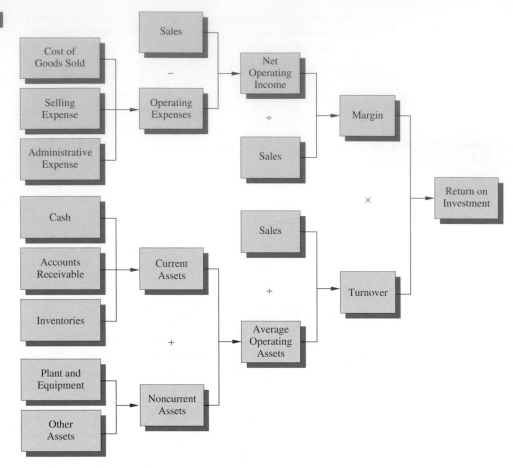

Du Pont was the first major corporation to recognize the importance of looking at both margin *and* turnover in assessing the performance of a manager. To it must go the credit for pioneering the ROI concept. Other major corporations have followed Du Pont's lead, and the ROI formula is now widely used as the key of a manager's performance when that manager has control of an investment centre. The ROI formula blends together many aspects of the manager's responsibilities into a single figure that can be compared against the returns of competing investment centres, as well as against that of other firms in the industry.

Net Operating Income and Operating Assets Defined

Note from Exhibit 12–7 that *net operating income,* rather than net income, is used in the ROI formula to compute the margin percentage. **Net operating income** is income before interest and taxes. In business jargon it is sometimes referred to as EBIT (earnings before interest and taxes). The reason for using net operating income in the formula is that the income figure used should be consistent with the base to which it is applied. Notice that the base in the turnover part of the formula consists of *operating assets.* Thus, to be consistent we use net operating income in computing the margin figure.

Operating assets include cash, accounts receivable, inventory, plant and equipment, and all other assets held for productive use in the organization. Examples of assets that would not be included in the operating assets category (that is, examples of nonoperating assets) would include land being held for future use, or a factory building being rented to someone else. The operating assets base used in the formula is typically computed as the average between the beginning and the end of the year.

CONTROLLING THE RATE OF RETURN

OBJECTIVE 9

Show how changes in sales, expenses, and assets affect an organization's ROI.

When being measured by the ROI formula as presented in Exhibit 12–7, an investment centre manager can improve profitability in three ways:

1. By increasing sales.
2. By reducing expenses.
3. By reducing assets.

To illustrate how the rate of return can be improved by each of these three actions, consider how the manager of the Lethbridge, Alberta, Burger Grill is evaluated. Burger Grill is a small chain of upscale casual restaurants that has been rapidly adding outlets via franchising. The Lethbridge franchise is owned by a group of local surgeons who have little time to devote to management and little expertise in business matters. Therefore, they delegate operating decisions—including decisions concerning investment in operating assets such as inventories—to a professional manager they have hired. The manager is evaluated largely based on the ROI the franchise generates.

The following data represent the results of operations for the most recent month:

Net operating income.	$ 10,000
Sales.	100,000
Average operating assets	50,000

The rate of return generated by the Burger Grill investment centre would be:

$$\frac{\text{Net operating income}}{\text{Sales}} \times \frac{\text{Sales}}{\text{Average operating assets}} = \text{ROI}$$

$$\frac{\$10,000}{\$100,000} \times \frac{\$100,000}{\$50,000} = \text{ROI}$$

$$10\% \times 2 = 20\%$$

As we stated above, to improve the ROI figure the manager must either (1) increase sales, (2) reduce expenses, or (3) reduce the operating assets.

Approach 1: Increase Sales.   Assume that the manager of the Burger Grill is able to increase sales from $100,000 to $110,000. Assume further that either because of good cost control or because most costs in the company are fixed, the net operating income increases even more rapidly, going from $10,000 to $12,000 per period. The operating assets remain constant.

$$\frac{\$12,000}{\$110,000} \times \frac{\$110,000}{\$50,000} = \text{ROI}$$

$$10.91\% \times 2.2 = 24\% \text{ (as compared to 20\% above)}$$

Approach 2: Reduce Expenses.   Assume that the manager is able to reduce expenses by $1,000, so that net operating income increases from $10,000 to $11,000. Both sales and operating assets remain constant.

$$\frac{\$11,000}{\$100,000} \times \frac{\$100,000}{\$50,000} = \text{ROI}$$

$$11\% \quad \times \quad 2 \quad = 22\% \text{ (as compared to 20\% above)}$$

Approach 3: Reduce Assets.   Assume that the manager is able to reduce operating assets from $50,000 to $40,000. Sales and net operating income remain unchanged.

$$\frac{\$10,000}{\$100,000} \times \frac{\$100,000}{\$40,000} = \text{ROI}$$

$$10\% \quad \times \quad 2.5 \quad = 25\% \text{ (as compared to 20\% above)}$$

A clear understanding of these three approaches to improving the ROI figure is critical to the effective management of an investment centre. We will now look at each approach in more detail.

Increase Sales

In first looking at the ROI formula, one is inclined to think that the sales figure is neutral, since it appears as the denominator in the margin computation and as the numerator in the turnover computation. We *could* cancel out the sales figure, but we don't do so for two reasons. First, this would tend to draw attention away from the fact that the rate of return is a function of *two* variables, margin and turnover. And second, it would tend to conceal the fact that a change in sales can affect *either* the margin or the turnover in an organization. To explain, a change in sales can affect the *margin* if expenses increase or decrease at a different rate than sales. For example, a company may be able to keep a tight control on its costs as its sales go up, thereby allowing the net operating income to increase more rapidly than sales and thus allowing the margin percentage to rise. Or a company may have many fixed expenses that will remain constant as sales go up, thereby again allowing a rapid increase in the net operating income and causing the margin percentage to rise. Either (or both) of these factors could have been responsible for the increase in the margin percentage from 10% to 10.91% illustrated in approach 1 above.

Further, a change in sales can affect the *turnover* if sales either increase or decrease without a proportionate increase or decrease in the operating assets. In the first approach above, for example, sales increased from $100,000 to $110,000, but the operating assets remained unchanged. As a result, the turnover increased from 2 to 2.2 for the period.

In summary, because a change in sales can affect either the margin or the turnover in a company, such changes are particularly significant to the manager in his or her attempts to control the ROI figure.

Reduce Expenses

Often the easiest route to increased profitability and to a stronger ROI figure is to simply cut the "fat" out of an organization through a concerted effort to control expenses. When profit margins begin to be squeezed, this is generally the first line of attack by a manager. The discretionary fixed costs usually come under scrutiny first, and various programs are either curtailed or eliminated in an effort to cut costs. Managers must be careful, however, lest they cut out muscle and bone along with the fat. Also, they must remember that frequent cost-cutting binges can be destructive to the morale of an organization. Most managers now agree that it is best to stay "lean and mean" all of the time.

Two prominent Canadian companies, Inco and Nova Corporation report on the importance of their cost cutting in maintaining their "low cost" competitive advantage.

Reduce Operating Assets

Managers have always been sensitive to the need to control sales, operating expenses, and operating margins. They have not always been equally sensitive, however, to the need to control investment in operating assets. Firms that have adopted the ROI approach to measuring managerial performance report that one of the first reactions on the part of investment centre managers is to trim down their investment in operating assets. The reason, of course, is that these managers soon realize that an excessive investment in operating assets will reduce the asset turnover and hurt the rate of return. As these managers pare down their investment in operating assets, funds are released that can be used elsewhere in the organization.

What approaches are open to an investment centre manager in his or her attempts to control the investment in operating assets? One approach is to pare out unneeded inventory. JIT purchasing and JIT manufacturing have been extremely helpful in reducing inventories of all types, with the result that ROI figures have improved dramatically in some companies. Another approach is to devise various methods of speeding up the collection of receivables. For example, many firms now permit customers to pay directly at a local bank. Others are using Electronic Data Interchange (E.D.I.) to speed payments of accounts. Credit card services and debit cards are also employed to facilitate payments of accounts. These practices speed up the collection process, thereby reducing the total investment required to carry accounts receivable. (The released funds are typically used to pay amounts due to short-term creditors.) As the accounts receivable balance is reduced, the asset turnover is increased.

The Problem of Allocated Expenses and Assets

In decentralized organizations such as General Products, Inc., it is common practice to allocate to the separate divisions the expenses incurred in operating corporate headquarters. When such allocations are made, a very thorny question arises as to whether these allocated expenses should be considered in the divisions' rate of return computations.

It can be argued on the one hand that allocated expenses should be included in rate of return computations, since they represent the value of services rendered to the divisions by central headquarters. On the other hand, it can be argued that they should not be included, since the divisional managers have no control over the incurrence of the expenses and since the "services" involved are often of questionable value, or are hard to pin down.

At the very least, *arbitrary* allocations should be avoided in rate of return computations. If arbitrary allocations are made, great danger exists of creating a bias for or against a particular division, as discussed earlier in the chapter. Expense allocations should be limited to the cost of those *actual* services provided by central headquarters that the divisions would *otherwise* have had to provide for themselves. The amount of expense allocated to a division should not exceed the cost that the division would have incurred if it had provided the service for itself.

These same guidelines apply to asset allocations from central corporate headquarters to the separate divisions. Assets relating to overall corporate operations should not be included as part of the divisional operating assets in divisional ROI computations, unless there are clear and traceable benefits to the divisions from the assets involved. As before, any type of arbitrary allocations (such as allocations on the basis of sales dollars) should be avoided.

Criticisms of ROI

Although ROI is widely used in evaluating performance, it is far from a perfect tool. The method is subject to the following criticisms:

1. ROI tends to emphasize short-run performance rather than long-run profitability. In an attempt to protect the current ROI, a manager may be motivated to reject otherwise profitable investment opportunities. (This point is discussed further in the following section.)
2. ROI is not consistent with the cash flow models used for capital expenditure analysis. (Cash flow models are discussed in Chapters 14 and 15.)
3. ROI may not be fully controllable by the division manager due to the presence of committed costs. This inability to control the ROI can make it difficult to distinguish between the performance of the manager and the performance of the division as an investment.

In an effort to overcome these problems, some companies use multiple criteria in evaluating performance rather than relying on ROI as a single measure. Other criteria used include the following:

Growth in market share.
Increases in productivity.
Dollar profits.
Receivables turnover.
Inventory turnover.
Product innovation.
Ability to expand into new and profitable areas.

It is felt that the use of multiple performance measures such as those above provide a more comprehensive picture of a manager's performance than can be obtained by relying on ROI alone.

RESIDUAL INCOME—ANOTHER MEASURE OF PERFORMANCE

OBJECTIVE 10
Compute the residual income and enumerate the strengths and weaknesses of this method of measuring performance.

We have assumed in our discussion that the purpose of an investment centre should be to maximize the rate of return that it is able to generate on operating assets. There is another approach to measuring performance in an investment centre that focuses on a concept known as *residual income*. **Residual income** is the net operating income that an investment centre is able to earn *above* some minimum return on its operating assets.

Economic value added (EVA) is a closely allied concept that differs in a few details from residual income. For example, under the economic value added concept, funds used for research and development are treated as investments rather than as expenses. However, for our purposes, we will not draw any distinction between residual income and economic value added.

When residual income or economic value added is used to measure performance, the purpose is to maximize the total amount of residual income or economic value added, *not* to maximize the overall ROI figure. Consider the following data for two comparable divisions:

	Performance Measured by—	
	Rate of Return (Division A)	Residual Income (Division B)
Average operating assets	$100,000 (a)	$100,000
Net operating income................................	$ 20,000 (b)	$ 20,000
ROI, (b) ÷ (a)...	20%	
Minimum required rate of return is assumed to be 15% (15% × $100,000).................		15,000
Residual income.....................................		$ 5,000

Notice that Division B has a positive residual income of $5,000. The performance of the manager of Division B is assessed according to how large or how small this residual income figure is from year to year. The larger the residual income figure, the better is the performance rating received by the division's manager.

FOCUS ON CURRENT PRACTICE

According to Fortune magazine, "Managers who run their businesses according to the precepts of EVA have hugely increased the value of their companies. Investors who know about EVA, and know which companies are employing it, have grown rich. Little wonder that highly regarded major corporations—Coca-Cola, AT&T, Quaker Oats, Briggs & Stratton, CSX, and many others—are flocking to the concept . . . Here's how Coca-Cola CEO Roberto Goizueta, a champion wealth creator, explains it: 'We raise capital to make concentrate, and sell it at an operating profit. Then we pay the cost of capital. Shareholders pocket the difference.' "[13]

[13]Shawn Tully, "The Real Key to Creating Wealth," *Fortune* (September 20 1993), pp. 38–50. Copyright © 1993 Time Inc. All rights reserved.

Motivation and Residual Income

Many companies believe that residual income is a better measure of performance than rate of return. They argue that the residual income approach encourages managers to make profitable investments that would be rejected by managers who are being measured by the ROI formula. To illustrate, assume that each of the divisions above is presented with an opportunity to make an investment of $25,000 in a new project that would generate a return of 18% on invested assets. The manager of Division A would probably reject this opportunity. Note from the tabulation that this division is already earning a return of 20% on its assets. If he takes on a new project that provides a return of only 18%, then his overall ROI will be reduced, as shown below:

	Present	New Project	Overall
Average operating assets (a)	$100,000	$25,000	$125,000
Net operating income (b)	$20,000	$4,500*	$24,500
ROI, (b) ÷ (a)	20%	18%	19.6%

*$25,000 × 18% = $4,500.

Since the performance of the manager of this division is being measured according to the *maximum* rate of return that he is able to generate on invested assets, he will be unenthused about any investment opportunity that reduces his current ROI figure. He will tend to think and act along these lines, even though the opportunity he rejects might have benefited the company *as a whole*.

FOCUS ON CURRENT PRACTICE

Quaker Oats provides an example of how use of EVA can change the way a company operates. "Until Quaker adopted the concept [of EVA] in 1991, its businesses had one overriding goal— increasing quarterly earnings. To do it, they guzzled capital. They offered sharp price discounts at the end of each quarter, so plants ran overtime turning out huge shipments of Gatorade, Rice-A-Roni, 100% Natural Cereal, and other products. Managers led the late rush, since their bonuses depended on raising operating profits each quarter . . . Pumping up sales requires many warehouses (capital) to hold vast temporary inventories (more capital). But who cared? Quaker's operating businesses paid no charge for capital in internal accounting, so they barely noticed. It took EVA to spotlight the problem . . . One plant has trimmed inventories from $15 million to $9 million, even though it is producing much more, and Quaker has closed five of 15 warehouses, saving $6 million a year in salaries and capital costs."[14]

On the other hand, the manager of Division B will be very anxious to accept the new investment opportunity. The reason is that she isn't concerned about maximizing her rate of return. She is concerned about maximizing her residual income. Any project that provides a return greater than the minimum required 15% will be attractive, since it will add to the *total amount* of the residual income figure. Under these circumstances, the new investment opportunity with its 18% return will clearly be attractive, as shown below:

---

[14]Shawn Tully, "The Real Key to Creating Wealth," *Fortune* (September 20, 1993), pp. 38–50. Copyright © 1993 Time Inc. All rights reserved.

	Present	New Project	Overall
Average operating assets..................	$100,000	$25,000	$125,000
Net operating income	$ 20,000	$ 4,500*	$ 24,500
Minimum required rate of return is again assumed to be 15%	15,000	3,750†	18,750
Residual income	$ 5,000	$ 750	$ 5,750

*$25,000 × 18% = $4,500.

†$25,000 × 15% = $3,750.

Thus, by accepting the new investment project, the manager of Division B will increase her division's overall residual income figure and thereby show an improved performance as a manager. The fact that her division's overall ROI might be lower as a result of accepting the project is immaterial, since performance is being evaluated by residual income, not ROI. The well-being of both the manager and the company as a whole will be maximized by accepting all investment opportunities down to the 15% cutoff rate.

Divisional Comparison and Residual Income

The residual income approach has one major disadvantage. It can't be used to compare the performance of divisions of different sizes, since by its very nature it creates a bias in favour of larger divisions. That is, one would expect larger divisions to have more residual income than smaller divisions, not necessarily because they are better managed but simply because of the bigger numbers involved.

As an example, consider the following residual income computations for Division X and Division Y:

	Division	
	X	Y
Average operating assets (a)	$1,000,000	$250,000
Net operating income............................	$ 120,000	$ 40,000
Minimum required return: 10% × (a)	100,000	25,000
Residual income	$ 20,000	$ 15,000

Observe that Division X has slightly more residual income than Division Y, but that Division X has $1,000,000 in operating assets as compared to only $250,000 in operating assets for Division Y. Thus, Division X's greater residual income is probably more a result of its size than the quality of its management. In fact, it appears that the smaller division is better managed, since it has been able to generate nearly as much residual income with only one-fourth as much in operating assets to work with.

BALANCED SCORECARDS

ROI and residual income measures of performance are financial in nature and they are applied to relatively large segments of a business. Segmentation and segment margins can be applied to smaller scale activities but they still reflect financial results and a period-by-period examination of results.

Reorganization of business on a cell-by-cell basis, the introduction of total quality control with continuous monitoring requires performance assessments that reflect the specific of each cell because each worker or small group must make continuous decisions that in turn affect the overall results of the organization. For example, a cell may need to choose between grade 1 or grade 2 materials which in turn affects delivery time, labour time, quality and overhead. Cells need to have information on a timely basis which suggests the implications of the alternatives and does not suggest solutions that are inappropriate for the achievement of the goals of the organization.

Senior managers need information that suggests alternatives that are appropriate for achieving the goals of the organization. Short and long-run goals must be balanced and consistent with the strategies set for the organization. Information of both a financial and nonfinancial nature needs to be consistent and should be able to be aggregated without introducing misleading results. However, how can worker satisfaction with a supervisor be identified and aggregated to a segment margin without losing the information? How can a lower segment margin this period be justified in favour of a higher future result especially if the lower current result causes bonuses to be lost? How can senior managers and junior managers follow the same path if the information they are using is inconsistent?

A **balanced scorecard** is an approach being used and studied by a number of well-known organizations in an effort to provide a performance report that is more comprehensive than the financial results determined in this chapter. In addition, this scorecard provides a vehicle to more clearly communicate strategies between various levels of an organization.

Balanced scorecards use four viewpoints within which to organize information. The customer view looks at, for example, sales of new products, on-time deliveries, and sales of proprietary products. The internal focus looks at cycle time, technology, unit costs, yields, and introduction time for new products. The innovation and learning focus examines time to develop the next generation product, process time, new product introduction versus the competition as a way of assessing how the organization innovates and learns. The fourth and final view is a financial one where aspects such as cash flow, sales growth, segment income growth and ROI are used as ways of viewing the financial affairs.

Each organization can adjust or modify the types of measures they wish to use under each of the viewpoints. This way they can keep the direction of the scorecard while adjusting it to suit their peculiarities. In each case measurements are linked to the strategy of the organization so that consistent results can be attained at the various organizations.[15]

Nova Corporation reports its balanced scorecard in its *1996 Annual Report.* Nova evaluates its activities in terms of customers, employees, communities and society, and shareholders. For customers, Nova reports the results of customer satisfaction ratings and relates these to employee activities. For employees, Nova used an employee climate survey, demographics and other human resource research. Nova targets areas for improvement and compares its results to other leading North American companies. In the section on Communities and Society, Nova cites its donations, taxes, safety, health and environment, and the development of a university course on community relations. For the shareholders, Nova mentions its dividends and shareholder returns. In addition, corporate directors are forced to take their fees in Nova shares to help assure a consistency of interests.[16]

---

[15]Robert S. Kaplan and David P. Norton, "The Balanced Scorecard—Measures that Drive Performance," *Harvard Business Review,* January–February 1992, pp. 71–79; Robert S. Kaplan and David P. Norton, "Putting the Balanced Scorecard to Work," *Harvard Business Review,* September–October 1993, pp. 134–42; Robert S. Kaplan and David P. Norton, "Using the Balanced Scorecard as a Strategic Management System," *Harvard Business Review,* January–February 1996, pp. 75–85.

[16]Nova Corporation, *1996 Annual Report,* pp. 62–63.

SUMMARY

The purpose of segment reporting is to provide information needed by the manager to determine the profitability of product lines, divisions, sales territories, and other segments of a company. Under the contribution approach to segment reporting, costs are classified as either traceable or common. Only those costs that are traceable are assigned to segments; common costs are not allocated to segments, since doing so might result in misleading data.

Costs that are traceable to a segment are further classified as either variable or fixed. Deducting variable costs from sales yields a contribution margin, which is highly useful in short-run planning and decision making. The traceable fixed costs of a segment are then deducted from the contribution margin to obtain a segment margin. The segment margin is highly useful in long-run planning and decision making.

Analysis provided by accountants can help managers view the important segment of marketing in a new light. Revenue and sales quantity analysis provide information about the effects of market changes or sales mix changes on profits. Association of marketing expenses with drivers that cause these expenses permits a review of how marketing activities cause expenses. Activity analysis is a powerful tool for assisting managers to understand marketing activities and their costs.

Segments are often divided into three levels of responsibility—cost centres, profit centres, and investment centres. The ROI formula is widely used as a method of evaluating performance in an investment centre because it summarizes in one figure many aspects of an investment centre manager's responsibilities. As an alternative to the ROI formula, some companies use residual income as a measure of investment centre performance. These companies argue that the residual income approach encourages profitable investment in many situations where the ROI approach might discourage investment.

Balanced scorecards presents one of the attempts used by organizations to evaluate performance on numerous activities that are not clearly visible in the ROI, RI or segmented financial results.

REVIEW PROBLEM 1: SEGMENTED STATEMENTS

The business staff of the legal firm Frampton, Davis & Smythe has constructed the following report which breaks down the firm's overall results for last month in terms of its two main business segments—family law and commercial law:

	Total	Family Law	Commercial Law
Revenues from clients....................	$1,000,000	$400,000	$600,000
Less variable expenses	220,000	100,000	120,000
Contribution margin	780,000	300,000	480,000
Less traceable fixed expenses...............	670,000	280,000	390,000
Segment margin	110,000	20,000	90,000
Less common fixed expenses	60,000	24,000	36,000
Net income	$ 50,000	$ (4,000)	$ 54,000

However, this report is not quite correct. The common fixed expenses such as the managing partner's salary, general administrative expenses, and general firm advertising have been allocated to the two segments based on revenues from clients.

Required

1. Redo the segment report, eliminating the allocation of common fixed expenses. Show both Amount and Percent columns for the firm as a whole and for each of the segments. Would the firm be better off financially if the family law segment were dropped? (Note: Many of the firm's commercial law clients also use the firm for their family law requirements such as drawing up wills.)

2. The firm's advertising agency has proposed an ad campaign targeted at boosting the revenues from the family law segment. The ad campaign would cost $20,000, and the advertising agency claims that it would increase family law revenues by $100,000. The managing partner of Frampton, Davis & Smythe believes this increase in business could be accommodated without any increase in fixed expenses. What effect would this ad campaign have on the family law segment margin and on overall net income of the firm?

Solution to Review Problem 1

1. The corrected segmented income statement appears below:

	Total		Family Law		Commercial Law	
	Amount	Percent	Amount	Percent	Amount	Percent
Revenues from clients	$1,000,000	100	$400,000	100	$600,000	100
Less variable expenses	220,000	22	100,000	25	120,000	20
Contribution margin	780,000	78	300,000	75	480,000	80
Less traceable fixed expenses	670,000	67	280,000	70	390,000	65
Segment margin........	110,000	11	$ 20,000	5	$ 90,000	15
Less common fixed expenses	60,000	6				
Net income	$ 50,000	5				

No, the firm would not be financially better off if the family law practice were dropped. The family law segment is covering all of its own costs and is contributing $20,000 per month to covering the common fixed expenses of the firm. While the segment margin as a percent of sales is much lower for family law than for commercial law, it is still profitable; and it is likely that family law is a service that the firm must provide to its commercial clients in order to remain competitive.

2. The ad campaign would be expected to add $55,000 to the family law segment as follows:

Increased revenues from clients	$100,000
Family law contribution margin ratio............	× 75%
Incremental contribution margin................	75,000
Less cost of the ad campaign	20,000
Increased segment margin.....................	$ 55,000

Since there would be no increase in fixed expenses (including common fixed expenses), the increase in overall net income would also be $55,000.

REVIEW PROBLEM 2: RETURN ON INVESTMENT (ROI) AND RESIDUAL INCOME

The Magnetic Imaging Division of Medical Diagnostics, Inc., has reported the following results for last year's operations:

$$\text{Sales.} \dots \dots \dots \$25 \text{ million}$$
$$\text{Net operating income} \dots \dots 3 \text{ million}$$
$$\text{Average operating assets} \dots \dots 10 \text{ million}$$

Required

1. Compute the margin, turnover, and ROI for the Magnetic Imaging Division.
2. Top management of Medical Diagnostics, Inc., has set a target minimum rate of return on average operating assets of 25%. What is the Magnetic Imaging Division's residual income for the year?

Solution to Review Problem 2

1. The required calculations appear below:

$$\text{Margin} = \frac{\text{Net operating income, } \$3,000,000}{\text{Sales, } \$25,000,000}$$

$$= 12\%$$

$$\text{Turnover} = \frac{\text{Sales, } \$25,000,000}{\text{Average operating assets, } \$10,000,000}$$

$$= 2.5$$

$$\text{ROI} = \text{Margin} \times \text{Turnover}$$

$$= 12\% \times 2.5$$

$$= 30\%$$

2. The residual income for the Magnetic Imaging Division is computed as follows:

Average operating assets	$10,000,000
Net operating income	$ 3,000,000
Minimum required return (25% × $10,000,000)	2,500,000
Residual income	$ 500,000

KEY TERMS FOR REVIEW

OBJECTIVE 11
Define or explain the key terms listed at the end of the chapter.

Balanced Scorecard   An approach to providing a comprehensive measure of performance. (p. 636)

Common fixed cost   A cost that can't be identified with any particular segment of a company. Such costs, which are also known as *indirect costs,* exist to serve overall operating activities. (p. 612)

Cost centre   A segment of a company that has control over the incurrence of cost but has no control over generating revenue or the use of investment funds. (p. 625)

Cross-subsidization   The result of improperly assigning costs between segments of an organization. (p. 607)

Decentralized organization   An organization in which decision making is not confined to a few top executives but rather is spread throughout the organization. (p. 623)

Economic value added (EVA)   A concept similar to residual income. In EVA, funds used for research and development are treated as investments rather than as expenses. (p. 633)

Investment centre   A segment that has control over the incurrence of cost and over the generating of revenue and that also has control over the use of investment funds. (p. 625)

Life cycle costing   A costing approach that focuses on all costs along the value chain that will be generated throughout the entire life of a product. (p. 606)

Margin   A measure of management's ability to control operating expenses in relation to sales. It is computed by dividing net operating income by the sales figure. (p. 627)

Market share variance   Actual sales volume minus the anticipated portion of the actual market volume all times budgeted contribution margin per unit. (p. 619)

Market volume variance   Actual market volume minus budget market volume times anticipated market share all times budget contribution margin. (p. 619)

Net operating income   The income of an organization before interest and income taxes have been deducted. (p. 628)

Operating assets   Cash, accounts receivable, inventory, plant and equipment, and all other assets held for productive use in an organization. (p. 628)

Profit centre   A segment that has control over the incurrence of cost and the generating of revenue but has no control over the use of investment funds. (p. 625)

Residual income   The net operating income that an investment centre is able to earn above some minimum return on its operating assets. (p. 633)

Responsibility centre   Any point in an organization that has control over the incurrence of cost, the generating of revenue, or the use of investment funds. (p. 626)

Return on investment (ROI)   A measure of profitability in an organization that is computed by multiplying the margin by the turnover. (p. 627)

Sales mix variance   Actual sales quantity minus actual sales quantity based on budgeted mix all times budgeted sales price. (p. 620)

Sales price variance   Actual sales price minus budgeted sales price all times actual sales quantity. (p. 619)

Sales quantity variance   Actual sales quantity based on budgeted mix minus budgeted sales quantity all times budgeted sales price. (p. 620)

Segment   Any part or activity of an organization about which the manager seeks cost, revenue, or profit data. (p. 605)

Segment margin   The amount computed by deducting the traceable fixed costs of a segment from the segment's contribution margin. It represents the margin available after a segment has covered all of its own costs. (p. 614)

Segment reporting   An income statement or other report in an organization in which data are divided according to product lines, divisions, territories, or similar organizational segments. (p. 605)

Traceable fixed cost   A cost that can be identified with a particular segment and that arises because of the existence of that segment. (p. 612)

Turnover   A measure of the amount of sales that can be generated in an investment centre for each dollar invested in operating assets. It is computed by dividing sales by the average operating assets figure. (p. 627)

Value chain   The major business functions that add value to a company's products and services. These functions consist of research and development, product design, manufacturing, marketing, distribution, and customer service. (p. 606)

APPENDIX 12A: TRANSFER PRICING

OBJECTIVE 12
Identify three ways that transfer prices can be set.

Special problems arise in evaluating segment performance when segments of a company do business with each other. The problems revolve around the question of what transfer price to charge between the segments. A **transfer price** is defined as the price charged when one segment of a company provides goods or services to another segment of the company. For example, when the petroleum refining division of a company such as Petro-Canada transfers gasoline to the division that sells to retail service stations, some transfer price must be agreed upon.

The Need for Transfer Prices

Assume that a vertically integrated firm has three divisions. The three divisions are:

Mining Division
Processing Division
Manufacturing Division

The Mining Division mines raw materials that are transferred to the Processing Division. After processing, the Processing Division transfers the processed materials to the Manufacturing Division. The Manufacturing Division then includes the processed materials as part of its finished product.

In this example, we have two transfers of goods between divisions within the same company. What price should control these transfers? Should the price be set so as to include some "profit" element to the selling division? Should it be set so as to include only the accumulated costs to that point? Or should it be set at yet another figure? The choice of a transfer price can be complicated by the fact that each division may be supplying portions of its output to outside customers, as well as to sister divisions. Another complication is that the price charged by one division becomes a cost to the other division, and the higher this cost, the lower will be the purchasing division's profit and rate of return. Thus, the purchasing division would like the transfer price to be low, whereas the selling division would like it to be high. The selling division may even want to charge the same "market" price internally as it charges to outside customers.

As the reader may guess, the problem of what transfer price to set between segments of a company has no easy solution and often leads to protracted and heated disputes between profit and investment centre managers. Yet some transfer price *must* be set if data are to be available for evaluating performance in the various parts or divisions of a company. In practice, three general approaches are used in setting transfer prices:

1. Set transfer prices at cost using:
    a.   Variable cost.
    b.   Full (absorption) cost.
2. Set transfer prices at the market price.
3. Set transfer prices at a negotiated price.

In the following discussion, we consider each of these approaches to the transfer pricing problem.

Transfer Prices at Cost

Many firms make transfers between divisions on a basis of the accumulated cost of the goods being transferred, thus ignoring any profit element to the selling division. A transfer price computed in this way might be based only on the variable costs involved, or fixed costs might also be considered and the transfer price thus based on full (absorption) costs accumulated to the point of transfer. Although the cost approach to setting transfer prices is relatively simple to apply, it has some major defects. These defects can be brought out by the following illustration:

Bradford Products, Inc., controls many companies, including Caswell Publishing and Regent Paper Company, both of which have been recently acquired. Regent Paper Company manufactures high-quality paper, which it sells for $30 per box. The paper costs $10 per box to manufacture. Caswell Publishing now purchases its paper, which is slightly lower in grade, from another paper company at a cost of $25 per box.

Top management at Bradford Products, Inc., wants Regent Paper Company to turn all of its capacity over to the manufacture of paper for Caswell Publishing. This paper would be slightly lighter in weight than the paper now being produced by Regent Paper Company, and it would cost $8 per box to manufacture. The same amount of time would be involved in the manufacture of a box of either type of paper.

Should Regent Paper Company give up its present business and produce paper for Caswell Publishing? On the surface this would seem to be a good decision, since the variable costs of the new paper would be only $8 per box as compared to $10 per box for the paper Regent is now manufacturing, and since Caswell Publishing is now paying $25 per box for its paper. Unfortunately, looking at cost alone (either variable cost or full absorption cost) will not provide management with the information it needs to make a wise decision. As stated, manufacturing the new paper *appears* to be a good decision, but appearances can sometimes be deceiving.

Herein lies one of the defects of the cost approach to setting transfer prices: Cost-based transfer prices can lead to dysfunctional decisions in a company because this approach has no built-in mechanism for telling the manager when transfers should and should not be made between segments. Thus, profits for the company as a whole can be adversely affected, and the manager may never know about it.

Another defect associated with cost-based transfer prices is that the only segment that will show any profits is the one that makes the final sale to an outside party. Other segments, such as Regent Paper Company in our example, will show no profits for their efforts because selling price and cost will be the same. Thus, evaluation by the ROI formula or by the residual income approach will not be possible.

A third criticism of cost-based transfer prices lies in their general inability to provide incentive for control of costs. If the costs of one division are simply passed on to the next, then there is little incentive for anyone to control costs. The final selling division is simply burdened with the accumulated waste and inefficiency of intermediate processors and will be penalized with a rate of return that is deficient in comparison to that of competitors. Experience has shown that unless costs are subject to some type of competitive pressures at transfer points, waste and inefficiency almost invariably develop.

FOCUS ON
CURRENT PRACTICE

Although cost-based transfer prices are in common use, studies show a trend toward greater use of market-based methods. A survey of 145 industrial companies in 1977 and of 132 industrial companies in 1990 showed the frequency of use of transfer pricing methods when domestic transfers were involved. The results of these surveys are shown in the table below. Note that the market-based approach was the only method to show an increase in use over the 13-year time period between the two surveys.[17]

	Percentage of Companies Using the Method	
	1990	1977
Cost-based transfer prices.................	46.2%	50.4%
Market-based transfer prices...............	36.7	31.5
Negotiated prices	16.6	18.1
Other.................................	0.5%	—
Total—all methods	100.0%	100.0%

---

[17]Roger Y. W. Tang, C. K. Walter, and Robert H. Raymond, "Transfer Pricing—Japanese vs. American Style," *Management Accounting* (January 1979), p. 14; and Roger Y. W. Tang, "Transfer Pricing in the 1990s," *Management Accounting* (February 1992), p. 25.

Despite these shortcomings, cost-based transfer prices are in fairly common use. Advocates argue that they are easily understood and highly convenient to use. If transfer prices are to be based on cost, then the costs should be standard costs rather than actual costs. This will at least avoid passing inefficiency on from one division to another.

A General Formula for Computing Transfer Prices

OBJECTIVE 13

Use the transfer pricing formula to compute an appropriate transfer price between segments, assuming the selling division (a) is operating at full capacity, and (b) has idle capacity.

A general formula exists that can be used by the manager as a starting point in computing the appropriate transfer price between divisions or segments in a multidivisional company.[18] The formula is that *the transfer price should be equal to the unit variable costs of the good being transferred, plus the contribution margin per unit that is lost to the selling division as a result of giving up outside sales.* The formula can be expressed as:

$$\text{Transfer} = \frac{\text{Variable costs}}{\text{per unit}} + \frac{\text{Lost contribution margin per}}{\text{unit on outside sales}}$$

To show the application of this formula, refer to the data for Regent Paper Company in the preceding section. The proper transfer price for Regent Paper Company to charge Caswell Publishing per box if the new paper is produced can be computed as follows:

Transfer price = $8 (the variable cost per box of the *new* paper) + $20 (the contribution margin *lost* per box of paper as a result of Regent Paper giving up its present sales: $30 selling price − $10 variable costs = $20)

Transfer price = $28 per box for the new paper

Upon seeing this transfer price, it becomes immediately obvious to the management of Bradford Products that no transfers should be made between the two companies, since Caswell Publishing can buy its paper from its outside supplier for only $25 per box. Thus, the transfer price enables management to reach the correct decision and to avoid any adverse effect on profits.

Two additional points should be noted before going on. First, *the price set by the transfer pricing formula always represents a lower limit for a transfer price, since the selling division must receive at least the amount shown by the formula in order to be as well off as if it sold only to outside customers.* Under certain conditions (discussed later), the price can be more than the amount shown by the formula, but it can't be less or the selling division and the company as a whole will suffer. Second, *the transfer price computed by using the formula is a price based on competitive market conditions.* The remainder of our discussion will focus on the setting of market-based transfer prices.

Transfers at Market Price: General Considerations

Some form of competitive **market price** (that is, the price charged for an item on the open market) is generally regarded as the best approach to the transfer pricing problem. The reason is that the use of market prices dovetails well with the profit centre concept and makes profit-based performance evaluation feasible at many levels of an organization. By using market prices to control transfers, *all* divisions or segments are able to show profits (if they *are* profitable) for their efforts—not just the final division in the chain of transfers. The market price approach also helps the manager to decide when

---

[18]For background discussion and generalizations, see Ralph L. Benke, Jr., and James Don Edwards, "Transfer Pricing: Techniques and Uses," *Management Accounting* (June 1980), pp. 44–46.

transfers should be made, as we saw earlier, and tends to lead to the best decisions involving transfer questions that may arise on a day-to-day basis.

The market price approach is designed for use in highly decentralized organizations. By this we mean that it is used in those organizations where divisional managers have enough autonomy in decision making so that the various divisions can be viewed as being virtually independent businesses with independent profit responsibility. The idea in using market prices to control transfers is to create the competitive market conditions that would exist if the various divisions were *indeed* separate firms and engaged in arm's-length, open-market bargaining. To the extent that the resulting transfer prices reflect actual market conditions, divisional operating results provide an excellent basis for evaluating managerial performance.

In addition to the formula given earlier, there are certain guidelines that should be followed when using market prices to control transfers between divisions. These guidelines are:

1. The buying division must purchase internally so long as the selling division meets all bona fide outside prices and wants to sell internally.
2. If the selling division does not meet all bona fide outside prices, then the buying division is free to purchase outside.
3. The selling division must be free to reject internal business if it prefers to sell outside.
4. An impartial board must be established to help settle disagreements between divisions over transfer prices.

Transfers at Market Price: Well-Defined Intermediate Market

Not all companies or divisions face the same market conditions. Sometimes the only customer a division has for its output is a sister division. In other situations, an **intermediate market** may exist for part or all of a division's output. By intermediate market, we mean that a market exists in which an item can be sold *immediately* and *in its present form* to outside customers, if desired, rather than being transferred to another division for use in its manufacturing process. Thus, if an intermediate market exists, a division will have a choice between selling its products to outside customers on the intermediate market or selling them to other divisions within the company. In the paragraphs that follow, we consider transfer pricing in those situations where intermediate markets are strong and well defined.

Let us assume that Division A or International Company has a product that can be sold either to Division B or to outside customers in an intermediate market. The cost and revenue structures of the two divisions are given below:

Division A		Division B	
Intermediate selling price		Final market price outside.	$100
if sold outside	$25	Transfer price from Division A	
Variable costs	15	(or outside purchase price)	25
		Variable costs added in Division B	40

What transfer price should control transfers between the two divisions? In this case, the answer is easy; the transfer price should be $25—the price that Division A can get by selling in the intermediate market and the price that Division B would otherwise have to pay to purchase the desired goods from en outside supplier in the intermediate market. This price can also be obtained by applying the formula developed earlier:

$$\text{Transfer price} = \frac{\text{Variable costs}}{\text{per unit}} + \frac{\text{Lost contribution margin per}}{\text{unit on outside sales}}$$

Transfer price = $15 + ($25 − $15 = $10)
Transfer price = $25

EXHIBIT 12-8   Transfers at Market Price: Well-Defined Intermediate Market

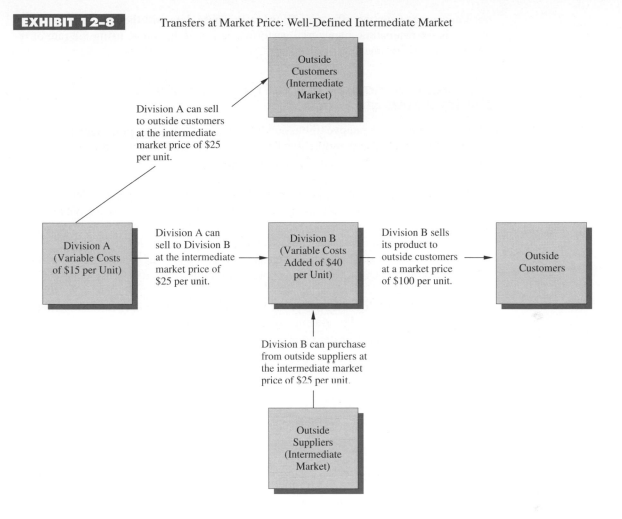

The choices facing the two divisions are shown graphically in Exhibit 12–8.

So long as Division A receives a transfer price of $25 per gallon from Division B, it will be willing to sell all of its output internally. In selling to Division B, Division A will be just as well off as if it has sold its product outside at the $25 price. In like manner, so long as the price charged by outside suppliers is not less than $25 per unit, Division B will be willing to pay that price to Division A. The $25 per unit intermediate market price therefore serves as an acceptable transfer price between the two divisions. The result of transfers at this price is summarized in the following table.

	Division A	Division B	Total Company
Sales price per unit	$25	$100	$100
Variable cost added per unit	15	40	55
Transfer cost per unit	—	25	—
Contribution margin per unit	$10	$ 35	$ 45

The contribution margin realized for the entire company is $45 per unit. By using the $25 intermediate market price to control intracompany transfers, the firm is able to show that a portion of this margin accrues from the efforts of Division A and that a portion accrues from the efforts of Division B. These data will then serve as an excellent basis for evaluating managerial performance in the divisions, using the rate of return or residual income approaches.

Transfers at Market Price: Price Changes in the Intermediate Market

We have assumed in the above discussion that there was complete price agreement in the intermediate market, and therefore that Division B could purchase the needed goods from an outside supplier at the same $25 price as being charged by Division A. In reality, complete price agreement often doesn't exist, or it may be upset by some suppliers deciding to cut their prices for various reasons. Returning to the preceding example, let us assume that an outside supplier has offered to supply the goods to Division B for only $20 per unit, rather than the at the normal $25 intermediate market price being charged by Division B. Should Division B accept this offer, or should Division A cut its price to $20 in order to get Division B's business? The answer will depend on whether Division A (the selling division) is operating at full or at partial (with idle) capacity.

Selling Division at Full Capacity.   If Division A (the selling division) is operating at capacity, then it will have to give up outside sales in order to sell to Division B. Under these circumstances, the transfer price will be computed in the same way as we computed it earlier:

$$\text{Transfer price} = \frac{\text{Variable costs}}{\text{per unit}} + \frac{\text{Lost contribution margin per}}{\text{unit on outside sales}}$$

$$\text{Transfer price} = \$15 + \left(\begin{array}{ccc}\$25 \text{ outside} & \$15 \text{ variable} & \$10 \text{ lost contribution} \\ \text{selling price} & - \text{ costs} & = \text{ margin per unit}\end{array}\right)$$

$$\text{Transfer price} = \$25$$

Recall that the price set by the formula always represents a *lower limit* for a transfer price, since the selling division must receive at least the amount shown by the formula in order to be as well off as if it sold only to outside customers. Therefore, Division A should not cut its price to $20 in order to continue to sell to Division B. If Division A cuts its price, it will lose $5 per unit in contribution margin, and both it and the company as a whole will be worse off.

In short, whenever the selling division must give up outside sales in order to sell internally, it has an opportunity cost that must be considered in setting the transfer price. As shown by the formula, this opportunity cost is the contribution margin that will be lost as a result of giving up outside sales. Unless the transfer price can be set high enough to cover this opportunity cost, along with the variable costs associated with the sale, no transfers should be made.

Selling Division with Idle Capacity.   If the selling division has idle capacity, then a different situation exists. Under these conditions, the selling division's opportunity cost *may* be zero (depending on what alternative uses it has for its idle capacity). Even if the opportunity cost is zero. many managers would argue that the transfer price should still be based on prevailing market prices, to the extent that these prices can be determined accurately and fairly. Other managers would argue that idle capacity combined with an opportunity cost of zero, or near zero, calls for a negotiation of the transfer price downward from prevailing market rates, so that both the buyer and the seller can profit from the intracompany business.

Under idle capacity conditions, so long as the selling division receives a price greater than its variable costs (at least in the short run), all parties will benefit by keeping business inside the company rather than having the buying division go outside. The accuracy of this statement can be shown by returning to the example in the preceding section. Assume again that an outside supplier offers to sell the concentrate to Division B for $20 per unit. In this case, however, we will assume that Division A has enough idle capacity to supply all of Division B's needs, with no prospects for additional outside sales at the current $25 intermediate market price. Using our formula, the transfer price between Divisions A and B would be:

$$\text{Transfer price} = \frac{\text{Variable costs}}{\text{per unit}} + \frac{\text{Lost contribution margin per}}{\text{unit on outside sales}}$$

$$\text{Transfer price} = \$15 + \$0$$
$$\text{Transfer price} = \$15$$

As stated before, the $15 figure represents a lower limit for a transfer price. Actually, the transfer price can be anywhere between this figure and the $20 price being quoted to Division B from the outside. In this situation, therefore, we have a transfer price *range* in which to operate, as shown below:

If Division A (the selling division) is hesitant to reduce its price, should it be required to meet the $20 figure in order to supply Division B's needs? The answer is no. The guidelines given earlier indicate that the selling division is not required to sell internally. Rather than accept a $20 price for its goods, Division A may prefer to let its capacity remain idle and search for other, more profitable products.

If Division A decides not to reduce its price to $20 to meet outside competition, should Division B be forced to continue to pay $25 and to buy internally? The answer again is no. The guidelines given earlier state that if the selling division is not willing to meet all bona fide outside prices, then the buying division is free to go outside to get the best price it can. However, if the selling division has idle capacity and the buying division purchases from an outside supplier, then *suboptimization* will result for the selling division, possibly for the buying division, and certainly for the company as a whole. By **suboptimization** we mean that the overall level of profitability will be less than the segment or the company is capable of earning. In our example, if Division A refuses to meet the $20 price, then *both it and the company as a whole will lose $5 per unit in potential contribution margin ($20 – $15 = $5).* In short, where idle capacity exists, every effort should be made to negotiate a price acceptable to both the buyer and the seller that will keep business within the company as a whole.

Negotiated Transfer Price

There are some situations where a transfer price below the intermediate market price can be justified. For example, selling and administrative expenses may be less when intracompany sales are involved, or the volume of units may be large enough to justify quantity discounts.

In addition, we have already seen that a price below the prevailing market price may be jus tified when the selling division has idle capacity. Situations such as these can probably be served best by some type of **negotiated transfer price.** A negotiated transfer price is one agreed on between the buying and selling divisions that reflects unusual or mitigating circumstances.

Possibly the widest use of negotiated transfer prices is in those situations where no intermediate market prices are available. For example, one division may require an item that is not available from any outside source and therefore must be produced internally. Under these circumstances, the buying division must negotiate with another division in the company and agree to a transfer price that is attractive enough to the other division to cause it to take on the new business. To provide an example of how a transfer price would be set in such a situation, consider the following data:

> Division X has developed a new product that requires a custom-made fitting. Another division in the company, Division Y, has both the experience and the equipment necessary to produce the fitting. Division X has approached Division Y for a quoted unit price based on the production of 5,000 fittings per year.
>
> Division Y has determined that the fitting would require variable costs of $8 per unit. However, in order to have time to produce the fitting, Division Y would have to reduce production of a different product, product A, by 3,500 units per year. Product A sells for $45 per unit and has variable costs of $25 per unit. What transfer price should Division Y quote to Division X for the new fittings? Employing our formula, we get:

$$\text{Transfer price} = \frac{\text{Variable costs}}{\text{per unit}} + \frac{\text{Lost contribution margin per}}{\text{unit on outside sales}}$$

The lost contribution margin per unit would be:

Selling price of product A	$ 45
Variable costs of product A	25
Contribution margin of product A	20
Unit sales of product A given up	× 3,500
Total lost contribution margin	$70,000

$$\frac{\$70,000 \text{ lost contribution margin on product A}}{5,000 \text{ fittings to be manufactured for Division X}} = \frac{\$14 \text{ lost contribution}}{\text{margin per fitting}}$$

Transfer price = $8 variable costs + $14 lost contribution margin
Transfer price = $22 per fitting

Thus, the transfer price quoted by Division Y should not be less than $22 per fitting. Division Y might quote a higher price if it wants to increase its overall profits (at the expense of Division X), but it should not quote less than $22, or the profits of the company as a whole will suffer. If Division X is not happy with the $22 price, it can get a quote from an outside manufacturer for the fitting.

If Division Y in our example has idle capacity, then the appropriate transfer price is less clear. The lower limit for a transfer price would be the $8 variable costs, as discussed earlier. However, no division wants to simply recover its costs, so the actual transfer price would undoubtedly be greater than $8, according to what could be negotiated between the two divisional managers. In situations such as this, the selling division will often add some "target" markup figure to its costs in quoting a transfer price to the buying division.

Divisional Autonomy and Suboptimization

A question often arises as to how much autonomy should be granted to divisions in setting their own transfer prices and in making decisions concerning whether to sell internally or to sell outside. Should the divisional heads have complete authority to make these decisions, or should top corporate management step in if it appears that a decision is about to be made that would result in suboptimization? For example, if idle capacity exists in the selling division and divisional managers are unable to agree on a transfer price, should top corporate management step in and *force* settlement of the dispute?

Efforts should always be made, of course, to bring disputing managers together. But the almost unanimous feeling among top corporate executives is that divisional heads should not be forced into an agreement over a transfer price. That is, if a particular divisional head flatly refuses to change his or her position in a dispute, *then this decision should be respected* even if it results in suboptimization. This is simply the price that is paid for the concept of divisional autonomy. If top corporate management steps in and forces the decisions in difficult situations, then the purposes of decentralization are defeated and the company simply becomes a centralized operation with decentralization of only minor decisions and responsibilities. In short, if a division is to be viewed as an autonomous unit with independent profit responsibility, then it must have control over its own destiny—even to the extent of having the right to make bad decisions.

We should note, however, that if a division consistently makes bad decisions, the results will soon have an impact on its rate of return, and the divisional manager may find that he or she has to defend the division's performance. Even so, the manager's right to get into an embarrassing situation must be respected if decentralization is to operate successfully. The overwhelming experience of multidivisional companies is that divisional autonomy and independent profit responsibility lead to much greater success and profitability than do closely controlled, centrally administered operations. Part of the price of this success and profitability is an occasional situation of suboptimization due to pettiness, bickering, or just plain managerial stubbornness.

International Aspects of Transfer Pricing

Transfer pricing is used worldwide to control the flow of goods and services between segments of an organization. However, the objectives of transfer pricing change when a multinational corporation (MNC) is involved and the goods and services being transferred must cross international borders. The objectives of international transfer pricing, as compared to domestic transfer pricing, are summarized in Exhibit 12–9.[19]

EXHIBIT 12-9

Domestic and International Transfer Pricing Objectives

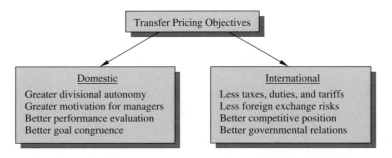

[19]Data in the exhibit are taken in part from Wagdy M. Abdallah, "Guidelines for CEOs in Transfer Pricing Policies," *Management Accounting* (September 1988), p. 61.

As shown in the exhibit, the objectives of international transfer pricing focus on minimizing taxes, duties, and foreign exchange risks, along with enhancing a company's competitive position and improving its relations with foreign governments. Although domestic objectives such as managerial motivation and divisional autonomy are always desirable in an organization, they usually become secondary when international transfers are involved. Companies will focus instead on charging a transfer price that will slash its total tax bill or that will strengthen a foreign subsidiary.

For example, charging a low transfer price for parts shipped to a foreign subsidiary may reduce customs duty payments as the parts cross international borders, or it may help the subsidiary to compete in foreign markets by keeping the subsidiary's costs low. On the other hand, charging a high transfer price may help an MNC draw profits out of a country that has stringent controls on foreign remittances, or it may allow an MNC to shift income from a country that has high income tax rates to a country that has low rates.

As previously mentioned, transfer prices can have a significant impact on a firm's income taxes. Firms prefer to shift products to countries which have lower tax rates by means of various transfer pricing schemes. On the other hand Revenue Canada seeks its fair share of the global tax pie, and its auditors demand hard documentary support of how transfer prices have been established. In general, Revenue Canada accepts fair-market value for determining the price of tangible products. For services such as management or marketing fees, transfer prices are generally based on costs with an appropriate markup added. Management, of course, has an incentive to set transfer prices to minimize its tax liability.[20]

The actual determination of transfer prices can become contentious. Alternative cost or revenue allocation methods can result in very different transfer prices. It is not surprising that disputes arise from time to time. For example, in a $200 million case, Revenue Canada claimed that Irving Oil owed taxes resulting from the sale of crude oil bought from its Bermuda subsidiary in 1971 to 1975. In February of 1991, the Federal Court of Appeal ruled in favour of Irving. The court acknowledged that Irving was practicing tax avoidance, not tax evasion. Acting within the law, Irving had paid fair market value for its crude.

In summary, managers must be sensitive to the geographic, political, and economic circumstances in which they are operating, and set transfer prices in such a way as to optimize total company performance.

REVIEW PROBLEM 3: TRANSFER PRICING

Situation A

Collyer Products, Inc., has a Valve Division that manufactures and sells a standard valve as follows:

Capacity in units................................	100,000
Selling price to outside customers on the intermediate market........................	$30
Variable costs per unit	16
Fixed costs per unit (based on capacity)	9

---

[20]Paul Glover, "Transfer Pricing: Are You Prepared?" *CMA Magazine* (October 1989), p. 24.

The company has a Pump Division that could use this valve in the manufacture of one of its pumps. The Pump Division is currently purchasing 10,000 valves per year from an overseas supplier at a cost of $29 per valve.

Required

1. Assume that the Valve Division has ample idle capacity to handle all of the Pump Division's needs. What should be the transfer price between the two divisions?
2. Assume that the Valve Division is selling all that it can produce to outside customers on the intermediate market. What should be the transfer price between the two divisions? At this price, will any transfers be made?
3. Assume again that the Valve Division is selling all that it can produce to outside customers on the intermediate market. Also assume that $3 in variable expenses can be avoided on intracompany sales, due to reduced selling costs. What should be the transfer price between the two divisions?

Solution to Situation A

1. Because the Valve Division has idle capacity, it does not have to give up any outside sales in order to take on the Pump Division's business. Therefore, applying the transfer pricing formula, we get:

$$\text{Transfer price} = \frac{\text{Variable costs}}{\text{per unit}} + \frac{\text{Lost contribution margin per}}{\text{unit on outside sales}}$$

Transfer price = $16 + $0
Transfer price = $16

However, a transfer price of $16 represents a minimum price to cover the Valve Division's variable costs. The actual transfer price would undoubtedly fall somewhere between this amount and the $29 price that the Pump Division is currently paying for its valves. Thus, we have a transfer price range in this case of from $16 to $29 per unit, depending on negotiations between the two divisions.

2. Because the Valve Division is selling all that it can produce on the intermediate market, it would have to give up some of these outside sales in order to take on the Pump Division's business. Applying the transfer pricing formula, we get:

$$\text{Transfer price} = \frac{\text{Variable costs}}{\text{per unit}} + \frac{\text{Lost contribution margin per}}{\text{unit on outside sales}}$$

Transfer price = $16 + $14 *
Transfer price = $30

*$30 selling−$16 variable costs = $14 contribution margin per unit.

Because the Pump Division can purchase valves from an outside supplier at only $29 per unit, no transfers will be made between the two divisions.

3. Applying the transfer pricing formula, we get:

$$\text{Transfer price} = \frac{\text{Variable costs}}{\text{per unit}} + \frac{\text{Lost contribution margin per}}{\text{unit on outside sales}}$$

Transfer price = $13* + $14
Transfer price = $27

*$16 variable costs − $3 variable costs avoided = $13.

In this case, we again have a transfer price range; it is between $27 (the lower limit) and $29 (the Pump Division's outside price) per unit.

Situation B

Refer to the original data in situation A above. Assume that the Pump Division needs 20,000 special valves per year that are to be supplied by the Valve Division. The Valve Division's variable costs to manufacture and ship the special valve would be $20 per unit. To produce these special valves, the Valve Division would have to give up one-half of its production of the regular valves (that is, cut its production of the regular valves from 100,000 units per year to 50,000 units per year). You can assume that the Valve Division is selling all of the regular valves that it can produce to outside customers on the intermediate market.

Required

If the Valve Division decides to produce the special valves for the Pump Division, what transfer price should it charge per valve?

Solution to Situation B

To produce the 20,000 special valves, the Valve Division will have to give up sales of 50,000 regular valves to outside customers. The lost contribution margin on the 50,000 regular valves will be as follows:

$$50,000 \text{ valves} \times \$14 \text{ per unit} = \$700,000$$

Spreading this lost contribution margin over the 20,000 special valves, we get:

$$\frac{\$700,000 \text{ lost contribution margin}}{20,000 \text{ special valves}} = \$35 \text{ per unit}$$

Using this amount in the transfer pricing formula, we get the following transfer price per unit on the special valves:

$$\text{Transfer price} = \frac{\text{Variable costs}}{\text{per unit}} + \frac{\text{Lost contribution margin per}}{\text{unit on outside sales}}$$

$$\text{Transfer price} = \$20 + \$35$$
$$\text{Transfer price} = \$55$$

Thus, the Valve Division must charge a transfer price of $55 per unit on the special valves in order to be as well off as if it just continued to manufacture and sell the regular valves on the intermediate market. If the Valve Division wishes to increase its profits, it could charge more than $55 per valve, but it must charge at least $55 in order to maintain its present level of profits.

KEY TERMS FOR REVIEW (APPENDIX 12A)

Intermediate market   A market in which an item can be sold immediately and in its present form to outside customers rather than just being transferred to another division for use in its manufacturing process. (p. 644)

Market price   The price being charged for an item on the open (intermediate) market. (p. 643)

Negotiated transfer price   A transfer price agreed on between buying and selling divisions that reflects unusual or mitigating circumstances. (p. 648)

Suboptimization   An overall level of profitability that is less than a segment or a company is capable of earning. (p. 647)

Transfer price   The price charged when one division or segment provides goods or services to another division or segment of an organization. (p. 640)

QUESTIONS

12–1 Identify three business practices that hinder proper cost assignment to segments of a company.

12–2 Define a segment of an organization. Give several examples of segments.

12–3 How does the contribution approach attempt to assign costs to segments of an organization?

12–4 Distinguish between a traceable cost and a common cost. Give several examples of each.

12–5 How does the manager benefit from having the income statement in a segmented format?

12–6 Explain how the segment margin differs from the contribution margin. Which concept is most useful to the manager? Why?

12–7 Why aren't common costs allocated to segments under the contribution approach?

12–8 How is it possible for a cost that is traceable under one segment arrangement to become a common cost under another segment arrangement?

12–9 What is meant by the term *decentralization*?

12–10 What benefits are felt to result from decentralization in an organization?

12–11 Distinguish between a cost centre, a profit centre, and an investment centre.

12–12 How is performance in a cost centre generally measured? Performance in a profit centre? Performance in an investment centre?

12–13 What is meant by the terms *margin* and *turnover*?

12–14 In what way is the ROI formula a more exacting measure of performance than the ratio of net income to sales?

12–15 When the ROI formula is being used to measure performance, what three approaches to improving the overall profitability are open to the manager?

12–16 The sales figure could be cancelled out in the ROI formula, leaving simply net operating income over operating assets. Since this abbreviated formula would yield the same ROI figure, why leave sales in?

12–17 A student once commented to one of the authors, "It simply is not possible for a decrease in operating assets to result in an increase in profitability. The way to increase profits is to *increase* the operating assets." Discuss.

12–18 X Company has high fixed expenses and is currently operating somewhat above the break-even point. From this point on, will percentage increases in net income tend to be greater than, about equal to, or less than percentage increases in total sales? Why? (Ignore income taxes.)

12–19 What is meant by residual income?

12–20 In what way can ROI lead to dysfunctional decisions on the part of the investment centre manager? How does the residual income approach overcome this problem?

12–21 Division A has operating assets of $100,000, and Division B has operating assets of $1,000,000. Can residual income be used to compare performance in the two divisions? Explain.

12–22 (Appendix 12A) What is meant by the term *transfer price*, and why are transfer pricing systems needed?

12–23 (Appendix 12A) Why are cost-based transfer prices in widespread use? What are the disadvantages of cost-based transfer prices?

12–24 (Appendix 12A) If a market price for a product can be determined, why is it generally considered to be the best transfer price?

12–25 (Appendix 12A) Under what circumstances might a negotiated price be a better approach to pricing transfers between divisions than the actual market price?

12–26 (Appendix 12A) In what ways can suboptimization result if divisional managers are given full autonomy in setting, accepting, and rejecting transfer prices?

EXERCISES

E12–1 Caltec, Inc., produces and sells two products. Revenue and cost information relating to the products follow:

	Product	
	A	**B**
Selling price per unit....................	$ 8.00	$ 25.00
Variable expenses per unit	3.20	17.50
Traceable fixed expenses per year	138,000	45,000

Common fixed expenses in the company total $105,000 annually. Last year, the company produced and sold 37,500 units of product A and 18,000 units of product B.

Required

Prepare an income statement for the year segmented by product lines. Show both Amount and Percent columns for the company as a whole and for each of the product lines. Carry percentage computations to one decimal place.

E12–2 Marple Company operates two divisions, X and Y. A segmented income statement for the company's most recent year is given below:

			Segment			
	Total Company		**Division X**		**Division Y**	
Sales	$750,000	100.0 %	$150,000	100 %	$600,000	100 %
Less variable expenses	405,000	54.0	45,000	30	360,000	60
Contribution margin	345,000	46.0	105,000	70	240,000	40
Less traceable fixed expenses.........	168,000	22.4	78,000	52	90,000	15
Divisional segment margin	177,000	23.6	$27,000	18 %	$150,000	25 %
Less common fixed expenses	120,000	16.0				
Net income	$57,000	7.6 %				

Required

1. By how much would the company's net income increase if Division Y increased its sales by $75,000 per year? Assume no change in cost behaviour patterns in the company.
2. Refer to the original data. Assume that sales in Division X increase by $50,000 next year and that sales in Division Y remain unchanged. Assume no change in fixed costs in the divisions or in the company.
   a. Prepare a new segmented income statement for the company, using the format above. Show both amounts and percentages.
   b. Observe from the income statement you have prepared that the CM ratio for Division X has remained unchanged at 70% (the same as in the data above) but that the segment margin ratio has changed. How do you explain the change in the segment margin ratio?

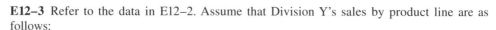

E12–3 Refer to the data in E12–2. Assume that Division Y's sales by product line are as follows:

			Segment			
	Division Y		**Product A**		**Product B**	
Sales	$600,000	100 %	$400,000	100 %	$200,000	100 %
Less variable expenses	360,000	60	260,000	65	100,000	50
Contribution margin	240,000	40	140,000	35	100,000	50
Less traceable fixed expenses.........	72,000	12	20,000	5	52,000	26
Product-line segment margin	168,000	28	$120,000	30 %	$48,000	24 %
Less common fixed expenses	18,000	3				
Divisional segment margin...........	$150,000	25 %				

The company would like to initiate an intensive advertising campaign on one of the two products during the next month. The campaign would cost $8,000. Marketing studies indicate that such a campaign would increase sales of product A by $70,000 or increase sales of product B by $60,000.

Required

1. On which of the products would you recommend that the company focus its advertising campaign? Show computations to support your answer.
2. In E12–2, Division Y shows $90,000 in traceable fixed expenses. What happened to the $90,000 in this exercise?

E12–4 You have a client who operates a large retail self-service grocery store that has a full range of departments. The management has encountered difficulty in using accounting data as a basis for decisions as to possible changes in departments operated, products, marketing methods, and so forth. List several overhead costs, or costs not applicable to a particular department, and explain how the existence of such costs (sometimes called *common costs* or *joint costs*) complicates and limits the use of accounting data in making decisions in such a store.

(CPA, adapted)

E12–5 Bovine Company has been experiencing losses for some time, as shown by its most recent monthly income statement below:

Sales..........................	$1,500,000
Less variable expenses............	588,000
Contribution margin..............	912,000
Less fixed expenses	945,000
Net loss......................	$ (33,000)

In an effort to isolate the problem, the president has asked for an income statement segmented by product lines. Accordingly, the accounting department has developed the following cost and revenue data:

	Product		
	A	**B**	**C**
Sales	$400,000	$600,000	$500,000
Variable expenses as a percentage			
of sales..................................	52%	30%	40%
Traceable fixed expenses....................	$240,000	$330,000	$200,000

Required

1. Prepare an income statement segmented by product lines, as desired by the president. Show both Amount and Percent columns for the company as a whole and for each product line. Carry percentage computations to one decimal place.
2. The company's sales manager believes that sales of product B could be increased by 15% if advertising were increased by $25,000 each month. Would you recommend the increased advertising? Show computations to support your answer.

E12–6 Selected operating data for two divisions of York Company are given below:

	Division	
	Eastern	**Western**
Sales	$1,000,000	$1,750,000
Average operating assets	500,000	500,000
Net operating income	90,000	105,000
Property, plant, and equipment..........	250,000	200,000

Required

1. Compute the rate of return for each division, using the ROI formula.
2. So far as you can tell from the available data, which divisional manager seems to be doing the better job? Why?

E12–7 Provide the missing data in the following tabulation:

	Division		
	A	**B**	**C**
Sales..............................	$800,000	$?	$?
Net operating income................	72,000	?	40,000
Average operating assets	?	130,000	?
Margin	?	4%	8%
Turnover..........................	?	5	?
ROI..............................	18%	?	20%

E12–8 Melbourne Company has two divisions, A and B, that operate in similar markets. Selected data on the two divisions follow:

	Division	
	A	**B**
Sales	$9,000,000	$20,000,000
Net operating income	630,000	1,800,000
Average operating assets	3,000,000	10,000,000

Required

1. Compute the ROI for each division.
2. Assume that the company evaluates performance by use of residual income and that the minimum required return for any division is 16%. Compute the residual income for each division.
3. Is Division B's greater residual income an indication that it is better managed? Explain.

E12–9 Supply the missing data in the tabulation below:

	Division		
	A	**B**	**C**
Sales.....................................	$400,000	$750,000	$600,000
Net operating income......................	?	45,000	?
Average operating assets	160,000	?	150,000
ROI......................................	20%	18%	?
Minimum required rate of return:			
Percentage	15%	?	12%
Dollar amount..........................	$?	$50,000	$?
Residual income..........................	?	?	6,000

E12–10 Selected sales and operating data for three companies are given below:

	Company		
	A	**B**	**C**
Sales.................................	$6,000,000	$10,000,000	$8,000,000
Average operating assets	1,500,000	5,000,000	2,000,000
Net operating income....................	300,000	900,000	180,000
Shareholders' equity.....................	1,000,000	3,500,000	1,500,000
Minimum required rate of return	15%	18%	12%

Required

1. Compute the ROI for each company.
2. Compute the residual income for each company.
3. Assume that each company is presented with an investment opportunity that would yield a rate of return of 17%.
    a. If performance is being measured by ROI, which company or companies will probably accept the opportunity? Reject? Why?
    b. If performance is being measured by residual income, which company or companies will probably accept the opportunity? Reject? Why?

E12–11 (Appendix 12A) Nelcro Company's Electrical Division produces a high-quality transformer. Sales and cost data on the transformer follow:

Selling price per unit on the intermediate market	$40
Variable costs per unit	21
Fixed costs per unit (based on capacity)	9
Capacity in units	60,000

Nelcro Company has an Audio Division that would like to begin purchasing this transformer from the Electrical Division. The Audio Division is currently purchasing 10,000 transformers each year from another manufacturer at a cost of $40 per transformer, less a 5% quantity discount.

Required

1. Assume that the Electrical Division is now selling only 50,000 transformers each year to outside customers on the intermediate market. If it begins to sell to the Audio Division, and if each division is to be treated as an independent investment centre, what transfer price would you recommend? Why?
2. Assume that the Electrical Division is selling all of the transformers it can produce to outside customers on the intermediate market. Would this change your recommended transfer price? Explain.

E12–12 (Appendix 12A) Division A manufactures picture tubes for TVs. The tubes can be sold either to Division B or to outside customers. Last year, the following activity was recorded in Division A:

Selling price per tube	$175
Production cost per tube	130
Number of tubes:	
Produced during the year	20,000
Sold to outside customers	16,000
Sold to Division B	4,000

Sales to Division B were at the same price as sales to outside customers. The tubes purchased by Division B were used in a TV set manufactured by that division. Division B incurred $300 in additional cost per TV and then sold the TVs for $600 each.

Required

1. Prepare income statements for last year for Division A, Division B, and the company as a whole.
2. Assume that Division A's manufacturing capacity is 20,000 tubes per year. Next year, Division B wants to purchase 5,000 tubes from Division A, rather than only 4,000 tubes as in last year. (Tubes of this type are not available from outside sources.) Should Division A sell the 1,000 additional tubes to Division B, or should it continue to sell them to outside customers? Explain why this would or would not make any difference from the point of view of the company as a whole.

E12–13 (Appendix 12A) In each of the cases below, assume that Division X has a product that can be sold either to outside customers on an intermediate market or to Division Y for use in its production process.

	Case	
	A	**B**
Division X:		
Capacity in units	100,000	100,000
Number of units being sold on the		
intermediate market	100,000	80,000
Selling price per unit on the		
intermediate market	$50	$35
Variable costs per unit	30	20
Fixed costs per unit (based on capacity)	8	6
Division Y:		
Number of units needed for production	20,000	20,000
Purchase price per unit now being paid		
to an outside supplier	$47	$34

Required

1. Refer to the data in case A above. Assume that $2 per unit in variable selling costs can be avoided on intracompany sales.
    a. Using the transfer pricing formula, determine the transfer price that Division X should charge on any sales to Division Y.
    b. Will any transfers be made between the two divisions? Explain.
2. Refer to the data in case B above. Within what range should the transfer price be set for any sales between the two divisions? (Use the transfer pricing formula as needed.)

PROBLEMS

P12–14 Segment Reporting The most recent monthly income statement for Reston Company is given below:

RESTON COMPANY
Income Statement
For the Month Ended May 31

Sales	$900,000	100.0%
Less variable expenses	408,000	45.3
Contribution margin	492,000	54.7
Less fixed expenses	465,000	51.7
Net income	$ 27,000	3.0%

Management is disappointed with the company's performance and is wondering what can be done to improve profits. By examining sales and cost records, you have determined the following:

a. The company is divided into two sales territories—Central and Eastern. The Central Territory recorded $400,000 in sales and $208,000 in variable expenses during May. The remaining sales and variable expenses were recorded in the Eastern Territory. Fixed expenses of $160,000 and $130,000 are traceable to the Central and Eastern Territories, respectively. The rest of the fixed expenses are common to the two territories.
b. The company sells two products—Awls and Pows. Sales of Awls and Pows totalled $100,000 and $300,00, respectively, in the Central Territory during May. Variable expenses are 25% of the selling price for Awls and 61% for Pows. Cost records show that $60,000 of the Central Territory's fixed expenses are traceable to Awls and $54,000 to Pows, with the remainder common to the two products.

Required

1. Prepare segmented income statements, first showing the total company broken down between sales territories and then showing the Central Territory broken down by product line. Show both Amount and Percent columns for the company in total and for each segment. Round percentage computations to one decimal place.
2. Look at the statement you have prepared showing the total company segmented by sales territory. What points revealed by this statement should be brought to the attention of management?
3. Look at the statement you have prepared showing the Central Territory segmented by product lines. What points revealed by this statement should be brought to the attention of management?

P12–15 Restructuring a Segmented Income Statement Brabant NV of the Netherlands is a wholesale distributor of Dutch cheeses that sells throughout the European Community. Unfortunately, the company's profits have been declining, which has caused considerable concern. To help understand the condition of the company, the managing director of the company has requested that the monthly income statement be segmented by sales territory. Accordingly, the company's accounting department has prepared the following statement for March, the most recent month. (The Dutch currency is the guilder, which is designated by the initials GLD.)

	Sales Territory		
	Southern Europe	Middle Europe	Northern Europe
Sales	300,000 GLD	800,000 GLD	700,000 GLD
Less territorial expenses (traceable):			
Cost of goods sold	93,000	240,000	315,000
Salaries	54,000	56,000	112,000
Insurance	9,000	16,000	14,000
Advertising	105,000	240,000	245,000
Depreciation	21,000	32,000	28,000
Shipping	15,000	32,000	42,000
Total territorial expenses	297,000	616,000	756,000
Territorial income (loss) before corporate expenses	3,000	184,000	(56,000)
Less corporate expenses:			
Advertising (general)	15,000	40,000	35,000
General administrative	20,000	20,000	20,000
Total corporate expenses	35,000	60,000	55,000
Net income (loss)	(32,000) GLD	124,000 GLD	(111,000) GLD

Cost of goods sold and shipping expenses are both variable; other costs are all fixed. Brabant NV purchases cheeses at auction and from farmers' cooperatives, and it distributes them in the three territories listed above. Each of the three sales territories has its own manager and sales staff. The cheeses vary widely in profitability; some have a high margin and some have a low margin. (Certain cheeses, after having been aged for long periods, are the most expensive and carry the highest margins.)

Required

1. List any disadvantages or weaknesses that you see to the statement format illustrated above.
2. Explain the basis that is apparently being used to allocate the corporate expenses to the sales territories. Do you agree with these allocations? Explain.
3. Prepare a new segmented income statement for March using the contribution approach. Show a Total column as well as data for each territory. Include percentages on your statement for all columns. Carry percentages to one decimal place.
4. Analyze the statement that you prepared in (3) above. What points that might help improve the company's performance would you be particularly anxious to bring to the attention of management?

P12–16   Basic Segmented Statement; Activity-Based Cost Assignment

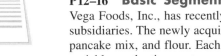

Vega Foods, Inc., has recently purchased a small mill that it intends to operate as one of its subsidiaries. The newly acquired mill has three products that it offers for sale—wheat cereal, pancake mix, and flour. Each product sells for $10 per package. Materials, labour, and other variable production costs are $3.00 per bag of wheat cereal, $4.20 per bag of pancake mix, and $1.80 per bag of flour. Sales commissions are 10% of sales for any product. All other costs are fixed.

The mill's income statement for the most recent month is given below:

	Total Company		Product Line		
			Wheat Cereal	Pancake Mix	Flour
Sales.	$600,000	100.0%	$200,000	$300,000	$100,000
Less expenses:					
Materials, labour, and other.	204,000	34.0	60,000	126,000	18,000
Sales commissions.	60,000	10.0	20,000	30,000	10,000
Advertising	123,000	20.5	48,000	60,000	15,000
Salaries	66,000	11.0	34,000	21,000	11,000
Equipment depreciation.	30,000	5.0	10,000	15,000	5,000
Warehouse rent	12,000	2.0	4,000	6,000	2,000
General administration	90,000	15.0	30,000	30,000	30,000
Total expenses	585,000	97.5	206,000	288,000	91,000
Net income (loss).	$ 15,000	2.5%	$ (6,000)	$ 12,000	$ 9,000

The following additional information is available about the company:

a. The same equipment is used to mill and package all three products. In the above income statement, equipment depreciation has been allocated on the basis of sales dollars. An analysis of the use of the equipment indicates that it is used 40% of the time to make wheat cereal, 50% of the time to make pancake mix, and 10% of the time to make flour.

b. All three products are stored in the same warehouse. In the above income statement, the warehouse rent has been allocated on the basis of sales dollars. The warehouse contains 24,000 square metres of space, of which 8,000 square metres are used for wheat cereal, 14,000 square metres are used for pancake mix, and 2,000 square metres are used for flour. The warehouse space costs the company $0.50 per square metre to rent.

c. The general administration costs relate to the administration of the company as a whole. In the above income statement, these costs have been divided equally among the three product lines.

d. All other costs are traceable to the product lines.

Vega Foods' management is anxious to improve on the mill's 2.5% margin on sales.

Required

1. Prepare a new segmented income statement for the month, using the contribution approach. Show both Amount and Percent columns for the company as a whole and for each product line. Adjust the allocation of equipment depreciation and warehouse rent as indicated by the additional information provided.

2. After seeing the income statement in the main body of the problem, management has decided to eliminate the wheat cereal, since it is not returning a profit, and to focus all available resources on promoting the pancake mix.
    a. Based on the statement you have prepared, do you agree with the decision to eliminate the wheat cereal? Explain.
    b. Based on the statement you have prepared, do you agree with the decision to focus all available resources on promoting the pancake mix? Explain. (You may assume that ample market is available for all three products.)

3. What additional points would you bring to the attention of management that might help to improve profits?

P12–17   ROI; Comparison of Company Performance   Comparative data on three companies in the same industry are given below:

| | Company | | |
	A	B	C
Sales........................	$4,000,000	$1,500,000	$?
Net operating income...........	560,000	210,000	?
Average operating assets	2,000,000	?	3,000,000
Margin	?	?	3.5%
Turnover....................	?	?	2
ROI........................	?	7%	?

Required

1. What advantages can you see in breaking down the ROI computation into two separate elements, margin and turnover?
2. Fill in the missing information above, and comment on the relative performance of the three companies in as much detail as the data permit. Make *specific recommendations* on steps to be taken to improve the return on investment, where needed.

(Adapted from National Association of Accountants, *Research Report No. 35,* p. 34)

P12–18   ROI and Residual Income   "I know headquarters wants us to add on that new product line," said Fred Halloway, manager of Kirsi Products' East Division. "But I want to see the numbers before I make a move. Our division has led the company for three years, and I don't want any letdown."

Kirsi Products is a decentralized company with four autonomous divisions. The divisions are evaluated on a basis of the return that they are able to generate on invested assets, with year-end bonuses given to the divisional managers who have the highest ROI figures. Operating results for the company's East Division for last year are given below:

Sales	$21,000,000
Less variable expenses	13,400,000
Contribution margin	7,600,000
Less fixed expenses................	5,920,000
Net operating income	$ 1,680,000
Divisional operating assets..........	$ 5,250,000

The company had an overall ROI of 18% last year (considering all divisions). The company's East Division has an opportunity to add a new product line that would require an investment of $3,000,000. The cost and revenue characteristics of the new product line per year would be as follows:

Sales	$9,000,000
Variable expenses	65% of sales
Fixed expenses	$2,520,000

Required

1. Compute the East Division's ROI for last year; also compute the ROI as it will appear if the new product line is added.
2. If you were in Fred Halloway's position, would you be inclined to accept or reject the new product line? Explain.
3. Why do you suppose "headquarters" is anxious for the East Division to add the new product line?
4. Suppose that the company views a return of 15% on invested assets as being the minimum that any division should earn and that performance is evaluated by the residual income approach.
    a.   Compute the East Division's residual income for last year; also compute the residual income as it will appear if the new product line is added.
    b.   Under these circumstances, if you were in Fred Halloway's position would you accept or reject the new product line? Explain.

P12–19 Variance Analysis The Leo Company produces and sells two product lines with the following budgeted revenues and expenses:

	Spars	Masts
Expected total industry sales.	48,000 units	85,000 units
Expected Leo Company sales.	4,200 units	17,000 units
Expected selling price.	$200 per unit	$300 per unit
Expected cost of manufacturing (40% fixed).	110 per unit	180 per unit
Expected selling and administration costs (70% fixed).	60 per unit	70 per unit
Expected product profit margin	$ 30 per unit	$ 50 per unit
Actual results for 19x9 included:		
Actual total industry sales.	60,000 units	100,000 units
Actual Leo Company sales.	6,000 units	18,000 units
Actual selling price.	$180 per unit	$300 per unit

All costs behaved exactly as expected.

W. Gallant, vice president of marketing and sales, has requested that the employees of his department be paid a bonus for the year based on the fact that they have been able to increase sales by 2,800 units over the budget level for the year, an increase of over 13%.

Required

1. Calculate the changes in overall company profits caused by the following factors:
    a. Sales price.
    b. Sales mix.
    c. Sales quantity.
    d. Market share.
    e. Market size.
2. Give two reasons why the marketing and sales employees should/should not receive the bonus suggested by Mr. Gallant.

(SMAC, adapted)

P12–20 The Appropriate Transfer Price; Well-Defined Intermediate Market (Appendix 12A) Galati Products, Inc., has just purchased a small company that specializes in the manufacture of electronic tuners that are used as a component part of TV sets. Galati Products, Inc., is a decentralized company, and it will treat the newly acquired company as an autonomous division with full profit responsibility. The new division, called the Tuner Division, has the following revenue and costs associated with each tuner that it manufactures and sells:

Selling price.		$20
Less expenses:		
Variable	$11	
Fixed (based on a capacity of 100,000 tuners per year).	6	17
Net income.		$ 3

Galati Products also has an Assembly Division that assembles TV sets. The division is currently purchasing 30,000 tuners per year from an overseas supplier at a cost of $20 per tuner, less a 10% quantity discount. The president of Galati Products is anxious to have the Assembly Division begin purchasing its tuners from the newly acquired Tuner Division in order to "keep the profits within the corporate family."

For (1) through (4) below, assume that the Tuner Division can sell all of its output to outside TV manufacturers at the normal $20 price.

Required

1. If the Assembly Division purchases 30,000 tuners each year from the Tuner Division, what price should control the transfers? Why?
2. Refer to the computations in (1) above. What are the lower limit and the upper limit for a transfer price? Is an upper limit relevant in this situation?
3. If the Tuner Division meets the price that the Assembly Division is currently paying to its overseas supplier and sells 30,000 tuners to the Assembly Division each year, what will be the effect on the profits of the Tuner Division, the Assembly Division, and the company as a whole?

4. If the intermediate market price for tuners is $20, is there any reason why the Tuner Division should sell to the Assembly Division for less than $20? Explain.

   For (5) through (8) below, assume that the Tuner Division is currently selling only 60,000 tuners each year to outside TV manufacturers at the stated $20 price.

5. If the Assembly Division purchases 30,000 tuners each year from the Tuner Division, what price should control the transfers? Why?
6. Suppose that the Assembly Division's overseas supplier drops its price (net of the quantity discount) to only $16 per tuner. Should the Tuner Division meet this price? Explain. If the Tuner Division does *not* meet this price, what will be the effect on the profits of the company as a whole?
7. Refer to (6) above. If the Tuner Division refuses to meet the $16 price, should the Assembly Division be required to purchase from the Tuner Division at a higher price, for the good of the company as a whole? Explain.
8. Refer to (6) above. Assume that due to inflexible management policies, the Assembly Division is required to purchase 30,000 tuners each year from the Tuner Division at $20 per tuner. What will be the effect on the profits of the company as a whole?

P12–21 Basic Transfer Pricing Computations   (Appendix 12A) In cases 1–3 below, assume that Division A has a product that can be sold either to Division B or to outside customers on an intermediate market. Treat each case independently.

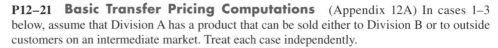

		Case		
	1	**2**	**3**	**4**
Division A:				
Capacity in units	50,000	300,000	100,000	200,000
Number of units now being sold to outside				
customers on the intermediate market	50,000	300,000	75,000	200,000
Selling price per unit on the intermediate market	$100	$40	$60	$45
Variable costs per unit	63	19	35	30
Fixed costs per unit (based on capacity)	25	8	17	6
Division B:				
Number of units needed annually	10,000	70,000	20,000	60,000
Purchase price now being paid to an outside				
supplier	$92	$39	$60*	—

*Before any quantity discount.

Required

1. Refer to case 1 above. A study has indicated that Division A can avoid $5 per unit in variable costs on any sales to Division B. Use the transfer pricing formula to determine what transfer price should be charged on any sales between the two divisions. Will any transfers be made? Explain.
2. Refer to case 2 above. Assume that Division A can avoid $4 per unit in variable costs on any sales to Division B.
    a. Again use the transfer pricing formula to compute an appropriate transfer price. Would you expect any disagreement between the two divisional managers over what transfer price should be paid? Explain.
    b. Assume that Division A offers to sell 70,000 units to Division B for $38 per unit and that Division B refuses this price. What will be the loss in potential profits for the company as a whole?
3. Refer to case 3 above. Assume that Division B is now receiving a 5% quantity discount from the outside supplier.
    a. Within what range should the transfer price be set for any sales between the two divisions?
    b. Assume that Division B offers to purchase 20,000 units from Division A at $52 per unit. If Division A accepts this price, would you expect its ROI to increase, decrease, or remain unchanged? Why?

4. Refer to case 4 above. Assume that Division B wants Division A to provide it with 60,000 units of a *different* product from the one that Division A is now producing. The new product would require $25 per unit in variable costs and would require that Division A cut back production of its present product by 30,000 units annually. Use the transfer pricing formula to determine what transfer price per unit Division A should charge Division B for the new product.

P12–22 Multiple Segmented Income Statements   Severo S.A. of Sao Paulo, Brazil, is organized into two divisions. The company's income statement (in terms of the Brazilian currency Real) for last month is given below:

	Total Company	Division Cloth	Division Leather
Sales..	R3,500,000	R2,000,000	R1,500,000
Less variable expenses.......................	1,721,000	960,000	761,000
Contribution margin.........................	1,779,000	1,040,000	739,000
Less traceable fixed expenses:			
Advertising..............................	612,000	300,000	312,000
Administration...........................	427,000	210,000	217,000
Depreciation.............................	229,000	115,000	114,000
Total traceable fixed expenses..............	1,268,000	625,000	643,000
Divisional segment margin	511,000	R 415,000	R 96,000
Less common fixed expenses..................	390,000		
Net income...............................	R 121,000		

Top management can't understand why the Leather Division has such a low segment margin when its sales are only 25% less than sales in the Cloth Division. As one step in isolating the problem, management has directed that the Leather Division be further segmented into product lines. The following information is available on the product lines in the Leather Division:

	Product Line Garments	Product Line Shoes	Product Line Handbags
Sales..........................	R500,000	R700,000	R300,000
Traceable fixed expenses:			
Advertising....................	80,000	112,000	120,000
Administration.................	30,000	35,000	42,000
Depreciation...................	25,000	56,000	33,000
Variable expenses as a percentage of sales..............	65%	40%	52%

Analysis shows that R110,000 of the Leather Division's administrative expenses are common to the product lines.

Required

1. Prepare a segmented income statement for the Leather Division, with segments defined as product lines. Use the contribution approach and the format shown in Exhibit 12–2. Show both Amount and Percent columns for the division in total and for each product line. Carry percentage figures to one decimal place.

2. Management is surprised by the handbag product line's poor showing and would like to have the product line segmented by market. The following information is available about the markets in which the handbag product line is sold:

	Market Domestic	Market Foreign
Sales..........................	R200,000	R100,000
Traceable fixed expenses:		
Advertising....................	40,000	80,000
Variable expenses as a percentage of sales..............	43%	70%

All of the handbag product line's administrative expenses and depreciation are common to the markets in which the product is sold. Prepare a segmented income statement for the handbag product line with segments defined as markets. Again use the format in Exhibit 12–2 and show both Amount and Percent columns.

3. Refer to the statement prepared in (1) above. The sales manager wants to run a special promotional campaign on one of the product lines over the next month. A marketing study indicates that such a campaign would increase sales of the garment product line by R200,000 or sales of the shoes product line by R145,000. The campaign would cost R30,000. Show computations to determine which product line should be chosen.

P12–23   ROI Analysis   The income statement for Westex, Inc., for its most recent period is given below:

	Total	Unit
Sales	$1,000,000	$50.00
Less variable expenses	600,000	30.00
Contribution margin	400,000	20.00
Less fixed expenses	320,000	16.00
Net operating income	80,000	4.00
Less income taxes (40%)	32,000	1.60
Net income	$ 48,000	$ 2.40

The company had average operating assets of $500,000 during the period.

Required

1. Compute the company's ROI for the period using the ROI formula.

For each of the following questions, indicate whether the margin and turnover will increase, decrease, or remain unchanged as a result of the events described, and then compute the new ROI figure. Consider each question separately, starting in each case from the original ROI computed in (1) above.

2. The company is able to achieve a cost savings of $10,000 per period by using less costly labour inputs.

3. By use of JIT to control the purchase of some items of raw materials, the company is able to reduce the average level of inventory by $100,000. (The released funds are used to pay off bank loans.)

4. Sales are increased by $100,000; operating assets remain unchanged.

5. The company issues bonds and uses the proceeds to purchase $125,000 in machinery and equipment. Interest on the bonds is $15,000 per period. Sales remain unchanged. The new, more efficient equipment reduces production costs by $5,000 per period.

6. The company invests $180,000 of cash (received on accounts receivable) in a plot of land that is to be held for possible future use as a plant site.

7. Obsolete items of inventory carried on the records at a cost of $20,000 are scrapped and written off as a loss, since they are unsalable.

P12–24   Segment Reporting; Activity-Based Cost Assignment   "Rats! We're still in the red," said Jana Andrews, executive vice president of the Ashland Company. "I know," said Steve Clark, the controller. "Just look at this income statement for March. We've got to forget about Districts A and B and zero in on District C." The statement to which Mr. Clark was referring is shown below:

	Total Company	Districts		
		A	B	C
Sales @ $20 per unit	$1,000,000	$300,000	$500,000	$200,000
Less cost of goods sold @ $9 per unit	450,000	135,000	225,000	90,000
Gross margin	550,000	165,000	275,000	110,000

Less operating expenses:
Marketing expenses:

Freight-out.	51,250	11,250	25,000	15,000
Warehouse rent	80,000	24,000	40,000	16,000
Sales commissions.	60,000	18,000	30,000	12,000
Sales salaries	30,000	12,000	10,000	8,000
District advertising.	75,000	20,000	25,000	30,000
National advertising*.	115,000	34,500	57,500	23,000
Total marketing expenses	411,250	119,750	187,500	104,000
Administrative expenses:				
District management salaries.	$ 40,000	$ 12,000	$ 15,000	$ 13,000
Central office administrative expenses*	100,000	30,000	50,000	20,000
Total administrative expenses	140,000	42,000	65,000	33,000
Total operating expenses	551,250	161,750	252,500	137,000
Net income (loss).	$ (1,250)	$ 3,250	$ 22,500	$ (27,000)

*Allocated on the basis of sales dollars.

The company is a retail organization that sells a single product. The product is sold in three districts, as shown above. Additional information on the company follows:

a. The sales and administrative offices are centrally located, being about the same distance from each district.

b. Each district specifies on the sales order what freight method is to be used (by truck, rail, or air). All goods are shipped from a central warehouse. Freight is a variable cost, and it is traceable to the districts; differences in amounts above are reflective of the different freight methods used.

c. All salespersons are paid a base salary of $500 per month, plus a commission of 6% of sales. There are 24 salespersons in District A, 20 in District B, and 16 in District C.

d. Each district manager must arrange his or her own district advertising program. The national advertising is provided by the central office.

e. The variable costs of processing orders, which have been included in the "Central office administrative expenses" above, amount to $25,000. During March, District A had 3,000 orders, District B had 1,500 orders, and District C had 500 orders. The remainder of the "Central office administrative expenses" are fixed and relate to general administrative assistance provided to all parts of the organization.

f. The warehouse contains 160,000 square metres of storage space. District A uses 60,000 square metres, District B uses 80,000 square metres, and District C uses 20,000 square metres.

Required

1. Garth Hansen, the president, has asked that the company's income statement be redone using the contribution format, which he heard about in a recent industry convention. Prepare the income statement as requested by Mr. Hansen. Show both an Amount and a Percent column for the company in total and for each district. (Carry computations to one decimal place.)

2. Compute the contribution margin per order for each district. What problems does this computation suggest?

3. The manager of District B would like to spend an extra $25,000 next month in a special promotional campaign. If sales increase by $100,000 as a result, would the expenditure be justified? No additional warehouse space would be required.

4. Analyze the data in the statement you prepared in (1) above. What points should be brought to the attention of management?

P12–25   ROI and Residual Income   Lawton Industries has manufactured prefabricated houses for over 20 years. The houses are constructed in sections to be assembled on customers' lots.

Lawton expanded into the kit housing market several years ago when it acquired Presser Company, one of its suppliers. In this market, various types of lumber are precut into the appropriate lengths, banded into packages, and shipped to customers' lots in the form of a kit for assembly. Lawton decided to maintain Presser's separate identity and therefore established the Presser Division as an investment centre of Lawton.

Lawton uses ROI as a performance measure. Management bonuses are based in part on ROI. All investments in operating assets are expected to earn a minimum return of 15% before income taxes.

Presser's ROI has ranged from 19% to 22%, since it was acquired by Lawton. During the past year, Presser had an investment opportunity that had an estimated ROI of 18%. Presser's management decided against the investment because it believed the investment would decrease the division's overall ROI.

Last year's income statement for Presser Division is given below. The division's operating assets employed were $15,500,000 at the end of the year, which represents a 24% increase over the previous year-end balance. (Several purchases of new equipment were made during the year.)

PRESSER DIVISION
Divisional Income Statement

Sales..............................		$35,000,000
Cost of goods sold		24,600,000
Gross margin		10,400,000
Less operating expenses:		
Selling expenses..................	$5,700,000	
Administrative expenses	1,900,000	7,600,000
Net operating income.................		$2,800,000

Required

1. Calculate the following performance measures for Presser Division:
    a. ROI. (Remember, ROI is based on the *average* operating assets, computed from the beginning-of-year and end-of-year balances.)
    b. Residual income.
2. Would the management of Presser Division have been more likely to accept the investment opportunity with an ROI of 18% if residual income were used as a performance measure instead of ROI? Explain.
3. The Presser Division is a separate investment centre within Lawton Industries. Identify the items Presser Division must be free to control if it is to be evaluated fairly by either the ROI or residual income performance measures.

(CMA, heavily adapted)

P12–26 Choosing an Appropriate Transfer Price (Appendix 12A) Top-Value Products, Inc., has just acquired a small company that manufactures electrical pumps. The company will operate as a division of Top-Value Products, Inc., under the name of the Pump Division. The pumps that are manufactured by the Pump Division are used primarily in dishwashers and are sold to various dishwasher manufacturers across the nation. The pumps sell for $60 each. Top-Value Products, Inc., has an Appliances Division that manufactures dishwashers, and the president of Top-Value Products, Inc., feels that the Appliances Division should begin to purchase its pumps from the newly acquired Pump Division.

The Appliances Division is currently purchasing 30,000 pumps each year from an outside supplier. The price is $57 per pump, which represents the normal $60 price less a 5% quantity discount.

The Pump Division's cost per pump is given below:

Direct materials................		$20
Direct labour		14
Variable overhead		6
Fixed overhead		5 *
Total cost per pump...........		$45

*Based on 100,000 units capacity.

The president of Top-Value Products, Inc., is unsure what transfer price should control sales between the two divisions.

Required

1. Assume that the Pump Division has sufficient idle capacity to supply 30,000 pumps each year to the Appliances Division. Explain why each of the following transfer prices would or would not be an appropriate price to charge the Appliances Division on the intracompany sales:
   a. $60.00.
   b. $57.00.
   c. $48.50.
   d. $45.00.
   e. $40.00.
2. Assume that the Pump Division is currently selling all the pumps it can produce to outside customers. Under these circumstances, explain why each of the transfer prices given in (1a) through (1e) above would or would not be an appropriate price to charge the Appliances Division on the intracompany sales.

P12–27 Cost Volume Profit Analysis; ROI; Transfer Pricing (Appendix 12A)

The Bearing Division of Timkin Company produces a small bearing that is used by a number of companies as a component part in the manufacture of their products. Timkin Company operates its divisions as autonomous units, giving its divisional managers great discretion in pricing and other decisions. Each division is expected to generate a return on its assets of at least 12%. The Bearing Division has operating assets as follows:

Cash.............................	$7,000
Accounts receivable	60,000
Inventories.......................	108,000
Plant and equipment, net............	125,000
Total assets	$300,000

The bearings are sold for $4 each. Variable costs are $2.50 per bearing, and fixed costs total $234,000 each period. The division's capacity is 200,000 bearings each period.

Required

1. How many bearings must be sold each period for the division to obtain the desired rate of return on its assets?
   a. What is the margin earned at this sales level?
   b. What is the turnover of assets at this sales level?
2. The divisional manager is considering two ways of increasing the ROI figure:
   a. Market studies suggest that an increase in price to $4.25 per bearing would result in sales of 160,000 units each period. The decrease in units sold would allow the division to reduce its investment in assets by $10,000, due to the lower level of inventories and receivables that would be needed to support sales. Compute the margin, turnover, and ROI if these changes are made.
   b. Other market studies suggest that a reduction in price to $3.75 per bearing would result in sales of 200,000 units each period. However, this would require an increase in total assets of $10,000, due to the somewhat larger inventories and receivables that would be carried. Compute the margin, turnover, and ROI if these changes are made.
3. Refer to the original data. Assume that the normal volume of sales is 180,000 bearings each period at a price of $4 per bearing. Another division of Timkin Company is currently purchasing 20,000 bearings each period from an overseas supplier at $3.25 per bearing. The manager of the Bearing Division says that this price is "ridiculous" and refuses to meet it, since doing so would result in a loss of $0.42 per bearing for her division:

Selling price		$ 3.25
Cost per bearing:		
Variable cost.....................................	$2.50	
Fixed cost ($234,000 ÷ 200,000 bearings)...........	1.17	3.67
Loss per bearing		$(0.42)

You may assume that sales to the other division would require an increase of $25,000 in the total assets carried by the Bearing Division. Would you recommend that the Bearing Division meet the $3.25 price and start selling 20,000 bearings per period to the other division? Support your answer with ROI computations.

P12–28   Negotiated Transfer Price   (Appendix 12A) Pella Company has several independent divisions. The company's Compressor Division produces a high-quality compressor that is sold to various users. The division's income statement for the most recent month, in which 500 compressors were sold, is given below:

	Total	Unit
Sales	$125,000	$250
Less cost of goods sold.	75,000	150
Gross margin.	50,000	100
Less selling and administrative expenses.	30,000	60
Divisional net income.	$ 20,000	$ 40

As shown above, it costs the division $150 to produce a compressor. This figure consists of the following costs:

Direct materials	$ 50
Direct labour.	60
Manufacturing overhead (50% fixed).	40
Total cost.	$150

The division has fixed selling and administrative expenses of $25,000 per month and variable selling and administrative expenses of $10 per compressor.

Another division of Pella Company, the Home Products Division, uses compressors as a component part of air-conditioning systems that it installs. The Home Products Division has asked the Compressor Division to sell it 40 compressors each month of a somewhat different design. The Compressor Division has estimated the following cost for each of the new compressors:

Direct materials	$ 60
Direct labour.	90
Manufacturing overhead (two-thirds fixed)	75
Total cost	$225

In order to produce the new compressors, the Compressor Division would have to reduce production of its present compressors by 100 units per month. However, all variable selling and administrative expenses could be avoided on the intracompany business. Total fixed overhead costs would not change.

Required

1. What price should be charged by the Compressor Division for the new compressor? Show all computations.
2. Suppose the Home Products Division has found a supplier that will provide the new compressors for only $350 each. If the Compressor Division meets this price, what will be the effect on the profits of the company as a whole?

P12–29   Impact of Transfer Price on Marketing Decisions   (Appendix 12A) Damico Company's Board Division manufactures an electronic control board that is widely used in compact disc (CD) players. The cost per control board is as follows:

Variable cost per board	$120
Fixed cost per board	30 *
Total cost per board	$150

*Based on a capacity of 80,000 boards per year.

Part of the Board Division's output is sold to outside manufacturers of CD players, and part is sold to Damico Company's Consumer Products Division, which produces a CD player under the Damico name. The Board Division charges a selling price of $190 per control board for all sales, both internally and externally.

The costs, revenues, and net income associated with the Consumer Products Division's CD player is given below:

Selling price per player		$580
Less variable costs per player:		
Cost of the control board	$190	
Variable cost of other parts	230	
Total variable costs		420
Contribution margin		160
Less fixed costs per player		85 *
Net income per player		$ 75

*Based on a capacity of 20,000 CD players per year.

The Consumer Products Division has an order from an overseas distributor for 5,000 CD players. The distributor wants to pay only $400 per CD player.

Required

1. Assume that the Consumer Products Division has enough idle capacity to fill the 5,000-unit order. Is the division likely to accept the $400 price, or to reject it? Explain.
2. Assume that both the Board Division and the Consumer Products Division have idle capacity. Under these conditions, would rejecting the $400 price be an advantage to the company as a whole, or would it result in the loss of potential profits? Show computations to support your answer.
3. Assume that the Board Division is operating at capacity and could sell all of its control boards to outside manufacturers of CD players. Assume, however, that the Consumer Products Division has enough idle capacity to fill the 5,000-unit order. Under these conditions, compute the dollar advantage or disadvantage of accepting the order at the $400 price.
4. What kind of transfer pricing information is needed by the Consumer Products Division in making decisions such as these?

P12–30   Segmented Statements; Product Line Analysis   "The situation is slowly turning around," declared Bill Aiken, president of Datex, Inc. "This $42,500 loss for June is our smallest yet. If we can just strengthen product lines A and C somehow, we'll soon be making a profit." Mr. Aiken was referring to the company's latest monthly income statement presented below (absorption costing basis):

DATEX, INC.
Income Statement

	Total	Line A	Line B	Line C
Sales	$1,000,000	$400,000	$250,000	$350,000
Cost of goods sold.	742,500	300,000	180,000	262,500
Gross margin.	257,500	100,000	70,000	87,500
Less operating expenses:				
Selling	150,000	60,000	22,500	67,500
Administrative.	150,000	60,000	37,500	52,500
Total operating expenses.	300,000	120,000	60,000	120,000
Net income (loss)	$ (42,500)	$ (20,000)	$ 10,000	$ (32,500)

"How's that new business graduate that we just hired doing?" asked Mr. Aiken. "He's supposed to be well trained in internal reporting; can he help us pinpoint what's wrong with lines A and C?" "He claims it's partly the way we make up our segmented statements," declared Margie Nelson, the controller. "Here are a lot of data he's prepared on what he calls traceable and common costs that he thinks we ought to be isolating in our reports." The data to which Ms. Nelson was referring are shown below:

	Line A	Line B	Line C
Variable costs:*			
Production (materials, labour,			
and variable overhead).	20%	30%	25%
Selling.	5%	5%	5%
Traceable fixed costs:			
Production	$107,000	$30,000	$63,000
Selling†.	40,000	10,000	50,000

*As a percentage of line sales.

†Salaries and advertising. Advertising contracts are signed annually.

a. Fixed production costs total $500,000 per month. Part of this amount is traceable directly to the product lines, as shown in the tabulation above. The remainder is common to the product lines.

b. All administrative costs are common to the three product lines.

c. Work in process and finished goods inventories are negligible and can be ignored.

d. Lines A and B each sell for $100 per unit, and line C sells for $80 per unit. Strong market demand exists for all three products.

"I don't get it," said Mr. Aiken. "Our CGA assures us that we're following good absorption costing methods, and we're segmenting our statements like they want us to do. So what could be wrong?"

At that moment, John Young, the production superintendent, came bursting into the room. "Word has just come that Fairchild Company, the supplier of our type B4 chips, has just gone out on strike. They'll be out for at least a month, and our inventory of B4 chips is low. We'll have to cut back production of either line A or B, since that chip is used in both products." (A single B4 chip is used per unit of each product.) Mr. Aiken looked at the latest monthly statement and declared, "Thank goodness for these segmented statements. It's pretty obvious that we should cut back production of line A. Pass the word, and concentrate all of our B4 chip inventory on production of line B."

Required

1. Prepare a new income statement segmented by product lines, using the contribution approach. Show both Amount and Percent columns for the company in total and for each of the product lines. (Carry percentages to one decimal place.)

2. Do you agree with Mr. Aiken's decision to cut back production of line A? Why or why not?

3. Assume that the company's executive committee is considering the elimination of line C, due to its poor showing. If you were serving on this committee, what points would you make for or against elimination of the line?

4. Line C is sold in both a home and a foreign market, with sales and cost data as follows:

	Home Market	Foreign Market
Sales	$300,000	$50,000
Traceable fixed costs:		
Selling	10,000	40,000

The fixed production costs of line C are considered to be common to the markets in which the product is sold. Variable expense relationships in the markets are the same as those shown in the main body of the problem for line C.

a. Prepare a segmented income statement showing line C segmented by markets. Show both Amount and Percent columns for line C in total and for both of the markets.

b. What points revealed by this statement would you be particularly anxious to bring to the attention of management?

P12–31   Transfer Pricing with and without Idle Capacity   (Appendix 12A) Division X manufactures an electronic relay device that can be sold either to outside customers or to Division Y. Selected operating data on the two divisions are given below:

Division X:

Unit selling price to outside customers	$ 30
Variable production cost per unit	16
Variable selling and administrative expense per unit	4
Fixed production cost in total.	500,000 *

Division Y:

Outside purchase price per unit (before any quantity discount)	30

*Capacity 100,000 units per year.

Division Y now purchases the relay from an outside supplier at the regular $30 intermediate price less a 10% quantity discount. Since the relay manufactured by Division X is of the same quality and type used by Division Y, consideration is being given to buying internally rather than from the outside supplier.

The controller of Division X has determined that half of the variable selling and administrative costs can be avoided on any intracompany sales. Top management wants to treat each division as an autonomous unit with independent profit responsibility.

Required

1. Assume that Division X is currently selling only 60,000 units per year to outside customers and that Division Y needs 40,000 units per year.
   a. What is the lowest transfer price that can be justified between the two divisions? Explain.
   b. What is the highest transfer price that can be justified between the two divisions? Explain.
   c. Assume that Division Y finds an outside supplier that will sell the needed relays for only $26 per unit. Should Division X be required to meet this price? Explain.
   d. Refer to the original data. Assume that Division X decides to raise its price to $35 per unit. If Division Y is forced to pay this price and to start purchasing from Division X, will this result in greater or less total corporate profits? How much per unit?
   e. Under the circumstances posed in (d) above, should Division Y be forced to purchase from Division X? Explain.
2. Assume that Division X can sell all that it produces to outside customers. Repeat (a) through (e) above.

CASES

C12–32   Service Organization; Segment Reporting   The American Association of Acupuncturists is a professional association for acupuncturists that has 10,000 members. The association operates from a central headquarters but has local chapters throughout North America. The association's monthly journal, *American Acupuncture,* features recent developments in the field. The association also publishes special reports and books, and it sponsors courses that qualify members for the continuing professional education credit required by state certification boards. The association's statement of revenues and expenses for the current year is presented on the following page.

AMERICAN ASSOCIATION OF ACUPUNCTURISTS
Statement of Revenues and Expenses
For the Year Ended December 31

Revenues......................................	$970,000
Less expenses:	
Salaries	440,000
Occupancy costs	120,000
Distributions to local chapters	210,000
Printing	82,000
Mailing	24,000
Continuing education instructors' fees	60,000
General and administrative.....................	27,000
Total expenses.............................	963,000
Excess of revenues over expenses	$ 7,000

The board of directors of the association has requested you to construct a segmented state-ment of operations that shows the financial contribution of each of the association's four major programs—membership service, journal, books and reports, and continuing education. The following data have been gathered to aid you:

a. Membership dues are $60 per year, of which $15 covers a one-year subscription to the as-sociation's journal. The other $45 pays for general membership services.

b. One-year subscriptions to *American Acupuncture* are sold to nonmembers and libraries at $20 per subscription. A total of 1,000 of these subscriptions were sold last year. In addition to subscriptions, the journal generated $50,000 in advertising revenues. The costs per journal subscription, for members as well as nonmembers, were $4 for printing and $1 for mailing.

c. A variety of technical reports and professional books were sold for a total of $70,000 during the year. Printing costs for these materials totalled $25,000, and mailing costs totalled $8,000.

d. The association offers a number of continuing education courses. The courses generated revenues of $230,000 last year.

e. Salary costs and space occupied by each program and the central staff follow:

	Salaries	Space Occupied (square metres)
Membership services	$170,000	333
Journal	60,000	111
Books and reports.............	40,000	111
Continuing education	50,000	222
Central staff	120,000	333
Total	$440,000	1,110

f. The $120,000 in occupancy costs incurred last year includes $20,000 in rental cost for a portion of a warehouse used by the Membership Services program for storage purposes. The association has a flexible rental agreement that allows it to pay rent only on the space it uses.

g. Printing costs other than for journal subscriptions and for books and reports relate to Con-tinuing Education.

h. Distributions to local chapters are for general membership services.

i. General and administrative expenses include costs relating to overall administration of the association as a whole. The association's central staff does some mailing of materials for general administrative purposes.

j. The expenses that can be traced or assigned to the central staff, as well as any other ex-penses that can't be logically assigned to the programs, will be treated as common costs. It is not necessary to distinguish between variable and fixed costs.

Required

1. Prepare a segmented statement of revenues and expenses for the American Association of Acupuncturists for last year. This statement should show the segment margin for each pro-gram as well as results for the association as a whole.

2. If segment reporting is adopted by the association for continuing usage, discuss the ways the information provided by the report can be used by management.

3. Give arguments for and against allocating all costs of the association to the four programs.

(CMA, adapted)

C12–33 Transfer Pricing; Divisional Performance; Behavioural Problems (Appendix 12A) Stanco, Inc., is a decentralized organization containing five divisions. The company's Electronics Division produces a variety of electronics items, including an XL5 circuit board. The division (which is operating at capacity) sells the XL5 circuit board to regular customers for $12.50 each. The circuit boards have a variable production cost of $8.25 each.

The company's Clock Division has asked the Electronics Division to supply it with a large quantity of XL5 circuit boards for only $9 each. The Clock Division, which is operating at only 60% of capacity, will put the circuit boards into a timing device that it will produce and sell to a large oven manufacturer. The cost of the timing device being manufactured by the Clock Division follows:

XL5 circuit board (desired cost)	$ 9.00
Other purchased parts (from outside vendors)	30.00
Direct labour	16.50
Variable overhead	4.25
Fixed overhead and administrative costs	10.00
Total cost per timing device	$69.75

The manager of the Clock Division feels that she can't quote a price greater than $70 per timing device to the oven manufacturer if her division is to get the job. As shown above, in order to keep the price at $70 or less, she can't pay more than $9 per unit to the Electronics Division for the XL5 circuit boards. Although the $9 price for the XL5 circuit boards represents a substantial discount from the normal $12.50 price, she feels that the price concession is necessary for her division to get the oven manufacturer contract and thereby keep its core of highly trained people.

The company uses ROI and dollar profits in measuring divisional performance.

Required

1. Assume that you are the manager of the Electronics Division. Would you recommend that your division supply the XL5 circuit boards to the Clock Division for $9 each as requested? Why or why not? Show all computations.

2. Would it be to the short-run economic advantage of the company as a whole for the Electronics Division to supply the Clock Division with the circuit boards for $9 each? Explain your answer.

3. Discuss the organizational and manager behaviour problems, if any, inherent in this situation. As the Stanco, Inc., company controller, what would you advise the company's president to do in this situation?

C12–34 Transfer Pricing Ms. Dundee was recently promoted to the position of executive vice president, finance, of CAM Company. Among several of her new responsibilities are (a) settling transfer price disputes, (b) reviewing sources, and (c) changing the transfer price rules where appropriate.

An immediate dispute Ms. Dundee has to settle involves two of the several divisions of CAM Company: engines division and jet fighter division. The Engines Division manufactures, on a full standard manufacturing cost-plus contract basis, a special engine, ETX, for the makers of single-engine executive jets. It has the physical capacity to produce and sell 60 ETX engines in any given year, but its actual annual capacity has been limited to only 45 because of a severe shortage of skilled labour. The standard cost of producing one ETX engine is as follows:

Materials	$200,000
Labour (4,000 hours)	160,000
Total manufacturing overhead	440,000
Total	$800,000

The variable portion of the total manufacturing overhead varies directly with labour-hours. The fixed portion is based on annual fixed manufacturing overhead of $10.8 million applied on the basis of annual denominator production volume of 45 EXT engines (or 180,000 labour-hours). Annual administrative expenses of $900,000 are all fixed. The division's only selling expenses are commissions of 2% of sales it pays to outside sales agents. Each contract for EXT engine stipulates a selling price that represents a markup of 40% over full standard manufacturing costs.

The jet fighter division assembles twin-engine jet fighter planes which it sells to foreign governments of small countries. It has been buying both the engines and the body for these jets from outside suppliers. The manager of the jet fighter division, Mr. Yankey, has become concerned recently about the decreasing number of outside suppliers of the engines. The outside suppliers appear to be embarking on diversification in anticipation of reduced demand for these engines as the relations among world superpowers are expected to continue to improve. Mr. Yankey has therefore approached the manager of the engine division, Mr. Maple, for a quote on 16 of these engines.

Mr. Maple feels that his division can make the necessary modifications easily to the EXT engine to suit the needs of the jet fighter division. He estimates that the materials would be slightly different and should cost about 10% less than those used in the EXT engine. Additional skilled labour would *not* be available. The present workforce would not work overtime, but the necessary labour-hours can be switched to work on the new engine without any problem. Each new engine would require 3,000 labour-hours. Total manufacturing overhead, consisting of fixed and variable, would be applied at the same rate per labour-hour as on the EXT engine but in order not to lose any profit, the markup on full cost would have to be at least 40%, the same as on the EXT engine.

Mr Yankey, the manager of the jet fighter division, agrees that Mr. Maple should not lose any profit on the quote. However, he also feels that this can be accomplished if Mr. Maple priced the new engine at its estimated variable manufacturing cost. As Mr. Yankey sees it, the Engine Division is after all operating at only 75% of physical capacity of plant and equipment.

Required

1. As an assistant to Ms. Dundee, compute the minimum price she could allow the manager of the Engines Division to charge for each new engine his division manufactures for the jet fighter division.
2. Does the situation in the engines division justify a transfer price based on estimated variable manufacturing cost? Why or why not?
3. What additional information would you recommend Ms. Dundee seek before arriving at a transfer price that will be in the overall best interest of CAM Company? Explain.

(CGA-Canada, adapted)

C12–35 Responsibility Accounting, and Transfer Pricing Peal Electronics Limited (PEL), a closely held Canadian corporation, was founded by Paul Peal to capitalize on the rapidly expanding personal computer market. He established PEL by acquiring several electronics manufacturing companies and organizing them into three divisions: processors, boards, and computers. The processors division produces and supplies processors to the boards division. The boards division produces and supplies electronic computer boards to the computers division.

Paul Peal established the divisions as investment centres and decided to pay the divisional managers a bonus based on their divisional ROIs in excess of the corporate target rate. Before he decided on an appropriate transfer pricing policy, Paul died suddenly, leaving the company to his daughter, Agnes.

Agnes was determined to operate PEL as her father had intended. One of her first actions was to establish a transfer pricing policy of actual full cost plus 20%.

Agnes' first year was a difficult one. Divisional managers argued increasingly with each other. Recently, the processors division manager formally complained that the boards division had started to purchase processors externally. While she was contemplating this problem, the computers division manager asked to meet with her on an urgent matter.

Computers Division Manager: I'm here to give you my letter of resignation. I just cannot perform my job under the current structure of the company. When your father hired me, I was assured that I could operate the division as a virtually independent company. There also was an understanding that divisions would give priority to sourcing and selling within the company. This policy sounded great, but it just has not worked out. Our salespeople had no problem getting business initially, but now customers are starting to complain that we can't deliver on time and our prices are too high. These problems occur because often we have to hold production waiting for boards to be delivered and the price charged by the boards division has been increasing steadily. Now I can buy boards externally, modified to our specifications, for a cost that is less than the price charged by the boards division.

Yesterday, I told the boards division manager that I wouldn't accept his price any longer. Despite the fact that we're his only customer, he still demands that we pay his price or he will stop supplying my division. The boards market is quite competitive and he thinks that he can sell his boards outside the company for a higher price than he's charging us. I tried to tell him that he'd be lucky to get the same price we're paying, but he was not willing to listen. He's also going against the informal rules by starting to source processors externally.

Agnes Peal: You're doing a good job and I'd hate to lose you. Please keep your letter of resignation for a few days while I see if the situation can be resolved.

Agnes immediately spoke with the boards division manager. He explained that processors always give better service and quality to outside customers since processors receive a higher markup on outside sales. Processors also refuses to absorb the cost of replacing defective processors; therefore, the boards division manager feels justified in sourcing processors externally even at a higher unit cost. He also defended his position with the computers division, stating that the transfer price is a set policy that computers has no right to refuse. There is no way he is going to help the computer divisions manager get a bonus by sacrificing his own.

Later that day, Agnes met with a management consultant. She outlined the problems voiced by the managers of the computers and boards divisions and indicated that the investment centre approach did not seem to be working. She asked the consultant for advice on how to resolve the problems and for any other suggestions which would help ensure a smoothly running and profitable operation in the future.

The consultant first assembled a chart which described the physical flows of input and output for the three divisions over the past year (see Exhibit 12–10).

Required

As the management consultant, analyze the operations of PEL and respond to Agnes Peal's request for advice.

(SMAC, adapted)

EXHIBIT 12-10

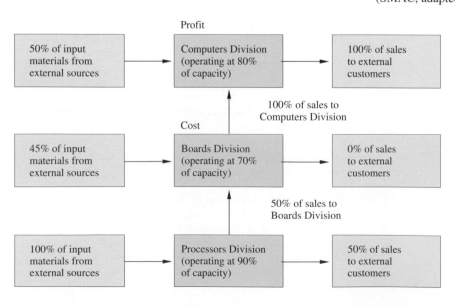

EXHIBIT 12-11

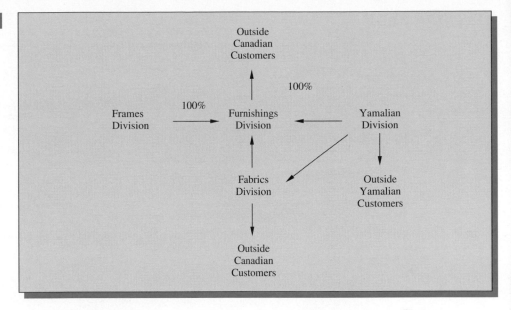

C12–36   Organizational Structure, Performance Evaluation, and International Transfer Pricing   Rupert Jones was recently hired as the corporate controller of Dreamland Manufacturing, a full-line manufacturer of fabric, beds, bed linens, and drapery. Dreamland is headquartered in a major Canadian city and has three nearby domestic operating divisions: fabrics, frames, and furnishings. A fourth division, Yamalian, is located in the country of Yamalia.

Currently, all divisions and divisional managers are evaluated based on maximizing divisional income. Except for the frames division, Dreamland's divisions have full freedom to source and sell any material or product in the outside market and to set their own transfer prices. An illustration of the product flows among divisions is shown in Exhibit 12–11.

The Yamalian division produces specialty fabrics; it transfers some to the fabrics and furnishings divisions in Canada and sells the rest in the Yamalian market. Transfers are subject to Canadian duty and excise taxes, as well as significant shipping costs.

The fabrics division produces fabric for the furnishings division and for large Canadian retail chains and wholesale distributors. The fabrics division also sews its fabric (or fabric transferred from the Yamalian division) into components for other Dreamland products that are assembled and finished by the furnishings division.

The frames division manufactures steel and wooden bed frames and box spring liners. All of the products manufactured by the frames division are transferred to the furnishings division.

The furnishings division is the main manufacturing and assembling centre of Dreamland's operations. This division manufactures and assembles mattresses and beds, and also sews bed linens and draperies. All of the output of the furnishings division is sold in the Canadian market.

Recently, the furnishings division negotiated a contract to produce specialty hospital mattresses for several large city hospitals at a price of $900 per mattress. Costs to fill this contract are $600 per mattress ($400 variable and $200 fixed) plus the cost of producing the special mattress covers needed for these mattresses. There are three options for sourcing the special fabric required for the mattress covers and two options for sewing and completing the mattress covers.

Fabric Sewing Options

1. Source the special fabric from the fabrics division at a transfer price of $92 per unit (see Exhibit 12–12)
2. Source the special fabric from the Yamalian division at a cost of $81.00 per unit (see Exhibit 12–12).
3. Purchase the special fabric from a reputable outside supplier at a price of $75 per unit.

(*Note:* 1 unit = the amount of fabric required to make one mattress cover.)

EXHIBIT 12-12

DREAMLAND MANUFACTURING
Calculation of Transfer Prices
For Special Mattress Covers
And Special Fabric

Fabrics Division

The proposed transfer price from the fabrics division for the special fabric needed
   to produce one mattress cover was computed as follows:

Direct materials	$ 15.00
Weaving labour	30.00
Variable overhead	5.00
Fixed overhead	30.00
Total manufacturing cost	80.00
Normal profit allowance (15%)	12.00
Transfer price of fabric	$ 92.00

The proposed transfer price from the fabrics division for a completed mattress
   cover was computed as follows:

Transfer price for fabric	$ 92.00
Cutting and sewing labour	15.00
Variable overhead	5.00
Fixed overhead	15.00
Total manufacturing cost	127.00
Normal profit allowance (15%)	19.05
Transfer price of fabric	$146.05

Yamalian Division

The proposed transfer price from the Yamalian division for the special fabric
   needed to produce one mattress cover was computed as follows (all costs
   represent translated Canadian currency):

Direct materials	$ 10.00
Weaving labour	8.00
Variable overhead	6.00
Fixed overhead	24.00
Total manufacturing cost	48.00
Normal profit allowance (25%)	12.00
Transfer price of fabric	$ 60.00
Other cost incurred by Dreamland:	
Canadian duty and excise taxes (based on 25% of fair market value of $62)	15.50
Shipping costs	5.50
Total cost of fabric	$ 81.00

Sewing and Completing Each Mattress Cover

1. The furnishings division can cut, sew, and complete each mattress cover for a cost which
   includes the fabric plus the following nonfabric items:

Cutting and sewing labour	$19.00
Variable overhead	5.00
Fixed overhead	18.00
Total conversion (nonfabric) costs	$42.00

2. The fabrics division has offered to cut, sew, and supply completed mattress covers to the
   furnishings division at a total transfer price of $146.05 per cover (see Exhibit 12–12).

   All divisions have enough capacity available to fulfill the requirements of the contract
without disrupting any of their other operations.

The furnishings division manager knows that the Fabrics and Yamalian divisions added standard markups to their costs in arriving at transfer prices (see Exhibit 12–12) and would prefer to deal with an internal division if he could convince one or the other to match the $75 price from the outside supplier. With this in mind, the furnishings division manager asked the president for his help in negotiating with the other internal divisions.

In response, the president asked Rupert Jones, the new corporate controller, to analyze the hospital mattress situation and recommend a production plan that would maximize overall company profitability. The president also asked Rupert to review the structure of Dreamland and to recommend an appropriate performance evaluation and transfer pricing system.

Required

As Rupert Jones, the newly appointed corporate controller, analyze the situation and recommend the best production plan for the hospital mattress covers. Also, as requested by the president, review the structure of Dreamland and recommend an appropriate performance evaluation and transfer pricing system.

(SMAC, adapted)

GROUP EXERCISES

GE12–37 Traditional Management Control and Performance Measurement Systems   Traditional management control and performance measurement systems (e.g., Du Pont's Financial Control System) were based on a set of assumptions, goals, and performance measures unique to the competitive environment of the 1920s through the 1960s. These performance measurement systems are still in widespread use today.

Required

For each of the levels of management listed below, typically, what are their overall goals, what performance measures are used to evaluate performance, what incentives do managers have to maximize their performance evaluation, and what types of suboptimizing behaviour or actions would likely result from such performance incentives?
1. Senior management.
2. Middle management (e.g., division managers, operating unit managers, and product-line managers).
3. Marketing management.
4. Plant management.

GE12–38 Performance Measurement at a Service Firm   How do service-oriented firms' performance measurement and compensation systems compare with those of manufacturing firms? To study one well-run service business, ask the manager of your local McDonald's if he or she could spend some time discussing what performance measures McDonald's uses to evaluate store managers and how these performance measures tie in with the compensation of the store managers.

Required

Organize your analysis into the following areas:
1. What are McDonald's goals, that is, the broad, long-range plans of the company (e.g., to increase market share)?
2. What are the critical success factors (CSF), that is, the key areas in which things must go right if the company is to be successful (e.g., low selling prices based on low production costs)?
3. What are the performance measures that help to motivate and monitor progress toward achieving each CSF (e.g., continuous reduction in cost of quality)?
4. Are performance measures consistent with the store manager's compensation plan? It might prove helpful if you read W. Sasser and S. Pettway, "The Case of Big Mac's Pay Plans," *Harvard Business Review* (July–August 1974), before you interview the store manager.

GE12–39 Evaluating Innovative and Standard Products Some firms choose a strategy that involves competing in established markets by selling high-volume standard products that have wide acceptance. Other firms choose a strategy that emphasizes competing in niche markets by selling low-volume innovative products that have a more narrow application.

Required

1. What criteria do customers use when choosing to purchase each type of product?
2. What measures should plant managers use to control and evaluate the performance of each product?
3. From your reading of Chapters 9–11, how do you think plant managers would control and evaluate the performance of each product?

GE12–40   Balanced Scorecard Consider the nature of the balanced scorecard as presented in the chapter. Read the references suggested.

Required

Can a scorecard really be balanced? Consider this question relative to your own experiences and those you might expect to occur in organizations.

PART III THE CAPSTONE:
Using Cost Data in Decision Making

13

RELEVANT COSTS FOR DECISION MAKING

LEARNING OBJECTIVES

After studying Chapter 13, you should be able to:

1 State a general rule for distinguishing between relevant and irrelevant costs in a decision-making situation.

2 Identify sunk costs and explain why they are not relevant in decision making, including decisions about whether to keep or replace old equipment.

3 Prepare an analysis showing whether a product line or other organizational segment should be dropped or retained.

4 Explain what is meant by a make or buy decision and prepare a well-organized make or buy analysis.

5 Prepare an analysis showing whether a special order should be accepted.

6 Make appropriate computations to determine the most profitable utilization of scarce resources.

7 Prepare an analysis showing whether joint products should be sold at the split-off point or processed further.

8 Explain why a manager should exercise caution in relevant cost analysis when activity-based costing is being used.

9 Define or explain the key terms listed at the end of the chapter.

10 (Appendix 13A) Compute the optimum inventory level and order size.

Mountain Goat Cycles, a manufacturer of a variety of high-quality bicycles, presently produces its own heavy-duty gear shifters. If an outside supplier should offer to provide the gear shifters, how would Mountain Goat Cycles determine whether to accept the offer?

D ecision making is one of the basic functions of a manager. Managers are constantly faced with problems of deciding what products to sell, what production methods to use, whether to make or buy component parts, what prices to charge, what channels of distribution to use, whether to accept special orders at special prices, and so forth. At best, decision making is a difficult and complex task. The difficulty of this task is usually increased by the existence of not just one or two but numerous courses of action that might be taken in any given situation facing a firm.

In decision making, *cost* is often a key factor. The costs of one alternative must be compared against the costs of other alternatives as one step in the decision-making process. The problem is that some costs associated with an alternative may not be *relevant* to the decision to be made. A **relevant cost** can be defined as a cost that is *applicable to a particular decision* in the sense that it will have a bearing on which alternative the manager selects.

To be successful in decision making, managers must have tools at their disposal to assist them in distinguishing between relevant and irrelevant costs so that the latter can be eliminated from the decision framework. The purpose of this chapter is to acquire these tools and to show their application in a wide range of decision-making situations.

COST CONCEPTS FOR DECISION MAKING

Four cost terms discussed in Chapter 2 are particularly applicable to this chapter. These terms are *differential costs, incremental costs, opportunity costs,* and *sunk costs.* You may find it helpful to turn back to Chapter 2 and refresh your memory concerning these terms before reading on.

Identifying Relevant Costs

OBJECTIVE 1

State a general rule for distinguishing between relevant and irrelevant costs in a decision-making situation.

What costs are relevant in decision making? The answer is easy. Any cost that is *avoidable* is relevant for decision purposes. An **avoidable cost** can be defined as a cost that can be eliminated (in whole or in part) as a result of choosing one alternative over another in a decision-making situation. *All* costs are considered to be avoidable, *except:*

1. Sunk costs.
2. Future costs that *do not differ* between the alternatives at hand.

As we learned in Chapter 2, a **sunk cost** is a cost that has already been incurred and that cannot be avoided regardless of which course of action a manager may decide to take. As such, sunk costs have no relevance to future events and must be ignored in decision making. Similarly, if a cost will be incurred regardless of which course of action a manager may take, then the cost cannot possibly be of any help in deciding which course of action is best. Such a cost is not avoidable, and hence it is not relevant to the manager's decision.

In managerial accounting, the term *avoidable cost* is synonymous with the term **differential cost** that we introduced in Chapter 2, and the terms are frequently used interchangeably. To identify the costs that are avoidable (differential) in a particular decision situation, the manager's approach to cost analysis should include the following steps:

1. Assemble *all* of the costs associated with *each* alternative being considered.
2. Eliminate those costs that are sunk.
3. Eliminate those costs that do not differ between alternatives.
4. Make a decision based on the remaining costs. These costs will be the *differential costs* or *avoidable costs,* and hence the costs relevant to the decision to be made.

Different Costs for Different Purposes

We need to recognize from the outset of our discussion that costs that are relevant in one decision situation are not necessarily relevant in another. Simply put, this means (as we've stated before) that *the manager needs different costs for different purposes.* For one purpose, a particular group of costs may be relevant; for another purpose, an entirely different group of costs may be relevant. Thus, in *each* decision situation the manager must examine the data at hand and then take the steps necessary to isolate the relevant costs. Otherwise, he or she runs the risk of being misled by irrelevant data.

The concept of "different costs for different purposes" is basic to managerial accounting; we shall see its application frequently in the pages that follow.

The Government of Canada had its first government-wide audit of material management in 1980. In 1996, it was learned that many of the problems discovered in 1980 had not yet been addressed. The Auditor General found that inadequate information for decision making was a reoccurring problem. For example, in the area of ship repair and overhaul, all relevant costs were not taken into account when a contract was awarded to the lowest bidder (lower by $71). Meanwhile, the ships in need of repair had to be shipped to the out-of-town shipyard at an additional cost of $30,000 while one of the unsuccessful bidders had facilities in town.[1]

SUNK COSTS ARE NOT RELEVANT COSTS

OBJECTIVE 2
Identify sunk costs and explain why they are not relevant in decision making, including decisions about whether to keep or replace old equipment.

One of the most difficult conceptual lessons that managers have to learn is that sunk costs are never relevant in decisions. The tendency to want to include sunk costs within the decision framework is especially strong in the case of book value of old equipment. We focus on book value of old equipment below, and then we consider other kinds of sunk costs in other parts of the chapter. We shall see that regardless of the kind of sunk cost involved, the conclusion is always the same—sunk costs are not avoidable, and therefore they must be eliminated from the manager's decision framework.

▼   ▼   ▼   ▼   ▼

MANAGERIAL ACCOUNTING IN ACTION—THE ISSUE

SoaringWings, Inc., is a small manufacturer of high-quality hang gliders. The most critical component of a hang glider is its metal frame, which must be very strong and yet very light. The frames are made by brazing together tubes of high-strength, but lightweight, metal alloys. Most of the brazing must be done by hand, but some can be done in an automated
Continued

---

[1]Gary Barber, "Material Must Be Better Managed," *CMA Management Accounting Magazine,* (March 1997), p. 35.

process by machine. Pete Kronski, the production manager of SoaringWings, Inc., has been trying to convince J. J. Marker, the company's president, to purchase a new brazing machine from Furimoro Industries. This machine would replace an old brazing machine from Bryston, Inc., that generates a large amount of scrap and waste.

On a recent blustery morning, Pete and J. J. happened to drive into the company's parking lot at the same time. The following conversation occurred as they walked together into the building.

PETE: Morning, J. J. Have you had a chance to look at the specifications on the new brazing machine from Furimoro Industries that I gave you last week?

J. J.: Are you still bugging me about the brazing machine?

PETE: You know it's almost impossible to keep that old Bryston brazing machine working within tolerances.

J. J.: I know, I know. But we're carrying the Bryston machine on the books for $140,000.

PETE: That's right. But I've done some investigating, and we could sell it for $90,000 to a plumbing company in town that doesn't require as tight tolerances as we do.

J. J.: Pete, that's just brilliant! You want me to sell a $140,000 machine for $90,000 and take a loss of $50,000. Do you have any other great ideas this morning?

PETE: J. J., I know it sounds far-fetched, but we would actually save money buying the new machine.

J. J.: I'm skeptical. However, if you can show me the hard facts, I'll listen.

PETE: Fair enough. I'll do it.

▼   ▼   ▼   ▼   ▼

SoaringWings' brazing machine represents a sunk cost that should not affect a manager's decision to purchase a new machine. Only relevant costs should be considered.

Book Value of Old Equipment

Pete first gathered the following data concerning the old machine and the proposed new machine:

Old Machine		**Proposed New Machine**	
Original cost	$175,000	List price new	$200,000
Remaining book value	140,000	Expected life	4 years
Remaining life	4 years	Disposal value in four years	$ –0–
Disposal value now	$ 90,000	Annual variable expenses	
Disposal value in four years	–0–	to operate	300,000
Annual variable expenses			
to operate	345,000	Annual revenue from sales	500,000
Annual revenue from sales	500,000		

Should the old machine be disposed of and the new machine purchased? The first reaction of SoaringWings' president was to say no, since disposal of the old machine would result in a "loss" of $50,000:

Old Machine

Remaining book value	$140,000
Disposal value now	90,000
Loss if disposed of now	$ 50,000

Given this potential loss if the old machine is sold, there is often an inclination for the manager to reason, "We've already made an investment in the old machine, so now we have no choice but to use it until our investment has been fully recovered." The manager will tend to think this way even though the new machine is clearly more efficient than the old machine. Although it may be appealing to think that an error of the past can be corrected by simply *using* the item involved, this, unfortunately, is not correct. The investment that has been made in the old machine is a sunk cost. The portion of this investment that remains on the company's books (the book value of $140,000) should not be considered in a decision about whether to buy the new machine. Pete Kronski verified this assertion by the following analysis:[2]

	Total Costs and Revenues— Four Years		
	Keep Old Machine	**Differential Costs**	**Purchase New Machine**
Sales	$ 2,000,000	$ –0–	$2,000,000
Variable expenses	(1,380,000)	180,000	(1,200,000)
Cost (depreciation) of the new machine	—	(200,000)	(200,000)
Depreciation of the old machine or book value write-off	(140,000)	–0–	(140,000)*
Disposal value of the old machine	—	90,000	90,000 *
Total net operating income over the four years	$ 480,000	$ 70,000	$ 550,000

*For external reporting purposes, the $140,000 remaining book value of the old machine and the $90,000 disposal value would be netted together and deducted as a single $50,000 "loss" figure.

Looking at all four years together, notice that the firm will be $70,000 better off by purchasing the new machine. Also notice that the $140,000 book value of the old machine had *no effect* on the outcome of the analysis. Since this book value is a sunk cost, it must

---

[2]The computations involved in this example are taken one step further in Chapters 14 and 15 where we discuss the time value of money and the use of present value in decision making.

be absorbed by the firm regardless of whether the old machine is kept and used or whether it is sold. If the old machine is kept and used, then the $140,000 book value is deducted in the form of depreciation. If the old machine is sold, then the $140,000 book value is deducted in the form of a lump-sum write-off. Either way, the company bears the same $140,000 cost.

Focusing on Relevant Costs.   What costs in the example above are relevant in the decision concerning the new machine? Following the steps outlined earlier and looking at the original cost data, we should eliminate (1) the sunk costs and (2) the future costs that do not differ between the alternatives at hand.

1. The sunk costs:
    a. The remaining book value of the old machine ($140,000).
2. The future costs that do not differ:
    a. The sales revenue ($500,000 per year).
    b. The variable expenses (to the extent of $300,000 per year).

The costs that remain will form the basis for a decision. The analysis is as follows:

	Differential Costs— Four Years
Reduction in variable expense promised by the new machine ($45,000* per year × 4 years)	$ 180,000
Cost of the new machine	(200,000)
Disposal value of the old machine	90,000
Net advantage of the new machine	$ 70,000

*$345,000 – $300,000 = $45,000.

Note that the items above are the same as those in the middle column of the earlier analysis and represent those costs and revenues that differ between the two alternatives. Armed with this analysis, Pete felt confident that he would be able to explain the financial advantages of the new machine to the president of the company.

▼   ▼   ▼   ▼   ▼

MANAGERIAL ACCOUNTING IN ACTION—WRAP-UP

Pete Kroneki took his analysis to the office of J. J. Marker, the president of SoaringWings, where the following conversation took place.

PETE: J. J., do you remember that discussion we had about the proposed new brazing machine?

J. J.: Sure I remember. Did you find out that I'm right?

PETE: Not exactly. Here's the analysis where I compare the profit with the old machine over the next four years to the profit with the new machine.

J. J.: I see you're claiming the profit is $70,000 higher with the new machine. Are you assuming higher sales with the new machine?

PETE: No, I have assumed total sales of $2,000,000 over the four years in either situation. The real advantage comes with the reduction in variable expenses of $180,000.

J. J.: Where are those reductions going to come from?

Continued

Pete: The new brazing machine should cut our scrap and rework rate at least in half. That results in substantial savings in materials and labour costs.

J. J.: What about the $50,000 loss on the old machine?

Pete: What really matters is the $200,000 cost of the new machine and the $90,000 salvage value of the old machine. The book value of the old machine is irrelevant. No matter what we do, that cost will eventually flow through the income statement as a charge in one form or another.

J. J.: I find that hard to accept, but it is difficult to argue with your analysis.

Pete: The analysis actually understates the advantages of the new machine. We don't catch all of the defects caused by the old machine. With the new machine, I expect our warranty costs to decrease and our repeat sales to increase. And I would hate to be held responsible for any accidents caused by defective brazing by our old machine.

J. J.: Okay, I'm convinced. Put together a formal proposal, and we'll present it at the next meeting of the board of directors.

Depreciation and Relevant Costs.   Since depreciation relating to the book value of old equipment is not a relevant cost in decision making, there is a tendency to assume that depreciation of *any* kind is irrelevant in the decision-making process. This is not a correct assumption. Depreciation is irrelevant in decisions *only* if it relates to a sunk cost. Notice from the comparative income statements at the beginning of this section that the $200,000 depreciation on the new machine appears in the middle column as a relevant item in trying to assess the desirability of the new machine's purchase. By contrast, depreciation on the old machine does not appear as a relevant cost. The difference is that the investment in the new machine has *not yet been made,* and therefore it does not represent depreciation of a sunk cost.

We must hasten to say that while accounting depreciation that relates to a sunk cost is irrelevant, the resale or disposal value of an existing asset will be relevant in any decision that involves disposing of the asset.

Yet another example of a supposed profitable project gone stale is that of the Sheppard subway in Metro Toronto—a project costing over $100 million. There is one possible way to salvage some of the sunk costs: convert the Sheppard subway into a light-rail line. This way, the light-rail line could utilize some of tunnels already dug for the Sheppard subway. It has been proposed that the savings from a light-rail system would enable the transport system to offer more routes than that of the Sheppard subway. To date, however, Toronto Transit Commission has rejected the light-rail option.[3]

---

[3]John Barber, "Light Rail Could Revive Sheppard Corpse," *The Globe and Mail,* August 13, 1996, p. A8.

FUTURE COSTS THAT DO NOT DIFFER
ARE NOT RELEVANT COSTS

Any future cost that does not differ between the alternatives in a decision situation is not a relevant cost so far as that decision is concerned. As stated earlier, if a company is going to sustain the same cost regardless of what decision it makes, then that cost can in no way tell the company which decision is best. The only way a future cost can help in the decision-making process is if it differs between the alternatives under consideration.

FOCUS ON
CURRENT PRACTICE

Not recognizing sunk costs for what they are can lead to poor decision making. A corporate plane can fly a passenger as well as a commercial airliner, but inappropriate cost allocation systems can make the commercial flight seem cheaper.

A failure to recognize the existence of sunk costs can lead to bad business decisions. As evidence, consider the following incident related by a business consultant after encountering a frustrated and angry fellow traveller ("Mr. Smith") whose flight home faced a lengthy delay:

Mr. Smith had recently flown into Calgary on a commercial airline for a two-day business trip. While there, he learned that his company's private airplane had flown in

the day before and would leave on the same day that he was scheduled to leave. Mr. Smith immediately cashed in his $200 commercial airline ticket and made arrangements to fly back on the company plane. He flew home feeling pretty good about saving his company the $200 fare and being able to depart on schedule.

About two weeks later, however, Mr. Smith's boss asked him why the department had been cross-charged $400 for his return trip when the commercial airfare was only $200. Mr. Smith explained that "the company plane was flying back regardless, and there were a number of empty seats."

How could Mr. Smith's attempt to save his company $200 end up "costing" his department $400? The problem is that Mr. Smith recognized something that his company's cost allocation system did not: namely, that the vast majority of the costs associated with flying the plane home were already sunk and, thus, unavoidable at the time he made the decision to fly home. By failing to distinguish between sunk (i.e., unavoidable) and avoidable costs, the cost allocation system was causing the firm and its managers to make uneconomic business decisions.

It is now clear why Mr. Smith was so frustrated the day I ran into him in Calgary. His company's plane was sitting on the runway with a number of empty seats and ready to take off for the very same destination. Yet there was no way Mr. Smith was going to fly on that plane even though doing so was the "best business decision."[4]

---

[4]Dennis L. Weisman, "How Cost Allocation Systems Can Lead Managers Astray," *Journal of Cost Management* (Spring 1991), p. 4. Used by permission.

FOCUS ON
CURRENT PRACTICE

In the early 1990s, General Motors Corp. laid off tens of thousands of its hourly workers who would nevertheless continue to receive full pay under union contracts. GM entered into an agreement with one of its suppliers, Android Industries, Inc., to use laid-off GM workers. GM agreed to pay the wages of the workers who would be supervised by Android Industries. In return, Android would subtract the wages from the bills it submitted to GM under their current contract. This reduction in contract price was pure gravy to GM, because it would have had to pay the laid-off workers in any case.[5]

An Example of Irrelevant Future Costs

To illustrate the irrelevance of future costs that do not differ, let us assume that a firm is contemplating the purchase of a new labour-saving machine. The machine will cost $30,000 and have a 10-year useful life. The company's sales and cost structure on an annual basis with and without the new machine are shown below:

	Present Costs	Expected Costs with the New Machine
Units produced and sold.	5,000	5,000
Selling price per unit	$ 40	$ 40
Direct materials cost per unit.	14	14
Direct labour cost per unit	8	5
Variable overhead cost per unit	2	2
Fixed costs, other	62,000	62,000
Fixed costs, new machine	—	3,000

The new machine promises a saving of $3 per unit in direct labour costs ($8 − $5 = $3), but it will increase fixed costs by $3,000 per year. All other costs, as well as the total number of units produced and sold, will remain the same. Following the steps outlined earlier, the analysis is as follows:

1. Eliminate the sunk costs. (No sunk costs are identified in this example.)
2. Eliminate the future costs (and revenues) that do not differ:
   a. The selling price per unit and the number of units sold do not differ between the alternatives. (Therefore, total future sales revenues will not differ.)
   b. The direct materials cost per unit, the variable overhead cost per unit, and the number of units produced do not differ between the alternatives. (Therefore, total future direct materials costs and variable overhead costs will not differ.)
   c. The "Fixed costs, other" do not differ between the alternatives.

This leaves just the direct labour costs and the fixed costs associated with the new machine as being differential costs:

Savings in direct labour costs (5,000 units at a cost saving of $3 per unit)	$15,000
Less increase in fixed costs	3,000
Net annual cost savings promised by the new machine	$12,000

[5]"GM Agrees to Allow a Parts Supplier to Use Some of Its Idled Employees," *The Wall Street Journal,* November 30, 1992, p. B3.

EXHIBIT 13-1

Differential Cost
Analysis

	5,000 Units Produced and Sold		
	Present Method	Differential Costs	New Machine
Sales.	$200,000	$ –0–	$200,000
Variable expenses:			
Direct materials	70,000	–0–	70,000
Direct labour	40,000	15,000	25,000
Variable overhead	10,000	–0–	10,000
Total variable expenses	120,000		105,000
Contribution margin	80,000		95,000
Less fixed expenses:			
Other	62,000	–0–	62,000
New machine	–0–	(3,000)	3,000
Total fixed expenses	62,000		65,000
Net operating income	$ 18,000	$12,000	$ 30,000

The accuracy of this solution can be proved by looking at *all* items of cost data (both those that are relevant and those that are not) under the two alternatives for a year and then comparing the net operating income results. This is done in Exhibit 13–1. Notice from the exhibit that we obtain the same $12,000 net advantage in favour of buying the new machine as we obtained above when we focused only on relevant costs. Thus, we can see that future costs that do not differ between alternatives are indeed irrelevant in the decision-making process and can be safely eliminated from the manager's decision framework.

Why Isolate Relevant Costs?

In the preceding example, we used two different approaches to show that the purchase of the new machine was desirable. First, we considered only the relevant costs; and second, we considered all costs, both those that were relevant and those that were not. We obtained the same answer under both approaches. When students see that the same answer can be obtained under either approach, they often ask, "Why bother to isolate relevant costs when total costs will do the job just as well?" The isolation of relevant costs is desirable for at least two reasons.

First, only rarely will enough information be available to prepare a detailed income statement such as we have done in the preceding examples. Since normally only limited data are available, the decision maker *must* know how to recognize which costs are relevant and which are not. Assume, for example, that you are called on to make a decision relating to a *single operation* of a multidepartmental, multiproduct firm. Under these circumstances, it would be virtually impossible to prepare an income statement of any type. You would have to rely on your ability to recognize which costs were relevant and which were not in order to assemble the data necessary to make a decision.

Second, the use of irrelevant costs mingled with relevant costs may confuse the picture and draw the decision maker's attention away from the matters that are really critical to the problem at hand. Furthermore, the danger always exists that an irrelevant piece of data may be used improperly, resulting in an incorrect decision. The best approach is to isolate the relevant items and to focus all attention directly on them and their impact on the decision to be made.

Relevant cost analysis, combined with the contribution approach to the income statement, provides a powerful tool for making decisions. We will investigate various uses of this tool in the remaining sections of this chapter.

ADDING AND DROPPING PRODUCT LINES AND OTHER SEGMENTS

OBJECTIVE 3
Prepare an analysis showing whether a product line or other organizational segment should be dropped or retained.

Decisions relating to whether old product lines or other segments of a company should be dropped and new ones added are among the most difficult that a manager has to make. In such decisions, many factors must be considered that are both qualitative and quantitative in nature. Ultimately, however, any final decision to drop an old segment or to add a new one is going to hinge primarily on the impact the decision will have on net operating income. To assess this impact, it is necessary to make a careful analysis of the costs involved.

 **FOCUS ON CURRENT PRACTICE**

McCain Foods Ltd. bought the Ore-Ida frozen French fries and potato specialties business from H. J. Heinz Co. in March 1997. New York analyst Bill Cummins, with Schroder Wertheim & Co., comments that this deal is good for both companies. Heinz will likely make a gain on the sale and can now focus its attention on brand-name foods while it gives McCain a stronger foothold in the U.S. market. According to Cummins, "Heinz was never really comfortable with the food service end of things, and didn't like the low margins it produced." McCain, on the other hand, acquired a "business it knows how to run well even if the margins are low."[6]

An Illustration of Cost Analysis

As a basis for discussion, let us consider the product lines of the Discount Drug Company. The company has three major product lines—drugs, cosmetics, and housewares. Sales and cost information for the preceding month for each separate product line and for the store in total are given in Exhibit 13–2.

What can be done to improve the company's overall performance? One product line—housewares—shows a net operating loss for the month. Perhaps dropping this line would cause profits in the company as a whole to improve. In deciding whether the line should be dropped, management will need to reason as follows:

If the housewares line is dropped, then the company will lose $20,000 per month in contribution margin that is now available to help cover the fixed costs. By dropping the line, however, it may be possible to avoid certain of these fixed costs. It may be possible, for example, to discharge certain employees, or it may be possible to reduce advertising costs. If by dropping the housewares line the company is able to avoid more in fixed

[6]Zena Olijnyk, "McCain Snaps Up Ore-Ida for US$500 M from Heinz," *The Financial Post,* March 15/17, 1997, pp. 1–2.

EXHIBIT 13–2

Discount Drug
Company Product
Lines

	Total	Drugs	Cosmetics	Housewares
			Product Line	
Sales	$250,000	$125,000	$75,000	$50,000
Less variable expenses	105,000	50,000	25,000	30,000
Contribution margin	145,000	75,000	50,000	20,000
Less fixed expenses:				
Salaries	50,000	29,500	12,500	8,000
Advertising	15,000	1,000	7,500	6,500
Utilities	2,000	500	500	1,000
Depreciation—fixtures	5,000	1,000	2,000	2,000
Rent.	20,000	10,000	6,000	4,000
Insurance.	3,000	2,000	500	500
General administrative	30,000	15,000	9,000	6,000
Total fixed expenses	125,000	59,000	38,000	28,000
Net operating income (loss)	$ 20,000	$ 16,000	$12,000	$ (8,000)

costs than it loses in contribution margin, then it will be better off if the line is eliminated, since overall net income should improve. On the other hand, if the company is not able to avoid as much in fixed costs as it loses in contribution margin, then the housewares line should be retained. In short, in order to identify the differential costs in decisions of this type, the manager must ask, "What costs can I avoid to offset my loss of revenue (or loss of contribution margin) if I drop this product line?"

As we have seen from our earlier discussion, not all costs are avoidable. For example, some of the costs associated with a product line may be sunk costs. Other costs may be allocated common costs that will not differ in total regardless of whether the product line is dropped or retained. To show how the manager should proceed in a product-line analysis, suppose that the management of the Discount Drug Company has analyzed the costs being charged to the three product lines and has determined the following:

1. The salaries represent salaries paid to employees working directly in each product-line area. All of the employees working in housewares can be discharged if the line is dropped.
2. The advertising represents direct advertising of each product line and is avoidable if the line is dropped.
3. The utilities represent utilities costs for the entire company. The amount charged to each product line represents an allocation based on space occupied.
4. The depreciation represents depreciation on fixtures used for display of the various product lines. Although the fixtures are nearly new, they are custom-built and will have little resale value if the housewares line is dropped.
5. The rent represents rent on the entire building housing the company; it is allocated to the product lines on the basis of sales dollars. The monthly rent of $20,000 is fixed under a long-term lease agreement.
6. The insurance represents insurance carried on inventories maintained within each of the three product-line areas.
7. The general administrative expense represents the costs of accounting, purchasing, and general management, which are allocated to the product lines on the basis of sales dollars. Total administrative costs will not change if the housewares line is dropped.

Even though the housewares department of a discount drugstore may appear to be losing money, careful cost analysis can lead to the conclusion that the department should be retained because eliminating it would reduce total profits.

With this information, management can identify those costs that are avoidable and those costs that are not avoidable if the product line is dropped:

	Total Cost	Not Avoidable*	Avoidable
Salaries	$ 8,000		$8,000
Advertising	6,500		6,500
Utilities	1,000	$1,000	
Depreciation—fixtures	2,000	2,000	
Rent	4,000	4,000	
Insurance	500		500
General administrative	6,000	6,000	
Total fixed expenses	$28,000	$13,000	$15,000

*These costs represent either (1) sunk costs or (2) costs that will not change regardless of whether the housewares line is retained or discontinued.

To determine how dropping the line will affect the overall profits of the company, we can compare the contribution margin that will be lost against the costs that can be avoided if the line is dropped:

Contribution margin lost if the housewares line is discontinued (see Exhibit 13–2)	$(20,000)
Less fixed costs that can be avoided if the housewares line is discontinued (see above)	15,000
Decrease in overall company net operating income	$ (5,000)

In this case, the fixed costs that can be avoided by dropping the product line are less than the contribution margin that will be lost. Therefore, based on the data given, the housewares line should not be discontinued unless a more profitable use can be found for the floor and counter space that it is occupying.

EXHIBIT 13-3

A Comparative
Format for Product-
Line Analysis

	Keep Housewares	Drop Housewares	Difference: Net Income Increase or (Decrease)
Sales................................	$50,000	$ –0–	$(50,000)
Less variable expenses	30,000	–0–	(30,000
Contribution margin	20,000	–0–	(20,000)
Less fixed expenses:			
Salaries	8,000	–0–	8,000
Advertising	6,500	–0–	6,500
Utilities	1,000	1,000	–0–
Depreciation—fixtures	2,000	2,000	–0–
Rent.............................	4,000	4,000	–0–
Insurance	500	–0–	500
General administrative	6,000	6,000	–0–
Total fixed expenses	28,000	13,000	15,000
Net operating income (loss)	$ (8,000)	$(13,000)	$(5,000)

A Comparative Format

Some managers prefer to approach decisions of this type by preparing comparative income statements showing the effects on the company as a whole of either keeping or dropping the product line in question. A comparative analysis of this type for the Discount Drug Company is shown in Exhibit 13–3.

As shown by column 3 in the exhibit, overall company net operating income will decrease by $5,000 each period if the housewares line is dropped. This is the same answer, of course, as we obtained in our earlier analysis.

Beware of Allocated Fixed Costs

Our conclusion that the housewares line should not be dropped seems to conflict with the data shown earlier in Exhibit 13–2. Recall from the exhibit that the housewares line is showing a loss rather than a profit. Why keep a line that is showing a loss? The explanation for this apparent inconsistency lies at least in part with the common fixed costs that are being allocated to the product lines. As we observed in Chapter 12, one of the great dangers in allocating common fixed costs is that such allocations can make a product line (or other segment of a business) *look* less profitable than it really is. Consider the actual business situation described in the Focus on Current Practice box on the following page.

The same thing has happened in the Discount Drug Company as happened in the bakery company in this actual business situation. That is, by allocating the common fixed costs among all product lines, the Discount Drug Company has made the housewares line *look* as if it were unprofitable, whereas, in fact, dropping the line would result in a decrease in overall company net operating income. This point can be seen clearly if we recast the data in Exhibit 13–2 and eliminate the allocation of the common fixed costs. This recasting of data —using the segmented approach from Chapter 12—is shown in Exhibit 13–4.

Exhibit 13–4 gives us a much different perspective of the housewares line than does Exhibit 13–2. As shown in Exhibit 13–4, the housewares line is covering all of its own traceable fixed costs and is generating a $3,000 segment margin toward covering the

FOCUS ON
CURRENT PRACTICE

A bakery distributed its products through route salespersons, each of whom loaded a truck with an assortment of products in the morning and spent the day calling on customers in an assigned territory. Believing that some items were more profitable than others, management asked for an analysis of product costs and sales. The accountants to whom the task was assigned allocated all manufacturing and marketing costs to products to obtain a net profit for each product. The resulting figures indicated that some of the products were being sold at a loss, and management discontinued these products. However, when this change was put into effect, the company's overall profit declined. It was then seen that by dropping some products, sales revenues had been reduced without commensurate reduction in costs because the common manufacturing costs and route sales costs had to be continued in order to make and sell the remaining products.

EXHIBIT 13-4

Discount Drug Company Product Lines—Recast in Contribution Format (from Exhibit 13-2)

		Product Line		
	Total	**Drugs**	**Cosmetics**	**Housewares**
Sales	$250,000	$125,000	$75,000	$50,000
Less variable expenses	105,000	50,000	25,000	30,000
Contribution margin	145,000	75,000	50,000	20,000
Less traceable fixed expenses:				
Salaries	50,000	29,500	12,500	8,000
Advertising	15,000	1,000	7,500	6,500
Depreciation—fixtures	5,000	1,000	2,000	2,000
Insurance...................	3,000	2,000	500	500
Total	73,000	33,500	22,500	17,000
Product-line segment margin	72,000	$ 41,500	$27,500	$ 3,000*
Less common fixed expenses:				
Utilities	2,000			
Rent.......................	20,000			
General administrative	30,000			
Total	52,000			
Net operating income	$ 20,000			

*If the housewares line is dropped, this $3,000 in segment margin will be lost to the company. In addition, we have seen that the $2,000 depreciation on the fixtures is a sunk cost that cannot be avoided. The sum of these two figures ($3,000 + $2,000 = $5,000) represents another way of obtaining the $5,000 figure that we found earlier would be the decrease in the company's overall profits if the housewares line were discontinued.

common fixed costs of the company. Unless another product line can be found that will generate a greater segment margin than this, the company will be better off keeping the housewares line. By keeping the line, the company will get at least some contribution toward the common fixed costs of the organization from the space it is occupying.

When we talk about another product to replace housewares, we are talking about the *opportunity cost* of space. As a next step, management should explore alternative uses for the space in the store, such as adding a new product, expanding the existing products, or even renting the space out that is now being occupied by housewares.

Any kind of merchandising outlet—from grocery stores to car dealerships—must carry items that provide little or no profit because customers expect to find the items available. Computer stores, for example, probably make very little profit selling mouse pads.

Additionally, we should note that even in those situations where the contribution of a particular product line is small in comparison with other products, managers will often retain the line instead of replacing it if the line is necessary to the sale of other products or if it serves as a "magnet" to attract customers. Bread, for example, is not an especially profitable line in food stores, but customers expect it to be available, and many would undoubtedly shift their buying elsewhere if a particular store decided to stop carrying it.

THE MAKE OR BUY DECISION

OBJECTIVE 4
Explain what is meant by a make or buy decision and prepare a well-organized make or buy analysis.

Many steps are involved in getting a finished product into the hands of a consumer. First, raw materials must be obtained through mining, drilling, growing crops, raising animals, and so forth. Second, these raw materials must be processed to remove impurities and to extract the desirable and usable materials. Third, the usable materials must be fabricated into desired form to serve as basic inputs for manufactured products such as textiles for clothing. Fourth, the actual manufacturing of the finished product must take place. And finally, the finished product must be distributed to the ultimate consumer.

When a company is involved in more than one of these steps in the entire value chain, it is following a policy of **vertical integration.** Vertical integration is very common. Some firms go so far as to control *all* of the activities in the value chain, from the mining of raw materials or the raising of crops right up to the final distribution of finished goods.

Sometimes, qualitative factors dictate that a company buy rather than make certain parts. Cummins Engine Company, a manufacturer of diesel engines, recently faced the problem of developing much more advanced piston designs in order to meet mandated emissions standards. Pistons are the very "guts" of the engine, so management was reluctant to outsource these parts. However, such advanced pistons could already be acquired from several outside suppliers whose cumulative volumes of piston production were many times larger than that of Cummins. This volume had allowed the suppliers to invest 20 times as much as Cummins in research and development and to build advanced manufacturing processes. Consequently, the suppliers were far ahead of Cummins and were likely to remain so without substantial investments that would be difficult to justify. Therefore, management decided to outsource the production of pistons.[7]

Other firms are content to integrate on a less grand scale by purchasing many of the parts and materials that go into their finished products.

A decision to produce a fabricated part internally, rather than to buy the part externally from a supplier, is often called a **make or buy decision.** Actually, any decision relating to vertical integration is a make or buy decision, since the company is deciding whether to meet its own needs internally or to buy externally.

Strategic Aspects of the Make or Buy Decision

Certain advantages arise from integration. The integrated firm is less dependent on its suppliers and may be able to ensure a smoother flow of parts and materials for production than the nonintegrated firm. For example, a strike against a major parts supplier might cause the operations of a nonintegrated firm to be interrupted for many months, whereas the integrated firm that is producing its own parts might be able to continue operations. Also, many firms feel that they can control quality better by producing their own parts and materials, rather than by relying on the quality control standards of outside suppliers. In addition, the integrated firm realizes profits from the parts and materials that it is "making" rather than "buying," as well as profits from its regular operations.

The advantages of integration are counterbalanced by a number of hazards. A firm that produces all of its own parts runs the risk of destroying long-run relationships with suppliers, which may prove harmful and disruptive to the firm. Once relationships with suppliers have been severed, they are often difficult to reestablish. If product demand becomes heavy, a firm may not have sufficient capacity to continue producing all of its own parts internally and may experience great difficulty in its efforts to secure assistance from a severed supplier. In addition, changing technology often makes continued production of one's own parts more costly than purchasing them from the outside, but this change in cost may not be obvious to the firm.

By pooling demand from a number of firms, a supplier may be able to enjoy economies of scale in research and development and in manufacturing. These economies of scale can result in higher quality and lower costs than would be possible if the firm

[7]Ravi Venkatesan, "Strategic Sourcing: To Make or Not to Make," *Harvard Business Review* (November–December 1992), p. 104.

were to attempt to make the parts on its own. A company must be careful, however, to re tain control over activities that are essential to maintaining its competitive position. For example, Hewlett-Packard controls the software for a laser printer it makes in coopera- tion with Canon Inc. of Japan to prevent Canon from coming out with a competing prod- uct. The present trend appears to be toward less vertical integration, with some companies like Sun Microsystems concentrating on hardware and software design and relying on outside supplies for almost everything else in the value chain.[8] Corel Corp. takes an inter- esting approach to its make or buy decisions. Corel may subcontract to learn from the specialists and then bring the activity back in-house to add value through integration and at a later date subcontract again.[9]

In sum, these factors suggest that although certain advantages may accrue to the inte- grated firm, the make or buy decision should be weighed very carefully before any move is undertaken that may prove to be costly in the long run.

An Example of Make or Buy

How should a manager approach the make or buy decision? Basically, the matters that must be considered fall into two broad categories—qualitative and quantitative. Qualita- tive matters deal with issues such as those raised in the preceding section. Quantitative matters deal with cost—what is the cost of producing as compared to the cost of buying? Several kinds of costs may be involved here, including opportunity costs.

To provide an illustration, consider Mountain Goat Cycles. The company is now producing the heavy-duty gear shifters used in its most popular line of mountain bikes. The company's accounting department reports the following "costs" of producing the shifter internally:

	Per Unit	8,000 Units
Direct materials................	$ 6	$ 48,000
Direct labour...................	4	32,000
Variable overhead	1	8,000
Supervisor's salary	3	24,000
Depreciation of special equipment..................	2	16,000
Allocated general overhead........	5	40,000
Total cost...................	$21	$168,000

Mountain Goat Cycles has just received an offer from an outside supplier who can provide 8,000 shifters a year at a price of only $19 each. Should the company stop pro- ducing the shifters internally and start purchasing them from the outside supplier? To ap- proach the decision from a financial point of view, the manager must again focus on the differential costs. As we have seen, the differential costs can be obtained by eliminating from the cost data those costs that are not avoidable—that is, by eliminating (1) the sunk costs and (2) the future costs that will continue regardless of whether the shifters are pro- duced internally or purchased outside. The costs that remain after making these elimina- tions will be the costs that are avoidable to the company by purchasing outside. If these costs are less than the outside purchase price, then the company should continue to manu- facture its own shifters and reject the outside supplier's offer. That is, the company should purchase outside only if the outside purchase price is less than the costs that can be avoided internally as a result of stopping production of the shifters.

---

[8]Ralph E. Drtina, "The Outsourcing Decision," *Management Accounting,* March 1994 (pp. 56–62).
[9]David K. Hurst, "Canada's Most Respected Corporations Managing for Excellence," *The Globe and Mail,* March 29, 1996, p. 56.

EXHIBIT 13–5

Mountain Goat
Cycles—Make or
Buy Analysis

	Production "Cost" per Unit	Per Unit Differential Costs		Total Differential Costs—8,000 Units	
		Make	Buy	Make	Buy
Direct materials	$6	$6		$48,000	
Direct labour	4	4		32,000	
Variable overhead.	1	1		8,000	
Supervisor's salary.	3	3		24,000	
Depreciation of special equipment.	2	—		—	
Allocated general overhead	5	—		—	
Outside purchase price.			$19		$152,000
Total cost	$21	$14	$19	$112,000	$152,000
Difference in favour of continuing to make.			$5		$40,000

Looking at the data above, notice first that depreciation of special equipment is one of the "costs" of producing the shifters internally. Since the equipment has already been purchased, this depreciation represents a sunk cost. Also notice that the company is allocating a portion of its general overhead costs to the shifters. Since these costs are common to all items produced in the factory, they will continue unchanged even if the shifters are purchased from the outside. These allocated costs, therefore, are not differential costs (since they will not differ between the make or buy alternatives), and they must be eliminated from the manager's decision framework along with the sunk costs.

The variable costs of producing the shifters (materials, labour, and variable overhead) are differential costs, since they can be avoided by buying the shifters from the outside supplier. If the supervisor can be discharged and his or her salary avoided by buying the shifters, then it too will be a differential cost and relevant to the decision. Assuming that both the variable costs and the supervisor's salary can be avoided by buying from the outside supplier, then the analysis takes the form shown in Exhibit 13–5.

Since it costs $5 less per unit to continue to make the shifters, Mountain Goat Cycles should reject the outside supplier's offer. There is one additional factor that the company may wish to consider before coming to a final decision, however. This factor is the opportunity cost of the space now being used to produce the shifters.

The Matter of Opportunity Cost

If the space now being used to produce the shifters *would otherwise be idle,* then Mountain Goat Cycles should continue to produce its own shifters and the supplier's offer should be rejected, as we stated above. Idle space that has no alternative use has an opportunity cost of zero.

But what if the space now being used to produce shifters would not sit idle but rather could be used for some other purpose? In that case, the space would have an opportunity cost that would have to be considered in assessing the desirability of the supplier's offer. What would this opportunity cost be? It would be the segment margin that could be derived from the best alternative use of the space.

To illustrate, assume that the space now being used to produce shifters could be used to produce a new cross-country bike that would generate a segment margin of $60,000 per year. Under these conditions, Mountain Goat Cycles would be better off to accept the supplier's offer and to use the available space to produce the new product line:

	Make	Buy
Differential cost per unit (see prior example)	$ 14	$ 19
Number of units needed annually	× 8,000	× 8,000
Total annual cost	112,000	152,000
Opportunity cost—segment margin foregone on a potential new product line.	60,000	
Total cost	$172,000	$152,000
Difference in favour of purchasing from the outside supplier		$20,000

Perhaps we should again emphasize that opportunity costs are not recorded in the accounts of an organization. They do not represent actual dollar outlays. Rather, they represent those economic benefits that are *foregone* as a result of pursuing some course of action. The opportunity costs of Mountain Goat Cycles are sufficiently large in this case to make continued production of the shifters very costly from an economic point of view.

FOCUS ON CURRENT PRACTICE

Deciding how much of a warranty to offer its customers was a decision a Canadian capital equipment supplier recently faced. Full guarantees are often offered on inexpensive consumer goods since the sunk cost of the sale is low. Offering a full guarantee on capital equipment when the sunk costs of installation and customization are so high is not such an easy decision. The Canadian capital equipment supplier hired the services of Hepworth and Company to help answer their warranty question. The Hepworth team learned that the supplier's customers would be more loyal if the supplier offered a more generous warranty on its equipment. The capital equipment supplier decided that the increased loyalty would turn into higher profits which would outweigh the additional expense of offering a better warranty. The supplier decided to offer the long-debated warranty.[10]

SPECIAL ORDERS

OBJECTIVE 5
Prepare an analysis showing whether a special order should be accepted.

Managers often must evaluate whether a *special order* should be accepted, or if the order is accepted, the price that should be charged. A **special order** is a one-time order that is not considered part of the company's normal ongoing business. To illustrate, Mountain Goat Cycles has just received a request from the Vancouver Police Department to produce 100 specially modified mountain bikes at a price of $179 each. The bikes would be used to patrol some of the more densely populated residential sections of the city. Mountain Goat Cycles can easily modify its City Cruiser model to fit the specifications of the Vancouver Police. The normal selling price of the City Cruiser bike is $249, and its unit product cost is $182 as shown below:

Direct materials.	$ 86
Direct labour	45
Manufacturing overhead	51
Unit product cost.	$182

---

[10]Peter Meyer, "Jigsaw Management: Getting to a Decision Quickly Saves Time, Energy, Staff and More," *Canadian Business Review* (Winter 1995), pp. 17–19.

The variable portion of the above manufacturing overhead is $6 per unit. The order would have no effect on the company's fixed manufacturing overhead costs.

The modifications to the bikes consist of welded brackets to hold radios, nightsticks, and other gear. These modifications would require $17 in incremental variable costs. In addition, the company would have to pay a graphics design studio $1,200 to design and cut stencils that would be used for spray painting the Vancouver Police Department's logo and other identifying marks on the bikes.

Should a company accept a special order, such as the Vancouver Police Department's order for mountain bikes from Mountain Goat Cycles? Some issues to consider include price, effect on other sales, modifications to a standard model, and regular production schedule.

This order should have no effect on the company's other sales. The production manager says that she can handle the special order without disrupting any of the regular scheduled production.

What effect would accepting this order have on the company's net operating income?

As in the earlier analyses, only the incremental costs are relevant. Since the existing fixed manufacturing overhead costs would not be affected by the order, they are not incremental costs and are therefore not relevant. The incremental net operating income can be computed as follows:

	Per Unit	Total 100 Bikes
Incremental revenue	$179	$17,900
Incremental costs:		
Variable costs:		
Direct materials	86	8,600
Direct labour	45	4,500
Variable manufacturing overhead	6	600
Special modifications	17	1,700
Total variable costs	$154	15,400
Fixed cost:		
Purchase of stencils		1,200
Total incremental costs		16,600
Incremental net operating income		$1,300

Therefore, even though the price on the special order ($179) is below the normal unit product cost ($182) and the order would require incurring additional costs, the order would result in an increase in net operating income. In general, a special order is profitable as long as the incremental revenue from the special order exceeds the incremental costs of the order. We must note, however, that it is important to make sure that there is indeed idle capacity and that the special order does not cut into normal sales. For example, if the company was operating at capacity, opportunity costs would have to be taken into account as well as the incremental costs that have already been detailed above.

UTILIZATION OF SCARCE RESOURCES

OBJECTIVE 6
Make appropriate computations to determine the most profitable utilization of scarce resources.

Managers are routinely faced with the problem of deciding how scarce resources are going to be utilized. A department store, for example, has a limited amount of floor space and therefore cannot stock every product that may be available. A manufacturing firm has a limited number of machine-hours and a limited number of direct labour-hours at its disposal. When capacity becomes pressed because of a scarce resource, the firm is said to have a **constraint.** Because of the constrained scarce resource, the company cannot fully satisfy demand, so the manager must decide how the scarce resource should be used. Fixed costs are usually unaffected by such choices, so the manager should select the course of action that will maximize the firm's *total* contribution margin.

Contribution in Relation to Scarce Resources

To maximize total contribution margin, a firm should not necessarily promote those products that have the highest *unit* contribution margins. Rather, total contribution margin will be maximized by promoting those products or accepting those orders that provide the highest unit contribution margin *in relation to the scarce resources of the firm.* To illustrate, Mountain Goat Cycles makes a line of paniers—a saddlebag for bicycles. There are two models of paniers—a touring model and a mountain model. Cost and revenue data for the two models of paniers are given below:

	Model	
	Mountain Panier	Touring Panier
Selling price per unit	$25	$30
Variable cost per unit	10	18
Contribution margin per unit	$15	$12
CM ratio	60%	40%

The mountain panier appears to be much more profitable than the touring panier. It has a $15 per unit contribution margin as compared to only $12 per unit for the touring model, and it has a 60% CM ratio as compared to only 40% for the touring model.

But now let us add one more piece of information—the plant that makes the paniers is operating at capacity. Ordinarily this does not mean that every machine and every person in the plant is working at the maximum possible rate. Because machines have different capacities, some machines will be operating at less than 100% of capacity. However, if the plant as a whole cannot produce any more units, some machine or process must be operating at capacity. The machine or process that is limiting overall output is called the **bottleneck.**

At Mountain Goat Cycles, the bottleneck is a particular stitching machine on which each unit of the mountain panier requires 2 minutes of processing time and each unit of the touring panier requires 1 minute of processing time. Since this stitching machine already has more work than it can handle, something will have to be cut back. In this situation, which product is more profitable? To answer this question, the manager should look at the *contribution margin per unit of the scarce resource.* This figure is computed by dividing the contribution margin for a unit of product by the amount of the scarce resource it requires. These calculations are carried out below for the mountain and touring paniers.

	Model	
	Mountain Panier	**Touring Panier**
Contribution margin per unit (above) (a)	$15.00	$12.00
Time on the stitching machine required to produce one unit (b)	2 min.	1 min.
Contribution margin per unit of the scarce resource, (a) ÷ (b).	$7.50/min.	$12.00/min.

With these data in hand, it is easy to decide which product is less profitable and should be de-emphasized. Each minute of processing time on the stitching machine that is devoted to the touring panier results in an increase of $12 in contribution margin and profits. The comparable figure for the mountain panier is only $7.50 per minute. Therefore, the touring model should be emphasized in this situation. Even though the mountain model has the larger per unit contribution margin and the larger CM ratio, the touring model provides the larger contribution margin in relation to the scarce resource.

To verify that the touring model is indeed the more profitable product in this situation, suppose an hour of additional processing time is available at the bottleneck and that there are unfilled orders for both products. The additional hour on the stitching machine could be used to make either 30 mountain paniers (60 minutes ÷ 2 minutes) or 60 touring paniers (60 minutes ÷ 1 minute), with the following consequences:

	Model	
	Mountain Panier	**Touring Panier**
Contribution margin per unit (above) (a).	$ 15	$ 12
Additional units that can be processed in one hour	× 30	× 60
Additional contribution margin	$450	$720

This example clearly shows that looking at unit contribution margins alone is not enough; the contribution margin must be viewed in relation to whatever resource constraint a firm may be working under.

Managing Constraints

Profits can be increased by effectively managing the constraints an organization faces. One aspect of managing constraints is to decide how to best utilize them. As discussed above, if the constraint is a bottleneck in the production process, the manager should select the product mix that maximizes the total contribution margin. In addition, the manager should take an active role in managing the constraint itself. Management should focus efforts on increasing the efficiency of the bottleneck operation and on increasing its capacity. Such efforts directly increase the output of finished goods and will often pay off in an almost immediate increase in profits.

It is often possible for a manager to effectively increase the capacity of the bottleneck, which is called **relaxing (or elevating) the constraint.** The stitching machine operator in the example could be asked to work overtime. This would result in more available processing time on the stitching machine and hence more finished goods that can be sold. The benefits from relaxing the constraint in such a manner are often enormous and can be easily quantified. The manager should first ask, "What would I do with additional capacity at the bottleneck if it were available?" In the example, if there are unfilled orders for both the touring and mountain paniers, the additional capacity would be used to process more touring paniers, since that would be a better use of the additional capacity. In that situation, the additional capacity would be worth $12 per minute or $720 per hour. This is because adding an hour of capacity would generate an additional $720 of contribution margin if it would be used solely to process more touring paniers. Since overtime pay for the operator is likely to be much less than $720 per hour, running the stitching machine on overtime would be an excellent way to increase the profits of the company while at the same time satisfying customers.

The bottleneck at Southwestern Ohio Steel is the blanking line. On the blanking line, large rolls of steel up to 60 inches wide are cut into flat sheets. Setting up the blanking line between jobs takes an average of 2.5 hours, and during this time, the blanking line is shut down.

Management estimates the opportunity cost of lost sales at $225 per hour, which is the contribution margin per hour of the blanking line for a typical order. Under these circumstances, a new loading device with an annual fixed cost of $36,000 that would save 720 setup hours per year looked like an excellent investment. The new loading device would have an average cost of only $50 per hour ($36,000 ÷ 720 hours = $50) compared to the $225 per hour the company would generate in added contribution margin.[11]

To reinforce this concept, suppose that making touring paniers has already been given top priority and consequently there are only unfilled orders for the mountain panier. How much would it be worth to the company to run the stitching machine overtime in this situation? Since the additional capacity would be used to make the mountain panier, the value of that additional capacity would drop to $7.50 per minute or $450 per hour. Nevertheless, the value of relaxing the constraint would still be quite high.

[11]Robert J. Campbell, "Steeling Time with ABC or TOC," *Management Accounting* (January 1995), pp. 31–36.

These calculations indicate that managers should pay great attention to bottleneck operations. If a bottleneck machine breaks down or is ineffectively utilized, the losses to the company can be quite large. In our example, for every minute the stitching machine is out of commission due to breakdowns or setups, the company loses between $7.50 and $12.00. The losses on an hourly basis are between $450 and $720! In contrast, there is no such loss of contribution margin if time is lost on a machine that is not a bottleneck—such machines have excess capacity anyway.

The implications are clear. Managers should focus much of their attention on managing bottlenecks. As we have discussed, managers should emphasize products that most profitably utilize the scarce resource. They should also make sure that products are processed smoothly through the bottlenecks, with minimal lost time due to breakdowns and setups. And they should try to find ways to increase the capacity at the bottlenecks.

There are a number of ways of effectively increasing the capacity of a bottleneck including:

- Working overtime on the bottleneck.
- Subcontracting some of the processing that would be done at the bottleneck.
- Investing in additional machines at the bottleneck.
- Shifting workers from processes that are not bottlenecks to the process that *is* a bottleneck.
- Rethinking the way the bottleneck resource is used and eliminating waste—particularly nonproductive time.
- Reducing defective units. Each defective unit that is processed through the bottleneck and subsequently scrapped takes the place of a good unit that could be sold.

The last three methods of increasing the capacity of the bottleneck are particularly attractive, since they are essentially free and may even yield additional cost savings.

With Mexico's economy on the rebound and Chile becoming one of Canada's latest free trade partners, many businesses are contemplating doing business in Latin America. One thing business persons should be aware of is the possibility of inefficiencies in the transportation of both finished goods and raw materials. The roads, port facilities, and railways are all underdeveloped compared to North American standards and may act as a bottleneck in one's operations.[12]

The Problem of Multiple Constraints

What does a firm do if it is operating under *several* scarce resource constraints? For example, a firm may have limited raw materials available, limited direct labour-hours available, limited floor space, and limited advertising dollars to spend on product promotion. How would it proceed to find the right combination of products to produce under such a

[12]"Toughened by the Experience: Latin America Could See a Period of Sustainable Growth after the Mexican Peso Crisis," *The Financial Post Daily,* February 11, 1997, p. 14.

EXHIBIT 13-6

Joint Products

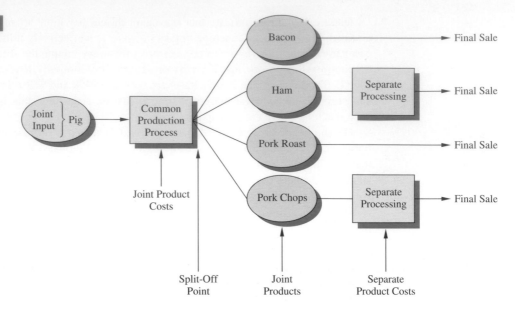

variety of constraints? The proper combination or "mix" of products can be found by use of a quantitative method known as *linear programming,* which is covered in quantitative methods and operations management courses.

JOINT PRODUCT COSTS AND THE CONTRIBUTION APPROACH

OBJECTIVE 7

Prepare an analysis showing whether joint products should be sold at the split-off point or processed further.

In some industries, a number of end products are produced from a single raw material input. A grisly, but apt, example is provided by the meat-packing industry. A great variety of end products—bacon, ham, spare ribs, pork roasts, and so on—are produced from a single pig. Firms that produce several end products from a common input (e.g., a pig) are faced with the problem of deciding how the cost of that input is going to be divided among the end products. Before we address this problem, it will be helpful to define three terms—joint products, joint product costs, and split-off point.

Two or more products that are produced from a common input are known as **joint products.** The term **joint product costs** is used to describe those manufacturing costs that are incurred in producing joint products up to the split-off point. The **split-off point** is that point in the manufacturing process at which the joint products (bacon, ham, spare ribs, and so on) can be recognized as separate products. At that point, some of the joint products will be in final form, ready to be marketed to the consumer. Others will still need further processing on their own before they are in marketable form. These concepts are presented graphically in Exhibit 13–6.

The Pitfalls of Allocation

Joint product costs are really common costs incurred to simultaneously produce a variety of end products. Traditional cost accounting books contain various approaches to allocating these common costs among the different products at the split-off point. A typical approach is to allocate the joint product costs according to the relative sales value of the end products.

Although allocation of joint product costs is needed for some purposes, such as balance sheet inventory valuation, allocations of this kind should be viewed with great caution *internally* in the decision-making process. Unless a manager proceeds with care, he or she may be led into incorrect decisions as a result of relying on allocated common costs. The Focus on Current Practice box below discusses an actual business situation illustrating an incorrect decision that resulted from using allocated costs.

FOCUS ON
CURRENT PRACTICE

A well-known international company is a producer of soap products. Its six main soap product lines are produced from common inputs. Joint product costs up to the split-off point constitute the bulk of the production costs for all six product lines. These joint product costs are allocated to the six product lines on the basis of the relative sales value of each line at the split-off point.

The company has a waste product that results from the production of the six main product lines. Until a few years ago, the company loaded the waste onto barges and dumped it, since the waste was thought to have no commercial value. The dumping was stopped, however, when the company's research division discovered that with some further processing the waste could be made commercially salable as a fertilizer ingredient. The further processing was initiated at a cost of $175,000 per year. The waste was then sold to fertilizer manufacturers at a total price of $300,000 per year.

The accountants responsible for allocating manufacturing costs included the sales value of the waste product along with the sales value of the six main product lines in their allocation of the joint product costs at the split-off point. This allocation resulted in the waste product being allocated $150,000 in joint product cost. This $150,000 allocation, when added to the further processing costs of $175,000 for the waste, caused the waste product to show the net loss computed in the table below.

When presented with this analysis, the company's management decided that further processing of the waste was not desirable after all. The company went back to dumping the waste. In addition to being unwise from an economic viewpoint, this dumping also raises questions regarding the company's social responsibility and the environmental impact of its actions.

Sales value of the waste product after further processing	$ 300,000
Less costs assignable to the waste product	325,000
Net loss	$ (25,000)

Sell or Process Further Decisions

Joint product costs are irrelevant in decisions regarding what to do with a product from the split-off point forward. The reason is that by the time one arrives at the split-off point, the joint product costs have already been incurred and therefore are sunk costs. In the case of the soap company (see the accompanying Focus on Current Practice box), the $150,000 in allocated joint product costs should not have been permitted to influence what was done with the waste product from the split-off point forward. The analysis should have been as follows:

EXHIBIT 13-7

Sell or Process
Further Decision

	Product		
	A	**B**	**C**
Sales value at the split-off point	$120,000	$150,000	$60,000
Sales value after further processing.......	160,000	240,000	90,000
Allocated joint product costs............	80,000	100,000	40,000
Cost of further processing	50,000	60,000	10,000
Analysis of sell or process further:			
Sales value after further processing.....	$160,000	$240,000	$90,000
Sales value at the split-off point	120,000	150,000	60,000
Incremental revenue from further			
processing	40,000	90,000	30,000
Cost of further processing	50,000	60,000	10,000
Profit (loss) from further processing	$(10,000)	$ 30,000	$ 20,000

	Dump in Gulf	Process Further
Sales value...............................	–0–	$300,000
Additional processing costs..................	–0–	175,000
Contribution margin	–0–	$125,000
Advantage of processing further..............		$125,000

Decisions of this type are known as **sell or process further decisions.** As a general guide, it will always be profitable to continue processing a joint product after the split-off point *so long as the incremental revenue from such processing exceeds the incremental processing costs.* Joint product costs that have already been incurred up to the split-off point are sunk costs, and are always irrelevant in decisions concerning what to do from the split-off point forward.

To provide a detailed example of a sell or process further decision, assume that three products are derived from a single raw material input. Cost and revenue data relating to the products are presented in Exhibit 13–7 along with an analysis of which products should be sold at the split-off point and which should be processed further. As shown in the exhibit, products B and C should both be processed further; product A should be sold at the split-off point.

ACTIVITY-BASED COSTING AND RELEVANT COSTS

OBJECTIVE 8
Explain why a manager should exercise caution in relevant cost analysis when activity-based costing is being used.

In various places throughout this text, we have discussed the growing use of activity-based costing as a means for assigning costs to products or other segments of a company. In our discussion, we have explained that the purpose of activity-based costing is to improve the traceability of costs through focusing on the activities in which a product or other segment is involved. Although improved traceability of costs does benefit a company in many ways, managers must exercise caution against reading more into this "traceability" than really exists. Why is caution needed? It is needed because there is a tendency to assume that if a cost is traceable to a segment through the activities in which it is involved, then the cost is automatically an avoidable cost in decision making.

Just because a cost is traceable to a product or other segment is no reason to assume that the cost can be avoided if the segment is dropped or if some other special decision is made regarding the segment. To illustrate, refer again to the data relating to the housewares line in Exhibit 13–4 on page 697. The $2,000 depreciation on fixtures is a traceable cost of the housewares line because it relates to activities in that department. We found, however, that the $2,000 is *not* avoidable if the housewares line is dropped. The key lesson here is that *the method used to assign a cost to a product or other segment does not change the basic nature of the cost.* A sunk cost such as depreciation of old equipment is still a sunk cost regardless of whether it is traced directly to a particular segment on an activity basis, allocated to all segments on a basis of labour-hours, or treated in some other way in the costing process.

Thus, managers must exercise care in relevant cost analysis when activity-based costing is in use, or they may be led into the trap of assuming that a traceable cost is automatically an avoidable cost. Regardless of the method used to assign costs to products or other segments, the manager still must apply the principles discussed in this chapter to determine the costs that are avoidable in each special-decision situation.[13]

SUMMARY

The accountant is responsible for seeing that relevant, timely data are available to guide management in all of its decisions, including those that relate to special, nonroutine situations. Reliance by management on irrelevant data can lead to incorrect decisions, reduced profitability, and inability to meet stated objectives. *All* costs are relevant in decision making, *except:*

1. Sunk costs.
2. Future costs that do not differ between the alternatives under consideration.

The concept of cost relevance has wide application. In this chapter, we have observed its use in equipment replacement decisions, in make or buy decisions, in discontinuance of product-line decisions, in joint product decisions, and in decisions relating to the effective use of scarce resources. This list does not include all of the possible applications of the relevant cost concept. Indeed, *any* decision involving costs hinges on the proper identification and use of those costs that are relevant, if the decision is to be made properly. For this reason, we shall continue to focus on the concept of cost relevance in the following two chapters, where we consider long-run investment decisions.

REVIEW PROBLEM: RELEVANT COSTS

Charter Sports Equipment manufactures round, rectangular, and octagonal trampolines. Data on sales and expenses for the past month follow:

| | | Trampoline | | |
	Total	Round	Rectangular	Octagonal
Sales	$1,000,000	$ 140,000	$500,000	$360,000
Less variable expenses	410,000	60,000	200,000	150,000
Contribution margin	590,000	80,000	300,000	210,000
Less fixed expenses:				
Advertising—traceable	216,000	41,000	110,000	65,000
Depreciation of special equipment	95,000	20,000	40,000	35,000
Line supervisors' salaries	19,000	6,000	7,000	6,000
General factory overhead*	200,000	28,000	100,000	72,000
Total fixed expenses	530,000	95,000	257,000	178,000
Net operating income (loss)	$ 60,000	$ (15,000)	$ 43,000	$ 32,000

*Allocated on the basis of sales dollars.

---

[13]For further discussion, see Douglas Sharp and Linda P. Christensen, "A New View of Activity-Based Costing," *Management Accounting* (September 1991), pp. 32–34; and Maurice L. Hirsch, Jr., and Michael C. Nibbelin, "Incremental, Separable, Sunk, and Common Costs in Activity-Based Costing," *Journal of Cost Management* (Spring 1992), pp. 39–47.

Management is concerned about the continued losses shown by the round trampolines and wants a recommendation as to whether or not the line should be discontinued. The special equipment used to produce the trampolines has no resale value. If the round trampoline model is dropped, the two line supervisors assigned to the model would be discharged.

Required

1. Should production and sale of the round trampolines be discontinued? You may assume that the company has no other use for the capacity now being used to produce the round trampolines. Show computations to support your answer.
2. Recast the above data in a format that would be more usable to management in assessing the long-run profitability of the various product lines.

Solution to Review Problem

1. No, production and sale of the round trampolines should not be discontinued. Computations to support this answer follow:

Contribution margin lost if the round trampolines are discontinued		$(80,000)
Less fixed costs that can be avoided:		
Advertising—traceable	$41,000	
Line supervisors' salaries	6,000	47,000
Decrease in net operating income for the company as a whole		$(33,000)

The depreciation of the special equipment represents a sunk cost, and therefore it is not relevant to the decision. The general factory overhead is allocated and will continue regardless of whether or not the round trampolines are discontinued; thus, it also is not relevant to the decision.

	Keep Round Tramps	Drop Round Tramps	Difference: Net Income Increase or Decrease)
Sales	$ 140,000	$ –0–	$(140,000)
Less variable expenses	60,000	–0–	60,000
Contribution margin	80,000	–0–	(80,000)
Less fixed expenses:			
Advertising—traceable	41,000	–0–	41,000
Depreciation of special equipment	20,000	20,000	–0–
Line supervisors' salaries	6,000	–0–	6,000
General factory overhead	28,000	28,000	–0–
Total fixed expenses	95,000	48,000	47,000
Net operating income (loss)	$ (15,000)	$(48,000)	$ (33,000)

2. If management wants a clear picture of the profitability of the segments, the general factory overhead should not be allocated. It is a common cost and therefore should be deducted from the total product-line segment margin, as we learned in the preceding chapter. The proper income statement format would be as follows:

		Trampoline		
	Total	Round	Rectangular	Octagonal
Sales	$1,000,000	$ 140,000	$500,000	$360,000
Less variable expenses	410,000	60,000	200,000	150,000
Contribution margin	590,000	80,000	300,000	210,000
Less traceable fixed expenses:				
Advertising—traceable	216,000	41,000	110,000	65,000
Depreciation of special equipment	95,000	20,000	40,000	35,000
Line supervisors' salaries	19,000	6,000	7,000	6,000
Total traceable fixed expenses	330,000	67,000	157,000	106,000
Product-line segment margin	260,000	$ 13,000	$143,000	$104,000
Less common fixed expenses	200,000			
Net operating income (loss)	$ 60,000			

KEY TERMS FOR REVIEW

Avoidable cost   Any cost that can be eliminated (in whole or in part) as a result of choosing one alternative over another in a decision-making situation. In managerial accounting, this term is synonymous with *relevant cost* and *differential cost.* (p. 684)

Bottleneck   A machine or process that limits total output because it is operating at capacity. (p. 705)

Constraint   A limitation under which a company must operate, such as limited machine time available or limited raw materials available. (p. 704)

Differential cost   Any cost that is present under one alternative in a decision-making situation but is absent in whole or in part under another alternative. In managerial accounting, this term is synonymous with *avoidable cost* and *relevant cost.* (p. 684)

Joint product costs   Those manufacturing costs that are incurred up to the split-off point in producing joint products. (p. 708)

Joint products   Two or more items that are produced from a common input. (p. 708)

Make or buy decision   A decision as to whether an item should be produced internally or purchased from an outside supplier. (p. 699)

Relaxing (or elevating) the constraint   An action that increases the capacity at a bottleneck. (p. 706)

Relevant cost   A cost that is applicable to a particular decision in the sense that it should have a bearing on which alternative the manager selects. In managerial accounting, this term is synonymous with *avoidable cost* and *differential cost.* (p. 684)

Sell or process further decision   A decision as to whether a joint product should be sold at the split-off point or processed further and sold at a later time in a different form. (p. 710)

Special order   A one-time order that is not considered part of the company's normal ongoing business. (p. 702)

Split-off point   That point in the manufacturing process where some or all of the joint products can be recognized as individual products. (p. 708)

Sunk cost   Any cost that has already been incurred and that cannot be changed by any decision made now or in the future. (p. 684)

Vertical integration   The involvement by a company in more than one of the steps from extracting or otherwise securing basic raw materials to the manufacture and distribution of a finished product. (p. 698)

APPENDIX 13A: INVENTORY DECISIONS

Inventory planning and control decisions are an important aspect of the management of many organizations. Inventory levels are not left to chance but rather are carefully planned. Major questions left unanswered are: How does the manager know what inventory level is right for the firm? and Won't the level that is right vary from organization to organization? The purpose of this section is to examine the inventory control methods available to the manager to answer these questions and the relevant costs for these decisions.

Costs Associated with Inventory

Three groups of costs are associated with inventory. The first group, known as **inventory ordering costs,** consists of costs associated with the acquisition of inventory. Examples include:

1. Clerical costs.
2. Transportation costs.

The second group, known as **inventory carrying costs,** consists of costs that arise from having inventory on hand. Examples include:

1. Storage space costs.
2. Handling costs.
3. Property taxes.
4. Insurance.
5. Obsolescence losses.
6. Interest on capital invested in inventory.

The third group, known as **costs of not carrying sufficient inventory,** consists of costs that result from not having enough inventory on hand to meet customers' needs. Costs in this group are more difficult to identify than costs in the other two groups, but nevertheless they can include items that are very significant to a firm. Examples of costs in this group are:

1. Customer ill will.
2. Quantity discounts foregone.
3. Erratic production (expediting of goods, extra setup, etc.)
4. Inefficiency of production runs.
5. Added transportation charges.
6. Lost sales.

In a broad conceptual sense, the right level of inventory to carry is the level that minimizes the total of these three groups of costs. Such a minimization is difficult to achieve, however, because certain of the costs involved are in direct conflict with one another. Notice, for example, that as inventory levels increase, the costs of carrying inventory also increase, but the costs of not carrying sufficient inventory decrease. In working toward total cost minimization, therefore, the manager must balance off the three groups of costs against one another. The problem really has two dimensions—how much to order (or how much to produce in a production run) and how often to do it.

Computing the Economic Order Quantity

The how-much-to-order question is commonly referred to as the **economic order quantity.** It is the order size that results in a minimization of the first two groups of costs just described. We consider two approaches to computing the economic order quantity—the tabular approach and the formula approach.

The Tabular Approach

Given a certain annual consumption of an item, a firm might place a few orders each year of a large quantity each, or it might place many orders of a small quantity each. Placing only a few orders will result in low inventory ordering costs but in high inventory carrying costs, as the average inventory level would be very large. On the other hand, placing many orders would result in high inventory ordering costs but in low inventory carrying costs; in this case the average inventory level would be quite small. As stated earlier, the economic order quantity seeks the order size that balances off these two groups of costs. To show how it is computed, assume that a manufacturer used 3,000 subassemblies (manufactured parts inserted in other manufactured items) in the manufacturing process each year. The subassemblies are purchased from a supplier at a cost of $20 each. Other cost data are given below:

Inventory carrying costs, per unit, per year	$ 0.80
Cost of replacing a purchase order	10.00

EXHIBIT 13-8   Tabulation of Costs Associated with Various Order Sizes

					Order Size in Units					
Symbol*		25	50	100	200	250	300	400	1,000	3,000
E/2	Average inventory in units............	12.5	25	50	100	125	150	200	500	1,500
Q/E	Number of purchase orders	120	60	30	15	12	10	7.5	3	1
C(E/2)	Annual carrying cost at									
	$0.80 per unit....................	$10	$20	$40	$80	$100	$120	$160	$400	$1,200
p(Q/E)	Annual purchase order cost									
	at $10 per order	1,200	600	300	150	120	100	75	30	10
T	Total annual cost	$1,210	$620	$340	$230	$220	$220	$235	$430	$1,210

*Symbols:

E = order size in units (see headings above).

Q = Annual quantity used in units (3,000 in this example).

C = Annual cost of carrying one unit in stock.

P = Cost of placing one order.

T = Total annual cost = $P(Q/E) + C(E/2)$

Exhibit 13–8 contains a tabulation of the total costs associated with various order sizes for the subassemblies. Notice the total annual cost is lowest (and is equal) at the 250- and 300-unit order sizes. The economic order quantity lies somewhere between these two points. We could locate it precisely by adding more columns to the tabulation, and we would in time zero in on 274 units as being the exact economic order quantity.

The cost relationships from this tabulation are shown graphically in Exhibit 13–9. Notice from the graph that total annual cost is minimized at that point when annual carrying costs and annual purchase order costs are equal. The same point identifies the economic order quantity, because the purpose of the computation is to find the point of exact trade-off between these two classes of costs.

EXHIBIT 13-9

Graphic Solution to
Economic Order Size

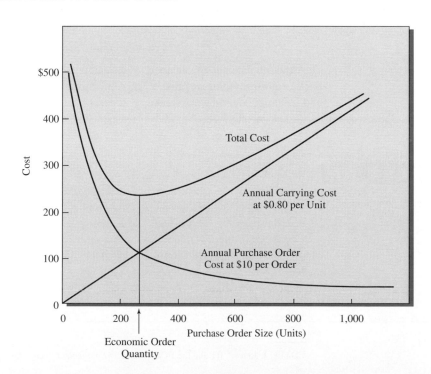

Observe from the graph that total cost shows a tendency to flatten out between 200 and 400 units. Most firms look for this minimum cost range and choose an order size that falls within it, rather than choosing the exact economic order quantity. The primary reason is that suppliers will often ship goods only in round-lot sizes.

The table in Exhibit 13–8 is based on the formula:

$$T = P(Q/E) + C(E/2)$$

where P is a constant cost per order, and C is a unit cost of carrying a unit of inventory for the period of time under consideration. If quantity discounts can be obtained for orders of a certain size, another term representing the purchase costs of the particular lot size should be added to the formula or another line to the table. Other complications arise where annual or period demand is not known, lead times vary, or multiple deliveries are necessary for each order.

The Formula Approach   The economic order quantity can also be found by means of a formula. The formula is derived by solving the minimization of $T = P(Q/E) + C(E/2)$ for E using calculus. The result is

$$E = \sqrt{\frac{2QP}{C}}$$

where

E = order size in units
Q = annual quantity used in units
P = cost of placing one order
C = annual cost of carrying one unit in stock

Substituting with the data used in our preceding example, we have:

Q = $3,000 subassemblies used per year
P = $10 cost to place one order
C = $0.80 cost to carry one subassembly in stock for one year

$$E = \sqrt{\frac{2(3,000)(\$10)}{\$0.80}} = \sqrt{\frac{\$60,000}{\$0.80}} = \sqrt{75,000}$$
$$E = 274 \text{ (the economic order quantity)}$$

Although data can be obtained very quickly using the formula approach, it has the drawback of not providing as great a range of information as the method discussed previously, and it cannot be used where changes in purchase prices occur with changes in lot sizes.

FOCUS ON
CURRENT PRACTICE

Research suggests that companies do, indeed, understate the cost of carrying a unit in stock. The reason for the understatement is that companies tend to consider only the variable costs of carrying goods and to ignore other costs such as depreciation (or rent) on facilities, material handling, accounting, and administration.[14] Yet these other costs can be more significant in the EOQ computation than the variable costs. Indeed, one factor that has propelled the Japanese toward JIT has been the extremely high cost of storage space in Japan. Real estate is so costly that companies can't afford to use valuable space to store inventory. In effect, the high inventory carrying costs in Japan have pushed the EOQ downward to the point where JIT is the only feasible alternative.

---

[14]Daniel J. Jones, "JIT and the EOQ Model," *Management Accounting* (February 1991), p. 57.

JIT and the Economic Order Quantity

The EOQ will decrease under either of these circumstances:

1. The cost of placing an order decreases.
2. The cost of carrying inventory in stock increases.

Managers who advocate JIT purchasing argue that the cost of carrying inventory in stock is much greater than generally realized because of the waste and inefficiency that inventories create. These managers argue that this fact, combined with the fact that JIT purchasing dramatically reduces the cost of placing an order, is solid evidence that companies should purchase more frequently in smaller amounts. Assume, for example, that a company has used the following data to compute its EOQ:

Q = 1,000 units needed each year

P = $60 cost to place one order

C = $3 cost to carry one unit in stock for one year

Given these data, the EOQ would be:

$$E = \sqrt{\frac{2QP}{C}} = \sqrt{\frac{2(1,000)(\$60)}{\$3}} = \sqrt{40,000}$$

$$E = 200 \text{ units}$$

Now assume that as a result of JIT purchasing the company is able to decrease the cost of placing an order to only $10. Also assume that because of the waste and inefficiency caused by inventories, the true cost of carrying a unit in stock is $8 per year. The revised EOQ would be:

$$E = \sqrt{\frac{2QP}{C}} = \sqrt{\frac{2(1,000)(\$10)}{\$8}} = \sqrt{2,500}$$

$$E = 50 \text{ units}$$

Under JIT purchasing, the company would *not* necessarily order in 50-unit lots since purchases would be geared to current demand. This example shows quite dramatically, however, the economics behind the JIT concept as far as the purchasing of goods is concerned.

Production Lot Size

The economic order quantity concept can also be applied to the problem of determining the **economic production lot size.** Deciding when to start and when to stop production runs is a problem that has plagued manufacturers for years. The problem can be solved quite easily by inserting the **setup cost** for a new production lot into the economic order quantity formula in place of the purchase order cost. The setup cost includes the labour and other costs involved in making facilities ready for a run of a different production item.

To illustrate, assume that Chittenden Company has determined that the following costs are associated with one of its product lines:

Q = 15,000 units produced each year

P = $150 setup costs to change production from one product to another

C = $2 to carry one unit in stock for one year

What is the optimal production lot size for this product line? It can be determined by using the same formula used to compute the economic order quantity:

$$O = \sqrt{\frac{2(15,000)(\$150)}{\$2}} = \sqrt{\frac{\$4,500,000}{\$2}} = \sqrt{2,250,000}$$

$$O = 1,500 \text{ (economic production lot size in units)}$$

The Chittenden Company will minimize its overall costs by producing in lots of 1,500 units each. Tabular analysis of the form presented in Exhibit 14–8 can be used to provide a more flexible model for the planning of production lot sizes.

JIT systems are being touted as a total manufacturing system for repetitive manufacturing environments such as those used to produce food and beverages, electrical products, textiles, and automobiles. Small lot production and flexible manufacturing are key elements to the system.[15] Distances in Canada may pose a problem for some industries but not necessarily for all. The seasonal nature of some businesses may preclude the use of JIT because additional production capacity is simply too costly to permit production only when the need is evident in the form of customer orders. However, the potential improvements in productivity and quality together with the reduction in needed investment in inventory make JIT production an option to be seriously investigated for manufacturers and processors.

JIT production philosophy, when it was originated, examined carefully the assumptions in economic production lot size analysis. The typical analysis as presented earlier assumes setup time is a known fixed cost, for example, $150 per setup in the preceding example. JIT approached this production lot size problem by attempting to reduce setup costs to zero. If setup costs in the Chittenden Company example were $0.0, the economic production lot size in units would be one, a JIT production approach. The less the setup cost, the smaller the production lots. Production approaches have been redesigned in some operations so that many different products can be manufactured at little or no setup costs. For example, a world-class automobile manufacturer has been noted as being able to change from one model to another in 2.5 minutes, a complete retooling operation.[16]

Reorder Point and Safety Stock

We stated earlier that the inventory problem has two dimensions—how much to order and how often to do it. How often to do it involves what are commonly termed the *reorder point* and the *safety stock,* and seeks to find the optimal tradeoff between the second two groups of inventory costs outlined earlier (the costs of carrying inventory and the costs of not carrying sufficient inventory). First, we will discuss the reorder point and the factors involved in its computation. Then, we discuss the circumstances under which a safety stock must be maintained.

The **reorder point** tells the manager when to place an order or when to initiate production to replenish depleted stocks. It is dependent on three factors—the economic order quantity (or economic production lot size), the *lead time,* and the rate of usage during the

---

[15]Alan T. G. Saipe, "Just-in-Time Holds Promise for Manufacturing Productivity," *Cost and Management,* May–June 1984, pp. 41–43.

[16]Robert D'Amore, "Just-Time-Systems," *Cost Accounting, Robotics, and the New Manufacturing Environment,* ed. Robert Capettini and Donald K. Clancy (Sarasota, Fla.: American Accounting Association, 1987), p. 8.2.

lead time. The **lead time** can be defined as the interval between the time that an order is placed and the time that the order is finally received from the supplier or from the production line.

Constant Usage during the Lead Time.   If the rate of usage during the lead time is known with certainty, the reorder point can be determined by the following formula:

$$\text{Reorder point} = \text{Lead time} \times \text{Average daily or weekly usage}$$

To illustrate the formula's use, assume that a company's economic order quantity is 500 units, that the lead time is 3 weeks, and that the average weekly usage is 50 units.

$$\text{Reorder point} = 3 \text{ weeks} \times 50 \text{ units per week} = 150 \text{ units}$$

The reorder point would be 150 units. That is, the company automatically places a new order for 500 units when inventory stock drops to a level of 150 units, or three weeks' supply, left on hand.

Variable Usage during the Lead Time.   The previous example assumed that the 50 units per week usage rate was constant and was known with certainty. Although some firms enjoy the luxury of certainty, the more common situation is to find considerable variation in the rate of usage of inventory items from period to period. If usage varies from period to period, the firm that reorders in the way computed earlier may soon find itself out of stock. A sudden spurt in demand, a delay in delivery, or a snag in processing an order may cause inventory levels to be depleted before a new shipment arrives.

Companies that experience problems in demand, delivery, or processing of orders have found that they need some type of buffer to guard against stock-outs. Such a buffer is usually called a **safety stock.** A safety stock serves as insurance against greater-than-usual demand and against problems in the ordering and delivery of goods. Its size is determined by deducting *average usage* from the *maximum usage* that can reasonably be expected during a period. For example, if the firm in the preceding example was faced with a situation of variable demand for its product, it would compute a safety stock as follows:

Maximum expected usage per week	73.3 units
Average usage per week	50
Excess	23.3 units
Lead time	× 3 weeks
Safety stock	70 units

The reorder point is then determined by *adding the safety stock to the average usage during the lead time.* In formula form, the reorder point will be:

$$\text{Reorder point} = (\text{Lead time} \times \text{Average daily or weekly usage}) + \text{Safety stock}$$

Computation of the reorder point by this approach is shown both numerically and graphically in Exhibit 13–10. As shown in the exhibit, the company places a new order for 500 units when inventory stocks drop to a level of 220 units left on hand.

If management does not wish to assume the worst-case situation by using the maximum expected usage per week, then a slightly more complex calculation of the safety stock is necessary as shown in Exhibit 13–11 and based on the data that follow. Assume management makes the following estimates for a yearly period:

Carrying cost per year, $1 per unit
Stock-out cost per unit, $0.60
Average usage per week, 50
Orders placed per year, 12

Demand	Probabilities
80	0.05
120	0.06
140	0.20
150	0.38
160	0.20
180	0.06
220	0.05
	1.00

EXHIBIT 13-10   Determining the Reorder Point—Variable Usage

Economic order quantity	500 units
Lead time	3 weeks
Average weekly usage	50 units
Maximum weekly usage	77.3 units
Safety stock	70 units

Reorder point = (3 weeks × 50 units per week) + 70 units = 220 units.

These estimates reflect the uncertainty experienced by management when they face the various demand possibilities. The table of demand levels and corresponding probabilities presents how management has described the uncertainty they face. This description will, as we shall see, be incorporated in the safety stock calculation.

The calculation of the optimal safety stock begins by computing the various inventory quantities that the demand probabilities indicate could be satisfied by the safety stock. These quantities are the demand quantities in excess of the expected demand during the lead time period. Calculation *a* in Exhibit 13–11 illustrates the amounts. Each unit of safety stock inventory will be on hand for the year (the typical time period used), so the carrying costs per unit of inventory per year is used to determine the first cost element, the total carrying cost and the safety stock per year.

EXHIBIT 13-11   Safety Stock Level

(a) Safety Stock Level in Units	Total Carrying Cost per Year	(b) Stock-Out in Units	(c) Stock-Out Cost per Order Time	Number of Times Orders Placed	Probability of Stock-Out	(d) Expected Stock-Out Cost per Year	(e) Total Cost per Year
–0–	$ –0–	10	$ 6.00	12	0.20	$14.40	
		30	18.00	12	0.06	12.96	
		70	42.00	12	0.05	25.20	$52.56
10	10	20	12.00	12	0.06	8.64	
		60	36.00	12	0.05	21.60	40.24
30	30	40	24.00	12	0.05	14.40	44.40
70	70	0	0.00	12	0.00	0.00	70.00

a. Safety stock level is possible demand minus expected demand (e.g., 180 – 150 = 30). Carrying cost of safety stock is units times cost per unit to carry (e.g., 30 × $1 = 30).

b. Stock-out in units is possible demand minus expected demand minus safety stocks (e.g., 200 – 150 – 10 = 60; 180 – 150 – 10 = 20).

c. Stock-out cost per order time is stock-out in unit times stock-out cost per unit (e.g., 30 × $0.60 = $18.00; 40 × 0.06 = $24.00).

d. Expected stock-out cost per year is stock-out cost per time the order is placed, times the number of orders placed per year, times the probability of a stock-out each time (e.g., $6 × 12 × 0.20 = $14.40; $12 × 12 × 0.06 = $8.64). The probability of a stock-out is obtained from the data for various demand levels in excess of the expected amount of 150 plus the safety stock.

e. Total cost per year is the carrying cost of the safety stock plus the expected stock-out cost per year for the appropriate demand levels (e.g., $0.0 + $14.40 + $12.96 + $25.20 = $52.56; $30 + $14.40 = $44.40).

The second set of calculations computes the stock-out costs caused because demand exceeds the safety stock quantity. Column *b* in Exhibit 13–11 reflects the excess demand possibilities above the safety stock and the average demand during the lead time, in other words, the stock-out quantity. The stock-out in units is multiplied by the stock-out cost per unit of 60 cents to give the stock-out cost for each time an order is placed. Knowledge of the average inventory usage per year and the order size is used to determine the number of times orders are placed in a year. To determine the stock-out total costs, the stock-out cost per order is multiplied by the number of orders per year by the probability of each possible demand level to yield column *d*. The sum of the total carrying cost for the safety stock and the expected stock-out costs give the cost for each safety stock level. The lowest expected total costs provide the optimal level of safety stock. Notice that Exhibit 13–11 suggests 10 is the optimal level, with a total cost of carrying the safety stock of $40.24. The conservative maximum safety stock level of 70 suggested earlier had an annual cost of $70 in this illustration.

Perishable Products

Inventory problems for perishable products or services such as hotel rooms pose an interesting and somewhat different inventory problem. Basically, if too much or many are ordered, the cost of the inventory is similar to a carrying cost, while ordering too few has the cost of contribution foregone from the lost sale. A firm cannot sell what it does not have, while it loses what it purchased but did not sell.

Assume the following:

Purchase cost $3 per unit.
Selling price $5 per unit.

Remember:

You cannot sell what you do not have.
What you buy but cannot sell is lost.

EXHIBIT 13-12

Calculation of
Optimal Inventory

	\$2	\$2	\$2	\$2	\$2	\$2.00

**Profitability of Order/Demand Combinations
and Probability/Demand**

	0.10	0.15	0.05	0.40	0.30	
Inventory	**1**	**2**	**3**	**4**	**5**	**Expected Profit**
1.	\$2	\$2	\$2	\$2	\$2	\$2.00
2.	– 1	4	4	4	4	3.50
3.	– 4	1	6	6	6	4.25
4.	– 7	–2	3	8	8	4.75
5.	–10	–5	–0–	5	10	3.25*

Note: Four units is the optimum level of inventory because it has the greatest profit, \$4.75.

*Profit × probability; for example, [0.10(–10) + 0.15(–5) + 0.05(0) + 0.40(5) + 0.30(10)] = \$3.25

Carefully review the calculations in Exhibit 13–12 to see how the information can be combined to select the optimum inventory level.

For perishable products, each unsold unit of inventory generally is lost; at best, it may receive a rebate from the inventory supplier. Comparison of the total revenue based on demand quantities time selling prices, with the purchase cost of the inventory adjusted for any rebates or returns, determines the cell profit or loss for each combination of demand and inventory shown in Exhibit 13–12. Because the demand levels are uncertain, each possible net income before income taxes for the particular inventory level is multiplied by the probability of the demand level to yield the expected profits. The maximum expected profit is considered to be the indicator of the optimum inventory level.

KEY TERMS FOR REVIEW (APPENDIX 13A)

Cost of not carrying sufficient inventory   Those costs that result from not having enough inventory in stock to meet customers' needs; such costs would include customer ill will, quantity discounts foregone, erratic production, added transportation charges, and lost sales. (p. 714)

Economic order quantity   The order size for materials that results in a minimization of the costs of ordering inventory and carrying inventory. (p. 714)

Economic production lot size   The number of units produced in a production lot that results in a minimization of setup costs and the costs of carrying inventory. (p. 717)

Inventory carrying costs   Those costs associated with the acquisition of inventory, such as rental or storage space, handling costs, property taxes, insurance, and interest on funds. (p. 714)

Inventory ordering costs   Those costs associated with the acquisition of inventory, such as clerical costs and transportation costs. (p. 713)

Lead time   The interval between the time that an order is placed and the time that the order is finally received from the supplier. (p. 719)

Reorder point   The point in time when an order must be placed to replenish depleted stocks; it is determined by multiplying the lead time by the average daily or weekly usage. (p. 718)

Safety stock   The difference between average usage of materials and maximum usage of materials that can reasonably be expected during the lead time. (p. 719)

Setup costs   Labour and other costs involved in getting facilities ready for a run of a different production item. (p. 717)

QUESTIONS

13–1   What is a *relevant cost?*

13–2   Define the following terms: *incremental cost, opportunity cost,* and *sunk cost.*

13–3   Are variable costs always relevant costs? Explain.

13–4   The book value of a machine (as shown on the balance sheet) is an asset to a company, but this same book value is irrelevant in decision making. Explain why this is so.

13–5   "Sunk costs are easy to spot—they're simply the fixed costs associated with a decision." Do you agree? Explain.

13–6   "My neighbour offered me $25 for the use of my boat over the weekend, but I decided that renting it out is just too risky." What cost term would you use to describe the $25? Explain.

13–7   "Variable costs and differential costs mean the same thing." Do you agree? Explain.

13–8   "All future costs are relevant in decision making." Do you agree? Why?

13–9   Prentice Company is considering dropping one of its product lines. What costs of the product line would be relevant to this decision? Irrelevant?

13–10   Why is the term *avoidable cost* used in connection with product line and make or buy decisions?

13–11   "If a product line is generating a loss, then that's pretty good evidence that the product line should be discontinued." Do you agree? Explain.

13–12   What is the danger in allocating common fixed costs among product lines or other segments of an organization?

13–13   What is meant by the term *make or buy?*

13–14   How does opportunity cost enter into the make or buy decision?

13–15   Give four examples of limiting or scarce factors that might be present in an organization.

13–16   How will the relating of product line contribution margins to scarce resources help a company ensure that profits will be maximized?

13–17   Define the following terms: *joint products, joint product costs,* and *split-off point.*

13–18   From a decision-making point of view, what pitfalls are there in allocating common costs among joint products?

13–19   What guideline can be used in determining whether a joint product should be sold at the split-off point or processed further?

13–20   Airlines sometimes offer reduced rates during certain times of the week to members of a businessperson's family if they accompany him or her on trips. How does the concept of relevant costs enter into the decision to offer reduced rates of this type?

13–21   Why must a manager exercise special caution in relevant cost analysis when activity-based costing is in use?

13–22   (Appendix 13A) What three classes of costs are associated with a company's inventory policy? Which of these classes of costs is the most difficult to quantify?

13–23   (Appendix 13A) List at least three costs associated with a company's inventory policy that do not appear as an expense on the income statement.

13–24   (Appendix 13A) What tradeoffs in costs are involved in computing the economic order quantity?

13–25   (Appendix 13A) "Managers are more interested in a minimum cost *range* than they are in a minimum cost point." Explain.

13–26   (Appendix 13A) Define *lead time* and *safety stock.*

13–27   (Appendix 13A) What implications exist when management can reduce setup costs?

13–28   (Appendix 13A) What modifications are necessary to the economic order quantity calculations when purchase discounts are possible?

13–29   (Appendix 13A) What are the inventory costs associated with perishable products?

EXERCISES

E13–1 Listed below are a number of "costs" that may be relevant in decisions faced by the management of Shelby Company:

	Case 1		Case 2	
Item 1	Relevant	Not Relevant	Relevant	Not Relevant
a. Sales revenue..............................				
b. Direct materials				
c. Direct labour				
d. Variable manufacturing overhead				
e. Depreciation—Model B100 machine				
f. Book value—Model B100 machine				
g. Disposal value—Model B100 machine.......				
h. Market value—Model B300 machine (cost)...				
i. Depreciation—Model B300 machine				
j. Fixed manufacturing overhead (general)				
k. Variable selling expense				
l. Fixed selling expense				
m. General administrative overhead............				

Required

Copy the information above onto your answer sheet, and place an X in the appropriate column to indicate whether each item is relevant or not relevant in the following situations (requirement 1 relates to Case 1 above, and requirement 2 relates to Case 2):

1. Management is considering purchasing a Model B300 machine to use in addition to the company's present Model B100 machine. This will increase the company's production and sales. The increase in volume will be large enough to require increases in fixed selling expenses and in general administrative overhead, but not in the fixed manufacturing overhead.
2. Management is instead considering replacing its present Model B100 machine with a new Model B300 machine. The Model B100 machine would be sold. This change will have no effect on production or sales, other than some savings in direct materials costs due to less waste.

E13–2 Samantha Ringer purchased a used automobile for $10,000 at the beginning of last year and incurred the following operating costs:

Depreciation ($10,000 ÷ 5 years)	$2,000
Insurance................................	960
Garage rent	480
Automobile tax and licence	60
Variable operating cost.................... 12¢ per kilometre	

The variable operating costs consist of gasoline, oil, tires, maintenance, and repairs. Samantha estimates that at her current rate of usage the car will have zero resale value in five years, so the annual straight-line depreciation is $2,000. The car is kept in a garage for a monthly fixed charge.

Required

1. Samantha drove the car 18,000 kilometres last year. Compute the average cost per kilometre of owning and operating the car.
2. Samantha is unsure about whether she should use her own car or rent a car to go on an extended cross-country trip for two weeks during spring break. What costs above are relevant in this decision?
3. Samantha is thinking about buying an expensive sports car to replace the car she bought last year. She would drive the same number of kilometres irrespective of which car she owns and would rent the same parking space. The sports car's variable operating costs would be roughly the same as the variable operating costs of her old car. However, her insurance and automobile tax and licence costs would go up. What costs are relevant in estimating the incremental cost of owning the more expensive car?

E13–3 Markham Company is considering the purchase of a high-speed lathe to replace a standard lathe that is now in use. Selected information on the two machines is given below:

	Standard Lathe	High-Speed Lathe
Original cost new	$40,000	$60,000
Accumulated depreciation to date	10,000	—
Current salvage value	8,000	—
Estimated cost per year to operate	36,000	21,000
Remaining years of useful life	5 years	5 years

Required

Prepare a computation covering the five-year period that will show the net advantage or disadvantage of purchasing the high-speed lathe. Use only relevant costs in your analysis.

E13–4 Dexter Products, Inc., manufactures and sells a number of items, including an overnight case. The company has been experiencing losses on the overnight case for some time, as shown on the following income statement:

DEXTER PRODUCTS, INC.
Income Statement—Overnight Cases
For the Quarter Ended June 30

Sales		$450,000
Less variable expenses:		
Variable manufacturing expenses	$130,000	
Sales commissions	48,000	
Freight-out	12,000	
Total variable expenses		190,000
Contribution margin		260,000
Less fixed expenses:		
Salary of product-line manager	21,000	
General factory overhead	104,000*	
Depreciation of equipment (no resale value)	36,000	
Advertising—traceable	110,000	
Insurance on inventories	9,000	
Purchasing department expenses	50,000†	
Total fixed expenses		330,000
Net operating loss		$ (70,000)

*Allocated on the basis of machine-hours.

†Allocated on the basis of sales dollars.

The discontinuance of the overnight cases would not affect sales of other product lines and would have no noticeable effect on the company's total general factory overhead or total purchasing department expenses.

Required

Would you recommend that the company discontinue the manufacture and sale of overnight cases? Support your answer with appropriate computations.

E13–5 Climate-Control, Inc., manufactures a variety of heating and air-conditioning units. The company is currently manufacturing all of its own component parts. An outside supplier has offered to produce and sell a particular part to the company at a cost of $20 per part. To evaluate this offer, Climate-Control, Inc., has gathered the following information relating to its own "cost" of producing the part internally:

	Per Part	15,000 Parts per Year
Direct materials	$ 6	$ 90,000
Direct labour	8	120,000
Variable manufacturing overhead	1	15,000
Fixed manufacturing overhead, traceable	5*	75,000
Fixed manufacturing overhead, common, but allocated	10	150,000
Total cost	$30	$450,000

*40% supervisory salaries; 60% depreciation of special equipment (no resale value).

Required

1. Assuming that the company has no alternative use for the facilities now being used to produce the part, should the outside supplier's offer be accepted? Show all computations.
2. Assuming that a new product that will generate a segment margin of $65,000 per year could be produced if the part were purchased, should the offer be accepted? Show computations.

E13–6 Solex Company manufactures three products from a common input in a joint processing operation. Joint processing costs up to the split-off point total $100,000 per year. The company allocates these costs to the joint products on the basis of their total sales value at the split-off point. These sales values are as follows: product X, $50,000; product Y, $90,000; and product Z, $60,000.

Each product may be sold at the split-off point or processed further. Additional processing requires no special facilities. The additional processing costs and the sales value after further processing for each product (on an annual basis) are shown below:

Product	Additional Processing Costs	Sales Value
X............	$35,000	$ 80,000
Y............	40,000	150,000
Z............	12,000	75,000

Required

1. Which product or products should be sold at the split-off point, and which product or products should be processed further? Show computations.
2. What general statement can be made with respect to joint costs and the decision to process further?

E13–7 Banner Company produces three products, A, B, and C. The selling price, variable costs, and contribution margin for one unit of each product follow:

	Product		
	A	B	C
Selling price	$60	$90	$80
Less variable expenses:			
Direct materials	27	14	40
Direct labour...........................	12	32	16
Variable manufacturing overhead............	3	8	4
Total	42	54	60
Contribution margin......................	$18	$36	$20
Contribution margin ratio..................	30%	40%	25%

Due to a strike in the plant of one of its competitors, demand for the company's products far exceeds its capacity to produce. Management is trying to determine which product(s) to concentrate on next week in filling its backlog of orders. The direct labour rate is $8 per hour, and only 3,000 hours of labour time are available each week.

Required

1. Compute the amount of contribution margin that will be obtained per hour of labour time spent on each product.
2. Which orders would you recommend that the company work on next week—the orders for product A, product B, or product C? Show computations.
3. By paying overtime wages, more than 3,000 hours of direct labour time can be made available next week. Up to how much should the company be willing to pay per hour in overtime wages as long as there is unfilled demand for the three products?

E13–8 Steve has just returned from salmon fishing. He was lucky on this trip and brought home two salmon. Steve's wife, Wendy, disapproves of fishing, and to discourage Steve from further fishing trips, she has presented him with the following cost data. The cost per fishing trip is based on an average of 10 fishing trips per year.

Cost per fishing trip:

Depreciation on fishing boat* (annual depreciation of
$1,500 ÷ 10 trips) $150

Boat moorage fees (annual rental of $1,200 ÷ 10 trips)   120

Expenditures on fishing gear, except for snagged lures
(annual expenditures of $200 ÷ 10 trips)   20

Fishing licence (yearly licence of $40 ÷ 10 trips)..................   4

Fuel and upkeep on boat per trip.................................   25

Junk food consumed during trip.................................   8

Snagged fishing lures   7

Total cost per fishing trip $334

Cost per salmon ($334 ÷ 2 salmon) $167

*The original cost of the boat was $15,000. It has an estimated useful life of 10 years, after which it will have no resale value. The boat does not wear out through use, but it does become less desirable for resale as it becomes older.

Required

1. Assuming that the salmon fishing trip Steve has just completed is typical, what costs are relevant to a decision as to whether he should go on another trip this year?
2. Suppose that on Steve's next fishing trip he gets lucky and catches three salmon in the amount of time it took him to catch two salmon on his last trip. How much would the third salmon have cost him to catch?
3. Discuss the costs that are relevant in a decision of whether Steve should give up fishing.

E13–9 (Appendix 13A) Classify the following as either (a) costs of carrying inventory or (b) costs of not carrying sufficient inventory:

1. Airfreight on a rush order of a critical part needed in production.
2. Interest paid on investment funds.
3. Municipal taxes on inventory.
4. Spoilage of perishable goods.
5. Excessive setup costs.
6. Customers lost through inability of the company to make prompt delivery.
7. Quantity discounts lost as a result of purchasing in small lots.
8. Fire insurance on inventory.
9. Loss sustained when a competitor comes out with a less expensive, more efficient product.
10. A general feeling of ill will among customers, due to broken delivery promises.

E13–10 Halifax County Senior Services is a nonprofit organization devoted to providing essential services to seniors who live in their own homes within the Halifax County area. Three services are provided for seniors—home nursing, meals on wheels, and housekeeping. In the home nursing program, nurses visit seniors on a regular basis to check on their general health and to perform tests ordered by their physicians. The meals on wheels program delivers a hot meal once a day to each senior enrolled in the program. The housekeeping service provides weekly housecleaning and maintenance services. Data on revenue and expenses for the past year follow:

	Total	Home Nursing	Meals on Wheels	House- keeping
Revenues	$900,000	$260,000	$400,000	$240,000
Less variable expenses........................	490,000	120,000	210,000	160,000
Contribution margin..........................	410,000	140,000	190,000	80,000
Less fixed expenses:				
Depreciation..............................	68,000	8,000	40,000	20,000
Liability insurance	42,000	20,000	7,000	15,000
Program administrators' salaries	115,000	40,000	38,000	37,000
General administrative overhead*	180,000	52,000	80,000	48,000
Total fixed expenses......................	405,000	120,000	165,000	120,000
Net operating income (loss)....................	$ 5,000	$ 20,000	$ 25,000	$ (40,000)

*Allocated on the basis of program revenues.

The head administrator of Halifax County Senior Services, Judith Miyama, is concerned about the organization's finances and considers the net income of $5,000 last year to be razor-thin. (Last year's results were very similar to the results for previous years and are representative of what would be expected in the future.) She feels that the organization should be building its financial reserves at a more rapid rate in order to prepare for the next inevitable recession. After seeing the above report, Ms. Miyama asked for more information about the financial advisability of perhaps discontinuing the housekeeping program.

The depreciation in housekeeping is for a small van that is used to carry the housekeepers and their equipment from job to job. If the program were discontinued, the van would be donated to a charitable organization. None of the general administrative overhead would be avoided if the housekeeping program were dropped, but the liability insurance and the salary of the program administrator would be avoided.

Required

1. Should the housekeeping program be discontinued? Show computations to support your answer.
2. Recast the above data in a format that would be more useful to management in assessing the long-run financial viability of the various services.

PROBLEMS

P13–11 Relevant Cost Analysis; Book Value   Natural Products, Ltd., is a manufacturer of various herb and vitamin capsules. One year ago the company purchased a new capsule press at a cost of $84,000. The press has been very satisfactory, but the company's production manager has just received information on a computer-operated press that is vastly superior to the press that has been purchased. The computer-operated press would slash annual operating costs by 70% as shown below:

	Present Press	Proposed New Press
Purchase cost when new	$84,000	$110,000
Estimated useful life when new	6 years	5 years
Annual straight-line depreciation	$14,000	$ 22,000
Remaining book value	70,000	—
Salvage value now	30,000	—
Annual costs to operate	40,000	12,000

The production manager would like to purchase the new press, but her enthusiasm has been dampened considerably by the following computation:

Remaining book value of the old press	$70,000
Less salvage value of the old press	30,000
Net loss from disposal	$40,000

After considering the matter, the production manager commented, "There's no way we can buy that new capsule press. If the front office found out that we took a loss on the old press, somebody's head would roll."

Sales of capsule products are expected to remain unchanged at $200,000 per year, and selling and administrative expenses are expected to be $116,000 per year, regardless of which press is used.

Required

1. Prepare a summary income statement covering the next five years, assuming:
   a. That the new press is not purchased.
   b. That the new press is purchased.
2. Determine the desirability of purchasing the new press using only relevant costs in your analysis.

P13–12   Dropping a Tour; Analysis of Operating Policy   Blueline Tours, Inc., operates a large number of tours throughout Canada. A careful study has indicated that some of the tours are not profitable, and consideration is being given to dropping these tours to improve the company's overall operating performance.

One such tour is a two-day Historic Mansions bus tour conducted in Nova Scotia. An income statement from a typical Historic Mansions tour is given below:

Ticket revenue (100 seats × 40% occupancy × $75 ticket price)	$3,000	100%
Less variable expenses ($22.50 per person)	900	30
Contribution margin	2,100	70%
Less tour expenses:		
Tour promotion	$ 600	
Salary of bus driver	350	
Fee, tour guide	800	
Fuel for bus	125	
Depreciation of bus	450	
Liability insurance, bus	200	
Overnight parking fee, bus	50	
Room and meals, bus driver and tour guide	75	
Bus maintenance and preparation	300	
Total tour expenses	2,950	
Net operating loss	$ (850)	

The following additional information is available about the tour:
a.   Bus drivers are paid fixed annual salaries; tour guides are paid for each tour conducted.
b.   The "Bus maintenance and preparation" cost above is an allocation of the salaries of mechanics and other service personnel who are responsible for keeping the company's fleet of buses in good operating condition.
c.   Depreciation is due to obsolescence. Depreciation due to wear and tear is negligible.
d.   Liability insurance premiums are based on the number of buses in the company's fleet.
e.   Dropping the Historic Mansions bus tour would not allow Blueline Tours to reduce the number of buses in its fleet, the number of bus drivers on the payroll, or the size of the maintenance and preparation staff.

Required

1.   Prepare an analysis showing what the impact will be on the company's profits if this tour is discontinued.
2.   The company's tour director has been criticized because only about 50% of the seats on Blueline's tours are being filled as compared to an average of 60% for the industry. The tour director has explained that Blueline's average seat occupancy could be improved considerably by eliminating about 10% of the tours, but that doing so would reduce profits. Explain how this could happen.

P13–13   Relevant Cost Potpourri   Unless otherwise indicated, each of the following parts is independent. In all cases, show computations to support your answer.
1.   Boyle's Home Centre has two departments, A and B. The most recent income statement for the company follows:

		Department	
	Total	A	B
Sales	$5,000,000	$1,000,000	$4,000,000
Less variable expenses	1,900,000	300,000	1,600,000
Contribution margin	3,100,000	700,000	2,400,00
Less fixed expenses	2,700,000	900,000	1,800,000
Net operating income (loss)	$ 400,000	$ (200,000)	$ 600,000

A study indicates that $370,000 of the fixed expenses being charged to department A are sunk costs and allocated costs that will continue even if department A is dropped. In addition, the elimination of department A would result in a 10% decrease in the sales of department B. If department A is dropped, what will be the effect on the income of the company as a whole?

2. Morrell Company produces several products from the processing of krypton, a rare mineral. Material and processing costs total $30,000 per tonne, one-third of which is allocable to product A. The amount of product A received from a tonne of krypton can either be sold at the split-off point or processed further at a cost of $13,000 and then sold for $60,000. The sales value of product A at the split-off point is $40,000. Should product A be processed further or sold at the split-off point?

3. Shelby Company produces three products, X, Y, and Z. Cost and revenue characteristics of the three products follow (per unit):

	Product		
	X	Y	Z
Selling price........................	$80	$56	$70
Less variable expenses:			
Direct materials	24	15	9
Labour and overhead..............	24	27	40
Total variable expenses	48	42	49
Contribution margin..................	$32	$14	$21
Contribution margin ratio	40%	25%	30%

Demand for the company's products is very strong, with far more orders on hand each month than the company has raw materials available to produce. The same material is used in each product. The material costs $3 per kilogram, with a maximum of 5,000 kilograms available each month. Which orders would you advise the company to accept first, those for X, for Y, or for Z? Which orders second? Third?

4. For many years, Diehl Company has produced a small electrical part that it uses in the production of its standard line of diesel tractors. The company's unit product cost, based on a production level of 60,000 parts per year, is as follows:

	Per Part	Total
Direct materials	$ 4.00	
Direct labour................................	2.75	
Variable manufacturing overhead.................	0.50	
Fixed manufacturing overhead, traceable...........	3.00	$180,000
Fixed manufacturing overhead, common		
(allocated on the basis of labour-hours)	2.25	135,000
Unit product cost	$12.50	

An outside supplier has offered to supply the electrical parts to the Diehl Company for only $10 per part. The company has determined that one-third of the traceable fixed manufacturing costs represent supervisory salaries and other costs that can be eliminated if the parts are purchased. The other two-thirds of the traceable fixed manufacturing costs represent depreciation of special equipment that has no resale value. The decision would have no effect on the common fixed costs of the company, and the space being used to produce the parts would otherwise be idle. Show the dollar advantage or disadvantage of accepting the supplier's offer.

5. Glade Company produces a single product. The cost of producing and selling a single unit of this product at the company's normal activity level of 8,000 units per month is as follows:

Direct materials	$2.50
Direct labour.......................................	3.00
Variable manufacturing overhead.....................	0.50
Fixed manufacturing overhead.......................	4.25
Variable selling and administrative expenses............	1.50
Fixed selling and administrative expenses..............	2.00

The normal selling price is $15 per unit. The company's capacity is 10,000 units per month. An order has been received from an overseas source for 2,000 units at a price of $12 per unit. This order would not disturb regular sales. If the order is accepted, by how much will monthly profits be increased or decreased? (The order would not change the company's total fixed costs.)

6. Refer to the data in (5) above. Assume that the company has 500 units of this product left over from last year that are inferior to the current model. The units must be sold through regular channels at reduced prices. What unit cost figure is relevant for establishing a minimum selling price for these units? Explain.

P13–14 Make or Buy Analysis   "That old equipment for producing subassemblies is worn out," said Paul Taylor, president of Timkin Company. "We need to make a decision quickly." The company is trying to decide whether it should purchase new equipment and continue to make its subassemblies internally or whether it should discontinue production of its subassemblies and purchase them from an outside supplier. The alternatives follow:

Alternative 1: New equipment for producing the subassemblies can be purchased at a cost of $350,000. The equipment would have a five-year useful life (the company uses straight-line depreciation) and a $50,000 salvage value.

Alternative 2: The subassemblies can be purchased from an outside supplier who has offered to provide them for $8 each under a five-year contract.

Timkin Company's present costs per unit of producing the subassemblies internally (with the old equipment) are given below. These costs are based on a current activity level of 40,000 subassemblies per year:

Direct materials	$ 2.75
Direct labour	4.00
Variable overhead	0.60
Fixed overhead ($0.75 supervision, $0.90 depreciation, and $2 general company overhead)	3.65
Total cost per unit	$11.00

The new equipment would be more efficient and, according to the manufacturer, would reduce direct labour costs and variable overhead costs by 25%. Supervision cost ($30,000 per year) and direct materials cost per unit would not be affected by the new equipment. The new equipment's capacity would be 60,000 subassemblies per year. The company has no other use for the space now being used to produce subassemblies.

The total general company overhead would be unaffected by this decision.

Required

1. The president is unsure what the company should do and would like an analysis showing what unit costs and what total costs would be under each of the two alternatives given above. Assume that 40,000 subassemblies are needed each year. Which course of action would you recommend to the president?

2. Would your recommendation in (1) above be the same if the company's needs were (a) 50,000 subassemblies per year, or (b) 60,000 subassemblies per year? Show computations in good form.

3. What other factors would you recommend that the company consider before making a decision?

P13–15 Make or Buy Decision   Bronson Company manufactures a variety of ballpoint pens. The company has just received an offer from an outside supplier to provide the ink cartridge for the company's Zippo pen line, at a price of $0.48 per dozen cartridges. The company is interested in this offer, since its own production of cartridges is at capacity.

Bronson Company estimates that if the supplier's offer were accepted, the direct labour and variable overhead costs of the Zippo pen line would be reduced by 10% and the direct materials cost would be reduced by 20%.

Under present operations, Bronson Company manufactures all of its own pens from start to finish. The Zippo pens are sold through wholesalers at $4 per box. Each box contains one dozen pens. Fixed overhead costs charged to the Zippo pen line total $50,000 each year. (The same equipment and facilities are used to produce several pen lines.) The present cost of producing one dozen Zippo pens (one box) is given below:

Direct materials.................	$1.50
Direct labour	1.00
Manufacturing overhead..........	0.80 *
Total cost....................	$3.30

*Includes both variable and fixed manufacturing overhead, based on production of 100,000 boxes of pens each year.

Required

1. Should Bronson Company accept the outside supplier's offer? Show computations.
2. What is the maximum price that Bronson Company would be willing to pay the outside supplier per dozen cartridges?
3. Due to the bankruptcy of a competitor, assume that Bronson Company expects to sell 150,000 boxes of Zippo pens next year. As stated above, the company presently has enough capacity to produce the cartridges for only 100,000 boxes of Zippo pens annually. By incurring $30,000 in added fixed cost each year, the company could expand its production of cartridges to satisfy the anticipated demand for Zippo pens. The variable cost per unit to produce the additional cartridges would be the same as at present. Under these circumstances, should all 150,000 boxes be purchased from the outside supplier, or should some of the 150,000 boxes be made by Bronson? Show computations to support your answer.
4. What qualitative factors should be considered before accepting the outside supplier's offer?

P13–16   Shutdown versus Continue-to-Operate Decision   (Note to the student: This type of decision is similar to that of dropping a product line, and the portion of the text dealing with that topic should be referred to, if needed.)

Hallas Company manufactures a fast-bonding glue in its Northwest plant. The company normally produces and sells 40,000 litres of the glue each month. This glue, which is known as MJ-7, is used in the wood industry in the manufacture of plywood. The selling price of MJ-7 is $35 per litre, variable expenses are $21 per litre, fixed manufacturing overhead costs in the plant total $230,000 per month, and the fixed selling costs total $310,000 per month.

Strikes in the mills that purchase the bulk of the MJ-7 glue have caused Hallas Company's sales to temporarily drop to only 11,000 litres per month. Hallas Company's management estimates that the strikes will last for about two months, after which sales of MJ-7 should return to normal. Due to the current low level of sales, however, Hallas Company's management is thinking about closing down the Northwest plant during the two months that the strikes are on.

If Hallas Company does close down the Northwest plant, it is estimated that fixed manufacturing overhead costs can be reduced to $170,000 per month and that fixed selling costs can be reduced by 10%. Start-up costs at the end of the shutdown period would total $14,000. Since Hallas Company uses JIT production methods, no inventories are on hand.

Required

1. Assuming that the strikes continue for two months, as estimated, would you recommend that Hallas Company close the Northwest plant? Show computations in good form to support your answer.
2. At what level of sales (in litres) for the two-month period would Hallas Company be indifferent between closing the plant or keeping it open? Show computations. (Hint: This is a type of break-even analysis, except that the fixed cost portion of your break-even computation should include only those fixed costs that are relevant [i.e., avoidable] over the two-month period.)

P13–17 Selected Relevant Cost Questions   Barker Company has a single product called a Zet. The company normally produces and sells 80,000 Zets each year at a selling price of $40 per unit. The company's unit costs at this level of activity are given below:

Direct materials.........................	$ 9.50
Direct labour...........................	10.00
Variable manufacturing overhead............	2.80
Fixed manufacturing overhead..............	5.00 ($400,000 total)
Variable selling expenses	1.70
Fixed selling expenses	4.50 ($360,000 total)
Total cost per unit.....................	$33.50

A number of questions relating to the production and sale of Zets are given below. Each question is independent.

Required

1. Assume that Barker Company has sufficient capacity to produce 100,000 Zets each year without any increase in fixed manufacturing overhead costs. The company could increase sales by 25% above the present 80,000 units each year if it were willing to increase the fixed selling expenses by $150,000. Would the increased fixed expenses be justified?

2. Assume again that Barker Company has sufficient capacity to produce 100,000 Zets each year. The company has an opportunity to sell 20,000 units in an overseas market. Import duties, foreign permits, and other special costs associated with the order would total $14,000. The only selling costs that would be associated with the order would be $1.50 per unit shipping cost. You have been asked by the president to compute the per unit break-even price on this order.

3. One of the materials used in the production of Zets is obtained from a foreign supplier. Civil unrest in the supplier's country has caused a cutoff in material shipments that is expected to last for three months. Barker Company has enough of the material on hand to continue to operate at 25% of normal levels for the three-month period. As an alternative, the company could close the plant down entirely for the three months. Closing the plant would reduce fixed overhead costs by 40% during the three-month period; the fixed selling costs would continue at two-thirds of their normal level while the plant was closed. What would be the dollar advantage or disadvantage of closing the plant for the three-month period?

4. The company has 500 Zets on hand that were produced last month and have small blemishes. Due to the blemishes, it will be impossible to sell these units at the regular price. If the company wishes to sell them through regular distribution channels, what unit cost figure is relevant for setting a minimum selling price?

5. An outside manufacturer has offered to produce Zets for Barker Company and to ship them directly to Barker's customers. If Barker Company accepts this offer, the facilities that it uses to produce Zets would be idle; however, fixed overhead costs would continue at 30% of their present level. Since the outside manufacturer would pay for all the costs of shipping, the variable selling costs would be reduced by 60%. Compute the unit cost figure that is relevant for comparison against whatever quoted price is received from the outside manufacturer.

P13–18 Discontinuance of a Store   Thrifty Markets, Inc., operates three stores in a large metropolitan area. The company's segmented income statement for the last quarter is given below.

THRIFTY MARKETS, INC.
Income Statement
For the Quarter Ended March 31

	Total	Uptown Store	Downtown Store	Westpark Store
Sales	$2,500,000	$900,000	$600,000	$1,000,000
Cost of goods sold	1,450,000	513,000	372,000	565,000
Gross margin	1,050,000	387,000	228,000	435,000

Operating expenses:
Selling expenses:

Direct advertising	118,500	40,000	36,000	42,500
General advertising*	20,000	7,200	4,800	8,000
Sales salaries	157,000	52,000	45,000	60,000
Delivery salaries	30,000	10,000	10,000	10,000
Store rent	215,000	70,000	65,000	80,000
Depreciation of store fixtures	46,950	18,300	8,800	19,850
Depreciation of delivery				
equipment	27,000	9,000	9,000	9,000
Total selling expenses	614,450	206,500	178,600	229,350
Administrative expenses:				
Store management salaries	63,000	20,000	18,000	25,000
General office salaries*	50,000	18,000	12,000	20,000
Utilities	89,800	31,000	27,200	31,600
Insurance on fixtures and inventory	25,500	8,000	9,000	8,500
Employment taxes	36,000	12,000	10,200	13,800
General office expenses—other*	25,000	9,000	6,000	10,000
Total administrative expenses	289,300	98,000	82,400	108,900
Total operating expenses	903,750	304,500	261,000	338,250
Net operating income (loss)	$ 146,250	$ 82,500	$ (33,000)	$ 96,750

*Allocated on the basis of sales dollars.

Management is very concerned about the Downtown Store's inability to show a profit, and consideration is being given to closing the store. The company has asked you to make a recommendation as to what course of action should be taken. The following additional information is available on the store:

a. The manager of the store has been with the company for many years; he would be retained and transferred to another position in the company if the store were closed. His salary is $6,000 per quarter.

b. The lease on the building housing the Downtown Store can be broken with no penalty.

c. The fixtures being used in the Downtown Store would be transferred to the other two stores if the Downtown Store were closed.

d. The company's employment taxes are 12% of salaries.

e. A single delivery crew serves all three stores. One delivery person could be discharged if the Downtown Store were closed; this person's salary is $3,000 per quarter. The delivery equipment would be distributed to the other stores. The equipment does not wear out through use, but it does eventually become obsolete.

f. One-third of the Downtown Store's insurance relates to its fixtures.

g. The general office salaries and other expenses relate to the general management of Thrifty Markets, Inc. The employee in the general office who is responsible for the Downtown Store's accounting records would be discharged if the store were closed. This employee's salary is $5,000 per quarter.

Required

1. Prepare a schedule showing the change in revenues and expenses and the impact on overall company net income that would result if the Downtown Store were closed.

2. Based on your computations in (1) above, what recommendation would you make to the management of Thrifty Markets, Inc.?

3. Assume that if the Downtown Store were closed, sales in the Uptown Store would increase by $200,000 per quarter due to loyal customers shifting their buying to the Uptown Store. The Uptown Store has ample capacity to handle the increased sales, and its gross profit rate is 43%. What effect would these factors have on your recommendation concerning the Downtown Store? Show computations.

P13–19 Breakeven; Eliminating an Unprofitable Line Mrs. Agatha Spencer-Atwood is managing director of the British company, Imperial Reflections, Ltd. The company makes reproductions of antique dressing room mirrors. Mrs. Spencer-Atwood would like guidance on the advisability of eliminating the Kensington line of mirrors. These mirrors have never been among the company's best-selling products, although their sales have been stable for many years.

Below is a condensed statement of operating income for the company and for the Kensington product line for the quarter ended June 30:

	Total Company	Kensington Product Line
Sales...	£5,000,000	£480,000
Cost of sales:		
Direct materials	420,000	32,000
Direct labour	1,600,000	200,000
Fringe benefits (30% of labour)......................	480,000	60,000
Variable manufacturing overhead	340,000	30,000
Building rent and maintenance	120,000	15,000
Depreciation...	80,000	10,000
Royalties (5% of sales)	250,000	24,000
Total cost of sales..............................	3,290,000	371,000
Gross margin	1,710,000	109,000
Selling and administrative expenses:		
Product-line managers' salaries	75,000	8,000
Sales commissions (10% of sales)	500,000	48,000
Fringe benefits (30% of salaries and commissions) ...	172,500	16,800
Shipping...	120,000	10,000
Advertising..	350,000	15,000
General administrative expenses	250,000	24,000
Total selling and administrative expenses	1,467,500	121,800
Net operating income (loss).........................	£ 242,500	£ (12,800)

The following additional data have been supplied by the company:

a. The company pays royalties to the owners of the original pieces of furniture from which the reproductions are copied.

b. All of the company's products are manufactured in the same facility and use the same equipment. The building rent and maintenance and the depreciation are allocated to products on the basis of direct labour dollars. The equipment does not wear out through use; rather it eventually becomes obsolete.

c. There is ample capacity to fill all orders.

d. Dropping the Kensington product line would have little (if any) effect on sales of other product lines.

e. All products are made to order, so there are no inventories.

f. Shipping costs are traced directly to the product lines.

g. Advertising costs are for ads to promote specific product lines. These costs have been traced directly to the product lines.

h. General administrative expenses are allocated to products on the basis of sales dollars. There would be no effect on the total general administrative expenses if the Kensington product line were dropped.

Required

1. Would you recommend that the Kensington product line be dropped, given the current level of sales? Prepare appropriate computations to support your answer.

2. What would sales of the Kensington product line have to be, at a minimum, to justify retaining the product line? (Hint: Set this up as a break-even problem in which only the relevant costs from requirement (1) above are considered. Assume costs are fixed or variable, as appropriate.)

P13–20 Sell or Process Further The Heather Honey Company purchases honeycombs from beekeepers for $4 per kilogram. The company produces two main products from the honeycombs—honey and beeswax. Honey is drained from the honeycombs, and then the honeycombs are melted down to form cubes of beeswax. The beeswax is sold for $3.00 per kilogram.

The honey can be sold in raw form for $2.80 per 500 gram bottle. However, some of the raw honey is used by the company to make honey drop candies. The candies are packed in a decorative container and are sold in gift and specialty shops. A container of honey drop candies sells for $3.80.

Each container of honey drop candies contains three quarters of a bottle of honey. The other variable costs associated with making the candies are as follows:

Decorative container.....................	$0.40
Other ingredients	0.25
Direct labour...........................	0.20
Variable manufacturing overhead...........	0.10
Total	$0.95

The monthly fixed manufacturing overhead costs associated with making the candies follow:

Master candy maker's salary.....................	$2,360
Depreciation of candy making equipment...........	400
Total.....................................	$2,760

The master candy maker has no duties other than to oversee production of the honey drop candies. The candy making equipment is special-purpose equipment that was constructed specifically to make this particular candy. The equipment has no resale value.

A salesperson is paid $1,000 per month plus a commission of 5% of sales to market the honey drop candies.

The company had enjoyed robust sales of the candies for several years, but the recent entrance of a competing product into the marketplace has depressed sales of the candies. The management of the company is now wondering whether it would be more profitable to sell all of the honey rather than converting some of it into candies.

Required

1. What is the incremental contribution margin per container from further processing the honey into candies?
2. What is the minimum number of containers of candy that must be sold each month to justify the continued processing of honey into candies? Show all computations in good form.

(CMA, heavily adapted)

P13–21 Accept or Reject Special Orders   Pietarsaari Oy, a Finnish company, produces cross-country ski poles that it sells for 32 mk a pair. (The Finnish unit of currency, the markka, is abbreviated as "mk.") Operating at capacity, the company can produce 50,000 pairs of ski poles a year. Costs associated with this level of production and sales are given below:

	Per Pair	Total
Direct materials.........................	12 mk	600,000 mk
Direct labour	3	150,000
Variable manufacturing overhead	1	50,000
Fixed manufacturing overhead	5	250,000
Variable selling expenses..................	2	100,000
Fixed selling expenses....................	4	200,000
Total cost...........................	27 mk	1,350,000 mk

Required

1. The Finnish army would like to make a one-time-only purchase of 10,000 pairs of ski poles for its mountain troops. The army would pay a fixed fee of 4 mk per pair, and in addition it would reimburse the Pietarsaari Oy company for its unit manufacturing costs (both fixed and variable). Due to a recession, the company would otherwise produce and sell only 40,000 pairs of ski poles this year. (Total fixed manufacturing overhead cost would be the same whether 40,000 pairs or 50,000 pairs of ski poles are produced.) The company would not incur its usual variable selling expenses with this special order.

    If the Pietarsaari Oy company accepts the army's offer, by how much would net operating income be increased or decreased from what they would be if only 40,000 pairs of ski poles were produced and sold during the year?

2. Assume the same situation as described in (1) above, except that the company is already operating at capacity and could sell 50,000 pairs of ski poles through regular channels. Thus, accepting the army's offer would require giving up sales of 10,000 pairs at the normal price of 32 mk a pair. If the army's offer is accepted, by how much will net operating income be increased or decreased from what it would be if the 10,000 pairs were sold through regular channels?

P13–22   Sell or Process Further   The joint process in which the Wedersen Co. is involved produces three separate products. The current estimated average cost of one batch of joint inputs is $1,000. Each of the products, Aferon, Beteron, and Ceteron, can be sold either at the split-off point or processed further and then sold. After the joint process, the processing of each product is independent of each other.

The manager of Wedersen has gathered the following information:

	Total	Variable Cost	Fixed But Avoidable with Shutdown of Process	Fixed, Not Avoidable with Shutdown of Process
Cost of joint process	$1,000	$600	$250	$150
Cost of separate process Aferon	40	30	8	2
Cost of separate process Beteron..........	60	40	15	5
Cost of separate process Ceteron..........	20	15	3	2

At the split-off point, Aferon can be sold for $450 or processed further at an incremental cost of $40 and then sold for $520.

At the split-off point, Beteron can be sold for $300 or processed further at an incremental cost of $60 and then sold for $350.

At the split-off point, Ceteron can be sold for $250 or processed further at an incremental cost of $20 and then sold for $265.

Required

1. Advise management of Wedersen whether they should sell the products at split-off, sell them in their fully processed form, discontinue production or employ some other course of action. See Note.
2. There is an opportunity for Wedersen to modify the units that result from the separate process Ceteron at an incremental cost of $140. These products (to be called Deteron) would be sold at a price of $400. Should Wedersen produce Deteron rather than Ceteron? Support your recommended courses of action with all relevant calculations.

(CGA-Canada, adapted)

P13–23   Break-Even Analysis and Relevant Costing   Humbug Enterprises produces electric motors. The following table shows the costs of manufacturing and marketing these electric motors at a normal volume of 2,500 motors per month. Each electric motor sells for $700. *The maximum production capacity is 4,000 motors per month.*

HUMBUG ENTERPRISES
Cost per unit for electric motors
Normal volume—2,500 per month

Manufacturing costs:		
Direct materials...	$75	
Direct labour..	125	
Variable overhead	20	
Fixed overhead	100	320
Marketing costs:		
Variable...	$30	
Fixed...	80	110
Total unit cost		$430

Required   The following questions are independent of each other *except where stated otherwise.*
1. Calculate the break-even point in units and in dollars.
2. The marketing research department of Humbug Enterprises believes that if the unit selling price is lowered to $630 that they could sell 3,200 motors. Would you recommend that the price be lowered to $630?
3. The National Defence Department wishes to purchase 600 motors during the month of May. The government is willing to pay a fixed fee of $240,000 plus reimbursement of all manufacturing costs incurred on behalf of the government in making the 600 motors. May is the busiest month for Humbug. During May Humbug's regular customers are willing to purchase 4,000 motors.

   On the government contract there will be no variable marketing costs.

   Should Humbug accept the government contract during May?

4. Humbug is trying to enter the Hong Kong market, where prices are very competitive. The company is trying to sell 1,000 motors in the months where there is idle capacity (not during May). Shipping costs will be $60 per unit, and the total costs of obtaining the contract will be $3,000.

   What is the minimum unit price Humbug should consider for this order of 1,000 motors? There will be no variable marketing costs.

5. Humbug has 300 units of an obsolete model in its warehouse. These will be sold through regular channels. What is the minimum selling price that Humbug should establish in selling these obsolete units? Give reasons for your answer.
6. An outside contractor has offered to supply 1,000 motors a month directly to Humbug's customers. Humbug's fixed marketing costs would be unaffected, its variable marketing costs would be reduced by 25% for these 1,000 motors. Its total fixed manufacturing costs would be reduced by 30%. The outside contractor is willing to do this for $310 per motor.

   Should Humbug accept this proposal?

7. Assume the same facts as in part (6) except that the idle facilities would be used to produce 750 special motors which would sell for $850 each. The variable manufacturing costs of these special motors would be $475 each, and the variable marketing costs would be $80 each. Fixed marketing and manufacturing costs would be unchanged whether the original 2,500 motors were manufactured or the mix of 1,500 regular motors plus 750 special motors were produced.

   Should the proposal be accepted for a price of $310 to the contractor?

(CGA-Canada, adapted)

P13–24   Economic Order Quantity, Safety Stock, and JIT Purchasing Impact
(Appendix 13A) Hillclimber, Inc. manufactures a four-wheeler, off-road vehicle. The company purchases one of the parts used in the manufacture of the vehicle from a supplier located in another province. In total, Hillclimber purchases 18,000 parts per year at a cost of $30 per part.

The parts are used evenly throughout the year in the production process on a 360-day-per-year basis. The company estimates that it costs $75 to place a single purchase order and about $1.20 to carry one part in inventory for a year.

Delivery from the supplier generally takes 9 days, but it can take as much as 13 days. The days of delivery time and the percentage of their occurrence are shown in the following tabulation:

Delivery Time (Days)	Percentage of Occurrence
9	70
10	12
11	6
12	6
13	6

Required

1. Compute the EOQ.
2. Assume that the company is willing to assume an 18% risk of being out of stock. What would be the safety stock? The reorder point?
3. Assume that the company is willing to assume only a 6% risk of being out of stock. What would be the safety stock? The reorder point?
4. Assume a 6% stock-out risk as stated in (3) above. What would be the total cost of ordering and carrying inventory for one year?
5. Refer to the original data. Assume that the company decides to adopt JIT purchasing policies, as stated in the chapter. This change allows the company to reduce its cost of placing a purchase order to only $6. Also, the company estimates that when the waste and inefficiency caused by inventories is considered, the true cost of carrying a unit in stock is $5.40 per year.
   a. Compute the new EOQ.
   b. How frequently would the company be placing an order, as compared to the old purchasing policy?
6. Using a computer spreadsheet and assuming a stock-out cost of $1.00 per unit, determine the optimal safety stock.

P13–25 Tabulation Approach, Economic Order Quantity, and Reorder Point (Appendix 13A) You have been engaged to install an inventory control system for Dexter Company. Among the inventory control features that Dexter desires in the system are indicators of "how much" to order "when." The following information is furnished for one item, called a *duosonic,* that is carried in inventory:

a. Duosonics are sold by the gross (12 dozen) at a list price of $500 per gross, FOB shipper. Dexter receives a 40% trade discount off list price on purchases in gross lots.
b. Freight cost is $20 per gross from the shipping point to Dexter's plant.
c. Dexter uses about 5,000 duosonics during a 259-day production year but must purchase a total of 36 gross per year to allow for normal breakage. Minimum and maximum usages are 12 and 28 duosonics per day, respectively.
d. Normal delivery time to receive an order is 20 working days from the date that a purchase request is initiated. A stock-out (complete exhaustion of the inventory) of duosonics would stop production, and Dexter would purchase duosonics locally at list price rather than shut down.
e. The cost of placing an order is $30.
f. Space storage cost is $24 per year per average gross in storage.
g. Insurance and taxes are approximately 12% of the net delivered cost of average inventory, and Dexter expects a return of at least 8% on its average investment. (Ignore ordering costs and carrying costs in making these computations.)

Required

1. Prepare a schedule computing the total annual cost of duosonics based on uniform order lot sizes of one, two, three, four, five, and six gross of duosonics. (The schedule should show the total annual cost according to each lot size.) Indicate the EOQ.
2. Prepare a schedule computing the minimum stock reorder point for duosonics. This is the point below which reordering is necessary to guard against a stock-out. Factors to be considered include average lead period usage and safety stock requirements.

(CPA, adapted)

P13–26 Economic Order Quantity, Safety Stock, and JIT Purchasing Impact (Appendix 13A) Stoffer Manufacturing Company uses 7,200 units of material X each year. The material is used evenly throughout th year in the company's production process. A recent cost study indicates that it costs $3.20 to carry one unit in stock for a year. The company estimates that the cost of placing an order for material X is $180.

On the average, it takes 7 days to receive an order from the supplier. Sometimes, orders do not arrive for 10 days, and at rare intervals (about 2% of the time) they do not arrive for 12 days. Each unit of material X costs the company $15. Stoffer works an average of 360 days per year.

Required

1   Compute the EOQ
2. What size safety stock would you recommend for material X? Why?
3. What is the reorder point for material X in units?
4. Compute the total cost associated with ordering and carrying material X in stock for a year. (Do *not* include the $15 purchase cost in this computation.)
5. Refer to the original data. Assume that as a result of adopting JIT purchasing policies, the company is able to reduce the cost of placing a purchase order to only $5. Also assume that after considering the waste and inefficiency caused by inventories, the actual cost of carrying one unit of material X in stock for a year is $18.
    a. Compute the new EOQ.
    b. How frequently would the company be placing a purchase order, as compared to the old purchasing policy?

P13–27   Integration of Purchases Budget, Reorder Point, and Safety Stock

(Appendix 13A) The Press Company manufactures and sells industrial components. The Whitmore Plant is responsible for producing two components. AD-5 and FX-3, Plastic, brass, and aluminum are used in the production of these two products.

Press Company has adopted a 13-period reporting cycle in all of its plants for budgeting purposes. Each period is four weeks long and has 20 working days. The projected inventory levels for AD-5 and FX-3 at the end of the current (seventh) period and the projected sales for these two products for the next three four-week periods are as follows:

| | | Projected Sales (in Units) | | |
| | Projected Inventory Level (in Units) End of 7th Period | 8 Period | 9 Period | 10 Period |
Component				
AD-5	3,000	7,500	8,750	9,500
FX-3.	2,800	7,000	4,500	4,000

Past experience has shown that adequate inventory levels for AD-5 and FX-3 can be maintained if 40% of the next period's projected sales are on hand at the end of a reporting period. Based on this experience and the projected sales, the Whitmore Plant has budgeted production of 8,000 units of AD-5 and 6,000 units of FX-3 in the eighth period. Production is assumed to be uniform for both products within each four-week period.

The raw material specifications for AD-5 an FX-3 are as follows:

	AD-5 (Kilograms)	FX-3 (Kilograms)
Plastic	2.0	1.0
Brass	0.5	—
Aluminum	—	1.5

Data relating to the purchase of raw materials are:

	Purchase Price per Kilogram	Standard Purchase Lot (Kilograms)	Reorder Point (Kilograms)	Projected Inventory Status at the End of the Seventh Period (Kilograms) On Hand	On Order	Lead Time in Working Days
Plastic	$0.40	15,000	12,000	16,000	15,000	10
Brass	0.95	5,000	7,500	9,000	—	30
Aluminum	0.55	10,000	10,000	14,000	10,000	20

The sales of AD-5 and FX-3 do not vary significantly from month to month. Consequently, the safety stock incorporated into the reorder point for each of the raw materials is adequate to compensate for variations in the sales of the finished products.

Raw material orders are placed the day the quantity on hand falls below the reorder point. Whitmore Plant's suppliers are very dependable so that the given lead times are reliable. The outstanding orders for plastic and aluminum are due to arrive on the 10th and 4th working days of the eighth period, respectively. Payments for all raw material orders are remitted in the month of delivery.

Required

Whitmore Plant is required to submit a report to corporate headquarters of Press Company summarizing the projected raw material activities before each period commences. The data for the eighth period report are being assembled. Determine the following items for plastic, brass, and aluminum for inclusion in the eighth period report:

1. Project quantities (in kilograms) of each raw material to be issued to production.
2. Projected quantities (in kilograms) of each raw material ordered and the date (in terms of working days) the order is to be placed.
3. The projected inventory balance (in kilograms) of each raw material at the end of the period.
4. The payments for purchases of each raw material.

(CMA, adapted)

P13–28 EOQ Computations (Appendix 13A) Sporting Goods Ltd. buys baseballs at $20 per dozen from its wholesaler. All purchase orders are authorized by the respective department managers who are paid weekly salaries of $600 to work 40 hours. On average, it takes a manager about 15 minutes to gather the information required to issue the purchase order. When not engaged in administrative duties, such as placing orders, hiring and scheduling staff, and attending meetings, the managers spend their time selling.

Once the purchase order information is gathered, it is typed onto a purchase order by a part-time employee hired on an hourly basis, at $12 per hour, to do typing. It takes this person 10 minutes to type the order. The order form costs $0.25 and mailing costs are $1.25.

When the order arrives, it is unloaded from the truck and placed in the stock room by the stock supervisor who is paid $12 per hour. It takes 20 minutes to unload and store each order. Rent, insurance, and taxes for each dozen baseballs in inventory amounts to $0.40 per year.

Sporting will sell about 36,000 dozen baseballs evenly throughout the year in its busy store where each salesperson generates weekly sales with a contribution margin of $2,000. In fact, the store is so busy that part-time staff, which is paid $10 per hour, is constantly used to help with sales.

Sporting desires a 10% return on any investment that it makes.

Required

1. What is the economic order quantity in dozens?
2. Assuming that Sporting ordered in order sizes of 800 dozen evenly throughout the year, what would be the total annual inventory expenses to sell 36,000 dozen baseballs?
3. Suppose that by streamlining its relationship with its supplier, Sporting can lower its total cost of placing each order to $1. What are the consequences of this reduction in order placing costs compared with the order size in (2)?

(CGA-Canada, adapted)

P13–29 Economic Order Quantity and Safety Stock (Appendix 13A) The Daffodil Co. Ltd. has obtained the following costs and other data pertaining to one of its raw materials.

> Working days per year, 250 days
> Normal use per day, 400 units
> Maximum use per day, 600 units
> Minimum use per day 100 units
> Lead time, 8 days
> Cost of placing one order, $20.00
> Carrying cost per unit per year, $0.30

You may need to use the following formula:

$$\sqrt{\frac{2QP}{C}}$$

Required

Compute the following:

1. Economic order quantity.
2. Safety stock.
3. Reorder point.
4. Normal maximum inventory.
5. Absolute minimum inventory.
6. Average inventory.
7. Assume use per day can occur with the following levels of chance.

Daily Demand	Probability
400..........	0.40
450..........	0.30
500..........	0.20
550..........	0.05
600..........	0.05

Stock-out costs are estimated to be $0.05 per unit. Determine the safety stock amount that minimizes the expected costs involved.

(CGA-Canada, adapted)

P13–30   Inventory of Perishable Products   (Appendix 13A) A newsstand receives its weekly order of *Glimpse* magazine on Monday and cannot reorder during the week. Each copy costs $0.90 and sells for $1.50. Unsold copies may be returned the following week for a $0.60 rebate. When the newsstand runs out of copies, the owner knows from past experience that customers will purchase *Glimpse* magazine elsewhere for an average of two weeks; therefore, the estimated goodwill loss for stock-outs is $1.20 per unsatisfied customer. Demand has been remarkably constant, ranging from 7 to 10 copies per week, as shown in the accompany table.

Demand (in copies)	7	8	9	10
Probability of time	0.03	0.04	0.20	0.10

Required

1. Determine the optimal number of copies to stock and the expected profit.
2. What is the expected opportunity loss from stocking seven copies?

(SMAC, adapted)

P13–31   Inventory of Perishable Products   (Appendix 13A) Bruno's Bakery stocks fresh baked doughnuts that sell for $6 per dozen and cost $4 per dozen to produce. Unsold day-old doughnuts are reduced in price to $3 per dozen and are always completely sold without affecting the current day's demand for fresh doughnuts. Bruno, the owner of the bakery, estimates daily demand characteristics for fresh doughnuts as follows:

Demand (Dozens)	Probability
20..........	0.1
22..........	0.2
24..........	0.3
26..........	0.3
28..........	0.1

Required

How many dozens of doughnuts should Bruno's Bakery produce each morning to maximize net income? Support your decision by preparing an appropriate payoff table.

(SMAC, adapted)

CASES

C13–32 Ethics and the Manager; Shut Down or Continue Operations

Marvin Braun had just been appointed vice president of the Atlantic Region of the Financial Services Corporation (FSC). The company provides cheque processing services for small banks. The banks send to FSC all cheques presented for deposit or payment. FSC then records the data on each cheque in a computerized database and sends the data electronically to the nearest chartered bank cheque clearing centre where the appropriate transfers of funds are made between banks. The Atlantic Region consists of three cheque processing centres in Moncton, Halifax, and St. John's. Prior to his promotion to vice president, Mr. Braun had been manager of a cheque processing centre in Ontario.

Immediately upon assuming his new position, Mr. Braun requested a complete financial report for the just-ended fiscal year from the region's controller, Lance Whiting. Mr. Braun specified that the financial report should follow the standardized format required by corporate headquarters for all regional performance reports. That report appears below:

Financial Performance
Great Basin Region

	Total	Moncton	Halifax	St. John's
		Cheque Processing Centres		
	Total	**Moncton**	**Halifax**	**St. John's**
Revenues........................	$20,000,000	$7,000,000	$8,000,000	$5,000,000
Operating expenses:				
Direct labour....................	12,200,000	4,400,000	4,700,000	3,100,000
Variable overhead	400,000	150,000	160,000	90,000
Equipment depreciation	2,100,000	700,000	800,000	600,000
Facility expenses.................	2,000,000	600,000	500,000	900,000
Local administrative expenses*	450,000	150,000	180,000	120,000
Regional administrative expenses†...	400,000	140,000	160,000	100,000
Corporate administrative expenses‡..	1,600,000	560,000	640,000	400,000
Total operating expenses.........	19,150,000	6,700,000	7,140,000	5,310,000
Net operating income	$ 850,000	$ 300,000	$ 860,000	$ (310,000)

*Local administrative expenses are the administrative expenses incurred at the cheque processing centres.

†Regional administrative expenses are allocated to the cheque processing centres based on sales revenues.

‡Corporate administrative expenses represent a standard 8% charge against revenues.

Upon seeing this report, Mr. Braun summoned Lance Whiting for an explanation.

BRAUN: What's the story on St. John's? It didn't have a loss the previous year, did it?

WHITING: No, the St. John's facility has had a nice profit every year since it was opened six years ago, but St. John's lost a big contract this year.

BRAUN: Why?

WHITING: One of our national competitors entered the local market and bid very aggressively on the contract. We couldn't afford to meet the bid. St. John's costs—particularly their facility expenses—are just too high. When St. John's lost the contract, we had to lay off a lot of employees, but we could not reduce the fixed costs of the St. John's facility.

BRAUN: Why is St. John's facility expense so high? It's a smaller facility than either Moncton or Halifax and yet its facility expense is higher.

WHITING: The problem is that we are able to rent suitable facilities very cheaply at Moncton and Halifax. No such facilities were available at St. John's, so we had them built. Unfortunately, there were big cost overruns. The contractor we hired was inexperienced at this kind of work and in fact went bankrupt before the project was completed. After hiring another contractor to finish the work, we were way over budget. The large depreciation charges on the facility didn't matter at first because we didn't have much competition at the time and could charge premium prices.

BRAUN: Well, we can't do that anymore. The St. John's facility will obviously have to be shut down. Its business can be shifted to the other two cheque processing centres in the region.

WHITING: I would advise against that. The $900,000 in depreciation charges on the St. John's facility are misleading. That facility should last indefinitely with proper maintenance. And it has no resale value; there is no other commercial activity around St. John's.

BRAUN: What about the other costs at St. John's?

WHITING: If we shifted St. John's business over to the other two processing centres in the region, we wouldn't save anything on direct labour or variable overhead costs. We might save $60,000 or so in local administrative expenses, but we would not save any regional administrative expense. And corporate headquarters would still charge us 8% of our revenues as corporate administrative expenses.

In addition, we would have to rent more space in Moncton and Halifax to handle the work transferred from St. John's; that would probably cost us at least $400,000 a year. And don't forget that it will cost us something to move the equipment from St. John's to Moncton and Halifax. And the move will disrupt service to customers.

BRAUN: I understand all of that, but a money-losing processing centre on my performance report is completely unacceptable.

WHITING: And if you do shut down St. John's, you are going to throw some loyal employees out of work.

BRAUN: That's unfortunate, but we have to face hard business realities.

WHITING: And you would have to write off the investment in the facilities at St. John's.

BRAUN: I can explain a write-off to corporate headquarters; hiring an inexperienced contractor to build the St. John's facility was my predecessor's mistake. But they'll have my head at headquarters if I show operating losses every year at one of my processing centres. St. John's has to go. At the next corporate board meeting, I am going to recommend that the St. John's facility be closed based on the loss in the financial performance report for the year.

Required

1. From the standpoint of the company as a whole, should the St. John's processing centre be shut down and its work redistributed to the other processing centres in the region? Explain.

2. Do you think Marvin Braun's decision to shut down the St. John's facility is ethical? Explain.

3. What influence should the depreciation on the facilities at St. John's have on prices charged by St. John's for its services?

C13–33   Decentralization and Relevant Costs   Whitmore Products consists of three decentralized divisions—Bayside Division, Cole Division, and Diamond Division. The president of Whitmore Products has given the managers of the three divisions the authority to decide whether they will sell to outside customers on the intermediate market or sell to other divisions within the company. The divisions are autonomous in that each divisional manager has power to set selling prices to outside customers and to set transfer prices to other divisions. (A transfer price is a price one division charges another division of the same company for a product or service it supplies to that division.) Each divisional manager is anxious to maximize his or her division's contribution margin.

To fill out capacity for the remainder of the current year, the manager of the Cole Division is considering two alternative orders. Data on the orders are provided below:

a. The Diamond Division is in need of 3,000 motors that can be supplied by the Cole Division at a transfer price of $2,000 per motor. To manufacture these motors, Cole would purchase component parts from the Bayside Division at a transfer price of $800 per part. (Each motor would require one part.) Bayside would incur variable costs for these parts of $400 each. In addition, each part would require 3.5 hours of machine time at a general fixed overhead rate of $40 per hour. Cole Division would then further process these parts and add other variable costs to the motors at a cost of $900 per motor. The motors would require seven hours of machine time each in Cole's plant at a general fixed overhead rate of $25 per hour.

If the Diamond Division can't obtain the motors from the Cole Division, it will purchase the motors from London Company, which has offered to supply the same motors to Diamond Division at a price of $2,000 per motor. To manufacture these motors, London Company would also have to purchase a component part from Bayside Division. This would be a different component part than that needed by the Cole Division. It would cost

Bayside $250 in variable cost to produce, and Bayside would sell it to London Company for $500 per part on an order of 3,000 parts. Because of its intricate design, this part would also require 3.5 hours of machine time to manufacture.

b.   The Wales Company wants to place an order with the Cole Division for 3,500 units of a motor that is similar to the motor needed by the Diamond Division. The Wales Company has offered to pay $1,800 per motor. To manufacture these motors, Cole Division would again have to purchase a component part from the Bayside Division. This part would cost Bayside Division $200 per part in variable cost to produce, and Bayside would sell it to Cole Division at a transfer price of $400 per part. This part would require three hours of machine time to manufacture in Bayside's plant. Cole Division would further process these parts and add other variable costs to the motors at a cost of $1,000 per motor. This work would require six hours of machine time per motor to complete.

The Cole Division's plant capacity is limited, and the division can accept only the order from the Diamond Division or the order from the Wales Company, but not both. The president of Whitmore Products and the manager of the Cole Division both agree that it would not be beneficial to increase capacity at this time.

Required

1.   If the manager of the Cole Division is anxious to maximize the division's profits, which order should be accepted—the order from the Diamond Division or the order from the Wales Company? Support your answer with appropriate computations.
2.   For the sake of discussion, assume that the Cole Division decides to accept the order from the Wales Company. Determine if this decision is in the best interests of Whitmore Products *as a whole*. Again support your answer with appropriate computations.

(CMA, heavily adapted)

C13–34 Sell or Process Further Decision   Midwest Mills has a plant that can either mill wheat grain into a cracked wheat cereal or further mill the cracked wheat into flour. The company can sell all the cracked wheat cereal that it can produce at a selling price of $490 per tonne. In the past, the company has sold only part of its cracked wheat as cereal and has retained the rest for further milling into the flour product. The flour has been selling for $700 per tonne, but recently the price has become unstable and has dropped to $625 per tonne. The costs and revenues associated with a tonne of flour follow:

		Per Tonne of Flour
Selling price.....................		$625
Cost to manufacture:		
Raw materials:		
Enrichment materials...........	$ 80	
Cracked wheat	470	
Total raw materials...........	550	
Direct labour	20	
Manufacturing overhead	60	630
Manufacturing profit (loss)		$ (5)

Because of the weak price for flour, the sales manager believes that the company should discontinue the milling of flour and concentrate its entire milling capacity on the milling of cracked wheat to sell as cereal. (The same milling equipment is used for both products.) Current cost and revenue data on the cracked wheat cereal follow:

		Per Tonne of Cracked Wheat
Selling price.....................		$490
Cost to manufacture:		
Wheat grain	$390	
Direct labour	20	
Manufacturing overhead	60	470
Manufacturing profit		$ 20

The sales manager argues that since the present $625 per tonne price for the flour results in a $5 per tonne loss, the milling of flour should be discontinued and should not be resumed until the price per tonne rises above $630.

The company assigns overhead cost to the two products on the basis of direct labour-hours. The same amount of time is required to either mill a tonne of cracked wheat or to further mill a tonne of cracked wheat into flour. Because of the nature of the plant, virtually all overhead costs are fixed. Materials and labour costs are variable.

Required

1. Do you agree with the sales manager that the company should discontinue milling flour and use the entire milling capacity to mill cracked wheat if the price of flour remains at $625 per tonne? Support your answer with appropriate comments and computations.

2. What is the lowest price that the company should accept for a tonne of flour? Again support your answer with appropriate comments and computations.

C13–35   Integrative Case: Relevant Costs; Pricing   Jenco, Inc., manufactures a combination fertilizer-weed killer under the name Fertikil. This is the only product that Jenco produces at present. Fertikil is sold nationwide through normal marketing channels to retail nurseries and garden stores.

Taylor Nursery plans to sell a similar fertilizer weed killer compound through its regional nursery chain under its own private label. Taylor does not have manufacturing facilities of its own, so it has asked Jenco (and several other companies) to submit a bid for manufacturing and delivering a 25,000-kilogram order of the private brand compound to Taylor. While the chemical composition of the Taylor compound differs from that of Fertikil, the manufacturing processes are very similar.

The Taylor compound would be produced in 1,000-kilogram lots. Each lot would require 60 direct labour-hours and the following chemicals:

Chemicals	Quantity in Kilograms
CW–3	400
JX–6	300
MZ–8	200
BE–7	100

The first three chemicals (CW–3, JX–6, and MZ–8) are all used in the production of Fertikil. BE–7 was used in another compound that Jenco discontinued several months ago. The supply of BE–7 that Jenco had on hand when the other compound was discontinued was not discarded. Jenco could sell its supply of BE–7 at the prevailing market price less $0.10 per kg selling and handling expenses.

Jenco also has on hand a chemical called CN–5, which was manufactured for use in another product that is no longer produced. CN–5, which cannot be used in Fertikil, can be substituted for CW–3 on a one-for-one basis without affecting the quality of the Taylor compound. The CN–5 in inventory has a salvage value of $500.

Inventory and cost data for the chemicals that can be used to produce the Taylor compound are as shown below:

Raw Material	Kg in Inventory	Actual Price per Kg When Purchased	Current Market Price per Kilogram
CW–3	22,000	$0.80	$0.90
JX–6	5,000	0.55	0.60
MZ–8	8,000	1.40	1.60
BE–7	4,000	0.60	0.65
CN–5	5,500	0.75	(Salvage)

The current direct labour rate is $7 per hour. The manufacturing overhead rate is established at the beginning of the year and is applied consistently throughout the year using direct labour-hours (DLH) as the base. The predetermined overhead rate for the current year, based on a two-shift capacity of 400,000 total DLH with no overtime, is as follows:

Variable manufacturing overhead	$2.25 per DLH
Fixed manufacturing overhead	3.75 per DLH
Combined rate	$6.00 per DLH

Jenco's production manager reports that the present equipment and facilities are adequate to manufacture the Taylor compound. Therefore, the order would have no effect on total fixed manufacturing overhead costs. However, Jenco is within 800 hours of its two-shift capacity this month before it must schedule overtime. If need be, the Taylor compound could be produced on regular time by shifting a portion of Fertikil production to overtime. Jenco's rate for overtime hours is 1½ times the regular pay rate, or $10.50 per hour. There is no allowance for any overtime premium in the manufacturing overhead rate.

Required

1. Assume that Jenco, Inc., has decided to submit a bid for a 25,000-kilogram order of Taylor's new compound. The order must be delivered by the end of the current month. Taylor has indicated that this is a one-time order that will not be repeated. Calculate the lowest price that Jenco could bid for the order without reducing its net income.
2. Refer to the original data. Assume that Taylor Nursery plans to place regular orders for 25,000-kg lots of the new compound during the coming year. Jenco expects the demand for Fertikil to remain strong again in the coming year. Therefore, the recurring orders from Taylor would put Jenco over its two-shift capacity. However, production could be scheduled so that 60% of each Taylor order could be completed during regular hours. As another option, some Fertikil production could be shifted temporarily to overtime so that the Taylor orders could be produced on regular time. Jenco's production manager has estimated that the prices of all chemicals will stabilize at the current market rates for the coming year; also, the variable and fixed overhead costs are expected to continue at the same rates per direct labour-hour.

   Jenco's standard markup policy for new products is 40% of the full manufacturing cost. Calculate the price that Jenco, Inc., would quote Taylor Nursery for each 25,000-kg lot of the new compound, assuming that it is to be treated as a new product.

(CMA, adapted)

C13–36 Economic Order Quantity Computations   (Appendix 13A) SaPane Company is a regional distributor of automobile window glass. With the introduction of the new subcompact car models and the expected high level of consumer demand, management recognizes a need to determine the total inventory cost associated with maintaining an optimal supply of replacement windshields for the new subcompact cars introduced by each of the three major manufacturers. SaPane is expecting a daily demand for 36 windshields. The purchase price of each windshield is $50.

Other costs associated with ordering and maintaining an inventory of these windshields are as follows:

a. The historical ordering costs incurred in the purchase order department for placing and processing orders are shown below:

Year	Orders Placed and Processed	Total Ordering Costs
1995.	20	$12,300
1996.	55	12,475
1997.	100	12,700

Management expects the ordering costs to increase 16% over the amounts and rates experienced during the last three years.

b. The windshield manufacturer charges SaPane a $75 shipping fee per order.
c. A clerk in the receiving department receives, inspects, and secures the windshields as they arrive from the manufacturer. This activity requires eight hours per order received. This

clerk has no other responsibilities and is paid at the rate of $9 per hour. Related variable overhead costs in this department are applied at the rate of $2.50 per hour.

d. Additional warehouse space will have to be rented to store the new windshields. Space can be rented as needed in a public warehouse at an estimated cost of $2,500 per year plus $5.25 per windshield.

e. Breakage cost is estimated to be 6% of the cost per windshield.

f. Taxes and fire insurance on the inventory are $1.15 per windshield.

g. The desired rate of return on the investment in inventory is 21% of the purchase price.

Six working days are required from the time an order is placed with the manufacturer until it is received. SaPane uses a 300-day workyear when making economic order quantity computations.

Required

Calculate the following values for SaPane Company.

1. Value for ordering cost that should be used in the EOQ formula.
2. Value for storage cost that should be used in the EOQ formula.
3. Economic order quantity.
4. Minimum annual cost as the economic order quantity point.
5. Reorder point in units.

(CMA, adapted)

GROUP EXERCISES

GE13–37 What's the Cost?   Nearly 70 years ago, eminent economist J. Maurice Clarke stated that "accountants use different costs because of their differing objectives." The business world has certainly become a lot more complicated since Professor Clarke's insightful comment. Management accountants today are expected to be a lot more conversant and knowledgeable about business operations. They are expected to add value to their company by their ability to bring the right information to bear on a decision. To do that, management accountants must be able to identify, analyze, and help solve problems. They have to operationalize Professor Clarke's statement.

Required

1. What are the different uses for accounting information? That is, for what purposes or functions is cost information used? Try to identify as many uses as you can and then try to group similar or related uses under some common heading, for example, external reporting.
2. Define each of the following cost or revenue concepts and give examples of decisions or situations where the concept would be used.
    a. Sunk cost.
    b. Avoidable cost.
    c. Opportunity cost.
    d. Joint cost.
    e. Contribution margin per unit of scarce resource.

GE13–38 Outsourcing May Be Hazardous to Your Health   Outsourcing, when a company contracts with third parties to produce some of its parts or products, has become commonplace among North American manufacturers. Thirty years ago, when direct labour costs were lower and factories were a lot less complex, factory burden rates of $0.50 or less per dollar of direct labour were deemed reasonable. But today, overhead burden rates of 500% of direct labour are common, and rates of 1,000% or more are not unusual. As a result, outsourcing has gained widespread acceptance over the past 15 years. Products with high direct labour content are especially susceptible to being outsourced to parts of the world where labour rates are a lot less than they are in North America.

Required

1. What is the meaning of manufacturing overhead rates of 500% or more of direct labour?
2. What implications do such high burden rates hold for products high in direct labour content?

3. If products with a high direct labour content are outsourced to low-wage areas of Canada or to less-developed, low-wage foreign countries, what impact will that have on the cost structure of the company? Please cite specific categories of costs affected by the outsourcing strategy.
4. What happens to the costs of the remaining products when a product is outsourced?
5. Can you think of any drawbacks to outsourcing in a less-developed foreign land or any limitations to a strategy dependent on labour cost savings?
6. Continuing with the line of thinking developed in (1)–(3), what happens next?

GE13–39 Productivity Paradox   In an award-winning article, Wickham Skinner wondered why " 'American manufacturers' near-heroic efforts to regain a competitive edge through productivity improvements have been disappointing." Why has the payoff from spending so much on productivity-enhancing programs amounted to so little? Skinner offers some insight into why so many productivity programs fail to produce the anticipated results. One of those insights is the "40/40/20" rule. Production experience regularly observes that approximately 40% of any competitive advantage derives from basic approaches to materials and workforce management and long-term changes in manufacturing structure—decisions concerning number, size, location, and capacity of facilities. Another 40% is the result of changes in equipment and process technology. And the final 20% comes from conventional approaches to productivity improvement. Source: Wickham Skinner, "The Productivity Paradox," *Harvard Business Review* (July–August 1986), pp. 55–59.

Required

1. From your study of Chapters 9–11, what do you think Skinner means by conventional approaches to productivity improvement?
2. Why do you think trying to wring additional productivity improvements from this area has restored no more than 20% of the competitive health of most firms?
3. If manufacturers were to focus on the 40% that derives from basic approaches to materials and workforce management, discuss this opportunity by contrasting traditional approaches and innovative ideas in these areas.
4. The other major opportunity for productivity improvements can be derived by making necessary investments in equipment and process technology. Is this nothing more than an investment in labour-replacing automation or is there something more to it than this? Explain.

GE13–40 We Have Seen the Enemy and He Is Us   It has been said that the true test of a manager's skill is how well he or she manages during times of distress. If that is the case, then economic recessions must present some real opportunities to show one's mettle as a manager. While some administrators always seem to be managing as if the next downturn were just around the corner, most would be guilty of not reacting soon enough and then overreacting when they do act.

Required

Following is a list of actions typically taken by experienced managers during recessions. These actions have usually failed to remedy the situation and may have made the circumstances worse. For each action, discuss the action's drawbacks and then offer suggestions about what actions could be taken to improve the company's overall competitive position—keeping in mind that this is a recession and funds are relatively scarce and expensive.

1. It's fair to "share the pain" and make cuts across the board.
2. Negotiate more aggressively with suppliers and try to get further price concessions.
3. Delay all major projects.
4. Please all customers at any cost.

14

CAPITAL BUDGETING DECISIONS

LEARNING OBJECTIVES

After studying Chapter 14, you should be able to:

1 Distinguish between capital budgeting screening and preference decisions, and identify the key characteristics of business investments.

2 Determine the acceptability of an investment project using the net present value method.

3 Enumerate the typical cash inflows and cash outflows that might be associated with an investment project, and explain how they would be used in a present value analysis.

4 Determine the acceptability of an investment project using the internal rate of return method (with interpolation, if needed).

5 Explain how the cost of capital is used as a screening tool.

6 Prepare a net present value analysis of two competing investment projects using either the incremental-cost approach or the total-cost approach.

7 Make a capital budgeting analysis involving automated equipment.

8 Determine the payback period for an investment using the payback formula.

9 Compute the simple rate of return for an investment using the simple rate of return formula.

10 Define or explain key terms listed at the end of the chapter.

11 (Appendix 14A) Explain the concept of present value, and make present value computations with and without the present value tables.

When evaluating large real estate
investments, such as office buildings in
a major metropolitan area, many
uncertainties must be considered:
interest rates, occupancy, and
construction costs to name just a few.

The term **capital budgeting** is used to describe actions relating to the planning and financing of capital outlays for such purposes as the purchase of new equipment, the introduction of new product lines, and the modernization of plant facilities. As such, capital budgeting decisions are a key factor in the long-run profitability of a firm. This is particularly true in situations where a firm has only limited investment funds available but has almost unlimited investment opportunities to choose from. The long-run profitability of the firm will depend on the skill of the manager in choosing those uses for limited funds that will provide the greatest return. This selection process is complicated by the fact that most investment opportunities are long term in nature, and the future is often hard to predict.

To make wise investment decisions, managers need tools that will guide them in comparing the relative advantages and disadvantages of various investment alternatives. We are concerned in this chapter with gaining understanding and skill in the use of such tools.

CAPITAL BUDGETING—AN INVESTMENT CONCEPT

OBJECTIVE 1

Distinguish between capital budgeting screening and preference decisions, and identify the key characteristics of business investments.

Capital budgeting is an *investment* concept, since it involves a commitment of funds now in order to receive some desired return in the future. When speaking of investments, one is inclined to think of a commitment of funds to purchase corporate shares and bonds. This is just one type of investment, however. The commitment of funds by a business to purchase inventory or equipment is also an investment. For example, Canadian Tire makes an investment when it opens a new store. McCain Food makes an investment when it installs a new computer to handle customer billing. Petro-Canada makes an investment when it expands exploration and development in Western Canada, Algeria and Norway. With a combination of private and public funding, Canadian universities such as the University of British Columbia, University of Toronto, McGill and Dalhousie make substantial investments in medical research in the search for new drugs and medical therapies. All of these investments are characterized by a commitment of funds today in the expectation of receiving a return in the future in the form of additional cash inflows or reduced cash outflows.

Typical Capital Budgeting Decisions

What types of business decisions require capital budgeting analysis? Virtually any decision that involves an outlay now in order to obtain some return (increase in revenue or reduction in costs) in the future. Typical capital budgeting decisions encountered by the manager are the following:

1. Cost reduction decisions. Should new equipment be purchased in order to reduce costs?
2. Plant expansion decisions. Should a new plant, warehouse, or other facility be acquired in order to increase capacity and sales?
3. Equipment selection decisions. Which of several available machines would be the most cost effective to purchase?
4. Lease or buy decisions. Should new plant facilities be leased or purchased?
5. Equipment replacement decisions. Should old equipment be replaced now or later?

Capital budgeting decisions tend to fall into two broad categories—*screening decisions* and *preference decisions*. **Screening decisions** are those relating to whether a proposed project meets some present standard of acceptance. For example, a firm may have a policy of accepting cost reduction projects only if they promise a return of, say, 20% before taxes.

Preference decisions, by contrast, relate to selecting from among several *competing* courses of action. To illustrate, a firm may be considering five different machines to replace an existing machine on the assembly line. The choice of which machine to purchase is a *preference* decision.

In this chapter, we discuss ways of making screening decisions. Preference decisions are discussed in the following chapter.

Characteristics of Business Investments

Most business investments have two key characteristics: (1) they involve *depreciable assets* and (2) the returns they provide extend over long periods of time.

Depreciable Assets.   An important feature of depreciable assets is that they generally have little or no resale value at the end of their useful lives. By contrast, the original sum invested in a *non*depreciable asset can be fully recovered when the project terminates. For example, if a firm purchases land (a nondepreciable asset) for $5,000 and rents it out at $750 a year for 10 years, at the end of the 10-year term the land will still be intact and should be salable for at least its purchase price. The computation of the rate of return on such an investment is fairly simple. Since the asset (the land) will still be intact at the end of the 10-year period, each year's $750 inflow is a return *on* the original $5,000 investment. The rate of return is therefore a straight 15% ($750 ÷ $5,000).

Computation of the rate of return on *depreciable* assets is more difficult, since the assets are "used up," so to speak, over their useful lives. Thus, any returns provided by such assets must be sufficient to do two things:

1.   Provide a return *on* the original investment.
2.   Return the total amount *of* the original investment itself.

To illustrate, assume that the $5,000 investment above was made in equipment rather than in land. Also assume that the equipment will reduce the firm's operating costs by $750 each year for 10 years. Is the return on the equipment a straight 15%, the same as it was on the land? The answer is no. The return promised by the equipment is much less than the return promised by the land. The reason is that part of the yearly $750 inflow from the equipment *must go to recoup the original $5,000 investment itself, since the equipment will be worthless at the end of its 10-year life.* Only what remains *after* recovery of this investment can be viewed as a return *on* the investment over the 10-year period.

The Time Value of Money.   As stated earlier, another common characteristic of business investments is that they promise returns that are likely to extend over fairly long periods of time. Therefore, in approaching capital budgeting decisions, it is necessary to employ techniques that recognize *the time value of money*. Any manager would rather receive a dollar today than a year from now. The same concept applies in choosing between investment projects. Those that promise returns earlier in time are preferable to those that promise returns later in time.

The capital budgeting techniques that recognize the above two characteristics of business investments most fully are those that involve *discounted cash flows*. We will spend most of this chapter illustrating the use of discounted cash flow methods in making capital budgeting decisions. If you are not already familiar with discounting and the use of present value tables, you should study Appendix 14A, The Concept of Present Value, at the end of this chapter before proceeding any further.

DISCOUNTED CASH FLOWS—THE NET PRESENT VALUE METHOD

There are two approaches to making capital budgeting decisions by means of discounted cash flow. One is the *net present value method,* and the other is the *internal rate of return method* (sometimes called the *time-adjusted rate of return method*). The net present value method is discussed in this section; the internal rate of return method is discussed in the next section.

The Net Present Value Method Illustrated

OBJECTIVE 2
Determine the acceptability of an investment project using the net present value method.

Under the net present value method, the present value of all cash inflows is compared to the present value of all cash outflows that are associated with an investment project. The difference between the present value of these cash flows, called the **net present value,** determines whether or not the project is an acceptable investment. To illustrate, let us assume the following data:

Example A

Harper Company is contemplating the purchase of a machine capable of performing certain operations that are now performed manually. The machine will cost $5,000, and it will last for five years. At the end of the five-year period, the machine will have a zero scrap value. Use of the machine will reduce labour costs by $1,800 per year. Harper Company requires a minimum return of 20% before taxes on all investment projects.[1]

Should the machine be purchased? To answer this question, it will be necessary first to isolate the cash inflows and cash outflows associated with the proposed project. To keep the example free of unnecessary complications, we have assumed only one cash inflow and one cash outflow. The cash inflow is the $1,800 annual reduction in labour costs. The cash outflow is the $5,000 initial investment in the machine.

The investment decision: Harper Company must determine whether a cash investment now of $5,000 can be justified if it will result in an $1,800 reduction in cost each year over the next five years, assuming that the company can get a 20% return on its money invested elsewhere.

---

[1]For simplicity, we assume in this chapter and in the next chapter that there is no inflation. The impact of inflation on discounted cash flow analysis is discussed in Appendix 14B to this chapter. Also, in this chapter we do not consider the matter of income taxes. The impact of income taxes on capital budgeting decisions will be covered in the next chapter.

EXHIBIT 14–1

Net Present Value
Analysis of a
Proposed Project

Initial cost.			$5,000	
Life of the project (years). . . .			5	
Annual cost savings			$1,800	
Salvage value			–0–	
Required rate of return			20%	

Item	Year(s)	Amount of Cash Flow	20% Factor	Present Value of Cash Flows
Annual cost savings	1–5	$ 1,800	2.991*	$5,384
Initial investment	Now	(5,000)	1.000	(5,000)
Net present value				$ 384

*From Table 14C–4 in Appendix 14C at the end of this chapter.

To determine whether the investment is desirable, it will be necessary to discount the stream of annual $1,800 cost reductions to its present value and to compare this discounted present value with the cost of the new machine. Since Harper Company requires a minimum return of 20% on all investment projects, we will use this rate in the discounting process. Exhibit 14–1 gives a net present value analysis of the desirability of purchasing the machine.

According to the analysis, Harper Company should purchase the new machine. The present value of the cost savings is $5,384, as compared to a present value of only $5,000 for the investment required (cost of the machine). Deducting the present value of the investment required from the present value of the cost savings gives a *net present value* of $384. Whenever the net present value is zero or greater, as in our example, an investment project is acceptable. Whenever the net present value is negative (the present value of the cash outflows exceeds the present value of the cash inflows), an investment project is not acceptable. In sum,

If the Net Present Value Is . . .	Then the Project Is . . .
Positive	Acceptable, since it promises a return greater than the required rate of return.
Zero	Acceptable, since it promises a return equal to the required rate of return.
Negative.	Not acceptable, since it promises a return less than the required rate of return.

A full interpretation of the solution would be as follows: The new machine promises slightly more than the required 20% rate of return. This is evident from the positive net present value of $384. Harper Company could spend up to $5,384 for the new machine and still obtain the 20% rate of return it desires. The net present value of $384, therefore, shows the amount of "cushion" or "margin of error" that the company has in estimating the cost of the new machine. Alternatively, it also shows the amount of error that can exist in the present value of the cost savings, with the project remaining acceptable. That is, if the present value of the cost savings were only $5,000 rather than $5,384, the project would still promise the required 20% rate of return.

Emphasis on Cash Flows

OBJECTIVE 3

Enumerate the typical cash inflows and cash outflows that might be associated with an investment project, and explain how they would be used in a present value analysis.

In capital budgeting decisions, the focus is on cash flows and not on accounting net income. The reason is that accounting net income is based on accrual concepts that ignore the timing of cash flows into and out of an organization. From a capital budgeting standpoint the timing of cash flows is important, since a dollar received today is more valuable than a dollar received in the future. Therefore, even though the accounting net income figure is useful for many things, it is not used in discounted cash flow analysis. Instead of determining accounting net income, the manager must concentrate on identifying the specific cash flows associated with various investment projects and on determining when these cash flows will take place.

In considering an investment project, what kinds of cash flows should the manager look for? Although the specific cash flows will vary from project to project, certain types of cash flows tend to recur as explained in the following paragraphs.

Typical Cash Outflows.   In most projects, there will be an immediate cash outflow in the form of an initial investment in equipment or other assets. Any salvage value realized from the sale of old equipment can be recognized as a cash inflow or as a reduction in the required investment. In addition, some projects require that a company expand its working capital. **Working capital** is the amount of current assets (cash, accounts receivable, and inventory) in excess of current liabilities that is available to meet day-to-day operating needs. When a company takes on a new project, the balances in the current asset accounts will often increase. For example, opening a new Eaton's department store would require additional cash to operate sales registers, increased accounts receivable to carry new customers, and more inventory to stock the shelves. Any such incremental working capital needs should be treated as part of the initial investment in a project. Also, many projects require periodic outlays for repairs and maintenance and for additional operating costs. These should all be treated as cash outflows for capital budgeting purposes.

Typical Cash Inflows.   On the cash inflow side, a project will normally either increase revenues or reduce costs. Either way, the amount involved should be treated as a cash inflow for capital budgeting purposes. (In regard to this point, notice that so far as cash flows are concerned, a *reduction in costs is equivalent to an increase in revenues.*) Cash inflows are also frequently realized from salvage of equipment when a project is terminated. In addition, upon termination of a project, any working capital that is released for use elsewhere should be treated as a cash inflow. Working capital is released, for example, when a company sells off its inventory, collects its receivables, and has the funds available for investment elsewhere. (If the released working capital is not shown as a cash inflow at the termination of a project, then the project will go on being charged for the use of the funds forever!)

In summary, the following types of cash flows are common in business investment projects:

> Cash outflows:
> Initial investment (including installation costs).
> Increased working capital needs.
> Repairs and maintenance.
> Incremental operating costs.
>   Cash inflows:
> Incremental revenues.
> Reduction in costs.
> Salvage value.
> Release of working capital.

Recovery of the Original Investment

When first introduced to present value analysis, students are often surprised by the fact that depreciation is not deducted in computing the present value of a project. There are two reasons for not deducting depreciation.

First, depreciation is an accounting concept not involving a current cash outflow.[2] As discussed above, discounted cash flow methods of making capital budgeting decisions focus on *flows of cash*. Although depreciation is a vital concept in computing accounting net income for financial statement purposes, it is not relevant in an analytical framework that focuses on flows of cash.

A second reason for not deducting depreciation is that discounted cash flow methods *automatically* provide for return of the original investment, thereby making a deduction for depreciation unnecessary. To demonstrate this point, let us assume the following data:

Example B

Carver Dental Clinic is considering the purchase of an attachment for its X-ray machine that will cost $3,170. The attachment will be usable for four years, after which time it will have no salvage value. It is estimated that the attachment will increase net cash inflows by $1,000 per year in the X-ray department. The clinic's board of directors has instructed that no investments are to be made unless they promise an annual return of at least 10%.

A present value analysis of the desirability of purchasing the attachment is presented in Exhibit 14–2. Notice that the attachment promises exactly a 10% return on the original investment, since the net present value is zero at a 10% discount rate.

Each annual $1,000 cash inflow arising from use of the attachment is made up of two parts. One part represents a recovery of a portion of the original $3,170 paid for the attachment, and the other part represents a return *on* this investment. The breakdown of each year's $1,000 cash inflow between recovery *of* investment and return *on* investment is shown in Exhibit 14–3.

EXHIBIT 14-2

Carver Dental Clinic—Net Present Value Analysis of X-Ray Attachment

Initial cost	$3,170
Life of the project (years)	4
Annual net cash inflow	$1,000
Salvage value	–0–
Required rate of return	10%

Item	Year(s)	Amount of Cash Flow	10% Factor	Present Value of Cash Flows
Annual net cash inflow	1–4	$ 1,000	3.170*	$ 3,170
Initial investment	Now	(3,170)	1.000	(3,170)
Net present value				$ –0–

*From Table 14C–4 in Appendix 14C.

---

[2]Although depreciation itself does not involve a cash outflow, it does have an effect on cash outflows for income taxes. Technically Revenue Canada does not permit the deduction of depreciation. Instead it allows businesses to deduct what is known as capital cost allowance. We shall take a look at this effect in the following chapter when we discuss the impact of income taxes on management planning.

EXHIBIT 14–3

Carver Dental
Clinic—
Breakdown of
Annual Cash Inflows

Year	(1) Investment Outstanding during the Year	(2) Cash Inflow	(3) Return on Investment (1) × 10%	(4) Recovery of Investment during the Year (2) – (3)	(5) Unrecovered Investment at the End of the Year (1) – (4)
1.............	$3,170	$1,000	$317	$ 683	$2,487
2.............	2,487	1,000	249	751	1,736
3.............	1,736	1,000	173	827	909
4.............	909	1,000	91	909	–0–
Total investment recovered.....				$3,170	

The first year's $1,000 cash inflow consists of a $317 interest return (10%) *on* the $3,170 original investment, plus a $683 return *of* that investment. Since the amount of the unrecovered investment decreases over the four years, the dollar amount of the interest return also decreases. By the end of the fourth year, all $3,170 of the original investment has been recovered.

Simplifying Assumptions

In working with discounted cash flows, at least two limiting assumptions are usually made. The first is that all cash flows occur at the end of a period. This is somewhat unrealistic in that cash flows typically occur somewhat uniformly *throughout* a period. The purpose of this assumption is just to simplify computations.

The second assumption is that all cash flows generated by an investment project are immediately reinvested in another project. It is further assumed that the second project will yield a rate of return at least as large as the discount rate used in the first project. Unless these conditions are met, the return computed for the first project will not be accurate. To illustrate, we used a discount rate of 10% for the Carver Dental Clinic in Exhibit 14–2. Unless the funds released each period are immediately reinvested in another project yielding at least a 10% return, the net present value computed for the X-ray attachment will be overstated.

Choosing a Discount Rate

In using the net present value method, it is necessary to choose some rate of return for discounting cash flows to present value. In Example A we used a rate of return of 20% before taxes, and in Example B we used a rate of return of 10%. These rates were chosen somewhat arbitrarily simply for the sake of illustration.

As a practical matter, firms put much time and study into the choice of a discount rate. The rate generally viewed as being most appropriate is a firm's *cost of capital*. A firm's cost of capital is not simply the interest rate that it must pay for long-term debt. Rather, **cost of capital** is a broad concept, involving a blending of the costs of *all* sources of investment funds, both debt and equity. The mechanics involved in cost of capital computations are covered in finance texts and will not be considered here. The cost of capital is known by various names. It is sometimes called the **hurdle rate,** the **cutoff rate,** or the **required rate of return.**

Most finance specialists would agree that a before-tax cost of capital of 16–20% would be typical for an average industrial corporation. The appropriate after-tax figure would depend on the corporation's tax circumstances, but it would probably average around 10–12%. Among the top Canadian wealth producers, this cost of capital is comparatively high. For example, Barrick Gold Corp's 16.6% cost of capital, and Placer Dome Inc's 17.2% well outpace the 11% average cost of 300 ranked Canadian companies.[3]

An Extended Example of the Net Present Value Method

To conclude our discussion of the net present value method, we present below an extended example of how it is used in analyzing an investment proposal. This example will also help to tie together (and to reinforce) many of the ideas developed thus far.

Example C

Under a special licensing arrangement, Swinyard Company has an opportunity to market a new product in Western Canada for a five-year period. The product would be purchased from the manufacturer, with Swinyard Company responsible for all costs of promotion and distribution. The licensing arrangement could be renewed at the end of the five-year period at the option of the manufacturer. After careful study, Swinyard Company has estimated that the following costs and revenues would be associated with the new product:

Cost of equipment needed	$ 60,000
Working capital needed	100,000
Overhaul of the equipment in four years	5,000
Salvage value of the equipment in five years	10,000
Annual revenues and costs:	
Sales revenues	200,000
Cost of goods sold	125,000
Out-of-pocket operating costs (for salaries,	
advertising, and other direct costs)	35,000

At the end of the five-year period, the working capital would be released for investment elsewhere if the manufacturer decided not to renew the licensing arrangement. Swinyard Company's cost of capital is 20%. Would you recommend that the new product be introduced? Ignore income taxes.

This example involves a variety of cash inflows and cash outflows. The solution is given in Exhibit 14–4.

Notice particularly how the working capital is handled in this exhibit. It is counted as a cash outflow at the beginning of the project and as a cash inflow when it is released at the end of the project. Also notice how the sales revenues, cost of goods sold, and out-of-pocket costs are handled. **Out-of-pocket costs** are actual cash outlays made during the period for salaries, advertising, and other operating expenses. Depreciation would not be an out-of-pocket cost, since it involves no current cash outlay.

Since the overall net present value is positive, the new product should be added, assuming that there is no better use for the investment funds involved.

---

[3]"The Financial Post MVA List," *The Financial Post,* June 22/24, 1996, pp. 43–47.

EXHIBIT 14-4

The Net Present
Value Method—An
Extended Example

		Sales revenues	$200,000	
		Less cost of goods sold.	125,000	
		Gross margin	75,000	
		Less out-of-pocket costs for		
		salaries, advertising, etc..	35,000	
		Annual net cash inflows	$ 40,000	

Item	Year(s)	Amount of Cash Flow	20% Factor	Present Value of Cash Flows
Purchase of equipment	Now	$ (60,000)	1.000	$(60,000)
Working capital needed.	Now	(100,000)	1.000	(100,000)
Overhaul of equipment	4	(5,000)	0.482*	(2,410)
Annual net cash inflows from				
sales of the product line	1–5	40,000	2.991†	119,640
Salvage value of the equipment . .	5	10,000	0.402*	4,020
Working capital released.	5	100,000	0.402*	40,200
Net present value.				$ 1,450

*From Table 14C–3 in Appendix 14C.

*From Table 14C–4 in Appendix 14C.

DISCOUNTED CASH FLOWS—THE INTERNAL RATE OF RETURN METHOD

OBJECTIVE 4
Determine the
acceptability of an
investment project
using the internal rate
of return method (with
interpolation, if
needed).

The **internal rate of return** (or **time-adjusted rate of return**) can be defined as the interest yield promised by an investment project over its useful life. It is sometimes referred to simply as the **yield** on a project. The internal rate of return is computed by finding the discount rate that equates the present value of a project's cash outflows with the present value of its cash inflows. In other words, the internal rate of return is that discount rate that will cause the net present value of a project to be equal to zero.

The Internal Rate of Return Method Illustrated

Finding a project's internal rate of return can be very helpful to a manager in making capital budgeting decisions. To illustrate, let us assume the following data:

Example D
Glendale School District is considering the purchase of a large tractor-pulled lawn mower. At present, the lawn is mowed using a small hand-pushed gas mower. The large, tractor-pulled mower will cost $16,950 and will have a life of 10 years. It will have only a negligible scrap value, which can be ignored. The tractor-pulled mower would do the job much more quickly than the old mower and would result in a labour savings of $3,000 per year.

To compute the internal rate of return promised by the new mower, it will be necessary to find the discount rate that will cause the net present value of the project to be zero. How do we do this? The simplest and most direct approach when the net cash inflow is the same every year is to divide the investment in the project by the expected net annual cash inflow. This computation will yield a factor from which the internal rate of return can be determined. The formula is as follows:

$$\text{Factor of the internal rate of return} = \frac{\text{Investment required}}{\text{Net annual cash inflow}} \qquad (1)$$

The factor derived from formula (1) is then located in the present value tables to see what rate of return it represents. We will now perform these computations for Glendale School District's proposed project. Using formula (1), we get:

$$\frac{\text{Investment required}}{\text{Net annual cash inflow}} = \frac{\$16,950}{\$3,000} = 5.650$$

Thus, the discount factor that will equate a series of $3,000 cash inflows with a present investment of $16,950 is 5.650. Now we need to find this factor in Table 14C–4 in Appendix 14C to see what rate of return it represents. If we refer to Table 14C–4 and scan along the 10-period line, we find that a factor of 5.650 represents a 12% rate of return. Therefore, the internal rate of return promised by the mower project is 12%. We can verify this by computing the project's net present value using a 12% discount rate. This computation is made in Exhibit 14–5.

Notice from Exhibit 14–5 that using a 12% discount rate equates the present value of the annual cash inflows with the present value of the investment required in the project, leaving a zero net present value. The 12% rate therefore represents the internal rate of return promised by the project.

Salvage Value and Other Cash Flows

The technique just demonstrated works very well if a project's cash flows are identical every year. But what if they are not? For example, what if a project will have some salvage value at the end of its life in addition to the annual cash inflows? Under these circumstances, a trial-and-error process is necessary to find the rate of return that will equate the cash inflows with the cash outflows. The trial-and-error process can be carried out by hand, or it can be carried out by means of computer software programs such as spreadsheets that perform the necessary computations in seconds. In short, simply because cash flows are erratic or uneven will not in any way prevent a manager from determining a project's internal rate of return.

EXHIBIT 14–5

Evaluation of the Mower Purchase Using a 12% Discount Rate

Initial cost	$16,950
Life of the project (years)	10
Annual cost savings	$3,000
Salvage value	–0–

Item	Year(s)	Amount of Cash Flow	12% Factor	Present Value of Cash Flows
Annual cost savings	1–10	$ 3,000	5.650*	$ 16,950
Initial investment	Now	(16,950)	1.000	(16,950)
Net present value				$ –0–

*From Table 14C–4 in Appendix 14C.

The Process of Interpolation

Interpolation is the process of finding rates of return that do not appear in published interest tables. It is an important concept, since published interest tables are usually printed in terms of whole percentages (10%, 12%, and so forth), whereas projects often have rates of return that involve fractional amounts. To illustrate the process of interpolation, assume the following data:

Investment required $6,000
Annual cost savings   1,500
Life of the project . . . .   10 years

What is the internal rate of return promised by this project? We can proceed as before and find that the relevant factor is 4.000:

$$\frac{\text{Investment required}}{\text{Annual cost savings}} = \frac{\$6,000}{\$1,500} = 4,000$$

Looking at Table 14C–4 in Appendix 14C and scanning along the 10-period line, we find that a factor of 4.000 represents a rate of return somewhere between 20% and 22%. To find the rate we are after, we must interpolate, as follows:

		Present Value Factors
20% factor	4.192	4.192
True factor	4.000	
22% factor		3.923
Difference	0.192	0.269

$$\text{Internal rate of return} = 20\% + \left(\frac{0.192}{0.269} \times 2\% \right)$$

$$\text{Internal rate of return} = 21.4\%$$

Although interpolation is an interesting exercise, it tends to imply a precision in the calculation of the internal rate of return that is difficult to justify. There are inherent uncertainties in the capital budgeting process. Future cash flows, for example, often are estimates. The internal rate of return calculated without interpolation may be just as good an estimate of the true IRR at the rate obtained through the interpolation process. It is unlikely that the difference in the IRR before and after the interpolation will lead to different decisions.

Using the Internal Rate of Return

Once the internal rate of return has been computed, what does the manager do with the information? The internal rate of return is compared to whatever rate of return (usually the cost of capital) the organization requires on its investment projects. If the internal rate of return is *equal* to or *greater* than the cost of capital, then the project is acceptable. If it is *less* than the cost of capital, then the project is rejected. A project is not a profitable undertaking if it can't provide a rate of return at least as great as the cost of the funds invested in it.

In the case of the Glendale School District example used earlier, let us assume that the district has set a minimum required rate of return of 10% on all projects. Since the large mower promises a rate of return of 12%, it clears this hurdle and would therefore be an acceptable investment.

THE COST OF CAPITAL AS A SCREENING TOOL

OBJECTIVE 5
Explain how the cost of capital is used as a screening tool.

As we have seen in preceding examples, the cost of capital operates as a *screening* tool, helping the manager screen out undesirable investment projects. This screening is accomplished in different ways, depending on whether the company is using the internal rate of return method or the net present value method in its capital budgeting analysis.

When the internal rate of return method is used, the cost of capital takes the form of a *hurdle rate* that a project must clear for acceptance. If the internal rate of return on a

EXHIBIT 14–6

Capital Budgeting
Screening Decisions

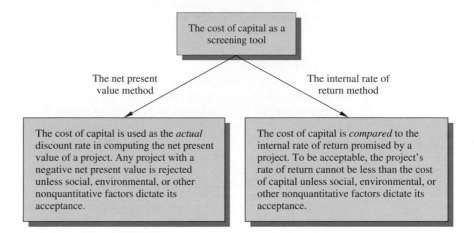

project is not great enough to clear the cost of capital hurdle, then the project is rejected. We saw the application of this idea in the Glendale School District example, where the hurdle rate was set at 10%.

When the net present value method is used, the cost of capital becomes the *actual discount rate* used to compute the net present value of a proposed project. Any project yielding a negative net present value is screened out and rejected unless nonquantitative factors such as social responsibility, employee morale, or improvements in a company's ability to compete are significant enough to require its acceptance. (This point is discussed further in a following section, Investments in Automated Equipment.)

The operation of the cost of capital as a screening tool is summarized in Exhibit 14–6.

COMPARISON OF THE NET PRESENT VALUE AND THE INTERNAL RATE OF RETURN METHODS

The net present value method has a number of advantages over the internal rate of return method of making capital budgeting decisions.

First, the net present value method is simpler to use. As explained earlier, the internal rate of return method often requires a trial-and-error process to find the exact rate of return that will equate a project's cash inflows and outflows. No such trial-and-error process is necessary when working with the net present value method.

Second, using the net present value method makes it easier to adjust for risk. The longer one has to wait for a cash inflow, the greater is the risk that the cash inflow will never materialize. To show the greater risk connected with cash flows that are projected to occur many years in the future, firms often discount such amounts at higher discount rates than the discount rates used for flows that are projected to occur earlier in time. For example, a firm might anticipate that a project will provide cash inflows of $10,000 per year for 15 years. If the firm's cost of capital is 18% before taxes, then it might discount the first five years' inflows at this rate. The discount rate might then be raised to, say, 20% for the next five years and then to 25% for the last five years. This successive raising of the discount rate is a way of adjusting for the greater risk connected with the cash flows that are projected to be received far into the future.

No such selective adjustment of discount rates is possible under the internal rate of return method. About the only way to adjust for risk is to raise the hurdle rate that the rate of return for a project must clear for acceptance. This is a somewhat crude approach to the risk problem in that it attaches the same degree of increased risk to *all* of the cash flows associated with a project—those that occur earlier in time as well as those that occur later in time.

Third, the net present value method provides more usable information than does the internal rate of return method. The dollar net present value figure generated by the net present value method is viewed as being particularly useful for decision-making purposes. This point is considered further in the following chapter.

EXPANDING THE NET PRESENT VALUE METHOD

OBJECTIVE 6
Prepare a net present value analysis of two competing investment projects using either the incremental-cost approach or the total-cost approach.

So far we have confined all of our examples to the consideration of a single investment alternative. We will now expand the net present value method to include two alternatives. In addition, we will integrate the concept of relevant costs into discounted cash flow analysis.

There are two ways that the net present value method can be used to compare competing investment projects. One is the *total-cost approach*, and the other is the *incremental-cost approach*. Each approach is illustrated below.

The Total-Cost Approach

The total-cost approach is the most flexible and perhaps the most widely used method of making a net present value analysis of competing projects. To illustrate the mechanics of the approach, let us assume the following data:

Example E

Harper Ferry Company provides a ferry service across the Halifax Harbour. One of its ferryboats is in poor condition. This ferry can be renovated at an immediate cost of $20,000. Further repairs and an overhaul of the motor will be needed five years from now at a cost of $8,000. In all, the ferry will be usable for 10 years if this work is done. At the end of 10 years, the ferry will have to be scrapped at a salvage value of approximately $6,000. The scrap value of the ferry right now is $7,000. It will cost $30,000 each year to operate the ferry, and revenues will total $40,000 annually.

Harper Ferry Company is a service company that must decide to renovate an old ferry or purchase a new one. The total-cost approach is one method that can provide an answer.

As an alternative, Harper Ferry Company can purchase a new ferryboat at a cost of $36,000. The new ferry will have a life of 10 years, but it will require some repairs at the end of 5 years. It is estimated that these repairs will amount to $3,000. At the end of 10 years, it is estimated that the ferry will have a scrap value of $6,000. It will cost $21,000 each year to operate the ferry, and revenues will total $40,000 annually.

Harper Ferry Company requires a return of at least 18% before taxes on all investment projects.

Should the company purchase the new ferry or renovate the old ferry? The solution is given in Exhibit 14–7.

Two points should be noted from the exhibit. First, observe that *all* cash inflows and *all* cash outflows are included in the solution under each alternative. No effort has been made to isolate those cash flows that are relevant to the decision and those that are not relevant. The inclusion of all cash flows associated with each alternative gives the approach its name—the *total-cost* approach.

Second, notice that a net present value figure is computed for each of the two alternatives. This is a distinct advantage of the total-cost approach in that an unlimited number of alternatives can be compared side by side to determine the most profitable course of action. For example, another alternative for Harper Ferry Company would be to get out of the ferry business entirely. If management desired, the net present value of this alternative could be computed to compare with the alternatives shown in Exhibit 14–7. Still other alternatives might be open to the company. Once management has determined the net present value of each alternative that it wishes to consider, it can select the course of action that promises to be the most profitable. In the case at hand, given only the two alternatives, the data indicate that the most profitable course is to purchase the new ferry.[4]

EXHIBIT 14–7

The Total-Cost Approach to Project Selection

	New Ferry	Old Ferry
Annual revenues	$40,000	$40,000
Annual cash operating costs	21,000	30,000
Net annual cash inflows	$19,000	$10,000

Item	Year(s)	Amount of Cash Flow	18% Factor	Present Value of Cash Flows
Buy the new ferry:				
Initial investment	Now	$(36,000)	1.000	$(36,000)
Repairs in five years	5	(3,000)	0.437	(1,311)
Net annual cash inflows	1–10	19,000	4.494	85,386
Salvage of the old ferry.	Now	7,000	1.000	7,000
Salvage of the new ferry	10	6,000	0.191	1,146
Net present value.				56,221
Keep the old ferry:				
Initial repairs.	Now	$(20,000)	1.000	(20,000)
Repairs in five years	5	(8,000)	0.437	(3,496)
Net annual cash inflows	1–10	10,000	4.494	44,940
Salvage of the old ferry.	10	6,000	0.191	1,146
Net present value.				22,590
Net present value in favour of buying the new ferry				$ 33,631

*All factors are from Tables 14C–3 and 14C–4 in Appendix 14C.

---

[4]The alternative with the highest net present value is not always the best choice, although it is the best choice in this case. For further discussion, see the section Preference Decisions—The Ranking of Investment Projects in Chapter 15.

EXHIBIT 14-8

The Incremental-
Cost Approach to
Project Selection

Item	Year(s)	Amount of Cash Flow	18% Factor	Present Value of Cash Flows
Incremental investment required to purchase the new ferry	Now	$(16,000)	1.000	$(16,000)
Repairs in five years avoided	5	5,000	0.437	2,185
Increased net annual cash inflows .	1–10	9,000	4.494	40,446
Salvage of the old ferry	Now	7,000	1.000	7,000
Difference in salvage value in 10 years	10	–0–	—	–0–
Net present value in favour of buying the new ferry				$ 33,631

*All factors are from Tables 14C–3 and 14C–4 in Appendix 14C.

The Incremental-Cost Approach

When only two alternatives are being considered, the incremental-cost approach offers a simpler and more direct route to a decision. Unlike the total-cost approach, it focuses only on differential costs.[5] The procedure is to include in the discounted cash flow analysis only those costs and revenues that *differ* between the two alternatives being considered. To illustrate, refer again to the data in Example E relating to Harper Ferry Company. The solution using only differential costs is presented in Exhibit 14–8.

Two things should be noted from the data in this exhibit. First, notice that the net present value of $33,631 shown in Exhibit 14–8 agrees with the net present value shown under the total-cost approach in Exhibit 14–7. This agreement should be expected, since the two approaches are just different roads to the same destination.

Should a company lease warehouse space or purchase its own building? The least-cost method is probably the best approach for making this decision.

---

[5]Technically, the incremental-cost approach is misnamed, since it focuses on differential costs (that is, on both cost increases and decreases) rather than just on incremental costs. As used here, the term *incremental costs* should be interpreted broadly to include both cost increases and cost decreases.

projects.[7] For nonprofit units such as schools and hospitals, it is generally recommended that the discount rate should "approximate the average rate of return on private sector investments."[8]

INVESTMENTS IN AUTOMATED EQUIPMENT

OBJECTIVE 7
Make a capital budgeting analysis involving automated equipment.

Investments in automated equipment tend to be very large in dollar amount, and their benefits are often indirect and intangible and therefore hard to quantify.

The cost involved in automating a process is much greater than the cost of purchasing conventional equipment. Single pieces of automated equipment, such as a robot or computerized numerically controlled machine, can cost $1 million or more. A flexible manufacturing system, involving one or more cells, can cost up to $50 million. Even more important, the front-end investment in machinery often constitutes less than half the total cost of automating. The nonhardware costs such as engineering, software development, and implementation of the system can equal or exceed the cost of the equipment itself. Clearly, it is important to realistically estimate such costs before embarking on an automation project.

FOCUS ON CURRENT PRACTICE

Rockwell International Corp.'s Herman M. Reininga wanted to buy an $80,000 laser to etch contract numbers on communications systems sold to the Pentagon. But the division's financial staff laughed him out of the meeting (in which he recommended the purchase). The laser would save only $4,000 in direct labour each year. At that rate, it would take 20 years to recover the cost.

Three years later, Reininga got his laser. He presented data showing that finished radios sat around for two weeks waiting for an antique etching operation to finish identity plates. The laser would do the job in 10 minutes, moving shipments out faster—and saving the company $200,000 a year in inventory-holding costs.[9]

Benefits from Automation

The benefits of automation roughly fall into two classes—tangible benefits and intangible benefits.

The tangible benefits are much easier to identify and measure than the intangible benefits. The tangible benefits of automation usually include decreased labour costs and a reduction in defective output. The reduction in defective output results in fewer inspections, and less scrap, waste, and rework. It can also result in less warranty work. General Electric reports, for example, that automating its dishwasher manufacturing plant resulted in a 50% reduction in its service call rate.

---

[7]Office of Management and Budget Circular No. A-94, March 1972. The U.S. Postal Service is exempted from the 10% rate as are all water resource projects and all lease or buy decisions.
[8]Robert N. Anthony and David W. Young, *Management Control in Nonprofit Organizations,* 5th ed. (Homewood, Ill.: Richard D. Irwin, Inc., 1994), p. 445.
[9]Reprinted from "The Productivity Paradox," *Business Week,* No. 3055 (June 6, 1988), p. 104, by special permission.

The intangible benefits of automated systems generally result from their greater speed, consistency, reliability, safety, and flexibility. These factors permit greater throughput and a greater variety of products, and they enhance product quality. In turn, the greater throughput, variety of products, and higher quality should lead to greater sales and profits, although the precise amount of the increase is very difficult to forecast. Automated processes also allow a company to reduce its inventories, since the company can more quickly respond to shifts in customer demand.

Finally, some managers argue that automation is necessary as a matter of self-preservation. When a company's competition is automating, the company faces the prospect of *capital decay* if it does not automate. **Capital decay** is the loss in market share that results from attempting to make do with technologically obsolete products and operations. Closely allied to this idea is the fear that if a company does not maintain its technical edge, it will lose the ability to catch up with the competition later on. Companies that hold back and do not automate may lose their ability to recognize and then implement the key elements of new technology that provide competitive advantage.

Note that the tangible benefits above represent potential *cost savings,* whereas the intangible benefits represent potential *revenue enhancements.* Generally, it's easier to measure the amount of cost savings associated with an investment project, and that's why items such as reduced direct labour cost always show up in a capital budgeting analysis. But it's harder to measure the impact of a potential revenue enhancement such as greater flexibility or faster market response. As a result, managers tend to overlook such items when evaluating the benefits from automated equipment. The intangible benefits must be explicitly considered, however, or faulty decisions will follow.

Decision Framework for Intangible Benefits

A fairly simple procedure can be followed when the intangible benefits are uncertain and significant. Suppose, for example, that a company with a 16% cost of capital is considering automated equipment that would have a 15-year useful life. Also suppose that a discounted cash flow analysis of just the tangible costs and benefits show a negative net present value of $223,000. Clearly, if the intangible benefits are large enough, they could turn this negative net present value into a positive net present value. In this case, the amount of additional cash flow per year from the intangible benefits that would be needed to make the project financially attractive can be computed as follows:

Net present value (negative) . . . . $(223,000)
Factor for an annuity of 16%
for 15 periods (from Table 14C–4
in Appendix 14C) 5.575

$$\frac{\text{Net present value, } \$(223,000)}{\text{Factor, } 5.575} = \$40,000$$

Thus, if intangible benefits such as greater flexibility, higher quality of output, and avoidance of capital decay are worth at least $40,000 a year to the company, then the automated equipment should be purchased. If, in the judgment of management, these intangible benefits are *not* worth $40,000 a year, then no purchase should be made.[10]

---

[10]Robert E. Bennett and James A. Hendricks suggest such a procedure in "Justifying the Acquisition of Automated Equipment," *Management Accounting* (July 1987), p. 46.

Consistency in the manufacturing of printing inks is the main reason Hostmann-Steinberg undertook to automate its production process with the help of Matrix Scale Systems, Inc. A fully-automated varnish plant and tank farm was planned for the newly purchased Brampton, Ontario site. The varnish plant is the beginning and is one of the highlights of Hostmann-Steinberg's automation project. Employees are healthier and happier and are now freed for more productive tasks, with no one laid off since the project began. The real benefits, however, lie in the area of production, which has increased at least 25%, and quality, an external benefit passed on to customers. George Zafiris, who has overseen the automation project on behalf of Matrix, points to the cooperation between Hostmann-Steinberg and Matrix as a key component in making the project a success. According to technical director David Daffern of Hostmann-Steinberg, involving outside help is a must in tackling any automation project.[11]

Several different techniques can be used to take into account uncertainties about future cash flows in capital budgeting. The uncertainties are particularly apparent in the drug business where it costs an average of $359 million and 10 years to bring a new drug through the governmental approval process and to market. And once on the market, 7 out of 10 products fail to return the company's cost of capital.

Merck & Co. manages the financial risks and uncertainties of drug research using a Research Planning Model they have developed. The model, which produces net present value estimates and other key statistics, is based on a wide range of scientific and financial variables—most of which are uncertain. For example, the future selling price of any drug resulting from current research is usually highly uncertain, but managers at Merck & Co. can at least specify a range within which the selling price is likely to fall. The computer is used to draw a value at random, within the permissible range, for each of the variables in the model. The model then computes a net present value. This process is repeated many times, and each time a new value of each of the variables is drawn at random. In this way, Merck is able to produce a probability distribution for the net present value. This can be used, for example, to estimate the probability that the project's net present value will exceed a certain level. "What are the payoffs of all this sophistication? In short, better decisions."[12]

OTHER APPROACHES TO CAPITAL BUDGETING DECISIONS

Discounted cash flow methods have gained widespread acceptance as decision-making tools. Other methods of making capital budgeting decisions are also available, however, and are preferred by some managers. In this section, we discuss two such methods known as *payback* and *simple rate of return*. Both methods have been in use for a hundred years or more, but they are now declining in popularity as primary tools for project evaluation.

---

[11]Green, Matt, "Written in Ink," *PEM-Plant-Engineering-and-Manufacturing* (September 1996), pp. 20–25.
[12]Nancy A. Nichols, "Scientific Management at Merck: An Interview with CFO Judy Lewent," *Harvard Business Review* (January–February 1994), pp. 89–99.

The Payback Method

The payback method centres on a span of time known as the *payback period*. The **payback period** can be defined as the length of time that it takes for an investment project to recoup its own initial cost out of the cash receipts that it generates. This period is sometimes spoken of as "the time that it takes for an investment to pay for itself." The basic premise of the payback method is that the more quickly the cost of an investment can be recovered, the more desirable is the investment.

The payback period is expressed in years. When the net annual cash inflow is the same every year, the following formula can be used to compute the payback period:

$$\text{Payback period} = \frac{\text{Investment required}}{\text{Net annual cash inflow*}} \qquad (2)$$

*If new equipment is replacing old equipment, this becomes incremental net annual cash inflow.

To illustrate the mechanics involved in payback computations, assume the following data:

Example G

York Company needs a new milling machine. The company is considering two machines: machine A and machine B. Machine A costs $15,000 and will reduce operating costs by $5,000 per year. Machine B costs only $12,000 but will also reduce operating costs by $5,000 per year.

Required

Which machine should be purchased? Make your calculations by the payback method.

$$\text{Machine A payback period} = \frac{\$15,000}{\$5,000} = 3.0 \text{ years}$$

$$\text{Machine B payback period} = \frac{\$12,000}{\$5,000} = 2.4 \text{ years}$$

According to the payback calculations, York Company should purchase machine B, since it has a shorter payback period than machine A.

Evaluation of the Payback Method

The payback method is not a true measure of the profitability of an investment. Rather, it is a measure of *time* in the sense that it simply tells the manager how many years will be required to recover the original investment. Unfortunately, a shorter payback period is not always an accurate guide as to whether one investment is more desirable than another.

To illustrate, consider again the two machines used in the example above. Since machine B has a shorter payback period than machine A, it *appears* that machine B is more desirable than machine A. But if we add one more piece of data, this illusion quickly disappears. Machine A has a projected 10-year life, and machine B has a projected 5-year life. It would take two purchases of machine B to provide the same length of service as would be provided by a single purchase of machine A. Under these circumstances, machine A would be a much better investment than machine B, even though machine B has a shorter payback period. Unfortunately, the payback method has no inherent mechanism for highlighting differences in useful life between investments for the decision maker. Such differences can be very important, and relying on payback alone can cause the manager to make incorrect decisions.

A further criticism of the payback method is that it does not consider the time value of money. A cash inflow to be received several years in the future is weighed equally with a cash inflow to be received right now. To illustrate, assume that for an investment of $8,000 you can purchase either of the two following streams of cash inflows:

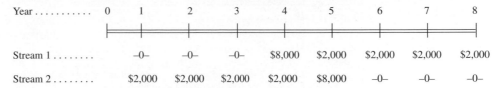

Year	0	1	2	3	4	5	6	7	8
Stream 1	–0–	–0–	–0–	$8,000	$2,000	$2,000	$2,000	$2,000	
Stream 2	$2,000	$2,000	$2,000	$2,000	$8,000	–0–	–0–	–0–	

Which stream of cash inflows would you prefer to receive in return for your $8,000 investment? Each stream has a payback period of 4.0 years. Therefore, if payback alone were relied on in making the decision, you would be forced to say that the streams are equally desirable. However, from the point of view of the time value of money, stream 2 is much more desirable than stream 1.

On the other hand, under certain conditions the payback method can be very useful to the manager. For one thing, it can help the manager identify which investment proposals are in the "ballpark." That is, it can be used as a screening tool to help answer the question, "Should I consider this proposal further?" If a proposal doesn't provide a payback within some specified period, then there may be no need to consider it further. In addition, the payback period is often of great importance to new firms that are "cash poor." When a firm is cash poor, a project with a short payback period but a low rate of return might be preferred over another project with a high rate of return but a long payback period. The reason is that the company may simply need a faster return of its cash investment. And finally, the payback method is sometimes used in industries where products become obsolete very rapidly—such as consumer electronics. Since products may last only a year or two, the payback period on investments must be very short.

An Extended Example of Payback

As shown by formula (2) given earlier, the payback period is computed by dividing the investment in a project by the net annual cash inflows that the project will generate. If new equipment is replacing old equipment, then any salvage to be received on disposal of the old equipment should be deducted from the cost of the new equipment, and only the *incremental* investment should be used in the payback computation. In addition, any depreciation deducted in arriving at the project's net income must be added back to obtain the project's expected net annual cash inflow. To illustrate, assume the following data:

Example H

Goodtime Fun Centres, Ltd., operates many outlets in eastern Canada. Some of the vending machines in one of its outlets provide very little revenue, so the company is considering the removal of the machines and the installation of equipment to dispense soft ice cream. The equipment would cost $80,000 and have an eight-year useful life. Incremental annual revenues and costs associated with the sale of ice cream would be as follows:

Sales	$150,000
Less cost of ingredients	90,000
Contribution margin	60,000
Less fixed expenses:	
Salaries	27,000
Maintenance	3,000
Depreciation	10,000
Total fixed expenses	40,000
Net income	$ 20,000

EXHIBIT 14–11

Computation of the
Payback Period

Step 1:   *Compute the net annual cash inflow.* Since the net annual cash inflow is not given, it must be
computed before the payback period can be determined.

Net income (given above)......................	$20,000
Add: Noncash deduction for depreciation	10,000
Net annual cash inflow	$30,000

Step 2:   *Compute the payback period.* Using the net annual cash inflow figure from above, the payback period can be determined as follows:

Cost of the new equipment	$80,000
Less salvage value of old equipment	5,000
Investment required...........................	$75,000

$$\text{Payback period} = \frac{\text{Investment required}}{\text{Net annual cash inflow}}$$

$$= \frac{\$75,000}{\$30,000} = 2.5 \text{ years}$$

The vending machines can be sold for a $5,000 scrap value. The company will not purchase
equipment unless it has a payback of three years or less. Should the equipment to dispense ice
cream be purchased?

An analysis as to whether the proposed equipment meets the company's payback requirements is given in Exhibit 14–11. Several things should be noted from the data in this
exhibit. First, notice that depreciation is added back to net income to obtain the net annual cash inflow promised by the new equipment. As stated earlier in the chapter, depreciation is not a present cash outlay; thus, it must be added back to net income in order to
adjust net income to a cash basis. Second, notice in the payback computation that the salvage value from the old machines has been deducted from the cost of the new equipment,
and that only the incremental investment has been used in computing the payback period.

Since the proposed equipment has a payback period of less than three years, the company's payback requirement has been met and the new equipment should be purchased.

Payback and Uneven Cash Flows

When the cash flows associated with an investment project change from year to year, the
simple payback formula that we outlined earlier is no longer usable, and the computations
involved in deriving the payback period can be fairly complex. Consider the following data:

Year	Investment	Cash Inflow
1	$4,000	$1,000
2		–0–
3		2,000
4	2,000	1,000
5		500
6		3,000
7		2,000
8		2,000

What is the payback period on this investment? The answer is 5.5 years, but to obtain
this figure it is necessary to balance off the cash inflows against the investment outflows

EXHIBIT 14-12

Payback and
Uneven Cash
Flows

Year	(1) Beginning Unrecovered Investment	(2) Additional Investment	(3) Total Unrecovered Investment (1) + (2)	(4) Cash Inflow	(5) Ending Unrecovered Investment (3) – (4)
1	$4,000		$4,000	$1,000	$3,000
2	3,000		3,000	–0–	3,000
3	3,000		3,000	2,000	1,000
4	1,000	$2,000	3,000	1,000	2,000
5	2,000		2,000	500	1,500
6	1,500		1,500	3,000	–0–
7	–0–		–0–	2,000	–0–
8	–0–		–0–	2,000	–0–

on a year-by-year basis. The steps involved in this process are shown in Exhibit 14–12. By the middle of the sixth year, sufficient cash inflows will have been realized to recover the entire investment of $6,000 ($4,000 + $2,000).

The Simple Rate of Return Method

OBJECTIVE 9
Compute the simple rate of return for an investment using the simple rate of return formula.

The **simple rate of return** method is another capital budgeting technique that does not involve discounted cash flows. The method is also known as the accounting rate of return, the unadjusted rate of return, and the financial statement method. It derives its popularity from the belief that it parallels conventional financial statements in its handling of investment data.

Unlike the other capital budgeting methods that we have discussed, the simple rate of return method does not focus on cash flows. Rather, it focuses on accounting net income. The approach is to estimate the revenues that will be generated by a proposed investment and then to deduct from these revenues all of the projected operating expenses associated with the project. This net income figure is then related to the initial investment in the project, as shown in the following formula:

$$\text{Simple rate of return} = \frac{\overbrace{\text{Incremental revenues}} - \overbrace{\substack{\text{Incremental expenses} \\ \text{including depreciation}}} = \overbrace{\substack{\text{Net} \\ \text{income}}}}{\text{Initial investment*}} \quad (3)$$

*The investment should be reduced by any salvage from the sale of old equipment.

Or, if a cost reduction project is involved, formula (3) becomes:

$$\text{Simple rate of return} = \frac{\overbrace{\substack{\text{Cost} \\ \text{savings}}} - \overbrace{\substack{\text{Depreciation on} \\ \text{new equipment}}}}{\text{Initial investment*}} \quad (4)$$

*The investment should be reduced by any salvage from the sale of old equipment.

Example 1
Brigham Tea, Ltd., is a processor of a nontannic acid tea product. The company is contemplating the purchase of equipment for an additional processing line. The additional processing line would increase revenues by $90,000 per year. Incremental cash operating expenses would be $40,000 per year. The equipment would cost $180,000 and have a nine-year life. No salvage value is projected.

Required

1. Compute the simple rate of return.
2. Compute the internal rate of return, and compare it to the simple rate of return.

Solution

1. By applying the formula for the simple rate of return found in equation (3), we can compute the simple rate of return to be 16.7%:

Simple rate of return

$$
= \frac{\left[\begin{array}{c} \$90,000 \\ \text{incremental} \\ \text{revenues} \end{array}\right] - \left[\begin{array}{c} \$40,000 \text{ cash operating expenses} \\ + \$20,000 \text{ depreciation} \end{array}\right] = \begin{array}{c} \$30,000 \\ \text{net income} \end{array}}{\$180,000 \text{ initial investment*}}
$$

Simple rate of return = 16.7%

2. The rate computed in (1) above, however, is far below the internal rate of return of approximately 24%:

$$
\text{Internal rate of return} = \frac{\$180,000}{\$50,000*} = \text{Factor of } 3.600
$$

$$
\text{Internal rate of return} = \begin{array}{c} \text{Approximately 24\% from Table 14C–4} \\ \text{in Appendix 14C, scanning} \\ \text{across the nine-year line} \end{array}
$$

*$30,000 net income + $20,000 depreciation = $50,000; or the annual cash inflow can be computed as $90,000 increased revenues – $40,000 cash expenses = $50,000.

Example J

Midwest Farms, Inc., hires people on a part-time basis to sort eggs. The cost of this hand-sorting process is $30,000 per year. The company is investigating the purchase of an egg-sorting machine that would cost $90,000 and have a 15-year useful life. The machine would have negligible salvage value, and it would cost $10,000 per year to operate and maintain. The egg-sorting equipment currently being used could be sold now for a scrap value of $2,500.

Required

Compute the simple rate of return on the new egg-sorting machine.

Solution

A cost reduction project is involved in this situation. By applying the formula for the simple rate of return found in equation (4), we can compute the simple rate of return as follows:

$$
\begin{array}{c} \text{Simple rate} \\ \text{of return} \end{array} = \frac{\begin{array}{c} \$20,000* \text{ cost} \\ \text{savings} \end{array} - \begin{array}{c} \$6,000^{\dagger} \text{ depreciation} \\ \text{on new equipment} \end{array}}{\$90,000 - \$2,500}
$$

$$
= 16.0\%
$$

*$30,000 – $10,000 = $20,000 cost savings.
†$90,000 ÷ 15 years = $6,000 depreciation.

Criticisms of the Simple Rate of Return

The most damaging criticism of the simple rate of return method is that it does not consider the time value of money. A dollar received 10 years from now is viewed as being just as valuable as a dollar received today. Thus, the manager can be misled in attempting to choose between competing courses of action if the alternatives being considered have different cash flow patterns. For example, assume that project A has a high simple rate of return but yields the bulk of its cash flows many years from now. Another project, B, has a somewhat lower simple rate of return but yields the bulk of its cash flows over the next few years. The manager would probably choose project A over project B because of its higher simple rate of return; however, project B might in fact be a much better investment if the time value of money were considered.

The Choice of an Investment Base

In our examples, we have defined the investment base for simple rate of return computations to be the entire initial investment in the project under consideration [see formula (3)]. Actual practice varies between using the entire initial investment, as we have done, and using only the *average* investment over the life of a project. As a practical matter, which approach one chooses to follow is unimportant so long as consistency is maintained between projects and between years. If the average investment is used rather than the entire initial investment, then the resulting rate of return will be approximately doubled.

A survey of 133 chief executive officers and chief financial officers of large Canadian companies revealed the following key conclusions:

1. Most of the firms used multiple evaluation criteria to assess capital investments.
2. Discounted cash flow methods were employed by more than 75% of respondents to evaluate projects such as expansion—existing operations, expansion—new operations, foreign operations, and leasing. The use of DCF methods, i.e., NPV, IRR, or both, varies from a low of 23.5% for social expenditures, to 66% for replacement projects, and to 84.9% for expansion—new operations. It appears, therefore, that the propensity to use DCF techniques increases with the complexity of the decision.
3. Of the DCF techniques, IRR was used more frequently then NPV.
4. The Accounting Rate of Return (ARR) had a usage rate below 20%. More than 50% use the payback method either alone or in conjunction with other techniques to evaluate various capital budgeting projects. Payback is used most frequently with DCF methods.[13]

POSTAPPRAISAL OF INVESTMENT PROJECTS

Postappraisal of an investment project means a follow-up after the project has been approved to see whether or not expected results are actually realized. This is a key part of the capital budgeting process in that it provides management with an opportunity, over time, to see how realistic the proposals are that are being submitted and approved. It also provides an opportunity to reinforce successful projects as needed, to strengthen or perhaps

---

[13]Vijay M. Jog and Ashwani K. Srivastave, "Capital Budgeting Practices in Canada," School of Business, Carleton University, Ottawa, 1993.

One way of applying the postappraisal process is through a process known as Economic Value Creation (EVC). Economic Value Creation is an increasingly popular concept which serves to provide a framework for valuing corporations, business units and the performance of managers. EVC is an entity's net operating profit after tax (NOPAT) minus a charge for its use of capital. In an earlier chapter we referred to this as residual income. Simply written in equation form,

$$EVC = NOPAT - \left[\text{weighted average cost of capital} \times \text{capital}\right]$$

Husky Injection Moulding, Imasco, and Domtar in Canada all use the EVC framework. In 1995, The Society of Management Accountants of Canada (SMAC) sponsored a survey of EVC practice in Canada. The survey was mailed to 942 of the top 1,000 Canadian organizations ranked by profits as reported in the July 1994 issue of the *Report on Business* magazine. The survey results indicated:

- EVC is at an early stage of development among Canadian corporations and different industry sectors are in different stages of EVC development.
- EVC has largely achieved the desired objectives of organizations that have adopted it.
- EVC is primarily used at the corporate or division level.
- The key reasons for adopting EVC relate to goal setting, accountability, performance analysis and compensation.
- The primary reasons for not adopting EVC relate to satisfaction with existing measures, low priority, and insufficient knowledge.

The research concluded that EVC concepts are just now being recognized and understood, and that we can expect increasing interest by Canadian organizations in learning more about and adopting EVC frameworks. Three reasons have been postulated to explain why EVC is increasingly being used by Canadian managers:

1. In contrast to the discounted cash flow or the net present value methods which provide a one time expected value of future investments, EVC allows for an annual measurement of actual (not estimated or forecasted) value creation performance.

2. EVC gains and losses track more closely with shareholder wealth than any traditional earnings or bottom line based measure.

3. EVC aligns desired organizational strategies with appropriate performance measurement and compensation procedures.[14]

salvage projects that are encountering difficulty, to terminate unsuccessful projects before losses become too great, and to improve the overall quality of future investment proposals.

Monitoring of capital budgeting projects may also help improve the quality of similar feature investment proposals. Care should be exercised, however, when trying to use past experience as a guide to future decisions because assumptions about the business environment may no longer be valid.

To avoid a liquidity crunch, the firm must respond quickly to significant overruns that require unplanned cash outflows. It may be necessary to arrange additional financing or to amend plans.

---

[14]Vijay Jog and Howard Armitage, "Economic Value Creation: What Every Management Accountant Should Know," *CMA Management Accounting Magazine* (October 1996), pp. 21–24.

Both firms and accounting bodies are placing increasing importance on the postappraisal process. *Management Accounting Guidelines* has a full section devoted to this process: Guideline No. 1— "Post-Appraisal of Capital Expenditure."[15]

The postappraisal should answer a variety of questions: Was the capital budgeting decision consistent with overall corporate strategy? Did the project meet the specifications that were set out in the appropriation request? Were the original specifications realistically and honestly determined? Were any additional expenditures properly authorized? A proper review may be tedious and time-consuming, and special care should be taken in making assertions about cause and effect. It is often difficult to relate particular costs and revenues to a particular project. This is especially true if there are several projects on-line simultaneously and is absolutely true if there is synergy among the projects.[16] A cost/benefit tradeoff is necessary when deciding how many company sources are to be devoted to the postappraisal.

To ensure objectivity, the postappraisal should be performed by an individual or team that has not been directly involved in the actual project. The postappraisal should not be a witch hunt aimed at placing blame, but should be an accountability process aimed at improving control and a learning process that will improve estimates of future projects.

In performing a postappraisal, the same technique should be used as was used in the original approval process. That is, if a project was approved on a basis of a net present value analysis, then the same procedure should be used in performing the postappraisal. However, the data going into the analysis should be *actual data* as observed in the actual operation of the project, rather than estimated data. This affords management with an opportunity to make a side-by-side comparison to see how well the project has worked out. It also helps assure that estimated data received on future proposals will be carefully prepared, since the persons submitting the data know that their estimates will be given careful scrutiny in the postappraisal process. Actual results that are far out of line with original estimates should be carefully reviewed by management, and corrective action taken as necessary. In accordance with the management by exception principle, those managers responsible for the original estimates should be required to provide a full explanation of any major differences between estimated and actual results.

SUMMARY

Decisions relating to the planning and financing of capital outlays are known as capital budgeting decisions. Such decisions are of key importance to the long-run profitability of a firm, since large amounts of money are usually involved and since whatever decisions are made may "lock in" a firm for many years.

A decision to make a particular investment hinges basically on whether the future returns promised by the investment can be justified in terms of the present cost outlay that must be made. A valid comparison between the future returns and the present cost outlay is difficult because of the difference in timing involved. This timing problem is overcome through use of the concept of present value and through employment of the technique of

---

[15]The Society of Management Accountants of Canada, *Management Accountants Handbook* (Hamilton, Ont.: 1984).

[16]Synergy occurs when the projects working together generate greater revenue than the sum of the revenues of all projects acting independently.

discounting. The future sums are discounted to their present value so that they can be compared on a valid basis with current cost outlays. The discount rate used may be the firm's cost of capital, or it may be some other rate of return that the firm requires on all investment projects.

There are two ways of using discounted cash flow in making capital budgeting decisions. One is the net present value method, and the other is the internal rate of return method. The net present value method involves choosing a discount rate, then discounting all cash flows to present value, as described in the preceding paragraph. If the present value of the cash inflows exceeds the present value of the cash outflows, then the net present value is positive and the project is acceptable. The opposite is true if the net present value is negative. The internal rate of return method finds the discount rate that equates the present value of the cash inflows and the present value of the cash outflows, leaving a zero net present value.

Instead of using discounted cash flow, some companies prefer to use either payback or the simple rate of return in evaluating investment proposals. Payback is determined by dividing a project's cost by the annual cash inflows that it will generate in order to find out how quickly the original investment can be recovered. The simple rate of return is determined by dividing a project's accounting net income either by the initial investment in the project or by the average investment over the life of the project. Both payback and the simple rate of return can be useful to the manager, so long as they are used with a full understanding of their limitations.

After an investment proposal has been approved, a postappraisal should be performed to see whether expected results are actually being realized. This is a key part of the capital budgeting process, since it tends to strengthen the quality of the estimates going into investment proposals and affords management with an early opportunity to recognize any developing problems or opportunities.

REVIEW PROBLEM 1: BASIC PRESENT VALUE COMPUTATIONS

Each of the following situations is independent. Work out your own solution to each situation, and then check it against the solution provided.

1. John has just reached age 58. In 12 years, he plans to retire. Upon retiring, he would like to take an extended vacation, which he expects will cost at least $4,000. What lump-sum amount must he invest now to have the needed $4,000 at the end of 12 years if the rate of return is:
   a.   8%?
   b.   12%?

2. The Morgans would like to send their daughter to an expensive music camp at the end of each of the next five years. The camp costs $1,000 each year. What lump-sum amount would have to be invested now in order to have the $1,000 at the end of each year if the rate of return is:
   a.   8%?
   b.   12%?

3. You have just received an inheritance from your father's estate. You can invest the money and either receive a $20,000 lump-sum amount at the end of 10 years or receive $1,400 at the end of each year for the next 10 years. If your minimum desired rate of return is 12%, which alternative would you prefer?

Solution to Review Problem 1

1. a.   The amount that must be invested now would be the present value of the $4,000, using a discount rate of 8%. From Table 14C–3 in Appendix 14C, the factor for a discount rate of 8% for 12 periods is 0.397. Multiplying this discount factor by the $4,000 needed in 12 years will give the amount of the present investment required: $4,000 × 0.397 = $1,588.

b. We will proceed as we did in (a) above, but this time we will use a discount rate of 12%. From Table 14C–3 in Appendix 14C, the factor for a discount rate of 12% for 12 periods is 0.257. Multiplying this discount factor by the $4,000 needed in 12 years will give the amount of the present investment required: $4,000 × 0.257 = $1,028.

Notice that as the discount rate (desired rate of return) increases, the present value decreases.

2. This part differs from (1) above in that we are now dealing with an annuity rather than with a single future sum. The amount that must be invested now will be the present value of the $1,000 needed at the end of each year for five years. Since we are dealing with an annuity, or a series of cash flows, we must refer to Table 14C–4 in Appendix 14C for the appropriate discount factor.

a. From Table 14C–4 in Appendix 14C, the discount factor for 8% for five periods is 3.993. Therefore, the amount that must be invested now in order to have $1,000 available at the end of each year for five years is $1,000 × 3.993 = $3,993.

b. From Table 14C–4 in Appendix 14C, the discount factor for 12% for five periods is 3.605. Therefore, the amount that must be invested now in order to have $1,000 available at the end of each year for five years is $1,000 × 3.605 = $3,605.

Again notice that as the discount rate (desired rate of return) increases, the present value decreases. This is logical, since at a higher rate of return we would expect to invest less than would have been needed if a lower rate of return were being earned.

3. For this part we will need to refer to both Tables 14C–3 and 14C–4 in Appendix 14C. From Table 14C–3, we will need to find the discount factor for 12% for 10 periods, then apply it to the $20,000 lump sum to be received in 10 years. From Table 14C–4, we will need to find the discount factor for 12% for 10 periods, then apply it to the series of $1,400 payments to be received over the 10-year period. Whichever alternative has the higher present value is the one that should be selected.

$$\$20,000 \times 0.322 = \$6,440$$

$$\$1,400 \times 5.650 = \$7,910$$

Thus, you would prefer to receive the $1,400 per year for 10 years, rather than the $20,000 lump sum.

REVIEW PROBLEM 2: COMPARISON OF CAPITAL BUDGETING METHODS

Lamar Company is studying a project that would have an eight-year life and require a $1,600,000 investment in equipment. At the end of eight years, the project would terminate and the equipment would have no salvage value. The project would provide net income each year as follows:

Sales		$3,000,000
Less variable expenses		1,800,000
Contribution margin		1,200,000
Less fixed expenses:		
Advertising, salaries, and other fixed out-of-pocket costs	$700,000	
Depreciation	200,000	
Total fixed expenses		900,000
Net income		$ 300,00

The company's cost of capital is 18%.

Required

1. Compute the net annual cash inflow promised by the project.
2. Compute the project's net present value. Is the project acceptable? Explain.
3. Compute the project's internal rate of return. Interpolate to one decimal place.

4. Compute the project's payback period. If the company requires a maximum payback of three years, is the project acceptable?

5. Compute the project's simple rate of return. Is the project acceptable? Explain.

Solution to Review Problem 2

1. The net annual cash inflow can be computed by deducting the cash expenses from sales:

Sales	$3,000,000
Less variable expenses	1,800,000
Contribution margin	1,200,000
Less advertising, salaries, and	
other fixed out-of-pocket costs	700,000
Net annual cash inflow	$ 500,00

Or it can be computed by adding depreciation back to net income:

Net income	$300,000
Add: Noncash deduction for depreciation.............	200,000
Net annual cash inflow	$500,000

2. The net present value can be computed as follows:

Items	Year(s)	Amount of Cash Flows	18% Factor	Present Value of Cash Flows
Cost of new equipment	Now	$(1,600,000)	1.000	$(1,600,000)
Net annual cash inflow	1–8	500,000	4.078	2,039,000
Net present value................				$ 439,000

Yes, the project is acceptable since it has a positive net present value.

3. The formula for computing the factor of the internal rate of return is:

$$\text{Factor of the internal rate of return} = \frac{\text{Investment required}}{\text{Net annual cash inflow}}$$

$$\frac{\$1,600,000}{\$500,000} = 3.200$$

Looking in Table 14C–4 in Appendix 14C at the end of the chapter and scanning along the 8-period line, we find that a factor of 3.200 represents a rate of return somewhere between 26% and 28%. To find the rate we are after, we must interpolate as follows:

26% factor	3.241	3.241
True factor	3.200	
28% factor		3.076
Difference	0.041	0.165

$$\text{Internal rate of return} = 26\% + \left(\frac{0.041}{0.165} \times 2\% \right)$$

$$= 26.5\%$$

4. The formula for the payback period is:

$$\text{Payback period} = \frac{\text{Investment required}}{\text{Net annual cash inflow}}$$

$$= \frac{\$1,600,000}{\$500,000}$$

$$= 3.2 \text{ years}$$

No, the project is not acceptable when measured by the payback method. The 3.2 years payback period is greater than the maximum 3 years set by the company.

5. The formula for the simple rate of return is:

$$\text{Simple rate of return} = \frac{\text{Incremental revenues} - \text{Incremental expenses, including depreciation} = \text{Net income}}{\text{Initial investment}}$$

$$= \frac{\$300,000}{\$1,600,000}$$

$$= 18.75\%$$

Yes, the project is acceptable when measured by the simple rate of return. The 18.75% return promised by the project is greater than the company's 18% cost of capital. Notice, however, that the simple rate of return greatly understates the true rate of return, which is 26.5% as shown in (3) above.

KEY TERMS FOR REVIEW

OBJECTIVE 10

Define or explain key terms listed at the end of the chapter.

Capital budgeting   Actions relating to the planning and financing of capital outlays for such purposes as the purchase of new equipment, the introduction of new product lines, and the modernization of plant facilities. (p. 752)

Capital decay   A loss in market share resulting from technologically obsolete products and operations. (p. 770)

Cost of capital   The overall cost to an organization of obtaining investment funds, including the cost of both debt sources and equity sources. This term is synonymous with *cutoff rate, hurdle rate,* and *required rate of return.* (p. 758)

Cutoff rate   This term is synonymous with *cost of capital, hurdle rate,* and *required rate of return.* (p. 759)

Hurdle rate   This term is synonymous with *cost of capital, cutoff rate,* and *required rate of return.* (p. 759)

Internal rate of return   The discount rate that will cause the net present value of an investment project to be equal to zero; thus, the internal rate of return represents the interest yield promised by a project over its useful life. This term is synonymous with *time-adjusted rate of return.* (p. 760)

Interpolation   The process of finding odd rates of return (such as 12.6% or 9.4%) that do not appear in published interest tables. (p. 761)

Net present value   The difference between the present value of the cash inflows and the cash outflows associated with an investment project. (p. 754)

Out-of-pocket costs   The actual cash outlays made during a period for salaries, advertising, repairs, and similar costs. (p. 759)

Payback period   The length of time that it takes for an investment project to recoup its own initial cost out of the cash receipts that it generates. (p. 772)

Postappraisal   The follow-up after a project has been approved and implemented to determine whether expected results are actually realized. (p. 777)

Preference decision   A decision as to which of several competing acceptable investment proposals is best. (p. 753)

Required rate of return   The minimum rate of return that an investment project must yield in order to be acceptable. This term is synonymous with *cost of capital, cutoff rate,* and *hurdle rate.* (p. 759)

Screening decision   A decision as to whether a proposed investment meets some preset standard of acceptance. (p. 752)

Simple rate of return   The rate of return promised by an investment project when the time value of money is not considered; it is computed by dividing a project's annual accounting net income by the initial investment required. (p. 775)

Time-adjusted rate of return   This term is synonymous with *internal rate of return.* (p. 760)

Working capital   The excess of current assets over current liabilities. (p. 756)

Yield   A term synonymous with *internal rate of return* and *time-adjusted rate of return.* (p. 760)

APPENDIX 14A: THE CONCEPT OF PRESENT VALUE

OBJECTIVE 11
Explain the concept of present value, and make present value computations with and without present value tables.

The point was made in the main body of the chapter that a manager would rather receive a dollar today than a year from now. There are two reasons why this is true. First, a dollar received today is more valuable than a dollar received a year from now. The dollar received today can be invested immediately, and by the end of the year it will have earned some return, making the total amount in hand at the end of the year *greater* than the investment started with. The person receiving the dollar a year from now will simply have a dollar in hand at that time.

Second, the future involves uncertainty. The longer people have to wait to receive a dollar, the more uncertain it becomes that they will ever get the dollar that they seek. As time passes, conditions change. The changes may be such as to make future payments of the dollar impossible.

Since money has a time value, the manager needs a method of determining whether a cash outlay made now in an investment project can be justified in terms of expected receipts from the project in future years. That is, the manager must have a means of expressing future receipts in present dollar terms so that the future receipts can be compared *on an equivalent basis* with whatever investment is required in the project under consideration. The theory of interest provides managers with the means of making such a comparison.

The Theory of Interest

If a bank pays $105 one year from now in return for a deposit of $100 now, we would say that the bank is paying interest at an annual rate of 5%. The relationships involved in this notion can be expressed in mathematical terms by means of the following equation:

$$F_1 = P(1 + r) \qquad\qquad (5)$$

where F_1 = the amount to be received in one year, P = the present outlay to be made, and r = the rate of interest involved.

If the present outlay is $100 deposited in a bank savings account that is to earn interest at 5%, then $P = \$100$ and $r = 0.05$. Under these conditions, $F_1 = \$105$, the amount to be received in one year.

The $100 present outlay is called the **present value** of the $105 amount to be received in one year. It is also known as the *discounted value* of the future $105 receipt. The $100 figure represents the value in present terms of a receipt of $105 to be received a year from now when the interest rate is 5%.

Compound Interest.   What if the investor leaves his or her money in the bank for a second year? In that case, by the end of the second year the original $100 deposit will have grown to $110.25:

Original deposit	$100.00
Interest for the first year:	
$100 × 0.05	5.00
Amount at the end of the first year	105.00
Interest for the second year:	
$105 × 0.05	5.25
Amount at the end of the second year	$110.25

Notice that the interest for the second year is $5.25, as compared to only $5 for the first year. The reason for the greater interest earned during the second year is that during the second year, interest is being paid *on interest*. That is, the $5 interest earned during the first year has been left in the account and has been added to the original $100 deposit in computing interest for the second year. This concept is known as **compound interest.** The compounding we have done is annual compounding. Interest can be compounded on a semiannual, quarterly, or even more frequent basis. Many savings institutions are now compounding interest on a daily basis. The more frequently compounding is done, the more rapidly the invested balance will grow.

How is the concept of compound interest expressed in equation form? It is expressed by taking equation (5) and adjusting it to state the number of years, n, that a sum is going to be left deposited in the bank:

$$F_n = P(1 + r)^n \qquad\qquad (6)$$

where n = years.

If $n = 2$ years, then our computation of the value of F in two years will be as follows:

$$F_2 = \$100(1 + 0.05)^2$$
$$F_2 = \$110.25$$

Present Value and Future Value.   Exhibit 14–13 shows the relationship between present value and future value as expressed in the theory of interest equations. As shown in the exhibit, if $100 is deposited in a bank at 5% interest, it will grow to $127.63 by the end of five years if interest is compounded annually.

EXHIBIT 14–13

The Relationship between Present Value and Future Value

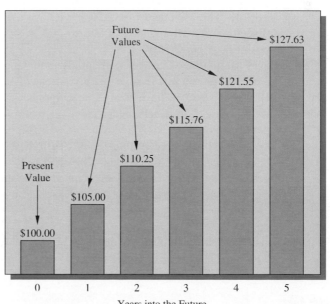

Computation of Present Value

An investment can be viewed in two ways. It can be viewed either in terms of its future value or in terms of its present value. We have seen from our computations above that if we know the present value of a sum (such as our $100 deposit), it is a relatively simple task to compute the sum's future value in n years by using equation (6). But what if the tables are reversed, and we know the *future* value of some amount but we do not know its present value?

For example, assume that you are to receive $200 two years from now. You know that the future value of this sum is $200, since this is the amount that you will be receiving in two years. But what is the sum's present value—what is it worth *right now?* The present value of any sum to be received in the future can be computed by turning equation (6) around and solving for P:

$$P = \frac{F_n}{(1 + r)^n} \qquad (7)$$

In our example, $F = \$200$ (the amount to be received in the future), $r = 0.05$ (the rate of interest), and $n = 2$ (the number of years in the future that the amount is to be received).

$$P = \frac{\$200}{(1 + 0.05)^2}$$

$$P = \frac{\$200}{1.1025}$$

$$P = \$181.40$$

As shown by the computation above, the present value of a $200 amount to be received two years from now is $181.40 if the interest rate is 5%. In effect, we are saying that $181.40 received *right now* is equivalent to $200 received two years from now if the rate of return is 5%. The $181.40 and the $200 are just two ways of looking at the same item.

The process of finding the present value of a future cash flow, which we have just completed, is called **discounting.** We have *discounted* the $200 to its present value of $181.40. The 5% interest figure that we have used to find this present value is called the **discount rate.** Discounting of future sums to their present value is a common practice in business. A knowledge of the present value of a sum to be received in the future can be very useful to the manager, particularly in making capital budgeting decisions.

If you have a power key (y^x) on your calculator, the above calculations are fairly easy. However, some of the present value formulas we will be using are more complex and difficult to use. Fortunately, tables are available in which the calculations have already been done for you. For example, Table 14C–3 in Appendix 14C shows the discounted present value of $1 to be received at various periods in the future at various interest rates. The table indicates that the present value of $1 to be received two periods from now at 5% is 0.907. Since in our example we want to know the present value of $200 rather than just $1, we need to multiply the factor in the table by $200:

$$\$200 \times 0.907 = \$181.40$$

The answer we obtain is the same answer as we obtained earlier using the formula in equation (7).

Example A

A purchaser promises to pay $96,800 two years from now for a lot of land. This amount includes interest at an annual rate of 10%. What is the selling price of the land today?

As indicated in Table 14C–3 (10% column, down two rows) the present value of $1 is $0.826. The present value of $96,800 is $79,956.80 ($96,800 times .826). A more accurate answer is found by using equation (3) as follows:

$$P = \$96,800(1 + .10)^{-2}$$
$$= \$80,000$$

Example B

A young lady in Vancouver plans to take a vacation trip four years from now. She estimates that she will need $18,000. At an annual interest rate of 16%, compounded quarterly, how much need be deposited in a bank account today to accumulate the required $18,000?

Because interest is compounded quarterly, the interest per period is 4% (the annual rate divided by four quarters). As shown in Table 14C–3, the present value of $1 to be received 16 periods in the future at 4% interest is $0.534. The present value of $18,000 is, therefore, $18,000 times .534 which is $9,612. The calculator solution is $18,000 \times (1 + .04)^{-16}$, which equals $9,610.35.

Present Value of a Series of Cash Flows (Annuity)

The present value of an **annuity** is the percent value of a series of equal payments or receipts discounted at compound interest and made at regular intervals. Stated differently, it is the sum that allows the withdrawal of a series of equal amounts at regular intervals if left at compound interest.

The present value of $1 to be received at the end of each of four periods at 8% interest per period is shown graphically in Exhibit 14–14.

Two points are important in connection with Exhibit 14–14. First, notice that the farther we go forward in time, the smaller is the present value of the $1 interest receipt. The present value of $1 received a year from now is $0.926, as compared to only $0.735 for the $1 interest payment to be received four periods from now. This point simply underscores the fact that money has a time value.

The second point is that even though the computations involved in Exhibit 14–14 are accurate, they have involved unnecessary work. The same present value of $3.312 could have been obtained more easily by referring to Table 14C–4 (8% column, down four rows). Table 14C–4 contains the present value of $1 to be received each year over a *series* of years at various interest rates. Table 14C–4 has been derived by simply adding together the factors from Table 14C–3.

The mathematical formula for the present value (P_n) of an annuity of $1 per period compounded at the rate of r for n periods is:

$$P_n = \frac{1 - (1 + r)^{-n}}{r} \quad or \quad \frac{1 - (1 + .08)^{-4}}{.08} = \$3.312$$

EXHIBIT 14-14

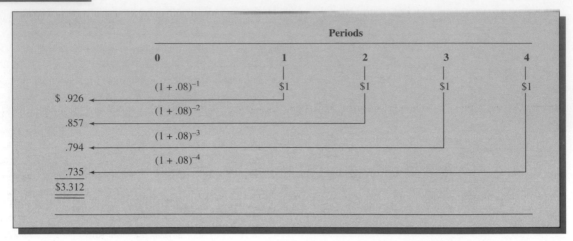

Example C

What is the present value of a series of six semiannual payments of $2,000 at 8% interest compounded annually? Assume that it is now January 1, 19x0, and the first payment is made on June 30, 19x0.

The purpose of solving this problem could be to determine (1) the sum that will provide for six semiannual withdrawals of $2,000 if invested at 4% per period (8% divided by two interest periods per year), and (2) the sum that is payable in settlement of a series of obligations of $2,000 that are due at six semiannual intervals and discounted at 4% per period. Using Table 14C–4 (4% column, down six periods) the value 5.242 is found. This present value of an annuity of $1 factor is then multiplied by $2,000 to give $10,484. Alternatively, using the present value of an ordinary annuity (annuity in arrears) formula:

$$P_n = \frac{1 - (1 + .04)^{-6}}{.04} \times \$2,000 = \$10,484.27$$

Example D

How much money would a company be willing to invest in a project that would return $3,000 every three months for three years, and in addition, a lump sum of $20,000 at the end of the third year? The receipts begin three months from now. Interest is 16% per annum.

The $3,000 to be received at the end of each three-month period is an ordinary annuity. The number of interest periods is 12 (4 per year for three years) and the quarterly interest rate is 4% (16%/4 periods). Using Table 14C–4 (4% column, down 12 rows) the value of 9.385 is found. The present value of this annuity is $28,155 (9.385 × $3,000). The present value of the single sum of $20,000 is .625 (Table 14C–3, 4% column, down 12 rows) times $20,000 or $12,500. The present value of the series of receipts and the single lump sum is, therefore, $28,155 plus $12,500, which totals $40,655.

Present Value of an Annuity Due

An annuity due is one in which the payments or receipts occur at the *beginning* of each period. Exhibit 14–15 compares the present value of an ordinary annuity of $1 for four periods with the present value of an annuity due for $1 for four periods. The interest rate is assumed to be 8%.

Note that Part B of Exhibit 14–15 can be interpreted as an ordinary annuity for $1 for three periods ($0.926 + $0.857 + $0.794) to which we add $1. We can calculate the present value of an annuity due by subtracting one period from n and calculating the present value of an ordinary annuity for $n - 1$ periods. We then add $1 to this annuity factor, which now gives the present value factor of an annuity due of $1.

Example E

On February 1, 1997, Vacon Company signed an 18-month lease with Aucoin Leasing Company. The lease payments begin immediately. Calculate the present value of the lease assuming that $2,000 is paid each quarter and that the annual interest rate is 16%.

We can solve this problem by first determining the present value of an ordinary annuity for $n - 1$ period where n is equal to six periods (18 months equals six quarters.)

EXHIBIT 14–15

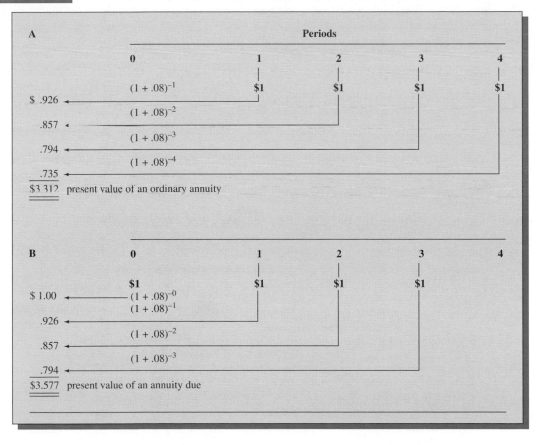

Using Table 14C–4, the present value of an annuity factor for 5 periods ($n - 1$) is 4.452 (4% column, 5 rows down). To this factor we add 1, resulting in an interest factor of 5.452. Next, we multiply the $2,000 payments by 5.452 to arrive at $10,904, the present value of the lease payments. Using the formula approach, the present value of an annuity due is as follows (calculator solution):

$$PV(\text{due}) = \$2,000 \times \left[1 + \frac{(1 - (1 + .04)^{-5}}{.04} \right]$$
$$= \$2,000 \times (1 + 4.4518223)$$
$$= \$2,000 \times 5.4518223$$
$$= \$10,903.65$$

Deferred Annuities

A deferred annuity is one in which the first payment or receipt does not begin until more than one interest period has expired. This is common for capital expenditure decisions that may take several periods to become operational.

Example F

What is the present value on January 1, 19x0, of a series of five receipts of $1,000, the first of which is expected to be received on January 1, 19x3? The interest rate is 10% per annum.

A graphical representation of the problem is as follows:

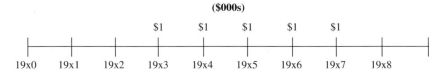

($000s)

One way of solving this problem is by the following two-step procedure:

Step 1.   Calculate the present value on January 1, 19x2, of an ordinary annuity of a series of five receipts of $1,000. This is $1,000 times 3.791 or $3,791.

Step 2.   The problem is now translated into a simple present value problem depicted as follows:

The present value on January 1, 19x0, can now be computed by discounting the $3,791 back two interest periods.

$$PV\text{January 1, 19x0} = \$3,791(1 + .10)^{-2}$$
$$= \$3,133$$

This problem could have also been solved by adding fictitious receipts on January 1, 19x1, and on January 1, 19x2, and calculating the present value of an ordinary annuity on January 1, 19x0, for 7 periods and then subtracting the present value of the receipts that did not occur:

Step 1:

$$\$1,000 \times \frac{(1 - (1 + .10)^{-7})}{.10}$$

$$= \$4,868$$

Step 2:

$$\$4,868 - \left(\$1,000 \times \frac{(1 - (1 + .10)^{-2})}{.10}\right)$$

$$= \$4,868 - \$1,735$$

$$= \$3,133$$

Future Value of an Annuity

Business transactions often involve a series of equal payments spaced evenly apart. As discussed earlier in the chapter, a series of equal payments at regular intervals is known as an annuity. The total that becomes due immediately after the last payment is the amount of an ordinary annuity or an annuity in arrears. If the payments are made or received at the beginning of the first interest period, the annuity is termed an annuity due or an annuity in advance.

The distinction between an ordinary annuity and an annuity due is presented graphically as follows:

Ordinary Annuity

	$1	$1	$1	$1
0	1	2	3	4

Annuity Due

$1	$1	$1	$1	$0
0	1	2	3	4

To illustrate how the future value of an ordinary annuity is determined, assume that $1 is deposited in a savings account at the end of each of four periods at 8% per period.

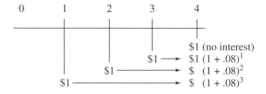

Thus, the value of an ordinary annuity of $1 due at the end of each period for four periods is:

$$\$1 + \$1(1 + .08)^1 + \$1(1 + .08)^2 + \$1(1 + .08)^3 =$$
$$\$1 + \quad \$1.08 \quad + \quad \$1.1664 \quad + \quad \$1.2597 \quad = \$4.5061$$

From the preceding illustration it can be seen that the $1 deposited at the end of the first year accumulates interest for a total of three periods, increasing to a value of

$1.2597. The deposit at the end of the second year grows to $1.1664, and the $1 deposited at the end of the third period accumulates to $1.08. The $1 deposited at the end of the fourth period has not yet earned any interest. The series of four payments of $1 each period grows to $4.5061 at the end of the fourth period.

This problem can be solved quickly by using a mathematical expression based on a geometric progression. The future value of an annuity in arrears (F_n) compounded at an interest rate (r) for a given number of periods (n) is:

$$F_n = \frac{(1+r)^n - 1}{r} \tag{5}$$

The value of a series of $1 deposits made at the end of each of four years compounded at 8% annually is

$$F_n = \$1 \times \frac{(1+.08)^4 - 1}{.08} = \$4.5061$$

The same calculation, rounded at three decimal places, can be determined by referring to Table 14C–2 (8% column, down four rows) and multiplying this factor by the amount of each receipt ($1).

It should be apparent that Tables 14C–1 and 14C–2 are related. We can treat each cash flow of the annuity separately and find the future value of each cash flow (Table 14C–1) and sum them. Alternatively, it is much faster to find the sum of the annuity using Table 14C–2.

To find the future value of an annuity of $1 per period for four periods if each payment is made at the *beginning* of each period (an annuity due), we can modify the formula as follows:

$$F_n(\text{due}) = \frac{(1+r)^n - 1}{r} \times (1+r)$$

$$= \frac{(1+.08)^4 - 1}{.08} \times (1+.08)$$

$$= \$4,867$$

The same result can be reached by looking up the interest factor in Table 14C–2 for one additional interest period and then subtracting 1 from this factor (8% column, five rows down, deduct 1 from the factor 5.867 to give 4.867). This problem is illustrated by the following diagram:

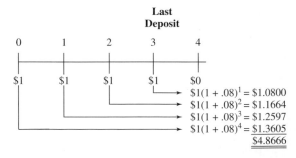

To summarize, the present value tables in Appendix C should be used as follows:

Table 14C–3: This table should be used to find the present value of a single cash flow (such as a single payment or receipt) occurring in the future.

Table 14C–4: This table should be used to find the present value of a series (or stream) of cash flows occurring in the future.

The use of both of these tables is illustrated in various exhibits in the main body of the chapter. *When a present value factor appears in an exhibit, the reader should take the time to trace it back into either Table 14C–3 or Table 14C–4 in order to get acquainted with the tables and how they work.* (Review Problem 1 at the end of this chapter was designed for those readers who would like some practice in present value analysis before attempting other homework exercises and problems.)

KEY TERMS FOR REVIEW (APPENDIX 14A)

Annuity   A series, or stream, of identical cash flows. (p. 787)
Compound interest   The process of paying interest on interest in an investment. (p. 785)
Discount rate   The rate of return that is used to find the present value of a future cash flow. (p. 786)
Discounting   The process of finding the present value of a future cash flow. (p. 786)
Present value   The estimated value now of an amount that will be received in some future period. (p. 784)

APPENDIX 14B: INFLATION AND CAPITAL BUDGETING

Doesn't inflation have an impact in a capital budgeting analysis? The answer is a qualified yes in that inflation does have an impact on the *numbers* that are used in a capital budgeting analysis, but it does not have an impact on the *results* of the analysis if certain conditions are satisfied. To show what we mean by this statement, we will use the following data:

Example A

Martin Company wants to purchase a new machine that costs $36,000. The machine would provide annual cost savings of $20,000, and it would have a three-year life with no salvage value. For each of the next three years, the company expects a 10% inflation rate in the cash flows associated with the new machine. If the company's cost of capital is 23.2%, should the new machine be purchased?

To answer this question, it is important to know how the cost of capital was derived. Ordinarily, it is based on the market rates of return on the company's various sources of financing—both debt and equity. This market rate of return includes expected inflation; the higher the expected rate of inflation, the higher the market rate of return on debt and equity. When the inflationary effect is removed from the market rate of return, the result is called a real rate of return. For example, if the inflation rate of 10% is removed from Martin's cost of capital of 23.2%, the "real cost of capital" is only 12%, as shown in Exhibit 14–16. (You can't simply subtract the inflation rate from the market cost of capital to obtain the real cost of capital. The computations are a bit more complex than that.)

When performing a net present value analysis, one must be consistent. The market-based cost of capital reflects inflation. Therefore, if a market-based cost of capital is used to discount cash flows, then the cash flows should be adjusted upwards to reflect the effects of inflation in forthcoming periods. Computations for Martin Company under this approach are given in solution B in Exhibit 14–16.

On the other hand, there is no need to adjust the cash flows upward if the "real cost of capital" is used in the analysis (since the inflationary effects have been taken out of the

EXHIBIT 14-16   Capital Budgeting and Inflation

Reconciliation of the Market-Based and Real Costs of Capital

The real cost of capital 12.0%
The inflation factor 10.0
The combined effect (12% × 10% = 1.2%) 1.2

The market-based cost of capital 23.2%

Solution A: Inflation Not Considered

Items	Year(s)	Amount of Cash Flows	12% Factor	Present Value of Cash Flows
Initial investment	Now	$(36,000)	1.000	$(36,000)
Annual cost savings	1–3	20,000	2.402	48,040
Net present value.............				$ 12,040‡

Solution B: Inflation Considered

Items	Year(s)	Amount of Cash Flows	Price Index Number*	Price-Adjusted Cash Flows	23.2% Factor†	Present Value of Cash Flows
Initial investment...............	Now	$(36,000)	1.000	$(36,000)	1.000	$(36,000)
Annual cost savings.............	1	20,000	1.100	22,000	0.812	17,864
	2	20,000	1.210	24,200	0.659	15,948
	3	20,000	1.331	26,620	0.535	14,242
						$ 12,054‡

*Computation of the price-index numbers, assuming a 10% inflation rate each year: year 1, $(1.10)^1 = 1.10$; year 2, $(1.10)^2 = 1.21$; and year 3, $(1.10)^3 = 1.331$.

†Discount formulas are computed using the formula $1/(1 + r)^n$, where r is the discount factor and n is the number of years. The computations are $1/1.232 = 0.812$ for year 1; $1/(1.232)^2 = 0.659$ for year 2; and $1/(1.232)^3 = 0.535$ for year 3.

‡These amounts are different only because of rounding error.

discount rate). Computations for Martin Company under this approach are given in solution A in Exhibit 14–16. Note that under solutions A and B that the answer will be the same (within rounding error) regardless of which approach is used, so long as one is consistent and all of the cash flows associated with the project are affected equally by inflation.

Several points should be noted about solution B, where the effects of inflation are explicitly taken into account. First, note that the annual cost savings are adjusted for the effects of inflation by multiplying each year's cash savings by a price-index number that reflects a 10% inflation rate. (Observe from the footnotes to the exhibit how the index number is computed for each year.) Second, note that the net present value obtained in solution B, where inflation is explicitly taken into account, is the same, within rounding error, to that obtained in solution A, where the inflation effects are ignored. This result may seem surprising, but it is logical. The reason is that we have adjusted both the cash flows and the discount rate so that they are consistent, and these adjustments cancel each other out across the two solutions.

Throughout the chapter we assumed for simplicity that there is no inflation. In that case, the market-based and real costs of capital are the same, and there is no reason to adjust the cash flows for inflation since there is none. When there is inflation, the unadjusted cash flows can be used in the analysis if all of the cash flows are affected equally by infla-tion and the real cost of capital is used to discount the cash flows. Otherwise, the cash flows should be adjusted for inflation and the market-based cost of capital should be used in the analysis.

APPENDIX 14C: FUTURE VALUE AND PRESENT VALUE TABLES

TABLE 14C-1

Future Value of $1;

$$F_n = P(1 + r)^n$$

Periods	4%	6%	8%	10%	12%	14%	20%
1	1.040	1.060	1.080	1.100	1.120	1.140	1.200
2	1.082	1.124	1.166	1.210	1.254	1.300	1.440
3	1.125	1.191	1.260	1.331	1.405	1.482	1.728
4	1.170	1.263	1.361	1.464	1.574	1.689	2.074
5	1.217	1.338	1.469	1.611	1.762	1.925	2.488
6	1.265	1.419	1.587	1.772	1.974	2.195	2.986
7	1.316	1.504	1.714	1.949	2.211	2.502	3.583
8	1.369	1.594	1.851	2.144	2.476	2.853	4.300
9	1.423	1.690	1.999	2.359	2.773	3.252	5.160
10	1.480	1.791	2.159	2.594	3.106	3.707	6.192
11	1.540	1.898	2.332	2.853	3.479	4.226	7.430
12	1.601	2.012	2.518	3.139	3.896	4.818	8.916
13	1.665	2.133	2.720	3.452	4.364	5.492	10.699
14	1.732	2.261	2.937	3.798	4.887	6.261	12.839
15	1.801	2.397	3.172	4.177	5.474	7.138	15.407
20	2.191	3.207	4.661	6.728	9.646	13.743	38.338
30	3.243	5.744	10.063	17.450	29.960	50.950	237.380
40	4.801	10.286	21.725	45.260	93.051	188.880	1469.800

TABLE 14C-2

Future Value of an Annuity of $1 in Arrears;

$$F_n = \frac{(1 + r)^n - 1}{r}$$

Periods	4%	6%	8%	10%	12%	14%	20%
1	1.000	1.000	1.000	1.000	1.000	1.000	1.000
2	2.040	2.060	2.080	2.100	2.120	2.140	2.220
3	3.122	3.184	3.246	3.310	3.374	3.440	3.640
4	4.247	4.375	4.506	4.641	4.779	4.921	5.368
5	5.416	5.637	5.867	6.105	6.353	6.610	7.442
6	6.633	6.975	7.336	7.716	8.115	8.536	9.930
7	7.898	8.394	8.923	9.487	10.089	10.730	12.916
8	9.214	9.898	10.637	11.436	12.300	13.233	16.499
9	10.583	11.491	12.488	13.580	14.776	16.085	20.799
10	12.006	13.181	14.487	15.938	17.549	19.337	25.959
11	13.486	14.972	16.646	18.531	20.655	23.045	32.150
12	15.026	16.870	18.977	21.385	24.133	27.271	39.580
13	16.627	18.882	21.495	24.523	28.029	32.089	48.497
14	18.292	21.015	24.215	27.976	32.393	37.581	59.196
15	20.024	23.276	27.152	31.773	37.280	43.842	72.035
20	29.778	36.778	45.762	57.276	75.052	91.025	186.690
30	56.085	79.058	113.283	164.496	241.330	356.790	1181.900
40	95.026	154.762	259.057	442.597	767.090	1342.000	7343.900

TABLE 14C-3   Present Value of $1; $P = \dfrac{F_n}{(1 + r)^n}$

Periods	4%	5%	6%	8%	10%	12%	14%	16%	18%	20%	22%	24%	26%	28%	30%	40%
1	0.962	0.952	0.943	0.926	0.909	0.893	0.877	0.862	0.847	0.833	0.820	0.806	0.794	0.781	0.769	0.714
2	0.925	0.907	0.890	0.857	0.826	0.797	0.769	0.743	0.718	0.694	0.672	0.650	0.630	0.610	0.592	0.510
3	0.889	0.864	0.840	0.794	0.751	0.712	0.675	0.641	0.609	0.579	0.551	0.524	0.500	0.477	0.455	0.364
4	0.855	0.823	0.792	0.735	0.683	0.636	0.592	0.552	0.516	0.482	0.451	0.423	0.397	0.373	0.350	0.260
5	0.822	0.784	0.747	0.681	0.621	0.567	0.519	0.476	0.437	0.402	0.370	0.341	0.315	0.291	0.269	0.186
6	0.790	0.746	0.705	0.630	0.564	0.507	0.456	0.410	0.370	0.335	0.303	0.275	0.250	0.227	0.207	0.133
7	0.760	0.711	0.665	0.583	0.513	0.452	0.400	0.354	0.314	0.279	0.249	0.222	0.198	0.178	0.159	0.095
8	0.731	0.677	0.627	0.540	0.467	0.404	0.351	0.305	0.266	0.233	0.204	0.179	0.157	0.139	0.123	0.068
9	0.703	0.645	0.592	0.500	0.424	0.361	0.308	0.263	0.225	0.194	0.167	0.144	0.125	0.108	0.094	0.048
10	0.676	0.614	0.558	0.463	0.386	0.322	0.270	0.227	0.191	0.162	0.137	0.116	0.099	0.085	0.073	0.035
11	0.650	0.585	0.527	0.429	0.350	0.287	0.237	0.195	0.162	0.135	0.112	0.094	0.079	0.066	0.056	0.025
12	0.625	0.557	0.497	0.397	0.319	0.257	0.208	0.168	0.137	0.112	0.092	0.076	0.062	0.052	0.043	0.018
13	0.601	0.530	0.469	0.368	0.290	0.229	0.182	0.145	0.116	0.093	0.075	0.061	0.050	0.040	0.033	0.013
14	0.577	0.505	0.442	0.340	0.263	0.205	0.160	0.125	0.099	0.078	0.062	0.049	0.039	0.032	0.025	0.009
15	0.555	0.481	0.417	0.315	0.239	0.183	0.140	0.108	0.084	0.065	0.051	0.040	0.031	0.025	0.020	0.006
16	0.534	0.458	0.394	0.292	0.218	0.163	0.123	0.093	0.071	0.054	0.042	0.032	0.025	0.019	0.015	0.005
17	0.513	0.436	0.371	0.270	0.198	0.146	0.108	0.080	0.060	0.045	0.034	0.026	0.020	0.015	0.012	0.003
18	0.494	0.416	0.350	0.250	0.180	0.130	0.095	0.069	0.051	0.038	0.028	0.021	0.016	0.012	0.009	0.002
19	0.475	0.396	0.331	0.232	0.164	0.116	0.083	0.060	0.043	0.031	0.023	0.017	0.012	0.009	0.007	0.002
20	0.456	0.377	0.312	0.215	0.149	0.104	0.073	0.051	0.037	0.026	0.019	0.014	0.010	0.007	0.005	0.001
21	0.439	0.359	0.294	0.199	0.135	0.093	0.064	0.044	0.031	0.022	0.015	0.011	0.008	0.006	0.004	0.001
22	0.422	0.342	0.278	0.184	0.123	0.083	0.056	0.038	0.026	0.018	0.013	0.009	0.006	0.004	0.003	0.001
23	0.406	0.326	0.262	0.170	0.112	0.074	0.049	0.033	0.022	0.015	0.010	0.007	0.005	0.003	0.002	
24	0.390	0.310	0.247	0.158	0.102	0.066	0.043	0.028	0.019	0.013	0.008	0.006	0.004	0.003	0.002	
25	0.375	0.295	0.233	0.146	0.092	0.059	0.038	0.024	0.016	0.010	0.007	0.005	0.003	0.002	0.001	
26	0.361	0.281	0.220	0.135	0.084	0.053	0.033	0.021	0.014	0.009	0.006	0.004	0.002	0.002	0.001	
27	0.347	0.268	0.207	0.125	0.076	0.047	0.029	0.018	0.011	0.007	0.005	0.003	0.002	0.001	0.001	
28	0.333	0.255	0.196	0.116	0.069	0.042	0.026	0.016	0.010	0.006	0.004	0.002	0.002	0.001	0.001	
29	0.321	0.243	0.185	0.107	0.063	0.037	0.022	0.014	0.008	0.005	0.003	0.002	0.001	0.001	0.001	
30	0.308	0.231	0.174	0.099	0.057	0.033	0.020	0.012	0.007	0.004	0.003	0.002	0.001	0.001		
40	0.208	0.142	0.097	0.046	0.022	0.011	0.005	0.003	0.001	0.001						

TABLE 14C-4   Present Value of an Annuity of $1 in Arrears; $P_n = \dfrac{1}{r}\left[1 - \dfrac{1}{(1+r)^n}\right]$

Periods	4%	5%	6%	8%	10%	12%	14%	16%	18%	20%	22%	24%	26%	28%	30%	40%
1	0.962	0.952	0.943	0.926	0.909	0.893	0.877	0.862	0.847	0.833	0.820	0.806	0.794	0.781	0.769	0.714
2	1.886	1.859	1.833	1.783	1.736	1.690	1.647	1.605	1.566	1.528	1.492	1.457	1.424	1.392	1.361	1.224
3	2.775	2.723	2.673	2.577	2.487	2.402	2.322	2.246	2.174	2.106	2.042	1.981	1.923	1.868	1.816	1.589
4	3.630	3.546	3.465	3.312	3.170	3.037	2.914	2.798	2.690	2.589	2.494	2.404	2.320	2.241	2.166	1.879
5	4.452	4.330	4.212	3.993	3.791	3.605	3.433	3.274	3.127	2.991	2.864	2.745	2.635	2.532	2.436	2.035
6	5.242	5.076	4.917	4.623	4.355	4.111	3.889	3.685	3.498	3.326	3.167	3.020	2.885	2.759	2.643	2.168
7	6.002	5.786	5.582	5.206	4.868	4.564	4.288	4.039	3.812	3.605	3.416	3.242	3.083	2.937	2.802	2.263
8	6.733	6.463	6.210	5.747	5.335	4.968	4.639	4.344	4.078	3.837	3.619	3.421	3.241	3.076	2.925	2.331
9	7.435	7.108	6.802	6.247	5.759	5.328	4.946	4.607	4.303	4.031	3.786	3.566	3.366	3.184	3.019	2.379
10	8.111	7.722	7.360	6.710	6.145	5.650	5.216	4.833	4.494	4.192	3.923	3.682	3.465	3.269	3.092	2.414
11	8.760	8.306	7.887	7.139	6.495	5.988	5.453	5.029	4.656	4.327	4.035	3.776	3.544	3.335	3.147	2.438
12	9.385	8.863	8.384	7.536	6.814	6.194	5.660	5.197	4.793	4.439	4.127	3.851	3.606	3.387	3.190	2.456
13	9.986	9.394	8.853	7.904	7.103	6.424	5.842	5.342	4.910	4.533	4.203	3.912	3.656	3.427	3.223	2.468
14	10.563	9.899	9.295	8.244	7.367	6.628	6.002	5.468	5.008	4.611	4.265	3.962	3.695	3.459	3.249	2.477
15	11.118	10.380	9.712	8.559	7.606	6.811	6.142	5.575	5.092	4.675	4.315	4.001	3.726	3.483	3.268	2.484
16	11.652	10.838	10.106	8.851	7.824	6.974	6.265	5.669	5.162	4.730	4.357	4.033	3.751	3.503	3.283	2.489
17	12.166	11.274	10.477	9.122	8.022	7.120	6.373	5.749	5.222	4.775	4.391	4.059	3.771	3.518	3.295	2.492
18	12.659	11.690	10.828	9.372	8.201	7.250	6.467	5.818	5.273	4.812	4.419	4.080	3.786	3.529	3.304	2.494
19	13.134	12.085	11.158	9.604	8.365	7.366	6.550	5.877	5.316	4.844	4.442	4.097	3.799	3.539	3.311	2.496
20	13.590	12.462	11.470	9.818	8.514	7.469	6.623	5.929	5.353	4.870	4.460	4.110	3.808	3.546	3.316	2.497
21	14.029	12.821	11.764	10.017	8.649	7.562	6.687	5.973	5.384	4.891	4.476	4.121	3.816	3.551	3.320	2.498
22	14.451	13.163	12.042	10.201	8.772	7.645	6.743	6.011	5.410	4.909	4.488	4.130	3.822	3.556	3.323	2.498
23	14.857	13.489	12.303	10.371	8.883	7.718	6.792	6.044	5.432	4.925	4.499	4.137	3.827	3.559	3.325	2.499
24	15.247	13.799	12.550	10.529	8.985	7.784	6.835	6.073	5.451	4.937	4.507	4.143	3.831	3.562	3.327	2.499
25	15.622	14.094	12.783	10.675	9.077	7.843	6.873	6.097	5.467	4.948	4.514	4.147	3.834	3.564	3.329	2.499
26	15.983	14.375	13.003	10.810	9.161	7.896	6.906	6.118	5.480	4.956	4.520	4.151	3.837	3.566	3.330	2.500
27	16.330	14.643	13.211	10.935	9.237	7.943	6.935	6.136	5.492	4.964	4.525	4.154	3.839	3.567	3.331	2.500
28	16.663	14.898	13.406	11.051	9.307	7.984	6.961	6.152	5.502	4.970	4.528	4.157	3.840	3.568	3.331	2.500
29	16.984	15.141	13.591	11.158	9.370	8.022	6.983	6.166	5.510	4.975	4.531	4.159	3.841	3.569	3.332	2.500
30	17.292	15.373	13.765	11.258	9.427	8.055	7.003	6.177	5.517	4.979	4.534	4.160	3.842	3.569	3.332	2.500
40	19.793	17.159	15.046	11.925	9.779	8.244	7.105	6.234	5.548	4.997	4.544	4.166	3.846	3.571	3.333	2.500

QUESTIONS

14–1   Distinguish between capital budgeting screening decisions and capital budgeting preference decisions.

14–2   What is meant by the term *time value of money?*

14–3   What is meant by the term *discounting,* and why is it important to the business manager?

14–4   Why can't accounting net income figures be used in the net present value and internal rate of return methods of making capital budgeting decisions?

14–5   Why are discounted cash flow methods of making capital budgeting decisions superior to other methods?

14–6   What is net present value? Can it ever be negative? Explain.

14–7   Identify two limiting assumptions associated with discounted cash flow methods of making capital budgeting decisions.

14–8   If a firm has to pay interest of 14% on long-term debt, then its cost of capital is 14%. Do you agree? Explain.

14–9   What is meant by an investment project's internal rate of return? How is the internal rate of return computed?

14–10 Explain how the cost of capital serves as a screening tool when dealing with (a) the net present value method and (b) the internal rate of return method.

14–11 Riskier investment proposals should be discounted at lower rates of return. Do you agree? Why or why not?

14–12 As the discount rate increases, the present value of a given future sum also increases. Do you agree? Explain.

14–13 Refer to Exhibit 14–4. Is the return promised by this investment proposal exactly 20%, slightly more than 20%, or slightly less than 20%? Explain.

14–14 Frontier Company is investigating the purchase of a piece of automated equipment, but after considering the savings in labour costs the machine has a negative net present value. If no other cost savings can be identified, should the company reject the equipment? Explain.

14–15 What is meant by the term *payback period?* How is the payback period determined?

14–16 In what ways can the payback method be useful to the manager?

14–17 What is the major criticism of the payback and simple rate of return methods of making capital budgeting decisions?

EXERCISES

E14–1 Consider each of the following situations independently. (Ignore income taxes.)

1. Annual cash inflows that will arise from two competing investment opportunities are given below. Each investment opportunity will require the same initial investment. You can invest money at a 20% rate of return. Compute the present value of the cash inflows for each investment.

	Investment	
Year	X	Y
1.........	$ 1,000	$ 4,000
2.........	2,000	3,000
3.........	3,000	2,000
4.........	4,000	1,000
	$10,000	$10,000

2. At the end of three years, when you graduate from college, your father has promised to give you a new car that will cost $12,000. What lump sum must he invest now to have the $12,000 at the end of three years if he can invest money at:
    a. 6%?
    b. 10%?

3. Mark has just won the grand prize on the "Hoot 'n' Holler" quiz show. He has a choice between (a) receiving $50,000 immediately and (b) receiving $6,000 per year for eight years plus a lump sum of $20,000 at the end of the eight-year period. If Mark can get a return of 10% on his investments, which option would you recommend that he accept? (Use present value analysis, and show all computations.)

4. You have just learned that you are a beneficiary in the will of your late Aunt Susan. The executrix of her estate has given you three options as to how you may receive your inheritance:
    a. You may receive $50,000 immediately.
    b. You may receive $75,000 at the end of six years.
    c. You may receive $12,000 at the end of each year for six years (a total of $72,000). If you can invest money at a 12% return, which option would you prefer?

E14–2 Each of the following parts is independent. (Ignore income taxes.)

1. Largo Freightlines plans to build a new garage in three years to have more space for repairing its trucks. The garage will cost $400,000. What lump-sum amount should the

company invest now to have the $400,000 available at the end of the three-year period? Assume that the company can invest money at:
   a. 8%.
   b. 12%.
2. Martell Products, Ltd., can purchase a new copier that will save $5,000 per year in copying costs. The copier will last for six years and have no salvage value. What is the maximum purchase price that Martell Products would be willing to pay for the copier if the company's required rate of return is:
   a. 10%.
   b. 16%.
3. Sally has just won the million-dollar Big Slam jackpot at a gambling casino. The casino will pay her $50,000 per year for 20 years as the payoff. If Sally can invest money at a 10% rate of return, what is the present value of her winnings? Did she really win a million dollars? Explain.

E14–3 On January 2, Fred Critchfield paid $18,000 for 900 common shares of Acme Company. Mr. Critchfield received an $0.80 per share dividend on the shares each year for four years. At the end of four years, he sold the shares for $22,500. Mr. Critchfield has a goal of earning a minimum return of 12% on all of his investments.

Required
(ignore income taxes)

Did Mr. Critchfield earn a 12% return on the shares? Use the net present value method and the general format shown in Exhibit 14–4 in determining your answer. (Round all computations to the nearest whole dollar.)

E14–4 Consider each case below independently.
1. Minden Company requires a minimum return of 18% on all investments. The company can purchase a new machine at a cost of $40,350. The new machine would generate cash inflows of $15,000 per year and have a four-year life with no salvage value. Compute the machine's net present value. (Use the format shown in Exhibit 14–1.) Is the machine an acceptable investment? Explain.
2. Leven Products, Inc., is investigating the purchase of a new grinding machine that has a projected life of 15 years. It is estimated that the machine will save $20,000 per year in cash operating costs. What is the machine's internal rate of return if it costs $93,500 new?
3. Sunset Press has just purchased a new trimming machine that cost $14,125. The machine is expected to save $2,500 per year in cash operating costs and to have a 10-year life. Compute the machine's internal rate of return. If the company's cost of capital is 16%, did it make a wise investment? Explain.

E14–5 Scalia's Cleaning Service is investigating the purchase of an ultrasound machine for cleaning window blinds. The machine would cost $136,700, including invoice cost, freight, and training of employees to operate it. Scalia's has estimated that the new machine would increase the company's cash flows, net of expenses, by $25,000 per year. The machine would have a 14-year useful life with no expected salvage value.

Required
(ignore income taxes)

1. Compute the machine's internal rate of return. (Do not round your computations.)
2. Compute the machine's net present value. Use a discount rate of 16%, and use the format shown in Exhibit 14–5. Why do you have a zero net present value? If the company's cost of capital is 15%, is this an acceptable investment? Explain.
3. Suppose that the new machine would increase the company's annual cash flows, net of expenses, by only $20,000 per year. Under these conditions, compute the internal rate of return. Interpolate as needed, and round your final answer to the nearest tenth of a percent.

E14–6 Pisa Pizza Parlor is investigating the purchase of a new delivery truck that would contain specially designed warming racks. The new truck would cost $22,300 and have a six-year useful life. It would save $1,400 per year over the present method of delivering pizzas.

In addition, it would result in delivery of about 1,800 more pizzas each year. The company realizes a contribution margin of $2 per pizza.

Required
(ignore income taxes)

1. What would be the total annual cash inflows associated with the new truck for capital budgeting purposes?
2. Compute the internal rate of return promised by the new truck. Interpolate to the nearest tenth of a percent.
3. In addition to the data above, assume that due to the unique warming racks, the truck will have a $13,000 salvage value at the end of six years. Under these conditions, compute the internal rate of return to the nearest whole percent. (Hint: You may find it helpful to use the net present value approach; find the discount rate that will cause the net present value to be closest to zero. Use the format shown in Exhibit 14–4.)

E14–7 Wriston Company has $300,000 to invest. The company is trying to decide between two alternative uses of the funds. The alternatives are as follows:

	A	B
Cost of equipment required	$300,000	$ —
Working capital investment required	—	300,000
Annual cash inflows	80,000	60,000
Salvage value of equipment in seven years	20,000	—
Life of the project	7 years	7 years

The working capital needed for project B will be released for investment elsewhere at the end of seven years. Wriston Company's cost of capital is 20%.

Required
(ignore income taxes)

Which investment alternative (if either) would you recommend that the company accept? Show all computations using the net present value format. (Prepare a separate computation for each project.)

E14–8 Sharp Company has $15,000 to invest. The company is trying to decide between two alternative uses of the funds. The alternatives are as follows:

	Invest in Project A	Invest in Project B
Investment required	$15,000	$15,000
Annual cash inflows	4,000	—
Single cash inflow at the end of 10 years	—	60,000
Life of the project	10 years	10 years

Sharp Company's cost of capital is 16%.

Required
(ignore income taxes)

Which investment would you recommend that the company accept? Show all computations using net present value. (Use the format shown in Exhibit 14–4. Prepare a separate computation for each investment.)

E14–9 Solve the three following present value exercises.
1. Mountain View Clinic has purchased new lab equipment that cost $134,650. The equipment is expected to last for three years and to provide cash inflows as follows:

> Year 1 .... $45,000
> Year 2   60,000
> Year 3 ....   ?

Assuming that the equipment will yield exactly a 16% rate of return, what is the expected cash inflow for year 3?

2. Lukow Products is investigating the purchase of a piece of automated equipment that will save $400,000 each year in direct labour and inventory carrying costs. This equipment costs $2,500,000 and is expected to have a 15-year useful life with no salvage value. The company requires a minimum 20% return on all equipment purchases. Management anticipates that this equipment will provide certain intangible benefits such as greater flexibility, higher quality of output, and a positive learning experience in automation. What dollar value per year would management have to attach to these intangible benefits in order to make the equipment an acceptable investment?

3. Worldwide Travel Service has made an investment in certain equipment that cost the company $307,100. The equipment is expected to generate cash inflows of $50,000 each year. How many years will the equipment have to be used in order to provide the company with a 14% return on its investment?

E14–10 Martin Company is considering the purchase of a new piece of equipment. Relevant information concerning the equipment follows:

Purchase cost.	$180,000
Annual cost savings that will be	
provided by the equipment	37,500
Life of the equipment	12 years
Cost of capital.	14%

**Required
(ignore income
taxes)**

1. Compute the payback period for the equipment. If the company requires a maximum payback period of four years, would you recommend purchase of the equipment? Explain.
2. Compute the simple rate of return on the equipment. Use straight-line depreciation based on the equipment's useful life. Would you recommend purchase of the equipment? Explain.

E14–11 The Heritage Amusement Park would like to construct a new ride called the Sonic Boom, which the park management feels would be very popular. The ride would cost $450,000 to construct, and it would have a 10% salvage value at the end of its 15-year useful life. It is estimated that the following annual costs and revenues would be associated with the ride:

Ticket revenues		$250,000
Less operating expenses:		
Maintenance	$40,000	
Salaries	90,000	
Depreciation	27,000	
Insurance	30,000	
Total operating expenses		187,000
Net income		$ 63,000

**Required
(ignore income
taxes)**

1. Assume that the Heritage Amusement Park will not construct a new ride unless the ride promises a payback period of six years or less. Does the Sonic Boom ride satisfy this requirement?
2. Compute the simple rate of return promised by the new ride. (Compute investment at initial cost.) If Heritage Amusement Park requires a simple rate of return of at least 12%, does the Sonic Boom ride meet this criterion?

PROBLEMS

P14–12 Basic Net Present Value Analysis   Renfree Mines, Ltd., owns the mining rights to a large tract of land in a mountainous area. The tract contains a mineral deposit that the company believes might be commercially attractive to mine and sell. An engineering and cost analysis has been made, and it is expected that the following cash flows would be associated with opening and operating a mine in the area:

Cost of equipment required.	$850,000
Net annual cash receipts	230,000*
Working capital required.	100,000
Cost of road repairs in three years	60,000
Salvage value of equipment in five years	200,000

*Receipts from sales of ore, less out-of-pocket costs for salaries, utilities,
insurance, and so forth.

It is estimated that the mineral deposit would be exhausted after five years of mining. At that point, the working capital would be released for reinvestment elsewhere. The company's cost of capital is 14%.

Required
(ignore income taxes)

Determine the net present value of the proposed mining project. Should the project be undertaken? Explain.

P14–13 Basic Net Present Value Analysis   Doughboy Bakery would like to buy a new machine for putting icing and other toppings on pastries. These are now put on by hand. The machine that the bakery is considering costs $90,000 new. It would last the bakery for eight years but would require a $7,500 overhaul at the end of the fifth year. After eight years, the machine could be sold for $6,000.

The bakery estimates that it will cost $14,000 per year to operate the new machine. The present hand method of putting toppings on the pastries costs $35,000 per year. In addition to reducing operating costs, the new machine will allow the bakery to increase its production of pastries by 5,000 packages per year. The bakery realizes a contribution margin of $0.60 per package. The bakery requires a 16% return on all investments in equipment.

Required
(ignore income taxes)

1. What are the net annual cash inflows that will be provided by the new machine?
2. Compute the new machine's net present value. Use the incremental cost approach, and round all dollar amounts to the nearest whole dollar.

P14–14 Opening a Small Business; Net Present Value   Frank White will retire in six years. He has $50,000 to invest, and he wants to open some type of small business operation that can be managed in the free time he has available from his regular occupation, but that can be closed easily when he retires. He is considering several investment alternatives, one of which is to open a laundromat.

After careful study, Mr. White has determined the following:

a. Washers, dryers, and other equipment needed to open the laundromat would cost $48,000. In addition, $2,000 in working capital investment would be required to purchase an inventory of soap, bleaches, and related items and to provide change for change machines. (The soap, bleaches, and related items would be sold to customers basically at cost.) After six years, the working capital would be released for investment elsewhere.
b. The laundromat would charge 50 cents per use for the washers and 25 cents per use for the dryers. (A regular wash cycle is 20 minutes, and a regular dryer cycle is 15 minutes.) Mr. White expects the laundromat to gross $600 each week from the washers and $375 each week from the dryers.
c. The only variable costs in the laundromat would be 7½ cents per use for water and electricity for the washers and 9 cents per use for gas and electricity for the dryers.
d. Fixed costs would be $1,000 per month for rent, $500 per month for cleaning, and $625 per month for maintenance, insurance, and other items.
e. The equipment would have a 10% disposal value in six years.

Mr. White will not open the laundromat unless it provides at least a 12% return, since this is the amount that he could earn from an alternative investment opportunity.

Required
(ignore income taxes)

1. Assuming that the laundromat would be open 52 weeks a year, compute the expected net annual cash receipts from its operation (gross cash receipts less cash disbursements). (Do not include the cost of the equipment, the working capital, or the salvage values in these computations.)
2. Would you advise Mr. White to open the laundromat? Show computations using the net present value method of investment analysis. Round all dollar amounts to the nearest whole dollar.

P14–15 Net Present Value Analysis; FMS/Automation Decision   Tiger Computers, Inc., of Singapore is considering the purchase of an automated etching machine for use in the production of its circuit boards. The machine would cost $900,000. (All currency amounts are in Singapore dollars.) An additional $650,000 would be required for installation costs and for software. Management believes that the automated machine would provide substantial annual reductions in costs, as shown below:

	Annual Reduction in Costs
Labour costs	$240,000
Material costs	96,000

The new machine would require considerable maintenance work to keep it in proper adjustment. The company's engineers estimate that maintenance costs would increase by $4,250 per month if the machine is purchased. In addition, the machine would require an overhaul at the end of the sixth year that the manufacturer estimates would cost $90,000.

The new etching machine would be usable for 10 years, after which it would be sold for its scrap value of $210,000. It would replace an old etching machine that can be sold now for its scrap value of $70,000. Tiger Computers, Inc., requires a return of at least 18% on investments of this type.

Required
(ignore income taxes)

1. Compute the net annual cost savings promised by the new etching machine.
2. Using the data from (1) above and other data from the problem, compute the new machine's net present value. (Use the incremental-cost approach.) Would you recommend purchase? Explain.
3. Assume that management can identify several intangible benefits associated with the new machine, including greater flexibility in shifting from one type of circuit board to another, improved quality of output, and faster delivery as a result of reduced throughput time. What dollar value per year would management have to attach to these intangible benefits in order to make the new etching machine an acceptable investment?

P14–16   Simple Rate of Return; Payback   Lugano's Pizza Parlor is considering the purchase of a large oven and related equipment for mixing and baking "crazy bread." The oven and equipment would cost $120,000 delivered and installed. It would be usable for about 15 years, after which it would have a 10% scrap value. The following additional information is available:

a. Mr. Lugano estimates that purchase of the oven and equipment would allow the pizza parlor to bake and sell 72,000 loaves of crazy bread each year. The bread sells for $1.25 per loaf.
b. The cost of the ingredients in a loaf of bread is 40% of the selling price. Mr. Lugano estimates that other costs each year associated with the bread would be the following: salaries, $18,000; utilities, $9,000; and insurance, $3,000.
c. The pizza parlor uses straight-line depreciation on all assets and considers salvage value in computing depreciation deductions.

Required
(ignore income taxes)

1. Prepare an income statement showing the net income each year from production and sale of the crazy bread. Use the contribution format.
2. Compute the simple rate of return promised by the new oven and equipment. If a simple rate of return above 12% is acceptable to Mr. Lugano, should the oven and equipment be purchased?
3. Compute the payback period on the oven and equipment. If Mr. Lugano wants a maximum six-year payback on any equipment, should the purchase be made?

P14–17   Net Present Value Analysis of Securities   Three years ago, Frank Vecci had $245,000 to invest. He used the funds to purchase the following three securities:

a. Preferred shares were purchased at their face value of $50,000. The share paid a 7% dividend (based on face value) each year for three years. At the end of three years, the shares were sold for $49,000.
b. Common shares were purchased at a cost of $95,000. The shares paid no dividends, but they were sold for $160,000 at the end of three years.

c. Bonds were purchased at a cost of $100,000. The bonds paid $6,000 in interest every six months. After three years, the bonds were sold for $113,400. (Note: In discounting a cash flow that occurs every six months, a common procedure is to halve the discount rate and double the number of periods. Use the same procedure in discounting the proceeds from the sale of the bonds.)

After all of the investments had been sold, Mr. Vecci's broker stated that the investments had earned more than a 16% return. The broker provided the following computations to support his claim:

Preferred shares:	
Dividends paid (7% × $50,000 × 3 years).	$ 10,500
Loss on sale ($49,000 − $50,000)	(1,000)
Common shares:	
Gain on sale ($160,000 − $95,000)	65,000
Bonds:	
Interest paid ($6,000 × 2 × 3 years).	36,000
Gain on sale ($113,400 − $100,000).	13,400
Net gain on all investments	$123,900

$$\frac{\$123,900 \div 3 \text{ years}}{\$245,000} = 16.9\% \text{ (rounded)}$$

Mr. Vecci's goal was to earn a before-tax return of at least 16% on his investments. In your answer to the following questions, round all dollar amounts to the nearest whole dollar.

Required
(ignore income taxes)

1. Compute the net present value of each of the three investments. On which investments did Mr. Vecci earn at least the desired 16% return?
2. Considering all three investments together, did Mr. Vecci earn the desired 16% return?
3. An insurance salesperson has approached Mr. Vecci with a proposal that Mr. Vecci invest the $322,400 proceeds from the sale of the securities ($49,000 + $160,000 + $113,400 = $322,400) in a 10-year annuity. The salesperson says that the annuity is guaranteed to yield an 18% return each year over the next 10 years. What annual cash inflow would Mr. Vecci have to receive from the annuity in order to earn an 18% return on his investment?

P14–18 Replacement Decision   Eastbay Care Centre has an auxiliary generator that is used when power failures occur. The generator is in bad repair and must be either overhauled or replaced with a new generator. The centre has assembled the following information:

	Present Generator	New Generator
Purchase cost new.	$16,000	$20,000
Remaining book value	9,000	—
Overhaul needed now	8,000	—
Annual cash operating costs	12,500	7,500
Salvage value—now	4,000	—
Salvage value—eight years from now	3,000	6,000

If the company keeps and overhauls its present generator, then the generator will be usable for eight more years. If a new generator is purchased, it will be used for eight years, after which it will be replaced. The new generator would be diesel-powered, resulting in a substantial reduction in annual operating costs, as shown above.

The centre computes depreciation on a straight-line basis. All equipment purchases are evaluated on the basis of a 16% rate of return.

Required
(ignore income taxes)

1. Should Eastbay Care Centre keep the old generator or purchase the new one? Use the total-cost approach to net present value in making your decision.
2. Redo (1) above, this time using the incremental-cost approach.

P14–19   Internal Rate of Return; Sensitivity Analysis   Dr. Heidi Black is the managing partner of the Crestwood Dental Clinic. Dr. Black is trying to determine whether or not the clinic should move patient files and other items out of a spare room in the clinic and use the room for dental work. She has determined that it would require an investment of $142,950 for equipment and related costs of getting the room ready for use. Based on receipts being generated from other rooms in the clinic, Dr. Black estimates that the new room would generate a net cash inflow of $37,500 per year. The equipment purchased for the room would have a seven-year estimated useful life.

Required
(ignore income taxes)

1. Compute the internal rate of return on the equipment for the new room. Verify your answer by computing the net present value of the equipment using the rate of return figure you have computed as the discount rate.
2. Assume that Dr. Black will not purchase the new equipment unless it promises a return of at least 14%. Compute the amount of annual cash inflow that would provide this return on the $142,950 investment.
3. Although seven years is the average life for dental equipment, Dr. Black knows that due to changing technology this life can vary substantially. Compute the internal rate of return if the life of the equipment were (a) five years and (b) nine years, rather than seven years. Interpolate to the nearest tenth of a percent. Is there any information provided by these computations that you would be particularly anxious to show Dr. Black?
4. Dr. Black is unsure about the estimated $37,500 annual cash inflow from the room. She thinks that the actual cash inflow could be as much as 20% greater or less than this figure.
    a. Assume that the actual cash inflow each year is 20% greater than estimated. Recompute the internal rate of return. Interpolate to the nearest tenth of a percent.
    b. Assume that the actual cash inflow each year is 20% less than estimated. Recompute the internal rate of return. Again interpolate to the nearest tenth of a percent.
5. Refer to the original data. Assume that the equipment is purchased and that the room is opened for dental use. However, due to an increasing number of dentists in the area, the clinic is able to generate only $30,000 per year in net cash receipts from the new room. At the end of five years, the clinic closes the room and sells the equipment to a newly licensed dentist for a cash price of $61,375. Compute the internal rate of return (to the nearest *whole* percent) that the clinic earned on its investment over the five-year period. Round all dollar amounts to the nearest whole dollar. (Hint: A useful way to proceed is to find the discount rate that will cause the net present value of the investment to be equal to, or near, zero).

P14–20   Simple Rate of Return; Payback   Nagoya Amusements Corporation places electronic games and other amusement devices in supermarkets and similar outlets throughout Japan. Nagoya Amusements is investigating the purchase of a new electronic game called Mystic Invaders. The manufacturer will sell 20 games to Nagoya Amusements for a total price of ¥180,000. (The Japanese currency is yen, which is denoted by the symbol ¥.) Nagoya Amusements has determined the following additional information about the game:
  a. The game would have a five-year useful life and only a negligible salvage value. The company uses straight-line depreciation.
  b. The game would replace other games that are unpopular and generating little revenue. These other games would be sold in bulk for a ¥30,000 sale price.
  c. Nagoya Amusements estimates that Mystic Invaders would generate incremental revenues of ¥200,000 per year (total for all 20 games). Incremental out-of-pocket costs each year would be (in total): maintenance, ¥50,000; and insurance, ¥10,000. In addition, Nagoya Amusements would have to pay a commission of 40% of total revenues to the supermarkets and other outlets in which the games were placed.

Required
(ignore income taxes)

1. Prepare an income statement showing the net income each year from Mystic Invaders. Use the contribution approach.
2. Compute the simple rate of return on Mystic Invaders. Should the game be purchased if Nagoya Amusements accepts any project with a simple rate of return greater than 14%?

3. Compute the payback period on Mystic Invaders. If the company requires a payback period of three years or less, should the game be purchased?

P14–21 Lease or Buy Decision   Blinko Products wants an airplane available for use by its corporate staff. The airplane that the company wishes to acquire, a Zephyr II, can be either purchased or leased from the manufacturer. The company has made the following evaluation of the two alternatives:

Purchase alternative. If the Zephyr II is purchased, then the costs incurred by the company would be as follows:

Purchase cost of the plane	$850,000
Annual cost of servicing,	
licences, and taxes	9,000
Repairs:	
First three years, per year	3,000
Fourth year	5,000
Fifth year	10,000

The plane would be sold after five years. Based on current resale values, the company would be able to sell it for about one-half of its original cost at the end of the five-year period.

Lease alternative. If the Zephyr II is leased, then the company would have to make an immediate deposit of $50,000 to cover any damage during use. The lease would run for five years, at the end of which time the deposit would be refunded. The lease would require an annual rental payment of $200,000 (the first payment is due at the end of year 1). As part of this lease cost, the manufacturer would provide all servicing and repairs, license the plane, and pay all taxes. At the end of the five-year period, the plane would revert to the manufacturer, as owner.

Blinko Products' cost of capital is 18%.

Required
(ignore income taxes)

1. Use the total-cost approach to determine the present value of the cash flows associated with each alternative.
2. Which alternative would you recommend that the company accept? Why?

P14–22 Simple Rate of Return; Payback; Internal Rate of Return   Chateau Beaune is a family-owned winery located in the Burgundy region of France, which is headed by Gerard Despinoy. The harvesting season in early fall is the busiest part of the year for the winery, and many part-time workers are hired to help pick and process grapes. Mr. Despinoy is investigating the purchase of a harvesting machine that would significantly reduce the amount of labour required in the picking process. The harvesting machine is built to straddle grapevines, which are laid out in low-lying rows. Two workers are carried on the machine just above ground level, one on each side of the vine. As the machine slowly crawls through the vineyard, the workers cut bunches of grapes from the vines, which then fall into a hopper. The machine separates the grapes from the stems and other woody debris. The debris are then pulverized and spread behind the machine as a rich ground mulch. Mr. Despinoy has gathered the following information relating to the decision of whether to purchase the machine:

a. The winery would save 190,000 FF per year in labour costs with the new harvesting machine. In addition, the company would no longer have to purchase and spread ground mulch—at an annual savings of 10,000 FF. (The French currency is the French franc, which is denoted by the symbol FF.)
b. The harvesting machine would cost 480,000 FF. It would have an estimated 12-year useful life and zero salvage value. The winery uses straight-line depreciation.
c. Annual out-of-pocket costs associated with the harvesting machine would be insurance, 1,000 FF; fuel, 9,000 FF; and a maintenance contract, 12,000 FF. In addition, an operator would be hired and trained for the machine, and this individual would be paid 70,000 FF per year.

d. Mr. Despinoy feels that the investment in the harvesting machine should earn at least a 16% rate of return.

Required
(ignore income taxes)

1. Determine the annual net savings in cash operating costs that would be realized if the harvesting machine were purchased.
2. Compute the simple rate of return expected from the harvesting machine. (Hint: This is a cost reduction project.)
3. Compute the payback period on the harvesting machine. Mr. Despinoy will not purchase equipment unless it has a payback period of five years or less. Under this criterion, should the harvesting machine be purchased?
4. Compute (to the nearest whole percent) the internal rate of return promised by the harvesting machine. Based on this computation, does it appear that the simple rate of return is an accurate guide in investment decisions?

P14–23   Comprehensive Problem: Simple Rate of Return; Payback   Bullrun Meatpackers is considering the purchase of two different items of equipment, as described below.

Machine A. A machine has come onto the market that would allow Bullrun Meatpackers to process and sell an item that was previously a waste product. The following information is available on the machine:
a. The machine would cost $350,000 and would have a 10% salvage value at the end of its 12-year useful life. The company uses straight-line depreciation and considers salvage value in computing depreciation deductions.
b. The new product from the machine would generate revenues of $500,000 per year. Variable manufacturing expenses would be 60% of sales.
c. Fixed expenses associated with the new product would be (per year) as follows: advertising, $36,000; salaries, $90,000; and insurance, $4,000.

Machine B. Another machine has come onto the market that would allow Bullrun Meatpackers to dispose of some antiquated, hand-operated wrapping equipment and replace it with a largely automatic wrapping process. The following information is available:
a. The new wrapping machine would cost $260,000 and would have negligible salvage value at the end of its 13-year useful life. The company would use straight-line depreciation on the new machine.
b. The old hand-operated wrapping equipment could be sold now for $10,000.
c. The new machine would provide substantial annual savings in cash operating costs. It would require an operator at an annual salary of $18,000, and it would require $4,500 in annual maintenance costs. The old hand-operated equipment costs $85,000 per year to operate.

Bullrun Meatpackers requires a simple rate of return of 15% on all equipment purchases. Also, it will not purchase equipment unless the equipment has a payback period of 4.0 years or less.

Required
(ignore income taxes)

1. For machine A:
    a. Prepare an income statement showing the expected net income each year from the new product. Use the contribution format.
    b. Compute the simple rate of return.
    c. Compute the payback period.
2. For machine B:
    a. Compute the simple rate of return.
    b. Compute the payback period.
3. According to the company's criteria, which machine, if either, should the company buy?

P14-24   Net Present Value; FMS/Automated Equipment; Postappraisal "If we can get that new robot to combine with our other automated equipment, we'll have a complete flexible manufacturing system in place in our Northridge plant," said Hal Swain, production manager for Diller Products.

"Let's just hope that reduced labour and inventory costs can justify its acquisition," replied Linda Wycoff, the controller. "Otherwise, we'll never get it. You know how the president feels about equipment paying for itself out of reduced costs."

Selected data relating to the robot are provided below:

Cost of the robot......................	$1,600,000
Software and installation	700,000
Annual savings in labour costs	?
Annual savings in inventory carrying costs.......................	190,000
Monthly increase in power and maintenance costs	2,500
Salvage value in 12 years................	90,000
Useful life............................	12 years

Engineering studies suggest that use of the robot will result in a savings of 40,000 direct labour-hours each year. The labour rate is $8 per hour. Also, the smoother work flow made possible by the FMS will allow the company to reduce the amount of inventory on hand by $300,000. The released funds will be available for use elsewhere in the company. This inventory reduction will take place in the first year of operation. The company requires a 20% return on all investments in automated equipment.

Required
(ignore income taxes)

1. Determine the net *annual* cost savings if the robot is purchased. (Do not include the $300,000 inventory reduction or the salvage value in this computation.)
2. Compute the net present value of the proposed investment in the robot. Based on these data, would you recommend that the robot be purchased? Explain.
3. Assume that the robot is purchased. At the end of the first year, Linda Wycoff has found that some items didn't work out as planned. Due to unforeseen problems, software and installation costs were $125,000 more than estimated, and direct labour has been reduced by only 35,000 hours per year, rather than by 40,000 hours. Assuming that all other items of cost data were accurate, does it appear that the company made a wise investment? Show computations, using the net percent value format as in (2) above. (Hint: It might be helpful to place yourself back at the beginning of the first year, with the new data.)
4. Upon seeing your analysis in (3) above, the president stated, "That robot is the worst investment we've ever made. And here we'll be stuck with it for years."
   a. Explain to the president what benefits other than cost savings might accrue from use of the new robot and FMS.
   b. Compute for the president the dollar amount of cash inflow that would be needed each year from the benefits in (a) above in order for the equipment to yield a 20% rate of return.

P14–25 Net Present Value; Analysis of a New Product Line   Atwood Company has an opportunity to produce and sell a revolutionary new smoke detector for homes. To determine whether this would be a profitable venture, the company has gathered the following data on probable costs and market potential:

a. New equipment would have to be acquired to produce the smoke detector. The equipment would cost $100,000 and be usable for 12 years. After 12 years, it would have a salvage value equal to 10% of the original cost.
b. Production and sales of the smoke detector would require a working capital investment of $40,000 to finance accounts receivable, inventories, and day-to-day cash needs. This working capital would be released for use elsewhere after 12 years.
c. An extensive marketing study projects sales in units over the next 12 years as follows:

Year	Sales in Units
1	4,000
2	7,000
3	10,000
4–12...........	12,000

d. The smoke detectors would sell for $45 each; variable costs for production, administration, and sales would be $25 per unit.

e. To gain entry into the market, the company would have to advertise heavily in the early years of sales. The advertising program follows:

Year	Amount of Advertising
1–2	$70,000
3	50,000
4–12	40,000

f. Other fixed costs for salaries, insurance, maintenance, and straight-line depreciation on equipment would total $127,500 per year. (Depreciation is based on cost less salvage value.)

g. Atwood Company views the smoke detector as a somewhat risky venture; therefore, the company would require a minimum 20% rate of return in order to accept it as a new product line.

Required
(ignore income taxes)

1. Compute the net cash inflow (cash receipts less yearly cash operating expenses) anticipated from sale of the smoke detectors for each year over the next 12 years.

2. Using the data computed in (1) above and other data provided in the problem, determine the net present value of the proposed investment. Would you recommend that Atwood Company accept the smoke detector as a new product line?

P14–26 Simple Rate of Return; Payback; Internal Rate of Return   Glenda's Place, a popular local doughnut and coffee shop, is owned and operated by Glenda Hunter. At present, the dough for doughnuts is rolled out by hand and then cut into the required shape with a simple handheld cutter. After cutting doughnuts from rolled-out dough, there is a great deal of dough left over around the edges and in the form of doughnut holes. This unused dough must be gathered together and then rerolled before cutting into doughnuts. A batch of dough may have to be gathered and rerolled up to half a dozen times before the waste has been reduced to negligible levels. Unfortunately, after being rerolled several times, the dough loses its elasticity and the quality deteriorates. Glenda discards the remaining dough when this happens.

To solve this problem, Glenda is considering the purchase of a machine that would roll out and cut the dough automatically, producing uniformly shaped doughnuts with no waste. She has gathered the following data concerning the decision:

a. The cost of the dough that is discarded at present is $5,000 per year. All of this waste would be eliminated with the new machine. In addition, the machine would save $2,000 per year in direct labour costs, since the rolling and cutting operation would take far less time.

b. The new machine would cost $18,000 installed, and it would have a 10-year useful life. The machine would have no salvage value.

c. Annual out-of-pocket costs associated with operating the machine are: supplies, $1,100; utilities, $1,500; and maintenance, $800.

d. Glenda feels that the investment in the machine should earn at least a 12% rate of return.

Required
(ignore income taxes)

1. Determine the annual net savings in cash operating costs that Glenda would realize if the machine were purchased.

2. Compute the simple rate of return expected from the machine. (Hint: This is a cost reduction project.)

3. Compute the payback period on the machine. Glenda will not purchase equipment unless it has a payback period of six years or less. Under this criterion, should the machine be purchased?

4. Compute (to the nearest whole percent) the internal rate of return promised by the machine. Based on this computation, does it appear that the simple rate of return is an accurate guide in investment decisions?

P14–27   Keep or Sell Rental Property   Wesco Products owns a tract of land on which there is a small factory building. The property was purchased several years ago at a cost of $350,000 with the intention of tearing down the old building and constructing a new building on the land. However, the company decided to construct the new building elsewhere. As a result, the old building is being rented to another company. Consideration is now being given to selling the old building and land, rather than continuing to rent it. Wesco Products has the following alternatives:

Keep the property. If Wesco Products keeps the property, it will continue to be rented. Annual revenues and expenses associated with the property follow:

Annual rental revenues		$90,000
Annual expenses:		
Property taxes	$16,500	
Insurance	8,900	
Repairs and maintenance	4,600	
Depreciation	20,000	50,000
Net income		$40,000

Wesco Products makes a $30,000 payment to its bank each year on a loan that was obtained to purchase the property. The loan will be paid off in seven more years. The building can be rented for only about 15 more years, after which the property could be sold for about $500,000.

Sell the property. A realty company has offered to purchase the property now. The realty company would pay $250,000 down on the property and then pay Wesco Products $32,500 per year for the next 15 years. If this option is accepted, Wesco Products would have to pay off its bank loan immediately. The remaining principal balance on the loan is $180,000.

**Required
(ignore income taxes)**

1. Assume that Wesco Products's cost of capital is 14%. Compute the present value of the cash flows associated with each alternative. Use the total-cost approach.
2. Would you advise Wesco Products to accept the realty company's offer, or would you advise it to wait for a better offer? Explain.

CASES

C14–28   Lease or Buy Decision   Wyndham Stores operates a regional chain of upscale department stores. The company is going to open another store soon in a prosperous and growing suburban area. In discussing how the company can acquire the desired building and other facilities needed to open the new store, Harry Wilson, the company's marketing vice president, stated, "I know most of our competitors are starting to lease facilities, rather than buy, but I just can't see the economics of it. Our development people tell me that we can buy the building site, put a building on it, and get all the store fixtures we need for $14 million. They also say that property taxes, insurance, maintenance, and repairs would run $200,000 a year. When you figure that we plan to keep a site for 20 years, that's a total cost of $18 million. But then when you realize that the building and property will be worth at least $5 million in 20 years, that's a net cost to us of only $13 million. Leasing costs a lot more than that."

"I'm not so sure," replied Erin Reilley, the company's executive vice president. "Guardian Insurance Company is willing to purchase the building site, construct a building and install fixtures to our specifications, and then lease the facility to us for 20 years for an annual lease payment of only $1 million."

"That's just my point," said Harry. "At $1 million a year, it would cost us $20 million over the 20 years instead of just $13 million. And what would we have left at the end? Nothing! The building would belong to the insurance company! I'll bet they would even want the first lease payment in advance."

"That's right," replied Erin. "We would have to make the first payment immediately and then one payment at the beginning of each of the following 19 years. However, you're overlooking a few things. For one thing, we would have to tie up a lot of our funds for 20 years under the purchase alternative. We would have to put $6 million down immediately if we buy the property, and then we would have to pay the other $8 million off over four years at $2 million a year."

"But that cost is nothing compared to $20 million for leasing," said Harry. "Also, if we lease, I understand we would have to put up a $400,000 security deposit that we wouldn't get back until the end. And besides that, we would still have to pay all the repair and maintenance costs just like we owned the property. No wonder those insurance companies are so rich if they can swing deals like this."

"Well, I'll admit that I don't have all the figures sorted out yet," replied Erin. "But I do have the operating cost breakdown for the building, which includes $90,000 annually for property taxes, $60,000 for insurance, and $50,000 for repairs and maintenance. If we lease, Guardian will handle its own insurance costs and will pay the property taxes, but we'll have to pay for the repairs and maintenance. I need to put all this together and see if leasing makes any sense with our 12% before-tax required rate of return. The president wants a presentation and recommendation in the executive committee meeting tomorrow."

**Required
(ignore income
taxes)**

1. By means of discounted cash flow analysis, determine whether Wyndham Stores should lease or buy the new store. Assume that you will be making your presentation before the company's executive committee, and remember that the president detests sloppy, disorganized reports.

2. What reply would you make in the meeting if Harry Wilson brings up the issue of the building's future sales value?

C14–29   Equipment Acquisition; Uneven Cash Flows   Woolrich Company's market research division has projected a substantial increase in demand over the next several years for one of the company's products. To meet this demand, the company will need to produce units as follows:

Year	Production in Units
1	20,000
2	30,000
3	40,000
4–10	45,000

At present, the company is using a single model 2600 machine to manufacture this product. To increase its productive capacity, the company is considering two alternatives:

Alternative 1. The company could purchase another model 2600 machine that would operate along with the one it now owns. The following information is available on this alternative:

a. The model 2600 machine now in use cost $165,000 four years ago. Its present book value is $99,000, and its present market value is $90,000.

b. A new model 2600 machine costs $180,000 now. The currently owned model 2600 machine will have to be replaced in six years at a cost of $200,000. The replacement machine will have a market value of about $100,000 when it is four years old.

c. The variable cost required to produce one unit of product using the model 2600 machine is given under the "general information" below.

d. Repairs and maintenance costs each year on a single model 2600 machine total $3,000.

Alternative 2. The company could purchase a model 5200 machine and use the currently owned model 2600 machine as standby equipment. The model 5200 machine is a high-speed unit with double the capacity of the model 2600 machine. The following information is available on this alternative:

a.   The cost of a new model 5200 machine is $250,000.

b.   The variable cost required to produce one unit of product using the model 5200 machine is given under the "general information" below.

c.   Due to its more complex operation, the model 5200 machine is more costly to maintain than the model 2600 machine. Repairs and maintenance on a model 5200 machine, with a model 2600 machine used as standby, would total $4,600 per year.

The following general information is available on the two alternatives:

a.   Both the model 2600 machine and the model 5200 machine have a 10-year life from the time they are first used in production. The scrap value of both machines is negligible and can be ignored. Straight-line depreciation is used by the company.

b.   The two machine models are not equally efficient in output. Comparative variable costs per unit of product are as follows:

	Model 2600	Model 5200
Direct materials per unit	$0.36	$0.40
Direct labour per unit	0.50	0.22
Supplies and lubricants per unit	0.04	0.08
Total variable cost per unit	$0.90	$0.70

c.   No other factory costs would change as a result of the decision between the two machines.

d.   Woolrich Company's cost of capital is 18%.

Required
(ignore income taxes)

1.   Which alternative should the company choose? Show computations using discounted cash flow. (Round to the nearest whole dollar.)

2.   Suppose that the cost of materials increases by 50%. Would this make the model 5200 machine more or less desirable? Explain. No computations are needed.

3.   Suppose that the cost of labour increases by 25%. Would this make the model 5200 machine more or less desirable? Explain. No computations are needed.

C14–30   Discontinuing a Department; Relevant Costs; Present Value   You have just been hired as a management trainee by Marley's Department Store. Your first assignment is to determine whether the store should discontinue its housewares department and expand its appliances department. The store's vice president believes that the housewares space could be better utilized selling appliances, since the appliances have a better markup and move more rapidly. The store's most recent income statement is presented below:

MARLEY'S DEPARTMENT STORE
Income Statement
For the Year Ended June 30

	Total	Department		
		Appliances	Housewares	Clothing
Sales	$8,000,000	$3,600,000	$2,000,000	$2,400,000
Less variable expenses	2,930,000	1,080,000	1,250,000	600,000
Contribution margin	5,070,000	2,520,000	750,000	1,800,000
Less fixed expenses:				
Advertising	1,450,000	650,000	370,000	430,000
Salaries	770,000	410,000	90,000	270,000
General administration	460,000	207,000	115,000	138,000
Insurance	33,000	13,000	8,000	12,000
Depreciation	242,000	80,000	72,000	90,000
Utilities	690,000	320,000	130,000	240,000
Total fixed expenses	3,645,000	1,680,000	785,000	1,180,000
Net income (loss)	$1,425,000	$ 840,000	$ (35,000)	$ 620,000

In the course of your analytical work, you have determined the following:

a. If the housewares department is discontinued, sales of appliances could be expanded by 25%. Sales of clothing would be unaffected.

b. The store fixtures being used in the housewares department could not be used in the expanded appliances department. These fixtures have a book value of $180,000, but they can be sold now for only $70,000. In 10 years they will have no salvage value.

c. Since appliances are much more expensive than housewares items, the store would have to expand its working capital investment in inventories and accounts receivable by $250,000.

d. The added level of appliance sales would carry the same percentage of variable expenses (for cost of goods sold and for commissions) as are carried by current appliance sales.

e. Expanding the appliances department would require extensive remodelling and the purchase of new fixtures at a cost of $1,560,000. The store's lease has 10 years to run, after which the fixtures would have a salvage value of $90,000. The company uses straight-line depreciation.

f. Only one employee of the housewares department will be retained if the housewares department is discontinued. This employee's salary is $25,000 per year. No additional employees would be needed in the expanded appliances department.

g. Since the appliances department already has an extensive advertising program, it would not need to increase its advertising if it moves into the new space. Also, utilities for the space would be the same regardless of whether it was occupied by the housewares or the appliances department. Insurance costs for the space, however, would be $15,000 per year if the space is used to sell appliances rather than housewares.

h. The general administration costs represent costs of top management that are allocated to the departments on the basis of sales dollars. Total general administration costs will not change if the housewares department is dropped.

i. The store requires a before-tax return of 16% on all investments.

Required
(ignore income taxes)

1. Compute the net *annual* change in cash flows if the housewares department is discontinued and the appliances department is expanded. (Do not include added investments or salvage values in this computation.)

2. Make a recommendation to the vice president as to whether the housewares department should be discontinued and the appliances department expanded. Use discounted cash flow and the incremental-cost approach. Show all computations in a neat, orderly form.

GROUP EXERCISES

GE14–31 Cost of Capital and the Market Value of the Firm   Capital budgeting decisions are among the most important decisions management can make. They will influence the direction of the company for years to come. Given the importance of such projects and the size of investment that is often required, it is crucial that management evaluate a capital investment proposal with a clear understanding of the underlying concepts.

Required

1. How does a firm's management go about the business of maximizing the value of the firm?
2. Explain the concept of cost of capital (i.e., the minimum required rate of return). How is the cost of capital for a particular project determined?
3. What role do common share equity and debt play in determining the cost of capital?
4. How is the cost of capital used to allocate capital among competing uses?
5. How would corporate management view an investment to maintain existing equipment or markets? An investment to expand present businesses or markets? An investment in an entirely new product, service, or market?
6. What practical difficulties or real-world problems does management confront in trying to implement capital budgeting decisions correctly?

GE14–32 Performance Measurement, Capital Budgeting, and Management Compensation Nearly every major decentralized Canadian business uses some measure of profitability or ROI to assess the performance of their divisional managers. Most companies evaluate managers over the short term (quarterly and annually) and tie their bonus compensation to exceeding a target level of profit or ROI for their business unit. This provides top management with a consistent basis for evaluating business unit managers and motivates business unit managers to make decisions that are consistent with the best interests of the company.

Furthermore, it is assumed that there is a high correlation between ROI and the market value or shareholder value of the firm. That is, the underlying assumption is that a high and growing ROI will result in an increase in the common share price and market value of the firm. This is a very important issue because the evaluation and compensation of most managers is determined by using accounting-based measures of performance.

Required

1. Are short-term accounting measures of performance consistent with the long-term interests of customers, employees, and shareholders? Explain and give examples.
2. This chapter indicated that discounted cash flow (DCF) models were best for determining the long-run impact of capital projects on the market value of the firm. The previous chapter indicated that most firms use quarterly and annual accounting measures of performance, like ROI, to evaluate the performance of managers once those assets have been acquired. Discuss the conflicts between short-term accounting-based measures of performance and the DCF models. Be sure to consider the role that risk plays in evaluation.
3. In an attempt to alleviate some of these conflicts, corporations could evaluate and compensate performance based on improvement in long-term (three to five years) accounting measures of performance like ROI. Evaluate this idea.
4. Historically, companies have used stock options (the right to buy shares at a certain price in the future, usually the price on the date the option was issued) to motivate management to take a long-term viewpoint. What are the advantages and disadvantages of this form of performance evaluation and compensation?
5. Canadian businesses have typically rewarded individual accomplishment rather than broader performance measures that reward team-based results. Evaluate each of these options.

GE14–33 Advanced Manufacturing Technologies and DCF In the early 1980s, the use of discounted cash flow (DCF) methods of analysis came under increasing criticism. In particular, DCF methods were found to be deficient when used to evaluate investments in new computer-integrated manufacturing (CIM) technologies. Critics claimed that DCF methods of analysis were biased against investments in CIM technology because DCF analysis did not consider the full range of benefits provided by CIM technology. Kaplan responded to this criticism in Robert Kaplan, "Must CIM Be Justified by Faith Alone," *Harvard Business Review* (March–April 1986), pp. 87–95.

Required

1. Briefly discuss the major technical issues that have led to the misapplication of the DCF analysis.
2. Discuss the more obvious or tangible benefits related to investments in CIM technology.
3. Discuss the less obvious or intangible benefits related to investments in CIM technology.
4. In other chapters of this textbook, the authors discuss the changing nature of competition and new global standards of performance that will determine success or failure. Do the tangible and intangible benefits from (2) and (3) above adequately address modern-day financial and nonfinancial performance standards outlined in earlier chapters?
5. Briefly explain how a capital budgeting analyst might approach quantifying the difficult-to-quantify intangible benefits.

15

FURTHER ASPECTS OF INVESTMENT DECISIONS

LEARNING OBJECTIVES

After studying Chapter 15, you should be able to:

1 Compute the after-tax cost of a tax-deductible cash expense and the after-tax benefit from a taxable cash receipt.

2 Explain how capital cost allowance is computed.

3 Compute the tax savings arising from the capital cost allowance tax shield.

4 Compute the after-tax net present value of an investment proposal.

5 Rank investment projects in order of preference using (1) the internal rate of return method and (2) the net present value method with the profitability index.

6 Define or explain the key terms listed at the end of the chapter.

7 (Appendix 15A) Measure risk in assessing capital budgeting projects.

The large and complex tax code can affect a capital budgeting decision in many ways. Companies often hire experts to study the tax ramifications of a capital budgeting decision.

W e continue our discussion of capital budgeting in this chapter by focusing on two new topics. First, we focus on income taxes and their impact on the capital budgeting decision. And second, we focus on methods of ranking competing capital investment projects according to their relative desirability.

INCOME TAXES AND CAPITAL BUDGETING

OBJECTIVE 1
Compute the after-tax cost of a tax-deductible cash expense and the after-tax benefit from a taxable cash receipt.

In our discussion of capital budgeting in the preceding chapter, the matter of income taxes was omitted for two reasons. First, many organizations have no taxes to pay. Such organizations include not-for- profit schools and hospitals, and governmental units on municipal, provincial, and federal levels. These organizations will always use capital budgeting techniques on a before-tax basis, as illustrated in the preceding chapter. Second, the topic of capital budgeting is somewhat complex, and it is best absorbed in small doses. Now that we have laid a solid groundwork in the concepts of present value and discounting, we can explore the effects of income taxes on capital budgeting decisions with little difficulty.

The Canadian Tax Regulations are enormously complex, and it requires many years of study to master even a portion of the regulations in any depth. We only scratch the surface in this text. To keep the subject within reasonable bounds, we have made many simplifying assumptions about the tax regulations throughout the chapter. The most important of these assumptions are that (1) with the exception of depreciation calculations, taxable income equals net income as computed for financial reports; and (2) the tax rate is a flat percentage of taxable income.[1] The reader should be aware that the actual tax regulations are far more complex than this. However, these and the other simplifications that we make throughout the chapter allow us to cover the most important implications of income taxes for capital budgeting, while suppressing details that are relatively unimportant in understanding the big picture.

No one person can be an expert on the entire Canadian Tax Regulations. Tax lawyers for corporations often end up in tax court wrestling with what the code means in a particular instance.

---

[1]Corporate taxes are taxed federally and provincially. Provincial rates vary from 5.9 to 17%. The basic federal rate is 28.8%, but this rate may be reduced for eligible manufacturing and processing companies and may be further reduced for Canadian-controlled private corporations by 16% on the first $200,000 of taxable income, bring the federal rate down to 12.8%.

The Concept of After-Tax Cost

If someone were to ask you how much the rent is on your apartment, you would probably answer with the dollar amount that you pay out each month. If someone were to ask a business executive how much the rent is on a factory building, he or she might answer by stating a lesser figure than the dollar amount being paid out each month. The reason is that rent is a tax-deductible expense to a business firm, and expenses such as rent are often looked at on an *after-tax* basis rather than on a before-tax basis. The true cost of a tax-deductible item is not the dollars paid out; rather, it is the amount of net cash outflow that results *after* taking into consideration any reduction in income taxes that the payment will bring about. An expenditure net of its tax effect is known as **after-tax cost.**

After-tax cost is not a difficult concept. To illustrate the ideas behind it, assume that two companies, A and B, have sales of $850,000 and cash expenses of $700,000 each month. Thus, the two companies are identical except that Company A is now considering an advertising program that will cost $60,000 each month. The tax rate is 40%. What will be the after-tax cost to Company A of the contemplated $60,000 monthly advertising expenditure? The computations needed to compute the after-tax cost figure are shown in Exhibit 15–1.

EXHIBIT 15-1

The Computation of
After-Tax Cost

	Company	
	A	**B**
Sales...	$850,000	$850,000
Less expenses:		
Salaries, insurance, and other..................	700,000	700,000
New advertising program.....................	60,000	—
Total expenses	760,000	700,000
Income before taxes...........................	90,000	150,000
Income taxes (40%)...........................	36,000	60,000
Net income...................................	$ 54,000	$90,000
After-tax cost of the new advertising program ($90,000 – $54,000)		$36,000

[2]Rob Norton, "Our Screwed-Up Tax Code," *Fortune* (September 6, 1993), p.34.

As shown in the exhibit, the after-tax cost of the advertising program would be only $36,000 per month. This figure, which is computed by finding the difference in net income between the two otherwise identical companies, represents the true cost of the advertising program of Company A. In effect, a $60,000 monthly advertising expenditure would *really* cost Company A only $36,000 *after taxes*.

A formula can be developed from these data that will give the after-tax cost of *any* tax-deductible cash expense.[3] The formula is as follows:

$$(1 - \text{Tax rate}) \times \text{Tax-deductible cash expense} = \begin{array}{c}\text{After-tax cost}\\ \text{(net cash outflow)}\end{array} \qquad (1)$$

We can verify the accuracy of this formula by applying it to Company A's $60,000 advertising expenditure:

$$(1 - 0.40) \times \$60,000 = \$36,000 \text{ after-tax cost of the advertising program}$$

The concept of after-tax cost is very useful to the manager, since it measures the *actual* amount of cash that will be leaving a company as a result of an expenditure decision. As we now integrate income taxes into capital budgeting decisions, it will be necessary to place all tax-deductible cash expense items on an after-tax basis by applying the formula above.

The same reasoning applies to revenues and other *taxable* cash receipts. When a cash receipt occurs, the amount of cash inflow realized by an organization will be the amount that remains after taxes have been paid. The **after-tax benefit,** or net cash inflow, realized from a particular cash receipt can be obtained by applying a simple variation of the cash expenditure formula used above:

$$(1 - \text{Tax rate}) \times \text{Taxable cash receipt} = \begin{array}{c}\text{After-tax benefit}\\ \text{(net cash inflow)}\end{array} \qquad (2)$$

We emphasize the term *taxable cash receipts* in our discussion because not all cash inflows are taxable. For example, the release of working capital at the termination of an investment project would not be a taxable cash inflow, since it simply represents a return of original investment.

The Concept of Capital Cost Allowance

The point was made in the preceding chapter that capital cost allowances do not involve cash flows. For this reason, capital cost allowances were ignored in Chapter 14 in all discounted cash flow computations.

Even though capital cost allowances do not involve cash flows, they have an impact on the amount of income taxes that a firm will pay, and income taxes *do* involve cash flows. Therefore, as we now integrate income taxes into capital budgeting decisions, it will be necessary to consider capital cost allowances to the extent that they affect tax payments.

A Cash Flow Comparison.   To illustrate the effect of capital cost allowance on tax payments, let us compare two companies, X and Y. Both companies have annual sales of $500,000 and cash operating expenses of $310,000. In addition, Company X has a depreciable asset on which the capital cost allowance is $90,000 the first year. The tax rate is 40%. A cash flow comparison of the two companies is given at the bottom of Exhibit 15–2.

---

[3]This formula assumes that a company is operating at a profit; if it is operating at a loss, the tax situation can be very complex. For simplicity, we assume in all examples, exercises, and problems that the involved company is operating at a profit.

EXHIBIT 15–2

The Impact of
Capital Cost
Allowance on Tax
Payments—
A Comparison of
Cash Flows

Income Statements

	Company	
	X	**Y**
Sales	$500,000	$500,000
Expenses:		
Cash operating expenses	310,000	310,000
Capital cost allowance	90,000	—
Total	400,000	310,000
Net income before taxes	100,000	190,000
Income taxes (40%)	40,000	76,000
Net income	$ 60,000	$114,000

Cash Flow Comparison

Cash inflow from operations:		
Net income, as above	$ 60,000	$114,000
Add: Noncash deduction for capital cost allowance	90,000	—
Net cash inflow	$150,000	$114,000
Greater amount of cash available to Company X	$36,000	

Notice from the exhibit that Company X's net cash inflow exceeds Company Y's by $36,000. Also notice that in order to obtain Company X's net cash inflow, it is necessary to add the $90,000 capital cost allowance back to the company's net income. This step is necessary since capital cost allowance is a noncash deduction on the income statement.

Exhibit 15–2 presents an interesting paradox. Notice that even though Company X's net cash inflow is $36,000 *greater* than Company Y's, its net income is much *lower* than Company Y's (only $60,000, as compared to Company Y's $114,000). The explanation for this paradox lies in the concept of the *capital cost allowance tax shield.*

The Capital Cost Allowance Tax Shield.   Company X's greater net cash inflow comes about as a result of the *shield* against tax payments that is provided by capital cost allowances. Although capital cost allowances involve no outflows of cash, they are fully deductible in arriving at taxable income. In effect, capital cost allowance *shield* revenues from taxation and thereby *lower* the amount of taxes that a company must pay.

In the case of Company X, the $90,000 capital cost allowance involved no current outflow of cash. Yet this capital cost allowance was fully deductible on the company's income statement and thereby *shielded* $90,000 in revenues from taxation. If the company did not have this capital cost allowance, its income taxes would have been $36,000 higher, since the entire $90,000 in shielded revenues would have been taxed at the regular tax rate of 40% (40% × $90,000 = $36,000). In effect, the capital cost allowance tax shield *has reduced Company X's taxes by $36,000,* permitting these funds to be retained within the company rather than going to the tax collector. Viewed another way, we can say that Company X has realized a $27,000 *cash inflow* (through reduced tax payments) as a result of its $90,000 capital cost allowance deduction.

Because capital cost allowance deductions shield revenues from taxation, they are generally referred to as a **capital cost allowance tax shield.**[4] The reduction in tax payments made possible by the capital cost allowance tax shield is equal to the amount of the capital cost allowance taken, multiplied by the tax rate. The formula is as follows:

Tax rate × Capital cost allowance
$\qquad$ = Tax savings from the capital cost allowance shield $\qquad$ (3)

We can verify this formula by applying it to the $90,000 capital cost allowance taken by Company X in our example:

0.40 × $90,000 = $36,000 reduction in tax payments (shown as "Greater
$\qquad\qquad\qquad$ amount of cash available to Company X" in Exhibit 15–2)

As we now integrate income taxes into capital budgeting computations, it will be necessary to consider the impact of capital cost allowances on tax payments by showing the tax savings provided by the capital cost allowance tax shield.

The concepts that we have introduced so far are not complex and can be mastered fairly quickly. A summary of these concepts is given in Exhibit 15–3.

The Capital Cost Allowance System

OBJECTIVE 2

Explain how capital cost allowance is computed.

Capital cost allowance is Revenue Canada's counterpart to depreciation. Depreciation is the allocation of the cost of an asset over its useful life. The amount deducted each period for financial statement reporting purposes is based on generally accepted accounting principles (GAAP). Any method that is systemic and rational falls within the bounds of GAAP. Although it is not possible to defend or refute such allocations, the amount deducted should be in proportion to the net revenue contributions expected to be generated by the asset. For income tax purposes, however, depreciation is not an allowable expense. Instead, an allowance commonly referred to as capital cost allowance or CCA is permitted by regulations that accompany the Canadian Income Tax Act.

EXHIBIT 15-3

Tax Adjustments Required in a Capital Budgeting Analysis

Item	Treatment
Tax-deductible cash expense*	Multiply by (1 – Tax rate) to get after-tax cost.
Taxable cash receipt*	Multiply by (1 – Tax rate) to get after-tax cash inflow.
CCA deduction	Multiply by the tax rate to get the tax savings from the CCA tax shield.

*When cash receipts and cash expenses recur *each year,* the expenses can be deducted from the receipts and the difference multiplied by (1 – Tax rate). See the example at the top of Exhibit 15–5.

---

[4]The term *capital cost allowance tax shield* may convey the impression that there is something underhanded about capital cost allowances—that companies are getting some sort of a special tax break. However, in order to use the capital cost allowance, a company must have already acquired a capital asset—which typically requires a cash outflow. Essentially, the tax regulation requires companies to delay recognizing the cash outflow as an expense until capital cost allowance charges are recorded.

The income tax regulations group assets into classes and each class is then assigned a maximum capital cost allowance rate for tax reporting purposes. Maximum capital cost allowance rates are prescribed by the tax regulations for 44 classes or pools of assets. A company has the option of deducting capital cost allowance for each asset class for any amount ranging from zero to the maximum amount prescribed by the act. These prescribed rates are subject to governmental change. Examples of these assets pools and prescribed rates follow:

Asset	Class	Prescribed Rate
Buildings	1	4%
Assets not included in other classes	8	20%
Computer equipment	10	30%
Vans, trucks and tractors	10	30%
Passenger automobiles.	10.1	Irregular
Small tools, certified films, nonsystem software	12	100%
Leasehold improvements.	13	Straight line
Rental cars and taxis	16	40%
Excavating equipment	22	30%

During the early years of an asset's life, CCA generally exceeds what depreciation would be and thus may be an incentive to encourage capital investment. One could also argue that these higher deductions are a partial compensation to taxpayers to help cope with rising inflationary prices of replacement assets. Without entirely removing the incentives, the current legislation now brings CCA rates fairly in line with depreciation for financial reporting purposes. Prescribed CCA rates, however, are and will likely continue to be influenced by a combination of social, economic and political pressures that are not analogous to the determinants of accounting-based depreciation.

OBJECTIVE 3
Compute the tax savings arising from the capital cost allowance tax shield.

Capital cost allowance is calculated essentially by applying the prescribed rate to a declining balance called **undepreciated capital cost (UCC).** Class 13 assets are an exception to the declining balance capital cost allowance write-off pattern. For net additions to each asset during the year, however, only one-half of the prescribed rate is permitted. Under Revenue Canada's half-year rule only half the normal CCA for most assets is allowed as a tax-deductible expense for the year the asset is put in use. Regardless of when during the year the asset is acquired the half-year rule will apply unless a particular exception is specified by the Tax Act. The act also specifies certain irregular write-off patterns, as in the case with passenger automobiles in Class 10.1. The management accountant may occasionally have to seek the advice of a tax expert to assist in capital budgeting analysis.

An asset becomes eligible for CCA during the year in which it is either put in use or ready for use. This is known as the "put in use" rule. An example illustrating the calculation of CCA for a Class 10 (30%) pool of assets follows:

UCC, January 1, 19x1		$20,000
Acquisition during the year		16,000
Disposal proceeds during the year		6,000
Thus:		
Beginning UCC.	$16,000	
Disposals.	(6,000)[5]	
Net additions	$10,000	
One-half of net additions		5,000
UCC for CCA purposes		$25,000
CCA at 30%		(7,500)
		$17,500
Add back one-half of net additions		5,000
UCC, December 31, 19x1		$22,500

---

[5]When there is a disposition of assets from the pool, the amount deducted is the lesser of the proceeds or the original capital cost of the asset.

EXHIBIT 15–4

The Tax
Consequences of
Asset Disposals

Beginning UCC.........	$90,000	$90,000	$90,000	$90,000	$90,000
Disposal of assets					
Capital cost..........	42,500	93,000	120,000	120,000	120,000
Proceeds............	20,000	98,000	100,000	55,000	140,000
Capital gain...........	–0–	5,000	–0–	–0–	20,000
UCC after disposition....	70,000	(3,000)	(10,000)	35,000	(30,000)
Recapture	–0–	3,000	10,000	–0–	30,000
Terminal loss...........	–0–	–0–	–0–	35,000	–0–
Ending UCC	$70,000	$ –0–	$ –0–	$ –0–	–0–

Exhibit 15–4 illustrates the tax consequences of asset disposals. On the disposal of assets, previously deducted CCA is **recaptured** if the proceeds of disposal exceed the UCC of the group of assets that make up the asset class. Cases 2, 3 and 5 all report negative UCC balances after disposal. These negative balances represent recaptured depreciation that is fully taxable income. There may also be a **capital gain** if disposal proceeds exceed the original cost of the particular disposed asset as is demonstrated in cases 2 and 5. A taxable gain is not fully taxable. The taxable portion of the capital gain has been increased from two-thirds to three-quarters effective since January 1, 1990. Referring to case 5 and assuming a 40% tax rate would result in a capital gains tax outflow of $6,000 ($20,000 × 3/4 × 40%). If all of the assets of a class have been disposed, any remaining *positive* UCC balance for the class is called a **terminal loss** and is fully deductible in computing taxable income (case 4).

Where a firm is profitable in some years but has losses in other years over the life of a project, then tax savings from the loss years may be available. A capital loss may be carried back up to three years (recovering taxes paid during profitable years) or carried forward against future capital gains thereby reducing future income taxes.

Example A

Toronto Ltd. has obtained a $30,000 loan to acquire a truck. Assuming that the company will have a taxable income definitely into the future, calculate the present value of the capital cost allowance tax shield for the first three years if the cost of capital is 10% and the tax rate is 40%.

(1)	(2)	(3)	(4)	(5)	(6)
Year	Undepreciated Capital Cost	CCA (2) × 30%	Tax Savings (3) × 40%	PV Factor at 10%	PV of Tax Savings (4) × (5)
1	$30,000	$4,500	$1,800	0.909	$1,636
2	25,500	7,650	3,060	0.826	2,528
3	17,850	5,355	2,142	0.751	1,609

Because the capital cost allowance is calculated on a declining balance of a pool of assets rather than on a single asset, a business is able to obtain tax savings from a project even after its disposition. So long as there are other assets in the pool and the proceeds from disposal are less than the UCC for the class, tax savings can be realized in perpetuity.

It can be shown mathematically that the present value of this infinite stream of tax savings from a declining balance capital cost allowance is calculated by what is referred to as the CCA *tax shield formula*.

$$PV = \frac{Cdt}{d + k} \times \frac{1 + 0.5k}{1 + k}$$

where

C = The capital cost of the asset added to the asset pool

d = CCA rate

t = The firm's marginal income tax rate

k = The cost of capital

$\dfrac{1 + 0.5k}{1 + k}$ = The correction factor to account for the provision that only one-half of the capital cost of an asset is included in UCC during the year of acquisition.

For the previous example, the present value of the CCA tax shield is

$$\frac{\$30,000 \times 0.30 \times 0.4}{0.30 + 0.10} \times \frac{1 + 0.5 \times 0.10}{1 + 0.10} = \begin{array}{l} \$9,000 \times 0.95455 \\ = \$8,591 \end{array}$$

Example B

Using the data in the previous example, calculate the present value of the CCA tax shield assuming that other assets remain in the pool and the asset is disposed of for $6,000 after five years use.

The sale of the truck results in a cash inflow at the beginning of year 6. This disposal results in the asset pool balance (UCC) being reduced by the $6,000 proceeds. The present value of the CCA tax shield is also reduced because from the end of year 5 onward CCA will be applied to a smaller UCC balance than it otherwise would have been without the asset disposal. If S represents salvage value the CCA tax shield formula must be adjusted by deducting

$$\frac{Sdt}{d + k} \times (1 + k)^{-n}$$

where

$$\frac{Sdt}{d + k}$$

calculates the present value of the lost tax shield at the end of year five ($n = 5$). This lost tax shield is then discounted to time period zero by multiplying $(1 + k)^{-n}$ or by using Table 14C–3. The present value of the tax shield is calculated to be $7,473.

▼ ▼ ▼ ▼ ▼

MANAGERIAL ACCOUNTING IN ACTION—THE ISSUE

E
agle Peak is a major Rocky Mountain destination ski resort managed by Chuck Redding. The company is considering the purchase of three 12-passenger Helimann SnoCats that would provide skier access to areas on the back of the mountain that are not served by ski lifts. The demand for such a service is very high—expert skiers are willing to pay over $100 a day for access to untracked powder snow. While Redding is familiar with net present value analysis, he is uncertain about the tax implications of the proposed purchases and has asked for advice from Marcia Sykes, a local public accountant and enthusiastic skier who provides accounting and business consulting services. The following discussion took place in Redding's office:

Continued

Snow skiers often like to ski in areas that have not been skied by others or that have powder snow. Many of these areas are not served by traditional ski lifts. Should Eagle Peak purchase Helimann SnoCats to meet this demand?

Chuck: It's good to see you, Marcia. I'm glad you could drop by.

Marcia: No problem. My skis are in the locker, and I'll hit the slope after we talk.

Chuck: You may have heard that we are thinking about buying some SnoCats to provide service to the back side of the mountain.

Marcia: From all the talk in town, I don't think you are going to have any trouble selling tickets.

Chuck: I know. Some of the local powder snow freaks have been trying to get us to sell them advance tickets.

Marcia: Does the economics of the SnoCats make sense?

Chuck: I'm not sure. I figured out the present value of all of the cash flows except for one thing and that's the capital cost allowance.

Marcia: Capital cost allowance isn't a cash flow.

Chuck: You're right. What I meant was that I haven't figured out what impact the capital cost allowance would have on our taxes.

Marcia: If you give me all of your data, I should have an answer for you within a day or two.

Chuck: Great. And by the way, Marcia, don't run over any of my ski patrollers out on the hill. They tell me you're a terror on skis.

Marcia: You ought to see my little sister.

▼   ▼   ▼   ▼   ▼

▼   ▼   ▼   ▼   ▼

MANAGERIAL ACCOUNTING IN ACTION—WRAP-UP

Two days later, Marcia Sykes drove up to Digby Pines Resort to see resort manager Chuck Redding.

Marcia: Here's the analysis you asked for. The present value of the tax savings from the capital cost allowance is $71,920.

Chuck: I see two terms in this analysis, one called depreciation and another called CCA. What is this CCA thing?

Marcia: CCA stands for confusing, contrived accounting.

Chuck: Really?

Marcia: No, just teasing. It's an acronym Revenue Canada uses to refer to its method for depreciation. For most classes of assets CCA is a method of accelerated depreciation as opposed to a straight-line method.

Chuck: This CCA thing looks confusing. Isn't there a simpler way?

Marcia: Sure, you could decide not to take any allowance. These capital cost allowances are maximum allowable deductions. But simplicity has a cost. The cost would be significantly higher taxes paid to Revenue Canada.

Chuck: On second thought, I think I'll forget about simplicity.

Marcia: For profitable companies like Digby Pines, CCA usually provides a better tax deal than if Revenue Canada permitted companies to deduct straight-line depreciation. You get more of the tax benefit earlier and can put the tax savings to work for you.

Chuck: With those tax savings and the rest of the cash flows, this investment looks like a winner. Would you like to be the first passenger on our new SnoCat service?

Marcia: Absolutely!

▼   ▼   ▼   ▼   ▼

Example of Income Taxes and Capital Budgeting

OBJECTIVE 4
Compute the after-tax net present value of an investment proposal.

Armed with an understanding of the CCA rules, and with an understanding of the concepts of after-tax cost, after-tax revenue, and capital cost allowance tax shield, we are now prepared to examine a comprehensive example of income taxes and capital budgeting. Assume the following data:

Holland Company owns the mineral rights to land on which there is a deposit of ore. The company is uncertain as to whether it should purchase equipment and open a mine on the property. After careful study, the following data have been assembled by the company:

Cost of land	$500,000
Cost of equipment needed	300,000
Working capital needed	75,000
Estimated annual cash receipts from sales of ore	350,000
Estimated annual cash expenses for salaries, insurance, utilities, and other cash expenses of mining the ore	170,000
Cost of road repairs needed in 6 years	40,000
Salvage value of the equipment in 10 years	100,000
Useful life of equipment	15 years

The ore in the mine would be exhausted after 10 years of mining activity, at which time the mine would be closed. The equipment would then be sold for its salvage value. The company's after-tax cost of capital is 12% and its tax rate is 30%. CCA is 30%. The land will be sold to the federal government for $600,000 at the end of year 10.

Should Holland Company purchase the equipment and open a mine on the property? The solution to the problem is given in Exhibit 15–5 on the next page. The reader should go through this solution item by item and note the following points:

1. *Cost of new equipment.* The initial investment of $300,000 in the new equipment is included in full, with no reductions for taxes. The tax effects of this investment are considered in the capital cost allowances.

2. *Working capital.* Observe that the working capital needed for the project is included in full, with no reductions for taxes. This represents an *investment*, not an expense, so no tax adjustment is needed. (Only revenues and expenses are adjusted for the effects of taxes.) Also observe that no tax adjustment is needed when the working capital is released at the end of the project's life. The release of working capital would not be a taxable cash flow, because it merely represents a return of investment funds back to the company.

3. *Net annual cash receipts.* The net annual cash receipts from sales of ore are adjusted for the effects of income taxes, as discussed earlier in the chapter. Note at the top of Exhibit 15–5 that the annual cash expenses are deducted from the annual cash receipts to obtain a net cash receipts figure. This just simplifies computations. (Many of the exercises and problems that follow already provide a net annual cash receipts figure, thereby eliminating the need to make this computation.)

4. *Road repairs.* Because the road repairs occur just once (in the sixth year), they are treated separately from other expenses. Road repairs would be a tax-deductible cash expense; therefore they are adjusted for the effects of income taxes, as discussed earlier in the chapter.

5. *Capital cost allowances.* The tax savings provided by CCA deductions are included earlier in the chapter. Note that capital cost includes only the portion of the total investment subject to capital cost allowance. The cost of land and working capital are excluded from this computation.

[6]"Easy Money: Business Speaks with Forked Tongue When It Comes to the Subject of Subsidies from Government," *BC Business Magazine* (February 1996), pp. 70–74.

EXHIBIT 15-5   Holland Company Example

	Per Year
Cash receipts from sales of ore	$350,000
Less payments for salaries, insurance,	
utilities, and other cash expenses	170,000
Net cash receipts	$180,000

	Years	**(1)** **Amount**	**(2)** **Tax Effect**	**After-Tax Cash Flows*** **(1 × 2)**	**12%** **Factor**	**Present Value of Cash Flows**
Cost of land.	Now	$(500,000)	—	$(500,000)	1.000	$(500,000)
Cost of new equipment	Now	$(300,000)	—	(300,000)	1.000	(300,000
Working capital needed.	Now	(75,000)	—	(75,000)	1.000	(75,000)
Net annual cash receipts	1–10	180,000	1–0.40	108,000	5.650	610,200
Road repairs	6	(40,000)	1–0.40	(24,000)	.507	(12,168)
Salvage value of equipment	10	100,000	—	100,000	.322	32,200
Release of working capital	10	75,000	—	75,000	.322	24,150
Proceeds from sale of land	10	600,000	—	600,000	.322	193,200
Subtotal.						$ (27,418)
Taxes paid on capital gain on sale of land (of which three-quarters is taxable)	10	100,000	—	(30,000)†	.322	(9,660)

Present value of CCA tax shield:

$$PV = \frac{Cdt}{d+k} \times \frac{(1+.5k)}{1+k} - \frac{S \times d \times t}{d+k} \times (1+k)^{-n}$$

$$PV = \frac{300,000 \times .3 \times .4}{.3+.12} \times \frac{1.06}{1.12} - \frac{100,000 \times .3 \times .4}{.3+.12} \times (1+.12)^{-10}$$

$$PV = \$85,714 \times .9464 - \$28,571 \times .322$$

	71,920
Net present value.	$ 34,842

*Taxable cash receipts and tax deductible cash expenses multiplied by (1 – Tax rate) to get the after-tax cash flow.

†($600,000 – $500,000) – ¾ × 40% tax rate.

6.   *Salvage value of equipment.* The salvage value of $100,000 results in a present value inflow of $32,200. However, later in the analysis note that the present value of the CCA tax shield is reduced. The value of $28,571 is the present value at the end of year 10 of the lost tax shield from the salvage. This amount, therefore, must be discounted to *now* by multiplying it by the present value factor of $1 at the end of 10 periods $(1 + 0.12)^{-10}$.

7.   *Capital gain.* Because the proceeds of $600,000 from the sale of land at the end of year 10 exceed the original cost of $500,000, there is a capital gain of $100,000. The portion of this capital gain to be included in taxable income is multiplied by the 40% tax rate to give $30,000. This $30,000 is then discounted back 10 periods to $9,660.

Because the net present value of the proposed mining project is positive, Holland Company should purchase the equipment and open the mine. The reader should study Exhibit 15–5 until all of its points are thoroughly understood. *Exhibit 15–5 is a key exhibit in this chapter!*

Replacement Cost Decisions with CCA and Income Taxes

As stated in the preceding chapter, the incremental approach is used to compare two or more competing investment proposals. To provide an example of this approach when income taxes are involved, assume the following data:

The *Daily Globe* has an auxiliary press that was purchased two years ago. The newspaper is thinking about replacing this old press with a newer, faster model. The alternatives are as follows:

Buy a new press. A new press could be purchased for $150,000. It would have a useful life of eight years, after which time it would be salable for $10,000. The old press could be sold now for $40,000. (The book value of the old press is $63,000.) The new press would cost $60,000 each year to operate.

Keep the old press. The old press was purchased two years ago at a cost of $90,000. The old press will last for eight more years, but it will need an overhaul in five years that will cost $20,000. Cash operating costs of the old press are $85,000 each year. The old press will have a salvage value of $5,000 at the end of eight more years.

The tax rate is 40%. The *Daily Globe* requires an after-tax return of 10% on all investments in equipment and the CCA rate is 30%.

Should the *Daily Globe* keep its old press or buy the new press? The solution using the incremental approach is presented in Exhibit 15–6. Most of the items in this exhibit have already been discussed in connection with Exhibit 15–5. Only a couple of points need elaboration:

EXHIBIT 15-6   *Daily Globe* Example

	Years	(1) Amount	(2) Tax Effect	After-Tax Cash Flows* (1 × 2)	10% Factor	Present Value of Cash Flows
Cost of the new press	Now	$(150,000)	—	$(150,000)	1.000	$(150,000)
Proceeds from sale of old press	Now	$40,000	—	40,000	1.000	40,000
Annual cash operating savings	1–8	25,000	1–0.40	15,000	5.335	80,025
Overhead avoided	5	20,000	1–0.40*	12,000	0.621	7,452
Difference in salvage in 8 years						
Salvage from the new press $10,000						
Salvage from the old press ....$ 5,000						
Difference ....$ 5,000		5,000	—	5,000	0.467	2,335

Present value of capital cost allowance

$$PV = \frac{110,000 \times .3 \times .4}{.3 + .10} \times \frac{1 + .5 \times .10}{1 + .10} - \frac{5,000 \times .3 \times .4}{.3 + .10} \times (1 + .10)^{-8}$$

$$= \$33,000 \times .95455 - 1,500 \times .467$$

$$= \$31,500 - 700$$

	30,800
Net present value in favour of purchasing the new press	$ 10,612

*Assumes fully deductible.

1. *Annual cash operating costs.* Because there are no revenues identified with the project, we simply place the cash operating costs on an after-tax basis and discount them as we did in Chapter 14.

2. *Sale of the old press.* The sale of the old press is deducted from the cost of the new press in the computation of the capital cost allowance tax shield. Note that we are making a *net addition* to the asset pool. The CCA half-year rule is applied to the incremental outlay to the asset class. It is the incremental cost of $110,000 ($150,000 minus $40,000) that is relevant in determining this benefit.

Qualitative factors are important in capital budgeting decisions. Technology assessment can help hospitals rank the importance of capital requests by providing crucial information both about existing equipment and about new equipment that has been requested. Integrating technology assessment into the capital budgeting process is the best way for hospitals to determine what equipment should be purchased each year. A case study of Hamilton Civic Hospitals (HCH) demonstrates how the capital budgeting process was modified by hiring an independent firm to assess HCH's imaging department's capital needs. By modifying the capital budgeting process, integrating a technology assessment component, and matching technology with need, HCH has created a needs-driven process that has permitted efficient allocation of its limited capital resources to match technology with need.[7]

PREFERENCE DECISIONS— THE RANKING OF INVESTMENT PROJECTS

OBJECTIVE 5
Rank investment projects in order of preference using (1) the internal rate of return method and (2) the net present value method with the profitability index.

In the preceding chapter, we indicated that there are two types of decisions that must be made relative to investment opportunities. These are screening decisions and preference decisions. Screening decisions have to do with whether or not some proposed investment is acceptable to a firm. We discussed ways of making screening decisions in the preceding chapter, where we studied the use of the cost of capital as a screening tool. Screening decisions are very important in that many investment proposals come to the attention of management, and those that are not worthwhile must be screened out.

Preference decisions come *after* screening decisions and attempt to answer the following question: "How do the remaining investment proposals, all of which have been screened and provide an acceptable rate of return, rank in terms of preference? That is, which one(s) would be *best* for the firm to accept?" Preference decisions are more difficult to make than screening decisions. The reason is that investment funds are usually limited, and this often requires that some (perhaps many) otherwise very profitable investment opportunities be foregone.

Preference decisions are sometimes called *ranking* decisions, or *rationing* decisions, because they attempt to ration limited investment funds among many competing invest-

---

[7]Dave Watts, Donna L. Finneu, and Brian Lovie, "Integrating Technology Assessment into the Capital Budgeting Process," *Healthcare Financial Management* (February 1993), pp. 21–29.

ment opportunities. The choice may be simply between two competing alternatives, or many alternatives may be involved that must be ranked according to their overall desir ability. Either the internal rate of return method or the net present value method can be used in making preference decisions.

Internal Rate of Return Method

When using the internal rate of return method to rank competing investment projects, the preference rule is: *The higher the internal rate of return, the more desirable the project.* If one investment project promises an internal rate of return of 18%, then it is preferable over another project that promises a return of only 15%.

Ranking projects according to internal rate of return is a widely used means of making preference decisions. The reasons are probably twofold. First, no additional computations are needed beyond those already performed in making the initial screening decisions. The rates of return themselves are used to rank acceptable projects. Second, the ranking data are easily understood by management. Rates of return are very similar to interest rates, which the manager works with every day.

Net Present Value Method

If the net present value method is being used to rank competing investment projects, the net present value of one project cannot be compared directly to the net present value of another project unless the investments in the projects are of equal size. For example, assume that a company is considering two competing investments, as shown below:

	Investment	
	A	**B**
Investment required	$(80,000)	$(5,000)
Present value of cash inflows	81,000	6,000
Net present value	$ 1,000	$ 1,000

Each project has a net present value of $1,000, but the projects are not equally desirable. A project requiring an investment of only $5,000 that produces cash inflows with a present value of $6,000 is much more desirable when funds are limited than a project requiring an investment of $80,000 that produces cash flows with a present value of only $81,000. To compare the two projects on a valid basis, it is necessary in each case to divide the present value of the cash inflows by the investment required. The ratio that this computation yields is called the **profitability index.** This method shows the present value of benefits per dollar of cost. An investment project should be undertaken only if the PI is greater than 1. The formula for the profitability index follows:

$$\frac{\text{Present value of cash inflows}}{\text{Investment required}} = \text{Profitability index} \qquad (4)$$

The profitability indexes for the two investments above would be as follows:

	Investment	
	A	**B**
Present value of cash inflows	$81,000 (a)	$6,000 (a)
Investment required	$80,000 (b)	$5,000 (b)
Profitability index, (a) ÷ (b)	1.01	1.20

When using the profitability index to rank competing investment projects, the preference rule is: *The higher the profitability index, the more desirable the project.* Applying this rule to the two investments above, and considering only the financial data provided in the example, investment B should be chosen over investment A.

The profitability index is an application of the techniques for utilizing scarce resources discussed in Chapter 13. In this case, the scarce resource is the limited funds available for investment, and the profitability index is similar to the contribution margin per unit of the scarce resource.

There are a few details to be clarified with respect to computation of the profitability index. The "Investment required" refers to any cash outflows that occur at the beginning of the project, reduced by any salvage value recovered from the sale of old equipment. The "Investment required" also includes any investment in working capital that the project may need. Finally, we should note that the "Present value of cash inflows" is net of all *out*flows that occur after the project starts.

Comparing the Preference Rules

The profitability index is conceptually superior to the internal rate of return as a method of making preference decisions. This is because the profitability index will always give the correct signal as to the relative desirability of alternatives, even if the alternatives have different lives and different patterns of earnings. By contrast, if lives are unequal, the internal rate of return method can lead the manager to make incorrect decisions.

Assume the following situation:

Parker Company is considering two investment proposals, only one of which can be accepted. Project A requires an investment of $5,000 and will provide a single cash inflow of $6,000 in one year. Therefore, it promises an internal rate of return of 20%. Project B also requires an investment of $5,000. It will provide cash inflows of $1,360 each year for six years. Its internal rate of return is 16%. Which project should be accepted?

Although project A promises an internal rate of return of 20%, as compared to only 16% for project B, project A is not necessarily preferable over project B. It is preferable *only* if the funds released at the end of the year under project A can be reinvested at a high rate of return in some *other* project for the five remaining years. Otherwise, project B, which promises a return of 16% over the *entire* six years, is more desirable.

Let us assume that the company in the example above has an after-tax cost of capital of 12%. The net present value method, with the profitability index, would rank the two proposals as follows:

	Project	
	A	**B**
Present value of cash inflows:		
$6,000 received at the end of one year at 12% factor (factor of 0.893)	$5,358 (a)	
$1,360 received at the end of each year for six years at 12% (factor of 4.111)		$5,591 (a)
Investment required	$5,000 (b)	$5,000 (b)
Profitability index, (a) ÷ (b)	1.07	1.12

The profitability index indicates that project B is more desirable than project A. This is in fact the case if the funds released from project A at the end of one year can be reinvested at only 12% (the cost of capital). Although the computations will not be shown here, in order for project A to be more desirable than project B, the funds released from project A would have to be reinvested at a rate of return greater than 14% for the remaining five years.

In short, the internal rate of return method of ranking tends to favour short-term, high-yield projects, whereas the net present value method of ranking (using the profitability index) tends to favour longer-term projects.

The internal rate of return method is problematic. It assumes that funds can be reinvested at a particular project's yield. The problem becomes apparent in the context of MacInnis Company of Kitchener, Ontario. If MacInnis has projects in Cambridge, Guelph, and Waterloo that have IRRs of 20%, 15%, and 10% respectively, it is nonsense to differentiate among the cash flows and assume that a dollar returned from the Waterloo project will earn less than a dollar returned from the Cambridge project. Obviously, a dollar is a dollar regardless of which project it comes from. The net present value method does not suffer from this flaw but assumes that funds can be reinvested at the firm's cost of capital. Because the net present value is conceptually superior, it should be used in ranking projects that are mutually exclusive. However, in choosing among projects that have the same net present values, the IRR should be used to rank them. Projects should then be chosen based on the highest internal rates of return.

Although the NPV method is conceptually superior to the IRR, these are practical reasons for decision makers to choose the latter. Managers typically make project investment decisions within a four- or five-year planning horizon. Faced with this time constraint, projects will be ranked according to their terminal values at the end of the planning horizon. Estimated cash flows after the planning period may be perceived by managers to be too uncertain to rely upon. Projects with larger IRR values will have cash flow patterns with higher short-term terminal values. In summary, although there are problems with the IRR method over the entire life of a project, it will accurately evaluate projects within the planning horizon.

FOCUS ON
CURRENT PRACTICE

Capital budgeting decisions are often put on hold during periods of economic decline. For pulp and paper companies, for example, capital spending has been negatively affected by poor economic conditions, below-average growth plans for capacity expansion, and slowdowns in environmental outlays. With improving economic conditions in the U.S., it was reported in *Pulp and Paper* magazine's Fall 1993 survey of investment that U.S. companies reported plans to spend $12 billion on mill improvements over the 1993–95 period. Environmental spending reported for U.S. mills totalled $1.4 billion in the survey. Spending plans were down in Canada for the fourth straight year, as the industry continues to retrench in response to lower earnings and severe overcapacity.[8]

Behavioural Considerations

The chapter thus far has emphasized the technical aspects of capital budgeting. The management accountant should also be cognizant of important behavioural considerations. An understanding of the functional and dysfunctional consequences of human input provides deeper insight into the whole capital budgeting process.

---

[8]Carl Bspe, "Capital Spending Plans, 1993–95," *Pulp and Paper* (January 1994), pp. 59–64.

Capital budgeting projects require creativity, judgment, and the ability to see ideas through to implementation. The entire capital budgeting process from idea generation to implementation can provide valuable training for managers. There may be nonfinancial reasons for accepting certain projects. Some marginal projects may be accepted because they provide good experience and training benefits.

Estimates of cash flows, discount rates, and salvage values may be affected by the attitudes of individual managers toward risk. Risk-averse managers tend to use more conservative figures in their estimates than those managers who tend to seek risk and take on more venturesome projects.

The micropolitics of the organizations may also affect the capital budgeting process. Key managers may favour their own pet projects. Self-identification with projects may obscure management judgment of when to abandon a particular project. Obtaining truthful estimates may become problematic. Internal politics may also influence how projects are awarded. With only limited company funds available for capital investments, a division with several good investment proposals may be denied acceptance of some proposals for less profitable projects of other divisions. Such sharing of projects may be seen as necessary to maintain harmony and to give the appearance of fairness.

The capital budgeting process itself may create additional pressure on top management. Projects often have to go through several layers of approval before reaching top management. It may be difficult to reject projects already approved by managers at lower levels. On the other hand, some projects rejected at lower levels, and thus never to reach the purview of top management, may actually be acceptable to top management because they help diversify the firm's overall risk.

Projects involving employee safety, environmental or consumer safety or which impact heavily on the firm's social environment may have to be evaluated by nonfinancial criteria. Other projects which cannot be justified on financial grounds may have to be undertaken in order to conform to municipal, provincial, or federal laws.

Unethical behaviour involving nepotism or kickbacks sometimes occur. The management accountant has an ethical responsibility to communicate information fairly and objectively. All relevant information, favourable or unfavourable, should be fully disclosed so as not to bias or undermine the decision-making process. Assumptions regarding cash flows, probabilities, salvage value etc. should be clearly communicated. The management accountant is expected to act with full integrity and should avoid situations which could prejudice his or her ability to perform capital budgeting analysis in an ethical manner.

Capital budgeting can also be affected by the firm's performance reward system. If too much weight is given to short-term performance measures, there is little incentive for managers to devote time and effort to long-term capital budgeting projects.

In summary, the capital budgeting process involves more factors than first meet the eye. A purely quantitative approach to capital budgeting is not sufficient. Any model developed to solve capital budgeting problems is not broad enough to encompass all decision variables. Important qualitative factors imposed on the process by the political and social environment within the firm may strongly influence capital budgeting decisions. All levels of management should take a broad view, and reward systems within the firm should be flexible enough to encourage the acceptance of projects leading to optimal capital investment decisions.

SUMMARY

Unless a company is a tax-exempt organization, such as a school or a governmental unit, income taxes should be considered in making capital budgeting computations. When income taxes are a factor in a company, tax-deductible cash expenditures must be placed on an after-tax basis by multiplying the expenditure by (1 – tax rate). Only the after-tax amount is used in determining the desirability of an investment proposal. Similarly, taxable cash flows must be placed on an after-tax basis by multiplying the cash inflow by the same formula.

Although capital cost allowances deductions do not involve a present outflow of cash, they are a valid expense for tax purposes and as such affect income tax payments. Capital cost allowances shield income from taxation, resulting in decreased taxes being paid. This shielding of income from taxation is commonly called a capital cost allowance tax shield. The savings in income taxes arising from the CCA tax shield are computed by multiplying the capital cost allowance deduction by the tax rate itself. Since capital cost allowances generally provide the bulk of their tax shield early in the life of an asset, they are superior to a straight-line method from a present value of tax savings point of view.

Preference decisions relate to ranking two or more investment proposals according to their relative desirability. This ranking can be performed using either the internal rate of return or the profitability index. The profitability index, which is the ratio of the present value of a proposal's cash inflows to the investment required, is generally regarded as the best way of making preference decisions when discounted cash flow is being used. Finally, behaviour considerations may play a strong role in the capital budgeting process. Important qualitative factors may reverse a decision made solely on a quantitative basis.

REVIEW PROBLEM: CAPITAL BUDGETING AND TAXES

A company is considering two investment projects. Relevant cost and cash inflow information on each project follows:

	Project	
	A	**B**
Investment in passenger bus.	$70,000	
Investment in working capital		$70,000
Net annual cash inflows	13,500	13,500
Life of the project.	8 years*	8 years

*Useful life of the buses.

The bus will have a $5,000 salvage value in eight years. The capital cost allowance is 30% and the income tax rate is 40%. At the end of eight years, the working capital in project B will be released for use elsewhere.

The company requires an after-tax return of 10% on all investments.

Required

1. Compute the net present value of each investment project.
2. Compute the profitability index for each investment project.

Solution to Review Problem

	Year(s)	Amount	Tax Effect	Cash Flows	Factor	Cash Flows
Investment in passenger buses	Now	$(70,000)	—	$(70,000)	1.000	$(70,000)
Net annual cash inflows	1–8	13,500	1 – 0.40	8,100	5.335	43,214
Present value of CCA tax shield:						

$$PV = \left(\frac{Cdt}{d+k}\right) \times \left(\frac{1+.5k}{1+k}\right) - \left(\frac{S \times d \times t}{d+k}\right) \times (1+k)^{-n}$$

$$= \frac{70{,}000 \times .3 \times .4}{.3+.10} \times \frac{1+.05}{1+.10} - \frac{5{,}000 \times .3 \times .4}{.3+.10} \times (1+.10)^{-8}$$

$$= (21{,}000 \times .9545) - (1{,}500 \times .467)$$

$$= 20{,}045 - 700 \qquad\qquad\qquad 19{,}345$$

Salvage value of the buses	8	5.000	—	5,000	.467	2,335
Net present value.						(5,106)

The formula for the profitability index is:

$$\frac{\text{Present value of cash flows}}{\text{Investment required}} = \text{Profitability index}$$

Applying this formula to the data in (1) above, we get:

	Project	
	A	**B**
Present value of cash inflows:		
Net annual cash inflows	$43,214	$43,214
Tax savings from CCA (totals)	19,345	—
Salvage value of the bus	2,335	—
Release of working capital	—	32,690
Total cash inflows (a)	$64,894	$75,904
Investment required (b).	$70,000	$70,000
Profitability index (a) – (b)	0.93	1.08

Note from (1) above that project A has a negative net present value and therefore is not an acceptable investment. This also can be seen in the profitability index computation in that project A has a profitability index of less than 1.00. If a project has a profitability index of less than 1.00, it means that the project is returning less than a dollar of cash inflow for each dollar of investment. By contrast, project B is returning $1.08 of cash inflow for each dollar of investment.

KEY TERMS FOR REVIEW

OBJECTIVE 6

Define or explain the key terms listed at the end of the chapter

After-tax benefit   The amount of net cash inflow realized by an organization from a taxable cash receipt after income tax effects have been considered. The amount is determined by multiplying the cash receipt by (1 – Tax rate). (p. 820)

After-tax cost   The amount of net cash outflow resulting from a tax-deductible cash expense after income tax effects have been considered. The amount is determined by multiplying the tax-deductible cash expense by (1 – Tax rate). (p. 819)

Capital cost allowance tax shield   A reduction in the amount of income subject to tax that results from the presence of capital cost allowance deductions on the income statement. The reduction in tax is computed by multiplying the depreciation deduction by the tax rate. (p. 822)

Capital gain   When the selling price of an asset exceeds its original cost, the excess is called a *capital gain*. The portion of this gain subject to tax is 75%. (p. 824)

Profitability index   The ratio of the present value of a project's cash inflows to the investment required. (p. 832)

Recapture   A negative undepreciated capital cost (UCC) balance for any pool or asset class. It is a recapture of previously claimed CCA and occurs when proceeds from dispositions exceed the predisposal UCC balance. This amount is fully taxable. (p. 824)

Terminal loss   The positive undepreciated capital cost (UCC) balance after all assets of a pool have been disposed of. This amount is fully deductible against other income. (p. 824)

Undepreciated capital cost (UCC)   The remaining book value of an asset class or pool of assets that is available for tax-deductible depreciation (capital cost allowance). The maximum amount of capital cost allowance that can be deducted in a taxation year of a particular CCA class is the UCC multiplied by the CCA rate for that asset class. (p. 823)

APPENDIX 15A: RISK AND UNCERTAINTY IN CAPITAL BUDGETING

OBJECTIVE 7
Measure risk in assessing capital budgeting projects.

The appendix to Chapter 6 introduced probabilities and discussed how a business decision may be influenced by a manager's assessment of the most likely outcomes. The same concepts can also be applied to capital budgeting.

Recall that a probability is a number between 0 and 1 which describes the likelihood that an event will take place. A probability of zero is assigned to an event which has no chance of occurring, while a probability of 1 denotes absolute certainty that an event will occur. An outcome with a 90% chance of occurring is assigned a probability of .9 indicating that it is expected to occur in 9 out of 10 times.

Assume that Lockwood Company in Vancouver is assessing which of two 5-year $12,000 investment projects to undertake. Lockwood uses expected value as its decision criterion. The cost of capital is estimated at 10%.

The analysis in Exhibit 15–7 shows that the expected returns for both project A and project B are $10,800 per year. The expected return of each project can be thought of as a return of $10,800 by the present value of an annuity factor of 3.791 and subtracting the initial investment of five-year period annuity. The net present value can now be calculated by multiplying the expected $12,000 ($10,800 × 3.791 – $12,000 = $28,943).

A limitation of using expected returns as a benchmark when deciding among competing projects is that it fails to account for the risk preferences of individual managers. A

EXHIBIT 15-7

Probable Outcome	Net Cash Flows	Probability	Probable Return
Project A:			
Pessimistic	$ 4,000	.20	$ 800
Most likely	10,000	.60	6,000
Optimistic	20,000	.20	4,000
		1.00	$10,800
Project B:			
Pessimistic	$ –0–	.20	$ –0–
Most likely	11,000	.60	6,600
Optimistic	21,000	.20	4,200
		1.00	$10,800

full discussion is beyond the scope of this book, but one should be cognizant that management's attitude toward risk may impact on the selection process. Risk takers may be willing to forego a project with a high expected return for another project with a lower expected return but with some probability of reaching a higher maximum.

A Statistical Measure of Risk

One way of measuring the risk of capital budgeting projects is to determine the extent to which actual returns deviate from the expected returns by calculating the **standard deviation.** The standard deviation of a project's return is the square root of the sum of the average squared deviations of actual returns from the expected return (EV) of the project. The formula for calculating the standard deviation is as follows:

$$\sigma = \sqrt{\sum_{i=1}^{N}(E_i - \overline{E})^2 P_i}$$

where σ = standard deviation
N = number of possible outcomes
E_i = the value of the ith possible outcome
$\overline{E}$ = the expected returns
P_i = probabilities that the ith outcome will occur

Statisticians have determined that for *normal* probability distributions, 68% of the outcomes are plus or minus one standard deviation from the expected value; 95% are plus or minus two standard deviations; and 99% of all outcomes lie between plus or minus three standard deviations away from the expected value. A normal probability distribution has one-half of the values in the distribution above the expected value and the other one-half below the expected value. Most statistics textbooks illustrate the normal distribution graphically as a bell-shaped curve and also provide tables that give the statistically calculated probabilities that are associated with various deviations from the expected values. Exhibit 15–8 shows the calculation of the standard deviation of projects A and B for Lockwood Company.

Although projects A and B have equal expected values of $10,800, it is clear from the foregoing analysis that there is more variation in the returns of project B. Standard deviation, a common statistical measure of this variation, is higher for project B than it is for project A.

Coefficient of Variation

The **coefficient of variation (CV)** is a measure of the relative risk of an investment project. It is calculated by dividing a project's standard deviation by its expected value. For Lockwood Company, the CVs for projects A and B are as follows:

$$\text{CV for project A} = \frac{\$5,154}{\$10,800} = .48$$

$$\text{CV for project B} = \frac{\$6,645}{\$10,800} = .62$$

The larger standard deviation is as a percentage of the expected value, the higher the risk is judged to be. Using CV as the decision criterion, project B is clearly riskier than project A. This is consistent with the conclusion reached by using the standard deviation

EXHIBIT 15-8

Probable Outcomes

Project A	E_i	$\bar{E}$	$(E_i - \bar{E})$	(In thousands of dollars) $(E_i - \bar{E})^2$	P_i	(In thousands of dollars) $(E_i - \bar{E})^2 P_i$
Pessimistic	$ 4,000	$10,800	$(6,800)	$46,240	.2	$ 9,248
Most likely	10,000	10,800	(800)	640	.6	384
Optimistic	20,000	10,800	9,200	84,640	.2	16,928
						Variance = $26,560

Standard deviation = $\sqrt{\text{variance}}$ = $\sqrt{\$26,560,000}$ = $5,154.00

Project B	E_i	$\bar{E}$	$(E_i - \bar{E})$	(In thousands of dollars) $(E_i - \bar{E})^2$	P_i	(In thousands of dollars) $(E_i - \bar{E})^2 P_i$
Pessimistic	$ -0-	$10,800	$(10,800)	$166,640	0.20	$23,328
Most likely	11,000	10,800	200	40	0.60	24
Optimistic	21,000	10,800	10,200	104,040	0.20	20,808
						Variance = $44,160

Standard deviation = $\sqrt{\text{variance}}$ = $\sqrt{\$44,160,000}$ = $6,645.30

alone. So long as the expected values of the projects are equal, the coefficient of variation does not add any additional information. When the expected values differ, however, the CV is a better measure of risk than the absolute measure that is provided by the standard deviation.

Example

To assist in choosing between two mutually exclusive investment projects (the selection of one precludes the selection of the other), the following information is available for Calgary Equipment Company:

	Project C	Project D
Expected cash returns ($\bar{E}$)	$20,000	$40,000
Standard deviation (SD)	$8,000	$12,000
Coefficient of variation (SD/$\bar{E}$)	.40	.30

On the basis of standard deviation alone the management of Calgary Equipment Company may be tempted to declare project D to be riskier than project C. The absolute measure of risk provided by the standard deviation can lead to an error in the selection process when the expected returns differ between the two projects. Using the coefficient of variation to measure the *relative* risk of projects, it is apparent that project C is riskier than project D.

From the perspective of an individual firm, it may be possible to reduce overall risk by selecting individual projects with returns that vary negatively with the firm's existing projects. **Correlation** is a statistical technique that measures the relationship of the returns of the project to those of another. A correlation of +1 indicates a perfect positive relationship. This means, for example, that when returns on project X are high, returns on project Y are also high. When returns on project X are low, returns on project Y are low as well. A correlation coefficient of –1 indicates a perfect negative correlation meaning, for example, that when returns are high for project X, they are low for project Y and vice versa. Most correlation coefficients fall somewhere in between +1 and –1. The essential point for the manager to bear in mind is that it may be less risky to select projects with returns that vary inversely with those of existing projects, so that a downturn for one project does not impact negatively on the returns on another project. In other words, by combining projects with returns that correlate negatively with the firm's existing portfolio of projects, the overall variability or risk for the firm may be reduced. In practice, these concepts are very hard to apply. In addition, there is strong theoretical support for choosing projects on their individual merits because the residual owners of the firm (common shareholders) can do their own diversifying by acquiring shares of a variety of companies.

Sensitivity Analysis

It is apparent that many estimates are required in the capital budgeting process. Managers may find it useful to prepare a what-if, or sensitivity, analysis to determine how sensitive the net present value or internal rate of return of a project is to changes in these estimates. Although **sensitivity analysis** does not actually quantify risk, it can provide management with useful insights into the effects of changes in such input variables such as cash flow estimates and discount rates. The more the net present value or internal rate of return changes in response to changes in input variables, the riskier the project is perceived to be.

KEY TERMS FOR REVIEW (APPENDIX15A)

Coefficient of variation   A relative measure of a project's dispersion calculated as the ratio of a project's standard deviation to its expected value. (p. 839)

Correlation   A number ranging from +1 to –1 that is a statistical measure of the degree of association of the returns of one project to those of another. (p. 840)

Sensitivity analysis   An analysis of the effect that changes in a project's input variables may have on its net present value or internal rate of return. (p. 841)

Standard deviation   A statistical tool used by the management accountant to determine the amount of variation in a project's actual returns from the project's expected returns. (p. 839)

QUESTIONS

15–1   Some organizations will always use capital budgeting techniques on a before-tax basis rather than on an after-tax basis. Name several such organizations.

15–2   What is meant by after-tax cost, and how is the concept used in capital budgeting decisions?

15–3   What is a capital cost allowance tax shield, and how does it affect capital budgeting decisions?

15–4   The three most widely used depreciation methods are straight line, sum-of-the-years' digits, and double-declining balance, with the depreciation period based on the asset's actual useful life. Explain why a company might use one or more of these methods, instead of the capital cost allowance, for computing depreciation expense in its published financial statements.

15–5   Why are accelerated methods of capital cost allowance superior to the straight-line method from an income tax point of view?

15–6   Ludlow Company is considering the introduction of a new product line. Would an increase in the income tax rate tend to make the new investment more or less attractive? Explain.

15–7   Assume that an old piece of equipment is sold at a loss. From a capital budgeting point of view, what two cash inflows will be associated with the sale?

15–8   Assume that a new piece of equipment costs $40,000 and that the tax rate is 30%. Should the new piece of equipment be shown in the capital budgeting analysis as a cash outflow of $40,000, or should it be shown as a cash outflow of $28,000 [$40,000 × (1 – 0.30)]? Explain.

15–9   Assume that a company has cash operating expenses of $15,000 and a capital cost allowance expense of $10,000. Can these two items be added together and treated as one in a capital budgeting analysis, or should they be kept separate? Explain.

15–10   Distinguish between capital budgeting screening decisions and capital budgeting preference decisions. Why are preference decisions more difficult to make than screening decisions?

15–11   Why are preference decisions sometimes called *rationing* decisions?

15–12   How is the profitability index computed, and what does it measure?

15–13   What is the preference rule for ranking investment projects under the net present value method?

15–14   Can an investment with a profitability index of less than 1.00 be an acceptable investment? Explain.

15–15   What is the preference rule for ranking investment projects using the internal rate of return?

15–16   Why might some capital budgeting projects be accepted even when they cannot be justified on a purely financial basis? Could there be some ethical issues involved?

EXERCISES

E15–1

a.   Sze Kam Fa's Company has hired a management consulting firm to review and make recommendations concerning Sze Kam Fa's organizational structure. The consulting firm's fee will be $120,000. What will be the after-tax cost of the consulting firm's fee if Sze Kam Fa's tax rate is 30%?

b.   The Green Hills Riding Club has redirected its advertising toward a different sector of the market. As a result of this change in advertising, the club's annual revenues have increased by $50,000. If the club's tax rate is 25%, what is the after-tax benefit from the increased revenues?

c.   The Sharp Shooters Basketball Team has just installed an electronic scoreboard in its playing arena at a cost of $210,000. The scoreboard has an estimated 15-year useful life and a salvage value of $14,000. Determine the first three years' tax savings from the CCA tax shield. Assume that the income tax rate is 30%. CCA is 30% and the cost of capital is 10%.

E15–2   Complete the following table:

Beginning UCC	$70,000	$70,000	$70,000	$70,000
Capital cost	30,000	50,000	80,000	80,000
Proceeds	20,00	85,000	75,000	50,000
Capital gain	_____	_____	_____	_____
UCC after dispositions	_____	_____	_____	_____
Recapture	_____	_____	_____	_____
Terminal loss	_____	_____	_____	_____
UCC for CCA purposes	_____	_____	_____	_____

E15–3   Swick Company would like to purchase equipment that would allow the company to penetrate a new market. The equipment would cost $65,000 and have a four-year useful life. CCA is 30% and salvage value is estimated at $9,000.

Use of the equipment would generate before-tax net cash receipts of $25,000 per year. The equipment would require repairs in the third year that would cost $12,000. The company's tax rate is 30%, and its after- tax cost of capital is 10%.

Required

1.   Compute the net present value of the proposed investment in new equipment. (Round all dollar amounts to the nearest whole dollar.)

2.   Would you recommend that the equipment be purchased? Explain.

E15–4 Kramer Corporation is considering two investment projects, each of which would require $50,000. Cost and cash flow data concerning the two projects are given below:

	Project A	Project B
Investment in high-speed photocopier	$50,000	
Investment in working capital.		$50,000
Net annual cash inflows	9,000	9,000
Life of the project	8 years	8 years

The high-speed photocopier will have a salvage value of $5,000 in eight years and will be depreciated for tax purposes using a CCA rate of 20%. At the end of eight years, the investment in working capital would be released for use elsewhere. The company requires an after-tax return of 10% on all investments. The tax rate is 30%.

Required

Compute the net present value of each investment project. (Round all dollar amounts to the nearest whole dollar.)

E15–5 (This exercise should be assigned only if E15–4 is also assigned.) Refer to the data in E15–4.

Required

1. Compute the profitability index for each investment project.
2. Is an investment project with a profitability index of less than 1.0 an acceptable project? Explain.

E15–6 Lam Publishing Company hires students from the local university to collate pages on various printing jobs. This collating is all done by hand, at a cost of $60,000 per year. A collating machine has just come onto the market that could be used in place of the student help. The machine would cost $170,000 and have a 15-year useful life. It would require an operator at an annual cost of $18,000 and have annual maintenance costs of $7,000. New roller pads would be needed on the machine in eight years at a total cost of $20,000. The salvage value of the machine in 15 years would be $40,000.

Management requires a 14% after-tax return on all equipment purchases. The company's tax rate is 40% The CCA rate is 30%.

Required

1. Determine the before-tax net annual cost savings that the new collating machine will provide.
2. Using the data from (1) above and other data from the exercise, compute the collating machine's net present value. (Round all dollar amounts to the nearest whole dollar.) Would you recommend that the machine be purchased?

E15–7 Information on four investment proposals is given below:

	Investment Proposal			
	A	**B**	**C**	**D**
Investment required	$ (90,000)	$(200,000)	$ (90,000)	$(170,000)
Present value of cash inflows.	126,000	184,000	135,000	221,000
Net present value	$ 34,000	$ (16,000)	$ 45,000	$ 51,000
Life of the project	5 years	7 years	6 years	6 years

Required

1. Compute the profitability index for each investment proposal.
2. Rank the proposals in terms of preference.

PROBLEMS

P15–8 Straightforward Net Present Value Analysis   The Crescent Drilling Company owns the drilling rights to several tracts of land on which natural gas has been found. The amount of gas on some of the tracts is somewhat marginal, and the company is unsure whether it would be profitable to extract and sell the gas that these tracts contain. One such tract is tract 410, on which the following information has been gathered:

Investment in equipment needed for extraction work	$600,000
Working capital investment needed	85,000
Annual cash receipts from sale of gas, net of related cash operating expenses (before taxes)	110,000
Cost of restoring land at completion of extraction work	70,000

The natural gas in tract 410 would be exhausted after 10 years of extraction work. The equipment would have a useful life of 15 years, but it could be sold for only 15% of its original cost when extraction was completed. The company uses a CCA rate of 20% in computing depreciation deductions for tax purposes. The tax rate is 40%, and the company's after-tax cost of capital is 10%. The working capital would be released for use elsewhere at the completion of the project.

Required

1. Compute the net present value of tract 410. Round all dollar amounts to the nearest whole dollar.
2. Would you recommend that the investment project be undertaken?

P15–9 Basic Net Present Value Analysis Rapid Parcel Service has been offered an eight-year contract to deliver mail and small parcels between army installations. To accept the contract, the company would have to purchase several new delivery trucks at a total cost of $450,000. Other data relating to the contract follow:

Net annual cash receipts (before taxes) from the contract	$108,000
Cost of overhauling the motors in the trucks in five years	45,000
Salvage value of the trucks at termination of the contract	20,000

The trucks would be in the "light truck" category for tax purposes. If the contract were accepted, several old, fully depreciated trucks would be sold at a total price of $30,000. These funds would be used in purchasing the new trucks. The company uses the MACRS tables to compute capital cost allowances for tax purposes and requires a 12% after-tax return on all equipment purchases. The tax rate is 30%.

Required

Compute the net present value of this investment opportunity. Round all dollar amounts to the nearest whole dollar. Would you recommend that the contract be accepted?

P15–10 Various Depreciation Methods; Net Present Value Vitro Company has been offered an eight-year contract to produce a key part for a government agency. Management has determined that the following costs and revenues would be associated with the contract:

Cost of special equipment	$700,000
Working capital needed to carry inventories	90,000
Annual revenues from the contract	450,000
Annual out-of-pocket costs for materials, salaries, and so forth	261,500
Salvage value of the equipment in eight years	25,000

Although the equipment would have a useful life of nine years, the company would sell it at the end of the contract period. Vitro Company's after-tax cost of capital is 14%, and its tax rate is 40%. At the end of the contract period, the working capital would be released for use elsewhere. CCA is 15%.

Required

Determine the present value of the proposed contract.

P15–11   Preference Ranking of Investment Projects   Austin Company is investigating five different investment opportunities. Information on the five projects under study is given below:

	Project Number				
	1	**2**	**3**	**4**	**5**
Investment required..........	$(480,000)	$(360,000)	$(270,000)	$(450,000)	$(400,000)
Present value of cash inflows at a 10% discount rate	567,270	433,400	336,140	522,970	379,760
Net present value............	$ 87,270	$ 73,400	$ 66,140	$ 72,970	$ (20,240)
Life of the project	6 years	12 years	6 years	3 years	5 years
Internal rate of return.........	16%	14%	18%	19%	8%

Since the company's cost of capital is 10%, a 10% discount rate has been used in the present value computations above. Limited funds are available for investment, so the company can't accept all of the projects available.

Required

1. Compute the profitability index for each investment project.
2. Rank the five projects according to preference, in terms of:
   a. Net present value.
   b. Profitability index.
   c. Internal rate of return.
3. Which ranking do you prefer? Why?

P15–12   Net Present Value Analysis   Fran's Travel Service is located in Quebec City. The company, which specializes in scenic tours, has an opportunity to purchase several buses that were recently repossessed by a bank. Although the buses cost $800,000 new and are only three years old, they can be purchased by Fran's for the remaining amount unpaid, which is only $610,000. Moreover, the bank will allow Fran's to pay $400,000 immediately and $70,000 each year for three years, without interest.

Fran's president, Vera Costeau, estimates that the buses could be operated 300 days per year, carrying 180 tourists per day. The company charges $7.50 per person for its tours. Ms. Costeau estimates that the following expenses would be associated with the buses each year:

Salaries for bus operators and tour guides........	$130,000
Insurance	9,000
Fuel	85,000
Bank payments	70,000*
Promotion for the tours	21,000
Rent for parking the buses...................	7,200
Maintenance..............................	53,000
Fees and highway taxes.....................	4,800
Depreciation..............................	37,333†
Total expenses	$417,333

*For the first three years only.

†$610,000 cost − $50,000 estimated salvage value = $560,000 depreciable cost; $560,000 ÷ 15 years = $37,333 per year

The owner of the property on which the buses would be parked at night would require a deposit of $1,800, which is equal to three months' rent. This deposit would be refunded at the end of the buses' 15-year remaining useful life. In nine years, the buses would need to have all seat coverings replaced at a cost of $35,000.

If the buses are purchased, Fran's will use a CCA rate of 30%. The company's after-tax cost of capital is 10%, and the tax rate is 30%.

Required

1. Compute the net cash receipts (before income taxes) each year from operating the buses.
2. By use of the net present value method, determine whether the buses should be purchased. (Round all dollar amounts to the nearest whole dollar.)

P15–13 Uneven Cash Flows; Net Present Value   "I know the salt in the Heber tract contains some contaminants, but I still think it's worth going after," said Bryce Wasser, chief engineer for Emory Mines.

"I'm not so sure," replied Erika Kretchow, the company's vice president. "The best we can hope to get for salt is $21 a tonne, and the accounting people say that it will cost at least $15 a tonne to remove the contaminants and process the salt into usable form. That doesn't leave much in the way of contribution margin."

"I know the contribution per tonne will be low," replied Bryce, "but our studies show that we have 1,275,000 tonnes of salt in the Heber tract. I figure we can extract 70,000, 100,000, and 160,000 tonnes the first three years, respectively, and then the remainder evenly over the next seven years. Even at only $21 a tonne, that will really enhance our cash flow."

"Yes, but what about all the other costs?" asked Erika. "Fixed costs for salaries, insurance, and so forth directly associated with the extraction of the salt would be $530,000 a year. In addition, we would have to pay out an additional $275,000 at the end of the project to level and fill the land. You know how tough those environmental people can be if a project isn't handled right. And all of this doesn't even consider the $800,000 cost of special equipment that we would need or the $90,000 in working capital that would be required to carry inventories and accounts receivable. I think we should just forget the whole idea and concentrate our resources on existing projects."

"You're suffering from tunnel vision," quipped Bryce. "The tax laws allow us to depreciate equipment with a 30% CCA rate, so we'll save tens of thousands of dollars in taxes at our 30% tax rate. Besides that, since the equipment would have a 15-year useful life, it would still have some use left when the salt was all extracted and we closed the area. Based on experience, I'm sure we could sell it to someone for at least 5% of its original cost."

"I'll admit the project has some tempting features, Bryce, but I'll still bet that it won't provide the 16% after-tax return we require on high-risk investments. Let's give our figures to the people in the New Projects Division and have them do a present value analysis for us."

Required

1. Compute the before-tax net cash receipts each year from the extraction, processing, and sale of the salt. (Do not include the cost of levelling and filling the land in this computation.)
2. Using the data from (1) above and other data from the problem as needed, prepare a net present value analysis to determine whether the company should purchase the equipment and extract the salt. (Round all dollar amounts to the nearest whole dollar.) You may assume that for the company *as a whole*, there will be a positive taxable income in every year, so that a tax benefit would be realized from any operating losses associated with the salt-extraction project.

P15–14 Various Depreciation Methods; Profitability Index   Stokes Broadcasting, Inc., operates several communications businesses, including a TV station. The company is considering the replacement of one of the cameras in the station with a more sophisticated model. Although the old camera is fully depreciated and has a negligible salvage value, it is in good operating condition and will be donated to a local university if the new camera is purchased. Management is considering two cameras as a replacement, only one of which can be purchased. Cost and other data on the two cameras are given below:

	Camera	
	1	2
Cost of the camera	$150,000	$225,000
Annual savings in cash operating costs	40,000	56,000
Parts replacement in four years..............	9,000	15,000
Salvage value	10,000	30,000
Useful life.............................	8 years	8 years
Depreciation method to be used	Straight line 30%	Straight line 30%

Stokes Company's after-tax cost of capital is 12%. The company's tax rate is 30%. Round all dollar amounts to the nearest whole dollar.

Required

1. Compute the net present value of each investment alternative. Based on these data, which camera should be purchased?
2. Compute the profitability index for each investment alternative. Based on these data, which camera should be purchased?

P15–15 Preference Ranking of Investment Projects Yancey Company has limited funds available for investment and must ration the funds among five competing projects. Selected information on the five projects follows:

Project		Investment Required	Net Present Value	Life of the Project (years)	Internal Rate of Return (percent)
A	....	$800,000	$221,615	7	18
B	....	675,000	210,000	12	16
C	....	500,000	175,175	7	20
D	....	700,000	152,544	3	22
E	....	900,000	(52,176)	6	8

Yancey Company's cost of capital is 10%. (The net present values above have been computed using a 10% discount rate.) The company wants your assistance in determining which project to accept first, which to accept second, and so forth. The company's investment funds are limited.

Required

1. Compute the profitability index for each project.
2. Rank the five projects in order of preference, in terms of:
   a. Net present value.
   b. Profitability index.
   c. Internal rate of return.
3. Which ranking do you prefer? Why?

P15–16 Comprehensive Problem: Various CCA Methods; Net Present Value Eric Giacardi, vice president of Dicer Products, would like to purchase an automated kiln for use in the manufacture of one of the company's product lines. Selected information about the kiln follows:

Cost of kiln	$900,000
Annual savings provided by the kiln in cash operating costs (before taxes)............................	230,000
Salvage value of the kiln (5% of cost)	45,000
Cost of relining the kiln in 5 years	130,000

The company would have to increase its working capital by $20,000 in order to support the operation of the new kiln.

An analysis that Mr. Giacardi has just received from his staff indicates that the new kiln will not provide the 14% after-tax return required by the company. In doing the analysis, Mr. Giacardi had instructed his staff to use the current maximum CCA rate of 20%. Dicer Products' tax rate is 40%. The useful life of the kiln is estimated to be nine years.

Upon seeing the analysis done by Mr. Giacardi's staff, Robyn Hafen, president of Dicer Products, suggested that the analysis be redone using a CCA rate at 60% proposed in new legislation. Somewhat surprised by this suggestion, Mr. Giacardi stated, "What difference does it make how we compute the CCA? We have the same total CCA either way. This new kiln simply doesn't meet our rate of return requirements."

Required

1. Compute the net present value of the kiln using a 20% CCA rate. (Round all dollar amounts to the nearest whole dollar.)
2. Compute the net present value of the kiln using a 60% CCA rate.

3. Explain to Mr. Giacardi how the CCA method used can affect the rate of return generated by an investment project.

P15–17 Equipment Replacement; Incremental-Cost Approach

"Those new golf carts are simply beautiful," exclaimed Bonnie Weskow, operations manager for Coral Lake Resort. "No wonder the board of directors is so anxious to buy them."

"All of the board except me," replied Harvey Delgado, chairman of the board. "Everyone seems to forget that we purchased our present carts just two years ago at a cost of $260,000. Those new carts will cost a cool $350,000. The worst part is that we can only get $110,000 out of our old carts if we sell them now. That's quite a loss for the resort to absorb."

"We can make up the loss very quickly," countered Bonnie. "Mountain Hills Resort in the northern part of the province says that usage of their carts increased by 20% when they purchased these new carts. I've gathered a lot of information about the new carts, and I'll have a recommendation ready for the board tomorrow."

The information to which Bonnie was referring is provided below:

a. Both the old and the new carts are eligible for a CCA rate of 30%. The new carts have an estimated useful life of eight years. Although the old carts have already been used for two years, Coral Lake's maintenance engineer is confident that with proper maintenance and with some extra care the old carts can be kept usable for an additional eight years.

b. The old carts are being rented an average of 45,000 hours per year. Coral Lake Resort charges $7 per hour for use of a cart.

c. To keep the new carts operating at peak efficiency, Coral Lake Resort would purchase a maintenance contract that would cost $8,000 more per year than the present maintenance contract. In addition, the resort would have to make a $4,000 maintenance deposit immediately. This deposit would be refunded at the end of the useful life of the carts.

d. The new carts have a unique, high-powered motor that would have to be rewound in five years at a total cost of $90,000.

e. Coral Lake Resort has a tax rate of 40% and requires an after-tax return of 10% on all investments. The old carts would have no salvage value at the end of eight years.

Required

1. Compute the incremental net annual cash receipts (before taxes) expected from use of the new carts. (Do not include the cost of rewinding the motors or any salvage value in this computation.)

2. Use discounted cash flow to determine whether the new carts should be purchased. Use the incremental-cost approach. (Round all dollar amounts to the nearest whole dollar.) Are there any nonquantitative factors that should be considered in this decision?

P15–18 Comparison of Total-Cost and Incremental-Cost Approaches

Viking Foods, Inc., provides hot, ready-to-eat dinners for airlines. The company is considering the purchase of several new trucks to replace an equal number of old trucks now in use in delivering dinners to flights at airports. The new trucks would cost $430,000, but they would require only one operator per truck (as compared to two operators for the trucks now being used), as well as provide other cost savings. A comparison of total annual cash operating costs between the old trucks that would be replaced and the new trucks is provided below:

	Old Trucks	New Trucks
Salaries—operators	$120,000	$ 60,000
Fuel.	80,000	75,000
Insurance	9,000	27,000
Maintenance	11,000	8,000
Total operating costs	$220,000	$170,000

If the new trucks are purchased, the old trucks will be sold to another company for $80,000. These trucks cost $350,000 when they were new, have a current book value of $105,000, and a UCC value of $102,042. They are in the 30% CCA property class, and the straight-line method is being used to depreciate these trucks for accounting purposes.

If the new trucks are not purchased, the old trucks will be used for eight more years and then sold for an estimated salvage value of $10,000. However, in order to keep the old trucks operating, extensive repairs would be needed in one year that will cost an estimated $100,000. These repairs will be expensed for tax purposes in the year incurred.

The new trucks would have a useful life of eight years. They would have an estimated $40,000 salvage value at the end of their useful life. The company's tax rate is 30%, and its after-tax cost of capital is 12%.

Required

1. By use of the total-cost approach to discounted cash flow, determine whether the new trucks should be purchased. (Round all dollar amounts to the nearest whole dollar.)
2. Repeat the computations in (1) above, this time using the incremental-cost approach to discounted cash flow.

P15–19   A Comparison of Investment Alternatives; Total-Cost Approach

Ms. Keri Lee, an expert in retro-fitting buildings to meet seismic safety standards, has just received a $200,000 after-tax bonus for the successful completion of a project on time and under budget. Business has been so good that she is planning to retire in 12 years, spending her time relaxing in the sun, skiing, and doing charitable work. Ms. Lee is considering two alternatives for investing her bonus.

Alternative 1. Municipal bonds can be purchased that mature in 12 years and that bear interest at 8%. Assume that this interest would be tax-free and paid semiannually. (In discounting a cash flow that occurs semiannually, the procedure is to halve the discount rate and double the number of periods. Use the same procedure for discounting the principal returned when the bonds reach maturity.)

Alternative 2. A small discount perfume shop is available for sale at a nearby factory outlet centre. The business can be purchased from its current owner for $200,000. The following information relates to this alternative:

a. Of the purchase price, $80,000 would be for fixtures and other depreciable items. The remainder would be for the company's working capital (inventory, accounts receivable, and cash). The fixtures and other depreciable items would have a remaining useful life of at least 12 years and a CCA rate of 20%. At the end of 12 years, these depreciable items would have a negligible salvage value; however, the working capital would be released for reinvestment elsewhere.
b. Store records indicate that sales have averaged $400,000 per year, and out-of-pocket costs have averaged $370,000 per year (*not* including income taxes). These out-of- pocket costs include rent on the building, cost of goods sold, utilities, and wages and salaries for the sales staff and the store manager. Ms. Lee plans to entrust the day-to- day operations of the store to the manager.
c. Ms. Lee's tax rate is 35%.
d. Ms. Lee wants an after-tax return on her investment of at least 8%.

Required

Advise Ms. Lee as to which alternative should be selected. Use the total-cost approach to discounted cash flow in your analysis. (Round all dollar amounts to the nearest whole dollar.)

P15–20   Ethics and the Manager

The Fore Corporation is an integrated food processing company that has operations in over two dozen countries. Fore's corporate headquarters is in Montreal, and the company's executives frequently travel to visit Fore's foreign and domestic facilities.

Fore has a fleet of aircraft that consists of two business jets with international range and six smaller turboprop aircraft that are used on shorter flights. Company policy is to assign aircraft to trips on the basis of minimizing cost, but the practice is to assign the aircraft based on the organizational rank of the traveller. Fore offers its aircraft for short-term lease or for charter by other organizations whenever Fore itself does not plan to use the aircraft. Fore surveys the market often in order to keep its lease and charter rates competitive.

William Earle, Fore's vice president of finance, has claimed that a third business jet can be justified financially. However, some people in the controller's office have surmised that the real reason for a third business jet was to upgrade the aircraft used by Earle. Presently, the people outranking Earle keep the two business jets busy, with the result that Earle usually flies in smaller turboprop aircraft.

The third business jet would cost $11 million. A capital expenditure of this magnitude requires a formal proposal with projected cash flows and net present value computations using Fore's minimum required rate of return. If Fore's president and the finance committee of the board of directors approve the proposal, it will be submitted to the full board of directors. The board has final approval on capital expenditures exceeding $5 million, and has established a firm policy of rejecting any discretionary proposal that has a negative net present value.

Earle asked Rachel Arnett, assistant corporate controller, to prepare a proposal on a third business jet. Arnett gathered the following data:

- Acquisition cost of the aircraft, including instrumentation and interior furnishing.
- Operating cost of the aircraft for company use.
- Projected avoidable commercial airfare and other avoidable costs from company use of the plane.
- Projected value of executive time saved by using the third business jet.
- Projected contribution margin from incremental lease and charter activity.
- Estimated resale value of the aircraft.
- Estimated income tax effects of the proposal.

When Earle reviewed Arnett's completed proposal and saw the large negative net present value figure, he returned the proposal to Arnett. With a glare, Earle commented, "You must have made an error. The proposal should look better than that."

Feeling some pressure, Arnett went back and checked her computations; she found no errors. However, Earle's message was clear. Arnett discarded her projections and estimates that she believed were reasonable and replaced them with figures that had a remote chance of actually occurring but were more favourable to the proposal. For example, she used first-class airfares to refigure the avoidable commercial airfare costs, even though company policy was to fly coach. She found revising the proposal to be distressing.

The revised proposal still had a negative net present value. Earle's anger was evident as he told Arnett to revise the proposal again, and to start with a $100,000 positive net present value and work backwards to compute supporting estimates and projections.

Required

1. Explain whether Rachel Arnett's revision of the proposal was in violation of ethical standards for management accountants.
2. Was William Earle ethically correct in telling Arnett specifically how to revise the proposal? Explain your answer.
3. Identify specific internal controls that Fore Corporation could implement to prevent unethical behaviour on the part of the vice president of finance.

(CMA, adapted)

P15–21   Risk and Net Present value Analysis   (Appendix 15A) Wolfville Ltd. is evaluating two mutually exclusive investment proposals. Edgar Scott, the firm's chief management accountant, has developed the following estimates for each project. The projects have estimated lifespans of 7 years and the firm's cost of capital is 10%.

		Cash Flows	
	Probability	A	B
Investment Outlay.........	1.0	$30,000	$30,000
Net cash flows			
Pessimistic.............	0.2	8,000	26,000
Most likely	0.6	10,000	11,000
Optimistic	0.2	42,000	21,000

Required

1. Calculate the net present value of each project for each probability.
2. Calculate the expected net present value for each alternative.
3. Calculate the standard deviation and coefficient of variation for each subject.
4. Which project would you recommend? Comment on the risk/return of these two projects.

P15–22 Expected Value, Standard Deviation, and Coefficient of Variation
(Appendix 15A) Fraser Company of Burnaby, British Columbia, is evaluting the expected returns of two 5-year projects. These projects are not mutually exclusive. The expected returns are expressed in thousands of dollars.

Year	X	Y
19x1................	$5.5	$12
19x2................	4	4
19x3................	6	4.5
19x4................	3.5	11
19x5................	12.5	5

Required

1. Calculate the expected value for each project.
2. Calculate the standard deviation and coefficient of variation for each project.
3. By observation, does there appear to be any correlation between the returns of the two projects?
4. As a management accountant consulting for Fraser Company, suggest how the company may diversify its risk. Support your comments.

P15–23 Capital Net Gain: Net Present Value Johnson Ltd. is considering the viability of erecting a new production facility on a piece of property. The land is presently vacant and can be acquired for the current market value of $800,000. The facility can be erected for $600,000, and equipment worth a further $450,000 needs to be acquired. Capital cost allowance rates on the building and equipment are 10% and 20% respectively. Operating savings from the new facility are expected to be $445,000 per year for the next 10 years. Johnson Ltd. expects to dispose of the property at the end of the 10 years for $1.4 million; this amount is solely the anticipated value of the land. The firm's tax rate is 45% and its cost of capital is 16%.

Required

Using the net present value approach, should Johnson Ltd. undertake the project? Show all calculations, and state any assumptions necessary.

(CGA-Canada, adapted)

CASES

C15–24 Integrative Case: Make or Buy; Discounted Cash Flow "According to my figures, it would be a mistake to buy those new tools and to continue manufacturing the K96 relay," said Allen Dusak, production manager for Midway Electronics. "If we do buy the new tools, then our cost for the K96 relay will jump from $38 to well over $40 per unit, and that's more than we would have to pay an outside supplier to manufacture the relay for us."

Midway Electronics manufactures several products, including many of the component parts (such as the K96 relay) that go into these products. The K96 relay requires specialized tools in its manufacture and the tools presently in use are worn out. Rather than replace the tools, management is considering whether the K96 relay should be purchased from an outside source. A supplier is willing to provide the relays at a unit sales price of $40 if at least 150,000 units are ordered each year. However, Midway Electronics is reluctant to accept this offer, since it has no alternative use for the space now being used to manufacture the K96 relay.

Midway Electronics has produced 160,000 K96 relays each year for the past four years. Sales forecasts suggest that this volume will remain constant for at least four more years. In the past, the relays have cost $38 each to manufacture, as shown by the following data:

Direct materials	$20.00
Direct labour	4.60
Variable manufacturing overhead	1.40
Fixed manufacturing overhead	12.00*
Total unit cost.	$38.00

*Depreciation of tools is one-fourth of the fixed
overhead. These tools must now be replaced. The
balance of this $12 is for general fixed overhead costs
of the factory that require cash expenditures.

If the specialized tools are purchased, they will cost $5,000,000 and will have a disposal value of $200,000 at the end of their four-year useful life. Straight-line depreciation would be used for financial reporting purposes, but a CCA rate of 30% would be used for tax purposes. Midway Electronics has a 40% tax rate, and management requires a 14% after-tax return on investment for any purchases of tools and equipment.

"I know the new tools are costly," said Marci Cantrell, sales representative for the manufacturer of the tools. "But they will allow direct labour and variable overhead to be reduced by $1.30 per unit for the K96 relay. I know this $1.30 figure is accurate because another company we sell to is using these same tools to produce a K96 relay of its own under operating conditions that are identical to Midway's."

"I agree that direct labour and variable overhead would be reduced by $1.30 per unit with the new tools," replied Allen Dusak. "The other company you mentioned was kind enough to provide me with a cost breakdown for its relay, as follows:

Direct materials	$21.80
Direct labour	4.00
Variable manufacturing overhead	0.70
Fixed manufacturing overhead	13.20
Total unit cost	$39.70

The thing you haven't mentioned, Marci, is that the other company's direct materials cost went up by $1.80 per unit, due to the higher quality of material that must be used with the new tools. Our materials cost would go up by the same amount, which would more than offset the $1.30 reduction in labour and variable overhead. Also, you haven't considered the difference in volume between the other company and us. They produce 200,000 relays a year. When you consider our lower volume, I'm sure that with the new tools our unit cost would jump well over $40."

Although the old tools being used by Midway Electronics have a negligible UCC balance, they have a salvage value of $30,000. These tools will be sold if the new tools are purchased. However, if the new tools are not purchased, then the old tools will be retained as standby equipment in case of a supply breakdown. Midway's accounting department has confirmed that total fixed overhead costs, other than depreciation, will not change regardless of the decision made concerning the relays. However, accounting has estimated that working capital needs will increase by $85,000 if the new tools are purchased due to the higher quality of material required in the manufacture of the relays.

Required

1. Prepare a discounted cash flow analysis that will help Midway Electronics' management decide whether the new tools should be purchased. Use the incremental-cost approach, and round all dollar amounts to the nearest whole dollar. Assume that Revenue Canada requires that the new tool be recorded in a separate asset class but the CCA rate remains at 30%.
2. Identify additional factors that Midway's management should consider before a decision is made about whether to manufacture or buy the K96 relays.

C15–25   Product Line Evaluation   John Able, the general manager of Western Products Inc., is reviewing revenue and cost data for product A which was added to Western's product line two years ago. These data are as follows:

	19x0	19x1
Units produced and sold	10,000	30,000
Unit selling price	$16.00	$15.00
Unit costs:		
Direct materials	$2.40	$2.30
Spoilage during fabrication	.28	.24
Direct labour	4.77	4.74
Department overhead —direct	2.44	1.48
—indirect.............	2.55	.85
Plant overhead*	1.59	1.58
Total plant cost..........................	$14.03	$11.19
General selling & administration†............	2.10	1.68
Total unit cost	$16.13	$12.87
Unit profit (loss)	$ (.13)	$ 2.13

*33⅓ percent of direct labour.
†15 percent of total plant cost.

Product A has been fabricated and assembled in one process in one department of the plant at a rate of four units per direct labour-hour. All of the direct materials are added during the fabrication process. Variable overhead is a function of direct labour-hours. Safety regulations restrict direct labour to a maximum of 40 hours per day, five days per week. All of Western's products are sold through a salaried sales force such that adding product A to the product line has not affected Western's total selling expense. Indirect department overhead costs, however, were increased by $6,000 annually when the assembly operation for product A was introduced in 19x0.

Able has initiated a number of studies concerned with lowering the cost of, and increasing the demand for, product A. The following information, proposals, and recommendations have resulted from these studies.

The purchasing department has located an outside supplier which would deliver the fabricated parts, ready for assembly, to Western's plant at a cost of $6.25 per unit. If Western purchases all of its requirements for fabricated parts from this supplier, the production process could be altered such that product A would be assembled at a rate of six units per direct labour-hour.

The engineering department has proposed that the company invest $800,000 to overhaul the existing general purpose requirement and to purchase new equipment designed to: (1) eliminate the safety regulation restriction on direct labour-hours; (2) eliminate the spoilage of direct materials in fabrication; and (3) reduce overall direct labour costs by 10%. The new equipment would be sold for $50,000 at the end of five years and the old equipment kept for other purposes. All of the equipment concerned is categorized as Class 8 assets for CCA purposes. The Class 8 rate is 20%.

The marketing department has made the following two recommendations designed to increase demand for product A:

1. The first recommendation essentially proposes to increase the annual marketing budget by $25,000 to increase expected demand from 30,000 units to 50,000 units annually.
2. The second recommendation is to increase the annual marketing budget by $25,000 and lower the unit price from $15 to $14. As a result, the marketing department expects that annual demand would be increased from 30,000 to 75,000 units.

The marketing department has carefully pointed out, however, that product A's life cycle will likely only extend for another five years with demand dropping off in the last year. The projected demand under each recommendation would be as follows:

	Projected demand for product A in units	
Year	Recommendation 1	Recommendation 2
19x2	50,000	75,000
19x3	50,000	75,000
19x4	50,000	75,000
19x5	50,000	75,000
19x6	37,500	37,500
19x7	Nil*	Nil*

Product A will be obsolete in 19x7.

Western Products Inc. has a marginal tax rate of 40% and an after-tax cost of capital of 16%.

Required

1. Determine by what amount Western's 19x1 net income before tax would have changed if product A had been dropped from the product line at the end of 19x0.
2. Identify and evaluate the alternatives open to Able, and recommend a course of action to be taken.

(SMAC, adapted)

C15–26   Break-Even and Net Present Value Analysis   VanDyk Enterprises has been operating a large gold mine for many years. The company wants to acquire equipment that will allow it to extract gold ore from a currently inaccessible area of the mine. Rich Salzman, VanDyk's controller, has gathered the following data to analyze the investment:

a. The initial cost of the extraction equipment is $2,500,000. In addition to this cost, the equipment will require a large concrete foundation at a cost of $300,000. The vendor has quoted an additional cost of $200,000 to install and test the equipment. All of these costs are considered part of the cost of acquiring the equipment.

b. The useful life of the equipment is 10 years with no salvage value at the end of this period. VanDyk uses a CCA rate of 20%.

c. Using the new equipment, 150 kilograms of gold can be extracted annually for the next 10 years from the previously inaccessible area of the mine.

d. The cost to extract and separate gold from the ore is $2,000 per kilogram of gold. After separation, the gold must undergo further processing and testing that costs $800 per kilogram of gold. These are all out-of-pocket variable costs.

e. Two skilled technicians will be hired to operate the new equipment. The total salary and fringe benefit expense for these two employees will be $110,000 annually over the 10 years.

f. Periodic maintenance on the equipment is expected to cost $50,000 per year.

g. The project would require an investment in additional working capital of $200,000. This working capital would be released for use elsewhere at the conclusion of the project in 10 years.

h. Environmental and safety regulations require that the mine be extensively restored at the conclusion of the project and toxic chemicals be safely disposed of. The cost of this restoration work is expected to be $4,000,000.

i. The current market price of gold is $11,200 per kilogram.

j. VanDyk's tax rate is 30%.

k. VanDyk uses a 12% after-tax minimum required rate of return.

Required

1. Determine the net present value of the extraction equipment assuming that the gold is sold for $11,200 per kilogram.
2. In reality, the future market value of gold is uncertain. What is the market price of gold at which VanDyk's acquisition of the extraction equipment will break even from a present value perspective?

(CMA, heavily adapted)

GROUP EXERCISES

GE15–27   Tax Incentives May Not Have Their Intended Effect   Quite often the government will use changes in the tax code to provide businesses with incentives to invest in new capital equipment. New legislation often offers the opportunity for faster CCA or investment tax credits to stimulate companies to make additional investments in modern equipment or worker training, or job tax credits to encourage firms to hire additional workers. The goal of tax reform is usually linked to attempts to resuscitate a lagging economy or to revitalize Canadian competitiveness. However, corporate response to these well-intended incentives may be uncertain because of the way business executives are evaluated and compensated.

Required

1.   Large, multidivisional companies like Magna or McCain tend to be decentralized. What is the process by which capital investment proposals are initiated and get recommended for funding in decentralized firms?
2.   What criteria are used to make capital investment decisions? What capital investment projects is senior-level (corporate-level) management willing to fund? Why?
3.   How do managers assess decisions? What influences how they will act?
4.   How are profit centre managers and divisional managers evaluated and compensated?
5.   Why wouldn't tax legislation of the type described above have its intended effect on divisional managers' investment decisions? What other conflicts exist between North American performance evaluation and compensation systems and capital budgeting models used to evaluate capital investments?
6.   What recommendations would you make to bring about greater consistency (congruence) between the models used to make capital budgeting decisions and the performance measures used to evaluate managers' performance?

GE15–28   Technology Is Changing the Face of Competition   Investments in leading-edge technology open up a whole new set of options never before experienced by manufacturers. Until recently, larger producers pursued a manufacturing strategy based on increased efficiency, higher volumes, lower unit costs, and the greater investments in economies of scale demanded by large markets. The high-margin niche markets were often left to the small manufacturers, who could service them more efficiently.

However, for more than a decade, the marketplace has been demanding greater variety and customization. To take advantage of the choices made available by such advanced process technologies, managers must recognize that the opportunities presented by these sophisticated technologies will require an entirely new way of thinking about markets and competition unrelated to the scale-based strategies of the past. Modern computer-based technologies make feasible economies of scope, the efficient production of variety without the necessity of high volumes. This increased flexibility poses a whole new set of demands to understanding the impact on strategy for those adopting these new technologies.

Required

What particular challenges to the effective use of newer process technologies arise in the following areas?
1.   Sales and marketing.
2.   Product design engineering.
3.   Process design engineering.
4.   Production.
5.   Accounting.

GE15–29   How Do Capital Markets Evaluate Performance?   Internally, companies usually use accounting measures to motivate and evaluate the performance of managers of corporate groups, divisions, product lines, and departments. How do investors use accounting information in determining whether to buy, sell, or hold onto a shares?

Most companies pay their top managers a salary and a bonus. The bonus part of their compensation is usually based on how well the executive performs against some accounting-based performance target. For example, some percentage of the CEO's bonus may be earned when he or she achieves a certain increase in earnings per share or, in the case of a division manager, when he or she exceeds a certain percentage increase in operating profits. Yet, there are numerous examples of CEOs and other top officers who have met their performance targets, but the stock price of the company lags or flounders for years on end. Top management prospers but shareholders may not.

Required

1. If a company consistently earns a profit year-in and year-out, do shareholders and prospective shareholders have a right to expect anything more than that from corporate management?
2. Is there any cost to holding large stocks of inventory? Is there any cost associated with the fixed assets—property, plant, and equipment—of capital-intensive businesses? Is there any cost of having idle assets or underutilized assets like buildings and equipment?
3. Is there any internal accounting charge for the money invested in working capital and fixed assets?
4. What is the cost of debt? Is there a similar cost associated with shareholders' equity? Explain.
5. Based on the discussion in (2) through (4), how does management create value (increase the share price)? Under what conditions would the share price languish or even decrease?
6. How would knowledge of this information influence how top management allocates the company's scarce cash resources within the firm?
7. Design a performance measurement system for senior-level officers and for divisional managers that is more consistent with enhancing a company's market value.
8. Do general economic conditions have any impact on a company's market value? How would you change the design of the performance measurement and compensation system to control for the fortune (or misfortune) of managing a company or division when general economic conditions were improving (or deteriorating)?

GE15–30 Cost-Benefit Analysis Applied to Governmental Programs Investment analysis is almost always thought of in terms of bricks, mortar, and machinery. Yet there are important social programs (e.g., hazardous waste, health and safety in the workplace, or jobs training) whose impact is nationwide and whose cost can easily run into the billions of dollars. Without putting a straightjacket around the evaluation of such programs or trying to evaluate such problems strictly in terms of financial considerations, such programs could nevertheless use some fresh thinking and a strong dose of cost-benefit analysis. Instead of viewing these problems in terms of whether we can afford to fix them, can we afford not to?

Required

Choose a government program and try to objectively identify the benefits of the program against the costs associated with its implementation. This may require reading or scanning some articles on political economy in order to grasp the basic objectives and projected costs of the program.

SERVICE DEPARTMENT COSTING: AN ACTIVITY APPROACH

LEARNING OBJECTIVES

After studying Chapter 16, you should be able to:

1 Explain what is meant by a service department, and explain why it is necessary to allocate service department costs to operating departments.

2 Select a first-stage allocation base (cost driver) for each service department that accurately measures consumption of services by other departments.

3 Allocate service department costs to other departments using (a) the direct method, (b) the step method, and (c) the reciprocal method.

4 Explain why variable and fixed service department costs should be allocated separately.

5 Explain how allocated service department costs are traced to operating department flexible budgets.

6 Enumerate the guidelines that should be followed in allocating service department costs.

7 Prepare an allocation schedule involving several service departments and several operating departments.

8 Define or explain the key terms listed at the end of the chapter.

Saint Mary's University in Halifax, Nova Scotia, has a number of service departments to support the teaching function. Computer services, athletics, library, and physical plant represent the larger ones. The Registrar, admissions, purchasing, art gallery, and the bookstore represent some of the other support service departments. Each of these service departments is part of the costs that is assigned to the education of students.

A s stated in Chapter 1, most organizations have one or more service departments that carry on critical auxiliary services for the entire organization. In this chapter, we look more closely at service departments and consider how their costs are allocated to the units they serve for planning, costing, and other purposes.

THE NEED FOR COST ALLOCATION

OBJECTIVE 1
Explain what is meant by a service department, and explain why it is necessary to allocate service department costs to operating departments.

Departments within an organization can be divided into two broad classes: (1) operating departments and (2) service departments. **Operating departments** include those departments or units where the central purposes of the organization are carried out. Examples of such departments or units would include the surgery department at QE II Hospital; the undergraduate and graduate programs at Saint Mary's; and producing departments such as milling, assembly, and painting in a manufacturing company such as Bombardier.

Service departments, by contrast, do not engage directly in operating activities. Rather, they provide services or assistance that facilitate the activities of the operating departments. Examples of such services include cafeteria, internal auditing, personnel, X ray, cost accounting, and purchasing. Although service departments do not engage directly in the operating activities of an organization, the costs that they incur are generally viewed as being part of the cost of the final product or service, the same as are materials, labour, and overhead in a manufacturing company or medications in a hospital.

The major question that we must consider in this chapter is: How does the manager determine how much of a service department's cost is to be allocated to each of the units that it serves? This is an important question, since the amount of service department cost allocated to a particular unit can have a significant impact on the computed cost of the goods or services that the unit is providing. As we shall see, many factors must be considered if allocations are to be equitable between departments or other units that receive services during a period.

GUIDELINES FOR COST ALLOCATION

Several basic guidelines should be followed in allocating service department costs. These guidelines relate to (1) selecting the proper allocation base, (2) allocating the costs of interdepartmental services, (3) allocating costs by behaviour, (4) avoiding certain allocation pitfalls, and (5) deciding whether to allocate budgeted or actual costs. These topics are covered in order in this section.

Selecting Allocation Bases

OBJECTIVE 2
Select a first-stage allocation base (cost driver) for each service department that accurately measures consumption of services by other departments.

In Chapter 5, we stated that many companies use a two-stage costing process. In the first stage, costs are assigned to the operating departments; in the second stage, costs are assigned from the operating departments to products and services. We focused most of our attention in Chapter 5 on the second stage and reserved discussion of first-stage costing procedures to this chapter. On the following pages we discuss the assignment of costs from service departments to operating departments, *which represents the first stage of the two-stage costing process.*

FOCUS ON
CURRENT PRACTICE

For many years, Hughes Aircraft allocated service department costs to operating departments using head count as the primary base because of its simplicity. Recently, the company has adopted an activity-based approach as it has taken dramatic steps to improve its costing system. Selected examples of service department allocations now made by the company are shown in the table below.

In describing the improved system, two Hughes managers stated, "For the first time operating units understand, and therefore can control, their level of cost absorption through an evaluation of their own activities. In addition, the metrics derived for each allocation serve as budgeting tools, [as] a method of communication between the providers and absorbers of an activity, and [as] a method for performance measurement in an era of continuous measurable improvement."[1]

Service Department	Allocation Bases (cost drivers)	Metrics
Human resources	Head count	$/head
	Hires	$/hire
	Union employees	$/head
	Training hours	$/training hour
Security	Square metres	$/square metre
Data processing	Lines printed	$/line
	CPU minutes	$/CPU minute
	Storage	$/storage unit

In our Chapter 5 discussion, we introduced activity-based costing and cited advantages for its use over volume measures such as direct labour-hours in assigning costs to products. Although some persons view activity-based costing as a new concept, only the term itself is new. This concept has been used for many years in the allocation of service department costs to other departments. Thus, the first-stage costing procedures we discuss in this chapter contain a healthy dose of what is now termed *activity-based costing*.

How are costs assigned from service departments to operating departments? This is accomplished by identifying the activity that drives costs in a service department, and then measuring the consumption of this activity by other departments. A cost-driving activity in a service department is generally referred to as an **allocation base.** Allocation bases may include number of employees, labour-hours, square metres of space occupied, or any other measure of activity in a department. Managers try to select allocation bases that reflect as accurately as possible the benefits that are being received by the various departments from the services involved. A number of such bases may be selected according to the nature of the service department. For example, data processing may have two bases—one consisting of CPU minutes and another consisting of lines printed or disk storage used. Examples of allocation bases that are frequently used by service departments are presented in Exhibit 16–1.

Once allocation bases have been chosen, they tend to remain unchanged for long periods unless it can be determined that some inequity exists that is resulting in costing errors. The criteria for selecting an allocation base may include the following:

1. Direct, traceable benefits from the service involved. Such benefits might be measured, for example, by the number of service orders handled.

[1]Jack Haedicke and David Feil, "Hughes Aircraft Sets the Standard for ABC,"*Management Accounting* (February 1991), pp. 31–32.

EXHIBIT 16-1

Bases Used in
Allocating Service
Department Costs

Service Department	Bases (cost drivers) Involved
Laundry	Kilograms of laundry, number of items processed
Airport ground services.	Number of flights
Cafeteria	Number of employees
Medical facilities.	Periodic analysis of cases handled, number of employees, hours worked
Materials handling	Hours of service, volume handled
Custodial services (building and grounds)	Measure of square metres occupied
Engineering.	Periodic analysis of services rendered, direct labour-hours
Production planning and control.	Periodic analysis of services rendered, direct labour-hours
Cost accounting.	Labour-hours, clients or patients serviced
Power	Measured usage (in kwh), capacity of machines
Personnel and employment.	Number of employees, turnover of labour, periodic analysis of time spent
Receiving, shipping, and stores	Units handled, number of requisition and issue slips, square or cubic metres occupied
Factory administration	Total labour-hours
Maintenance	Machine-hours, total labour-hours (in order of preference)

2. The extent to which space or equipment is made available to a department. This availability might be measured, for example, by the square metres of space occupied in a building.

In addition to these criteria, the manager must be sure that allocations are clear and straightforward, since complex allocation computations run the risk of being more effort than they are worth. Allocation methods should be simple and easily understood by all involved, particularly by the managers to whom the costs are being allocated.

OBJECTIVE 3

Allocate service
department costs to
other departments
using (a) the direct
method, (b) the step
method, and (c) the
reciprocal method.

Interdepartmental Services

Many service departments provide services for each other, as well as for operating departments. The cafeteria, for example, provides food for all employees, including those assigned to other service departments. In turn, the cafeteria may receive services from other service departments, such as from custodial services or from personnel. Services provided between service departments are known as **interdepartmental services** or **reciprocal services.**

Three approaches are used to allocate the costs of service departments to other departments. These are known as the *direct method,* the *step method,* and the *reciprocal method.* All three methods are discussed in the following sections.

Direct Method.   The **direct method** is a very simple allocation approach in that it ignores the costs of services between service departments and allocates all costs directly to operating departments. Even if a service department (such as personnel) renders a large amount of service to another service department (such as the cafeteria), no allocations are made between the two departments. Rather, all costs would go directly to the operating departments of the company. Hence the term *direct method.*

To provide a numerical example of the direct method, assume that the QE II Hospital has two service departments and two operating departments as shown below:

	Service Department		Operating Department		
	Hospital Administration	Custodial Services	Laboratory	Daily Patient Care	Total
Departmental costs before allocation....................	$360,000	$90,000	$261,000	$689,000	$1,400,000
Labour-hours....................	—	6,000	18,000	30,000	54,000
Proportion of labour-hours..........	—	$\frac{1}{9}$	$\frac{3}{9}$	$\frac{5}{9}$	$\frac{9}{9}$
Space occupied—square metres......	10,000	—	5,000	45,000	60,000
Proportion of space occupied........	$\frac{2}{12}$	—	$\frac{1}{12}$	$\frac{9}{12}$	$\frac{12}{12}$

Allocation of the hospital's service department costs by the direct method to the operating departments is shown in Exhibit 16–2. Note that after all allocations have been made, all of the departmental costs are contained in the two operating departments. These costs will form the basis for preparing overhead rates and for determining the overall profitability of the operating departments in the hospital.

Step Method.   Unlike the direct method, the **step method** provides for allocation of a service department's costs to other service departments, as well as to operating departments, in a sequential manner. The sequence typically begins with the department that provides the greatest amount of service to other departments. After its costs have been allocated, the process continues, step by step, ending with the department that provides the least amount of services to other service departments.

A numeric example of the step method is provided in Exhibit 16–3. The data in this exhibit are the same as those used earlier in connection with the direct method in Exhibit 16–2.

Since hospital administration provides the greatest amount of service to other departments, its costs are allocated first. This allocation is on the basis of labour-hours in other departments. The costs of custodial services are then allocated on a basis of square metres of space occupied.

An alternative way to view the ordering is that the step method should begin with the department that receives the least amount of service from other departments. In this way the inaccuracy caused by failing to back allocate would be minimized because there would

---

EXHIBIT 16-2   Direct Method of Allocation

	Service Department		Operating Department		
	Hospital Administration	Custodial Services	Laboratory	Daily Patient Care	Total
Departmental costs before allocation...............	$ 360,000	$ 90,000	$261,000	$689,000	$1,400,000
Allocation:					
Hospital administration costs ($\frac{3}{8}$, $\frac{5}{8}$)*...............	(360,000)		135,000	225,000	
Custodial services costs ($\frac{1}{10}$, $\frac{9}{10}$)†.............		(90,000)	9,000	81,000	
Total costs after allocation....	$ –0–	$ –0–	$405,000	$995,000	$1,400,000

*Allocation based on the labour-hours in the two operating departments, which are 18,000 hours + 30,000 hours = 48,000 hours.

†Allocation based on the space occupied by the two operating departments, which is 5,000 square metres + 45,000 square metres = 50,000 square metres.

EXHIBIT 16–3   Step Method of Allocation

| | Service Department | | Operating Department | | |
	Hospital Administration	Custodial Services	Laboratory	Daily Patient Care	Total
Departmental costs before allocation	$ 360,000	$ 90,000	$261,000	$ 689,000	$1,400,000
Allocation:					
Hospital administration costs ($\frac{1}{9}$, $\frac{3}{9}$, $\frac{5}{9}$)	(360,000)	40,000	120,000	200,000	
Custodial services costs ($\frac{1}{10}$, $\frac{9}{10}$)*		(130,000)	13,000	117,000	
Total costs after allocation	$ –0–	$ –0–	$394,000	$1,006,000	$1,400,000

*This allocation is based on the space occupied by the two operating departments, which is 5,000 square metres + 45,000 square metres = 50,000 square metres.

be little service to justify a back allocation. In the event that such a department cannot be found, the reciprocal method should be examined as to the appropriateness of its approach.

Two things should be noted about these allocations. First, the costs of hospital administration are borne by another service department (custodial services) as well as by the operating departments. Second, those hospital administration costs that have been allocated to custodial services *are included with custodial services costs,* and the total ($90,000 + $40,000 = $130,000) is allocated only to subsequent departments. That is, no part of custodial services' costs is reallocated back to hospital administration, even though custodial services may have provided services to hospital administration during the period. This is a key idea associated with the step method: After the allocation of a service department's costs has been completed, costs of other service departments are not reallocated back to it.

Reciprocal Method.   Where one service department performs services for another service department and the second department also works for the first service department, the step method does not account for the services going in both directions. However, if the amounts do not materially affect the results, then the step or direct method may be sufficient. The **reciprocal allocation approach** can deal with these reciprocal services by using simultaneous allocations of each of the departments involved. Although the approach may seem awkward, computers can handle such allocations with relative ease. To illustrate reciprocal allocation, consider the following illustration in Exhibit 16–4 based on Exhibit 16–2 and the data provided about QE II Hospital.

Note the amount allocated by hospital administration had to be determined outside the schedule before the allocation was made. Similarly the custodial services total costs of $132,453 include what was charged from administration. These two new amounts include the effect of the reciprocal services each department performed for the other. Once the simultaneous solutions are determined, the allocations proceed like the step method except allocations can go backward rather than proceed in sequence as required by the step method. Once the allocations are completed, totals for the operating departments are checked to ensure that the total overhead of $1.4 million was actually allocated. If more than two service departments exist, the solution procedure to determine the amount to be allocated commonly uses matrix inversion, which is beyond the scope of this book.

EXHIBIT 16–4   Reciprocal Allocation

Hospital Administration (HA)

$$HA = 360,000 + \tfrac{2}{12}\,CS$$

where HA denotes the costs to be allocated; that is, the direct costs plus those allocated from custodial services.

Custodial Services (CS)

$$CS = 90,000 + \tfrac{1}{9}\,HA$$

where CS denotes the costs to be allocated; that is, the direct costs plus those allocated from hospital administration.

To solve (1) –360,000 = – HA + $\tfrac{2}{12}$ CS

(2) – 90,000 = $\tfrac{1}{9}$ HA – CS

Multiply (2) by 9 (1) –360,000 = –HA + $\tfrac{2}{12}$ CS

(2) –810,000 = $\underline{\ \ HA – 9\ CS}$

Add (1) and (2)   –1,170,000 = 0 – 8 ($\tfrac{10}{12}$) CS

CS = \$132,453

Substitute in (1) –360,000 = –HA + $\tfrac{2}{12}$(132,453)

HA = \$360,000 + \$22,076

HA = \$382,076

	Service Department		Operating Department		
	Hospital Administration	**Custodial Services**	**Laboratory**	**Daily Patient Care**	**Total**
Departmental costs before allocation	\$ 360,000	\$ 90,000	\$261,000	\$ 689,000	\$1,400,000
Allocation:					
Hospital administration costs ($\tfrac{1}{9}, \tfrac{3}{9}, \tfrac{5}{9}$)	(382,076)	42,453	127,359	212,264	
Custodial services costs ($\tfrac{2}{12}, \tfrac{1}{12}, \tfrac{9}{12}$)	22,076	(132,453)	11,038	99,339	
Totals	\$ 0.0	\$ 0.0	\$399,397	\$1,000,603	\$1,400,000

Revenue Producing Departments. Before concluding our discussion of allocation methods, it is important to note that even though most service departments are cost centres and therefore generate no revenues, a few service departments such as the cafeteria may charge for the services they perform. If a service department generates revenues, these revenues should be offset against the department's costs, and only the net amount of cost remaining after this offset should be allocated to other departments within the organization. In this manner, the other departments will not be required to bear costs for which the service department has already been reimbursed.

Allocating Costs by Behaviour

OBJECTIVE 4

Explain why variable and fixed service department costs should be allocated separately.

Whenever possible, service department costs should be separated into fixed and variable classifications and allocated separately. Extending this distinction somewhat further, the usual approach is to group costs according to what causes them. Costs generated by one activity base such as usage should be separated from those generated by capacity. This approach is necessary to avoid possible inequities in allocation, as well as to provide more useful data for planning and control of departmental operations.

Variable Costs.   Variable costs represent direct costs of providing services and will generally vary in total in proportion to fluctuations in the level of service consumed. Food cost in a cafeteria would be a variable cost, for example, and one would expect this cost to vary proportionately with the number of persons using the cafeteria over a given period of time.

As a general rule, variable costs should be charged to consuming departments according to whatever activity base controls the incurrence of the cost involved. If, for example, the variable costs of a service department such as maintenance are incurred according to the number of machine-hours worked in the producing departments, then variable maintenance costs should be allocated to the producing departments on a machine-hours basis. By this means, the departments directly responsible for the incurrence of servicing costs are required to bear them in proportion to their actual usage of the service involved.

Technically, the assigning of variable servicing costs to consuming departments can more accurately be termed *charges* than allocations, since the service department is actually charging the consuming departments at some fixed rate per unit of service provided. In effect, the service department is saying, "I'll charge you X dollars for every unit of my service that you consume. You can consume as much or as little as you desire; the total charge you bear will vary proportionately."

Fixed Costs.   The fixed costs of service departments represent the cost of having long-run service capacity available. As such, these costs are most equitably allocated to consuming departments on a basis of *predetermined lump-sum amounts.* By predetermined lump-sum amounts we mean that the amount charged to each consuming department is determined in advance and, once determined, does not change from period to period without due cause. Typically, the lump-sum amount charged to a department is based either on the department's peak-period or long-run average servicing needs. The logic behind lump-sum allocations of this type is as follows:

When a service department is first established, some basic capacity is built into it according to the observed needs of the other departments that it services. This basic capacity may reflect the peak-period needs of the other departments, or it may reflect their long-run average or normal servicing needs. Depending on how much servicing capacity is provided for, it is necessary to make a commitment of resources to the servicing unit, which is reflected in its fixed costs. Generally, these fixed costs should be borne by the consuming departments whose servicing needs have made the creation of the service department necessary, and the costs should be borne in proportion to the individual servicing needs provided. That is, if available capacity in the service department has been provided to meet the peak-period needs of consuming departments, then the fixed costs of the service department should be allocated in predetermined lump-sum amounts to consuming departments on this basis. If available capacity has been provided only to meet normal or long-run average needs, then the fixed costs should be allocated on this basis.

Once set, allocations should not vary from period to period, because they represent each consuming department's fair share of having a certain level of service capacity available and on line. The fact that a consuming department does not need a peak level or even a normal level of servicing every period is immaterial; if it requires such servicing at certain times, then the capacity to deliver it must be available. It is the responsibility of the consuming departments to bear the cost of that availability.

To illustrate this idea, assume that Novak Company has just organized a maintenance department to service all machines in the cutting, assembly, and finishing departments. In determining the capacity that should be built into the newly organized maintenance department, the company recognized that the various producing departments would have the following peak-period needs for maintenance:

Department	Peak-Period Maintenance Needs in Hours of Maintenance Work Required	Percent of Total Hours
Cutting	900	30
Assembly	1,800	60
Finishing	300	10
	3,000	100

Therefore, in allocating the maintenance department fixed costs to the producing departments, 30% should be allocated to the cutting department, 60% to the assembly department, and 10% to the finishing department. These lump-sum allocations *will not change* from period to period unless there is some shift in servicing needs due to structural changes in the organization.

Pitfalls in Allocating Fixed Costs

Rather than allocate fixed costs in predetermined lump-sum amounts, some firms allocate them by use of a *variable* allocation base. What's wrong with this practice? The answer is that it can create serious inequities between departments. The inequities will arise from the fact that the fixed costs allocated to one department are heavily influenced by what happens in *other* departments or segments of the organization.

To illustrate, assume that Kolby Products has an auto service centre that provides maintenance work on the fleet of autos used in the company's two sales territories. The auto service centre costs are all fixed. Contrary to good practice, the company allocates these fixed costs to the sales territories on the basis of kilometres driven (a variable base). Selected cost data for the last two years are as follows:

	Year 1	Year 2
Auto service centre costs (all fixed)	$120,000 (a)	$120,000 (a)
Sales territory A—kilometres driven.	1,500,000	1,500,000
Sales territory B—kilometres driven.	1,500,000	900,000
Total kilometres driven	3,000,000 (b)	2,400,000 (b)
Allocation rate per kilometre, (a) ÷ (b)	$0.04	$0.05

Notice that sales territory A maintained an activity level of 1.5 million kilometres driven in both years. On the other hand, sales territory B allowed its activity to drop off from 1.5 million kilometres in year 1 to only 900,000 kilometres in year 2. The auto service centre costs that would have been allocated to the two sales territories over the two-year span are as follows:

Year 1:
    Sales territory A: 1,500,000 kilometres at $0.04. . . . . $ 60,000
    Sales territory B: 1,500,000 kilometres at $0.04.   60,000
      Total cost allocated $120,000

Year 2:
    Sales territory A: 1,500,000 kilometres at $0.05. . . . . $ 75,000
    Sales territory B: 900,000 kilometres at $0.05   45,000
      Total cost allocated $120,000

In year 1, the two sales territories share the service department costs equally. In year 2, however, the bulk of the service department costs are allocated to sales territory A. This is not because of any increase in activity in sales territory A; rather, it is because of the *decrease* in activity in sales territory B, during year 2. Even though sales territory A maintained the same level of activity in both years, the use of a variable allocation base has caused it to be penalized with a heavier cost allocation in year 2 because of what has happened in *another* territory of the company.

This kind of inequity is almost inevitable when a variable allocation base is used to allocate fixed costs. The manager of sales territory A undoubtedly will be upset about the inequity forced on his territory, but feel powerless to do anything about it. The result would be a loss of confidence in the system and the accumulation of a considerable back log of ill feeling.

Should Actual or Budgeted Costs Be Allocated?

Should a service department allocate its *actual* costs to operating departments, or should it allocate its *budgeted* costs? The usual answer is that budgeted costs should be allocated. What's wrong with allocating actual costs? Allocating actual costs burdens the operating departments with the inefficiencies of the service department managers. If actual costs are allocated, then any lack of cost control on the part of the service department manager is simply buried in a routine allocation to other departments.

Any variance over budgeted costs should be retained in the service department and closed out at year-end against the company's revenues or against cost of goods sold, along with other variances. Operating department managers rarely complain about being allocated a portion of service department costs, but they complain bitterly if they are forced to absorb service department inefficiencies.

Like most generalities, exceptions exist. Management may want a specific job carried out by the service department without its being restricted by the budget estimates used in setting the budgeted costs. For example, maintenance may have to be done to prevent shutdowns in the operations. If variances from budgets are kept in the service department, operations may suffer when the service department feels it cannot absorb a variance. Similarly, developmental departments such as computers or research may not be able to estimate costs accurately enough to permit them to avoid variances. Operations may want the service regardless of the cost. Pricing may want the total costs charged to be reflected in prices. Rate-regulated firms may want all costs in their expenses. Any one of the preceding reasons can mean that actual cost, or at least the actual activity base, should be used to charge operations.

EFFECT OF ALLOCATIONS ON OPERATING DEPARTMENTS

OBJECTIVE 5
Explain how allocated service department costs are traced to operating department flexible budgets.

Once allocations have been completed, what do the operating departments do with the allocated service department costs? Since the amounts allocated are presumed to represent each department's fair share of the cost of services provided for it, the allocations are included in performance evaluations of the operating departments and also included in determining their individual profitability.

In addition, if the operating departments are responsible for developing overhead rates for costing of products or billing of services, the allocated costs are combined with the other costs of the operating departments, and the total is used as a basis for rate computations. This rate development process is illustrated in Exhibit 16–5. Observe from the exhibit that the term *allocated* describes the movement of service department costs to operating departments, whereas the term *applied* describes the attaching of these costs (along with operating department costs) to products and services.

EXHIBIT 16–5

Effect of Allocations on Products and Services

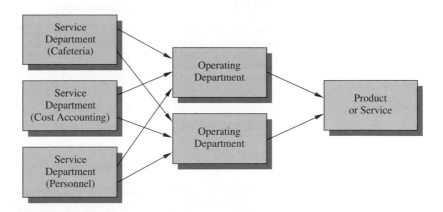

The flexible budget serves as the means for combining allocated service department costs with operating department costs and for computing overhead rates. An example of the combining of these costs on a flexible budget is presented in Exhibit 16–6. Note from the exhibit that both variable and fixed service department costs have been allocated to Superior Company's milling department and are included on the latter's flexible budget. Since allocated service department costs become an integral part of the flexible budget, they are automatically included in overhead rate computations, as shown at the bottom of the exhibit.

EXHIBIT 16–6

Flexible Budget Containing Allocated Service Department Costs

SUPERIOR COMPANY
Flexible Budget—Milling Department

Budgeted direct labour-hours   50,000

Overhead Costs	Cost Formula (per hour)	40,000	50,000	60,000
Variable costs:				
Indirect labour.	$1.45	$58,000	$72,500	$87,000
Indirect material	0.90	36,000	45,000	54,000
Utilities	0.10	4,000	5,000	6,000
Allocation—cafeteria	0.15	6,000	7,500	9,000
Total variable costs	$2.60	104,000	130,000	156,000
Fixed costs:				
Depreciation		85,000	85,000	85,000
Supervisory salaries		110,000	110,000	110,000
Property taxes		9,000	9,000	9,000
Allocation—cafeteria		21,000	21,000	21,000
Allocation—human resources.		45,000	45,000	45,000
Total fixed costs		270,000	270,000	270,000
Total overhead costs		$374,000	$400,000	$426,000

$$\text{Predetermined overhead rate} = \frac{\$400,000}{50,000 \text{ DLH}} = \$8 \text{ per direct labour-hour}$$

A SUMMARY OF SERVICE DEPARTMENT COST ALLOCATION GUIDELINES

OBJECTIVE 6
Enumerate the guidelines that should be followed in allocating service department costs.

To summarize the material covered in preceding sections, we can note five key points to remember about allocating service department costs:

1. If possible, the distinction between variable and fixed costs in service departments should be maintained.
2. Variable costs should be allocated at the budgeted rate, according to whatever activity (kilometres driven, direct labour-hours, number of employees) controls the incurrence of the cost involved.
   a. If the allocations are being made at the beginning of the year, they should be based on the budgeted activity level planned for the consuming departments. The allocation formula would be:

   $$\text{Budgeted rate} \times \text{Budgeted activity} = \text{Cost allocated}$$

   b. If the allocations are being made at the end of the year, they should be based on the actual activity level that has occurred during the year. The allocation formula would be:

   $$\text{Budgeted rate} \times \text{Actual activity} = \text{Cost allocated}$$

   Allocations made at the beginning of the year would be to provide data for computing overhead rates for costing of products and billing of services in the operating departments. Allocations made at the end of the year would be to provide data for comparing actual performance against planned performance.
3. Fixed costs represent the costs of having service capacity available. Where feasible, these costs should be allocated in predetermined lump-sum amounts. The lump-sum amount going to each department should be in proportion to the servicing needs that gave rise to the investment in the service department in the first place. (This might be either peak-period needs for servicing or long-run average needs.) Budgeted fixed costs, rather than actual fixed costs, should always be allocated.
4. If it is not feasible to maintain a distinction between variable and fixed costs in a service department, then the costs of the department should be allocated to consuming departments according to the base that appears to provide the best measure of benefits received.
5. Where possible, reciprocal services between departments should be recognized.

IMPLEMENTING THE ALLOCATION GUIDELINES

OBJECTIVE 7
Prepare an allocation schedule involving several service departments and several operating departments.

We will now show the implementation of these guidelines by the use of specific examples. We will focus first on the allocation of costs for a single department, and then develop a more extended example where multiple departments are involved.

Basic Allocation Techniques

Seaboard Airlines is divided into a Freight Division and a Passenger Division. The company has a single aircraft maintenance department that provides servicing to both divisions. Variable servicing costs are budgeted at $10 per flight-hour. The fixed costs of the maintenance department are budgeted based on the peak-period demand, which occurs during the late November to New Year's holiday period. The airline wants to make sure that none of its aircraft are grounded during this key period due to unavailability of maintenance facilities. Approximately 40% of the maintenance during this period is performed on the Freight Division's equipment, and 60% is performed on the Passenger Division's equipment. These figures and the budgeted flight-hours for the coming year appear below:

	Percent of Peak Period Capacity Required	Budgeted Flight-Hours
Freight Division	40	9,000
Passenger Division	60	15,000
Total	100	24,000

Given these data, the amount of cost that would be allocated to each division from the aircraft maintenance department at the beginning of the coming year would be as follows:

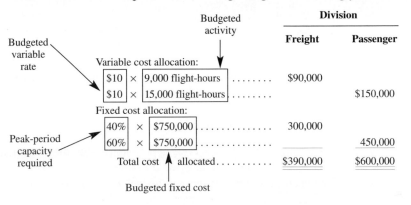

As explained earlier, these allocated costs would be included in the flexible budgets of the respective divisions and included in the computation of divisional overhead rates.

At the end of the year, Seaboard Airlines' management may want to make a second allocation, this time based on actual activity, in order to compare actual performance for the year against planned performance. To illustrate, year-end records show that actual costs in the aircraft maintenance department for the year were variable costs, $260,000; and fixed costs, $780,000. One division logged more flight-hours during the year than planned, and the other division logged less flight-hours than planned, as shown below:

	Flight-Hours	
	Budgeted (see above)	Actual
Freight Division.	9,000	8,000
Passenger Division.	15,000	17,000
Total flight-hours	24,000	25,000

The amount of actual service department cost charged to each division for the year would be as follows:

		Division	
		Freight	Passenger
Budgeted variable rate	Actual activity		
Variable cost allocation:			
$10 × 8,000 flight-hours		$80,000	
$10 × 17,000 flight-hours			$170,000
Fixed cost allocation:			
40% × $750,000		300,000	
Peak-period capacity required 60% × $750,000			450,000
Total cost allocated		$380,000	$620,000
Budgeted fixed cost			

Notice that the variable cost is allocated according to the budgeted rate ($10 per hour) times the *actual activity* for the year, and that the fixed cost is allocated according to the original budgeted amount. As stated in the guidelines given earlier, allocations should be based on budgeted rates and amounts in order to avoid passing on costs due to inefficiency from one department to another. Thus, a portion of the actual costs of the aircraft maintenance department for the year will not be allocated, as shown below:

	Variable	Fixed
Total actual costs incurred	$260,000	$780,000
Costs allocated (above)	250,000*	750,000
Spending variance—not allocated	$ 10,000	$ 30,000

*$10 per flight-hour × 25,000 actual flight-hours = $250,000.

These variances will be closed out against the company's overall revenues for the year, along with any other variances that may occur.

An Extended Example

Proctor Company has three service departments—building maintenance, cafeteria, and inspection. The company also has two operating departments—shipping and assembly. The service departments provide services to each other, as well as to the operating departments. Types of costs in the service departments and bases for allocation are given below:

Department	Type of Cost	Base for Allocation
Building maintenance	Fixed costs	Square metres occupied
Cafeteria	Variable costs Fixed costs	Number of employees 10% to inspection, 40% to shipping, and 50% to assembly
Inspection	Variable costs Fixed costs	Direct labour-hours 70% to shipping and 30% to assembly

Proctor Company allocates service department costs by the step method in the following order:

1. Building maintenance.
2. Cafeteria.
3. Inspection.

Assume the following budgeted cost and operating data for the year:

Department	Variable Cost	Fixed Cost
Building maintenance	—	$130,000
Cafeteria	$200 per employee	250,000
Inspection	$0.06 per direct labour-hour	548,000

Department	Number of Employees	Direct Labour-Hours	Square Metres of Space Occupied (square metres)
Building maintenance	6*	—	3,000
Cafeteria	9*	—	4,000
Inspection	30	—	1,000
Shipping	190	300,000	8,000
Assembly	250	500,000	13,000
Total	485	800,000	29,000

*Although there are employees in both of these service departments, under the step method costs are only allocated *forward*—never backward. For this reason, the costs of the cafeteria will be allocated *forward* on the basis of the number of employees in the inspection, shipping, and assembly departments.

In addition to the service department costs listed above, the company's shipping department has budgeted $1,340,000 in overhead costs, and its assembly department has budgeted $1,846,000 in overhead costs.

Cost allocations from the service departments to the operating departments are as shown in Exhibit 16–7 on page 874. To save space, we have computed the operating department's predetermined overhead rates at the bottom of the exhibit.

No Distinction Made between Fixed and Variable Costs

As stated in the guidelines given earlier, in some cases it may not be feasible to maintain a distinction between fixed and variable service department costs. We noted that in such cases the costs should be allocated to operating departments according to the base that appears to provide the best measure of benefits received. An example of such allocation was given earlier in Exhibit 16–4, where we first illustrated the step method. The reader may wish to turn back and review this example before reading on.

Should All Costs Be Allocated?

As a general rule, any service department costs that are incurred as a result of specific services provided to operating departments should be allocated back to these departments and used to compute overhead rates and to measure profitability. The only time when this general rule is not followed is in those situations where, in the view of the management, allocation would result in an undesirable behavioural response from people in the operating departments. Some servicing costs, for example, are clearly beneficial to operating departments but may not be utilized fully, particularly in times of cost economizing. Systems design is a good example of such a cost. Utilization of systems design services may be very beneficial to operating departments in terms of improving overall efficiency, reducing waste, and assuring adherence to departmental policies. But if a department knows that it will be charged for the systems design services it uses, it

---

FOCUS ON
CURRENT PRACTICE

It can be unwise for a service department to offer "free" services to other departments, as shown by the following experience:

> [A hospital] established a policy of allowing its employees to eat all they wanted in the cafeteria, free of charge. The administration believed that the hospital's cost of providing this employee benefit would be low because the kitchen facilities were a fixed cost. Labour costs also would be low because of the mass production of food for the hospital's patients.
>
> However, the hospital's food services costs shot up. An investigation revealed that the employees were wasting large amounts of food. Some were taking several entrees, tasting them, and throwing the rest away.
>
> When the policy was changed and the employees were charged a token amount—about a third of a diner's prices—the wasting of food declined dramatically. In fact, the decrease in the food service department's costs was greater than the revenue generated by the nominal charge.[2]

---

[2]Leon B. Hoshower and Robert P. Crum, "Controlling Service Center Costs," *Management Accounting* (November 1987), p. 44. Used by permission.

EXHIBIT 16-7

THE PROCTOR COMPANY
Beginning-of-Year Cost Allocations for Purposes of
Preparing Predetermined Overhead Rates

	Building Maintenance	Cafeteria	Inspection	Shipping	Assembly
Variable costs to be allocated	$ –0–	$ 94,000	$ 42,000	$ —	$ —
Cafeteria allocation at $200 per employee:					
30 employees × $200	—	(6,000)	6,000	—	—
190 employees × $200	—	(38,000)	—	38,000	—
250 employees × $200	—	(50,000)	—	—	50,000
Inspection allocation at $0.06 per direct labour-hour:					
300,000 DLH × $0.06.	—	—	(18,000)	18,000	—
500,000 DLH × $0.06.	—	—	(30,000)	—	30,000
Total	–0–	–0–	–0–	56,000	80,000
Fixed costs to be allocated	130,000	250,000	548,000		
Building maintenance allocation at $5 per square metre:*					
4,000 square metres × $5	(20,000)	20,000	—	—	—
1,000 square metres × $5	(5,000)	—	5,000	—	—
8,000 square metres × $5	(40,000)	—	—	40,000	—
13,000 square metres × $5	(65,000)	—	—	—	65,000
Cafeteria allocation:†					
10% × $270,000	—	(27,000)	27,000	—	—
40% × $270,000	—	(108,000)	—	108,000	—
50% × $270,000	—	(135,000)	—	—	135,000
Inspection allocation:‡					
70% × $580,000	—	—	(406,000)	406,000	—
30% × $580,000	—	—	(174,000)	—	174,000
Total	–0–	–0–	–0–	554,000	374,000
Total allocated costs	$ –0–	$ –0–	$ –0–	610,000	454,000
Other flexible budget costs at the planned activity level				1,340,000	1,846,000
Total overhead costs				$1,950,000	$2,300,000 (a)
Budgeted direct labour-hours				300,000	500,000 (b)
Predetermined overhead rate, (a) ÷ (b).				$6.50	$4.60

*Square metres of space . . . . 29,000 square metres
Less building maintenance space . . . . 3,000 square metres

Net space for allocation . . . . 26,000 square metres

$$\frac{\text{Building maintenance fixed costs, } \$130,000}{\text{Net space for allocation, } 26,000 \text{ square metres}} = \$5 \text{ per squ}$$

†Cafeteria fixed costs	$250,000
Allocated from building maintenance	20,000
Total cost to be allocated	$270,000

Allocation percentages are given in the problem.

‡Inspection fixed costs	$548,000
Allocated from building maintenance	5,000
Allocated from cafeteria	27,000
Total cost to be allocated	$580,000

Allocation percentages are given in the problem.

may be less inclined to take advantage of the benefits involved, especially if the department is feeling some pressure to trim costs. In short, the departmental manager may opt for the near-term benefit of avoiding a direct charge, in lieu of the long-term benefit of reduced waste and greater efficiency.

To avoid discouraging use of a service that is beneficial to the entire organization, some firms do not charge for the service at all. These managers feel that by making such services a "free" commodity, departments will be more inclined to take full advantage of their benefits.

Other firms take a somewhat different approach. They agree that charging according to usage may discourage utilization of such services as systems design, but they argue that such services should not be free. Instead of providing free services, these firms take what is sometimes called a **retainer fee approach.** Each department is charged a flat amount each year, regardless of how much or how little of the service it utilizes. The thought is that if a department knows it is going to be charged a certain amount for systems design services, *regardless of usage,* then it will probably utilize the services at least to that extent.

Beware of Sales Dollars as an Allocation Base

Over the years, sales dollars have been a favourite allocation base for service department costs. One reason is that a sales dollars base is simple, straightforward, and easy to work with. Another reason is that people tend to view sales dollars as a measure of well-being, or "ability to pay," and, hence, as a measure of how readily costs can be absorbed from other parts of the organization.

Unfortunately, sales dollars often constitute a very poor allocation base, for the reason that sales dollars vary from period to period, whereas the costs being allocated are often largely *fixed* in nature. As discussed earlier, if a variable base is used to allocate fixed costs, inequities can result between departments, since the costs being allocated to one department will depend in large part on what happens in *other* departments. For example, a letup in sales effort in one department will shift allocated costs off that department and onto other, more productive departments. In effect, the departments putting forth the best sales efforts are penalized in the form of higher allocations, simply because of inefficiencies elsewhere that are beyond their control. The result is often bitterness and resentment on the part of the managers of the better departments.

Consider the following situation encountered by one of the authors:

A large men's clothing store has one service department and three sales departments—suits, shoes, and accessories. The service department's costs total $60,000 per period and are allocated to the three sales departments according to sales dollars. A recent period showed the following allocation:

Sales dollars can be a poor allocation tax base because sales may vary from department to department while the services required remain constant in each department.

	Department			
	Suits	**Shoes**	**Accessories**	**Total**
Sales by department.....................	$260,000	$40,000	$100,000	$400,000
Percentage of total sales...................	65%	10%	25%	100%
Allocation of service department costs,				
based on percentage of total sales...........	$ 39,000	$ 6,000	$ 15,000	$ 60,000

In a following period, the manager of the suit department launched a very successful program to expand sales by $100,000 in his department. Sales in the other two departments remained unchanged. Total service department costs also remained unchanged, but the allocation of these costs changed substantially, as shown below:

	Department			
	Suits	**Shoes**	**Accessories**	**Total**
Sales by department.....................	$360,000	$40,000	$100,000	$500,000
Percentage of total sales...................	72%	8%	20%	100%
Allocation of service department costs,				
based on percentage of total sales...........	$ 43,200	$ 4,800	$ 12,000	$ 60,000
Increase (or decrease) from				
prior allocation........................	4,200	(1,200)	(3,000)	—

The manager of the suit department complained that as a result of his successful effort to expand sales in his department, he was being forced to carry a larger share of the service department costs. On the other hand, the managers of the departments that showed no improvement in sales were being relieved of a portion of the costs that they had been carrying. Yet there had been no change in the amount of services provided for any department.

The manager of the suit department viewed the increased service department cost allocation to his department as a penalty for his outstanding performance, and he wondered whether his efforts had really been worthwhile after all in the eyes of top management.

Sales dollars should be used as an allocation base only in those cases where there is a direct causal relationship between sales dollars and the service department costs being allocated. In those situations where service department costs are fixed in nature, they should be allocated according to the guidelines discussed earlier in the chapter.

SUMMARY

Service departments are organized to provide some needed service in a single, centralized place, rather than to have all units within the organization provide the service for themselves. Although service departments do not engage directly in production or other operating activities, the costs that they incur are vital to the overall success of an organization and therefore are properly included as part of the cost of its products and services.

Service department costs are charged to operating departments by an allocation process. In turn, the operating departments include the allocated costs within their flexible budgets, from which overhead rates are computed for purposes of costing of products or billing of services.

To avoid inequity in allocations, variable and fixed service department costs should be allocated separately. The variable costs should be allocated according to whatever activity causes their incurrence. The fixed costs should be allocated in predetermined lump-sum amounts according to either the peak-period or the long-run average servicing needs of the consuming departments. Budgeted costs, rather than actual costs, should always be allocated in order to avoid the passing on of inefficiency between departments. Any variances between budgeted and actual service department costs should be kept within the service departments for analysis purposes, then written off against revenues or against cost of goods sold, along with other variances.

REVIEW PROBLEM: DIRECT AND STEP METHODS

Kovac Printing Company has three service departments and two operating departments. Selected data for the five departments relating to the most recent period follow:

	Service Department			Operating Department		
	Train-ing	Jani-torial	Mainte-nance	Offset Printing	Lithog-raphy	Total
Overhead costs........	$360,000	$210,000	$96,000	$400,000	$534,000	$1,600,000
Number of employees	120	70	280	630	420	1,520
Square metres of space occupied......	10,000	20,000	40,000	80,000	200,000	350,000
Hours of press time	—	—	—	30,000	60,000	90,000

The company allocates service department costs in the following order and using the bases indicated: training (number of employees), janitorial (space occupied), and maintenance (hours of press time). The company makes no distinction between variable and fixed service department costs.

Required

1. Use the direct method to allocate service department costs to the operating departments.
2. Use the step method to allocate service department costs to the operating departments.

Solution to Review Problem

1. Under the direct method, service department costs are allocated directly to the operating departments. Supporting computations for these allocations follow:

	Allocation Bases					
	Training		Janitorial		Maintenance	
Offset printing data...........	630 employees	$\frac{3}{5}$	80,000 square metres	$\frac{2}{7}$	30,000 hours	$\frac{1}{3}$
Lithography data.............	420 employees	$\frac{2}{5}$	200,000 square metres	$\frac{5}{7}$	60,000 hours	$\frac{2}{3}$
Total	1,050 employees	$\frac{5}{5}$	280,000 square metres	$\frac{7}{7}$	90,000 hours	$\frac{3}{3}$

Given these allocation rates, the allocations to the operating departments would be as follows:

	Service Department			Operating Department		
	Train-ing	Jani-torial	Mainte-nance	Offset Printing	Lithog-raphy	Total
Overhead costs........	$360,000	$ 210,000	$ 96,000	$400,000	$534,000	$1,600,000
Allocation:						
Training ($\frac{3}{5}$; $\frac{2}{5}$).........	(360,000)			216,000	144,000	
Janitorial ($\frac{2}{7}$; $\frac{5}{7}$)		(210,000)		60,000	150,000	
Maintenance ($\frac{1}{3}$; $\frac{2}{3}$)			(96,000)	32,000	64,000	
Total overhead cost after allocations	$ –0–	$ –0–	$ –0–	$708,000	$892,000	$1,600,000

2. Under the step method, services rendered between service departments are recognized when costs are allocated to other departments. Starting with the training service department, supporting computations for these allocations follow:

	Allocation Bases					
	Training		Janitorial		Maintenance	
Janitorial data	70 employees	5 %	—		—	
Maintenance data	280 employees	20	40,000 square metres	$\frac{1}{8}$	—	
Offset printing data.	630 employees	45	80,000 square metres	$\frac{2}{8}$	30,000 hours	$\frac{1}{3}$
Lithography data.	420 employees	30	200,000 square metres	$\frac{5}{8}$	60,000 hours	$\frac{2}{3}$
Total	1,400 employees	100 %	320,000 square metres	$\frac{8}{8}$	90,000 hours	$\frac{3}{3}$

Given these allocation rates, the allocations to the various departments would be as follows:

	Service Department			Operating Department		
	Train-ing	Jani-torial	Mainte-nance	Offset Printing	Lithog-raphy	Total
Overhead costs.	$360,000	$ 210,000	$ 96,000	$400,000	$534,000	$1,600,000
Allocation:						
Training (5%; 20%; 45%; 30%)*	(360,000)	18,000	72,000	162,000	108,000	
Janitorial ($\frac{1}{8}$; $\frac{2}{8}$; $\frac{5}{8}$).		(228,000)	28,500	57,000	142,500	
Maintenance ($\frac{1}{3}$; $\frac{2}{3}$)			(196,500)	65,500	131,000	
Total overhead cost after allocations	$ –0–	$ –0–	$ –0–	$684,500	$915,500	$1,600,000

*Allocation rates can be shown either in percentages, in fractions, or as a dollar rate per unit of activity. Both percentages and fractions are shown in this problem for sake of illustration. *It is better to use fractions if percentages would result in odd decimals.*

KEY TERMS FOR REVIEW

Allocation base   Any measure of activity (such as labour-hours, number of employees, or square metres of space) that is used to charge service department costs to other departments. (p. 861)

Direct method   The allocation of all of a service department's costs directly to operating departments without recognizing services provided to other service departments. (p. 862)

Interdepartmental services   Services provided between service departments. Also see *Reciprocal services.* (p. 862)

Operating department   A department or similar unit in an organization within which the central purposes of the organization are carried out. (p. 860)

Reciprocal allocation approach   A method of allocating service department costs that gives full recognition to interdepartmental services. (p. 864)

Reciprocal services   Services provided between service departments. Also see *Interdepartmental services.* (p. 862)

Retainer fee approach   A method of allocating service department costs in which other departments are charged a flat amount each period regardless of usage of the service involved. (p. 875)

Service department   A department that provides support or assistance to operating departments and that does not engage directly in production or in other operating activities of an organization. (p. 860)

Step method   The allocation of a service department's costs to other service departments, as well as to operating departments, in a sequential manner. The sequence starts with the service department that provides the greatest amount of service to other departments. (p. 863)

QUESTIONS

16–1   What is the difference between a service department and an operating department? Give several examples of service departments.

16–2   In what way are service department costs similar to costs such as lubricants, utilities, and factory supervision?

16–3   "Products and services can be costed equally well with or without allocations of service department costs." Do you agree? Why or why not?

16–4   How do service department costs enter into the final cost of products and services?

16–5   What criteria are relevant to the selection of allocation bases for service department costs?

16–6   What are interdepartmental service costs? How are such costs allocated to other departments under the step method?

16–7   How are service department costs allocated to other departments under the direct method?

16–8   If a service department generates revenues of some type, how do these revenues enter into the allocation of the department's costs to other departments?

16–9   What guidelines should govern the allocation of fixed service department costs to other departments? The allocation of variable service department costs?

16–10   "A variable base should never be used in allocating fixed service department costs to operating departments." Explain.

16–11   Why might it be desirable not to allocate some service department costs to operating departments?

16–12   What is the purpose of the retainer fee approach to cost allocation?

16–13   How does the reciprocal method allocate interdepartmental services? How does the approach differ from the step method?

16–14   When is it proper to pass on variances from budget in a service department to departments using the services?

16–15   Why are arbitrary allocations a practice that should be avoided whenever possible?

16–16   When are arbitrary allocations necessary?

EXERCISES

E16–1   Arbon Company has three service departments and two operating departments. Selected data on the five departments are presented below:

| | Service Department | | | Operating Department | | |
	X	Y	Z	1	2	Total
Overhead costs........	$84,000	$67,800	$36,000	$256,100	$498,600	$942,500
Number of employees ..	80	60	240	600	300	1,280
Square metres of space occupied......	3,000	12,000	10,000	20,000	70,000	115,000
Machine-hours........	—	—	—	10,000	30,000	40,000

The company allocates service department costs by the step method in the following order: X (number of employees), Y (space occupied), and Z (machine-hours). The company makes no distinction between fixed and variable service department costs.

Required

Using the step method, make the necessary allocations of service department costs.

E16–2 Refer to the data for Arbon Company in E16–1. Assume that the company allocates service department costs by the direct method, rather than by the step method.

Required

Assuming that the company uses the direct method, how much overhead cost would be chargeable to each operating department? Show computations in good form.

E16–3 Gutherie Oil Company has a transport services department that provides trucks to transport crude oil from east coast docks to the company's Arbon Refinery and Beck Refinery. Budgeted costs for the transport services consist of $0.075 per litre variable cost and $200,000 fixed cost. The level of fixed cost is determined by peak-period requirements. During the peak period, Arbon Refinery requires 60% of the capacity and the Beck Refinery requires 40%.

During the coming year, 1,080,000 litres of crude oil are budgeted to be hauled to the Arbon Refinery and 520,000 litres of crude oil to the Beck Refinery.

Required

Compute the amount of transport services cost that should be allocated to each refinery at the beginning of the year for purposes of computing predetermined overhead rates. (The company allocates variable and fixed costs separately.)

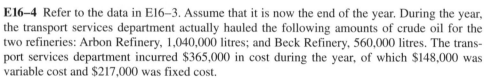

E16–4 Refer to the data in E16–3. Assume that it is now the end of the year. During the year, the transport services department actually hauled the following amounts of crude oil for the two refineries: Arbon Refinery, 1,040,000 litres; and Beck Refinery, 560,000 litres. The transport services department incurred $365,000 in cost during the year, of which $148,000 was variable cost and $217,000 was fixed cost.

Management wants end-of-year service department cost allocations in order to compare actual performance against planned performance.

Required

1. Determine how much of the $148,000 in variable cost should be allocated to each refinery.
2. Determine how much of the $217,000 in fixed cost should be allocated to each refinery.
3. Will any of the $365,000 in transport services cost not be allocated to the refineries? Explain.

E16–5 Reed Company operates a medical services department for its employees. The variable costs of the department are allocated to operating departments on the basis of the number of employees in each department. Budgeted and actual data for last year are given below:

	Variable Costs	
	Budgeted	**Actual**
Medical services department............	$60 per employee	$72 per employee

The budgeted and actual number of employees in each operating department during the year appear below.

	Department		
	Cutting	**Milling**	**Assembly**
Budgeted number of employees............	600	300	900
Actual number of employees..............	500	400	800

Required

Determine the amount of medical services department variable cost that should have been allocated to each of the three operating departments at the end of the year, for purposes of comparing actual performance against planned performance.

E16–6 Refer to Reed Company in E16–5. In addition to the medical services department, the company also has a janitorial services department that provides services to all other departments in the company. The fixed costs of the two service departments are allocated on the following bases:

Department	Basis for Allocation
Janitorial services	Square metres of space occupied:
	Medical services department .... 6,000 square metres
	Cutting department.................. 30,000 square metres
	Milling department.................. 24,000 square metres
	Assembly department................ 90,000 square metres
Medical services	Long-run average number of employees:
	Janitorial services department .... 20 employees
	Cutting department.................. 600 employees
	Milling department.................. 400 employees
	Assembly department................ 1,000 employees

Budgeted and actual fixed costs in the two service departments for the year follow:

	Janitorial Services	Medical Services
Budgeted fixed costs	$350,000	$596,000
Actual fixed costs..............	361,000	605,000

Required

1. Show the allocation of the fixed costs of the two service departments at the beginning of the year for purposes of computing overhead rates in the operating departments. The company uses the step method of allocation, starting with the janitorial services department.
2. Show the allocation of the fixed costs of the two service departments at the end of the year for purposes of comparing actual performance against planned performance.

E16–7 Lacey's Department Store allocates its fixed administrative expenses to its four departments on the basis of sales dollars. During 19x6, the fixed administrative expenses totalled $900,000. These expenses were allocated as follows:

	Department				
	1	2	3	4	Total
Total sales—19x6............	$600,000	$1,500,000	$2,100,000	$1,800,000	$6,000,000
Percent of total sales	10%	25%	35%	30%	100%
Allocation (based on the above percents)	$90,000	$225,000	$315,000	$270,000	$900,000

During 19x7, the following year, department 2 doubled its sales. The sales levels in the other three departments remained unchanged. As a result of department 2's sales increase, the company's 19x7 sales data appeared as follows:

	Department				
	1	2	3	4	Total
Total sales—19x7............	$600,000	$3,000,000	$2,100,000	$1,800,000	$7,500,000
Percent of total sales	8%	40%	28%	24%	100%

Fixed administrative expenses in the company remained unchanged at $900,000 during 19x7.

Required

1. Using sales dollars as an allocation base, show the allocation of the fixed administrative expenses between the four departments for 19x7.
2. Compare your allocation from (1) above to the allocation for 19x6. As the manager of department 2, how would you feel about the allocation that has been charged to you for 19x7?
3. Comment on the usefulness of sales dollars as an allocation base.

PROBLEMS

P16–8 Cost Allocation: Step Method versus Direct Method Petah, Ltd., of Tel Aviv, Israel, has budgeted costs in its various departments as follows for the coming year:

Factory administration	w 540,000
Custodial services	137,520
Personnel.	57,680
Maintenance	90,400
Stamping—overhead.	752,600
Assembly—overhead	351,800
Total cost	w1,930,000

(The Israeli currency is the shekel, symbolized by *w*.)

The company allocates service department costs to other departments, *in the order listed below.* Bases for allocation are to be chosen from the following:

	Number of Employees	Total Labour- Hours	Square Metres of Space Occupied	Direct Labour- Hours	Machine- Hours
Factory administration	22	—	5,000	—	—
Custodial services	8	6,000	2,000	—	—
Personnel	10	10,000	3,000	—	—
Maintenance	50	44,000	10,000	—	—
Stamping—overhead	80	60,000	70,000	40,000	140,000
Assembly—overhead	120	180,000	20,000	160,000	20,000
	290	300,000	110,000	200,000	160,000

Stamping and assembly are operating departments; the other departments all act in a service capacity. The company does not make a distinction between fixed and variable service department costs. Allocations are made to using departments according to the base that appears to provide the best measure of benefits received. (Factory administration is allocated on the basis of labour-hours.)

Required

1. Allocate service department costs to using departments by the step method. Then compute predetermined overhead rates in the operating departments, using a machine-hours basis in stamping and a direct labour-hours basis in assembly.
2. Repeat (1) above, this time using the direct method. Again compute predetermined overhead rates in stamping and assembly.
3. Assume that the company doesn't want to bother with allocating service department costs but simply wants to compute a single plantwide overhead rate based on total overhead costs (both service department and operating department) divided by total direct labour-hours. Compute the appropriate overhead rate.
4. Suppose a job requires machine and labour time as follows:

	Direct Machine Hours	Labour- Hours
Stamping department	190	25
Assembly department	10	75
Total hours.	200	100

Using the overhead rates computed in (1), (2), and (3) above, compute the amount of overhead cost that would be assigned to the job if the overhead rates were developed using the step method, the direct method, and the plantwide method. (Round allocations to the nearest whole shekel.)

P16–9 Various Allocation Methods   Northstar Company consists of a Machine Tools Division and a Special Products Division. The company has a maintenance department that services the equipment in both divisions. The costs of operating the maintenance department are budgeted at $80,000 per month plus $0.50 per machine-hour. The fixed costs of the maintenance department are determined by peak-period requirements. The Machine Tools Division requires 65% of the peak-period capacity, and the Special Products Division requires 35%.

For October, the Machine Tools Division has estimated that it will operate at a 90,000 machine-hours level of activity and the Special Products Division has estimated that it will operate at a 60,000 machine-hours level of activity.

Required

1. At the beginning of October, how much maintenance department cost should be allocated to each division for flexible budget planning purposes?
2. Assume that it is now the end of October. Cost records in the maintenance department show that actual fixed costs for the month totalled $85,000 and that actual variable costs totalled $78,000. Due to labour unrest and an unexpected strike, the Machine Tools Division worked only 60,000 machine-hours during the month. The Special Products Division also worked 60,000 machine-hours, as planned. How much of the actual maintenance department costs for the month should be allocated to each division? (Management uses these end-of-month allocations to compare actual performance against planned performance.)
3. Refer to the data in (2) above. Assume that the company follows the practice of allocating *all* maintenance department costs each month to the divisions in proportion to the actual machine-hours recorded in each division for the month. On this basis, how much cost would be allocated to each division for October?
4. What criticisms can you make of the allocation method used in (3) above?
5. If managers of producing departments know that fixed service department costs are going to be allocated on the basis of long-run average usage of the service involved, what will be their probable strategy as they report their estimate of this usage to the company's budget committee? As a member of top management, what would you do to neutralize any such strategies?

P16–10 Cost Allocation in a Hospital; Step Method   Pleasant View Hospital has three service departments—food services, administrative services, and X-ray services. The costs of these departments are allocated by the step method, using the bases and in the order shown below:

Service Department	Costs Incurred	Base for Allocation
Food services	Variable Fixed	Meals served Peak-period needs
Administrative services.............	Variable Fixed	Files processed 10% X-ray services, 20% Outpatient Clinic, 30% OB Care, and 40% General Hospital
X-ray services	Variable Fixed	X rays taken Peak-period needs

Estimated cost and operating data for all departments in the hospital for the forthcoming month are presented in the following table:

	Food Services	Admin. Services	X-Ray Services	Outpatient Clinic	OB Care	General Hospital	Total
Variable costs........................	$ 73,150	$ 6,800	$38,100	$11,700	$ 14,850	$ 53,400	$198,000
Fixed costs...........................	48,000	33,040	59,520	26,958	99,738	344,744	612,000
Total costs	$121,150	$39,840	$97,620	$38,658	$114,588	$398,144	$810,000
Files processed........................	—	—	1,500	3,000	900	12,000	17,400
X rays taken...........................	—	—	—	1,200	350	8,400	9,950
Percent of peak-period X-ray needs	—	—	—	13%	3%	84%	100%
Meals served	—	1,000	500	—	7,000	30,000	38,500
Percent of peak-period needs—meals........................	—	2%	1%	—	17%	80%	100%

All billing in the hospital is done through the Outpatient Clinic, OB Care, or General Hospital. The hospital's administrator wants the costs of the three service departments allocated to those three billing centres.

Required

Prepare the cost allocation desired by the hospital administrator. Include under each billing centre the direct costs of the centre as well as the costs allocated from the service departments.

P16–11 Beginning- and End-of-Year Allocations Björnson A/S of Norway has only one service department—a cafeteria, in which meals are provided for employees in the company's milling and finishing departments. The costs of the cafeteria are all paid by the company as a fringe benefit to its employees. These costs are allocated to the milling and finishing departments on the basis of meals served in each department. Cost and other data relating to the cafeteria and to the milling and finishing departments for 19x7 are provided below. (The Norwegian unit of currency is the krone, which is indicated below by K.)

Cafeteria:

	19x7	
	Budget	**Actual**
Variable costs for food	300,000 K*	384,000 K
Fixed costs	200,000	215,000

*Budgeted at 20K per meal served.

Milling and finishing departments:

		Number of Meals Served	
	Percent of Peak-Period Capacity Required	19x7	
		Budget	**Actual**
Milling department.	70	10,000	12,000
Finishing department	30	5,000	4,000
Total	100	15,000	16,000

The company allocates variable and fixed costs separately. The level of fixed costs is determined by peak-period requirements.

Required

1. Assume that it is the beginning of 19x7. An allocation of cafeteria costs must be made to the milling and finishing departments to assist in computing predetermined overhead rates. How much of the budgeted cafeteria cost above would be allocated to each department?
2. Assume that it is now the end of 19x7. Management would like data to assist in comparing actual performance against planned performance in the cafeteria and in the other departments.
   a. How much of the actual cafeteria costs above would be allocated to the milling department and to the finishing department?
   b. Would any portion of the actual cafeteria costs not be allocated to the other departments? If so, compute the amount that would not be allocated, and explain why it would not be allocated.

P16–12 Cost Allocation in a Hotel; Step Method The Coral Lake Hotel has three service departments—grounds and maintenance, general administration, and laundry. The costs of these departments are allocated by the step method using the bases and in the order shown below:

Grounds and maintenance:
  Fixed costs—allocated on the basis of square metres of space occupied.

General administration:
  Variable costs—allocated on the basis of number of actual employees.
  Fixed costs—allocated 20% to laundry, 14% to convention centre, 36% to food services, and 30% to lodging.

Laundry:
  Variable costs—allocated on the basis of number of items processed.
  Fixed costs—allocated on the basis of the percentage of peak-period needs.

Cost and operating data for all departments in the hotel for a recent month are presented in the table below:

	Grounds and Maintenance	General Administration	Laundry	Convention Centre	Food Services	Lodging	Total
Variable costs	$ –0–	$ 915	$13,725	$ –0–	$ 48,000	$ 36,450	$ 99,090
Fixed costs	17,500	12,150	18,975	28,500	64,000	81,000	222,125
Total overhead costs	$17,500	$13,065	$32,700	$28,500	$112,000	$117,450	$321,215
Square metres of space	2,000	2,500	3,750	15,000	6,250	97,500	127,000
Number of employees	9	5	10	5	25	21	75
Laundry items processed	—	—	—	1,000	5,250	40,000	46,250
Percent of peak-period laundry requirements	—	—	—	3%	13%	84%	100%

All billing in the hotel is done through the convention centre, food services, and lodging. The hotel's general manager wants the costs of the three service departments allocated to these three billing centres.

Required

Prepare the cost allocation desired by the hotel's general manager. Include under each billing centre the direct costs of the centre, as well as the costs allocated from the service departments.

P16–13   Allocating Costs Equitably between Divisions   Precision Plastics maintains its own computer to service the needs of its three divisions. The company assigns the costs of the computer centre to the three divisions on the basis of the number of lines of print prepared for each division during the month.

In July, Carol Benz, manager of Division A, came to the company's controller seeking an explanation as to why her division had been charged a larger amount for computer services in June than in May, although her division had used the computer less in June. During the course of the discussion, the following data were referred to by the controller:

		Division		
	Total	A	B	C
May actual results:				
Lines of print	200,000	80,000	20,000	100,000
Percent of total	100%	40%	10%	50%
Computer cost assigned	$182,000	$72,800	$18,200	$91,000
June actual results:				
Lines of print	150,000	75,000	30,000	45,000
Percent of total	100%	50%	20%	30%
Computer cost assigned	$179,000	$89,500	$35,800	$53,700

"You see," said Eric Weller, the controller, "the computer centre has large amounts of fixed costs that continue regardless of how much the computer is used. We have built into the computer enough capacity to handle the divisions' peak-period needs, and this cost must be absorbed by someone. I know it hurts, but the fact is that during June your division received a greater share of the computer's output than it did during May; therefore, it has been allocated a greater share of the cost."

Carol Benz was unhappy with this explanation. "I still don't understand why I would be charged more for the computer, when I used it less," she said. "There must be a better way to handle these cost allocations."

An analysis of the divisions' peak-period needs shows that Division A requires 40% of the computer's peak-period capacity, Division B requires 12%, and Division C requires 48%.

Required

1. Is there any merit to Carol Benz's complaint? Explain.
2. By use of the high-low method, determine the monthly cost of the computer in terms of a variable rate per line of print and total fixed cost.

3. Reallocate the computer centre costs for May and June in accordance with the cost allocation principles discussed in the chapter. Allocate the variable and fixed costs separately.

P16–14 Multiple Departments; Step Method; Predetermined Overhead Rates; Unit Costs   Apsco Products has two service departments and two producing departments. The service departments are medical services and maintenance. Estimated monthly cost and operating data for the coming year are given below. These data have been prepared for purposes of computing predetermined overhead rates in the producing departments.

	Medical Services	Maintenance	Producing A	Producing B
Direct labour cost....................	—	—	$ 30,000	$ 40,000
Maintenance labour cost	—	$ 5,000	—	—
Direct materials	—	—	50,000	80,000
Maintenance materials.................	—	7,536	—	—
Medical supplies	$ 3,630	—	—	—
Miscellaneous overhead costs	7,500	6,000	104,000	155,000
Total costs	$11,130	$18,536	$184,000	$275,000
Direct labour-hours	—	—	6,000	10,000
Number of employees:				
Currently employed.................	3	8	38	64
Long-run employee needs	3	10	60	80
Floor space occupied—square metres......	800	1,500	8,000	12,000

Apsco Products allocates service department costs to producing departments for product costing purposes. The step method is used, starting with medical services. Allocation bases for the service departments are as follows:

Department	Costs Incurred	Base for Allocation
Medical services.........	Variable	Currently employed workers
	Fixed	Long-run employee needs
Maintenance............	Variable	Direct labour-hours
	Fixed	Square metres of floor space occupied

The behaviour of various costs is shown below:

	Medical Services	Maintenance
Maintenance labour cost	—	V
Maintenance materials................	—	V
Medical supplies	V	—
Miscellaneous overhead costs	F	F

V = Variable.
F = Fixed.

Required

1. Show the allocation of the service department costs for the purpose of computing predetermined overhead rates. Round all allocations to the nearest whole dollar.
2. Compute the predetermined overhead rate to be used in each of the producing departments (overhead rates are based on direct labour-hours).
3. Assume that production in department B is planned at 20,000 units for the month. Compute the planned cost of one unit of product in department B.

P16–15 Direct and Reciprocal Methods   At the beginning of this year, a group of lawyers and accountants in Calgary decided to join efforts in providing one-stop legal and accounting consulting services to industry and the government. The group established a consulting company, rented office space, and hired both professional and clerical staff.

Following several initial organizational meetings, the partners decided to divide the operation into three parts: the consulting department, the legal department, and the accounting department.

The consulting department dealt directly with the clients, providing two somewhat distinct services, accounting consulting (AC) and legal consulting (LC). In its first full month of operations, this department recorded its own identifiable costs as $20,000, 30% attributed to accounting consultations and 70% to legal work. Billings to clients amounted to $30,000 and $20,500 for accounting and legal consultations, respectively. This department made use of the other two departments' services in preparing work for the external clients.

The accounting and legal departments provided professional services for each other and for the consulting department on the basis of time according to the following schedule:

	Accounting Department	Legal Department	Consulting AC	Consulting LC
Accounting services	—	20%	60%	20%
Legal services	50%	—	10	40

The accounting department incurred $8,000 in costs in the first month and the legal department incurred $10,000. Neither department directly bills external clients.

Having completed the first month's activity, the partners are ready to evaluate the performance of the group and of the individual areas. The managing partner is concerned that his organizational structure may be a major determinant of success and has asked you, as an outside consultant, to prepare some performance information for him.

Required

1. Prepare an income statement for each consulting branch separately under each of the following allocation approaches:
   a. Direct
   b. Reciprocal
2. Prepare a brief memorandum to the managing partner on the performance of the group and the individual areas. In your memorandum, comment on the usefulness of standard costing for this service organization.

(SMAC, adapted)

CASES

C16–16   Direct Method; Plantwide Overhead Rates versus Departmental Overhead Rates   Sun Concepts, Inc., manufactures and markets a complete line of surfboards. Sun Concepts has three manufacturing departments—molding, assembly, and finishing—and two service departments—quality control and maintenance.

The basic fiberglass boards are fabricated in the molding department. Fittings are attached to the boards in the assembly department. The boards are painted, surfaces are sanded and polished, and the completed boards are disassembled and packed in the finishing department. Varying amounts of materials, time, and effort are required for each of the various surfboards produced by the company. The quality control department and maintenance department provide services to the manufacturing departments.

Sun Concepts has always used a plantwide overhead rate. Direct labour-hours are used to assign the overhead to products. The overhead rate is computed by dividing the company's total estimated overhead cost by the total estimated direct labour-hours to be worked in the three manufacturing departments.

Pui Lan Lee, manager of cost accounting, has recommended that the company use departmental overhead rates rather than a single, plantwide rate. Planned operating costs and expected levels of activity for the coming year have been developed by Lee and are presented below:

	Service Department Costs	
	Quality Control	**Maintenance**
Variable costs	$ 60,000	$ 8,000
Fixed costs	140,000	78,000
Total service department costs	$200,000	$86,000

	Manufacturing Department		
	Molding	**Assembly**	**Finishing**
Departmental activity measures:			
Direct labour-hours.............................	10,000	40,000	30,000
Machine-hours	–0–	8,000	50,000
Department costs:			
Raw materials...................................	$800,000	$2,000,000	$100,000
Direct labour...................................	150,000	600,000	450,000
Variable overhead..............................	100,000	200,000	50,000
Fixed overhead.................................	1,200,300	702,300	597,400
Total department costs	$2,250,300	$3,502,300	$1,197,400

	Manufacturing Department		
	Molding	**Assembly**	**Finishing**
Use of service departments:			
Quality control:			
Estimated quality control hours	4,000	3,000	1,000
Percentage of peak-period requirements	50%	35%	15%
Maintenance:			
Estimated maintenance hours.....................	200	600	800
Percentage of peak-period requirements	15%	40%	45%

Required

1. Assume that the company will use a single, plantwide overhead rate for the coming year, the same as in the past. Under these conditions, compute the plantwide rate that would be used.
2. Assume that Pui Lan Lee has been asked to develop departmental overhead rates for the three manufacturing departments for comparison with the plantwide rate. To develop these rates, do the following:
   a. By use of the direct method, allocate the service department costs to the manufacturing departments. In each case, allocate the variable and fixed costs separately. The fixed portion of the service department costs are incurred in order to support peak-period activity.
   b. Compute overhead rates for the three manufacturing departments for the coming year. In computing the rates, use a machine-hours basis in the finishing department and a direct labour-hours basis in the other two departments.
3. Assume that the Pipeline model surfboard has the following annual requirements for machine time and direct labour time in the various departments:

	Machine-Hours	Direct Labour-Hours
Molding department............	–0–	500
Assembly department...........	200	1,000
Finishing department	1,500	800
Total hours	1,700	2,300

   a. Compute the amount of overhead cost that would be allocated to the Pipeline model if a plantwide overhead rate is used. Repeat the computation, this time assuming that departmental overhead rates are used.
   b. Management is concerned because the Pipeline model is priced well below competing products of competitors. On the other hand, certain other of Sun Concepts' products

are priced well above the prices of competitors with the result that profits in the company are deteriorating because of declining sales. Looking at the computations in (a) above, what effect is the use of a plantwide rate having on the costing of products and therefore on selling prices?

4. What additional steps could Sun Concepts, Inc., take to improve its overhead costing?

(CMA, heavily adapted)

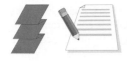

C16–17 Step Method versus Direct Method "I can't understand what's happening here," said Mike Holt, president of Severson Products, Inc. "We always seem to bid too high on jobs that require a lot of labour time in the finishing department, and we always seem to get every job we bid on that requires a lot of machine time in the milling department. Yet we don't seem to be making much money on those milling department jobs. I wonder if the problem is in our overhead rates."

Severson Products manufactures high-quality wood products to customers' specifications. Some jobs take a large amount of machine work in the milling department, and other jobs take a large amount of hand finishing work in the finishing department. In addition to the milling and finishing departments, the company has three service departments. The costs of these service departments are allocated to other departments *in the order listed below.* (For each service department, use the allocation base that provides the best measure of service provided, as discussed in the chapter.)

	Total Labour-Hours	Square Metres of Space Occupied	Number of Employees	Machine-Hours	Direct Labour-Hours
Cafeteria.	16,000	12,000	25	—	—
Custodial services	9,000	3,000	40	—	—
Maintenance.	15,000	10,000	60	—	—
Milling	30,000	40,000	100	160,000	20,000
Finishing	100,000	20,000	300	40,000	70,000
	170,000	85,000	525	200,000	90,000

Budgeted overhead costs in each department for the current year are as follows (no distinction is made between variable and fixed costs):

Cafeteria.	$ 320,000 *
Custodial services	65,400
Maintenance.	93,600
Milling	416,000
Finishing	166,000
Total budgeted costs.	$1,061,000

*This represents the amount of cost subsidized by the company.

The company has always allocated service department costs to the producing departments (milling and finishing) using the direct method of allocation, because of its simplicity.

Required

1. Allocate service department costs to using departments by the step method. Then compute predetermined overhead rates in the producing departments for the current year, using a machine-hours basis in the milling department and a direct labour-hours basis in the finishing department.

2. Repeat (1) above, this time using the direct method. Again compute predetermined overhead rates in the milling and finishing departments.

3. Assume that during the current year the company bids on a job that requires machine and labour time as follows:

	Machine-Hours	Direct Labour-Hours
Milling department.	2,000	1,600
Finishing department	800	13,000
Total hours	2,800	14,600

    a. Determine the amount of overhead that would be assigned to the job if the company used the overhead rates developed in (1) above. Then determine the amount of overhead that would be assigned to the job if the company used the overhead rates developed in (2) above.

    b. Explain to the president why the step method would provide a better basis for computing predetermined overhead rates than the direct method.

C16–18 Comprehensive St. Mary's College, founded under the Provincial Colleges and Universities Act, is a nonprofit organization involved in the delivery of educational programs. St. Mary's is multi-faceted. Its activities are separated into four categories: academic programs, federal government programs, profit centres, and support services. (See Exhibit 16–8 for a macro-version of its organizational chart.)

Academic Programs

St. Mary's College delivers post-secondary academic educational programs on a trimester basis. These trimesters run from September to December, January to April and May to August. This activity accounts for 70% of the college's operations and is funded by the provincial government. These funds are provided by the government at the beginning of every trimester and are based on a formula, with an allowance for inflation and overhead, applied to student enrollment for the same trimester two years previous. For example, if the enrollment for the September to December trimester in 1995 was 750 students, the inflation/overhead-adjusted funding received for September to December 1997 is based on 750 students even if the actual enrollment is 800 students or 700 students. In addition to the government funds, the college charges a government-regulated student fee to each student.

    This funding formula allows the college, in planning for the academic programs being offered in a particular trimester, to know how much revenue it will receive. If the college has a cash shortage in any particular trimester due to increased enrollment, it can use its reserve fund or it can apply to the government for emergency funds.

    The reserve fund is closely monitored by the government to ensure that the reserves are maintained at a certain level. The reserves which have been built up over the years are the result of actual enrollments being lower than the base enrollment used in the government funding formula. For example, if actual enrollment for September to December 1997 is 650 students and if the college conducts its affairs in a fiscally responsible manner, excess funds received based on the 1995 trimester enrollment of 750 would be added to the reserve fund. These reserves are to be used for expansion, replacement of capital assets, or as a buffer against hard times.

Federal Government Programs

St. Mary's College delivers, on an "as required" basis, adult skills training and apprenticeship programs for the federal government. This government service activity accounts for 20% of the college's operations and, unlike the academic programs, does not run on a trimester basis. The federal government directly, and indirectly through local Industry Training Committees, purchases these programs from the college. The purchase price is a per diem rate per student enrolled in the program. For example, if the federal government directly purchases a computer skills training program from the college for 50 students for a period of four weeks (20 days) at $55 per day per student, the total purchase price is $55,000. Calculation of the per diem rate is based on a target of recovering all direct costs plus 8% of direct costs to cover overhead. The duration of the skills training programs can vary from 4 to 52 weeks. The apprenticeship programs can run from 2 to 4 years and require the students to attend classes part of the time and gain work experience through co-op placement with local businesses the rest of the time.

    Negotiations for purchasing and running all federal government programs are conducted in November and December and are finalized in March. Courses commence in April. Some of these programs could have a small surplus and some a small deficit, but overall they achieve their target.

EXHIBIT 16-8   St. Mary's College Organization Chart

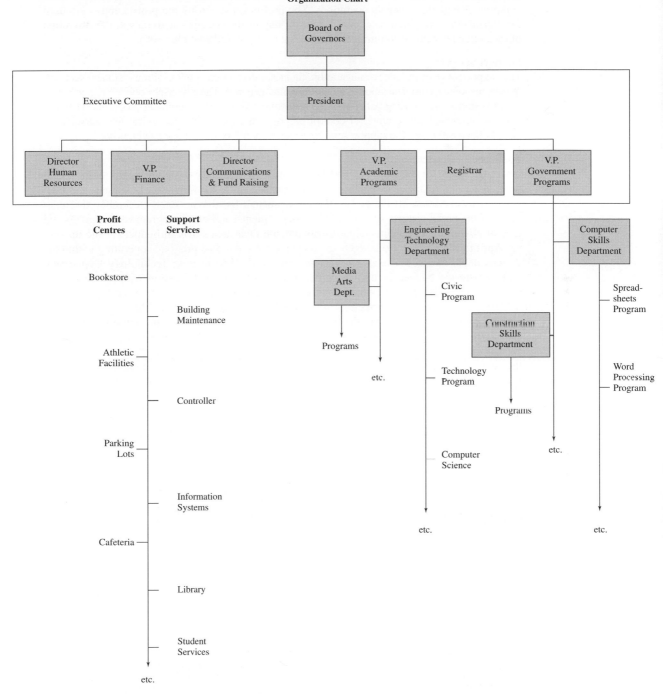

Profit Centres

The bookstore, athletic facilities, cafeteria and parking lots are operated as profit centres and are synchronized with the delivery of the academic programs. These profit centre activities comprise 5% of the college's operations. The profits generated by the profit centres are used for expansion or to purchase capital assets for any of the college's activities at the discretion of the college executive committee. The pricing policy is full cost plus 30%.

Support Services

The support services include administration, finance, information systems, library, student services, human resources, communications and building maintenance. These services operate regardless of the time frames and funding patterns of the academic and federal government programs. They operate as individual cost centres for control purposes, but their costs are completely allocated to other college activities. The support services account for 5% of the college's operations.

Budgets and Reports

Under the terms of the Colleges and Universities Act, each year the college is obligated to provide audited financial statements and an annual report to the Ministry of Colleges and Universities as at March 31, the end of the government's fiscal year. Each December, the managers of the profit centres, support services departments, academic programs departments and federal government programs departments prepare their area's overall budget for the upcoming April to March year. No budgets are prepared for individual programs operating within the various departments. For example, the manager of the Engineering Technology Department will prepare the budget for his whole department after some discussion with the individual program heads. The managers then go through a negotiation process with the college's executive committee and the department/profit centre budgets are finalized in February.

For control purposes during the year, the managers are provided with monthly accounting reports. (See Exhibit 16–9 for an example.) Although individual program data is not provided, department managers are informally aware of what is going on in the programs. At the end of the year, comparative accounting statements are prepared for each profit centre/department for evaluation purposes. (See Exhibit 16–10 for an example of a year-end profit centre report.)

EXHIBIT 16–9

Engineering Technology Department
Accounting Report
For the Period April 1 to April 30, 1998

	Current Month Actual	Year to Date Actual	Annual Budget
Salaries and benefits:			
Full-time faculty...........................	$65,408	$65,408	$780,000
Part-time faculty...........................	–0–	–0–	45,000
Administrative staff........................	18,400	18,400	216,000
Support staff..............................	9,317	9,317	120,000
	93,125	93,125	1,161,000
Instructional materials......................	32,000	32,000	35,000
Equipment rental...........................	200	200	2,400
Supplies...................................	421	421	2,000
Meetings and seminars.......................	–0–	–0–	2,000
Overhead*.................................	150	150	10,000
Printing and publications....................	65	65	1,000
Honorariums..............................	–0–	–0–	10,000
Total operating costs.......................	$125,961	$125,961	$1,223,400

*Overhead represents both direct departmental overhead and the support services costs. The support services costs are allocated at the end of the year.

EXHIBIT 16-10

Bookstore
Statement of Revenues and Expenses
For the Year Ended March 31, 1998

	1998	1997
Sales revenue	$5,750,000	$6,145,000
Cost of sales	4,515,000	4,620,000
	1,235,000	1,525,000
Operating expenses	520,000	525,000
Net profit	$715,000	$1,000,000

In 1997, the standard mark-up was reduced with the hope of increasing sales volume. In 1996 and prior years, the bookstore maintained a markup of 30% on full cost. The bookstore accounts for 25% of the revenue generated by the profit centres.

Executive Committee Meeting, March 31, 1998

PRESIDENT: I presume all those present have had an opportunity to review the preliminary set of financial statements. This is the second year in a row that we are showing a deficit in the operating fund. Fortunately, we still have enough in the reserve fund to cover this deficit, but how are we going to explain continuous deficits to the board of governors? More importantly, what are we going to do for the future since the pie and our slice of it are shrinking? Are we spending more than we get? If so, how are we going to control spending? Remember, nowhere is it stated that we cannot run certain types of operations at a profit.

VICE PRESIDENT, FINANCE: I have been with the college for only six months and, as I see it, the issue is not the deficit, but rather whether the college is achieving its mission and objectives of providing and promoting high-quality education in the most economic, effective, and efficient manner possible. We have been concentrating on getting information for financial audits and external reports, while the more important aspect of regularly using information for management planning and control has been nonexistent.

VICE PRESIDENT, ACADEMIC PROGRAMS: I have to agree. The monthly reports my department managers get make no sense to them. More often than not, these reports are neatly filed away for review at a later date. The accounting reports we receive provide no insights as to how a program is doing financially or whether it is achieving its goal of providing students with the skills and education that will make them competitive and marketable in the workplace. If I want to find out how a program is doing, I have to call the registrar's office for enrollment information and the student placement office for information as to how many graduates of the program were successful in obtaining employment.

VICE PRESIDENT, GOVERNMENT PROGRAMS: While reviewing the accounting records of one of my departments, I noticed that a major purchase of computer equipment was included in the expenses. Correct me if I am wrong, but isn't this a capital item? Expensing this item has put that department in a deficit position.

VICE PRESIDENT, FINANCE: The issues raised and problems confronting us arise from a basic flaw in our information system. Accounting records and budget information are being prepared and maintained solely for the purpose of satisfying the legal requirement of audited financial statements at the end of the year. According to the manager of information systems, the present information system is inflexible and not integrated. The main computer system is geared only to the financial reporting and audit function. Other information is recorded on individual department's personal computers. My counterpart at DEF College told me that they have installed a computerized information system that serves both management and financial audit requirements. I have arranged to meet with him together with our controller and manager of information systems.

EXHIBIT 16-11

GHI Motor Company
Projected Annual Costs
Mechanics Training Program

Salaries and benefits:

Full-time faculty	$200,000
Part-time faculty	50,000
Administrative staff*	100,000
Support staff	40,000
	390,000
Instructional materials	36,000
Supplies	12,000
Utilities and building maintenance	11,000
Equipment maintenance	8,000
Overhead†	11,000
Total operating costs	$468,000

*Includes administrator's salary of $75,000 to be paid by GHI Motor Company.

†Overhead represents direct program overhead plus $10,000 of allocated support services costs.

THE REGISTRAR: We need a computerized student information system that will eliminate duplication and errors that occur in the current system of recording student enrollments. At present, the registrar's office records student enrollments in its own computer system which is not connected to the accounting system. Then enrollment data has to be manually input separately into the accounting system. This has led to discrepancies and errors.

DIRECTOR, COMMUNICATIONS AND FUND RAISING: We need to go through all this and come up with a plan that enables us to function in a fiscally responsible manner while at the same time not forgetting our main objective. It appears that programs are not being reviewed for their effectiveness and program heads are not being held accountable for the efficient running of their programs. Department managers are preparing budgets without senior management guidance or input. There does not seem to be any uniformity or consistency throughout the college in the preparation of budgets.

PRESIDENT: I have been concerned about the accounting reports that are sent to me every month. I receive every department's report and I do not have the time to go through them all. What I require is one report that will enable me to see total college activities.

Furthermore, these reports are of a purely financial nature. This is well and good, but we are a nonprofit organization whose success is also evaluated based on nonmonetary factors such as the quality of our services, and the need for the services we offer.

One opportunity has arisen for the college. I recently met with the board of directors of GHI Motors Company. They would like us to run a mechanics training program for their employees and they have offered to donate to the college the building, equipment and services of an administrator that we would need to run the program. The building could be built on the currently unused grounds by the northeast student parking lot. The duration of a training session would be 20 days. The company wants 11 such sessions in the course of a year. Each session would be attended by at least 40 employees.

The company is willing ot pay the college a per diem rate per student, adjusted for inflation each year. I would like to know how much the per diem rate per student should be if we are to cover the additional costs to the college of this program. I am also looking into the possibility of running this program as a profit centre. What is the maximum per diem rate per student we could charge given our pricing policy? Here is a breakdown of the projected annual costs to run this program (see Exhibit 16–11). Since this is the first time the college has received such a donation, some clarification as to the accounting/ financial treatment of the donation and its impact on the college is essential.

I'd like you, Mary (Vice President, Finance), to analyze all of the concerns raised at today's meeting and make recommendations for next Thursday's meeting.

Required

Assume the role of Mary Wise, Vice President, Finance, and prepare the requested report for Peter Smith, President of St. Mary's College.

(SMAC, adapted)

GROUP EXERCISES

GE16–19 Understanding the Cost of Complexity Service departments (or production support departments in the case of a manufacturer) make up a large and growing part of the cost structure of most businesses. This is as true in hospitals, financial institutions, universities, and other service industries as it is in manufacturing. The overall costs of service departments are high and rising. In many manufacturing firms, production support department costs can average 40% or more of total manufacturing costs. Yet, in reality, very little is known about the source or behaviour of these discretionary fixed costs. If you don't know where these costs came from and you don't have a good understanding of how the costs behave, it is going to be very difficult to control and reduce these costs.

In an effort to reduce costs, many companies think all they have to do is reduce head count, a demoralizing and debilitating experience not only for those who lose their jobs but also for those who remain employed. One sure sign of problems with this head-count-reduction approach is that more than half of firms refill these positions within a year after eliminating them.

Required

1. Choose an industry with which you are somewhat familiar (or know someone who is familiar with the industry) and list seven or eight major production support or service departments in a factory or other facility in this industry. What is the output of each of these support or service departments?
2. Assume a relatively uncomplicated factory (facility) where just a single, standard product (or service) is mass produced. Describe the activity or work being done in each of the service areas of this focused firm.
3. Now assume a more complicated operation for another factory located close by where a wide range of products are made or services are offered—some are standard products/ services while others are made to order, some are high-volume products/services while others are low volume, and some are fairly complex products/services while others are relatively simple. Describe the activity or work being done in the various service functions for this full-service firm.
4. Which factory or facility has higher production support costs? Why?
5. Explain the relationship between the range of products produced and the size of the support departments. When does the output of each of these support departments increase? When does the cost of each of these support departments increase?
6. Most firms are under increasing pressure to reduce costs. How would you go about logically reversing this explosive growth in overhead costs and bringing the overall level of service department costs down?

GE16–20 TQM and Service Quality Total quality management is just as applicable to service functions and service businesses as it is to manufacturing activities and manufacturing businesses. Applying TQM to service functions, for example, management accounting, is an approach that focuses on customer requirements. Customer satisfaction is at the forefront of TQM techniques.

Required

Choose one of the service areas of an organization. By seeking the views of others and drawing from as many different sources as you can, complete the following series of questions:

Stage 1:   Who is the customer?
Stage 2:   What does the customer expect from us?
Stage 3:   What are the customer's decision-making requirements?
Stage 4:   What problem areas do we perceive in the decision-making process?
Stage 5:   Identify improvement opportunities.

What perceptions did you uncover in your research?

This five-stage process is a modification of an eight-step process utilized by Alcoa of Australia and discussed in Malcolm Smith, "Improving Management Accounting Reporting Practices: A 'Total Quality Management' Approach (Part 1)," *Journal of Cost Management* (Winter 1994), pp. 50–57.

GE16–21   Complexity and Cost Drivers in the Purchasing Function

Have several different groups contact the purchasing department of a number of local manufacturers (one per group), a chain of grocery or retail stores, and at least one large hospital (or, if you can find a purchasing manager willing to speak to your class, that could be almost as effective). Indicate that your management accounting class is studying the purchasing function and would like to interview someone who has an in-depth knowledge of all the department's activities. The interviews should be designed to help you understand how complex purchasing has become—how many employees work in purchasing, what are their major activities, how many different parts (or items) does the company purchase, how many purchase orders are prepared during a year, how many vendors does the company deal with, how many shipments are received, what is the average size of a purchase order, how many purchase orders are for less than $500, and so forth. Once the interview is completed, organize the information in a form that can be reported to the rest of the class in an understandable fashion.

The purchasing representative may not know all of this information, especially if his or her company has not undergone a study in preparation for reducing the cost of the procurement process. That's OK. The objective here is to gain an understanding of all the complexities involved and their impact on cost. If you like, you could study almost any support department of a large firm. Have your instructor help you develop a set of questions appropriate for the service activity your group wishes to study.

GE16–22   Reengineering Purchasing

Each group should take the information developed from GE16–19 above and begin to consider how to reduce the cost of the purchasing function while maintaining (or even improving) the quality and service level of the various activities performed. Again, it could prove helpful at some point to speak with someone who has either reengineered his or her company's purchasing function or is applying continuous improvement techniques to reduce the time spent on low-value activities.

It would be even better if one of these individuals could speak to the class about his or her experiences in redesigning the purchasing function. (Note to the Instructor: Be sure that students complete their assignments before they hear the experiences of the speaker.)

Required

1. Who are the customers of purchasing and accounts payable and what are their requirements?
2. With the help of your instructor and starting with the preparation of a materials requisition, map out or document the process flow. Identify as many steps or tasks in the entire procurement/accounts payable process as you can.
3. Prepare a process flowchart or workflow diagram (with boxes and circles) for each step in the process. This provides a good visual reference of the order as it moves through the entire procurement cycle.
4. Determine whether each step or task is value-added (VA) or non-value-added (NVA). To determine whether a step is VA or NVA, ask if eliminating that step or task would in any way cause customer satisfaction to decline.

While you will be unable to complete the additional steps in this process value analysis, they would include costing each step in the process, a determination of why that step or task is performed, and an evaluation of alternative courses of action (e.g., continuous improvement of the existing process, or redesign and change the process entirely). Completion of these steps would result in permanent improvements.

GE16–23   Necessity Is the Mother of Invention

In an effort to reduce spending in areas where the value added is low, many companies are looking to reduce or eliminate the "paper chase" so endemic to the purchasing and accounts payable process. Corporate management is putting pressure on purchasing and finance to cut costs of processing transactions by anywhere from 35% to 90%.

Many companies have found that purchases of less than $2,500 make up the majority of purchase orders. On average, more than half of all purchases are for less than $500. A phenomenon often observed in business—called Pareto's Law—holds forth here too: 80% of the purchases account for only 20% of the dollar volume. Most of these are for so-called MRO purchases (maintenance, repairs, and operations) for things like office supplies, replacement machine parts, machine lubrication, and other relatively low-cost items incidental to production. It can cost a company anywhere from $15 to $150 to process a purchase order (PO) and another $100 to manage the purchase. No company can afford to spend this much to process a PO of $500 or less. By some estimates, the cost to process a PO is far more costly than this once you consider the requestor's time, purchasing's time, receiving's time, accounts payable's time, and the treasury office's time, not to mention the supplier's time.

Required   If you have answered (4) of GE16–22 above, you have completed all the steps preliminary to improving or re-engineering the purchasing of MRO items. How could you significantly reduce the cost of processing MRO items? Think boldly and identify all activities that can be either reduced or eliminated altogether.

17

"HOW WELL AM I DOING?" FINANCIAL STATEMENT ANALYSIS

LEARNING OBJECTIVES

After studying Chapter 17, you should be able to:

1 Explain the need for and limitations of financial statement analysis.

2 Prepare financial statements in comparative form, and explain how such statements are used.

3 Place the balance sheet and the income statement in common-size form, and properly interpret the results.

4 Identify the ratios used to measure the well-being of the common shareholder, and state each ratio's formula and interpretation.

5 Explain what is meant by the term *financial leverage,* and show how financial leverage is measured.

6 Identify the ratios used to measure the well-being of the short-term creditor, and state each ratio's formula and interpretation.

7 Identify the ratios used to measure the well-being of the long-term creditor, and state each ratio's formula and interpretation.

8 Define or explain the key terms listed at the end of the chapter.

A company's annual report can provide a wealth of information about its financial health, provided you know where to look and how to analyze the numbers.

All financial statements are essentially historical documents. They tell what *has happened* during a particular period of time. However, most users of financial statements are concerned about what *will happen* in the future. Shareholders are concerned with future earnings and dividends. Creditors are concerned with the company's future ability to repay its debts. Managers are concerned with the company's ability to finance future expansion. Despite the fact that financial statements are historical documents, they can still provide valuable information bearing on all of these concerns.

Financial statement analysis involves careful selection of data from financial statements for the primary purpose of forecasting the financial health of the company. This is accomplished by examining trends in key financial data, comparing financial data across companies, and analyzing key financial ratios. In this chapter, we consider some of the more important ratios and other analytical tools that analysts use in attempting to predict the future course of events in business organizations.

LIMITATIONS OF FINANCIAL STATEMENT ANALYSIS

OBJECTIVE 1

Explain the need for and limitations of financial statement analysis.

The Internal Use of Ratios

From the perspective of top management, ratio analysis can serve as a useful tool for performance evaluation, analysis of threats, constraints, and opportunities, and for strategic planning.

As was discussed in Chapter 12, ratios such as ROI combined with other measures can aid in evaluating the performance of individual unit managers. Further, ratios such as the current ratio and debt ratio can be calculated to determine whether managers are operating in accordance with contractual agreements regarding restrictions such as minimum working capital requirements and borrowing limitations.

Ratios can be helpful in formulating policy and in developing an ongoing organizational plan. A deeper awareness of the total business environment is essential for long-term growth and survival. Key business ratios of competitors, customers, and suppliers can be calculated to provide input data for marketing strategy. Indeed, regular monitoring of competitors may help to predict competitors' reactions to pricing and production decisions. Key ratios of customers can prove valuable in assessing their ability to honour purchase commitments. Ratios of suppliers can provide signals on their ability to meet deadlines and other contractual provisions. In summary, ratios of competitors, customers, and suppliers can be of great potential value in the competitive struggle for business survival and growth.

Benchmarking

Financial statements are not only historical documents but also essentially static documents. They speak only of the events of a single period of time. However, statement users are concerned about more than just the present; they are also concerned about the *trend* of events over time. For this reason, financial statement analysis directed toward a single period is of limited usefulness. The results of financial statement analysis for a particular period are of value only when viewed in *comparison* with the results of other periods (intrafirm analysis) and, in some cases, with the results of other firms (interfirm analysis). It is only through comparison that one can gain insight into trends and make intelligent judgements as to their significance.

Ratios of other firms in the same industry can serve as standards by which to make comparisons. Industry ratios are available from a number of sources such as Dun & Bradstreet, which provides statistics on the median, upper quartile, and lower quartile for 14 key ratios. (See Exhibit 17–9 at the end of this chapter for a list of sources.) Rather than industry averages, the ratios of the most successful firms may be chosen as standards of comparison. This is known as **benchmarking,** a process of continuously measuring a firm against the best firms in the industry. In today's increasingly competitive international environment, successful firms set benchmarks based on the highest industry standards. The most successful companies emphasize the highest standards in terms of cost efficiency, quality products and services, and customer focus. Once benchmarks are chosen a manager can make individual comparisons. Depending on the direction and extent of any deviation from a ratio's benchmark, a judgment is made as to whether a particular ratio is good, bad, or satisfactory. Plans should then be put in place by management to address any weak spots while maintaining strengths. This requires looking beyond ratios and seeking out detailed information on what best practices successful firms use. It is not always easy to obtain sensitive information from competitors but much can be learned by visiting both competing and noncompeting firms and by keeping up to date with recent industry and trade publications and talking with knowledgeable industry experts, discriminating customers, and discerning suppliers.

Industry benchmarks should be interpreted with caution. For example, structural or technological change in an industry can cause a benchmark to become outdated and limit its usefulness. Used properly, benchmarks should lead both production and service firms to continuous quality improvements. The aim is to be the best in all value-added activities in terms of lower costs, better quality, and greater customer satisfaction. This may necessitate major changes to value chain activities and the elimination of non-value-added activities. Such major changes are referred to as re-engineering and may involve 30% or more of a firm's activities. At the least, however, there should be ongoing incremental improvement.

Comparisons with best firms within an industry can sometimes be made difficult by differences in accounting methods used by firms being compared. Accounting methods for inventory valuation, depreciation of capital assets, and recognition of sales revenue can vary widely among firms. For example, if one firm values its inventories by FIFO and another values its inventories by average cost, then direct comparisons of financial data such as inventory valuations and cost of goods sold between the two firms may be misleading. Sometimes enough data is presented in footnotes to the financial statements to restate data to a comparable basis. When footnotes are not available, the analyst should keep in mind the lack of comparability of the data before drawing any definite conclusions. Nevertheless, even with this limitation in mind, comparisons of key ratios with other companies and with industry averages often suggest avenues for further investigation. Although the analytical work required here might be tougher, it is often necessary if the manager is to have useful data available for comparative purposes. At no time should accounting methods be chosen for the sake of bringing ratios closer to benchmarks. This is a misuse of the benchmarking concept. The aim is for superior value-added improvements and ratios to reflect whether or not a firm is meeting its targets.

Ratios should be interpreted in the context of management's chosen competitive strategy. If the chosen strategy is high turnover/low profit margin, benchmarks should reflect performance of companies with a similar strategic focus and may not be comparable to firms that employ a lower turnover/high profit margin strategy. For example, a successful company with a low turnover/high profit margin strategy would react with less concern to ratios reflecting lower cost control. This is because it can recover its cost through the relatively higher prices it charges for its goods or services. Customers are willing to pay more because of real or perceived differences in the firm's product or services. On the other hand, a company with a high turnover/low profit margin strategy would be unable to pass these costs on to customers. Such companies are no-frill operations that attempt to keep costs as low as possible. Successful companies using this strategy are profitable as a consequence of their high sales volume. Even a small change in unit cost will make a relatively large impact on total cost because many units are affected. High cost for a firm following this strategy translates into lower profits and may severely threaten a firm's ability to compete.

The Need to Look beyond Ratios

There is a tendency for the inexperienced analyst to assume that ratios are sufficient in themselves as a basis for judgments about the future. Nothing could be further from the truth. The experienced analyst realizes that conclusions based on ratio analysis must be regarded as tentative in nature. Ratios should not be viewed as an end, but rather they should be viewed as a *starting point,* as indicators of what to pursue in greater depth. They raise many questions, but they rarely answer any questions by themselves.

In addition to looking at ratios, the analyst should look at other sources of data in order to make judgments about the future of an organization. The analyst should look, for example, at industry trends, technological changes, changes in consumer tastes, changes in broad economic factors, and changes that are taking place within the firm itself. A recent change in a key management position, for example, might provide a basis for optimism about the future, even though the past performance of the firm (as shown by its ratios) may have been mediocre.

STATEMENTS IN COMPARATIVE AND COMMON-SIZE FORM

As stated earlier, few figures appearing on financial statements have much significance standing by themselves. It is the relationship of one figure to another and the amount and direction of change from one point in time to another that are important in financial statement analysis. How does the analyst key in on significant relationships? How does the analyst dig out the important trends and changes in a company? Three analytical techniques are in widespread use:

1. Dollar and percentage changes on statements.
2. Common-size statements.
3. Ratios.

The first and second techniques are discussed in this section; the third technique is discussed in the next section.

Dollar and Percentage Changes on Statements

OBJECTIVE 2

Prepare financial statements in comparative form, and explain how such statements are used.

A good place to begin in financial statement analysis is to put statements in comparative form. This consists of little more than putting two or more years' data side by side. Statements cast in comparative form underscore movements and trends and may give the analyst valuable clues as to what to expect in the way of financial and operating performance in the future.

An example of financial statements placed in comparative form is given in Exhibits 17–1 and 17–2. These are the statements of Brickey Electronics, a hypothetical firm that has been experiencing substantial growth. The data on these statements are used as a basis for discussion throughout the remainder of the chapter.

EXHIBIT 17-1

BRICKEY ELECTRONICS
Comparative Balance Sheet
December 31, 19x2, and 19x1
(dollars in thousands)

	19x2	19x1	Increase (Decrease) Amount	Percent
Assets				
Current assets:				
Cash..................................	$1,200	$2,350	$(1,150)	(48.9)*
Accounts receivable, net...................	6,000	4,000	2,000	50.0
Inventory...............................	8,000	10,000	(2,000)	(20.0)
Prepaid expenses........................	300	120	180	150.0
Total current assets	15,500	16,470	(970)	(5.9)
Capital assets:				
Land	4,000	4,000	–0–	–0–
Buildings and equipment, net...............	12,000	8,500	3,500	41.2
Total property and equipment.............	16,000	12,500	3,500	28.0
Total assets	$31,500	$28,970	$ 2,530	8.7
Liabilities and Shareholders' Equity				
Current liabilities:				
Accounts payable	$5,800	$4,000	$ 1,800	45.0
Accrued payables	900	400	500	125.0
Notes payable, short term................	300	600	(300)	(50.0)
Total current liabilities	7,000	5,000	2,000	40.0
Long-term liabilities:				
Bonds payable, 8%......................	7,500	8,000	(500)	(6.3)
Total liabilities	14,500	13,000	1,500	11.5
Shareholders' equity:				
6% Preferred shares, $100 liquidation value,				
20,000 shares issued	2,000	2,000	–0–	–0–
Common shares, 500,000 shares.............	6,000	6,000	–0–	–0–
Contributed surplus......................	1,000	1,000	–0–	0
Total paid-in capital	9,000	9,000	–0–	–0–
Retained earnings	8,000	6,970	1,030	14.8
Total shareholders' equity...............	17,000	15,970	1,030	6.4
Total liabilities and shareholders' equity	$31,500	$28,970	$2,530	8.7

*Since we are measuring the amount of change between 19x1 and 19x2, the dollar amounts for 19x1 become the "base" figures for expressing these changes in percentage form. For example, Cash decreased by $1,150 between 19x1 and 19x2. This decrease expressed in percentage form is computed as follows: $1,150 ÷ $2,350 = 48.9%. Other percentage figures in this exhibit and in Exhibit 17–2 are computed in the same way.

Horizontal Analysis. Comparison of two or more years' financial data is known as **horizontal analysis** or **trend analysis.** Horizontal analysis is greatly facilitated by showing changes between years in both dollar *and* percentage form, as has been done in Exhibits 17–1 and 17–2. Showing changes in dollar form helps the analyst focus on key factors that have affected profitability or financial position. For example, observe in Exhibit 17–2 that sales for 19x2 were up $4 million over 19x1, but that this increase in sales was more than negated by a $4.5 million increase in cost of goods sold.

Brickey Electronics provides electronic components for companies in the computer and television industries. In this chapter we analyze the financial statements of Brickey Electronics, using a variety of analytical tools.

EXHIBIT 17–2

BRICKEY ELECTRONICS
Comparative Income Statement and Reconciliation of Retained Earnings
For the Years Ended December 31, 19x2, and 19x1
(dollars in thousands)

	19x2	19x1	Increase (Decrease) Amount	Percent
Sales	$52,000	$48,000	$4,000	8.3
Cost of goods sold..........................	36,000	31,500	4,500	14.3
Gross margin..............................	16,000	16,500	(500)	(3.0)
Operating expenses:				
Selling expenses	7,000	6,500	500	7.7
Administrative expenses	5,860	6,100	(240)	(3.9)
Total operating expenses.................	12,860	12,600	260	2.1
Net operating income	3,140	3,900	(760)	(19.5)
Interest expense............................	640	700	(60)	(8.6)
Net income before taxes	2,500	3,200	(700)	(21.9)
Less income taxes (30%)	750	960	(210)	(21.9)
Net income	1,750	2,240	$ (490)	(21.9)
Dividends to preferred shareholders, $6 per share (see Exhibit 17–1)...............	120	120		
Net income remaining for common shareholders	1,630	2,120		
Dividends to common shareholders, $1.20 per share	600	600		
Net income added to retained earnings...........	1,030	1,520		
Retained earnings, beginning of year	6,970	5,450		
Retained earnings, end of year	$ 8,000	$ 6,970		

Showing changes between years in percentage form helps the analyst to gain *perspective* and to gain a feel for the *significance* of the changes that are taking place. One would have a different perspective of a $1 million increase in sales if the prior year's sales were $2 million than if the prior year's sales were $20 million. In the first situation, the increase would be 50%—undoubtedly a significant increase for any firm. In the second situation, the increase would be only 5%—perhaps just a reflection of normal growth.

Trend Percentages. Horizontal analysis of financial statements can also be carried out by computing *trend percentages*. **Trend percentages** state several years' financial data in terms of a base year. The base year equals 100%, with all other years stated as some percentage of this base. To illustrate, consider Compaq Computer Corporation which vies with IBM and Apple Computer for the number one position in personal computer sales. Compaq has enjoyed tremendous growth in recent years, as evidenced by the following data:

	1993	1992	1991	1990	1989
Sales (millions)	$7,191	$4,000	$3,271	$3,599	$2,876
Net income (millions)	462	213	131	455	333

By simply looking at these data, one can see that sales have increased more or less steadily over the five-year period. But how rapidly have sales been increasing, and have the increases in net income kept pace with the increases in sales? By looking at the raw data alone, it is difficult to answer these questions. The increases in sales and the increases in net income can be put into better perspective by stating them in terms of trend percentages, with 1989 as the base year. These percentages (all rounded) are given below:

	1993	1992	1991	1990	1989
Sales (millions)*	250%	139%	114%	125%	100%
Net income (millions)	139%	64%	39%	137%	100%

*For 1990, $3,599 ÷ $2,876 = 125%; for 1991, $3,271 ÷ $2,876 = 114%; and so forth.

While Compaq's sales growth has been impressive and even spectacular in some years, there is no clearly discernible trend in its net income. The roller-coaster-like performance of net income is likely due to a combination of intense competitive pressures and rapid technological change in the personal computer industry, general trends in the economy, and strategic decisions made by management. *The Wall Street Journal* reported that:

> Two years ago, Compaq jettisoned its strategy of charging premium prices, after experiencing slumping sales and plummeting earnings in 1991. Under its new chief executive officer . . . the company initiated a price war, slashed its costs to offset plunging margins and broadened its product line. Sales have been surging ever since.[1]

Common-Size Statements

OBJECTIVE 3

Place the balance sheet and the income statement in common-size form, and properly interpret the results.

Key changes and trends can also be highlighted by the use of *common-size statements*. A **common-size statement** is one that shows the items appearing on it in percentage form as well as in dollar form. Each item is stated as a percentage of some total of which that item is a part. The preparation of common-size statements is known as **vertical analysis.**

Common-size statements are particularly useful when comparing data from different companies. For example, Wendy's net income was about $65 million in 1992, whereas McDonald's was $959 million. This comparison is somewhat misleading because of the

_____

[1]Jim Carlton, "Compaq PCs Outsold IBM and Apple World-Wide during the First Quarter," *The Wall Street Journal,* Wednesday, May 25, 1994, p. A3.

dramatically different sizes of the two companies. To put this in better perspective, the net income figures can be expressed as a percentage of the sales of each company. Since Wendy's sales were $3.9 billion in 1992 and McDonald's were $21.9 billion, Wendy's net income as a percentage of sales was about 1.7% and McDonald's was about 4.4%. While the comparison still favours McDonald's, the contrast between the two companies has been placed on a more comparable basis.

The Balance Sheet.   One application of the vertical analysis idea is to state the separate assets of a company as percentages of total assets. A common-size statement of this type is shown in Exhibit 17–3 for Brickey Electronics.

Notice from Exhibit 17–3 that placing all assets in common-size form clearly shows the relative importance of the current assets as compared to the noncurrent assets. It also shows that significant changes have taken place in the *composition* of the current assets over the last year. Notice, for example, that the receivables have increased in relative importance and that both cash and inventory have declined in relative importance. Judging from the sharp increase in receivables, the deterioration in the cash position may be a result of inability to collect from customers.

McDonald's net income is almost 15 times that of Wendy's, $959 million compared to $65 million. Such differences in raw numbers make comparisons between the two companies difficult. Common-size statements resolve this problem.

The Income Statement.   Another application of the vertical analysis idea is to place all items on the income statement in percentage form in terms of sales. A common-size statement of this type is shown in Exhibit 17–4.

By placing all items on the income statement in common size in terms of sales, it is possible to see at a glance how each dollar of sales is distributed between the various costs, expenses, and profits. For example, notice from Exhibit 17–4 that 69.2 cents out of every dollar of sales was needed to cover cost of goods sold in 19x2, as compared to only

EXHIBIT 17–3

BRICKEY ELECTRONICS
Common-Size Comparative Balance Sheet
December 31, 19x2, and 19x1
(dollars in thousands)

	19x2	19x1	Common-Size Percentages 19x2	Common-Size Percentages 19x1
Assets				
Current assets:				
Cash....................................	$1,200	$2,350	3.8*	8.1
Accounts receivable, net...................	6,000	4,000	19.0	13.8
Inventory.............................	8,000	10,000	25.4	34.5
Prepaid expenses........................	300	120	1.0	0.4
Total current assets.....................	15,500	16,470	49.2	56.9
Capital assets:				
Land	4,000	4,000	12.7	13.8
Buildings and equipment, net...............	12,000	8,500	38.1	29.3
Total capital assets.....................	16,000	12,500	50.8	43.1
Total assets	$31,500	$28,970	100.0	100.0
Liabilities and Shareholders' Equity				
Current liabilities:				
Accounts payable	$5,800	$4,000	18.4	13.8
Accrued payables	900	400	2.8	1.4
Notes payable, short term.................	300	600	1.0	2.1
Total current liabilities..................	7,000	5,000	22.2	17.3
Long-term liabilities:				
Bonds payable, 8%.......................	7,500	8,000	23.8	27.6
Total liabilities.......................	14,500	13,000	46.0	44.9
Shareholders' equity:				
6% Preferred shares;				
$100 liquidation value, 20,000 shares issued ..	2,000	2,000	6.4	6.9
Common shares, 500,000 no-par shares........	6,000	6,000	19.0	20.7
Contributed surplus........................	1,000	1,000	3.2	3.5
Total contributed in capital...............	9,000	9,000	28.6	31.1
Retained earnings	8,000	6,970	25.4	24.0
Total shareholders' equity..............	17,000	15,970	54.0	55.1
Total liabilities and shareholders' equity	$31,500	$28,970	100.0	100.0

*Each asset account on a common-size statement is expressed in terms of total assets, and each liability and equity account is expressed in terms of total liabilities and shareholders' equity. For example, the percentage figure above for Cash in 19x2 is computed as follows: $1,200 ÷ $31,500 = 3.8%.

65.7 cents in the prior year; also notice that only 3.4 cents out of every dollar of sales remained for profits in 19x2—down from 4.6 cents in the prior year.

Common-size statements are also very helpful in pointing out efficiencies and inefficiencies that might otherwise go unnoticed. To illustrate, in 19x2, Brickey Electronics' selling expenses increased by $500,000 over 19x1. A glance at the common-size income statement shows, however, that on a relative basis selling expenses were no higher in 19x2 than in 19x1. In each year, they represented 13.5% of sales.

EXHIBIT 17–4

BRICKEY ELECTRONICS
Common-Size Comparative Income Statement
For the Years Ended December 31, 19x2, and 19x1
(dollars in thousands)

			Common-Size Percentages	
	19x2	19x1	19x2	19x1
Sales	$52,000	$48,000	100.0	100.0
Cost of goods sold	36,000	31,500	69.2*	65.7
Gross margin	16,000	16,500	30.8	34.3
Operating expenses:				
Selling expenses	7,000	6,500	13.5	13.5
Administrative expenses	5,860	6,100	11.2	12.7
Total operating expenses	12,860	12,600	24.7	26.2
Net operating income	3,140	3,900	6.0	8.1
Interest expense	640	700	1.2	1.5
Net income before taxes	2,500	3,200	4.8	6.6
Income taxes (30%)	750	960	1.4	2.0
Net income	$ 1,750	$ 2,240	3.4	4.6

*Note that the percentage figures for each year are expressed in terms of total sales for the year. For example, the percentage figure for cost of goods sold in 19x2 is computed as follows: $36,000 ÷ $52,000 = 69.2%.

RATIO ANALYSIS—THE COMMON SHAREHOLDER

OBJECTIVE 4
Identify the ratios used to measure the well-being of the common shareholder, and state each ratio's formula and interpretation.

A number of financial ratios are used to assess how well the company is doing from the standpoint of the shareholders. These ratios naturally focus on net income, dividends, and shareholders' equities.

Earnings per Share

An investor buys and retains shares with the expectation of realizing a return in the form of either dividends or future increases in the value of the shares. Since earnings form the basis for dividend payments, as well as the basis for any future increases in the value of shares, investors are always interested in a company's reported *earnings per share*. Probably no single statistic is more widely quoted or relied on in investor actions than earnings per share, although it has some inherent limitations, as discussed below.

Earnings per share is computed by dividing net income remaining for common shareholders by the number of common shares outstanding. "Net income remaining for common shareholders" is equal to the net income of a company, reduced by preferred share dividends.

$$\frac{\text{Net income} - \text{Preferred dividends}}{\text{Number of common shares outstanding}} = \text{Earnings per share}$$

Using the deta in Exhibits 17–1 and 17–2, we see that the earnings per share for Brickey Electronics for 19x2 would be computed as follows:

$$\frac{\$1,750,000 - \$120,000}{500,000 \text{ shares*}} = \$3.26 \qquad\qquad (1)$$

*6,000,000 ÷ $12 = 500,000 shares

Note that the denominator in the earnings per share formula uses the weighted average number of common shares outstanding for the year. Using a weighted average is appropriate because it recognizes that common shareholders may contribute varying amounts of capital for varying amounts of time. A weighted average number of shares reflects earnings per share during the period and is not a measure of entitlement to earnings at period-end. Assume that a company began operations on January 2, 19x1 by issuing 10,000 common shares, and on October 1, 19x1, an additional 10,000 shares were issued. The company obviously has 20,000 shares outstanding at year-end. However, the weighted average number of shares outstanding for the year is calculated as follows:

$$
\begin{array}{rcl}
10,000 \text{ shares} \times 9 \text{ months} &=& 90,000 \text{ share months} \\
20,000 \text{ shares} \times \underline{3} \text{ months} &=& \underline{60,000} \text{ share months} \\
12 & & 150,000 \text{ share months}
\end{array}
$$

The 10,000 shares issued on January 2 were outstanding for nine months before any new shares were issued. On October 1 another 10,000 shares were issued, bringing the total outstanding to 20,000 for the last three months of the year. The weighted average can now be determined by dividing the number of share months (150,000) by the number of months in a year (12) to give a weighted average of 12,500 shares.

Two complications can arise in connection with the computation of earnings per share. The first arises whenever an extraordinary gain or loss appears as part of net income. The second arises whenever a company has convertible securities on its balance sheet. These complications are discussed in the following paragraphs.

Extraordinary Items and Earnings per Share

Extraordinary items are items which result from transactions or events that have all of the following characteristics:

1. They are not expected to occur frequently over several years.
2. They do not typify the normal business activities of the entity.
3. They do not depend primarily on the decisions of management or determinations by management or owners.

If a company has extraordinary gains or losses appearing as part of net income, *two* earnings per share figures must be computed—one showing the earnings per share resulting from *normal* operations and one showing the earnings per share impact of the *extraordinary* items. This approach to computing earnings per share accomplishes three things. First, it helps statement users to recognize extraordinary items for what they are—unusual events that probably will not recur. Second, it eliminates the distorting influence of the extraordinary items from the basic earnings per share figure. And third, it helps statement users to properly assess the *trend* of *normal* earnings per share over time. Since one would not expect the extraordinary or unusual items to be repeated year after year, they should be given less weight in judging earnings performance than is given to profits resulting from normal operations.

In addition to reporting extraordinary items separately, the accountant also reports them *net of their tax effect*. This means that whatever impact the unusual item has on

EXHIBIT 17–5

Reporting
Extraordinary Items
Net of Their Tax
Effects

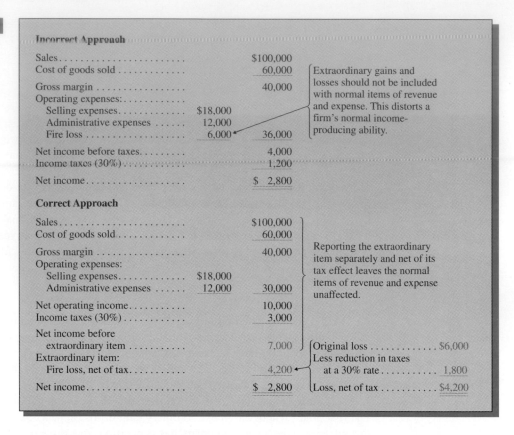

Incorrect Approach

Sales		$100,000
Cost of goods sold		60,000
Gross margin		40,000
Operating expenses:		
Selling expenses	$18,000	
Administrative expenses	12,000	
Fire loss	6,000	36,000
Net income before taxes		4,000
Income taxes (30%)		1,200
Net income		$ 2,800

Extraordinary gains and losses should not be included with normal items of revenue and expense. This distorts a firm's normal income-producing ability.

Correct Approach

Sales		$100,000
Cost of goods sold		60,000
Gross margin		40,000
Operating expenses:		
Selling expenses	$18,000	
Administrative expenses	12,000	30,000
Net operating income		10,000
Income taxes (30%)		3,000
Net income before extraordinary item		7,000
Extraordinary item:		
Fire loss, net of tax		4,200
Net income		$ 2,800

Reporting the extraordinary item separately and net of its tax effect leaves the normal items of revenue and expense unaffected.

Original loss	$6,000
Less reduction in taxes at a 30% rate	1,800
Loss, net of tax	$4,200

income taxes is *deducted from* the unusual item on the income statement. Only the net, after-tax gain or loss is used in earnings per share computations.

To illustrate these ideas, let us assume that Amata Company has suffered a fire loss of $6,000 and that management is wondering how the loss should be reported on the company's income statement. The correct and incorrect approaches to reporting the loss are shown in Exhibit 17–5.

As shown under the Correct Approach in the exhibit, the $6,000 loss is reduced to only $4,200 after tax effects are taken into consideration. The reasoning behind this computation is as follows: The fire loss is fully deductible for tax purposes. Therefore, this deduction will reduce the firm's taxable income by $6,000. If taxable income is $6,000 lower, then income taxes will be $1,800 *less* (30% × $6,000) than they *otherwise* would have been. In other words, the fire loss of $6,000 saves the company $1,800 in taxes that otherwise would have been paid. The $1,800 savings in taxes is deducted from the loss that caused it, leaving a net loss of only $4,200. This same $4,200 figure could have been obtained by multiplying the original loss by the formula (1 – Tax rate): [$6,000 × (1 – 0.30) = $4,200]

This same procedure is used in reporting extraordinary gains. The only difference is that extraordinary gains *increase* taxes; thus, any tax resulting from a gain must be deducted from it, with only the net gain reported on the income statement.

To continue our illustration, assume that the company in Exhibit 17–5 has 2,000 common shares outstanding. Earnings per share would be reported as follows:

Earnings per share on common stock:	
On net income before extraordinary item ($7,000 ÷ 2,000 shares)	$ 3.50
On extraordinary item, net of tax ($4,200 ÷ 2,000 shares)	(2.10)
Net earnings per share	$ 1.40

In summary, clearly segregating extraordinary items as we have done above is necessary to avoid misunderstanding a company's normal income-producing ability. Reporting *only* the flat $1.40 per share figure would be misleading and perhaps cause investors to regard the company less favourably than they should.

Fully Diluted Earnings per Share

A problem sometimes arises in trying to determine the number of common shares to use in computing earnings per share. Until recent years, the distinctions between common shares, preferred shares, and debt were quite clear. However, these distinctions have become murkier due to a growing tendency to issue convertible securities of various types. Rather than simply issuing common shares, firms today often issue preferred stock or bonds that carry a **conversion feature** allowing the purchaser to convert the preferred shares or bonds into common shares at some future time.

When convertible securities are present in the financial structure of a firm, the question arises as to whether these securities should be retained in their unconverted form or treated as common shares in computing earnings per share. The generally accepted position is that convertible securities should be treated *both* in their present and prospective forms. This requires the presentation of *two* earnings per share figures, one showing earnings per share assuming no conversion into common shares and the other showing full conversion into common shares. The latter figure is known as the **fully diluted earnings per share.**

To illustrate the computation of a company's fully diluted earnings per share, let us assume that the preferred shares of Brickey Electronics in Exhibit 17–1 is convertible into common on the basis of five shares of common for each share of preferred. Since 20,000 shares of preferred are outstanding, conversion would require issuing an additional 100,000 shares of common stock. Earnings per share on a fully diluted basis would be computed as follows:

$$\frac{\text{Net income}}{\text{(Weighted average number of common shares outstanding + potential shares issued on convertible securities)}} = \frac{\text{Fully diluted earnings per share}}{}$$

$$\frac{\text{Net income}}{(500{,}000 \text{ shares outstanding} + 100{,}000 \text{ converted shares})}$$

$$= \frac{\$1{,}750{,}000}{600{,}000 \text{ shares}} = \$2.92 \qquad (2)$$

In comparing equation (2) with equation (1) on page 909, we can note that the earnings per share figure has dropped by 34 cents. Although the impact of full dilution is relatively small in this case, it can be very significant in situations where large amounts of convertible securities are present.

Earnings per Share and Profitability

Earnings per share can be a misleading measure of profitability. To illustrate, assume that Simyar Company has 100,000 shares outstanding over a three-year period. Simyar Company has total assets for 19x1 of $1 million and it is company policy to pay out 50% of its after-tax income as dividends. Note from the following data that earnings per share increased each period. This increase may be misinterpreted as improved operating performance when in fact it is totally attributable to Simyar Company reinvesting 50% of its earnings. Return on investment has actually remained at 10%. For this illustration, it is assumed that ROI is calculated on total assets at the beginning of the year.

Year	Assets	Earnings Available for Common Shareholders	Return on Investment	Earnings per Share
19x1	$1,000,000	$100,000	10%	$1.0000
19x2	1,050,000	105,000	10%	1.0500
19x3	1,102,500	110,250	10%	1.1025

Price-Earnings Ratio

The relationship between the market price of a share and current earnings per share is often quoted in terms of a **price-earnings ratio.** If we assume that the current market price for Brickey Electronics' share is $40 per share, the company's price-earnings ratio would be computed as follows:

$$\frac{\text{Market price per share}}{\text{Earnings per share}} = \text{Price-earnings ratio}$$

$$\frac{\$40}{\$3.26 \text{ [see equation (1)]}} = 12.3 \tag{3}$$

The price-earnings ratio is 12.3; that is, the shares are selling for about 12.3 times its current earnings per share.

The price-earnings ratio is widely used by investors as a general guideline in gauging share values. Investors increase or decrease the price-earnings ratio that they are willing to accept for a share according to how they view its *future prospects.* Companies with ample opportunities for growth generally have high price-earnings ratios, with the opposite being true for companies with limited growth opportunities. The price-earnings ratio is a measure of investor confidence. If investors decided that Brickey Electronics had greater than average growth prospects, then undoubtedly the price of the company's shares would begin to rise. If the price increased to, say, $52 per share, then the price-earnings ratio would rise to 16 ($52 price ÷ $3.26 EPS = 16.0 P-E ratio).

Dividend Payout and Yield Ratios

Investors hold shares of one company in preference to shares of another company because they anticipate that the first will provide them with a more attractive return. The return sought isn't always dividends. Many investors prefer not to receive dividends. Instead, they prefer to have the company retain all earnings and reinvest them internally in order to support growth. The shares of companies that adopt this approach, loosely termed *growth stocks,* often enjoy rapid upward movement in market price. Other investors prefer to have a dependable, current source of income through regular dividend payments. Such investors seek out shares with consistent dividend records and payout ratios.

The Dividend Payout Ratio.   The **dividend payout ratio** gauges the portion of current earnings being paid out in dividends. Investors who seek growth in market price would like this ratio to be small, whereas investors who seek dividends prefer it to be large. This ratio is computed by relating dividends per share to earnings per share for common shares:

$$\frac{\text{Dividends per share}}{\text{Earnings per share}} = \text{Dividend payout ratio}$$

For Brickey Electronics, the dividend payout ratio for 19x2 is computed as follows:

$$\frac{\$1.20 \text{ (see Exhibit 17–2)}}{\$3.26 \text{ [see equation (1)]}} = 36.8\% \tag{4}$$

There is no such thing as a "right" payout ratio, even though it should be noted that the ratio tends to be somewhat the same for the bulk of firms within a particular industry. Industries with ample opportunities for growth at high rates of return on assets tend to have low payout ratios, whereas payout ratios tend to be high in industries with limited reinvestment opportunities.

The Dividend Yield Ratio.   The **dividend yield ratio** is obtained by dividing the current dividends per share by the current market price per share:

$$\frac{\text{Dividends per share}}{\text{Market price per share}} = \text{Dividend yield ratio}$$

If we continue the assumption of a market price of \$40 per share for Brickey Electronics, the dividend yield is computed as follows:

$$\frac{\$1.20}{\$40} = 3.0\% \tag{5}$$

Note that we used the current market price of the shares rather than the price the investor paid for the shares initially (which might be above or below the current market price). By using current market price, we recognize the opportunity cost of the investment in terms of its yield. That is, this is the yield that would be lost or sacrificed if the investor sold the shares for \$40 and bought a new security in its place.

It should be noted, however, that the dividend yield is only a partial measure of an investor's return. The total return consists of the dividend yield plus a capital gains yield from holding the shares during the period. For example, if the price of the shares jumped from \$32 at the beginning of the year to the current \$40 the capital gains yield would be (\$40 − \$32)/\$32 to yield 25%. The total return would be the sum of the dividend yield and the capital gains yield amounting to 28%.

Return on Total Assets

Managers have both *financing* and *operating* responsibilities. Financing responsibilities relate to how one *obtains* the funds needed to provide for the assets in an organization. Operating responsibilities relate to how one *uses* the assets once they have been obtained. Proper discharge of both responsibilities is vital to a well-managed firm. However, care must be taken not to confuse or mix the two when assessing the performance of a manager. That is, whether funds have been obtained from creditors or from shareholders should not be allowed to influence one's assessment of *how well* the assets have been employed since being received by the firm.

The **return on total assets** is a measure of how well assets have been employed; that is, it is a measure of operating performance. The formula is as follows:

$$\frac{\text{Net income} + [\text{Interest expense} \times (1 - \text{Tax rate})]}{\text{Average total assets}} = \text{Return on total assets}$$

Adding interest expense back to net income results in an adjusted earnings figure that shows what earnings would have been if the assets had been acquired solely by selling shares. With this adjustment, the return on total assets can be compared for companies with differing amounts of debt or for a single company that changes its mix of debt and equity over time. Thus, the measurement of how well the assets have been employed is not influenced by how the assets were financed. Notice that before being added back to net income, the interest expense must be placed on an after-tax basis by multiplying the interest figure by the formula (1 – Tax rate).

In other words, the rate of return on total assets measures a firm's profitability before payments are made to those who supply capital. Return on total assets is a function of returns to creditors, preferred shareholders, and common shareholders as in the following schematic:

$$\text{Return on total assets} = \int \left(\begin{array}{ccc} \text{Return to} & \text{Return to preferred} & \text{Return to common} \\ \text{creditors,} & \text{shareholders,} & \text{shareholders *} \end{array} \right)$$

*Before extraordinary items.

Each dollar of return can be attributed to those who provide funds to the firm. Returns to suppliers of capital represent costs to the firm. Creditors receive interest, preferred shareholders receive dividends, and any residual return accrues to the common shareholders. Some sources of capital have no explicit costs. This is the case with such liabilities as accounts payable and salaries payable. These points can be summarized as follows:

$$\text{Return on total assets is influenced by} = \left(\frac{\text{After-tax interest expense}}{\text{Average total liability}}, \frac{\text{Preferred dividends}}{\text{Average equity of preferred shareholders}}, \frac{\text{Net income less preferred dividends}}{\text{Average equity of common shareholders}} \right)$$

The return on total assets for Brickey Electronics for 19x2 would be computed as follows (from Exhibits 17–1 and 17–2):

Net income	$ 1,750,000
Add back interest expense: $640,000 × (1 – 0.30)	448,000
Total	$ 2,198,000 (a)
Assets, beginning of year	$28,970,000
Assets, end of year	31,500,000
Total	$60,470,000
Average total assets: $60,470,000 ÷ 2.	$30,235,000 (b)
Return on total assets, (a) ÷ (b).	7.3% (6)

Brickey Electronics has earned a return of 7.3% on average assets employed over the last year.

Return on Common Shareholders' Equity

One of the primary reasons for operating a corporation is to generate income for the benefit of the common shareholders. One measure of a company's success in this regard is the **return on common shareholders' equity.** The formula is as follows:

$$\frac{\text{Net income} - \text{Preferred dividends}}{\begin{array}{c} \text{Average common shareholders'equity} \\ \text{(Average total shareholders'equity} \\ -\text{Average preferred shares)} \end{array}} = \begin{array}{c} \text{Return on common} \\ \text{shareholders'equity} \end{array}$$

For Brickey Electronics, the return on common shareholders' equity is 11.3% for 19x2, as shown below:

Net income	$ 1,750,000	
Deduct preferred dividends.............................	120,000	
Net income remaining for common shareholders.............	$ 1,630,000	(a)
Average shareholders' equity	$16,485,000*	
Deduct average preferred shares........................	2,000,000†	
Average common shareholders' equity....................	$14,485,000	(b)
Return on common shareholders' equity, (a) ÷ (b)............	11.3%	(7)

*$15,970,000 + $17,000,000 = $32,970,000; $32,970,000 ÷ 2 = $16,485,000.

†$2,000,000 + $2,000,000 = $4,000,000; $4,000,000 ÷ 2 = $2,000,000.

Compare the return on common shareholders' equity above (11.3%) with the return on total assets computed in the preceding section (7.3%). Why is the return on common shareholders' equity so much higher? The answer lies in the principle of *financial leverage* (sometimes called trading on the equity). Financial leverage is discussed in the following paragraphs.

Financial Leverage

OBJECTIVE 5

Explain what is meant by the term *financial leverage,* and show how financial leverage is measured

Financial leverage (often called *leverage* for short) involves acquiring assets with funds that have been obtained from creditors or from preferred shareholders at a fixed rate of return. If the assets in which the funds are invested are able to earn a rate of return *greater* than the fixed rate of return required by the funds' suppliers, then we have **positive financial leverage** and the common shareholders benefit.

For example, suppose that Regina Cablevision is able to earn an after-tax return of 12% on its broadcasting assets. If the company can borrow from creditors at a 10% interest rate in order to expand its assets, then the common shareholders can benefit from positive leverage. The borrowed funds invested in the business will earn an after-tax return of 12%, but the after-tax interest cost of the borrowed funds will be only 7% [10% interest rate × (1 − 0.30) = 7%]. The difference will go to the common shareholders.

We can see this concept in operation in the case of Brickey Electronics. Notice from Exhibit 17–1 that the company's bonds payable bear a fixed interest rate of 8%. The after-tax interest cost of these bonds is only 5.6% [8% interest rate × (1 − 0.30) = 5.6%]. The company's assets (which would contain the proceeds from the original sale of these bonds) are generating an after-tax return of 7.3%, as we computed earlier. Since this return on assets is greater than the after-tax interest cost of the bonds, leverage is positive, and the difference accrues to the benefit of the common shareholders. This explains in part why the return on common shareholders' equity (11.3%) is greater than the return on total assets (7.3%).

Sources of Financial Leverage.   Financial leverage can be obtained from several sources. One source is long-term debt, such as bonds payable or notes payable. Two additional sources are current liabilities and preferred shares. Current liabilities are always a source of positive leverage in that funds are provided for use in a company with no interest return required by the short-term creditors involved. For example, when a company acquires inventory from a supplier on account, the inventory is available for use in the business, yet the supplier requires no interest return on the amount owed.

Preferred shares can also be a source of positive leverage so long as the dividend payable to the preferred shareholders is less than the rate of return being earned on the total assets employed. In the case of Brickey Electronics, positive leverage is being realized on the preferred shares. Notice from Exhibit 17-1 that the preferred dividend rate is only 6% ($2 million ÷ 20,000 shares = $100; $6 ÷ $100 = 6%), whereas the assets in the company are earning at a rate of 7.3%, as computed earlier. Again, the difference goes to the common shareholders, thereby helping to bolster their return to the 11.3% computed earlier.

To solidify your understanding of leverage refer back to Exhibit 17–3. Note that current creditors provided average assets of $6,000 [($7,000 + $5,000)/2]. Since these assets have no explicit cost but generate a return of 7.3%, this entire percentage accrues to the common shareholders. Bondholders supplied average funds of $7,750 $\left(\dfrac{\$7,500 + \$8,000}{2}\right)$. The after-tax costs of bonds is 5.6%; this leaves an excess return to the common shareholders of 1.7% (7.3 minus 5.6). Similarly, the excess return on funds provided by preferred shareholders is 1.3%. The return on funds provided by the common shareholders is simply 7.3% of the $14,485 average capital that they provided. This brings the total return to common shareholders to $1,653.16, yielding a rate of return on common equity of 11.4%. The 0.1% difference from our earlier calculation is a result of rounding.

Excess return from short-term creditors (7.3% of $6,000)	$438.00
Excess return from bondholders [7.3 – (5.6% × $7,750)]	131.75
Excess return from preferred shareholders [(7.3 – 6) × $2,000]	26.00
Return from common shareholder funds (7.3% of $14,485)	1,057.41
Return accruing to common shareholders	$1,653.16
Return on common shareholders' equity: $1,653/$14,485	11.4%

Unfortunately, leverage is a two-edged sword. If assets are unable to earn a high enough rate to cover the interest costs of debt, or to cover the preferred dividend due to the preferred shareholders, *then the common shareholder suffers.* The reason is that part of the earnings from the assets that the common shareholder has provided to the company will have to make up the deficiency to the long-term creditors or to the preferred shareholders, and the common shareholder is left with a smaller return than would otherwise have been earned. Under these circumstances, we have **negative financial leverage.**

The Impact of Income Taxes.   Debt and preferred shares are not equally efficient in generating positive leverage. The reason is that interest on debt is tax deductible, whereas preferred dividends are not. This usually makes debt a much more effective source of positive leverage than preferred shares.

To illustrate this point, suppose that Tim Hortons is considering three ways of financing a $100 million expansion of its chain of donut shops:

1. $100 million from an issue of common shares.
2. $50 million from an issue of common shares, and $50 million from an issue of preferred shares bearing a dividend rate of 8%.
3. $50 million from an issue of common shares, and $50 million from an issue of bonds bearing an interest rate of 8%.

Assuming that Tim Hortons can earn an additional $15 million each year before interest and taxes as a result of the expansion, the operating results under each of the three alternatives are shown in Exhibit 17–6.

EXHIBIT 17-6

Leverage from
Preferred Shares and
Long-Term Debt

	Alternatives: $100,000,000 Issue of Securities		
	Alternative 1: $100,000,000 Common Shares	Alternative 2: $50,000,000 Common Shares; $50,000,000 Preferred Shares	Alternative 3: $50,000,0000 Common Shares; $50,000,000 Bonds
Earnings before interest and taxes	$ 15,000,000	$15,000,000	$15,000,000
Deduct interest expense (8% × $50,000,000)	—	—	4,000,000
Net income before taxes	15,000,000	15,000,000	11,000,000
Deduct income taxes (30%)	4,500,000	4,500,000	3,300,000
Net income	10,500,000	10,500,000	7,700,000
Deduct preferred dividends (8% × $50,000,000)	—	4,000,000	—
Net income remaining for common (a).	$ 10,500,000	$ 6,500,000	$ 7,700,000
Common shareholders' equity (b)	$100,000,000	$50,000,000	$50,000,000
Return on common shareholders' equity, (a) ÷ (b)	10.5%	13.0%	15.4%

If the entire $100 million is raised from an issue of common share, then the return to the common shareholders will be only 10.5%, as shown under alternative 1 in the exhibit. If half of the funds are raised from an issue of preferred shares, then the return to the common shareholders increases to 13%, due to the positive effects of leverage. However, if half of the funds are raised from an issue of bonds, then the return to the common shareholders jumps to 15.4%, as shown under alternative 3. Thus, long-term debt is much more efficient in generating positive leverage than is preferred shares. The reason is that the interest expense on long-term debt is tax deductible, whereas the dividends on preferred shares are not.

The Desirability of Leverage. Because of leverage, having some debt in the capital structure can substantially benefit the common shareholder. For this reason, most companies today try to maintain a certain level of debt—a level at least equal to that which is considered to be "normal" within the industry. Some companies have no debt, but in view of the benefits that can be gained from positive leverage, the possibility always exists that such a company is shortchanging its shareholders. As a practical matter, many companies, such as commercial banks and other financial institutions, rely heavily on leverage to provide an attractive return on their common shares.

Book Value per Share

Another statistic frequently used in attempting to assess the well-being of the common shareholder is book value per share. The **book value per share** measures the amount that would be distributed to holders of each common share if all assets were sold at their balance sheet carrying amounts and if all creditors were paid off. Thus, book value per share is based entirely on historical costs. The formula for computing it is as follows:

$$\frac{\text{Common shareholders' equity (Total shareholders' equity} - \text{Preferred shares)}}{\text{Number of common shares outstanding}} = \text{Book value per share}$$

Total shareholders' equity (see Exhibit 17–1)	$17,000,000
Deduct preferred shares (see Exhibit 17–1)	2,000,000
Common shareholders' equity	$15,000,000

The book value per share of Brickey Electronics' common shares is computed as follows:

$$\frac{\$15,000,000}{500,000 \text{ shares}} = \$30 \tag{8}$$

If this book value is compared with the $40 market value of Brickey Electronics shares, then the shares appear to be somewhat overpriced. However, as we discussed earlier, market prices reflect expectations about future earnings and dividends, whereas book value largely reflects the results of events that occurred in the past. Ordinarily, the market value of a share exceeds its book value. For example, at the end of 1996, the market value of George Weston Ltd. common shares was $66.85 while its book value was $35.62 and Coca-Cola sells at a multiple of 19.

FOCUS ON CURRENT PRACTICE

McDonald's Corporation provides an interesting illustration of the use of financial ratios. Data for the 1992 fiscal year appear below:

Net income	$ 958.6 million
Interest expense	373.6 million
Tax rate	33.8%
Average total assets	$11,515.2 million
Preferred share dividends	14.7 million
Average common shareholders' equity	4,874.6 million
Common share dividends—per share	$0.39
Earnings per share	2.60
Market price per share—end of year	48.75
Book value per share	14.77

Some key financial ratios are computed below:

$$\frac{\text{Return on}}{\text{total assets}} = \frac{\$958.6 + [\$373.6 \times (1 - .338)]}{\$11,515.2} = 10.5\%$$

$$\frac{\text{Return on common}}{\text{shareholders' equity}} = \frac{\$958.6 - \$14.7}{\$4,874.6} = 19.4\%$$

$$\text{Dividend payout ratio} = \frac{\$0.39}{\$2.60} = 15\%$$

$$\text{Dividend yield ratio} = \frac{\$0.39}{\$48.75} = 0.8\%$$

The return on common shareholders' equity of 19.4% is higher than the return on total assets of 10.5%, and therefore the company has positive financial leverage. (About half of the company's financing is provided by creditors; the rest is provided by common and preferred shareholders.) According to the company's annual report, "Given McDonald's high return on equity and assets, management believes it is prudent to reinvest a significant portion of earnings back into the business. Accordingly, the common share [dividend] yield is relatively modest." Indeed, only 15% of earnings are paid out in dividends. In relation to the share price, this is a dividend yield of less than 1%. Finally, note that the market value per share is over three times as large as the book value per share. This premium over book value reflects the market's perception that McDonald's earnings will continue to grow in the future.

The book value per common share probably finds its greatest application in situations where large amounts of liquid assets are being held in anticipation of liquidation. Occasionally some use is also made of book value per share in attempting to set a price on the shares of closely held corporations.

RATIO ANALYSIS—THE SHORT-TERM CREDITOR

OBJECTIVE 6
Identify the ratios used to measure the well-being of the short-term creditor, and state each ratio's formula and interpretation.

Short-term creditors, such as suppliers, want to be repaid on time. Therefore, they focus on the company's cash flows and on its working capital, since these are the company's primary sources of cash in the short run.

Working Capital

The excess of current assets over current liabilities is known as **working capital.** The working capital for Brickey Electronics is computed below:

Current assets – Current liabilities = Working capital		
	19x2	**19x1**
Current assets	$15,500,000	$16,470,000
Current liabilities	7,000,000	5,000,000
Working capital.	$8,500,000	$11,470,000

(9)

The amount of working capital available to a firm is of considerable interest to short-term creditors, *since it represents assets financed from long-term capital sources that do not require near-term repayment.* Therefore, the greater the working capital, the greater is the cushion of protection available to short-term creditors and the greater is the assurance that short-term debts will be paid when due.

Although it is always comforting to short-term creditors to see a large working capital balance, a large balance by itself is no assurance that debts will be paid when due. Rather than being a sign of strength, a large working capital balance may simply mean that obsolete inventory is being accumulated. Therefore, to put the working capital figure into proper perspective, it must be supplemented with other analytical work. The following four ratios (the current ratio, the acid-test ratio, the accounts receivable turnover, and the inventory turnover) should all be used in connection with an analysis of working capital.

Current Ratio

The elements involved in the computation of working capital are frequently expressed in ratio form. A company's current assets divided by its current liabilities is known as the **current ratio:**

$$\frac{\text{Current assets}}{\text{Current liabilities}} = \text{Current ratio}$$

For Brickey Electronics, the current ratios for 19x1 and 19x2 would be computed as follows:

19x2	**19x1**
$\frac{\$15,000,000}{\$7,000,000} = 2.21 \text{ to } 1$	$\frac{\$16,470,000}{\$5,000,000} = 3.29 \text{ to } 1$

(10)

Although widely regarded as a measure of short-term debt-paying ability, the current ratio must be interpreted with great care. A *declining* ratio, as above, might be a sign of a deteriorating financial condition. On the other hand, it might be the result of a paring of obsolete inventories or other stagnant current assets. An *improving* ratio might be the result of an unwise stockpiling of inventory, or it might indicate an improving financial situation. In short, the current ratio is useful, but tricky to interpret. To avoid a blunder, the analyst must take a hard look at the individual assets and liabilities involved.

The general rule of thumb calls for a current ratio of 2 to 1. This rule, of course, is subject to many exceptions, depending on the industry and the firm involved. Some industries can operate quite successfully on a current ratio of slightly over 1 to 1. The adequacy of a current ratio depends heavily on the *composition* of the assets involved. For example, as we see in the table on the next page, both Worthington Corporation and Greystone, Inc., have current ratios of 2 to 1. However, they are not in comparable financial condition. Greystone is likely to have difficulty meeting its current financial obligations, since almost all of its current assets consist of inventory rather than more liquid assets such as cash and accounts receivable.

	Worthington Corporation	Greystone, Inc.
Current assets:		
Cash..........................	$ 25,000	$ 2,000
Accounts receivable, net..........	60,000	8,000
Inventory......................	85,000	160,000
Prepaid expenses................	5,000	5,000
Total current assets	$175,000	$175,000 (a)
Current liabilities	$ 87,500	$ 87,500 (b)
Current ratio, (a) ÷ (b).............	2 to 1	2 to 1

Acid-Test (Quick) Ratio

The **acid-test (quick) ratio** is a much more rigorous test of a company's ability to meet its short-term debts. Inventories and prepaid expenses are excluded from total current assets, leaving only the more liquid (or "quick") assets to be divided by current liabilities.

$$\frac{\text{Cash} + \text{Marketable securities} + \text{Current receivables *}}{\text{Current liabilities}} = \text{Acid-test ratio}$$

*Current receivables include both accounts receivable and any short-term notes receivable.

The acid-test ratio is designed to measure how well a company can meet its obligations without having to liquidate or depend too heavily on its inventory. Since inventory is not an immediate source of cash and may not even be salable in times of economic stress, it is generally felt that to be properly protected each dollar of liabilities should be backed by at least $1 of quick assets. Thus, an acid-test ratio of 1 to 1 is broadly viewed as being adequate in many firms.

The acid-test ratios for Brickey Electronics for 19x1 and 19x2 are computed below:

	19x2	19x1	
Cash (see Exhibit 17–1)	$1,200,000	$2,350,000	
Accounts receivable (see Exhibit 17–1)	6,000,000	4,000,000	
Total quick assets	$7,200,000	$6,350,000	(a)
Current liabilities (see Exhibit 17–1)	$7,000,000	$5,000,000	(b)
Acid-test ratio, (a) ÷ (b)	1.03 to 1	1.27 to 1	(11)

Although Brickey Electronics has an acid-test ratio for 19x2 that is within the acceptable range, an analyst might be concerned about several disquieting trends revealed in the company's balance sheet. Notice in Exhibit 17–1 that short-term debts are rising, while the cash position seems to be deteriorating. Perhaps the weakened cash position is a result of the greatly expanded volume of accounts receivable. One wonders why the accounts receivable have been allowed to increase so rapidly in so brief a time.

In short, as with the current ratio, the acid-test ratio should be interpreted with one eye on its basic components.

Accounts Receivable Turnover

The **accounts receivable turnover** is a rough measure of how many times a company's accounts receivable have been turned into cash during the year. It is frequently used in conjunction with an analysis of working capital, since a smooth flow from accounts receivable into cash is an important indicator of the "quality" of a company's working capital and is critical to its ability to operate. The accounts receivable turnover is computed by dividing sales on account (i.e., credit sales) by the average accounts receivable balance for the year.

$$\frac{\text{Sales on account}}{\text{Average accounts receivable balance}} = \text{Accounts receivable turnover}$$

Assuming that all sales for the year were on account, the accounts receivable turnover for Brickey Electronics for 19x2 would be computed as follows:

$$\frac{\text{Sales on account}}{\text{Average accounts receivable balance}} = \frac{\$52,000,000}{\$5,000,000*} = 10.4 \text{ times} \tag{12}$$

*4,000,000 + $6,000,000 = $10,000,000; $10,000,000 ÷ 2 = $5,000,000 average

The turnover figure can then be divided into 365 to determine the average number of days being taken to collect an account (known as the **average collection period**).

$$\frac{365 \text{ days}}{\text{Accounts receivable turnover}} = \text{Average collection period}$$

The average collection period for Brickey Electronics for 19x2 is computed as follows:

$$\frac{365}{10.4 \text{ times}} = 35 \text{ days} \tag{13}$$

This simply means that on average it takes 35 days to collect on a credit sale. Whether the average of 35 days taken to collect an account is good or bad depends on the credit terms Brickey Electronics is offering its customers. If the credit terms are 30 days, then a 35-day average collection period would usually be viewed as very good. Most customers will tend to withhold payment for as long as the credit terms will allow and may even go over a few days. This factor, added to ever-present problems with a few slow-paying customers, can cause the average collection period to exceed normal credit terms by a week or so and should not cause great alarm.

On the other hand, if the company's credit terms are 10 days, then a 35-day average collection period may cause some concern. The long collection period may be a result of the presence of many old accounts of doubtful collectibility, or it may be a result of poor day-to-day credit management. The firm may be making sales with inadequate credit checks on customers, or perhaps no follow-ups are being made on slow accounts.

Inventory Turnover

The **inventory turnover ratio** measures how many times a company's inventory has been sold and replaced during the year. It is computed by dividing the cost of goods sold by the average level of inventory on hand:

$$\frac{\text{Cost of goods sold}}{\text{Average inventory balance}} = \text{Inventory turnover}$$

The average inventory figure is computed by taking the average of the beginning and ending inventory figures. Since Brickey Electronics has a beginning inventory figure of $10,000,000 and an ending inventory figure of $8,000,000, its average inventory for the year would be $9,000,000. The company's inventory turnover for 19x2 would be computed as follows:

$$\frac{\text{Cost of goods sold}}{\text{Average inventory balance}} = \frac{\$36,000,000}{\$9,000,000} = 4 \text{ times} \tag{14}$$

The number of days being taken to sell the entire inventory one time (called the **average sale period**) can be computed by dividing 365 by the inventory turnover figure:

$$\frac{365 \text{ days}}{\text{Inventory turnover}} = \text{Average sale period}$$

$$\frac{365}{4 \text{ times}} = 91\,\tfrac{1}{4} \text{ days} \tag{15}$$

The average sale period varies from industry to industry. Grocery stores tend to turn their inventory over very quickly, perhaps as often as every 12 to 15 days. On the other hand, jewellery stores tend to turn their inventory over very slowly, perhaps only a couple of times each year.

If a firm has a turnover that is much slower than the average for its industry, then there may be obsolete goods on hand, or inventory stocks may be needlessly high. Excessive inventories tie up funds that could be used elsewhere in operations. Managers sometimes argue that they must buy in very large quantities in order to take advantage of the best discounts being offered. But these discounts must be carefully weighed against the added costs of insurance, taxes, financing, and risks of obsolescence and deterioration that result from carrying added inventories.

A below average inventory turnover is a signal that managerial action is needed. By taking action to increase the inventory turnover ratio, working capital tied up in this asset can be released for more productive use. It may be necessary, for example, to install a new inventory control system or develop strategies to increase sales to achieve a faster turnover.

Also, management should carefully examine its financial policy when evaluating the firm's short-term liquidity risk. For example, it is generally wise to finance short-term assets with short-term debt and to finance capital assets with long-term debt. It is usually considered risky to finance capital assets by increasing short-term borrowing unless the capital assets are likely to quickly generate operating cash flows or short-term interest rates are substantially less than long-term rates. There is a long legacy of firms that have violated this basic financial policy only to end in bankruptcy.

Inventory turnover has been increasing in recent years as companies have adopted just-in-time (JIT) methods. Under JIT, inventories are purposely kept low, and thus a company utilizing JIT methods may have a very high inventory turnover as compared to other companies. Indeed, one of the goals of JIT is to increase inventory turnover by systematically reducing the amount of inventory on hand.

Cash Flow Ratios

In analyzing the firm's short-term liquidity risk, the manager may find it useful to refer to the statement of cash flows in conjunction with a firm's balance sheet and income statement to compute various ratios. The ratio of cash flow from operations (CFO) to current liabilities can provide valuable clues to management on how best to finance business operations. This ratio is an indicator of the amount of cash the firm has derived from operations after meeting current debt and working capital obligations. In calculating this ratio it is best to use cash flow from continuing operations so as not to be mislead by unusual or nonrecurring items. A ratio of .40 or more is considered good for a manufacturing or retailing firm.[2]

In addition to short-term ratio analysis, a manager may also find it useful to do a trend analysis comparing net income over several periods with cash flow from operations. To reduce the effect of noncash items, such as depreciation and accruals of revenue and expenses, one could use the following ratio:

$$\frac{\text{CFO before interest and taxes}}{\text{Operating income before interest,}}$$
$$\text{taxes and depreciation}$$

Any evidence of the CFO and operating income not moving in parallel could signal trouble and the cause should be investigated in time to take corrective action.

Other cash flow ratios may also be of interest. In assessing the quality of earnings, for example, insight can be gained by dividing cash flow from operations by sales. A high ratio signals high-quality earnings. Cash flow from operations is used in lieu of operating income because the latter is more subject to judgment regarding cost allocation and revenue recognition. Another indicator of quality of earnings is cash flow from operations divided by operating income. Because of noncash expenses such as depreciation and noncash revenues such as credit sales or the recognition of previously deferred revenue, a substantial difference may exist between CFO and operating income.

In addition to assessing quality of earnings, CFO can also be used to compute other ratios of interest to management. A manager may be interested, for example, in determining the firm's ability to make capital expenditures from internally generated funds. A helpful ratio is CFO divided by capital asset acquisitions. Dividends are usually deducted from CFO under the assumption that current dividends will not be cut.

$$\frac{\text{CFO} - \text{Dividends}}{\text{Cash paid for capital assets}}$$

Although it is likely that a firm will seek long-run sources of financing for major acquisitions, CFO has information content. CFO can be interpreted as an indicator of the firm's ability to service debt. However, this ratio does have limitations as do cash flow ratios generally. Because managers often have considerable discretion regarding capital

---

[2]C. Casey and N. Bartzcak, "Cash Flow—It's Not the Bottom Line," *Harvard Business Review* (July–August), pp. 61–66.

asset decisions, the CFO to capital expenditures ratio can be easily manipulated. One should look for trends and seek explanations for changes in these trends.

Caution should be exercised in the use and interpretation of all cash flow ratios. Cash flow ratios, for example, should not be interpreted as a measure of the firm's ability to distribute cash. This is because cash flow ratios do not include some critical information that has future cash flow effects. Cash flow ratios, for example, do not include provision for asset replacement or for contingencies. When used in conjunction with other ratios, however, cash flow ratios may provide useful insights for managerial decisions.

RATIO ANALYSIS—THE LONG-TERM CREDITOR

OBJECTIVE 7
Identify the ratios used to measure the well-being of the long-term creditor, and state each ratio's formula and interpretation.

The position of long-term creditors differs from that of short-term creditors in that they are concerned with both the near-term *and* the long-term ability of a firm to meet its commitments. They are concerned with the near term since the interest they are entitled to is normally paid on a current basis. They are concerned with the long term from the point of view of the eventual retirement of their holdings.

Since the long-term creditor is usually faced with somewhat greater risks than the short-term creditor, firms are often required to agree to various restrictive covenants, or rules, for the long-term creditor's protection. Examples of such restrictive covenants include the maintenance of minimum working capital levels and restrictions on payment of dividends to common shareholders. Although these restrictive covenants are in widespread use, they must be viewed as a poor second to adequate future *earnings* from the point of view of assessing protection and safety. Creditors do not want to go to court to collect their claims; they would much prefer staking the safety of their claims for interest and eventual repayment of principal on an orderly and consistent flow of funds from operations.

Times Interest Earned Ratio

The most common measure of the ability of a firm's operations to provide protection to the long-term creditor is the **times interest earned ratio.** It is computed by dividing earnings *before* interest expense and income taxes by the yearly interest charges that must be met:

$$\frac{\text{Earnings before interest expense and income taxes (Net operating income)}}{\text{Interest expense}} = \text{Times interest earned}$$

For Brickey Electronics, the times interest earned ratio for 19x2 would be computed as follows:

$$\frac{\$3,140,000}{\$640,000} = 4.9 \text{ times} \tag{16}$$

Earnings before income taxes must be used in the computation, since interest expense deductions come *before* income taxes are computed. Income taxes are secondary to interest payments in that the latter have first claim on earnings. Only those earnings remaining after all interest charges have been provided for are subject to income taxes.

Generally, earnings are viewed as adequate to protect long-term creditors if the times interest earned ratio is 2 or more. Before making a final judgment, however, it would be necessary to look at a firm's long-run *trend* of earnings and evaluate how vulnerable the firm is to cyclical changes in the economy.

Debt-to-Equity Ratio

Long-term creditors are also concerned with keeping a reasonable balance between the portion of assets being provided by creditors and the portion of assets being provided by the shareholders of a firm. This balance is measured by the **debt-to-equity ratio:**

$$\frac{\text{Total liabilities}}{\text{Shareholders' equity}} = \text{Debt-to-equity ratio}$$

	19x2	19x1	
Total liabilities	$14,500,000	$13,000,000	(a)
Shareholders' equity	17,000,000	15,970,000	(b)
Debt-to-equity ratio, (a) ÷ (b)	0.85 to 1	0.81 to 1	(17)

The debt-to-equity ratio indicates the amount of assets being provided by creditors for each dollar of assets being provided by the owners of a company. In 19x1, creditors of Brickey Electronics were providing 81 cents of assets for each $1 of assets being provided by shareholders; the figure increased only slightly to 85 cents by 19x2.

It should come as no surprise that creditors would like the debt-to-equity ratio to be relatively low. The lower the ratio, the greater the amount of assets being provided by the owners of a company and the greater is the buffer of protection to creditors. By contrast, common shareholders would like the ratio to be relatively high, since through leverage common shareholders can benefit from the assets being provided by creditors.

In most industries, norms have developed over the years that serve as guides to firms in their decisions as to the "right" amount of debt to include in the capital structure. Different industries face different risks. For this reason, the level of debt that is appropriate for firms in one industry is not necessarily a guide to the level of debt that is appropriate for firms in a different industry.

Monitoring Productivity

The importance of productivity has taken on a heightened awareness among Canadian business firms. In the manufacturing sector, Canadian firms have not kept pace with U.S. and Japanese competitors. To help reverse this trend, management must alert to new production techniques that result in long-term productivity gains and must make use of measurement methods that help the firm assess its relative position. Long-term productivity gains can result from the early adoption of more efficient production techniques. The development and application of knowledge and new ideas are the primary drivers of productivity. Improved productivity may manifest itself in savings in material, labour, capital and energy costs. Productivity benefits could also include improved quality or more variety, faster cycle time, faster and more efficient production runs and better customer service.

To management, improving productivity can mean obtaining higher profitability and greater assurance of survival in an ever more competitive business environment. The management accountant can play an important role in the assessment of a firm's productivity.

Productivity can be determined as a ratio of some measure of output to some measure of input. Outputs can be expressed in physical units or by dollar values corresponding to the firm's objectives. Inputs consist of materials, labour, overhead, and capital. Corporate annual reports typically provide physical data useful for measuring a company's productivity.

Numerous methods can be used to measure productivity. They range from sophisticated computer models that perform sensitivity analysis on productivity (profitability) as any or all of the elements of the input mix are changed, to the simple utilization of financial data readily available from the firm's existing accounting system. Both performance and productivity of invested capital can be measured by calculating financial ratios that help to relate production inputs to production outputs.

One measurement ratio useful in assessing productivity is the return on investment formula calculated in Chapter 12 as follows:

$$ROI = \frac{\text{Net operating income}}{\text{Sales}} = \frac{\text{Sales}}{\text{Average operating assets}} = \frac{\text{Net operating income}}{\text{Average operating assets}}$$

Other financial ratios which may help assess productivity include such ratios as manufacturing cost to sales, selling cost to sales, and administrative cost to sales. More detailed productivity analysis can be extended, for example, to analyze the individual components of manufacturing cost. Separate ratios can be computed for raw materials, labour, and manufacturing overhead as percentages of the market value of production (manufacturing cost times the ratio of sales to cost of sales).

Other partial measures of productivity can be computed by expressing components of the balance sheet as percentages of sales. The lower the investment for a given level of sales, the more productive is the business in the utilization of its resources. For example, taking the ratio of capital assets to sales, the higher the sales that can be generated for each dollar invested in capital assets, the greater is the productivity of the firm's fixed assets.

Key business leaders believe the commitment to quality is essential to Canadian competitiveness. With the recent removal of tariff protection Canadian business is forced to compete with world standards in terms of cost, quality, and engineering and administrative capability. Companies such as IBM Canada have developed key principles that are critical for success in the new global competitive business environment. One such principle is benchmarking. IBM measures itself against American Express for billing, Imperial Oil for planning and benchmarks its telemarketing against Land's End. Other key principles are customer focus and a commitment to total quality management and continuous improvement. At IBM Canada management believes that strong leadership and communication from senior management is essential to putting these principles into practice and making real improvements in productivity.

The management accountant should be cautious, however, in interpreting productivity ratios. The interrelationships among the various measures of productivity and their ultimate effect on the firm's profitability must be clearly understood. For example, labour may be decreasing as a percentage of manufacturing cost as a result of the purchase of higher-quality raw materials. Careful analysis may reveal that increased productivity of labour was more than offset by the increased cost of the raw materials. Nevertheless, partial productivity ratios can provide information on how output is affected by a given input factor, and changes in these ratios can serve as a signal for investigation that might otherwise go unnoticed.

Productivity analysis is as important to service industries as it is to manufacturing firms. Measures such as the number of customers served per day or the number of transactions completed per week for a given staff complement are examples of productivity measures for service industries.

In spite of the fact that productivity can be measured for any input factor, labour-hours have been the most commonly used input in measuring productivity. Productivity measures derived from labour no doubt can be useful to management in assessing learning curve effects and the motivational level of employees. However, as firms face stiffer competition both nationally and internationally, it seems prudent for management to assess the interrelationships among several productivity measures. This is especially true in the new manufacturing environment where costs are mostly fixed. Even the direct labour that remains can be interpreted as fixed in the sense that employee skills are essential to a firm's success. The amount invested in training and development may be a critical performance measure in this environment in assessing current position and as an indicator of future productivity. Since workers need multiple skills in the high-tech environment, a measure such as percent cross-trained could be a revealing statistic in monitoring productivity. Other useful measures could include number of defects, percentage passing first inspection, work in process turnover, scrap as a percentage of output, and percentage of on-time shipments. What is measured and reported should be determined by the measure's relationship to the firm's operating and strategic goals. For example, if a major objective of a company is to increase market share, measures of delivery and quality improvements may provide useful strategic information. By using **productivity ratios** and new performance indicators to help understand key interrelationships, management may be able to more quickly adopt cost-reducing innovations that lead to improvements in total productivity and to increased long-term profitability.

Ratios and Profit Planning

Profit planning and the projection of budgeted financial statements were discussed in Chapters 7–9. Ratios can be linked to the budgeting process to help project financial statement account balances as well as to assist in estimating cash flows. In addition, using ratios in the forecasting process allows a complete articulation of the balance sheet, income statement, and statement of changes in financial position.

To illustrate, consider the accounts receivable turnover. Recalling that the accounts receivable turnover is equal to sales on account divided by accounts receivable, a simple manipulation of the formula solves for accounts receivable. Note that because we are projecting for the *end* of 19x2, we are not using *average* accounts receivable in the turnover formula.

$$\text{Accounts receivable turnover} = \frac{\text{Sales on account}}{\text{Accounts receivable}}$$

$$\text{Accounts receivable} = \frac{\text{Sales on account}}{\text{Accounts receivable turnover}}$$

Budgeted accounts receivable can, therefore, be estimated by dividing projected sales on account by the accounts receivable turnover. For example, if projected sales for 19x2 for Brickey Electronics, from Exhibit 17–2, is $52,000 and if the accounts receivable turnover is forecasted to be 8.67, then estimated accounts receivable for 19x2 is $6,000 ($52,000/8.67 rounded).

Similarly, inventory for 19x2 can be projected by manipulating the inventory turnover formula. Recall that:

$$\text{Inventory turnover} = \frac{\text{Costs of goods sold}}{\text{Inventory}}$$

Then:

$$\text{Inventory} = \frac{\text{Cost of goods sold}}{\text{Inventory turnover}}$$

If the cost of goods sold is estimated at 69% of sales and the inventory turnover is expected to be 4.5, then inventory is projected to be 7,973 [($52,000 × 0.69)/4.5].

Accounts payable can be projected by linking budgeted purchases to a new ratio called the accounts payable turnover.

$$\text{Accounts payable turnover} = \frac{\text{Purchases on account}}{\text{Accounts payable}}$$

Therefore:

$$\text{Accounts payable} = \frac{\text{Purchases on account}}{\text{Accounts payable turnover}}$$

However, because purchases on account is not disclosed, it too must be estimated. A convenient way to project purchases is through the algebraic manipulation of the cost of goods sold (CGS) formula.

$$\text{Beginning inventory} + \text{Purchases} - \text{Ending inventory} = \text{CGS}$$

Therefore:

$$\text{Purchases} = \text{CGS} - \text{Beginning inventory} + \text{Ending inventory}$$
$$= \$35,880 - \$10,000 + \$7,973$$
$$= \$33,853$$

If 5.8 times is the accounts payable turnover, then accounts payable is projected to equal $5,837 ($33,854/5.8).

A full integration of the sales forecast for 19x2 is presented in Exhibit 17–7, which incorporates the following additional assumptions. Prepaid expenses are projected to be $500 at December 31, 19x2. The Land account balance is expected not to change, and buildings and equipment are forecasted at $12,000 net of depreciation. The expected balance of accrued payables is $900; $500 will be used to retire bonds and contributed capital accounts are not expected to change. Where amounts in Exhibit 17–7 differ with corresponding items in Exhibits 17–1 and 17–2, it is a result of rounding.

EXHIBIT 17-7

Estimated Income Statement*

Sales revenue (given).	$52,000
Cost of goods sold	35,880
Gross margin on sales	16,120
Operating expenses:	
Selling expenses (13.5%).	7,000
Administrative expenses (11.2%)	5,860
Total operating expenses	12,860
Net operating income.	3,260
Interest expense (1.2%)	640
Net income before taxes	2,620
Income tax (30%)	786
Net income.	$ 1,834

EXHIBIT 17-7

(concluded)

Estimated Statement of Changes in Financial Position

Operating activities:

Net income.	$ 1,834
Increase in accounts receivable (52,000/8.67–4,000)	(1,998)
Decrease in inventory (35,880/4.5–10,000).	2,026
Increase in prepaid expenses (given).	(300)
Depreciation expense (given)	1,500
Increase in accounts payable (33,853/5.8–4,000.	1,837
Increase in accrued payables (900 given – 400)	500
Cash flow from operations.	$ 5,399

Financing activities:

Retired bonds (given).	(500)
Paid dividends (given)	(800)

Investing activities:

Purchased equipment (given).		(5,000)
Net change in cash and cash equivalents		$ (901)
Cash balance 19x1.	$2,270	
Less: Short-term note 19x1	600	
Cash and cash equivalents		$ 1,670
Balance of cash and cash equivalents		$ 769

Estimated Balance Sheet, December 31, 19x2

Assets

Current Assets:

Cash and cash equivalents	$ 769
Accounts receivable (52,000 ÷ 8.67).	5,998
Inventory (35,880 ÷ 4.5)	7,973
Prepaid expenses	500
Total.	$15,240

Capital assets:

Land.	4,000
Buildings and equipment, net	12,000
Total assets.	$31,240

Liabilities

Current liabilities:

Accounts payable (33,853 ÷ 5.8).	$ 5,837
Accrued payables (given)	900
Total.	6,737

Long-term liabilities:

Bonds payable, 8% (8,000 – 500)	7,500
Total.	$14,237

Shareholders' Equity

Preferred shares, $100 liquidation value 6%.	$ 2,000
Common shares	6,000
Contributed surplus	1,000
Total contributed capital	9,000
Retained earnings (6,970 + 1,834 – 800 given).	8,004
Total shareholders' equity	17,004
Total liabilities and shareholders' equity	$31,241

*Assumes depreciation of $1,500 is included in selling and administrative expenses.

SUMMARY OF RATIOS AND SOURCES OF COMPARATIVE RATIO DATA

As an aid to the reader, Exhibit 17–8 contains a summary of the ratios discussed in this chapter. Included in the exhibit are the formula for each ratio and a summary comment on each ratio's significance to the manager.

EXHIBIT 17–8   Summary of Ratios

Ratio	Formula	Significance
Cash flow from operations to current liabilities	CFO ÷ CL	Shows the amount of cash derived from operations after meeting short-term obligations.
Cash flow from operation to operating income	CFO before interest and taxes ÷ Operating income before interest, taxes, and depreciation	Shows the relationship of CFO to operating income. Changes in the pattern over time signal need for management investigation.
Cash flow from operations to sales	CFO ÷ Sales	Helps assess the quality of a firm's earnings.
Cash flow from operations to operating income	CFO ÷ Operating income	Used as a measure of the quality of a firm's income before operations.
Cash flow from operations to capital asset acquisitions	CFO – Dividends ÷ Cash paid for capital assets	Shows the ability of the firm to assume capital expenditures from internally generated funds.
Earnings per share (of common stock)	(Net income – Preferred dividends) ÷ Number of common shares outstanding	Tends to have an effect on the market price per share, as reflected in the price-earnings ratio.
Fully diluted earnings pr share	Net income ÷ (The average number of common shares outstanding + Average number of common shares issued on the assumed conversion of convertible securities)	Shows the potential effect on earnings per share of converting convertible securities into common shares.
Price-earnings ratio	Market price per share ÷ Earnings per share	An index of whether a share is relatively cheap or relatively expensive and a measure of investor confidence.
Dividend payout ratio	Dividends per share ÷ Earnings per share	An index showing whether a company pays out most of its earnings in dividends or reinvests the earnings internally.
Dividend yield ratio	Dividends per share ÷ Market price per share	Shows the dividend return being provided by a share, which can be compared to the return being provided by other shares.
Return on total assets	Net income + [Interest expense × (1 – Tax rate)] ÷ Average total assets	Measure of how well assets have been employed by management.
Return on common shareholders' equity	(Net income – Preferred dividends) ÷ Average common shareholders' equity	When compared to the return on total assets, measures the extent to which financial leverage is working for or against common shareholders.
Book value per share	Common shareholders' equity ÷ Number of common shares outstanding	Measures the amount that would be distributed to holders of common stock if all assets were sold at their balance sheet carrying amounts and if all creditors were paid off.
Working capital	Current assets – Current liabilities	Represents current assets financed from long-term capital sources that do not require near-tern repayment.
Current ratio	Current assets ÷ Current liabilities	Test of short-term debt-paying ability
Acid-test (quick) ratio	(Cash + Marketable securities + Current receivables) ÷ Current liabilities	Test of short-term debt-paying ability without having to rely on inventory.

EXHIBIT 17-8 *(concluded)*

Ratio	Formula	Significance
Accounts receivable turnover	Sales on account ÷ Average accounts receivable balance	Measure of how many times a company's accounts receivable have been turned into cash during the year.
Average collection period (age of receivables)	365 days + Accounts receivable turnover	Measure of the average number of days taken to collect an account receivable.
Inventory turnover	Cost of goods sold + Average inventory balance	Measure of how many times a company's inventory has been sold during the year.
Average sale period (turnover in days)	365 days ÷ Inventory turnover	Measure of the average number of days taken to sell the inventory one time.
Times interest earned	Earnings before interest expense and income taxes + Interest expense	Measure of the likelihood that creditors will continue to receive their interest payments.
Debt-to-equity ratio	Total liabilities ÷ Shareholders' equity	Measure of the amount of assets being provided by creditors for each dollar of assets being provided by the shareholders.

Exhibit 17–9 contains a listing of published sources that provide comparative ratio data organized by industry. These sources are used extensively by managers, investors, and analysts in doing comparative analyses and in attempting to assess the well-being of companies.

As a final caution, recall that judgment must be exercised in interpreting variations from industry benchmarks. Managerial evaluation of a ratio hinges very much on how such information will be used. For example, if the intent is to approach a creditor for a loan, then a liquidity ratio which is higher than its industry benchmark would be desirable. On the other hand, if an evaluation is being made of how well a firm is managing its working capital, this high liquidity ratio may signal that current assets and current liabilities are not being well managed.

EXHIBIT 17-9

Published Sources of Financial Ratios

Source	Content
Canadian Statistics	
Industrial Corporations, Financial Statistics	Financial statements of different sectors.
Financial Institutions, Financial Statistics	Financial statements for financial sectors.
Corporate Financial Statistics	Financial statements of different stores.
Corporation Taxation Statistics	Taxable income and taxes payable by Canadian corporations
Dun & Bradstreet's Canadian Key Directory	Business profile on top 3% of Canadian companies.
Dun & Bradstreet's Key Business Ratios	Ratio analysis of top 3% of Canadian companies.
Financial Post's Corporation Service	Individual companies' financial statements.
Financial Post's Dividend Record	Record of dividends.
Financial Post's "500"	Largest 500 companies, by sales, in Canada.
Financial Post's "Surveys of . . ."	Performance of industry sectors.
Moody's Handbook of Common Stock	Canadian companies on the New York Stock Exchange, dividend and share performance.
Moody's Bond Record	Performance of corporate, convertible, government, and municipal bonds.
Moody's Dividend Record	List of dividends.
Toronto Stock Exchange *TSE Review*	Stock market activity of the Toronto Stock Exchange.
Blue Book of Canadian Business	Survey of individual companies.

(continued)

EXHIBIT 17-9

(concluded)

Federal Publications

Federal Corporation Index	Annual reports of private companies.
Bank of Canada *Annual Report*	Canada's balance of payments, bank operations.
Bank of Canada *Review*	Monetary, banking, and other financial statistics.

Other

Consumer and Corporate Affairs *Annual Report*	Funding of consumer groups, patents, trademarks.
Consumer and Corporate Affairs *Canada Corporations Bulletin*	Statistical data on Canadian corporations.
Consumer and Corporate Affairs *Insolvency Bulletin*	Statistics on all bankruptcies.
Finance Canada Economic Review	Reviews of economic developments in Canada, main economic indicators.
Industry, Trade and Commerce *Small Business in Canada*	Statistical profile of the small business sector.
Insurance Canada *List of Securities*	Market value of all securities owned by Canadian insurance companies.

SUMMARY

The data contained in financial statements represent a quantitative summary of a firm's operations and activities. Someone who is skillful at analyzing these statements can learn much about a company's strengths, weaknesses, emerging problems, operating efficiency, profitability, and so forth.

Starbucks Coffee Company has experienced phenomenal growth in recent years. One source of its success has been its ability to exploit financial leverage.

Many techniques are available to analyze financial statements and to assess the direction and importance of trends and changes. In this chapter, we have discussed three such analytical techniques—dollar and percentage changes in statements, common-size statements, and ratio analysis. The reader should refer to Exhibit 17–7 for a detailed listing of the ratios that we have discussed. This listing also contains a brief statement as to the significance of each ratio.

REVIEW PROBLEM: SELECTED RATIOS AND FINANCIAL LEVERAGE

Starbucks Coffee Company is a leading retailer and roaster of specialty coffee in North America with over 250 stores in 10 different markets. Data from recent year-end financial statements are given below:

STARBUCKS COFFEE COMPANY
Comparative Balance Sheet
October 3, 19x2, and September 27, 19x1
(dollars in thousands)

	Oct. 3, 19x2	Sept. 27, 19x1
Assets		
Current assets:		
Cash	$ 34,496	$37,740
Accounts receivable, net	2,862	1,571
Inventory	24,247	11,720
Other current assets	4,626	2,138
Total current assets	66,231	53,169
Investment in marketable debt securities	56,918	–0–
Capital assets, net	65,753	33,568
Other assets	4,069	1,129
Total assets	$192,971	$87,866
Liabilities and Shareholders' Equity		
Current liabilities:		
Accounts payable	$ 5,650	$ 4,012
Accrued payables	12,524	3,986
Other current liabilities	6,224	4,580
Total current liabilities	24,398	12,578
Long-term liabilities:		
Bonds payable	80,500	–0–
Total liabilities	104,898	12,578
Shareholders' equity:		
Preferred shares	–0–	–0–
Common shares	78,636	73,934
Additional contributed capital	–0–	–0–
Total contributed capital	78,636	73,934
Retained earnings	9,437	1,354
Total shareholders' equity	88,073	75,288
Total liabilities and shareholders' equity	$192,971	$87,866

Note: The bonds payable were sold to creditors in August of 19x2 and carried an interest rate of 4 ½%. Most of the proceeds were temporarily invested by the company in marketable debt securities. The company did not classify this marketable debt as a current asset.

STARBUCKS COFFEE COMPANY
Comparative Income Statement
For the Years Ended October 3, 19x2, and September 27, 19x1
(dollars in thousands)

	19x2	19x1
Sales	$163,477	$93,078
Cost of goods sold	73,572	41,854
Gross margin	89,905	51,224
Operating expenses:		
Store operating expenses	53,263	31,234
General and administrative expenses	12,470	7,706
Other operating expenses	11,197	5,890
Total operating expenses	76,930	44,830
Net operating income	12,975	6,394
Plus interest income	1,680	651
Less interest expense	736	465
Net income before taxes	13,919	6,580
Less income taxes (about 38%)	5,416	2,476
Net income	$ 8,503	$ 4,104

Required

1. Compute the return on total assets.
2. Compute the return on common shareholders' equity.
3. Is Starbucks' financial leverage positive or negative? Explain.
4. Compute the current ratio.
5. Compute the inventory turnover.
6. Compute the average sale period.
7. Compute the debt-to-equity ratio.

Solution to Review Problem

1. Return on total assets:

$$\frac{\text{Net income} + [\text{Interest expense} \times (1 - \text{Tax rate})]}{\text{Average total assets}} = \frac{\text{Return on}}{\text{total assets}}$$

$$\frac{8,503 + [\$736 \times (1 - .38)]}{\frac{1}{2}\,(\$192,971 + \$87,866)} = 6.4\% \text{ (rounded)}$$

2. Return on common shareholders' equity:

$$\frac{\text{Net income} - \text{Preferred dividends}}{\text{Average shareholders' equity}} = \frac{\text{Return on common}}{\text{shareholders' equity}}$$

$$\frac{\$8,503 - \$0}{\frac{1}{2}\,(\$88,073 + \$75,288)} = 10.4\% \text{ (rounded)}$$

3. The company has positive financial leverage, since the return on common shareholders' equity (10.4%) is greater than the return on total assets (6.4%). The positive financial leverage was obtained from current liabilities and the bonds payable. The interest rate on the bonds is very low and is substantially less than the return on total assets.

4. Current ratio:

$$\frac{\text{Current assets}}{\text{Current liabilities}} = \text{Current ratio}$$

$$\frac{\$66,231}{\$24,398} = 2.71 \text{ (rounded)}$$

Note that the current ratio would have been even larger if the company had classified its marketable debt securities as a current asset.

5. Inventory turnover:

$$\frac{\text{Cost of goods sold}}{\text{Average inventory balance}} = \text{Inventory turnover}$$

$$\frac{\$73,572}{\frac{1}{2}\,(\$24,247 + \$11,720)} = 4.09 \text{ (rounded)}$$

6. Average sale period:

$$\frac{365 \text{ days}}{\text{Inventory turnover}} = \text{Average sale period}$$

$$\frac{365 \text{ days}}{4.09} = 89 \text{ days (rounded)}$$

7. Debt-to-equity ratio

$$\frac{\text{Total liabilities}}{\text{Shareholders' equity}} = \text{Debt-to-equity ratio}$$

$$\frac{\$104,898}{\$88,073} = 1.19 \text{ (rounded)}$$

KEY TERMS FOR REVIEW

OBJECTIVE 8
Define or explain the key terms listed at the end of the chapter.

(Note: Significance and formulas for all financial ratios are given in Exhibit 17–8 and are not included here.)

Accounts receivable turnover   A rough measure of how many times a company's accounts receivable have been turned into cash during the year. (p. 921)

Benchmarking   The process of measuring a firm against the most successful firms in the industry. (p. 901)

Common-size statements   A statement that shows the items appearing on it in percentage form rather than in dollar form. On the income statement, the percentages are based on total sales; on the balance sheet, the percentages are based on total assets or total equities. (p. 905)

Conversion feature   The ability to exchange either bonds or preferred shares for common shares at some future time. (p. 911)

Financial leverage   The financing of assets in a company with funds that have been acquired from creditors or from preferred shareholders at a fixed rate of return. (p. 915)

Horizontal analysis   A comparison of two or more years' financial statements (also called *trend analysis*). (p. 903)

Negative financial leverage   A situation in which the fixed return to a company's creditors and preferred shareholders is greater than the return on total assets. In this situation, the return on common shareholders' equity is *less* than the return on total assets. (p. 916)

Positive financial leverage   A situation in which the fixed return to a company's creditors and preferred shareholders is less than the return on total assets. In this situation, the return on common shareholders' equity is *greater* than the return on total assets. (p. 915)

Productivity ratios   Ratios that measure output in relation to some measure of input, such as direct labour-charges. (p. 927)

Trend percentages   The expression of several years' financial data in percentage form in terms of a base year. (p. 905)

Vertical analysis   The presentation of a company's financial statements in common-size form. (p. 905)

QUESTIONS

17–1 What three analytical techniques are used in financial statement analysis?

17–2   Distinguish between horizontal and vertical analysis of financial statement data.

17–3 What is the basic objective in looking at trends in financial ratios and other data? Rather than looking at trends, to what other standard of comparison might a statement user turn?

17–4 In financial analysis, why does the analyst compute financial ratios rather than simply studying raw financial data? What dangers are there in the use of ratios?

17–5 What pitfalls are involved in computing earnings per share? How can these pitfalls be avoided?

17–6 What is meant by reporting an extraordinary item on the income statement net of its tax effect? Give an example of both an extraordinary gain and an extraordinary loss net of its tax effect. Assume a tax rate of 30%.

17–7 Assume that two companies in the same industry have equal earnings. Why might these companies have different price-earnings ratios? If a company has a price-earnings ratio of 20 and reports earnings per share for the current year of $4, at what price would you expect to find the shares selling on the market?

17–8 Armcor, Inc., is in a rapidly growing technological industry. Would you expect the company to have a high or low dividend payout ratio?

17–9 Distinguish between a manager's *financing* and *operating* responsibilities. Which of these responsibilities is the return on total assets ratio designed to measure?

17–10 What is meant by the dividend yield on a common share investment? In computing dividend yield, why do you use current market value rather than original purchase price?

17–11 What is meant by the term *financial leverage?*

17–12 The president of a medium-sized plastics company was recently quoted in a business journal as stating, "We haven't had a dollar of interest-paying debt in over 10 years. Not many companies can say that." As a shareholder in this firm, how would you feel about its policy of not taking on interest-paying debt?

17–13 Why is it more difficult to obtain positive financial leverage from preferred shares than from long-term debt?

17–14 If a share's market value exceeds its book value, then the share is overpriced. Do you agree? Explain.

17–15 Weaver Company experiences a great deal of seasonal variation in its business activities. The company's high point in business activity is in June; its low point is in January. During which month would you expect the current ratio to be highest? At what point would you advise the company to end its fiscal year? Why?

17–16 A company seeking a line of credit at a bank was turned down. Among other things, the bank stated that the company's 2 to 1 current ratio was not adequate. Give reasons why a 2 to 1 current ratio might not be adequate.

17–17 If you were a long-term creditor of a firm, would you be more interested in the firm's long-term or short-term debt-paying ability? Why?

17–18 A young college student once complained to one of the authors, "The reason that corporations are such big spenders is that the government always picks up part of the tab." What did he mean by this statement?

17–19 "Earnings per share this year is higher than last year. Profitability is definitely improving." Comment.

17–20 How can cash flow ratios be used to access earnings quality? Explain.

EXERCISES

E17–1 A comparative income statement is given below for Ryder Company:

RYDER COMPANY
Comparative Income Statement
For the Years Ended June 30, 19x2, and 19x1

	19x2	19x1
Sales	$5,000,000	$4,000,000
Less cost of goods sold.	3,160,000	2,400,000
Gross margin.	1,840,000	1,600,000
Selling expenses	900,000	700,000
Administrative expenses.	680,000	584,000
Total expenses.	1,580,000	1,284,000
Net operating income	260,000	316,000
Interest expense	70,000	40,000
Net income before taxes	$ 190,000	$ 276,000

The president is concerned that net income is down in 19x2 even though sales have increased during the year. The president is also concerned that administrative expenses have increased, since the company made a concerted effort during 19x2 to pare "fat" out of the organization.

Required

1. Express each year's income statement in common-size percentages. Carry computations to one decimal place.
2. Comment briefly on the changes between the two years.

E17–2 Starkey Company's sales, current assets, and current liabilities (all in thousands of dollars) have been reported as follows over the last five years:

	19x6	19x5	19x4	19x3	19x2
Sales	$5,625	$5,400	$4,950	$4,725	$4,500
Current assets:					
Cash.	$ 64	$ 72	$ 84	$ 88	$ 80
Accounts receivable	560	496	432	416	400
Inventory.	896	880	816	864	800
Total current assets	$1,520	$1,448	$1,332	$1,368	$1,280
Current liabilities	$ 390	$ 318	$ 324	$ 330	$ 300

Required

1. Express all of the asset, liability, and sales data in trend percentages. (Show percentages for each item.) Use 19x2 as the base year, and carry computations to one decimal place.
2. Comment on the results of your analysis.

E17–3 Recent financial statements for Madison Company are given below:

MADISON COMPANY
Balance Sheet
June 30, 19x4

Assets

Current assets:	
Cash	$ 21,000
Accounts receivable, net.	160,000
Merchandise inventory.	300,000
Prepaid expenses	9,000
Total current assets.	490,000
Capital assets, net.	810,000
Total assets	$1,300,000

Liabilities and Shareholders' Equity

Liabilities:		
Current liabilities		$ 200,000
Bonds payable, 10%		300,000
Total liabilities		500,000
Shareholders' equity:		
Common shares, 20,000 outstanding	$100,000	
Retained earnings	700,000	
Total shareholders' equity		800,000
Total liabilities and shareholders' equity		$1,300,000

MADISON COMPANY
Income Statement
For the Year Ended June 30, 19x4

Sales	$2,100,000
Less cost of goods sold	1,260,000
Gross margin	840,000
Less operating expenses..................................	660,000
Net operating income....................................	180,000
Less interest expense	30,000
Net income before taxes.................................	150,000
Less income taxes	45,000
Net income..	$ 105,000

Account balances at the beginning of the company's fiscal year (July 1, 19x3) were: accounts receivable, $140,000; and inventory, $260,000. All sales were on account.

Required

Compute financial ratios as follows:
1. Current ratio. (Industry average: 2.3 to 1.)
2. Acid-test ratio. (Industry average: 1.2 to 1.)
3. Accounts receivable turnover in days. (Terms: $2/_{10}$, n/30.)
4. Inventory turnover in days. (Industry average: 72 days.)
5. Debt-to-equity ratio.
6. Times interest earned.
7. Book value per share. (Market price: $63.)

E17–4 Refer to the financial statements for Madison Company in E17–3. In addition to the data in these statements, assume that Madison Company paid dividends of $3.15 per share during the year ended June 30, 19x4. Also assume that the company's common shares had a market price of $60 per share on June 30, 19x3.

Required

Compute the following:
1. Earnings per share.
2. Dividend payout ratio.
3. Dividend yield ratio.
4. Price-earnings ratio. (Industry average: 10.)
5. Capital gains yield.

E17–5 Refer to the financial statements for Madison Company in E17–3. Assets at the beginning of the year totalled $1,100,000, and the shareholders' equity totalled $725,000.

Required

Compute the following:
1. Return on total assets.
2. Return on common shareholders' equity.
3. Was financial leverage positive or negative for the year? Explain.

E17–6 Rightway Products had a current ratio of 2.5 to 1 on June 30 of the current year. On that date, the company's assets were as follows:

Cash		$ 80,000
Accounts receivable	$530,000	
Less allowance for doubtful accounts	70,000	460,000
Inventory.		750,000
Prepaid expenses		10,000
Capital assets, net		1,900,000
Total assets		$3,200,000

Required

1. What was the company's working capital on June 30?
2. What was the company's acid-test ratio on June 30?
3. The company paid an account payable of $100,000 immediately after June 30.
   a. What effect did this transaction have on working capital? Show computations.
   b. What effect did this transaction have on the current ratio? Show computations.

E17–7 Midwest Products, Inc., reported income as follows for the past year:

MIDWEST PRODUCTS, INC.
Income Statement
For the Year Ended May 31

Sales	$800,000
Cost of goods sold	500,000
Gross margin	300,000
Operating expenses.	210,000
Net income before taxes.	90,000
Income taxes (30%)	27,000
Net income	$ 63,000

Included in the operating expenses above is a $30,000 loss resulting from a fire in the company's warehouse.

Required

1. Redo the company's income statement by showing the loss net of tax.
2. Assume that the company has 20,000 common shares outstanding. Compute the earnings per share as it should appear in the company's annual report to its shareholders.

E17–8 Selected financial data from the September 30 year-end statements of Kosanka Company are given below:

Total assets	$5,000,000
Long-term debt (12% interest rate).	750,000
Preferred shares, 7%.	800,000
Total shareholders' equity	3,100,000
Interest paid on long-term debt	90,000
Net income	470,000

Total assets at the beginning of the year were $4,800,000; total shareholders' equity was $2,900,000. There has been no change in the preferred shares during the year. The company's tax rate is 30%.

Required

1. Compute the return on total assets.
2. Compute the return on common shareholders' equity.
3. Is the company's financial leverage positive or negative? Explain.

PROBLEMS

P17–9   Ratio Analysis and Common-Size Statements   Modern Building Supply sells various building materials to retail outlets. The company has just approached Toronto

Dominion Bank requesting a $300,000 loan to strengthen the Cash account and to pay certain pressing short-term obligations. The company's financial statements for the most recent two years follow:

MODERN BUILDING SUPPLY
Comparative Balance Sheet

	This Year	Last Year
Assets		
Current assets:		
Cash....................................	$ 90,000	$ 200,000
Temporary investments	—	50,000
Accounts receivable, net	650,000	400,000
Inventory	1,300,000	800,000
Prepaid expenses	20,000	20,000
Total current assets	2,060,000	1,470,000
Capital assets, net	1,940,000	1,830,000
Total assets..............................	$4,000,000	$3,300,000

Liabilities and Shareholders' Equity

	This Year	Last Year
Liabilities:		
Current liabilities........................	$1,100,000	$ 600,000
Bonds payable, 12%	750,000	750,000
Total liabilities.......................	1,850,000	1,350,000
Shareholders' equity:		
Preferred shares, 8%	200,000	200,000
Common shares	500,000	500,000
Retained earnings	1,450,000	1,250,000
Total shareholders' equity	2,150,000	1,950,000
Total liabilities and shareholders' equity.........	$4,000,000	$3,300,000

MODERN BUILDING SUPPLY
Comparative Income Sheet

	This Year	Last Year
Sales.....................................	$7,000,000	$6,000,000
Less cost of goods sold	5,400,000	4,800,000
Gross margin	1,600,000	1,200,00
Less operating expenses	970,000	710,000
Net operating income	630,000	490,000
Less interest expense.......................	90,000	90,000
Net income before taxes	540,000	400,000
Less income taxes (40%)....................	216,000	160,000
Net income	324,000	240,000
Dividends paid:		
Preferred dividends	16,000	16,000
Common dividends	108,000	60,000
Total dividends paid.....................	124,000	76,000
Net income retained........................	200,000	164,000
Retained earnings, beginning of year	1,250,000	1,086,000
Retained earnings, end of year	$1,450,000	$1,250,000

The preferred shares and common shares were issued for $50 and $10 respectively. During the past year, the company has expanded the number of lines that it carries in order to stimulate sales and increase profits. It has also moved aggressively to acquire new customers. Sales terms are 2/10, n/30. All sales are on account.

Assume that the following ratios are typical of firms in the building supply industry:

Current ratio	2.5 to 1
Acid-test ratio	1.2 to 1
Average age of receivables	18 days
Inventory turnover in days	50 days
Debt-to-equity ratio	0.75 to 1
Times interest earned	6.0 times
Return on total assets	10%
Price-earnings ratio	9
Net income as a percentage	
of sales	4%

Required

1. Toronto Dominion Bank is uncertain whether the loan should be made. To assist it in making a decision, you have been asked to compute the following ratios for both this year and last year:
   a.   The amount of working capital.
   b.   The current ratio.
   c.   The acid-test ratio.
   d.   The average age of receivables. (The accounts receivable at the beginning of last year totalled $350,000.)
   e.   The inventory turnover in days. (The inventory at the beginning of last year totalled $720,000.)
   f.   The debt-to-equity ratio.
   g.   The number of times interest was earned.
2. For both this year and last year (carry computations to one decimal place):
   a.   Present the balance sheet in common-size form.
   b.   Present the income statement in common-size form down through net income.
3. From your analysis in (1) and (2) above, what problems or strengths do you see existing in Modern Building Supply? Make a recommendation as to whether the loan should be approved.

P17–10   Investor Ratios; Analysis of Whether to Retain or Sell Shares
Refer to the financial statements and other data in P17–9. Assume that you have just inherited several hundred shares of Modern Building Supply stock. Not being acquainted with the company, you decide to do some analytical work before making a decision about whether to retain or sell the shares you have inherited.

Required

1. You decide first to assess the well-being of the common shareholders. For both this year and last year, compute the following:
   a.   The earnings per share.
   b.   The fully diluted earnings per share. The preferred shares are convertible into common stock at the rate of 2.5 shares of common for each share of preferred. The bonds are not convertible.
   c.   The dividend yield ratio for common. The company's common shares are currently selling for $45 per share; last year it sold for $36 per share.
   d.   The dividend payout ratio for common.
   e.   The price-earnings ratio. How do investors regard Modern Building Supply as compared to other firms in the industry? Explain.
   f.   The book value per share of common. Does the difference between market value and book value suggest that the stock at its current price is too high? Explain.
2. You decide next to assess the rate of return that the company is generating. Compute the following for both this year and last year:
   a.   The return on total assets. (Total assets at the beginning of last year were $2,700,000.)
   b.   The return on common equity. (Shareholders' equity at the beginning of last year was $1,786,000.)
   c.   Is the company's financial leverage positive or negative? Explain.
3. Based on your analytical work (and assuming that you have no immediate need for cash), would you retain or sell the shares you have inherited? Explain.

P17–11 Effect of Leverage on the Return on Common Equity Vince Zolta and several other investors are in the process of organizing a new company to produce and distribute a household cleaning product. Mr. Zolta and his associates feel that $500,000 would be adequate to finance the new company's operations, and the group is studying three methods of raising this amount of money. The three methods are as follows:

Method A: All $500,000 obtained through issue of common shares.

Method B: $250,000 obtained through issue of common shares and the other $250,000 obtained through issue of 10% preferred shares.

Method C: $250,000 obtained through issue of common shares and the other $250,000 obtained through issue of bonds carrying an interest rate of 10%.

Mr. Zolta and his associates are confident that the company can earn $100,000 each year before interest and taxes. The tax rate is 30%.

Required

1. Assuming that Mr. Zolta and his associates are correct in their earnings estimate, compute the net income that would go to the common shareholders under each of the three financing methods listed above.
2. Using the income data computed in (1) above, compute the return on common equity under each of the three methods.
3. Why do methods B and C provide a greater return on common equity than does method A? Why does method C provide a greater return on common equity than method B?

P17–12 Effect of Transactions on Various Ratios Selected amounts from Reingold Company's December 31, 19x1, balance sheet follow:

Cash	$70,000
Temporary investments	12,000
Accounts receivable, net	350,000
Inventory	460,000
Prepaid expenses	8,000
Plant and equipment, net	950,000
Accounts payable	200,000
Accrued liabilities	60,000
Notes due within one year	100,000
Bonds payable in five years	140,000

During the next year (19x2), the company completed the following transactions:

x. Purchased inventory on account, $50,000.
a. Declared a cash dividend, $30,000.
b. Paid accounts payable, $100,000.
c. Collected cash on accounts receivable, $80,000.
d. Purchased equipment for cash, $75,000.
e. Paid a cash dividend previously declared, $30,000.
f. Borrowed cash on a short-term note with the bank, $60,000.
g. Sold inventory costing $70,000 for $100,000, on account.
h. Wrote off uncollectible accounts in the amount of $10,000. The company uses the allowance method of accounting for bad debts.
i. Sold temporary investments costing $12,000 for cash, $9,000.
j. Issued additional shares of capital stock for cash, $200,000.
k. Paid off all short-term notes due, $160,000.

Required

1. Compute the following amounts and ratios as of December 31, 19x1:
    a. Working capital.
    b. Current ratio.
    c. Acid-test ratio.

2. For 19x2, indicate the effect of each of the transactions given above on working capital, the current ratio, and the acid-test ratio. Give the effect in terms of increase, decrease, or none. Item (x) is given below as an example of the format to use:

		The Effect on	
Transaction	**Working Capital**	**Current Ratio**	**Acid-Test Ratio**
(x) Purchased inventory on account	None	Decrease	Decrease

P17–13   Effect of Transactions on Various Financial Ratios   In the right-hand column below, certain financial ratios are listed. To the left of each ratio is a business transaction or event relating to the operating activities of Graham Company.

1. Inventory was sold for cash at a profit.	Debt-to-equity ratio
2. Land was purchased for cash.	Earnings per share
3. The company sold inventory.	Acid-test ratio
4. The company paid off some accounts payable.	Working capital
5. A customer paid an overdue bill.	Average collection period
6. The company declared, but did not yet pay, a cash dividend.	Current ratio
7. A previously declared cash dividend was paid.	Current ratio
8. The company's common share price increased.	Book value per share
9. The company's common share price increased. Earnings per share remained unchanged.	Dividend yield ratio
10. Property was sold for a profit.	Return on total assets
11. Obsolete inventory was written off as a loss.	Inventory turnover ratio
12. The company issued bonds with an interest rate less than the company's return on assets.	Return on common shareholders' equity
13. The company's common share price decreased. The dividend paid per share remained the same.	Dividend payout ratio
14. The company's net income decreased, but long-term debt remained unchanged.	Times interest earned
15. An uncollectible account was written off against the Allowance for Bad Debts.	Current ratio
16. Inventory was purchased on credit.	Acid-test ratio
17. The company's common share price increased. Earnings per share remained unchanged.	Price-earnings ratio
18. The company paid off some accounts payable.	Debt-to-equity ratio

Required

Indicate the effect that each transaction or event would have on the ratio listed opposite to it. State the effect in terms of increase, decrease, or no effect on the ratio involved, and give the reason for your choice. In all cases, assume that the current assets exceed current liabilities both before and after the event or transaction. Use the following format for your answers:

Effect on Ratio   **Reason for Increase, Decrease, or No Effect**

1.
2.
Etc.

P17–14   Interpretation of Already Completed Ratios   Being a prudent investor, Sally Perkins always investigates a company thoroughly before purchasing shares of its stock for investment. At present, Ms. Perkins is interested in the common shares of Plunge Enterprises. All she has available on the company is a copy of its annual report for the current year (19x3), which contains the 19x3 financial statements and the summary of ratios given below:

	19x3	19x2	19x1
Current ratio	2.8 to 1	2.5 to 1	2.0 to 1
Acid-test ratio	0.7 to 1	0.9 to 1	1.2 to 1
Accounts receivable turnover	8.6 times	9.5 times	10.4 times
Inventory turnover.............	5.0 times	5.7 times	6.8 times
Sales trend...................	130.0	118.0	100.0
Dividends paid per share*........	$2.50	$2.50	$2.50
Dividend yield ratio.............	5%	4%	3%
Dividend payout ratio	40%	50%	60%
Return on total assets	13.0%	11.8%	10.4%
Return on common equity........	16.2%	14.5%	9.0%

*There were no issues or retirements of common shares over the three-year period.

Ms. Perkins would like answers to a number of questions about the trend of events over the last three years in Plunge Enterprises. Her questions are as follows:

a. Is the market price of the company's shares going up or down?
b. Is the amount of the earnings per share increasing or decreasing?
c. Is the price-earnings ratio going up or down?
d. Is the company employing financial leverage to the advantage of the common shareholders?
e. Is it becoming easier for the company to pay its bills as they come due?
f. Are customers paying their bills at least as fast now as they did in 19x1?
g. Is the total of the accounts receivable increasing, decreasing, or remaining constant?
h. Is the level of inventory increasing, decreasing, or remaining constant?

Required

Answer each of Ms. Perkins' questions using the data given above. In each case, explain how you arrived at your answer.

P17–15   Comprehensive Problem on Ratio Analysis   You have just been hired as a loan officer at Fairfield Bank. Your supervisor has given you a file containing a request from Hedrick Company for a $1,000,000 five-year loan. Financial statement data on the company for the last two years are given below:

HEDRICK COMPANY
Comparative Balance Sheet

	This Year	Last Year
Assets		
Current assets:		
Cash.....................................	$ 320,000	$ 420,000
Temporary investments.....................	–0–	100,000
Accounts receivable, net....................	900,000	600,000
Inventory................................	1,300,000	800,000
Prepaid expenses..........................	80,000	60,000
Total current assets	2,600,000	1,980,000
Capital, net	3,100,000	2,980,000
Total assets	$5,700,000	$4,960,000
Liabilities and Shareholders' Equity		
Liabilities:		
Current liabilities	$1,300,000	$ 920,000
Bonds payable, 10%	1,200,000	1,000,000
Total liabilities	2,500,000	1,920,000
Shareholders' equity:		
Preferred shares, 8%, ...	600,000	600,000
Common shares...........................	2,000,000	2,000,000
Retained earnings	600,000	440,000
Total shareholders' equity.................	3,200,000	3,040,000
Total liabilities and shareholders' equity	$5,700,000	$4,960,000

HEDRICK COMPANY
Comparative Income Statement

	This Year	Last Year
Sales (all on account)	$5,250,000	$4,160,000
Less cost of goods sold	4,200,000	3,300,000
Gross margin	1,050,000	860,000
Less operating expenses	530,000	520,000
Net operating income	520,000	340,000
Less interest expense	120,000	100,000
Net income before taxes	400,000	240,000
Less income taxes (30%)	120,000	72,000
Net income	280,000	168,000
Dividends paid:		
Preferred shares	48,000	48,000
Common shares	72,000	36,000
Total dividends paid	120,000	84,000
Net income retained	160,000	84,000
Retained earnings, beginning of year	440,000	356,000
Retained earnings, end of year	$ 600,000	$ 440,000

Marva Rossen, who just two years ago was appointed president of Hedrick Company, admits that the company has been "inconsistent" in its performance over the past several years. But Rossen argues that the company has its costs under control and is now experiencing strong sales growth, as evidenced by the more than 25% increase in sales over the last year. Rossen also argues that investors have recognized the improving situation at Hedrick Company, as shown by the jump in the price of its common shares from $20 per share last year to $36 per share this year. Rossen believes that with strong leadership and with the modernized equipment that the $1,000,000 loan will permit the company to buy, profits will be even stronger in the future.

Anxious to impress your supervisor, you decide to generate all the information you can about the company. You determine that the following ratios are typical of companies in Hedrick's industry:

Current ratio	2.3 to 1
Acid-test ratio	1.2 to 1
Average age of receivables	31 days
Inventory turnover	60 days
Return on assets	9.5%
Debt-to-equity ratio	0.65 to 1
Times interest earned	5.7
Price-earnings ratio	10

Required

1. You decide first to assess the rate of return that the company is generating. The preferred and common shares were issued for $30 and $40 respectively. Compute the following for both this year and last year:
   a. The return on total assets. (Total assets at the beginning of last year were $4,320,000.)
   b. The return on common equity. (Shareholders' equity at the beginning of last year totalled $3,016,000, and preferred shares were $600,000.)
   c. Is the company's leverage positive or negative? Explain.

2. You decide next to assess the well-being of the common shareholders. For both this year and last year, compute:
   a. The earnings per share.
   b. The fully diluted earnings per share. The preferred shares are convertible into common at the rate of two shares of common for each share of preferred.
   c. The dividend yield ratio for common.
   d. The dividend payout ratio for common.

e. The price-earnings ratio. How do investors regard Hedrick Company as compared to other firms in the industry? Explain.

f. The book value per share of common. Does the difference between market value per share and book value per share suggest that the shares at its current price are a bargain? Explain.

3. You decide, finally, to assess creditor ratios to determine both short-term and long-term debt paying ability. For both this year and last year, compute:

a. Working capital.

b. The current ratio.

c. The acid-test ratio.

d. The average age of receivables. (The accounts receivable at the beginning of last year totalled $520,000.)

e. The inventory turnover. (The inventory at the beginning of last year totalled $640,000.)

f. The debt-to-equity ratio.

g. The number of times interest was earned.

4. Evaluate the data computed in (1) to (3) above, and using any additional data provided in the problem, make a recommendation to your supervisor as to whether the loan should be approved.

P17–16 Common-Size Financial Statements   Refer to the financial statement data for Hedrick Company given in P17–15.

Required

For both this year and last year:

1. Present the balance sheet in common-size format.

2. Present the income statement in common-size format down through net income.

3. Comment on the results of your analysis.

P17–17 Comprehensive Problem—Part 1: Investor Ratios   (P17–18 and P17–19 delve more deeply into the data presented below. Each problem is independent.) Microswift, Inc., was organized several years ago to develop and market computer software programs. The company is small but growing, and you are considering the purchase of some of its common shares as an investment. The following data on the company are available for the past two years:

MICROSWIFT, INC.
Comparative Income Statement
For the Years Ended December 31, 19x2, and 19x1

	19x2	19x1
Sales.	$10,000,000	$7,500,000
Less cost of goods sold	6,500,000	4,500,000
Gross margin	3,500,000	3,000,000
Less operating expenses	2,630,000	2,280,000
Net operating income.	870,000	720,000
Less interest expense	120,000	120,000
Net income before taxes	750,000	600,000
Less income taxes (30%).	225,000	180,000
Net income.	$ 525,000	$ 420,000

MICROSWIFT, INC.
Comparative Retained Earnings Statement
For the Years Ended December 31, 19x2, and 19x1

	19x2	19x1
Retained earnings, January 1	$1,200,000	$ 980,000
Add net income (above)	525,000	420,000
Total	1,725,000	1,400,000
Deduct cash dividends paid:		
Preferred dividends	60,000	60,000
Common dividends	180,000	140,000
Total dividends paid	240,000	200,000
Retained earnings, December 31	$1,485,000	$1,200,000

MICROSWIFT, INC.
Comparative Balance Sheet
December 31, 19x2, and 19x1

	19x2	19x1
Assets		
Current assets:		
Cash	$ 100,000	$ 200,000
Accounts receivable, net	750,000	400,000
Inventory	1,500,000	600,000
Prepaid expenses	50,000	50,000
Total current assets	2,400,000	1,250,000
Capital assets, net	2,585,000	2,700,000
Total assets	$4,985,000	$3,950,000
Liabilities and Shareholders' Equity		
Liabilities:		
Current liabilities	$1,250,000	$ 500,000
Bonds payable, 12%	1,000,000	1,000,000
Total liabilities	2,250,000	1,500,000
Shareholders' equity:		
Preferred shares, 8%, ...	750,000	750,000
Common shares	500,000	500,000
Retained earnings	1,485,000	1,200,000
Total shareholders' equity	2,735,000	2,450,000
Total liabilities and shareholders' equity	$4,985,000	$3,950,000

After some research, you have determined that the following ratios are typical of companies in the computer software industry:

Dividend yield ratio	3%
Dividend payout ratio	40%
Price-earnings ratio	16
Return on total assets	13.5%
Return on common equity	20%

The company's common shares are currently selling for $60 per share. During 19x1, the shares sold for $45 per share. The preferred and common shares were issued at $10 and $5 respectively.

Required

1. In analyzing the company, you decide first to compute the earnings per share and related ratios. For both 19x1 and 19x2, compute:
   a. The earnings per share.
   b. The fully diluted earnings per share. Assume that each share of the preferred stock is convertible into two common shares. The bonds are not convertible.

    c. The dividend yield ratio.

    d. The dividend payout ratio.

    e. The price-earnings ratio.

    f. The book value per share of common stock.

2. You decide next to determine the rate of return that the company is generating. For both 19x1 and 19x2, compute:

    a. The return on total assets. (Total assets were $3,250,000 on January 1, 19x1.)

    b. The return on common shareholders' equity. (Common shareholders' equity was $1,450,000 on January 1, 19x1.)

    c. Is financial leverage positive or negative? Explain.

3. Based on your work in (1) and (2) above, does the company's common stock seem to be an attractive investment? Explain.

P17–18   Comprehensive Problem—Part 2: Creditor Ratios Refer to the data in P17–17. Although Microswift, Inc., has been very profitable since it was organized several years ago, the company is beginning to experience some difficulty in paying its bills as they come due. Management has approached Guaranty National Bank requesting a two-year $250,000 loan to bolster the Cash account.

    Guaranty National Bank has assigned you to evaluate the loan request. You have gathered the following data relating to companies in the computer software industry:

Current ratio.	2.4 to 1
Acid-test ratio	1.2 to 1
Average age of receivables	16 days
Inventory turnover in days	40 days
Times interest earned	7 times
Debt-to-equity ratio	0.70 to 1

The following additional information is available on Microswift, Inc.:

a. All sales are on account.

b. On January 1, 19x1, the accounts receivable balance was $300,000 and the inventory balance was $500,000.

Required

1. Compute the following amounts and ratios for both 19x1 and 19x2:

    a. The working capital.

    b. The current ratio.

    c. The acid-test ratio.

    d. The accounts receivable turnover (average collection period) in days.

    e. The inventory turnover (average sale period) in days.

    f. The times interest earned.

    g. The debt-to-equity ratio.

2. Comment on the results of your analysis in (1) above.

3. Would you recommend that the loan be approved? Explain.

P17–19   Comprehensive Problem—Part 3: Common-Size Statements Refer to the data in P17–17. The president of Microswift, Inc., is very concerned. Sales increased by $2.5 million during 19x2, yet the company's net income increased by only $105,000. Also, the company's operating expenses went up in 19x2, even though a major effort was launched during the year to cut costs.

Required

1. For both 19x1 and 19x2, prepare the income statement and the balance sheet in common-size form. (Round computations to one decimal place.)

2. From your work in (1) above, explain to the president why the increase in profits was so small in 19x2. Were any benefits realized from the company's cost-cutting efforts? Explain.

P17–20 Incomplete Statements; Analysis of Ratios Incomplete financial statements for Tanner Company are given below:

TANNER COMPANY
Income Statement
For the Year Ended December 31

Sales	$2,700,000
Less cost of goods sold	?
Gross margin	?
Less operating expenses	?
Net operating income	?
Less interest expense	45,000
Net income before taxes	?
Less income taxes (40%)	?
Net income	$?

TANNER COMPANY
Balance Sheet
December 31

Current assets:	
Cash	$?
Accounts receivable, net	?
Inventory	?
Total current assets	?
Capital assets, net	?
Total assets	$?
Current liabilities	$250,000
Bonds payable, 10%	?
Total liabilities	?
Shareholders' equity:	
Common shares	?
Retained earnings	?
Total shareholders' equity	?
Total liabilities and shareholders' equity	$?

The following additional information is available about the company:
a. Selected financial ratios computed from the statements above are given below:

Current ratio	2.40 to 1
Acid-test ratio	1.12 to 1
Accounts receivable turnover	15.0 times
Inventory turnover	6.0 times
Debt-to-equity ratio	0.875 to 1
Times interest earned	7.0 times
Earnings per share	$4.05
Return on total assets	14%

b. All sales during the year were on account.
c. The interest expense on the income statement relates to the bonds payable; the amount of bonds outstanding did not change throughout the year.
d. There were no issues or retirements of common shares during the year.
e. Selected balances at the *beginning* of the current year (January 1) were as follows:

Accounts receivable	$ 160,000
Inventory	280,000
Total assets	1,200,000

f. Common shares were issued at $2.50 each.

Required

Compute the missing amounts on the company's financial statements. (Hint: You may find it helpful to think about the difference between the current ratio and the acid-test ratio.)

P17–21 Forecast Financial Statements: Computer Spreadsheet   Koberg Company has just prepared the comparative annual financial statements for 19B given below:

KOBERG COMPANY
Income Statement
For the Years Ended
December 31, 19B, 19A

	For the Year Ended	
	19B	**19A**
Sales revenue (one half on credit)	$100,000	$95,000
Cost of goods sold		46,000
Gross margin		49,000
Expenses (including $3,000 interest expense each year)		33,000
Pretax income		16,000
Income tax on operations (22%)		3,520
Net income		12,480

KOBERG COMPANY
Balance Sheet
At December 31, 19B, 19A

	19B	**19A**
Assets		
Cash	$	$20,000
Accounts receivable (net)		30,000
Inventory		40,000
Operational assets (net)		100,000
Total assets		$190,000
Liabilities		
Accounts payable		$50,000
Income tax payable		1,000
Note payable, long-term		25,000
Shareholder's Equity		
Capital stock		80,000
Retained earnings		34,000
Total liabilities and shareholders' equity		$190,000

Additional information: Depreciation expense was $20,000 in 19B; no long-term notes payable were paid during 19B; $1,50 of income tax was unpaid at the end of 19B; $12,000 was paid in dividends during 19B; $10,000 was spent for additions to operational assets during 19B; $40,000 was in inventory, January 1, 19A.

Required

Using a computer spreadsheet, prepare forecasts of the 19B income statement, Statement of Cash Flows, and December 31, 19B balance sheet. (Hint: Use 19A turnovers as estimates for 19B.)

GROUP EXERCISES

GE17–22 How Useful Are Financial Statements?   There is little doubt that the data contained in financial statements is an important source of information.

Required

1. What are the major limitations of financial statements as a source of information for making investment or credit decisions?

2. How would you judge the timeliness of financial statements as a source of useful information?

3. What recommendations would you make for improving current financial reporting?

4. What other sources of information would prospective investors and creditors need to make informed judgments about a company? How would you rank these different sources of information in terms of their perceived usefulness?

GE17–23 What Information Do the Experts Use? Who better to consult than the experienced professionals whose job it is to ferret out information about a company's value or creditworthiness?

Required

1. Have students volunteer to contact an experienced securities analyst from a local brokerage firm and a credit analyst from a local financial institution and invite them to speak to the class about what sources of information they use and how they use that information in making informed decisions about companies. It would be helpful if the class prepared a set of questions far enough in advance of their scheduled presentation that the guest speakers had time to think about the questions and prepare any relevant materials.

2. Capital markets appear to adjust very rapidly to new information about a company, an industry, or general economic conditions—both domestic and international. For this to happen, there must be nearly continuous communication and exchange of information between financial analysts, companies, and investors/credit grantors. Ask the guest analysts to explain this information exchange process and the relatively free flow of information between the different groups.

3. As sophisticated as this information system is, sometimes professional analysts and investors get "fooled." How does this happen? What can be done to minimize this problem?

GE17–24 A Case of Less Than Full Disclosure Have students read the following article: "Old Game, New Twist," *Forbes* (January 12, 1987).

Required

1. Why was *Forbes* critical of Patten Corporation?

2. Compare the share price of Patten shares during the month before publication of the article to the behaviour of its share price during the week that the *Forbes* article was published. What impact did *Forbes*'s criticism have on Patten's share price?

3. Assuming Patten's management disagreed with *Forbes*'s assessment of the situation, what could Patten management have done to improve the credibility of their financial reporting and alleviate some of the uncertainty surrounding the company's financial reports?

4. Are there any risks associated with your recommendations in (3) above?

5. What could Patten management have done to convince investors that Patten's receivables have a higher value than indicated by the *Forbes*'s article? (If you want to know more about the facts surrounding this fascinating situation, read Krishna Palepu, *Patten Corporation,* Case 9-188-027 [Boston, Mass.: Harvard Business School, 1988]).

GE17–25 Striving for Quality on the Earnings Statement How successful a company has been over a period of time usually involves some assessment of the firm's earnings. When evaluating profits, investors should consider the quality and sources of the company's earnings as well as their amount. In other words, the source of earnings is as important a consideration as the size of earnings.

For this series of questions, students will need the financial statements of a firm. The financial statements of BCE Inc., Paragon Entertainment, Alcan, Seagram Co. Ltd., Royal Bank of Canada, George Weston Ltd., and Canadian Airlines are just a few that might prove helpful for answering the following questions:

Required

1. What products or services is this business selling? With this in mind, discuss the differences between operating profits and the bottom line—profits after all revenues and expenses.

2. Do you think a dollar of earnings coming from operations is any more or less valuable than a dollar of earnings generated from some other source below operating profits (e.g., one-time gains from selling assets or one-time write-offs for charges related to closing a plant)? Explain.

3. What is the concept of operating leverage and operating risk? What is the relationship between operating leverage, operating risk, and operating profits, and return on assets?

4. What is the concept of financial leverage and financial risk? What is the relationship between financial leverage, financial risk, profits, and return on common share equity?

5. Looking through the eyes of an investor, how would the above factors influence the share price of a firm over an entire economic cycle?

GE17–26 Has GE Conquered the Business Cycle?   A recent article in *The Wall Street Journal* alleges that General Electric, the industrial and financial-services conglomerate, manages its earnings to smooth out the high-earnings years and to fill in the low-earnings years. The end result of this smoothing is that the company is able to report steady earnings growth year after year. It is alleged that investors don't like uncertainty and are willing to pay a premium for the stock of companies whose earnings grow at a steady and predictable rate.

There are a variety of manoeuvres that practitioners of earnings management can use to show a steady upward trend in earnings. These manoeuvres include timing gains and losses to smooth out earnings and timing the acquisitions of other companies so as to use their earnings to cover blips in the acquiring company's own earnings. Source: Randall Smith, Steven Lipin, and Amal Kumar Naj, "How General Electric Damps Fluctuations in Its Annual Earnings," *The Wall Street Journal,* November 3, 1994, pp. A1, A11.

Required

1. Why would companies "manage earnings"?

2. Are there any risks of having business decisions (e.g., the acquisition of another business or taking a gain or loss) influenced by the decision's impact on the profits of the company?

3. Do you see any ethics issues involved in managing earnings? Explain.

4. How would investors and financial analysts view the financial statements of companies known to manage earnings?

PRICING PRODUCTS AND SERVICES

LEARNING OBJECTIVES

After studying this Appendix, you should be able to:

1 Compute the target selling price of a product by use of cost-plus pricing under either the absorption or the contribution approach.

2 Derive the markup percentage needed to achieve a target ROI for a product under either the absorption or the contribution approach.

3 Explain how target costing is used in developing new products.

4 Compute and use the billing rates used in time and material pricing in service organizations.

5 Define or explain the key terms listed at the end of the appendix.

The Swiss Corporation for Microelectronics and Watchmaking manufactures watches from the inexpensive Swatch to the prestigious Omega. Target costing is one key to its success.

Some businesses have no pricing problems at all. They make a product that is in competition with other, identical products for which a market price already exists. Customers will not pay more than this price, and there is no reason for any firm to charge less. Under these circumstances, no price calculations are necessary. Every firm charges the prevailing market price. Markets for basic raw materials such as farm products and minerals follow this pattern.

In this appendix, we are concerned with the more common situation in which the firm is faced with the problem of setting its own prices. The pricing decision in such situations can be critical. Since the prices charged for a firm's products largely determine the quantities customers are willing to purchase, the setting of prices dictates the inflows of revenues into the firm. If these revenues consistently fail to cover all the costs of the firm, then in the long run the firm cannot survive. This is true regardless of how carefully costs may be controlled or how innovative managers and employees are in carrying out their responsibilities.

Bell Canada did not enter a price war over long distance rates in 1994. The suggestion is that they had the most to lose because they were the incumbent. Instead, Bell attempted to win back customers who left for price reasons by selling value to the customers. This strategy is possible because Bell has more services to offer than the competition along with its support facilities and its reliability. A "prices only" strategy is suggested as a way to promote customer disloyalty.[1]

A subsequent assessment of Bell's strategy suggests that pricing by Sprint Canada Inc. resulted in Bell announcing it had to cut costs by laying off 2,200 employees because of a loss of two percentage points of market share in Quebec and Ontario over the first three months of 1997.[2]

COST-PLUS PRICING

OBJECTIVE 1
Compute the target selling price of a product by use of cost-plus pricing under either the absorption or the contribution approach.

At the most basic level, the price of a product or service should cover all of the costs that are *traceable* to the product or service. When we say traceable, we mean the traceable fixed costs as well as the traceable variable costs. If revenues are not sufficient to cover these costs, then the firm would be better off without the product or service.[3] In addition to the traceable costs, all products and services must assist in covering the common costs of the organization. These common costs include such items as general factory, advertising, and top management salaries.

In practice, the most common approach to the pricing of products is to employ some type of cost-plus pricing formula. Typically, **cost-plus pricing** involves determination of

---

[1]Sean Silcoff, "The Price is (Really) Right," *Canadian Business* (February 1997), p. 62.
[2]Philip DeMont, "Bell on the Defensive," *The Financial Post,* July 19–21, 1997, p. 1.
[3]There are exceptions. These exceptions most often occur when there are interdependencies among products—sales of one product affect sales of another or making one product affects the costs of making another.

a cost base and then adding to this base a predetermined **markup** to arrive at a target selling price. The formula is expressed simply by:

$$\text{Target selling price} = \left[\text{Cost} + (\text{Markup percentage} \times \text{Cost})\right]$$

In Chapters 3 and 8, we found that products can be costed in at least two different ways—by the absorption approach or by the contribution approach (with variable costing). The most common method followed in cost-plus pricing is to add a percentage markup to product cost computed using the absorption method, but we consider both costing methods below.[4]

The Absorption Approach

Under the absorption approach to cost-plus pricing, the cost base is defined as the cost to manufacture one unit. Selling, general, and administrative (SG&A) expenses are not included in this cost base, but rather are provided for through the markup. Thus, the markup must be high enough to cover SG&A expenses as well as to provide the company with a "satisfactory" profit margin.

To illustrate, let us assume that Ritter Company is in the process of setting a selling price on a product that has just undergone some modifications in design. The accounting department has provided cost estimates for the redesigned product as shown below:

	Per Unit	Total
Direct materials	$6	
Direct labour	4	
Variable manufacturing overhead	3	
Fixed manufacturing overhead	—	$70,000
Variable selling, general, and administrative expenses	2	
Fixed selling, general, and administrative expenses	—	60,000

The first step in the absorption costing approach to cost-plus pricing is to compute the unit manufacturing cost. For Ritter Company, this amounts to $20 per unit at a volume of 10,000 units, as computed in Exhibit A–1.

EXHIBIT A-1

Ritter Company:
Cost to Manufacture
10,000 Units

	Per Unit	Total
Direct materials	$ 6.00	$ 60,000
Direct labour	4.00	40,000
Variable manufacturing overhead	3.00	30,000
Fixed manufacturing overhead	7.00*	70,000
Total manufacturing cost	$20.00	$200,000

*$70,000 ÷ 10,000 units = $7.

---

[4]One study found that 83% of the 504 companies surveyed used some form of full cost (either absorption cost or absorption cost plus selling, general, and administrative expenses) as a basis for pricing. The remaining 17% used only variable costs as a basis for pricing decisions. See V. Govindarajan and Robert N. Anthony, "How Firms Use Cost Data in Pricing Decisions," *Management Accounting* (July 1983), pp. 30–36. A more recent, but less extensive, survey by Eunsup Shim and Ephraim F. Sudit, "How Manufacturers Price Products," *Management Accounting* (February 1995), pp. 37–39, found similar results.

EXHIBIT A-2

Price Quotation
Sheet—Absorption
Basis (10,000 Units)

Direct materials	$ 6
Direct labour	4
Variable manufacturing overhead	3
Fixed manufacturing overhead (based on 10,000 units)	7
Unit manufacturing cost	20
Markup to cover selling, general, and administrative expenses and desired profit—50% of unit manufacturing cost	10
Target selling price	$30

Let us assume that to obtain its target price, Ritter Company has a general policy of marking up the unit manufacturing cost by 50%. A price quotation sheet for the company prepared using the absorption approach is presented in Exhibit A–2. Note that even though this pricing approach is termed cost-plus, SG&A costs are not included in the cost base. Instead, the markup is made large enough to hopefully cover the SG&A expenses. Later we will see how some companies compute these markup percentages.

If Ritter Company produces and sells 10,000 units of the product at a price of $30 per unit, net income will be $20,000 as illustrated in Exhibit A–3.

EXHIBIT A-3

RITTER COMPANY
Income Statement
Absorption Basis

Sales (10,000 units at $30)	$300,000
Cost of goods sold (10,000 units at $20)	200,000
Gross margin	100,000
Selling, general, and administrative expenses (10,000 units at $2 variable plus $60,000 fixed)	80,000
Net income	$ 20,000

The Contribution Approach

The contribution approach to cost-plus pricing differs from the absorption approach in that it emphasizes costs by behaviour rather than by function. Thus, under the contribution approach, the cost base consists of all of the variable costs associated with a product including variable SG&A expenses. Since fixed costs are not included in the base, the markup must be adequate to cover those costs.

To illustrate, refer again to the cost data for Ritter Company. The base to use in cost-plus pricing under the contribution approach would be $15, as computed below:

Direct materials	$ 6
Direct labour	4
Variable manufacturing overhead	3
Variable selling, general, and administrative expenses	2
Total variable expenses	$15

Let us assume Ritter Company uses a markup of 100% of variable expenses to arrive at its target prices. A price quotation sheet prepared using this method is shown in Exhibit A–4.

EXHIBIT A-4

Price Quotation
Sheet—
Contribution Basis

Direct materials	$ 6
Direct labour	4
Variable manufacturing overhead	3
Variable selling, general, and administrative expenses	2
Total variable costs	15
Markup to cover fixed costs and desired profit—	
100% of variable costs	15
Target selling price	$30

Notice again that even though this pricing method is termed cost-plus pricing, some of the costs are left out of the cost base. In this case, the cost base does not include fixed costs, so it is hoped that the markup is sufficient to cover those costs.

To conclude the Ritter Company example, let us again assume the company produces and sells 10,000 units at a selling price of $30 per unit. The company's income statement as it would appear under a contribution format is shown in Exhibit A–5.

The contribution approach is essentially the approach favoured by economists. The rule advocated by economists—"set marginal revenue equal to marginal cost"—can be interpreted as "mark up variable cost by a factor reflecting how sensitive customers are to price changes." However, computing the *ideal* markup on variable cost using this rule would involve estimating demand schedules, which is beyond the scope of this text.

EXHIBIT A-5

RITTER COMPANY
Income Statement
Contribution Basis

Sales (10,000 units at $30)		$300,000
Less variable expenses (10,000 units at $15)		150,000
Contribution margin		150,000
Less fixed expenses:		
Manufacturing	$70,000	
Selling, general, and administrative	60,000	130,000
Net income		$ 20,000

DETERMINING THE MARKUP PERCENTAGE

OBJECTIVE 2
Derive the markup percentage needed to achieve a target ROI for a product under either the absorption or the contribution approach.

How did Ritter Company arrive at its markup percentage of 50% of per unit manufacturing cost under the absorption approach? This figure could be a widely used rule of thumb in the industry or just a company tradition that seems to work. The markup percentage may also be the result of an explicit computation by a manager. As we have discussed, the markup over cost ideally should be largely determined by market conditions. However, a popular approach is to at least start with a markup based on cost and desired profit. The reasoning goes like this. The markup must be large enough to cover SG&A expenses and to provide at least an adequate return on investment (ROI). The firm should therefore set a target ROI figure and then structure the markup so that this target figure is achieved.

Markup on an Absorption Basis

Formulas can be used to determine the appropriate markup percentage, given the ROI figure that management wishes to obtain for the organization and the assumed unit sales volume. Under the absorption approach to cost-plus pricing, the formula is as follows:

$$\text{Markup percentage on absorption cost} = \frac{\text{Desired return on assets employed} + \text{SG\&A expenses}}{\text{Volume in units} \times \text{Unit manufacturing cost}}$$

To show how the basic formula above is applied, assume Hart Company has determined that an investment of $2,000,000 is necessary to produce and market 50,000 units of a product each year. The $2,000,000 investment would cover purchase of equipment and provide funds needed to carry inventories and accounts receivable. The company's accounting department estimates that the following costs would be associated with the manufacture and sale of the product:

Anticipated annual unit sales.....................	50,000
Required investment in assets	$2,000,000
Unit manufacturing cost	30
Selling, general, and administrative expenses.........	700,000

If Hart Company desires a 25% ROI, then the required markup for the product would be as follows:

$$\text{Markup percentage on absorption cost} = \frac{\text{Desired return on assets employed} + \text{SG\&A expenses}}{\text{Volume in units} \times \text{Unit manufacturing cost}}$$

$$= \frac{(25\% \times \$2,000,000) + \$700,000}{50,000 \text{ units} \times \$30}$$

$$= \frac{\$1,200,000}{\$1,500,000} = 80\%$$

Using this markup percentage and the absorption cost approach to setting target prices, the selling price would be set at $54 (as shown in the top portion of Exhibit A–6).

Exhibit A–6 demonstrates that the $54 selling price would permit Hart Company to achieve a 25% ROI, *providing that 50,000 units are sold.* If it turns out that more than 50,000 units are sold, the ROI will be greater than 25%; if less than 50,000 units are sold, the ROI will be less than 25%. *The target ROI will be attained only if the budgeted sales volume is attained.*

Markup on a Contribution Basis

A similar approach can be taken to establishing a markup percentage if the contribution approach to cost-plus pricing is used. In that case, the formula becomes the following:

$$\text{Markup percentage on variable costs} = \frac{\text{Desired return on assets employed} + \text{Fixed costs}}{\text{Volume in units} \times \text{Unit variable costs}}$$

EXHIBIT A-6

Income Statement
and ROI Analysis—
Hart Company

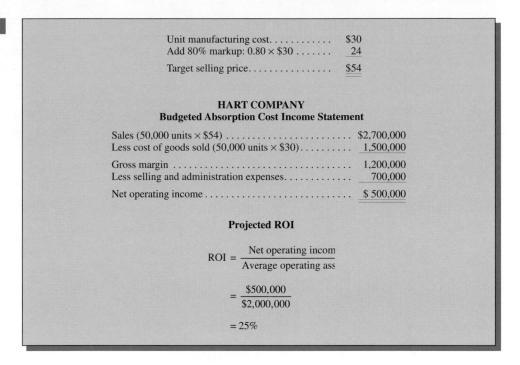

Unit manufacturing cost.	$30
Add 80% markup: 0.80 × $30	24
Target selling price.	$54

HART COMPANY
Budgeted Absorption Cost Income Statement

Sales (50,000 units × $54)	$2,700,000
Less cost of goods sold (50,000 units × $30)	1,500,000
Gross margin	1,200,000
Less selling and administration expenses.	700,000
Net operating income	$ 500,000

Projected ROI

$$ROI = \frac{\text{Net operating income}}{\text{Average operating assets}}$$

$$= \frac{\$500,000}{\$2,000,000}$$

$$= 25\%$$

Like the absorption cost basis however, the target ROI will be attained only if the budgeted sales volume is attained. In reality, neither of these methods guarantees a certain level of profits or a certain return on assets. A manager should only feel secure when market conditions make it reasonably certain that the budgeted sales volume will be reached at the target selling price.

TARGET COSTING

OBJECTIVE 3
Explain how target costing is used in developing new products.

Our discussion thus far has presumed that a product has already been developed, has been costed, and is ready to be marketed as soon as a price is set. In many cases, the sequence of events is just the reverse. That is, the company will already *know* what price should be charged, and the problem will be to *develop* a product that can be marketed profitably at the desired price. Even in this situation, where the normal sequence of events is reversed, cost is still a crucial factor. The company's approach will be to employ *target costing*. **Target costing** is the process of determining the maximum allowable cost for a new product and then developing a prototype that can be profitably manufactured and distributed for that maximum target cost figure. The target cost for a product is computed by starting with the product's anticipated selling price and deducting the desired profit, as follows:

Target cost = Anticipated selling price – Desired profit

The product development team is directed to design the product so that it can be made for no more than the target cost.

Target costing is widely used in Japan. In the automobile industry, the target cost for a new model is decomposed into target costs for each of the elements of the car—down to a target cost for each of the individual parts. The designers draft a trial blueprint, and a check is made to see if the estimated cost of the car is within reasonable distance of the target cost. If not, design changes are made, and a new trial blueprint is drawn up. This process continues until there is sufficient confidence in the design to make a prototype car according to the trial blueprint. If there is still a gap between the target cost and estimated cost, the design of the car will be further modified.

After repeating this process a number of times, the final blueprint is drawn up and turned over to the production department. In the first several months of production, the target costs will ordinarily not be achieved due to problems in getting a new model into production. However, after that initial period, target costs are compared to actual costs and discrepancies between the two are investigated with the aim of eliminating the discrepancies and achieving target costs.[5]

Nicolas G. Hayek, the head of the Swiss Corporation for Microelectronics and Watchmaking, has led the remarkable resurgence of the Swiss watch industry. The company makes watches spanning the market from the low-end fashion Swatch to the high-end prestigious Omega. Hayek explains the company's manufacturing strategy as follows:

We must build where we live . . . We have to change . . . the instinctive reaction that if a company has a mass-market consumer product, the only place to build it is Asia or Mexico. CEOs must say to their people: "We will build this product in our country at a lower cost and with higher quality than anywhere else in the world." Then we have to figure out how to do it.

We do this all the time. We agree on the performance specifications of a new product—a watch, a pager, a telephone. Then we assemble a project team. We present the team with some target economics: this is how much the product can sell for, not one penny more; this is the margin we need to support advertising, promotion, and so on. Thus these are the costs we can afford. Now go design a product and a production system that allows us to build it at those costs—in Switzerland.

That means focusing on labour. If we can design a manufacturing process in which direct labour accounts for less than 10% of total costs, there is nothing to stop us from building a product in Switzerland, the most expensive country in the world. Nothing.[6]

---

[5]Yasuhiro Monden and Kazuki Hamada, "Target Costing and Kaizen Costing in Japanese Automobile Companies," *Journal of Management Accounting Research* (Fall 1991), pp. 16–34.
[6]Reprinted by permission of *Harvard Business Review*. Excerpt from William Taylor, "Message and Muscle: An Interview with Swatch Titan Nicolas Hayek," *Harvard Business Review* (March–April 1993). Copyright © 1993 by the President and Fellows of Harvard College. All rights reserved.

Boeing has set a goal of reducing the costs of its new aircraft by 25% to 30%.[7] This is not an arbitrary goal. Boeing views its major competitor to be the existing fleet of aircraft already flying routes worldwide rather than Airbus or McDonnel Douglas. As long as airlines believe it is cheaper to keep old aircraft in service rather than to replace them with new aircraft, Boeing's sales will suffer. By cutting its costs 25% to 30% and passing on the savings to its customers in the form of lower selling prices, Boeing expects to generate more demand for replacement aircraft. "Boeing's 25% to 30% cost-reduction target isn't guesswork. It's the precise saving needed to drive out the old planes." Kenneth Raff of American Airlines says: "If Boeing can cut its costs 25%, a lot of old planes will turn into beer cans."

Reasons for Using Target Costing

The target costing approach was developed in recognition of two important characteristics of markets and costs. The first is that many firms really have less control over price than they would like to think. The market (i.e., supply and demand) really determines prices, and a firm that attempts to ignore this does so at its peril. Therefore, the anticipated market price is taken as a given in target costing. The second observation is that most of the cost of a product is determined in the design stage. Once a product has been designed and has gone into production, there is not much that can be done to significantly reduce its cost. Most of the opportunities to reduce cost come from designing the product so that it is simple to make, uses inexpensive parts, and is robust and reliable. If the firm has little control over market price and little control over cost once the product has gone into production, then it follows that the major opportunities for affecting profit come in the design stage where valuable features that customers are willing to pay for can be added and where most of the costs are really determined. So that is where the effort is concentrated—in designing and developing the product. The difference between target costing and other approaches to product development is profound. Instead of designing the product and then finding out how much it costs, the target cost is first set and then the product is designed so that the target cost is attained.

An Example of Target Costing

To provide a simple numerical example of target costing, assume the following situation: Handy Appliance Company feels that there is a market niche for a hand mixer with certain new features. Surveying the features and prices of hand mixers already on the market, the marketing department believes that a price of $30 would be about right for the new mixer. At that price, marketing estimates that 40,000 of the new mixers could be sold annually. To design, develop, and produce these new mixers, an investment of $2,000,000 would be required. The company desires a 15% ROI. Given these data, the target cost to manufacture, sell, distribute, and service one mixer is $22.50 as shown below:

Projected sales (40,000 mixers × $30).........	$1,200,000
Less desired profit (15% × $2,000,000)........	300,000
Target cost for 40,000 mixers	$ 900,000
Target cost per mixer	
($900,000 ÷ 40,000 mixers)	$22.50

[7]Shawn Tully, "Can Boeing Reinvent Itself?" *Fortune* (March 8, 1993), pp. 66–73.

This $22.50 target cost would be broken down into target costs for the various functions: manufacturing, marketing, distribution, after sales service, and so on. Each functional area would be responsible for keeping its actual costs within target.

SERVICE COMPANIES—TIME AND MATERIAL PRICING

OBJECTIVE 4
Compute and use the billing rates used in time and material pricing in service organizations.

Some companies—particularly in service industries—use a variation on cost-plus pricing called **time and material pricing**. Under this method, two pricing rates are established—one based on direct labour time and the other based on the cost of direct material used. The rates include allowances for selling, general, and administrative expenses; for other direct costs; and for a desired profit. This pricing method is widely used in repair shops, home renovators, in printing shops, and by many professionals such as accountants, lawyers, physicians, and consultants.

Time Component

The time component is typically expressed as a rate per hour of labour. The rate is computed by adding together three elements: (1) the direct costs of the employee, including salary and fringe benefits; (2) a pro rata allowance for selling, general, and administrative expenses of the organization; and (3) an allowance for a desired profit per hour of employee time. In some organizations (such as a repair shop), the same hourly rate will be charged regardless of which employee actually works on the job; in other organizations, the rate may vary by employee. For example, in a public accounting firm, the rate charged for a new assistant accountant's time will generally be less than the rate charged for an experienced senior accountant or for a partner.

Material Component

The material component is determined by adding a **material loading charge** to the invoice price of any materials used on the job. The material loading charge is designed to cover the costs of ordering, handling, and carrying materials in stock, plus a profit margin on the materials themselves.

An Example of Time and Material Pricing

To provide a numerical example of time and material pricing, assume the following data:

The Quality Auto Shop uses time and material pricing for all of its repair work. The following costs have been budgeted for the coming year:

	Repairs	Parts
Mechanics' wages	$300,000	$ —
Service manager—salary	40,000	—
Parts manager—salary	—	36,000
Clerical assistant—salary	18,000	15,000
Retirement and insurance—		
16% of salaries and wages	57,280	8,160
Supplies	720	540
Utilities	36,000	20,800
Property taxes	8,400	1,900
Depreciation	91,600	37,600
Invoice cost of parts used	—	400,000
Total budgeted cost	$552,000	$520,000

EXHIBIT A–7   Time and Material Pricing

	Time Component: Repairs		Parts: Material Loading Charge	
	Total	**Per Hour***	**Total**	**Percent†**
Cost of mechanics' time:				
Mechanics' wages.....................	$300,000			
Retirement and insurance (16% of wages)....	48,000			
Total costs........................	348,000	$14.50		
For repairs—other cost of repair service. For parts—costs of ordering, handling, and storing parts:				
Repairs service manager—salary...........	40,000		$ —	
Parts manager—salary..................	—		36,000	
Clerical assistant—salary................	18,000		15,000	
Retirement and insurance (16% of salaries)...	9,280		8,160	
Supplies	720		540	
Utilities............................	36,000		20,800	
Property taxes........................	8,400		1,900	
Depreciation	91,600		37,600	
Total costs........................	204,000	8.50	120,000	30
Desired profit:				
24,000 hours × $7.....................	168,000	7.00	—	
15% × $400,000	—		60,000	15
Total amount to be billed	$720,000	$30.00	$180,000	45

*Based on 24,000 hours.

†Based on $400,000 invoice cost of parts. The charge for ordering, handling, and storing parts, for example, is computed as follows: $120,000 cost ÷ $400,000 invoice cost = 30%.

The company expects to bill customers for 24,000 hours of repair time. A profit of $7 per hour of repair time is considered to be feasible, given the competitive conditions in the market. For parts, the competitive markup on the invoice cost of parts used is 15%.

Computations showing the billing rate and the material loading charge to be used over the next year are presented in Exhibit A–7. Note that the billing rate, or time component, is $30 per hour of repair time and the material loading charge is 45% of the invoice cost of parts used. Using these rates, a repair job that requires 4.5 hours of mechanic's time and $200 in parts would be billed as follows:

Labour time: 4.5 hours × $30..................		$135
Parts used:		
Invoice cost..............................	$200	
Material loading charge: 45% × $200	90	290
Total price of the job.........................		$425

Rather than using labour-hours as a basis for computing the time rate, a machine shop, a printing shop, or a similar organization might use machine-hours. Some organizations also charge different machine-hour rates depending on the type of machine used.

Pricing and "The Law"

Canadian legislation forbids certain forms of price discrimination. Price discrimination is illegal in Canada, however, only if different prices are charged for goods of like quality and quantity. Price fixing is also illegal in Canada. A manufacturer may suggest a list price but it cannot be mandated. According to the Federal Bureau of Competition Policy for the period covering 1985 to 1989 there were 15 companies and two individuals convicted of bid-rigging offences in Canada. In contrast to other countries, it is rare in Canada for individuals to be charged in such cases. However, it is individuals who ultimately commit these offences, and unless these individuals are held personally responsible, such criminal actions may be difficult to deter. Other illegal acts include false or misleading advertising, agreements not to bid on contracts that are not revealed to customers, and pyramid selling. Pyramid selling is the process of paying a fee to participate in selling and receiving the right to charge others for the right to sell.

International restrictions relating to pricing exist in the form of the antidumping laws. These laws prohibit the sale of products below cost in international markets. Again, cost is interpreted as full cost, including fully allocated fixed costs. Such laws are designed to protect a domestic manufacturer in its home market in those instances where it is in direct competition with a foreign supplier.

KEY TERMS FOR REVIEW

OBJECTIVE 5
Define or explain the key terms at the end of the appendix.

Cost-plus pricing   A pricing method in which a predetermined markup is applied to a cost base to determine a target selling price. (p. 956)

Markup   The difference between the selling price of a product or service and its cost. The markup is usually expressed as a percentage of cost. (p. 957)

Material loading charge   A markup applied to the cost of materials that is designed to cover the costs of ordering, handling, and carrying materials in stock and to provide for some profit. (p. 964)

Target costing   The process of determining the maximum allowable cost for a new product and then developing a prototype that can be profitably manufactured and distributed for that maximum target cost figure. (p. 961)

Time and material pricing   A pricing method, often used in service firms, in which two pricing rates are established—one based on direct labour time and the other based on direct materials used. (p. 964)

QUESTIONS

A–1   What is meant by *cost-plus pricing?* What is the difference between the absorption and contribution approaches to cost-plus pricing?

A–2   In what sense is the term *cost-plus pricing* a misnomer?

A–3   Discuss the following statement: "Full cost can be viewed as a floor of protection. If a firm always sets its prices above full cost, it will never have to worry about operating at a loss."

A–4   In cost-plus pricing, what elements must be covered by the markup when the cost base consists of the cost to manufacture a product? What elements must be covered when the cost base consists of a product's variable costs?

A–5   What is *target costing?* How do target costs enter into the pricing decision?

A–6   What is time and material pricing? What type of organization would be most likely to use time and material pricing?

A–7   What is a material loading charge in time and material pricing?

EXERCISES

EA–1 Meridian Company must determine a target selling price for one of its products. Cost data relating to the product are as follows:

	Per Unit	Total
Direct materials	$6	
Direct labour	10	
Variable manufacturing overhead	3	
Fixed manufacturing overhead	5	$450,000
Variable selling, general, and administrative expenses	1	
Fixed selling, general, and administrative expenses	4	360,000

The costs above are based on an anticipated volume of 90,000 units produced and sold each period. The company uses cost-plus pricing, and it has a policy of obtaining target selling prices by adding a markup of 50% of unit manufacturing cost or by adding a markup of 80% of variable costs.

Required

1. Assuming that the company uses absorption costing, compute the target selling price for one unit of product.
2. Assuming that the company uses the contribution approach to costing, compute the target selling price for one unit of product.

EA–2 Naylor Company is considering the introduction of a new product. As one step in its study of the new product, the company has gathered the following information:

Number of units to be produced and sold each year	12,500
Unit manufacturing cost	$ 30
Projected annual selling and administrative expenses	60,000
Estimated investment required by the company	500,000
Desired ROI	18%

The company uses the absorption approach to cost-plus pricing.

Required

1. Compute the markup the company will have to use to achieve the desired ROI.
2. Compute the target selling price per unit.

EA–3 Romer, Inc., is anxious to introduce a new product on the market and is trying to determine what price to charge. The new product has required a $500,000 investment in equipment and working capital. The company wants a 10% ROI on all products. The following costs are traceable to the new product:

	Per Unit	Annual Total
Variable production costs (direct materials, direct labour, and variable manufacturing overhead)	$19	—
Fixed manufacturing overhead costs	—	$250,000
Variable selling, general, and administrative expenses	1	—
Fixed selling, general, and administrative expenses	—	150,000

The company uses the contribution approach to cost-plus pricing.

Required

1. Assume that the company expects to sell 50,000 units each year. What percentage markup would be required to achieve the target ROI? Using this markup, what would be the selling price per unit?
2. Repeat the computations in (1) above, assuming that the company expects to sell 30,000 units each year.

EA–4 Riteway Plumbing Company provides plumbing repair services and uses time and material pricing. The company has budgeted the following costs for next year:

Plumbers' wages and fringe benefits	$340,000
Other repair costs, except for	
parts-related costs......................	160,000
Costs of ordering, handling, and	
storing parts	15% of invoice cost

In total, the company expects to log 20,000 hours of billable repair time next year. According to competitive conditions, the company believes it should aim for a profit of $5 per hour of plumber's time. The competitive markup on parts is 30% of invoice cost.

Required

1. Compute the time rate and the material loading charge that would be used to bill jobs.
2. One of the company's plumbers has just completed a repair job that required three hours of time and $40 in parts (invoice cost). Compute the amount that would be billed for the job.

EA–5 Eastern Auto Supply, Inc., is a producer and distributor of auto supplies. The company is anxious to enter the rapidly growing market for long-life batteries that is based on lithium technology. Management believes that to be fully competitive, the new battery that the company is planning can't be priced at more than $65. At this price, management is confident that the company can sell 50,000 batteries per year. The batteries would require a permanent investment of $2,500,000, and the desired ROI is 20%.

Required

Compute the target cost of one battery.

PROBLEMS

PA–6   Time and Material Pricing   Superior TV Repair, Inc., uses time and material pricing, and each year it reviews its rates in light of the actual costs incurred in the prior year. Actual costs incurred last year in connection with repair work and in connection with the company's parts inventory are given below:

	Repairs	**Parts**
Repair technicians—wages....................	$280,000	$ —
Repair service manager—salary................	30,000	—
Parts manager—salary	—	26,000
Repairs and parts assistant—salary..............	16,000	4,000
Retirement benefits (20% of salaries		
and wages)	65,200	6,000
Health insurance (5% of salaries		
and wages)	16,300	1,500
Utilities	71,000	15,700
Truck operating costs	11,600	—
Property taxes	5,200	3,200
Liability and fire insurance....................	3,800	1,800
Supplies...................................	$ 900	$ 300
Rent—Building.............................	24,000	16,500
Depreciation—trucks and equipment	36,000	—
Invoice cost of parts used	—	300,000
Total costs for the year	$560,000	$375,000

Customers were billed for 20,000 hours of repair work last year.

The company has a target profit of $4 per hour of repair service time and a target profit of 15% of the invoice cost of parts used. During the past year, the company billed repair service time at $27.50 per hour and added a material loading charge of 35% to parts. There is some feeling in the company that these rates may now be inadequate, since costs have risen somewhat over the last year.

Required

1. Using the data above, compute the following:
   a. The rate that would be charged per hour of repair service time using time and material pricing. Your rate should contain three cost elements, as discussed in the body of this Appendix.

b. The material loading charge that would be used in billing jobs. The material loading charge should be expressed as a percentage of the invoice cost of parts and should contain two elements, as discussed in the body of this Appendix.

2. Are the time and material rates that the company has been using adequate to cover its costs and yield the desired profit margins? Explain. (No computations are necessary.)

3. Assume that the company adopts the rates that you have computed in (1) above. What should be the total price charged on a repair job that requires 1½ hours of service time and parts with an invoice cost of $69.50?

PA–7 Integrative Problem: Standard Costs; Markup Computations; Pricing Decisions   Euclid Fashions, Inc., has designed a sports jacket that is about to be introduced on the market. A standard cost card has been prepared for the new jacket, as shown below:

	Standard Quantity or Hours	Standard Price or Rate	Standard Cost
Direct materials.........................	2.0 metres	$ 4.60 per metre	$9.20
Direct labour	1.4 hours	10.00 per hour	14.00
Manufacturing overhead (⅙ variable).........	1.4 hours	12.00 per hour	16.80
Total standard cost per jacket			$40.00

The following additional information relating to the new jacket is available:

a. The only variable selling, general, or administrative costs on the jackets will be $4 per jacket for shipping. Fixed selling, general, and administrative costs will be (per year):

Salaries	$ 90,000
Advertising and other	384,000
Total	$474,000

b. Since the company manufactures many products, it is felt that no more than 21,000 hours of labour time per year can be devoted to production of the new jackets.

c. An investment of $900,000 will be necessary to carry inventories and accounts receivable and to purchase some new equipment. The company desires a 24% ROI in new product lines.

d. Manufacturing overhead costs are allocated to products on the basis of direct labour-hours.

Required

1. Assume that the company uses the absorption approach to cost-plus pricing.
   a. Compute the markup that the company needs on the jackets to achieve a 24% ROI.
   b. Using the markup you have computed, prepare a price quote sheet for a single jacket.
   c. Assume that the company is able to sell all of the jackets that it can produce. Prepare an income statement for the first year of activity, and compute the company's ROI for the year on the jackets, using the ROI formula from Chapter 12.

2. Assume that the company uses the contribution approach to cost-plus pricing.
   a. Compute the markup that the company needs on the jackets to achieve a 24% ROI.
   b. Using the markup you have computed, prepare a price quote sheet for a single jacket.
   c. Prepare an income statement for the first year of activity.

3. After marketing the jackets for several years, the company is experiencing a falloff in demand due to an economic recession. A large retail outlet will make a bulk purchase of jackets if its label is sewn in and if an acceptable price can be worked out. What is the minimum acceptable price for this order?

PA–8 Pricing Potpourri   Unless otherwise indicated, each of the following parts is independent. In all cases, show computations to support your answer.

1. Rockwell Company incurs the following unit costs in producing and selling 10,000 units of one of its products each year:

Production costs:	
Direct materials	$20
Direct labour	7
Variable manufacturing overhead	5
Fixed manufacturing overhead...................	13
Selling, general, and administrative costs:	
Variable	4
Fixed..	9

Assume that the company uses the absorption approach to cost-plus pricing and desires a markup of 40%. Compute the target selling price per unit.

2. Refer to the data in (1) above. Assume that the company uses the contribution approach to cost-plus pricing and desires a markup of 75%. Compute the target selling price per unit.

3. Refer to the data in (1) above. What is the absolute minimum price below which the Rockwell Company should not price its product, even in special situations involving the use of idle capacity?

4. Caldwell, Inc., estimates that the following costs and activity would be associated with the manufacture and sale of a product:

Number of units sold annually...........................	40,000
Required investment in assets	$850,000
Unit manufacturing cost.....................................	15
Annual selling, general, and administrative expenses.............	250,000

The company uses the absorption approach to cost-plus pricing and desires a 20% ROI. What is the required markup in percentage terms?

5. Rohr Company desires a 16% ROI. The company estimates that an investment of $2,500,000 would be needed to produce and sell 30,000 units of a product each year. Other costs associated with the product would be as follows:

	Variable (per unit)	Fixed (total)
Production (materials, labour, and overhead)	$50	$200,000
Selling, general, and administrative....................	10	600,000

The company uses the contribution approach to cost-plus pricing. Given these data, what markup would be required for the company to achieve its target ROI?

6. You have just received a bill for $360 for materials used in doing some plumbing repair work on your home. You feel that this charge is unreasonable, and at your insistence the company has given you the following breakdown:

Invoice cost of materials	$225
Charge for ordering, handling, and storing materials	45
Profit margin on the materials..............................	90
Total charge for materials	$360

Compute the material loading charge (in percentage terms) being used by the company.

7. Barker Company uses time and material pricing. The time rate is $36 per hour. The material loading charge is 20% for ordering, handling, and storing material and 30% for the desired profit on materials. Given these data, what is the total charge on a job that requires 2.5 hours of labour time and $140 in materials?

8. Dumas Company, a manufacturer of consumer products, wants to introduce a new hair dryer. To compete effectively, the dryer should not be priced at more than $40. The company requires a 16% ROI on all new products. To produce and sell 50,000 dryers each year, the company would need to make an investment of $750,000. Compute the target cost per dryer.

PA–9 Integrative Problem: Missing Data; Markup Computations; Return on Investment; Pricing   Rest Easy, Inc., has designed a new puncture-proof, self-inflating sleeping pad that is unlike anything on the market. Because of the unique properties of the new sleeping pad, the company anticipates that it will be able to sell all the pads that it can produce. On this basis, the following budgeted income statement for the first year of activity is available:

Sales (___?___ pads at ___?___ per pad)	$?
Less cost of goods sold (___?___ pads at ___?___ per pad).....	4,000,000
Gross margin.......................................	?
Less selling, general, and administrative expenses.................	2,160,000
Net income	$?

Additional information on the new sleeping pad is given below:

a. The company will hire enough workers to commit 100,000 direct labour-hours to the manufacture of the pads.

b. A partially completed standard cost card for the new sleeping pad follows:

	Standard Quantity or Hours	Standard Price or Rate	Standard Cost
Direct materials..................	5 metres	$6 per metre	$30
Direct labour....................	2 hours	? per hour	?
Manufacturing overhead...........	?	? per hour	?
Total standard cost per sleeping pad................			$?

c. An investment of $3,500,000 will be necessary to carry inventories and accounts receivable and to purchase some new equipment needed in the manufacturing process. Management has decided that the design of the new pad is unique enough that the company should set a selling price that will yield a 24% ROI.

d. Other information relating to production and costs follows:

Variable manufacturing overhead cost (per pad)................	$ 7
Variable selling cost (per pad)...............................	5
Fixed manufacturing overhead cost (total)....................	1,750,000
Fixed selling, general, and administrative cost (total)...........	?
Number of pads produced and sold (per year).................	?

e. Manufacturing overhead costs are allocated to production on the basis of direct labour-hours.

Required

1. Complete the standard cost card for a single pad.
2. Assume that the company uses the absorption approach to cost-plus pricing.
   a. Compute the markup that the company needs on the pads to achieve a 24% ROI.
   b. Using the markup you have computed, prepare a price quotation sheet for a single pad.
   c. Assume, as stated, that the company can sell all the pads that it can produce. Complete the income statement for the first year of activity, and then compute the company's ROI for the year using the ROI formula from Chapter 12.
3. Assume that the company uses the contribution approach to cost-plus pricing.
   a. Compute the markup that the company needs on the pads to achieve a 24% ROI.
   b. Using the markup you have computed, prepare a price quotation sheet for a single pad.
   c. Prepare an income statement for the first year.

INDEX

PHOTO CREDITS